three testaments

praise for *Three Testaments*

"This is an unusual, ambitious and groundbreaking book that seeks to discover the threads that connect the sacred texts of Judaism, Christianity and Islam." —*The Bible Today*

"This work brings together in one volume scholarly and gender-inclusive translations and interpretations of Judaism's Torah, Christianity's New Testament and Islam's Qur'an. . . . Intimately connected, the sacred scriptures of Judaism, Christianity and Islam are 'possibly the most spiritually significant trilogy in the history of literature.' This work not only introduces each scriptural text but also serves as a foundation for greater understanding among the three traditions." —*Booklist*

"Brian Arthur Brown (Noah's Other Son), a United Church of Canada minister, was surprised that the sacred scriptures of Judaism, Christianity and Islam are not usually included in a single volume. He includes all three here, emphasizing the common ground among these monotheistic religions and their texts . . . what is here is useful for comparative analysis as persons from each tradition may not have read the other texts or studied them as is possible here. VERDICT: General readers and undergraduates with an interest in these monotheistic religions and their sacred writings will find this book to be very helpful." —*Library Journal*

"Brown has assembled Muslim, Christian and Jewish scholars to introduce modern, readable translations of the three texts. The scholars explain how the holy books of each community are used and understood within the faith they represent." —*The Catholic Register*

"Demonstrating the many ways in which Jewish, Christian and Islamic sacred texts manifest influences and parallels, Brown and his associates here turn to a deeper investigation of the common as well as the distinctive features of the monotheistic world faiths present in the Torah, the Gospel and the Quran, including some possible influence in each by Zoroastrianism." —**Max L. Stackhouse**, professor of theology and public life emeritus, Princeton Theological Seminary

"What an interesting read! I am delighted to see the use of the calligraphy by Mohamed Zakariya in balance with the evocative Irving Kligfield collection of engravings in this splendid book." —**Serene Jones**, president, Union Theological Seminary, New York

"*Three Testaments* suggests new paradigms that could considerably enrich interfaith discussions for each of these three faiths: a new paradigm for Jews about the origin of monotheism in world religion, a new paradigm for Christians about the savior of the world and a new paradigm for Muslims about the people of the book." —**Mark G. Toulouse**, Emmanuel College, University of Toronto

"*Three Testaments* invites readers to study the interdependence of the Scriptures claiming the tradition of Abraham, Sarah and Hagar as their heritage. I especially appreciate the use of inclusive language and the voice of wo/men scholars in part I and III introducing the progressive edge of Jewish and Muslim Scriptures. This volume is a very unique and helpful resource for introductory Scripture courses and interreligious dialogue. I highly recommend it." —**Elisabeth Schüssler Fiorenza**, Krister Stendahl Professor, Harvard Divinity School

three testaments

Torah, Gospel, and Quran

Brian Arthur Brown

ROWMAN AND LITTLEFIELD
Lanham • Boulder • New York • Toronto • Plymouth, UK

Published by Rowman & Littlefield
4501 Forbes Boulevard, Suite 200, Lanham, Maryland 20706
www.rowman.com

10 Thornbury Road, Plymouth PL6 7PP, United Kingdom

British Library Cataloguing in Publication Information Available

Library of Congress Cataloging-in-Publication Data
The hardback edition of this book was originally cataloged by the Library of Congress as follows:

Brown, Brian A., 1942–
  Three testaments : Torah, Gospel, and Quran / Brian Arthur Brown.
    p. cm.
  Includes bibliographical references (p.   ) and index.
  1. Religions—Relations. 2. Abrahamic religions. 3. Sacred books—Comparative studies. 4. Torah.
5. Bible. O.T. Pentateuch—Criticism, interpretation, etc. 6. Bible. N.T.—Criticism, interpretation, etc.
7. Koran—Criticism, interpretation, etc. I. Title.
  BL410.B75 2012
  208'.2—dc23   2012009166

  ISBN 978-1-4422-1492-7 (cloth : alk. paper)
  ISBN 978-1-4422-1493-4 (pbk : alk. paper)
  ISBN 978-1-4422-1494-1 (electronic)

Printed in the United States of America

∞™ The paper used in this publication meets the minimum requirements of American National Standard for Information Sciences—Permanence of Paper for Printed Library Materials, ANSI/NISO Z39.48-1992.

To the Winberg Foundation of Toronto,
and to Milton and Florence Winberg,
lifelong patrons of the arts and letters,
and sponsors of the religious, academic, media and public 2012 book tour and launch events in
seven cities: New York, Washington, Dallas, Los Angeles, San Francisco, Chicago and Toronto

Shalom, Peace and Salam to participants in these events and to all readers subsequently engaged

Cyrus, God's Anointed, according to the Bible,
Under the Sign of Zoroastrianism, Sponsor of the
Jewish Return in Conjunction with a Written Torah

contents

foreword

Amir Hussain,
editor of the *Journal of the American Academy of Religion*

THE BOOK THAT YOU HOLD IN YOUR HANDS IS REVOLUTIONARY. IT PRESENTS TOGETHER THE texts of the Torah, the New Testament and the Quran, inviting the reader to examine the interdependence of the Scriptures that are central to Jews, Christians and Muslims. That shared presentation in and of itself gives *Three Testaments* its name and makes it extraordinary. What makes it revolutionary are the connections that Brian Arthur Brown and the other contributors to this volume make among these three great traditions.

In speaking about itself, as it often does, the Quran says that those whose knowledge is sound will say that "we have faith that what is in it is all from God. But only those who have wisdom understand."[1] This book provides both the wisdom and the understanding.

To show the deep connections in our religious history, my mentor, Professor Wilfred Cantwell Smith, began one of his books, *Towards a World Theology*, with a story of Leo Tolstoy—his *Confession* from 1879, published in 1884. How many readers are familiar with Tolstoy and the story of his "conversion" from a worldly life to a life of ascetic service? The story that converted him was the story of Barlaam (the hermit) and Josaphat (the Indian prince). In the story, Josaphat is converted from a life of worldly power to the search for moral and spiritual truths by Barlaam, a Sinai desert monk. Tolstoy learned the story from the Russian Orthodox Church. However, it was not a Russian story, as the Russian Church got it from the Byzantine Church. It was not a Byzantine story either, as it came to the Byzantine Church from the Muslims. The story did not originate with Muslims, as Muslims in Central Asia learned it from Manichees. In the end, finally, it was not a Manichean story, as the Manichees got it from Buddhists. The tale of Barlaam and Josaphat is in fact a story of the Buddha. Bodhisattva becomes Bodasaf in Manichee, and Josaphat in later tellings of the tale.

However, Smith's genius was not in simply pointing to the history of this story but to how it moved forward in time. Those who remember Tolstoy know that he was an influence on a young Indian lawyer, Mohandas Gandhi, who founded Tolstoy Farm in South Africa in 1910. Those who remember Gandhi know that the story does not end with him. Gandhi was an influence on a young African American minister, the Reverend Martin Luther King Jr. The story shows that we are connected to each other, both forward and backward in time.

We see that connection when we study our Scriptures. Our best scholarly evidence tells us that the Torah was first written down during the Babylonian Exile and in the Return to Jerusalem, as sponsored by Cyrus the Great and his successors. We know that their Zoroastrian tradition, present in Babylon during the Exile, influenced the Bible. In this book, Brian Brown credibly reestablishes the traditional understanding that Jewish monotheism predates that of Zoroaster, despite popular and esoteric predilections placing him thousands of years earlier. Moses, or one of the more contemporary Hebrew prophets, may even have been a source of inspiration for Zoroaster, whose dates we now believe to be early seventh century BCE. At a later time, Zoroastrians may have helped the Jews in their midst to recognize God's own self as the only "Redeemer" of Israel.

Brian Brown then shows how possible exposure to Zoroastrianism may have been a revelation to Jesus about his messianic destiny, not only to restore the Davidic kingdom, according to his spiritual understanding of it, but also to be the "Redeemer" or Savior of the whole world—a distinctly Zoroastrian concept. Finally, Brown presents the Quran's self-understanding as confirming both the Jewish monotheistic heritage and the messiahship of Jesus. He commends the Quran as confirming many other Scriptures, including Zoroastrian, in addition to those of the Hebrew and Christian communities by using a traditional Islamic perspective that may be a welcome affirmation for Muslims and helpfully insightful for Jews and Christians in particular.

Ellen Frankel and Marc Brettler present their portrayals of the resolute dedication of Jews to their covenant relationship with God and with each other, as well as certain incongruities in the Torah's articulation of the monotheistic heritage since at least the time of Moses. Henry Carrigan and David Bruce describe the devotional aspect of the stories of Jesus in Christian tradition and the intricacies associated with the texts of the Christian Scriptures. Laleh Bakhtiar and Nevin Reda bring the cutting edges of both classical and progressive Islamic scholarship to bear on challenges associated with presenting the Quran in the context of twenty-first-century investigations.

Far from simply ignoring the profound differences among and within religious traditions, *Three Testaments* is committed to engaging the very differences that we have to gain a deeper sense of each other's commitments. This, for me, is the goal of interfaith dialogue as advanced by this book—not that we seek to convert each other, but that we help each other to find what is meaningful in our own traditions.

Christian and Jewish readers will gain better understandings of their own intertwined traditions and also learn a great deal about Muslims and Islam. Muslim readers will benefit from understanding the Quran in its historical and cultural contexts—asking when and why and how the verses were revealed to Muhammad. They can also learn about the truth of metaphor in the discussion of the work of Northrop Frye. Just as an increasing number of Jews and Christians believe the truth of the Bible to be in the way it provides meaning for their lives and puts them in touch with the Divine, so Muslims can experience their "truth" in new ways. What once might have been understood as literally true is now seen as metaphorically true at the deepest level of meaning. The Quran seems to give some allowance for such understandings in the first part of the verse quoted earlier: "It is God who has revealed the Book to you. In it are clear revelations which are the foundation of the Book, while others are metaphorical."[2]

Important as they are in every North American community, with Jewish, Muslim and "other" populations now equal to small nations in size, interfaith relations here are affected by the numerical dominance of Christians. With a population of 460 million people in North America, there are approximately six million Jews, six million Muslims, six million "other" and perhaps twelve million currently "unaffiliated" in a sea of 430 million Christians, active or nominal. Several contributors to this book are members, adherents or affiliates of the United Church of Canada, the largest Protestant church in Canada. Just before Canada's centennial in 1967, the University of Toronto Press published *The Vertical Mosaic*, a defining analysis of one hundred years of evolving national identity, in which John Porter described the United Church as being "as Canadian as the maple leaf and the beaver."[3] Since then the maple leaf has survived the threat of acid rain, the beaver has adapted to climate change and the United Church has adjusted to the changing demographics of immigration and the testing of organized religion by a "secular spiritualism" in much of Canadian society. However, Jews and Muslims are not alone in recognizing that the United Church has played a leading role in fashioning the egalitarian society that makes Canada a much-needed model for the world in the twenty-first century. How much is this needed in the era of *Little Mosque on the Prairie*, the CBC sitcom hit televised in every English-speaking country in the world except one? In this book, eminent American religious scholars join the initiative of Canadian academics and spiritual leaders in support of this model as exemplified by the contributors associated with the United Church.

At a minimum, we have here a model for a Christianity that can coexist peacefully and fruitfully with its neighbors. Other Christians, including people who do not know the United Church as well as I do, sometimes mistake its inclusive, gracious and generous ethos for a mere superficial adherence to orthodox Christian belief. Nothing could be further from the truth, so in response to Brian Arthur Brown, a Christian faithfully articulating Islamic beliefs, allow me, as a Muslim, to present a creedal summary of United Church beliefs as part of the context of this study. These are articulated in *A New Creed* (1994), now used around the world in a number of languages:

> We are not alone,
> we live in God's world.
> We believe in God:
> who has created and is creating,
> who has come in Jesus,
> the Word made flesh,
> to reconcile and make new,
> who works in us and others
> by the Spirit.
> We trust in God.
> We are called to be the Church:
> to celebrate God's presence,
> to live with respect in Creation,
> to love and serve others,
> to seek justice and resist evil,
> to proclaim Jesus, crucified and risen,
> our judge and our hope.
> In life, in death, in life beyond death,
> God is with us.
> We are not alone.
> Thanks be to God.[4]

Except for being "called to be the Church," none of that, properly understood, is particularly difficult for a Muslim, although the crucified part does present some issues. Clearly, Muslims and Christians need to talk, and they need to include Jews in the kind of conversation found in this book. The unity of God that Jews express in repeating the words of the *Shema*, "Hear O Israel, the Lord our God is One,"[5] is mirrored in the first line of the *shahadah* or faith statement for Muslims, "There is no god except God."[6] It is also instructive to remember that it is the Hebrew *Shema* that Jesus quotes as the Great Commandment.[7]

Three Testaments also opens up one final intriguing insight. While the Scriptures of Judaism, Christianity and Islam may all contain revelations received earlier in some form by Zoroaster, he himself may be seen as not merely the axis in the Axial Age but also as the reformer of ancient Vedic religion. In my view, recent opinion regarding the late dates for Zoroaster's life and influence, as documented here, are important, since his reforms affected the old Hinduism and the newer Buddhism as profoundly as his spiritual insights influenced Judaism, Christianity and Islam. This realization is a "game-changer" for interfaith studies. Not only are the traditions of Oriental and Occidental religions required to tolerate and learn to appreciate each other in the world culture that is emerging, but they are also meant to embrace each other as long-lost relatives, distant cousins many times removed. This provides a new basis for scholarly discourse that may occupy many of us in the years to come.

"And They Shall Beat Their Swords into Plowshares": The Vision of Peace Prophesied by Both Isaiah and Micah

illustrations

REPRESENTATIONAL ART EXHIBITED IN *THREE TESTAMENTS* IS STRICTLY LIMITED TO THE PERSONAL collection of the late Irving Kligfield. This compilation of a lifetime, which became legally registered as the *Counsel Collection*, was never shared with the public except for a short-lived exposition in *The Family Bible Encyclopedia* published by Curtis Books in 1972, shortly before Curtis Publishing disappeared along with the *Saturday Evening Post* and other Kligfield publications. Kligfield began this particular collection by acquiring woodcuts, etchings and metal engravings in the public domain from the sixteenth, seventeenth, eighteenth and nineteenth centuries, including evocative black-and-white illustrations by William Blake, Horace Castelli, W. J. Linton and Gustav Doré, supplemented by other works that Kligfield himself commissioned various artists to execute in this same ancient and redolent style. In particular, we exhibit one drawing *in situ*, illustrating a stele among the current ruins of Persepolis, which depicts the throne of Cyrus and the Zoroastrian symbol better than any photograph could portray. While historical details of a few scenes in the Kligfield etchings may be open to question, the collection's ethos reflects a traditional religiosity that may be closer to the spiritual animus of the ancient world than is modern analysis.

The maps are original to Brian Arthur Brown, with research assistance from "newmapper" Ward Kaiser and cartographer Len Guelke. The one chart is again from the author, but it is produced with technical assistance from Karen Arbour, and the calligraphy is by Mohamed Zakariya. All are more adequately recognized in the "Acknowledgments" section.

Readers are encouraged to download two color charts from www.BrianArthurBrown.com identified as *A Diagram of the Sources of the Pentateuch* and *A Diagram of Previously Revealed Scriptures Confirmed in the Quran.*

Mercy Is Extended to Hagar in the Desert as She Looks to God for Grace

acknowledgments

THE NINE SUPPLEMENTAL ESSAYISTS IN THIS COMPENDIUM, WHOSE CREDENTIALS ARE ACKNOWLEDGED elsewhere, include Amir Hussain, Ellen Frankel, Marc Zvi Brettler, Henry L. Carrigan Jr., David Bruce, Nevin Reda and Laleh Bakhtiar, the latter writing both the preface to *The Sublime Quran* and the translator's notes, like those of David Stein and Joe Dearborn for the Hebrew and Christian Scriptures, respectively. The twelve chapters I have written are thereby matched by twelve essays of significant weight, including my own prologue and epilogue, in the sections of the volume where I have been merely the "contributing editor."

Four other contributions deserve special acknowledgment. Karen Arbour, a former administrator in both United and Catholic churches in Toronto, currently associated with the Sunnybrook Research Institute for Clinical Evaluative Sciences, should be added to that list for her painstaking production of the graphic diagram of previous revelations confirmed in the Quran. Researched by seminary students in the global south, it is modeled on my own Diagram of the Sources of the Pentateuch and the classic gospel Diagram of Synoptic Relationships by Allan Barr from T&T Clark, all three of which are available for download at www.BrianArthurBrown.com in various sizes for personal or classroom usage.

The rest of the graphics throughout the text as a whole come from three sources, Christian, Muslim and Jewish by chance. Paul and Roy Kligfield of New York and Colorado are warmly acknowledged for their decision and kind permission for exclusive access to the artworks in the estate of their late father, Irving Kligfield, described in the "Illustrations" section as the sole source of representational art used throughout this entire volume. Mohamed Zakariya, the preeminent Islamic calligrapher of North America, has generously provided appropriate examples of this art form from his portfolio, which includes U.S. postage stamps, works that President Obama has presented to foreign heads of state and other projects executed for the Smithsonian Institution and the National Jewish Museum in Washington. In cartography I was privileged to have had guidance from Ward Kaiser, the author of *How Maps Change Things* (2012), who published the first English-language version of the now-standard Peters Projection World Map in 1983. He also engaged the assistance of fellow cartographer Len Guelke to touch up my original maps with graphic techniques acceptable to the publisher. The maps are copyrighted in my name and available for download from my website free of charge for noncommercial reproduction by anyone who owns a copy of this book.

Our online community of some two hundred and seventy collaborators and monitors of the work is entirely appreciated, acknowledging senior scholars from Carol Meyers through Serene Jones to Mahmoud Ayoub, and even including childhood mentors, my Sunday School teacher Dr. Earle Reid (who died during this project), my summer camp counselor Grant Chisholm, and my grade four teacher, Earle Brown. None of these or any of the others are responsible for aspects of the work that might be challenged, but to collaborating scholars as well as to all of these who did the "test driving" of this production, I owe a deep debt of gratitude.

Carleton United Church in St. Catharines, Ontario, provided time and collegial support for my work, in conjunction with an appointment by Niagara Presbytery of the United Church of Canada. Members of the congregation studied the manuscript chapters with friends from the synagogue of B'Nai Israel and the mosque of the Niagara Peninsula Islamic Society, again "test driving" the material. We studied under the leadership of Rabbi Eli Courante, who had been briefly chief rabbi of Siberia and All Eastern Russia before coming to Canada, and Imam Murtaza Najmudin. Dr. Najmudin's wife, Samah Marei, a scholar and author in her own right, had been my tutor in Islamic research beginning a decade ago, a role assumed more recently by Dr. Faud Sahin of Niagara-on-the-Lake—both of them dedicated to minimizing any egregious errors on my part relating to Muslim cultural application of Islamic principles.

Under the gracious aegis of Principal Mark Toulouse and with the involvement of senior and graduate students, Emmanuel College at the University of Toronto provided academic research and library support, meeting space and encouragement for this project as a complement to its pioneering interfaith developments, maintaining its own denominational roots and accreditation while also providing credibility and recognition for professional training of Muslim chaplains and academics. This development, in cooperation with sister seminaries (the Toronto School of Theology, the Canadian Yeshiva & Rabbinical School and the Centre for the Study of Religion), is taking place at a university where enrollments in religion classes in 2012 stand at three thousand students, as compared with well under one thousand in the year 2000—a token of the times.

During my brief tenure there in 2009, the faculty and students of St. Andrew's Theological College (Presbyterian) in Trinidad also contributed immensely to the research for this book as described in chapter 12. Mawlana Siddiq Nasir of the Ahlus Sunnah Wal Jama'ah Institute has been helpful in visiting my home in Niagara Falls and during my working visits to Trinidad.

It should be said here that support from the best scholarship in the world cannot relieve me from complete responsibility for the more speculative theses of this volume, such as that of Book One—that Zoroaster's monotheism was influenced by that of early Israeli exiles in his Scythian birthplace, which came full circle later in the Jewish-Zoroastrian interface in Babylon. Likewise for Book Two—that the Gospel reports of Jesus traveling in the countries we know as Lebanon, Syria and Jordan were related to possible contacts with Zoroastrian influences even further east—and Book Three—that the Quran has a Zoroastrian subtext similar to its amplifications of the Torah and the Gospel in which the monotheism of Jews and the messiahship of Jesus are confirmed.

My wife, Jenny Brown, is my associate in all things literary, and with her family's expatriate Indian worldview, as articulated to me by her late father, Bajnath Gosine, and her mother, Lily (Ram), it was she who convinced me to revisit and reexamine the view, widespread in India and elsewhere outside the West, that Jesus either visited India as a young man or was influenced by Buddhism, Zoroastrianism or both in those areas he visited beyond the borders of Israel. This tradition is usually spurned by Western Christians because their Scriptures make no direct mention of such travels during the three years of Jesus' ministry, but as we have seen, Jesus was engaged in more international travel than commonly recognized, as demonstrated by those very Scriptures. In that regard I also acknowledge the particular influence of three of my professors at McGill University some fifty years ago. Wilfred Cantwell Smith, Willard Gurdon Oxtoby and John Hatfield were all aware of the potential in the Jesus in India folklore, though while Oxtoby in particular mused about it aloud in class, none of them were yet prepared to develop this hypothesis.

Finally, I am particularly grateful to God for conversations with Mary Boyce in 2004 and especially in the winter of 2005 to 2006, only a few months before she died. As professor emerita at the School of African and Oriental Studies, University of London, and perhaps the world's leading authority in Zoroastrian studies, she recapitulated the controversy and scholarly debates concerning the dating of the life of Zoroaster and shared my pursuit of Zoroastrian echoes in the Quran. We had many lengthy and profitable conversations, and although she was bedridden toward the end, she remained kindly informative and enthusiastic. Those conversations form perhaps the perfect backdrop for much of this work.

prologue

The People of the Book

I S *THREE TESTAMENTS* A BIBLE THAT INCLUDES THE QURAN IN PLACE OF MAPS, CONCORDANCE, A STUDY guide or the Dead Sea Scrolls? Or is this the Quran, now prefaced by the previously revealed Scriptures that it purports to confirm, critique and amplify, instead of the usual copious footnotes about Hebrew and Christian Scriptures?[1] The answers are "neither," "both" and "something more than either."

The three testaments of Abraham, Sarah and Hagar's family are the sacred Scriptures of Judaism, Christianity and Islam. Obvious links between the three Scriptures include such things as revelations through the angel Gabriel in all three, the positioning of Matthew as a deliberate connector between the Hebrew and Christian Testaments, and the appearance of the Quran following Revelation at the end of the Christian Scriptures in the same apocalyptic style. Other links also manifest themselves.

The goal of this work is to develop mutual respect based on a reciprocated appreciation of Abraham's family Scriptures, published together for the first time, almost an antidote to the burning of the Quran. This book is a compendium of scriptures complete with commentary by reputable scholars, and background related to the latest findings on Scriptural context unfolding in the twenty first century.

the contributors

Ellen Frankel, herself a respected author, is editor emerita of the Jewish Publication Society, where, until recently, she was CEO and editor-in-chief for nearly twenty years. Henry Carrigan, senior editor at Northwestern University Press, is also an author and one of America's most highly regarded literary critics. Laleh Bakhtiar, having edited *The Encyclopedia of Islamic Law* and other compendia, has authored several books and is the acclaimed translator of *The Sublime Quran*. These three esteemed editors have written the prefaces to Book One, Book Two and Book Three, providing a perspective on each.

As among the most senior editors in their own traditions, they also took the lead in the careful selection of the three Jewish, Christian and Muslim scholars who have contributed substantial introductions to the three Scriptural texts. This was done to ensure the highest level of confidence in the three religious communities and by others addressed in this work.

First among these scholars is Professor Marc Zvi Brettler of Brandeis University, the editor of the *Oxford Jewish Study Bible*, who presents the "Introduction to the Torah." The "Introduction to the Gospel" in Book Two is presented by David Bruce, best known in Canada as the sole author of the four-volume *Jesus 24/7* series from the United Church Publishing House. The "Introduction to the Quran" is written by Nevin Reda, who holds an MA in biblical Hebrew language and literature, in addition to her PhD in Islamic studies from the University of Toronto, where Dr. Reda is the founding coordinator of the Muslim studies program at Emmanuel College. Shia and Sunni Muslim perspectives are represented in *Three Testaments*, as well as both liberal and more conservative Jewish views. Protestant positions are evident and Roman Catholic perspectives are here in the debut of David Bruce, writing now as a Catholic scholar.

the collaborators

This project was commissioned at a conference co-sponsored by seminaries and institutes from the three traditions at the Riverside Church in New York in 2009. The conference was called to consider this theme in embryonic form as presented in my earlier books, *Noah's Other Son* and *Forensic Scriptures*. Frankel, Carrigan and Bakhtiar were among the lead presenters, along with Amir Hussain, editor of the *Journal of the American Academy of Religion*. Over the three days I moderated six panels of six scholars each, for some two hundred conference participants. The panels included interfaith stalwarts such as Max Stackhouse, Ann Holmes Redding, Hussein Rashid, Phyllis Trible and Judith Plaskow, plus other outstanding presenters. Canadian Muslim feminist Raheel Raza led us in Muslim prayers on Friday evening; Rabbi Arthur Waskow presented a grandly inclusive Shabbat service on Saturday; and we all worshipped with the great Riverside Christian congregation on Sunday in an interfaith service.

In the final Sunday session of that conference I was encouraged to edit this book with an assurance that a significant community of scholars would be supportively involved. It was agreed from the outset that I would also write some chapters of commentary on the influence exerted by Zoroastrianism on all three monotheistic Scriptures, a newer discipline perhaps destined for a more significant role in the twenty-first century than is yet realized by many.

In that discussion, Professor Mahmoud Ayoub of Hartford initially objected to a possible "homogenization" of the Scriptures. Others shared his concern that a presentation of "parallel texts," or an emphasis on the harmony to be found, might obscure the richness in the differences, thus sacrificing the potential for growth in understanding we were seeking. Ayoub was answered by Professor Fred Weidmann, then director of the Center for Church Life and professor of biblical studies at Auburn Theological Seminary, who suggested that the book should appear in three parts, in which the sacred texts are close enough to appreciate the connection, but separate enough to achieve Ayoub's desire that they enhance our appreciation of their diversity. Hence the decision to publish as Book One, Book Two and Book Three, all within one volume but each with separate prefaces, contextual chapters, introductions, translator's notes and Scriptural texts.

Carol Meyers of Duke had spoken earlier of the common connections of all three traditions to literatures or revelations in pre-biblical times, which we applied then to the quest for a fuller understanding of the Zoroastrian role. Serene Jones, president of Union Theological Seminary, initiated the idea that judicious use of appropriate art and Islamic calligraphy could balance any predilection to excessive dependence on Western critical methods. Rod Hutton of Trinity Lutheran Seminary urged that we honor the place of the Septuagint version of the Hebrew Scriptures and indeed the spectrum of translations and versions. Whitney Bodman of the Austin Theological Seminary called for as much cross-referencing, footnoting and indexing as possible. Over the three years of work, these concerns have been taken into consideration in an ongoing online conversation.

The Global South was represented at that gathering by, among others, Principal Joy Abdul-Mohan of the St. Andrew's Theological College in Trinidad. She suggested that if the consultation were to continue online, some of her faculty and students should be included, since they had done significant background research in preparation for the conference. This led to support for an online collaboration including everyone present, later developed further with the inclusion of other nominees.

Some 270 scholars, students and laypeople from the three traditions participated as an online community of collaborating consultants, solving textual conundrums and other puzzles as we worked. As the publication date drew near and excitement mounted, this online community was invited to nominate additional colleagues. The final year included one thousand scholars, students and "monitors," some of whom just wished to be "along for the ride" but most finding themselves engaged at various levels.

Ellen Frankel raised questions about the book's bold title and gave her opinion from a Jewish perspective: "To Jews, the word *testament* usually conjures up the New Testament, whose appearance suddenly re-labeled our own Bible as the Old Testament (and implied that it had been superseded)." I and others are aware of the freight attached to the word *testaments*, but we have stuck with it in the hope that the name of the book might be seen as an appropriate challenge to any easy Christian assumptions, a challenge that a book from a Jewish or Muslim source alone could not make as credibly.

The subtitle is derived from the use of the Torah alone to represent the Hebrew Scriptures, as in the *Contemporary Torah*, which, like some other versions, stands on its own, much as the Torah does in synagogues where its scrolls are uniquely cherished in the *Aron Kodesh*, the Holy Ark of the Scrolls, from which they are paraded in the weekly Shabbat services. *Gospel* is a word that connotes the "good news" of God's love, sometimes referring to one of the first four books of the New Testament, but it is also used as a reference to the Christian Scriptures as a whole, as in this case. There is no other term to describe the Muslim Scriptures except *Quran*, "the recitation."

Three Testaments does facilitate an articulation of the views that the Torah is basic or fundamental, that the Gospel is a unique and special revelation, and that the Quran is final and complete, confirming the truths of both, and other revelations as well. For Jews, the Word of God is embodied in the living community of the covenant. For Christians the Living Word is embodied in Jesus Christ. For Muslims, both positions are confirmed in the Quran in a manner we hope to elucidate. The ways in which these traditions can inform and assist each other is elaborated as part of the essence of this project.

the texts

Readers do not need to read every word of each Scripture in order to fully engage the *Three Testaments* as a book. We would hope that many have done so previously and that others will do so in the future, perhaps encouraged to consider the twenty-first-century versions included in this compendium. This book presents the full texts of these three Scriptures together as a "statement" regarding the intimate connection among them, possibly the most spiritually significant trilogy in history.

There are two recognized methods of translation, known as *formal equivalence* and *dynamic equivalence*.[2] The first requires the translator to use the nearest linguistic equivalent words in translating the original text into another language. The second conveys the essential thought or idea of a sentence or paragraph in words and images understood by readers but divorced from cultural mores of the past, if they appear to distort or detract from the essential meaning of the passage.

Suppose a writer today used a figurative phrase like "hit a home run," and years from now that author's book was to be translated into the language of people who had never heard of baseball. The translator might render the words exactly as they are, which would be a correct formal equivalence but make little sense. Alternatively, the translator might be more true to the original meaning by using a culturally equivalent phrase like "succeeded spectacularly," a dynamic equivalent interpretation. The first method may sometimes produce a translation that is technically accurate but somewhat stilted, while the second relies more on the translator's prayerful perspective and may be dated in its application to the time, place and circumstances of the translator and the intended readership. For these and other reasons, we offer here two versions of each Scripture under consideration. We begin with the most trusted twentieth-century scholarly versions in the extensive quotations found in the chapters and essays. We then present newer versions produced by the best twenty-first-century scholarship to date in the full-text versions to show some of the directions in which these three religions are moving in relation to understanding and applying their Scriptures.

Accordingly, the "scholarly" quotations from the Hebrew Scriptures in Book One of this volume are from the widely respected 1985 Tanakh translation of the Torah, published by the Jewish

Publication Society,[3] while the full-text version presented here is that of 2006 in *The Contemporary Torah: A Gender-Sensitive Adaptation of the JPS Translation*.

Permission was granted by the National Council of Churches of Christ (USA) for our use of the New Revised Standard Version (NRSV) of the New Testament, which is the established standard in the academic community. We use that version in Book Two,[4] but for the full text we present the New Testament from *The Inclusive Bible* of 2007, which unabashedly uses dynamic equivalence in the matter of removing the diversionary gender bias, except where gender is the point of the text. Both the NRSV and the more conservative New International Version had made progress in the matter of gender inclusion late in the twentieth century, mainly by "spot cleaning" the excessive use of male pronouns, but *The Inclusive Bible* from Sheed & Ward moves the matter to a new level. Rather than "spot clean" for extraneous male pronouns, *The Inclusive Bible* purposes to "re-image" the scriptures in a true dynamic equivalence, and it succeeds admirably in doing so.

A similar inclusive agenda may be found in our selection of Islamic Scriptures, although the movement here is from the dynamic equivalence of earlier "interpretations" to support for a progressive position actually based on formal equivalence, which is harder for literalists to argue against. Accordingly, Book Three contains quotes from the 1938 edition of *The Holy Qur'an* by Yusuf Ali, beloved by Muslims and perhaps the most familiar version for Jews and Christians who have read the Quran. The full-text portion presents the 2011 English translation of *The Sublime Quran*, a Kazi (USA) publication. Yusuf Ali's older interpretation was a dynamic equivalent translation, through his generous addition of (bracketed) phrases in mid-sentence, supplemented by several thousand footnotes, presenting both the scholarly opinions and the devotional instincts of the translator. Yet in the twenty-first century, perhaps surprisingly, it is formal equivalence that is used by Laleh Bakhtiar to make the radical point, for example, that Quran 4:34 has been mistranslated for centuries, when it instructs men to "beat" their wives as a last resort in disputes. Her incisive exegesis of other uses of this controversial word from within the Quran, and then from other Arabic writing of an early time, confirms an alternative translation, based on a formal equivalence of the words in question. In this key verse, Dr. Bakhtiar's translation finds its place in history as she provides textual evidence that the traditional interpretation is simply wrong linguistically and philologically, suggesting that the error may be based on very early cultural perversions of pronouncing the text prior to the addition of diacritical marks.

The translator's notes are excerpted from the separate original publications, but they present an unexpected harmony of agendas within the progressive elements of all three communities. For those used to the phrase *Judeo-Christian*, we introduce the term *Judeo-X-Islamic* (*juDAYO-chrisLAMic*), asking Christians to accept the ancient *X* monogram as standing for Christian. Scholarly readers will be familiar with the formal distinctions between the Near East, Middle East and Far East, but for the convenience of the general reader we have designated the area from Egypt to Afghanistan, including Turkey, as the more familiar "Middle East." We drop "Near East" as archaic in reference to North Africa, and we refer to the former "Far East" as the Orient and South Asia. In this we accept the judgment of the late Edward Saïd that such terms denote a Eurocentric "orientalism" of the nineteenth century, although the term *Middle East* seems destined to endure.

A similar awkwardness pertains to the use of the term *Western*, since Islam is usually described as one of the religions of "Western monotheism" and both Europe and North America now have sizable Muslim populations. However, while all three of these religions originated on the Asian side of the tiny "hinge" of three continents, Judaism and Christianity have a longer history in Europe and the Western hemisphere, giving their traditions a "Western" label in the context of scholarship that is difficult to avoid. So in a few instances where we might usefully experiment with such a term, we "test drive" the phrase *Middle West* to denote these traditional Western perspectives prior to the recent westward expansion of Islam. We recognize also that Christianity now has a "non-Western" majority in its membership, and that Judaism itself has relocated its center of gravity to the east of this great divide.

Finally, with respect to the texts, let us again reiterate the value of the reader downloading the two charts associated with this study. They may be obtained free from www.BrianArthurBrown. com. *A Diagram of the Sources of the Pentateuch* is the result of 130 years of research by Jewish and Christian scholars, though the chart itself has been evolving in my hands for just fifty years. The identification of sources on that chart is based primarily on the work of Stanley B. Frost, former dean of graduate studies at McGill University. Just after his one hundredth birthday in 2013, he renewed permission for this work found in his 1960 publication, *The Beginning of the Promise*, though his model has been modestly supplemented by suggested updates of the documentary hypothesis by Richard Elliott Friedman, *The Anchor Bible*, *The Interpreters Bible* and others. In contrast, research for *A Diagram of Previous Revelations Confirmed in the Quran*, still in early stages of refinement by experts, is based on my own work, initially assisted by faculty and students of St. Andrew's Theological College in Trinidad in 2009.

the "z" factor

If any or all of these religions actually do have an "Old Testament," it might be the Zoroastrian Scriptures, known as the Avesta, which is something of a subtext in the contextual background chapters in this volume. The discovery (by Muslim folk) of the Dead Sea Scrolls opened a new era in the study of Hebrew Scriptures, and the discovery of the Nag Hammadi Library (again by Muslims) reopened the question of the relationship between the Christian Scriptures and Gnosticism. In a similar way, the key to our understanding, and a principal feature of this compendium, is the current and ongoing "unearthing" of lost material from the Zoroastrian Avesta, much of it buried between the lines of the Quran. In this instance, Jews and Christians are involved in the search. The Rosetta Stone, erected in Memphis, Egypt, in 196 BCE on behalf of King Ptolemy V, was used in 1799 by Napoleon's expedition to crack the code of ancient Egyptian hieroglyphics by comparing its three inscriptions in hieroglyphic, proto-Coptic and Greek scripts. Zoroastrianism might now be seen as a "Rosetta Stone" key to a deeper understanding of the three texts before us in this study.

The hardcover version of *Three Testaments* was well received in almost all quarters, but several reviewers expressed initial surprise at "the amount of ink" expended on the Zoroastrian connection in a book about the Torah, the Gospel and the Quran. By actual word count, this book is 70 percent Hebrew, Christian and Muslim Scripture (in approximately equal thirds), 15 percent commentary by learned colleagues, about 10 percent my study of linkages, and just 5 percent Zoroastrian. Much of the Z material is near the beginning of the book, so the bewilderment of critics is understandable. Some slight restructuring attends this new printing.

Though presented as having significant value in contextualizing all three Scriptures, Zoroastrianism is but a subtext in this volume. It is the third of three principal elements that are (1) the texts of the three Scriptures themselves, (2) the exposition of their meaning, purpose and value in the three religious communities and (3) considerations of the influence of Zoroaster as the progenitor of the Axial Age. In Book One we consider the late dates now increasingly accepted for Zoroaster (628–551 BCE), suggesting that his often-vaunted monotheism, coming hundreds of years after Moses, was derived from Israelite exiles in his Scythian-Azerbaijani birthplace. In Book Two, in a manner similar to recent reconsideration of information about early Christianity in the Gnostic Gospels, we reassess ancient legends that Jesus traveled the Silk Road to India during his "missing years," postulating that his travels at least into Syrian Zoroastrian territory, as recorded in the Gospels,[5] may have had more significance than has been traditionally understood. In Book Three we use a traditional Muslim understanding of the Quran as confirming, critiquing and amplifying previous revelations, noting how the Zoroastrian Avesta possibly foreshadows the Quran, both positively and negatively, in much the same manner as the Hebrew and Christian Scriptures.

As a major religion, Zoroastrianism is little known because its Persian base became almost completely Islamicized in the ninth and tenth centuries CE. Although much Zoroastrian material has otherwise disappeared, it would now appear that significant portions of the Quran were also revealed earlier in the Zoroastrian Avesta, and may now be recovered there. Parsees in India, Iran, the United Kingdom, Australia and North America use hundreds of ancient Zoroastrian hymns. Computer-generated analyses appear to reveal word clusters found in these scriptural hymns that may correlate with certain sections in a manner consistent with a traditional Muslim understanding of the origins of the Quran. Such material had been "previously revealed" and was embedded in Middle Eastern lore, to be revealed again to Muhammad (as opposed to being copied) in a fresh, correct and evocative manner.

Zoroastrianism has enjoyed a certain vogue status in recent years, and it is frequently cited as the world's first monotheistic religion by those who mistakenly date its origins to a time before Moses, or even well before Abraham. Because so much of its history was obliterated, first by Alexander the Great and then, after its dualistic revival, by the rise of Islam, Zoroastrianism's origins and theology have perplexed many. Competing claims and theories about Zoroaster's birth date and birthplace; his teachings; the conversion of his patron, King Vishtaspa; his relationship to Vishtaspa's son, Darius I (a successor to Cyrus the Great, both of whom might well have known this prophet); and the number of his marriages and children are all tentatively but neatly resolved by the unifying principles of the theses of this book, supported by new evidence of correlation within the three testaments themselves, which will be exhibited as the story unfolds.

Words freighted with specific theological meaning and particular phrases first seen in the Zoroastrian Avesta can now be correlated with similar or identical words, phrases and verses in the Torah, the Gospel and the Quran, a phenomenon we designate as "the Z factor." For years, Torah scholars using some version of the popular "documentary hypothesis" have gone through the first five books of the Hebrew Scriptures with a degree of confidence, identifying those verses that came from "P" (the priestly source), "D" (the Deuteronomist) or the earliest sources, "J" and "E." New Testament scholars can likewise go through the Gospels of Matthew and Luke, underlining passages identified as "Q" (an early church document many believe they both used) with some confidence.

As a result of this study, future students may be able to identify the Z-related passages, as, for example, when Isaiah directly answers specific questions posed by Zoroaster, when Leviticus opens with ten chapters introducing fire sacrifices (including "perpetual fire" on the altar, unique in the Torah), or when Ezekiel prophesies in a "valley of dry bones,[6]" an area where Zoroastrians were bleaching the bones of the dead according to their tradition (as Jenny Rose suggests in her book, Zoroastrianism[7]), unless the Jews had by then adopted the practice themselves. In gospel passages, Jesus defines the Messiah as more like the Zoroastrian "Savior of the World" than the one who would restore the throne of Israel, and in the Quran, Muhammad hears God's voice confirming the pristine monotheistic prophecies of Zoroaster. Like recent "Green Bibles" with God's commands to protect the creation printed in green, or "red letter" editions of the New Testament highlighting the words of Jesus, we considered printing the Z passages of *Three Testaments* in bold, but we concluded that our hypotheses need refinement before offering such a graphic presentation. We offer Z passages from the Avesta itself in paraphrases with a modern ring to them, designed to evoke the same excitement in contemporary readers that they must have done for many in the Axial Age of the ancient world, from Buddha and Plato to Isaiah, Jesus and Muhammad.

apología

No author could consider publishing the three "Abrahamic" Scriptures together today, with his or her own background commentary, without input and validation from commentators, scholars and editors of high reputation in all three faith communities. From the beginning I have been supported and guided in this work by leading Jewish, Christian and Muslim academics, as acknowledged above. Their endorsements of my work and the contributions by these commentators of renown not only authenticate this project for Jewish, Christian, Muslim and other readers but also free me to offer my own personal faith perspective as part of the integrity of the work, without disguising my own position behind a facade of "objective scholarship." Though I am also eager to acknowledge the enrichment of my faith perspective through a growing appreciation of Jewish and Muslim perceptions, it is rare for an author of this type of work to be given such personal license by colleagues from obviously diverse viewpoints. I trust that readers will find the confidence of my colleagues is not misplaced as I express personal convictions as well as scholarly observations in the context of mutual respect. But while I acknowledge and appreciate the frank freedom my colleagues have given me in the privilege of expressing my own religious convictions in the sections in which I am the author, I believe they are unanimous in recognizing that, as editor of their sections, I have given them the same opportunity. We believe we are providing a new model for relationships appropriate to the twenty-first century, sharing with humility and listening with respect.

book one

TORAH

King Solomon Supervises Construction of the First Temple in Jerusalem

preface to the torah

Ellen Frankel

"In the beginning, two thousand years before the heaven and the earth, seven things were created: [first] the Torah, written with black fire on white fire, and lying in the lap of God."[1]

"God consulted the Torah and created the world."[2]

S O CENTRAL IS THE TORAH TO JEWISH LIFE AND TRADITION THAT IT HAS BECOME SYNONYMOUS with Judaism itself. Although the word generally refers to a specific book—also known as the Five Books of Moses and the Pentateuch—it also functions as metaphor, symbol and metonym, the trademark and crest of the Jewish people. Dating back some 2,500 years as a unitary written work and many centuries before that as a valued legacy of oral traditions, the Torah has served the Jewish people in many capacities: as constitution, foundational covenant, divine-human wedding contract, national narrative, ritual operating manual, lexicon and grammar, educational curriculum and moral guidebook.

For much of its history, the Torah—as interpreted by Jews—has remained essentially unfamiliar to two of its daughter religions, Christianity and Islam. In part, this is a consequence of prejudice and religious triumphalism, which for centuries marginalized Jewish and other minority cultures and communities. But the Jewish community also contributed to its own cultural segregation as a way to safeguard itself from the threat of cultural absorption by the host societies. In modern times, a new peril has emerged—critical Bible scholarship—that threatens to undermine historic devotional attitudes toward sacred texts.

This current volume is meant to mitigate these threats: first, by presenting each faith tradition on its own terms; second, by highlighting kinship rather than contention among the Scriptures; and third, by addressing the issues of critical scholarship within a purely religious context. So, for example, in the case of Jewish tradition, what the Christian community calls the "Old Testament" is here called by its normative Jewish names—the Hebrew Bible or Tanakh (a Hebrew acronym referring to the three traditional divisions of the Hebrew Bible—Torah, Prophets and Writings). By renaming the Hebrew Bible the "Old" as opposed to the "New" Testament, Christianity effectively appropriated the authority of Jewish Scripture, supplanting it with its own new covenant. Now, two thousand years later, this volume serves as a needed corrective to this ancient displacement.

By publishing the Torah in the authoritative English translation of the Jewish Publication Society, alongside the sacred Scriptures of Christianity and Islam, this volume also acknowledges the unique identities of these three holy texts. True, the Torah emerged first, passing on some of its own

DNA to three branching traditions: Zoroastrianism, Christianity and Islam. Indeed, by situating Zoroaster in the seventh century BCE, Brian Arthur Brown proposes Zoroastrian monotheism as the earliest of what are actually Judaism's three "daughter" religions, along with Christianity and Islam, at least in terms of time lines regarding the adoption of monotheism in the respective texts. Once transmitted, that material took on a destiny of its own within each new scriptural context, and it must be read by that tradition's interpretive protocols. Though separated by as much as a thousand years, each Scripture serves as the rootstock of its own faith tradition.

Unlike the classic works of ancient Near Eastern cultures—the Epic of Gilgamesh, the Law of Hammurabi, the Hymn to Inanna,[3] and other literature of Sumer, Akkad, Ugarit, Babylonia and Canaan—the Torah has survived as living Scripture for twenty-five centuries and remains the core text of Judaism to this day. Even in this digital age, Jews continue to chant, just as their ancestors did, from an unvocalized, handwritten parchment scroll of the Torah during worship services three times every week and on all Jewish holidays. Every time the Torah scroll is returned to the Holy Ark after being read, the congregation stands and sings the verse from Proverbs 3:18: "She [the Torah] is a tree of life to all who hold fast to it, and all of its supporters are happy."

Throughout the world, synagogue websites post weekly the Torah portion (lectionary reading) for the coming Sabbath. Many rabbis, teachers, leaders and even congregants blog about the weekly portion online. In thousands of pulpits, thirteen-year-old boys and girls offer their own interpretations of the weekly Torah reading as they become bar and bat mitzvah. Rabbis of all stripes base their sermons on the weekly portion, as do members of numerous Jewish nonprofit boards. At a time of increasing balkanization within the Jewish world, one common thread continues to unite all Jews the world over: the Torah. The calendar of Torah readings is universally synchronized—in Brooklyn, Buenos Aires, Katmandu and Jerusalem.

To paraphrase the Russian Jewish writer, Ahad Ha'am, who once wrote that "more than the Jews have kept the Sabbath, the Sabbath has kept the Jews," history has proven that the Torah has kept the Jews alive. Even the most marginal Jews, if they connect at all with formal Judaism, will inevitably encounter the Torah—a few of its words at a bar mitzvah or wedding, a passage from the Haggadah at a Seder, an epitaph on a Jewish gravestone.

The Torah has served both as a central organizing principle of Jewish culture and as a symbol of Judaism itself. Through these two means, the Torah has kept Judaism and the Jewish people alive during two thousand years of exile. How has this been accomplished?

Although the ancient rabbis of Israel and Babylonia did not want to serve as religious innovators, history gave them no choice. In 70 CE, the Roman Empire destroyed every institution essential to Jewish life: the Holy Temple with its sacrificial system and priestly infrastructure; the city of Jerusalem, royal and economic capital of Israel; the sanctuary of a homeland, complete with language and culture; a measure of political and legal autonomy. To weather this national catastrophe, called in Jewish tradition the *churban* (Hebrew for "total destruction"), the handful of rabbis who remained in Israel after the Roman conquest invented a radical survival strategy. Their secret weapon was the biblical prooftext.

A prooftext is nothing more than a citation from the Bible, mustered to validate a rabbi's statement or argument. The rabbis endowed that citation with extraordinary authority. Based on the creative fiction that their own religious innovations and reinterpretations were not new but rather originated in the Bible, they set about redesigning biblical Judaism to suit the new postchurban realities. Practically all Jews of the twenty-first century are Rabbinic Jews, heirs to the new Judaism created by these rabbis. The only pre-Rabbinic Jews who still survive—although they long ago diverged from the Jewish mainstream—are a few thousand Karaites, living primarily in Europe, Israel and the San Francisco Bay Area, who rejected the Talmud in the eighth century.

The genius of the ancient rabbis was to recognize that the Torah must remain the indisputable foundation of Jewish law and tradition but that it had to change to meet the changing needs of its adherents. By anchoring their own readings, stories, legislation, moral teachings and ideas with authoritative biblical prooftexts, the rabbis provided continuity to the scattered people of Israel. Fashioning a portable Judaism out of linked texts and stories, they ensured that the inevitable diversity born out of diaspora—cultural, linguistic, culinary, musical and sociological—would not fragment the Jewish people. The Torah would act as a unifying force, providing a framework for a dynamic, ever-changing supranational culture.

As a result of the rabbis' bold gambit, Judaism and the Jewish people continued to thrive and develop in exile, accommodating controversy, diverse points of view, intellectual creativity and religious flexibility—all because of the canny stratagem of the prooftext. As long as all Jews could claim a common patrimony, the Torah, they could regard themselves as members of the same family, descended from the same clan.

Between the seventh and eleventh centuries CE, a dedicated group of scribes known as the Masoretes (from *masorah*, meaning "tradition") centered in Tiberias and strengthened the rabbis' plan by stabilizing and standardizing the Torah text by adding vowels, cantillation marks, punctuation, decorative crowns, mysterious dots and readers' notes to the unadorned ancient text. Today there exist two rival variant manuscripts of the Masoretic Bible, known as the Aleppo Codex and the Leningrad Codex, but their differences are minimal, and they mostly involve punctuation. Recently, a new edition of the Masoretic text, known as the Jerusalem Crown, has been published in Israel, which artfully merges Aleppo and Leningrad (along with a few other variant manuscripts). This edition appears to be on its way to being recognized, at least in Israel, as *the* authoritative text of the Hebrew Bible, supplanting earlier codices.

A more serious challenge to the Torah's continuing role as unifying principle has come in modern times. The documentary hypothesis, which disputes the single authorship of the Five Books, threatens to create a rift between traditional and liberal branches of Judaism. After two thousand years, it seems that the rabbis' ingenious stratagem is being put to the test.

The rabbis themselves were careful to make a distinction between their own authority and that of Scripture, which is why their idea of the prooftext so quickly gained acceptance in the Jewish community. They asserted that a teaching that was *d'oraita*, "from the Torah," overrode that which was *de-rabbanan*, the teachings of the rabbis. No Jewish figure of authority openly dared to question the divine character of the Torah, which according to Jewish tradition was dictated whole and perfect to Moses at Sinai.

But beginning in the seventeenth century with Baruch Spinoza, Thomas Hobbes and others and fully developed in the nineteenth century by Julius Wellhausen and German Higher Criticism, European scholars began to unravel the documentary strands making up the Hebrew Bible, claiming evidence of multiple hands at work. It was not long before certain German Jewish intellectuals followed suit, leading to a schism within the Jewish community—and the birth of Orthodox and Reform branches of Judaism. Today that rift continues to widen, although there is also some movement the other way as many traditional Jews are exposed to critical Bible scholarship in college and through the media. The jury is still out as to whether the Torah can continue its historic role as unifier. If it cannot, it is possible that the Jewish people will splinter as never before.

In the minds and hearts of the Jewish people, the Torah is much more than a precious document. It is also a sacred talisman. Throughout the generations, Jews have risked and sometimes given their lives in order to teach the Torah or to save Torah scrolls from desecration. According to Jewish tradition, ten revered Talmudic sages, among them the great Rabbi Akiva, defied Hadrian's decree in the second century CE against teaching the Torah and were publicly martyred. One of the ten, Hananiah ben Teradyon, was burned alive wrapped in a Torah scroll, crying out in death that he saw the Hebrew letters flying up to heaven.

During the Crusades in the twelfth century, the Spanish Inquisition in the fifteenth and countless pogroms throughout Europe since then, Jews risked and sometimes gave their lives to save Torah scrolls. During World War II, the Nazis seized more than 1,500 Torah scrolls from Jewish communities, intending to display them in Hitler's infamous "Museum of an Extinct Race" in Prague.

Now most of these "Holocaust Torahs" serve as memorials in synagogues throughout the world, proxies for whole communities destroyed.

But it is as a positive symbol, a Tree of Life, that the Torah is most often regarded. In the Jewish worship service, the Torah is arrayed as royalty, dressed in a velvet mantle, silver crown and breastplate, and bearing a silver scepter ending in a miniature human hand, which readers use to follow the lines in the parchment scroll as they chant. When the scroll is taken out of the ark and again when it is returned, it is marched around the sanctuary in a royal procession. As the Torah passes by, congregants salute or kiss it; no one sits until the scroll is set down. At the end of the Torah service, a congregant raises the open scroll aloft for all to see, and another dresses it for its recessional to the ark.

Another sign of communal reverence for the Torah's physical body is the manner in which a new Torah is written. Jewish law prescribes precise rules for preparing the sheets of parchment, making the quill and ink, and the calligraphy of the Hebrew words. The trained scribe, who spends up to eighteen months writing a Torah scroll, must not only be accomplished in scribal skills but must also be pious and learned. If the scribe makes a mistake when writing the name of God, the entire sheet of parchment must be cut out of the scroll and buried; a new sheet is then sewn in and a new text penned.

Tradition dictates the precise shape of each letter. Illustrations or artistic decorations are strictly forbidden, except for a prescribed set of special markings. Among the 304,805 letters contained in a Torah scroll are about one hundred letters that are nonstandard in size, placement, or orientation. These special characters must be reproduced exactly. In addition, seven letters of the Hebrew alphabet are decorated with three-pronged "crowns" known as *tagim*, which are found only in the handwritten scroll, not in printed editions of the Torah. Finally, there are ten places in the Torah (and five more in the other two divisions of the Bible) where a mysterious series of dots is added above or below certain Hebrew words. An ancient tradition dating back almost two thousand years, the meaning of these unusual features remains a mystery to this day.

The rabbis well understood the need to balance a reverence for immutable Scripture with the need for interpretation and new understandings of ancient teachings. And so, as much as Jews have respected the Torah and preserved every jot and tittle in the parchment scroll, they have also been encouraged to add their own readings to the text so that it remains intelligible and usable in their own lives.

A well-known midrash illustrates the rabbis' thinking about this balancing act:

> When Moses ascended Mount Sinai to receive the Torah, he found God busy decorating the letters of the Torah with elaborate crowns. He asked God what these crowns meant.
>
> God told him, "In later years there shall live a man named Akiva, who will fashion a mountain of laws based on every dot crowning these letters." Moses said, "Show me this man!"
>
> So God transported Moses to the classroom of Rabbi Akiva, and he took a seat on one of the back benches. He listened to the master and his students discussing the law, but could not follow a word they said.
>
> One of the students asked Rabbi Akiva, "Master, how do you know that this is so?"
>
> Akiva replied, "This is the law given to Moses on Mount Sinai."

In this simple and ironic tale, the ancient rabbis reveal their sophisticated understanding of the dynamic of constancy and change in religious tradition. Clearly, Akiva was inventing something new, but he knew he needed to root it in the old. And so, he called upon Moses's authority to bolster his own, and in so doing, appropriated the former's authority as his own. Yet this midrash is not intended to demonstrate the cleverness of the rabbis at the Torah's expense. Rather, we are meant to learn from it that we own the past as much as it owns us, and that only in dialogue and dialectic with it do we honor those who came before us.

This volume is designed to encourage members of three faith traditions to read each other's Scriptures and to open a dialogue between their own Scripture and those of other traditions. Although Jews and Christians have been studying each other's sacred texts for centuries, especially in more recent times, neither community knows very much about the Quran. Nor are today's Muslims generally familiar with the Hebrew Bible and the New Testament in their own right. This project holds great promise to advance the cause of interfaith understanding.

I feel privileged to participate in this current groundbreaking project. *Three Testaments* has the potential to break down walls and to launch a fruitful dialogue among members of three great world religions. The last time such a three-way conversation happened was during the so-called Golden Age of Spain, in the period known as *La Convivencia* ("The Coexistence," which occurred between the tenth and twelfth centuries), when Jews, Christians and Muslims lived together in relative harmony, fraternizing with each other, studying and even writing books together. The world is long overdue for a reprise.

Let me end with an ancient teaching from the Talmud. Commenting on the constant legal quarreling between the students of Hillel and those of his rival Shammai, the rabbis state that Hillel and Shammai always argued "for the sake of heaven"—that is, to achieve the highest good—which is why both their viewpoints will last forever. Boldly, the rabbis declare, *"Elu v'elu divrei Elohim hayim"* ("The words of both are those of the living God").4 So, too, are the words in this book. May we who engage with them do so for the sake of heaven.

Nebuchadnezzar Pardons Jeremiah during the Prophet's Visit to Exiles in Babylon

1

also sprach zarathustra

S PORTIONS OF THE HEBREW TORAH WERE BEING EDITED BY PRUDENT AND PIOUS SCHOLARS IN Jerusalem during the sixth century BCE, word of these developments may have triggered ramifications among Israelites exiled earlier (740–722 BCE) by Assyria. This may have produced a chain of events that expanded the eventual reach of certain Torah teachings to the whole world, Christian and Muslim, Hindu and Buddhist, philosophical and humanistic, from Greece to China. From the ancient Babylonian Talmud and early Arab Christian records to Arnold Toynbee speculating in the twentieth century, there are hints that Jewish prophets and profiteers both visited these exiles. A recent consensus on Zoroaster's birthplace and dates, summarized below, suggests the possibility of a convergence with a significance only now recognized, in which the Hebrew prophet Jeremiah might be one of the pivotal figures.

The word of the LORD came to me:
Before I created you in the womb, I selected you;
Before you were born, I consecrated you;
I appointed you a prophet concerning the nations.

I replied: Ah, LORD God!
I don't know how to speak, for I am still a boy.
And the LORD said to me: Do not say, "I am still a boy,"
But go wherever I send you and speak whatever I command you.
Have no fear, for I am with you to deliver you.[1]

Our story begins around 610 BCE in Scythia (today's Azerbaijan), the birthplace of Zoroaster in 628 BCE, where Israelite exiles had settled down, intermarried and were possibly beginning to lose their religion. Jeremiah is well known as a prophet of Judah, and specifically to Jerusalem, but there could be more to his career than is found in the Scriptural record. Born about 646 BCE, he began to prophesy in Jerusalem in 626 BCE, but we do not know much about his activities until he was joined mid-career by his secretary, Baruch, in 605. By then he already possessed some knowledge about Scythians, as reflected in his later prophetic utterances, and a passion about exiles that led him to travel and prophesy among Judah's own exiles in later times in Babylon and Egypt. Indeed, Jeremiah seems fixated on the threat of exile hanging over Judah from the time he appears in Scripture. He may have known the implications of that danger from firsthand observations earlier in Scythia.

The LORD said: I have abandoned my people,
I have deserted my precious possession, the people I have loved.

I have given over My dearly beloved into the hands of her enemies.
My own people acted toward Me like a lion in the forest;
She raised her voice against me—therefore I rejected her in those days.[2]

We cannot yet know with any certainty which prophet might have taken a scroll of the JE Torah document to the exiles. Richard Elliott Friedman, among current scholars, is persuasive in *Who Wrote the Bible* when he argues that the northern Israelite E document had been brought south to Jerusalem after the Assyrian deportations. There it was edited into the southern J document by Levite refugees who used this joint edition of Hebrew history and religious experience as their entrée into southern Jewish society. The exiles may have already been familiar with JE long before a copy of Deuteronomy was discovered in Jerusalem during a 658 temple renovation, a scroll of speeches by Moses, memorized and handed down by the Levites, something still practiced with startling expertise in the Middle East.

It seems relatively likely that a scribe or a prophet might have taken it upon himself to deliver a copy of the Deuteronomy scroll to the exiles, to encourage them to keep the faith. Although the trip to the Scythian region of the Assyrian Empire is a two-month journey on foot, such journeys were not unusual in ancient times. Zoroaster appears to have spent his teen years training for the Vedic priesthood, and our study opens with us picturing him possibly sitting among a crowd of Israelite in-laws or friends around a campfire, listening to a spellbinding prophet from far away.

Hear, O Israel. The LORD our God is one. Love the LORD your God
with all your heart, with all your soul and with all your strength.
Take to heart these instructions with which I charge you this day.
Impress them upon your children and recite them when you stay at home,
When you are away, when you lie down and when you get up.[3]

Given his now accepted dates and birthplace, we should be open to the possibility that in such circumstances Zoroaster first heard of One God who rules the universe, and the invitation and responsibility to join that God in the fight between good and evil, neither idea being current in the communal religion of his Vedic ancestors. Understanding how Zoroaster may have digested this inspiring message and later preached it from one end of the Silk Road to the other sets the stage for a new appreciation of events in the Axial Age.

Thus said the LORD: Inquire among the nations.
Who has heard of what has transpired in olden times?
Maiden Israel has done a most horrible thing.
But who would go beyond Lebanon's snow to these mountain rocks?
Does anyone abandon the cool waters of the Jordan for this desert?[4]

Hebrew monotheism had been in the air throughout neighboring nations since the time of Moses, and the activities of a prophet like Jeremiah may well have included such addresses to Israelites exiled by Assyria a hundred years earlier. Many were then living in communities eventually absorbed into the Median Empire, as mentioned in Zoroaster's own story in the Avesta. Twentieth-century historian Arnold J. Toynbee said of Zoroaster that "we cannot say for certain whether his religious discovery was independent . . . or whether his voice was a mere echo of the cry of forgotten Israelite prophets who had been marooned in the cities of the Medes."[5]

The LORD commanded me to thus warn the people of God in Jerusalem.
They say to me: "Where is the prediction of the LORD? Let it come to pass."[6]
But you here know these things. The utterance of my lips is ever before you.
And now the LORD God of Israel calls out to you to return to him alone.
It is to you, O Israel among the nations, that God has sent me in mercy and love.

The Scriptural evidence for a direct connection of Jeremiah to Zoroaster's homeland is slender, but such a link would help explain several features of his prophetic corpus. Israel's lamenting prophet had something of a fixation with the exiles, wherever they were, visiting many such communities, as attested by several references in Scripture. He even prophesied that if the Northern and Southern Kingdoms of Israel and Judah reunited, they would be rejoined by the exiles from "the north."[7] He also demonstrated personal knowledge of the Scythians when he describes "rising waters of the north," their ability and possible interest in flooding the enemies of Israel with "galloping steeds and rumbling chariots."[8] By Jeremiah's time, many exiles may have intermarried with the Scythians in northern Assyria, Media and elsewhere, so Zoroaster may have even had Israelite relatives.

Jeremiah did have a calling to prophesy to the nations, but such allusions are more easily understood when the references to "nations" are understood as including the tribes of Israel in various configurations: the northern nation, the southern nation, the nation in Assyrian exile, the nation in Babylon and the nation in Egypt. Moreover, throughout his ministry, Jeremiah exhibits a longing for Ephraim, the "tribe" that eventually came to stand for the Israelite diaspora, mentioned in seven of his prophecies. His father, Hilkiah, was from the tribe of Benjamin, on the border between the Northern and Southern Kingdoms. He was appointed high priest in Jerusalem, perhaps to consolidate the divided loyalties of Benjamin, next to Ephraim in geography and, after the Assyrian exile, next to Ephraim in the hearts of Hilkiah's people. After he "found" the scroll of Deuteronomy during the temple renovations, did Hilkiah pass a passion to his son to share this treasure with the exiles? Indeed, Jeremiah's whole prophetic ministry, which is known to us only after Baruch began to write it up in 605 BCE, suddenly looks quite different if we imagine that he prophesied among the earlier exiles. Once the idea is contemplated, the stamp of his northern experience is clearly seen in his later prophecies. The arc of his message now takes on a new trajectory, with a quality of completeness.

> The LORD roars from on high, He makes His voice heard from His holy dwelling:
> He roars aloud over His earthly abode, shouting to dwellers of the earth afar.
> Thus said the LORD: I will be God to all the clans of Israel, and they shall be My people.
> Those who escaped from the sword have found favor in the wilderness.
> I continue My grace to you. I will build you firmly again, O Maiden Israel.[7]

Jeremiah's speech to the exiles, as imagined above, would have been revolutionary in the polytheistic ancient world, and it begs for us to imagine the passion of the prophet and the potential impact on the listeners. Did he read from the scroll? Did he rehearse the Shema with them again and again? Did they ask questions? Was the sense of individual responsibility in the commandments as new to the descendants of the exiles as to the in-laws and neighbors who came with them to the campfire? Did Jeremiah elaborate on the commandments and explain that, in addition to communal religious duty, God expects individuals to take personal responsibility in the fight against evil?

Was there a student for the priesthood in the crowd, an eighteen-year-old who could not sleep when he got home? Given the meshing of their dates, as we now understand the overlap, it is entirely possible that a teenage Zoroaster could have heard Jeremiah, his elder contemporary, preaching the monotheistic faith and issuing a plea for the descendents of the exiles to return to their homeland. At a minimum, he might have heard the thirty-year-old prophet urging them to keep the faith and rededicate themselves to obeying God's commandments, perhaps especially those ten commandments uniquely directed toward individuals.

The appeal of monotheism could well have had significance at a time when young Zoroaster was deeply troubled by the religious and political situations as they affected his community. Given hints in the Talmud and early Arab Christian references, the Jeremiah connection to Scythians and the exile communities in Zoroaster's homeland may be a promising area of future study in support of this thesis. At the very least, if Zoroaster's initiation into awareness of monotheism was not through a connection with Jeremiah, it seems reasonable that it could well have been through one of the other prophets, or from Jewish merchants, or Jews visiting relatives in the exile community, energizing the descendents of Israelite exiles and attempting to rekindle their devotion to the God of Abraham and the commandments given to Moses.

Israel is now among the nations, and Israel is in Jerusalem.
Her children in the holy temple need to hear of your travail and to prepare for their own.
I bring this scroll of the Law of Moses so that everyone who hears my voice may know.
These commandments are addressed to God's people, and to each one in particular.
Each one of you must decide for the LORD, and choose to serve and join with Him alone.

Ten years later, times were tough and the people of his religious community were oppressed. The brilliant priest was himself now thirty years old and thinking of Jeremiah. He went down to the river to prepare the water sacrifice and to meditate on his need, and that of his people, to hear a word from God. As he waded out of the river in reverie, quite unexpectedly an angel appeared in the shining form of a man who both confronted and instructed him.[8]

This pensive priest, approaching his prime, had waded into the river and immersed himself, almost distracted from his improvisational incantations by the social disintegration all around him. As he emerged, a vision came to him in which he was personally addressed by a specter he could only identify as one of the Immortals, beings then identified with the seven major celestial bodies visible to the naked eye in the universe, a story so important that it is repeated three times in the Avesta Scriptures.[9]

After establishing rapport, the shining figure led him in the spirit into an audience with the Lord of Wisdom, *Ahura Mazda*, who was also the diva of justice and who was attended by six Immortals. Ahura Mazda (Or/mazd in the later Avestan dialect) was both immanent and entirely lucid in authorizing Zoroaster to energize his people to oppose violence and to confront the terror of the times. He had gone into the water a priest and come out a prophet.

Zoroaster learned in this revelation that even divinities had to choose between order and disorder in support of either harmony or chaos. The human race was being enlisted to join the forces of nature in a new era that would lead to eventual victory of good over evil. Zoroaster experienced the immanence of the transcendent Lord of Wisdom, and the glory of the moment triggered his immediate realization that this Ahura Mazda should be identified as the Creator of the Universe. The ultimate divinity is "uncreated," before whom all the forces of nature must become subservient, an apparition of God so similar to a vision he had experienced previously.

Ahura Mazda is not alone in the universe, but he alone is God. Some suggest this was not technically monotheism at first, since the Immortals participated in divinity, but they are correctly understood as angels in the service of the only One worthy of worship. It was also revealed or became clear that the LORD had an evil counterpart whose status appeared great, although his purpose was less lofty and he was destined to fail, as humans joined the struggle on the side of goodness. Zoroaster put the choices this clearly to his people and all people for the rest of his life.

Zoroaster had been born laughing, according to the Avestas (as the Scriptures of Zoroastrianism are known), not hidden like Moses in the Hebrew Scriptures or talking from the cradle as the Quran reports of Jesus. His family may have had roots among the nomads, for they named their son Camel Herder (or Shining Camel or even Golden Camel). His infant narratives record that Zoroaster was born among the beasts, but a stallion shielded him from horses' hooves, a bull stood over him to prevent him being trampled by stampeding cattle, and a she-wolf nurtured him among her cubs. In a manner not very different from the development of these Scriptures, the latter story foreshadows the birth of Romulus and Remus, founders of Rome, recounted in an era when the influences of Zoroastrianism were almost universal.

Spiritually precocious, even as a child, Zoroaster had trained to be a priest from the age of seven and was recognized early for his ability to improvise incantations during sacrificial ceremonies.[10] Following the revelation at the river, Zoroaster continued his studies and was ready to commence his mission in earnest by the age of thirty, but through the first several years he gained only one reliable disciple, in the person of a cousin. He also earned the enmity of the religious establishments, until his opportunity came, regarded as a godsend by his later followers. After years of frustration in Media, Zoroaster was given an opportunity to discuss his mission with the priests of a royal court some distance to the east in the kingdom of Bactria (northern Afghanistan and contiguous Islamic republics today). After three days they dismissed him and had him jailed as a fraud, but he had caught the eye of King Vishtaspa, who must have seen the divine spark in the prophet priest, now forty years old.

When Vishtaspa's favorite horse became paralyzed and unable to rise, the established priests could do nothing, so the king took the opportunity to send for Zoroaster, who prayed over the beast and raised him to renewed vigor, to the delight of the king, the queen and the royal household. They converted to the cause of peace and justice for possibly both spiritual and political reasons (sometimes inseparable), and Zoroaster flourished, with influence growing throughout the region. He trained three orders of disciples who fanned out across the ancient world and organized the community of faith in the Lord of Wisdom. The horse itself became an enduring symbol of the Zoroastrian religion, and, as trends sometimes do, Zoroaster's spiritual influence galloped all along the Silk Road from Greece to China.

Zoroaster married, possibly more than once, and established his home and religious headquarters in the city of Balkh, then the capital of Bactria, some twenty kilometers to the northwest of Mazar-e-Sharif in today's Afghanistan. He had three sons who took the lead in reorganizing society into three classes: priests, warriors and farmers, aligning closely with the three principal castes organized in India by related Aryan migrants many generations earlier. The reformation of Hinduism triggered by Zoroaster, and his stimulation of the spiritual climate leading to the establishment of Buddhism, should be the subject or another book by another author, as the basis for discussion between Eastern and Western religions.

As had been revealed to Zoroaster, the mighty prince of darkness, introduced as Ahriman (later known as Satan or Lucifer), also had a retinue of six additional Anti-mortals, including Indra and other forces that served the cause of evil in the world. Following the revelation at the river, the cosmic battle was to be joined by those prepared to struggle on earth. Zoroaster was inspired to understand that in the battle between the divas representing good and evil, the Lord of Wisdom was destined for the final victory and that mortals who joined his cause should acknowledge him as the only true God. This rapid blossoming of monotheism is reflected in the extant Avestas, preserved by the modern Parsees and other Zoroastrians, though seeds of a transitory flowering of spiritual dualism in much of that community were also there from the beginning in Zoroaster's own "ethical dualism" of good and evil.

All of this and the subsequent Avestan Scriptures are presented in dramatic apocalyptic language, the first appearance of this style in the world. We meet this style again in Daniel and a few other places in the Hebrew Scriptures. The apocalyptic style dominates the book of Revelation, concluding the Christian Scriptures, prior to its predominant use again through almost the whole of the Quran. This is the first hint of the closeness between the Avesta and the Quran, a core thesis of this book, which will unfold throughout this text.

Zoroaster lived long and well and saw the influence of his mission spread throughout all areas of Persian influence and well beyond, the harbinger of what many scholars now call the Axial Age of religion and philosophy. Peasants and royal families alike flocked to his banner. Until recently, it was believed that he died a mysterious and violent death at the hands of assassins in the fire-temple at Balkh at seventy-seven years of age. On the basis of the dialect used in these reports, suspicions have arisen that this story was a fabrication by detractors some centuries later. He probably died at a great age, having seen his revelations transform his religion and all religions and his reforms transform his society and all societies throughout the ancient world. In the twenty-first century we are beginning to recognize his prophetic career as the epicenter of an eruption of religious fervor in an epoch now identified as the Axial Age. The reverberations of this era are still being felt, with lessons for today.

His name was *Zarathustra* in Persian, but the Greeks called him *Zorastres*, the Romans called him *Zoroastres*, and the anglicized *Zoroaster* has now become almost universal. Exceptions are the German title from Friedrich Nietzsche's book, *Also Sprach Zarathustra*, and the music by Richard Strauss that used that title for music that was popularized by Stanley Kubrick's movie, *2001: A Space Odyssey*, which was used as the introduction to every Elvis Presley show from 1969 until his death in 1977. Even in an era before research had revealed as much as we now know, Zoroaster appears as Sarastro in Mozart's opera *The Magic Flute*, in which he represents moral order in opposition to the "Queen of the Night." He is also the subject of the 1749 opera *Zoroastre* by Jean-Philippe Rameau, set in the ancient kingdom of Bactria, where the forces of Good, led by Zoroastre, the "founder of the Magi," struggle against the forces of Evil. During the Enlightenment, Voltaire and other encyclopaedists promoted research into Zoroastrianism, considering it to be a rational deism more acceptable than Christianity. In essence, Zoroaster was a reformer of the older Vedic religion that provided the raw materials for all emerging religions at the Middle Eastern hinge of continents, the area where monotheism also took root. Until recently, his dates were a mystery, at least in the West, but the period of one hundred years after Zoroaster, when all of this happened, has now come to be identified as the Axial Age, a subject to which we shall return.

In a world of warlord "kingdoms," Azerbaijan, Syria, Media, Lydia, Bactria and 122 others that all became provinces of the Persian Empire, Zoroaster had been born in the city of Urmiah, now known as Rizaijeh, in the Shiz district of present-day Azerbaijan. Arabic and Persian sources mark his birth date as 628 BCE by noting that the sacking of the Persian capital of Persepolis by Alexander the Great in 330 BCE took place 258 years after the "appearance of Zoroaster." This is possibly a reference to his birth, but it more likely refers to the establishment of the Zoroastrian religion under King Vishtaspa, and Avesta records show that Zoroaster was some forty years old at that time.[11]

An alternate ancient tradition reported by Xanthus of Lydia in about 450 BCE and adopted by Greek and Roman historians places the birth of Zoroaster a full six thousand years before Xerxes. This pushes Zoroaster's dates back to about 6,500 BCE, a popular mythology that survived until very recently, although it makes Zoroaster appear approximately twelve times as ancient in the Persian record.[11] This is the basis of the mythical "new age" image of Zoroaster, rather than the historical reality, so an accurate dating of Zoroaster's impact on the world is key to the argument in this story.

Whenever we see what appear to be fantastic or impossible dates and ages in the ancient world, the first question we must ask is if these numbers are divisible by twelve. Most primitive societies measured time by moons, from early civilizations regulated by astronomy, including early Hebrew, contiguous and related societies, and even aboriginal societies surviving into the modern era. Methuselah[12] may have lived to a very old age for his times, but it is obvious that, if divided by twelve, the 969 cycles of the moon are but some 80 cycles of the sun. We would call this eighty solar years, a method of time measurement that was adopted shortly before the Common Era. By this computation, Noah was 950 moons[13] when he died, and was six hundred when the flood came, or fifty years old by our calculations. After the adoption of solar time measurement, we are given to understand that Jesus lived approximately thirty years and Muhammad some sixty-three years, both ages described in the system used in the current era. The confusion might be illustrated by the current switch in temperature measurement. The United States continues to use the Fahrenheit scale, while the rest of the world has switched to Celsius. A thousand years from now, when the whole world has been using Celsius for centuries, at first glance a study would reveal that while temperatures peaked at thirty or forty degrees everywhere else, a hot day in America was represented by one hundred degrees, misunderstood as the hottest place on earth with unbelievable heat.[14]

So when the ancient Greek historian, Xanthus, reported that Zoroaster was born six thousand "cycles" before Persian King Xerxes invaded Asia Minor and Greece in 480 BCE, probably quoting older Asian sources, we may presume that he meant six thousand cycles of the moon. The Roman historian Diogenes Laertius, among others, took this to be six thousand cycles of the sun, since he lived in the solar era, placing the birth of Zoroaster at a seemingly impossibly remote date in relation to the Aryan activities that preceded him and the religious developments in Persia and elsewhere that succeeded him. When Xanthus recorded that period as six thousand cycles, he meant five hundred of our solar years before 480 BCE, or the year 930 BCE, according to our calculations. This is not exactly the same as the Persian record, but a difference measured in two or three centuries, not many thousands of years. The choices for birth dates of Zoroaster are, first, 6,500 BCE if you believe Xanthus really meant solar years rather than moons; second, somewhere between 1100 and 930 BCE if you adjust this Greek and Roman account from moons to solar years; or third, 628 BCE if you accept the Arabic and Persian records.

We use the slightly later Arabic and Persian date of 628 BCE partly because it fits with our thesis regarding Persian Zoroastrianism as the direct and immediate predecessor of Scriptural Judaism in Babylon as represented by the Torah as we have it. The slightly earlier Greek and Roman date would not be a major problem, since it, too, follows Moses by some centuries, but it does not work quite as well. However, impressive corroboration of our position is bolstered by research now widely accepted about the birth of Darius I, shortly before 550 BCE.[15] This son of the first royal convert, King Vishtaspa, grew up to succeed to the Persian throne in 522, eight years after the death of Cyrus, and he would have known Zoroaster as the revered priest and prophet in his father's court.

The evidence for a birth date of around 628 BCE is convincing and important for our thesis that Zoroaster was exposed to Jewish influence less than two decades later, and received his own revelation at the river shortly before 600 BCE. Zoroaster's prophetic ministry flowered ten years later and dramatically impacted the ancient Middle East and beyond for the next fifty years. Then Cyrus, the rising Zoroastrian conqueror, marched into Babylon in 539 to establish that faith at the heart of the first realm in history to be appropriately described as a superpower. The significance of the Zoroastrian Cyrus establishing the Persian Empire in this manner just twenty years after the death of Zoroaster (or a century after his birth) has yet to be entirely digested in either academic circles or the popular imagination.

As indicated, the late date for Zoroaster's birth (either before 930 or in 628 BCE) places the revelation that was given to him well after the establishment of monotheism in Israel. Future chapters will establish beyond doubt that religious and other ideas traveled in a fluid dynamic all through the ancient east. While Zoroastrianism may have facilitated the spread of monotheism and the Torah concept of personal responsibility to God throughout the Persian Empire, the fact that these seminal beliefs had flourished for hundreds of years in the Jewish community almost next door to Zoroaster's birthplace can hardly be mere coincidence. We may regard the revelation to Zoroaster as genuine, but monotheism was not exactly new to him. His worldview was Vedic, but Zoroaster's inspiration with respect to monotheism was Jewish. The exceptional Zoroastrian influence on Judaism during the Persian years of Israel's exile in Babylon may now be understood as but the closing of the circle. Monotheism came to Zoroaster and to the world from the Jews, and the Hebrew Torah was facilitated and financed by Zoroastrian monarchs in Babylon and through the return to Jerusalem.

Zoroaster's people had been part of a vast migration of Hittite-related Aryans who were in the final stages of moving *en masse* from the steppes of Eastern Europe and southern Russia into India. A significant offshoot of this migration had detoured into Greater Mesopotamia, where they became dominant, and some of these tribes also eventually continued on into India. The Avestan-speaking Persian Aryans were Indo-European cousins of their Sanskrit-speaking kinsmen in language, culture and religion in the Indus River valley. Earlier migrations of this dynamic polyglot of mixed races and tribes from the Caucasian steppes had pushed into Greece, Italy, Germany and even Scandinavia, establishing the Caucasian-Aryan stamp as firmly on Europe as on other parts of their whole Indo-European swath of influence.[16] As such, the Zoroastrian Vedic reforms are a connecting link between East and West for which the world has been waiting, although until recently we did not know enough about Zoroaster's life or his teachings to make this assertion with confidence.

Research a hundred years ago demonstrated that, well before their migrations began prior to 1,500 BCE, the Aryans worshipped *Dyaus Pitr*, the "Divine Father," who created the universe.[17] Known as *Gitchi Manitou* on the Great Central Plains of North America, and called *Shang Di* in ancient China, *Altjira* in the Australian Outback, *Nyambe* in the west tropics of Africa and *Brahman* among the group arriving later in India, this religious instinct was shared by aboriginal peoples around the world. By 1,500 BCE the seeming remoteness of God resulted in a growing adulation of life forces called *devas* (from which we get both "divinities" and "devils") that were nearer at hand in the thinking of these spirited Aryans. *Agni*, the fire spirit, existed in balance with other forces of nature that needed to be harnessed. *Varuna*, representing the night, the waters, the underworld and the unconscious, maintained order. *Indra*, the divine warrior, defended the people from their foes. *Mythra*, the diva of sun and rain, would nourish and replenish the earth. *Mazda*, whose name means "wisdom," would engender the cult of wisdom and all the wisdom traditions that form subtexts of many religions down through the ages.

It was the Lord of Wisdom, *Ahura Mazda*, who rose in Zoroastrianism to represent the Dyaus Pitr, though closer at hand and available to those seeking guidance in the midst of chaos. Chaos came with a new stirring of the spirit of adventure and even conflict in the era of migration. Mythra would develop from a peaceful fertility deva to become the favorite mascot-god of the Roman Legion, as that army became Aryanized. More dramatically, and much earlier, the Aryans had adopted bronze weapons from the Armenians and learned to hitch their wild horses to wagons acquired from Kazakh neighbors, leading to their invention of the war chariot. In their sweep into India, Indra was transformed from defensive patron to a spirit of the scourge: "Heroes with noble horses ready for war, and chosen warriors, call upon me! I am Indra, Lord of plunder. I excite the conflict. I stir up the dust. I am the Lord of unsurpassed vigor."[18]

The movement of these peoples into Persia appears less violent than the move into India in some respects. The migration to Persia included gentler elements of the Aryan culture, including many who sought to simply maintain the old pastoral ways. Others in their midst were stirred by the spirit of plunder and adventure, even to preying on their fellow Aryans in the name of strife that brings victory and reward to the strong. "Dog eat dog" and "every man for himself" were slogans appropriate for the times. The price was high for women and children, farmers settling into production, the elderly and anyone with cattle that could be rustled. What kind of gods were these devas now? This question would have been uppermost in the mind of the young Zoroaster.

The account of the revelation he received at the river may sound just like the biblical story of Daniel at the River Ulai, also in Persia,[19] but the young prophet Zoroaster, in the first instance, was a hundred years earlier. No one need doubt the meaning or the significance of the reported appearance of the archangel Gabriel to Daniel just because that epiphany is identical in format to the earlier appearance to Zoroaster, as recorded in the ancient but still extant Avesta Scriptures of Zoroastrianism. Daniel's epiphany did occur at the beginning of the reign of Cyrus II, Persia's first Zoroastrian monarch, but similar appearances by Gabriel heralded the births of John the Baptist[20] and Jesus Christ[21] in the Gospel according to Luke.

The unexpected appearance of Gabriel to Muhammad in the Cave of Hera[22] also bears a striking resemblance to the angelic appearances to Zoroaster and to Daniel, Zechariah and Mary, and it was this same archangel who appeared time and again to Muhammad over the next twenty-three years, always unannounced and unexpected, to present the recitations that stand now as the final chapters of Scripture in this family compendium. This is not the forum in which to address skeptics who are unable to rationally fathom the reality or meaning of angelic appearances. Suffice it to say that the powerful phenomenological occurrences reported in Zoroastrianism bear a striking resemblance to critical embryonic junctures in the three religions whose Scriptures are the substance of this study.

The moment when Zoroaster was confronted and instructed by the archangel was not the last occasion when religion changed from ritual, from philosophy and even from theology into experience and a personal encounter with the Divine. God's call for Abraham to leave home,[23] the story of Jacob's ladder[24] and his wrestling all night that changed him into Israel,[25] and Moses at the burning bush[26] and on Mount Sinai[27] are all later examples of this phenomenon. Saint Paul, knocked off his horse on the road to Damascus,[28] and Muhammad, embraced by the angel Gabriel in the Hera Cave, were far off in the future when Zoroaster's heart was first stirred by some Hebrew prophet, preparing him for his own such moment at the river.

Ritual, philosophy and theology have also continued elsewhere, in formal religious guise and otherwise, but what Karl Jaspers has helped us recognize as the Axial Age[29] of reform may be attributed to that moment of personal intimacy with God experienced by Zoroaster at the river. Within a hundred years of the churning wake of that river episode, to the east the Buddha transformed Hinduism and founded his religion of enlightenment, and even further east Confucius taught philosophy and Lao Tse introduced the Tao, both focused on the rights and wrongs of life. To the west the classical age of prophecy blossomed with dramatic impact in Judah, while even further west the philosophers of Greece swept away an old mythology with the new concepts of justice and truth. These all made their contributions, but we have now identified the axis of the Axial Age.

The significance of the dates 628 to 551 for Zoroaster has been recognized partly as a result of growing acceptance of the Axial Age theory, popularized now by writers such as Karen Armstrong in *The Great Transformation*. Sometimes called the Pivotal Age in English,[30] Karl Jaspers originally used his "axistime" to describe a slightly broader era of a few centuries, and he was unable to identify a specific "pivot." He locates Zoroaster just prior to Cyrus in Persia, but the connection of the two insights depends on a complex examination of dates, upon which an important thesis of this book is based, a story worth pursuing through controversy and intrigue.

In the nineteenth century an investigation into the links between Zoroastrianism and Judaism had been undertaken by the German History of Religions School (Religionsgeschichtliche Schule) with considerable optimism, but too many imponderables still remained about Zoroaster, and the trail ran cold. The twentieth century opened with investigations less interested in connections to other religions. An article on Zoroaster in the eleventh edition of the Encyclopedia Britannia (1910-1911) by Dr. Karl Friederich Geldner, professor of Sanskrit and comparative philology at the University of Marburg, became the standard reference on all things Zoroastrian until 1977. This classic was typical of the preeminent edition of that encyclopedia and is still available in most first-rate libraries.

Other twentieth-century attempts were hamstrung by scholarly disputes on how to read the surviving material and the external references. However, near the end of that century a consensus on many such issues emerged around the findings of Mary Boyce at the University of London's School of Oriental and African Studies. Her *A Persian Stronghold of Zoroastrianism* was published in 1977 after a year of life "on the ground" in the Zoroastrian villages of Iran. In the welter of mysteries solved, she was initially somewhat ambivalent about Zoroaster's precise dates, but she did succeed in establishing that his "mythical" European dates of 6,500 or 6,000 BCE are to be replaced by dates somewhere between 1,200 and 1,000 BCE at a minimum. These dates work plausibly with the thesis of this book, though not as well as the traditional Persian dates placing him in the seventh century BCE, with his followers interfacing with Jews in Babylon in the sixth century BCE. By the beginning of the twenty-first century, a number of leading Italian, British and German experts coalesced around support for the old Persian-Arabic dates, after dramatic politicking among scholars of Zoroastrianism who recognized the impact this issue could have on world history. This led to the consolidation of the position of this book, with some guidance from Mary Boyce herself in the last years of her life, the ramifications of which will become clear.

In spite of this consensus, there are still respected scholars of Zoroastrianism who cling to dates around or before 1000 BCE, mainly for philological reasons, since it is clear that the Gatha poem prayers composed by Zoroaster himself employ a dialect of the Avesta language from that earlier era. The answer to that is found in twentieth-century Christian hymns and prayers written in Shakespearian English, the "noble" form of the language as employed in the beloved King James Version of the Bible, seen almost as the language of God. For that matter, when semi-modern Mormon or Baha'i scriptures sought authenticity, they were presented in the language of the King James Version from hundreds of years before their formation. In precisely this manner, as Zoroaster re-interpreted the sacred Vedic traditions of his time, he would have been moved to authenticate his words by the use of the still revered Vedic dialect and cadence from earlier than the 1000 BCE date.

A mainstream appreciation of Zoroastrianism and its influence on our three religions, and Judaism in particular, is overdue. In this quest, the current study will unfold by working backward from Judaism to Zoroastrianism, the opposite approach to that of nineteenth-century scholars who tried in vain to locate and define Zoroaster, and who could therefore see little direct connection between him and Judaism or anything else. We will start with Judaism in Babylon and see how rapidly and dramatically it developed there in tension with "something" that looks like Z, sounds like Z, and walks like Z, so it must be Z, or something that looks too much like Z to ignore. Some work has been done in Jewish circles, working forward from the Exile to note the interplay between Z and the Jews in Babylon, Jerusalem and elsewhere in the Parthian and Sasanian eras. We will be working backward to show evidence positioning Zoroaster immediately before Cyrus the Great, just before consolidation of the Torah, with all that means to Jews, as well as to Christians, Muslims and the world at large.

In the meantime, the Avesta itself will almost certainly be found during the lifetime of current students of these matters. Why? Because it did not fall into disuse or get lost through disinterest. Rather, twice there were attempts to destroy every scroll and book, surely prompting devotees to hide some copies. The precious Gathas and early parts of the Avesta were burned in an official program at Persepolis by Alexander the Great, who wished to "civilize" Asia, but what would happen to the copies in Bactria when people heard what the conquerors were doing? The whole reconstituted corpus was again "destroyed" in Baghdad and Damascus by Muslims objecting to the mixture of monotheism and dualism in the melange of writings they found there, but what would happen in such circumstances to the copies cherished by Zoroastrians among the Sogdian merchants in western China? In both of these cases and many more, at least some few of those devotees would hide their Avesta Scriptures with as much care as those who hid the Dead Sea Scrolls and the Nag Hammadi Library, both concealed in similar circumstances. As satellite infra-red scanners turn up more and more treasure troves of archaeological caches, the trail gets warmer. When the discovery is announced, even the supermarket tabloids will be hard pressed to find words to describe this unearthing of previous revelations related to most of the Scriptures in use in the world today.

Our purposes here are not only to display the three Scriptures from the family of Abraham, Sarah and Hagar as a "statement" of their inter-relatedness, and as a catalyst for mutual respect among Jews, Christians and Jews. *Three Testaments: Torah, Gospel and Quran* is both those things and more, but it is also a preeminent beginning of a twenty-first-century understanding of revelation and God's engagement with all people in love, challenge, demand and call to fulfill God's purpose. This begins with the Torah as the original touchstone of God's revelation to the family of Abraham, Sarah and Hagar, and through them to the nations, to subsequent religions, and to individual people, as Zoroaster discovered.

Cyrus En Route to Babylon to Establish the Persian Superpower and a Zoroastrian Spiritual Base for World Religion

2

monotheism

IT WOULD NOW APPEAR THAT ZOROASTER DIED ABOUT A DOZEN YEARS BEFORE CYRUS THE GREAT occupied Babylon and began Persian rule over some 127 former kingdoms of various sizes. This empire covered one quarter of the world's landmass, equal to the Roman Empire at its height, the British Empire at its zenith and the Soviet Union before its collapse. The state religion was Zoroastrian monotheism, and this era represents the Axial Age in full bloom. The influence and the power of the Zoroastrian movement over the next thousand years is difficult to picture or imagine for many now because, even at its zenith when Persia was the world's first superpower, it was the religion of an Oriental culture outside the mainstream of Western historical reportage. It reached great heights, but was eventually decimated both militarily and politically by Alexander the Great and then vigorously revived for hundreds of years more in a degraded form. Finally, it was practically eliminated by Islam, except for elements of its culture and religion that lived on in Iran and India, surviving today both there and in pockets of the United Kingdom, Canada, Australia and the United States.

However, the once pervasive sway of this movement, which may have contributed key elements to the spiritual foundation of the whole world, can be glimpsed in the politics and theological development of ancient Israel and in historical accounts of its near domination of Europe in the failed Persian invasions of Greece. A more objective appraisal of these events than that found in Hollywood presentations and the biased reports in Greek history, or in the adulation of Cyrus in Hebrew literature, might be seen in a brief overview of the reigns of Zoroastrian monarchs whom we know at least peripherally. From both the Bible and ancient historical writers we know something about a line of such monarchs who ruled the Persian Empire at the apex of the Zoroastrian era in a world just beyond the horizon of the West. The relevance of their rule to the development of the Torah will become apparent in this chapter.

Vishtaspa, the first Zoroastrian monarch, is mainly known to us because of his relationship to Zoroaster. Not a lot is known about his rule beyond that connection, although the record perhaps serves to introduce life in the court of a typical monarchy of minor status in an era and in a part of the world unfamiliar to many. Cyrus, however, is well known both to historians and to readers of the Hebrew Scriptures. In 559 BCE, almost a decade before Zoroaster died, Cyrus succeeded to the throne of Anshan, a vassal kingdom of Media (now northern Iran), which was then ruled by his grandfather, another early Zoroastrian monarch. Within two decades Cyrus had subdued Media itself, conquered Asia Minor and marched into India. After a period of consolidation, in 539 his forces fought their way into the great city of Babylon, the vast urban center of the ancient world.

The supreme potentate of Babylonia, King Belshazzar, was killed, and Cyrus assumed rule of the entire Babylonian Empire. This was prophesied by Daniel, as the account appears in the Hebrew Scriptures, when Belshazzar and his court were feasting out of the sacred vessels stolen from the

Temple in Jerusalem. This travesty resulted in their guilty vision of the *Mene, Mene, Tekel, Parsin* "writing on the wall," interpreted for them by Daniel in terms of God's judgment.[1] Babylon's time was up: it was found wanting, divided and ready to be conquered. In assuming and extending his control, Cyrus ruled the largest and most powerful empire the world would see until that of Alexander the Great and the later Roman Empire.

The success of Cyrus was built on combining military strategy with enlightened diplomacy and Zoroastrian spirituality. For example, the kingdom of Lydia had been difficult to conquer on the way to hegemony, but upon finally defeating the wealthy King Croesus, instead of killing him Cyrus made him prime minister, and even one of his "Companions of the Garden,"[2] an inner circle of advisors to the Zoroastrian monarch. Everywhere he conquered, in addition to graciousness toward the vanquished, Cyrus allied himself with those who had been oppressed by their former rulers. A famous but not entirely unique example relates to his relationship with the elite Jewish exiles, who were highly placed in the civil service of Babylon. His sponsorship of their return to Jerusalem and his funding of the rebuilding of their temple and culture won him the loyalty of a new province on his Egyptian flank, a buffer facing a power that would not be integrated into the Persian Empire until the rule of Cyrus's son and successor.

The new religion of Cyrus was Zoroastrianism in its pristine, complete and uncorrupted manifestation, articulated at the core of his brilliantly successful policy toward enemies and subjects alike. This Zoroastrian monotheism was undiluted at first, again suggesting chronological closeness to the monotheistic originator of the faith. In a time subsequent to Cyrus, an altered form of the religion did shift the balance toward dualism in the struggle between good and evil, light and darkness. While he recognized the necessity of the struggle with evil forces, which are real in human experience, Zoroaster himself believed fervently in the ultimate exclusivity of the prerogatives and final reign of the Lord of Wisdom, and in the goodness that the religion he founded was commissioned to promote. Cyrus appears to have embraced the pristine Zoroastrian religion much as it was first promulgated by its founding prophet. The Jewish exiles recognized the affinity of this religion with their own, possibly even before Cyrus ascended to the throne of Babylon.

The pristine Zoroastrian appearance of edicts and documents from the reign of Cyrus and their similarity to prophetic pronouncements of Zoroaster, in both extant Avestas and those emerging from and confirmed by the Quran, is one more aid in dating Zoroaster's life and ministry. The convergence of these monotheistic and justice elements is among the most persuasive arguments for a new level of understanding of the Zoroastrian contribution to world culture that is emerging in our time. A reasonably complete picture may become achievable as we add the Quranic appreciations, new perspectives that Jewish sources can teach us, unique Christian Gospel material from a Zoroastrianism not acquired from Jewish sources and material from sources in the related religious traditions much further east. This may be seen as a quest appropriate to elements of a world culture emerging in the twenty-first century.

The British Museum is in possession of a clay cylinder ordered to be made and circulated by Cyrus as king of Persia and which is said to represent the first "bill of rights" in human history and to encapsulate his policy of religious toleration. A replica resides at the United Nations headquarters in New York. This "Cyrus Cylinder" was discovered in Babylon in 1878, just after archaeologists made the discovery of Troy. In a manner similar to the way that the discovery of Troy disproved the view that Homer's *Iliad* was fiction, the finding of the Cyrus Cylinder gave substance to echoes in classical literature that ascribed the highest ideals to this leader of the world's first superpower, principles that were regarded as mere idealizations until the cylinder was found. It is difficult to imagine that such important information from such relatively recent times was lost for two and a half millennia, but we are now realizing that Zoroaster himself has been that close all along, although hidden from our sight.

His combination of firm stability and enlightened diplomacy has caused some political observers to regard Cyrus as a leader almost without equal in history. The monotheism of the monarch was generous in spirit toward the many people who had not yet reached that level of theological sophistication. At the same time, no doubt, Cyrus knew who his friends were, and his unique relationship with his Jewish subjects was also made feasible under policies described by the Cyrus

Cylinder. His influence and that of his successors is felt today primarily through their actions that facilitated the completion of the Torah as we know it.

While his policy toward the Jews was consistent with its manifestation toward other people, it should not be surprising if it appears that Cyrus displayed something of a special delight and favor toward his Jewish subjects. This would have been because of his recognition of the absolute monotheism they eschewed at that particular time. The Jews may have vacillated in their monotheism at times since Moses was confronted by God at the burning bush, and there may have also been monotheistic tendencies among related nomadic desert tribes, but the Hebrews appear unique in their monotheistic steadfastness in this respect among the national client groupings at the time they were all dominated by the Zoroastrians. The priests and rulers of the Persian Empire's Zoroastrian monotheist tradition would have taken pleasure in the discovery of an established elder ally, of whom they may have had some previous knowledge. The response of the Hebrews to the dynamic vigor of the monotheism of their rulers would have set this relationship apart, with an impact that has reverberated throughout history.

For that matter, this relationship with Cyrus, his administration and his Zoroastrianism, was of such "watershed" dimensions that one could almost say the Hebrews themselves practically divided history into a BC and AD of "Before Cyrus" and "After Death" of Cyrus in the writings of the Chronicler. The Scriptural Books of Chronicles begins with Adam and closes with a purported edict by Cyrus.

> Thus says King Cyrus of Persia: The LORD God of Heaven has given me all the kingdoms of the earth, and has charged me with building Him a House in Jerusalem, which is in Judah. Any one of you, of all His people, the LORD his God be with him and let him go up.[3]

That is where the old history of Israel and the world ends, and it is clear that the writer believes that Cyrus is not only a monotheist but also that the God of Cyrus is the God of Israel, and on that basis the same writer moves on to the new era in the books of Ezra and Nehemiah.

The interface between the Zoroastrian rulers and the Jewish civil service, and presumably between the Zoroastrian and Jewish priesthoods, continued for decades in Persia, even while the Return to Israel began and the rebuilding of the temple got underway. That work began well but ground to a halt eventually, resulting in a second wave of the Return to Israel with a renewed mandate. According to the Jewish account, objections by Israel's neighbors in this "Province-beyond-the-River" resulted in a search of Persian archives to confirm the original decree.[4] This resulted in the publication by Darius I of a scroll found in the citadel in Ecbatana, capital of Media, the first stronghold of Cyrus:

> Memorandum: In the first year of King Cyrus, King Cyrus issued an order concerning the house of God in Jerusalem: "Let the house be built, a place for offering sacrifices, with a base built up high. Let it be sixty cubits high and sixty cubits wide, with a course of unused timber for each three courses of hewn stone. The expenses shall be paid by the palace. And the gold and silver vessels of the House of God which Nebuchadnezzar had taken away from the temple in Jerusalem and transported to Babylon shall be returned, and let each go back to the temple in Jerusalem where it belongs; you shall deposit it in the House of God."[5]

It may be difficult to confidently assign an exact level of historical credibility to these reports, but it is impossible to ignore the impact of what transpired, and it is important to understand why these things happened. Leaping ahead to circumstances that facilitated Ezra's work, resulting in the final editing of the Torah as we have it during and following the Return to Israel, we find a complementary declaration from the next monarch, describing the resources for that immense undertaking.

> The following is the text of the letter which King Artaxerxes gave Ezra the priest-scribe, a scholar in matters concerning the commandments of the LORD and His laws to Israel:
> "Artaxerxes king of kings, to Ezra the priest, scholar in the law of the God of heaven, and so forth. And now, I hereby issue an order that anyone in my kingdom who is of the people of Israel and its priests

and Levites who feels impelled to go to Jerusalem may go with you. For you are commissioned by the king and his seven advisors to regulate Judah and Jerusalem according to the law of your God, which is in your care, and to bring the freewill offering of silver and gold, which the king and his advisors made to the God of Israel, whose dwelling is in Jerusalem, and whatever silver and gold that you find throughout the province of Babylon, together with the freewill offerings that the people and the priests will give for the House of their God, which is in Jerusalem. You shall, therefore, with dispatch acquire with this money bulls, rams, and lambs, with their meal offerings and libations, and offer them on the altar of the House of your God in Jerusalem. And whatever you wish to do with the leftover silver and gold, you and your kinsmen may do, in accord with the will of your God. The vessels for the service of the House of your God that are given to you, deliver to God in Jerusalem, and any other needs of the House of your God that it falls to you to supply, do so from the royal treasury."[6]

Given the reference to Ezra as a scholar in the "law" of God, we may reasonably presume that the final clauses funded final editing and publication of the Torah in Jerusalem.

Other client nations may have found their religions respected and their cultures encouraged, even though they usually did eventually fall under the influence of the Zoroastrian religion and the Persian cultural sovereignty that came with political and military subjugation. Only the Jews were treated as religious equals and even permitted to co-opt the Zoroastrian religion to their own ends, and only the Jews were not just set free but also generously funded, not once but twice, in rebuilding their national homeland and its temple in particular.

While the evidence for the Hebrew people even being in Egypt is limited to one-sided Hebrew records, and while the proof of Babylonian influence in Israel is sketchy and between the lines of the Torah, the details of the Persian sponsorship of the renewal of the Hebrew national entity is well preserved and witnessed both in Hebrew Scriptures and independently. In the first instance, "Exhibit A" is not merely what is in the Scriptures, but the Torah itself. In reference to an "Exhibit B," recent, current and ongoing archaeological digs show the foundation stones of the temple, rebuilt at Persian Zoroastrian expense in Jerusalem and resting on stones of the original Solomon's Temple, both now supporting the famous Western Wall of the temple substructure. We are not talking about hints between the lines of a text here, or potsherds discovered in a dig. The Torah that came out of that vortex is a cornerstone of Western, and now world, culture. The remnants of that temple are all open to the public in the Hall of Eras, an ancient street excavated along the western edge of the Western Wall in Jerusalem today.

The more massive foundation stones of the Western Wall, with which many of us are familiar, are part of Herod's renovation of the temple in 19–20 BCE, but while the original Second Temple he inherited was not as high, he was renovating rather than building something new. Herod himself suggested that Cyrus and his successors dictated the original measurements of the temple built under Persian sponsorship. Herod's speech inaugurating the project is preserved by Josephus (37–100 CE), the Romano-Jewish historian who had no reason to curry favor with any Persian readers. Yet this record from outside Scripture agrees entirely with the Bible in ascribing responsibility for that earlier construction to the Persian monarchs. Josephus quotes Herod to wit:

Our fathers, indeed, when they were returned from Babylon, built this temple to God Almighty, yet does it want sixty cubits of its largeness in altitude; for so much did that first temple which Solomon built exceed this temple; nor let anyone condemn our fathers for their negligence or want of piety herein, for it was not their fault that the temple was no higher; for it was Cyrus, and Darius the son of Hystaspes, who determined the measures for its rebuilding; and it hath been by reason of the subjection of those fathers of ours to them and to their posterity, and after them to the Macedonians, that they had not the opportunity to follow the original model of this pious edifice, nor could raise it to its ancient altitude; but since I am now, by God's will, your governor, and I have had peace a long time, and have gained great riches and large revenues, and, what is the principal filing of all, I am at amity with and well regarded by the Romans, who, if I may so say, are the rulers of the whole world, I will do my endeavor to correct that imperfection, which hath arisen from the necessity of our affairs, and the slavery we have been under formerly, and to make a thankful return, after the most pious manner, to God, for what blessings I have received from him, by giving me this kingdom, and that by rendering his temple as complete as I am able.[7]

The Cyrus Cylinder actually states, "I (Cyrus) gathered all their former inhabitants and returned to them their habitations," but only one other example has come to light of the Persian rulers in fact funding the specifically spiritual aspirations of their subjects. Elamite tablets have been found in the ruins at Persepolis showing that, in a time subsequent to Cyrus, Darius I encouraged these non-Persian subjects to worship their ancestral gods in addition to the Lord of Wisdom, and that he made grants from the royal treasury for this purpose. But this was nothing on the scale of the resources provided to the Jews, and nothing even remotely comparable to the reconstructed temple or to the completed Torah remains to show Zoroastrian support of any other religion. The time may be right for Torah scholarship to recognize Zoroastrianism as a support and a source like no other except for the Hebrew people's own traditions, reflecting their own desert, tribal and national experiences of God.

What is needed is a rationale to explain what motivated the exceptional relationship that resulted in the enduring evidence provided by the existence of the Torah as we have it and the foundation stones of the Second Temple. From the beginning, the keen affection of Cyrus was reciprocated by the Jews, and what happened in the dynamic years between the end of Babylonian rule and the Return to Jerusalem put an indelible Zoroastrian stamp on the Judeo-X-Islamic future. With Muslim material now possibly illustrating more about the Zoroastrian side of that conversation, we are able to understand more completely what motivated the refining and final editing of the Torah that took place following the reign of Cyrus and the rebuilding of the Temple under Persian Zoroastrian financial sponsorship.

Nefertiti, the Semitic wife of Akhenaton, perhaps briefly brought into the Egyptian court the protomonotheism of Abraham, which had become the shared property of related desert peoples. Monotheism had been refined and was well articulated by Moses after the burning bush experience. While it also experienced corruption from time to time in the Hebrew communal expression, it remained the hallmark of this people right into their captivity in Babylon. Various biblical expressions about "other gods" may be seen as Israel's "shorthand" reference to "false gods" in accommodation to accepted local reference. When the Jews found favor with their new Persian monotheistic ruler, they were sure the hand of God must have anointed him as a world leader and as their savior. Until then, the Hebrew concept of the messiah had been developed in general outline, related only to a restoration of the Davidic monarchy. It was a short step from there to the concept of the Zoroastrian *Saoshyant*,[8] a "Redeemer" who was seen as a universal messiah.

Mentioned remarkably some twenty-two times in the Hebrew Scriptures (as often as Adam is mentioned), Cyrus himself was briefly proclaimed there to be the expected messiah, especially by one particular prophetic writer in the Hebrew exile community. He is known to scholars as Isaiah or perhaps "Second Isaiah" because some think he had been a young associate of Isaiah back in the homeland, or that he considered himself to stand in the tradition of that great prophet, and because his work was appended to the scroll of Isaiah.

Concerning Cyrus and Israel's monotheistic God, this Second Isaiah proclaimed:

Thus said the LORD to Cyrus, His anointed one—
Whose right hand He has grasped,
Treading down nations before him,
Opening doors before him and letting no gate stay shut:
I will march before you
And level the hills that loom up;
I will shatter doors of bronze
And cut down iron bars.
I will give you treasures concealed in the dark
And secret hoards—
So that you may know that it is I the LORD,
The God of Israel, who call you by name.

For the sake of my servant Jacob,
Israel my chosen one,
I call you by name,
I hail you by title, though you have not known me,
I am the LORD and there is none else;
Beside Me, there is no god.
I engird you, though you have not known Me,
So that they may know, from east to west,
That there is none but Me.
I am the LORD and there is none else,
I form light and create darkness,
I make weal and create woe—
I the LORD do all these things.[9]

It is impossible to conceive of the God of Israel praising Cyrus in such absolute terms and having "anointed" him unless Cyrus was indeed a genuine believer in monotheism, as opposed to the dualism many later scholars have associated with Zoroastrianism, a flaw that became a reality within a few generations. The danger of Zoroastrianism crediting Ahriman (Satan) with too high a standing may have been apparent to Second Isaiah, so his exaltation is tempered by the reminder that the LORD God, the Lord of Wisdom worshipped by the monarch, actually created both the light and the darkness. Known as YHWH to the Jews, it is this same God who rewards with benefits and punishes with misfortune in both religions. If it was the divine purpose to redeem Israel from bondage, Cyrus was merely an agent of the one worshipped by both Persians and Jews, known by either name.

We have here an indication of the dynamic discussion going on between Jewish and Zoroastrian priests in the court of Cyrus, who were delighted with each other and each refined the theological concepts of the other. Cyrus himself may or may not have known God by the name the Jews were using, but there could be no doubt that the Jews believed it was the same one God. In this context, the Jews were then apparently eager for their God to be known universally as such, from east to west, a new concept developed through the interface with the Zoroastrians.

The edict of Cyrus, restoring the Jewish community to Palestine and authorizing the rebuilding of the Temple, was early in his reign in Babylon.[10] The putative acknowledgment of him as the Anointed, the *Messiah*, was not a flattery that resulted in the edict, but a response to it. The Return to Jerusalem did not pick up the momentum it needed to truly succeed until the reign of Artaxerxes, later in the succession of these Zoroastrian monarchs. Therefore the theological discussion and work toward the final editing of the Torah may have begun during a couple of generations in Zoroastrian Babylon itself. The results of this spiritual fermentation are becoming more apparent.

To anticipate what we can now know in the wider connection, we will realize that certain sections of the Quran are focused upon angels, creation, light and darkness, law and order, the coming universal messiah, and especially judgment, resurrection and heaven. These sections are interlaced with Zoroastrian hymn phrases to do with the number seven, swift horses, rolling thunder, clear paths, flowing water and beautiful gardens, plus Persian words transliterated into Arabic. Such phrases may occur in other religious imagery and various languages, but their frequency in clusters of relational patterns mark their appearance in the Quran as separate and distinct from other Quranic material. What this may tell us about the Torah has yet to be appreciated. The details of this new awareness that the Quran possibly critiques lost sections of the Avesta, and more about their potential impact, will be discussed in Book Three of this compendium. Some of these key concepts, such as *paradise*, a word introducing the concept of heaven, have been identified through linguistic studies as Persian and Zoroastrian in origin long before this. In the meanwhile, the creation story provides a profound illustration of the importance of this growing insight.

The sense of that story is made clear by its use in Zoroastrian parables, and the meaning of the story is developed by divine inspiration as it appears in the Torah,[11] but few realize that the bare bones of this material came to the world first in the Vedic Scriptures in India, and even earlier during their development prior to the migration era. The component parts of creation in seven stages are traceable through the voluminous Vedas, but they are more easily accessed through the existing books of the Zoroastrian Avesta where the old devas carried out the creative process of the Lord of Wisdom in seven stages that have become familiar to us all.

First, they made the sky out of the kind of rock that still falls from time to time, but as a solid sphere. Second, they filled the sphere half full of water, and third, they floated the earth upon the water, as a saucer-like disk. The creations of flora and fauna followed, first a single plant, then a single animal and finally one man, each of which generated a crop of similar productions. The seventh phase of creation put the sun in the sky, a ball of fire that became the sacred symbol of the divine hearth, the spiritual warmth needed by humanity in particular.[12] It was when this symbol replaced the divine reality as the object of adoration that Agni was transformed from the sacred deva of Zoroastrian worship to the hellfire of Christianity. Zoroastrian sacred fire was also presented as a symbol of pagan degeneration in the Quran.

The title of Gore Vidal's novel, *Creation*, reflects a holistic aspect of an ongoing environmental concern that is among the elements of this prophet's message that continues to make Zoroastrianism attractive to New Agers and others. It is instructive to realize that Zoroastrianism got these concepts from ancient Vedic lore, and it is important to identify this source. But let us remind ourselves that Israel had an understanding of creation in seven stages imbedded in the Sabbath of the Ten Commandments, long before the Hebrew priestly scholars sat down with the Persian Zoroastrian scholars to refine the creation story as they then presented it for the first chapter of Genesis. The compilers of the priestly material in the Torah possibly began their work earlier in the first Jerusalem temple,[13] continuing it through the Exile, prior to completion of the Torah upon the Return to Jerusalem. The possibility of even earlier connections of the Hebraic traditions to a Vedic source, through Zoroastrianism or independently, continues to lurk just beneath our current understanding, but the trail is getting warmer.

Earlier generations of critical studies realized that the Torah included material gathered during the Babylonian captivity. These materials were then given inspired spiritual meaning by the Jewish compilers. Their editors or redactors, often identified as R, were closely identified with the "priestly" source, known as P, among the array of such sources to be identified in some detail by Marc Brettler in his introduction to the Torah in this compendium. Our awareness of such sources often tended to lump highly sophisticated Persian material from Zoroastrianism in with a broad spectrum of "Babylonian" and other material acquired over the ages and in the earlier years of the Exile. This might include things as diverse as the influence of the Hammurabi Code to the biblical understanding of dreams. But the first chapter of Genesis, with material adopted by Jewish priests late in the P process and prefixed to the existing body of Torah material, shows a theological sophistication the Babylonians never knew. The Jewish priestly school built this chapter on a Hebrew foundation of revealed, received and instinctive material, but the bricks were Zoroastrian refinements of ancient Vedic material. The better we understand the Zoroastrian contribution, the better we understand the biblical Torah. The value of fine-tuning our understanding of the source and the meaning of the creation story will become more apparent as we recognize the implications for world culture. We can then extend the principle to the judgment day, the struggle against evil, the salvation quest, the resurrection and life in paradise, all found in the three religions related to Zoroastrianism.

Even the idea that the era of final victory and judgment would be heralded and facilitated by a messianic savior was first revealed to Zoroaster by the Lord of Wisdom and was promulgated in the Zoroastrian religion. This was long before Judaism, Christianity and Islam had fully developed their own messianic expectations, which were either modeled on Zoroastrianism or based on identical revelations that came later. When Second Isaiah called Cyrus "God's Anointed," the Zoroastrian priests knew exactly what he meant because they had developed the concept in universal application long before they shared those intimate decades with their Jewish civil service, coreligionist priests and dreaming royalists. Again, as in the cases of monotheism and creation, the Hebrews had a messianic hope before the appearance of Zoroaster, but it was refined and strengthened during the final years in Babylon with a speed that indicated active stimulation in a manner entirely compatible with Zoroastrian belief.

We will return to these theological considerations, but for now, we continue the present investigation. Cambyses, who followed Cyrus on the throne of the greatest empire in the world, finally succeeded in enfolding Egypt into it, although his reign lasted only eight years. He was succeeded by Darius, the youngest son of old Vishtaspa, the first Zoroastrian monarch, who was identified as Hystaspes in Greek history by Herodotus, the Greek historian of the fifth century BCE, from whom we get much of this information.[14] Darius extended the empire still further in practically every direction, except for his failed attempt to invade Greece, having his army stopped in its tracks at Marathon by a party of Athenians who initially hoped for nothing more than to delay the presumed Persian conquest. Darius also believed in the Lord of Wisdom as the great God, as attested to by a helpful collection of inscriptions:[15]

> Saith Darius the King: This which I did, in one and the same year, I did by the favour of Ahura Mazda. Ahura Mazda provided aid to me, as did the other divinities. A great God is Ahura Mazda, who created this earth, who created yonder sky, who created man, who created happiness for man, and who made Darius king.

As we see, there were already hints here that strict monotheism was tempered, if not compromised, by the continued recognition of the importance of immortal forces in the universe, "divinities," or angelic spirits. This continued until eventually the change led to fundamental dualism in which Ahura Mazda's power for good was practically matched by the power of Angra Manyu, also known as Ahriman, the chief of demons, described in terms equivalent to the later emerging Satan of Jews, Christians and Muslims. From the same source we read the ambivalent testimony of Darius's successor, Xerxes.

> Saith Xerxes the King: Among these countries there was a place where previous devas were worshipped. Afterwards, by the favour of Ahura Mazda, I destroyed that sanctuary of demons and I made proclamation,—The demons shall not be worshipped! Where previously the demons had been worshipped, there I worshipped Ahura Mazda and Arta.

His successor, Artaxerxes, while loyal to Ahura Mazda, was even more forthcoming with respect to the lesser deva forces:

> Saith Artaxerxes the Great King: By the favour of Ahura Mazda, Anaitis and Mithras I built this palace. A great God is Ahura Mazda, the greatest of gods, who created this earth, who created yonder sky, who created man and who created happiness for man.

Xerxes and Artaxerxes ruled at the apex era of Zoroastrian influence in the world, just beyond the horizon of the West. Xerxes determined to complete the conquest of Greece and move on to Europe, leading a force of 1,700,000 troops, the largest army in world history until the twentieth century. Herodotus tells us that it was Xerxes's infantry alone that numbered 1,700,000 men. There were also 100,000 cavalry, camel corps and chariot corps, plus 300,000 Thracian and Greek mercenaries in his employ, for a total of 2,100,000. There were 541,610 men manning the fleet, for a total armed force of 2,641,610 men. He then adds noncombatants such as cooks, laundry and drivers, to double the total and reach the awesome number of 5,283,220 in the entire military establishment.[16] The last part might be inflated since we do not know the military life of the time, but the proportions are similar to modern armies, and most of these men were present at the battles of Thermopylae and Artemisium in 480 BCE.

The Greeks had learned at Marathon that the Persians could actually be stopped. Between bad logistical planning by Persian generals and the vagaries of weather and luck, not to mention the determined resistance of three hundred elite Spartan troops at the head of a miniscule Greek force, the invaders of Europe from Asia were stalled again at Thermopylae, while the Greek navy, under Athenian leadership, outmaneuvered the Persian armada at Artemisium. Historians tend to regard these two battles as a central turning point in world history, after which Persian fortunes reversed. The Athenian navy actually decimated the Persian navy later that year at the Battle of Salamis, and the following spring the Greek forces led by Sparta caught the Persian army unaware and defeated them soundly at Plataea, leading to general withdrawal. Xerxes is, of course, the Ahasuerus of the biblical book of Esther, in which the monarchy, now focused on conquering Greece and dominating Europe, appeared to have either forgotten about the Jews, still in positions of influence and causing jealousy, or mistakenly assumed that most of them had by now returned to Jerusalem.

Xerxes's son Artaxerxes reigned for forty-one years over what was still by far the dominant world power, though in imperceptible decline as so often happens with great empires. During his reign, Zoroastrianism continued as the state religion but with its monotheism increasingly blurred by both acknowledgment of the other deva forces as lesser gods and by a further slide into dualism in its theology. Artaxerxes became again aware of the Jewish situation when it came to his attention that the rebuilding of the city and its temple had slowed down and that his own capital still had more Jews than did Jerusalem. Highly placed Jewish civil service personnel and theological scholars of the first rank had not seen fit to give up their sinecure. This would change when Artaxerxes appointed Nehemiah, a prominent Jew at the imperial court, as provincial governor[17] with ample resources to finish the job, and Ezra,[18] another prominent Jew, to restore the Temple to its former glory, not merely physically but also academically and theologically, and to do whatever he wanted to do in these regards—resulting in the final editing of the Torah, at least in the reasoned opinion of many Jewish scholars.

The story of the revised and carefully reedited Torah emerging from these events, presented and accepted as "The Law of Moses,"[19] is another epic of significance in world history. This was dealt with in *Forensic Scriptures*, written prior to this compendium, and in the introduction to the Torah by Professor Marc Brettler in the present volume. Suffice it to say here that best-selling fictional intrigues like *The Da Vinci Code* by Dan Brown or the Hollywood presentation by George Lucas of Indiana Jones searching for the Ark of the Covenant in *Raiders of the Lost Ark* pale in comparison with the Bible and the story behind its final composition and our current understanding of how all that came about.[20]

Xerxes II was succeeded by Darius II, who was followed by Artaxerxes II, the empire declining in each case and Zoroastrian religion becoming further removed from its roots in the revelation to its prophet. Upon assassination after two years, Artaxerxes III was next succeeded by Darius III, who lasted not much longer. Then, before Xerxes III could mount the Peacock throne, Alexander the Great had crossed the Hellespont in 334 BCE. He subdued the whole empire within two years and sacked the then capital, Persepolis, in 330. This began an era of Hellenization in which all the Avesta Scriptures that could be confiscated were destroyed, beginning with the burning of thousands of its texts in the library of that once great capital built by the Zoroastrian monarchs.

In summarizing the history of the Persian Empire, we may note that Persia is the European name, based on the name of the best-known province, Fars. Internally it has always been the nation or empire of Aryans or "Iranians" in "Iran." The Achaemenid dynasty, named for Achmenid, the grandfather of Cyrus, lasted from Cyrus in 550 BCE to Alexander in 330 BCE and stretched from Thrace, north of Greece in Europe, across southern Russia to China and from North Africa through Egypt and the Levant to eastern parts of India. It had stable government, wise diplomacy, highly developed arts and culture, a mighty military and Zoroastrian religion.

After a decade in the Macedonian Empire, when Alexander died his general, Seleucus, withdrew from that structure and revived the Persian Empire, initiating the Selucid dynasty. It lasted from 313 BCE to 224 BCE, although the Greek generals were succeeded by Parthian rulers for the last twenty-five years of that era. They expanded the grip of the empire in Turkey and Armenia and extended its reach into Turkmenistan, Tajikistan and Uzbekistan, even while diluting its culture and religion.

In 224 BCE a coup led by a Persian named Ardashir initiated the Sassanian dynasty, named typically for his grandfather, Sassan. The Sassanians revived both Persian culture and the Zoroastrian religion, although the latter had continued the evolution toward a dualistic theology, perhaps latent in

Zoroastrianism from the beginning. Monotheism appears to have survived in its Bactrian stronghold as well as in the rural villages of Fars, but it was in this era that Zoroastrian thought developed in a multitude of directions through previously existing religions like Sabaean and Magian, and also evolved into the Manichean and Mithraic religions. Its influence in Judaism, Christianity and Islam bore the distinct marks of monotheism as revealed and accepted by all three, and also the scars of controversy with dualistic Gnosticism and other seeming aberrations. The Sassanian era ended in 637 CE when Islamic Arabs conquered that empire. They respected and kept much of the Persian style of government, art, architecture and culture that is characteristic of Iran today. Protection was extended to the old monotheistic elements of Zoroastrianism remaining in Bactria and Fars, similar to the protection initially provided for monotheistic Jews and Christians. Although it was the state religion in various forms, dualistic Zoroastrianism was practically annihilated by Islam and its strict monotheism in the seventh and eighth centuries CE, a development perhaps even welcomed by some—at least any who longed for the pure monotheism of bygone days.

Cyrus Returns to the Jews the Temple Vessels Looted by Nebuchadnezzar

3

fROM ZOROASTER to ZOROBABEL

I T HAS BEEN WELL KNOWN AND WIDELY ACCEPTED FOR THE PAST TWO HUNDRED YEARS THAT THE
Hebrew Scriptures, and most particularly the Torah, show clear influences from many
surrounding cultures—Akkadian, Sumerian, Chaldean, Assyrian, Babylonian, possibly
Coptic-Egyptian and even Hittite. There is less evidence of any reciprocal Hebrew influence on those cultures, not because it did not take place, but because Israel survived and the
other cultures did not.

While taking nothing away from Israel's own unique and definitive encounters with the Divine, or
from Israel's own interface with other neighbors, it is now increasingly apparent that these external
influences on Hebrew Scriptural development may have been significantly reinforced through the
encounter with Zoroastrianism in a dynamic interchange under Persian rule during Israel's Exile
in Babylon. Many such influences were embedded in Zoroastrianism.

Likewise, perhaps the most significant of neighborly influences on Zoroastrianism itself, in its
adoption of monotheism, may have been Israel. Nearly a hundred years after the birth of Zoroaster,
as that influence came full circle, the powerful Persian Zoroastrians appropriately respected the
Jews, and the Jews benefited from this theological convergence with those who had taken up the
monotheistic cause and promoted it beyond the borders of Israel.

The Hebrews assimilated and co-opted much of this Zoroastrian influence in the century between
the ascendency of Cyrus in Babylon in 539 BCE and the reading of the final text of the revised,
edited and integrated Torah by Ezra in the Jerusalem public square in 444 BCE. The impact of the
Babylonian Captivity, often referred to simply as the Exile, can hardly be overstated in reference
to Jewish history, sociology, theology and literature. Along with the founding of the modern state
of Israel, the Exile ranks with the sojourn in Egypt, the crossing of the Red Sea and the giving of
the Law at Sinai. Its impact was equal to the Wilderness experience, the Conquest of Canaan and
the more recent Holocaust (Shoah). Israel went into the Exile experience with traditions, liturgy,
law, literature, historic legends, monotheism and foundational theology, and it came out of the
experience with the Torah, which defines Israel in all the ways indicated by Ellen Frankel in her
insightful preface to this study.

The Zoroastrian influence may now be seen as also one explanation for the ways in which the
Torah has profoundly influenced the shape of our still emerging world culture. To set the scene for
a new or renewed appreciation of the Torah and other Hebrew Scriptures, it may be helpful at this
point to offer the reader a word picture of the Avesta itself, or what remains of it. Originally it was
considerably more voluminous than all the classical Hebrew writings in our possession—Scriptural,
apocryphal texts and noncanonical materials combined. Like the Bible itself, the Avesta was (and
what remains of it is still) a compendium of documents written in various related languages. The
oldest portions contain material that is revised from Vedic sources that were somewhat previous

to Abraham, down to final texts composed just prior to the closing of the canon of the Christian Scriptures. The Avesta as a whole may therefore be regarded as a slightly older contemporary of the entire Bible and a powerful background context for it.

Mention has been made of the deliberate destruction of the Avesta in a conflagration under the direction of Alexander the Great in 330 BCE. This desecration was part of a program to "Hellenize" his empire, the first of many European attempts to "civilize" the rest of the world. Following the break-up of that empire, the Parthians governed Persia from 150 to 250 CE and revived the vigor of the Zoroastrian religion. This was especially evident under King Vologese, who commissioned an attempt to recover Avesta materials from scattered fragments, to write down the oral traditions and liturgies, and to gather Zoroastrian quotations from Greek manuscripts. A brief disruption of the project by political and military upheavals was followed by a revival of the Persian Empire itself in the Sassanian era, 250–650 CE, in which Zoroastrianism became again the state religion. Its high priests succeeded in collecting the surviving Avesta documents into twelve volumes called *nasks*, producing the first official Zoroastrian canon not long after the establishment of the Hebrew canon and just shortly before the closing of the Christian canon.

Sadly, from Jewish and Christian perspectives, new materials produced in these popular revivals were increasingly dualistic in nature, so that by the time of Muhammad, Zoroastrian monotheism was largely a memory. The surviving portions of the Avesta itself were ambivalent in this regard, so most of what remained was eventually obliterated by the fervently monotheistic Muslims when they took over Persia in the seventh century CE. Both confirmation of the early monotheistic truths of the Avesta and condemnation of its latter dualism are almost certainly to be found in the Quran, as we hope to discover in Book Three of this compendium.

What remains today of the original documents consists of portions from several religious nasks, both monotheistic and mixed, and one lawbook of social regulations. These have been put together from documents and fragments hidden by the few remaining Zoroastrian believers in Persia/Iran, or spirited out of the country by refugees fleeing to India at that time and later. They were supplemented by well-known and much-loved hymns, dating back to Zoroaster himself, which could be reproduced by believers at any time. There is just enough that we can outline the development of the Avesta as a whole, prior to tracing its influence on the Torah, and also considering its influence in the world of the Torah, in which the rest of the Hebrew Scriptures were produced in the form we know.

Europeans were actually unaware of the Avesta until after the seventeenth century, when, with the growth of trade with India, manuscript copies began to reach Europe. The French scholar A. H. Anquetil du Perron (1731–1805) went to India, learned to read the Avestan language from a Parsi priest in Surat, acquired manuscripts and produced a translation. European study of the Avesta subsequently paralleled and drew support from the study of the earliest Sanskrit literature, which was linguistically related. More recent translations are more reliable, using tools produced by Mary Boyce, who had a Sanskrit scholastic background and became fluent in the Persian Avestan cognate languages as preserved in the rural Zoroastrian communities of Iran.

The core of the surviving or extant Avesta is a small collection of writings called the Gathas, universally recognized as prophetic utterances by Zoroaster himself. We refer to their language as Gathic Avestan, an ancient Indo-European language that serves as a link between Sanskrit and Hindi to the southeast and Greek and Latin to the northwest, each with their own linguistic offshoots. At each stage of the Avesta's development, it also displays a linguistic affinity with Aramaic, its linguistic contemporary as spoken in Persia, and a link with Hebrew. The Gathas have an oracular quality, somewhat cryptic, rhetorical, and poetically melodic—an apocalyptic literature, the first in the world. Like other ancient linguistic traditions, these factors make them difficult to translate, so they are cherished by Zoroastrians today in the original as memorized. There are only about six thousand words in the Gathas, recorded in five distinct poems, each with its own meter. They present Zoroaster's sublime expression of belief in one uncreated Lord of Wisdom, and they outline what this God expects of people in the universal and the personal struggle between good and evil, between truth and falsehood. God's will is presented as both invitation and command, detailed equally in worship and in good deeds as opposed to false gods and bad deeds.

The second surviving "text" of the Avesta was possibly written by a school of Zoroaster's disciples, probably during his lifetime or soon after, although Mary Boyce, as the world's leading academic authority on the Gathic Avestan dialect, believed it, too, may have been composed entirely by Zoroaster later in his life.[1] Titled "Worship in Seven Chapters" in translation, it is known in the Zoroastrian community as the Yasna Haptanhaiti. The prayers in these seven chapters are more like hymns than poems, invoking the Lord of Wisdom as well as the sacred devas or "guardian angels" who protect the earth, sky and sea. In direct correspondence to the prophet's teaching, they profess devotion to the truth and seek the happiness and fulfillment of the believers in serving God in good thoughts (worship) and in good deeds (action).

The third book, simply known as Yasna, "Worship," begins at chapter 28, implying that the seven chapters of the Yasna Haptanhaiti was once preceded by twenty-one poems, chapters or other materials by Zoroaster and/or his disciples (including his five Gathas), all of which would have existed in the Persian community when Jewish exiles were in dialogue with Zoroastrian priests. Yasna, too, is primarily liturgical, consisting of rubrics and instructions for worship. The Yasna has seventy-two chapters at present and appears rather complete. Written somewhat later in a dialect known as "Younger Avestan," in it we catch a glimpse of creationism and cosmological inferences from its introduction of the old devas of the Vedic pantheon. They are called *yazatas*, and they are regarded as spirits whose only purpose now is to serve and glorify the Lord of Wisdom.

A fourth collection, titled the Visparad, is much smaller at this point, also written in a Younger Avestan dialect. Its purpose is to simply comment on much of what we find in the first three collections.

The fifth series of documents is called the Yashts, or "Services" of worship. There are twenty-one complete Yashts, and other bits and pieces, all based on ancient Vedic hymns. These have been thoroughly reworked to conform with Zoroastrian monotheism, as they laud the yazatas as models for humans to emulate in service to the Lord of Wisdom. Ahura Mazda is extolled, using the Younger Avestan translation of his name, *Ormazd*, which came into use even before the Common Era, although modern Zoroastrians have largely maintained the use of *Ahuramazda*.

In the Yashts, in spite of their beauty, the Zoroastrian religion appears to begin the transition toward dualism, a form of Zoroastrianism that did not ultimately survive. There are yasht hymns to specific yazatas or reinvigorated Vedic devas, like *Mah*, the Moonlight, or *Tir*, the Starshine, and *Aban*, the Waterfall. The latter features a recycled Vedic hymn to the river goddess Ardvi Sura Anahita, a hymn still in use among Hindus in the twenty-first century. These days, a similar concept of angelic presences, long associated with Catholic and orthodox Christian tradition, appears to be undergoing a popular revival among Jews, Protestants and Muslims in our popular culture. Such hymn poems are among the most sublime passages in the Avesta, and they may remind us of the romantic devotion to nature found in new age greeting cards and recordings used for meditation today. We may find some of them represented in the Quran in a more theologically complete form.

The danger was always in compromising the rigorous abstraction of Zoroaster's original monotheistic vision. That danger is illustrated in Yashts extolling the beauty of green pastures and still waters, but without the shepherd. Others extol the endurance of the *Fravashis*, the souls of good people, but with no reference to the goodness of God. The fire may give a certain charm to the hearth, but without the warmth of God's spirit that it represents, the most beautiful moments are but fleeting illusions. This Zoroastrianism resembled a greeting card religion, with beautiful sentiment but few demands, subject only, if we are correct, to such sentiments being revealed to Muhammad in an appropriate form acceptable to God—much like the re-presentation of Hebrew and Christian revelations.

The balance needed for the use of such imagery to experience and to reflect God's glory was about to be lost in Zoroastrianism. Once the power of these aesthetic devas was no longer used to serve and glorify God, and as they themselves became the object of meditation or worship, the direct encounter between humans and God was gone. With it went the impetus for personal morality and the imperative for social justice, both lost in the loveliness and beauty of an antiseptic religion that never dirties its hands—a precursor to sermons and discussions in many synagogues, churches and masjids today, distinguishing between the demands of the Creator and the desires of the created.

The sixth and concluding section in the extant Avesta material is the Vendidad, intended to exorcise demons, but in confirming their power, the Vendidad reinforces many of the negative stereotypes of Zoroastrianism that have existed in many quarters. Published sometime after 300 CE, halfway between the lifetimes of Jesus and Muhammad, it continues the momentum of Vedic revival in the service of a dualistic worldview Zoroaster would have found abhorrent.

Without a solid monotheistic underpinning, Zoroastrianism by this time bore little resemblance to the pristine faith encountered by the Jews in Babylon. The Vendidad appears to be a recapitulation of earlier texts, now lost, but the clumsy use of the Avestan language gives it a strained tone. Its prescriptions for the purification of women in menstruation, priests *in flagrante*, animals and corpses are said to be still observed in remote rural Zoroastrian villages in Iran and India. The Vendidad is either ignored or scorned by many urbane Zoroastrians today in Tehran, Mumbai, London, Toronto, New York and Sydney.

However, even the Vendidad contains traces of the original revelation that could not be entirely expunged from Zoroastrianism and which accounts for the strict monotheism of Zoroastrians in the twenty-first century. Such chapters in this section are called *Fargards* (singular *Fargan*), where the "requirements" (commandments or criterion) of God are both elucidated and confused. This was too late for clarification or correction by Jews or Christians, both of whom were indifferent in any event, but the Zoroastrian situation was ripe for reform. Purification came by the Muslims in the zeal of their ascendency. The name of the Fargan commandments in the latter Zoroastrian Avesta appears to materialize again in a "corrected" version as *Furqan* in Arabic, translated as the *Criterion* of God in the fresh revelation given to Muhammad in the Quran.

In addition to these large and significant Zoroastrian Avesta texts, there is also the Khordah Avesta, the "Little Avesta" still in use as the prayer book by Zoroastrians today. Composed and collected at an undetermined time during one of the attempts to recover texts and summarize the teachings in a worshipful context, the Khordah Avesta contains quotes from all the other collections, as well as fragments not found anywhere else. In one part of this Little Avesta, Zoroaster presents a revelation in which Ahura Mazda, the Lord of Wisdom, or simply God, repeatedly uses the phrase I AM as a title. In detail, God says:

> I AM the Keeper.
> I AM the Creator.
> I AM the Maintainer.
> I AM the Discerner.
> I AM the Beneficent.

Taken with other tenuous connections, some yet to be presented, we have here the clearest indication so far of a specific linkage between Zoroastrianism and the much earlier Hebrew tradition of God speaking from the burning bush to Moses. The Zoroastrian I AM passages are an obvious throwback to and an elaboration of the seminal utterance in which God asserts an identity as "the One who is," the I AM.[2] The full meaning and impact of this tantalizing allusion can only be realized when taken as part of a larger picture, but it begins to emerge that Zoroastrianism owed a great debt to Israel as the first major religion to draw from that monotheistic source.

The messianic references in Deuteronomy were touched up during the Exile to give them a more universal cast,[3] no doubt under Zoroastrian influence. Even more important, and more readily apparent now, is the certainty that the Jewish priests somehow maintained the cohesion of their work that began in Jerusalem, through the earlier years of the Exile in Babylon, until that dynamic epoch when they worked intimately in an inspired interplay with the Zoroastrian priests of the Persian regime. A result of this hybrid moment in religious history was the Hebrew spiritualization of the pristine Zoroastrian view of creation, structured around older Vedic cosmologies and Babylonian "science," which we have in Genesis, chapter 1.

The whole of the book of Leviticus might even be seen as a Zoroastrian sacrifice manual that overlays the Hebrew experience of forty years in the wilderness. However, if the priestly material in the Torah frequently displays such Zoroastrian subtexts, nothing herein is meant to undermine the importance of the whole patriarchal period as represented by the preexilic sources of the Pentateuch, all brilliantly integrated by Ezra and his team of Zoroastrian-funded scholars following the Return to Jerusalem from the Exile.

Along with Zoroaster's articulation of creation in seven days and his descriptions of a messianic savior of the world, social justice, personal salvation and a highly developed system of sacrifice, mainstream Judaism was suddenly inundated by Zoroastrian concepts such as Satan, judgment, resurrection and paradise, each with a prominence unlike anything preexilic. In some respects, pristine Zoroastrianism may be regarded as an "Old Testament" of the Torah and as a principal source of the theology of the Christian Scriptures. It also underlies the Quran in a textual dialogue we have yet to examine in depth. In its language and in certain basic concepts, Zoroastrianism even links these three religions to their more distant cousins further east, all descended from Vedic ancestors.

The Zoroastrians had already assimilated the religious and cultural traditions of the whole Mesopotamian region into their own wider Aryan worldview, inherited through Vedic traditions. In his moments of revelation from God, these resources were purified, refined and inspired by Zoroaster, as we see by their appearance in the Avesta Scriptures, both those surviving and those we are now in the process of recovering from the Quran. The Jewish priests took this hybrid "knowledge" (*gnosis*) and "wisdom" (*sophia*) of the universe, integrated it into their cherished tribal collections of religious folk stories, legends and history, and gave it the final meanings we find in the Bible, all at the dictation of the Divine One.

Just as there was a plurality of expressions of Christianity competing in the early centuries CE, before the theology of the Orthodox/Catholic church became predominant, so also there were competing visions of Judaism, especially in the era before the destruction of Jerusalem in 70 CE. These were represented by various parties and sects, some of which were eventually subsumed into Rabbinic Judaism, itself sometimes described as a new religion at that point. Others have maintained "underground" connections, communities and literatures down to the present day. Most of the latter display distinct Zoroastrian influences.

Herodotus first described the Magi, for example, as a priestly caste of the Medes. When the Persian Zoroastrians defeated Medes, the Magi converted to become Zoroastrian priests. When the Zoroastrians were eventually supplanted, it appears that the Magi continued their spiritual perambulations by adapting further, rather than disappearing. In *Three Testaments* we do not attempt to define or track the Magi evolution or its integration with other movements, except to point to a whole underground of such Eastern traditions that still continue in Judaism and elsewhere.

The Gnostic movement, to give a similar example, appears to have developed the Persian Zoroastrian cosmology, itself forged out of earlier Vedic and later Babylonian material, into a hybrid union emphasizing the conflict between the forces of light and the forces of darkness. Both the cosmology and the conflict derive from Zoroastrianism, but in this context they combine to look like pages right out of the Dead Sea Scrolls and the Nag Hammadi Library. There was thus a Zoroastrian subtext for most of the literature in the area, emerging in many movements that appear heterodox to orthodox Jews, Christians and Muslims, although they themselves exhibit Zoroastrian traits in their own material.

This pervasiveness of Zoroastrianism is only surprising to the modern reader because it is largely outside the tradition of European literatures from Greece and Rome and off the radar screen of Western history. Before the dominant Roman Empire, and previous to Alexander the Great, the only ancient "superpower" was that Persian Empire that was twice thrown back at Europe's borders. It remained over the horizon from the West, except that its religion seeped into everything that came westward, especially through Persia's client state, Israel. This included much of what developed as mature orthodoxy, as well as heterodox elements on the fringes of Judaism. The importance and value of all these traditions is being reexamined today, not only to expand our understanding of the context of the Torah and other Scriptures, but also for intrinsic spiritual values they may possess in their own right.

Zoroastrian-inspired cognate religions and sects are also of interest today for what light they may now shed on our quest to understand and recover information about Zoroastrianism itself. This task is doubly complicated by the fact that in addition to never really registering in the Western consciousness, both the Persian Empire and its Zoroastrian state religion were later obliterated by Islam, which destroyed most of the remaining literature of the latter. The exceptions are Scriptural fragments and hymns in the extant Avesta, references in the work of ancient Western historians and gleanings from quotations in early Western literature. To this we may add the information we are now unearthing from between the lines of the Quran, which may lead to possible new spinoff intimations about Zoroastrianism from the Torah and the Gospel as well. In addition to its thousand-year regional influence, it may be important to recall that Persian rule influenced Israel for over two hundred years from 539 until 330 BCE in a specific and direct manner. Only part of this time was during the Exile, with Torah production extending well into the later client state era in which cordial relations with Persia, its religion and its literature, continued.

The overlaps with noncanonical traditions of Jewish literature are also instructive. For example, these days, from Hollywood to Bollywood, Cabalism increasingly replaces Scientology as the religious vogue of movie stars, many of whom prefer to dabble outside the religious mainstream. It is sometimes spelled "Kabbalah" in Jewish circles, with the smaller Christian and Muslim offshoots seeming to prefer "Cabala" and "Qaballah," respectively.

This ancient esoteric Jewish mystical tradition of philosophy, containing strong elements of pantheism, is often accused of practicing "magic" from the Magi tradition, although it is also compared to neo-Platonism. Cabalistic writing reached its peak between the thirteenth and sixteenth centuries CE. Although largely rejected by modern Judaic thought as medieval superstition, Cabalism has greatly influenced ultra-Orthodox Hasidic and Lubavitch sects, and it had a certain cachet among Theosophists in New York in the twentieth century. The latter are members of a wealthy philosophical sect who have regarded themselves as the new Zoroastrians, perhaps with some justification.

As a leading theosophist has put it, "The hidden wisdom of the Hebrew rabbis of the middle ages was derived from older secret doctrines concerning divine things and cosmogony. These were combined into a theology after the time of the captivity of the Jews in Babylon. All works that fall under this esoteric category are termed kabalistic."[4]

According to H. P. Blavatsky, who was one of the founders of Theosophy, these disseminators of the Zoroastrian tradition, in the early centuries of the Common Era, were known as *Tanaim*. "The kabalist is a student of 'secret science,' one who interprets the hidden meaning of the Scriptures with the help of the symbolical Kabala. . . . The Tanaim were the first kabalists among the Jews; they appeared at Jerusalem about the beginning of the third century before the Christian era. . . . This secret doctrine is identical with Persian wisdom, or 'magic.'"[5] According to the Jewish Encyclopedia, Cabalists claim to have received their traditions of numbers and incantations, not from ancient Chaldeans through the Zoroastrians, but actually from the Patriarchs and Prophets "by the power of the Holy Spirit"; that is, orally, rather than in a written form like the Torah.

Because of its heretical nature, the Cabala was not generally promulgated among the Jews but remained the "secret doctrine" of "elect" members of the Jewish community. That is to say, certain Jews who were deemed worthy could comprehend hidden teachings in the written Torah and, through mystical techniques, make direct contact with God. Among these practices are rapid recitation of the "Holy Name of God" (YHWH, the "Tetragrammaton"); meditation on the eleven Sephiroth of the Tree of Life, which are believed to be emanations of God; learning to use the twenty-two letters of the Hebrew alphabet as force-carrying energy patterns that serve as the building blocks of the cosmos; and, finally, transcending the space/time limitations of the physical world to realize one's "inner divinity."

This "secret doctrine" has been preserved throughout the ages to the present time by a spiritual community whose members progress individually to various stages of enlightenment and proficiency in the hidden wisdom—from "elect" to "adepts" to "wise men" (or magi) and finally to those "adept in grace." Cabalism projects a connectedness of the Jewish, Christian and Muslim religions and their Scriptures, as well as Zoroastrianism. For example, it refers to the "tree of life" found in both Genesis 1 and Revelation 22 (the first and last chapters of most Bibles) as the "Lote tree," which emanates power before God's throne in both the Quran and Zoroastrian hymns.

A fourth example of the pervasiveness of Zoroastrian influence would be "Wisdom Literature." In Judaism, Wisdom is a body of Scriptural writings consisting of Job, Proverbs, Ecclesiastes, Song of Solomon, plus certain Wisdom Psalms in the Ketubin writings of Hebrew Scriptures, as well as Ecclesiasticus, the Wisdom of Solomon, Books of Esdras, Tobit and Baruch in the Apocrypha (which is Jewish but counted as Scripture by only Roman Catholic and Orthodox Christians). Wisdom Literature also includes a large body of material from Egypt, ancient Greece and many Mesopotamian cultures, including Akkadian, Sumerian, Ugaritic and Babylonian. Along with Gnosticism and Cabala, Wisdom also enjoys a trendy vogue early in the twenty-first century, as liberal Jews, mainstream Christians, Sufi Muslims and others increasingly explore writings related to but outside their canonical traditions.

Wisdom literature in the Bible lacks the grandeur of the Torah and the power of the Prophets of Israel, both of which may have counterparts in the Avestas. But Wisdom teaches the basics of right and wrong and the importance of good deeds as opposed to evil deeds, both high on the Zoroastrian agenda. The Wisdom literature of Israel was produced mainly in the postexilic period, and Daniel itself has elements of the Wisdom style, perhaps developed in embryonic format while the community was still in Persia. The spirituality of Israel's monotheistic Wisdom exceeds its counterparts in the Wisdom literature of practically all cultures in the vicinity, with the possible exception of Zoroastrianism, whose Wisdom texts are among the missing parts of that once vast compendia. Because Ahura Mazda is the "Lord of Wisdom," the expectation might be that Zoroastrianism was a major contributor to the Wisdom genre. In extant literature, only the Book of Job could possibly qualify as an example of Wisdom material from Zoroastrianism, a subject to which we shall return.

Before the discovery of the Dead Sea Scrolls, there was broad scholarly interest in the group who Greek and Latin authors called *Essenes*. In the years since the discovery of those scrolls, interest in the Essenes has been reduced to almost a single issue: their identity as the people living at Qumran who wrote the scrolls and stored them near that site. Early in the twenty-first century, understanding of the Essenes has broadened again to the ways in which they were described by Philo, Pliny, Josephus and the encyclopedic Dio of Prusa, in the light of recent research on these authors.[6] It would now appear that the scrolls may have been written by an entirely different group living at Qumran. The only real link between the Essenes and that group may be their separate but substantial connections to Zoroastrianism, which impacted most things Judaic during and after the Exile, as noted, and which also influenced Israel's neighbors until the Muslim era.

Whatever the connection between the two groups at Qumran, they both wore the white gowns of the Zoroastrian tradition for initiation, as did candidates for baptism in the church and other sectarian offshoots of Judaism. It has been suggested that a Jewish high priest named Onias, or some members of the Zadokite house, may have founded the other Qumran community, whoever they were. In the Rule of the Community, the Dead Sea Scrolls themselves suggest a central role for the descendants of Zadok the Priest,[7] and the name of the "Teacher of Righteousness" (*Moreh Zedek*) may point to a Zadokite. This was one of several parties rising to prominence following the Exile due to Persian Zoroastrian influence, which had elevated this particular priestly group earlier in Babylon.

Finally, in reference to the Torah, special consideration should be given to the Pharisee movement that had its origins in the Persian era of Babylon. This Farsi, Parsee, Pharisee or "Persian" party appeared first during the latter years of the Exile, adopted the Zoroastrian doctrines of judgment, resurrection and paradise, and promoted these theological concepts in the Return to Jerusalem. They maintained and defended these doctrines all through the subsequent Maccabean era, the occupations that followed, the fall and destruction of Jerusalem, the defining of the canon of Jewish Scripture with the Torah at its core, and the establishment of the Rabbinical Judaism that remains the dominant form of the religion to this day. The Pharisee tradition was therefore one of the most influential forces in putting the Persian stamp of Zoroastrianism on Judaism then and now.

Beyond this survey one might expect to find evidence for or against Zoroastrian influence in Jewish literature in the Talmud, especially since it appears in two important versions, the Jerusalem Talmud and the Babylonian Talmud. The latter is actually the more senior, as a fulsome written record of conversations going back more than a thousand years into the Exile. However, experts in this field are sharply divided. The opinion of Jacob Neusner, regarded by many as the scholar with the greatest knowledge of Babylonia during the Sassanian era, was typical until recently. In his opinion, what the rabbis of the Talmud knew of Zoroastrianism amounted to virtually nothing at all.[8] However, a 2007 Jewish conference at the University of California in Los Angeles advertised its interest in this question as a new discipline.

> For several decades, scholars of rabbinic literature have looked towards Rome, and Greco-Roman culture more generally, in order to provide a framework for understanding rabbinic texts of Palestinian provenance. This attempt to reach beyond the strictures of the literature itself has opened up avenues of inquiry and has yielded a more nuanced understanding of how Jews as a minority participated within the Greco-Roman world. More recently, scholars of the Babylonian Talmud have turned to the orbit of Iranian civilization. Undoubtedly, the notion that the rabbis of the Talmud may have been exposed to the theological and liturgical discourse of the Zoroastrian religion, or more directly affected by Sasanian legal practices, has many significant implications for scholars of Rabbinics, as well as for Iranists.[9]

Echoing our present study, this new level of interest in Zoroastrianism may produce results, but at the present time the investigations are at an early stage of a new phase. This is but one of several indications that Zoroastrian studies may occupy much of our attention in the twenty-first century, including less scholarly but insightful popular forays into the topic such as the recent biography of Zoroaster under the title *The Man Who Sent the Magi*,[10] currently popular in Catholic Christian circles.

Zoroastrianism also impacted the Nevi'im, or Prophecies of Israel, as we will see clearly in the instances of at least four prophets considered in the next chapter, but its main influence on Israel was in the final stages of Torah development. Possibly this happened through minor amendments to the final text of Deuteronomy, and it had a major impact on the priestly material with which the Torah opens. This material is scattered through Genesis, Exodus and Numbers, and possibly underlies Leviticus in its entirety.

The extended family of Abraham, Sarah and Hagar may now begin to give greater weight to Zoroastrianism as a background contributor to Hebrew, Christian and Muslim Scriptures, based partly on new appreciations of Avestan Scriptural material reflected in the Quran and as supported by the reasonable presumption of a unique mutuality between Jewish and Zoroastrian priests in Babylon. But it would help with the apparent lack of hard evidence from the Torah itself if we could find a direct reference to Zoroaster somewhere in the Hebrew Scriptures. The student hoping to find such a reference might start with a biblical encyclopedia. No entry exists under the name of Zoroaster in any such resource, but the eye might be led to the word *Zerubbabel*, an entry about the grandson of King Jehoiachin, the last monarch of the southern kingdom of Judah.

Born in Babylon and thoroughly immersed in its culture, even the name of Zerubbabel was not Hebrew but Babylonian or Persian, a strange name for the presumptive heir to the throne of the homesick exiles. It was Zerubbabel who would be called upon by the new Persian Zoroastrian rulers of Babylon to lead the people back to Jerusalem, and it was he who would be entrusted with considerable treasure in the form of a government grant large enough to rebuild the city and resettle the inhabitants. He also rebuilt the "sanctuary" in Jerusalem, not exactly as a Zoroastrian fire-temple, but as a place of sacrifice influenced by the temples and possibly the liturgies of the benefactor. Its worship services were implemented in a manner described for the first time in the Book of Leviticus, where the multiplication of fire sacrifices is exponential and immediate, relying on information now "remembered" by the Jewish priests during the Exile or "revealed" to them there, with fire sacrifices in chapters 1–10 including "perpetual fire" unique in the Torah.

The curious student might then note that the alternate spelling of his name in English is "Zorobabel," used in the New Testament and the Apocrypha, among other places. Easily translated as "Zoro of Babylon," this name might be seen as an obvious eponym for Zoroaster in the genealogy of the royal family of Judah. It may be a linguistic connection to the name of the Zoroastrian founder and prophet, notwithstanding more complicated explanations of the name of this prince in various respected commentaries. The traditional Hebrew view is that Zerubbabel's name embeds the name of Babylon, or *Babel*, and that the prefix *zeru* infers the verb phrase *to disperse*, but in the words of an old song debunking religious myths, "It ain't necessarily so." An elucidation of a possible connection to Zoroastrianism even solves a long-standing problem of the dating of Zorobabel's activities, since placing his birth somewhat later than is usually suggested works better in several regards in relation to his relationship with Ezra and others.

"Zorobabel" is the spelling rendered in the Greek Septuagint version of the Hebrew Scriptures, as adopted in the Latin, French and most other languages, while only English Bibles follow the Hebrew tradition with a transliteration of the Persian spelling. This commentary will make frequent use of the more universal spelling, "Zorobabel," inferring a connection to Zoroaster, the Greek spelling of "Zarathustra," as the Septuagint translators must have almost certainly intended. They appear to have deliberately devised a Greek spelling of Zorobabel's name that conveniently matches with the Greek spelling of the old prophet, Zoroaster.

To concede the possibility of a scholastic oversight in this regard, it may be helpful to develop the argument further with assistance from Carol and Eric Meyers, who touch upon the etymology in a review of the name *Zarubbabel* in their studies of the postexilic prophets, particularly Haggai and Zechariah.[11] Though they had no intention of connecting the name of Zorobabel with Zoroaster, a possibility they never addressed, their background information about difficulties with the name helps to open up this possibility.

Apparently various forms of names similar to this one were common in Babylon before the Persian conquest. They are found in some form in inscriptions before the Achaemenid period, in which the spelling might be rendered in English as "Zerbabili."[12] These earlier cognate forms of the name are usually taken to mean "offspring of Babylon" or "seed of Babylon." Carol and Eric Meyers suggest that later occurrences which incorporate *bbl* may do so in deference to a god of the city, "perhaps the chief god of Babylon,"[13] hardly a suitable connection for the name of a presumptive future king of Israel. Actually, no exact parallel of his name, as found in postexilic Hebrew Scripture, appears anywhere in Babylonian script. It is no stretch to recognize a possible ingratiating intention on the part of the Jewish royal family in exile as they adapted this name to honor and connect with new and powerful monotheistic Zoroastrian allies approaching the city.

Academic traditions ignoring this connection are themselves weak, depending on an early date for the birth of Zorobabel, long prior to the arrival of the Persians, whereas recent archaeological evidence suggests he remained as governor until almost 500 BCE.[14] However, even if he was born as early as 559 BCE, the Jewish royal family in exile, with its sophisticated priesthood intact and well-placed administrators in the Babylonian civil service, could have been heartened by the rise of the Zoroastrian autocrat, Cyrus, to the east of Babylon. They might well have named a child in honor or anticipation of the rising influence of Zoroastrian monotheism, whose leader, Cyrus, was causing Babylon to tremble. Of course, the spellings using the prefix *Zoro* relate to Greek spellings, as in *Zoroaster* and *Zorobabel*. In the original texts we would be looking for prefixes such as the Persian *Zara*, as in *Zarathustra*, possibly rendered *Zaru* in Hebrew, as suggested by the Meyers team regarding Zerubbabel.[15] The likelihood of a deliberate connection between Zarathustra and Zerubbabel in Hebrew, or Zoroaster and Zorobabel in the Greek of the Septuagint, deserves further consideration.

Zoroastrianism continued, overshadowing Judaism in certain respects, into the Common Era, when, in addition to the Persian state religion, it was manifested in two particular mutant forms as Mithraism and Manichaeism. The first was a muscular religion associated with the Roman military, and the second a Zoroastrian-Gnostic hybrid of Christianity and Buddhism founded by the Persian prophet, Mani, whose followers believed him to be the Saoshyant or Messiah. In these forms it was both engaged and co-opted by the rise of Christianity and confronted and quashed by Islam.

Recent scholarship has advanced the practice of looking to the future unfolding of an idea as much as to its past in understanding its tradition. *Zara* as a name meaning "Shining" or "Radiance" has been used for millennia for both men and women in Hindi, Farsi and Kurdish, a linguistic marker among those cultures of former Zoroastrian ethos. Spelled "Al-Zarah" in Arabic, could this middle name Muhammad gave to his favored daughter, Fatima, reflect a respect the Prophet had developed for Zarathustra himself as he traveled among the Zoroastrians as a teen and as a youthful caravan boss, exposed to both the pristine beauty of the tradition as well as its later disintegration? Names continue to be chosen with care by families both humble and exalted. The Persian origin of the name Zara Phillips, suggested by Prince Charles, did not escape notice by the British press at her baptism in 1981 or at the wedding in 2011 of this granddaughter of Queen Elizabeth II, twelfth in line to the British throne.

Popular culture may also offer as much instinctive *sophia* or *gnosis* as formal scholarship, whereby we might recognize the name Zara Zara from the theme song in the 2008 Bollywood movie, *Race*—just one more Zoroastrian "coincidence" in a world in which Zarathustra may be coming back into his own. For that matter, a recognition of God by the name of Ahura Mazda appeared in the twentieth century in a similar way among a few ingenious souls. Thomas Edison had named the two companies he merged to become General Electric as Mazda Electric and the Mazda Service and Development Company.[16] In 1931 the Toyo Cork Kogyo Company called its first three-wheeled truck Mazda "after the all-knowing God of Zarathustra," the name used for the line of cars popular since the 1960s.[17]

The "Tomb" of Cyrus, a Zoroastrian "Astodan" Facility for Bone Storage

4

ísrael's redeemer

THE HEBREW, CHRISTIAN AND MUSLIM SCRIPTURES ALL OPEN AND CLOSE WITH CHAPTERS THAT are not directly from the Avesta but are clearly related to Zoroastrian sources. The proof of this assertion will be presented in reference to The Gospel in Book Two of this compendium and in reference to the Quran in Book Three. For our present purposes in Book One, we examine chapter 1 of Genesis and the postexilic Book of Malachi, first and last in the traditional arrangement of Hebrew Scriptures, along with other postexilic prophets and related material.

The priestly material that forms the opening chapter of Genesis includes earlier Babylonian references as well as Vedic sources from Zoroastrian antecedents, both subsumed into a uniquely Hebrew wisdom-type theological interpretation. Valid as these observations from traditional scholarship may be, by the time of the Exile such external references were both integral to Zoroastrian teaching and sweeping the entire region. The first chapter of Genesis is implicitly couched in terms of the creation story as contained in the most ancient available Zoroastrian texts with ancient and intrinsic Vedic references and is explicitly framed in the Babylonian cosmology adopted by the Persians. The material lacked only the deeply inspirational touches added through God's grace by the Hebrew priests, out of Israel's experience and from the Jewish perspective.

During the Exile or soon after the Return, this refined Zoroastrian creation motif was prepended to the Hebrew compendium as the opening chapter of the Torah. It was to serve as a background for what was to come from distinctly Hebrew sources in chapter 2. The Zoroastrian sense of the personal responsibility given by God to each person was strengthened in references to the first humans, who were mandated to both develop the resources of the earth and to replenish it. By the time the Hebrew prophets joined their efforts to the Scriptural enterprise, the struggle between good and evil was expressed in terms of light and darkness, apocalyptic language had entered the biblical idiom, and the role of Messiah was expanded to some degree from the hope for renewal of the national monarchy to some expectation of a universal Savior. During the Exile, Satan also achieved his biblical persona, and the concepts of judgment, resurrection, paradise and the Kingdom of God were all introduced, extrapolated and subsumed into the Hebrew corpus, from which they extended into Christian and Muslim revelations.

Illustration and validation of the hypothesis regarding the enrichment and refining of Israel's theology is found in regulations for worship in the Book of Leviticus. It is framed by the tabernacle activities that are introduced at the end of Exodus and concluded at the beginning of Numbers, an introduction and a conclusion that serve as figurative bookends for Leviticus. The fact is that tabernacle sacrifices are never even mentioned in the preexilic Torah sections of Hebrew Scripture. Remarkably, the tabernacle itself is not even mentioned in Deuteronomy, except for a single verse later inserted into chapter 31. There and elsewhere in the Torah, except for Leviticus, only the tabernacle's physical description is given, with no hints whatsoever of what went on in its inner sanctum. That was introduced only after the encounter with Zoroastrianism.

The details of sacrificial and liturgical aspects of worship were not recorded by the earlier writers, J and E, were forgotten or omitted from the oral history, or were so simple in format as to be without substance until "remembered" during the exile,[1] almost certainly under Zoroastrian influence. This is so amazing that if the traditional preexilic sources are accurate depictions of the Wilderness experience from three eyewitness traditions (J, E and D), it justifies the offsetting of Leviticus as unique and of a different genre, even though it is shorter than the usual scroll length, encapsulating a sacrificial system that was just one of the many spiritual gifts of Zoroastrianism to Judaism and the world.

It was also Zoroaster who bequeathed to us the concept of linear time that is so fundamental to the understanding of progress in the life of Western civilization and is now integral to world culture. Ancient civilizations from Egypt to India and China had been limited by the sense that the order of things had been decreed by the gods of a bygone mythical era, a Golden Age to which they aspired to return by never deviating from the established precepts. In his vision of the Kingdom of God, Zoroaster gave Persian rulers a teleological concept of time, which provided a purpose to history and goals for their rule. He taught that all humans were warriors in the cosmic battle between light and darkness, good and evil. The earth was the field of battle, and every person's physical body was the site of a firefight that was part of a campaign that would finally result in victory and the establishment of the Kingdom of God.

Persia never did successfully conquer Europe militarily, but the particular Zoroastrian principle of progress toward a teleological goal became a defining characteristic of Greek philosophy in a conquest of Europe that would be permanent. This spiritual and philosophical conquest was supported by subsequent legions of Jews and Christians, who also followed Zoroaster in this regard, a conquest that placed Europe in the lead of the column of progress for much of human history. In spite of Islam's objections to other elements of Zoroastrian religion in its time, in the Quran this concept of progress is revealed as true to Muhammad as well, so that Muslims share a concept of time and purpose with other members of their extended family.

In a way similar to the Greek and European experiences, but developed more directly in the Exile, the theology of Judaism was affected by several such Zoroastrian concepts. It is clear that the creative theological tension in the latter era of the Exile resulted in the adoption of demonology and angelology by the Jews, for whom such concepts previously had been vague at best. Until the encounter with Zoroastrianism, the Jewish concepts of heaven and hell had also been ill defined—a shadow life in Sheol, an underworld land of the dead, where both the good and the bad might reside. Zoroaster preached the resurrection of the body after death, followed by a Day of Judgment, both communal and individual, leading to either reward or punishment. Presented as an advisor to the Persian monarch, as if by then a respected colleague of the Zoroastrian priests of the realm, Daniel was the first of the Jewish prophets to write of resurrection, judgment, reward and punishment in the Zoroastrian vein: "Many of those that sleep in the dust of the earth will awake, some to eternal life, others to reproaches, to everlasting abhorrence."[2]

The belief in resurrection was promoted in Judaism by the Pharisees, who were, as noted, the Persian party in Judaism. Their dispute with the Sadducees over Zoroastrian theology lasted into early Christian times[3] when their position found acceptance in Judaism and into the religions that followed. But it was possibly in the concept of the Messiah that Zoroaster affected Jewish and subsequent religions most profoundly. More than a hope for another great king in the Davidic monarchy, they now appeared to adopt aspects of the Zoroastrian prophecy of a universal savior or Saoshyant, who would be born of a virgin, and who would lead believers in the final apocalyptic battle against dark forces of evil at the end of time.

As we seek to uncover authentic passages of the Avesta Scriptures, including dualistic portions, condemned and represented in corrected, amended or amplified form in the Quran, we should ask if there is any substantial volume of material directly from the Avestas in the Torah as well. We have identified substantial portions of the priestly material scattered throughout the Pentateuch and focused on chapter 1 of Genesis and the Book of Leviticus as falling into this category. Is there anything else of Zoroastrian substance in the Hebrew Scriptures, more broadly speaking?

In its present form, the Book of Job cannot be said to be merely a translation of a Zoroastrian Avesta Scripture, but if the same license granted to the Quran in amplifying previously revealed Scripture were to apply to the Bible, there is enough evidence, or at least enough suspicion, to treat this ancient Scripture, from somewhere east of Israel, in a similarly significant manner. We will shortly consider Job in conjunction with other Torah texts that contain linguistic markers connecting them to Zoroastrian provenance.

Some of the preexilic prophets who saw the decline of Israel and Judah coming predated Zoroaster. Their prophecies are included primarily in First Isaiah, Joel and the oracles of a few other prophets such as Obadiah, Nahum and Habakkuk, who joined in to sound the warning. The prophetic figures who lived during the Exile included Second Isaiah, Daniel, Esther and Ezekiel, with prophetic utterance in a Zoroastrian-style bone yard, and Jeremiah connecting the two groups, with a possible significance of his own with respect to Zoroaster.

The first postexilic prophet to make an impact was Haggai. Born in Babylon, and part of the first migration back to the homeland, Haggai was probably a devout layperson, not a priest, judging by his request for advice from the priests regarding the laws of purity,[4] though he may have been a Levite, as pious and as zealous as those of old. His prophecies from 520 to 516 BCE, all dated in the text by the Persian calendar, were focused exhortations that stressed the importance of rebuilding the Temple. His first and fourth oracles were addressed to the young prince, Zorobabel, first commissioning him for the task of rebuilding and later holding out the possibility of future kingship. The first was achieved but the second was not, except in hints that the messianic vision may have had a universal meaning,[5] as later articulated in detail in the Epistle to the Hebrews of the Christian Scriptures.[6]

Haggai joyfully attended the dedication of the Second Temple in 516 BCE, as did his colleague, Zechariah,[7] a true priest, descended from a priestly father and grandfather in Babylon. Zechariah was operating now in a new era with a new societal consciousness, at least within the Jewish community itself. Having been part of the first wave of the Return[8] and possibly inspired by Haggai, he began to prophesy in Jerusalem in 520, a few months after his mentor.

More visionary and mystical than his older contemporary, Zechariah's oracles are intensely spiritual and emotional. Zechariah continued to revere Persia as an instrument of God's ultimate sovereignty, to be exercised not merely through a new king of Israel, but by the community's spiritual leadership acting in concert with the respected civil authority. More even than Haggai, Zechariah successfully transferred the messianic expectations of Israelites longing for a restored monarchy to the end time.[9] Zechariah's oracles were delivered in the apocalyptic style associated with the oracles of Zoroaster, and he featured the role of Satan in a manner unknown among the preexilic prophets but similar to his appearance in the Book of Job.

His own oracles are confined to what we call Zechariah 1–8. "Second Zechariah," as we may call the rest of the book, comprises chapters 9–14, written by a later disciple or group, applying his theology to another era (possibly the time of the Maccabees). This portion displays even greater apocalyptic rapture, a focus on the Day of Judgment and a new creation in which God's justice will finally triumph. The Zoroastrian imprint had not diminished.

The stern intransigence of the final postexilic prophet, "Malachi," is reflected in his decision to remain anonymous behind that nickname, meaning "Messenger." He chastised the priests for their slackness and immorality in the era between the first and second terms of Nehemiah as governor. He preached that sacrifices were of no avail unless the people's hearts were right with God, harking back to the preexilic Amos, as if the whole Zoroastrian interface had never taken place, except that now Malachi's message was strengthened by the certainty that Judgment Day is coming. When Malachi was preaching in the years 423 and 424 BCE, the Temple had been up and operating again for some time. This prophet's disillusionment was related to his belief that the Exile and Return were connected to God's wrath and God's grace. His vigorous prophetic ministry may have led to the reforms of Nehemiah in that governor's second term, although it is of interest that Mary Boyce has given a second, possibly compatible rationale for those reforms. She pointed to Zoroastrian purity laws featuring abhorrence of dead bodies and female menstruation as the source of Nehemiah's concern with matters of purity. She believed the biblical injunctions could be traced to his acquaintance with the Zoroastrian practices he observed in his role as cupbearer to Artaxerxes I.[10]

Malachi provides us with a perfect example of the way scholarship and tradition have too easily combined in the past to draw conclusions that fit their presuppositions to the exclusion of the Zoroastrian perspective we are now beginning to appreciate. For example, Malachi's favorable comments on worship in many parts of the world[11] have been taken by Jews to refer to the future Diaspora and by Christians to refer to their future worldwide mission. We see now that the plain sense of the passage is a reference to the Zoroastrian early insinuation of monotheism into the worship and practice of all the religions of the Persian realm. While this was happening, in the opinion of Malachi, the Jews, as the very people most naturally inclined toward monotheism, were corrupt in their worship and an embarrassment to the God who had restored their destiny.

Overshadowing all these prophetic utterances was the even more refined theology of Isaiah, the preeminent prophet of the Exile community, or the several prophets writing under that illustrious name, now identified by many scholars as First, Second and possibly Third Isaiah. It is unnecessary as well as impossible to imagine one writer spanning this passage of two centuries of solar time, during which, for example, the Temple was described as standing in splendor, lying in ruins and standing again as the Second Temple. The lack of a name for the author of "Second Isaiah," or even a third writer of that appellation, is insignificant, since writers of Scripture usually declined to sign their work. They presented it as the inspired Word of God, and the author was the Divine One.

While the Temple in Jerusalem was still standing, First Isaiah[12] denounces Judah's apostasy and anticipates the virgin birth of a savior, as shortly thereafter also foretold by Zoroaster. In relation to the prophecies of a messiah, Josephus reports that Cyrus was said to be flattered to learn that Isaiah prophesied the coming of such a leader, even before he was born.[13] Any such preexilic "mutual awareness" hints at an interplay of ideas and personalities that is greater than previously realized but which is increasingly recognized. The dates ascribed to this First Isaiah are 740–681 BCE.

Before the current consensus about the later birth date of Zoroaster began to emerge it was commonly supposed that some Zoroastrian ideas are found in First Isaiah. Given the new picture of this relationship, it is more likely that Hebrew ideas articulated by First Isaiah influenced Zoroaster at an early stage of his priestly training. That fits with the view that chapters 1–39 are indeed written sometime before 700 BCE by First Isaiah. Zoroaster's Saoshyant, to be born of a virgin, may actually reference Israelite heritage from First Isaiah, rather than mere "Middle Eastern lore."

Second Isaiah[14] begins, in the words of the version familiar from Handel's *Messiah*, "Comfort ye, comfort ye my people"[15] (addressed to the exiles), as Cyrus draws near in an era of hope in which the royal family might well have given a Zoroastrian name to their prince-in-waiting. This section proclaims that God "has roused a victor from the east,"[16] a liberator who is coming to set the captives free, and it develops into joy at the liberation, even while the Temple still lies in rubble.

> Raise a shout together, O ruins of Jerusalem! The LORD will comfort his people and will redeem Jerusalem. The LORD will bare His holy arm in the sight of all the nations, and the very ends of the earth shall see the victory of our God.[17]

There is also a word of caution. Those returning with the stolen Temple vessels, again in their possession, must not loot or steal as they go:

> Turn away, touch naught unclean as you depart from there; keep pure as you go forth from there, you who bear the vessels of the LORD.[18]

The Return for which they were longing has begun.

Third Isaiah[19] may be written by yet another prophet, though even scholars convinced of the multiple authorship are divided as to whether this is Second Isaiah, having returned to Jerusalem at a great old age, a group of poetic prophets who emulated his style, or indeed a third writer. The Temple is standing again, and the power, insight and beauty of these chapters is qualitatively equal to the strident alarm in First Isaiah and to the transformative insights of Second Isaiah. The message of God's purpose and plan is the same, whether we have one, two or three writers, but our interest has already been directed to the recognition of Cyrus as Yahweh's anointed by Second Isaiah. There are other indications that this literary giant was party to, or witnessed, one of the most amazing theological encounters in the history of the world—the interface between Hebrew and Zoroastrian priests that lasted for two full generations at least.

For example, while the priests continue to flesh out their portion of the creation story, Second Isaiah is meditating upon and providing direct answers to the questions asked rhetorically by Zoroaster in the creation chapter of the Gathas:

Zoroaster: "Who made the routes of the sun and stars? By whom does the moon wax and wane?"[20]

Isaiah: "Lift high your eyes and see who created these. He who sends out their host by count and who calls them by name. Because of his great might and vast power, not one fails to appear."[21]

Zoroaster: "Who fixed the earth below and kept the sky above from falling?"[22]

Isaiah: "He who measured the waters with the hollow of his hand and gauged the skies with a span."[23]

Zoroaster: "What craftsman made light and darkness, good and evil?"[24]

Isaiah: "I form light and create darkness, I make weal and create woe—I, the LORD, do all these things."[25]

Both the content and the style match in these and other apparent answers to Zoroaster's rhetorical questions.

The final personas to be considered in these connections are those postexilic figures previously mentioned, Nehemiah and Ezra. We have little knowledge of any specifically Zoroastrian influence on Nehemiah except that his reforms may reflect some Zoroastrian practices, and we know that Zoroastrian monarchs were open to Jewish influence and entreaty in general. So when Nehemiah approached the throne for a special hearing, like Esther, perhaps at about the same time but in different circumstances, he, too, was well received. Reporting that the Return had not been entirely successful in rebuilding either Jerusalem or its Temple, and perhaps acknowledging that a majority of Jewish professionals and educated leaders were still in Persia, Nehemiah obtained generous funding for a second wave of the Return and for substantial public works improvements to Jerusalem, its infrastructure and especially the Temple and its functions.[26]

One of those functions was the scholarship behind the final editing of the Torah material, to be collectively known as "The Law of Moses," and the moving of that enterprise to Jerusalem from Babylon under the leadership of Ezra. This worthy individual would become known as the Second Moses for his brilliance in producing what many regard as the greatest literary masterpiece in the history of the world: the Hebrew Torah. In it, universal experiences before Abraham, the Patriarchal era, the encounters of Moses with God and the experiences of the Hebrew people down through their history were refined through the monotheistic filter of pristine Zoroastrianism and the revelations given to its prophetic founder. This resulted in an inspired composite work reflecting both the spiritual experience of the Hebrew people and that of humanity as a whole, the particular and the universal. This Torah would later bless Christians and Muslims and become a cornerstone of world culture, even as we acknowledge the broader perspective of humanity in the spiritual quest we all share. The complexity of the Torah in its completeness is now to be elaborated by Marc Brettler, a twenty-first-century scholar who continues the vocation of the team that stretches back to those who worked with Ezra so very long ago, and even before.

Some believers prefer to think of the Torah arriving holus-bolus from heaven or dictated in pieces by God, perhaps to Moses, much as Muslims regard the composition of the Quran. Ellen Frankel has raised the specter of a split in Judaism if many Jews were to adopt something we might call "progressive revelation." A good example of progressive revelation might be the doctrine of the Trinity as understood by Christians, for whom the Hebrew Scriptures allude to the doctrine, which is elaborated in the Christian Scriptures but not named until fully developed by the church. Professor Brettler shows how God's grace is manifest in the process of Scriptural development, and we will apply the hypothesis to the wider community forum of faith.

The oral sources presented the intuitive wisdom of the believing community in cadences of camp-fire recitations, powerfully gripping as coming from God. The first writers are sometimes called "pencils in the hand of God," but they were not necessarily more inspired than those who came before them or the editors who followed, weaving the warp and woof of threads into the fabric of whole cloth. The rabbis who voted to decide which scrolls went into the final collection prayed for divine guidance and received it. The translators into Greek, English and other languages often worked in committees and felt certain that God was in the deliberations. Printers, publishers and distributors got the word out. Scholars in the seminary and teachers in the synagogue prepared lectors and cantors for the service and listeners in the pew until even the individual reading alone at home was able to hear God speaking in his or her own heart as surely as Moses on the mountain or Muhammad in the cave. Let no one presume that God's dictation to one person, however holy, is necessarily the only significant manner in which God can speak. God also speaks through the whole community in ways that are profound and powerful. There may be ways of perceiving the Torah in which both elements are present, and the meaning of the Word may be the same in either case. Professor Brettler will illustrate the progressive or community revelation as it pertains specifically to the text of the Torah in particular.

Before he does so, we will explore one final consideration, an important linguistic marker connecting Judaism and Zoroastrianism, justifying the pattern of speculation to this point and demonstrating the wider sweep of the divine communication.

Perhaps it is possible that Cyrus and other Persian monarchs successfully pursued a policy of progressive engagement toward all of their subject peoples, and that the Jews were not a special case just because they were monotheists. That is not supported by the archaeological evidence to the contrary, witnessed by anyone who has seen the stones supporting the Western Wall in Jerusalem, a foundation wall of the Second Temple, some of which was put in place at Persian expense in the first rebuilding of that temple. Where else is such Zoroastrian largess to be found?

Our suggestion that Zerubbabel was named in anticipation of Zoroastrian rule by a politically astute Jewish royal family, or that he was given his name as a second name to honor the monotheistic rulers, may be impossible to document. Somebody should have explained that to the translators of the Greek Septuagint version of the Hebrew Scriptures, since they appear to have gone to some lengths to make the spelling of his name in Greek, Zorobabel, correspond with the Greek version of Zoroaster, not very many years later.

No doubt a monkey with a word processor could answer the questions posed by Zoroaster, given unlimited time and enough bananas, but it is Second Isaiah who answers those questions in the biblical text. Perhaps there is another explanation for the long-delayed presentation of tabernacle liturgies in Leviticus, and the Jews could have developed their theologies of angels, Satan, creation, judgment, salvation and paradise during the Exile on their own or by direct inspiration from the Divine, without reference to the Zoroastrian priests who believed in these things at the same time and in the same place where the Jews were writing. Perhaps the Vedic context for the order of creation reached the Jews by some other means.

All of these caveats notwithstanding, I believe the case for regarding Zoroastrianism as raw material for the Torah has been made. Herein lies significant potential for greater understanding, not only of the Torah, but also of Christian and Islamic Scriptures, with evidence of their own connections yet to come. However, since Book Three is largely based on the importance of linguistic markers connecting parts of the Quran to Zoroastrianism, it would be of more than passing interest to discover if any clear examples of such linguistic markers exist in the Hebrew and Christian Scriptures.

Just such an example in the Hebrew Scriptures was discovered with the help of our online collaborators, some of whom are members of the Jewish research facility H-Judiac, which kindly provided access to an even wider group of Jewish scholars who joined in the pursuit of an answer to this puzzle. Many of these people in Europe, South Africa, Australia and Israel joined with the Jewish community in North America to find a linguistic marker connecting the Torah to the Avesta.

We found what we were looking for after intense research by several scholars examining the biblical use of the Hebrew word *gaol*, which is usually translated "nearest *kinsman*," "blood *avenger*" or even *"vindicator."* In no translation of the Torah itself, from the old King James Version to the respected Jewish Tanakh and everything in between, is *gaol* ever translated as *Redeemer*. That word is reserved almost exclusively for translations of Second Isaiah. *Redeemer*, as a noun referring to God, is not found even once in the Torah! Nor is it found in First Isaiah or any other prophet, with one exception (coincidently, Jeremiah). It is found three times in wisdom writings, possibly connected to Zoroastrian precedents themselves. But such a specific use of *gaol* in the sense of *Redeemer* appears thirteen times in Second Isaiah alone. We are quite certain that we know the reason, given the time and place of his writing, and a cluster of that magnitude becomes a "linguistic marker" if the context holds up in some unique pattern.

Not only was Second Isaiah active as a prophet during the interface between Zoroastrian and Hebrew priests, but he also showed his special interest in the Zoroastrian concept of the *Saoshyant*, as evidenced by his description of the Zoroastrian monarch, Cyrus, as possibly "God's Anointed" or Messiah. Saoshyant is a figure of Zoroastrian eschatology that brings about the final renovation of the world for good. In popular literature, the word *Saoshyant* is often translated by the Hebrew word *Messiah*, somewhat erroneously. A more correct translation of the Persian/Avestan word *Saoshyant* in English is *Redeemer*.[27] The Hebrew and Christian translators in every age all caught that meaning from the context in Second Isaiah, and *Gaol/Redeemer* as a noun, and as a name for God, is the "linguistic marker" that establishes a literal connection between the Hebrew Torah and the Zoroastrian Avestas in a manner similar to the twenty or more such examples connecting the Quran to previous Zoroastrian revelations.

An examination of every occurrence of *Redeemer* in the Tanakh shows clearly how this title for the Zoroastrian "messiah" is adopted by Second Isaiah. It is even adapted by him in terms of a more sophisticated Jewish theology, showing God himself to be the one who "redeems" Israel. The theological sophistication of this concept in this context cannot be overstated. Second Isaiah is surely party to the growing understanding among Jews that the Saoshyant/Messiah will appear at the end-time of history, but as if to argue the point of redemption here and now with Zoroastrian priestly colleagues, he insists on the point that *God is Israel's Redeemer*. This is a point that Jews have had to pursue in later conversations with Christians and others, but one initially established at the moment Israel first adopted the Redeemer imagery from Zoroastrianism.

Second Isaiah 41:14: "I will help you, declares the Lord. I, your Redeemer, the Holy One of Israel." *(God has a new name in all these texts, although deliberately connected to God's old name, especially in the phrase "the Holy One of Israel," an earlier appellation by none other than First Isaiah.)*

Second Isaiah 43:14: "Thus said the Lord, Your Redeemer, the Holy One of Israel: 'For your sake I send to Babylon . . .'" *(Babylon is frequently the scene of the action of this Redeemer God.)*

Second Isaiah 44:6: "Thus said the Lord, the King of Israel, Their Redeemer, the Lord of Hosts: I am the first and the last, And there is no God but me." *(In this context, there is also an affirmation of monotheism, as might be expected.)*

Second Isaiah 44:24: "Thus said the Lord, your Redeemer, Who formed you in the womb: It is I, the Lord, who made everything." *(An equally prominent answer to the Zoroastrian question about the source of creation.)*

Second Isaiah 47:4: "Our Redeemer—the Lord of Hosts is his name, Is the Holy One of Israel." *(It would be impossible to be more direct in this regard than this affirmation. When Second Isaiah attributes worship of Israel's God to Cyrus, the single identity of the Hebrew and Zoroastrian God is made possible in a phrase like the one above.)*

Second Isaiah 48:17: "Thus said the Lord, your Redeemer, The Holy One of Israel: I am the Lord your God." *(Driving the point home, this identification of the title* Redeemer *with Israel's God is a deliberate campaign by Second Isaiah. He has an agenda not found elsewhere in the Hebrew Scriptures.)*

Second Isaiah 49:7: "Thus said the Lord, The Redeemer of Israel. . . . The Holy One of Israel chose you." *(The people are assured that the broader context takes nothing away from Israel's sense of uniqueness.)*

Second Isaiah 49:26: "I, the Lord, am your savior, The Mighty One of Jacob, your Redeemer." *(A more messianic thrust, combining Jewish history with Zoroastrian vision.)*

Second Isaiah 54:5: "The Holy One of Israel will redeem you [most other translations: "will be your Redeemer"], He is called God of all the Earth." *(Taking the universality of the Saoshyant and attributing the role of redemption to God himself.)*

Second Isaiah 54:8: "I will take you back in love, said the LORD, your Redeemer." *(A connection of love with redemption, rare for Hebrew Scriptures to this point, but germane to the identification of Zoroastrian influence.)*

Second Isaiah 59:20: "He shall come as a Redeemer to Zion." *(The universal agenda notwithstanding, the particular agenda of Israel is specifically supported.)*

Second Isaiah 60:16: "You shall know that I the LORD am your Saviour, I, the Mighty One of Jacob, am your Redeemer." *(The concepts of Savior and Redeemer are again closely associated, except that where Zoroastrians place the messianic vision into the future work of a divinely appointed individual and Christians pick up messianic themes as referring to Christ, the theological understanding of Second Isaiah comes through again, identifying God himself as the Savior and Redeemer Messiah, a theological sophistication perhaps more typical of Jewish tradition generally.)*

Second Isaiah 63:16: "You, O LORD, are our Father. From of old, Your name is Our Redeemer." *(Except that "from of old" in Israel, God's name was never any such thing! To the Jews, this is a new name for God, and the direct source is now obvious.)*

I have attributed this use of the Zoroastrian name *Redeemer* for the messiah to Second Isaiah, though a Third Isaiah or group of Isaiah's later disciples may have stood in that tradition in postexilic times, reflected in the last three examples above. The few other rare uses of this name for God may also actually connect with the Zoroastrian identity. The Tanakh gives us *Redeemer* as a name for God once in Jeremiah and in twice in the Psalms. Some translations find that usage also once in a Proverb.

Jeremiah 50:34: "Their Redeemer is mighty, His name is the LORD of Hosts. He will champion their cause—So as to give rest to the earth, And unrest to the inhabitants of Babylon."

Among the oracles in the book of Jeremiah, chapters 30 and 31 have such a marked similarity to the style of Isaiah 40–55 and such a clear dissimilarity from the rest of Jeremiah that they may even be an insertion from something written by Second Isaiah, according to certain text experts.[28] More likely, given what we know now about Zoroaster's dates and Jeremiah's ministry among exiles in Babylon, Egypt and possibly earlier among the Scythians, this is a final clue that there was interplay between Zoroaster's ministry and that of Jeremiah.

Psalm 19:15: "May the words of my mouth And the prayer of my heart Be acceptable to You, O LORD, my rock and my Redeemer."

Psalm 78:35: "They remembered that God was their rock, God most high, their Redeemer."

In both cases these psalms may indicate random usage, innocent of awareness of Zoroastrianism, although we should not be too sure. That is where the critical interface took place, but these Psalms are of undetermined date, and wisdom literature in particular may reflect a longer connection with Zoroastrianism and even the Saoshyant doctrine, translated as *Redeemer*, possibly a usage of an acceptable idiom from outside Israel.

A traditional concordance also lists another Wisdom example in Proverbs 23:11 as an instance of *gaol* being translated as *Redeemer* in the King James Version, which is followed by the Revised Standard Version and the New Revised Standard Version, but not the Tanakh or other translations. The point is that *gaol* as a noun, capitalized and used as a title for God in the divine role as *Saoshyant/Redeemer*, is extremely rare, and it is never found in the Torah in any version. It is confined almost exclusively to Second Isaiah, but there it is repeated again and again in the writing of the very prophet who answers Zoroaster's questions, suggests Cyrus as a candidate for messiahship, and then develops the sophisticated theological concept of God himself acting as the Redeemer. The clustering of this particular usage of *gaol*, the manner in which it is used and its parallels in the dominant religious culture surrounding the Jews at the time of its writing make it a genuine linguistic marker, establishing a linkage between the Hebrew Scriptures and a uniquely Zoroastrian expression at a most significant level.

Finally, beyond the specialized usage of *gaol/Redeemer* in Second Isaiah, there is one other dramatic usage of this word in the wisdom writings of Hebrew Scripture. It qualifies as a connecting "linguistic marker" if we can be persuaded that the Book of Job may itself be Zoroastrian in origin. This particular usage is the clincher in any case, as either an instance of Redeemer as a loan word in a loaned book or as an example of a concept shared with the community of wisdom references, which are related to the Zoroastrian Lord of Wisdom.

The story of Job is not among the Zoroastrian treasures buried in the Quran, but it is preserved in Hebrew Scriptures in much the same manner, and after a similar transformation of its contents.

The biblical picture of God in the Book of Job presiding over a council of lesser beings in His heavenly entourage, none of whom were "divine," does match with that of the yazatas in Zoroastrianism.[29] The reference to the "sons of God"[30] in Job is an easy connection to "the Immortals." The appearance of Satan gives the book a Zoroastrian stamp. The general Zoroastrian ethos is brought to a head in two particular verses.

Job 19:25: "I know that my Redeemer liveth, and that he shall stand at the latter day upon the earth."[31]

It is impossible to ignore the strength of the Zoroastrian connection in Job, traditionally regarded as Eastern and ancient anyway, but with a resurrection motif, this passage continues:

Job 19:26: "Though after my skin, worms destroy this body, yet in my flesh I shall see God."[32]

There is additional supporting evidence or at least hints corroborating the hypotheses that Job originated in the lost Zoroastrian Avesta, which were still circulating when Israel was in Babylon. Despite its universally agreed non-Hebraic context, the story uses the name *Yahweh* for God, a parallel to the suggestion in Isaiah[33] of an association between the Eastern God of Cyrus and "YHWH," the latter making Zoroastrianism the only other non-Hebraic usage of the holy name in the Hebrew Scriptures. These are all indications that Job is originally Zoroastrian, possibly reworked for Hebrew readers in the mode of the creation story reworked in chapter 1 of Genesis.

We may presume that the prologue and the epilogue of Job are lifted directly from the Avesta original and that the dialogue is produced in freestyle translation, enhancing the Zoroastrian original with Hebrew spiritual sensitivity and theological sophistication. It would be easy to find objections, but Job came from somewhere, and its use of *Redeemer* as a title for God or for the Messiah/Saoshyant in the context of resurrection at the last day is too much for even Muslims to ignore from a greater distance, much less Christians or Jews. We will find some similar examples of linguistic markers linking the Gospel and Zoroastrianism, but it is in the relationship of the Quran to Zoroastrianism that we will use this method of identification with greatest profit for the study of all three related sacred texts.

The Zoroastrian link is by no means the whole story of Torah studies in the twenty-first century, but that particular connection may now be studied in three phases. In preexilic times it is more than probable that Hebrew monotheism fed into Zoroastrian spiritual formation as its most defining characteristic and contributed to such expectations as a messiah born of a virgin and an ideal Kingdom of God. To think otherwise is to unnecessarily diminish the probable influence of the Hebrew religion, as indeed the only major religion of the ancient Middle East to prove durable, and which confirmed its power to influence others again later in the rise of Christianity and Islam.

The second phase of the interface took place during the Exile when Zoroastrian refinements of Vedic and other neighboring religions combined with earlier Hebrew theological concepts to impact on the Jews themselves. This resulted in more sharply defined angelology and demonology and theologies of judgment, salvation, resurrection, paradise and more universal concepts of creation. These fully developed concepts are all then integrated into the Torah, which assumed its final form under Zoroastrian financial sponsorship. The evidence for each of these assertions is itself somewhat circumstantial, but taken all together as a pattern, in conjunction with the Arabian and Persian dates for Zoroaster's prophetic ministry and the events of the Axial Age, we have here the outline of a new understanding of the symbiosis between Zoroastrianism and Judaism in the dynamics of Middle Eastern religious developments.

In the third phase, the relationship may have continued in respectful ways that resulted in Zoroastrian influence in several Jewish subcultures, including earliest Christianity. The relationship may have faded under the increasing impact of Greek and Roman influences until it disappeared with the near total demise of Zoroastrianism under Islamic domination. However, it is now clear that spiritual ideas and theology from Zoroastrianism lie buried in the Torah. If we can find some other places where parts of the Avesta are interred, we may have a more complete picture of the amazing phenomenon triggered by Zoroaster that resulted in the spiritual flowering of the Axial Age. Some greater appreciation of the Zoroastrian contribution to Western religious thought, and a more fulsome articulation of Western linkages to the Orient through Zoroastrianism, may now emerge as a unifying religious principle, or at least a shared quest for scholars in the twenty-first century. Our next step along that path is to consider the Torah itself in all its complexity and splendor.

Job Seeks Answers from on High

introduction to the torah

Marc Zvi Brettler

THE WORD *TORAH*, OFTEN TRANSLATED AS "LAW," IS BETTER RENDERED "INSTRUCTION" OR "teaching." It derives from the Hebrew root *y-r-h*, "to shoot (an arrow)" or "to hit the mark." The Torah is the text that allows a person to live properly. It does so by combining two main genres: law and story. The first third is largely narrative, while much of the rest comprises laws of different types. Thus understanding the Torah simply as law, or calling it "The Law," is inaccurate, and in some circumstances it reflects an erroneous Christian understanding of Judaism as essentially a religion of law.

The Torah, which contains five books (Genesis, Exodus, Leviticus, Numbers and Deuteronomy), is the first part of the tripartite Jewish Bible, known by the acronym TNK, or Tanakh, for Torah, Nevi'im ("prophets") and Khetuvim ("writings"). The Christian Old Testament is not identical to the Jewish Hebrew Bible in format. The Catholic Bible actually contains several Jewish books (the Apocrypha), such as the Wisdom of Solomon, that are not part of the Jewish Bible. In addition, Christian Bibles divide the Old Testament into four sections: the Torah, Historical Books, Poetic Books and Prophetic Books. This four-part division was likely originally Jewish as well, but it was abandoned by the Jewish community sometime after it was adopted by early Christianity. The fact that the Torah is first in all orders known of the Hebrew Bible—that used now by Jews, Catholics, Protestants and all branches of the Eastern Church—indicates its lofty status as first among equals.

We are not certain what the oldest name of the Torah was. Although the word *torah* appears in the Torah, it means "instruction" or "set of instructions" there, never the collection of the five books from Genesis to Deuteronomy. This is because the Torah came together gradually and so cannot refer to itself as a finished product. Later biblical literature, however, refers to "the Torah," "the Torah of Moses," "the Torah of God" and "the Torah of the LORD." The term *Pentateuch*, from the Greek for "five (*penta*) books (*teuchos*)," is used in English (by way of Latin) as another designation for the Torah, which is also sometimes called "The Five Books of Moses," after its putative author.

Within Judaism, the term *Torah* is used much more widely than as a title of the Bible's first five books. It may refer to the Tanakh or the Hebrew Bible in its entirety. In addition, according to the classical rabbis, much of rabbinic law derives from divine revelation as well, and they therefore distinguish between "the written Torah"—namely, the Pentateuch—and "the oral Torah"—rabbinic laws that are not recorded in the Pentateuch, or rabbinic interpretations of Pentateuchal laws. This chapter will focus on the Torah in the sense of the Pentateuch, although it will conclude with some general observations concerning the relation of the Torah to the broader Hebrew Bible.

The Torah is not a book in our sense of the word—a single, unified composition by one author. Modern scholarship has persuasively argued that each of these books is composite, consisting of many sources from different periods in Israel's history. It is also difficult to find a single theme that unifies the Torah. Although Moses is the central human character of much of the Torah, he is only introduced in chapter 2 of Exodus, its second book. Nor is the early development of Israel as a people the Pentateuch's unifying theme, as may be seen from the first eleven chapters of the Bible, which are concerned with the world from creation to the birth of Abraham.[1] Various other suggested unifying themes for the Pentateuch, such as the covenant, are also incorrect, since they do not explicitly appear at the beginning of the Pentateuch and are continued well beyond it. The notion that the promise of the land unifies the Pentateuch is especially problematic, since this theme, although introduced in Genesis 12, is only fulfilled with the conquest of the land in the book of Joshua, the Bible's sixth book, in which case the Hexateuch ("six books": the Pentateuch plus Joshua) rather than the Pentateuch should be seen as the decisive unit. Some have suggested that this six-book unit is more original than the current Pentateuch and that the current structuring reflects the idea that law is more important than the land of Israel, or at least that observance of God's law is independent of the land.

This idea is consistent with the fact that law, although it is not the only genre of the Torah, is its predominant genre. The Torah contains not only the Decalogue[2] in Exodus 20 and Deuteronomy 5 but also extensive legal collections in Exodus 21–23, Leviticus 17–26 and Deuteronomy 12–26, as well as selected laws within various narratives, such as the law of circumcision in the narrative about Abraham in Genesis 17, or the law concerning inheritance of the land by women in Numbers 36, both embedded within narratives about the possession of the land.

Many narrative sections also contain material that is of legal significance. For example, the first creation account in Genesis culminates with the "creation" of the Sabbath,[3] although this would only be legislated in Exodus, first in chapter 16 and then as part of the Decalogue, in Exodus 20:8–11. Similarly, the account of the construction of the tabernacle,[4] a temporary temple for God in the wilderness, is not narrated for its own sake but as an introduction to the various laws of sacrifice, narrated in the following book of Leviticus.

Thus the Torah contains sections that represent the two main uses of the word *torah* in the Bible. Sections of it are legal, representing the use of the word *torah* in places such as Leviticus 6:7: "This is the law (*torah*) concerning the meal offering." Other parts use stories to teach, representing a use found, for example, in the third part of the Jewish canon (Khetuvim, or Writings), in the book of Proverbs: "Hear, my child, your father's instruction, and do not reject your mother's teaching [Heb *torah*]."[5] Although ancient Near Eastern law collections sometimes had narrative preambles or conclusions, the Torah is exceptional in its context in the manner in which it combines, and sometimes even intertwines, legal and narrative material.

The Torah contains traditions that Moses wrote down in parts of the Torah, as in Exodus 24:4—"Moses then wrote down all the commands of the LORD" (referring perhaps to the preceding laws)—and in Deuteronomy 31:9—"Moses then wrote down all the commands of the LORD" (referring probably to all or part of the Book of Deuteronomy). This does not explicitly suggest that it was compiled by Moses himself, and even these traditions about sections of the Torah as Mosaic are not viewed as historically accurate by most scholars. The phrase *the Torah* in passages such as Deuteronomy 4.44, "This is the law [Heb *torah*] that Moses set before the Israelites," never refers to the complete Pentateuch. Yet it is easy to see how the tradition ascribing these five books in their entirety to Moses developed. As noted, several large sections were explicitly attributed to him at some point in history, and in several places the Hebrew Scriptures suggest that Moses stayed on Mount Sinai for forty days and forty nights.[6] Clearly, this was too long a time for short legal collections such as Exodus 21–23 to have been conveyed to him, and traditions developed that Moses received the entire written Torah from God at that point.

According to the classical rabbis, Moses simultaneously received the oral law, which served as the authoritative interpretation of the written law. The written Torah included, according to all rabbinic sources (which are followed by the early church), even the Book of Genesis, which thus represents God's narration to Moses of the early history of the world and of Abraham and his family. Some rabbinic sources even suggest that the final chapter of the Torah, Deuteronomy 34, which narrates the death of Moses, was dictated by God to Moses, who wrote them with his tears. The view that the Torah should be understood as the divine word mediated by Moses was the accepted view among Jews and Christians in synagogues and churches throughout the Renaissance.

This perspective of Mosaic authorship of the entire Torah is contradicted by the Torah's narrative, as was only rarely recognized in the Jewish Middle Ages. Abraham ibn Ezra, a scholar active in the twelfth century CE, noted that Genesis 12:6 states in reference to Abraham that "at that time the Canaanites were in the land." The words *at that time* suggest that for the author, the Canaanites were no longer in the land; in other words, it appears that the text was written after the time of Moses, because during his time the Canaanites were still in the land. A small number of other places that suggest authorship later than Moses were pointed out by a few medieval Jewish scholars, but these were not systematized into a thesis that could challenge the dominant view concerning Moses's authorship of the Torah.[7]

modern source theories

Slowly, with the rise of European rationalism, particularly as associated with figures such as Thomas Hobbes (1588–1679) and Benedict (Baruch) Spinoza (1632–1677), the view that the Torah was a unified whole, written by Moses, began to be questioned.[8] Various theories developed. Some saw the Torah as composed of various fragments (the fragmentary hypothesis), others of a main document that was supplemented by various hands (the supplementary hypothesis) and still others that it was composed of various long documents that were intertwined (the documentary hypothesis). By the late nineteenth century, the documentary hypothesis was dominant, especially in the form popularized in 1878 by the German scholar Julius Wellhausen, that the Pentateuch (or Hexateuch) is composed of four main sources or documents that were edited or redacted together: J, E, P and D.[9] Each of these sources or documents is embedded in a (relatively) complete form in the current Pentateuch, and each has a distinct vocabulary and theological perspective.

J and E are so called after the names for God that each of them uses in Genesis and early in Exodus. J uses the name *Yahweh* (German "Jahwe," hence "J"), translated in the New Jewish Publication Society (the Tanakh used in this volume) as "Lord," even though it is really a personal name, whose exact meaning is unknown, from the root *to be* (or perhaps "the one who causes all to be"). E prefers to call the deity *Elohim* (translated as "God"), an epithet that also serves as the generic term for God or gods in the Bible.[10] P, which also uses *Elohim* (and other names, such as the enigmatic El Shaddai), identifies the Priestly material. D refers to Deuteronomy, a recapitulation of the speeches of Moses.

The difference in divine names, however, is not the main criterion used by scholars for suggesting that the Torah is not a unified composition. Much more significant are doublets and contradictions, in both narrative and legal material. For example, it has long been noted that chapters 1–3 of Genesis twice narrate the creation of the world. People are created first in 1:27—"So God created humankind in his image, in the image of God he created them; male and female he created them"—and then again in 2:7—"Then the Lord God formed man from the dust of the ground, and breathed into his nostrils the breath of life; and the man became a living being."

Furthermore, the second creation account does not simply mirror or repeat the first but differs from the first both in outline and in detail. Genesis 1:1–2.4a,[11] the first account, narrates the creation of a highly symmetrical world by a very powerful deity who creates through the word. In this account man and woman are created together (1:27) after the creation of the land animals (1:25). In contrast, the second story, in Genesis 2:4b–3:24, says that man was created (2:7), then the animals (2:19) and then woman (2:21–22). Its focus is on the creation of humanity, not of the entire physical world, and God anthropomorphically "forms" various beings, rather than creating them with the word. The Hebrew word *bara'*, which is used only of God as "creator," typifies the first story, but it is totally absent in the second. Genesis 1–3 contains two separate accounts, written by two authors, representing different worldviews about the nature of creation, humanity and God.

While the two creation accounts appear as two totally separate blocks of material in Genesis 1:1–2:4a and 2:4b–3:24, in several other cases such a clear-cut division of sources is impossible for narrative reasons. For example, the flood story culminates in a tradition that God will never again bring a flood on the land;[12] for this reason, the J and P narratives cannot appear as separate and complete narratives, so they are intertwined. Similarly, the story of the plague of blood in Exodus 7:14–24 contains two intertwined accounts; for example, in J Moses is the protagonist, and the blood affects only the Nile (vv. 17–18), while in P Aaron appears as well, and the flood affects all Egyptian water sources (vv. 19, 24). The following frog plague is similar. In such cases, the narratives are combined skillfully. Careful attention to plot and vocabulary help modern scholars discern the original building blocks or sources of the story, although this is sometimes obscured by the English translation, which often levels the different versions in an attempt to create a more unified final text that reads well.

The legal material in the Torah is also the product of several sources. For example, slave laws concerning Hebrew or Israelite slaves are found in the Torah in Exodus 21:1–6, Leviticus 25:39–46 and Deuteronomy 15:12–18. These laws cannot be reconciled in a straightforward fashion since three different notions of slavery underlie them. For example, Exodus differentiates between the treatment of male and female slaves, whereas Deuteronomy insists that they should both be treated similarly. While Exodus and Deuteronomy agree that a slave who loves his master may opt to remain a slave "for life"[13] or "forever,"[14] Leviticus[15] insists that slavery does not really exist, since slaves must be treated "as hired or bound laborers," and they may only serve "until the year of the Jubilee," which occurred every fifty years.[16] Such legal differences are not surprising given that the Torah is composite and that the different legal collections reflect norms or ideals of different groups living in different times.

In fact, it is possible to trace distinctive styles and theological notions that typify individual Pentateuchal sources. For example, the J source is well known for its highly anthropomorphic God, who has a close relationship with humans, as seen in Genesis 2:4b–3:24, which includes, for example, a description of the LORD God "walking in the garden,"[17] and says that the LORD God "made garments of skins for the man and for his wife, and clothed them."[18] On the other hand, in E, the Elohist source, God is more distant from people, typically communicating with them by dreams or through intermediaries, such as heavenly messengers or "angels" and prophets.

The P or Priestly source is characterized by a strong interest in order and boundaries,[19] as well as an overriding concern with the priestly family of Aaron and the Temple-based religious system. D, Deuteronomy, is characterized by its focus on Moses and its unique, preaching-like style, which insists strongly that God cannot be seen, as in this source's description of revelation: "Then the LORD spoke to you out of the fire. You heard the sound of words but saw no form; there was only a voice."[20] This explains why this source, uniquely, insists that God does not physically dwell in the Temple or tabernacle; rather, the Temple is "the place that the LORD your God will choose as a dwelling for his name."[21] In contrast, Priestly literature suggests that God's "Presence" (Hebrew *kavod*) dwells there. D also emphasizes that this one God must be worshipped in one place only;[22] this place is later understood to be Jerusalem.

The narrative sources J, E, P and D also have legal collections associated with them. Many scholars refer to these as "codes," but this is imprecise. As far as we know, Israel and its neighbors did not have legal codes in the sense of documents intended for use in the law-court, organized with such a use in mind.[23] The Covenant Collection in Exodus 20:22–23:33 is associated with J or E. The Holiness Collection (or "H") of Leviticus 17–26 is so named because of its central injunction: "You shall be holy, for I the LORD your God am holy."[24] It is a later reformulation of priestly law and thought, influenced by P, certain prophetic ideals and other texts. The Deuteronomic law collection appears in Deuteronomy 12–26.

We know nothing about the authors of the sources as individuals. Only a small elite of males (perhaps 5 percent) in the ancient Near East, the area that is now called the Middle East, were literate; the sources' authors were likely among these, unless of course the sources were first oral literature, as some think, and were later recorded. Most ancient Eastern documents were written anonymously—as were their sources. Although the Torah may contain some documents written by women or that circulated in women's groups—such as the *Song of the Sea* in Exodus 15, a typical victory song written by women after their men returned from battle[25]—the vast majority of the Torah, both legal and narrative sections, was written by men, and it reflects the ideas and aspirations of male elites. It is therefore important not to confuse "ancient Israel" (what ancient Israel really looked like from a broad perspective) and "biblical Israel" (the picture that is depicted in the Bible, including the Torah; much of this is prescriptive, by and to a small community, and it represents various ideals rather than the reality).

Critical biblical scholarship through much of the twentieth century was quite confident in dating each of the Pentateuchal sources along with the legal collections they incorporated. J was seen as the earliest collection, often dated to the period of David and Solomon in the tenth century BCE, followed by E, which was often associated with the early history of the Northern Kingdom of Israel. D was connected to the reform of King Josiah of Judah in the late seventh century, and P was seen as deriving from the sixth century. Scholars now agree that the reasons given for assigning these dates are problematic, and a lively debate has developed concerning such fundamental issues as the relative order of these sources and the extent to which any of them are as early as previous scholars had suggested. The existence of E as a complete source has been questioned as well, especially since E first appears well after the beginning of the Torah and is very difficult to disentangle from J after the beginning of Exodus. Thus, many scholars now talk of JE together as an early narrative source, incorporating diverse traditions.[26]

Additionally, most scholars now do not see D and P as representative of a single author writing at one particular time but recognize that each was produced by a group or "school" over a long time. Thus, it is best in some cases to speak of streams or strands of tradition and to contrast their basic underpinnings, rather than to speak of a source as a single document deriving from a single author, period and locale. For example, as noted above, in D Yahweh's name (Hebrew *shem*) resides in the Temple, while in P the Divine Presence (Hebrew *kavod*) is there. To offer another example that differentiates between these two great streams of tradition, Deuteronomy views Israel as intrinsically holy—as seen, for example, in Deuteronomy 7:6, "For you are a people holy to the LORD your God"—while the Priestly view, articulated most clearly in the Holiness Collection, suggests that Israel must aspire to holiness—as in Leviticus 19:2, "You shall be holy."

The last few decades have seen some erosion of the classical documentary hypothesis. The very early dating of the J and E sources has been questioned, with much justification. Some have returned to a type of supplementary hypothesis, viewing the Torah as an original core that has been added to over time. Others have seen P as earlier than D, while still others have claimed that J is the latest of the sources. Yet, within scholarly circles, the idea that the Torah is a composite text with a long and complex history is the dominant model. Even most scholars who read the Torah as a single literary text acknowledge that this unity is the result of the book's redaction, rather than it being authored by a single individual. The concepts of JED and P thus remain useful, if not as "documents," then at least as an important starting point for understanding the prehistory of the Torah.

compilation and redaction of the torah

It is unclear how these various sources and legal collections, which now comprise the Torah, came together to form a single book. Scholars posit an editor or series of editors or redactors, conveniently called R, who combined the various sources, perhaps in several stages. Certainly not all ancient Israelite legal and narrative traditions were collected and redacted as part of the Torah, as the Torah itself occasionally indicates when it refers to other sources.[27] Much was certainly lost. Without access to this lost material, it is impossible to fully reconstruct how and why the redactor(s), R, functioned in a particular way.

It is sufficient to note two fundamental ways that the redaction of the Torah differs from modern editing. (1) Modern works typically reflect a unified viewpoint, yet the redaction of the Torah, like the editing of other ancient works, was not interested in creating a purely consistent, singular perspective, but incorporated a variety of voices and perspectives and wished to preserve them despite their repetitions and contradictions. (2) Unlike modern works, where there are legal copyright protections for authors so that their works may not be reused or reworked without permission, the Torah is an anonymous compilation. In many ways the Torah is like a document on the Internet that has had many authors and has gone through much editing and reediting, often with no attribution.

It is unclear exactly when the Torah was redacted—namely, when various sources became the Torah. Some scholars believe that this took place during the Babylonian Exile, after the destruction of the First Temple in 586 by the Babylonians, as Judaism developed from a Temple-centered religion to a book-centered one—a development unique in the ancient Near Eastern world. Others believe that Ezra the scribe, who according to the Bible lived in the fifth century, was empowered with creating the Torah following the Return, as may be suggested in Ezra 7:14, where the Persian King Artaxerxes tells Ezra, "For you are commissioned by the king and his seven advisers to regulate Judah and Jerusalem according to the law of your God, which is in your care."[28] The result of this final redaction was the creation of a very long book (really a scroll or set of scrolls, since books in our sense were not yet invented), narrating what must have been felt to be the formative period of Israel, from the period of the creation of the world through the death of Moses. Perhaps the events narrated in Genesis 1–11 were included as a justification of the choosing of Abraham, describing in detail the failures of humanity, as seen especially in the Garden of Eden story,[29] the flood narrative[30] and the Tower of Babel episode,[31] which necessitated the choosing of a particular nation by God.

the content of the torah

According to both Jewish and Christian tradition, the Torah is divided into the five books of Genesis, Exodus, Leviticus, Numbers and Deuteronomy. In some, but not all cases, these are framed as separate books—this is especially the case with Deuteronomy, which is introduced as speeches by Moses shortly before his death, as distinct from the end of the previous book, Numbers, which claims to contain "the commandments and regulations that the LORD enjoined upon the Israelites, through Moses, on the steppes of Moab, at the Jordan near Jericho."[32] Many of the other books are not separated as clearly, and thus it is proper to read the Torah as a single narrative rather than several separate sections, as the Christian Gospels or the Chapters of the Quran are typically read.

Genesis, called *Bereishit* in Hebrew after its first word ("In the beginning"), is really a story of several beginnings. The focus of chapters 1–11 is by and large, but not totally, universal, and contains such well-known stories as the six-day creation, the Garden of Eden, the flood and the Tower of Babel. At the beginning of chapter 12, Abram, later called Abraham, is commanded by the LORD, "Go forth from your native land and from your father's house to the land that I will show you. I will make of you a great nation, and I will bless you; I will make your name great, and you shall be a blessing. I will bless those who bless you and curse him that curses you; and all the families of the earth shall bless themselves by you."[33] This begins the ancestral stories, concerning Abraham and Sarah, Isaac and Rebecca, and Jacob (also called Israel), Rachel, Leah and the two concubines. Much of the end of Genesis focuses on Jacob's son, Joseph, who is the ultimate cause for the family's migration from the land of Israel—a central theme of the other ancestral narratives—to Egypt. Genesis ends with the death of Joseph.

Many scholars differentiate between the first third of Genesis and the rest. This is not accurate, since even though the beginning chapters appear universal, they are told from an Israelite perspective, and the latter section is no more historically accurate than the initial chapters. The chapters about the ancestors are not interested in what actually happened, but like many mythological texts, they are validating present institutions and order by anchoring them in the deep past.

Exodus, the English name of the Torah's second book, is a misnomer; although the exodus from Egypt is narrated in chapters 14–15, the book has many other foci as well. In Hebrew it is named *shemot*, "the names of," after the book's first words—all the other books of the Torah are named similarly after an important first word, following an ancient Semitic tradition for naming literary works. It includes stories of the early life of Moses and his appointment as Yahweh's prophet from the different sources, followed by accounts of plagues against the Egyptians, which in the redacted version total ten. Israel flees from Egypt as the Reed Sea, often mistakenly called the Red Sea, parts to let them through, drowning the Egyptians who were chasing after them. Soon thereafter, Israel arrives at Sinai, where they are given the Decalogue (the Ten Commandments), and then another set of laws, the Covenant Collection. The importance of the Decalogue is highlighted through its description as unmediated divine revelation, but it is nowhere depicted as the center of the Bible or as the core moral principles of Israel. The remainder of the book narrates in great detail the construction of the tabernacle (Hebrew *mishkan*), which is to be constructed as a place where Yahweh or his Presence (*kavod*) will dwell (from the Hebrew root *sh-k-n*). This is narrated in great detail by the Priestly author, since it serves as a prototype of the Jerusalem Temple, where the priests would serve. The story of the golden calf is intertwined with the beginning of the tabernacle construction narrative.

Leviticus, laws concerning priests, is the Bible's third book. It is in its entirety P or Priestly. It begins with a description of various sacrifices, and then contains regulations concerning ritual purity and impurity. This issue is of paramount importance to the priests, since ritual impurity may defile the Temple, causing Yahweh, or the Divine Presence, to abandon it. The laws of Yom Kippur, the Day of Atonement, in chapter 16 are aimed at assuring that Yahweh will stay in the Temple, protecting Israel. A subsection called H, for Holiness, in chapters 17–25 presents a variety of cultic and moral laws, including the famous "Love your fellow as yourself: I am the LORD."[34] H concludes with a series of (short) blessings and (long) curses.[35] Chapter 27 is a later addition; in antiquity, before word-processing programs were developed, additional material that was found was typically added to the end of a book.

Numbers, the Torah's fourth book (named after the census at the book's beginning), is largely but not entirely Priestly. The beginning is all Priestly, but then it turns to the story of spies or scouts, who were sent to determine how to best conquer the land of Israel. Their report is about how the Canaanite residents of Israel scared the Israelites, who were then punished—almost that entire generation was to die in the wilderness, and only their children would possess the land. Stories of other rebellions against Yahweh follow. Most of the final chapters narrate the conquest of the Trans-Jordan, the land to the east of the Jordan River. In that context, Balaam, a seer, is hired to curse Israel, but he instead blesses them. The poetry of that blessing is very difficult, but it highlights Israel as Yahweh's cherished people, whom its God will protect.

Deuteronomy, the Torah's final book, is named from the Greek *deutero nomos*, or second law, since Deuteronomy presents itself as Moses retelling the laws (and the history of Israel) to the generation about to enter the land of Israel. However, this retelling is quite different from what is narrated in Exodus and Numbers—even the Decalogue in Deuteronomy 5 differs in significant details from that found in Exodus 20. The first eleven chapters are mostly a retelling of history, while the next fifteen or so are largely legal. The legislation of Deuteronomy is quite distinctive, emphasizing the centralization of worship, the importance of total obedience to Yahweh and a particular concern for the lower classes. It concludes with the death of Moses, the main (human) character of much of the Torah, and his succession by Joshua, the protagonist of the following book. Its final verses emphasize the incomparable greatness of both Yahweh and his messenger Moses: "Never again did there arise in Israel a prophet like Moses—whom the LORD singled out, face to face, for the various signs and portents that the LORD sent him to display in the land of Egypt, against Pharaoh and all his courtiers and his whole country, and for all the great might and awesome power that Moses displayed before all Israel."[36]

the torah as an ancient eastern text

Given that the Torah is an ancient Near Eastern text, it should come as no surprise that it partakes in many of the motifs and conventions of surrounding civilizations, including the great civilizations of Mesopotamia and Egypt and the smaller Phoenician and Aramean states to the north, its neighbors Ammon and Moab to the east, and Edom, to the south.[37] In some cases, we can see that its authors knew other ancient Eastern texts, and in others that they knew and imitated the forms of ancient Eastern literature. The importance of the Bible, including the Torah, is not in its originality but in the manner in which it combined various preexisting ideas and added some novel ones, serving as a core text for religious civilizations for such a long time.

The clearest cases of ancient Eastern influence come from Canaanite literature and from Mesopotamia. We do not have the Canaanite literature that Israel would have known directly, although we have many texts that were excavated in the twentieth century from ancient Ugarit, modern Ras-Shamra in Syria. Most come from the fourteenth century BCE, and scholars believe that they are more or less representative of the Canaanite culture that Israel encountered in the land of Israel. We also have a number of texts from Mesopotamia—from both Assyria (northern Mesopotamia) and Babylon (southern Mesopotamia). Israel and Judah were often vassals of one or the other of these prestigious civilizations, and elites would have known, and been influenced by, its literature. In addition, the Judeans spent part of the sixth century in exile in Babylon, where many came into direct contact with Babylonian literature and traditions. Surprisingly, given the tradition of Israel having been enslaved for many years in Egypt early in its history, the influence of Egyptian literature is much less evident. Later in the biblical period, authors were influenced by Persian theology, and then by Greek ideas.

Most of the influences of Ugaritic literature are found outside the Torah, especially in biblical poetry. One example in the Torah is Numbers 12:13, where, after Moses's sister is afflicted with a serious skin disease (typically mistranslated as leprosy), the text reads, "So Moses cried out to the LORD, saying, 'O God, pray heal her!'" The Hebrew word used for *God* unexpectedly is *el*—this reflects the Canaanite deity El or Il, whose portfolio included healing the sick. The idea that this appeal for healing is to God as El rather than Yahweh reflects Canaanite influence.

The clearest cases of influence of Mesopotamian texts on the Bible are from the Epic of Gilgamesh and the flood story in Genesis and from the laws of the goring ox in the Laws of Hammurabi and the Covenant Collection in the Book of Exodus.

The Epic of Gilgamesh was an ancient bestseller, telling of the search of Gilgamesh, whom we know was a historical king, for immortality. In the process of that quest, he sought out Utnapishtim—literally, "the one who found life"—who survived a cataclysmic flood with his family and others in an ark. The parallels between this story and the story of Noah in Genesis 6–9 are striking, including the way in which the ark is constructed, the landing of the ark on a mountain, the use of birds to determine if the flood had subsided, sacrifice to God/gods after the flood and a divine promise that such a flood would not recur. There is even a "smoking gun" that indicates that the biblical author knew the flood story from Gilgamesh tablet eleven. Genesis 6:14 uses the word *kofer* for pitch, used to caulk the wood of the ark. This is not the Hebrew word for pitch but a borrowing from Akkadian, the Semitic language of Gilgamesh: the likely explanation of why this unexpected word was used is because the author was influenced by its use in the Mesopotamian epic.[38] When the Torah copies other traditions, it changes them—it "Israelizes" them. Thus, in the Israelite flood story, a single God brings forth the waters due to people's grave sins; in Gilgamesh XI it is the noise of the population that bothers the gods. In Genesis, God fully controls the waters, and all of nature, while in Gilgamesh (as in Mesopotamian culture as a whole) nature sometimes stands above the deities, and thus in Gilgamesh the gods are frightened by the flood that they unleash.

The Hammurabi Law collection, now found in the Louvre, derives from the king of that name, who reigned in eighteenth-century BCE Babylonia. It contains several laws about what happens if an ox gores a person or a slave. Contrary to the image that we may have from the running of the bulls, however, oxen do not typically gore people, especially to death. Yet, the same legal situation is presented in the Book of Exodus, in the same order found in Hammurabi. From this and other similarities, it is clear that the author of the Covenant Collection knew the Hammurabi Law and "Israelized" it as well. Here, too, he made significant changes; these most likely reflect the absolute value of human life within ancient Israel.

The Book of Deuteronomy, both in its general structure and in the structure of its parts, reveals clear Assyrian influence. Unlike Leviticus, which contains laws and then curses, Deuteronomy contains a lengthy historical prologue, followed by laws, curses and other features. In its structure, Deuteronomy is similar to treaties the great Assyrian kings made with the people they conquered—

Assyrian vassal treaties. There are also very close literary correspondences between these treaties and Deuteronomy. For example, in these treaties the vassal was commanded to "love" the crown prince just as in Deuteronomy 6:5 (which later became part of the Jewish *Shema* prayer[39]) Israel was commanded to love Yahweh. These similarities make it likely that Deuteronomy as a whole should be read as a theologized treaty (Hebrew *berit*), in which Yahweh replaces the Assyria overlord.

Many genres and ideas that people think are unique to ancient Israel were well known in antiquity. Morality, prayer, law, even prophecy were known among Israel's neighbors. The seer Balaam, central to the second half of the Book of Numbers, is attested to in a nonbiblical inscription. The idea that gods are very involved in history and in the day-to-day affairs of the world, which was once thought to be an Israelite innovation, is found often among Israel's neighbors.

Given the date of composition of the Torah, soon after the conquest of Babylon by Cyrus the Great of Persia, it is not surprising that Persian words and ideas are hardly found in it and that Greek notions are totally absent—in contrast to later books of the Hebrew Bible, where they are found in abundance. To offer here but a single later example, the Persian-period text Isaiah 45:7, "I form light and create darkness, I make weal and create woe," likely reflects the vigorous dialogue with Persian Zoroastrianism of that era.[40] The text from Isaiah makes it clear that Yahweh is responsible for both good and evil.

It is often pointed out that the Torah is unique in the ancient Near Eastern world in its monotheistic beliefs. Monotheism is very difficult to define, and there are several Torah texts that suggest that Yahweh was a high, even an incomparable deity, though not the only god. This is clearest in the early text from Exodus 15:11: "Who is like You, O LORD, among the celestials [better: 'gods'— Hebrew *elim*]." Yet even in these texts Yahweh is much more powerful than other deities, who are subservient to Him. What is stated in the Decalogue—"You shall have no other gods besides Me"[41] rather than "There is no other God besides Me"—is more typical. It is almost better, therefore, to speak of monotheizing tendencies in the Torah rather than to speak of the Torah, or the Hebrew Bible as a whole, as a totally monotheistic corpus. However, certain late Torah texts teach that Yahweh alone is God: "It has been clearly demonstrated to you that the LORD alone is God; there is none beside Him."[42]

One idea that is unique to ancient Israel within the ancient world is the idea that law derives from God. Some other civilizations such as the Hittites and the Mesopotamians had legal collections, but these were never attributed to the deity. In Mesopotamia, in particular, the king was responsible for establishing justice, and the Laws of Hammurabi were presented *to* the deities, not received *from* them. This meant that in ancient Israel, at least as reflected in the Torah, law had a different force, and both tort law and cultic law were understood as divine. For example, in the rest of the ancient Eastern world, if a man committed adultery, he was seen as committing a civil crime against the woman's husband, while in ancient Israel, as reflected in the story of the attempt of Joseph's master's wife to seduce him, adultery was seen as a crime against Yahweh: "How then could I do this most wicked thing, and sin before God?"[43] The idea that law was of divine origin made Israel fundamentally different from its neighbors (with, again, the possible exception of the Zoroastrians, perhaps known later than the other neighbors in a relationship in which influence may have run both ways).

the torah and the rest of the hebrew bible

As noted above, the word *Torah* has many uses—the first five books of the Bible, the entire (written) Hebrew Bible and the entire corpus of (originally oral) rabbinic literature in addition to the Bible. This essay has focused on the Torah in the sense of the Pentateuch, since it is first among equals.

In the Jewish order of the Hebrew Bible, the tripartite Tanakh, the Torah is followed by the canonical section Nevi'im, the prophets, which is further subdivided into two parts: the former prophets and the latter prophets. The former prophets—Joshua, Judges, Samuel and Kings—are historical books that tell the history of the conquest of Israel through the destruction of the First Temple in Jerusalem in 586 BCE. They are not historical books in the sense of accurately describing the past;

they contain internal contradictions, and they are sometimes contradicted by contemporaneous ancient sources. Like other premodern texts about the past, they are highly ideological and rarely represent eyewitness accounts.

When the Hebrew Bible was translated into Greek as the Septuagint, the translation of the "seventy," beginning in the third century BCE, the long books of Samuel and Kings were divided in half; this explains why in English Bibles we now have First Samuel, Second Samuel, First Kings and Second Kings. The designation of Joshua–Kings as former prophets is somewhat misleading. Although these books mention prophets such as Joshua, Samuel and Nathan, their main focus is on the military and political leadership of figures such as Joshua, the judges and the kings. The books of Joshua–Kings share many stylistic and theological similarities with the preceding Book of Deuteronomy, and many biblical scholars call Deuteronomy–Kings the Deuteronomic History, in the sense of five books that adhere to the ideas and language found in Deuteronomy.

The latter prophets contain Isaiah, Jeremiah, Ezekiel and the Twelve Minor (in the sense of short, not insignificant) prophets. These books reflect a selection from several centuries of prophecy in ancient Israel. Given the complicated way that biblical books were edited and supplemented over time, it is often difficult to know exactly what in these books is from the named prophet or what might have been added by his disciples or later editors. It is likely that the canonical section of Nevi'im was closed by the fourth century or so.

The final canonical section has the rather vague name Khetuvim (Writings), reflecting the broad range of literature it encompasses. It was probably canonized by the first century CE. Its order in different manuscripts is highly variable, but in the JPS Tanakh it appears in the following order. Psalms is a collection of prayers of the individual and the community, from many different times and places. Proverbs is a collection of longer and shorter sayings. Job is a work reflecting on theodicy, the presence of evil given a good God. The five *megillot* (scrolls) that were read on various festivals or holy days include Song of Songs, which is a love poem; Ruth, which is a polemical work, emphasizing that kindness is more important than Jewish ethnicity; Lamentations, which is a collection of five poems reflecting on the destruction of the First Temple in 586 BCE; Ecclesiastes, which is a wisdom work, insisting on Yahweh's great power in relation to people; and Esther, a burlesque tale explaining the origin of the Purim festival. Daniel is an apocalyptic work, Ezra–Nehemiah (separated into two books in the Septuagint) is a "history" of the period after Cyrus the Great conquered Babylon in 539, and Chronicles (also divided into two books in the Septuagint) is a retelling of history from Adam through Cyrus.

How the Bible became the Bible—what is often called the process of canonization—is a complex and debated question. It is likely that this took place in stages, with the Torah canonized first, in or soon after the Babylonian Exile, the Prophets several centuries later and the Writings last, late in the Second Temple period.[44] This process does not mean, however, that all sections of the Nevi'im are later than all parts of the Torah and that all of Khetuvim are later than all parts of Nevi'im. In fact, much of the literature in the Torah and the Nevi'im (and to a lesser extent, Khetuvim) came into being at the same time. For example, the author of Amos 5:25, "Did you offer sacrifice and oblation to Me those forty years in the wilderness, O House of Israel?" does not know the Priestly stories that insist that sacrifice was an important part of the worship of Yahweh in the wilderness. So Amos, among the Prophetic writings, is earlier than the Priestly texts now found in the Torah.

Even though the Jewish canon is divided into three sections, which may seem to be of equal authority, the beginning of the Nevi'im and Khetuvim sections each refer to the Torah as authoritative. Joshua 1:7–8 reads, "But you must be very strong and resolute to observe faithfully all the Torah that My servant Moses enjoined upon you. Do not deviate from it to the right or to the left, that you may be successful wherever you go. Let not this Book of the Torah cease from your lips, but recite it day and night, so that you may observe faithfully all that is written in it. Only then will you prosper in your undertakings and only then will you be successful." The first psalm, at the beginning of Khetuvim, notes that for the righteous individual, "The Torah of the LORD is his delight, and he studies that teaching day and night."[45] Thus, the structure of the Bible suggests that the Torah is its most important section.

Like the Torah, most of the rest of the Bible is also elite male literature—just like most other writing from the ancient East. The Book of Ruth, which focuses on the relationship between two women, is likely one of the exceptions. I Samuel 1 and 2 contain prayers by Hannah, a woman, the mother of the prophet Samuel, and a prayer in I Samuel 2 is reflected in Psalm 113, suggesting that women could declaim psalms. However, we must be very careful in using the Torah and the rest of the Bible to reconstruct ancient Israelite culture—the Bible is but a fragment of the literature from that much broader ancient society.

conclusions

Although the Bible shares many ideas with surrounding civilizations, in its final form the Bible, and even the Torah, are unique within their ancient context, which produced no other work of comparable length or inclusiveness in terms of the time covered and the sources systematically incorporated. This extensive, inclusive nature of the Torah has created a fundamental and interesting challenge with which all serious biblical interpreters have either consciously or subconsciously grappled: Do we concentrate on interpreting the individual sources, on hearing the voices of the component parts of the text before redaction took place? Or do we focus on the final product, an approach that has been called holistic reading?

Finally, within this volume, we must consider the role that interpretation within each faith community should play in how we understand the Torah and in determining which sections of the Hebrew Bible are the most important. The three great monotheistic religions all view the Hebrew Bible as significant, but we must remember that it is of different significance to each, that each considers different parts of it to be especially significant, and that each interprets it differently. For these reasons, it is possible to consider the Torah as a book that both unifies and separates Judaism, Christianity and Islam.

Ezra Expounds on the Completed Torah, the "Law of Moses"

torah text:
the contemporary torah

translator's notes

THE PRESENT TRANSLATION ADAPTS THE NEW JEWISH PUBLICATION SOCIETY (NJPS)* VERSION with respect to *social gender* only. My adaptation effort has followed the pioneering trail of the translation committee that produced NJPS. The driving force behind NJPS was the late Harry M. Orlinsky, who served as editor-in-chief of its first section, *The Torah*. He stated with justifiable pride that NJPS was "the first translation of the Hebrew Bible that went behind all previous translations"—looking afresh at the original Hebrew text in order to take full account of the tremendous advances in knowledge about the ancient Near East made possible by the modern study of the distant past. At the same time as it drew upon the findings of history and science, it took stock of those traditional rabbinic interpretations of the biblical text that accorded with the translators' plain-sense approach.

Orlinsky explained that NJPS relied rigorously on philology: "the meaning and nuance of every word and phrase and verse, in context, was considered anew and carefully before its equivalent in the idiom of the English language was decided upon." Its translators did not strive, as some do, to show how ambiguous the original text is, or to convey how the text made meaning via rhetorical stratagems. Rather, their aims were to convey the plain-sense meaning, to value clarity of expression, to employ idioms familiar to the contemporary audience and to emphasize a religious message. That distinctive set of characteristics has made NJPS the ideal basis for a gender-sensitive translation.

Shortly thereafter, Orlinsky began to address a new topic in translation: gender. Lecturing widely, he would point out that the best-known Bible versions had too often rendered certain Hebrew nouns mechanically as referring to men—thus making women appear relatively invisible. For example, the Decalogue in the classic King James Version (KJV) of 1611 had God "visiting the iniquity of the fathers (*'avot*) upon the children" (Exod. 20:5) even though logic dictated—and other biblical passages indicated—that also in view were mothers and *their* sins. Orlinsky saw such customary renderings as misrepresenting the biblical text, and in his view, the solution lay in a contextual, idiomatic approach to translation—of which NJPS was the exemplar (NJPS reads, "visiting the guilt of the parents upon the children"). He would reiterate that its philological approach has no inherent ideological bias, but rather "seeks to determine within the context and in the light of pertinent data elsewhere in the Bible and in related extra-biblical societies what the author meant to convey."

---

*JPS Tanakh version used in commentary sections of this book.

Where the Torah's language suggested a neutral sense, NJPS avoided misleadingly ascribing gender, not only by rendering inclusively some "male" nouns, but also by rendering masculine inflections and pronouns idiomatically rather than literally. Thus, for example, what KJV had rendered as "thou shalt not wrest the judgment of thy poor in *his* cause" appears in NJPS as "you shall not subvert the rights of your needy in *their* disputes" (Exod. 23:6). In short, NJPS inadvertently led the way among contemporary translations in "gender-sensitive" rendering, but despite its overall strengths, the gender ascriptions in NJPS can still be called into question on a number of counts. I will now discuss, as two distinct categories, how NJPS handled the biblical text's references to human beings and to divine beings.

references to human beings

Like every translation, NJPS contains some internal inconsistencies. For example, the Hebrew wording in Numbers 14 is ambiguous as to who is to be punished for brazen faithlessness: the men or the people as a whole. Seeking the plain sense, the translators quite reasonably opted for the latter view (in contrast to some classic midrashic readings). Yet, to render two Hebrew phrases that do not themselves specify gender, they employed English idioms at odds with their overall interpretation. We read that Moses urges an incensed God not to "slay the people to a *man*" (14:15), and that God then condemns a generation of Israelites to die in the wilderness "to the last *man*" (14:35). Ironically, in some other cases NJPS reads neutrally where a *non*-inclusive rendering was actually called for.

Three examples should suffice. First, NJPS could render *yeled* contextually as "lad, boy" (e.g., Gen. 4:23, 37:30); yet it unconventionally cast the plural *yeladim* as "children" in Gen. 32:23 even though in that context the term can refer only to Jacob's sons (not to his daughter, Dinah). Similarly, NJPS rendered the noun *'edah* five different ways in the Torah; yet its rendering states that Moses was instructed to take a census of the Israelite "community" (*'edah*, Num. 1:2), although ancient censuses counted men only. And unlike prior translations, NJPS renders *banim* as "children" in Lev. 10:1315, although the topic is donations that are restricted to priests—that is, Aaron's "sons."

In a number of other instances, the NJPS translators appear to have based their rendering on an inaccurate understanding of social gender in the biblical setting. For example, where God referred to Abram's eventual death as going "to your *avot*" (Gen. 15:15; cf. 47:30), NJPS seems to have relied on a modern scholarly opinion that the Israelites counted only their male forebears ("fathers") as kin. Yet that view appears to be based on an etymological fallacy, ignoring ample circumstantial evidence that suggests ancient Israelites also viewed their deceased mother and even her forebears as kin. The weight of the evidence argues for rendering *'avot* inclusively here as "ancestors" or the like.

Contemporary readers make their way through a translation at a vast remove from the biblical setting. Many of us misconstrue that setting, perceiving the translated Bible as more male-oriented than the original audience probably perceived the Hebrew text to be. We imagine the Israelite past as having been so "patriarchal" that, for example, in the context of ritual animal sacrifices and male-only priests, some of us infer that women were not part of the scene. Thus, when NJPS relates that if someone eats sacrificial meat while ritually impure, "that *person* shall be cut off from *his* kin" (Lev. 7:20b), we may take the word "his" not as gender neutral but as referring to a male—discounting "person" as if it were a falsely generic term. That is, we may well understand NJPS to mean "that *man* shall be cut off from *his* kin." In such ways the standard English style has put a stumbling block before readers.

Often we found that a common noun's lexical domains significantly affected the social-gender sense in ways not recognized by NJPS or other English translations that we consulted. Of such words, the term *'ish* deserves special mention, because (together with its effective plural, *'anashim*) it is one of the most common nouns in biblical Hebrew—occurring about 570 times in the Torah and 2,200 times throughout the Bible. Lexicographers and grammarians customarily gloss *'ish* as "man," but the import of this assigned equivalence is often misunderstood: the word "man" in English has more than a dozen senses that correspond to the usage of *'ish* in the Bible, and only *one* of those senses is emphatically male. For most instances of *'ish* in the Torah, social gender is not at issue; while its use may correspond to that of "man" in English, the foreground sense is something other than "adult male."

NJPS recognized that 'ish has a wide semantic range by rendering it variously according to context. In Genesis, for example, I count fourteen different renderings of the singular form alone. Still, in the majority of instances in that book, NJPS renders 'ish as "man" (and 'anashim as "men"). A gender-sensitive translation, however, warrants even more precision as to the contextual sense of 'ish, because the audience for such a translation tends to expect clarity as to which gender is in view. To avoid giving the wrong impression, my adaptation restricts the use of "man" to mean "adult male," employing other words to cover the additional senses of 'ish that traditionally are also rendered as "man." This policy has turned out to be far-reaching: the present adaptation employs the words "man" or "men" only about a third as often as *The Torah* of NJPS.

That difference is not only dramatic but also revealing. It demonstrates that the Torah did not constantly emphasize social gender and maleness—as readers of NJPS (not to mention a more literal translation) might imagine. What the biblical text is attending to most often are matters of social roles, social station and the like. While the Torah frequently refers to men, their social gender is supposed to be apparent from the topic or other wording; it usually goes without saying explicitly. The precise treatment of 'ish is one way that the present translation reflects more accurately the degree of the text's attention (or inattention) to social gender, relative to other factors. It takes the text on its own terms. It serves to put gender in perspective.

Ancient "inclusive" language cannot be dismissed as, say, a figment of a postmodern feminist imagination. Rather, it was part of the biblical ethos. This can be seen even in mundane conversation, as when the Bible's characters matter-of-factly refer to females using the grammatically masculine interrogative pronoun *mi* (Gen. 19:12; Job 38:29; Songs 3:6, 6:10, 8:5; Ruth 3:9, 16).

The same consideration applied when faced with wording that had morally binding force. In the book of Judges, the chieftain Jephthah makes an infamous vow to God that refers to its object in grammatically masculine terms. Even so, he and his daughter understand that his vow applies to *her* after she otherwise fulfills its conditions (Judg. 11:30–31, 34–40). It could hardly be true that the text's audience was expected to react by saying, "What a fool Jephthah was! He could have spared his daughter simply by claiming that he had only a *male* in mind when he made his vow." Rather, we can safely infer that the audience shared not only the biblical characters' sense of tragedy but also their understanding of the gender-inclusive sense of indefinite masculine language.

The Bible also expected Israelites to allow for "inclusive" language in the realm of civil law. The book of Jeremiah recounts how the king and Jerusalem's elite covenanted to free their male and female slaves (Jer. 34:8–16). Yet when the narrator quotes God's restatement of the relevant directive to Jeremiah, it reads, "[E]ach of you shall let his *brother* Hebrew go free who has been sold to you and has served you for six years—you must set *him* free" (Jer. 34:14, my translation; cf. Deut. 15:12). Grammatically speaking, the divine language is again decidedly masculine (even more so than my rendering reflects). But obviously Jeremiah is supposed to construe that language as gender-inclusive, as is the reader.

References to divine beings

In the Torah, God's gender basically goes without saying. Whether maleness is to be understood, then, is a matter of assumption. Many contemporary scholars of biblical theology and Israelite history doubt whether the Torah presented a non-gendered deity to its *original* audience. Rather, those scholars say, the text's grammatically masculine language and male imagery (lord, father, king and warrior) referred to what everyone at the time understood to be a *male* deity. The issue is thorny because, while all language is metaphoric at its root, language relating to a deity is especially so.

When pointing toward a Reality that is beyond words, the language necessarily remains ambiguous. One could hardly have composed a text in ancient Hebrew that presented God as non-gendered any better than the Torah. Even beyond stating that God has neither male nor female form (Deut. 4:16), and in sharp contrast to other ancient Near Eastern literature, the Torah never ascribes to its deity anatomical sex characteristics or sexual activity.

Further, such grammatically masculine language was the only real option for referring to a non-gendered deity. And only in poetic or otherwise obviously figurative passages does the text depict God in terms of gendered social status terms; outside of those cases, the social gender of God—as a question of the deity's nature—is never germane to the text's foreground sense. Like nearly all English translations of the Bible, NJPS employed masculine language for the references to God. Arguably, it meant such wording in a gender-neutral sense. Those scholars who claim that the Torah's composer(s) could only have construed its deity as male contend that the most historically accurate way to render the text's God-language is indeed in masculine terms.

However, those who differ with that version of history, or who read a Bible translation in order to reckon with the monotheistic God of Judaism, have grounds for discontent with the gendered God language of NJPS. Such readers are well aware that "lord" is a male title by common usage; for them, rendering God's personal name as "the Lord" can function like wearing male sunglasses to view the invisible deity: "I'm not sure what I'm seeing—but it appears to be masculine." Furthermore, the translation's masculine pronouns may conjure for them an image of a male deity, even though as a matter of logic or belief they would insist that God has no gender. In short, the NJPS style hinders their appreciation of the Torah text.

To represent the Name (the four-letter "personal" name of God that is traditionally not pronounced as it is spelled), NJPS adopted a practice that has long been widespread: rendering the Name impersonally as "the Lord." That custom dates back more than two thousand years to the first translation of the Hebrew Bible—the ancient Jewish version in Greek called the Septuagint. (The audience for that translation lived in the polytheistic milieu of Hellenistic Egypt. The translation's producers apparently wanted to make an ideological point, emphasizing that their Deity was not merely one more named god among many. As a substitute name, *kyrios* ["Lord"] put this particular deity in the spotlight.)

At the same time, however, some ancient Septuagint copyists employed another approach as well: they consistently inscribed the Name using Hebrew letters—in what was otherwise a Greek translation. Meanwhile, in the land of Israel, some copyists of Hebrew manuscripts were employing a similar approach by writing the Name in a special way. For the latter, they took to using the archaic Hebrew script that Jewish scribes had abandoned several hundred years earlier in favor of an alphabet used by Aramaic speakers.

In the view of those scribes, not only could the Name not be translated into *another* language, it could not even be properly presented in the standard script in the *same* language! In short, the Name has long been treated not like any ordinary Hebrew word but like something totally different. Such distinctive treatment appears to be a reflex of the monotheistic concept of God as unique and transcendent. Ellen Frankel and I asked certain scholars, rabbis and leaders for suggestions on how best to represent the Name in this translation. We received thoughtful input from two dozen respondents.

Although we began by seeking an English rendering, we came to see that no rendering could do justice to the Name, neither as presented in the Bible nor as treated thereafter in Jewish lore. The Torah employs the Name primarily *as a name* (not an attribute, not as a declaration and not in terms of etymology), which surely is how the original audience experienced it. All things considered, we decided to represent the Name un-translated, in (un-vocalized) Hebrew letters as יהוה. This styling enables the word to function as a name, without limiting the conception of God to a single quality. *We invite those who read this translation aloud to pronounce the Name via whatever term that they customarily use for it.*

To mention shortcomings of NJPS is not to censure what remains as the Jewish translation of choice for those who value contextual precision and modern idiom. Rather, my point is that gender is such a complex and far-reaching cultural category that NJPS could not do it justice without a comprehensive and focused review of gender ascriptions both in the ancient text and in its translation. I undertook such a review as the core of the present project. It showed me where to redress some

NJPS oversights, how to take advantage of more recent scholarship and where to reduce imprecision in NJPS's English style. I then proceeded to test (and hopefully prove) Orlinsky's 1991 assertion that "the English language has resources that allow a translator faithfully to translate biblical texts and be inclusive where the text is inclusive, and exclusive where the original is exclusive."

Often I and the consulting editors spent many hours (and sometimes days) in order to fully grasp the gender implications of a single Hebrew word—even a term that appeared only once or applied to the most minor of characters. Next came a review of how well NJPS conveyed the Torah's gender ascription in each passage. Where I found warrant to modify NJPS, I tried to employ the same rendering techniques as those that the NJPS translators had used as a matter of course. Not for nothing have I quipped that this adaptation is "just like NJPS, only more so."

By now it should be clear that this adaptation is *not* a "gender-neutral" translation. On the contrary, it pays close attention to the nuances of social gender in the Torah. It reflects the depictions of an ancient text composed for an audience in which gender mattered a great deal. As revising editor I did not pass judgment on how Israelite society and the Torah constructed gender. My renderings neither commend nor condemn the ancient perception of the text. They take the text on its own terms, and they attempt to convey it accurately.

David E. S. Stein

the five books of moses

When God began to create heaven and earth—²the earth being unformed and void, with darkness over the surface of the deep and a wind from God sweeping over the water—³God said, "Let there be light"; and there was light. ⁴God saw that the light was good, and God separated the light from the darkness. ⁵God called the light Day and called the darkness Night. And there was evening and there was morning, a first day.

⁶God said, "Let there be an expanse in the midst of the water, that it may separate water from water." ⁷God made the expanse, and it separated the water which was below the expanse from the water which was above the expanse. And it was so. ⁸God called the expanse Sky. And there was evening and there was morning, a second day.

⁹God said, "Let the water below the sky be gathered into one area, that the dry land may appear." And it was so. ¹⁰God called the dry land Earth and called the gathering of waters Seas. And God saw that this was good. ¹¹And God said, "Let the earth sprout vegetation: seed-bearing plants, fruit trees of every kind on earth that bear fruit with the seed in it." And it was so. ¹²The earth brought forth vegetation: seed-bearing plants of every kind, and trees of every kind bearing fruit with the seed in it. And God saw that this was good. ¹³And there was evening and there was morning, a third day.

¹⁴God said, "Let there be lights in the expanse of the sky to separate day from night; they shall serve as signs for the set times—the days and the years; ¹⁵and they shall serve as lights in the expanse of the sky to shine upon the earth." And it was so. ¹⁶God made the two great lights, the greater light to dominate the day and the lesser light to dominate the night, and the stars. ¹⁷And God set them in the expanse of the sky to shine upon the earth, ¹⁸to dominate the day and the night, and to separate light from darkness. And God saw that this was good. ¹⁹And there was evening and there was morning, a fourth day.

²⁰God said, "Let the waters bring forth swarms of living creatures, and birds that fly above the earth across the expanse of the sky." ²¹God created the great sea monsters, and all the living creatures of every kind that creep, which the waters brought forth in swarms, and all the winged birds of every kind. And God saw that this was good. ²²God blessed them, saying, "Be fertile and increase, fill the waters in the seas, and let the birds increase on the earth." ²³And there was evening and there was morning, a fifth day.

²⁴God said, "Let the earth bring forth every kind of living creature: cattle, creeping things, and wild beasts of every kind." And it was so. ²⁵God made wild beasts of every kind and cattle of every kind, and all kinds of creeping things of the earth. And God saw that this was good. ²⁶And God said, "Let us make humankind in our image, after our likeness. They shall rule the fish of the sea, the birds of the sky, the cattle, the whole earth, and all the creeping things that creep on earth." ²⁷And God created humankind in the divine image, creating it in the image of God—creating them male and female. ²⁸God blessed them and God said to them, "Be fertile and increase, fill the earth and master it; and rule the fish of the sea, the birds of the sky, and all the living things that creep on earth."

²⁹God said, "See, I give you every seed-bearing plant that is upon all the earth, and every tree that has seed-bearing fruit; they shall be yours for food. ³⁰And to all the animals on land, to all the birds of the sky, and to everything that creeps on earth, in which there is the breath of life, [I give] all the green plants for food." And it was so. ³¹And God saw all that had been made, and found it very good. And there was evening and there was morning, the sixth day.

2 ¹The heaven and the earth were finished, and all their array. ²On the seventh day God finished the work that had been undertaken: [God] ceased on the seventh day from doing any of the work. ³And God blessed the seventh day and declared it holy—having ceased on it from all the work of creation that God had done. ⁴Such is the story of heaven and earth when they were created.

When God יהוה made earth and heaven—⁵when no shrub of the field was yet on earth and no grasses of the field had yet sprouted, because God יהוה had not sent rain upon the earth and there were no human beings to till the soil, ⁶but a flow would well up from the ground and water the whole surface of the earth—⁷God יהוה formed the Human from the soil's humus, blowing into his nostrils the breath of life: the Human became a living being.

⁸God יהוה planted a garden in Eden, in the east, and placed there the Human who had been fashioned. ⁹And from the ground God יהוה caused to grow every tree that was pleasing to the sight and good for food, with the tree of life in the middle of the garden, and the tree of knowledge of good and bad.

¹⁰A river issues from Eden to water the garden, and it then divides and becomes four branches. ¹¹The name of the first is Pishon, the one that winds through the whole land of Havilah, where the gold is. (¹²The gold of that land is good; bdellium is there, and lapis lazuli.) ¹³The name of the second river is Gihon, the one that winds through the whole land of Cush. ¹⁴The name of the third river is Tigris, the one that flows east of Asshur. And the fourth river is the Euphrates.

¹⁵God יהוה settled the Human in the garden of Eden, to till it and tend it. ¹⁶And God יהוה commanded the Human, saying, "Of every tree of the garden you are free to eat; ¹⁷but as for the tree of knowledge of good and bad, you must not eat of it; for as soon as you eat of it, you shall die."

¹⁸God יהוה said, "It is not good for the Human to be alone; I will make a fitting counterpart for him." ¹⁹And God יהוה formed out of the earth all the wild beasts and all the birds of the sky, and brought them to the Human to see what he would call them; and whatever the Human called each living creature, that would be its name. ²⁰And the Human gave names to all the cattle and to the birds of the sky and to all the wild beasts; but no fitting counterpart for a human being was found. ²¹So God יהוה cast a deep sleep upon the Human; and, while he slept, [God] took one of his sides and closed up the flesh at that site. ²²And God יהוה fashioned the side that had been taken from the Human into a woman, bringing her to the Human.

²³Then the Human said,

"This one at last
Is bone of my bones
And flesh of my flesh.
This one shall be called Woman,
For from a Human was she taken."

²⁴Hence a man leaves his father and mother and clings to his wife, so that they become one flesh. ²⁵The two of them were naked, the Human and his wife, yet they felt no shame.

3 ¹Now the serpent was the shrewdest of that God יהוה had made. It said to the woman, "Did God really say: You shall not eat of any tree of the garden?" ²The woman replied to the serpent, "We may eat of the fruit of the other trees of the garden. ³It is only about fruit of the tree in the middle of the garden that God said: 'You shall not eat of it or touch it, lest you die.'" ⁴And the serpent said to the woman, "You are not going to die, ⁵but God knows that as soon as you eat of it your eyes will be opened and you will be like divine beings who know good and bad." ⁶When the woman saw that the tree was good for eating and a delight to the eyes, and that the tree was desirable as a source of wisdom, she took of its fruit and ate. She also gave some to her husband, and he ate. ⁷Then the eyes of both of them were opened and they perceived that they were naked; and they sewed together fig leaves and made themselves loincloths.

⁸They heard the sound of God יהוה moving about in the garden at the breezy time of day; and the Human and his wife hid from God יהוה among the trees of the garden. ⁹God יהוה called out to the Human and said to him, "Where are you?" ¹⁰He replied, "I heard the sound of You in the garden, and I was afraid because I was naked, so I hid."

¹¹"Who told you that you were naked? Did you eat of the tree from which I had forbidden you to eat?" ¹²The Human said, "The woman You put at my side—she gave me of the tree, and I ate." ¹³And God יהוה said to the woman, "What is this you have done!" The woman replied, "The serpent duped me, and I ate." ¹⁴Then God יהוה said to the serpent,

"Because you did this,
More cursed shall you be
Than all cattle
And all the wild beasts:
On your belly shall you crawl
And dirt shall you eat
All the days of your life.
¹⁵ I will put enmity
Between you and the woman,
And between your offspring and hers;
They shall strike at your head,
And you shall strike at their heel."

¹⁶And to the woman [God] said,

"I will greatly expand
Your hard labor—and your pregnancies;
In hardship shall you bear children.
Yet your urge shall be for your husband,
And he shall rule over you."

¹⁷To Adam [God] said, "Because you did as your wife said and ate of the tree about which I commanded you, 'You shall not eat of it,'

Cursed be the ground because of you;
By hard labor shall you eat of it
All the days of your life:
¹⁸ Thorns and thistles shall it sprout for you.
But your food shall be the grasses of the field;
¹⁹ By the sweat of your brow
Shall you get bread to eat,
Until you return to the ground—
For from it you were taken.
For dust you are,
And to dust you shall return."

²⁰The Human named his wife Eve, because she was the mother of all the living. ²¹And God יהוה made garments of skins for Adam and his wife, and clothed them.

²²And God יהוה said, "Now that humankind has become like any of us, knowing good and bad, what if one should stretch out a hand and take also from the tree of life and eat, and live forever!" ²³So God יהוה banished humankind from the garden of Eden, to till the soil from which it was taken; ²⁴it was driven out; and east of the garden of Eden were stationed the cherubim and the fiery ever-turning sword, to guard the way to the tree of life.

4 ¹Now the Human knew his wife Eve, and she conceived and bore Cain, saying, "I have created a person with the help of יהוה." ²She then bore his brother Abel. Abel became a keeper of sheep, and Cain became a tiller of the soil. ³In the course of time, Cain brought an offering to יהוה from the fruit of the soil; ⁴and Abel, for his part, brought the choicest of the firstlings of his flock. יהוה paid heed to Abel and his offering, ⁵but to Cain and his offering [God] paid no heed. Cain was much distressed and his face fell. ⁶And יהוה said to Cain,

"Why are you distressed,
And why is your face fallen?
⁷ Surely, if you do right,
There is uplift.
But if you do not do right
Sin couches at the door;
Its urge is toward you,
Yet you can be its master."

⁸Cain said to his brother Abel . . . and when they were in the field, Cain set upon his brother Abel and killed him. ⁹ יהוה said to Cain, "Where is your brother Abel?" And he said, "I do not know. Am I my brother's keeper?" ¹⁰"What have you done? Hark, your brother's blood cries out to Me from the ground! ¹¹Therefore, you shall be more cursed than the ground, which opened its mouth to receive your brother's blood from your hand. ¹²If you till the soil, it shall no longer yield its strength to you. You shall become a ceaseless wanderer on earth." ¹³Cain said to יהוה, "My punishment is too great to bear! ¹⁴Since You have banished me this day from the soil, and I must avoid Your presence and become a restless wanderer on earth—anyone who meets me may kill me!" ¹⁵ יהוה said to him, "I promise, if anyone kills Cain, sevenfold vengeance shall be exacted." And יהוה put a mark on Cain, lest anyone who met him should kill him. ¹⁶Cain left the presence of יהוה and settled in the land of Nod, east of Eden.

¹⁷Cain knew his wife, and she conceived and bore Enoch. And he then founded a city, and named the city after his son Enoch. ¹⁸To Enoch was born Irad, and Irad begot Mehujael, and Mehujael begot Methusael, and Methusael begot Lamech. ¹⁹Lamech took to himself two wives: the name of the one was Adah, and the name of the other was Zillah. ²⁰Adah bore Jabal; he was the ancestor of those who dwell in tents and amidst herds. ²¹And the name of his brother was Jubal; he was the ancestor of all who play the lyre and the pipe. ²²As for Zillah, she bore Tubalcain, who forged all implements of copper and iron. And the sister of Tubalcain was Naamah. ²³And Lamech said to his wives,

"Adah and Zillah, hear my voice;
O wives of Lamech, give ear to my speech.
I have slain a person for wounding me,
And a lad for bruising me.
²⁴ If Cain is avenged sevenfold,
Then Lamech seventy-sevenfold."

²⁵Adam knew his wife again, and she bore a son and named him Seth, meaning, "God has provided me with another

offspring in place of Abel," for Cain had killed him. ²⁶And to Seth, in turn, a son was born, and he named him Enosh. It was then that יהוה began to be invoked by name.

5 ¹This is the record of Adam's line.—When God created humankind, it was made in the likeness of God; ²male and female were they created. And when they were created, [God] blessed them and called them Humankind.—³When Adam had lived 130 years, he begot a son in his likeness after his image, and he named him Seth. ⁴After the birth of Seth, Adam lived 800 years and begot sons and daughters. ⁵All the days that Adam lived came to 930 years; then he died.

⁶When Seth had lived 105 years, he begot Enosh. ⁷After the birth of Enosh, Seth lived 807 years and begot sons and daughters. ⁸All the days of Seth came to 912 years; then he died.

⁹When Enosh had lived 90 years, he begot Kenan. ¹⁰After the birth of Kenan, Enosh lived 815 years and begot sons and daughters. ¹¹All the days of Enosh came to 905 years; then he died.

¹²When Kenan had lived 70 years, he begot Mahalalel. ¹³After the birth of Mahalalel, Kenan lived 840 years and begot sons and daughters. ¹⁴All the days of Kenan came to 910 years; then he died.

¹⁵When Mahalalel had lived 65 years, he begot Jared. ¹⁶After the birth of Jared, Mahalalel lived 830 years and begot sons and daughters. ¹⁷All the days of Mahalalel came to 895 years; then he died.

¹⁸When Jared had lived 162 years, he begot Enoch. ¹⁹After the birth of Enoch, Jared lived 800 years and begot sons and daughters. ²⁰All the days of Jared came to 962 years; then he died.

²¹When Enoch had lived 65 years, he begot Methuselah. ²²After the birth of Methuselah, Enoch walked with God 300 years; and he begot sons and daughters. ²³All the days of Enoch came to 365 years. ²⁴Enoch walked with God; then he was no more, for God took him.

²⁵When Methuselah had lived 187 years, he begot Lamech. ²⁶After the birth of Lamech, Methuselah lived 782 years and begot sons and daughters. ²⁷All the days of Methuselah came to 969 years; then he died.

²⁸When Lamech had lived 182 years, he begot a son. ²⁹And he named him Noah, saying, "This one will provide us relief from our work and from the toil of our hands, out of the very soil which יהוה placed under a curse." ³⁰After the birth of Noah, Lamech lived 595 years and begot sons and daughters. ³¹All the days of Lamech came to 777 years; then he died.

³²When Noah had lived 500 years, Noah begot Shem, Ham, and Japheth.

6 ¹When humankind began to increase on earth and daughters were born to them, ²the [males among the] divine beings saw how pleasing the human women were and took wives from among those who delighted them.—יהוה said, "My breath shall not abide in humankind forever, since it too is flesh; let the days allowed them be one hundred and twenty years."—⁴It was then, and later too, that the Nephilim appeared on earth—when divine beings cohabited with the human women, who bore them offspring. Such were the heroes of old, the renowned ones.

⁵יהוה saw how great was human wickedness on earth—how every plan devised by the human mind was nothing but evil all the time. ⁶And יהוה regretted having made humankind on earth. With a sorrowful heart, ⁷יהוה said, "I will blot out from the earth humankind whom I created—humans together with beasts, creeping things, and birds of the sky; for I regret that I made them." ⁸But Noah found favor with יהוה.

⁹This is the line of Noah.—Noah was a righteous personage; he was blameless in his age; Noah walked with God.—¹⁰Noah begot three sons: Shem, Ham, and Japheth.

¹¹The earth became corrupt before God; the earth was filled with lawlessness. ¹²When God saw how corrupt the earth was, for all flesh had corrupted its ways on earth, ¹³God said to Noah, "I have decided to put an end to all flesh, for the earth is filled with lawlessness because of them: I am about to destroy them with the earth. ¹⁴Make yourself an ark of *gopher* wood; make it an ark with compartments, and cover it inside and out with pitch. ¹⁵This is how you shall make it: the length of the ark shall be three hundred cubits, its width fifty cubits, and its height thirty cubits. ¹⁶Make an opening for daylight in the ark, and terminate it within a cubit of the top. Put the entrance to the ark in its side; make it with bottom, second, and third decks.

¹⁷"For My part, I am about to bring the Flood—waters upon the earth—to destroy all flesh under the sky in which there is breath of life; everything on earth shall perish. ¹⁸But I will establish My covenant with you, and you shall enter the ark, with your sons, your wife, and your sons' wives. ¹⁹And of all that lives, of all flesh, you shall take two of each into the ark to keep alive with you; they shall be male and female. ²⁰From birds of every kind, cattle of every kind, every kind of creeping thing on earth, two of each shall come to you to stay alive. ²¹For your part, take of everything that is eaten and store it away, to serve as food for you and for them." ²²Noah did so; just as God commanded him, so he did.

7 ¹Then יהוה said to Noah, "Go into the ark, with all your household, for you alone have I found righteous before Me in this generation. ²Of every pure animal you shall take seven pairs, males and their mates, and of every animal that is not pure, two, a male and its mate; ³of the birds of the sky also, seven pairs, male and female, to keep seed alive upon all the earth. ⁴For in seven days' time I will make it rain upon the earth, forty days and forty nights, and I will blot out from the earth all existence that I created." ⁵And Noah did just as יהוה commanded him.

⁶Noah was six hundred years old when the Flood came, waters upon the earth. ⁷Noah, with his sons, his wife, and his sons' wives, went into the ark because of the waters of the Flood. ⁸Of the pure animals, of the animals that are not pure, of the birds, and of everything that creeps on the ground, ⁹two of each, male and female, came to Noah into the ark, as God had commanded Noah. ¹⁰And on the seventh day the waters of the Flood came upon the earth.

¹¹In the six hundredth year of Noah's life, in the second month, on the seventeenth day of the month, on that day

All the fountains of the great deep burst apart,

And the floodgates of the sky broke open.

(¹²The rain fell on the earth forty days and forty nights.) ¹³That same day Noah and Noah's sons, Shem, Ham, and Japheth, went into the ark, with Noah's wife and the three wives of his sons—¹⁴they and all beasts of every kind, all cattle of every kind, all creatures of every kind that creep on the earth, and all birds of every kind, every bird, every winged thing. ¹⁵They came to Noah into the ark, two each of all flesh in which there was breath of life. ¹⁶Thus they that entered comprised male and female of all flesh, as God had commanded him. And יהוה shut him in.

¹⁷The Flood continued forty days on the earth, and the waters increased and raised the ark so that it rose above the earth. ¹⁸The waters swelled and increased greatly upon the earth, and the ark drifted upon the waters. ¹⁹When the waters had swelled much more upon the earth, all the highest

mountains everywhere under the sky were covered. ²⁰Fifteen cubits higher did the waters swell, as the mountains were covered. ²¹And all flesh that stirred on earth perished—birds, cattle, beasts, and all the things that swarmed upon the earth, and all humankind. ²²All in whose nostrils was the merest breath of life, all that was on dry land, died. ²³All existence on earth was blotted out—humans, cattle, creeping things, and birds of the sky; they were blotted out from the earth. Only Noah was left, and those with him in the ark. ²⁴And when the waters had swelled on the earth one hundred and fifty days,

8 ¹God remembered Noah and all the beasts and all the cattle that were with him in the ark, and God caused a wind to blow across the earth, and the waters subsided. ²The fountains of the deep and the floodgates of the sky were stopped up, and the rain from the sky was held back; ³the waters then receded steadily from the earth. At the end of one hundred and fifty days the waters diminished, ⁴so that in the seventh month, on the seventeenth day of the month, the ark came to rest on the mountains of Ararat. ⁵The waters went on diminishing until the tenth month; in the tenth month, on the first of the month, the tops of the mountains became visible.

⁶At the end of forty days, Noah opened the window of the ark that he had made ⁷and sent out the raven; it went to and fro until the waters had dried up from the earth. ⁸Then he sent out the dove to see whether the waters had decreased from the surface of the ground. ⁹But the dove could not find a resting place for its foot, and returned to him to the ark, for there was water over all the earth. So putting out his hand, he took it into the ark with him. ¹⁰He waited another seven days, and again sent out the dove from the ark. ¹¹The dove came back to him toward evening, and there in its bill was a plucked-off olive leaf! Then Noah knew that the waters had decreased on the earth. ¹²He waited still another seven days and sent the dove forth; and it did not return to him any more.

¹³In the six hundred and first year, in the first month, on the first of the month, the waters began to dry from the earth; and when Noah removed the covering of the ark, he saw that the surface of the ground was drying. ¹⁴And in the second month, on the twenty-seventh day of the month, the earth was dry.

¹⁵God spoke to Noah, saying, ¹⁶"Come out of the ark, together with your wife, your sons, and your sons' wives. ¹⁷Bring out with you every living thing of all flesh that is with you: birds, animals, and everything that creeps on earth; and let them swarm on the earth and be fertile and increase on earth." ¹⁸So Noah came out, together with his sons, his wife, and his sons' wives. ¹⁹Every animal, every creeping thing, and every bird, everything that stirs on earth came out of the ark by families.

²⁰Then Noah built an altar to יהוה and, taking of every pure animal and of every pure bird, he offered burnt offerings on the altar. ²¹יהוה smelled the pleasing odor, and יהוה resolved: "Never again will I doom the earth because of humankind, since the devisings of the human mind are evil from youth; nor will I ever again destroy every living being, as I have done.

²² So long as the earth endures,
Seedtime and harvest,
Cold and heat,
Summer and winter,
Day and night
Shall not cease."

9 ¹God blessed Noah and his sons, and said to them, "Be fertile and increase, and fill the earth. ²The fear and the dread of you shall be upon all the beasts of the earth and

upon all the birds of the sky—everything with which the earth is astir—and upon all the fish of the sea; they are given into your hand. ³Every creature that lives shall be yours to eat; as with the green grasses, I give you all these. ⁴You must not, however, eat flesh with its lifeblood in it. ⁵But for your own lifeblood I will require a reckoning: I will require it of every beast; of humankind, too, will I require a reckoning for human life, of everyone for each other!

⁶ Whoever sheds human blood,
By human [hands] shall that one's blood be shed;
For in the image of God
Was humankind made.

⁷Be fertile, then, and increase; abound on the earth and increase on it."

⁸And God said to Noah and to his sons with him, ⁹"I now establish My covenant with you and your offspring to come, ¹⁰and with every living thing that is with you—birds, cattle, and every wild beast as well—all that have come out of the ark, every living thing on earth. ¹¹I will maintain My covenant with you: never again shall all flesh be cut off by the waters of a flood, and never again shall there be a flood to destroy the earth."

¹²God further said, "This is the sign that I set for the covenant between Me and you, and every living creature with you, for all ages to come. ¹³I have set My bow in the clouds, and it shall serve as a sign of the covenant between Me and the earth. ¹⁴When I bring clouds over the earth, and the bow appears in the clouds, ¹⁵I will remember My covenant between Me and you and every living creature among all flesh, so that the waters shall never again become a flood to destroy all flesh. ¹⁶When the bow is in the clouds, I will see it and remember the everlasting covenant between God and all living creatures, all flesh that is on earth. ¹⁷That," God said to Noah, "shall be the sign of the covenant that I have established between Me and all flesh that is on earth."

¹⁸The sons of Noah who came out of the ark were Shem, Ham, and Japheth—Ham being the father of Canaan. ¹⁹These three were the sons of Noah, and from these the whole world branched out.

²⁰Noah, the tiller of the soil, was the first to plant a vineyard. ²¹He drank of the wine and became drunk, and he uncovered himself within his tent. ²²Ham, the father of Canaan, saw his father's nakedness and told his two brothers outside. ²³But Shem and Japheth took a cloth, placed it against both their backs and, walking backward, they covered their father's nakedness; their faces were turned the other way, so that they did not see their father's nakedness. ²⁴When Noah woke up from his wine and learned what his youngest son had done to him, ²⁵he said,

"Cursed be Canaan;
The lowest of slaves
Shall he be to his brothers."

²⁶And he said,

"Blessed be יהוה,
The God of Shem;
Let Canaan be a slave to them.
²⁷ May God enlarge Japheth,
And let him dwell in the tents of Shem;
And let Canaan be a slave to them."

²⁸Noah lived after the Flood 350 years. ²⁹And all the days of Noah came to 950 years; then he died.

10 ¹These are the lines of Shem, Ham, and Japheth, the sons of Noah: sons were born to them after the Flood.

²The descendants of Japheth: Gomer, Magog, Madai, Javan, Tubal, Meshech, and Tiras. ³The descendants of Gomer: Ashkenaz, Riphath, and Togarmah. ⁴The descendants of Javan: Elishah and Tarshish, the Kittim and the Dodanim. ⁵From these the maritime nations branched out. [These are the descendants of Japheth] by their lands—each with its language—their clans and their nations.

⁶The descendants of Ham: Cush, Mizraim, Put, and Canaan. ⁷The descendants of Cush: Seba, Havilah, Sabtah, Raamah, and Sabteca. The descendants of Raamah: Sheba and Dedan.

⁸Cush also begot Nimrod, who was the first mighty figure on earth. ⁹He was a mighty hunter by the grace of יהוה; hence the saying, "Like Nimrod a mighty hunter by the grace of יהוה." ¹⁰The mainstays of his kingdom were Babylon, Erech, Accad, and Calneh in the land of Shinar. ¹¹From that land Asshur went forth and built Nineveh, Rehobothir, Calah, ¹²and Resen between Nineveh and Calah, that is the great city.

¹³And Mizraim begot the Ludim, the Anamim, the Lehabim, the Naphtuhim, ¹⁴the Pathrusim, the Casluhim, and the Caphtorim, whence the Philistines came forth.

¹⁵Canaan begot Sidon, his firstborn, and Heth; ¹⁶and the Jebusites, the Amorites, the Girgashites, ¹⁷the Hivites, the Arkites, the Sinites, ¹⁸the Arvadites, the Zemarites, and the Hamathites. Afterward the clans of the Canaanites spread out. (¹⁹The [original] Canaanite territory extended from Sidon as far as Gerar, near Gaza, and as far as Sodom, Gomorrah, Admah, and Zeboiim, near Lasha.) ²⁰These are the descendants of Ham, according to their clans and languages, by their lands and nations.

²¹Sons were also born to Shem, ancestor of all the descendants of Eber and older brother of Japheth. ²²The descendants of Shem: Elam, Asshur, Arpachshad, Lud, and Aram. ²³The descendants of Aram: Uz, Hul, Gether, and Mash. ²⁴Arpachshad begot Shelah, and Shelah begot Eber. ²⁵Two sons were born to Eber: the name of the first was Peleg, for in his days the earth was divided; and the name of his brother was Joktan. ²⁶Joktan begot Almodad, Sheleph, Hazarmaveth, Jerah, ²⁷Hadoram, Uzal, Diklah, ²⁸Obal, Abimael, Sheba, ²⁹Ophir, Havilah, and Jobab; all these were the descendants of Joktan. ³⁰Their settlements extended from Mesha as far as Sephar, the hill country to the east. ³¹These are the descendants of Shem according to their clans and languages, by their lands, according to their nations.

³²These are the groupings of Noah's descendants, according to their origins, by their nations; and from these the nations branched out over the earth after the Flood.

11 ¹Everyone on earth had the same language and the same words. ²And as they migrated from the east, they came upon a valley in the land of Shinar and settled there. ³They said to one another, "Come, let us make bricks and burn them hard."—Brick served them as stone, and bitumen served them as mortar.—⁴And they said, "Come, let us build us a city, and a tower with its top in the sky, to make a name for ourselves; else we shall be scattered all over the world." ⁵יהוה came down to look at the city and tower that humanity had built, ⁶and יהוה said, "If, as one people with one language for all, this is how they have begun to act, then nothing that they may propose to do will be out of their reach. ⁷Let us, then, go down and confound their speech there, so that they shall not understand one another's speech." ⁸Thus יהוה scattered them from there over the face of the whole earth; and they stopped building the city. ⁹That is why it was called Babel, because there יהוה confounded the speech of the whole earth; and from there יהוה scattered them over the face of the whole earth.

¹⁰This is the line of Shem. Shem was 100 years old when he begot Arpachshad, two years after the Flood. ¹¹After the birth of Arpachshad, Shem lived 500 years and begot sons and daughters.

¹²When Arpachshad had lived 35 years, he begot Shelah. ¹³After the birth of Shelah, Arpachshad lived 403 years and begot sons and daughters.

¹⁴When Shelah had lived 30 years, he begot Eber. ¹⁵After the birth of Eber, Shelah lived 403 years and begot sons and daughters.

¹⁶When Eber had lived 34 years, he begot Peleg. ¹⁷After the birth of Peleg, Eber lived 430 years and begot sons and daughters.

¹⁸When Peleg had lived 30 years, he begot Reu. ¹⁹After the birth of Reu, Peleg lived 209 years and begot sons and daughters.

²⁰When Reu had lived 32 years, he begot Serug. ²¹After the birth of Serug, Reu lived 207 years and begot sons and daughters.

²²When Serug had lived 30 years, he begot Nahor. ²³After the birth of Nahor, Serug lived 200 years and begot sons and daughters.

²⁴When Nahor had lived 29 years, he begot Terah. ²⁵After the birth of Terah, Nahor lived 119 years and begot sons and daughters.

²⁶When Terah had lived 70 years, he begot Abram, Nahor, and Haran. ²⁷Now this is the line of Terah: Terah begot Abram, Nahor, and Haran; and Haran begot Lot. ²⁸Haran died in the lifetime of his father Terah, in his native land, Ur of the Chaldeans. ²⁹Abram and Nahor took wives for themselves, the name of Abram's wife being Sarai and that of Nahor's wife Milcah, the daughter of Haran, the father of Milcah and Iscah. ³⁰Now Sarai was barren; she had no child.

³¹Terah took his son Abram, his grandson Lot the son of Haran, and his daughter-in-law Sarai, the wife of his son Abram, and they set out together from Ur of the Chaldeans for the land of Canaan; but when they had come as far as Haran, they settled there. ³²The days of Terah came to 205 years; and Terah died in Haran.

12 ¹יהוה said to Abram, "Go forth from your native land and from your father's house to the land that I will show you.

²   I will make of you a great nation,
    And I will bless you;
    I will make your name great,
    And you shall be a blessing.
³   I will bless those who bless you
    And curse the one who curses you;
    And all the families of the earth
    Shall bless themselves by you."

⁴Abram went forth as יהוה had commanded him, and Lot went with him. Abram was seventy-five years old when he left Haran. ⁵Abram took his wife Sarai and his brother's son Lot, and all the wealth that they had amassed, and the persons that they had acquired in Haran; and they set out for the land of Canaan. When they arrived in the land of Canaan, ⁶Abram passed through the land as far as the site of Shechem, at the terebinth of Moreh. The Canaanites were then in the land.

⁷יהוה appeared to Abram and said, "I will assign this land to your offspring." And he built an altar there to יהוה who had appeared to him. ⁸From there he moved on to the hill country east of Bethel and pitched his tent, with Bethel on the west and Ai on the east; and he built there an altar to

יהוה and invoked יהוה by name. 9Then Abram journeyed by stages toward the Negeb.

10There was a famine in the land, and Abram went down to Egypt to sojourn there, for the famine was severe in the land. 11As he was about to enter Egypt, he said to his wife Sarai, "I know what a beautiful woman you are. 12If the Egyptians see you, and think, 'She is his wife,' they will kill me and let you live. 13Please say that you are my sister, that it may go well with me because of you, and that I may remain alive thanks to you."

14When Abram entered Egypt, the Egyptians saw how very beautiful the woman was. 15Pharaoh's courtiers saw her and praised her to Pharaoh, and the woman was taken into Pharaoh's palace. 16And because of her, it went well with Abram; he acquired sheep, oxen, asses, male and female slaves, she-asses, and camels.

17But יהוה afflicted Pharaoh and his household with mighty plagues on account of Sarai, the wife of Abram. 18Pharaoh sent for Abram and said, "What is this you have done to me! Why did you not tell me that she was your wife? 19Why did you say, 'She is my sister,' so that I took her as my wife? Now, here is your wife; take her and be gone!" 20And Pharaoh put deputies in charge of him, and they sent him off with his wife and all that he possessed.

13 1From Egypt, Abram went up into the Negeb, with his wife and all that he possessed, together with Lot. 2Now Abram was very rich in cattle, silver, and gold. 3And he proceeded by stages from the Negeb as far as Bethel, to the place where his tent had been formerly, between Bethel and Ai, 4the site of the altar that he had built there at first; and there Abram invoked יהוה by name.

5Lot, who went with Abram, also had flocks and herds and tents, 6so that the land could not support them staying together; for their possessions were so great that they could not remain together. 7And there was quarreling between the herders of Abram's cattle and those of Lot's cattle.—The Canaanites and Perizzites were then dwelling in the land.— 8Abram said to Lot, "Let there be no strife between you and me, between my herders and yours, for we are kin. 9Is not the whole land before you? Let us separate: if you go north, I will go south; and if you go south, I will go north." 10Lot looked about him and saw how well watered was the whole plain of the Jordan, all of it—this was before יהוה had destroyed Sodom and Gomorrah—all the way to Zoar, like the garden of יהוה, like the land of Egypt. 11So Lot chose for himself the whole plain of the Jordan, and Lot journeyed eastward. Thus they parted from each other; 12Abram remained in the land of Canaan, while Lot settled in the cities of the Plain, pitching his tents near Sodom. 13Now the inhabitants of Sodom were very wicked sinners against יהוה.

14And יהוה said to Abram, after Lot had parted from him, "Raise your eyes and look out from where you are, to the north and south, to the east and west, 15for I give all the land that you see to you and your offspring forever. 16I will make your offspring as the dust of the earth, so that if one can count the dust of the earth, then your offspring too can be counted. 17Up, walk about the land, through its length and its breadth, for I give it to you." 18And Abram moved his tent, and came to dwell at the terebinths of Mamre, which are in Hebron; and he built an altar there to יהוה.

14 1Now, when King Amraphel of Shinar, King Arioch of Ellasar, King Chedorlaomer of Elam, and King Tidal of Goiim 2made war on King Bera of Sodom, King Birsha of Gomorrah, King Shinab of Admah, King Shemeber of Zeboiim, and the king of Bela, which is Zoar, 3all the latter joined forces at the Valley of Siddim, now the Dead Sea. 4Twelve years they served Chedorlaomer, and in the thirteenth year they rebelled. 5In the fourteenth year Chedorlaomer and the kings who were with him came and defeated the Rephaim at Ashterothkarnaim, the Zuzim at Ham, the Emim at Shaveh-kiriathaim, 6and the Horites in their hill country of Seir as far as Elparan, which is by the wilderness. 7On their way back they came to Enmishpat, which is Kadesh, and subdued all the territory of the Amalekites, and also the Amorites who dwelt in Hazazontamar. 8Then the king of Sodom, the king of Gomorrah, the king of Admah, the king of Zeboiim, and the king of Bela, which is Zoar, went forth and engaged them in battle in the Valley of Siddim: 9King Chedorlaomer of Elam, King Tidal of Goiim, King Amraphel of Shinar, and King Arioch of Ellasar—four kings against those five.

10Now the Valley of Siddim was dotted with bitumen pits; and the kings of Sodom and Gomorrah, in their flight, threw themselves into them, while the rest escaped to the hill country. 11[The invaders] seized all the wealth of Sodom and Gomorrah and all their provisions, and went their way. 12They also took Lot, the son of Abram's brother, and his possessions, and departed; for he had settled in Sodom.

13A fugitive brought the news to Abram the Hebrew, who was dwelling at the terebinths of Mamre the Amorite, kinsman of Eshkol and Aner, these being Abram's allies. 14When Abram heard that his kinsman's [household] had been taken captive, he mustered his retainers born into his household, numbering three hundred and eighteen, and went in pursuit as far as Dan. 15At night, he and his servants deployed against them and defeated them; and he pursued them as far as Hobah, which is north of Damascus. 16He brought back all the possessions; he also brought back his kinsman Lot and his possessions, and the women and the rest of the people.

17When he returned from defeating Chedorlaomer and the kings with him, the king of Sodom came out to meet him in the Valley of Shaveh, which is the Valley of the King. 18And King Melchizedek of Salem brought out bread and wine; he was a priest of God Most High, 19He blessed him, saying,

"Blessed be Abram of God Most High,
Creator of heaven and earth.
20 And blessed be God Most High,
Who has delivered your foes into your hand."

And [Abram] gave him a tenth of everything. 21Then the king of Sodom said to Abram, "Give me the persons, and take the possessions for yourself." 22But Abram said to the king of Sodom, "I swear to יהוה, God Most High, Creator of heaven and earth: 23I will not take so much as a thread or a sandal strap of what is yours; you shall not say, 'It is I who made Abram rich.' 24For me, nothing but what my servants have used up; as for the share of the notables who went with me—Aner, Eshkol, and Mamre—let them take their share."

15 1Some time later, the word of יהוה came to Abram in a vision:

"Fear not, Abram,
I am a shield to you;
Your reward shall be very great."

2But Abram said, "O lord יהוה, what can You give me, seeing that I shall die childless, and the one in charge of my household is Dammesek Eliezer!" 3Abram said further, "Since You have granted me no offspring, my steward will be my heir." 4The word of יהוה came to him in reply, "That one shall not be your heir; none but your very own issue shall be your heir." 5[Then in the vision, God] took him outside and said,

"Look toward heaven and count the stars, if you are able to count them"—continuing, "So shall your offspring be." [6]And he put his trust in יהוה, who reckoned it to his merit.

[7]Then [God] said to him, "I am יהוה who brought you out from Ur of the Chaldeans to assign this land to you as a possession." [8]And he said, "O lord יהוה, how shall I know that I am to possess it?" [9]Came the reply, "Bring Me a three year old heifer, a three year old she-goat, a three year old ram, a turtledove, and a young bird." [10]He brought all these and cut them in two, placing each half opposite the other; but he did not cut up the bird. [11]Birds of prey came down upon the carcasses, and Abram drove them away. [12]As the sun was about to set, a deep sleep fell upon Abram, and a great dark dread descended upon him. [13]And [God] said to Abram, "Know well that your offspring shall be strangers in a land not theirs, and they shall be enslaved and oppressed four hundred years; [14]but I will execute judgment on the nation they shall serve, and in the end they shall go free with great wealth.

[15] As for you,
You shall go to your ancestors in peace;
You shall be buried at a ripe old age.

[16]And they shall return here in the fourth generation, for the iniquity of the Amorites is not yet complete."

[17]When the sun set and it was very dark, there appeared a smoking oven, and a flaming torch which passed between those pieces. [18]On that day יהוה made a covenant with Abram: "To your offspring I assign this land, from the river of Egypt to the great river, the river Euphrates—[19]the Kenites, the Kenizzites, the Kadmonites, [20]the Hittites, the Perizzites, the Rephaim, [21]the Amorites, the Canaanites, the Girgashites, and the Jebusites."

16 [1]Sarai, Abram's wife, had borne him no children. She had an Egyptian maidservant whose name was Hagar. [2]And Sarai said to Abram, "Look, יהוה has kept me from bearing. Consort with my maid; perhaps I shall have a child through her." And Abram heeded Sarai's request. [3]So Sarai, Abram's wife, took her maid, Hagar the Egyptian—after Abram had dwelt in the land of Canaan ten years—and gave her to her husband Abram as concubine. [4]He cohabited with Hagar and she conceived; and when she saw that she had conceived, her mistress was lowered in her esteem. [5]And Sarai said to Abram, "The wrong done me is your fault! I myself put my maid in your bosom; now that she sees that she is pregnant I am lowered in her esteem. יהוה decide between you and me!" [6]Abram said to Sarai, "Your maid is in your hands. Deal with her as you think right." Then Sarai treated her harshly, and she ran away from her.

[7]A messenger of יהוה found her by a spring of water in the wilderness, the spring on the road to Shur, [8]and said, "Hagar, slave of Sarai, where have you come from, and where are you going?" And she said, "I am running away from my mistress Sarai."

[9]And the messenger of יהוה said to her, "Go back to your mistress, and submit to her harsh treatment." [10]And the messenger of יהוה said to her,

"I will greatly increase your offspring,
And they shall be too many to count."

[11]The messenger of יהוה said to her further,

"Behold, you are pregnant
And shall bear a son;
You shall call him Ishmael,
For יהוה has paid heed to your suffering."

[12] He shall be a wild ass of a person;
His hand against everyone,
And everyone's hand against him;
He shall dwell alongside of all his kin."

[13]And she called יהוה who spoke to her, "You Are Elroi," by which she meant, "Have I not gone on seeing after my being seen!" [14]Therefore the well was called Beerlahairoi; it is between Kadesh and Bered.—[15]Hagar bore a son to Abram, and Abram gave the son that Hagar bore him the name Ishmael. [16]Abram was eighty-six years old when Hagar bore Ishmael to Abram.

17 [1]When Abram was ninety-nine years old, יהוה appeared to Abram and said to him, "I am El Shaddai. Walk in My ways and be blameless. [2]I will establish My covenant between Me and you, and I will make you exceedingly numerous."

[3]Abram threw himself on his face; and God spoke to him further, [4]"As for Me, this is My covenant with you: You shall be the father of a multitude of nations. [5]And you shall no longer be called Abram, but your name shall be Abraham, for I make you the father of a multitude of nations. [6]I will make you exceedingly fertile, and make nations of you; and kings shall come forth from you. [7]I will maintain My covenant between Me and you, and your offspring to come, as an everlasting covenant throughout the ages, to be God to you and to your offspring to come. [8]I assign the land you sojourn in to you and your offspring to come, all the land of Canaan, as an everlasting holding. I will be their God."

[9]God further said to Abraham, "As for you, you and your offspring to come throughout the ages shall keep My covenant. [10]Such shall be the covenant between Me and you and your offspring to follow which you shall keep: every male among you shall be circumcised. [11]You shall circumcise the flesh of your foreskin, and that shall be the sign of the covenant between Me and you. [12]And throughout the generations, every male among you shall be circumcised at the age of eight days. As for the home-born slave and the one bought from an outsider who is not of your offspring, [13]they must be circumcised, home-born, and purchased alike. Thus shall My covenant be marked in your flesh as an everlasting pact. [14]And if any male who is uncircumcised fails to circumcise the flesh of his foreskin, that person shall be cut off from kin; he has broken My covenant."

[15]And God said to Abraham, "As for your wife Sarai, you shall not call her Sarai, but her name shall be Sarah. [16]I will bless her; indeed, I will give you a son by her. I will bless her so that she shall give rise to nations; rulers of peoples shall issue from her." [17]Abraham threw himself on his face and laughed, as he said to himself, "Can a child be born to a man a hundred years old, or can Sarah bear a child at ninety?" [18]And Abraham said to God, "O that Ishmael might live by Your favor!" [19]God said, "Nevertheless, Sarah your wife shall bear you a son, and you shall name him Isaac; and I will maintain My covenant with him as an everlasting covenant for his offspring to come. [20]As for Ishmael, I have heeded you. I hereby bless him. I will make him fertile and exceedingly numerous. He shall be the father of twelve chieftains, and I will make of him a great nation. [21]But My covenant I will maintain with Isaac, whom Sarah shall bear to you at this season next year." [22]Done speaking with him, God was gone from Abraham.

[23]Then Abraham took his son Ishmael, and all his home-born slaves and all those he had bought, every male in Abraham's household, and he circumcised the flesh of their foreskins on that very day, as God had spoken to him. [24]Abraham was ninety-nine years old when he circumcised the flesh of his foreskin, [25]and his son Ishmael was thirteen years old

when he was circumcised in the flesh of his foreskin . ²⁶Thus Abraham and his son Ishmael were circumcised on that very day; ²⁷and all [men of] his household, his home-born slaves and those that had been bought from outsiders, were circumcised with him.

18 ¹יהוה appeared to him by the terebinths of Mamre; he was sitting at the entrance of the tent as the day grew hot. ²Looking up, he saw three [divine] envoys standing near him. Perceiving this, he ran from the entrance of the tent to greet them and, bowing to the ground, ³he said, "My lords! If it please you, do not go on past your servant. ⁴Let a little water be brought; bathe your feet and recline under the tree. ⁵And let me fetch a morsel of bread that you may refresh yourselves; then go on—seeing that you have come your servant's way." They replied, "Do as you have said." ⁶Abraham hastened into the tent to Sarah, and said, "Quick, three *seahs* of choice flour! Knead and make cakes!" ⁷Then Abraham ran to the herd, took a calf, tender and choice, and gave it to a servant-boy, who hastened to prepare it. ⁸He took curds and milk and the calf that had been prepared and set these before them; and he waited on them under the tree as they ate.

⁹They said to him, "Where is your wife Sarah?" And he replied, "There, in the tent." ¹⁰Then one said, "I will return to you next year, and your wife Sarah shall have a son!" Sarah was listening at the entrance of the tent, which was behind him. ¹¹Now Abraham and Sarah were old, advanced in years; Sarah had stopped having her periods. ¹²And Sarah laughed to herself, saying, "Now that I've lost the ability, am I to have enjoyment—with my husband so old?" ¹³Then יהוה said to Abraham, "Why did Sarah laugh, saying, 'Shall I in truth bear a child, old as I am?' ¹⁴Is anything too wondrous for יהוה? I will return to you at the same season next year, and Sarah shall have a son." ¹⁵Sarah lied, saying, "I did not laugh," for she was frightened. Came the reply, "You did laugh."

¹⁶The envoys set out from there and looked down toward Sodom, Abraham walking with them to see them off. ¹⁷Now יהוה had said, "Shall I hide from Abraham what I am about to do, ¹⁸since Abraham is to become a great and populous nation and all the nations of the earth are to bless themselves by him? ¹⁹For I have singled him out, that he may instruct his children and his posterity to keep the way of יהוה by doing what is just and right, in order that יהוה may bring about for Abraham what has been promised him." ²⁰Then יהוה said, "The outrage of Sodom and Gomorrah is so great, and their sin so grave! ²¹I will go down to see whether they have acted altogether according to the outcry that has reached Me; if not, I will take note."

²²The envoys went on from there to Sodom, while Abraham remained standing before יהוה. ²³Abraham came forward and said, "Will You sweep away the innocent along with the guilty? ²⁴What if there should be fifty innocent within the city; will You then wipe out the place and not forgive it for the sake of the innocent fifty who are in it? ²⁵Far be it from You to do such a thing, to bring death upon the innocent as well as the guilty, so that innocent and guilty fare alike. Far be it from You! Shall not the Judge of all the earth deal justly?" ²⁶And יהוה answered, "If I find within the city of Sodom fifty innocent ones, I will forgive the whole place for their sake." ²⁷Abraham spoke up, saying, "Here I venture to speak to my lord, I who am but dust and ashes: ²⁸What if the fifty innocent should lack five? Will You destroy the whole city for want of the five?"

"I will not destroy if I find forty-five there."

²⁹But he spoke up again, and said, "What if forty should be found there?"

"I will not do it, for the sake of the forty."

³⁰And he said, "Let not my lord be angry if I go on: What if thirty should be found there?"

"I will not do it if I find thirty there."

³¹And he said, "I venture again to speak to my lord: What if twenty should be found there?"

"I will not destroy, for the sake of the twenty."

³²And he said, "Let not my lord be angry if I speak but this last time: What if ten should be found there?"

"I will not destroy, for the sake of the ten."

³³Having finished speaking to Abraham, יהוה departed; and Abraham returned to his place.

19 ¹The two messengers arrived in Sodom in the evening, as Lot was sitting in the gate of Sodom. When Lot saw them, he rose to greet them and, bowing low with his face to the ground, ²he said, "Please, my lords, turn aside to your servant's house to spend the night, and bathe your feet; then you may be on your way early." But they said, "No, we will spend the night in the square." ³But he urged them strongly, so they turned his way and entered his house. He prepared a feast for them and baked unleavened bread, and they ate.

⁴They had not yet lain down, when the town council [and] the militia of Sodom,—insignificant and influential alike, the whole assembly without exception—gathered about the house. ⁵And they shouted to Lot and said to him, "Where are the envoys [of יהוה] who came to you tonight? Bring them out to us, that we may be intimate with them." ⁶So Lot went out to them to the entrance, shut the door behind him, ⁷and said, "I beg you, my friends, do not commit such a wrong. ⁸Look, I have two daughters who have not known a man. Let me bring them out to you, and you may do to them as you please; but do not do anything to these envoys, since they have come under the shelter of my roof." ⁹But they said, "Stand back! The fellow," they said, "came here as an alien, and already he acts the ruler! Now we will deal worse with you than with them." And they pressed hard against that householder—against Lot—and moved forward to break the door. ¹⁰But the envoys stretched out their hands and pulled Lot into the house with them, and shut the door. ¹¹And the people who were at the entrance of the house, low and high alike, they struck with blinding light, so that they were helpless to find the entrance.

¹²Then the envoys said to Lot, "Whom else have you here? Sons-in-law, your sons and daughters, or anyone else that you have in the city—bring them out of the place. ¹³For we are about to destroy this place; because the outcry against them before יהוה has become so great that יהוה has sent us to destroy it." ¹⁴So Lot went out and spoke to his sons-in-law, who had married his daughters, and said, "Up, get out of this place, for יהוה is about to destroy the city." But he seemed to his sons-in-law as one who jests.

¹⁵As dawn broke, the messengers urged Lot on, saying, "Up, take your wife and your two remaining daughters, lest you be swept away because of the iniquity of the city." ¹⁶Still he delayed. So the envoys seized his hand, and the hands of his wife and his two daughters—in יהוה's mercy on him—and brought him out and left him outside the city. ¹⁷When they had brought them outside, one said, "Flee for your life! Do not look behind you, nor stop anywhere in the Plain; flee to

the hills, lest you be swept away." ¹⁸But Lot said to them, "Oh no, my lord! ¹⁹You have been so gracious to your servant, and have already shown me so much kindness in order to save my life; but I cannot flee to the hills, lest the disaster overtake me and I die. ²⁰Look, that town there is near enough to flee to; it is such a little place! Let me flee there—it is such a little place—and let my life be saved." ²¹He replied, "Very well, I will grant you this favor too, and I will not annihilate the town of which you have spoken. ²²Hurry, flee there, for I cannot do anything until you arrive there." Hence the town came to be called Zoar.

²³As the sun rose upon the earth and Lot entered Zoar, ²⁴יהוה rained upon Sodom and Gomorrah sulfurous fire from יהוה out of heaven—²⁵annihilating those cities and the entire Plain, and all the inhabitants of the cities and the vegetation of the ground. ²⁶Lot's wife looked back, and she thereupon turned into a pillar of salt.

²⁷Next morning, Abraham hurried to the place where he had stood before יהוה, ²⁸and, looking down toward Sodom and Gomorrah and all the land of the Plain, he saw the smoke of the land rising like the smoke of a kiln.

²⁹Thus it was that, when God destroyed the cities of the Plain and annihilated the cities where Lot dwelt, God was mindful of Abraham and removed Lot from the midst of the upheaval.

³⁰Lot went up from Zoar and settled in the hill country with his two daughters, for he was afraid to dwell in Zoar; and he and his two daughters lived in a cave. ³¹And the older one said to the younger, "Our father is old, and there is not a man on earth to consort with us in the way of all the world. ³²Come, let us make our father drink wine, and let us lie with him, that we may maintain life through our father." ³³That night they made their father drink wine, and the older one went in and lay with her father; he did not know when she lay down or when she rose. ³⁴The next day the older one said to the younger, "See, I lay with Father last night; let us make him drink wine tonight also, and you go and lie with him, that we may maintain life through our father." ³⁵That night also they made their father drink wine, and the younger one went and lay with him; he did not know when she lay down or when she rose.

³⁶Thus the two daughters of Lot became pregnant by their father. ³⁷The older one bore a son and named him Moab; he is the father of the Moabites of today. ³⁸And the younger also bore a son, and she called him Benammi; he is the father of the Ammonites of today.

20 ¹Abraham journeyed from there to the region of the Negeb and settled between Kadesh and Shur. While he was sojourning in Gerar, ²Abraham said of Sarah his wife, "She is my sister." So King Abimelech of Gerar had Sarah brought to him. ³But God came to Abimelech in a dream by night and said to him, "You are to die because of the woman that you have taken, for she is a married woman." ⁴Now Abimelech had not approached her. He said, "O lord, will You slay people even though innocent? ⁵He himself said to me, 'She is my sister!' And she also said, 'He is my brother.' When I did this, my heart was blameless and my hands were clean." ⁶And God said to him in the dream, "I knew that you did this with a blameless heart, and so I kept you from sinning against Me. That was why I did not let you touch her. ⁷Therefore, restore the wife of this householder—since he is a prophet, he will intercede for you—to save your life. If you fail to restore her, know that you shall die, you and all that are yours."

⁸Early next morning, Abimelech called his servants and told them all that had happened. Those officials were greatly frightened. ⁹Then Abimelech summoned Abraham and said to him, "What have you done to us? What wrong have I done that you should bring so great a guilt upon me and my kingdom? You have done to me things that ought not to be done. ¹⁰What, then," Abimelech demanded of Abraham, "was your purpose in doing this thing?" ¹¹"I thought," said Abraham, "surely there is no fear of God in this place, and they will kill me because of my wife. ¹²And besides, she is in truth my sister, my father's daughter though not my mother's; and she became my wife. ¹³So when God made me wander from my father's house, I said to her, 'Let this be the kindness that you shall do me: whatever place we come to, say there of me: He is my brother.'"

¹⁴Abimelech took sheep and oxen, and male and female slaves, and gave them to Abraham; and he restored his wife Sarah to him. ¹⁵And Abimelech said, "Here, my land is before you; settle wherever you please." ¹⁶And to Sarah he said, "I herewith give your brother a thousand pieces of silver; this will serve you as vindication before all who are with you, and you are cleared before everyone." ¹⁷Abraham then prayed to God, and God healed Abimelech and his wife and his slave girls, so that they bore children; ¹⁸for יהוה had closed fast every womb of the household of Abimelech because of Sarah, the wife of Abraham.

21 ¹יהוה took note of Sarah as promised, and יהוה did for Sarah what had been announced. ²Sarah conceived and bore a son to Abraham in his old age, at the set time of which God had spoken. ³Abraham gave his newborn son, whom Sarah had borne him, the name of Isaac. ⁴And when his son Isaac was eight days old, Abraham circumcised him, as God had commanded him. ⁵Now Abraham was a hundred years old when his son Isaac was born to him. ⁶Sarah said, "God has brought me laughter; everyone who hears will laugh with me." ⁷And she added,

> "Who would have said to Abraham
> That Sarah would suckle children!
> Yet I have borne a son in his old age."

⁸The child grew up and was weaned, and Abraham held a great feast on the day that Isaac was weaned.

⁹Sarah saw the son whom Hagar the Egyptian had borne to Abraham playing. ¹⁰She said to Abraham, "Cast out that slave-woman and her son, for the son of that slave shall not share in the inheritance with my son Isaac." ¹¹The matter distressed Abraham greatly, for it concerned a son of his. ¹²But God said to Abraham, "Do not be distressed over the boy or your slave; whatever Sarah tells you, do as she says, for it is through Isaac that offspring shall be continued for you. ¹³As for the son of the slave-woman, I will make a nation of him, too, for he is your seed."

¹⁴Early next morning Abraham took some bread and a skin of water, and gave them to Hagar. He placed them over her shoulder, together with the child, and sent her away. And she wandered about in the wilderness of Beersheba. ¹⁵When the water was gone from the skin, she left the child under one of the bushes, ¹⁶and went and sat down at a distance, a bowshot away; for she thought, "Let me not look on as the child dies." And sitting thus afar, she burst into tears.

¹⁷God heard the cry of the boy, and a messenger of God called to Hagar from heaven and said to her, "What troubles you, Hagar? Fear not, for God has heeded the cry of the boy where he is. ¹⁸Come, lift up the boy and hold him by the hand, for I will make a great nation of him." ¹⁹Then God opened her eyes and she saw a well of water. She went and filled the skin with water, and let the boy drink. ²⁰God was with the boy and he grew up; he dwelt in the wilderness and became

skilled with a bow. ²¹He lived in the wilderness of Paran; and his mother got a wife for him from the land of Egypt.

²²At that time Abimelech and Phicol, chief of his troops, said to Abraham, "God is with you in everything that you do. ²³Therefore swear to me here by God that you will not deal falsely with me or with my kith and kin, but will deal with me and with the land in which you have sojourned as loyally as I have dealt with you." ²⁴And Abraham said, "I swear it."

²⁵Then Abraham reproached Abimelech for the well of water which the servants of Abimelech had seized. ²⁶But Abimelech said, "I do not know who did this; you did not tell me, nor have I heard of it until today." ²⁷Abraham took sheep and oxen and gave them to Abimelech, and the two of them made a pact. ²⁸Abraham then set seven ewes of the flock by themselves, ²⁹and Abimelech said to Abraham, "What mean these seven ewes which you have set apart?" ³⁰He replied, "You are to accept these seven ewes from me as proof that I dug this well." ³¹Hence that place was called Beersheba, for there the two of them swore an oath. ³²When they had concluded the pact at Beersheba, Abimelech and Phicol, chief of his troops, departed and returned to the land of the Philistines. ³³[Abraham] planted a tamarisk at Beersheba, and invoked there the name of יהוה, the Everlasting God. ³⁴And Abraham resided in the land of the Philistines a long time.

22 ¹Some time afterward, God put Abraham to the test, saying to him, "Abraham." He answered, "Here I am." ²"Take your son, your favored one, Isaac, whom you love, and go to the land of Moriah, and offer him there as a burnt offering on one of the heights that I will point out to you."

³So early next morning, Abraham saddled his ass and took with him two of his servants and his son Isaac. He split the wood for the burnt offering, and he set out for the place of which God had told him. ⁴On the third day Abraham looked up and saw the place from afar. ⁵Then Abraham said to his servants, "You stay here with the ass. The boy and I will go up there; we will worship and we will return to you."

⁶Abraham took the wood for the burnt offering and put it on his son Isaac. He himself took the firestone and the knife; and the two walked off together. ⁷Then Isaac said to his father Abraham, "Father!" And he answered, "Yes, my son." And he said, "Here are the firestone and the wood; but where is the sheep for the burnt offering?" ⁸And Abraham said, "It is God who will see to the sheep for this burnt offering, my son." And the two of them walked on together.

⁹They arrived at the place of which God had told him. Abraham built an altar there; he laid out the wood; he bound his son Isaac; he laid him on the altar, on top of the wood. ¹⁰And Abraham picked up the knife to slay his son. ¹¹Then a messenger of יהוה called to him from heaven: "Abraham! Abraham!" And he answered, "Here I am."

¹²"Do not raise your hand against the boy, or do anything to him. For now I know that you fear God, since you have not withheld your son, your favored one, from Me."

¹³When Abraham looked up, his eye fell upon a ram, caught in the thicket by its horns. So Abraham went and took the ram and offered it up as a burnt offering in place of his son. ¹⁴And Abraham named that site Adonaiyireh, whence the present saying, "On the mount of יהוה there is vision."

¹⁵The messenger of יהוה called to Abraham a second time from heaven, ¹⁶and said, "By Myself I swear, יהוה declares: Because you have done this and have not withheld your son, your favored one, ¹⁷I will bestow My blessing upon you and make your descendants as numerous as the stars of heaven and the sands on the seashore; and your descendants shall seize the gates of their foes. ¹⁸All the nations of the earth shall bless themselves by your descendants, because you

have obeyed My command." ¹⁹Abraham then returned to his servants, and they departed together for Beersheba; and Abraham stayed in Beersheba.

²⁰Some time later, Abraham was told, "Milcah too has borne sons to your brother Nahor: ²¹Uz the firstborn, and Buz his brother, and Kemuel the father of Aram; ²²and Chesed, Hazo, Pildash, Jidlaph, and Bethuel"—²³Bethuel being the father of Rebekah. These eight Milcah bore to Nahor, Abraham's brother. ²⁴And his concubine, whose name was Reumah, also bore [sons]—Tebah, Gaham, and Tahash—and [a daughter,] Maacah.

23 ¹Sarah's lifetime—the span of Sarah's life—came to one hundred and twenty-seven years. ²Sarah died in Kiriatharba—now Hebron—in the land of Canaan; and Abraham proceeded to mourn for Sarah and to bewail her. ³Then Abraham rose from beside his dead, and spoke to the Hittites, saying, ⁴"I am a resident alien among you; sell me a burial site among you, that I may remove my dead for burial." ⁵And the Hittites replied to Abraham, saying to him, ⁶"Hear us, my lord: you are the elect of God among us. Bury your dead in the choicest of our burial places; none of us will withhold his burial place from you for burying your dead." ⁷Thereupon Abraham bowed low to the land owning citizens, the Hittites, ⁸and he said to them, "If it is your wish that I remove my dead for burial, you must agree to intercede for me with Ephron son of Zohar. ⁹Let him sell me the cave of Machpelah that he owns, which is at the edge of his land. Let him sell it to me, at the full price, for a burial site in your midst."

¹⁰Ephron was present among the Hittites; so Ephron the Hittite answered Abraham in the hearing of the Hittites, the assembly in his town's gate, saying, ¹¹"No, my lord, hear me: I give you the field and I give you the cave that is in it; I give it to you in the presence of my people. Bury your dead." ¹²Then Abraham bowed low before the land owning citizens, ¹³and spoke to Ephron in the hearing of the land owning citizens, saying, "If only you would hear me out! Let me pay the price of the land; accept it from me, that I may bury my dead there." ¹⁴And Ephron replied to Abraham, saying to him, ¹⁵"My lord, do hear me! A piece of land worth four hundred shekels of silver—what is that between you and me? Go and bury your dead." ¹⁶Abraham accepted Ephron's terms. Abraham paid out to Ephron the money that he had named in the hearing of the Hittites—four hundred shekels of silver at the going merchants' rate.

¹⁷So Ephron's land in Machpelah, near Mamre—the field with its cave and all the trees anywhere within the confines of that field—passed ¹⁸to Abraham as his possession, in the presence of the Hittites, of the assembly in his town's gate. ¹⁹And then Abraham buried his wife Sarah in the cave of the field of Machpelah, facing Mamre—now Hebron—in the land of Canaan. ²⁰Thus the field with its cave passed from the Hittites to Abraham, as a burial site.

24 ¹Abraham was now old, advanced in years, and יהוה had blessed Abraham in all things. ²And Abraham said to the senior servant of his household, who had charge of all that he owned, "Put your hand under my thigh ³and I will make you swear by יהוה, the God of heaven and the God of the earth, that you will not take a wife for my son from the daughters of the Canaanites among whom I dwell, ⁴but will go to the land of my birth and get a wife for my son Isaac." ⁵And the servant said to him, "What if the woman does not consent to follow me to this land, shall I then take your son back to the land from which you came?" ⁶Abraham answered him, "On no account must you take my son back there! יהוה,

the God of heaven—who took me from my father's house and from my native land, who promised me on oath, saying, 'I will assign this land to your offspring'—will send a messenger before you, and you will get a wife for my son from there. ⁸And if the woman does not consent to follow you, you shall then be clear of this oath to me; but do not take my son back there." ⁹So the servant put his hand under the thigh of his master Abraham and swore to him as bidden.

¹⁰Then the servant took ten of his master's camels and set out, taking with him all the bounty of his master; and he made his way to Aramnaharaim, to the city of Nahor. ¹¹He made the camels kneel down by the well outside the city, at evening time, the time when women come out to draw water. ¹²And he said, "O יהוה God of my master Abraham's [house], grant me good fortune this day, and deal graciously with my master Abraham: ¹³Here I stand by the spring as the daughters of the town's householders come out to draw water; ¹⁴let the maiden to whom I say, 'Please, lower your jar that I may drink,' and who replies, 'Drink, and I will also water your camels'—let her be the one whom You have decreed for Your servant Isaac. Thereby shall I know that You have dealt graciously with my master."

¹⁵He had scarcely finished speaking, when Rebekah, who was born to Bethuel, the son of Milcah the wife of Abraham's brother Nahor, came out with her jar on her shoulder. ¹⁶The maiden was very beautiful—[and] a virgin, no man having known her. She went down to the spring, filled her jar, and came up. ¹⁷The servant ran toward her and said, "Please, let me sip a little water from your jar." ¹⁸"Drink, my lord," she said, and she quickly lowered her jar upon her hand and let him drink. ¹⁹When she had let him drink his fill, she said, "I will also draw for your camels, until they finish drinking." ²⁰Quickly emptying her jar into the trough, she ran back to the well to draw, and she drew for all his camels.

²¹The emissary, meanwhile, stood gazing at her, silently wondering whether יהוה had made his errand successful or not. ²²When the camels had finished drinking, the emissary took a gold nose-ring weighing a half-shekel, and two gold bands for her arms, ten shekels in weight. ²³"Pray tell me," he said, "whose daughter are you? Is there room in your father's house for us to spend the night?" ²⁴She replied, "I am the daughter of Bethuel the son of Milcah, whom she bore to Nahor." ²⁵And she went on, "There is plenty of straw and feed at home, and also room to spend the night." ²⁶The emissary bowed low in homage to יהוה ²⁷and said, "Blessed be יהוה, the God of my master Abraham's [house], who has not withheld steadfast faithfulness from my master. For I have been guided on my errand by יהוה, to the house of my master's kin."

²⁸The maiden ran and told all this to her mother's household. ²⁹Now Rebekah had a brother whose name was Laban. Laban ran out to the emissary at the spring—³⁰when he saw the nose-ring and the bands on his sister's arms, and when he heard his sister Rebekah say, "Thus the emissary spoke to me." He went up to the emissary, who was still standing beside the camels at the spring. ³¹"Come in, O blessed of יהוה," he said, "why do you remain outside, when I have made ready the house and a place for the camels?" ³²So the emissary entered the house, and the camels were unloaded. The camels were given straw and feed, and water was brought to bathe his feet and the feet of the entourage under him. ³³But when food was set before him, he said, "I will not eat until I have told my tale." He said, "Speak, then."

³⁴"I am Abraham's servant," he began. ³⁵"יהוה has greatly blessed my master, who has become rich—giving him sheep and cattle, silver and gold, male and female slaves, camels and asses. ³⁶And Sarah, my master's wife, bore my master a son in her old age, and he has assigned to him everything he owns. ³⁷Now my master made me swear, saying, 'You shall not get a wife for my son from the daughters of the Canaanites in whose land I dwell; ³⁸but you shall go to my father's house, to my kindred, and get a wife for my son.' ³⁹And I said to my master, 'What if the woman does not follow me?' ⁴⁰He replied to me, 'יהוה, whose ways I have followed, will send a messenger with you and make your errand successful; and you will get a wife for my son from my kindred, from my father's house. ⁴¹Thus only shall you be freed from my adjuration: if, when you come to my kindred, they refuse you—only then shall you be freed from my adjuration.'

⁴²"I came today to the spring, and I said: O יהוה, God of my master Abraham's [house], if You would indeed grant success to the errand on which I am engaged! ⁴³As I stand by the spring of water, let the young woman who comes out to draw and to whom I say, 'Please, let me drink a little water from your jar,' ⁴⁴and who answers, 'You may drink, and I will also draw for your camels'—let her be the wife whom יהוה has decreed for my master's son.' ⁴⁵I had scarcely finished praying in my heart, when Rebekah came out with her jar on her shoulder, and went down to the spring and drew. And I said to her, 'Please give me a drink.' ⁴⁶She quickly lowered her jar and said, 'Drink, and I will also water your camels.' So I drank, and she also watered the camels. ⁴⁷I inquired of her, 'Whose daughter are you?' And she said, 'The daughter of Bethuel, son of Nahor, whom Milcah bore to him.' And I put the ring on her nose and the bands on her arms. ⁴⁸Then I bowed low in homage to יהוה and blessed יהוה, the God of my master Abraham's [house], who led me on the right way to get the daughter of my master's brother for his son. ⁴⁹And now, if you mean to treat my master with true kindness, tell me; and if not, tell me also, that I may turn right or left."

⁵⁰Then Laban and Bethuel answered, "The matter was decreed by יהוה; we cannot speak to you bad or good. ⁵¹Here is Rebekah before you; take her and go, and let her be a wife to your master's son, as יהוה has spoken." ⁵²When Abraham's servant heard their words, he bowed low to the ground before יהוה. ⁵³The servant brought out objects of silver and gold, and garments, and gave them to Rebekah; and he gave presents to her brother and her mother. ⁵⁴Then he and the entourage under him ate and drank, and they spent the night. When they arose next morning, he said, "Give me leave to go to my master." ⁵⁵But her brother and her mother said, "Let the maiden remain with us some ten days; then you may go." ⁵⁶He said to them, "Do not delay me, now that יהוה has made my errand successful. Give me leave that I may go to my master." ⁵⁷And they said, "Let us call the girl and ask for her reply." ⁵⁸They called Rebekah and said to her, "Will you go with this emissary?" And she said, "I will." ⁵⁹So they sent off their sister Rebekah and her nurse along with Abraham's servant and his entourage. ⁶⁰And they blessed Rebekah and said to her,

> "O sister!
> May you grow
> Into thousands of myriads;
> May your descendants seize
> The gates of their foes."

⁶¹Then Rebekah and her maids arose, mounted the camels, and followed the emissary. So the servant took Rebekah and went his way. ⁶²Isaac had just come back from the vicinity of Beerlahairoi, for he was settled in the region of the Negeb. ⁶³And Isaac went out walking in the field toward evening and, looking up, he saw camels approaching. ⁶⁴Raising her eyes, Rebekah saw Isaac. She alighted from the camel ⁶⁵and said to the servant, "Who is that dignitary walking in the

field toward us?" And the servant said, "That is my master." So she took her veil and covered herself. ⁶⁶The servant told Isaac all the things that he had done. ⁶⁷Isaac then brought her into the tent of his mother Sarah, and he took Rebekah as his wife. Isaac loved her, and thus found comfort after his mother's death.

25 ¹Abraham took another wife, whose name was Keturah. ²She bore him Zimran, Jokshan, Medan, Midian, Ishbak, and Shuah. ³Jokshan begot Sheba and Dedan. The descendants of Dedan were the Asshurim, the Letushim, and the Leummim. ⁴The descendants of Midian were Ephah, Epher, Enoch, Abida, and Eldaah. All these were descendants of Keturah. ⁵Abraham willed all that he owned to Isaac; ⁶but to Abraham's sons by concubines Abraham gave gifts while he was still living, and he sent them away from his son Isaac eastward, to the land of the East.

⁷This was the total span of Abraham's life: one hundred and seventy-five years. ⁸And Abraham breathed his last, dying at a good ripe age, old and contented; and he was gathered to his kin. ⁹His sons Isaac and Ishmael buried him in the cave of Machpelah, in the field of Ephron son of Zohar the Hittite, facing Mamre, ¹⁰the field that Abraham had bought from the Hittites; there Abraham was buried, and Sarah his wife. ¹¹After the death of Abraham, God blessed his son Isaac. And Isaac settled near Beerlahairoi.

¹²This is the line of Ishmael, Abraham's son, whom Hagar the Egyptian, Sarah's slave, bore to Abraham. ¹³These are the names of the sons of Ishmael, by their names, in the order of their birth: Nebaioth, the firstborn of Ishmael, Kedar, Adbeel, Mibsam, ¹⁴Mishma, Dumah, Massa, ¹⁵Hadad, Tema, Jetur, Naphish, and Kedmah. ¹⁶These are the sons of Ishmael and these are their names by their villages and by their encampments: twelve chieftains of as many tribes.— ¹⁷These were the years of the life of Ishmael: one hundred and thirtyseven years; then he breathed his last and died, and was gathered to his kin.—¹⁸They dwelt from Havilah, by Shur, which is close to Egypt, all the way to Asshur; they camped alongside all their kin.

¹⁹This is the story of Isaac, son of Abraham. Abraham begot Isaac. ²⁰Isaac was forty years old when he took to wife Rebekah, daughter of Bethuel the Aramean of Paddanaram, sister of Laban the Aramean. ²¹Isaac pleaded with יהוה on behalf of his wife, because she was barren; and יהוה responded to his plea, and his wife Rebekah conceived. ²²But the children struggled in her womb, and she said, "If so, why do I exist?" She went to inquire of יהוה, ²³and יהוה answered her,

> "Two nations are in your womb,
> Two separate peoples shall issue from your body;
> One people shall be mightier than the other,
> And the older shall serve the younger."

²⁴When her time to give birth was at hand, there were twins in her womb. ²⁵The first one emerged red, like a hairy mantle all over; so they named him Esau. ²⁶Then his brother emerged, holding on to the heel of Esau; so they named him Jacob. Isaac was sixty years old when they were born. ²⁷When the boys grew up, Esau became a skillful hunter, the wild sort; but Jacob became the mild type, raising livestock. ²⁸Isaac favored Esau because he had a taste for game; but Rebekah favored Jacob. ²⁹Once when Jacob was cooking a stew, Esau came in from the open, famished. ³⁰And Esau said to Jacob, "Give me some of that red stuff to gulp down, for I am famished"—which is why he was named Edom. ³¹Jacob said, "First sell me your birthright." ³²And Esau said, "I am at the point of death, so of what use is my birthright to me?" ³³But Jacob said, "Swear to me first." So he swore to him, and

sold his birthright to Jacob. ³⁴Jacob then gave Esau bread and lentil stew; he ate and drank, and he rose and went away. Thus did Esau spurn the birthright.

26 ¹There was a famine in the land—aside from the previous famine that had occurred in the days of Abraham—and Isaac went to Abimelech, king of the Philistines, in Gerar. ²יהוה had appeared to him and said, "Do not go down to Egypt; stay in the land which I point out to you. ³Reside in this land, and I will be with you and bless you; I will assign all these lands to you and to your heirs, fulfilling the oath that I swore to your father Abraham. ⁴I will make your heirs as numerous as the stars of heaven, and assign to your heirs all these lands, so that all the nations of the earth shall bless themselves by your heirs—⁵inasmuch as Abraham obeyed Me and kept My charge: My commandments, My laws, and My teachings."

⁶So Isaac stayed in Gerar. ⁷When the local leaders asked him about his wife, he said, "She is my sister," for he was afraid to say "my wife," thinking, "The local leaders might kill me on account of Rebekah, for she is beautiful." ⁸When some time had passed, Abimelech king of the Philistines, looking out of the window, saw Isaac fondling his wife Rebekah. ⁹Abimelech sent for Isaac and said, "So she is your wife! Why then did you say: 'She is my sister?'" Isaac said to him, "Because I thought I might lose my life on account of her." ¹⁰Abimelech said, "What have you done to us! One of the men might have lain with your wife, and you would have brought guilt upon us." ¹¹Abimelech then charged all the people, saying, "Anyone who molests this householder or his wife shall be put to death."

¹²Isaac sowed in that land and reaped a hundredfold the same year. יהוה blessed the householder, ¹³and he grew richer and richer until he was very wealthy: ¹⁴he acquired flocks and herds, and a large household, so that the Philistines envied him. ¹⁵And the Philistines stopped up all the wells which his father's servants had dug in the days of his father Abraham, filling them with earth. ¹⁶And Abimelech said to Isaac, "Go away from us, for you have become far too big for us."

¹⁷So Isaac departed from there and encamped in the wadi of Gerar, where he settled. ¹⁸Isaac dug anew the wells which had been dug in the days of his father Abraham and which the Philistines had stopped up after Abraham's death; and he gave them the same names that his father had given them. ¹⁹But when Isaac's servants, digging in the wadi, found there a well of spring water, ²⁰the herdsmen of Gerar quarreled with Isaac's herdsmen, saying, "The water is ours." He named that well Esek, because they contended with him. ²¹And when they dug another well, they disputed over that one also; so he named it Sitnah. ²²He moved from there and dug yet another well, and they did not quarrel over it; so he called it Rehoboth, saying, "Now at last יהוה has granted us ample space to increase in the land."

²³From there he went up to Beersheba. ²⁴That night יהוה appeared to him and said, "I am the God of your father Abraham's [house]. Fear not, for I am with you, and I will bless you and increase your offspring for the sake of My servant Abraham." ²⁵So he built an altar there and invoked יהוה by name. Isaac pitched his tent there and his servants started digging a well. ²⁶And Abimelech came to him from Gerar, with Ahuzzath his councilor and Phicol chief of his troops. ²⁷Isaac said to them, "Why have you come to me, seeing that you have been hostile to me and have driven me away from you?" ²⁸And they said, "We now see plainly that יהוה has been with you, and we thought: Let there be a sworn treaty between our two parties, between you and us. Let us make a pact with you ²⁹that you will not do us

harm, just as we have not molested you but have always dealt kindly with you and sent you away in peace. From now on, be you blessed of יהוה!" ³⁰Then he made for them a feast, and they ate and drank.

³¹Early in the morning, they exchanged oaths. Isaac then bade them farewell, and they departed from him in peace. ³²That same day Isaac's servants came and told him about the well they had dug, and said to him, "We have found water!" ³³He named it Shibah; therefore the name of the city is Beersheba to this day.

³⁴When Esau was forty years old, he took to wife Judith daughter of Beeri the Hittite, and Basemath daughter of Elon the Hittite; ³⁵and they were a source of bitterness to Isaac and Rebekah.

27 ¹When Isaac was old and his eyes were too dim to see, he called his older son Esau and said to him, "My son." He answered, "Here I am." ²And he said, "I am old now, and I do not know how soon I may die. ³Take your gear, your quiver and bow, and go out into the open and hunt me some game. ⁴Then prepare a dish for me such as I like, and bring it to me to eat, so that I may give you my innermost blessing before I die."

⁵Rebekah had been listening as Isaac spoke to his son Esau. When Esau had gone out into the open to hunt game to bring home, ⁶Rebekah said to her son Jacob, "I overheard your father speaking to your brother Esau, saying, ⁷'Bring me some game and prepare a dish for me to eat, that I may bless you, with יהוה's approval, before I die.' ⁸Now, my son, listen carefully as I instruct you. ⁹Go to the flock and fetch me two choice kids, and I will make of them a dish for your father, such as he likes. ¹⁰Then take it to your father to eat, in order that he may bless you before he dies." ¹¹Jacob answered his mother Rebekah, "But my brother Esau is the hairy type and I am smooth-skinned. ¹²If my father touches me, I shall appear to him as a trickster and bring upon myself a curse, not a blessing." ¹³But his mother said to him, "Your curse, my son, be upon me! Just do as I say and go fetch them for me."

¹⁴He got them and brought them to his mother, and his mother prepared a dish such as his father liked. ¹⁵Rebekah then took the best clothes of her older son Esau, which were there in the house, and had her younger son Jacob put them on; ¹⁶and she covered his hands and the hairless part of his neck with the skins of the kids. ¹⁷Then she put in the hands of her son Jacob the dish and the bread that she had prepared.

¹⁸He went to his father and said, "Father." And he said, "Yes, which of my sons are you?" ¹⁹Jacob said to his father, "I am Esau, your firstborn; I have done as you told me. Pray sit up and eat of my game, that you may give me your innermost blessing." ²⁰Isaac said to his son, "How did you succeed so quickly, my son?" And he said, "Because your God יהוה granted me good fortune." ²¹Isaac said to Jacob, "Come closer that I may feel you, my son—whether you are really my son Esau or not." ²²So Jacob drew close to his father Isaac, who felt him and wondered. "The voice is the voice of Jacob, yet the hands are the hands of Esau." ²³He did not recognize him, because his hands were hairy like those of his brother Esau; and so he blessed him.

²⁴He asked, "Are you really my son Esau?" And when he said, "I am," ²⁵he said, "Serve me and let me eat of my son's game that I may give you my innermost blessing." So he served him and he ate, and he brought him wine and he drank. ²⁶Then his father Isaac said to him, "Come close and kiss me, my son"; ²⁷and he went up and kissed him. And he smelled his clothes and he blessed him, saying, "Ah, the smell of my son is like the smell of the fields that יהוה has blessed.

²⁸ "May God give you
Of the dew of heaven and the fat of the earth,
Abundance of new grain and wine.

²⁹ Let peoples serve you,
And nations bow to you;
Be master over your brothers,
And let your mother's sons bow to you.
Cursed be they who curse you,
Blessed they who bless you."

³⁰No sooner had Jacob left the presence of his father Isaac—after Isaac had finished blessing Jacob—than his brother Esau came back from his hunt. ³¹He too prepared a dish and brought it to his father. And he said to his father, "Let my father sit up and eat of his son's game, so that you may give me your innermost blessing." ³²His father Isaac said to him, "Who are you?" And he said, "I am your son, Esau, your firstborn!" ³³Isaac was seized with very violent trembling. "Who was it then," he demanded, "that hunted game and brought it to me? Moreover, I ate of it before you came, and I blessed him; now he must remain blessed!" ³⁴When Esau heard his father's words, he burst into wild and bitter sobbing, and said to his father, "Bless me too, Father!" ³⁵But he answered, "Your brother came with guile and took away your blessing." ³⁶[Esau] said, "Was he, then, named Jacob that he might supplant me these two times? First he took away my birthright and now he has taken away my blessing!" And he added, "Have you not reserved a blessing for me?" ³⁷Isaac answered, saying to Esau, "But I have made him master over you: I have given him all his brothers for servants, and sustained him with grain and wine. What, then, can I still do for you, my son?" ³⁸And Esau said to his father, "Have you but one blessing, Father? Bless me too, Father!" And Esau wept aloud. ³⁹And his father Isaac answered, saying to him,

"See, your abode shall enjoy the fat of the earth
And the dew of heaven above.

⁴⁰ Yet by your sword you shall live,
And you shall serve your brother;
But when you grow restive,
You shall break his yoke from your neck."

⁴¹Now Esau harbored a grudge against Jacob because of the blessing which his father had given him, and Esau said to himself, "Let but the mourning period of my father come, and I will kill my brother Jacob." ⁴²When the words of her older son Esau were reported to Rebekah, she sent for her younger son Jacob and said to him, "Your brother Esau is consoling himself by planning to kill you. ⁴³Now, my son, listen to me. Flee at once to Haran, to my brother Laban. ⁴⁴Stay with him a while, until your brother's fury subsides ⁴⁵until your brother's anger against you subsides—and he forgets what you have done to him. Then I will fetch you from there. Let me not lose you both in one day!"

⁴⁶Rebekah said to Isaac, "I am disgusted with my life because of the Hittite women. If Jacob marries a Hittite woman like these, from among the native women, what good will life be to me?"

28 ¹So Isaac sent for Jacob and blessed him. He instructed him, saying, "You shall not take a wife from among the Canaanite women. ²Up, go to Paddanaram, to the house of Bethuel, your mother's father, and take a wife there from among the daughters of Laban, your mother's brother. ³May El Shaddai bless you, make you fertile and numerous, so that you become an assembly of peoples. ⁴May you and your offspring be granted the blessing of Abraham, that you may possess the land where you are sojourning, which

God assigned to Abraham." 5Then Isaac sent Jacob off, and he went to Paddanaram, to Laban the son of Bethuel the Aramean, the brother of Rebekah, mother of Jacob and Esau.

6When Esau saw that Isaac had blessed Jacob and sent him off to Paddanaram to take a wife from there, charging him, as he blessed him, "You shall not take a wife from among the Canaanite women," 7and that Jacob had obeyed his father and mother and gone to Paddanaram, 8Esau realized that the Canaanite women displeased his father Isaac. 9So Esau went to Ishmael and took to wife, in addition to the wives he had, Mahalath the daughter of Ishmael son of Abraham, sister of Nebaioth.

10Jacob left Beersheba, and set out for Haran. 11He came upon a certain place and stopped there for the night, for the sun had set. Taking one of the stones of that place, he put it under his head and lay down in that place. 12He had a dream; a stairway was set on the ground and its top reached to the sky, and messengers of God were going up and down on it. 13And standing beside him was יהוה, who said, "I am יהוה, the God of your father Abraham's [house] and the God of Isaac's [house]: the ground on which you are lying I will assign to you and to your offspring. 14Your descendants shall be as the dust of the earth; you shall spread out to the west and to the east, to the north and to the south. All the families of the earth shall bless themselves by you and your descendants. 15Remember, I am with you: I will protect you wherever you go and will bring you back to this land. I will not leave you until I have done what I have promised you."

16Jacob awoke from his sleep and said, "Surely יהוה is present in this place, and I did not know it!" 17Shaken, he said, "How awesome is this place! This is none other than the abode of God, and that is the gateway to heaven." 18Early in the morning, Jacob took the stone that he had put under his head and set it up as a pillar and poured oil on the top of it. 19He named that site Bethel; but previously the name of the city had been Luz.

20Jacob then made a vow, saying, "If God remains with me, protecting me on this journey that I am making, and giving me bread to eat and clothing to wear, 21and I return safe to my father's house—יהוה shall be my God. 22And this stone, which I have set up as a pillar, shall be God's abode; and of all that You give me, I will set aside a tithe for You."

29 1Jacob resumed his journey and came to the land of the Easterners. 2There before his eyes was a well in the open. Three flocks of sheep were lying there beside it, for the flocks were watered from that well. The stone on the mouth of the well was large. 3When all the flocks were gathered there, the stone would be rolled from the mouth of the well and the sheep watered; then the stone would be put back in its place on the mouth of the well. 4Jacob said to them, "My friends, where are you from?" And they said, "We are from Haran." 5He said to them, "Do you know Laban the son of Nahor?" And they said, "Yes, we do." 6He continued, "Is he well?" They answered, "Yes, he is; and there is his daughter Rachel, coming with the flock." 7He said, "It is still broad daylight, too early to round up the animals; water the flock and take them to pasture." 8But they said, "We cannot, until all the flocks are rounded up; then the stone is rolled off the mouth of the well and we water the sheep."

9While he was still speaking with them, Rachel came with her father's flock—for she was its shepherd. 10And when Jacob saw Rachel, the daughter of his uncle Laban, and the flock of his uncle Laban, Jacob went up and rolled the stone off the mouth of the well, and watered the flock of his uncle Laban. 11Then Jacob kissed Rachel, and broke into tears. 12Jacob told Rachel that he was her father's kinsman, that he was Rebekah's son; and she ran and told her father. 13On hearing the news of his sister's son Jacob, Laban ran to greet him; he embraced him and kissed him, and took him into his house. He told Laban all that had happened, 14and Laban said to him, "You are truly my bone and flesh."

When he had stayed with him a month's time, 15Laban said to Jacob, "Just because you are a kinsman, should you serve me for nothing? Tell me, what shall your wages be?" 16Now Laban had two daughters; the name of the older one was Leah, and the name of the younger was Rachel. 17Leah had weak eyes; Rachel was shapely and beautiful. 18Jacob loved Rachel; so he answered, "I will serve you seven years for your younger daughter Rachel." 19Laban said, "Better that I give her to you than that I should give her to an outsider. Stay with me." 20So Jacob served seven years for Rachel and they seemed to him but a few days because of his love for her.

21Then Jacob said to Laban, "Give me my wife, for my time is fulfilled, that I may cohabit with her." 22And Laban gathered all the people of the place and made a feast. 23When evening came, he took his daughter Leah and brought her to him; and he cohabited with her.—24Laban had given his maidservant Zilpah to his daughter Leah as her maid.—25When morning came, there was Leah! So he said to Laban, "What is this you have done to me? I was in your service for Rachel! Why did you deceive me?" 26Laban said, "It is not the practice in our place to marry off the younger before the older. 27Wait until the bridal week of this one is over and we will give you that one too, provided you serve me another seven years." 28Jacob did so; he waited out the bridal week of the one, and then he gave him his daughter Rachel as wife.—29Laban had given his maidservant Bilhah to his daughter Rachel as her maid.—30And Jacob cohabited with Rachel also; indeed, he loved Rachel more than Leah. And he served him another seven years.

31Seeing that Leah was unloved, יהוה opened her womb; but Rachel was barren. 32Leah conceived and bore a son, and named him Reuben; for she declared, "It means: 'יהוה has seen my affliction'; it also means: 'Now my husband will love me.'" 33She conceived again and bore a son, and declared, "This is because יהוה heard that I was unloved and has given me this one also"; so she named him Simeon. 34Again she conceived and bore a son and declared, "This time my husband will become attached to me, for I have borne him three sons." Therefore he was named Levi. 35She conceived again and bore a son, and declared, "This time I will praise יהוה." Therefore she named him Judah. Then she stopped bearing.

30 1When Rachel saw that she had borne Jacob no children, she became envious of her sister; and Rachel said to Jacob, "Give me children, or I shall die." 2Jacob was incensed at Rachel, and said, "Can I take the place of God, who has denied you fruit of the womb?" 3She said, "Here is my maid Bilhah. Consort with her, that she may bear on my knees and that through her I too may have children." 4So she gave him her maid Bilhah as concubine, and Jacob cohabited with her. 5Bilhah conceived and bore Jacob a son. 6And Rachel said, "God has vindicated me; indeed, [God] has heeded my plea and given me a son." Therefore she named him Dan. 7Rachel's maid Bilhah conceived again and bore Jacob a second son. 8And Rachel said, "A fateful contest I waged with my sister; yes, and I have prevailed." So she named him Naphtali.

9When Leah saw that she had stopped bearing children, she took her maid Zilpah and gave her to Jacob as concubine. 10And when Leah's maid Zilpah bore Jacob a son, 11Leah said, "What luck!" So she named him Gad. ¹²When Leah's maid Zilpah bore Jacob a second son, ¹³Leah declared, "What fortune!" meaning, "Women will deem me fortunate." So she named him Asher. ¹⁴Once, at the time of the wheat harvest, Reuben came upon some mandrakes in the field and brought them to his mother Leah. Rachel said to Leah, "Please give me some of your son's mandrakes." ¹⁵But she said to her, "Was it not enough for you to take away my husband, that you would also take my son's mandrakes?" Rachel replied, "I promise, he shall lie with you tonight, in return for your son's mandrakes." ¹⁶When Jacob came home from the field in the evening, Leah went out to meet him and said, "You are to sleep with me, for I have hired you with my son's mandrakes." And he lay with her that night. ¹⁷God heeded Leah, and she conceived and bore him a fifth son. ¹⁸And Leah said, "God has given me my reward for having given my maid to my husband." So she named him Issachar. ¹⁹When Leah conceived again and bore Jacob a sixth son, ²⁰Leah said, "God has given me a choice gift; this time my husband will exalt me, for I have borne him six sons." So she named him Zebulun. ²¹Last, she bore him a daughter, and named her Dinah.

²²Now God remembered Rachel; God heeded her and opened her womb. ²³She conceived and bore a son, and said, "God has taken away my disgrace." ²⁴So she named him Joseph, which is to say, "May יהוה add another son for me."

²⁵After Rachel had borne Joseph, Jacob said to Laban, "Give me leave to go back to my own homeland. ²⁶Give me my wives and my children, for whom I have served you, that I may go; for well you know what services I have rendered you." ²⁷But Laban said to him, "If you will indulge me, I have learned by divination that יהוה has blessed me on your account." ²⁸And he continued, "Name the wages due from me, and I will pay you." ²⁹But he said, "You know well how I have served you and how your livestock has fared with me. ³⁰For the little you had before I came has grown to much, since יהוה has blessed you wherever I turned. And now, when shall I make provision for my own household?" ³¹He said, "What shall I pay you?" And Jacob said, "Pay me nothing! If you will do this thing for me, I will again pasture and keep your flocks: ³²let me pass through your whole flock today, removing from there every speckled and spotted animal—every dark-colored sheep and every spotted and speckled goat. Such shall be my wages. ³³In the future when you go over my wages, let my honesty toward you testify for me: if there are among my goats any that are not speckled or spotted or any sheep that are not dark-colored, they got there by theft." ³⁴And Laban said, "Very well, let it be as you say."

³⁵But that same day he removed the streaked and spotted he-goats and all the speckled and spotted she-goats—every one that had white on it—and all the dark-colored sheep, and left them in the charge of his sons. ³⁶And he put a distance of three days' journey between himself and Jacob, while Jacob was pasturing the rest of Laban's flock.

³⁷Jacob then got fresh shoots of poplar, and of almond and plane, and peeled white stripes in them, laying bare the white of the shoots. ³⁸The rods that he had peeled he set up in front of the goats in the troughs, the water receptacles, that the goats came to drink from. Their mating occurred when they came to drink, ³⁹and since the goats mated by the rods, the goats brought forth streaked, speckled, and spotted young. ⁴⁰But Jacob dealt separately with the sheep; he made these animals face the streaked or wholly dark-colored animals in Laban's flock. And so he produced special flocks for himself, which he did not put with Laban's flocks. ⁴¹Moreover, when the sturdier animals were mating, Jacob would place the rods in the troughs, in full view of the animals, so that they mated by the rods; ⁴²but with the feebler animals he would not place them there. Thus the feeble ones went to Laban and the sturdy to Jacob. ⁴³So as a householder he grew exceedingly prosperous, and came to own large flocks, maidservants and menservants, camels and asses.

31 ¹Now he heard the things that Laban's sons were saying: "Jacob has taken all that was our father's, and from that which was our father's he has built up all this wealth." ²Jacob also saw that Laban's manner toward him was not as it had been in the past. ³Then יהוה said to Jacob, "Return to your ancestors' land—where you were born—and I will be with you." ⁴Jacob had Rachel and Leah called to the field, where his flock was, ⁵and said to them, "I see that your father's manner toward me is not as it has been in the past. But the God of my father's [house] has been with me. ⁶As you know, I have served your father with all my might; ⁷but your father has cheated me, changing my wages time and again. God, however, would not let him do me harm. ⁸If he said thus, 'The speckled shall be your wages,' then all the flocks would drop speckled young; and if he said thus, 'The streaked shall be your wages,' then all the flocks would drop streaked young. ⁹God has taken away your father's livestock and given it to me.

¹⁰"Once, at the mating time of the flocks, I had a dream in which I saw that the he-goats mating with the flock were streaked, speckled, and mottled. ¹¹And in the dream a messenger of God said to me, 'Jacob!' 'Here,' I answered. ¹²And the messenger said, 'Note well that all the he-goats which are mating with the flock are streaked, speckled, and mottled; for I have noted all that Laban has been doing to you. ¹³I am the God of Bethel, where you anointed a pillar and where you made a vow to Me. Now, arise and leave this land and return to your native land.'"

¹⁴Then Rachel and Leah answered him, saying, "Have we still a share in the inheritance of our father's house? ¹⁵Surely, he regards us as outsiders, now that he has sold us and has used up our purchase price. ¹⁶Truly, all the wealth that God has taken away from our father belongs to us and to our children. Now then, do just as God has told you."

¹⁷Thereupon Jacob put his children and wives on camels; ¹⁸and he drove off all his livestock and all the wealth that he had amassed, the livestock in his possession that he had acquired in Paddanaram, to go to his father Isaac in the land of Canaan. ¹⁹Meanwhile Laban had gone to shear his sheep, and Rachel stole her father's household idols. ²⁰Jacob kept Laban the Aramean in the dark, not telling him that he was fleeing, ²¹and fled with all that he had. Soon he was across the Euphrates and heading toward the hill country of Gilead.

²²On the third day, Laban was told that Jacob had fled. ²³So he took his kinsmen with him and pursued him a distance of seven days, catching up with him in the hill country of Gilead. ²⁴But God appeared to Laban the Aramean in a dream by night and said to him, "Beware of attempting anything with Jacob, good or bad."

²⁵Laban overtook Jacob. Jacob had pitched his tent on the Height, and Laban with his kinsmen encamped in the hill country of Gilead. ²⁶And Laban said to Jacob, "What did you mean by keeping me in the dark and carrying off my daughters like captives of the sword? ²⁷Why did you flee in secrecy and mislead me and not tell me? I would have sent you off with festive music, with timbrel and lyre. ²⁸You did not even let me kiss my sons and daughters goodbye! It was a foolish thing for you to do. ²⁹I have it in my power to do you harm; but the God of your father's [house] said to me last night, 'Beware of attempting anything with Jacob, good or bad.' ³⁰Very well, you had to leave because you were longing for your father's house; but why did you steal my gods?"

³¹Jacob answered Laban, saying, "I was afraid because I thought you would take your daughters from me by force. ³²But anyone with whom you find your gods shall not remain alive! In the presence of our kin, point out what I have of yours and take it." Jacob, of course, did not know that Rachel had stolen them.

³³So Laban went into Jacob's tent and Leah's tent and the tents of the two maidservants; but he did not find them. Leaving Leah's tent, he entered Rachel's tent. ³⁴Rachel, meanwhile, had taken the idols and placed them in the camel cushion and sat on them; and Laban rummaged through the tent without finding them. ³⁵For she said to her father, "Let not my lord take it amiss that I cannot rise before you, for I am in a womanly way." Thus he searched, but could not find the household idols.

³⁶Now Jacob became incensed and took up his grievance with Laban. Jacob spoke up and said to Laban, "What is my crime, what is my guilt that you should pursue me? ³⁷You rummaged through all my things; what have you found of all your household objects? Set it here, before my kin and yours, and let them decide between us two.

³⁸"These twenty years I have spent in your service, your ewes and she-goats never miscarried, nor did I feast on rams from your flock. ³⁹That which was torn by beasts I never brought to you; I myself made good the loss; you exacted it of me, whether snatched by day or snatched by night. ⁴⁰Often, scorching heat ravaged me by day and frost by night; and sleep fled from my eyes. ⁴¹Of the twenty years that I spent in your household, I served you fourteen years for your two daughters, and six years for your flocks; and you changed my wages time and again. ⁴²Had not the God of my father's [house]—the God of Abraham and the Fear of Isaac—been with me, you would have sent me away empty-handed. But it was my plight and the toil of my hands that God took notice of—and gave judgment on last night."

⁴³Then Laban spoke up and said to Jacob, "The daughters are my daughters, the children are my children, and the flocks are my flocks; all that you see is mine. Yet what can I do now about my daughters or the children they have borne? ⁴⁴Come, then, let us make a pact, you and I, that there may be a witness between you and me." ⁴⁵Thereupon Jacob took a stone and set it up as a pillar. ⁴⁶And Jacob said to his kinsmen, "Gather stones." So they took stones and made a mound; and they partook of a meal there by the mound. ⁴⁷Laban named it Yegar-sahadutha, but Jacob named it Galed. ⁴⁸And Laban declared, "This mound is a witness between you and me this day." That is why it was named Galed; ⁴⁹and [it was called] Mizpah, because he said, "May יהוה watch between you and me, when we are out of sight of each other. ⁵⁰If you ill treat my daughters or take other wives besides my daughters—though no one else be about, remember, it is God who will be witness between you and me."

⁵¹And Laban said to Jacob, "Here is this mound and here the pillar which I have set up between you and me: ⁵²this mound shall be witness and this pillar shall be witness that I am not to cross to you past this mound, and that you are not to cross to me past this mound and this pillar, with hostile intent. ⁵³May the God of Abraham's [house] and the god of Nahor's [house]—their ancestral deities—"judge between us." And Jacob swore by the Fear of his father Isaac's [house]. ⁵⁴Jacob then offered up a sacrifice on the Height, and invited his kinsmen to partake of the meal. After the meal, they spent the night on the Height.

32 ¹Early in the morning, Laban kissed his sons and daughters and bade them goodbye; then Laban left on his journey homeward. ²Jacob went on his way, and messengers of God encountered him. ³When he saw them, Jacob said, "This is God's camp." So he named that place Mahanaim.

⁴Jacob sent messengers ahead to his brother Esau in the land of Seir, the country of Edom, ⁵and instructed them as follows, "Thus shall you say, 'To my lord Esau, thus says your servant Jacob: I stayed with Laban and remained until now; ⁶I have acquired cattle, asses, sheep, and male and female slaves; and I send this message to my lord in the hope of gaining your favor.'" ⁷The messengers returned to Jacob, saying, "We came to your brother Esau; he himself is coming to meet you, and his retinue numbers four hundred." ⁸Jacob was greatly frightened; in his anxiety, he divided the people with him, and the flocks and herds and camels, into two camps, ⁹thinking, "If Esau comes to the one camp and attacks it, the other camp may yet escape."

¹⁰Then Jacob said, "O God of my father Abraham's [house] and God of my father Isaac's [house], O יהוה, who said to me, 'Return to your native land and I will deal bountifully with you'! ¹¹I am unworthy of all the kindness that You have so steadfastly shown Your servant: with my staff alone I crossed this Jordan, and now I have become two camps. ¹²Deliver me, I pray, from the hand of my brother, from the hand of Esau; else, I fear, he may come and strike me down, mothers and children alike. ¹³Yet You have said, 'I will deal bountifully with you and make your offspring as the sands of the sea, which are too numerous to count.'"

¹⁴After spending the night there, he selected from what was at hand these presents for his brother Esau: ¹⁵200 she-goats and 20 he-goats; 200 ewes and 20 rams; ¹⁶30 milch camels with their colts; 40 cows and 10 bulls; 20 she-asses and 10 he-asses. ¹⁷These he put in the charge of his servants, drove by drove, and he told his servants, "Go on ahead, and keep a distance between droves." ¹⁸He instructed the one in front as follows, "When my brother Esau meets you and asks you, 'Who's your master? Where are you going? And whose [animals] are these ahead of you?' ¹⁹you shall answer, 'Your servant Jacob's; they are a gift sent to my lord Esau; and [Jacob] himself is right behind us.'" ²⁰He gave similar instructions to the second one, and the third, and all the others who followed the droves, namely, "Thus and so shall you say to Esau when you reach him. ²¹And you shall add, 'And your servant Jacob himself is right behind us.'" For he reasoned, "If I propitiate him with presents in advance, and then face him, perhaps he will show me favor." ²²And so the gift went on ahead, while he remained in camp that night.

²³That same night he arose, and taking his two wives, his two maidservants, and his eleven sons, he crossed the ford of the Jabbok. ²⁴After taking them across the stream, he sent across all his possessions. ²⁵Jacob was left alone. And a figure wrestled with him until the break of dawn. ²⁶When he saw that he had not prevailed against him, he wrenched Jacob's hip at its socket, so that the socket of his hip was strained as he wrestled with him. ²⁷Then he said, "Let me go, for dawn is breaking." But he answered, "I will not let you go, unless you bless me." ²⁸Said the other, "What is your name?" He replied, "Jacob." ²⁹Said he, "Your name shall no longer be Jacob, but Israel, for you have striven with beings divine and human, and have prevailed." ³⁰Jacob asked, "Pray tell me your name." But he said, "You must not ask my name!" And he took leave of him there. ³¹So Jacob named the place Peniel, meaning, "I have seen a divine being face to face, yet my life has been preserved." ³²The sun rose upon him as he passed Penuel, limping on his hip. ³³That is why the children of Israel to this day do not eat the thigh muscle that is on the socket of the hip, since Jacob's hip socket was wrenched at the thigh muscle.

33 ¹Looking up, Jacob saw Esau coming, with a retinue of four hundred. He divided the children among Leah, Rachel, and the two maids, ²putting the maids and their children first, Leah and her children next, and Rachel and Joseph last. ³He himself went on ahead and bowed low to the ground seven times until he was near his brother. ⁴Esau ran to greet him. He embraced him and, falling on his neck, he kissed him; and they wept. ⁵Looking about, he saw the women and the children. "Who," he asked, "are these with you?" He answered, "The children with whom God has favored your servant." ⁶Then the maids, with their children, came forward and bowed low; ⁷next Leah, with her children, came forward and bowed low; and last, Joseph and Rachel came forward and bowed low. ⁸And he asked, "What do you mean by all this company which I have met?" He answered, "To gain my lord's favor." ⁹Esau said, "I have enough, my brother; let what you have remain yours." ¹⁰But Jacob said, "No, I pray you; if you would do me this favor, accept from me this gift; for to see your face is like seeing the face of God, and you have received me favorably. ¹¹Please accept my present which has been brought to you, for God has favored me and I have plenty." And when he urged him, he accepted.

¹²And [Esau] said, "Let us start on our journey, and I will proceed at your pace." ¹³But he said to him, "My lord knows that the children are frail and that the flocks and herds, which are nursing, are a care to me; if they are driven hard a single day, all the flocks will die. ¹⁴Let my lord go on ahead of his servant, while I travel slowly, at the pace of the cattle before me and at the pace of the children, until I come to my lord in Seir."

¹⁵Then Esau said, "Let me assign to you some of the people who are with me." But he said, "Oh no, my lord is too kind to me!" ¹⁶So Esau started back that day on his way to Seir. ¹⁷But Jacob journeyed on to Succoth, and built a house for himself and made stalls for his cattle; that is why the place was called Succoth.

¹⁸Jacob arrived safe in the city of Shechem which is in the land of Canaan—having come thus from Paddanaram—and he encamped before the city. ¹⁹The parcel of land where he pitched his tent he purchased from the kin of Hamor, Shechem's father, for a hundred *kesitah*s. ²⁰He set up an altar there, and called it Eleloheyisrael.

34 ¹Now Dinah, the daughter whom Leah had borne to Jacob, went out to visit the daughters of the land. ²Shechem son of Hamor the Hivite, chief of the country, saw her, and took her and lay with her and disgraced her. ³Being strongly drawn to Dinah daughter of Jacob, and in love with the maiden, he spoke to the maiden tenderly. ⁴So Shechem said to his father Hamor, "Get me this girl as a wife."

⁵Jacob heard that he had defiled his daughter Dinah; but since his sons were in the field with his cattle, Jacob kept silent until they came home. ⁶Then Shechem's father Hamor came out to Jacob to speak to him. ⁷Meanwhile Jacob's sons, having heard the news, came in from the field. As the representatives [of Jacob's house], they were distressed and very angry, because he had committed an outrage in Israel by lying with Jacob's daughter—a thing not to be done.

⁸And Hamor spoke with them, saying, "My son Shechem longs for your daughter. Please give her to him in marriage. ⁹Intermarry with us: give your daughters to us, and take our daughters for yourselves: ¹⁰You will dwell among us, and the land will be open before you; settle, move about, and acquire holdings in it." ¹¹Then Shechem said to her father and brothers, "Do me this favor, and I will pay whatever you tell me. ¹²Ask of me a brideprice ever so high, as well

as gifts, and I will pay what you tell me; only give me the maiden for a wife."

¹³Jacob's sons answered Shechem and his father Hamor—speaking with guile because he had defiled their sister Dinah—¹⁴and said to them, "We cannot do this thing, to give our sister to someone uncircumcised, for that is a disgrace among us. ¹⁵Only on this condition will we agree with you; that you will become like us in that every male among you is circumcised. ¹⁶Then we will give our daughters to you and take your daughters to ourselves; and we will dwell among you and become as one kindred. ¹⁷But if you will not listen to us and become circumcised, we will take our daughter and go."

¹⁸Their words pleased Hamor and Hamor's son Shechem. ¹⁹And the youth lost no time in doing the thing, for he wanted Jacob's daughter. Now he was the most respected in his father's house. ²⁰So Hamor and his son Shechem went to the public place of their town and spoke to their town council, saying, ²¹"These people are our friends; let them settle in the land and move about in it, for the land is large enough for them; we will take their daughters to ourselves as wives and give our daughters to them. ²²But only on this condition will their representatives agree with us to dwell among us and be as one kindred: that all our males become circumcised as they are circumcised. ²³Their cattle and substance and all their beasts will be ours, if we only agree to their terms, so that they will settle among us." ²⁴All his fellow townsmen heeded Hamor and his son Shechem, and all males, all his fellow townsmen, were circumcised.

²⁵On the third day, when they were in pain, Simeon and Levi, two of Jacob's sons, brothers of Dinah, took each his sword, came upon the city unmolested, and slew all the males. ²⁶They put Hamor and his son Shechem to the sword, took Dinah out of Shechem's house, and went away. ²⁷The other sons of Jacob came upon the slain and plundered the town, because their sister had been defiled. ²⁸They seized their flocks and herds and asses, all that was inside the town and outside; ²⁹all their wealth, all their children, and their wives, all that was in the houses, they took as captives and booty.

³⁰Jacob said to Simeon and Levi, "You have brought trouble on me, making me odious among the inhabitants of the land, the Canaanites and the Perizzites; my fighters are few in number, so that if they unite against me and attack me, I and my house will be destroyed." ³¹But they answered, "Should our sister be treated like a whore?"

35 ¹God said to Jacob, "Arise, go up to Bethel and remain there; and build an altar there to the God who appeared to you when you were fleeing from your brother Esau." ²So Jacob said to his household and to all who were with him, "Rid yourselves of the alien gods in your midst, purify yourselves, and change your clothes. ³Come, let us go up to Bethel, and I will build an altar there to the God who answered me when I was in distress and who has been with me wherever I have gone." ⁴They gave to Jacob all the alien gods that they had, and the rings that were in their ears, and Jacob buried them under the terebinth that was near Shechem. ⁵As they set out, a terror from God fell on the cities round about, so that they did not pursue the sons of Jacob.

⁶Thus Jacob came to Luz—that is, Bethel—in the land of Canaan, he and all the people who were with him. ⁷There he built an altar and named the site Elbethel, for it was there that God had been revealed to him when he was fleeing from his brother.

⁸Deborah, Rebekah's nurse, died, and was buried under the oak below Bethel; so it was named Allonbacuth.

9God appeared again to Jacob on his arrival from Paddanaram. God blessed him, 10saying to him,

"You whose name is Jacob,
You shall be called Jacob no more,
But Israel shall be your name."

Thus he was named Israel.
11And God said to him,

"I am El Shaddai.
Be fertile and increase;
A nation, yea an assembly of nations,
Shall descend from you.
Kings shall issue from your loins.
12 The land that I assigned to Abraham and Isaac
I assign to you;
And to your offspring to come
Will I assign the land."

13God parted from him at the spot where [God] had spoken to him; 14and Jacob set up a pillar at the site where [God] had spoken to him, a pillar of stone, and he offered a libation on it and poured oil upon it. 15Jacob gave the site, where God had spoken to him, the name of Bethel.

16They set out from Bethel; but when they were still some distance short of Ephrath, Rachel was in childbirth, and she had hard labor. 17When her labor was at its hardest, the midwife said to her, "Have no fear, for it is another boy for you." 18But as she breathed her last—for she was dying—she named him Benoni; but his father called him Benjamin. 19Thus Rachel died. She was buried on the road to Ephrath—now Bethlehem. 20Over her grave Jacob set up a pillar; it is the pillar at Rachel's grave to this day. 21Israel journeyed on, and pitched his tent beyond Migdaleder.

22While Israel stayed in that land, Reuben went and lay with Bilhah, his father's concubine; and Israel found out.

Now the sons of Jacob were twelve in number. 23The sons of Leah: Reuben—Jacob's firstborn—Simeon, Levi, Judah, Issachar, and Zebulun. 24The sons of Rachel: Joseph and Benjamin. 25The sons of Bilhah, Rachel's maid: Dan and Naphtali. 26And the sons of Zilpah, Leah's maid: Gad and Asher. These are the sons of Jacob who were born to him in Paddanaram.

27And Jacob came to his father Isaac at Mamre, at Kiriatharba—now Hebron—where Abraham and Isaac had sojourned. 28Isaac was a hundred and eighty years old 29when he breathed his last and died. He was gathered to his kin in ripe old age; and he was buried by his sons Esau and Jacob.

36 1This is the line of Esau—that is, Edom. 2Esau took his wives from among the Canaanite women—Adah daughter of Elon the Hittite, and Oholibamah daughter of Anah daughter of Zibeon the Hivite—3and also Basemath daughter of Ishmael and sister of Nebaioth. 4Adah bore to Esau Eliphaz; Basemath bore Reuel; 5and Oholibamah bore Jeush, Jalam, and Korah. Those were the sons of Esau, who were born to him in the land of Canaan.

6Esau took his wives, his sons and daughters, and all the members of his household, his cattle and all his livestock, and all the property that he had acquired in the land of Canaan, and went to another land because of his brother Jacob. 7For their possessions were too many for them to dwell together, and the land where they sojourned could not support them because of their livestock. 8So Esau settled in the hill country of Seir—Esau being Edom. 9This, then, is the line of Esau, the ancestor of the Edomites, in the hill country of Seir.

10These are the names of Esau's sons: Eliphaz, the son of Esau's wife Adah; Reuel, the son of Esau's wife Basemath.

11The sons of Eliphaz were Teman, Omar, Zepho, Gatam, and Kenaz. 12Timna was a concubine of Esau's son Eliphaz; she bore Amalek to Eliphaz. Those were the descendants of Esau's wife Adah. 13And these were the sons of Reuel: Nahath, Zerah, Shammah, and Mizzah. Those were the descendants of Esau's wife Basemath. 14And these were the sons of Esau's wife Oholibamah, daughter of Anah daughter of Zibeon: she bore to Esau Jeush, Jalam, and Korah.

15These are the clans of the sons of Esau. The descendants of Esau's firstborn Eliphaz: the clans Teman, Omar, Zepho, Kenaz, 16Korah, Gatam, and Amalek; these are the clans of Eliphaz in the land of Edom. Those are the descendants of Adah. 17And these are the descendants of Esau's son Reuel: the clans Nahath, Zerah, Shammah, and Mizzah; these are the clans of Reuel in the land of Edom. Those are the descendants of Esau's wife Basemath. 18And these are the descendants of Esau's wife Oholibamah: the clans Jeush, Jalam, and Korah; these are the clans of Esau's wife Oholibamah, the daughter of Anah. 19Those were the sons of Esau—that is, Edom—and those are their clans.

20These were the sons of Seir the Horite, who were settled in the land: Lotan, Shobal, Zibeon, Anah, 21Dishon, Ezer, and Dishan. Those are the clans of the Horites, the descendants of Seir, in the land of Edom.

22The sons of Lotan were Hori and Hemam; and Lotan's sister was Timna. 23The sons of Shobal were these: Alvan, Manahath, Ebal, Shepho, and Onam. 24The sons of Zibeon were these: Aiah and Anah—that was the Anah who discovered the hot springs in the wilderness while pasturing the asses of his father Zibeon. 25The children of Anah were these: Dishon and Anah's daughter Oholibamah. 26The sons of Dishon were these: Hemdan, Eshban, Ithran, and Cheran. 27The sons of Ezer were these: Bilhan, Zaavan, and Akan. 28And the sons of Dishan were these: Uz and Aran.

29These are the clans of the Horites: the clans Lotan, Shobal, Zibeon, Anah, 30Dishon, Ezer, and Dishan. Those are the clans of the Horites, clan by clan, in the land of Seir.

31These are the kings who reigned in the land of Edom before any king reigned over the Israelites. 32Bela son of Beor reigned in Edom, and the name of his city was Dinhabah. 33When Bela died, Jobab son of Zerah, from Bozrah, succeeded him as king. 34When Jobab died, Husham of the land of the Temanites succeeded him as king. 35When Husham died, Hadad son of Bedad, who defeated the Midianites in the country of Moab, succeeded him as king; the name of his city was Avith. 36When Hadad died, Samlah of Masrekah succeeded him as king. 37When Samlah died, Saul of Rehoboth-on-the-river succeeded him as king. 38When Saul died, Baalhanan son of Achbor succeeded him as king. 39And when Baalhanan son of Achbor died, Hadar succeeded him as king; the name of his city was Pau, and his wife's name was Mehetabel daughter of Matred daughter of Mezahab.

40These are the names of the clans of Esau, each with its families and locality, name by name: the clans Timna, Alvah, Jetheth, 41Oholibamah, Elah, Pinon, 42Kenaz, Teman, Mibzar, 43Magdiel, and Iram. Those are the clans of Edom—that is, of Esau, father of the Edomites—by their settlements in the land which they hold.

37 1Now Jacob was settled in the land where his father had sojourned, the land of Canaan. 2This, then, is the line of Jacob:

At seventeen years of age, Joseph tended the flocks with his brothers, as a helper to the sons of his father's wives Bilhah and Zilpah. And Joseph brought bad reports of them to their father. 3Now Israel loved Joseph best of all his sons—he was his child of old age; and he had made him an ornamented tunic. 4And when his brothers saw that their father loved him more than any of his brothers, they hated him so that they could not speak a friendly word to him.

5Once Joseph had a dream which he told to his brothers; and they hated him even more. 6He said to them, "Hear this dream which I have dreamed: 7There we were binding sheaves in the field, when suddenly my sheaf stood up and remained upright; then your sheaves gathered around and bowed low to my sheaf." 8His brothers answered, "Do you mean to reign over us? Do you mean to rule over us?" And they hated him even more for his talk about his dreams.

9He dreamed another dream and told it to his brothers, saying, "Look, I have had another dream: And this time, the sun, the moon, and eleven stars were bowing down to me." 10And when he told it to his father and brothers, his father berated him. "What," he said to him, "is this dream you have dreamed? Are we to come, I and your mother and your brothers, and bow low to you to the ground?" 11So his brothers were wrought up at him, and his father kept the matter in mind.

12One time, when his brothers had gone to pasture their father's flock at Shechem, 13Israel said to Joseph, "Your brothers are pasturing at Shechem. Come, I will send you to them." He answered, "I am ready." 14And he said to him, "Go and see how your brothers are and how the flocks are faring, and bring me back word." So he sent him from the valley of Hebron. When he reached Shechem, 15someone came upon him wandering in the fields. The man asked him, "What are you looking for?" 16He answered, "I am looking for my brothers. Could you tell me where they are pasturing?" 17The man said, "They have gone from here, for I heard them say: Let us go to Dothan." So Joseph followed his brothers and found them at Dothan.

18They saw him from afar, and before he came close to them they conspired to kill him. 19They said to on another, "Here comes that dreamer! 20Come now, let us kill him and throw him into one of the pits; and we can say, 'A savage beast devoured him.' We shall see what comes of his dreams!" 21But when Reuben heard it, he tried to save him from them. He said, "Let us not take his life." 22And Reuben went on, "Shed no blood! Cast him into that pit out in the wilderness, but do not touch him yourselves"—intending to save him from them and restore him to his father. 23When Joseph came up to his brothers, they stripped Joseph of his tunic, the ornamented tunic that he was wearing, 24and took him and cast him into the pit. The pit was empty; there was no water in it.

25Then they sat down to a meal. Looking up, they saw a caravan of Ishmaelites coming from Gilead, their camels bearing gum, balm, and ladanum to be taken to Egypt. 26Then Judah said to his brothers, "What do we gain by killing our brother and covering up his blood? 27Come, let us sell him to the Ishmaelites, but let us not do away with him ourselves. After all, he is our brother, our own flesh." His brothers agreed. 28When Midianite traders passed by, they pulled Joseph up out of the pit. They sold Joseph for twenty pieces of silver to the Ishmaelites, who brought Joseph to Egypt.

29When Reuben returned to the pit and saw that Joseph was not in the pit, he rent his clothes. 30Returning to his brothers, he said, "The boy is gone! Now, what am I to do?" 31Then they took Joseph's tunic, slaughtered a kid, and dipped the tunic in the blood. 32They had the ornamented tunic taken to their father, and they said, "We found this. Please examine it; is it your son's tunic or not?" 33He recognized it, and said, "My son's tunic! A savage beast devoured him! Joseph was torn by a beast!" 34Jacob rent his clothes, put sackcloth on his loins, and observed mourning for his son many days. 35All his sons and daughters sought to comfort him; but he refused to be comforted, saying, "No, I will go down mourning to my son in Sheol." Thus his father bewailed him. 36The Midianites, meanwhile, sold him in Egypt to Potiphar, a courtier of Pharaoh and his chief prefect.

38 1About that time Judah left his brothers and camped near a prominent Adullamite whose name was Hirah. 2There Judah saw the daughter of a prominent Canaanite whose name was Shua, and he took her [into his household as wife] and cohabited with her. 3She conceived and bore a son, and he named him Er. 4She conceived again and bore a son, and named him Onan. 5Once again she bore a son, and named him Shelah; he was at Chezib when she bore him.

6Judah got a wife for Er his firstborn; her name was Tamar. 7But Er, Judah's firstborn, was displeasing to יהוה, and יהוה took his life. 8Then Judah said to Onan, "Join with your brother's wife and do your duty by her as a brother-in-law, and provide offspring for your brother." 9But Onan, knowing that the offspring would not count as his, let [the semen] go to waste whenever he joined with his brother's wife, so as not to provide offspring for his brother. 10What he did was displeasing to יהוה, who took his life also. 11Then Judah said to his daughter-in-law Tamar, "Stay as a widow in your father's house until my son Shelah grows up"—for he thought, "He too might die like his brothers." So Tamar went to live in her father's house.

12A long time afterward, Shua's daughter, the wife of Judah, died. When his period of mourning was over, Judah went up to Timnah to his sheepshearers, together with his friend Hirah the Adullamite. 13And Tamar was told, "Your father-in-law is coming up to Timnah for the sheep-shearing." 14So she took off her widow's garb, covered her face with a veil, and, wrapping herself up, sat down at the entrance to Enaim, which is on the road to Timnah; for she saw that Shelah was grown up, yet she had not been given to him as wife. 15When Judah saw her, he took her for a harlot; for she had covered her face. 16So he turned aside to her by the road and said, "Here, let me sleep with you"—for he did not know that she was his daughter-in-law. "What," she asked, "will you pay for sleeping with me?" 17He replied, "I will send a kid from my flock." But she said, "You must leave a pledge until you have sent it." 18And he said, "What pledge shall I give you?" She replied, "Your seal and cord, and the staff which you carry." So he gave them to her and slept with her, and she conceived by him. 19Then she went on her way. She took off her veil and again put on her widow's garb.

20Judah sent the kid by his friend the Adullamite, to redeem the pledge from the woman; but he could not find her. 21He inquired of the council of that locale, "Where is the prostitute, the one at Enaim, by the road?" But they said, "There has been no prostitute here." 22So he returned to Judah and said, "I could not find her; moreover, the local council said: There has been no prostitute here." 23Judah said, "Let her keep them, lest we become a laughingstock. I did send her this kid, but you did not find her."

24About three months later, Judah was told, "Your daughter-in-law Tamar has played the harlot; in fact, she is pregnant from harlotry." "Bring her out," said Judah. "She should be burned!" 25As she was being brought out, she sent this message to her father-in-law, "I am pregnant by the dignitary to whom these belong." And she added, "Examine these: whose seal and cord and staff are these?" 26Judah recognized them, and said, "She is more in the right than I, inasmuch as I did not give her to my son Shelah." And he was not intimate with her again.

27When the time came for her to give birth, there were twins in her womb! 28While she was in labor, one of them put out a hand, and the midwife tied a crimson thread on that hand, to signify: This one came out first. ²⁹But just then it drew back its hand, and out came its brother; and she said, "What a breach you have made for yourself!" So he was named Perez. ³⁰Afterward his brother came out, on whose hand was the crimson thread; he was named Zerah.

39 ¹When Joseph was taken down to Egypt, Potiphar, a courtier of Pharaoh and his chief prefect—an Egyptian official—bought him from the Ishmaelites who had brought him there. ²יהוה was with Joseph, and he proved highly capable; and he stayed in the house of his Egyptian master. ³And when his master saw that יהוה was with him and that יהוה lent success to everything he undertook, ⁴he took a liking to Joseph. He made him his personal attendant and put him in charge of his household, placing in his hands all that he owned. ⁵And from the time that the Egyptian put him in charge of his household and of all that he owned, יהוה blessed his house for Joseph's sake, so that the blessing of יהוה was upon everything that he owned, in the house and outside. ⁶He left all that he had in Joseph's hands and, with him there, he paid attention to nothing save the food that he ate. Now Joseph was well built and handsome.

⁷After a time, his master's wife cast her eyes upon Joseph and said, "Lie with me." ⁸But he refused. He said to his master's wife, "Look, with me here, my master gives no thought to anything in this house, and all that he owns he has placed in my hands. ⁹He wields no more authority in this house than I, and he has withheld nothing from me except yourself, since you are his wife. How then could I do this most wicked thing, and sin before God?" ¹⁰And much as she coaxed Joseph day after day, he did not yield to her request to lie beside her, to be with her.

¹¹One such day, he came into the house to do his work. None of the household being there inside, ¹²she caught hold of him by his garment and said, "Lie with me!" But he left his garment in her hand and got away and fled outside. ¹³When she saw that he had left it in her hand and had fled outside, ¹⁴she called out to her servants and said to them, "Look, he had to bring us a Hebrew to dally with us! This one came to lie with me; but I screamed loud. ¹⁵And when he heard me screaming at the top of my voice, he left his garment with me and got away and fled outside." ¹⁶She kept his garment beside her, until his master came home. ¹⁷Then she told him the same story, saying, "The Hebrew slave whom you brought into our house came to me to dally with me; ¹⁸but when I screamed at the top of my voice, he left his garment with me and fled outside."

¹⁹When his master heard the story that his wife told him, namely, "Thus and so your slave did to me," he was furious. ²⁰So Joseph's master had him put in prison, where the king's prisoners were confined. But even while he was there in prison, ²¹יהוה was with Joseph—extending kindness to him and disposing the chief jailer favorably toward him. ²²The chief jailer put in Joseph's charge all the prisoners who were in that prison, and he was the one to carry out everything that was done there. ²³The chief jailer did not supervise anything that was in Joseph's charge, because יהוה was with him, and whatever he did יהוה made successful.

40 ¹Some time later, the cupbearer and the baker of the king of Egypt gave offense to their lord the king of Egypt. ²Pharaoh was angry with his two courtiers, the chief cupbearer and the chief baker, ³and put them in custody, in the house of the chief prefect, in the same prison house where Joseph was confined. ⁴The chief prefect assigned Joseph to them, and he attended them. When they had been

in custody for some time, ⁵both of them—the cupbearer and the baker of the king of Egypt, who were confined in the prison—dreamed in the same night, each his own dream and each dream with its own meaning. ⁶When Joseph came to them in the morning, he saw that they were distraught. ⁷He asked Pharaoh's courtiers, who were with him in custody in his master's house, saying, "Why do you appear downcast today?" ⁸And they said to him, "We had dreams, and there is no one to interpret them." So Joseph said to them, "Surely God can interpret! Tell me [your dreams]."

⁹Then the chief cupbearer told his dream to Joseph. He said to him, "In my dream, there was a vine in front of me. ¹⁰On the vine were three branches. It had barely budded, when out came its blossoms and its clusters ripened into grapes. ¹¹Pharaoh's cup was in my hand, and I took the grapes, pressed them into Pharaoh's cup, and placed the cup in Pharaoh's hand." ¹²Joseph said to him, "This is its interpretation: The three branches are three days. ¹³In three days Pharaoh will pardon you and restore you to your post; you will place Pharaoh's cup in his hand, as was your custom formerly when you were his cupbearer. ¹⁴But think of me when all is well with you again, and do me the kindness of mentioning me to Pharaoh, so as to free me from this place. ¹⁵For in truth, I was kidnapped from the land of the Hebrews; nor have I done anything here that they should have put me in the dungeon."

¹⁶When the chief baker saw how favorably he had interpreted, he said to Joseph, "In my dream, similarly, there were three openwork baskets on my head. ¹⁷In the uppermost basket were all kinds of food for Pharaoh that a baker prepares; and the birds were eating it out of the basket above my head." ¹⁸Joseph answered, "This is its interpretation: The three baskets are three days. ¹⁹In three days Pharaoh will lift off your head and impale you upon a pole; and the birds will pick off your flesh."

²⁰On the third day—his birthday—Pharaoh made a banquet for all his officials, and he singled out his chief cupbearer and his chief baker from among his officials. ²¹He restored the chief cupbearer to his cup-bearing, and he placed the cup in Pharaoh's hand; ²²but the chief baker he impaled—just as Joseph had interpreted to them. ²³Yet the chief cupbearer did not think of Joseph; he forgot him.

41 ¹After two years' time, Pharaoh dreamed that he was standing by the Nile, ²when out of the Nile there came up seven cows, handsome and sturdy, and they grazed in the reed grass. ³But presently, seven other cows came up from the Nile close behind them, ugly and gaunt, and stood beside the cows on the bank of the Nile; ⁴and the ugly gaunt cows ate up the seven handsome sturdy cows. And Pharaoh awoke.

⁵He fell asleep and dreamed a second time: Seven ears of grain, solid and healthy, grew on a single stalk. ⁶But close behind them sprouted seven ears, thin and scorched by the east wind. ⁷And the thin ears swallowed up the seven solid and full ears. Then Pharaoh awoke: it was a dream!

⁸Next morning, his spirit was agitated, and he sent for all the magician-priests of Egypt, and all its sages; and Pharaoh told them his dreams, but none could interpret them for Pharaoh. ⁹The chief cupbearer then spoke up and said to Pharaoh, "I must make mention today of my offenses. ¹⁰Once Pharaoh was angry with his servants, and placed me in custody in the house of the chief prefect, together with the chief baker. ¹¹We had dreams the same night, he and I, each of us a dream with a meaning of its own. ¹²A Hebrew youth was there with us, a servant of the chief prefect; and when we told him our dreams, he interpreted them for us, telling each of the meaning of his dream. ¹³And as he interpreted for us, so it came to pass: I was restored to my post, and the other was impaled."

[14]Thereupon Pharaoh sent for Joseph, and he was rushed from the dungeon. He had his hair cut and changed his clothes, and he appeared before Pharaoh. [15]And Pharaoh said to Joseph, "I have had a dream, but no one can interpret it. Now I have heard it said of you that for you to hear a dream is to tell its meaning." [16]Joseph answered Pharaoh, saying, "Not I! God will see to Pharaoh's welfare."

[17]Then Pharaoh said to Joseph, "In my dream, I was standing on the bank of the Nile, [18]when out of the Nile came up seven sturdy and well-formed cows and grazed in the reed grass. [19]Presently there followed them seven other cows, scrawny, ill-formed, and emaciated—never had I seen their likes for ugliness in all the land of Egypt! [20]And the seven lean and ugly cows ate up the first seven cows, the sturdy ones; [21]but when they had consumed them, one could not tell that they had consumed them, for they looked just as bad as before. And I awoke. [22]In my other dream, I saw seven ears of grain, full and healthy, growing on a single stalk; [23]but right behind them sprouted seven ears, shriveled, thin, and scorched by the east wind. [24]And the thin ears swallowed the seven healthy ears. I have told my magician-priests, but none has an explanation for me."

[25]And Joseph said to Pharaoh, "Pharaoh's dreams are one and the same: Pharaoh has been told what God is about to do. [26]The seven healthy cows are seven years, and the seven healthy ears are seven years; it is the same dream. [27]The seven lean and ugly cows that followed are seven years, as are also the seven empty ears scorched by the east wind; they are seven years of famine. [28]It is just as I have told Pharaoh: Pharaoh has been shown what God is about to do. [29]Immediately ahead are seven years of great abundance in all the land of Egypt. [30]After them will come seven years of famine, and all the abundance in the land of Egypt will be forgotten. As the land is ravaged by famine, [31]no trace of the abundance will be left in the land because of the famine thereafter, for it will be very severe. [32]As for Pharaoh having had the same dream twice, it means that the matter has been determined by God, and that God will soon carry it out.

[33]"Accordingly, let Pharaoh select an official who's discerning and wise, and set him over the land of Egypt. [34]And let Pharaoh take steps to appoint overseers over the land, and organize the land of Egypt in the seven years of plenty. [35]Let all the food of these good years that are coming be gathered, and let the grain be collected under Pharaoh's authority as food to be stored in the cities. [36]Let that food be a reserve for the land for the seven years of famine which will come upon the land of Egypt, so that the land may not perish in the famine."

[37]The plan pleased Pharaoh and all his courtiers. [38]And Pharaoh said to his courtiers, "Could we find an [existing] official like him one in whom is the spirit of God?" [39]So Pharaoh said to Joseph, "Since God has made all this known to you, there is none so discerning and wise as you. [40]You shall be in charge of my court, and by your command shall all my people be directed; only with respect to the throne shall I be superior to you." [41]Pharaoh further said to Joseph, "See, I put you in charge of all the land of Egypt." [42]And removing his signet ring from his hand, Pharaoh put it on Joseph's hand; and he had him dressed in robes of fine linen, and put a gold chain about his neck. [43]He had him ride in the chariot of his second-in-command, and they cried before him, "Abrek!" Thus he placed him over all the land of Egypt.

[44]Pharaoh said to Joseph, "I am Pharaoh; yet without you, no one shall lift up hand or foot in all the land of Egypt." [45]Pharaoh then gave Joseph the name Zaphenathpaneah; and he gave him for a wife Asenath daughter of Potiphera, priest of On. Thus Joseph emerged in charge of the land of Egypt.—[46]Joseph was thirty years old when he entered the service of Pharaoh king of Egypt.—Leaving Pharaoh's presence, Joseph traveled through all the land of Egypt.

[47]During the seven years of plenty, the land produced in abundance. [48]And he gathered all the grain of the seven years that the land of Egypt was enjoying, and stored the grain in the cities; he put in each city the grain of the fields around it. [49]So Joseph collected produce in very large quantity, like the sands of the sea, until he ceased to measure it, for it could not be measured.

[50]Before the years of famine came, Joseph became the father of two sons, whom Asenath daughter of Potiphera, priest of On, bore to him. [51]Joseph named the firstborn Manasseh, meaning, "God has made me forget completely my hardship and my parental home." [52]And the second he named Ephraim, meaning, "God has made me fertile in the land of my affliction." [53]The seven years of abundance that the land of Egypt enjoyed came to an end, [54]and the seven years of famine set in, just as Joseph had foretold. There was famine in all lands, but through out the land of Egypt there was bread. [55]And when all the land of Egypt felt the hunger, the people cried out to Pharaoh for bread; and Pharaoh said to all the Egyptians, "Go to Joseph; whatever he tells you, you shall do."—[56]Accordingly, when the famine became severe in the land of Egypt, Joseph laid open all that was within, and rationed out grain to the Egyptians. The famine, however, spread over the whole world. [57]So all the world came to Joseph in Egypt to procure rations, for the famine had become severe throughout the world.

42 [1]When Jacob saw that there were food rations to be had in Egypt, he said to his sons, "Why do you keep looking at one another? [2]Now I hear," he went on, "that there are rations to be had in Egypt. Go down and procure rations for us there, that we may live and not die." [3]So ten of Joseph's brothers went down to get grain rations in Egypt; [4]for Jacob did not send Joseph's brother Benjamin with his brothers, since he feared that he might meet with disaster. [5]Thus the sons of Israel were among those who came to procure rations, for the famine extended to the land of Canaan.

[6]Now Joseph was the vizier of the land; it was he who dispensed rations to all the people of the land. And Joseph's brothers came and bowed low to him, with their faces to the ground. [7]When Joseph saw his brothers, he recognized them; but he acted like a stranger toward them and spoke harshly to them. He asked them, "Where do you come from?" And they said, "From the land of Canaan, to procure food." [8]For though Joseph recognized his brothers, they did not recognize him. [9]Recalling the dreams that he had dreamed about them, Joseph said to them, "You are spies, you have come to see the land in its nakedness." [10]But they said to him, "No, my lord! Truly, your servants have come to procure food. [11]We are all of us members of the same household; we are honest people; your servants have never been spies!" [12]And he said to them, "No, you have come to see the land in its nakedness!" [13]And they replied, "We your servants were twelve brothers, sons of a certain householder in the land of Canaan; the youngest, however, is now with our father, and one is no more." [14]But Joseph said to them, "It is just as I have told you: You are spies! [15]By this you shall be put to the test: unless your youngest brother comes here, by Pharaoh, you shall not depart from this place! [16]Let one of you go and bring your brother, while the rest of you remain confined, that your words may be put to the test whether there is truth in you. Else, by Pharaoh, you are nothing but spies!" [17]And he confined them in the guardhouse for three days.

18On the third day Joseph said to them, "Do this and you shall live, for I fear God. 19If you are 'honest people,' let one of you brothers be held in your place of detention, while the rest of you go and take home rations for your starving households; 20but you must bring me your youngest brother, that your words may be verified and that you may not die." And they did accordingly. 21They said to one another, "Alas, we are being punished on account of our brother, because we looked on at his anguish, yet paid no heed as he pleaded with us. That is why this distress has come upon us." 22Then Reuben spoke up and said to them, "Did I not tell you, 'Do no wrong to the boy'? But you paid no heed. Now comes the reckoning for his blood." 23They did not know that Joseph understood, for there was an interpreter between him and them. 24He turned away from them and wept. But he came back to them and spoke to them; and he took Simeon from among them and had him bound before their eyes. 25Then Joseph gave orders to fill their bags with grain, return each one's money to his sack, and give them provisions for the journey; and this was done for them. 26So they loaded their asses with the rations and departed from there.

27As one of them was opening his sack to give feed to his ass at the night encampment, he saw his money right there at the mouth of his bag. 28And he said to his brothers, "My money has been returned! It is here in my bag!" Their hearts sank; and, trembling, they turned to one another, saying "What is this that God has done to us?"

29When they came to their father Jacob in the land of Canaan, they told him all that had befallen them, saying, 30"The official who is lord of the land spoke harshly to us and accused us of spying on the land. 31We said to him, 'We are honest people; we have never been spies! 32There were twelve of us brothers, sons by the same father; but one is no more, and the youngest is now with our father in the land of Canaan.' 33But the official who is lord of the land said to us, 'By this I shall know that you are "honest people": leave one of your brothers with me, and take something for your starving households and be off. 34And bring your youngest brother to me, that I may know that you are not spies but honest people. I will then restore your brother to you, and you shall be free to move about in the land.'"

35As they were emptying their sacks, there, in each one's sack, was his moneybag! When they and their father saw their moneybags, they were dismayed. 36Their father Jacob said to them, "It is always me that you bereave: Joseph is no more and Simeon is no more, and now you would take away Benjamin. These things always happen to me!" 37Then Reuben said to his father, "You may kill my two sons if I do not bring him back to you. Put him in my care, and I will return him to you." 38But he said, "My son must not go down with you, for his brother is dead and he alone is left. If he meets with disaster on the journey you are taking, you will send my white head down to Sheol in grief."

43 1But the famine in the land was severe. 2And when they had eaten up the rations which they had brought from Egypt, their father said to them, "Go again and procure some food for us." 3But Judah said to him, "The official warned us, 'Do not let me see your faces unless your brother is with you.' 4If you will let our brother go with us, we will go down and procure food for you; 5but if you will not let him go, we will not go down, for that official said to us, 'Do not let me see your faces unless your brother is with you.'" 6And Israel said, "Why did you serve me so ill as to tell the official that you had another brother?" 7They replied, "But the official kept asking about us and our family, saying, 'Is your father still living? Have you another brother?' And we answered him accordingly. How were we to know that he would say, 'Bring your brother here'?"

8Then Judah said to his father Israel, "Send the boy in my care, and let us be on our way, that we may live and not die—you and we and our children. 9I myself will be surety for him; you may hold me responsible: if I do not bring him back to you and set him before you, I shall stand guilty before you forever. 10For we could have been there and back twice if we had not dawdled."

11Then their father Israel said to them, "If it must be so, do this: take some of the choice products of the land in your baggage, and carry them down as a gift for the official—some balm and some honey, gum, ladanum, pistachio nuts, and almonds. 12And take with you double the money, carrying back with you the money that was replaced in the mouths of your bags; perhaps it was a mistake. 13Take your brother too; and go back at once to that official. 14And may El Shaddai dispose that official to mercy toward you, that he may release to you your other brother, as well as Benjamin. As for me, if I am to be bereaved, I shall be bereaved."

15So the emissaries took that gift, and they took with them double the money, as well as Benjamin. They made their way down to Egypt, where they presented themselves to Joseph. 16When Joseph saw Benjamin with them, he said to his house steward, "Take the emissaries into the house; slaughter and prepare an animal, for those emissaries will dine with me at noon." 17The steward did as Joseph said, and he brought those emissaries into Joseph's house. 18But the emissaries were frightened at being brought into Joseph's house. "It must be," they thought, "because of the money replaced in our bags the first time that we have been brought inside, as a pretext to attack us and seize us as slaves, with our pack animals." 19So they went up to Joseph's house steward and spoke to him at the entrance of the house. 20"If you please, my lord," they said, "we came down once before to procure food. 21But when we arrived at the night encampment and opened our bags, there was each one's money in the mouth of his bag, our money in full. So we have brought it back with us. 22And we have brought down with us other money to procure food. We do not know who put the money in our bags." 23He replied, "All is well with you; do not be afraid. Your God, the God of your father, must have put treasure in your bags for you. I got your payment." And he brought out Simeon to them.

24Then the steward brought the emissaries into Joseph's house; he gave them water to bathe their feet, and he provided feed for their asses. 25They laid out their gifts to await Joseph's arrival at noon, for they had heard that they were to dine there.

26When Joseph came home, they presented to him the gifts that they had brought with them into the house, bowing low before him to the ground. 27He greeted them, and he said, "How is your aged father of whom you spoke? Is he still in good health?" 28They replied, "It is well with your servant our father; he is still in good health." And they bowed and made obeisance.

29Looking about, he saw his brother Benjamin, his mother's son, and asked, "Is this your youngest brother of whom you spoke to me?" And he went on, "May God be gracious to you, my boy." 30With that, Joseph hurried out, for he was overcome with feeling toward his brother and was on the verge of tears; he went into a room and wept there. 31Then he washed his face, reappeared, and—now in control of himself—gave the order, "Serve the meal." 32They served him by himself, and them by themselves, and the Egyptians who ate with him by themselves; for the Egyptians could not dine with the Hebrews, since that would be abhorrent to the Egyptians. ³³As they were seated by his direction, from the oldest in the order of his seniority to the youngest in the order of his youth, the emissaries looked at one another in astonishment. ³⁴Portions were served them from his table; but Benjamin's portion was several times that of anyone else. And they drank their fill with him.

44 ¹Then he instructed his house steward as follows, "Fill these emissaries' bags with food, as much as they can carry, and put each one's money in the mouth of his bag. ²Put my silver goblet in the mouth of the bag of the youngest one, together with his money for the rations." And he did as Joseph told him.

³With the first light of morning, the emissaries were sent off with their pack animals. ⁴They had just left the city and had not gone far, when Joseph said to his house steward, "Up, go after those emissaries! And when you overtake them, say to them, 'Why did you repay good with evil? ⁵It is the very one from which my master drinks and which he uses for divination. It was a wicked thing for you to do!'"

⁶He overtook them and spoke those words to them. ⁷And they said to him, "Why does my lord say such things? Far be it from your servants to do anything of the kind! ⁸Here we brought back to you from the land of Canaan the money that we found in the mouths of our bags. How then could we have stolen any silver or gold from your master's house! ⁹Whichever of your servants it is found with shall die; the rest of us, moreover, shall become slaves to my lord." ¹⁰He replied, "Although what you are proposing is right, only the one with whom it is found shall be my slave; but the rest of you shall go free."

¹¹So each one hastened to lower his bag to the ground, and each one opened his bag. ¹²He searched, beginning with the oldest and ending with the youngest; and the goblet turned up in Benjamin's bag. ¹³At this they rent their clothes. Each reloaded his pack animal, and they returned to the city.

¹⁴When Judah and his brothers reentered the house of Joseph, who was still there, they threw themselves on the ground before him. ¹⁵Joseph said to them, "What is this deed that you have done? Do you not know that someone in my position practices divination?" ¹⁶Judah replied, "What can we say to my lord? How can we plead, how can we prove our innocence? God has uncovered the crime of your servants. Here we are, then, slaves of my lord, the rest of us as much as he in whose possession the goblet was found." ¹⁷But he replied, "Far be it from me to act thus! Only the one in whose possession the goblet was found shall be my slave; the rest of you go back in peace to your father."

¹⁸Then Judah went up to him and said, "Please, my lord, let your servant appeal to my lord, and do not be impatient with your servant, you who are the equal of Pharaoh. ¹⁹My lord asked his servants, 'Have you a father or another brother?' ²⁰We told my lord, 'We have an old father, and there is a child of his old age, the youngest; his full brother is dead, so that he alone is left of his mother, and his father dotes on him.' ²¹Then you said to your servants, 'Bring him down to me, that I may set eyes on him.' ²²We said to my lord, 'The boy cannot leave his father; if he were to leave him, his father would die.' ²³But you said to your servants, 'Unless your youngest brother comes down with you, do not let me see your faces.' ²⁴When we came back to your servant my father, we reported my lord's words to him.

²⁵"Later our father said, 'Go back and procure some food for us.' ²⁶We answered, 'We cannot go down; only if our youngest brother is with us can we go down, for we may not show our faces to the official unless our youngest brother is with us.' ²⁷Your servant my father said to us, 'As

you know, my wife bore me two sons. ²⁸But one is gone from me, and I said: Alas, he was torn by a beast! And I have not seen him since. ²⁹If you take this one from me, too, and he meets with disaster, you will send my white head down to Sheol in sorrow.'

³⁰"Now, if I come to your servant my father and the boy is not with us—since his own life is so bound up with his—³¹when he sees that the boy is not with us, he will die, and your servants will send the white head of your servant our father down to Sheol in grief. ³²Now your servant has pledged himself for the boy to my father, saying, 'If I do not bring him back to you, I shall stand guilty before my father forever.' ³³Therefore, please let your servant remain as a slave to my lord instead of the boy, and let the boy go back with his brothers. ³⁴For how can I go back to my father unless the boy is with me? Let me not be witness to the woe that would overtake my father!"

45 ¹Joseph could no longer control himself before all his attendants, and he cried out, "Have all of the staff withdraw from me!" So none of the staff was about when Joseph made himself known to his brothers. ²His sobs were so loud that the Egyptians could hear, and so the news reached Pharaoh's palace.

³Joseph said to his brothers, "I am Joseph. Is my father still well?" But his brothers could not answer him, so dumfounded were they on account of him. ⁴Then Joseph said to his brothers, "Come forward to me." And when they came forward, he said, "I am your brother Joseph, he whom you sold into Egypt. ⁵Now, do not be distressed or reproach yourselves because you sold me hither; it was to save life that God sent me ahead of you. ⁶It is now two years that there has been famine in the land, and there are still five years to come in which there shall be no yield from tilling. ⁷God has sent me ahead of you to ensure your survival on earth, and to save your lives in an extraordinary deliverance. ⁸So, it was not you who sent me here, but God—who has made me a father to Pharaoh, lord of all his household, and ruler over the whole land of Egypt.

⁹"Now, hurry back to my father and say to him: Thus says your son Joseph, 'God has made me lord of all Egypt; come down to me without delay. ¹⁰You will dwell in the region of Goshen, where you will be near me—you and your children and your grandchildren, your flocks and herds, and all that is yours. ¹¹There I will provide for you—for there are yet five years of famine to come—that you and your household and all that is yours may not suffer want.' ¹²You can see for yourselves, and my brother Benjamin for himself, that it is indeed I who am speaking to you. ¹³And you must tell my father everything about my high station in Egypt and all that you have seen; and bring my father here with all speed."

¹⁴With that he embraced his brother Benjamin around the neck and wept, and Benjamin wept on his neck. ¹⁵He kissed all his brothers and wept upon them; only then were his brothers able to talk to him.

¹⁶The news reached Pharaoh's palace: "Joseph's brothers have come." Pharaoh and his courtiers were pleased. ¹⁷And Pharaoh said to Joseph, "Say to your brothers, 'Do as follows: load up your beasts and go at once to the land of Canaan. ¹⁸Take your father and your households and come to me; I will give you the best of the land of Egypt and you shall live off the fat of the land.' ¹⁹And you are bidden [to add], 'Do as follows: take from the land of Egypt wagons for your children and your wives, and bring your father here. ²⁰And never mind your belongings, for the best of all the land of Egypt shall be yours.'"

²¹The sons of Israel did so; Joseph gave them wagons as Pharaoh had commanded, and he supplied them with

provisions for the journey. ²²To each of them, moreover, he gave a change of clothing; but to Benjamin he gave three hundred pieces of silver and several changes of clothing. ²³And to his father he sent the following: ten heasses laden with the best things of Egypt, and ten sheasses laden with grain, bread, and provisions for his father on the journey. ²⁴As he sent his brothers off on their way, he told them, "Do not be quarrelsome on the way."

²⁵They went up from Egypt and came to their father Jacob in the land of Canaan. ²⁶And they told him, "Joseph is still alive; yes, he is ruler over the whole land of Egypt." His heart went numb, for he did not believe them. ²⁷But when they recounted all that Joseph had said to them, and when he saw the wagons that Joseph had sent to transport him, the spirit of their father Jacob revived. ²⁸"Enough!" said Israel. "My son Joseph is still alive! I must go and see him before I die."

46

¹So Israel set out with all that was his, and he came to Beersheba, where he offered sacrifices to the God of his father Isaac. ²God called to Israel in a vision by night: "Jacob! Jacob!" He answered, "Here."

³"I am God, the God of your father. Fear not to go down to Egypt, for I will make you there into a great nation. ⁴I Myself will go down with you to Egypt, and I Myself will also bring you back; and Joseph's hand shall close your eyes."

⁵So Jacob set out from Beersheba. The sons of Israel put their father Jacob and their children and their wives in the wagons that Pharaoh had sent to transport him; ⁶and they took along their livestock and the wealth that they had amassed in the land of Canaan. Thus Jacob and all his offspring with him came to Egypt: ⁷he brought with him to Egypt his sons and grandsons, his daughters and granddaughters—all his offspring.

⁸These are the names of the Israelites, Jacob and his descendants, who came to Egypt. Jacob's firstborn Reuben; ⁹Reuben's sons: Enoch, Pallu, Hezron, and Carmi. ¹⁰Simeon's sons: Jemuel, Jamin, Ohad, Jachin, Zohar, and Saul the son of a Canaanite woman. ¹¹Levi's sons: Gershon, Kohath, and Merari. ¹²Judah's sons: Er, Onan, Shelah, Perez, and Zerah—but Er and Onan had died in the land of Canaan; and Perez's sons were Hezron and Hamul. ¹³Issachar's sons: Tola, Puvah, Iob, and Shimron. ¹⁴Zebulun's sons: Sered, Elon, and Jahleel. ¹⁵Those were the sons whom Leah bore to Jacob in Paddanaram, in addition to his daughter Dinah. Persons in all, male and female: 33.

¹⁶Gad's sons: Ziphion, Haggi, Shuni, Ezbon, Eri, Arodi, and Areli. ¹⁷Asher's sons: Imnah, Ishvah, Ishvi, and Beriah, and their sister Serah. Beriah's sons: Heber and Malchiel. ¹⁸These were the descendants of Zilpah, whom Laban had given to his daughter Leah. These she bore to Jacob—16 persons.

¹⁹The sons of Jacob's wife Rachel were Joseph and Benjamin. ²⁰To Joseph were born in the land of Egypt Manasseh and Ephraim, whom Asenath daughter of Potiphera priest of On bore to him. ²¹Benjamin's sons: Bela, Becher, Ashbel, Gera, Naaman, Ehi, Rosh, Muppim, Huppim, and Ard. ²²These were the descendants of Rachel who were born to Jacob—14 persons in all.

²³Dan's son: Hushim. ²⁴Naphtali's sons: Jahzeel, Guni, Jezer, and Shillem. ²⁵These were the descendants of Bilhah, whom Laban had given to his daughter Rachel. These she bore to Jacob—7 persons in all.

²⁶All the persons belonging to Jacob who came to Egypt—his own issue, aside from the wives of Jacob's sons—all these persons numbered 66. ²⁷And Joseph's sons who were born to him in Egypt were two in number. Thus the total of Jacob's household who came to Egypt was seventy persons.

²⁸He had sent Judah ahead of him to Joseph, to point the way before him to Goshen. So when they came to the region of Goshen, ²⁹Joseph ordered his chariot and went to Goshen to meet his father Israel; he presented himself to him and, embracing him around the neck, he wept on his neck a good while. ³⁰Then Israel said to Joseph, "Now I can die, having seen for myself that you are still alive."

³¹Then Joseph said to his brothers and to his father's household, "I will go up and tell the news to Pharaoh, and say to him, 'My brothers and my father's household, who were in the land of Canaan, have come to me. ³²These householders are shepherds; they have always been breeders of livestock, and they have brought with them their flocks and herds and all that is theirs.' ³³So when Pharaoh summons you and asks, 'What is your occupation?' ³⁴you shall answer, 'Your servants have been breeders of livestock from the start until now, both we and our fathers'—so that you may stay in the region of Goshen. For all shepherds are abhorrent to Egyptians."

47

¹Then Joseph came and reported to Pharaoh, saying, "My father and my brothers, with their flocks and herds and all that is theirs, have come from the land of Canaan and are now in the region of Goshen." ²And having selected from among his brothers a few representatives, he presented them to Pharaoh. ³Pharaoh said to his brothers, "What is your occupation?" They answered Pharaoh, "We your servants are shepherds, as were also our fathers. ⁴We have come," they told Pharaoh, "to sojourn in this land, for there is no pasture for your servants' flocks, the famine being severe in the land of Canaan. Pray, then, let your servants stay in the region of Goshen." ⁵Then Pharaoh said to Joseph, "As regards your father and your brothers who have come to you, ⁶the land of Egypt is open before you: settle your father and your brothers in the best part of the land; let them stay in the region of Goshen. And if you know any capable administrators among them, put them in charge of my livestock."

⁷Joseph then brought his father Jacob and presented him to Pharaoh; and Jacob greeted Pharaoh. ⁸Pharaoh asked Jacob, "How many are the years of your life?" ⁹And Jacob answered Pharaoh, "The years of my sojourn [on earth] are one hundred and thirty. Few and hard have been the years of my life, nor do they come up to the life spans of my ancestors during their sojourns." ¹⁰Then Jacob bade Pharaoh farewell, and left Pharaoh's presence.

¹¹So Joseph settled his father and his brothers, giving them holdings in the choicest part of the land of Egypt, in the region of Rameses, as Pharaoh had commanded. ¹²Joseph sustained his father, and his brothers, and all his father's household with bread, down to the little ones.

¹³Now there was no bread in all the world, for the famine was very severe; both the land of Egypt and the land of Canaan languished because of the famine. ¹⁴Joseph gathered in all the money that was to be found in the land of Egypt and in the land of Canaan, as payment for the rations that were being procured, and Joseph brought the money into Pharaoh's palace. ¹⁵And when the money gave out in the land of Egypt and in the land of Canaan, all the Egyptians came to Joseph and said, "Give us bread, lest we die before your very eyes; for the money is gone!" ¹⁶And Joseph said, "Bring your livestock, and I will sell to you against your livestock, if the money is gone." ¹⁷So they brought their livestock to Joseph, and Joseph gave them bread in exchange for the horses, for the stocks of sheep and cattle, and the asses; thus he provided them with bread that year in exchange for all their livestock. ¹⁸And when that year was ended, they came to him the next year and said to him, "We cannot hide from my lord that, with all the money and animal stocks consigned to my lord, nothing is left at my lord's disposal save our persons and

our farmland. ¹⁹Let us not perish before your eyes, both we and our land. Take us and our land in exchange for bread, and we with our land will be serfs to Pharaoh; provide the seed, that we may live and not die, and that the land may not become a waste."

²⁰So Joseph gained possession of all the farm land of Egypt for Pharaoh, all the Egyptians having sold their fields because the famine was too much for them; thus the land passed over to Pharaoh. ²¹And he removed the population town by town, from one end of Egypt's border to the other. ²²Only the land of the priests he did not take over, for the priests had an allotment from Pharaoh, and they lived off the allotment which Pharaoh had made to them; therefore they did not sell their land. ²³Then Joseph said to the people, "Whereas I have this day acquired you and your land for Pharaoh, here is seed for you to sow the land. ²⁴And when harvest comes, you shall give one-fifth to Pharaoh, and four-fifths shall be yours as seed for the fields and as food for you and those in your households, and as nourishment for your children." ²⁵And they said, "You have saved our lives! We are grateful to my lord, and we shall be serfs to Pharaoh." ²⁶And Joseph made it into a land law in Egypt, which is still valid, that a fifth should be Pharaoh's; only the land of the priests did not become Pharaoh's.

²⁷Thus Israel settled in the country of Egypt, in the region of Goshen; they acquired holdings in it, and were fertile and increased greatly.

²⁸Jacob lived seventeen years in the land of Egypt, so that the span of Jacob's life came to one hundred and forty-seven years. ²⁹And when the time approached for Israel to die, he summoned his son Joseph and said to him, "Do me this favor, place your hand under my thigh as a pledge of your steadfast loyalty: please do not bury me in Egypt. ³⁰When I lie down with my ancestors, take me up from Egypt and bury me in their burial-place." He replied, "I will do as you have spoken." ³¹And he said, "Swear to me." And he swore to him. Then Israel bowed at the head of the bed.

48 ¹Some time afterward, Joseph was told, "Your father is ill." So he took with him his two sons, Manasseh and Ephraim. ²When Jacob was told, "Your son Joseph has come to see you," Israel summoned his strength and sat up in bed.

³And Jacob said to Joseph, "El Shaddai, who appeared to me at Luz in the land of Canaan, blessed me—⁴and said to me, 'I will make you fertile and numerous, making of you a community of peoples; and I will assign this land to your offspring to come for an everlasting possession.' ⁵Now, your two sons, who were born to you in the land of Egypt before I came to you in Egypt, shall be mine; Ephraim and Manasseh shall be mine no less than Reuben and Simeon. ⁶But progeny born to you after them shall be yours; they shall be recorded instead of their brothers in their inheritance.

⁷I [do this because], when I was returning from Paddan, Rachel died, to my sorrow, while I was journeying in the land of Canaan, when still some distance short of Ephrath; and I buried her there on the road to Ephrath"—now Bethlehem.

⁸Noticing Joseph's sons, Israel asked, "Who are these?" ⁹And Joseph said to his father, "They are my sons, whom God has given me here." "Bring them up to me," he said, "that I may bless them." ¹⁰Now Israel's eyes were dim with age; he could not see. So [Joseph] brought them close to him, and he kissed them and embraced them. ¹¹And Israel said to Joseph, "I never expected to see you again, and here God has let me see your children as well."

¹²Joseph then removed them from his knees, and bowed low with his face to the ground. ¹³Joseph took the two of them, Ephraim with his right hand—to Israel's left—and

Manasseh with his left hand—to Israel's right—and brought them close to him. ¹⁴But Israel stretched out his right hand and laid it on Ephraim's head, though he was the younger, and his left hand on Manasseh's head—thus crossing his hands—although Manasseh was the firstborn. ¹⁵And he blessed Joseph, saying,

> "God in whose ways my fathers Abraham and Isaac walked,
> God who has been my shepherd from my birth to this day—
> ¹⁶ The Messenger who has redeemed me from all harm—
> Bless the lads.
> In them may my name be recalled,
> And the names of my fathers Abraham and Isaac,
> And may they be teeming multitudes upon earth."

¹⁷When Joseph saw that his father was placing his right hand on Ephraim's head, he thought it wrong; so he took hold of his father's hand to move it from Ephraim's head to Manasseh's. ¹⁸"Not so, Father," Joseph said to his father, "for the other is the firstborn; place your right hand on his head." ¹⁹But his father objected, saying, "I know, my son, I know. He too shall become a people, and he too shall be great. Yet his younger brother shall be greater than he, and his offspring shall be plentiful enough for nations." ²⁰So he blessed them that day, saying, "By you shall Israel invoke blessings, saying: God make you like Ephraim and Manasseh." Thus he put Ephraim before Manasseh.

²¹Then Israel said to Joseph, "I am about to die; but God will be with you and bring you back to the land of your ancestors. ²²And now, I assign to you one portion more than to your brothers, which I wrested from the Amorites with my sword and bow."

49 ¹And Jacob called his sons and said, "Come together that I may tell you what is to befall you in days to come.

> ² Assemble and hearken, O sons of Jacob;
> Hearken to Israel your father:
> ³ Reuben, you are my firstborn,
> My might and first fruit of my vigor,
> Exceeding in rank
> And exceeding in honor.
> ⁴ Unstable as water, you shall excel no longer;
> For when you mounted your father's bed,
> You brought disgrace—my couch he mounted!
> ⁵ Simeon and Levi are a pair;
> Their weapons are tools of lawlessness.
> ⁶ Let not my person be included in their council,
> Let not my being be counted in their assembly.
> For when angry they slay a man,
> And when pleased they maim an ox.
> ⁷ Cursed be their anger so fierce,
> And their wrath so relentless.
> I will divide them in Jacob,
> Scatter them in Israel.
> ⁸ You, O Judah, your brothers shall praise;
> Your hand shall be on the nape of your foes;
> Your father's sons shall bow low to you.
> ⁹ Judah is a lion's whelp;
> On prey, my son, have you grown.
> He crouches, lies down like a lion,
> Like a lioness—who dare rouse him?
> ¹⁰ The scepter shall not depart from Judah,
> Nor the ruler's staff from between his feet;
> So that tribute shall come to him
> And the homage of peoples be his.

11 He tethers his ass to a vine,
His ass's foal to a choice vine;
He washes his garment in wine,
His robe in blood of grapes.

12 His eyes are darker than wine;
His teeth are whiter than milk.

13 Zebulun shall dwell by the seashore;
He shall be a haven for ships,
And his flank shall rest on Sidon.

14 Issachar is a strong-boned ass,
Crouching among the sheepfolds.

15 When he saw how good was security,
And how pleasant was the country,
He bent his shoulder to the burden,
And became a toiling serf.

16 Dan shall govern his people,
As one of the tribes of Israel.

17 Dan shall be a serpent by the road,
A viper by the path,
That bites the horse's heels
So that his rider is thrown backward.

18 I wait for Your deliverance, O יהוה!

19 Gad shall be raided by raiders,
But he shall raid at their heels.

20 Asher's bread shall be rich,
And he shall yield royal dainties.

21 Naphtali is a hind let loose,
Which yields lovely fawns.

22 Joseph is a wild ass,
A wild ass by a spring
—Wild colts on a hillside.

23 Archers bitterly assailed him;
They shot at him and harried him.

24 Yet his bow stayed taut,
And his arms were made firm
By the hands of the Mighty One of Jacob—
There, the Shepherd, the Rock of Israel—

25 The God of your father's [house], who helps you,
And Shaddai who blesses you
With blessings of heaven above,
Blessings of the deep that couches below,
Blessings of the breast and womb.

26 The blessings of your father
Surpass the blessings of my ancestors,
To the utmost bounds of the eternal hills.
May they rest on the head of Joseph,
On the brow of the elect of his brothers.

27 Benjamin is a ravenous wolf;
In the morning he consumes the foe,
And in the evening he divides the spoil."

28All these were the tribes of Israel, twelve in number, and this is what their father said to them as he bade them farewell, addressing to each a parting word appropriate to him. 29Then he instructed them, saying to them, "I am about to be gathered to my kin. Bury me with my ancestors in the cave which is in the field of Ephron the Hittite, 30the cave which is in the field of Machpelah, facing Mamre, in the land of Canaan, the field that Abraham bought from Ephron the Hittite for a burial site—31there Abraham and his wife Sarah were buried; there Isaac and his wife Rebekah were buried; and there I buried Leah—32the field and the cave in it, bought from the Hittites." 33When Jacob finished his instructions to his sons, he drew his feet into the bed and, breathing his last, he was gathered to his kin.

50 1Joseph flung himself upon his father's face and wept over him and kissed him. 2Then Joseph ordered the physicians in his service to embalm his father, and the physicians embalmed Israel. 3It required forty days, for such is the full period of embalming. The Egyptians bewailed him seventy days; 4and when the wailing period was over, Joseph spoke to Pharaoh's court, saying, "Do me this favor, and lay this appeal before Pharaoh: 5'My father made me swear, saying, "I am about to die. Be sure to bury me in the grave which I made ready for myself in the land of Canaan." Now, therefore, let me go up and bury my father; then I shall return.'" 6And Pharaoh said, "Go up and bury your father, as he made you promise on oath."

7So Joseph went up to bury his father; and with him went up all the officials of Pharaoh, the senior members of his court, and all of Egypt's dignitaries, 8together with all of Joseph's household, his brothers, and his father's household; only their children, their flocks, and their herds were left in the region of Goshen. 9Chariots, too, and horsemen went up with him; it was a very large troop.

10When they came to Goren ha-Atad, which is beyond the Jordan, they held there a very great and solemn lamentation; and he observed a mourning period of seven days for his father. 11And when the Canaanite inhabitants of the land saw the mourning at Goren ha-Atad, they said, "This is a solemn mourning on the part of the Egyptians." That is why it was named Abelmizraim, which is beyond the Jordan. 12Thus his sons did for him as he had instructed them. 13His sons carried him to the land of Canaan, and buried him in the cave of the field of Machpelah, the field near Mamre, which Abraham had bought for a burial site from Ephron the Hittite. 14After burying his father, Joseph returned to Egypt, he and his brothers and all who had gone up with him to bury his father.

15When Joseph's brothers saw that their father was dead, they said, "What if Joseph still bears a grudge against us and pays us back for all the wrong that we did him!" 16So they sent this message to Joseph, "Before his death your father left this instruction: 17So shall you say to Joseph, 'Forgive, I urge you, the offense and guilt of your brothers who treated you so harshly.' Therefore, please forgive the offense of the servants of the God of your father." And Joseph was in tears as they spoke to him.

18His brothers went to him themselves, flung themselves before him, and said, "We are prepared to be your slaves." 19But Joseph said to them, "Have no fear! Am I a substitute for God? 20Besides, although you intended me harm, God intended it for good, so as to bring about the present result—the survival of many people. 21And so, fear not. I will sustain you and your dependents." Thus he reassured them, speaking kindly.

22So Joseph and his father's household remained in Egypt. Joseph lived one hundred and ten years. 23Joseph lived to see children of the third generation of Ephraim; the children of Machir son of Manasseh were likewise born upon Joseph's knees. 24At length, Joseph said to his brothers, "I am about to die. God will surely take notice of you and bring you up from this land to the land promised on oath to Abraham, to Isaac, and to Jacob." 25So Joseph made the sons of Israel swear, saying, "When God has taken notice of you, you shall carry up my bones from here." 26Joseph died at the age of one hundred and ten years; and he was embalmed and placed in a coffin in Egypt.

exodus

1 ¹These are the names of the sons of Israel who came to Egypt with Jacob, each coming with his household: ²Reuben, Simeon, Levi, and Judah; ³Issachar, Zebulun, and Benjamin; ⁴Dan and Naphtali, Gad and Asher. ⁵The total number of persons that were of Jacob's issue came to seventy, Joseph being already in Egypt. ⁶Joseph died, and all his brothers, and all that generation. ⁷But the Israelites were fertile and prolific; they multiplied and increased very greatly, so that the land was filled with them.

⁸A new king arose over Egypt who did not know Joseph. ⁹And he said to his people, "Look, the Israelite people are much too numerous for us. ¹⁰Let us deal shrewdly with them, so that they may not increase; otherwise in the event of war they may join our enemies in fighting against us and rise from the ground." ¹¹So they set taskmasters over them to oppress them with forced labor; and they built garrison cities for Pharaoh: Pithom and Rameses. ¹²But the more they were oppressed, the more they increased and spread out, so that the [Egyptians] came to dread the Israelites.

¹³The Egyptians ruthlessly imposed upon the Israelites ¹⁴the various labors that they made them perform. Ruthlessly they made life bitter for them with harsh labor at mortar and bricks and with all sorts of tasks in the field.

¹⁵The king of Egypt spoke to the Hebrew midwives, one of whom was named Shiphrah and the other Puah, ¹⁶saying, "When you deliver the Hebrew women, look at the birthstool: if it is a boy, kill him; if it is a girl, let her live." ¹⁷The midwives, fearing God, did not do as the king of Egypt had told them; they let the boys live. ¹⁸So the king of Egypt summoned the midwives and said to them, "Why have you done this thing, letting the boys live?" ¹⁹The midwives said to Pharaoh, "Because the Hebrew women are not like the Egyptian women: they are vigorous. Before the midwife can come to them, they have given birth." ²⁰And God dealt well with the midwives; and the people multiplied and increased greatly. ²¹And [God] established households for the midwives, because they feared God. ²²Then Pharaoh charged all his people, saying, "Every boy that is born you shall throw into the Nile, but let every girl live."

2 ¹A certain member of the house of Levi went and took [into his household as his wife] a woman of Levi. ²The woman conceived and bore a son; and when she saw how beautiful he was, she hid him for three months. ³When she could hide him no longer, she got a wicker basket for him and caulked it with bitumen and pitch. She put the child into it and placed it among the reeds by the bank of the Nile. ⁴And his sister stationed herself at a distance, to learn what would befall him.

⁵The daughter of Pharaoh came down to bathe in the Nile, while her maidens walked along the Nile. She spied the basket among the reeds and sent her slave girl to fetch it. ⁶When she opened it, she saw that it was a child, a boy crying. She took pity on it and said, "This must be a Hebrew child." ⁷Then his sister said to Pharaoh's daughter, "Shall I go and get you a Hebrew nurse to suckle the child for you?" ⁸And Pharaoh's daughter answered, "Yes." So the girl went and called the child's mother. ⁹And Pharaoh's daughter said to her, "Take this child and nurse it for me, and I will pay your wages." So the woman took the child and nursed it. ¹⁰When the child grew up, she brought him to Pharaoh's daughter, who made him her son. She named him Moses, explaining, "I drew him out of the water."

¹¹Some time after that, when Moses had grown up, he went out to his kinsfolk and witnessed their labors. He saw an Egyptian beating a Hebrew, one of his kinsmen. ¹²He turned this way and that and, seeing no one about, he struck down the Egyptian and hid him in the sand. ¹³When he went out the next day, he found two Hebrews fighting; so he said to the offender, "Why do you strike your fellow?" ¹⁴He retorted, "Who made you chief and ruler over us? Do you mean to kill me as you killed the Egyptian?" Moses was frightened, and thought: Then the matter is known! ¹⁵When Pharaoh learned of the matter, he sought to kill Moses; but Moses fled from Pharaoh. He arrived in the land of Midian, and sat down beside a well.

¹⁶Now the priest of Midian had seven daughters. They came to draw water, and filled the troughs to water their father's flock; ¹⁷but shepherds came and drove them off. Moses rose to their defense, and he watered their flock. ¹⁸When they returned to their father Reuel, he said, "How is it that you have come back so soon today?" ¹⁹They answered, "An Egyptian rescued us from the shepherds; he even drew water for us and watered the flock." ²⁰He said to his daughters, "Where is he then? Why did you leave the [Egyptian]? Ask him in to break bread." ²¹Moses consented to stay in that household, and [Reuel] gave Moses his daughter Zipporah as wife. ²²She bore a son whom he named Gershom, for he said, "I have been a stranger in a foreign land."

²³A long time after that, the king of Egypt died. The Israelites were groaning under the bondage and cried out; and their cry for help from the bondage rose up to God. ²⁴God heard their moaning, and God remembered the covenant with Abraham and Isaac and Jacob. ²⁵God looked upon the Israelites, and God took notice of them.

3 ¹Now Moses, tending the flock of his father-in-law Jethro, the priest of Midian, drove the flock into the wilderness, and came to Horeb, the mountain of God. ²A messenger of יהוה appeared to him in a blazing fire out of a bush. He gazed, and there was a bush all aflame, yet the bush was not consumed. ³Moses said, "I must turn aside to look at this marvelous sight; why doesn't the bush burn up?" ⁴When יהוה saw that he had turned aside to look, God called to him out of the bush: "Moses! Moses!" He answered, "Here I am." ⁵And [God] said, "Do not come closer! Remove your sandals from your feet, for the place on which you stand is holy ground!" ⁶and continued, "I am the God of your father's [house]—the God of Abraham, the God of Isaac, and the God of Jacob." And Moses hid his face, for he was afraid to look at God.

⁷And יהוה continued, "I have marked well the plight of My people in Egypt and have heeded their outcry because of their taskmasters; yes, I am mindful of their sufferings. ⁸I have come down to rescue them from the Egyptians and to bring them out of that land to a good and spacious land, a land flowing with milk and honey, the region of the Canaanites, the Hittites, the Amorites, the Perizzites, the Hivites, and the Jebusites. ⁹Now the cry of the Israelites has reached Me; moreover, I have seen how the Egyptians oppress them. ¹⁰Come, therefore, I will send you to Pharaoh, and you shall free My people, the Israelites, from Egypt."

¹¹But Moses said to God, "Who am I that I should go to Pharaoh and free the Israelites from Egypt?" ¹²And [God] said, "I will be with you; that shall be your sign that it was I who sent you. And when you have freed the people from Egypt, you shall worship God at this mountain."

¹³Moses said to God, "When I come to the Israelites and say to them, 'The God of your ancestors has sent me to you,' and they ask me, 'What is his name?' what shall I say to them?" ¹⁴And God said to Moses, "Ehyeh-Asher-Ehyeh," continuing, "Thus shall you say to the Israelites, 'Ehyeh sent me to you.'" ¹⁵And God said further to Moses, "Thus shall you speak to the Israelites: יהוה, the God of your ancestors—the God of Abraham, the God of Isaac, and the God of Jacob—has sent me to you:

This shall be My name forever,
This My appellation for all eternity.

¹⁶"Go and assemble the elders of Israel and say to them: יהוה, the God of your ancestors—the God of Abraham, Isaac, and Jacob—has appeared to me and said, 'I have taken note of you and of what is being done to you in Egypt, ¹⁷and I have declared: I will take you out of the misery of Egypt to the land of the Canaanites, the Hittites, the Amorites, the Perizzites, the Hivites, and the Jebusites, to a land flowing with milk and honey.' ¹⁸They will listen to you; then you shall go with the elders of Israel to the king of Egypt and you shall say to him, 'יהוה, the God of the Hebrews, became manifest to us. Now therefore, let us go a distance of three days into the wilderness to sacrifice to our God יהוה.' ¹⁹Yet I know that the king of Egypt will let you go only because of a greater might. ²⁰So I will stretch out My hand and smite Egypt with various wonders which I will work upon them; after that he shall let you go. ²¹And I will dispose the Egyptians favorably toward this people, so that when you go, you will not go away empty-handed. ²²Each woman shall borrow from her neighbor and the lodger in her house objects of silver and gold, and clothing, and you shall put these on your sons and daughters, thus stripping the Egyptians."

4 ¹But Moses spoke up and said, "What if they do not believe me and do not listen to me, but say: יהוה did not appear to you?" ²יהוה said to him, "What is that in your hand?" And he replied, "A rod." ³[God] said, "Cast it on the ground." He cast it on the ground and it became a snake; and Moses recoiled from it. ⁴Then יהוה said to Moses, "Put out your hand and grasp it by the tail"—he put out his hand and seized it, and it became a rod in his hand—⁵"that they may believe that יהוה, the God of their ancestors, the God of Abraham, the God of Isaac, and the God of Jacob, did appear to you."

⁶יהוה said to him further, "Put your hand into your bosom." He put his hand into his bosom; and when he took it out, his hand was encrusted with snowy scales! ⁷And [God] said, "Put your hand back into your bosom."—He put his hand back into his bosom; and when he took it out of his bosom, there it was again like the rest of his body.—⁸"And if they do not believe you or pay heed to the first sign, they will believe the second. ⁹And if they are not convinced by both these signs and still do not heed you, take some water from the Nile and pour it on the dry ground, and it—the water that you take from the Nile—will turn to blood on the dry ground."

¹⁰But Moses said to יהוה, "Please, O my lord, I have never been good with words, either in times past or now that You have spoken to Your servant; I am slow of speech and slow of tongue." ¹¹And יהוה said to him, "Who gives humans speech? Who makes them dumb or deaf, seeing or blind? Is it not I, יהוה ? ¹²Now go, and I will be with you as you speak and will instruct you what to say." ¹³But he said, "Please, O my lord, make someone else Your agent." ¹⁴יהוה became angry with Moses and said, "There is your brother Aaron the Levite. He, I know, speaks readily. Even now he is setting out to meet you, and he will be happy to see you.

¹⁵You shall speak to him and put the words in his mouth—I will be with you and with him as you speak, and tell both of you what to do—¹⁶and he shall speak for you to the people. Thus he shall serve as your spokesman, with you playing the role of God to him, ¹⁷and take with you this rod, with which you shall perform the signs."

¹⁸Moses went back to his father-in-law Jethro and said to him, "Let me go back to my kinsfolk in Egypt and see how they are faring." And Jethro said to Moses, "Go in peace." ¹⁹יהוה said to Moses in Midian, "Go back to Egypt, for all the authorities who sought to kill you are dead." ²⁰So Moses took his wife and sons, mounted them on an ass, and went back to the land of Egypt; and Moses took the rod of God with him.

²¹And יהוה said to Moses, "When you return to Egypt, see that you perform before Pharaoh all the marvels that I have put within your power. I, however, will stiffen his heart so that he will not let the people go. ²²Then you shall say to Pharaoh, 'Thus says יהוה: Israel is My firstborn son. ²³I have said to you, "Let My son go, that he may worship Me," yet you refuse to let him go. Now I will slay your firstborn son.'"

²⁴At a night encampment on the way, יהוה encountered him and sought to kill him. ²⁵So Zipporah took a flint and cut off her son's foreskin, and touched his legs with it, saying, "You are truly a bridegroom of blood to me!" ²⁶And when [God] let him alone, she added, "A bridegroom of blood because of the circumcision."

²⁷יהוה said to Aaron, "Go to meet Moses in the wilderness." He went and met him at the mountain of God, and he kissed him. ²⁸Moses told Aaron about all the things that יהוה had committed to him and all the signs about which he had been instructed. ²⁹Then Moses and Aaron went and assembled all the elders of the Israelites. ³⁰Aaron repeated all the words that יהוה had spoken to Moses, and he performed the signs in the sight of the people, ³¹and the people were convinced. When they heard that יהוה had taken note of the Israelites and that [God] had seen their plight, they bowed low in homage.

5 ¹Afterward Moses and Aaron went and said to Pharaoh, "Thus says יהוה, the God of Israel: Let My people go that they may celebrate a festival for Me in the wilderness." ²But Pharaoh said, "Who is יהוה that I should heed him and let Israel go? I do not know יהוה, nor will I let Israel go." ³They answered, "The God of the Hebrews has become manifest to us. Let us go, we pray, a distance of three days into the wilderness to sacrifice to our God יהוה, lest [God] strike us with pestilence or sword." ⁴But the king of Egypt said to them, "Moses and Aaron, why do you distract the people from their tasks? Get to your labors!" ⁵And Pharaoh continued, "The people of the land are already so numerous, and you would have them cease from their labors!"

⁶That same day Pharaoh charged the taskmasters and overseers of the people, saying, ⁷"You shall no longer provide the people with straw for making bricks as heretofore; let them go and gather straw for themselves. ⁸But impose upon them the same quota of bricks as they have been making heretofore; do not reduce it, for they are shirkers; that is why they cry, 'Let us go and sacrifice to our God!' ⁹Let heavier work be laid upon the laborers; let them keep at it and not pay attention to deceitful promises."

¹⁰So the taskmasters and overseers of the people went out and said to the people, "Thus says Pharaoh: I will not give you any straw. ¹¹You must go and get the straw yourselves wherever you can find it; but there shall be no decrease whatever in your work." ¹²Then the people scattered throughout the land of Egypt to gather stubble for straw. ¹³And the taskmasters

pressed them, saying, "You must complete the same work assignment each day as when you had straw." ¹⁴And the overseers of the Israelites, whom Pharaoh's taskmasters had set over them, were beaten. "Why," they were asked, "did you not complete the prescribed amount of bricks, either yesterday or today, as you did before?"

¹⁵Then the overseers of the Israelites came to Pharaoh and cried: "Why do you deal thus with your servants? ¹⁶No straw is issued to your servants, yet they demand of us: Make bricks! Thus your servants are being beaten, when the fault is with your own people." ¹⁷He replied, "You are shirkers, shirkers! That is why you say, 'Let us go and sacrifice to יהוה.' ¹⁸Be off now to your work! No straw shall be issued to you, but you must produce your quota of bricks!"

¹⁹Now the overseers of the Israelites found themselves in trouble because of the order, "You must not reduce your daily quantity of bricks." ²⁰As they left Pharaoh's presence, they came upon Moses and Aaron standing in their path, ²¹and they said to them, "May יהוה look upon you and punish you for making us loathsome to Pharaoh and his courtiers—putting a sword in their hands to slay us." ²²Then Moses returned to יהוה and said, "O my lord, why did You bring harm upon this people? Why did You send me? ²³Ever since I came to Pharaoh to speak in Your name, he has dealt worse with this people; and still You have not delivered Your people."

6 ¹Then יהוה said to Moses, "You shall soon see what I will do to Pharaoh: he shall let them go because of a greater might; indeed, because of a greater might he shall drive them from his land." ²God spoke to Moses and said to him, "I am יהוה. ³I appeared to Abraham, Isaac, and Jacob as El Shaddai, but I did not make Myself known to them by My name יהוה. ⁴I also established My covenant with them, to give them the land of Canaan, the land in which they lived as sojourners. ⁵I have now heard the moaning of the Israelites because the Egyptians are holding them in bondage, and I have remembered My covenant. ⁶Say, therefore, to the Israelite people: I am יהוה. I will free you from the labors of the Egyptians and deliver you from their bondage. I will redeem you with an outstretched arm and through extraordinary chastisements. ⁷And I will take you to be My people, and I will be your God. And you shall know that I, יהוה, am your God who freed you from the labors of the Egyptians. ⁸I will bring you into the land which I swore to give to Abraham, Isaac, and Jacob, and I will give it to you for a possession, I יהוה." ⁹But when Moses told this to the Israelites, they would not listen to Moses, their spirits crushed by cruel bondage.

¹⁰יהוה spoke to Moses, saying, ¹¹"Go and tell Pharaoh king of Egypt to let the Israelites depart from his land." ¹²But Moses appealed to יהוה, saying, "The Israelites would not listen to me; how then should Pharaoh heed me, me—who gets tongue-tied!" ¹³So יהוה spoke to both Moses and Aaron in regard to the Israelites and Pharaoh king of Egypt, instructing them to deliver the Israelites from the land of Egypt.

¹⁴The following are the heads of their respective clans. The sons of Reuben, Israel's firstborn: Enoch and Pallu, Hezron and Carmi; those are the families of Reuben. ¹⁵The sons of Simeon: Jemuel, Jamin, Ohad, Jachin, Zohar, and Saul the son of a Canaanite woman; those are the families of Simeon. ¹⁶These are the names of Levi's sons by their lineage: Gershon, Kohath, and Merari; and the span of Levi's life was 137 years. ¹⁷The sons of Gershon: Libni and Shimei, by their families. ¹⁸The sons of Kohath: Amram, Izhar, Hebron, and Uzziel; and the span of Kohath's life was 133 years. ¹⁹The sons of Merari: Mahli and Mushi. These are the families of the Levites by their lineage.

²⁰Amram took into his [household] as wife his father's sister Jochebed, and she bore him Aaron and Moses; and the span of Amram's life was 137 years. ²¹The sons of Izhar: Korah, Nepheg, and Zichri. ²²The sons of Uzziel: Mishael, Elzaphan, and Sithri. ²³Aaron took into his [household] as wife Elisheba, daughter of Amminadab and sister of Nahshon, and she bore him Nadab and Abihu, Eleazar and Ithamar. ²⁴The sons of Korah: Assir, Elkanah, and Abiasaph. Those are the families of the Korahites. ²⁵And Aaron's son Eleazar took into his [household] as wife one of Putiel's daughters, and she bore him Phinehas. Those are the heads of the ancestral houses of the Levites by their families.

²⁶It is the same Aaron and Moses to whom יהוה said, "Bring forth the Israelites from the land of Egypt, troop by troop." ²⁷It was they who spoke to Pharaoh king of Egypt to free the Israelites from the Egyptians; these are the same Moses and Aaron. ²⁸For when יהוה spoke to Moses in the land of Egypt ²⁹and יהוה said to Moses, "I am יהוה; speak to Pharaoh king of Egypt all that I will tell you," ³⁰Moses appealed to יהוה, saying, "See, I get tongue-tied; how then should Pharaoh heed me!"

7 ¹יהוה replied to Moses, "See, I place you in the role of God to Pharaoh, with your brother Aaron as your prophet. ²You shall repeat all that I command you, and your brother Aaron shall speak to Pharaoh to let the Israelites depart from his land. ³But I will harden Pharaoh's heart, that I may multiply My signs and marvels in the land of Egypt. ⁴When Pharaoh does not heed you, I will lay My hand upon Egypt and deliver My ranks, My people the Israelites, from the land of Egypt with extraordinary chastisements. ⁵And the Egyptians shall know that I am יהוה, when I stretch out My hand over Egypt and bring out the Israelites from their midst." ⁶This Moses and Aaron did; as יהוה commanded them, so they did. ⁷Moses was eighty years old and Aaron eighty-three, when they made their demand on Pharaoh.

⁸יהוה said to Moses and Aaron, ⁹"When Pharaoh speaks to you and says, 'Produce your marvel,' you shall say to Aaron, 'Take your rod and cast it down before Pharaoh.' It shall turn into a serpent." ¹⁰So Moses and Aaron came before Pharaoh and did just as יהוה had commanded: Aaron cast down his rod in the presence of Pharaoh and his courtiers, and it turned into a serpent. ¹¹Then Pharaoh, for his part, summoned the sages and the sorcerers; and the Egyptian magician-priests, in turn, did the same with their spells: ¹²each cast down his rod, and they turned into serpents. But Aaron's rod swallowed their rods. ¹³Yet Pharaoh's heart stiffened and he did not heed them, as יהוה had said.

¹⁴And יהוה said to Moses, "Pharaoh is stubborn; he refuses to let the people go. ¹⁵Go to Pharaoh in the morning, as he is coming out to the water, and station yourself before him at the edge of the Nile, taking with you the rod that turned into a snake. ¹⁶And say to him, 'יהוה, the God of the Hebrews, sent me to you to say, "Let My people go that they may worship Me in the wilderness." But you have paid no need until now. ¹⁷Thus says יהוה, "By this you shall know that I am יהוה." See, I shall strike the water in the Nile with the rod that is in my hand, and it will be turned into blood; ¹⁸and the fish in the Nile will die. The Nile will stink so that the Egyptians will find it impossible to drink the water of the Nile.'"

¹⁹And יהוה said to Moses, "Say to Aaron: Take your rod and hold out your arm over the waters of Egypt—its rivers, its canals, its ponds, all its bodies of water—that they may turn to blood; there shall be blood throughout the land of Egypt, even in vessels of wood and stone." ²⁰Moses and Aaron did just as יהוה commanded: he lifted up the rod and struck the water in the Nile in the sight of Pharaoh and

his courtiers, and all the water in the Nile was turned into blood ²¹and the fish in the Nile died. The Nile stank so that the Egyptians could not drink water from the Nile; and there was blood throughout the land of Egypt. ²²But when the Egyptian magician-priests did the same with their spells, Pharaoh's heart stiffened and he did not heed them—as יהוה had spoken. ²³Pharaoh turned and went into his palace, paying no regard even to this. ²⁴And all the Egyptians had to dig round about the Nile for drinking water, because they could not drink the water of the Nile.

²⁵When seven days had passed after יהוה struck the Nile, ²⁶יהוה said to Moses, "Go to Pharaoh and say to him, 'Thus says יהוה: Let My people go that they may worship Me. ²⁷If you refuse to let them go, then I will plague your whole country with frogs. ²⁸The Nile shall swarm with frogs, and they shall come up and enter your palace, your bedchamber and your bed, the houses of your courtiers and your people, and your ovens and your kneading bowls. ²⁹The frogs shall come up on you and on your people and on all your courtiers.'"

8 ¹And יהוה said to Moses, "Say to Aaron: Hold out your arm with the rod over the rivers, the canals, and the ponds, and bring up the frogs on the land of Egypt." ²Aaron held out his arm over the waters of Egypt, and the frogs came up and covered the land of Egypt. ³But the magician-priests did the same with their spells, and brought frogs upon the land of Egypt.

⁴Then Pharaoh summoned Moses and Aaron and said, "Plead with יהוה to remove the frogs from me and my people, and I will let the people go to sacrifice to יהוה." ⁵And Moses said to Pharaoh, "You may have this triumph over me: for what time shall I plead in behalf of you and your courtiers and your people, that the frogs be cut off from you and your houses, to remain only in the Nile?" ⁶"For tomorrow," he replied. And [Moses] said, "As you say—that you may know that there is none like our God יהוה; ⁷the frogs shall retreat from you and your courtiers and your people; they shall remain only in the Nile." ⁸Then Moses and Aaron left Pharaoh's presence, and Moses cried out to יהוה in the matter of the frogs which had been inflicted upon Pharaoh. ⁹And יהוה did as Moses asked; the frogs died out in the houses, the courtyards, and the fields. ¹⁰And they piled them up in heaps, till the land stank. ¹¹But when Pharaoh saw that there was relief, he became stubborn and would not heed them, as יהוה had spoken.

¹²Then יהוה said to Moses, "Say to Aaron: Hold out your rod and strike the dust of the earth, and it shall turn to lice throughout the land of Egypt." ¹³And they did so. Aaron held out his arm with the rod and struck the dust of the earth, and vermin came upon human and beast; all the dust of the earth turned to lice throughout the land of Egypt. ¹⁴The magician-priests did the like with their spells to produce lice, but they could not. The vermin remained upon human and beast; ¹⁵and the magician-priests said to Pharaoh, "This is the finger of God!" But Pharaoh's heart stiffened and he would not heed them, as יהוה had spoken.

¹⁶And יהוה said to Moses, "Early in the morning present yourself to Pharaoh, as he is coming out to the water, and say to him, 'Thus says יהוה: Let My people go that they may worship Me. ¹⁷For if you do not let My people go, I will let loose swarms of insects against you and your courtiers and your people and your houses; the houses of the Egyptians, and the very ground they stand on, shall be filled with swarms of insects. ¹⁸But on that day I will set apart the region of Goshen, where My people dwell, so that no swarms of insects shall be there, that you may know that I יהוה am in the midst of the land. ¹⁹And I will make a distinction between

My people and your people. Tomorrow this sign shall come to pass.'" ²⁰And יהוה did so. Heavy swarms of insects invaded Pharaoh's palace and the houses of his courtiers; throughout the country of Egypt the land was ruined because of the swarms of insects.

²¹Then Pharaoh summoned Moses and Aaron and said, "Go and sacrifice to your God within the land." ²²But Moses replied, "It would not be right to do this, for what we sacrifice to our God יהוה is untouchable to the Egyptians. If we sacrifice that which is untouchable to the Egyptians before their very eyes, will they not stone us! ²³So we must go a distance of three days into the wilderness and sacrifice to יהוה as our God may command us." ²⁴Pharaoh said, "I will let you go to sacrifice to your God יהוה in the wilderness; but do not go very far. Plead, then, for me." ²⁵And Moses said, "When I leave your presence, I will plead with יהוה that the swarms of insects depart tomorrow from Pharaoh and his courtiers and his people; but let not Pharaoh again act deceitfully, not letting the people go to sacrifice to יהוה."

²⁶So Moses left Pharaoh's presence and pleaded with יהוה. ²⁷And יהוה did as Moses asked—removing the swarms of insects from Pharaoh, from his courtiers, and from his people; not one remained. ²⁸But Pharaoh became stubborn this time also, and would not let the people go.

9 ¹יהוה said to Moses, "Go to Pharaoh and say to him, 'Thus says יהוה, the God of the Hebrews: Let My people go to worship Me. ²For if you refuse to let them go, and continue to hold them, ³then the hand of יהוה will strike your livestock in the fields—the horses, the asses, the camels, the cattle, and the sheep—with a very severe pestilence. ⁴But יהוה will make a distinction between the livestock of Israel and the livestock of the Egyptians, so that nothing shall die of all that belongs to the Israelites. ⁵יהוה has fixed the time: tomorrow יהוה will do this thing in the land.'" ⁶And יהוה did so the next day: all the livestock of the Egyptians died, but of the livestock of the Israelites not a beast died. ⁷When Pharaoh inquired, he found that not a head of the livestock of Israel had died; yet Pharaoh remained stubborn, and he would not let the people go.

⁸Then יהוה said to Moses and Aaron, "Each of you take handfuls of soot from the kiln, and let Moses throw it toward the sky in the sight of Pharaoh. ⁹It shall become a fine dust all over the land of Egypt, and cause an inflammation breaking out in boils on human and beast throughout the land of Egypt." ¹⁰So they took soot of the kiln and appeared before Pharaoh; Moses threw it toward the sky, and it caused an inflammation breaking out in boils on human and beast. ¹¹The magician-priests were unable to confront Moses because of the inflammation, for the inflammation afflicted the magician-priests as well as all the other Egyptians. ¹²But יהוה stiffened the heart of Pharaoh, and he would not heed them, just as יהוה had told Moses.

¹³יהוה said to Moses, "Early in the morning present yourself to Pharaoh and say to him, 'Thus says יהוה, the God of the Hebrews: Let My people go to worship Me. ¹⁴For this time I will send all My plagues upon your person, and your courtiers, and your people, in order that you may know that there is none like Me in all the world. ¹⁵I could have stretched forth My hand and stricken you and your people with pestilence, and you would have been effaced from the earth. ¹⁶Nevertheless I have spared you for this purpose: in order to show you My power, and in order that My fame may resound throughout the world. ¹⁷Yet you continue to thwart My people, and do not let them go! ¹⁸This time tomorrow I will rain down a very heavy hail, such as has not been in Egypt from the day it was founded until now. ¹⁹Therefore,

order your livestock and everything you have in the open brought under shelter; every human and beast that is found outside, not having been brought indoors, shall perish when the hail comes down upon them!'" 20Those among Pharaoh's courtiers who feared יהוה's word brought their slaves and livestock indoors to safety; 21but those who paid no regard to the word of יהוה left their slaves and livestock in the open.

22יהוה said to Moses, "Hold out your arm toward the sky that hail may fall on all the land of Egypt, upon human and beast and all the grasses of the field in the land of Egypt." 23So Moses held out his rod toward the sky, and יהוה sent thunder and hail, and fire streamed down to the ground, as יהוה rained down hail upon the land of Egypt. 24The hail was very heavy—fire flashing in the midst of the hail—such as had not fallen on the land of Egypt since it had become a nation. 25Throughout the land of Egypt the hail struck down all that were in the open, both human and beast; the hail also struck down all the grasses of the field and shattered all the trees of the field. 26Only in the region of Goshen, where the Israelites were, there was no hail.

27Thereupon Pharaoh sent for Moses and Aaron and said to them, "I stand guilty this time. יהוה is in the right, and I and my people are in the wrong. 28Plead with יהוה that there may be an end of God's thunder and of hail. I will let you go; you need stay no longer." 29Moses said to him, "As I go out of the city, I shall spread out my hands to יהוה; the thunder will cease and the hail will fall no more, so that you may know that the earth is יהוה's. 30But I know that you and your courtiers do not yet fear God יהוה."—31Now the flax and barley were ruined, for the barley was in the ear and the flax was in bud; 32but the wheat and the emmer were not hurt, for they ripen late.—33Leaving Pharaoh, Moses went outside the city and spread out his hands to יהוה: the thunder and the hail ceased, and no rain came pouring down upon the earth. 34But when Pharaoh saw that the rain and the hail and the thunder had ceased, he became stubborn and reverted to his guilty ways, as did his courtiers. 35So Pharaoh's heart stiffened and he would not let the Israelites go, just as יהוה had foretold through Moses.

10 1Then יהוה said to Moses, "Go to Pharaoh. For I have hardened his heart and the hearts of his courtiers, in order that I may display these My signs among them, 2and that you may recount in the hearing of your children and of your children's children how I made a mockery of the Egyptians and how I displayed My signs among them—in order that you may know that I am יהוה. 3So Moses and Aaron went to Pharaoh and said to him, "Thus says יהוה, the God of the Hebrews, 'How long will you refuse to humble yourself before Me? Let My people go that they may worship Me. 4For if you refuse to let My people go, tomorrow I will bring locusts on your territory. 5They shall cover the surface of the land, so that no one will be able to see the land. They shall devour the surviving remnant that was left to you after the hail; and they shall eat away all your trees that grow in the field. 6Moreover, they shall fill your palaces and the houses of all your courtiers and of all the Egyptians—something that neither your fathers nor fathers' fathers have seen from the day they appeared on earth to this day.'" With that he turned and left Pharaoh's presence.

7Pharaoh's courtiers said to him, "How long shall this one be a snare to us? Let their notables go to worship their God יהוה! Are you not yet aware that Egypt is lost?" 8So Moses and Aaron were brought back to Pharaoh and he said to them, "Go, worship your God יהוה! Who are the ones to go?" 9Moses replied, "We will all go—regardless of social station—we will go with our sons and daughters, our flocks

and herds; for we must observe יהוה's festival." 10But he said to them, "יהוה be with you—the same as I mean to let your dependents go with you! Clearly, you are bent on mischief. 11No! You men folk go and worship יהוה, since that is what you want." And they were expelled from Pharaoh's presence.

12Then יהוה said to Moses, "Hold out your arm over the land of Egypt for the locusts, that they may come upon the land of Egypt and eat up all the grasses in the land, whatever the hail has left." 13Moses held out his rod over the land of Egypt, and יהוה drove an east wind over the land all that day and all night; and when morning came, the east wind had brought the locusts. 14Locusts invaded all the land of Egypt and settled within all the territory of Egypt in a thick mass; never before had there been so many, nor will there ever be so many again. 15They hid all the land from view, and the land was darkened; and they ate up all the grasses of the field and all the fruit of the trees which the hail had left, so that nothing green was left, of tree or grass of the field, in all the land of Egypt.

16Pharaoh hurriedly summoned Moses and Aaron and said, "I stand guilty before your God יהוה and before you. 17Forgive my offense just this once, and plead with your God יהוה that this death but be removed from me." 18So he left Pharaoh's presence and pleaded with יהוה. 19יהוה caused a shift to a very strong west wind, which lifted the locusts and hurled them into the Sea of Reeds; not a single locust remained in all the territory of Egypt. 20But יהוה stiffened Pharaoh's heart, and he would not let the Israelites go.

21Then יהוה said to Moses, "Hold out your arm toward the sky that there may be darkness upon the land of Egypt, a darkness that can be touched." 22Moses held out his arm toward the sky and thick darkness descended upon all the land of Egypt for three days. 23People could not see one another, and for three days no one could move about; but all the Israelites enjoyed light in their dwellings.

24Pharaoh then summoned Moses and said, "Go, worship יהוה! Only your flocks and your herds shall be left behind; even your dependents may go with you." 25But Moses said, "You yourself must provide us with sacrifices and burnt offerings to offer up to our God יהוה; 26our own livestock, too, shall go along with us—not a hoof shall remain behind: for we must select from it for the worship of our God יהוה; and we shall not know with what we are to worship יהוה until we arrive there." 27But יהוה stiffened Pharaoh's heart and he would not agree to let them go. 28Pharaoh said to him, "Be gone from me! Take care not to see me again, for the moment you look upon my face you shall die." 29And Moses replied, "You have spoken rightly. I shall not see your face again!"

11 1And יהוה said to Moses, "I will bring but one more plague upon Pharaoh and upon Egypt; after that he shall let you go from here; indeed, when he lets you go, he will drive you out of here one and all. 2Tell the people to borrow, each man from his neighbor and each woman from hers, objects of silver and gold." 3יהוה disposed the Egyptians favorably toward the people. Moreover, their leader Moses was much esteemed in the land of Egypt, among Pharaoh's courtiers and among the people.

4Moses said, "Thus says יהוה: Toward midnight I will go forth among the Egyptians, 5and every [male] firstborn in the land of Egypt shall die, from the firstborn of Pharaoh who sits on his throne to the firstborn of the slave girl who is behind the millstones; and all the firstborn of the cattle. 6And there shall be a loud cry in all the land of Egypt, such as has never been or will ever be again; 7but not a dog shall snarl at any of the Israelites, at human or beast—in order that you may know that יהוה makes a distinction between Egypt and Israel.

8"Then all these courtiers of yours shall come down to me and bow low to me, saying, 'Depart, you and all the people who follow you!' After that I will depart." And he left Pharaoh's presence in hot anger.

9Now יהוה had said to Moses, "Pharaoh will not heed you, in order that My marvels may be multiplied in the land of Egypt." 10Moses and Aaron had performed all these marvels before Pharaoh, but יהוה had stiffened the heart of Pharaoh so that he would not let the Israelites go from his land.

12 יהוה said to Moses and Aaron in the land of Egypt: 2This month shall mark for you the beginning of the months; it shall be the first of the months of the year for you. 3Speak to the whole community of Israel and say that on the tenth of this month each of them shall take a lamb to a family, a lamb to a household. 4But if the household is too small for a lamb, let it share one with a neighbor who dwells nearby, in proportion to the number of persons: you shall contribute for the lamb according to what each household will eat. 5Your lamb shall be without blemish, a yearling male; you may take it from the sheep or from the goats. 6You shall keep watch over it until the fourteenth day of this month; and all the assembled congregation of the Israelites shall slaughter it at twilight. 7They shall take some of the blood and put it on the two doorposts and the lintel of the houses in which they are to eat it. 8They shall eat the flesh that same night; they shall eat it roasted over the fire, with unleavened bread and with bitter herbs. 9Do not eat any of it raw, or cooked in any way with water, but roasted—head, legs, and entrails—over the fire. 10You shall not leave any of it over until morning; if any of it is left until morning, you shall burn it.

11This is how you shall eat it: your loins girded, your sandals on your feet, and your staff in your hand; and you shall eat it hurriedly: it is a passover offering to יהוה. 12For that night I will go through the land of Egypt and strike down every [male] firstborn in the land of Egypt, both human and beast; and I will mete out punishments to all the gods of Egypt, I יהוה. 13And the blood on the houses where you are staying shall be a sign for you: when I see the blood I will pass over you, so that no plague will destroy you when I strike the land of Egypt.

14This day shall be to you one of remembrance: you shall celebrate it as a festival to יהוה throughout the ages; you shall celebrate it as an institution for all time. 15Seven days you shall eat unleavened bread; on the very first day you shall remove leaven from your houses, for whoever eats leavened bread from the first day to the seventh day, that person shall be cut off from Israel. 16You shall celebrate a sacred occasion on the first day, and a sacred occasion on the seventh day; no work at all shall be done on them; only what every person is to eat, that alone may be prepared for you. 17You shall observe the [Feast of] Unleavened Bread, for on this very day I brought your ranks out of the land of Egypt; you shall observe this day throughout the ages as an institution for all time. 18In the first month, from the fourteenth day of the month at evening, you shall eat unleavened bread until the twenty-first day of the month at evening. 19No leaven shall be found in your houses for seven days. For whoever eats what is leavened, that person—whether a stranger or a citizen of the country—shall be cut off from the community of Israel. 20You shall eat nothing leavened; in all your settlements you shall eat unleavened bread.

21Moses then summoned all the elders of Israel and said to them, "Go, pick out lambs for your families, and slaughter the passover offering. 22Take a bunch of hyssop, dip it in the blood that is in the basin, and apply some of the blood that is in the basin to the lintel and to the two doorposts. None of you shall go outside the door of your house until morning. 23For יהוה, when going through to smite the Egyptians, will see the blood on the lintel and the two doorposts, and יהוה will pass over the door and not let the Destroyer enter and smite your home.

24"You shall observe this as an institution for all time, for you and for your descendants. 25And when you enter the land that יהוה will give you, as promised, you shall observe this rite. 26And when your children ask you, 'What do you mean by this rite?' 27you shall say, 'It is the passover sacrifice to יהוה, who passed over the houses of the Israelites in Egypt when smiting the Egyptians, but saved our houses.'"

The people then bowed low in homage. 28And the Israelites went and did so; just as יהוה had commanded Moses and Aaron, so they did.

29In the middle of the night יהוה struck down all the [male] firstborn in the land of Egypt, from the firstborn of Pharaoh who sat on the throne to the firstborn of the captive who was in the dungeon, and all the firstborn of the cattle. 30And Pharaoh arose in the night, with all his courtiers and all the Egyptians—because there was a loud cry in Egypt; for there was no house where there was not someone dead. 31He summoned Moses and Aaron in the night and said, "Up, depart from among my people, you and the Israelites with you! Go, worship יהוה as you said! 32Take also your flocks and your herds, as you said, and begone! And may you bring a blessing upon me also!"

33The Egyptians urged the people on, impatient to have them leave the country, for they said, "We shall all be dead." 34So the people took their dough before it was leavened, their kneading bowls wrapped in their cloaks upon their shoulders. 35The Israelites had done Moses' bidding and borrowed from the Egyptians objects of silver and gold, and clothing. 36And יהוה had disposed the Egyptians favorably toward the people, and they let them have their request; thus they stripped the Egyptians.

37The Israelites journeyed from Rameses to Succoth, about six hundred thousand men on foot, aside from dependents. 38Moreover, a mixed multitude went up with them, and very much livestock, both flocks and herds. 39And they baked unleavened cakes of the dough that they had taken out of Egypt, for it was not leavened, since they had been driven out of Egypt and could not delay; nor had they prepared any provisions for themselves. 40The length of time that the Israelites lived in Egypt was four hundred and thirty years; 41at the end of the four hundred and thirtieth year, to the very day, all the ranks of יהוה departed from the land of Egypt. 42That was for יהוה a night of vigil to bring them out of the land of Egypt; that same night is יהוה's, one of vigil for all the children of Israel throughout the ages.

43יהוה said to Moses and Aaron: This is the law of the Passover offering: No foreigner shall eat of it. 44But any householder's purchased male slave may eat of it once he has been circumcised. 45No bound or hired laborer shall eat of it. 46It shall be eaten in one house: you shall not take any of the flesh outside the house; nor shall you break a bone of it. 47The whole community of Israel shall offer it. 48If a male stranger who dwells with you would offer the passover to יהוה, all his males must be circumcised; then he shall be admitted to offer it; he shall then be as a citizen of the country. But no uncircumcised man may eat of it. 49There shall be one law for the citizen and for the stranger who dwells among you.

50And all the Israelites did so; as יהוה had commanded Moses and Aaron, so they did. 51That very day יהוה freed the Israelites from the land of Egypt, troop by troop.

13 ¹יהוה spoke further to Moses, saying ²"Consecrate to Me every male firstborn; human and beast, the first [male] issue of every womb among the Israelites is Mine."

³And Moses said to the people, "Remember this day, on which you went free from Egypt, the house of bondage, how יהוה freed you from it with a mighty hand: no leavened bread shall be eaten. ⁴You go free on this day, in the month of Abib. ⁵So, when יהוה has brought you into the land of the Canaanites, the Hittites, the Amorites, the Hivites, and the Jebusites, which was sworn to your fathers to be given you, a land flowing with milk and honey, you shall observe in this month the following practice:

⁶"Seven days you shall eat unleavened bread, and on the seventh day there shall be a festival of יהוה. ⁷Throughout the seven days unleavened bread shall be eaten; no leavened bread shall be found with you, and no leaven shall be found in all your territory. ⁸And you shall explain to your child on that day, 'It is because of what יהוה did for me when I went free from Egypt.'

⁹"And this shall serve you as a sign on your hand and as a reminder on your forehead—in order that the Teaching of יהוה may be in your mouth—that with a mighty hand יהוה freed you from Egypt. ¹⁰You shall keep this institution at its set time from year to year.

¹¹"And when יהוה has brought you into the land of the Canaanites, as [God] swore to you and to your fathers, and has given it to you, ¹²you shall set apart for יהוה every first issue of the womb: every male firstling that your cattle drop shall be יהוה's. ¹³But every firstling ass you shall redeem with a sheep; if you do not redeem it, you must break its neck. And you must redeem every male firstborn among your children. ¹⁴And when, in time to come, a child of yours asks you, saying, 'What does this mean?' you shall reply, 'It was with a mighty hand that יהוה brought us out from Egypt, the house of bondage. ¹⁵When Pharaoh stubbornly refused to let us go, יהוה slew every [male] firstborn in the land of Egypt, the firstborn of both human and beast. Therefore I sacrifice to יהוה every first male issue of the womb, but redeem every male firstborn among my children.' ¹⁶"And so it shall be as a sign upon your hand and as a symbol on your forehead that with a mighty hand יהוה freed us from Egypt."

¹⁷Now when Pharaoh let the people go, God did not lead them by way of the land of the Philistines, although it was nearer; for God said, "The people may have a change of heart when they see war, and return to Egypt." ¹⁸So God led the people round about, by way of the wilderness at the Sea of Reeds. Now the Israelites went up armed out of the land of Egypt. ¹⁹And Moses took with him the bones of Joseph, who had exacted an oath from the children of Israel, saying, "God will be sure to take notice of you: then you shall carry up my bones from here with you." ²⁰They set out from Succoth, and encamped at Etham, at the edge of the wilderness. ²¹יהוה went before them in a pillar of cloud by day, to guide them along the way, and in a pillar of fire by night, to give them light, that they might travel day and night. ²²The pillar of cloud by day and the pillar of fire by night did not depart from before the people.

14 ¹יהוה said to Moses: ²Tell the Israelites to turn back and encamp before Pi-hahiroth, between Migdol and the sea, before Baal-zephon; you shall encamp facing it, by the sea. ³Pharaoh will say of the Israelites, "They are astray in the land; the wilderness has closed in on them." ⁴Then I will stiffen Pharaoh's heart and he will pursue them, that I may gain glory through Pharaoh and all his host; and the Egyptians shall know that I am יהוה. And they did so.

⁵When the king of Egypt was told that the people had fled, Pharaoh and his courtiers had a change of heart about the people and said, "What is this we have done, releasing Israel from our service?" ⁶He ordered his chariot and took his force with him; ⁷he took six hundred of his picked chariots, and the rest of the chariots of Egypt, with officers in all of them. ⁸יהוה stiffened the heart of Pharaoh king of Egypt, and he gave chase to the Israelites. As the Israelites were departing defiantly, ⁹the Egyptians gave chase to them, and all the chariot horses of Pharaoh, his riders, and his warriors overtook them encamped by the sea, near Pi-hahiroth, before Baal-zephon.

¹⁰As Pharaoh drew near, the Israelites caught sight of the Egyptians advancing upon them. Greatly frightened, the Israelites cried out to יהוה. ¹¹And they said to Moses, "Was it for want of graves in Egypt that you brought us to die in the wilderness? What have you done to us, taking us out of Egypt? ¹²Is this not the very thing we told you in Egypt, saying, 'Let us be, and we will serve the Egyptians, for it is better for us to serve the Egyptians than to die in the wilderness'?" ¹³But Moses said to the people, "Have no fear! Stand by, and witness the deliverance which יהוה will work for you today; for the Egyptians whom you see today you will never see again. ¹⁴יהוה will battle for you; you hold your peace!"

¹⁵Then יהוה said to Moses, "Why do you cry out to Me? Tell the Israelites to go forward. ¹⁶And you lift up your rod and hold out your arm over the sea and split it, so that the Israelites may march into the sea on dry ground. ¹⁷And I will stiffen the hearts of the Egyptians so that they go in after them; and I will gain glory through Pharaoh and all his warriors, his chariots, and his riders. ¹⁸Let the Egyptians know that I am יהוה, when I gain glory through Pharaoh, his chariots, and his riders."

¹⁹The messenger of God, who had been going ahead of the Israelite army, now moved and followed behind them; and the pillar of cloud shifted from in front of them and took up a place behind them, ²⁰and it came between the army of the Egyptians and the army of Israel. Thus there was the cloud with the darkness, and it cast a spell upon the night, so that the one could not come near the other all through the night.

²¹Then Moses held out his arm over the sea and יהוה drove back the sea with a strong east wind all that night, and turned the sea into dry ground. The waters were split, ²²and the Israelites went into the sea on dry ground, the waters forming a wall for them on their right and on their left. ²³The Egyptians came in pursuit after them into the sea, all of Pharaoh's horses, chariots, and riders. ²⁴At the morning watch, יהוה looked down upon the Egyptian army from a pillar of fire and cloud, and threw the Egyptian army into panic. ²⁵[God] locked the wheels of their chariots so that they moved forward with difficulty. And the Egyptians said, "Let us flee from the Israelites, for יהוה is fighting for them against Egypt."

²⁶Then יהוה said to Moses, "Hold out your arm over the sea, that the waters may come back upon the Egyptians and upon their chariots and upon their riders." ²⁷Moses held out his arm over the sea, and at daybreak the sea returned to its normal state, and the Egyptians fled at its approach. But יהוה hurled the Egyptians into the sea. ²⁸The waters turned back and covered the chariots and the riders—Pharaoh's entire army that followed them into the sea; not one of them remained. ²⁹But the Israelites had marched through the sea on dry ground, the waters forming a wall for them on their right and on their left.

³⁰Thus יהוה delivered Israel that day from the Egyptians. Israel saw the Egyptians dead on the shore of the sea. ³¹And when Israel saw the wondrous power which יהוה had wielded

against the Egyptians, the people feared יהוה; they had faith in יהוה and in God's servant Moses.

15 ¹Then Moses and the Israelites sang this song to יהוה. They said:

I will sing to יהוה, for He has triumphed gloriously;
Horse and driver He has hurled into the sea.
² יהוה is my strength and might;
He is become my deliverance.
This is my God and I will enshrine Him;
The God of my ancestors, and I will exalt Him.
³ יהוה, the Warrior—
יהוה is His name!
⁴ Pharaoh's chariots and his army
He has cast into the sea;
And the pick of his officers
Are drowned in the Sea of Reeds.
⁵ The deeps covered them;
They went down into the depths like a stone.
⁶ Your right hand, יהוה, glorious in power,
Your right hand, יהוה, shatters the foe!
⁷ In Your great triumph You break Your opponents;
You send forth Your fury, it consumes them like
straw.
⁸ At the blast of Your nostrils the waters piled up,
The floods stood straight like a wall;
The deeps froze in the heart of the sea.

⁹The foe said,

"I will pursue, I will overtake,
I will divide the spoil;
My desire shall have its fill of them.
I will bare my sword—
My hand shall subdue them."
¹⁰ You made Your wind blow, the sea covered them;
They sank like lead in the majestic waters.
¹¹ Who is like You, יהוה, among the celestials;
Who is like You, majestic in holiness,
Awesome in splendor, working wonders!
¹² You put out Your right hand,
The earth swallowed them.
¹³ In Your love You lead the people You redeemed;
In Your strength You guide them to Your holy abode.
¹⁴ The peoples hear, they tremble;
Agony grips the dwellers in Philistia.
¹⁵ Now are the clans of Edom dismayed;
The tribes of Moab—trembling grips them;
All the dwellers in Canaan are aghast.
¹⁶ Terror and dread descend upon them;
Through the might of Your arm they are still as
stone—
Till Your people cross over, יהוה,
Till Your people cross whom You have ransomed.
¹⁷ You will bring them and plant them in Your own
mountain,
The place You made to dwell in, יהוה,
The sanctuary, יהוה, which Your hands established.
¹⁸ יהוה will reign for ever and ever!

¹⁹For the horses of Pharaoh, with his chariots and riders, went into the sea; and יהוה turned back on them the waters of the sea; but the Israelites marched on dry ground in the midst of the sea. ²⁰Then Miriam the prophet, Aaron's sister, picked up a hand-drum, and all the women went out after her in dance with hand-drums. ²¹And Miriam chanted for them:

Sing to יהוה, for He has triumphed gloriously;
Horse and driver He has hurled into the sea.

²²Then Moses caused Israel to set out from the Sea of Reeds. They went on into the wilderness of Shur; they traveled three days in the wilderness and found no water. ²³They came to Marah, but they could not drink the water of Marah because it was bitter; that is why it was named Marah. ²⁴And the people grumbled against Moses, saying, "What shall we drink?" ²⁵So he cried out to יהוה, and יהוה showed him a piece of wood; he threw it into the water and the water became sweet. There [God] made for them a fixed rule; there they were put to the test. ²⁶[God] said, "If you will heed your God יהוה diligently, doing what is upright in God's sight, giving ear to God's commandments and keeping all God's laws, then I will not bring upon you any of the diseases that I brought upon the Egyptians, for I יהוה am your healer."

²⁷And they came to Elim, where there were twelve springs of water and seventy palm trees; and they encamped there beside the water.

16 ¹Setting out from Elim, the whole Israelite community came to the wilderness of Sin, which is between Elim and Sinai, on the fifteenth day of the second month after their departure from the land of Egypt. ²In the wilderness, the whole Israelite community grumbled against Moses and Aaron. ³The Israelites said to them, "If only we had died by the hand of יהוה in the land of Egypt, when we sat by the fleshpots, when we ate our fill of bread! For you have brought us out into this wilderness to starve this whole congregation to death."

⁴And יהוה said to Moses, "I will rain down bread for you from the sky, and the people shall go out and gather each day that day's portion—that I may thus test them, to see whether they will follow My instructions or not. ⁵But on the sixth day, when they apportion what they have brought in, it shall prove to be double the amount they gather each day." ⁶So Moses and Aaron said to all the Israelites, "By evening you shall know it was יהוה who brought you out from the land of Egypt; ⁷and in the morning you shall behold the Presence of יהוה, because [God] has heard your grumblings against יהוה. For who are we that you should grumble against us? ⁸Since it is יהוה," Moses continued, "who will give you flesh to eat in the evening and bread in the morning to the full—because יהוה has heard the grumblings you utter—what is our part? Your grumbling is against יהוה, not against us!"

⁹Then Moses said to Aaron, "Say to the whole Israelite community: Advance toward יהוה, who has heard your grumbling." ¹⁰And as Aaron spoke to the whole Israelite community, they turned toward the wilderness, and there, in a cloud, appeared the Presence of יהוה.

¹¹יהוה spoke to Moses: ¹²"I have heard the grumbling of the Israelites. Speak to them and say: By evening you shall eat flesh, and in the morning you shall have your fill of bread; and you shall know that I יהוה am your God."

¹³In the evening quail appeared and covered the camp; in the morning there was a fall of dew about the camp. ¹⁴When the fall of dew lifted, there, over the surface of the wilderness, lay a fine and flaky substance, as fine as frost on the ground. ¹⁵When the Israelites saw it, they said to one another, "What is it?"—for they did not know what it was. And Moses said to them, "That is the bread which יהוה has given you to eat. ¹⁶This is what יהוה has commanded: Gather as much of it as each of you requires to eat, an *omer* to a person for as many of you as there are; you shall each fetch for those in your tent."

[17]The Israelites did so, some gathering much, some little. [18]But when they measured it by the *omer*, anyone who had gathered much had no excess, and anyone who had gathered little had no deficiency: they had gathered as much as they needed to eat. [19]And Moses said to them, "Let no one leave any of it over until morning." [20]But they paid no attention to Moses; some of them left of it until morning, and it became infested with maggots and stank. And Moses was angry with them.

[21]So they gathered it every morning, as much as each one needed to eat; for when the sun grew hot, it would melt. [22]On the sixth day they gathered double the amount of food, two *omers* for each; and when all the chieftains of the community came and told Moses, [23]he said to them, "This is what יהוה meant: Tomorrow is a day of rest, a holy sabbath of יהוה. Bake what you would bake and boil what you would boil; and all that is left put aside to be kept until morning." [24]So they put it aside until morning, as Moses had ordered; and it did not turn foul, and there were no maggots in it. [25]Then Moses said, "Eat it today, for today is a Sabbath of יהוה; you will not find it today on the plain. [26]Six days you shall gather it; on the seventh day, the sabbath, there will be none."

[27]Yet some of the people went out on the seventh day to gather, but they found nothing. [28]And יהוה said to Moses, "How long will you all refuse to obey My commandments and My teachings? [29]Mark that it is יהוה who, having given you the sabbath, therefore gives you two days' food on the sixth day. Let everyone remain in place: let no one leave the vicinity on the seventh day." [30]So the people remained inactive on the seventh day.

[31]The house of Israel named it manna; it was like coriander seed, white, and it tasted like wafers in honey. [32]Moses said, "This is what יהוה has commanded: Let one *omer* of it be kept throughout the ages, in order that they may see the bread that I fed you in the wilderness when I brought you out from the land of Egypt." [33]And Moses said to Aaron, "Take a jar, put one *omer* of manna in it, and place it before יהוה, to be kept throughout the ages." [34]As יהוה had commanded Moses, Aaron placed it before the Pact, to be kept. [35]And the Israelites ate manna forty years, until they came to a settled land; they ate the manna until they came to the border of the land of Canaan. [36]The *omer* is a tenth of an *ephah*.

17 [1]From the wilderness of Sin the whole Israelite community continued by stages as יהוה would command. They encamped at Rephidim, and there was no water for the people to drink. [2]The people quarreled with Moses. "Give us water to drink," they said; and Moses replied to them, "Why do you quarrel with me? Why do you try יהוה?" [3]But the people thirsted there for water; and the people grumbled against Moses and said, "Why did you bring us up from Egypt, to kill us and our children and livestock with thirst?" [4]Moses cried out to יהוה, saying, "What shall I do with this people? Before long they will be stoning me!" [5]Then יהוה said to Moses, "Pass before the people; take with you some of the elders of Israel, and take along the rod with which you struck the Nile, and set out. [6]I will be standing there before you on the rock at Horeb. Strike the rock and water will issue from it, and the people will drink." And Moses did so in the sight of the elders of Israel. [7]The place was named Massah and Meribah, because the Israelites quarreled and because they tried יהוה, saying, "Is יהוה present among us or not?"

[8]Amalek came and fought with Israel at Rephidim. [9]Moses said to Joshua, "Pick some troops for us, and go out and do battle with Amalek. Tomorrow I will station myself on the top of the hill, with the rod of God in my hand." [10]Joshua did as Moses told him and fought with Amalek, while Moses, Aaron, and Hur went up to the top of the hill. [11]Then, whenever Moses held up his hand, Israel prevailed; but whenever he let down his hand, Amalek prevailed. [12]But Moses' hands grew heavy; so they took a stone and put it under him and he sat on it, while Aaron and Hur, one on each side, supported his hands; thus his hands remained steady until the sun set. [13]And Joshua overwhelmed the people of Amalek with the sword.

[14]Then יהוה said to Moses, "Inscribe this in a document as a reminder, and read it aloud to Joshua: I will utterly blot out the memory of Amalek from under heaven!" [15]And Moses built an altar and named it Adonainissi. [16]He said, "It means, 'Hand upon the throne of יהוה!' יהוה will be at war with Amalek throughout the ages."

18 [1]Jethro priest of Midian, Moses' father-in-law, heard all that God had done for Moses and for Israel, God's people, how יהוה had brought Israel out from Egypt. [2]So Jethro, Moses' father-in-law, took Zipporah, Moses' wife, after she had been sent home, [3]and her two sons—of whom one was named Gershom, that is to say, "I have been a stranger in a foreign land"; [4]and the other was named Eliezer, meaning, "My ancestors' God was my help, delivering me from the sword of Pharaoh." [5]Jethro, Moses' father-in-law, brought Moses' sons and wife to him in the wilderness, where he was encamped at the mountain of God. [6]He sent word to Moses, "I, your father-in-law Jethro, am coming to you, with your wife and her two sons." [7]Moses went out to meet his father-in-law; he bowed low and kissed him; each asked after the other's welfare, and they went into the tent.

[8]Moses then recounted to his father-in-law everything that יהוה had done to Pharaoh and to the Egyptians for Israel's sake, all the hardships that had befallen them on the way, and how יהוה had delivered them. [9]And Jethro rejoiced over all the kindness that יהוה had shown Israel when delivering them from the Egyptians. [10]"Blessed be יהוה," Jethro said, "who delivered you from the Egyptians and from Pharaoh, and who delivered the people from under the hand of the Egyptians. [11]Now I know that יהוה is greater than all gods, yes, by the result of their very schemes against [the people]." [12]And Jethro, Moses' father-in-law, brought a burnt offering and sacrifices for God; and Aaron came with all the elders of Israel to partake of the meal before God with Moses' father-in-law.

[13]Next day, Moses sat as magistrate among the people, while the people stood about Moses from morning until evening. [14]But when Moses' father-in-law saw how much he had to do for the people, he said, "What is this thing that you are doing to the people? Why do you act alone, while all the people stand about you from morning until evening?" [15]Moses replied to his father-in-law, "It is because the people come to me to inquire of God. [16]When they have a dispute, it comes before me, and I decide between one person and another, and I make known the laws and teachings of God."

[17]But Moses' father-in-law said to him, "The thing you are doing is not right; [18]you will surely wear yourself out, and these people as well. For the task is too heavy for you; you cannot do it alone. [19]Now listen to me. I will give you counsel, and God be with you! You represent the people before God: you bring the disputes before God, [20]and enjoin upon them the laws and the teachings, and make known to them the way they are to go and the practices they are to follow. [21]You shall also seek out, from among all the people, capable individu-

als who fear God—trustworthy ones who spurn ill-gotten gain. Set these over them as chiefs of thousands, hundreds, fifties, and tens, and ²²let them judge the people at all times. Have them bring every major dispute to you, but let them decide every minor dispute themselves. Make it easier for yourself by letting them share the burden with you. ²³If you do this—and God so commands you—you will be able to bear up; and all these people too will go home unwearied." ²⁴Moses heeded his father-in-law and did just as he had said. ²⁵Moses chose capable individuals out of all Israel, and appointed them heads over the people—chiefs of thousands, hundreds, fifties, and tens; ²⁶and they judged the people at all times: the difficult matters they would bring to Moses, and all the minor matters they would decide themselves. ²⁷Then Moses bade his father-in-law farewell, and he went his way to his own land.

19 ¹On the third new moon after the Israelites had gone forth from the land of Egypt, on that very day, they entered the wilderness of Sinai. ²Having journeyed from Rephidim, they entered the wilderness of Sinai and encamped in the wilderness. Israel encamped there in front of the mountain, ³and Moses went up to God. יהוה called to him from the mountain, saying, "Thus shall you say to the house of Jacob and declare to the children of Israel: ⁴'You have seen what I did to the Egyptians, how I bore you on eagles' wings and brought you to Me. ⁵Now then, if you will obey Me faithfully and keep My covenant, you shall be My treasured possession among all the peoples. Indeed, all the earth is Mine, ⁶but you shall be to Me a kingdom of priests and a holy nation.' These are the words that you shall speak to the children of Israel."

⁷Moses came and summoned the elders of the people and put before them all that יהוה had commanded him. ⁸All the people answered as one, saying, "All that יהוה has spoken we will do!" And Moses brought back the people's words to יהוה. ⁹And יהוה said to Moses, "I will come to you in a thick cloud, in order that the people may hear when I speak with you and so trust you ever after." Then Moses reported the people's words to יהוה, ¹⁰and יהוה said to Moses, "Go to the people and warn them to stay pure today and tomorrow. Let them wash their clothes. ¹¹Let them be ready for the third day; for on the third day יהוה will come down, in the sight of all the people, on Mount Sinai. ¹²You shall set bounds for the people round about, saying, 'Beware of going up the mountain or touching the border of it. Whoever touches the mountain shall be put to death ¹³without being touched—by being either stoned or shot; beast or person, a trespasser shall not live.' When the ram's horn sounds a long blast, they may go up on the mountain."

¹⁴Moses came down from the mountain to the people and warned the people to stay pure, and they washed their clothes. ¹⁵And he said to the people, "Be ready for the third day: [the men among] you should not go near a woman."

¹⁶On the third day, as morning dawned, there was thunder, and lightning, and a dense cloud upon the mountain, and a very loud blast of the horn; and all the people who were in the camp trembled. ¹⁷Moses led the people out of the camp toward God, and they took their places at the foot of the mountain.

¹⁸Now Mount Sinai was all in smoke, for יהוה had come down upon it in fire; the smoke rose like the smoke of a kiln, and the whole mountain trembled violently. ¹⁹The blare of the horn grew louder and louder. As Moses spoke, God answered him in thunder. ²⁰יהוה came down upon Mount Sinai, on the top of the mountain, and יהוה called Moses to the top of the mountain and Moses went up. ²¹יהוה said to Moses, "Go down, warn the people not to break through to יהוה to gaze, lest many of them perish. ²²The priests also, who come near יהוה, must stay pure, lest יהוה break out against them." ²³But Moses said to יהוה, "The people cannot come up to Mount Sinai, for You warned us saying, 'Set bounds about the mountain and sanctify it.'" ²⁴So יהוה said to him, "Go down, and come back together with Aaron; but let not the priests or the people break through to come up to יהוה, lest [God] break out against them." ²⁵And Moses went down to the people and spoke to them.

20 ¹God spoke all these words, saying:
²I יהוה am your God who brought you out of the land of Egypt, the house of bondage: ³You shall have no other gods besides Me.

⁴You shall not make for yourself a sculptured image, or any likeness of what is in the heavens above, or on the earth below, or in the waters under the earth. ⁵You shall not bow down to them or serve them. For I your God יהוה am an impassioned God, visiting the guilt of the parents upon the children, upon the third and upon the fourth generations of those who reject Me, ⁶but showing kindness to the thousandth generation of those who love Me and keep My commandments.

⁷You shall not swear falsely by the name of your God יהוה; for יהוה will not clear one who swears falsely by God's name.

⁸Remember the sabbath day and keep it holy. ⁹Six days you shall labor and do all your work, ¹⁰but the seventh day is a Sabbath of your God יהוה: you shall not do any work—you, your son or daughter, your male or female slave, or your cattle, or the stranger who is within your settlements. ¹¹For in six days יהוה made heaven and earth and sea—and all that is in them—and then rested on the seventh day; therefore יהוה blessed the sabbath day and hallowed it.

¹²Honor your father and your mother, that you may long endure on the land that your God יהוה is assigning to you.

¹³You shall not murder. You shall not commit adultery. You shall not steal. You shall not bear false witness against your neighbor.

¹⁴You shall not covet your neighbor's house: you shall not covet your neighbor's wife, nor male or female slave, nor ox or ass, nor anything that is your neighbor's.

¹⁵All the people witnessed the thunder and lightning, the blare of the horn and the mountain smoking; and when the people saw it, they fell back and stood at a distance. ¹⁶"You speak to us," they said to Moses, "and we will obey; but let not God speak to us, lest we die." ¹⁷Moses answered the people, "Be not afraid; for God has come only in order to test you, and in order that the fear of God may be ever with you, so that you do not go astray." ¹⁸So the people remained at a distance, while Moses approached the thick cloud where God was.

¹⁹יהוה said to Moses:
Thus shall you say to the Israelites: You yourselves saw that I spoke to you from the very heavens: ²⁰With Me, therefore, you shall not make any gods of silver, nor shall you make for yourselves any gods of gold. ²¹Make for Me an altar of earth and sacrifice on it your burnt offerings and your sacrifices of wellbeing, your sheep and your oxen; in every place where I cause My name to be mentioned I will come to you and bless you. ²²And if you make for Me an altar of stones, do not build it of hewn stones; for by wielding your tool upon them you have profaned them. ²³Do not ascend My altar by steps, that your nakedness may not be exposed upon it.

21 ¹These are the rules that you shall set before them: ²When you acquire a Hebrew slave, that person shall serve six years—and shall go free in the seventh year, without payment. ³If [a male slave] came single, he shall leave single; if he had a wife, his wife shall leave with him. ⁴If his master gave him a wife, and she has borne him children, the wife and her children shall belong to the master, and he shall leave alone. ⁵But if the slave declares, "I love my master, and my wife and children: I do not wish to go free," ⁶his master shall take him before God. He shall be brought to the door or the doorpost, and his master shall pierce his ear with an awl; and he shall then remain his master's slave for life.

⁷When a parent sells a daughter as a slave, she shall not go free as male slaves do. ⁸If she proves to be displeasing to her (male) master, who designated her for himself, he must let her be redeemed; he shall not have the right to sell her to outsiders, since he broke faith with her. ⁹And if the master designated her for a son, he shall deal with her as is the practice with free maidens. ¹⁰If he takes another [into the household as his wife], he must not withhold from this one her food, her clothing, or her conjugal rights. ¹¹If he fails her in these three ways, she shall go free, without payment.

¹²One who fatally strikes another person shall be put to death. ¹³If [a male killer] did not do it by design, but it came about by an act of God, I will assign you a place to which he can flee.

¹⁴When a person schemes against another and kills through treachery, you shall take that person from My very altar to be put to death.

¹⁵One who strikes one's father or mother shall be put to death.

¹⁶One who kidnaps a person—whether having sold or still holding the victim—shall be put to death.

¹⁷One who insults one's father or mother shall be put to death.

¹⁸When individuals quarrel and one strikes the other with stone or fist, and the victim does not die but has to take to bed: ¹⁹if that victim then gets up and walks outdoors upon a staff, the assailant shall go unpunished—except for paying for the idleness and the cure.

²⁰When a person [who is a slave owner] strikes a slave, male or female, with a rod, who dies there and then, it must be avenged. ²¹But if the victim survives a day or two, it is not to be avenged, since the one is the other's property.

²²When individuals fight, and one of them pushes a pregnant woman and a miscarriage results, but no other damage ensues, the one responsible shall be fined according as the woman's husband may exact, the payment to be based on reckoning. ²³But if other damage ensues, the penalty shall be life for life, ²⁴eye for eye, tooth for tooth, hand for hand, foot for foot, ²⁵burn for burn, wound for wound, bruise for bruise.

²⁶When a person [who is a slave owner] strikes the eye of a slave, male or female, and destroys it, that person shall let the slave go free on account of the eye. ²⁷If the owner knocks out the tooth of a slave, male or female, that person shall let the slave go free on account of the tooth.

²⁸When an ox gores a man or a woman to death, the ox shall be stoned and its flesh shall not be eaten, but the owner of the ox is not to be punished. ²⁹If, however, that ox has been in the habit of goring, and its owner, though warned, has failed to guard it, and it kills a man or a woman—the ox shall be stoned and its owner, too, shall be put to death. ³⁰If ransom is imposed, the owner must pay whatever is imposed to redeem the owner's own life. ³¹So, too, if it gores a minor, male or female, [its owner] shall be dealt with according to the same rule. ³²But if the ox gores a slave, male or female, [its owner] shall pay thirty shekels of silver to the master, and the ox shall be stoned.

³³When a person opens a pit, or digs a pit and does not cover it, and an ox or an ass falls into it, ³⁴the one responsible for the pit must make restitution—paying the price to the owner, but keeping the dead animal.

³⁵When a person's ox injures a neighbor's ox and it dies, they shall sell the live ox and divide its price; they shall also divide the dead animal. ³⁶If, however, it is known that the ox was in the habit of goring, and its owner has failed to guard it, that person must restore ox for ox, but shall keep the dead animal.

³⁷When a person steals an ox or a sheep, and slaughters it or sells it, that person shall pay five oxen for the ox, and four sheep for the sheep.

22 ¹If the thief is seized while tunneling and beaten to death, there is no bloodguilt in that case. ²If the sun had already risen, there is bloodguilt in that case.—The thief must make restitution, and if lacking the means, shall be sold for the theft. ³But if what was stolen—whether ox or ass or sheep—is found alive and in hand, that person shall pay double.

⁴When a person who owns livestock lets it loose to graze in another's land, and so allows a field or a vineyard to be grazed bare, restitution must be made for the impairment of that field or vineyard.

⁵When a fire is started and spreads to thorns, so that stacked, standing, or growing grain is consumed, the one who started the fire must make restitution.

⁶When a person gives money or goods to another for safekeeping, and they are stolen from that other person's house: if caught, the thief shall pay double; ⁷if the thief is not caught, the owner of the house shall depose before God and deny laying hands on the other's property. (⁸In all charges of misappropriation—pertaining to an ox, an ass, a sheep, a garment, or any other loss, whereof one party alleges, "This is it"—the case of both parties shall come before God: the one whom God declares guilty shall pay double to the other.)

⁹When a person gives to another an ass, an ox, a sheep or any other animal to guard, and it dies or is injured or is carried off, with no witness about, ¹⁰an oath before יהוה shall decide between the two of them that the one has not laid hands on the property of the other; the owner must acquiesce, and no restitution shall be made. ¹¹But if [the animal] was stolen from the guardian, restitution shall be made to its owner. ¹²If it was torn by beasts, the guardian shall bring it as evidence—not needing to replace what has been torn by beasts.

¹³When a person borrows [an animal] from another and it dies or is injured, its owner not being with it, that person must make restitution. ¹⁴If its owner was with it, no restitution need be made; but if it was hired, that payment is due.

¹⁵If a man seduces a virgin for whom the bride-price has not been paid, and lies with her, he must make her his wife by payment of a bride-price. ¹⁶If her father refuses to give her to him, he must still weigh out silver in accordance with the bride-price for virgins.

¹⁷You shall not tolerate a sorceress.

¹⁸Whoever lies with a beast shall be put to death.

¹⁹Whoever sacrifices to a god other than יהוה alone shall be proscribed.

²⁰You shall not wrong or oppress a stranger, for you were strangers in the land of Egypt.

²¹You [communal leaders] shall not ill treat any widow or orphan. ²²If you do mistreat them, I will heed their outcry as soon as they cry out to Me, ²³and My anger shall blaze forth and I will put you to the sword, and your own wives shall become widows and your children orphans.

24If you lend money to My people, to the poor among you, do not act toward them as a creditor; exact no interest from them. 25If you take your neighbor's garment in pledge, you must return it before the sun sets; 26it is the only available clothing—it is what covers the skin. In what else shall [your neighbor] sleep? Therefore, if that person cries out to Me, I will pay heed, for I am compassionate.

27You shall not revile God, nor put a curse upon a chieftain among your people.

28You shall not put off the skimming of the first yield of your vats. You shall give Me the male firstborn among your children. 29You shall do the same with your cattle and your flocks: seven days it shall remain with its mother; on the eighth day you shall give it to Me.

30You shall be holy people to Me: you must not eat flesh torn by beasts in the field; you shall cast it to the dogs.

23 1You must not carry false rumors; you shall not join hands with the guilty to act as a malicious witness: 2You shall neither side with the mighty to do wrong—you shall not give perverse testimony in a dispute so as to pervert it in favor of the mighty—3nor shall you show deference to a poor person in a dispute.

4When you encounter your enemy's ox or ass wandering, you must take it back.

5When you see the ass of your enemy lying under its burden and would refrain from raising it, you must nevertheless help raise it.

6You shall not subvert the rights of your needy in their disputes. 7Keep far from a false charge; do not bring death on those who are innocent and in the right, for I will not acquit the wrongdoer. 8Do not take bribes, for bribes blind the clearsighted and upset the pleas of those who are in the right.

9You shall not oppress a stranger, for you know the feelings of the stranger, having yourselves been strangers in the land of Egypt.

10Six years you shall sow your land and gather in its yield; 11but in the seventh you shall let it rest and lie fallow. Let the needy among your people eat of it, and what they leave let the wild beasts eat. You shall do the same with your vineyards and your olive groves.

12Six days you shall do your work, but on the seventh day you shall cease from labor, in order that your ox and your ass may rest, and that your home-born slave and the stranger may be refreshed.

13Be on guard concerning all that I have told you. Make no mention of the names of other gods; they shall not be heard on your lips.

14Three times a year you shall hold a festival for Me: 15You shall observe the Feast of Unleavened Bread—eating unleavened bread for seven days as I have commanded you—at the set time in the month of Abib, for in it you went forth from Egypt; and none shall appear before Me empty-handed; 16and the Feast of the Harvest, of the first fruits of your work, of what you sow in the field; and the Feast of Ingathering at the end of the year, when you gather in the results of your work from the field. 17Three times a year all your males shall appear before the Sovereign, יהוה.

18You shall not offer the blood of My sacrifice with anything leavened; and the fat of My festal offering shall not be left lying until morning.

19The choice first fruits of your soil you shall bring to the house of your God יהוה.

You shall not boil a kid in its mother's milk.

20I am sending a messenger before you to guard you on the way and to bring you to the place that I have made ready. 21Pay heed to him and obey him. Do not defy him, for he will not pardon your offenses, since My Name is in him; 22but if you obey him and do all that I say, I will be an enemy to your enemies and a foe to your foes.

23When My messenger goes before you and brings you to theAmorites, the Hittites, the Perizzites, the Canaanites, the Hivites, and the Jebusites, and I annihilate them, 24you shall not bow down to their gods in worship or follow their practices, but shall tear them down and smash their pillars to bits. 25You shall serve your God יהוה, who will bless your bread and your water. And I will remove sickness from your midst. 26No woman in your land shall miscarry or be barren. I will let you enjoy the full count of your days.

27I will send forth My terror before you, and I will throw into panic all the people among whom you come, and I will make all your enemies turn tail before you. 28I will send a plague ahead of you, and it shall drive out before you the Hivites, the Canaanites, and the Hittites. 29I will not drive them out before you in a single year, lest the land become desolate and the wild beasts multiply to your hurt. 30I will drive them out before you little by little, until you have increased and possess the land. 31I will set your borders from the Sea of Reeds to the Sea of Philistia, and from the wilderness to the Euphrates; for I will deliver the inhabitants of the land into your hands, and you will drive them out before you. 32You shall make no covenant with them and their gods. 33They shall not remain in your land, lest they cause you to sin against Me; for you will serve their gods—and it will prove a snare to you.

24 1Then [God] said to Moses, "Come up to יהוה, with Aaron, Nadab and Abihu, and seventy elders of Israel, and bow low from afar. 2Moses alone shall come near יהוה; but the others shall not come near, nor shall the people come up with him." 3Moses went and repeated to the people all the commands of יהוה and all the rules; and all the people answered with one voice, saying, "All the things that יהוה has commanded we will do!"

4Moses then wrote down all the commands of יהוה.

Early in the morning, he set up an altar at the foot of the mountain, with twelve pillars for the twelve tribes of Israel. 5He designated some assistants among the Israelites, and they offered burnt offerings and sacrificed bulls as offerings of wellbeing to יהוה. 6Moses took one part of the blood and put it in basins, and the other part of the blood he dashed against the altar. 7Then he took the record of the covenant and read it aloud to the people. And they said, "All that יהוה has spoken we will faithfully do!" 8Moses took the blood and dashed it on the people and said, "This is the blood of the covenant that יהוה now makes with you concerning all these commands."

9Then Moses and Aaron, Nadab and Abihu, and seventy elders of Israel ascended; 10and they saw the God of Israel—under whose feet was the likeness of a pavement of sapphire, like the very sky for purity. 11Yet [God] did not raise a hand against the leaders of the Israelites; they beheld God, and they ate and drank.

12יהוה said to Moses, "Come up to Me on the mountain and wait there, and I will give you the stone tablets with the teachings and commandments which I have inscribed to instruct them." 13So Moses and his attendant Joshua arose, and Moses ascended the mountain of God. 14To the elders he had said, "Wait here for us until we return to you. You have Aaron and Hur with you; let anyone who has a legal matter approach them."

15When Moses had ascended the mountain, the cloud covered the mountain. 16The Presence of יהוה abode on Mount Sinai, and the cloud hid it for six days. On the seventh day

[God] called to Moses from the midst of the cloud. ¹⁷Now the Presence of יהוה appeared in the sight of the Israelites as a consuming fire on the top of the mountain. ¹⁸Moses went inside the cloud and ascended the mountain; and Moses remained on the mountain forty days and forty nights.

25 יהוה spoke to Moses, saying: ²Tell the Israelite people to bring Me gifts; you shall accept gifts for Me from every person whose heart is so moved. ³And these are the gifts that you shall accept from them: gold, silver, and copper; ⁴blue, purple, and crimson yarns, fine linen, goats' hair; ⁵tanned ram skins, dolphin skins, and acacia wood; ⁶oil for lighting, spices for the anointing oil and for the aromatic incense; ⁷lapis lazuli and other stones for setting, for the ephod and for the breast-piece. ⁸And let them make Me a sanctuary that I may dwell among them. ⁹Exactly as I show you—the pattern of the Tabernacle and the pattern of all its furnishings—so shall you make it.

¹⁰They shall make an ark of acacia wood, two and a half cubits long, a cubit and a half wide, and a cubit and a half high. ¹¹Overlay it with pure gold—overlay it inside and out—and make upon it a gold molding round about. ¹²Cast four gold rings for it, to be attached to its four feet, two rings on one of its side walls and two on the other. ¹³Make poles of acacia wood and overlay them with gold; ¹⁴then insert the poles into the rings on the side walls of the ark, for carrying the ark. ¹⁵The poles shall remain in the rings of the ark: they shall not be removed from it. ¹⁶And deposit in the Ark [the tablets of] the Pact which I will give you.

¹⁷You shall make a cover of pure gold, two and a half cubits long and a cubit and a half wide. ¹⁸Make two cherubim of gold—make them of hammered work—at the two ends of the cover. ¹⁹Make one cherub at one end and the other cherub at the other end; of one piece with the cover shall you make the cherubim at its two ends. ²⁰The cherubim shall have their wings spread out above, shielding the cover with their wings. They shall confront each other, the faces of the cherubim being turned toward the cover. ²¹Place the cover on top of the Ark, after depositing inside the Ark the Pact that I will give you. ²²There I will meet with you, and I will impart to you—from above the cover, from between the two cherubim that are on top of the Ark of the Pact—all that I will command you concerning the Israelite people.

²³You shall make a table of acacia wood, two cubits long, one cubit wide, and a cubit and a half high. ²⁴Overlay it with pure gold, and make a gold molding around it. ²⁵Make a rim of a hand's breadth around it, and make a gold molding for its rim round about. ²⁶Make four gold rings for it, and attach the rings to the four corners at its four legs. ²⁷The rings shall be next to the rim, as holders for poles to carry the table. ²⁸Make the poles of acacia wood, and overlay them with gold; by these the table shall be carried. ²⁹Make its bowls, ladles, jars and jugs with which to offer libations; make them of pure gold. ³⁰And on the table you shall set the bread of display, to be before Me always.

³¹You shall make a lamp-stand of pure gold; the lamp-stand shall be made of hammered work; its base and its shaft, its cups, calyxes, and petals shall be of one piece. ³²Six branches shall issue from its sides; three branches from one side of the lamp-stand and three branches from the other side of the lampstand. ³³On one branch there shall be three cups shaped like almond blossoms, each with calyx and petals, and on the next branch there shall be three cups shaped like almond blossoms, each with calyx and petals; so for all six branches issuing from the lamp-stand. ³⁴And on the lamp-stand itself there shall be four cups shaped like almond blossoms, each with calyx and petals: ³⁵a calyx, of one piece with it, under a pair of branches; and a calyx, of one piece with it, under the second pair of branches, and a calyx, of one piece with it, under the last pair of branches; so for all six branches issuing from the lamp-stand. ³⁶Their calyxes and their stems shall be of one piece with it, the whole of it a single hammered piece of pure gold. ³⁷Make its seven lamps—the lamps shall be so mounted as to give the light on its front side—³⁸and its tongs and fire pans of pure gold. ³⁹It shall be made, with all these furnishings, out of a talent of pure gold. ⁴⁰Note well, and follow the patterns for them that are being shown you on the mountain.

26 ¹As for the tabernacle, make it of ten strips of cloth; make these of fine twisted linen, of blue, purple, and crimson yarns, with a design of cherubim worked into them. ²The length of each cloth shall be twenty-eight cubits, and the width of each cloth shall be four cubits, all the cloths to have the same measurements. ³Five of the cloths shall be joined to one another, and the other five cloths shall be joined to one another. ⁴Make loops of blue wool on the edge of the outermost cloth of the one set; and do likewise on the edge of the outermost cloth of the other set: ⁵make fifty loops on the one cloth, and fifty loops on the edge of the end cloth of the other set, the loops to be opposite one another. ⁶And make fifty gold clasps, and couple the cloths to one another with the clasps, so that the Tabernacle becomes one whole.

⁷You shall then make cloths of goats' hair for a tent over the Tabernacle; make the cloths eleven in number. ⁸The length of each cloth shall be thirty cubits, and the width of each cloth shall be four cubits, the eleven cloths to have the same measurements. ⁹Join five of the cloths by themselves, and the other six cloths by themselves; and fold over the sixth cloth at the front of the tent. ¹⁰Make fifty loops on the edge of the outermost cloth of the one set, and fifty loops on the edge of the cloth of the other set. ¹¹Make fifty copper clasps, and fit the clasps into the loops, and couple the tent together so that it becomes one whole. ¹²As for the overlapping excess of the cloths of the tent, the extra half-cloth shall overlap the back of the Tabernacle, ¹³while the extra cubit at either end of each length of tent cloth shall hang down to the bottom of the two sides of the Tabernacle and cover it. ¹⁴And make for the tent a covering of tanned ram skins, and a covering of dolphin skins above.

¹⁵You shall make the planks for the Tabernacle of acacia wood, upright. ¹⁶The length of each plank shall be ten cubits and the width of each plank a cubit and a half. ¹⁷Each plank shall have two tenons, parallel to each other; do the same with all the planks of the Tabernacle. ¹⁸Of the planks of the Tabernacle, make twenty planks on the south side: ¹⁹making forty silver sockets under the twenty planks, two sockets under the one plank for its two tenons and two sockets under each following plank for its two tenons; ²⁰and for the other side wall of the Tabernacle, on the north side, twenty planks, ²¹with their forty silver sockets, two sockets under the one plank and two sockets under each following plank. ²²And for the rear of the Tabernacle, to the west, make six planks; ²³and make two planks for the corners of the Tabernacle at the rear. ²⁴They shall match at the bottom, and terminate alike at the top inside one ring; thus shall it be with both of them: they shall form the two corners. ²⁵Thus there shall be eight planks with their sockets of silver: sixteen sockets, two sockets under the first plank, and two sockets under each of the other planks.

²⁶You shall make bars of acacia wood: five for the planks of the one side wall of the Tabernacle, ²⁷five bars for the planks of the other side wall of the Tabernacle, and five bars for the planks of the wall of the Tabernacle at the rear to the west.

²⁸The center bar halfway up the planks shall run from end to end. ²⁹Overlay the planks with gold, and make their rings of gold, as holders for the bars; and overlay the bars with gold. ³⁰Then set up the Tabernacle according to the manner of it that you were shown on the mountain.

³¹You shall make a curtain of blue, purple, and crimson yarns, and fine twisted linen; it shall have a design of cherubim worked into it. ³²Hang it upon four posts of acacia wood overlaid with gold and having hooks of gold, [set] in four sockets of silver. ³³Hang the curtain under the clasps, and carry the Ark of the Pact there, behind the curtain, so that the curtain shall serve you as a partition between the Holy and the Holy of Holies. ³⁴Place the cover upon the Ark of the Pact in the Holy of Holies. ³⁵Place the table outside the curtain, and the lamp-stand by the south wall of the Tabernacle opposite the table, which is to be placed by the north wall.

³⁶You shall make a screen for the entrance of the Tent, of blue, purple, and crimson yarns, and fine twisted linen, done in embroidery. ³⁷Make five posts of acacia wood for the screen and overlay them with gold—their hooks being of gold—and cast for them five sockets of copper.

27 ¹You shall make the altar of acacia wood, five cubits long and five cubits wide—the altar is to be square—and three cubits high. ²Make its horns on the four corners, the horns to be of one piece with it; and overlay it with copper. ³Make the pails for removing its ashes, as well as its scrapers, basins, flesh hooks, and fire pans—make all its utensils of copper. ⁴Make for it a grating of meshwork in copper; and on the mesh make four copper rings at its four corners. ⁵Set the mesh below, under the ledge of the altar, so that it extends to the middle of the altar. ⁶And make poles for the altar, poles of acacia wood, and overlay them with copper. ⁷The poles shall be inserted into the rings, so that the poles remain on the two sides of the altar when it is carried. ⁸Make it hollow, of boards. As you were shown on the mountain, so shall they be made.

⁹You shall make the enclosure of the Tabernacle: On the south side, a hundred cubits of hangings of fine twisted linen for the length of the enclosure on that side—¹⁰with its twenty posts and their twenty sockets of copper, the hooks and bands of the posts to be of silver.

¹¹Again a hundred cubits of hangings for its length along the north side—with its twenty posts and their twenty sockets of copper, the hooks and bands of the posts to be of silver. ¹²For the width of the enclosure, on the west side, fifty cubits of hangings, with their ten posts and their ten sockets. ¹³For the width of the enclosure on the front, or east side, fifty cubits: ¹⁴fifteen cubits of hangings on the one flank, with their three posts and their three sockets; ¹⁵fifteen cubits of hangings on the other flank, with their three posts and their three sockets; ¹⁶and for the gate of the enclosure, a screen of twenty cubits, of blue, purple, and crimson yarns, and fine twisted linen, done in embroidery, with their four posts and their four sockets.

¹⁷All the posts round the enclosure shall be banded with silver and their hooks shall be of silver; their sockets shall be of copper. ¹⁸The length of the enclosure shall be a hundred cubits, and the width fifty throughout; and the height five cubits—[with hangings] of fine twisted linen. The sockets shall be of copper: ¹⁹all the utensils of the Tabernacle, for all its service, as well as all its pegs and all the pegs of the court, shall be of copper.

²⁰You shall further instruct the Israelites to bring you clear oil of beaten olives for lighting, for kindling lamps regularly. ²¹Aaron and his sons shall set them up in the Tent of Meeting, outside the curtain which is over [the Ark of] the Pact,

[to burn] from evening to morning before יהוה. It shall be a due from the Israelites for all time, throughout the ages.

28 ¹You shall bring forward your brother Aaron, with his sons, from among the Israelites, to serve Me as priests: Aaron, Nadab and Abihu, Eleazar and Ithamar, the sons of Aaron. ²Make sacral vestments for your brother Aaron, for dignity and adornment. ³Next you shall instruct all who are skillful, whom I have endowed with the gift of skill, to make Aaron's vestments, for consecrating him to serve Me as priest. ⁴These are the vestments they are to make: a breast-piece, an ephod, a robe, a fringed tunic, a headdress, and a sash. They shall make those sacral vestments for your brother Aaron and his sons, for priestly service to Me; ⁵they, therefore, shall receive the gold, the blue, purple, and crimson yarns, and the fine linen.

⁶They shall make the ephod of gold, of blue, purple, and crimson yarns, and of fine twisted linen, worked into designs. ⁷It shall have two shoulder-pieces attached; they shall be attached at its two ends. ⁸And the decorated band that is upon it shall be made like it, of one piece with it: of gold, of blue, purple, and crimson yarns, and of fine twisted linen. ⁹Then take two lazuli stones and engrave on them the names of the sons of Israel: ¹⁰six of their names on the one stone, and the names of the remaining six on the other stone, in the order of their birth. ¹¹On the two stones you shall make seal engravings—the work of a lapidary—of the names of the sons of Israel. Having bordered them with frames of gold, ¹²attach the two stones to the shoulder-pieces of the ephod, as stones for remembrance of the Israelite people, whose names Aaron shall carry upon his two shoulder-pieces for remembrance before יהוה.

¹³Then make frames of gold ¹⁴and two chains of pure gold; braid these like corded work, and fasten the corded chains to the frames.

¹⁵You shall make a breast-piece of decision, worked into a design; make it in the style of the ephod: make it of gold, of blue, purple, and crimson yarns, and of fine twisted linen. ¹⁶It shall be square and doubled, a span in length and a span in width. ¹⁷Set in it mounted stones, in four rows of stones. The first row shall be a row of carnelian, chrysolite, and emerald; ¹⁸the second row: a turquoise, a sapphire, and an amethyst; ¹⁹the third row: a jacinth, an agate, and a crystal; ²⁰and the fourth row: a beryl, a lapis lazuli, and a jasper. They shall be framed with gold in their mountings. ²¹The stones shall correspond [in number] to the names of the sons of Israel: twelve, corresponding to their names. They shall be engraved like seals, each with its name, for the twelve tribes.

²²On the breast-piece make braided chains of corded work in pure gold. ²³Make two rings of gold on the breast-piece, and fasten the two rings at the two ends of the breast-piece, ²⁴attaching the two golden cords to the two rings at the ends of the breast-piece. ²⁵Then fasten the two ends of the cords to the two frames, which you shall attach to the shoulder-pieces of the ephod, at the front. ²⁶Make two rings of gold and attach them to the two ends of the breast-piece, at its inner edge, which faces the ephod. ²⁷And make two other rings of gold and fasten them on the front of the ephod, low on the two shoulder-pieces, close to its seam above the decorated band. ²⁸The breast-piece shall be held in place by a cord of blue from its rings to the rings of the ephod, so that the breast-piece rests on the decorated band and does not come loose from the ephod. ²⁹Aaron shall carry the names of the sons of Israel on the breast-piece of decision over his heart, when he enters the sanctuary, for remembrance before יהוה at all times. ³⁰Inside the breast-piece of decision you

shall place the Urim and Thummim, so that they are over Aaron's heart when he comes before יהוה. Thus Aaron shall carry the instrument of decision for the Israelites over his heart before יהוה at all times.

³¹You shall make the robe of the ephod of pure blue. ³²The opening for the head shall be in the middle of it; the opening shall have a binding of woven work round about—it shall be like the opening of a coat of mail—so that it does not tear. ³³On its hem make pomegranates of blue, purple, and crimson yarns, all around the hem, with bells of gold between them all around: ³⁴a golden bell and a pomegranate, a golden bell and a pomegranate, all around the hem of the robe. ³⁵Aaron shall wear it while officiating, so that the sound of it is heard when he comes into the sanctuary before יהוה and when he goes out—that he may not die.

³⁶You shall make a frontlet of pure gold and engrave on it the seal inscription: "Holy to יהוה." ³⁷Suspend it on a cord of blue, so that it may remain on the headdress; it shall remain on the front of the headdress. ³⁸It shall be on Aaron's forehead, that Aaron may take away any sin arising from the holy things that the Israelites consecrate, from any of their sacred donations; it shall be on his forehead at all times, to win acceptance for them before יהוה.

³⁹You shall make the fringed tunic of fine linen.
You shall make the headdress of fine linen.
You shall make the sash of embroidered work.

⁴⁰And for Aaron's sons also you shall make tunics, and make sashes for them, and make turbans for them, for dignity and adornment. ⁴¹Put these on your brother Aaron and on his sons as well; anoint them and ordain them and consecrate them to serve Me as priests.

⁴²You shall also make for them linen breeches to cover their nakedness; they shall extend from the hips to the thighs. ⁴³They shall be worn by Aaron and his sons when they enter the Tent of Meeting or when they approach the altar to officiate in the sanctuary, so that they do not incur punishment and die. It shall be a law for all time for him and for his offspring to come.

29 ¹This is what you shall do to them in consecrating them to serve Me as priests: Take a young bull of the herd and two rams without blemish; ²also unleavened bread, unleavened cakes with oil mixed in, and unleavened wafers spread with oil—make these of choice wheat flour. ³Place these in one basket and present them in the basket, along with the bull and the two rams. ⁴Lead Aaron and his sons up to the entrance of the Tent of Meeting, and wash them with water. ⁵Then take the vestments, and clothe Aaron with the tunic, the robe of the ephod, the ephod, and the breast-piece, and gird him with the decorated band of the ephod. ⁶Put the headdress on his head, and place the holy diadem upon the headdress. ⁷Take the anointing oil and pour it on his head and anoint him. ⁸Then bring his sons forward; clothe them with tunics ⁹and wind turbans upon them. And gird both Aaron and his sons with sashes. And so they shall have priesthood as their right for all time.

You shall then ordain Aaron and his sons. ¹⁰Lead the bull up to the front of the Tent of Meeting, and let Aaron and his sons lay their hands upon the head of the bull. ¹¹Slaughter the bull before יהוה, at the entrance of the Tent of Meeting, ¹²and take some of the bull's blood and put it on the horns of the altar with your finger; then pour out the rest of the blood at the base of the altar. ¹³Take all the fat that covers the entrails, the protuberance on the liver, and the two kidneys with the fat on them, and turn them into smoke upon the altar. ¹⁴The rest of the flesh of the bull, its hide, and its dung shall be put to the fire outside the camp; it is a sin offering.

¹⁵Next take the one ram, and let Aaron and his sons lay their hands upon the ram's head. ¹⁶Slaughter the ram, and take its blood and dash it against all sides of the altar. ¹⁷Cut up the ram into sections, wash its entrails and legs, and put them with its quarters and its head. ¹⁸Turn all of the ram into smoke upon the altar. It is a burnt offering to יהוה, a pleasing odor, an offering by fire to יהוה.

¹⁹Then take the other ram, and let Aaron and his sons lay their hands upon the ram's head. ²⁰Slaughter the ram, and take some of its blood and put it on the ridge of Aaron's right ear and on the ridges of his sons' right ears, and on the thumbs of their right hands, and on the big toes of their right feet; and dash the rest of the blood against every side of the altar round about. ²¹Take some of the blood that is on the altar and some of the anointing oil and sprinkle upon Aaron and his vestments, and also upon his sons and his sons' vestments. Thus shall he and his vestments be holy, as well as his sons and his sons' vestments.

²²You shall take from the ram the fat parts—the broad tail, the fat that covers the entrails, the protuberance on the liver, the two kidneys with the fat on them, and the right thigh; for this is a ram of ordination. ²³Add one flat loaf of bread, one cake of oil bread, and one wafer, from the basket of unleavened bread that is before יהוה. ²⁴Place all these on the palms of Aaron and his sons, and offer them as an elevation offering before יהוה. ²⁵Take them from their hands and turn them into smoke upon the altar with the burnt offering, as a pleasing odor before יהוה; it is an offering by fire to יהוה.

²⁶Then take the breast of Aaron's ram of ordination and offer it as an elevation offering before יהוה; it shall be your portion. ²⁷You shall consecrate the breast that was offered as an elevation offering and the thigh that was offered as a gift offering from the ram of ordination—from that which was Aaron's and from that which was his sons'—²⁸and those parts shall be a due for all time from the Israelites to Aaron and his descendants. For they are a gift; and so shall they be a gift from the Israelites, their gift to יהוה out of their sacrifices of wellbeing.

²⁹The sacral vestments of Aaron shall pass on to his sons after him, for them to be anointed and ordained in. ³⁰He among his sons who becomes priest in his stead, who enters the Tent of Meeting to officiate within the sanctuary, shall wear them seven days.

³¹You shall take the ram of ordination and boil its flesh in the sacred precinct; ³²and Aaron and his sons shall eat the flesh of the ram, and the bread that is in the basket, at the entrance of the Tent of Meeting. ³³These things shall be eaten only by those for whom expiation was made with them when they were ordained and consecrated; they may not be eaten by a lay person, for they are holy. ³⁴And if any of the flesh of ordination, or any of the bread, is left until morning, you shall put what is left to the fire; it shall not be eaten, for it is holy.

³⁵Thus you shall do to Aaron and his sons, just as I have commanded you. You shall ordain them through seven days, ³⁶and each day you shall prepare a bull as a sin offering for expiation; you shall purge the altar by performing purification upon it, and you shall anoint it to consecrate it. ³⁷Seven days you shall perform purification for the altar to consecrate it, and the altar shall become most holy; whatever touches the altar shall become consecrated.

³⁸Now this is what you shall offer upon the altar: two yearling lambs each day, regularly. ³⁹You shall offer the one lamb in the morning, and you shall offer the other lamb at twilight. ⁴⁰There shall be a tenth of a measure of choice flour with a quarter of a *hin* of beaten oil mixed in, and a libation of a quarter *hin* of wine for one lamb; ⁴¹and you shall offer the other lamb at twilight, repeating with it the

meal offering of the morning with its libation—an offering by fire for a pleasing odor to יהוה, [42]a regular burnt offering throughout the generations, at the entrance of the Tent of Meeting before יהוה.

For there I will meet with you, and there I will speak with you, [43]and there I will meet with the Israelites, and it shall be sanctified by My Presence. [44]I will sanctify the Tent of Meeting and the altar, and I will consecrate Aaron and his sons to serve Me as priests. [45]I will abide among the Israelites, and I will be their God. [46]And they shall know that I יהוה am their God, who brought them out from the land of Egypt that I might abide among them—I, their God יהוה.

30 [1]You shall make an altar for burning incense; make it of acacia wood. [2]It shall be a cubit long and a cubit wide—it shall be square—and two cubits high, its horns of one piece with it. [3]Overlay it with pure gold: its top, its sides round about, and its horns; and make a gold molding for it round about. [4]And make two gold rings for it under its molding; make them on its two side walls, on opposite sides. They shall serve as holders for poles with which to carry it. [5]Make the poles of acacia wood, and overlay them with gold.

[6]Place it in front of the curtain that is over the Ark of the Pact—in front of the cover that is over the Pact—where I will meet with you. [7]On it Aaron shall burn aromatic incense: he shall burn it every morning when he tends the lamps, [8]and Aaron shall burn it at twilight when he lights the lamps—a regular incense offering before יהוה throughout the ages. [9]You shall not offer alien incense on it, or a burnt offering or a meal offering; neither shall you pour a libation on it. [10]Once a year Aaron shall perform purification upon its horns with blood of the sin offering of purification; purification shall be performed upon it once a year throughout the ages. It is most holy to יהוה.

[11]יהוה spoke to Moses, saying: [12]When you take a census of the Israelite men according to their army enrollment, each shall pay יהוה a ransom for himself on being enrolled, that no plague may come upon them through their being enrolled. [13]This is what everyone who is entered in the records shall pay: a half-shekel by the sanctuary weight—twenty *gerahs* to the shekel—a half-shekel as an offering to יהוה. [14]Everyone who is entered in the records, from the age of twenty years up, shall give יהוה's offering. [15]the rich shall not pay more and the poor shall not pay less than half a shekel when giving יהוה's offering as expiation for your persons. [16]You shall take the expiation money from the Israelites and assign it to the service of the Tent of Meeting; it shall serve the Israelites as a reminder before יהוה, as expiation for your persons.

[17]יהוה spoke to Moses, saying: [18]Make a laver of copper and a stand of copper for it, for washing; and place it between the Tent of Meeting and the altar. Put water in it, [19]and let Aaron and his sons wash their hands and feet [in water drawn] from it. [20]When they enter the Tent of Meeting they shall wash with water, that they may not die; or when they approach the altar to serve, to turn into smoke an offering by fire to יהוה, [21]they shall wash their hands and feet, that they may not die. It shall be a law for all time for them—for him and his offspring—throughout the ages.

[22]יהוה spoke to Moses, saying: [23]Next take choice spices: five hundred weight of solidified myrrh, half as much—two hundred and fifty—of fragrant cinnamon, two hundred and fifty of aromatic cane, [24]five hundred—by the sanctuary weight—of cassia, and a *hin* of olive oil. [25]Make of this a sacred anointing oil, a compound of ingredients expertly blended, to serve as sacred anointing oil. [26]With it anoint the Tent of Meeting, the Ark of the Pact, [27]the table and all its utensils, the lamp-stand and all its fittings, the altar of

incense, [28]the altar of burnt offering and all its utensils, and the laver and its stand. [29]Thus you shall consecrate them so that they may be most holy; whatever touches them shall be consecrated. [30]You shall also anoint Aaron and his sons, consecrating them to serve Me as priests.

[31]And speak to the Israelite people, as follows: This shall be an anointing oil sacred to Me throughout the ages. [32]It must not be rubbed on any person's body, and you must not make anything like it in the same proportions; it is sacred, to be held sacred by you. [33]Whoever compounds its like, or puts any of it on a lay person, shall be cut off from kin.

[34]And יהוה said to Moses: Take the herbs stacte, onycha, and galbanum—these herbs together with pure frankincense; let there be an equal part of each. [35]Make them into incense, a compound expertly blended, refined, pure, sacred. [36]Beat some of it into powder, and put some before the Pact in the Tent of Meeting, where I will meet with you; it shall be most holy to you. [37]But when you make this incense, you must not make any in the same proportions for yourselves; it shall be held by you sacred to יהוה. [38]Whoever makes any like it, to smell of it, shall be cut off from kin.

31 [1]יהוה spoke to Moses: [2]See, I have singled out by name Bezalel son of Uri son of Hur, of the tribe of Judah. [3]I have endowed him with a divine spirit of skill, ability, and knowledge in every kind of craft; [4]to make designs for work in gold, silver, and copper, [5]to cut stones for setting and to carve wood—to work in every kind of craft. [6]Moreover, I have assigned to him Oholiab son of Ahisamach, of the tribe of Dan; and I have also granted skill to all who are skillful, that they may make everything that I have commanded you: [7]the Tent of Meeting, the Ark for the Pact and the cover upon it, and all the furnishings of the Tent; [8]the table and its utensils, the pure lamp-stand and all its fittings, and the altar of incense; [9]the altar of burnt offering and all its utensils, and the laver and its stand; [10]the service vestments, the sacral vestments of Aaron the priest and the vestments of his sons, for their service as priests; [11]as well as the anointing oil and the aromatic incense for the sanctuary. Just as I have commanded you, they shall do.

[12]And יהוה said to Moses: [13]Speak to the Israelite people and say: Nevertheless, you must keep My sabbaths, for this is a sign between Me and you throughout the ages, that you may know that I יהוה have consecrated you. [14]You shall keep the sabbath, for it is holy for you. One who profanes it shall be put to death: whoever does work on it, that person shall be cut off from among kin. [15]Six days may work be done, but on the seventh day there shall be a sabbath of complete rest, holy to יהוה; whoever does work on the sabbath day shall be put to death. [16]The Israelite people shall keep the sabbath, observing the sabbath throughout the ages as a covenant for all time: [17]it shall be a sign for all time between Me and the people of Israel. For in six days יהוה made heaven and earth, and on the seventh day [God] ceased from work and was refreshed.

[18]Upon finishing speaking with him on Mount Sinai, [God] gave Moses the two tablets of the Pact, stone tablets inscribed with the finger of God.

32 [1]When the people saw that Moses was so long in coming down from the mountain, the people gathered against Aaron and said to him, "Come, make us a god who shall go before us, for that fellow Moses—the leader who brought us from the land of Egypt—we do not know what has happened to him." [2]Aaron said to them, "[You men,] take off the gold rings that are on the ears of your wives, your sons, and your daughters, and bring them to me." [3]And all the people took off the gold rings that were in their ears and brought them to Aaron. 4This he took from them and cast in a mold, and made it into a molten calf. And they exclaimed, "This is your god, O Israel, who brought you out of the land of Egypt!" 5When Aaron saw this, he built an altar before it; and Aaron announced: "Tomorrow shall be a festival of יהוה." 6Early next day, the people offered up burnt offerings and brought sacrifices of wellbeing; they sat down to eat and drink, and then rose to dance.

7יהוה spoke to Moses, "Hurry down, for your people, whom you brought out of the land of Egypt, have acted basely. 8They have been quick to turn aside from the way that I enjoined upon them. They have made themselves a molten calf and bowed low to it and sacrificed to it, saying: 'This is your god, O Israel, who brought you out of the land of Egypt!'"

9יהוה further said to Moses, "I see that this is a stiff-necked people. 10Now, let Me be, that My anger may blaze forth against them and that I may destroy them, and make of you a great nation." 11But Moses implored his God יהוה, saying, "Let not Your anger, יהוה, blaze forth against Your people, whom You delivered from the land of Egypt with great power and with a mighty hand. 12Let not the Egyptians say, 'It was with evil intent that he delivered them, only to kill them off in the mountains and annihilate them from the face of the earth.' Turn from Your blazing anger, and renounce the plan to punish Your people. 13Remember Your servants, Abraham, Isaac, and Israel, how You swore to them by Your Self and said to them: I will make your offspring as numerous as the stars of heaven, and I will give to your offspring this whole land of which I spoke, to possess forever." 14And יהוה renounced the punishment planned for God's people.

15Thereupon Moses turned and went down from the mountain bearing the two tablets of the Pact, tablets inscribed on both their surfaces: they were inscribed on the one side and on the other. 16The tablets were God's work, and the writing was God's writing, incised upon the tablets. 17When Joshua heard the sound of the people in its boisterousness, he said to Moses, "There is a cry of war in the camp." 18But he answered,

"It is not the sound of the tune of triumph,
Or the sound of the tune of defeat;
It is the sound of song that I hear!"

19As soon as Moses came near the camp and saw the calf and the dancing, he became enraged; and he hurled the tablets from his hands and shattered them at the foot of the mountain. 20He took the calf that they had made and burned it; he ground it to powder and strewed it upon the water and so made the Israelites drink it.

21Moses said to Aaron, "What did this people do to you that you have brought such great sin upon them?" 22Aaron said, "Let not my lord be enraged. You know that this people is bent on evil. 23They said to me, 'Make us a god to lead us; for that fellow Moses—the leader who brought us from the land of Egypt—we do not know what has happened to him.' 24So I said to them, 'Whoever has gold, take it off!' They gave it to me and I hurled it into the fire and out came this calf!"

25Moses saw that the people were out of control—since Aaron had let them get out of control—so that they were a menace to any who might oppose them. 26Moses stood up in the gate of the camp and said, "Whoever is for יהוה, come here!" And all the men of Levi rallied to him. 27He said to them, "Thus says יהוה, the God of Israel: Each of you put sword on thigh, go back and forth from gate to gate throughout the camp, and slay sibling, neighbor, and kin." 28The men of Levi did as Moses had bidden; and some three thousand of the people fell that day. 29And Moses said, "Dedicate yourselves

to יהוה this day—for each of you has been against blood relations—that [God] may bestow a blessing upon you today."

30The next day Moses said to the people, "You have been guilty of a great sin. Yet I will now go up to יהוה; perhaps I may win forgiveness for your sin." 31Moses went back to יהוה and said, "Alas, this people is guilty of a great sin in making for themselves a god of gold. 32Now, if You will forgive their sin [well and good]; but if not, erase me from the record which You have written!" 33But יהוה said to Moses, "Only one who has sinned against Me will I erase from My record. 34Go now, lead the people where I told you. See, My messenger shall go before you. But when I make an accounting, I will bring them to account for their sins." 35Then יהוה sent a plague upon the people, for what they did with the calf that Aaron made.

33 1Then יהוה said to Moses, "Set out from here, you and the people that you have brought up from the land of Egypt, to the land of which I swore to Abraham, Isaac, and Jacob, saying, 'To your offspring will I give it'—2I will send a messenger before you, and I will drive out the Canaanites, the Amorites, the Hittites, the Perizzites, the Hivites, and the Jebusites—3a land flowing with milk and honey. But I will not go in your midst, since you are a stiff-necked people, lest I destroy you on the way."

4When the people heard this harsh word, they went into mourning, and none put on finery. 5יהוה said to Moses, "Say to the Israelite people, 'You are a stiff-necked people. If I were to go in your midst for one moment, I would destroy you. Now, then, leave off your finery, and I will consider what to do to you.'" 6So the Israelites remained stripped of the finery from Mount Horeb on.

7Now Moses would take the Tent and pitch it outside the camp, at some distance from the camp. It was called the Tent of Meeting, and whoever sought יהוה would go out to the Tent of Meeting that was outside the camp. 8Whenever Moses went out to the Tent, all the people would rise and stand, at the entrance of each tent, and gaze after Moses until he had entered the Tent. 9And when Moses entered the Tent, the pillar of cloud would descend and stand at the entrance of the Tent, while [God] spoke with Moses. 10When all the people saw the pillar of cloud poised at the entrance of the Tent, all the people would rise and bow low, at the entrance of each tent. 11יהוה would speak to Moses face to face, as one person speaks to another. And he would then return to the camp; but his attendant, Joshua son of Nun, [serving as] deputy, would not stir out of the Tent.

12Moses said to יהוה, "See, You say to me, 'Lead this people forward,' but You have not made known to me whom You will send with me. Further, You have said, 'I have singled you out by name, and you have, indeed, gained My favor.' 13Now, if I have truly gained Your favor, pray let me know Your ways, that I may know You and continue in Your favor. Consider, too, that this nation is Your people." 14And [God] said, "I will go in the lead and will lighten your burden." 15And he replied, "Unless You go in the lead, do not make us leave this place. 16For how shall it be known that Your people have gained Your favor unless You go with us, so that we may be distinguished, Your people and I, from every people on the face of the earth?"

17And יהוה said to Moses, "I will also do this thing that you have asked; for you have truly gained My favor and I have singled you out by name." 18He said, "Oh, let me behold Your Presence!" 19And [God] answered, "I will make all My goodness pass before you, and I will proclaim before you the name יהוה, and the grace that I grant and the compassion that I show," 20continuing, "But you cannot see My face, for a human being may not see Me and live." ²¹And יהוה said, "See, there is a place near Me. Station yourself on the rock ²²and, as My Presence passes by, I will put you in a cleft of the rock and shield you with My hand until I have passed by. ²³Then I will take My hand away and you will see My back; but My face must not be seen."

34 ¹יהוה said to Moses: "Carve two tablets of stone like the first, and I will inscribe upon the tablets the words that were on the first tablets, which you shattered. ²Be ready by morning, and in the morning come up to Mount Sinai and present yourself there to Me, on the top of the mountain. ³No one else shall come up with you, and no one else shall be seen anywhere on the mountain; neither shall the flocks and the herds graze at the foot of this mountain."

⁴So Moses carved two tablets of stone, like the first, and early in the morning he went up on Mount Sinai, as יהוה had commanded him, taking the two stone tablets with him. ⁵יהוה came down in a cloud—and stood with him there, proclaiming the name יהוה. ⁶יהוה passed before him and proclaimed: "יהוה! יהוה! a God compassionate and gracious, slow to anger, abounding in kindness and faithfulness, ⁷extending kindness to the thousandth generation, forgiving iniquity, transgression, and sin—yet not remitting all punishment, but visiting the iniquity of parents upon children and children's children, upon the third and fourth generations."

⁸Moses hastened to bow low to the ground in homage, ⁹and said, "If I have gained Your favor, O my lord, pray, let my lord go in our midst, even though this is a stiff-necked people. Pardon our iniquity and our sin, and take us for Your own!"

¹⁰[God] said: I hereby make a covenant. Before all your people I will work such wonders as have not been wrought on all the earth or in any nation; and all the people who are with you shall see how awesome are יהוה's deeds which I will perform for you. ¹¹Mark well what I command you this day. I will drive out before you the Amorites, the Canaanites, the Hittites, the Perizzites, the Hivites, and the Jebusites. ¹²Beware of making a covenant with the inhabitants of the land against which you are advancing, lest they be a snare in your midst. ¹³No, you must tear down their altars, smash their pillars, and cut down their sacred posts; ¹⁴for you must not worship any other god, because יהוה, whose name is Impassioned, is an impassioned God. ¹⁵You must not make a covenant with the inhabitants of the land, for they will lust after their gods and sacrifice to their gods and invite you, and you will eat of their sacrifices. ¹⁶And when you take [wives into your households] from among their daughters for your sons, their daughters will lust after their gods and will cause your sons to lust after their gods.

¹⁷You shall not make molten gods for yourselves.

¹⁸You shall observe the Feast of Unleavened Bread—eating unleavened bread for seven days, as I have commanded you—at the set time of the month of Abib, for in the month of Abib you went forth from Egypt.

¹⁹Every first issue of the womb is Mine, from all your livestock that drop a male as firstling, whether cattle or sheep. ²⁰But the firstling of an ass you shall redeem with a sheep; if you do not redeem it, you must break its neck. And you must redeem every male firstborn among your children.

None shall appear before Me empty-handed.

²¹Six days you shall work, but on the seventh day you shall cease from labor; you shall cease from labor even at plowing time and harvest time.

²²You shall observe the Feast of Weeks, of the first fruits of the wheat harvest; and the Feast of Ingathering at the turn of the year. ²³Three times a year all your males shall appear before the Sovereign יהוה, the God of Israel. ²⁴I will drive

out nations from your path and enlarge your territory; no one will covet your land when you go up to appear before your God יהוה three times a year.

²⁵You shall not offer the blood of My sacrifice with anything leavened; and the sacrifice of the Feast of Passover shall not be left lying until morning.

²⁶The choice first fruits of your soil you shall bring to the house of your God יהוה.

You shall not boil a kid in its mother's milk.

²⁷And יהוה said to Moses: Write down these commandments, for in accordance with these commandments I make a covenant with you and with Israel.

²⁸And he was there with יהוה forty days and forty nights; he ate no bread and drank no water; and he wrote down on the tablets the terms of the covenant, the Ten Commandments.

²⁹So Moses came down from Mount Sinai. And as Moses came down from the mountain bearing the two tablets of the Pact, Moses was not aware that the skin of his face was radiant, since he had spoken with God. ³⁰Aaron and all the Israelites saw that the skin of Moses' face was radiant; and they shrank from coming near him. ³¹But Moses called to them, and Aaron and all the chieftains in the assembly returned to him, and Moses spoke to them. ³²Afterward all the Israelites came near, and he instructed them concerning all that יהוה had imparted to him on Mount Sinai. ³³And when Moses had finished speaking with them, he put a veil over his face.

³⁴Whenever Moses went in before יהוה to converse, he would leave the veil off until he came out; and when he came out and told the Israelites what he had been commanded, ³⁵the Israelites would see how radiant the skin of Moses' face was. Moses would then put the veil back over his face until he went in to speak with God.

35 ¹Moses then convoked the whole Israelite community and said to them:

These are the things that יהוה has commanded you to do: ²On six days work may be done, but on the seventh day you shall have a sabbath of complete rest, holy to יהוה; whoever does any work on it shall be put to death. ³You shall kindle no fire throughout your settlements on the sabbath day.

⁴Moses said further to the whole community of Israelites: This is what יהוה has commanded: ⁵Take from among you gifts to יהוה; everyone whose heart is so moved shall bring them—gifts for יהוה: gold, silver, and copper; ⁶blue, purple, and crimson yarns, fine linen, and goats' hair; ⁷tanned ram skins, dolphin skins, and acacia wood; ⁸oil for lighting, spices for the anointing oil and for the aromatic incense; ⁹lapis lazuli and other stones for setting, for the ephod and the breast-piece.

¹⁰And let all among you who are skilled come and make all that יהוה has commanded: ¹¹the Tabernacle, its tent and its covering, its clasps and its planks, its bars, its posts, and its sockets; ¹²the ark and its poles, the cover, and the curtain for the screen; ¹³the table, and its poles and all its utensils; and the bread of display; ¹⁴the lamp-stand for lighting, its furnishings and its lamps, and the oil for lighting; ¹⁵the altar of incense and its poles; the anointing oil and the aromatic incense; and the entrance screen for the entrance of the Tabernacle; ¹⁶the altar of burnt offering, its copper grating, its poles, and all its furnishings; the laver and its stand; ¹⁷the hangings of the enclosure, its posts and its sockets, and the screen for the gate of the court; ¹⁸the pegs for the Tabernacle, the pegs for the enclosure, and their cords; ¹⁹the service vestments for officiating in the sanctuary, the sacral vestments of Aaron the priest and the vestments of his sons for priestly service.

²⁰So the whole community of the Israelites left Moses' presence. ²¹And everyone who excelled in ability and everyone

whose spirit was moved came, bringing to יהוה an offering for the work of the Tent of Meeting and for all its service and for the sacral vestments. 22Men and women, all whose hearts moved them, all who would make an elevation offering of gold to יהוה, came bringing brooches, earrings, rings, and pendants—gold objects of all kinds. 23And everyone who possessed blue, purple, and crimson yarns, fine linen, goats' hair, tanned ram skins, and dolphin skins, brought them; 24everyone who would make gifts of silver or copper brought them as gifts for יהוה; and everyone who possessed acacia wood for any work of the service brought that. 25And all the skilled women spun with their own hands, and brought what they had spun, in blue, purple, and crimson yarns, and in fine linen. 26And all the women who excelled in that skill spun the goats' hair. 27And the chieftains brought lapis lazuli and other stones for setting, for the ephod and for the breast-piece; 28and spices and oil for lighting, for the anointing oil, and for the aromatic incense. 29Thus the Israelites, all the men and women whose hearts moved them to bring anything for the work that יהוה, through Moses, had commanded to be done, brought it as a freewill offering to יהוה.

30And Moses said to the Israelites: See, יהוה has singled out by name Bezalel, son of Uri son of Hur, of the tribe of Judah, 31endowing him with a divine spirit of skill, ability, and knowledge in every kind of craft, 32and inspiring him to make designs for work in gold, silver, and copper, 33to cut stones for setting and to carve wood—to work in every kind of designer's craft—34and to give directions. He and Oholiab son of Ahisamach of the tribe of Dan 35have been endowed with the skill to do any work—of the carver, the designer, the embroiderer in blue, purple, crimson yarns, and in fine linen, and of the weaver—as workers in all crafts and as makers of designs.

36 1Let, then, Bezalel and Oholiab and all the skilled persons whom יהוה has endowed with skill and ability to perform expertly all the tasks connected with the service of the sanctuary carry out all that יהוה has commanded.

2Moses then called Bezalel and Oholiab, and every skilled person whom יהוה had endowed with skill, everyone who excelled in ability, to undertake the task and carry it out. 3They took over from Moses all the gifts that the Israelites had brought, to carry out the tasks connected with the service of the sanctuary. But when these continued to bring freewill offerings to him morning after morning, 4all the artisans who were engaged in the tasks of the sanctuary came, from the task upon which each one was engaged, 5and said to Moses, "The people are bringing more than is needed for the tasks entailed in the work that יהוה has commanded to be done." 6Moses thereupon had this proclamation made throughout the camp: "Let no man or woman make further effort toward gifts for the sanctuary!" So the people stopped bringing: 7their efforts had been more than enough for all the tasks to be done.

8Then all the skilled among those engaged in the work made the Tabernacle of ten strips of cloth, which they made of fine twisted linen, blue, purple, and crimson yarns; into these they worked a design of cherubim. 9The length of each cloth was twentyeight cubits, and the width of each cloth was four cubits, all cloths having the same measurements. 10They joined five of the cloths to one another, and they joined the other five cloths to one another. 11They made loops of blue wool on the edge of the outermost cloth of the one set, and did the same on the edge of the outermost cloth of the other set: 12they made fifty loops on the one cloth, and they made fifty loops on the edge of the end cloth of the other set, the loops being opposite one another. 13And they made fifty gold clasps and coupled the units to one another with the clasps, so that the Tabernacle became one whole.

14They made cloths of goats' hair for a tent over the Tabernacle; they made the cloths eleven in number. 15The length of each cloth was thirty cubits, and the width of each cloth was four cubits, the eleven cloths having the same measurements. 16They joined five of the cloths by themselves, and the other six cloths by themselves. 17They made fifty loops on the edge of the outermost cloth of the one set, and they made fifty loops on the edge of the end cloth of the other set. 18They made fifty copper clasps to couple the Tent together so that it might become one whole. 19And they made a covering of tanned ram skins for the tent, and a covering of dolphin skins above.

20They made the planks for the Tabernacle of acacia wood, upright. 21The length of each plank was ten cubits, the width of each plank a cubit and a half. 22Each plank had two tenons, parallel to each other; they did the same with all the planks of the Tabernacle. 23Of the planks of the Tabernacle, they made twenty planks for the south side, 24making forty silver sockets under the twenty planks, two sockets under one plank for its two tenons and two sockets under each following plank for its two tenons; 25and for the other side wall of the Tabernacle, the north side, twenty planks, 26with their forty silver sockets, two sockets under one plank and two sockets under each following plank. 27And for the rear of the Tabernacle, to the west, they made six planks; 28and they made two planks for the corners of the Tabernacle at the rear. 29They matched at the bottom, but terminated as one at the top into one ring; they did so with both of them at the two corners. 30Thus there were eight planks with their sockets of silver: sixteen sockets, two under each plank.

31They made bars of acacia wood, five for the planks of the one side wall of the Tabernacle, 32five bars for the planks of the other side wall of the Tabernacle, and five bars for the planks of the wall of the Tabernacle at the rear, to the west; 33they made the center bar to run, halfway up the planks, from end to end. 34They overlaid the planks with gold, and made their rings of gold, as holders for the bars; and they overlaid the bars with gold.

35They made the curtain of blue, purple, and crimson yarns, and fine twisted linen, working into it a design of cherubim. 36They made for it four posts of acacia wood and overlaid them with gold, with their hooks of gold; and they cast for them four silver sockets. 37They made the screen for the entrance of the Tent, of blue, purple, and crimson yarns, and fine twisted linen, done in embroidery; 38and five posts for it with their hooks. They overlaid their tops and their bands with gold; but the five sockets were of copper.

37 1Bezalel made the ark of acacia wood, two and a half cubits long, a cubit and a half wide, and a cubit and a half high. 2He overlaid it with pure gold, inside and out; and he made a gold molding for it round about. 3He cast four gold rings for it, for its four feet: two rings on one of its side walls and two rings on the other. 4He made poles of acacia wood, overlaid them with gold, 5and inserted the poles into the rings on the side walls of the ark for carrying the ark.

6He made a cover of pure gold, two and a half cubits long and a cubit and a half wide. 7He made two cherubim of gold; he made them of hammered work, at the two ends of the cover: 8one cherub at one end and the other cherub at the other end; he made the cherubim of one piece with the cover, at its two ends. 9The cherubim had their wings spread out above, shielding the cover with their wings. They faced each other; the faces of the cherubim were turned toward the cover.

¹⁰He made the table of acacia wood, two cubits long, one cubit wide, and a cubit and a half high; ¹¹he overlaid it with pure gold and made a gold molding around it. ¹²He made a rim of a hand's breadth around it and made a gold molding for its rim round about. ¹³He cast four gold rings for it and attached the rings to the four corners at its four legs. ¹⁴The rings were next to the rim, as holders for the poles to carry the table. ¹⁵He made the poles of acacia wood for carrying the table, and overlaid them with gold. ¹⁶The utensils that were to be upon the table—its bowls, ladles, jugs, and jars with which to offer libations—he made of pure gold.

¹⁷He made the lamp-stand of pure gold. He made the lamp-stand—its base and its shaft—of hammered work; its cups, calyxes, and petals were of one piece with it. ¹⁸Six branches issued from its sides: three branches from one side of the lamp-stand, and three branches from the other side of the lamp stand. ¹⁹There were three cups shaped like almond blossoms, each with calyx and petals, on one branch; and there were three cups shaped like almond blossoms, each with calyx and petals, on the next branch; so for all six branches issuing from the lamp-stand. ²⁰On the lamp-stand itself there were four cups shaped like almond blossoms, each with calyx and petals: ²¹a calyx, of one piece with it, under a pair of branches; and a calyx, of one piece with it, under the second pair of branches; and a calyx, of one piece with it, under the last pair of branches; so for all six branches issuing from it. ²²Their calyxes and their stems were of one piece with it, the whole of it a single hammered piece of pure gold. ²³He made its seven lamps, its tongs, and its fire pans of pure gold. ²⁴He made it and all its furnishings out of a talent of pure gold.

²⁵He made the incense altar of acacia wood, a cubit long and a cubit wide—square—and two cubits high; its horns were of one piece with it. ²⁶He overlaid it with pure gold: its top, its sides round about, and its horns; and he made a gold molding for it round about. ²⁷He made two gold rings for it under its molding, on its two walls—on opposite sides—as holders for the poles with which to carry it. ²⁸He made the poles of acacia wood, and overlaid them with gold. ²⁹He prepared the sacred anointing oil and the pure aromatic incense, expertly blended.

38 ¹He made the altar for burnt offering of acacia wood, five cubits long and five cubits wide—square—and three cubits high. ²He made horns for it on its four corners, the horns being of one piece with it; and he overlaid it with copper. ³He made all the utensils of the altar—the pails, the scrapers, the basins, the flesh hooks, and the fire pans; he made all these utensils of copper. ⁴He made for the altar a grating of meshwork in copper, extending below, under its ledge, to its middle. ⁵He cast four rings, at the four corners of the copper grating, as holders for the poles. ⁶He made the poles of acacia wood and overlaid them with copper; ⁷and he inserted the poles into the rings on the side walls of the altar, to carry it by them. He made it hollow, of boards.

⁸He made the laver of copper and its stand of copper, from the mirrors of the women who performed tasks at the entrance of the Tent of Meeting.

⁹He made the enclosure:

On the south-side, a hundred cubits of hangings of fine twisted linen for the enclosure—¹⁰with their twenty posts and their twenty sockets of copper, the hooks and bands of the posts being silver.

¹¹On the north side, a hundred cubits—with their twenty posts and their twenty sockets of copper, the hooks and bands of the posts being silver.

¹²On the west side, fifty cubits of hangings—with their ten posts and their ten sockets, the hooks and bands of the posts being silver.

¹³And on the front side, to the east, fifty cubits: ¹⁴fifteen cubits of hangings on the one flank, with their three posts and their three sockets, ¹⁵and fifteen cubits of hangings on the other flank—on each side of the gate of the enclosure—with their three posts and their three sockets.

¹⁶All the hangings around the enclosure were of fine twisted linen. ¹⁷The sockets for the posts were of copper, the hooks and bands of the posts were of silver, the overlay of their tops was of silver; all the posts of the enclosure were banded with silver.—¹⁸The screen of the gate of the enclosure, done in embroidery, was of blue, purple, and crimson yarns, and fine twisted linen. It was twenty cubits long. Its height—or width—was five cubits, like that of the hangings of the enclosure. ¹⁹The posts were four; their four sockets were of copper, their hooks of silver; and the overlay of their tops was of silver, as were also their bands.—²⁰All the pegs of the Tabernacle and of the enclosure round about were of copper.

²¹These are the records of the Tabernacle, the Tabernacle of the Pact, which were drawn up at Moses' bidding—the work of the Levites under the direction of Ithamar son of Aaron the priest. ²²Now Bezalel, son of Uri son of Hur, of the tribe of Judah, had made all that יהוה had commanded Moses; ²³at his side was Oholiab son of Ahisamach, of the tribe of Dan, carver and designer, and embroiderer in blue, purple, and crimson yarns and in fine linen.

²⁴All the gold that was used for the work, in all the work of the sanctuary—the elevation offering of gold—came to 29 talents and 730 shekels by the sanctuary weight. ²⁵The silver of those of the community who were recorded came to 100 talents and 1,775 shekels by the sanctuary weight: ²⁶a half-shekel a head, half a shekel by the sanctuary weight, for each one who was entered in the records, from the age of twenty years up, 603,550 men. ²⁷The 100 talents of silver were for casting the sockets of the sanctuary and the sockets for the curtain, 100 sockets to the 100 talents, a talent a socket. ²⁸And of the 1,775 shekels he made hooks for the posts, overlay for their tops, and bands around them.

²⁹The copper from the elevation offering came to 70 talents and 2,400 shekels. ³⁰Of it he made the sockets for the entrance of the Tent of Meeting; the copper altar and its copper grating and all the utensils of the altar; ³¹the sockets of the enclosure round about and the sockets of the gate of the enclosure; and all the pegs of the Tabernacle and all the pegs of the enclosure round about.

39 ¹Of the blue, purple, and crimson yarns they also made the service vestments for officiating in the sanctuary; they made Aaron's sacral vestments—as יהוה had commanded Moses.

²The ephod was made of gold, blue, purple, and crimson yarns, and fine twisted linen. ³They hammered out sheets of gold and cut threads to be worked into designs among the blue, the purple, and the crimson yarns, and the fine linen. ⁴They made for it attaching shoulder-pieces; they were attached at its two ends. ⁵The decorated band that was upon it was made like it, of one piece with it; of gold, blue, purple, and crimson yarns, and fine twisted linen—as יהוה had commanded Moses.

⁶They bordered the lazuli stones with frames of gold, engraved with seal engravings of the names of the sons of Israel. ⁷They were set on the shoulder-pieces of the ephod, as stones of remembrance for the Israelites—as יהוה had commanded Moses.

8The breast-piece was made in the style of the ephod: of gold, blue, purple, and crimson yarns, and fine twisted linen. 9It was square; they made the breast-piece doubled—a span in length and a span in width, doubled. 10They set in it four rows of stones. The first row was a row of carnelian, chrysolite, and emerald; 11the second row: a turquoise, a sapphire, and an amethyst; 12the third row: a jacinth, an agate, and a crystal; 13and the fourth row: a beryl, a lapis lazuli, and a jasper. They were encircled in their mountings with frames of gold. 14The stones corresponded [in number] to the names of the sons of Israel: twelve, corresponding to their names; engraved like seals, each with its name, for the twelve tribes.

15On the breast-piece they made braided chains of corded work in pure gold. 16They made two frames of gold and two rings of gold, and fastened the two rings at the two ends of the breast-piece, 17attaching the two golden cords to the two rings at the ends of the breast-piece. 18They then fastened the two ends of the cords to the two frames, attaching them to the shoulder-pieces of the ephod, at the front. 19They made two rings of gold and attached them to the two ends of the breast-piece, at its inner edge, which faced the ephod. 20They made two other rings of gold and fastened them on the front of the ephod, low on the two shoulder-pieces, close to its seam above the decorated band. 21The breast-piece was held in place by a cord of blue from its rings to the rings of the ephod, so that the breast-piece rested on the decorated band and did not come loose from the ephod—as יהוה had commanded Moses.

22The robe for the ephod was made of woven work, of pure blue. 23The opening of the robe, in the middle of it, was like the opening of a coat of mail, with a binding around the opening, so that it would not tear. 24On the hem of the robe they made pomegranates of blue, purple, and crimson yarns, twisted. 25They also made bells of pure gold, and attached the bells between the pomegranates, all around the hem of the robe, between the pomegranates: 26a bell and a pomegranate, a bell and a pomegranate, all around the hem of the robe for officiating in—as יהוה had commanded Moses.

27They made the tunics of fine linen, of woven work, for Aaron and his sons; 28and the headdress of fine linen, and the decorated turbans of fine linen, and the linen breeches of fine twisted linen; 29and sashes of fine twisted linen, blue, purple, and crimson yarns, done in embroidery—as יהוה had commanded Moses.

30They made the frontlet for the holy diadem of pure gold, and incised upon it the seal inscription: "Holy to יהוה." 31They attached to it a cord of blue to fix it upon the headdress above—as יהוה had commanded Moses.

32Thus was completed all the work of the Tabernacle of the Tent of Meeting. The Israelites did so; just as יהוה had commanded Moses, so they did.

33Then they brought the Tabernacle to Moses, with the Tent and all its furnishings: its clasps, its planks, its bars, its posts, and i ts sockets; 34the covering of tanned ram skins, the covering of dolphin skins, and the curtain for the screen; 35the Ark of the Pact and its poles, and the cover; 36the table and all its utensils, and the bread of display; 37the pure lamp-stand, its lamps—lamps in due order—and all its fittings, and the oil for lighting; 38the altar of gold, the oil for anointing, the aromatic incense, and the screen for the entrance of the Tent; 39the copper altar with its copper grating, its poles and all its utensils, and the laver and its stand; 40the hangings of the enclosure, its posts and its sockets, the screen for the gate of the enclosure, its cords and its pegs—all the furnishings for the service of the Tabernacle, the Tent of Meeting; 41the service vestments for officiating in the sanctuary, the sacral vestments of Aaron the priest, and the vestments of his sons for priestly service. 42Just as יהוה had commanded Moses, so the Israelites had done all the work. 43And when Moses saw that they had performed all the tasks—as יהוה had commanded, so they had done—Moses blessed them.

40 1And יהוה spoke to Moses, saying:
2On the first day of the first month you shall set up the Tabernacle of the Tent of Meeting. 3Place there the Ark of the Pact, and screen off the ark with the curtain. 4Bring in the table and lay out its due setting; bring in the lampstand and light its lamps; 5and place the gold altar of incense before the Ark of the Pact. Then put up the screen for the entrance of the Tabernacle.

6You shall place the altar of burnt offering before the entrance of the Tabernacle of the Tent of Meeting. 7Place the laver between the Tent of Meeting and the altar, and put water in it. 8Set up the enclosure round about, and put in place the screen for the gate of the enclosure.

9You shall take the anointing oil and anoint the Tabernacle and all that is in it to consecrate it and all its furnishings, so that it shall be holy. 10Then anoint the altar of burnt offering and all its utensils to consecrate the altar, so that the altar shall be most holy. 11And anoint the laver and its stand to consecrate it.

12You shall bring Aaron and his sons forward to the entrance of the Tent of Meeting and wash them with the water. 13Put the sacral vestments on Aaron, and anoint him and consecrate him, that he may serve Me as priest. 14Then bring his sons forward, put tunics on them, 15and anoint them as you have anointed their father, that they may serve Me as priests. This their anointing shall serve them for everlasting priesthood throughout the ages.

16This Moses did; just as יהוה had commanded him, so he did.

17In the first month of the second year, on the first of the month, the Tabernacle was set up. 18Moses set up the Tabernacle, placing its sockets, setting up its planks, inserting its bars, and erecting its posts. 19He spread the tent over the Tabernacle, placing the covering of the tent on top of it—just as יהוה had commanded Moses.

20He took the Pact and placed it in the ark; he fixed the poles to the ark, placed the cover on top of the ark, 21and brought the ark inside the Tabernacle. Then he put up the curtain for screening, and screened off the Ark of the Pact—just as יהוה had commanded Moses.

22He placed the table in the Tent of Meeting, outside the curtain, on the north side of the Tabernacle. 23Upon it he laid out the setting of bread before יהוה—as יהוה had commanded Moses. 24He placed the lamp-stand in the Tent of Meeting opposite the table, on the south side of the Tabernacle. 25And he lit the lamps before יהוה—as יהוה had commanded Moses. 26He placed the altar of gold in the Tent of Meeting, before the curtain. 27On it he burned aromatic incense—as יהוה had commanded Moses.

28Then he put up the screen for the entrance of the Tabernacle. 29At the entrance of the Tabernacle of the Tent of Meeting he placed the altar of burnt offering. On it he offered up the burnt offering and the meal offering—as יהוה had commanded Moses. 30He placed the laver between the Tent of Meeting and the altar, and put water in it for washing. 31From it Moses and Aaron and his sons would wash their hands and feet; 32they washed when they entered the Tent of Meeting and when they approached the altar—as יהוה had commanded Moses. 33And he set up the enclosure around the Tabernacle and the altar, and put up the screen for the gate of the enclosure.

When Moses had finished the work, 34the cloud covered the Tent of Meeting, and the Presence of יהוה filled the Tabernacle. 35Moses could not enter the Tent of Meeting, because the cloud had settled upon it and the Presence of יהוה filled the Tabernacle. 36When the cloud lifted from the Tabernacle, the Israelites would set out, on their various journeys; 37but if the cloud did not lift, they would not set out until such time as it did lift. 38For over the Tabernacle a cloud of יהוה rested by day, and fire would appear in it by night, in the view of all the house of Israel throughout their journeys.

leviticus

1 1יהוה called to Moses and spoke to him from the Tent of Meeting, saying: 2Speak to the Israelite people, and say to them:

When any of you presents an offering of cattle to יהוה: You shall choose your offering from the herd or from the flock. 3If your offering is a burnt offering from the herd, you shall make your offering a male without blemish. You shall bring it to the entrance of the Tent of Meeting, for acceptance in your behalf before יהוה. 4You shall lay a hand upon the head of the burnt offering, that it may be acceptable in your behalf, in expiation for you. 5The bull shall be slaughtered before יהוה; and Aaron's sons, the priests, shall offer the blood, dashing the blood against all sides of the altar which is at the entrance of the Tent of Meeting. 6The burnt offering shall be flayed and cut up into sections. 7The sons of Aaron the priest shall put fire on the altar and lay out wood upon the fire; 8and Aaron's sons, the priests, shall lay out the sections, with the head and the suet, on the wood that is on the fire upon the altar. 9Its entrails and legs shall be washed with water, and the priest shall turn the whole into smoke on the altar as a burnt offering, an offering by fire of pleasing odor to יהוה.

10If your offering for a burnt offering is from the flock, of sheep or of goats, you shall make your offering a male without blemish. 11It shall be slaughtered before יהוה on the north side of the altar, and Aaron's sons, the priests, shall dash its blood against all sides of the altar. 12When it has been cut up into sections, the priest shall lay them out, with the head and the suet, on the wood that is on the fire upon the altar. 13The entrails and the legs shall be washed with water; the priest shall offer up and turn the whole into smoke on the altar. It is a burnt offering, an offering by fire, of pleasing odor to יהוה.

14If your offering to יהוה is a burnt offering of birds, you shall choose your offering from turtledoves or pigeons. 15The priest shall bring it to the altar, pinch off its head, and turn it into smoke on the altar; and its blood shall be drained out against the side of the altar. 16He shall remove its crop with its contents, and cast it into the place of the ashes, at the east side of the altar. 17The priest shall tear it open by its wings, without severing it, and turn it into smoke on the altar, upon the wood that is on the fire. It is a burnt offering, an offering by fire, of pleasing odor to יהוה.

2 1When a person presents an offering of meal to יהוה: The offering shall be of choice flour; the offerer shall pour oil upon it, lay frankincense on it, 2and present it to Aaron's sons, the priests. The priest shall scoop out of it a handful of its choice flour and oil, as well as all of its frankincense; and this token portion he shall turn into smoke on the altar, as an offering by fire, of pleasing odor to יהוה. 3And the remainder of the meal offering shall be for Aaron and his sons, a most holy portion from יהוה's offerings by fire.

4When you present an offering of meal baked in the oven, [it shall be of] choice flour: unleavened cakes with oil mixed in, or unleavened wafers spread with oil.

5If your offering is a meal offering on a griddle, it shall be of choice flour with oil mixed in, unleavened. 6Break it into bits and pour oil on it; it is a meal offering.

7If your offering is a meal offering in a pan, it shall be made of choice flour in oil.

8When you present to יהוה a meal offering that is made in any of these ways, it shall be brought to the priest who shall take it up to the altar. 9The priest shall remove the token portion from the meal offering and turn it into smoke on the altar as an offering by fire, of pleasing odor to יהוה. 10And the remainder of the meal offering shall be for Aaron and his sons, a most holy portion from יהוה's offerings by fire.

11No meal offering that you offer to יהוה shall be made with leaven, for no leaven or honey may be turned into smoke as an offering by fire to יהוה. 12You may bring them to יהוה as an offering of choice products; but they shall not be offered up on the altar for a pleasing odor. 13You shall season your every offering of meal with salt; you shall not omit from your meal offering the salt of your covenant with God; with all your offerings you must offer salt.

14If you bring a meal offering of first fruits to יהוה, you shall bring new ears parched with fire, grits of the fresh grain, as your meal offering of first fruits. 15You shall add oil to it and lay frankincense on it; it is a meal offering. 16And the priest shall turn a token portion of it into smoke: some of the grits and oil, with all of the frankincense, as an offering by fire to יהוה.

3 1If your offering is a sacrifice of wellbeing—If you offer of the herd, whether a male or a female, you shall bring before יהוה one without blemish. 2You shall lay a hand upon the head of your offering and slaughter it at the entrance of the Tent of Meeting; and Aaron's sons, the priests, shall dash the blood against all sides of the altar. 3Then present from the sacrifice of wellbeing, as an offering by fire to יהוה, the fat that covers the entrails and all the fat that is about the entrails; 4the two kidneys and the fat that is on them, that is at the loins; and the protuberance on the liver, which you shall remove with the kidneys. 5Aaron's sons shall turn these into smoke on the altar, with the burnt offering which is upon the wood that is on the fire, as an offering by fire, of pleasing odor to יהוה.

6And if your offering for a sacrifice of wellbeing to יהוה is from the flock, whether a male or a female, you shall offer one without blemish. 7If you present a sheep as your offering, you shall bring it before יהוה 8and lay a hand upon the head of your offering. It shall be slaughtered before the Tent of Meeting, and Aaron's sons shall dash its blood against all sides of the altar. 9Then present, as an offering by fire to יהוה, the fat from the sacrifice of wellbeing: the whole broad tail, which you shall remove close to the backbone; the fat that covers the entrails and all the fat that is about the entrails; 10the two kidneys and the fat that is on them, that is at the loins; and the protuberance on the liver, which you shall remove with the kidneys. 11The priest shall turn these into smoke on the altar as food, an offering by fire to יהוה.

¹²And if your offering is a goat, you shall bring it before יהוה ¹³and lay a hand upon its head. It shall be slaughtered before the Tent of Meeting, and Aaron's sons shall dash its blood against all sides of the altar. ¹⁴Then present as your offering from it, as an offering by fire to יהוה, the fat that covers the entrails and all the fat that is about the entrails; ¹⁵the two kidneys and the fat that is on them, that is at the loins; and the protuberance on the liver, which you shall remove with the kidneys. ¹⁶The priest shall turn these into smoke on the altar as food, an offering by fire, of pleasing odor. All fat is יהוה's. ¹⁷It is a law for all time throughout the ages, in all your settlements: you must not eat any fat or any blood.

4 ¹יהוה spoke to Moses, saying: ²Speak to the Israelite people thus:

When a person unwittingly incurs guilt in regard to any of יהוה's commandments about things not to be done, and does one of them—³If it is the anointed priest who has incurred guilt, so that blame falls upon the people, he shall offer for the sin of which he is guilty a bull of the herd without blemish as a sin offering to יהוה. ⁴He shall bring the bull to the entrance of the Tent of Meeting, before יהוה, and lay a hand upon the head of the bull. The bull shall be slaughtered before יהוה, ⁵and the anointed priest shall take some of the bull's blood and bring it into the Tent of Meeting. ⁶The priest shall dip his finger in the blood, and sprinkle of the blood seven times before יהוה, in front of the curtain of the Shrine. ⁷The priest shall put some of the blood on the horns of the altar of aromatic incense, which is in the Tent of Meeting, before יהוה; and all the rest of the bull's blood he shall pour out at the base of the altar of burnt offering, which is at the entrance of the Tent of Meeting. ⁸He shall remove all the fat from the bull of sin offering: the fat that covers the entrails and all the fat that is about the entrails; ⁹the two kidneys and the fat that is on them, that is at the loins; and the protuberance on the liver, which he shall remove with the kidneys—¹⁰just as it is removed from the ox of the sacrifice of wellbeing. The priest shall turn them into smoke on the altar of burnt offering. ¹¹But the hide of the bull, and all its flesh, as well as its head and legs, its entrails and its dung—¹²all the rest of the bull—he shall carry to a pure place outside the camp, to the ash heap, and burn it up in a wood fire; it shall be burned on the ash heap.

¹³If it is the community leadership of Israel that has erred and the matter escapes the notice of the congregation, so that they do any of the things which by יהוה's commandments ought not to be done, and they realize guilt—¹⁴when the sin through which they incurred guilt becomes known, the congregation shall offer a bull of the herd as a sin offering, and bring it before the Tent of Meeting. ¹⁵The elders of the community shall lay their hands upon the head of the bull before יהוה, and the bull shall be slaughtered before יהוה. ¹⁶The anointed priest shall bring some of the blood of the bull into the Tent of Meeting, ¹⁷and the priest shall dip his finger in the blood and sprinkle of it seven times before יהוה, in front of the curtain. ¹⁸Some of the blood he shall put on the horns of the altar which is before יהוה in the Tent of Meeting, and all the rest of the blood he shall pour out at the base of the altar of burnt offering, which is at the entrance of the Tent of Meeting. ¹⁹He shall remove all its fat from it and turn it into smoke on the altar. ²⁰He shall do with this bull just as is done with the [priest's] bull of sin offering; he shall do the same with it. The priest shall thus make expiation for them, and they shall be forgiven. ²¹He shall carry the bull outside the camp and burn it as he burned the first bull; it is the sin offering of the congregation.

²²In case it is a chieftain who incurs guilt by doing unwittingly any of the things which by the commandment of his God יהוה ought not to be done, and he realizes guilt—²³or the sin of which he is guilty is made known—he shall bring as his offering a male goat without blemish. ²⁴He shall lay a hand upon the goat's head, and it shall be slaughtered at the spot where the burnt offering is slaughtered before יהוה; it is a sin offering. ²⁵The priest shall take with his finger some of the blood of the sin offering and put it on the horns of the altar of burnt offering; and the rest of its blood he shall pour out at the base of the altar of burnt offering. ²⁶All its fat he shall turn into smoke on the altar, like the fat of the sacrifice of wellbeing. The priest shall thus make expiation on his behalf for his sin, and he shall be forgiven.

²⁷If any person from among the populace unwittingly incurs guilt by doing any of the things which by יהוה's commandments ought not to be done, and realizes guilt—²⁸or the sin of which one is guilty is made known—that person shall bring a female goat without blemish as an offering for the sin of which that one is guilty. ²⁹The offerer shall lay a hand upon the head of the sin offering. The sin offering shall be slaughtered at the place of the burnt offering. ³⁰The priest shall take with his finger some of its blood and put it on the horns of the altar of burnt offering; and all the rest of its blood he shall pour out at the base of the altar. ³¹The offerer shall remove all its fat, just as the fat is removed from the sacrifice of wellbeing; and the priest shall turn it into smoke on the altar, for a pleasing odor to יהוה. The priest shall thus make expiation for that person, who shall be forgiven.

³²If the offering one brings as a sin offering is a sheep, that person shall bring a female without blemish. ³³The offerer shall lay a hand upon the head of the sin offering, and it shall be slaughtered as a sin offering at the spot where the burnt offering is slaughtered. ³⁴The priest shall take with his finger some of the blood of the sin offering and put it on the horns of the altar of burnt offering, and all the rest of its blood he shall pour out at the base of the altar. ³⁵And all its fat the offerer shall remove, just as the fat of the sheep of the sacrifice of wellbeing is removed; and this the priest shall turn into smoke on the altar, over יהוה's offering by fire. For the sin of which one is guilty, the priest shall thus make expiation on behalf of that person, who shall be forgiven.

5 ¹If a person incurs guilt—

When one has heard a public imprecation but (although able to testify as having either seen or learned of the matter) has not given information and thus is subject to punishment;

²Or when a person touches any impure thing (be it the carcass of an impure beast or the carcass of impure cattle or the carcass of an impure creeping thing) and the fact has escaped notice, and then, being impure, that person realizes guilt;

³Or when one touches human impurity (any such impurity whereby someone becomes impure) and, though having known about it, the fact has escaped notice, but later that person realizes guilt;

⁴Or when a person utters an oath to bad or good purpose (whatever a human being may utter in an oath) and, though having known about it, the fact has escaped notice, but later that person realizes guilt in any of these matters—⁵upon realizing guilt in any of these matters, one shall confess having sinned in that way. ⁶And one shall bring as a penalty to יהוה, for the sin of which one is guilty, a female from the flock, sheep or goat, as a sin offering; and the priest shall make expiation for the sin, on that person's behalf.

⁷But if one's means do not suffice for a sheep, that person shall bring to יהוה, as the penalty for that of which one is

guilty, two turtledoves or two pigeons—one for a sin offering and the other for a burnt offering. ⁸The offerer shall bring them to the priest, who shall offer first the bird for the sin offering, pinching its head at the nape without severing it. ⁹He shall sprinkle some of the blood of the sin offering on the side of the altar, and what remains of the blood shall be drained out at the base of the altar; it is a sin offering. ¹⁰And the second bird he shall prepare as a burnt offering, according to regulation. For the sin of which one is guilty, the priest shall thus make expiation on behalf of that person, who shall be forgiven.

¹¹And if one's means do not suffice for two turtledoves or two pigeons, that person shall bring as an offering for that of which one is guilty a tenth of an *ephah* of choice flour for a sin offering; one shall not add oil to it or lay frankincense on it, for it is a sin offering. ¹²The offerer shall bring it to the priest, and the priest shall scoop out of it a handful as a token portion and turn it into smoke on the altar, with יהוה's offerings by fire; it is a sin offering. ¹³For whichever of these sins one is guilty, the priest shall thus make expiation on behalf of that person, who shall be forgiven. It shall belong to the priest, like the meal offering.

¹⁴And יהוה spoke to Moses, saying:

¹⁵When a person commits a trespass, being unwittingly remiss about any of יהוה's sacred things: One shall bring as a penalty to יהוה a ram without blemish from the flock, convertible into payment in silver by the sanctuary weight, as a guilt offering. ¹⁶That person shall make restitution for the remission regarding the sacred things, adding a fifth part to it and giving it to the priest. The priest shall make expiation with the ram of the guilt offering on behalf of that person, who shall be forgiven.

¹⁷And a person who, without knowing it, sins in regard to any of יהוה's commandments about things not to be done, and then realizes guilt: Such a person shall be subject to punishment. ¹⁸That person shall bring to the priest a ram without blemish from the flock, or the equivalent, as a guilt offering. For the error committed unwittingly, the priest shall make expiation on behalf of that person, who shall be forgiven. ¹⁹It is a guilt offering; guilt has been incurred before יהוה.

²⁰יהוה spoke to Moses, saying: ²¹When a person sins and commits a trespass against יהוה—by dealing deceitfully with another in the matter of a deposit or a pledge, or through robbery, or by defrauding another, ²²or by finding something lost and lying about it; if one swears falsely regarding any one of the various things that someone may do and sin thereby—²³when one has thus sinned and, realizing guilt, would restore either that which was gotten through robbery or fraud, or the entrusted deposit, or the lost thing that was found, ²⁴or anything else about which one swore falsely, that person shall repay the principal amount and add a fifth part to it. One shall pay it to its owner upon realizing guilt. ²⁵Then that person shall bring to the priest, as a penalty to יהוה, a ram without blemish from the flock, or the equivalent, as a guilt offering. ²⁶The priest shall make expiation before יהוה on behalf of that person, who shall be forgiven for whatever was done to draw blame thereby.

6 ¹יהוה spoke to Moses, saying: ²Command Aaron and his sons thus:

This is the ritual of the burnt offering: The burnt offering itself shall remain where it is burned upon the altar all night until morning, while the fire on the altar is kept going on it. ³The priest shall dress in linen raiment, with linen breeches next to his body; and he shall take up the ashes to which the fire has reduced the burnt offering on the altar and place them beside the altar. ⁴He shall then take off his vestments and put on other vestments, and carry the ashes outside the camp to a pure place. ⁵The fire on the altar shall be kept burning, not to go out: every morning the priest shall feed wood to it, lay out the burnt offering on it, and turn into smoke the fat parts of the offerings of wellbeing. ⁶A perpetual fire shall be kept burning on the altar, not to go out.

⁷And this is the ritual of the meal offering: Aaron's sons shall present it before יהוה, in front of the altar. ⁸A handful of the choice flour and oil of the meal offering shall be taken from it, with all the frankincense that is on the meal offering, and this token portion shall be turned into smoke on the altar as a pleasing odor to יהוה. ⁹What is left of it shall be eaten by Aaron and his sons; it shall be eaten as unleavened cakes, in the sacred precinct; they shall eat it in the enclosure of the Tent of Meeting. ¹⁰It shall not be baked with leaven; I have given it as their portion from My offerings by fire; it is most holy, like the sin offering and the guilt offering. ¹¹Only the males among Aaron's descendants may eat of it, as their due for all time throughout the ages from יהוה's offerings by fire. Anything that touches these shall become holy.

¹²יהוה spoke to Moses, saying: ¹³This is the offering that Aaron and his sons shall offer to יהוה on the occasion of his anointment: a tenth of an *ephah* of choice flour as a regular meal offering, half of it in the morning and half of it in the evening, ¹⁴shall be prepared with oil on a griddle. You shall bring it well soaked, and offer it as a meal offering of baked slices, of pleasing odor to יהוה. ¹⁵And so shall the priest, anointed from among his sons to succeed him, prepare it; it is יהוה's—a law for all time—to be turned entirely into smoke. ¹⁶So, too, every meal offering of a priest shall be a whole offering: it shall not be eaten.

¹⁷יהוה spoke to Moses, saying: ¹⁸Speak to Aaron and his sons thus: This is the ritual of the sin offering: the sin offering shall be slaughtered before יהוה, at the spot where the burnt offering is slaughtered: it is most holy. ¹⁹The priest who offers it as a sin offering shall eat of it; it shall be eaten in the sacred precinct, in the enclosure of the Tent of Meeting. ²⁰Anything that touches its flesh shall become holy; and if any of its blood is spattered upon a garment, you shall wash the bespattered part in the sacred precinct. ²¹An earthen vessel in which it was boiled shall be broken; if it was boiled in a copper vessel, [the vessel] shall be scoured and rinsed with water. ²²Only the males in the priestly line may eat of it: it is most holy. ²³But no sin offering may be eaten from which any blood is brought into the Tent of Meeting for expiation in the sanctuary; any such shall be consumed in fire.

7 ¹This is the ritual of the guilt offering: it is most holy. ²The guilt offering shall be slaughtered at the spot where the burnt offering is slaughtered, and the blood shall be dashed on all sides of the altar. ³All its fat shall be offered: the broad tail; the fat that covers the entrails; ⁴the two kidneys and the fat that is on them at the loins; and the protuberance on the liver, which shall be removed with the kidneys. ⁵The priest shall turn them into smoke on the altar as an offering by fire to יהוה; it is a guilt offering. ⁶Only the males in the priestly line may eat of it; it shall be eaten in the sacred precinct: it is most holy.

⁷The guilt offering is like the sin offering. The same rule applies to both: it shall belong to the priest who makes expiation thereby. ⁸So, too, the priest who offers a person's burnt offering shall keep the skin of the burnt offering that was offered. ⁹Further, any meal offering that is baked in an oven, and any that is prepared in a pan or on a griddle, shall belong to the priest who offers it. ¹⁰But every other meal offering, with oil mixed in or dry, shall go to the sons of Aaron all alike.

¹¹This is the ritual of the sacrifice of wellbeing that one may offer to יהוה:

¹²One who offers it for thanksgiving shall offer, together with the sacrifice of thanksgiving, unleavened cakes with oil mixed in—unleavened wafers spread with oil—and cakes of choice flour with oil mixed in, well soaked. ¹³This offering, with cakes of leavened bread added, shall be offered along with one's thanksgiving sacrifice of wellbeing. ¹⁴Out of this the person shall offer one of each kind as a gift to יהוה; it shall go to the priest who dashes the blood of the offering of wellbeing. ¹⁵And the flesh of the thanksgiving sacrifice of wellbeing shall be eaten on the day that it is offered; none of it shall be set aside until morning.

¹⁶If, however, the sacrifice offered is a votive or a freewill offering, it shall be eaten on the day that one offers the sacrifice, and what is left of it shall be eaten on the morrow. ¹⁷What is then left of the flesh of the sacrifice shall be consumed in fire on the third day. ¹⁸If any of the flesh of the sacrifice of wellbeing is eaten on the third day, it shall not be acceptable; it shall not count for the one who offered it. It is an offensive thing, and the person who eats of it shall bear the guilt.

¹⁹Flesh that touches anything impure shall not be eaten; it shall be consumed in fire. As for other flesh, only one who is pure may eat such flesh. ²⁰But the person who, in a state of impurity, eats flesh from יהוה's sacrifices of wellbeing, that person shall be cut off from kin. ²¹When a person touches anything impure, be it human impurity or an impure animal or any impure creature, and eats flesh from יהוה's sacrifices of wellbeing, that person shall be cut off from kin.

²²And יהוה spoke to Moses, saying: ²³Speak to the Israelite people thus: You shall eat no fat of ox or sheep or goat. ²⁴Fat from animals that died or were torn by beasts may be put to any use, but you must not eat it. ²⁵If anyone eats the fat of animals from which offerings by fire may be made to יהוה, the person who eats it shall be cut off from kin. ²⁶And you must not consume any blood, either of bird or of animal, in any of your settlements. ²⁷Anyone who eats blood shall be cut off from kin.

²⁸And יהוה spoke to Moses, saying: ²⁹Speak to the Israelite people thus: The offering to יהוה from a sacrifice of wellbeing must be presented by the one who offers that sacrifice of wellbeing to יהוה: ³⁰one's own hands shall present יהוה's offerings by fire. The offerer shall present the fat with the breast, the breast to be elevated as an elevation offering before יהוה; ³¹the priest shall turn the fat into smoke on the altar, and the breast shall go to Aaron and his sons. ³²And the right thigh from your sacrifices of wellbeing you shall present to the priest as a gift; ³³he from among Aaron's sons who offers the blood and the fat of the offering of wellbeing shall get the right thigh as his portion. ³⁴For I have taken the breast of elevation offering and the thigh of gift offering from the Israelites, from their sacrifices of wellbeing, and given them to Aaron the priest and to his sons as their due from the Israelites for all time.

³⁵Those shall be the perquisites of Aaron and the perquisites of his sons from יהוה's offerings by fire, once they have been inducted to serve יהוה as priests; ³⁶these יהוה commanded to be given them, once they had been anointed, as a due from the Israelites for all time throughout the ages.

³⁷Such are the rituals of the burnt offering, the meal offering, the sin offering, the guilt offering, the offering of ordination, and the sacrifice of wellbeing, ³⁸with which יהוה charged Moses on Mount Sinai, when commanding that the Israelites present their offerings to יהוה, in the wilderness of Sinai.

8 יהוה spoke to Moses, saying: ²Take Aaron along with his sons, and the vestments, the anointing oil, the bull of sin offering, the two rams, and the basket of unleavened bread; ³and assemble the community leadership at the entrance of the Tent of Meeting. ⁴Moses did as יהוה commanded him. And when the leadership was assembled at the entrance of the Tent of Meeting, ⁵Moses said to the leadership, "This is what יהוה has commanded to be done."

⁶Then Moses brought Aaron and his sons forward and washed them with water. ⁷He put the tunic on him, girded him with the sash, clothed him with the robe, and put the ephod on him, girding him with the decorated band with which he tied it to him. ⁸He put the breast-piece on him, and put into the breast-piece the Urim and Thummim. ⁹And he set the headdress on his head; and on the headdress, in front, he put the gold frontlet, the holy diadem—as יהוה had commanded Moses.

¹⁰Moses took the anointing oil and anointed the Tabernacle and all that was in it, thus consecrating them. ¹¹He sprinkled some of it on the altar seven times, anointing the altar, all its utensils, and the laver with its stand, to consecrate them. ¹²He poured some of the anointing oil upon Aaron's head and anointed him, to consecrate him. ¹³Moses then brought Aaron's sons forward, clothed them in tunics, girded them with sashes, and wound turbans upon them, as יהוה had commanded Moses.

¹⁴He led forward the bull of sin offering. Aaron and his sons laid their hands upon the head of the bull of sin offering, ¹⁵and it was slaughtered. Moses took the blood and with his finger put some on each of the horns of the altar, purifying the altar; then he poured out the blood at the base of the altar. Thus he consecrated it in order to make expiation upon it.

¹⁶Moses then took all the fat that was about the entrails, and the protuberance of the liver, and the two kidneys and their fat, and turned them into smoke on the altar. ¹⁷The rest of the bull, its hide, its flesh, and its dung, he put to the fire outside the camp—as יהוה had commanded Moses.

¹⁸Then he brought forward the ram of burnt offering. Aaron and his sons laid their hands upon the ram's head, ¹⁹and it was slaughtered. Moses dashed the blood against all sides of the altar. ²⁰The ram was cut up into sections and Moses turned the head, the sections, and the suet into smoke on the altar; ²¹Moses washed the entrails and the legs with water and turned all of the ram into smoke. That was a burnt offering for a pleasing odor, an offering by fire to יהוה—as יהוה had commanded Moses.

²²He brought forward the second ram, the ram of ordination. Aaron and his sons laid their hands upon the ram's head, ²³and it was slaughtered. Moses took some of its blood and put it on the ridge of Aaron's right ear, and on the thumb of his right hand, and on the big toe of his right foot. ²⁴Moses then brought forward the sons of Aaron, and put some of the blood on the ridges of their right ears, and on the thumbs of their right hands, and on the big toes of their right feet; and the rest of the blood Moses dashed against every side of the altar. ²⁵He took the fat—the broad tail, all the fat about the entrails, the protuberance of the liver, and the two kidneys and their fat—and the right thigh. ²⁶From the basket of unleavened bread that was before יהוה, he took one cake of unleavened bread, one cake of oil bread, and one wafer, and placed them on the fat parts and on the right thigh. ²⁷He placed all these on the palms of Aaron and on the palms of his sons, and elevated them as an elevation offering before יהוה. ²⁸Then Moses took them from their hands and turned them into smoke on the altar with the burnt offering. This was an ordination offering for a pleasing odor; it was an offering by fire to יהוה. ²⁹Moses took the breast and elevated it as an elevation offering before יהוה; it was Moses' portion of the ram of ordination—as יהוה had commanded Moses.

³⁰And Moses took some of the anointing oil and some of the blood that was on the altar and sprinkled it upon Aaron and upon his vestments, and also upon his sons and upon their vestments. Thus he consecrated Aaron and his vestments, and also his sons and their vestments.

³¹Moses said to Aaron and his sons: Boil the flesh at the entrance of the Tent of Meeting and eat it there with the bread that is in the basket of ordination—as I commanded: Aaron and his sons shall eat it; ³²and what is left over of the flesh and the bread you shall consume in fire. ³³You shall not go outside the entrance of the Tent of Meeting for seven days, until the day that your period of ordination is completed. For your ordination will require seven days. ³⁴Everything done today, יהוה has commanded to be done [seven days], to make expiation for you. ³⁵You shall remain at the entrance of the Tent of Meeting day and night for seven days, keeping יהוה's charge—that you may not die—for so I have been commanded.

³⁶And Aaron and his sons did all the things that יהוה had commanded through Moses.

9 ¹On the eighth day Moses called Aaron and his sons, and the elders of Israel. ²He said to Aaron: "Take a calf of the herd for a sin offering and a ram for a burnt offering, without blemish, and bring them before יהוה. ³And speak to the Israelites, saying: Take a hegoat for a sin offering; a calf and a lamb, yearlings without blemish, for a burnt offering; ⁴and an ox and a ram for an offering of wellbeing to sacrifice before יהוה; and a meal offering with oil mixed in. For today יהוה will appear to you."

⁵They brought to the front of the Tent of Meeting the things that Moses had commanded, and the community leadership came forward and stood before יהוה. ⁶Moses said: "This is what יהוה has commanded that you do, that the Presence of יהוה may appear to you." ⁷Then Moses said to Aaron: "Come forward to the altar and sacrifice your sin offering and your burnt offering, making expiation for yourself and for the people; and sacrifice the people's offering and make expiation for them, as יהוה has commanded."

⁸Aaron came forward to the altar and slaughtered his calf of sin offering. ⁹Aaron's sons brought the blood to him; he dipped his finger in the blood and put it on the horns of the altar; and he poured out the rest of the blood at the base of the altar. ¹⁰The fat, the kidneys, and the protuberance of the liver from the sin offering he turned into smoke on the altar—as יהוה had commanded Moses; ¹¹and the flesh and the skin were consumed in fire outside the camp. ¹²Then he slaughtered the burnt offering. Aaron's sons passed the blood to him, and he dashed it against all sides of the altar. ¹³They passed the burnt offering to him in sections, as well as the head, and he turned it into smoke on the altar. ¹⁴He washed the entrails and the legs, and turned them into smoke on the altar with the burnt offering.

¹⁵Next he brought forward the people's offering. He took the goat for the people's sin offering, and slaughtered it, and presented it as a sin offering like the previous one. ¹⁶He brought forward the burnt offering and sacrificed it according to regulation. ¹⁷He then brought forward the meal offering and, taking a handful of it, he turned it into smoke on the altar—in addition to the burnt offering of the morning. ¹⁸He slaughtered the ox and the ram, the people's sacrifice of wellbeing. Aaron's sons passed the blood to him—which he dashed against every side of the altar—¹⁹and the fat parts of the ox and the ram: the broad tail, the covering [fat], the kidneys, and the protuberances of the livers. ²⁰They laid these fat parts over the breasts; and Aaron turned the fat parts into smoke on the altar, ²¹and elevated the breasts and the right thighs as an elevation offering before יהוה—as Moses had commanded.

²²Aaron lifted his hands toward the people and blessed them; and he stepped down after offering the sin offering, the burnt offering, and the offering of wellbeing. ²³Moses and Aaron then went inside the Tent of Meeting. When they came out, they blessed the people; and the Presence of יהוה appeared to all the people. ²⁴Fire came forth from before יהוה and consumed the burnt offering and the fat parts on the altar. And all the people saw, and shouted, and fell on their faces.

10 ¹Now Aaron's sons Nadab and Abihu each took his fire pan, put fire in it, and laid incense on it; and they offered before יהוה alien fire, which had not been enjoined upon them.

²And fire came forth from יהוה and consumed them; thus they died at the instance of יהוה. ³Then Moses said to Aaron, "This is what יהוה meant by saying:

> Through those near to Me I show Myself holy,
> And gain glory before all the people."

And Aaron was silent.

⁴Moses called Mishael and Elzaphan, sons of Uzziel the uncle of Aaron, and said to them, "Come forward and carry your kinsmen away from the front of the sanctuary to a place outside the camp." ⁵They came forward and carried them out of the camp by their tunics, as Moses had ordered. ⁶And Moses said to Aaron and to his sons Eleazar and Ithamar, "Do not bare your heads and do not rend your clothes, lest you die and anger strike the whole community. But your kin, all the house of Israel, shall bewail the burning that יהוה has wrought. ⁷And so do not go outside the entrance of the Tent of Meeting, lest you die, for יהוה's anointing oil is upon you." And they did as Moses had bidden.

⁸And יהוה spoke to Aaron, saying: ⁹Drink no wine or other intoxicant, you or your sons, when you enter the Tent of Meeting, that you may not die. This is a law for all time throughout the ages, ¹⁰for you must distinguish between the sacred and the profane, and between the impure and the pure; ¹¹and you must teach the Israelites all the laws which יהוה has imparted to them through Moses.

¹²Moses spoke to Aaron and to his remaining sons, Eleazar and Ithamar: Take the meal offering that is left over from יהוה's offerings by fire and eat it unleavened beside the altar, for it is most holy. ¹³You shall eat it in the sacred precinct, inasmuch as it is your due, and that of your sons, from יהוה's offerings by fire; for so I have been commanded. ¹⁴But the breast of elevation offering and the thigh of gift offering you [and your wife], and your sons and daughters with you, may eat in any pure place, for they have been assigned as a due to you and your sons from the Israelites' sacrifices of wellbeing. ¹⁵Together with the fat of fire offering, they must present the thigh of gift offering and the breast of elevation offering, which are to be elevated as an elevation offering before יהוה, and which are to be your due and that of your sons with you for all time—as יהוה has commanded.

¹⁶Then Moses inquired about the goat of sin offering, and it had already been burned! He was angry with Eleazar and Ithamar, Aaron's remaining sons, and said, ¹⁷"Why did you not eat the sin offering in the sacred area? For it is most holy, and it is what was given to you to remove the guilt of the community and to make expiation for them before יהוה. ¹⁸Since its blood was not brought inside the sanctuary, you should certainly have eaten it in the sanctuary, as I commanded." ¹⁹And Aaron spoke to Moses, "See, this day they brought their sin offering and their burnt offering before יהוה, and such things have befallen me! Had I eaten sin

offering today, would יהוה have approved?" ²⁰And when Moses heard this, he approved.

11 ¹יהוה spoke to Moses and Aaron, saying to them: ²Speak to the Israelite people thus:

These are the creatures that you may eat from among all the land animals: ³any animal that has true hoofs, with clefts through the hoofs, and that chews the cud—such you may eat. ⁴The following, however, of those that either chew the cud or have true hoofs, you shall not eat: the camel—although it chews the cud, it has no true hoofs: it is impure for you; ⁵the daman—although it chews the cud, it has no true hoofs: it is impure for you; ⁶the hare—although it chews the cud, it has no true hoofs: it is impure for you; ⁷and the swine—although it has true hoofs, with the hoofs cleft through, it does not chew the cud: it is impure for you. ⁸You shall not eat of their flesh or touch their carcasses; they are impure for you.

⁹These you may eat of all that live in water: anything in water, whether in the seas or in the streams, that has fins and scales—these you may eat. ¹⁰But anything in the seas or in the streams that has no fins and scales, among all the swarming things of the water and among all the other living creatures that are in the water—they are an abomination for you ¹¹and an abomination for you they shall remain: you shall not eat of their flesh and you shall abominate their carcasses. ¹²Everything in water that has no fins and scales shall be an abomination for you.

¹³The following you shall abominate among the birds—they shall not be eaten, they are an abomination: the eagle, the vulture, and the black vulture; ¹⁴the kite, falcons of every variety; ¹⁵all varieties of raven; ¹⁶the ostrich, the nighthawk, the sea gull; hawks of every variety; ¹⁷the little owl, the cormorant, and the great owl; ¹⁸the white owl, the pelican, and the bustard; ¹⁹the stork; herons of every variety; the hoopoe, and the bat.

²⁰All winged swarming things that walk on fours shall be an abomination for you. ²¹But these you may eat among all the winged swarming things that walk on fours: all that have, above their feet, jointed legs to leap with on the ground—²²of these you may eat the following: locusts of every variety; all varieties of bald locust; crickets of every variety; and all varieties of grasshopper. ²³But all other winged swarming things that have four legs shall be an abomination for you.

²⁴And the following shall make you impure—whoever touches their carcasses shall be impure until evening, ²⁵and whoever carries the carcasses of any of them shall wash those clothes and be impure until evening—²⁶every animal that has true hoofs but without clefts through the hoofs, or that does not chew the cud. They are impure for you; whoever touches them shall be impure. ²⁷Also all animals that walk on paws, among those that walk on fours, are impure for you; whoever touches their carcasses shall be impure until evening. ²⁸And anyone who carries their carcasses shall wash those clothes and remain impure until evening. They are impure for you.

²⁹The following shall be impure for you from among the things that swarm on the earth: the mole, the mouse, and great lizards of every variety; ³⁰the gecko, the land crocodile, the lizard, the sand lizard, and the chameleon. ³¹Those are for you the impure among all the swarming things; whoever touches them when they are dead shall be impure until evening. ³²And anything on which one of them falls when dead shall be impure: be it any article of wood, or a cloth, or a skin, or a sack—any such article that can be put to use shall be dipped in water, and it shall remain impure until evening; then it shall be pure. ³³And if any of those falls into an earthen vessel, everything inside it shall be impure and

[the vessel] itself you shall break. ³⁴As to any food that may be eaten, it shall become impure if it came in contact with water; as to any liquid that may be drunk, it shall become impure if it was inside any vessel. ³⁵Everything on which the carcass of any of them falls shall be impure: an oven or stove shall be smashed. They are impure—and impure they shall remain for you. ³⁶However, a spring or cistern in which water is collected shall be pure, but whoever touches such a carcass in it shall be impure. ³⁷If such a carcass falls upon seed grain that is to be sown, it is pure; ³⁸but if water is put on the seed and any part of a carcass falls upon it, it shall be impure for you.

³⁹If an animal that you may eat has died, anyone who touches its carcass shall be impure until evening; ⁴⁰anyone who eats of its carcass shall wash those clothes and remain impure until evening; and anyone who carries its carcass shall wash those clothes and remain impure until evening.

⁴¹All the things that swarm upon the earth are an abomination; they shall not be eaten. ⁴²You shall not eat, among all things that swarm upon the earth, anything that crawls on its belly, or anything that walks on fours, or anything that has many legs; for they are an abomination. ⁴³You shall not draw abomination upon yourselves through anything that swarms; you shall not make yourselves impure therewith and thus become impure. ⁴⁴For יהוה am your God: you shall sanctify yourselves and be holy, for I am holy. You shall not make yourselves impure through any swarming thing that moves upon the earth. ⁴⁵For I יהוה am the One who brought you up from the land of Egypt to be your God: you shall be holy, for I am holy.

⁴⁶These are the instructions concerning animals, birds, all living creatures that move in water, and all creatures that swarm on earth, ⁴⁷for distinguishing between the impure and the pure, between the living things that may be eaten and the living things that may not be eaten.

12 ¹יהוה spoke to Moses, saying: ²Speak to the Israelite people thus: When a woman at childbirth bears a male, she shall be impure seven days; she shall be impure as at the time of her condition of menstrual separation.—³On the eighth day the flesh of his foreskin shall be circumcised.—⁴She shall remain in a state of blood purification for thirty-three days: she shall not touch any consecrated thing, nor enter the sanctuary until her period of purification is completed. ⁵If she bears a female, she shall be impure two weeks as during her menstruation, and she shall remain in a state of blood purification for sixty-six days.

⁶On the completion of her period of purification, for either son or daughter, she shall bring to the priest, at the entrance of the Tent of Meeting, a lamb in its first year for a burnt offering, and a pigeon or a turtledove for a sin offering. ⁷He shall offer it before יהוה and make expiation on her behalf; she shall then be pure from her flow of blood. Such are the rituals concerning her who bears a child, male or female. ⁸If, however, her means do not suffice for a sheep, she shall take two turtledoves or two pigeons, one for a burnt offering and the other for a sin offering. The priest shall make expiation on her behalf, and she shall be pure.

13 ¹יהוה spoke to Moses and Aaron, saying:
²When a person has on the skin of the body a swelling, a rash, or a discoloration, and it develops into a scaly affection on the skin of the body, it shall be reported to Aaron the priest or to one of his sons, the priests. ³The priest shall examine the affection on the skin of the body: if hair in the affected patch has turned white and the affection appears to be deeper than the skin of the body, it is a leprous affection;

when the priest sees it, he shall pronounce the person impure. [4]But if it is a white discoloration on the skin of the body which does not appear to be deeper than the skin and the hair in it has not turned white, the priest shall isolate the affected person for seven days. [5]On the seventh day the priest shall conduct an examination, and if the affection has remained unchanged in color and the disease has not spread on the skin, the priest shall isolate that person for another seven days. [6]On the seventh day the priest shall again conduct an examination: if the affection has faded and has not spread on the skin, the priest shall pronounce the person pure. It is a rash; after washing those clothes, that person shall be pure. [7]But if the rash should spread on the skin after the person has been seen by the priest and pronounced pure, that person shall again report to the priest. [8]And if the priest sees that the rash has spread on the skin, the priest shall pronounce that person impure; it is leprosy.

[9]When a person has a scaly affection, it shall be reported to the priest. [10]If the priest finds on the skin a white swelling which has turned some hair white, with a patch of undiscolored flesh in the swelling, [11]it is chronic leprosy on the skin of the body, and the priest shall pronounce the person impure; being impure, that person need not be isolated. [12]If the eruption spreads out over the skin so that it covers all the skin of the affected person from head to foot, wherever the priest can see—[13]if the priest sees that the eruption has covered the whole body—he shall pronounce as pure the affected person, who is pure from having turned all white. [14]But as soon as undiscolored flesh appears in it, that person shall be impure; [15]when the priest sees the undiscolored flesh, he shall pronounce the person impure. The undiscolored flesh is impure; it is leprosy. [16]But if the undiscolored flesh again turns white, that person shall come to the priest, [17]and the priest shall conduct an examination: if the affection has turned white, the priest shall pronounce as pure the affected person, who is then pure.

[18]When an inflammation appears on the skin of one's body and it heals, [19]and a white swelling or a white discoloration streaked with red develops where the inflammation was, that person shall report to the priest. [20]If the priest finds that it appears lower than the rest of the skin and that the hair in it has turned white, the priest shall pronounce the person impure; it is a leprous affection that has broken out in the inflammation. [21]But if the priest finds that there is no white hair in it and it is not lower than the rest of the skin, and it is faded, the priest shall isolate that person for seven days. [22]If it should spread in the skin, the priest shall pronounce the person impure; it is an affection. [23]But if the discoloration remains stationary, not having spread, it is the scar of the inflammation; the priest shall pronounce that person pure.

[24]When the skin of one's body sustains a burn by fire, and the patch from the burn is a discoloration, either white streaked with red, or white, [25]the priest shall examine it. If some hair has turned white in the discoloration, which itself appears to go deeper than the skin, it is leprosy that has broken out in the burn. The priest shall pronounce the person impure; it is a leprous affection. [26]But if the priest finds that there is no white hair in the discoloration, and that it is not lower than the rest of the skin, and it is faded, the priest shall isolate that person for seven days. [27]On the seventh day the priest shall conduct an examination: if it has spread in the skin, the priest shall pronounce the person impure; it is a leprous affection. [28]But if the discoloration has remained stationary, not having spread on the skin, and it is faded, it is the swelling from the burn. The priest shall pronounce that person pure, for it is the scar of the burn.

[29]If a man or a woman has an affection on the head or in his beard, [30]the priest shall examine the affection. If it appears to go deeper than the skin and there is thin yellow hair in it, the priest shall pronounce the person impure; it is a scall, a scaly eruption in the hair or beard. [31]But if the priest finds that the scall affection does not appear to go deeper than the skin, yet there is no black hair in it, the priest shall isolate the person with the scall affection for seven days. [32]On the seventh day the priest shall examine the affection. If the scall has not spread and no yellow hair has appeared in it, and the scall does not appear to go deeper than the skin, [33]the person with the scall shall shave—but without shaving the scall; the priest shall isolate that person for another seven days. [34]On the seventh day the priest shall examine the scall. If the scall has not spread on the skin, and does not appear to go deeper than the skin, the priest shall pronounce the person pure; after washing those clothes, that person shall be pure. [35]If, however, the scall should spread on the skin after the person has been pronounced pure, [36]the priest shall conduct an examination. If the scall has spread on the skin, the priest need not look for yellow hair: the person is impure. [37]But if the scall has remained unchanged in color, and black hair has grown in it, the scall is healed; the person is pure. The priest shall pronounce that person pure.

[38]If a man or a woman has the skin of the body streaked with white discolorations, [39]and the priest sees that the discolorations on the skin of the body are of a dull white, it is a tetter broken out on the skin; that person is pure.

[40]If a man loses the hair of his head and becomes bald, he is pure. [41]If he loses the hair on the front part of his head and becomes bald at the forehead, he is pure. [42]But if a white affection streaked with red appears on the bald part in the front or at the back of the head, it is a scaly eruption that is spreading over the bald part in the front or at the back of the head. [43]The priest shall examine him: if the swollen affection on the bald part in the front or at the back of his head is white streaked with red, like the leprosy of body skin in appearance, [44]he is among the leprous; he is impure. The priest shall pronounce him impure; he has the affection on his head.

[45]As for the person with a leprous affection: the clothes shall be rent, the head shall be left bare, and the upper lip shall be covered over; and that person shall call out, "Impure! Impure!" [46]The person shall be impure as long as the disease is present. Being impure, that person shall dwell apart—in a dwelling outside the camp.

[47]When an eruptive affection occurs in a cloth of wool or linen fabric, [48]in the warp or in the woof of the linen or the wool, or in a skin or in anything made of skin; [49]if the affection in the cloth or the skin, in the warp or the woof, or in any article of skin, is streaky green or red, it is an eruptive affection. It shall be shown to the priest; [50]and the priest, after examining the affection, shall isolate the affected article for seven days. [51]On the seventh day he shall examine the affection: if the affection has spread in the cloth—whether in the warp or the woof, or in the skin, for whatever purpose the skin may be used—the affection is a malignant eruption; it is impure. [52]The cloth—whether warp or woof in wool or linen, or any article of skin—in which the affection is found, shall be burned, for it is a malignant eruption; it shall be consumed in fire. [53]But if the priest sees that the affection in the cloth—whether in warp or in woof, or in any article of skin—has not spread, [54]the priest shall order the affected article washed, and he shall isolate it for another seven days. [55]And if, after the affected article has been washed, the priest sees that the affection has not changed color and that it has not spread, it is impure. It shall be consumed in fire; it is a fret, whether

on its inner side or on its outer side. ⁵⁶But if the priest sees that the affected part, after it has been washed, is faded, he shall tear it out from the cloth or skin, whether in the warp or in the woof; ⁵⁷and if it occurs again in the cloth—whether in warp or in woof—or in any article of skin, it is a wild growth; the affected article shall be consumed in fire. ⁵⁸If, however, the affection disappears from the cloth—warp or woof—or from any article of skin that has been washed, it shall be washed again, and it shall be pure. ⁵⁹Such is the procedure for eruptive affections of cloth, woolen or linen, in warp or in woof, or of any article of skin, for pronouncing it pure or impure.

14 יהוה spoke to Moses, saying: ²This shall be the ritual for a leper at the time of being purified.

When it has been reported to the priest, ³the priest shall go outside the camp. If the priest sees that the leper has been healed of the scaly affection, ⁴the priest shall order two live pure birds, cedar wood, crimson stuff, and hyssop to be brought for the one to be purified. ⁵The priest shall order one of the birds slaughtered over fresh water in an earthen vessel; ⁶and he shall take the live bird, along with the cedar wood, the crimson stuff, and the hyssop, and dip them together with the live bird in the blood of the bird that was slaughtered over the fresh water. ⁷He shall then sprinkle it seven times on the one to be purified of the eruption and effect the purification; and he shall set the live bird free in the open country. ⁸The one to be purified shall wash those clothes, shave off all hair, and bathe in water—and then shall be pure. After that, the camp may be entered but one must remain outside one's tent seven days. ⁹On the seventh day all hair shall be shaved off—of head, beard [if any], and eyebrows. Having shaved off all hair, the person shall wash those clothes and bathe the body in water—and then shall be pure. ¹⁰On the eighth day that person shall take two male lambs without blemish, one ewe lamb in its first year without blemish, three-tenths of a measure of choice flour with oil mixed in for a meal offering, and one *log* of oil. ¹¹These shall be presented before יהוה, with the person to be purified, at the entrance of the Tent of Meeting, by the priest who performs the purification.

¹²The priest shall take one of the male lambs and offer it with the *log* of oil as a guilt offering, and he shall elevate them as an elevation offering before יהוה. ¹³The lamb shall be slaughtered at the spot in the sacred area where the sin offering and the burnt offering are slaughtered. For the guilt offering, like the sin offering, goes to the priest; it is most holy. ¹⁴The priest shall take some of the blood of the guilt offering, and the priest shall put it on the ridge of the right ear of the one who is being purified, and on the thumb of the right hand, and on the big toe of the right foot. ¹⁵The priest shall then take some of the *log* of oil and pour it into the palm of his own left hand. ¹⁶And the priest shall dip his right finger in the oil that is in the palm of his left hand and sprinkle some of the oil with his finger seven times before יהוה. ¹⁷Some of the oil left in his palm shall be put by the priest on the ridge of the right ear of the one being purified, on the thumb of the right hand, and on the big toe of the right foot—over the blood of the guilt offering. ¹⁸The rest of the oil in his palm the priest shall put on the head of the one being purified. Thus the priest shall make expiation for that person before יהוה. ¹⁹The priest shall then offer the sin offering and make expiation for the one being purified of defilement. Last, the burnt offering shall be slaughtered, ²⁰and the priest shall offer the burnt offering and the meal offering on the altar; the priest shall make expiation for that person, who shall then be pure.

²¹If, however, one is poor and without sufficient means, that person shall take one male lamb for a guilt offering, to be elevated in expiation, one-tenth of a measure of choice flour with oil mixed in for a meal offering, and a *log* of oil; ²²and two turtledoves or two pigeons—depending on that person's means—the one to be the sin offering and the other the burnt offering. ²³On the eighth day of purification, the person shall bring them to the priest at the entrance of the Tent of Meeting, before יהוה. ²⁴The priest shall take the lamb of guilt offering and the *log* of oil, and elevate them as an elevation offering before יהוה. ²⁵When the lamb of guilt offering has been slaughtered, the priest shall take some of the blood of the guilt offering and put it on the ridge of the right ear of the one being purified, on the thumb of the right hand, and on the big toe of the right foot. ²⁶The priest shall then pour some of the oil into the palm of his own left hand, ²⁷and with the finger of his right hand the priest shall sprinkle some of the oil that is in the palm of his left hand seven times before יהוה. ²⁸Some of the oil in his palm shall be put by the priest on the ridge of the right ear of the one being purified, on the thumb of the right hand, and on the big toe of the right foot, over the same places as the blood of the guilt offering; ²⁹and what is left of the oil in his palm the priest shall put on the head of the one being purified, to make expiation for that person before יהוה. ³⁰That person shall then offer one of the turtledoves or pigeons, depending on the person's means—³¹whichever that person can afford—the one as a sin offering and the other as a burnt offering, together with the meal offering. Thus the priest shall make expiation before יהוה for the one being purified. ³²Such is the ritual for one who has a scaly affection and whose means for purification are limited.

³³יהוה spoke to Moses and Aaron, saying:

³⁴When you enter the land of Canaan that I give you as a possession, and I inflict an eruptive plague upon a house in the land you possess, ³⁵the owner of the house shall come and tell the priest, saying, "Something like a plague has appeared upon my house." ³⁶The priest shall order the house cleared before the priest enters to examine the plague, so that nothing in the house may become impure; after that the priest shall enter to examine the house. ³⁷If, when he examines the plague, the plague in the walls of the house is found to consist of greenish or reddish streaks that appear to go deep into the wall, ³⁸the priest shall come out of the house to the entrance of the house, and close up the house for seven days. ³⁹On the seventh day the priest shall return. If he sees that the plague has spread on the walls of the house, ⁴⁰the priest shall order the stones with the plague in them to be pulled out and cast outside the city into an impure place. ⁴¹The house shall be scraped inside all around, and the coating that is scraped off shall be dumped outside the city in an impure place. ⁴²They shall take other stones and replace those stones with them, and take other coating and plaster the house.

⁴³If the plague again breaks out in the house, after the stones have been pulled out and after the house has been scraped and replastered, ⁴⁴the priest shall come to examine: if the plague has spread in the house, it is a malignant eruption in the house; it is impure. ⁴⁵The house shall be torn down—its stones and timber and all the coating on the house—and taken to an impure place outside the city.

⁴⁶Whoever enters the house while it is closed up shall be impure until evening. ⁴⁷Whoever sleeps in the house must wash those clothes, and whoever eats in the house must wash those clothes.

⁴⁸If, however, the priest comes and sees that the plague has not spread in the house after the house was replastered,

the priest shall pronounce the house pure, for the plague has healed. 49To purge the house, he shall take two birds, cedar wood, crimson stuff, and hyssop. 50He shall slaughter the one bird over fresh water in an earthen vessel. 51He shall take the cedar wood, the hyssop, the crimson stuff, and the live bird, and dip them in the blood of the slaughtered bird and the fresh water, and sprinkle on the house seven times. 52Having purged the house with the blood of the bird, the fresh water, the live bird, the cedar wood, the hyssop, and the crimson stuff, 53he shall set the live bird free outside the city in the open country. Thus he shall make expiation for the house, and it shall be pure.

54Such is the ritual for every eruptive affection—for scalls, 55for an eruption on a cloth or a house, 56for swellings, for rashes, or for discolorations—57to determine when they are impure and when they are pure. Such is the ritual concerning eruptions.

15 יהוה spoke to Moses and Aaron, saying: 2Speak to the Israelite people and say to them:

When any man has a discharge issuing from his member, he is impure. 3The impurity from his discharge shall mean the following—whether his member runs with the discharge or is stopped up so that there is no discharge, his impurity means this: 4Any bedding on which the one with the discharge lies shall be impure, and every object on which he sits shall be impure. 5Those who touch his bedding shall wash their clothes, bathe in water, and remain impure until evening. 6All those who sit on an object on which the one with the discharge has sat shall wash their clothes, bathe in water, and remain impure until evening. 7Those who touch the body of the one with the discharge shall wash their clothes, bathe in water, and remain impure until evening. 8If the one with a discharge spits on someone who is pure, the latter shall wash those clothes, bathe in water, and remain impure until evening. 9Any means for riding that the one with a discharge has mounted shall be impure; 10all those who touch anything that was under him shall be impure until evening; and all those who carry such things shall wash their clothes, bathe in water, and remain impure until evening. 11All those whom the one with a discharge touches, without having rinsed his hands in water, shall wash their clothes, bathe in water, and remain impure until evening. 12An earthen vessel that the one with a discharge touches shall be broken; and any wooden implement shall be rinsed with water.

13When the one with a discharge becomes purified of his discharge he shall count off seven days for his purification, wash those clothes, and bathe his body in fresh water; then he shall be pure. 14On the eighth day he shall take two turtledoves or two pigeons and come before יהוה at the entrance of the Tent of Meeting and give them to the priest. 15The priest shall offer them, the one as a sin offering and the other as a burnt offering. Thus the priest shall make expiation on his behalf, for his discharge, before יהוה. 16When a man has an emission of semen, he shall bathe his whole body in water and remain impure until evening. 17All cloth or leather on which semen falls shall be washed in water and remain impure until evening. 18Likewise for a woman: when a man has carnal relations with her, both shall bathe in water and remain impure until evening.

19When a woman has a discharge, her discharge being blood from her body, she shall remain in her menstrual separation seven days; whoever touches her shall be impure until evening. 20Anything that she lies on during her menstrual separation shall be impure; and anything that she sits on shall be impure. 21All those who touch her bedding shall wash their clothes, bathe in water, and remain impure until

evening; 22and all those who touch any object on which she has sat shall wash their clothes, bathe in water, and remain impure until evening. 23Be it the bedding or be it the object on which she has sat, on touching it one shall be impure until evening. 24And if a man lies with her, her menstrual separation applies to him; he shall be impure seven days, and any bedding on which he lies shall become impure.

25When a woman has had a discharge of blood for many days, not at the time of her menstrual separation, or when she has a discharge beyond her period of menstrual separation, she shall be impure, as though at the time of her menstrual separation, as long as her discharge lasts. 26Any bedding on which she lies while her discharge lasts shall be for her like bedding during her menstrual separation; and any object on which she sits shall become impure, as it does during her menstrual separation: 27All those who touch them shall be impure—and shall wash their clothes, bathe in water, and remain impure until evening. 28When she becomes purified of her discharge, she shall count off seven days, and after that she shall be pure. 29On the eighth day she shall take two turtledoves or two pigeons, and bring them to the priest at the entrance of the Tent of Meeting. 30The priest shall offer the one as a sin offering and the other as a burnt offering; and the priest shall make expiation on her behalf, for her impure discharge, before יהוה.

31You shall put the Israelites on guard against their impurity, lest they die through their impurity by defiling My Tabernacle which is among them.

32Such is the ritual concerning one who has a discharge: concerning him who has an emission of semen and becomes impure thereby; 33and concerning her whose condition is that of menstrual separation; and concerning anyone, male or female, who has a discharge; and concerning a man who lies with an impure woman.

16 יהוה spoke to Moses after the death of the two sons of Aaron who died when they drew too close to the presence of יהוה. 2 יהוה said to Moses:

Tell your brother Aaron that he is not to come at will into the Shrine behind the curtain, in front of the cover that is upon the ark, lest he die; for I appear in the cloud over the cover. 3Thus only shall Aaron enter the Shrine: with a bull of the herd for a sin offering and a ram for a burnt offering.—4He shall be dressed in a sacral linen tunic, with linen breeches next to his flesh, and be girt with a linen sash, and he shall wear a linen turban. They are sacral vestments; he shall bathe his body in water and then put them on.—5And from the Israelite community he shall take two he-goats for a sin offering and a ram for a burnt offering.

6Aaron is to offer his own bull of sin offering, to make expiation for himself and for his household. 7Aaron shall take the two he-goats and let them stand before יהוה at the entrance of the Tent of Meeting; 8and he shall place lots upon the two goats, one marked for יהוה and the other marked for Azazel. 9Aaron shall bring forward the goat designated by lot for יהוה, which he is to offer as a sin offering; 10while the goat designated by lot for Azazel shall be left standing alive before יהוה, to make expiation with it and to send it off to the wilderness for Azazel.

11Aaron shall then offer his bull of sin offering, to make expiation for himself and his household. He shall slaughter his bull of sin offering, 12and he shall take a panful of glowing coals scooped from the altar before יהוה, and two handfuls of finely ground aromatic incense, and bring this behind the curtain. 13He shall put the incense on the fire before יהוה, so that the cloud from the incense screens the cover that is over [the Ark of] the Pact, lest he die. 14He shall take some of the blood of the bull and sprinkle it with his finger over the cover on the east side; and in front of the cover he shall sprinkle some of the blood with his finger seven times. [15]He shall then slaughter the people's goat of sin offering, bring its blood behind the curtain, and do with its blood as he has done with the blood of the bull: he shall sprinkle it over the cover and in front of the cover.

[16]Thus he shall purge the Shrine of the impurity and transgression of the Israelites, whatever their sins; and he shall do the same for the Tent of Meeting, which abides with them in the midst of their impurity. [17]When he goes in to make expiation in the Shrine, nobody else shall be in the Tent of Meeting until he comes out. When he has made expiation for himself and his household, and for the whole congregation of Israel, [18]he shall go out to the altar that is before יהוה and purge it: he shall take some of the blood of the bull and of the goat and apply it to each of the horns of the altar; [19]and the rest of the blood he shall sprinkle on it with his finger seven times. Thus he shall purify it of the defilement of the Israelites and consecrate it.

[20]When he has finished purging the Shrine, the Tent of Meeting, and the altar, the live goat shall be brought forward. [21]Aaron shall lay both his hands upon the head of the live goat and confess over it all the iniquities and transgressions of the Israelites, whatever their sins, putting them on the head of the goat; and it shall be sent off to the wilderness through a designated agent. [22]Thus the goat shall carry on it all their iniquities to an inaccessible region; and the goat shall be set free in the wilderness.

[23]And Aaron shall go into the Tent of Meeting, take off the linen vestments that he put on when he entered the Shrine, and leave them there. [24]He shall bathe his body in water in the holy precinct and put on his vestments; then he shall come out and offer his burnt offering and the burnt offering of the people, making expiation for himself and for the people. [25]The fat of the sin offering he shall turn into smoke on the altar.

[26]The one who set the Azazel goat free shall wash those clothes and bathe the body in water—and after that may reenter the camp.

[27]The bull of sin offering and the goat of sin offering whose blood was brought in to purge the Shrine shall be taken outside the camp; and their hides, flesh, and dung shall be consumed in fire. [28]The one who burned them shall wash those clothes and bathe the body in water—and after that may reenter the camp.

[29]And this shall be to you a law for all time: In the seventh month, on the tenth day of the month, you shall practice selfdenial; and you shall do no manner of work, neither the citizen nor the alien who resides among you. [30]For on this day atonement shall be made for you to purify you of all your sins; you shall be pure before יהוה. [31]It shall be a sabbath of complete rest for you, and you shall practice self-denial; it is a law for all time. [32]The priest who has been anointed and ordained to serve as priest in place of his father shall make expiation. He shall put on the linen vestments, the sacral vestments. [33]He shall purge the innermost Shrine; he shall purge the Tent of Meeting and the altar; and he shall make expiation for the priests and for all the people of the congregation.

[34]This shall be to you a law for all time: to make atonement for the Israelites for all their sins once a year.

And Moses did as יהוה had commanded him.

17 [1]יהוה spoke to Moses, saying: [2]Speak to Aaron and his sons and to all the Israelite people and say to them: This is what יהוה has commanded: [3]if anyone of the house of Israel slaughters an ox or sheep or goat in the camp, or does so outside the camp, [4]and does not bring it to the entrance of the Tent of Meeting to present it as an offering to יהוה, before יהוה's Tabernacle, bloodguilt shall be imputed to that person: having shed blood, that person shall be cut off from among this people. [5]This is in order that the Israelites may bring the sacrifices which they have been making in the open—that they may bring them before יהוה, to the priest, at the entrance of the Tent of Meeting, and offer them as sacrifices of wellbeing to יהוה; [6]that the priest may dash the blood against the altar of יהוה at the entrance of the Tent of Meeting, and turn the fat into smoke as a pleasing odor to יהוה; [7]and that they may offer their sacrifices no more to the goatdemons after whom they stray. This shall be to them a law for all time, throughout the ages.

[8]Say to them further: If anyone of the house of Israel or of the strangers who reside among them offers a burnt offering or a sacrifice, [9]and does not bring it to the entrance of the Tent of Meeting to offer it to יהוה, that person shall be cut off from this people.

[10]And if anyone of the house of Israel or of the strangers who reside among them partakes of any blood, I will set My face against the person who partakes of the blood; I will cut that person off from among kin. [11]For the life of the flesh is in the blood, and I have assigned it to you for making expiation for your lives upon the altar; it is the blood, as life, that effects expiation. [12]Therefore I say to the Israelite people: No person among you shall partake of blood, nor shall the stranger who resides among you partake of blood.

[13]And if any Israelite or any stranger who resides among them hunts down an animal or a bird that may be eaten, that person shall pour out its blood and cover it with earth. [14]For the life of all flesh—its blood is its life. Therefore I say to the Israelite people: You shall not partake of the blood of any flesh, for the life of all flesh is its blood. Anyone who partakes of it shall be cut off.

[15]Any person, whether citizen or stranger, who eats what has died or has been torn by beasts shall wash those clothes, bathe in water, remain impure until evening—and shall then be pure. [16]But if the clothes are not washed and the body is not bathed, that person shall bear the guilt.

18 [1]יהוה spoke to Moses, saying: [2]Speak to the Israelite people and say to them:

I יהוה am your God. [3]You shall not copy the practices of the land of Egypt where you dwelt, or of the land of Canaan to which I am taking you; nor shall you follow their laws. [4]My rules alone shall you observe, and faithfully follow My laws: I יהוה am your God.

[5]You shall keep My laws and My rules, by the pursuit of which human beings shall live: I am יהוה.

[6]None of you men shall come near anyone of his own flesh to uncover nakedness: I am יהוה.

[7]Your father's nakedness, that is, the nakedness of your mother, you shall not uncover; she is your mother—you shall not uncover her nakedness.

[8]Do not uncover the nakedness of your father's wife; it is the nakedness of your father.

[9]The nakedness of your sister—your father's daughter or your mother's, whether born into the household or outside—do not uncover their nakedness.

[10]The nakedness of your son's daughter, or of your daughter's daughter—do not uncover their nakedness; for their nakedness is yours.

[11]The nakedness of your father's wife's daughter, who was born into your father's household—she is your sister; do not uncover her nakedness.

[12]Do not uncover the nakedness of your father's sister; she is your father's flesh.

¹³Do not uncover the nakedness of your mother's sister; for she is your mother's flesh.

¹⁴Do not uncover the nakedness of your father's brother: do not approach his wife; she is your aunt.

¹⁵Do not uncover the nakedness of your daughter-in-law: she is your son's wife; you shall not uncover her nakedness.

¹⁶Do not uncover the nakedness of your brother's wife; it is the nakedness of your brother.

¹⁷Do not uncover the nakedness of a woman and her daughter; nor shall you take [into your household as a wife] her son's daughter or her daughter's daughter and uncover her nakedness: they are kindred; it is depravity.

¹⁸Do not take [into your household as a wife] a woman as a rival to her sister and uncover her nakedness in the other's lifetime.

¹⁹Do not come near a woman during her menstrual period of impurity to uncover her nakedness.

²⁰Do not have carnal relations with your neighbor's wife and defile yourself with her.

²¹Do not allow any of your offspring to be offered up to Molech, and do not profane the name of your God: I am יהוה.

²²Do not lie with a male as one lies with a woman; it is an abhorrence.

²³Do not have carnal relations with any beast and defile yourself thereby. Likewise for a woman: she shall not lend herself to a beast to mate with it; it is perversion.

²⁴Do not defile yourselves in any of those ways, for it is by such that the nations that I am casting out before you defiled themselves. ²⁵Thus the land became defiled; and I called it to account for its iniquity, and the land spewed out its inhabitants. ²⁶But you must keep My laws and My rules, and you must not do any of those abhorrent things, neither the citizen nor the stranger who resides among you; ²⁷for all those abhorrent things were done by the people who were in the land before you, and the land became defiled. ²⁸So let not the land spew you out for defiling it, as it spewed out the nation that came before you. ²⁹All who do any of those abhorrent things—such persons shall be cut off from their people. ³⁰You shall keep My charge not to engage in any of the abhorrent practices that were carried on before you, and you shall not defile yourselves through them: I יהוה am your God.

19 ¹יהוה spoke to Moses, saying: ²Speak to the whole Israelite community and say to them:

You shall be holy, for I, your God יהוה, am holy.

³You shall each revere your mother and your father, and keep My sabbaths: I יהוה am your God.

⁴Do not turn to idols or make molten gods for yourselves: I יהוה am your God.

⁵When you sacrifice an offering of wellbeing to יהוה, sacrifice it so that it may be accepted on your behalf. ⁶It shall be eaten on the day you sacrifice it, or on the day following; but what is left by the third day must be consumed in fire. ⁷If it should be eaten on the third day, it is an offensive thing, it will not be acceptable. ⁸And one who eats of it shall bear the guilt for having profaned what is sacred to יהוה; that person shall be cut off from kin.

⁹When you reap the harvest of your land, you shall not reap all the way to the edges of your field, or gather the gleanings of your harvest. ¹⁰You shall not pick your vineyard bare, or gather the fallen fruit of your vineyard; you shall leave them for the poor and the stranger: I יהוה am your God.

¹¹You shall not steal; you shall not deal deceitfully or falsely with one another. ¹²You shall not swear falsely by My name, profaning the name of your God: I am יהוה.

¹³You shall not defraud your fellow [Israelite]. You shall not commit robbery. The wages of a laborer shall not remain with you until morning.

¹⁴You shall not insult the deaf, or place a stumbling block before the blind. You shall fear your God: I am יהוה.

¹⁵You shall not render an unfair decision: do not favor the poor or show deference to the rich; judge your kin fairly. ¹⁶Do not deal basely with members of your people. Do not profit by the blood of your fellow [Israelite]: I am יהוה.

¹⁷You shall not hate your kinsfolk in your heart. Reprove your kin but incur no guilt on their account. ¹⁸You shall not take vengeance or bear a grudge against members of your people. Love your fellow [Israelite] as yourself: I am יהוה.

¹⁹You shall observe My laws.

You shall not let your cattle mate with a different kind; you shall not sow your field with two kinds of seed; you shall not put on cloth from a mixture of two kinds of material.

²⁰If a man has carnal relations with a woman who is a slave and has been designated for another man, but has not been redeemed or given her freedom, there shall be an indemnity; they shall not, however, be put to death, since she has not been freed. ²¹But he must bring to the entrance of the Tent of Meeting, as his guilt offering to יהוה, a ram of guilt offering. ²²With the ram of guilt offering the priest shall make expiation for him before יהוה for the sin that he committed; and the sin that he committed will be forgiven him.

²³When you enter the land and plant any tree for food, you shall regard its fruit as forbidden. Three years it shall be forbidden for you, not to be eaten. ²⁴In the fourth year all its fruit shall be set aside for jubilation before יהוה; ²⁵and only in the fifth year may you use its fruit—that its yield to you may be increased: I יהוה am your God.

²⁶You shall not eat anything with its blood. You shall not practice divination or soothsaying. ²⁷You [men] shall not round off the side-growth on your head, or destroy the sidegrowth of your beard. ²⁸You shall not make gashes in your flesh for the dead, or incise any marks on yourselves: I am יהוה.

²⁹Do not degrade your daughter and make her a harlot, lest the land fall into harlotry and the land be filled with depravity. ³⁰You shall keep My sabbaths and venerate My sanctuary: I am יהוה.

³¹Do not turn to ghosts and do not inquire of familiar spirits, to be defiled by them: I יהוה am your God.

³²You shall rise before the aged and show deference to the old; you shall fear your God: I am יהוה.

³³When strangers reside with you in your land, you shall not wrong them. ³⁴The strangers who reside with you shall be to you as your citizens; you shall love each one as yourself, for you were strangers in the land of Egypt: I יהוה am your God.

³⁵You shall not falsify measures of length, weight, or capacity. ³⁶You shall have an honest balance, honest weights, an honest *ephah*, and an honest *hin*. I יהוה am your God who freed you from the land of Egypt. ³⁷You shall faithfully observe all My laws and all My rules: I am יהוה.

20 ¹And יהוה spoke to Moses: ²Say further to the Israelite people:

Anyone among the Israelites, or among the strangers residing in Israel, who gives any offspring to Molech, shall be put to death; the people of the land shall pelt the person with stones. ³And I will set My face against that person, whom I will cut off from among the people for having given offspring to Molech and so defiled My sanctuary and profaned My holy name. ⁴And if the people of the land should shut their eyes to that person's giving offspring to Molech, and should not put the person to death, ⁵I Myself will set My face against that person's kin as well; and I will cut off from among their people both that person and all who follow in going astray after Molech. 6And if any person turns to ghosts and familiar spirits and goes astray after them, I will set My face against that person, whom I will cut off from among the people.

7You shall sanctify yourselves and be holy, for I יהוה am your God. 8You shall faithfully observe My laws: I יהוה make you holy.

9If anyone insults either father or mother, that person shall be put to death; that person has insulted father and mother—and retains the bloodguilt.

10If a man commits adultery with another's wife—committing adultery with the wife of his fellow [Israelite]—the adulterer and the adulteress shall be put to death. 11If a man lies with his father's wife, it is the nakedness of his father that he has uncovered; the two shall be put to death—and they retain the bloodguilt. 12If a man lies with his daughter-in-law, both of them shall be put to death; they have committed incest—and they retain the bloodguilt. 13If a man lies with a male as one lies with a woman, the two of them have done an abhorrent thing; they shall be put to death—and they retain the bloodguilt. 14If a man takes a woman and her mother [into his household as his wives], it is depravity; both he and they shall be put to the fire, that there be no depravity among you. 15If a man has carnal relations with a beast, he shall be put to death; and you shall kill the beast. 16If a woman approaches any beast to mate with it, you shall kill the woman and the beast; they shall be put to death—and they retain the bloodguilt.

17If a man takes his sister [into his household as a wife], the daughter of either his father or his mother, so that he sees her nakedness and she sees his nakedness, it is a disgrace; they shall be excommunicated in the sight of their kinsfolk. He has uncovered the nakedness of his sister, he shall bear the guilt. 18If a man lies with a woman during her menstrual condition and uncovers her nakedness, he has laid bare her flow and she has exposed her blood flow; both of them shall be cut off from among their people. 19You [males] shall not uncover the nakedness of your mother's sister or of your father's sister, for that is laying bare one's own flesh; they shall bear their guilt. 20If a man lies with his uncle's wife, it is his uncle's nakedness that he has uncovered. They shall bear their guilt: they shall die childless. 21If a man takes the wife of his brother [into his household as a wife], it is indecency. It is the nakedness of his brother that he has uncovered; they shall remain childless.

22You shall faithfully observe all My laws and all My regulations, lest the land to which I bring you to settle in spew you out. 23You shall not follow the practices of the nation that I am driving out before you. For it is because they did all these things that I abhorred them 24and said to you: You shall possess their land, for I will give it to you to possess, a land flowing with milk and honey. I יהוה am your God who has set you apart from other peoples. 25So you shall set apart the pure beast from the impure, the impure bird from the pure. You shall not draw abomination upon yourselves through beast or bird or anything with which the ground is alive, which I have set apart for you to treat as impure. 26You shall be holy to Me, for I יהוה am holy, and I have set you apart from other peoples to be Mine.

27A man or a woman who has a ghost or a familiar spirit shall be put to death; they shall be pelted with stones—and they shall retain the bloodguilt.

21 יהוה said to Moses: Speak to the priests, the sons of Aaron, and say to them:

None shall defile himself for any [dead] person among his kin, 2except for the relatives that are closest to him: his mother, his father, his son, his daughter, and his brother; 3also for a virgin sister, close to him because she has not become someone's [wife], for her he may defile himself. 4But he shall not defile himself for his wife as kin, and so profane himself.

5They shall not shave smooth any part of their heads, or cut the side-growth of their beards, or make gashes in their flesh. 6They shall be holy to their God and not profane the name of their God; for they offer יהוה's offerings by fire, the food of their God, and so must be holy.

7They shall not take [into their household as their wife] a woman defiled by harlotry, nor shall they take one divorced from her husband. For they are holy to their God 8and you must treat them as holy, since they offer the food of your God; they shall be holy to you, for I יהוה who sanctify you am holy.

9When the daughter of a priest defiles herself through harlotry, it is her father whom she defiles; she shall be put to the fire.

10The priest who is exalted above his fellows, on whose head the anointing oil has been poured and who has been ordained to wear the vestments, shall not bare his head or rend his vestments.

11He shall not go in where there is any dead body; he shall not defile himself even for his father or mother. 12He shall not go outside the sanctuary and profane the sanctuary of his God, for upon him is the distinction of the anointing oil of his God, Mine יהוה's. 13He may take [into his household as his wife] only a woman who is a virgin. 14A widow, or a divorced woman, or one who is degraded by harlotry—such he may not take. Only a virgin of his own kin may he take as his wife—15that he may not profane his offspring among his kin, for I יהוה have sanctified him.

16יהוה spoke further to Moses: 17Speak to Aaron and say: No man of your offspring throughout the ages who has a defect shall be qualified to offer the food of his God. 18No one at all who has a defect shall be qualified: no man who is blind, or lame, or has a limb too short or too long; 19no man who has a broken leg or a broken arm; 20or who is a hunchback, or a dwarf, or who has a growth in his eye, or who has a boilscar, or scurvy, or crushed testes. 21No man among the offspring of Aaron the priest who has a defect shall be qualified to offer יהוה's offering by fire; having a defect, he shall not be qualified to offer the food of his God. 22He may eat of the food of his God, of the most holy as well as of the holy; 23but he shall not enter behind the curtain or come near the altar, for he has a defect. He shall not profane these places sacred to Me, for I יהוה have sanctified them. 24Thus Moses spoke to Aaron and his sons and to all the Israelites.

22 יהוה spoke to Moses, saying: 2Instruct Aaron and his sons to be scrupulous about the sacred donations that the Israelite people consecrate to Me, lest they profane My holy name, Mine יהוה's. 3Say to them:

Throughout the ages, if any man among your offspring, while in a state of impurity, partakes of any sacred donation that the Israelite people may consecrate to יהוה, that person shall be cut off from before Me: I am יהוה. 4No man of Aaron's offspring who has an eruption or a discharge shall eat of the sacred donations until he is pure. If one touches anything made impure by a corpse, or if a man has an emission of semen, 5or if a man touches any swarming thing by which he is made impure or any human being by whom he is made impure—whatever his impurity—6the person who touches such shall be impure until evening and shall not eat of the sacred donations unless he has washed his body in water.

7As soon as the sun sets, he shall be pure; and afterward he may eat of the sacred donations, for they are his food. 8He shall not eat anything that died or was torn by beasts, thereby becoming impure: I am יהוה. 9They shall keep My charge, lest they incur guilt thereby and die for it, having committed profanation: I יהוה consecrate them.

10No lay person shall eat of the sacred donations. No bound or hired laborer of a priest shall eat of the sacred donations; 11but a person who is a priest's property by purchase may eat of them; and those that are born into his household may eat of his food. 12If a priest's daughter becomes a layman's [wife], she may not eat of the sacred gifts; 13but if the priest's daughter is widowed or divorced and without offspring, and is back in her father's house as in her youth, she may eat of her father's food. No lay person may eat of it: 14but if a person eats of a sacred donation unwittingly, the priest shall be paid for the sacred donation, adding one-fifth of its value. 15But [the priests] must not allow the Israelites to profane the sacred donations that they set aside for יהוה, 16or to incur guilt requiring a penalty payment, by eating such sacred donations: for it is I יהוה who make them sacred.

17יהוה spoke to Moses, saying: 18Speak to Aaron and his sons, and to all the Israelite people, and say to them: When any person of the house of Israel or of the strangers in Israel presents a burnt offering as the offering for any of the votive or any of the freewill offerings that they offer to יהוה, 19it must, to be acceptable in your favor, be a male without blemish, from cattle or sheep or goats. 20You shall not offer any that has a defect, for it will not be accepted in your favor.

21And when a person offers, from the herd or the flock, a sacrifice of wellbeing to יהוה for an explicit vow or as a freewill offering, it must, to be acceptable, be without blemish; there must be no defect in it. 22Anything blind, or injured, or maimed, or with a wen, boil-scar, or scurvy—such you shall not offer to יהוה; you shall not put any of them on the altar as offerings by fire to יהוה. 23You may, however, present as a freewill offering an ox or a sheep with a limb extended or contracted; but it will not be accepted for a vow. 24You shall not offer to יהוה anything [with its testes] bruised or crushed or torn or cut. You shall have no such practices in your own land, 25nor shall you accept such [animals] from a foreigner for offering as food for your God, for they are mutilated, they have a defect; they shall not be accepted in your favor.

26יהוה spoke to Moses, saying: 27When an ox or a sheep or a goat is born, it shall stay seven days with its mother, and from the eighth day on it shall be acceptable as an offering by fire to יהוה. 28However, no animal from the herd or from the flock shall be slaughtered on the same day with its young.

29When you sacrifice a thanksgiving offering to יהוה, sacrifice it so that it may be acceptable in your favor. 30It shall be eaten on the same day; you shall not leave any of it until morning: I am יהוה.

31You shall faithfully observe My commandments: I am יהוה. 32You shall not profane My holy name, that I may be sanctified in the midst of the Israelite people—I יהוה who sanctify you, 33I who brought you out of the land of Egypt to be your God, I יהוה.

23 יהוה spoke to Moses, saying: 2Speak to the Israelite people and say to them: These are My fixed times, the fixed times of יהוה, which you shall proclaim as sacred occasions.

3On six days work may be done, but on the seventh day there shall be a sabbath of complete rest, a sacred occasion. You shall do no work; it shall be a sabbath of יהוה throughout your settlements.

4These are the set times of יהוה, the sacred occasions, which you shall celebrate each at its appointed time: 5In the first month, on the fourteenth day of the month, at twilight, there shall be a passover offering to יהוה, 6and on the fifteenth day of that month יהוה's Feast of Unleavened Bread. You shall eat unleavened bread for seven days. 7On the first day you shall celebrate a sacred occasion: you shall not work at your occupations. 8Seven days you shall make offerings by fire to יהוה. The seventh day shall be a sacred occasion: you shall not work at your occupations.

9יהוה spoke to Moses, saying: 10Speak to the Israelite people and say to them:

When you enter the land that I am giving to you and you reap its harvest, you shall bring the first sheaf of your harvest to the priest. 11He shall elevate the sheaf before יהוה for acceptance in your behalf; the priest shall elevate it on the day after the sabbath. 12On the day that you elevate the sheaf, you shall offer as a burnt offering to יהוה a lamb of the first year without blemish. 13The meal offering with it shall be two-tenths of a measure of choice flour with oil mixed in, an offering by fire of pleasing odor to יהוה; and the libation with it shall be of wine, a quarter of a *hin*. 14Until that very day, until you have brought the offering of your God, you shall eat no bread or parched grain or fresh ears; it is a law for all time throughout the ages in all your settlements.

15And from the day on which you bring the sheaf of elevation offering—the day after the sabbath—you shall count off seven weeks. They must be complete: 16you must count until the day after the seventh week—fifty days; then you shall bring an offering of new grain to יהוה. 17You shall bring from your settlements two loaves of bread as an elevation offering; each shall be made of two-tenths of a measure of choice flour, baked after leavening, as first fruits to יהוה. 18With the bread you shall present, as burnt offerings to יהוה, seven yearling lambs without blemish, one bull of the herd, and two rams, with their meal offerings and libations, an offering by fire of pleasing odor to יהוה. 19You shall also offer one he-goat as a sin offering and two yearling lambs as a sacrifice of wellbeing. 20The priest shall elevate these—the two lambs—together with the bread of first fruits as an elevation offering before יהוה; they shall be holy to יהוה, for the priest. 21On that same day you shall hold a celebration; it shall be a sacred occasion for you; you shall not work at your occupations. This is a law for all time in all your settlements, throughout the ages.

22And when you reap the harvest of your land, you shall not reap all the way to the edges of your field, or gather the gleanings of your harvest; you shall leave them for the poor and the stranger: I יהוה am your God.

23יהוה spoke to Moses, saying: 24Speak to the Israelite people thus: In the seventh month, on the first day of the month, you shall observe complete rest, a sacred occasion commemorated with loud blasts. 25You shall not work at your occupations; and you shall bring an offering by fire to יהוה.

26יהוה spoke to Moses, saying: 27Mark, the tenth day of this seventh month is the Day of Atonement. It shall be a sacred occasion for you: you shall practice self-denial, and you shall bring an offering by fire to יהוה; 28you shall do no work throughout that day. For it is a Day of Atonement, on which expiation is made on your behalf before your God יהוה. 29Indeed, any person who does not practice self-denial throughout that day shall be cut off from kin; 30and whoever does any work throughout that day, I will cause that person to perish from among the people. 31Do no work whatever; it is a law for all time, throughout the ages in all your settlements. 32It shall be a sabbath of complete rest for you, and you shall practice self-denial; on the ninth day of the month at evening, from evening to evening, you shall observe this your sabbath.

יהוה 33spoke to Moses, saying: 34Say to the Israelite people: On the fifteenth day of this seventh month there shall be the Feast of Booths to יהוה, [to last] seven days. 35The first day shall be a sacred occasion: you shall not work at your occupations; 36seven days you shall bring offerings by fire to יהוה. On the eighth day you shall observe a sacred occasion and bring an offering by fire to יהוה; it is a solemn gathering: you shall not work at your occupations.

37Those are the set times of יהוה that you shall celebrate as sacred occasions, bringing offerings by fire to יהוה—burnt offerings, meal offerings, sacrifices, and libations, on each day what is proper to it—38apart from the sabbaths of יהוה, and apart from your gifts and from all your votive offerings and from all your freewill offerings that you give to יהוה.

39Mark, on the fifteenth day of the seventh month, when you have gathered in the yield of your land, you shall observe the festival of יהוה [to last] seven days: a complete rest on the first day, and a complete rest on the eighth day. 40On the first day you shall take the product of *hadar* trees, branches of palm trees, boughs of leafy trees, and willows of the brook, and you shall rejoice before your God יהוה seven days. 41You shall observe it as a festival of יהוה for seven days in the year; you shall observe it in the seventh month as a law for all time, throughout the ages. 42You shall live in booths seven days; all citizens in Israel shall live in booths, 43in order that future generations may know that I made the Israelite people live in booths when I brought them out of the land of Egypt—I, your God יהוה. 44So Moses declared to the Israelites the set times of יהוה.

24 יהוה spoke to Moses, saying: 2Command the Israelite people to bring you clear oil of beaten olives for lighting, for kindling lamps regularly. 3Aaron shall set them up in the Tent of Meeting outside the curtain of the Pact [to burn] from evening to morning before יהוה regularly; it is a law for all time throughout the ages. 4He shall set up the lamps on the pure lamp-stand before יהוה [to burn] regularly.

5You shall take choice flour and bake of it twelve loaves, two-tenths of a measure for each loaf. 6Place them on the pure table before יהוה in two rows, six to a row. 7With each row you shall place pure frankincense, which is to be a token offering for the bread, as an offering by fire to יהוה. 8He shall arrange them before יהוה regularly every sabbath day—it is a commitment for all time on the part of the Israelites. 9They shall belong to Aaron and his sons, who shall eat them in the sacred precinct; for they are his as most holy things from יהוה's offerings by fire, a due for all time.

10There came out among the Israelites a man whose mother was Israelite and whose father was Egyptian. And a fight broke out in the camp between that half Israelite and a certain Israelite. 11The son of the Israelite woman pronounced the Name in blasphemy, and he was brought to Moses—now his mother's name was Shelomith daughter of Dibri of the tribe of Dan—12and he was placed in custody, until the decision of יהוה should be made clear to them.

13And יהוה spoke to Moses, saying: 14Take the blasphemer outside the camp; and let all who were within hearing lay their hands upon his head, and let the community leadership stone him.

15And to the Israelite people speak thus: Anyone who blasphemes God shall bear the guilt; 16and one who also pronounces the name יהוה shall be put to death. The community leadership shall stone that person; stranger or citizen—having thus pronounced the Name—shall be put to death.

17If anyone kills any human being, that person shall be put to death. 18One who kills a beast shall make restitution for it: life for life. 19If anyone maims another [person]: what was done shall be done in return—20fracture for fracture, eye for eye, tooth for tooth. The injury inflicted on a human being shall be inflicted in return. 21One who kills a beast shall make restitution for it; but one who kills a human being shall be put to death. 22You shall have one standard for stranger and citizen alike: for I יהוה am your God.

23Moses spoke thus to the Israelites. And they took the blasphemer outside the camp and pelted him with stones. The Israelites did as יהוה had commanded Moses.

25 יהוה spoke to Moses on Mount Sinai: 2Speak to the Israelite people and say to them:

When you enter the land that I assign to you, the land shall observe a sabbath of יהוה. 3Six years you may sow your field and six years you may prune your vineyard and gather in the yield. 4But in the seventh year the land shall have a sabbath of complete rest, a sabbath of יהוה: you shall not sow your field or prune your vineyard. 5You shall not reap the after-growth of your harvest or gather the grapes of your untrimmed vines; it shall be a year of complete rest for the land. 6But you may eat whatever the land during its sabbath will produce—you, your male and female slaves, the hired and bound laborers who live with you, 7and your cattle and the beasts in your land may eat all its yield.

8You shall count off seven weeks of years—seven times seven years—so that the period of seven weeks of years gives you a total of forty-nine years. 9Then you shall sound the horn loud; in the seventh month, on the tenth day of the month—the Day of Atonement—you shall have the horn sounded throughout your land 10and you shall hallow the fiftieth year. You shall proclaim release throughout the land for all its inhabitants. It shall be a jubilee for you: each of you shall return to your holding and each of you shall return to your family. 11That fiftieth year shall be a jubilee for you: you shall not sow, neither shall you reap the after-growth or harvest the untrimmed vines, 12for it is a jubilee. It shall be holy to you: you may only eat the growth direct from the field.

13In this year of jubilee, each of you shall return to your holding. 14When you sell property to your neighbor, or buy any from your neighbor, you shall not wrong one another. 15In buying from your neighbor, you shall deduct only for the number of years since the jubilee; and in selling to you, that person shall charge you only for the remaining crop years: 16the more such years, the higher the price you pay; the fewer such years, the lower the price; for what is being sold to you is a number of harvests. 17Do not wrong one another, but fear your God; for I יהוה am your God.

18You shall observe My laws and faithfully keep My rules, that you may live upon the land in security; 19the land shall yield its fruit and you shall eat your fill, and you shall live upon it in security. 20And should you ask, "What are we to eat in the seventh year, if we may neither sow nor gather in our crops?" 21I will ordain My blessing for you in the sixth year, so that it shall yield a crop sufficient for three years. 22When you sow in the eighth year, you will still be eating old grain of that crop; you will be eating the old until the ninth year, until its crops come in.

23But the land must not be sold beyond reclaim, for the land is Mine; you are but strangers resident with Me. 24Throughout the land that you hold, you must provide for the redemption of the land.

25If one of your kin is in straits and has to sell part of a holding, the nearest redeemer shall come and redeem what that relative has sold. 26If a person has no one to be redeemed but prospers and acquires enough to redeem with, ²⁷the years since its sale shall be computed and the difference shall be refunded to the person to whom it was sold, so that the person returns to that holding. ²⁸If that person lacks sufficient means to recover it, what was sold shall remain with the purchaser until the jubilee; in the jubilee year it shall be released, so that the person returns to that holding.

²⁹If someone sells a dwelling house in a walled city, it may be redeemed until a year has elapsed since its sale; the redemption period shall be a year. ³⁰If it is not redeemed before a full year has elapsed, the house in the walled city shall pass to the purchaser beyond reclaim throughout the ages; it shall not be released in the jubilee. ³¹But houses in villages that have no encircling walls shall be classed as open country: they may be redeemed, and they shall be released through the jubilee. ³²As for the cities of Levi, the houses in the cities it holds: Levi shall forever have the right of redemption. ³³Such property as may be redeemed from Levi—houses sold in a city it holds—shall be released through the jubilee; for the houses in the cities of Levi are its holding among the Israelites. ³⁴But the unenclosed land about its cities cannot be sold, for that is its holding for all time.

³⁵If your kin, being in straits, come under your authority, and are held by you as though resident aliens, let them live by your side: ³⁶do not exact advance or accrued interest, but fear your God. Let your kin live by your side as such. ³⁷Do not lend your money at advance interest, nor give your food at accrued interest. ³⁸I יהוה am your God, who brought you out of the land of Egypt, to give you the land of Canaan, to be your God.

³⁹If your kin under you continue in straits and must be given over to you, do not subject them to the treatment of a slave. ⁴⁰Remaining with you as a hired or bound laborer, they shall serve with you only until the jubilee year. ⁴¹Then they, along with any children, shall be free of your authority; they shall go back to their family and return to the ancestral holding.—⁴²For they are My servants, whom I freed from the land of Egypt; they may not give themselves over into servitude.—⁴³You shall not rule over them ruthlessly; you shall fear your God. ⁴⁴Such male and female slaves as you may have—it is from the nations round about you that you may acquire male and female slaves. ⁴⁵You may also buy them from among the children of aliens resident among you, or from their families that are among you, whom they begot in your land. These shall become your property: ⁴⁶you may keep them as a possession for your children after you, for them to inherit as property for all time. Such you may treat as slaves. But as for your Israelite kin, no one shall rule ruthlessly over another.

⁴⁷If a resident alien among you has prospered, and your kin, being in straits, comes under that one's authority and is given over to the resident alien among you, or to an off-shoot of an alien's family, ⁴⁸[your kin] shall have the right of redemption even after having been given over. [Typically,] a brother shall do the redeeming, ⁴⁹or an uncle or an uncle's son shall do the redeeming—anyone in the family who is of the same flesh shall do the redeeming; or, having prospered, [your formerly impoverished kin] may do the redeeming. ⁵⁰The total shall be computed with the purchaser as from the year of being given over to the other until the jubilee year; the price of sale shall be applied to the number of years, as though it were for a term as a hired laborer under the other's authority. ⁵¹If many years remain, [your kin] shall pay back for the redemption in proportion to the purchase price; ⁵²and if few years remain until the jubilee year, so shall it be computed: payment shall be made for the redemption according to the years involved. ⁵³One shall be under the other's authority as a laborer hired by the year; the other shall not rule ruthlessly in your sight. ⁵⁴If not redeemed in any of those ways, that person, along with any children, shall go free in the jubilee year. ⁵⁵For it is to Me that the Israelites are servants: they are My servants, whom I freed from the land of Egypt—I, your God יהוה.

26

¹You shall not make idols for yourselves, or set up for yourselves carved images or pillars, or place figured stones in your land to worship upon, for I יהוה am your God. ²You shall keep My sabbaths and venerate My sanctuary, Mine, יהוה's.

³If you follow My laws and faithfully observe My commandments, ⁴I will grant your rains in their season, so that the earth shall yield its produce and the trees of the field their fruit. ⁵Your threshing shall overtake the vintage, and your vintage shall overtake the sowing; you shall eat your fill of bread and dwell securely in your land.

⁶I will grant peace in the land, and you shall lie down untroubled by anyone; I will give the land respite from vicious beasts, and no sword shall cross your land. ⁷[Your army] shall give chase to your enemies, and they shall fall before you by the sword. ⁸Five of you shall give chase to a hundred, and a hundred of you shall give chase to ten thousand; your enemies shall fall before you by the sword. ⁹I will look with favor upon you, and make you fertile and multi ply you; and I will maintain My covenant with you. ¹⁰You shall eat old grain long stored, and you shall have to clear out the old to make room for the new.

¹¹I will establish My abode in your midst, and I will not spurn you. ¹²I will be ever present in your midst: I will be your God, and you shall be My people. ¹³I יהוה am your God who brought you out from the land of the Egyptians to be their slaves no more, who broke the bars of your yoke and made you walk erect.

¹⁴But if you do not obey Me and do not observe all these commandments, ¹⁵if you reject My laws and spurn My rules, so that you do not observe all My commandments and you break My covenant, ¹⁶I in turn will do this to you: I will wreak misery upon you—consumption and fever, which cause the eyes to pine and the body to languish; you shall sow your seed to no purpose, for your enemies shall eat it. ¹⁷I will set My face against you: you shall be routed by your enemies, and your foes shall dominate you. You shall flee though none pursues.

¹⁸And if, for all that, you do not obey Me, I will go on to discipline you sevenfold for your sins, ¹⁹and I will break your proud glory. I will make your skies like iron and your earth like copper, ²⁰so that your strength shall be spent to no purpose. Your land shall not yield its produce, nor shall the trees of the land yield their fruit.

²¹And if you remain hostile toward Me and refuse to obey Me, I will go on smiting you sevenfold for your sins. ²²I will loose wild beasts against you, and they shall bereave you of your children and wipe out your cattle. They shall decimate you, and your roads shall be deserted.

²³And if these things fail to discipline you for Me, and you remain hostile to Me, ²⁴I too will remain hostile to you: I in turn will smite you sevenfold for your sins. ²⁵I will bring a sword against you to wreak vengeance for the covenant; and if you withdraw into your cities, I will send pestilence among you, and you shall be delivered into enemy hands. ²⁶When I break your staff of bread, ten women shall bake your bread in a single oven; they shall dole out your bread by weight, and though you eat, you shall not be satisfied.

²⁷But if, despite this, you disobey Me and remain hostile to Me, ²⁸I will act against you in wrathful hostility; I, for My

part, will discipline you sevenfold for your sins. ²⁹You shall eat the flesh of your sons and the flesh of your daughters. ³⁰I will destroy your cult places and cut down your incense stands, and I will heap your carcasses upon your lifeless fetishes. I will spurn you. ³¹I will lay your cities in ruin and make your sanctuaries desolate, and I will not savor your pleasing odors. ³²I will make the land desolate, so that your enemies who settle in it shall be appalled by it. ³³And you I will scatter among the nations, and I will unsheath the sword against you. Your land shall become a desolation and your cities a ruin.

³⁴Then shall the land make up for its sabbath years throughout the time that it is desolate and you are in the land of your enemies; then shall the land rest and make up for its Sabbath years. ³⁵Through out the time that it is desolate, it shall observe the rest that it did not observe in your sabbath years while you were dwelling upon it. ³⁶As for those of you who survive, I will cast a faintness into their hearts in the land of their enemies. The sound of a driven leaf shall put them to flight. Fleeing as though from the sword, they shall fall though none pursues. ³⁷With no one pursuing, they shall stumble over one another as before the sword. You shall not be able to stand your ground before your enemies, ³⁸but shall perish among the nations; and the land of your enemies shall consume you.

³⁹Those of you who survive shall be heartsick over their iniquity in the land of your enemies; more, they shall be heartsick over the iniquities of their forebears; ⁴⁰and they shall confess their iniquity and the iniquity of their forebears, in that they trespassed against Me, yea, were hostile to Me. ⁴¹When I, in turn, have been hostile to them and have removed them into the land of their enemies, then at last shall their obdurate heart humble itself, and they shall atone for their iniquity. ⁴²Then will I remember My covenant with Jacob; I will remember also My covenant with Isaac, and also My covenant with Abraham; and I will remember the land.

⁴³For the land shall be forsaken of them, making up for its sabbath years by being desolate of them, while they atone for their iniquity; for the abundant reason that they rejected My rules and spurned My laws. ⁴⁴Yet, even then, when they are in the land of their enemies, I will not reject them or spurn them so as to destroy them, annulling My covenant with them: for I יהוה am their God. ⁴⁵I will remember in their favor the covenant with the ancients, whom I freed from the land of Egypt in the sight of the nations to be their God: I, יהוה. ⁴⁶These are the laws, rules, and instructions that יהוה established, through Moses on Mount Sinai, with the Israelite people.

27 ¹יהוה spoke to Moses, saying: ²Speak to the Israelite people and say to them: When anyone explicitly vows to יהוה the equivalent for a human being, ³the following scale shall apply: If it is a male from twenty to sixty years of age, the equivalent is fifty shekels of silver by the sanctuary weight; ⁴if it is a female, the equivalent is thirty shekels. ⁵If the age is from five years to twenty years, the equivalent is twenty shekels for a male and ten shekels for a female. ⁶If the age is from one month to five years, the equivalent for a male is five shekels of silver, and the equivalent for a female is three shekels of silver. ⁷If the age is sixty years or over, the equivalent is fifteen shekels in the case of a male and ten shekels for a female. ⁸But if one cannot afford the

equivalent, that person shall be presented before the priest, and the priest shall make an assessment; the priest shall make the assessment according to what the vower can afford.

⁹If [the vow concerns] any animal that may be brought as an offering to יהוה, any such that may be given to יהוה shall be holy. ¹⁰One may not exchange or substitute another for it, either good for bad, or bad for good; if one does substitute one animal for another, the thing vowed and its substitute shall both be holy. ¹¹If [the vow concerns] any impure animal that may not be brought as an offering to יהוה, the animal shall be presented before the priest, ¹²and the priest shall assess it. Whether high or low, whatever assessment is set by the priest shall stand; ¹³and if one wishes to redeem it, one-fifth must be added to its assessment.

¹⁴If anyone consecrates a house to יהוה, the priest shall assess it. Whether high or low, as the priest assesses it, so it shall stand; ¹⁵and if the one who has consecrated the house wishes to redeem it, onefifth must be added to the sum at which it was assessed, and then it shall be returned.

¹⁶If anyone consecrates to יהוה any landholding, its assessment shall be in accordance with its seed requirement: fifty shekels of silver to a *chomer* of barley seed. ¹⁷If the land is consecrated as of the jubilee year, its assessment stands. ¹⁸But if the land is consecrated after the jubilee, the priest shall compute the price according to the years that are left until the jubilee year, and its assessment shall be so reduced; ¹⁹and if the one who consecrated the land wishes to redeem it, one-fifth must be added to the sum at which it was assessed, and it shall be passed back. ²⁰But if the one [who consecrated it] does not redeem the land, and the land is sold to another, it shall no longer be redeemable: ²¹when it is released in the jubilee, the land shall be holy to יהוה, as land proscribed; it becomes the priest's holding.

²²If one consecrates to יהוה land that was purchased, which is not one's landholding, ²³the priest shall compute the proportionate assessment up to the jubilee year, and the assessment shall be paid as of that day, a sacred donation to יהוה. ²⁴In the jubilee year the land shall revert to the one from whom it was bought, whose holding the land is. ²⁵All assessments shall be by the sanctuary weight, the shekel being twenty *gerahs*.

²⁶A firstling of animals, however, which—as a firstling—is יהוה's, cannot be consecrated by anybody; whether ox or sheep, it is יהוה's. ²⁷But if it is of impure animals, it may be ransomed as its assessment, with one-fifth added; if it is not redeemed, it shall be sold at its assessment.

²⁸But of all that anyone owns, be it human or beast or landholding, nothing that has been proscribed for יהוה may be sold or redeemed; every proscribed thing is totally consecrated to יהוה. ²⁹No human being who has been proscribed can be ransomed: that person shall be put to death.

³⁰All tithes from the land, whether seed from the ground or fruit from the tree, are יהוה's; they are holy to יהוה. ³¹If anyone wishes to redeem any tithes, one-fifth must be added to them. ³²All tithes of the herd or flock—of all that passes under the shepherd's staff, every tenth one—shall be holy to יהוה. ³³One must not look out for good as against bad, or make substitution for it. If one does make substitution for it, then it and its substitute shall both be holy: it cannot be redeemed.

³⁴These are the commandments that יהוה gave Moses for the Israelite people on Mount Sinai.

numbers

1 ¹On the first day of the second month, in the second year following the exodus from the land of Egypt, יהוה spoke to Moses in the wilderness of Sinai, in the Tent of Meeting, saying: ²Take a census of the whole Israelite company [of fighters] by the clans of its ancestral houses, listing the names, every male, head by head. ³You and Aaron shall record them by their groups, from the age of twenty years up, all those in Israel who are able to bear arms. ⁴Associated with you shall be a representative of each tribe, each one the head of his ancestral house.

⁵These are the names of the representatives who shall assist you:

From Reuben, Elizur son of Shedeur.
⁶From Simeon, Shelumiel son of Zurishaddai.
⁷From Judah, Nahshon son of Amminadab.
⁸From Issachar, Nethanel son of Zuar.
⁹From Zebulun, Eliab son of Helon.
¹⁰From the sons of Joseph:
from Ephraim, Elishama son of Ammihud;
from Manasseh, Gamaliel son of Pedahzur.
¹¹From Benjamin, Abidan son of Gideoni.
¹²From Dan, Ahiezer son of Ammishaddai.
¹³From Asher, Pagiel son of Ochran.
¹⁴From Gad, Eliasaph son of Deuel.
¹⁵From Naphtali, Ahira son of Enan.

¹⁶Those are the elected of the assembly, the chieftains of their ancestral tribes: they are the heads of the contingents of Israel.

¹⁷So Moses and Aaron took those representatives, who were designated by name, ¹⁸and on the first day of the second month they convoked the whole company [of fighters], who were registered by the clans of their ancestral houses—the names of those aged twenty years and over being listed head by head. ¹⁹As יהוה had commanded Moses, so he recorded them in the wilderness of Sinai.

²⁰They totaled as follows: The descendants of Reuben, Israel's firstborn, the registration of the clans of their ancestral house, as listed by name, head by head, all males aged twenty years and over, all who were able to bear arms—²¹those enrolled from the tribe of Reuben: 46,500.

²²Of the descendants of Simeon, the registration of the clans of their ancestral house, their enrollment as listed by name, head by head, all males aged twenty years and over, all who were able to bear arms—²³those enrolled from the tribe of Simeon: 59,300. ²⁴Of the descendants of Gad, the registration of the clans of their ancestral house, as listed by name, aged twenty years and over, all who were able to bear arms—²⁵those enrolled from the tribe of Gad: 45,650.

²⁶Of the descendants of Judah, the registration of the clans of their ancestral house, as listed by name, aged twenty years and over, all who were able to bear arms—²⁷those enrolled from the tribe of Judah: 74,600.

²⁸Of the descendants of Issachar, the registration of the clans of their ancestral house, as listed by name, aged twenty years and over, all who were able to bear arms—²⁹those enrolled from the tribe of Issachar: 54,400.

³⁰Of the descendants of Zebulun, the registration of the clans of their ancestral house, as listed by name, aged twenty years and over, all who were able to bear arms—³¹those enrolled from the tribe of Zebulun: 57,400.

³²Of the descendants of Joseph: Of the descendants of Ephraim, the registration of the clans of their ancestral house, as listed by name, aged twenty years and over, all

who were able to bear arms—³³those enrolled from the tribe of Ephraim: 40,500.

³⁴Of the descendants of Manasseh, the registration of the clans of their ancestral house, as listed by name, aged twenty years and over, all who were able to bear arms—³⁵those enrolled from the tribe of Manasseh: 32,200.

³⁶Of the descendants of Benjamin, the registration of the clans of their ancestral house, as listed by name, aged twenty years and over, all who were able to bear arms—³⁷those enrolled from the tribe of Benjamin: 35,400.

³⁸Of the descendants of Dan, the registration of the clans of their ancestral house, as listed by name, aged twenty years and over, all who were able to bear arms—³⁹those enrolled from the tribe of Dan: 62,700.

⁴⁰Of the descendants of Asher, the registration of the clans of their ancestral house, as listed by name, aged twenty years and over, all who were able to bear arms—⁴¹those enrolled from the tribe of Asher: 41,500.

⁴²[Of] the descendants of Naphtali, the registration of the clans of their ancestral house as listed by name, aged twenty years and over, all who were able to bear arms—⁴³those enrolled from the tribe of Naphtali: 53,400.

⁴⁴Those are the enrollments recorded by Moses and Aaron and by the chieftains of Israel, who were twelve in number, one representative of each ancestral house. ⁴⁵All the Israelite males, aged twenty years and over, enrolled by ancestral houses, all those in Israel who were able to bear arms—⁴⁶all who were enrolled came to 603,550.

⁴⁷The Levites, however, were not recorded among them by their ancestral tribe. ⁴⁸For יהוה had spoken to Moses, saying: ⁴⁹Do not on any account enroll the tribe of Levi or take a census of them with the Israelites. ⁵⁰You shall put the Levites in charge of the Tabernacle of the Pact, all its furnishings, and everything that pertains to it: they shall carry the Tabernacle and all its furnishings, and they shall tend it; and they shall camp around the Tabernacle. ⁵¹When the Tabernacle is to be set out, the Levites shall take it down, and when the Tabernacle is to be pitched, the Levites shall set it up; any outsider who encroaches shall be put to death. ⁵²The Israelites shall encamp troop by troop, each man with his division and each under his standard. ⁵³The Levites, however, shall camp around the Tabernacle of the Pact, that wrath may not strike the Israelite community; the Levites shall stand guard around the Tabernacle of the Pact. ⁵⁴The Israelites did accordingly; just as יהוה had commanded Moses, so they did.

2 יהוה spoke to Moses and Aaron, saying: ²The Israelites shall camp each man with his standard, under the banners of their ancestral house; they shall camp around the Tent of Meeting at a distance.

³Camped on the front, or east side: the standard of the division of Judah, troop by troop. Chieftain of the Judites: Nahshon son of Amminadab. ⁴His troop, as enrolled: 74,600.

⁵Camping next to it: The tribe of Issachar. Chieftain of the Issacharites: Nethanel son of Zuar. ⁶His troop, as enrolled: 54,400.

⁷The tribe of Zebulun. Chieftain of the Zebulunites: Eliab son of Helon. ⁸His troop, as enrolled: 57,400.

⁹The total enrolled in the division of Judah: 186,400, for all troops. These shall march first.

¹⁰On the south: the standard of the division of Reuben, troop by troop. Chieftain of the Reubenites: Elizur son of Shedeur. ¹¹His troop, as enrolled: 46,500.

¹²Camping next to it: The tribe of Simeon. Chieftain of the Simeonites: Shelumiel son of Zurishaddai. ¹³His troop, as enrolled: 59,300.

¹⁴And the tribe of Gad. Chieftain of the Gadites: Eliasaph son of Reuel. ¹⁵His troop, as enrolled: 45,650. ¹⁶The total enrolled in the division of Reuben: 151,450, for all troops. These shall march second.

¹⁷Then, midway between the divisions, the Tent of Meeting, the division of the Levites, shall move. As they camp, so they shall march, each in position, by their standards.

¹⁸On the west: the standard of the division of Ephraim, troop by troop. Chieftain of the Ephraimites: Elishama son of Ammihud. ¹⁹His troop, as enrolled: 40,500.

²⁰Next to it: The tribe of Manasseh. Chieftain of the Manassites: Gamaliel son of Pedahzur. ²¹His troop, as enrolled: 32,200.

²²And the tribe of Benjamin. Chieftain of the Benjaminites: Abidan son of Gideoni. ²³His troop, as enrolled: 35,400.

²⁴The total enrolled in the division of Ephraim: 108,100 for all troops. These shall march third.

²⁵On the north: the standard of the division of Dan, troop by troop. Chieftain of the Danites: Ahiezer son of Ammishaddai. ²⁶His troop, as enrolled: 62,700.

²⁷Camping next to it: The tribe of Asher. Chieftain of the Asherites: Pagiel son of Ochran. ²⁸His troop, as enrolled: 41,500.

²⁹And the tribe of Naphtali. Chieftain of the Naphtalites: Ahira son of Enan. ³⁰His troop, as enrolled: 53,400. ³¹The total enrolled in the division of Dan: 157,600. These shall march last, by their standards.

³²Those are the enrollments of the Israelites by ancestral houses. The total enrolled in the divisions, for all troops: 603,550. ³³The Levites, however, were not recorded among the Israelites, as יהוה had commanded Moses.

³⁴The Israelites did accordingly; just as יהוה had commanded Moses, so they camped by their standards, and so they marched, each man with his clan according to his ancestral house.

3 ¹This is the line of Aaron and Moses at the time that יהוה spoke with Moses on Mount Sinai. ²These were the names of Aaron's sons: Nadab, the firstborn, and Abihu, Eleazar and Ithamar; ³those were the names of Aaron's sons, the anointed priests who were ordained for priesthood. ⁴But Nadab and Abihu died by the will of יהוה, when they offered alien fire before יהוה in the wilderness of Sinai; and they left no sons. So it was Eleazar and Ithamar who served as priests in the lifetime of their father Aaron.

⁵יהוה spoke to Moses, saying: ⁶Advance the tribe of Levi and place [its men] in attendance upon Aaron the priest to serve him. ⁷They shall perform duties for him and for the whole community before the Tent of Meeting, doing the work of the Tabernacle. ⁸They shall take charge of all the furnishings of the Tent of Meeting—a duty on behalf of the Israelites—doing the work of the Tabernacle. ⁹You shall assign the Levites to Aaron and to his sons: they are formally assigned to him from among the Israelites. ¹⁰You shall make Aaron and his sons responsible for observing their priestly duties; and any outsider who encroaches shall be put to death.

¹¹יהוה spoke to Moses, saying: ¹²I hereby take the Levites from among the Israelites in place of all the male firstborn, the first issue of the womb among the Israelites: the Levites shall be Mine. ¹³For every male firstborn is Mine: at the time that I smote every [male] firstborn in the land of Egypt, I consecrated every male firstborn in Israel, human and beast, to Myself, to be Mine, יהוה's.

¹⁴יהוה spoke to Moses in the wilderness of Sinai, saying: ¹⁵Record the descendants of Levi by ancestral house and by clan; record every male among them from the age of one

month up. ¹⁶So Moses recorded them at the command of יהוה, as he was bidden. ¹⁷These were the sons of Levi by name: Gershon, Kohath, and Merari. ¹⁸These were the names of the sons of Gershon by clan: Libni and Shimei. ¹⁹The sons of Kohath by clan: Amram and Izhar, Hebron and Uzziel. ²⁰The sons of Merari by clan: Mahli and Mushi.

These were the clans of the Levites within their ancestral houses:

²¹To Gershon belonged the clan of the Libnites and the clan of the Shimeites; those were the clans of the Gershonites. ²²The recorded entries of all their males from the age of one month up, as recorded, came to 7,500. ²³The clans of the Gershonites were to camp behind the Tabernacle, to the west. ²⁴The chieftain of the ancestral house of the Gershonites was Eliasaph son of Lael. ²⁵The duties of the Gershonites in the Tent of Meeting comprised: the tabernacle, the tent, its covering, and the screen for the entrance of the Tent of Meeting; ²⁶the hangings of the enclosure, the screen for the entrance of the enclosure which surrounds the Tabernacle, the cords thereof, and the altar—all the service connected with these.

²⁷To Kohath belonged the clan of the Amramites, the clan of the Izharites, the clan of the Hebronites, and the clan of the Uzzielites; those were the clans of the Kohathites. ²⁸All the listed males from the age of one month up came to 8,600, attending to the duties of the sanctuary. ²⁹The clans of the Kohathites were to camp along the south side of the Tabernacle. ³⁰The chieftain of the ancestral house of the Kohathite clans was Elizaphan son of Uzziel. ³¹Their duties comprised: the ark, the table, the lamp-stand, the altars, and the sacred utensils that were used with them, and the screen—all the service connected with these. ³²The head chieftain of the Levites was Eleazar son of Aaron the priest, in charge of those attending to the duties of the sanctuary.

³³To Merari belonged the clan of the Mahlites and the clan of the Mushites; those were the clans of Merari. ³⁴The recorded entries of all their males from the age of one month up came to 6,200. ³⁵The chieftain of the ancestral house of the clans of Merari was Zuriel son of Abihail. They were to camp along the north side of the Tabernacle. ³⁶The assigned duties of the Merarites comprised: the planks of the Tabernacle, its bars, posts, and sockets, and all its furnishings—all the service connected with these; ³⁷also the posts around the enclosure and their sockets, pegs, and cords.

³⁸Those who were to camp before the Tabernacle, in front—before the Tent of Meeting, on the east—were Moses and Aaron and his sons, attending to the duties of the sanctuary, as a duty on behalf of the Israelites; and any outsider who encroached was to be put to death. ³⁹All the Levites who were recorded, whom at יהוה's command Moses and Aaron recorded by their clans, all the males from the age of one month up, came to 22,000.

⁴⁰יהוה said to Moses: Record every firstborn male of the Israelite people from the age of one month up, and make a list of their names; ⁴¹and take the Levites for Me, יהוה, in place of every male firstborn among the Israelite people, and the cattle of the Levites in place of every male firstborn among the cattle of the Israelites. ⁴²So Moses recorded all the male firstborn among the Israelites, as יהוה had commanded him. ⁴³All the firstborn males as listed by name, recorded from the age of one month up, came to 22,273.

⁴⁴יהוה spoke to Moses, saying: ⁴⁵Take the Levites in place of all the male firstborn among the Israelite people, and the cattle of the Levites in place of their cattle; and the Levites shall be Mine, יהוה's. ⁴⁶And as the redemption price of the 273 Israelite male firstborn over and above the number of the Levites, ⁴⁷take five shekels per head—take this by the sanctuary weight, twenty *gerahs* to the shekel—⁴⁸and give

the money to Aaron and his sons as the redemption price for those who are in excess. ⁴⁹So Moses took the redemption money from those over and above the ones redeemed by the Levites; ⁵⁰he took the money from the male firstborn of the Israelites, 1,365 sanctuary shekels. ⁵¹And Moses gave the redemption money to Aaron and his sons at יהוה's bidding, as יהוה had commanded Moses.

4 ¹יהוה spoke to Moses and Aaron, saying: ²Take a [separate] census of the Kohathites among the Levites, by the clans of their ancestral house, ³from the age of thirty years up to the age of fifty, all who are subject to service, to perform tasks for the Tent of Meeting. ⁴This is the responsibility of the Kohathites in the Tent of Meeting: the most sacred objects.

⁵At the breaking of camp, Aaron and his sons shall go in and take down the screening curtain and cover the Ark of the Pact with it. ⁶They shall lay a covering of dolphin skin over it and spread a cloth of pure blue on top; and they shall put its poles in place.

⁷Over the table of display they shall spread a blue cloth; they shall place upon it the bowls, the ladles, the jars, and the libation jugs; and the regular bread shall rest upon it. ⁸They shall spread over these a crimson cloth which they shall cover with a covering of dolphin skin; and they shall put the poles in place.

⁹Then they shall take a blue cloth and cover the lampstand for lighting, with its lamps, its tongs, and its fire pans, as well as all the oil vessels that are used in its service. ¹⁰They shall put it and all its furnishings into a covering of dolphin skin, which they shall then place on a carrying frame.

¹¹Next they shall spread a blue cloth over the altar of gold and cover it with a covering of dolphin skin; and they shall put its poles in place. ¹²They shall take all the service vessels with which the service in the sanctuary is performed, put them into a blue cloth and cover them with a covering of dolphin skin, which they shall then place on a carrying frame. ¹³They shall remove the ashes from the [copper] altar and spread a purple cloth over it. ¹⁴Upon it they shall place all the vessels that are used in its service: the fire pans, the flesh hooks, the scrapers, and the basins—all the vessels of the altar—and over it they shall spread a covering of dolphin skin; and they shall put its poles in place.

¹⁵When Aaron and his sons have finished covering the sacred objects and all the furnishings of the sacred objects at the breaking of camp, only then shall the Kohathites come and lift them, so that they do not come in contact with the sacred objects and die. These things in the Tent of Meeting shall be the porterage of the Kohathites.

¹⁶Responsibility shall rest with Eleazar son of Aaron the priest for the lighting oil, the aromatic incense, the regular meal offering, and the anointing oil—responsibility for the whole Tabernacle and for everything consecrated that is in it or in its vessels.

¹⁷יהוה spoke to Moses and Aaron, saying: ¹⁸Do not let the group of Kohathite clans be cut off from the Levites. ¹⁹Do this with them, that they may live and not die when they approach the most sacred objects: let Aaron and his sons go in and assign each of them to his duties and to his porterage. ²⁰But let not [the Kohathites] go inside and witness the dismantling of the sanctuary, lest they die.

²¹יהוה spoke to Moses: ²²Take a census of the Gershonites also, by their ancestral house and by their clans. ²³Record them from the age of thirty years up to the age of fifty, all who are subject to service in the performance of tasks for the Tent of Meeting. ²⁴These are the duties of the Gershonite clans as to labor and porterage: ²⁵they shall carry the cloths

of the Tabernacle, the Tent of Meeting with its covering, the covering of dolphin skin that is on top of it, and the screen for the entrance of the Tent of Meeting; ²⁶the hangings of the enclosure, the screen at the entrance of the gate of the enclosure that surrounds the Tabernacle, the cords thereof, and the altar, and all their service equipment and all their accessories; and they shall perform the service. ²⁷All the duties of the Gershonites, all their porterage and all their service, shall be performed on orders from Aaron and his sons; you shall make them responsible for attending to all their porterage. ²⁸Those are the duties of the Gershonite clans for the Tent of Meeting; they shall attend to them under the direction of Ithamar son of Aaron the priest.

²⁹As for the Merarites, you shall record them by the clans of their ancestral house; ³⁰you shall record them from the age of thirty years up to the age of fifty, all who are subject to service in the performance of the duties for the Tent of Meeting. ³¹These are their porterage tasks in connection with their various duties for the Tent of Meeting: the planks, the bars, the posts, and the sockets of the Tabernacle; ³²the posts around the enclosure and their sockets, pegs, and cords—all these furnishings and their service: you shall list by name the objects that are their porterage tasks. ³³Those are the duties of the Merarite clans, pertaining to their various duties in the Tent of Meeting under the direction of Ithamar son of Aaron the priest.

³⁴So Moses, Aaron, and the chieftains of the community recorded the Kohathites by the clans of their ancestral house, ³⁵from the age of thirty years up to the age of fifty, all who were subject to service for work relating to the Tent of Meeting. ³⁶Those recorded by their clans came to 2,750. ³⁷That was the enrollment of the Kohathite clans, all those who performed duties relating to the Tent of Meeting, whom Moses and Aaron recorded at the command of יהוה through Moses.

³⁸The Gershonites who were recorded by the clans of their ancestral house, ³⁹from the age of thirty years up to the age of fifty, all who were subject to service for work relating to the Tent of Meeting—⁴⁰those recorded by the clans of their ancestral house came to 2,630. ⁴¹That was the enrollment of the Gershonite clans, all those performing duties relating to the Tent of Meeting whom Moses and Aaron recorded at the command of יהוה.

⁴²The enrollment of the Merarite clans by the clans of their ancestral house, ⁴³from the age of thirty years up to the age of fifty, all who were subject to service for work relating to the Tent of Meeting—⁴⁴those recorded by their clans came to 3,200. ⁴⁵That was the enrollment of the Merarite clans which Moses and Aaron recorded at the command of יהוה through Moses.

⁴⁶All the Levites whom Moses, Aaron, and the chieftains of Israel recorded by the clans of their ancestral houses, ⁴⁷from the age of thirty years up to the age of fifty, all who were subject to duties of service and porterage relating to the Tent of Meeting—⁴⁸those recorded came to 8,580. ⁴⁹Each one was given responsibility for his service and porterage at the command of יהוה through Moses, and each was recorded as יהוה had commanded Moses.

5 ¹יהוה spoke to Moses, saying: ²Instruct the Israelites to remove from camp anyone with an eruption or a discharge and any one defiled by a corpse. ³Remove male and female alike; put them outside the camp so that they do not defile the camp of those in whose midst I dwell.

⁴The Israelites did so, putting them outside the camp; as יהוה had spoken to Moses, so the Israelites did.

⁵יהוה spoke to Moses, saying: ⁶Speak to the Israelites: When men or women individually commit any wrong toward a

fellow human being, thus breaking faith with יהוה, and they realize their guilt, 7they shall confess the wrong that they have done. They shall make restitution in the principal amount and add one-fifth to it, giving it to the one who was wronged. 8If the person [is deceased and] has no kin to whom restitution can be made, the amount repaid shall go to יהוה for the priest—in addition to the ram of expiation with which expiation is made on their behalf. 9So, too, any gift among the sacred donations that the Israelites offer shall be the priest's. 10And each shall retain his sacred donations: each priest shall keep what is given to him.

11יהוה spoke to Moses, saying: 12Speak to the Israelite people and say to them:

If any wife has gone astray and broken faith with her husband, 13in that a man has had carnal relations with her unbeknown to her husband, and she keeps secret the fact that she has defiled herself without being forced, and there is no witness against her—14but a fit of jealousy comes over him and he is wrought up about the wife who has defiled herself; or if a fit of jealousy comes over one and he is wrought up about his wife although she has not defiled herself—15the husband shall bring his wife to the priest. And he shall bring as an offering for her one-tenth of an *ephah* of barley flour. No oil shall be poured upon it and no frankincense be laid on it, for it is a meal offering of jealousy, a meal offering of remembrance which recalls wrong-doing.

16The priest shall bring her forward and have her stand before יהוה. 17The priest shall take sacral water in an earthen vessel and, taking some of the earth that is on the floor of the Tabernacle, the priest shall put it into the water. 18After he has made the wife stand before יהוה, the priest shall bare the wife's head and place upon her hands the meal offering of remembrance, which is a meal offering of jealousy. And in the priest's hands shall be the water of bitterness that induces the spell. 19The priest shall adjure the wife, saying to her, "If no man has lain with you, if you have not gone astray in defilement while living in your husband's household, be immune to harm from this water of bitterness that induces the spell. 20But if you have gone astray while living in your husband's household and have defiled yourself, if a man other than your husband has had carnal relations with you"—21here the priest shall administer the curse of adjuration to the wife, as the priest goes on to say to the wife—"may יהוה make you a curse and an imprecation among your people, as יהוה causes your thigh to sag and your belly to distend; 22may this water that induces the spell enter your body, causing the belly to distend and the thigh to sag." And the wife shall say, "Amen, amen!"

23The priest shall put these curses down in writing and rub it off into the water of bitterness. 24He is to make the wife drink the water of bitterness that induces the spell, so that the spell-inducing water may enter into her to bring on bitterness. 25Then the priest shall take from the wife's hand the meal offering of jealousy, elevate the meal offering before יהוה, and present it on the altar. 26The priest shall scoop out of the meal offering a token part of it and turn it into smoke on the altar. Last, he shall make the wife drink the water.

27Once he has made her drink the water—if she has defiled herself by breaking faith with her husband, the spell-inducing water shall enter into her to bring on bitterness, so that her belly shall distend and her thigh shall sag; and the wife shall become a curse among her people. 28But if the wife has not defiled herself and is pure, she shall be unharmed and able to retain seed.

29This is the ritual in cases of jealousy, when a wife goes astray while living in her husband's household, and defiles

herself, 30or when a fit of jealousy comes over a husband and he is wrought up over his wife: the wife shall be made to stand before יהוה and the priest shall carry out all this ritual with her. 31The husband shall be clear of guilt; but that wife shall suffer for her guilt.

6 1יהוה spoke to Moses, saying: 2Speak to the Israelites and say to them: If any men or women explicitly utter a nazirite's vow, to set themselves apart for יהוה, 3they shall abstain from wine and any other intoxicant; they shall not drink vinegar of wine or of any other intoxicant, neither shall they drink anything in which grapes have been steeped, nor eat grapes fresh or dried. 4Throughout their term as nazirite, they may not eat anything that is obtained from the grapevine, even seeds or skin.

5Throughout the term of their vow as nazirite, no razor shall touch their head; it shall remain consecrated until the completion of their term as nazirite of יהוה, the hair of their head being left to grow untrimmed. 6Throughout the term that they have set apart for יהוה, they shall not go in where there is a dead person. 7Even if their father or mother, or their brother or sister should die, they must not become defiled for any of them, since hair set apart for their God is upon their head; 8throughout their term as nazirite they are consecrated to יהוה.

9If someone dies suddenly nearby, defiling the consecrated hair, the person shall shave the head at the time of becoming pure, shaving it on the seventh day. 10On the eighth day the person shall bring two turtledoves or two pigeons to the priest, at the entrance of the Tent of Meeting. 11The priest shall offer one as a sin offering and the other as a burnt offering, and make expiation on the person's behalf for the guilt incurred through the corpse. That same day the head shall be reconsecrated; 12and the person shall rededicate to יהוה the term as nazirite, bringing a lamb in its first year as a penalty offering. The previous period shall be void, since the consecrated hair was defiled.

13This is the ritual for the nazirite: On the day that the term as nazirite is completed, the person shall be brought to the entrance of the Tent of Meeting. 14As an offering to יהוה the person shall present: one male lamb in its first year, without blemish, for a burnt offering; one ewe lamb in its first year, without blemish, for a sin offering; one ram without blemish for an offering of wellbeing; 15a basket of unleavened cakes of choice flour with oil mixed in, and unleavened wafers spread with oil; and the proper meal offerings and libations.

16The priest shall present them before יהוה and offer the sin offering and the burnt offering. 17He shall offer the ram as a sacrifice of wellbeing to יהוה, together with the basket of unleavened cakes; the priest shall also offer the meal of-ferings and the libations. 18The nazirite shall then shave the consecrated hair, at the entrance of the Tent of Meeting, and take those locks of consecrated hair and put them on the fire that is under the sacrifice of wellbeing.

19The priest shall take the shoulder of the ram when it has been boiled, one unleavened cake from the basket, and one unleavened wafer, and place them on the hands of the nazirite after the consecrated hair has been shaved. 20The priest shall elevate them as an elevation offering before יהוה; and this shall be a sacred donation for the priest, in addition to the breast of the elevation offering and the thigh of gift offering. After that the nazirite may drink wine.

21Such is the obligation of a nazirite; except that those who vow an offering to יהוה of what they can afford, beyond their nazirite requirements, must do exactly according to the vow that they have made beyond their obligation as nazirites.

²²יהוה spoke to Moses: ²³Speak to Aaron and his sons: Thus shall you bless the people of Israel. Say to them:

²⁴יהוה bless you and protect you!

²⁵יהוה deal kindly and graciously with you!

²⁶יהוה bestow [divine] favor upon you and grant you peace!

²⁷Thus they shall link My name with the people of Israel, and I will bless them.

7 ¹On the day that Moses finished setting up the Tabernacle, he anointed and consecrated it and all its furnishings, as well as the altar and its utensils. When he had anointed and consecrated them, ²the chieftains of Israel, the heads of ancestral houses, namely, the chieftains of the tribes, those who were in charge of enrollment, drew near ³and brought their offering before יהוה: six draught carts and twelve oxen, a cart for every two chieftains and an ox for each one.

When they had brought them before the Tabernacle, ⁴יהוה said to Moses: ⁵Accept these from them for use in the service of the Tent of Meeting, and give them to the Levites according to their respective services.

⁶Moses took the carts and the oxen and gave them to the Levites. ⁷Two carts and four oxen he gave to the Gershonites, as required for their service, ⁸and four carts and eight oxen he gave to the Merarites, as required for their service—under the direction of Ithamar son of Aaron the priest. ⁹But to the Kohathites he did not give any; since theirs was the service of the [most] sacred objects, their porterage was by shoulder.

¹⁰The chieftains also brought the dedication offering for the altar upon its being anointed. As the chieftains were presenting their offerings before the altar, ¹¹יהוה said to Moses: Let them present their offerings for the dedication of the altar, one chieftain each day.

¹²The one who presented his offering on the first day was Nahshon son of Amminadab of the tribe of Judah. ¹³His offering: one silver bowl weighing 130 shekels and one silver basin of 70 shekels by the sanctuary weight, both filled with choice flour with oil mixed in, for a meal offering; ¹⁴one gold ladle of 10 shekels, filled with incense; ¹⁵one bull of the herd, one ram, and one lamb in its first year, for a burnt offering; ¹⁶one goat for a sin offering; ¹⁷and for his sacrifice of wellbeing: two oxen, five rams, five he-goats, and five yearling lambs. That was the offering of Nahshon son of Amminadab.

¹⁸On the second day, Nethanel son of Zuar, chieftain of Issachar, made his offering. ¹⁹He presented as his offering: one silver bowl weighing 130 shekels and one silver basin of 70 shekels by the sanctuary weight, both filled with choice flour with oil mixed in, for a meal offering; ²⁰one gold ladle of 10 shekels, filled with incense; ²¹one bull of the herd, one ram, and one lamb in its first year, for a burnt offering; ²²one goat for a sin offering; ²³and for his sacrifice of wellbeing: two oxen, five rams, five hegoats, and five yearling lambs. That was the offering of Nethanel son of Zuar.

²⁴On the third day, it was the chieftain of the Zebulunites, Eliab son of Helon. ²⁵His offering: one silver bowl weighing 130 shekels and one silver basin of 70 shekels by the sanctuary weight, both filled with choice flour with oil mixed in, for a meal offering; ²⁶one gold ladle of 10 shekels, filled with incense; ²⁷one bull of the herd, one ram, and one lamb in its first year, for a burnt offering; ²⁸one goat for a sin offering; ²⁹and for his sacrifice of wellbeing: two oxen, five rams, five hegoats, and five yearling lambs. That was the offering of Eliab son of Helon.

³⁰On the fourth day, it was the chieftain of the Reubenites, Elizur son of Shedeur. ³¹His offering: one silver bowl weighing 130 shekels and one silver basin of 70 shekels by the sanctuary weight, both filled with choice flour with oil mixed in, for a meal offering; ³²one gold ladle of 10 shekels, filled with incense; ³³one bull of the herd, one ram, and one lamb in its first year, for a burnt offering; ³⁴one goat for a sin offering; ³⁵and for his sacrifice of wellbeing: two oxen, five rams, five hegoats, and five yearling lambs. That was the offering of Elizur son of Shedeur.

³⁶On the fifth day, it was the chieftain of the Simeonites, Shelumiel son of Zurishaddai. ³⁷His offering: one silver bowl weighing 130 shekels and one silver basin of 70 shekels by the sanctuary weight, both filled with choice flour with oil mixed in, for a meal offering; ³⁸one gold ladle of 10 shekels, filled with incense; ³⁹one bull of the herd, one ram, and one lamb in its first year, for a burnt offering; ⁴⁰one goat for a sin offering; ⁴¹and for his sacrifice of wellbeing: two oxen, five rams, five hegoats, and five yearling lambs. That was the offering of Shelumiel son of Zurishaddai.

⁴²On the sixth day, it was the chieftain of the Gadites, Eliasaph son of Deuel. ⁴³His offering: one silver bowl weighing 130 shekels and one silver basin of 70 shekels by the sanctuary weight, both filled with choice flour with oil mixed in, for a meal offering; ⁴⁴one gold ladle of 10 shekels, filled with incense; ⁴⁵one bull of the herd, one ram, and one lamb in its first year, for a burnt offering; ⁴⁶one goat for a sin offering; ⁴⁷and for his sacrifice of wellbeing: two oxen, five rams, five he-goats, and five yearling lambs. That was the offering of Eliasaph son of Deuel.

⁴⁸On the seventh day, it was the chieftain of the Ephraimites, Elishama son of Ammihud. ⁴⁹His offering: one silver bowl weighing 130 shekels and one silver basin of 70 shekels by the sanctuary weight, both filled with choice flour with oil mixed in, for a meal offering; ⁵⁰one gold ladle of 10 shekels, filled with incense; ⁵¹one bull of the herd, one ram, and one lamb in its first year, for a burnt offering; ⁵²one goat for a sin offering; ⁵³and for his sacrifice of wellbeing: two oxen, five rams, five he-goats, and five yearling lambs. That was the offering of Elishama son of Ammihud.

⁵⁴On the eighth day, it was the chieftain of the Manassites, Gamaliel son of Pedahzur. ⁵⁵His offering: one silver bowl weighing 130 shekels and one silver basin of 70 shekels by the sanctuary weight, both filled with choice flour with oil mixed in, for a meal offering; ⁵⁶one gold ladle of 10 shekels, filled with incense; ⁵⁷one bull of the herd, one ram, and one lamb in its first year, for a burnt offering; ⁵⁸one goat for a sin offering; ⁵⁹and for his sacrifice of wellbeing: two oxen, five rams, five he-goats, and five yearling lambs. That was the offering of Gamaliel son of Pedahzur.

⁶⁰On the ninth day, it was the chieftain of the Benjaminites, Abidan son of Gideoni. ⁶¹His offering: one silver bowl weighing 130 shekels and one silver basin of 70 shekels by the sanctuary weight, both filled with choice flour with oil mixed in, for a meal offering; ⁶²one gold ladle of 10 shekels, filled with incense; ⁶³one bull of the herd, one ram, and one lamb in its first year, for a burnt offering; ⁶⁴one goat for a sin offering; ⁶⁵and for his sacrifice of wellbeing: two oxen, five rams, five hegoats, and five yearling lambs. That was the offering of Abidan son of Gideoni.

⁶⁶On the tenth day, it was the chieftain of the Danites, Ahiezer son of Ammishaddai. ⁶⁷His offering: one silver bowl weighing 130 shekels and one silver basin of 70 shekels by the sanctuary weight, both filled with choice flour with oil mixed in, for a meal offering; ⁶⁸one gold ladle of 10 shekels, filled with incense; ⁶⁹one bull of the herd, one ram, and one lamb in its first year, for a burnt offering; ⁷⁰one goat for a sin offering; ⁷¹and for his sacrifice of wellbeing: two oxen, five rams, five he-goats, and five yearling lambs. That was the offering of Ahiezer son of Ammishaddai.

⁷²On the eleventh day, it was the chieftain of the Asherites, Pagiel son of Ochran. ⁷³His offering: one silver bowl weighing

130 shekels and one silver basin of 70 shekels by the sanctuary weight, both filled with choice flour with oil mixed in, for a meal offering; 74one gold ladle of 10 shekels, filled with incense; 75one bull of the herd, one ram, and one lamb in its first year, for a burnt offering; 76one goat for a sin offering; 77and for his sacrifice of wellbeing: two oxen, five rams, five hegoats, and five yearling lambs. That was the offering of Pagiel son of Ochran.

78On the twelfth day, it was the chieftain of the Naphtalites, Ahira son of Enan. 79His offering: one silver bowl weighing 130 shekels and one silver basin of 70 shekels by the sanctuary weight, both filled with choice flour with oil mixed in, for a meal offering; 80one gold ladle of 10 shekels, filled with incense; 81one bull of the herd, one ram, and one lamb in its first year, for a burnt offering; 82one goat for a sin offering; 83and for his sacrifice of wellbeing: two oxen, five rams, five hegoats, and five yearling lambs. That was the offering of Ahira son of Enan.

84This was the dedication offering for the altar from the chieftains of Israel upon its being anointed: silver bowls, 12; silver basins, 12; gold ladles, 12. 85Silver per bowl, 130; per basin, 70. Total silver of vessels, 2,400 sanctuary shekels. 86The 12 gold ladles filled with incense—10 sanctuary shekels per ladle—total gold of the ladles, 120.

87Total of herd animals for burnt offerings, 12 bulls; of rams, 12; of yearling lambs, 12—with their proper meal offerings; of goats for sin offerings, 12. 88Total of herd animals for sacrifices of wellbeing, 24 bulls; of rams, 60; of he-goats, 60; of yearling lambs, 60. That was the dedication offering for the altar after its anointing.

89When Moses went into the Tent of Meeting to speak with [God], he would hear the Voice addressing him from above the cover that was on top of the Ark of the Pact between the two cherubim; thus [God] spoke to him.

8 1יהוה spoke to Moses, saying: 2Speak to Aaron and say to him, "When you mount the lamps, let the seven lamps give light at the front of the lamp-stand." 3Aaron did so; he mounted the lamps at the front of the lamp-stand, as יהוה had commanded Moses.—4Now this is how the lamp-stand was made: it was hammered work of gold, hammered from base to petal. According to the pattern that יהוה had shown Moses, so was the lamp-stand made.

5יהוה spoke to Moses, saying: 6Take the Levites from among the Israelites and purify them. 7This is what you shall do to them to purify them: sprinkle on them water of purification, and let them go over their whole body with a razor, and wash their clothes; thus they shall be purified. 8Let them take a bull of the herd, and with it a meal offering of choice flour with oil mixed in, and you take a second bull of the herd for a sin offering. 9You shall bring the Levites forward before the Tent of Meeting. Assemble the Israelite community leadership, 10and bring the Levites forward before יהוה. Let the Israelites lay their hands upon the Levites, 11and let Aaron designate the Levites before יהוה as an elevation offering from the Israelites, that they may perform the service of יהוה. 12The Levites shall now lay their hands upon the heads of the bulls; one shall be offered to יהוה as a sin offering and the other as a burnt offering, to make expiation for the Levites.

13You shall place the Levites in attendance upon Aaron and his sons, and designate them as an elevation offering to יהוה. 14Thus you shall set the Levites apart from the Israelites, and the Levites shall be Mine. 15Thereafter the Levites shall be qualified for the service of the Tent of Meeting, once you have purified them and designated them as an elevation offering. 16For they are formally assigned to Me from among the Israelites: I have taken them for Myself in place of all the first issue of the womb, of all the male firstborn of the Israelites. 17For every male firstborn among the Israelites, human as well as beast, is Mine; I consecrated them to Myself at the time that I smote every [male] firstborn in the land of Egypt. 18Now I take the Levites instead of every male firstborn of the Israelites; 19and from among the Israelites I formally assign the Levites to Aaron and his sons, to perform the service for the Israelites in the Tent of Meeting and to make expiation for the Israelites, so that no plague may afflict the Israelites for coming too near the sanctuary.

20Moses, Aaron, and the Israelite community leadership did with the Levites accordingly; just as יהוה had commanded Moses in regard to the Levites, so the Israelites did with them. 21The Levites purified themselves and washed their clothes; and Aaron designated them as an elevation offering before יהוה, and Aaron made expiation for them to purify them. 22Thereafter the Levites were qualified to perform their service in the Tent of Meeting, under Aaron and his sons. As יהוה had commanded Moses in regard to the Levites, so they did to them.

23יהוה spoke to Moses, saying: 24This is the rule for the Levites. From twenty-five years of age up they shall participate in the work force in the service of the Tent of Meeting; 25but at the age of fifty they shall retire from the work force and shall serve no more. 26They may assist their brother Levites at the Tent of Meeting by standing guard, but they shall perform no labor. Thus you shall deal with the Levites in regard to their duties.

9 1יהוה spoke to Moses in the wilderness of Sinai, on the first new moon of the second year following the exodus from the land of Egypt, saying: 2Let the Israelite people offer the Passover sacrifice at its set time; 3you shall offer it on the fourteenth day of this month, at twilight, at its set time; you shall offer it in accordance with all its rules and rites.

4Moses instructed the Israelites to offer the passover sacrifice; 5and they offered the passover sacrifice in the first month, on the fourteenth day of the month, at twilight, in the wilderness of Sinai. Just as יהוה had commanded Moses, so the Israelites did.

6But there were some householders who were impure by reason of a corpse and could not offer the passover sacrifice on that day. Appearing that same day before Moses and Aaron, 7those householders said to them, "Impure though we are by reason of a corpse, why must we be debarred from presenting יהוה's offering at its set time with the rest of the Israelites?" 8Moses said to them, "Stand by, and let me hear what instructions יהוה gives about you."

9And יהוה spoke to Moses, saying: 10Speak to the Israelite people, saying: When any of you or of your posterity who are defiled by a corpse or are on a long journey would offer a passover sacrifice to יהוה—11they shall offer it in the second month, on the fourteenth day of the month, at twilight. They shall eat it with unleavened bread and bitter herbs, 12and they shall not leave any of it over until morning. They shall not break a bone of it. They shall offer it in strict accord with the law of the passover sacrifice. 13But if a householder who is pure and not on a journey refrains from offering the passover sacrifice, that person shall be cut off from kin, for יהוה's offering was not presented at its set time; that householder shall bear his guilt.

14And when a stranger who resides with you would offer a passover sacrifice to יהוה, it must be offered in accordance with the rules and rites of the passover sacrifice. There shall be one law for you, whether stranger or citizen of the country.

¹⁵On the day that the Tabernacle was set up, the cloud covered the Tabernacle, the Tent of the Pact; and in the evening it rested over the Tabernacle in the likeness of fire until morning. ¹⁶It was always so: the cloud covered it, appearing as fire by night. ¹⁷And whenever the cloud lifted from the Tent, the Israelites would set out accordingly; and at the spot where the cloud settled, there the Israelites would make camp. ¹⁸At a command of יהוה the Israelites broke camp, and at a command of יהוה they made camp: they remained encamped as long as the cloud stayed over the Tabernacle. ¹⁹When the cloud lingered over the Tabernacle many days, the Israelites observed יהוה's mandate and did not journey on. ²⁰At such times as the cloud rested over the Tabernacle for but a few days, they remained encamped at a command of יהוה, and broke camp at a command of יהוה. ²¹And at such times as the cloud stayed from evening until morning, they broke camp as soon as the cloud lifted in the morning. Day or night, whenever the cloud lifted, they would break camp. ²²Whether it was two days or a month or a year—however long the cloud lingered over the Tabernacle—the Israelites remained encamped and did not set out; only when it lifted did they break camp. ²³On a sign from יהוה they made camp and on a sign from יהוה they broke camp; they observed יהוה's mandate at יהוה's bidding through Moses.

10 ¹יהוה spoke to Moses, saying: ²Have two silver trumpets made; make them of hammered work. They shall serve you to summon [military bodies of] the community and to set the divisions in motion. ³When both are blown in long blasts, the whole company [of fighters] shall assemble before you at the entrance of the Tent of Meeting; ⁴and if only one is blown, the chieftains, heads of Israel's contingents, shall assemble before you. ⁵But when you sound short blasts, the divisions encamped on the east shall move forward; ⁶and when you sound short blasts a second time, those encamped on the south shall move forward. Thus short blasts shall be blown for setting them in motion, ⁷while to convoke [military bodies of] the congregation you shall blow long blasts, not short ones. ⁸The trumpets shall be blown by Aaron's sons, the priests; they shall be for you an institution for all time throughout the ages.

⁹When you are at war in your land against an aggressor who attacks you, you shall sound short blasts on the trumpets, that you may be remembered before your God יהוה and be delivered from your enemies. ¹⁰And on your joyous occasions—your fixed festivals and new moon days—you shall sound the trumpets over your burnt offerings and your sacrifices of wellbeing. They shall be a reminder of you before your God: I, יהוה, am your God.

¹¹In the second year, on the twentieth day of the second month, the cloud lifted from the Tabernacle of the Pact ¹²and the Israelites set out on their journeys from the wilderness of Sinai. The cloud came to rest in the wilderness of Paran. ¹³When the march was to begin, at יהוה's command through Moses, ¹⁴the first standard to set out, troop by troop, was the division of Judah. In command of its troops was Nahshon son of Amminadab; ¹⁵in command of the tribal troop of Issachar, Nethanel son of Zuar; ¹⁶and in command of the tribal troop of Zebulun, Eliab son of Helon.

¹⁷Then the Tabernacle would be taken apart; and the Gershonites and the Merarites, who carried the Tabernacle, would set out.

¹⁸The next standard to set out, troop by troop, was the division of Reuben. In command of its troop was Elizur son of Shedeur; ¹⁹in command of the tribal troop of Simeon, Shelumiel son of Zurishaddai; ²⁰and in command of the tribal troop of Gad, Eliasaph son of Deuel.

²¹Then the Kohathites, who carried the sacred objects, would set out; and by the time they arrived, the Tabernacle would be set up again.

²²The next standard to set out, troop by troop, was the division of Ephraim. In command of its troop was Elishama son of Ammihud; ²³in command of the tribal troop of Manasseh, Gamaliel son of Pedahzur; ²⁴and in command of the tribal troop of Benjamin, Abidan son of Gideoni.

²⁵Then, as the rear guard of all the divisions, the standard of the division of Dan would set out, troop by troop. In command of its troop was Ahiezer son of Ammishaddai; ²⁶in command of the tribal troop of Asher, Pagiel son of Ochran; ²⁷and in command of the tribal troop of Naphtali, Ahira son of Enan.

²⁸Such was the order of march of the Israelites, as they marched troop by troop.

²⁹Moses said to Hobab son of Reuel the Midianite, Moses' father-in-law, "We are setting out for the place of which יהוה has said, 'I will give it to you.' Come with us and we will be generous with you; for יהוה has promised to be generous to Israel."

³⁰"I will not go," he replied to him, "but will return to my native land." ³¹He said, "Please do not leave us, inasmuch as you know where we should camp in the wilderness and can be our guide. ³²So if you come with us, we will extend to you the same bounty that יהוה grants us."

³³They marched from the mountain of יהוה a distance of three days. The Ark of the Covenant of יהוה traveled in front of them on that three days' journey to seek out a resting place for them; ³⁴and יהוה's cloud kept above them by day, as they moved on from camp.

³⁵When the Ark was to set out, Moses would say:

Advance, O יהוה!
May Your enemies be scattered,
And may Your foes flee before You!

³⁶And when it halted, he would say:

Return, O יהוה,
You who are Israel's myriads of thousands!

11 ¹The people took to complaining bitterly before יהוה. יהוה heard and was incensed: a fire of יהוה broke out against them, ravaging the outskirts of the camp. ²The people cried out to Moses. Moses prayed to יהוה, and the fire died down. ³That place was named Taberah, because a fire of יהוה had broken out against them.

⁴The riffraff in their midst felt a gluttonous craving; and then the Israelites wept and said, "If only we had meat to eat! ⁵We remember the fish that we used to eat free in Egypt, the cucumbers, the melons, the leeks, the onions, and the garlic. ⁶Now our gullets are shriveled. There is nothing at all! Nothing but this manna to look to!"

⁷Now the manna was like coriander seed, and in color it was like bdellium. ⁸The people would go about and gather it, grind it between millstones or pound it in a mortar, boil it in a pot, and make it into cakes. It tasted like rich cream. ⁹When the dew fell on the camp at night, the manna would fall upon it.

¹⁰Moses heard the people weeping, every clan apart, at the entrance of each tent. יהוה was very angry, and Moses was distressed. ¹¹And Moses said to יהוה, "Why have You dealt ill with Your servant, and why have I not enjoyed Your favor, that You have laid the burden of all this people upon me? ¹²Did I produce all this people, did I engender them, that You should say to me, 'Carry them in your bosom as a caretaker carries an infant,' to the land that You have promised on oath to their fathers? ¹³Where am I to get meat to give to all this people, when they whine before me and

say, 'Give us meat to eat!' ¹⁴I cannot carry all this people by myself, for it is too much for me. ¹⁵If You would deal thus with me, kill me rather, I beg You, and let me see no more of my wretchedness!"

¹⁶Then יהוה said to Moses, "Gather for Me seventy of Israel's elders of whom you have experience as elders and officers of the people, and bring them to the Tent of Meeting and let them take their place there with you. ¹⁷I will come down and speak with you there, and I will draw upon the spirit that is on you and put it upon them; they shall share the burden of the people with you, and you shall not bear it alone. ¹⁸And say to the people: Purify yourselves for tomorrow and you shall eat meat, for you have kept whining before יהוה and saying, 'If only we had meat to eat! Indeed, we were better off in Egypt!' יהוה will give you meat and you shall eat. ¹⁹You shall eat not one day, not two, not even five days or ten or twenty, ²⁰but a whole month, until it comes out of your nostrils and becomes loathsome to you. For you have rejected יהוה who is among you, by whining before [God] and saying, 'Oh, why did we ever leave Egypt!'"

²¹But Moses said, "The people who are with me number six hundred thousand foot soldiers; yet You say, 'I will give them enough meat to eat for a whole month.' ²²Could enough flocks and herds be slaughtered to suffice them? Or could all the fish of the sea be gathered for them to suffice them?" ²³And יהוה answered Moses, "Is there a limit to יהוה's power? You shall soon see whether what I have said happens to you or not!"

²⁴Moses went out and reported the words of יהוה to the people. He gathered seventy of the people's elders and stationed them around the Tent. ²⁵Then, after coming down in a cloud and speaking to him, יהוה drew upon the spirit that was on him and put it upon the seventy representative elders. And when the spirit rested upon them, they spoke in ecstasy, but did not continue.

²⁶Two of the elders, one named Eldad and the other Medad, had remained in camp; yet the spirit rested upon them—they were among those recorded, but they had not gone out to the Tent—and they spoke in ecstasy in the camp. ²⁷An assistant ran out and told Moses, saying, "Eldad and Medad are acting the prophet in the camp!" ²⁸And Joshua son of Nun, Moses' attendant from his youth, spoke up and said, "My lord Moses, restrain them!" ²⁹But Moses said to him, "Are you wrought up on my account? Would that all יהוה's people were prophets, that יהוה put [the divine] spirit upon them!" ³⁰Moses then reentered the camp together with the elders of Israel.

³¹A wind from יהוה started up, swept quail from the sea and strewed them over the camp, about a day's journey on this side and about a day's journey on that side, all around the camp, and some two cubits deep on the ground. ³²The people set to gathering quail all that day and night and all the next day—even the one who gathered least had ten *chom-ers*—and they spread them out all around the camp. ³³The meat was still between their teeth, not yet chewed, when the anger of יהוה blazed forth against the people and יהוה struck the people with a very severe plague. ³⁴That place was named Kibroth-hattaavah, because the people who had the craving were buried there. ³⁵Then the people set out from Kibroth-hattaavah for Hazeroth.

12 ¹When they were in Hazeroth, Miriam and Aaron spoke against Moses because of the Cushite woman he had taken [into his household as his wife]: "He took a Cushite woman!"

²They said, "Has יהוה spoken only through Moses? Has [God] not spoken through us as well?" יהוה heard it. ³Now

Moses was a very humble leader, more so than any other human being on earth. ⁴Suddenly יהוה called to Moses, Aaron, and Miriam, "Come out, you three, to the Tent of Meeting." So the three of them went out. ⁵יהוה came down in a pillar of cloud, stopped at the entrance of the Tent, and called out, "Aaron and Miriam!" The two of them came forward; ⁶and [God] said, "Hear these My words: When prophets of יהוה arise among you, I make Myself known to them in a vision, I speak with them in a dream. ⁷Not so with My servant Moses; he is trusted throughout My household. ⁸With him I speak mouth to mouth, plainly and not in riddles, and he beholds the likeness of יהוה. How then did you not shrink from speaking against My servant Moses!" ⁹Still incensed with them, יהוה departed.

¹⁰As the cloud withdrew from the Tent, there was Miriam stricken with snow-white scales! When Aaron turned toward Miriam, he saw that she was stricken with scales. ¹¹And Aaron said to Moses, "O my lord, account not to us the sin which we committed in our folly. ¹²Let her not be like a stillbirth which emerges from its mother's womb with half its flesh eaten away!" ¹³So Moses cried out to יהוה, saying, "O God, pray heal her!"

¹⁴But יהוה said to Moses, "If her father spat in her face, would she not bear her shame for seven days? Let her be shut out of camp for seven days, and then let her be readmitted." ¹⁵So Miriam was shut out of camp seven days; and the people did not march on until Miriam was readmitted. ¹⁶After that the people set out from Hazeroth and encamped in the wilderness of Paran.

13 ¹יהוה spoke to Moses, saying, ²"Send emissaries to scout the land of Canaan, which I am giving to the Israelite people; send one representative from each of their ancestral tribes, each one a chieftain among them." ³So Moses, by יהוה's command, sent them out from the wilderness of Paran, all of them being notables, leaders of the Israelites. ⁴And these were their names:

From the tribe of Reuben, Shammua son of Zaccur. ⁵From the tribe of Simeon, Shaphat son of Hori. ⁶From the tribe of Judah, Caleb son of Jephunneh. ⁷From the tribe of Issachar, Igal son of Joseph. ⁸From the tribe of Ephraim, Hosea son of Nun. ⁹From the tribe of Benjamin, Palti son of Rafu. ¹⁰From the tribe of Zebulun, Gaddiel son of Sodi. ¹¹From the tribe of Joseph, namely, the tribe of Manasseh, Gaddi son of Susi. ¹²From the tribe of Dan, Ammiel son of Gemalli. ¹³From the tribe of Asher, Sethur son of Michael. ¹⁴From the tribe of Naphtali, Nahbi son of Vophsi. ¹⁵From the tribe of Gad, Geuel son of Machi. ¹⁶Those were the names of the emissaries whom Moses sent to scout the land; but Moses changed the name of Hosea son of Nun to Joshua.

¹⁷When Moses sent them to scout the land of Canaan, he said to them, "Go up there into the Negeb and on into the hill country, ¹⁸and see what kind of country it is. Are the people who dwell in it strong or weak, few or many? ¹⁹Is the country in which they dwell good or bad? Are the towns they live in open or fortified? ²⁰Is the soil rich or poor? Is it wooded or not? And take pains to bring back some of the fruit of the land."—Now it happened to be the season of the first ripe grapes.

²¹They went up and scouted the land, from the wilderness of Zin to Rehob, at Lebo-hamath. ²²They went up into the Negeb and came to Hebron, where lived Ahiman, Sheshai, and Talmai, the Anakites.—Now Hebron was founded seven years before Zoan of Egypt.—²³They reached the

wadi Eshcol, and there they cut down a branch with a single cluster of grapes—it had to be borne on a carrying frame by two of them—and some pomegranates and figs. ²⁴That place was named the wadi Eshcol because of the cluster that the Israelites cut down there.

²⁵At the end of forty days they returned from scouting the land. ²⁶They went straight to Moses and Aaron and the whole Israelite community at Kadesh in the wilderness of Paran, and they made their report to them and to the whole community, as they showed them the fruit of the land. ²⁷This is what they told him: "We came to the land you sent us to; it does indeed flow with milk and honey, and this is its fruit. ²⁸However, the people who inhabit the country are powerful, and the cities are fortified and very large; moreover, we saw the Anakites there. ²⁹Amalekites dwell in the Negeb region; Hittites, Jebusites, and Amorites inhabit the hill country; and Canaanites dwell by the Sea and along the Jordan."

³⁰Caleb hushed the people before Moses and said, "Let us by all means go up, and we shall gain possession of it, for we shall surely overcome it."

³¹But the emissaries who had gone up with him said, "We cannot attack that people, for it is stronger than we." ³²Thus they spread calumnies among the Israelites about the land they had scouted, saying, "The country that we traversed and scouted is one that devours its settlers. All the people that we saw in it are of great size; ³³we saw the Nephilim there—the Anakites are part of the Nephilim—and we looked like grasshoppers to ourselves, and so we must have looked to them."

14 ¹The whole community broke into loud cries, and the people wept that night. ²All the Israelites railed against Moses and Aaron. "If only we had died in the land of Egypt," the whole community shouted at them, "or if only we might die in this wilderness!" ³"Why is יהוה taking us to that land to fall by the sword?" "Our wives and children will be carried off! It would be better for us to go back to Egypt!" ⁴And they said to one another, "Let us head back for Egypt."

⁵Then Moses and Aaron fell on their faces before all the assembled congregation of Israelites. ⁶And Joshua son of Nun and Caleb son of Jephunneh, of those who had scouted the land, rent their clothes ⁷and exhorted the whole Israelite community: "The land that we traversed and scouted is an exceedingly good land. ⁸If pleased with us, יהוה will bring us into that land, a land that flows with milk and honey, and give it to us; ⁹only you must not rebel against יהוה. Have no fear then of the people of the country, for they are our prey: their protection has departed from them, but יהוה is with us. Have no fear of them!" ¹⁰As the whole community threatened to pelt them with stones, the Presence of יהוה appeared in the Tent of Meeting to all the Israelites.

¹¹And יהוה said to Moses, "How long will this people spurn Me, and how long will they have no faith in Me despite all the signs that I have performed in their midst? ¹²I will strike them with pestilence and disown them, and I will make of you a nation far more numerous than they!" ¹³But Moses said to יהוה, "When the Egyptians, from whose midst You brought up this people in Your might, hear the news, ¹⁴they will tell it to the inhabitants of that land. Now they have heard that You, יהוה, are in the midst of this people; that You, יהוה, appear in plain sight when Your cloud rests over them and when You go before them in a pillar of cloud by day and in a pillar of fire by night. ¹⁵If then You slay this people wholesale, the nations who have heard Your fame will say, ¹⁶'It must be because יהוה was powerless to bring that people into the land promised them on oath that [that god]

slaughtered them in the wilderness.' ¹⁷Therefore, I pray, let my lord's forbearance be great, as You have declared, saying, ¹⁸'יהוה! slow to anger and abounding in kindness; forgiving iniquity and transgression; yet not remitting all punishment, but visiting the iniquity of parents upon children, upon the third and fourth generations.' ¹⁹Pardon, I pray, the iniquity of this people according to Your great kindness, as You have forgiven this people ever since Egypt."

²⁰And יהוה said, "I pardon, as you have asked. ²¹Nevertheless, as I live and as יהוה's Presence fills the whole world, ²²none of the adults who have seen My Presence and the signs that I have performed in Egypt and in the wilderness, and who have tried Me these many times and have disobeyed Me, ²³shall see the land that I promised on oath to their fathers; none of those who spurn Me shall see it. ²⁴But My servant Caleb, because he was imbued with a different spirit and remained loyal to Me—him will I bring into the land that he entered, and his offspring shall hold it as a possession. ²⁵Now the Amalekites and the Canaanites occupy the valleys. Start out, then, tomorrow and march into the wilderness by way of the Sea of Reeds."

²⁶יהוה spoke further to Moses and Aaron, ²⁷"How much longer shall that wicked community keep muttering against Me? Very well, I have heeded the incessant muttering of the Israelites against Me. ²⁸Say to them: 'As I live,' says יהוה, 'I will do to you just as you have urged Me. ²⁹In this very wilderness shall your carcasses drop. Of all of you [men] who were recorded in your various lists from the age of twenty years up, you who have muttered against Me, ³⁰not one shall enter the land in which I swore to settle you—save Caleb son of Jephunneh and Joshua son of Nun. ³¹Your children who, you said, would be carried off—these will I allow to enter; they shall know the land that you have rejected. ³²But your carcasses shall drop in this wilderness, ³³while your children roam the wilderness for forty years, suffering for your faithlessness, until the last of your carcasses is down in the wilderness. ³⁴You shall bear your punishment for forty years, corresponding to the number of days—forty days—that you scouted the land: a year for each day. Thus you shall know what it means to thwart Me. ³⁵I יהוה have spoken: Thus will I do to all that wicked band that has banded together against Me: in this very wilderness they shall die and so be finished off.'"

³⁶As for the emissaries whom Moses sent to scout the land, those who came back and caused the whole community to mutter against him by spreading calumnies about the land— ³⁷those who spread such calumnies about the land died of plague, by the will of יהוה. ³⁸Of those emissaries who had gone to scout the land, only Joshua son of Nun and Caleb son of Jephunneh survived.

³⁹When Moses repeated these words to all the Israelites, the people were overcome by grief. ⁴⁰Early next morning [their fighting force] set out toward the crest of the hill country, saying, "We are prepared to go up to the place that יהוה has spoken of, for we were wrong." ⁴¹But Moses said, "Why do you transgress יהוה's command? This will not succeed. ⁴²Do not go up, lest you be routed by your enemies, for יהוה is not in your midst. ⁴³For the Amalekites and the Canaanites will be there to face you, and you will fall by the sword, inasmuch as you have turned from following יהוה and יהוה will not be with you."

⁴⁴Yet defiantly they marched toward the crest of the hill country, though neither יהוה's Ark of the Covenant nor Moses stirred from the camp. ⁴⁵And the Amalekites and the Canaanites who dwelt in that hill country came down and dealt them a shattering blow at Hormah.

15 יהוה spoke to Moses, saying: ²Speak to the Israelite people and say to them:

When you enter the land that I am giving you to settle in, ³and would present an offering by fire to יהוה from the herd or from the flock, be it burnt offering or sacrifice, in fulfillment of a vow explicitly uttered, or as a freewill offering, or at your fixed occasions, producing an odor pleasing to יהוה:

⁴The person who presents the offering to יהוה shall bring as a meal offering: a tenth of a measure of choice flour with a quarter of a *hin* of oil mixed in. ⁵You shall also offer, with the burnt offering or the sacrifice, a quarter of a *hin* of wine as a libation for each sheep.

⁶In the case of a ram, you shall present as a meal offering: two-tenths of a measure of choice flour with a third of a *hin* of oil mixed in; ⁷and a third of a *hin* of wine as a libation—as an offering of pleasing odor to יהוה.

⁸And if it is an animal from the herd that you offer to יהוה as a burnt offering or as a sacrifice, in fulfillment of a vow explicitly uttered or as an offering of wellbeing, ⁹there shall be offered a meal offering along with the animal: three-tenths of a measure of choice flour with half a *hin* of oil mixed in; ¹⁰and as libation you shall offer half a *hin* of wine—these being offerings by fire of pleasing odor to יהוה.

¹¹Thus shall be done with each ox, with each ram, and with any sheep or goat, ¹²as many as you offer; you shall do thus with each one, as many as there are. ¹³Every citizen, when presenting an offering by fire of pleasing odor to יהוה, shall do so with them.

¹⁴And when, throughout the ages, a stranger who has taken up residence with you, or one who lives among you, would present an offering by fire of pleasing odor to יהוה—as you do, so shall it be done by ¹⁵the rest of the congregation. There shall be one law for you and for the resident stranger; it shall be a law for all time throughout the ages. You and the stranger shall be alike before יהוה; ¹⁶the same ritual and the same rule shall apply to you and to the stranger who resides among you.

¹⁷יהוה spoke to Moses, saying: ¹⁸Speak to the Israelite people and say to them:

When you enter the land to which I am taking you ¹⁹and you eat of the bread of the land, you shall set some aside as a gift to יהוה: ²⁰as the first yield of your baking, you shall set aside a loaf as a gift; you shall set it aside as a gift like the gift from the threshing floor. ²¹You shall make a gift to יהוה from the first yield of your baking, throughout the ages.

²²If you unwittingly fail to observe any one of the commandments that יהוה has declared to Moses—²³anything that יהוה has enjoined upon you through Moses—from the day that יהוה gave the commandment and on through the ages: ²⁴If this was done unwittingly, through the inadvertence of the community, the community leaders shall present one bull of the herd as a burnt offering of pleasing odor to יהוה, with its proper meal offering and libation, and one he-goat as a sin offering. ²⁵The priest shall make expiation for the whole Israelite community and they shall be forgiven; for it was an error, and for their error they have brought their offering, an offering by fire to יהוה and their sin offering before יהוה. ²⁶The whole Israelite community and the stranger residing among them shall be forgiven, for it happened to the entire people through error.

²⁷In case it is an individual who has sinned unwittingly, that person shall offer a she-goat in its first year as a sin offering. ²⁸The priest shall make expiation before יהוה on behalf of the person who erred, for having sinned unwittingly, making such expiation that the person may be forgiven. ²⁹For the citizen among the Israelites and for the stranger who resides among them—you shall have one ritual for anyone who acts in error. ³⁰But the person, whether citizen or stranger, who acts defiantly reviles יהוה; that person shall be cut off from among the people. ³¹Because it was the word of יהוה that was spurned and [God's] commandment that was violated, that person shall be cut off—and bears the guilt.

³²Once, when the Israelites were in the wilderness, they came upon a man gathering wood on the sabbath day. ³³Those who found him as he was gathering wood brought him before Moses, Aaron, and the community leadership. ³⁴He was placed in custody, for it had not been specified what should be done to him. ³⁵Then יהוה said to Moses, "This fellow shall be put to death: the community leadership shall pelt him with stones outside the camp." ³⁶So the community leadership took him outside the camp and stoned him to death—as יהוה had commanded Moses.

³⁷יהוה said to Moses as follows: ³⁸Speak to the Israelite people and instruct them to make for themselves fringes on the corners of their garments throughout the ages; let them attach a cord of blue to the fringe at each corner. ³⁹That shall be your fringe; look at it and recall all the commandments of יהוה and observe them, so that you do not follow your heart and eyes in your lustful urge. ⁴⁰Thus you shall be reminded to observe all My commandments and to be holy to your God. ⁴¹I יהוה am your God, who brought you out of the land of Egypt to be your God: I, your God יהוה.

16 ¹Now Korah, son of Izhar son of Kohath son of Levi, betook himself, along with Dathan and Abiram sons of Eliab, and On son of Peleth—descendants of Reuben—²to rise up against Moses, together with two hundred and fifty Israelite notables—chieftains of the community, chosen in the assembly, with fine reputations. ³They combined against Moses and Aaron and said to them, "You have gone too far! For all the community are holy, all of them, and יהוה is in their midst. Why then do you raise yourselves above יהוה's congregation?"

⁴When Moses heard this, he fell on his face. ⁵Then he spoke to Korah and all his company, saying, "Come morning, יהוה will make known who is [God's] and who is holy, and will grant him direct access; the one whom [God] has chosen will be granted access. ⁶Do this: You, Korah and all your band, take fire pans, ⁷and tomorrow put fire in them and lay incense on them before יהוה. Then the candidate whom יהוה chooses, he shall be the holy one. You have gone too far, sons of Levi!"

⁸Moses said further to Korah, "Hear me, sons of Levi. ⁹Is it not enough for you that the God of Israel has set you apart from the community of Israel and given you direct access, to perform the duties of יהוה's Tabernacle and to minister to the community and serve them? ¹⁰Now that [God] has advanced you and all your fellow Levites with you, do you seek the priesthood too? ¹¹Truly, it is against יהוה that you and all your company have banded together. For who is Aaron that you should rail against him?"

¹²Moses sent for Dathan and Abiram, sons of Eliab; but they said, "We will not come! ¹³Is it not enough that you brought us from a land flowing with milk and honey to have us die in the wilderness, that you would also lord it over us? ¹⁴Even if you had brought us to a land flowing with milk and honey, and given us possession of fields and vineyards, should you gouge out those subordinates' eyes? We will not come!"

¹⁵Moses was much aggrieved and he said to יהוה, "Pay no regard to their oblation. I have not taken the ass of any one of them, nor have I wronged any one of them."

¹⁶And Moses said to Korah, "Tomorrow, you and all your company appear before יהוה, you and they and Aaron. ¹⁷Each of you take his fire pan and lay incense on it, and each of

you bring his fire pan before יהוה, two hundred and fifty fire pans; you and Aaron also [bring] your fire pans." [18]Each of them took his fire pan, put fire in it, laid incense on it, and took his place at the entrance of the Tent of Meeting, as did Moses and Aaron. [19]Korah gathered the whole community against them at the entrance of the Tent of Meeting.

Then the Presence of יהוה appeared to the whole community, [20]and יהוה spoke to Moses and Aaron, saying, [21]"Stand back from this community that I may annihilate them in an instant!" [22]But they fell on their faces and said, "O God, Source of the breath of all flesh! When one member sins, will You be wrathful with the whole community?"

[23]יהוה spoke to Moses, saying, [24]"Speak to the community and say: Withdraw from about the abodes of Korah, Dathan, and Abiram."

[25]Moses rose and went to Dathan and Abiram, the elders of Israel following him. [26]He addressed the community, saying, "Move away from the tents of these wicked fellows and touch nothing that belongs to them, lest you be wiped out for all their sins." [27]So they withdrew from about the abodes of Korah, Dathan, and Abiram.

Now Dathan and Abiram had come out and they stood at the entrance of their tents, with their wives, their [grown] children, and their little ones. [28]And Moses said, "By this you shall know that it was יהוה who sent me to do all these things; that they are not of my own devising: [29]if these people's death is that of all humankind, if their lot is humankind's common fate, it was not יהוה who sent me. [30]But if יהוה brings about something unheard-of, so that the ground opens its mouth and swallows them up with all that belongs to them, and they go down alive into Sheol, you shall know that these fellows have spurned יהוה." [31]Scarcely had he finished speaking all these words when the ground under them burst asunder, [32]and the earth opened its mouth and swallowed them up with their households, all Korah's people and all their possessions. [33]They went down alive into Sheol, with all that belonged to them; the earth closed over them and they vanished from the midst of the congregation. [34]All Israel around them fled at their shrieks, for they said, "The earth might swallow us!" [35]And a fire went forth from יהוה and consumed the two hundred and fifty notables offering the incense.

17 [1]יהוה spoke to Moses, saying: [2]Order Eleazar son of Aaron the priest to remove the fire pans—for they have become sacred—from among the charred remains; and scatter the coals abroad. [3][Remove] the fire pans of those who have sinned at the cost of their lives, and let them be made into hammered sheets as plating for the altar—for once they have been used for offering to יהוה, they have become sacred—and let them serve as a warning to the people of Israel. [4]Eleazar the priest took the copper fire pans which had been used for offering by those who died in the fire; and they were hammered into plating for the altar, [5]as יהוה had ordered him through Moses. It was to be a reminder to the Israelites, so that no outsider—one not of Aaron's offspring—should presume to offer incense before יהוה and suffer the fate of Korah and his band.

[6]Next day the whole Israelite community railed against Moses and Aaron, saying, "You two have brought death upon יהוה's people!" [7]But as the community gathered against them, Moses and Aaron turned toward the Tent of Meeting; the cloud had covered it and the Presence of יהוה appeared.

[8]When Moses and Aaron reached the Tent of Meeting, [9]יהוה spoke to Moses, saying, [10]"Remove yourselves from this community, that I may annihilate them in an instant." They fell on their faces. [11]Then Moses said to Aaron, "Take the fire pan, and put on it fire from the altar. Add incense

and take it quickly to the community and make expiation for them. For wrath has gone forth from יהוה: the plague has begun!" [12]Aaron took it, as Moses had ordered, and ran to the midst of the congregation, where the plague had begun among the people. He put on the incense and made expiation for the people; [13]he stood between the dead and the living until the plague was checked. [14]Those who died of the plague came to fourteen thousand and seven hundred, aside from those who died on account of Korah. [15]Aaron then returned to Moses at the entrance of the Tent of Meeting, since the plague was checked.

[16]יהוה spoke to Moses, saying: [17]Speak to the Israelite people and take from them—from the chieftains of their ancestral houses—one staff for each chieftain of an ancestral house: twelve staffs in all. Inscribe each one's name on his staff, [18]there being one staff for each head of an ancestral house; also inscribe Aaron's name on the staff of Levi. [19]Deposit them in the Tent of Meeting before the Pact, where I meet with you. [20]The staff of the candidate whom I choose shall sprout, and I will rid Myself of the incessant mutterings of the Israelites against you.

[21]Moses spoke thus to the Israelites. Their chieftains gave him a staff for each chieftain of an ancestral house, twelve staffs in all; among these staffs was that of Aaron. [22]Moses deposited the staffs before יהוה, in the Tent of the Pact. [23]The next day Moses entered the Tent of the Pact, and there the staff of Aaron of the house of Levi had sprouted: it had brought forth sprouts, produced blossoms, and borne almonds. [24]Moses then brought out all the staffs from before יהוה to all the Israelites; each identified and recovered his staff.

[25]יהוה said to Moses, "Put Aaron's staff back before the Pact, to be kept as a lesson to rebels, so that their mutterings against Me may cease, lest they die." [26]This Moses did; just as יהוה had commanded him, so he did.

[27]But the Israelites said to Moses, "Lo, we perish! We are lost, all of us lost! [28]Everyone who so much as ventures near יהוה's Tabernacle must die. Alas, we are doomed to perish!"

18 [1]יהוה said to Aaron: You and your sons and the ancestral house under your charge shall bear any guilt connected with the sanctuary; you and your sons alone shall bear any guilt connected with your priesthood. [2]You shall also associate with yourself your kinsmen the tribe of Levi, your ancestral tribe, to be attached to you and to minister to you, while you and your sons under your charge are before the Tent of the Pact. [3]They shall discharge their duties to you and to the Tent as a whole, but they must not have any contact with the furnishings of the Shrine or with the altar, lest both they and you die. [4]They shall be attached to you and discharge the duties of the Tent of Meeting, all the service of the Tent; but no outsider shall intrude upon you [5]as you discharge the duties connected with the Shrine and the altar, that wrath may not again strike the Israelites.

[6]I hereby take your fellow Levites from among the Israelites; they are assigned to you in dedication to יהוה, to do the work of the Tent of Meeting; [7]while you and your sons shall be careful to perform your priestly duties in everything pertaining to the altar and to what is behind the curtain. I make your priesthood a service of dedication; any outsider who encroaches shall be put to death.

[8]יהוה spoke further to Aaron: I hereby give you charge of My gifts, all the sacred donations of the Israelites; I grant them to you and to your sons as a perquisite, a due for all time. [9]This shall be yours from the most holy sacrifices, the offerings by fire: every such offering that they render to Me as most holy sacrifices, namely, every meal offering, sin offering, and guilt offering of theirs, shall belong to you

and your sons. ¹⁰You shall partake of them as most sacred donations: only males may eat them; you shall treat them as consecrated.

¹¹This, too, shall be yours: the gift offerings of their contributions, all the elevation offerings of the Israelites, I give to you [and your wives], to your sons, and to the daughters that are with you, as a due for all time; everyone of your household who is pure may eat it.

¹²All the best of the new oil, wine, and grain—the choice parts that they present to יהוה—I give to you. ¹³The first fruits of everything in their land, that they bring to יהוה, shall be yours; everyone of your household who is pure may eat them. ¹⁴Everything that has been proscribed in Israel shall be yours. ¹⁵The first [male] issue of the womb of every being, human or beast, that is offered to יהוה, shall be yours; but you shall have the male firstborn of human beings redeemed, and you shall also have the firstling of impure animals redeemed. ¹⁶Take as their redemption price, from the age of one month up, the money equivalent of five shekels by the sanctuary weight, which is twenty *gerahs*. ¹⁷But the firstlings of cattle, sheep, or goats may not be redeemed; they are consecrated. You shall dash their blood against the altar, and turn their fat into smoke as an offering by fire for a pleasing odor to יהוה. ¹⁸But their meat shall be yours: it shall be yours like the breast of elevation offering and like the right thigh.

¹⁹All the sacred gifts that the Israelites set aside for יהוה I give to you, to your sons, and to the daughters that are with you, as a due for all time. It shall be an everlasting covenant of salt before יהוה for you and for your offspring as well. ²⁰And יהוה said to Aaron: You shall, however, have no territorial share among them or own any portion in their midst; I am your portion and your share among the Israelites.

²¹And to the Levites I hereby give all the tithes in Israel as their share in return for the services that they perform, the services of the Tent of Meeting. ²²Henceforth, Israelites shall not trespass on the Tent of Meeting, and thus incur guilt and die: ²³only Levites shall perform the services of the Tent of Meeting; others would incur guilt. It is the law for all time throughout the ages. But they shall have no territorial share among the Israelites; ²⁴for it is the tithes set aside by the Israelites as a gift to יהוה that I give to the Levites as their share. Therefore I have said concerning them: They shall have no territorial share among the Israelites.

²⁵יהוה spoke to Moses, saying: ²⁶Speak to the Levites and say to them: When you receive from the Israelites their tithes, which I have assigned to you as your share, you shall set aside from them one-tenth of the tithe as a gift to יהוה. ²⁷This shall be accounted to you as your gift. As with the new grain from the threshing floor or the flow from the vat, ²⁸so shall you on your part set aside a gift for יהוה from all the tithes that you receive from the Israelites; and from them you shall bring the gift for יהוה to Aaron the priest. ²⁹You shall set aside all gifts due to יהוה from everything that is donated to you, from each thing its best portion, the part thereof that is to be consecrated.

³⁰Say to them further: When you have removed the best part from it, you Levites may consider it the same as the yield of threshing floor or vat. ³¹You and your households may eat it anywhere, for it is your recompense for your services in the Tent of Meeting. ³²You will incur no guilt through it, once you have removed the best part from it; but you must not profane the sacred donations of the Israelites, lest you die.

19 ¹יהוה spoke to Moses and Aaron, saying: ²This is the ritual law that יהוה has commanded:
Instruct the Israelite people to bring you a red cow without blemish, in which there is no defect and on which no yoke

has been laid. ³You shall give it to Eleazar the priest. It shall be taken outside the camp and slaughtered in his presence. ⁴Eleazar the priest shall take some of its blood with his finger and sprinkle it seven times toward the front of the Tent of Meeting. ⁵The cow shall be burned in his sight—its hide, flesh, and blood shall be burned, its dung included—⁶and the priest shall take cedar wood, hyssop, and crimson stuff, and throw them into the fire consuming the cow. ⁷The priest shall wash his garments and bathe his body in water; after that the priest may reenter the camp, but he shall be impure until evening. ⁸He who performed the burning shall also wash his garments in water, bathe his body in water, and be impure until evening. ⁹A man who is pure shall gather up the ashes of the cow and deposit them outside the camp in a pure place, to be kept for water of lustration for the Israelite community. It is for purgation. ¹⁰He who gathers up the ashes of the cow shall also wash his clothes and be impure until evening. This shall be a permanent law for the Israelites and for the strangers who reside among you.

¹¹Those who touch the corpse of any human being shall be impure for seven days. ¹²They shall purify themselves with [the ashes] on the third day and on the seventh day, and then be pure; if they fail to purify themselves on the third and seventh days, they shall not be pure. ¹³Those who touch a corpse, the body of a person who has died, and do not purify themselves, defile יהוה's Tabernacle; those persons shall be cut off from Israel. Since the water of lustration was not dashed on them, they remain impure; their impurity is still upon them.

¹⁴This is the ritual: When a person dies in a tent, whoever enters the tent and whoever is in the tent shall be impure seven days; ¹⁵and every open vessel, with no lid fastened down, shall be impure. ¹⁶And in the open, anyone who touches a person who was killed or who died naturally, or human bone, or a grave, shall be impure seven days. ¹⁷Some of the ashes from the fire of purgation shall be taken for the impure person, and fresh water shall be added to them in a vessel. ¹⁸A person who is pure shall take hyssop, dip it in the water, and sprinkle on the tent and on all the vessels and people who were there, or on the one who touched the bones or the person who was killed or died naturally or the grave. ¹⁹The pure person shall sprinkle it upon the impure person on the third day and on the seventh day, thus purifying that person by the seventh day. [The one being purified] shall then wash those clothes and bathe in water—and at nightfall shall be pure. ²⁰If anyone who has become impure fails to undergo purification, that person shall be cut off from the congregation for having defiled יהוה's sanctuary. The water of lustration was not dashed on that person, who is impure.

²¹That shall be for them a law for all time. Further, the one who sprinkled the water of lustration shall wash those clothes; and whoever touches the water of lustration shall be impure until evening. ²²Whatever that impure person touches shall be impure; and the person who touches the impure one shall be impure until evening.

20 ¹The Israelites arrived in a body at the wilderness of Zin on the first new moon, and the people stayed at Kadesh. Miriam died there and was buried there.

²The community was without water, and they joined against Moses and Aaron. ³The people quarreled with Moses, saying, "If only we had perished when our brothers perished at the instance of יהוה! ⁴Why have you brought יהוה's congregation into this wilderness for us and our beasts to die there? ⁵Why did you make us leave Egypt to bring us to this wretched place, a place with no grain or figs or vines or pomegranates? There is not even water to drink!"

⁶Moses and Aaron came away from the congregation to the entrance of the Tent of Meeting, and fell on their faces. The Presence of יהוה appeared to them, 7and יהוה spoke to Moses, saying, 8"You and your brother Aaron take the rod and assemble the community, and before their very eyes order the rock to yield its water. Thus you shall produce water for them from the rock and provide drink for the congregation and their beasts."

⁹Moses took the rod from before יהוה, as he had been commanded. ¹⁰Moses and Aaron assembled the congregation in front of the rock; and he said to them, "Listen, you rebels, shall we get water for you out of this rock?" ¹¹And Moses raised his hand and struck the rock twice with his rod. Out came copious water, and the community and their beasts drank.

¹²But יהוה said to Moses and Aaron, "Because you did not trust Me enough to affirm My sanctity in the sight of the Israelite people, therefore you shall not lead this congregation into the land that I have given them." ¹³Those are the Waters of Meribah—meaning that the Israelites quarreled with יהוה—whose sanctity was affirmed through them.

¹⁴From Kadesh, Moses sent messengers to the king of Edom: "Thus says your brother, Israel: You know all the hardships that have befallen us; ¹⁵that our ancestors went down to Egypt, that we dwelt in Egypt a long time, and that the Egyptians dealt harshly with us and our ancestors. ¹⁶We cried to יהוה who heard our plea, sending a messenger who freed us from Egypt. Now we are in Kadesh, the town on the border of your territory. ¹⁷Allow us, then, to cross your country. We will not pass through fields or vineyards, and we will not drink water from wells. We will follow the king's highway, turning off neither to the right nor to the left until we have crossed your territory."

¹⁸But Edom answered him, "You shall not pass through us, else we will go out against you with the sword." ¹⁹"We will keep to the beaten track," the Israelites said to them, "and if we or our cattle drink your water, we will pay for it. We ask only for passage on foot—it is but a small matter." ²⁰But they replied, "You shall not pass through!" And Edom went out against them in heavy force, strongly armed. ²¹So Edom would not let Israel cross their territory, and Israel turned away from them.

²²Setting out from Kadesh, the Israelites arrived in a body at Mount Hor. ²³At Mount Hor, on the boundary of the land of Edom, יהוה said to Moses and Aaron, ²⁴"Let Aaron be gathered to his kin: he is not to enter the land that I have assigned to the Israelite people, because you disobeyed my command about the waters of Meribah. ²⁵Take Aaron and his son Eleazar and bring them up on Mount Hor. ²⁶Strip Aaron of his vestments and put them on his son Eleazar. There Aaron shall be gathered unto the dead."

²⁷Moses did as יהוה had commanded. They ascended Mount Hor in the sight of the whole community. ²⁸Moses stripped Aaron of his vestments and put them on his son Eleazar, and Aaron died there on the summit of the mountain. When Moses and Eleazar came down from the mountain, ²⁹the whole community knew that Aaron had breathed his last. All the house of Israel bewailed Aaron thirty days.

21 ¹When the Canaanite, king of Arad, who dwelt in the Negeb, learned that Israel was coming by the way of Atharim, he engaged Israel in battle and took some of them captive. ²Then Israel made a vow to יהוה and said, "If You deliver this people into our hand, we will proscribe their towns." ³יהוה heeded Israel's plea and delivered up the Canaanites; and they and their cities were proscribed. So that place was named Hormah.

⁴They set out from Mount Hor by way of the Sea of Reeds to skirt the land of Edom. But the people grew restive on the journey, ⁵and the people spoke against God and against Moses, "Why did you make us leave Egypt to die in the wilderness? There is no bread and no water, and we have come to loathe this miserable food." ⁶יהוה sent *seraph* serpents against the people. They bit the people and many of the Israelites died. ⁷The people came to Moses and said, "We sinned by speaking against יהוה and against you. Intercede with יהוה to take away the serpents from us!" And Moses interceded for the people. ⁸Then יהוה said to Moses, "Make a *seraph* figure and mount it on a standard. And anyone who was bitten who then looks at it shall recover." ⁹Moses made a copper serpent and mounted it on a standard; and when bitten by a serpent, anyone who looked at the copper serpent would recover.

¹⁰The Israelites marched on and encamped at Oboth. ¹¹They set out from Oboth and encamped at Iyeabarim, in the wilderness bordering on Moab to the east. ¹²From there they set out and encamped at the wadi Zered. ¹³From there they set out and encamped beyond the Arnon, that is, in the wilderness that extends from the territory of the Amorites. For the Arnon is the boundary of Moab, between Moab and the Amorites. ¹⁴Therefore the Book of the Wars of יהוה speaks of "...Waheb in Suphah, and the wadis: the Arnon ¹⁵with its tributary wadis, stretched along the settled country of Ar, hugging the territory of Moab . . ."

¹⁶And from there to Beer, which is the well where יהוה said to Moses, "Assemble the people that I may give them water." ¹⁷Then Israel sang this song:

Spring up, O well—sing to it—
¹⁸ The well which the chieftains dug,
 Which the nobles of the people started
 With maces, with their own staffs.

And from Midbar to Mattanah, ¹⁹and from Mattanah to Nahaliel, and from Nahaliel to Bamoth, ²⁰and from Bamoth to the valley that is in the country of Moab, at the peak of Pisgah, overlooking the wasteland.

²¹Israel now sent messengers to Sihon king of the Amorites, saying, ²²"Let me pass through your country. We will not turn off into fields or vineyards, and we will not drink water from wells. We will follow the king's highway until we have crossed your territory." ²³But Sihon would not let Israel pass through his territory. Sihon gathered all his people and went out against Israel in the wilderness. He came to Jahaz and engaged Israel in battle. ²⁴But Israel put them to the sword, and took possession of their land, from the Arnon to the Jabbok, as far as [Az] of the Ammonites, for Az marked the boundary of the Ammonites. ²⁵Israel took all those towns. And Israel settled in all the towns of the Amorites, in Heshbon and all its dependencies.

²⁶Now Heshbon was the city of Sihon king of the Amorites, who had fought against a former king of Moab and taken all his land from him as far as the Arnon. ²⁷Therefore the bards would recite:

"Come to Heshbon; firmly built
 And well founded is Sihon's city.
²⁸ For fire went forth from Heshbon,
 Flame from Sihon's city,
 Consuming Ar of Moab,
 The lords of Bamoth by the Arnon.
²⁹ Woe to you, O Moab!
 You are undone, O people of Chemosh!
 His sons are rendered fugitive
 And his daughters captive
 By an Amorite king, Sihon."

30 Yet we have cast them down utterly,
Heshbon along with Dibon;
We have wrought desolation at Nophah,
Which is hard by Medeba.

31So Israel occupied the land of the Amorites. 32Then Moses sent to spy out Jazer, and they captured its dependencies and dispossessed the Amorites who were there.

33They marched on and went up the road to Bashan, and King Og of Bashan, with all his people, came out to Edrei to engage them in battle. 34But יהוה said to Moses, "Do not fear him, for I give him and all his people and his land into your hand. You shall do to him as you did to Sihon king of the Amorites who dwelt in Heshbon." 35They defeated him and his sons and all his people, until no remnant was left him; and they took possession of his country.

22 1The Israelites then marched on and encamped in the steppes of Moab, across the Jordan from Jericho.

2Balak son of Zippor saw all that Israel had done to the Amorites. 3Moab was alarmed because that people was so numerous. Moab dreaded the Israelites, 4and Moab said to the elders of Midian, "Now this horde will lick clean all that is about us as an ox licks up the grass of the field."

Balak son of Zippor, who was king of Moab at that time, 5sent messengers to Balaam son of Beor in Pethor, which is by the Euphrates, in the land of his kinsfolk, to invite him, saying, "There is a people that came out of Egypt; it hides the earth from view, and it is settled next to me. 6Come then, put a curse upon this people for me, since they are too numerous for me; perhaps I can thus defeat them and drive them out of the land. For I know that he whom you bless is blessed indeed, and he whom you curse is cursed."

7The elders of Moab and the elders of Midian, versed in divination, set out. They came to Balaam and gave him Balak's message. 8He said to them, "Spend the night here, and I shall reply to you as יהוה may instruct me." So the Moabite dignitaries stayed with Balaam.

9God came to Balaam and said, "What do these envoys want of you?" 10Balaam said to God, "Balak son of Zippor, king of Moab, sent me this message: 11Here is a people that came out from Egypt and hides the earth from view. Come now and curse them for me; perhaps I can engage them in battle and drive them off." 12But God said to Balaam, "Do not go with them. You must not curse that people, for they are blessed."

13Balaam arose in the morning and said to Balak's dignitaries, "Go back to your own country, for יהוה will not let me go with you." 14The Moabite dignitaries left, and they came to Balak and said, "Balaam refused to come with us."

15Then Balak sent other dignitaries, more numerous and distinguished than the first. 16They came to Balaam and said to him, "Thus says Balak son of Zippor: Please do not refuse to come to me. 17I will reward you richly and I will do anything you ask of me. Only come and damn this people for me." 18Balaam replied to Balak's officials, "Though Balak were to give me his house full of silver and gold, I could not do anything, big or little, contrary to the command of my God יהוה. 19So you, too, stay here over night, and let me find out what else יהוה may say to me." 20That night God came to Balaam and said to him, "If these envoys have come to invite you, you may go with them. But whatever I command you, that you shall do." 21When he arose in the morning, Balaam saddled his ass and departed with the Moabite dignitaries.

22But God was incensed at his going; so a messenger of יהוה took a position in his way as an adversary.

He was riding on his sheass, with his two servants alongside, 23when the ass caught sight of the messenger of יהוה standing in the way, with his drawn sword in his hand. The ass swerved from the road and went into the fields; and Balaam beat the ass to turn her back onto the road. 24The messenger of יהוה then stationed himself in a lane between the vineyards, with a fence on either side. 25The ass, seeing the messenger of יהוה, pressed herself against the wall and squeezed Balaam's foot against the wall; so he beat her again. 26Once more the messenger of יהוה moved forward and stationed himself on a spot so narrow that there was no room to swerve right or left. 27When the ass now saw the messenger of יהוה, she lay down under Balaam; and Balaam was furious and beat the ass with his stick. 28Then יהוה opened the ass's mouth, and she said to Balaam, "What have I done to you that you have beaten me these three times?" 29Balaam said to the ass, "You have made a mockery of me! If I had a sword with me, I'd kill you." 30The ass said to Balaam, "Look, I am the ass that you have been riding all along until this day! Have I been in the habit of doing thus to you?" And he answered, "No."

31Then יהוה uncovered Balaam's eyes, and he saw the messenger of יהוה standing in the way, his drawn sword in his hand; thereupon he bowed right down to the ground. 32The messenger of יהוה said to him, "Why have you beaten your ass these three times? It is I who came out as an adversary, for the errand is obnoxious to me. 33And when the ass saw me, she shied away because of me those three times. If she had not shied away from me, you are the one I should have killed, while sparing her." 34Balaam said to the messenger of יהוה, "I erred because I did not know that you were standing in my way. If you still disapprove, I will turn back." 35But the messenger of יהוה said to Balaam, "Go with those envoys. But you must say nothing except what I tell you." So Balaam went on with Balak's dignitaries.

36When Balak heard that Balaam was coming, he went out to meet him at Irmoab, which is on the Arnon border, at its farthest point. 37Balak said to Balaam, "When I first sent to invite you, why didn't you come to me? Am I really unable to reward you?" 38But Balaam said to Balak, "And now that I have come to you, have I the power to speak freely? I can utter only the word that God puts into my mouth."

39Balaam went with Balak and they came to Kiriathhuzoth. 40Balak sacrificed oxen and sheep, and had them served to Balaam and the dignitaries with him. 41In the morning Balak took Balaam up to Bamothbaal. From there he could see a portion of the people.

23 1Balaam said to Balak, "Build me seven altars here and have seven bulls and seven rams ready here for me." 2Balak did as Balaam directed; and Balak and Balaam offered up a bull and a ram on each altar. 3Then Balaam said to Balak, "Stay here beside your offerings while I am gone. Perhaps יהוה will grant me a manifestation, and whatever is revealed to me I will tell you." And he went off alone.

4God became manifest to Balaam, who stated, "I have set up the seven altars and offered up a bull and a ram on each altar." 5And יהוה put a word in Balaam's mouth and said, "Return to Balak and speak thus."

6So he returned to him and found him standing beside his offerings, and all the Moabite dignitaries with him. 7He took up his theme, and said:

From Aram has Balak brought me,
Moab's king from the hills of the East:
Come, curse me Jacob,
Come, tell Israel's doom!
8 How can I damn whom God has not damned,
How doom when יהוה has not doomed?
9 As I see them from the mountain tops,

Gaze on them from the heights,
There is a people that dwells apart,
Not reckoned among the nations,
10 Who can count the dust of Jacob,
Number the dust cloud of Israel?
May I die the death of the upright,
May my fate be like theirs!

11Then Balak said to Balaam, "What have you done to me? Here I brought you to damn my enemies, and instead you have blessed them!" 12He replied, "I can only repeat faithfully what יהוה puts in my mouth." 13Then Balak said to him, "Come with me to another place from which you can see them—you will see only a portion of them; you will not see all of them—and damn them for me from there." 14With that, he took him to Sedehzophim, on the summit of Pisgah. He built seven altars and offered a bull and a ram on each altar. 15And [Balaam] said to Balak, "Stay here beside your offerings, while I seek a manifestation yonder."

16יהוה became manifest to Balaam and put a word in his mouth, saying, "Return to Balak and speak thus." 17He went to him and found him standing beside his offerings, and the Moabite dignitaries with him. Balak asked him, "What did יהוה say?" 18And he took up his theme, and said:

Up, Balak, attend,
Give ear unto me, son of Zippor!
19 God is not human to be capricious,
Or mortal to have a change of heart.
Would [God] speak and not act,
Promise and not fulfill?
20 My message was to bless:
When [God] blesses, I cannot reverse it.
21 No harm is in sight for Jacob,
No woe in view for Israel.
Their God יהוה is with them,
And their King's acclaim in their midst.
22 God who freed them from Egypt
Is for them like the horns of the wild ox.
23 Lo, there is no augury in Jacob,
No divining in Israel:
Jacob is told at once,
Yea Israel, what God has planned.
24 Lo, a people that rises like a lioness,
Leaps up like a lion,
Rests not till it has feasted on prey
And drunk the blood of the slain.

25Thereupon Balak said to Balaam, "Don't curse them and don't bless them!" 26In reply, Balaam said to Balak, "But I told you: Whatever יהוה says, that I must do." 27Then Balak said to Balaam, "Come now, I will take you to another place. Perhaps God will deem it right that you damn them for me there." 28Balak took Balaam to the peak of Peor, which overlooks the wasteland. 29Balaam said to Balak, "Build me here seven altars, and have seven bulls and seven rams ready for me here." 30Balak did as Balaam said: he offered up a bull and a ram on each altar.

24 1Now Balaam, seeing that it pleased יהוה to bless Israel, did not, as on previous occasions, go in search of omens, but turned his face toward the wilderness. 2As Balaam looked up and saw Israel encamped tribe by tribe, the spirit of God came upon him. 3Taking up his theme, he said:

Word of Balaam son of Beor,
Word of the man whose eye is true,
4 Word of one who hears God's speech,

Who beholds visions from the Almighty,
Prostrate, but with eyes unveiled:
5 How fair are your tents, O Jacob,
Your dwellings, O Israel!
6 Like palm groves that stretch out,
Like gardens beside a river,
Like aloes planted by יהוה,
Like cedars beside the water;
7 Their boughs drip with moisture,
Their roots have abundant water.
Their ruler shall rise above Agag,
Their sovereignty shall be exalted.
8 God who freed them from Egypt
Is for them like the horns of the wild ox.
They shall devour enemy nations,
Crush their bones,
And smash their arrows.
9 They crouch, they lie down like a lion,
Like a lioness; who dares rouse them?
Blessed are they who bless you,
Accursed they who curse you!

10Enraged at Balaam, Balak struck his hands together. "I called you," Balak said to Balaam, "to damn my enemies, and instead you have blessed them these three times! 11Back with you at once to your own place! I was going to reward you richly, but יהוה has denied you the reward." 12Balaam replied to Balak, "But I even told the messengers you sent to me, 13'Though Balak were to give me his house full of silver and gold, I could not of my own accord do anything good or bad contrary to יהוה's command. What יהוה says, that I must say.' 14And now, as I go back to my people, let me inform you of what this people will do to your people in days to come." 15He took up his theme, and said:

Word of Balaam son of Beor,
Word of the man whose eye is true,
16 Word of one who hears God's speech,
Who obtains knowledge from the Most High,
And beholds visions from the Almighty,
Prostrate, but with eyes unveiled:
17 What I see for them is not yet,
What I behold will not be soon:
A star rises from Jacob,
A scepter comes forth from Israel;
It smashes the brow of Moab,
The foundation of all children of Seth.
18 Edom becomes a possession,
Yea, Seir a possession of its enemies;
But Israel is triumphant.
19 A victor issues from Jacob
To wipe out what is left of Ir.

20He saw Amalek and, taking up his theme, he said:

A leading nation is Amalek;
But its fate is to perish forever.

21He saw the Kenites and, taking up his theme, he said:

Though your abode be secure,
And your nest be set among cliffs,
22 Yet shall Kain be consumed,
When Asshur takes you captive.

23He took up his theme and said:

Alas, who can survive except God has willed it!
24 Ships come from the quarter of Kittim;
They subject Asshur, subject Eber.
They, too, shall perish forever.

25Then Balaam set out on his journey back home; and Balak also went his way.

25

1While Israel was staying at Shittim, the menfolk profaned themselves by whoring with the Moabite women, 2who invited the men folk to the sacrifices for their god. The men folk partook of them and worshiped that god. 3Thus Israel attached itself to Baalpeor, and יהוה was incensed with Israel. 4יהוה said to Moses, "Take all the ringleaders and have them publicly impaled before יהוה, so that יהוה's wrath may turn away from Israel." 5So Moses said to Israel's officials, "Each of you slay those of his men who attached themselves to Baalpeor."

6Just then one of the Israelite notables came and brought a Midianite woman over to his companions, in the sight of Moses and of the whole Israelite community who were weeping at the entrance of the Tent of Meeting. 7When Phinehas, son of Eleazar son of Aaron the priest, saw this, he left the assembly and, taking a spear in his hand, 8he followed the Israelite notable into the chamber and stabbed both of them, the Israelite notable and the woman, through the belly. Then the plague against the Israelites was checked. 9Those who died of the plague numbered twenty-four thousand.

10יהוה spoke to Moses, saying, 11"Phinehas, son of Eleazar son of Aaron the priest, has turned back My wrath from the Israelites by displaying among them his passion for Me, so that I did not wipe out the Israelite people in My passion. 12Say, therefore, 'I grant him My pact of friendship. 13It shall be for him and his descendants after him a pact of priesthood for all time, because he took impassioned action for his God, thus making expiation for the Israelites.'"

14The name of the Israelite notable who was killed, the one who was killed with the Midianite woman, was Zimri son of Salu, chieftain of a Simeonite ancestral house. 15The name of the Midianite woman who was killed was Cozbi daughter of Zur; he was the tribal head of an ancestral house in Midian.

16יהוה spoke to Moses, saying, 17"Assail the Midianites and defeat them—18for they assailed you by the trickery they practiced against you—because of the affair of Peor and because of the affair of their kinswoman Cozbi, daughter of the Midianite chieftain, who was killed at the time of the plague on account of Peor." 19When the plague was over,

26

1יהוה said to Moses and to Eleazar son of Aaron the priest, 2"Take a census of the whole Israelite company [of fighters] from the age of twenty years up, by their ancestral houses, all Israelite males able to bear arms." 3So Moses and Eleazar the priest, on the steppes of Moab, at the Jordan near Jericho, gave instructions about them, namely, 4those from twenty years up, as יהוה had commanded Moses.

The [eligible male] descendants of the Israelites who came out of the land of Egypt were:

5Reuben, Israel's firstborn. Descendants of Reuben: [of] Enoch, the clan of the Enochites; of Pallu, the clan of the Palluites; 6of Hezron, the clan of the Hezronites; of Carmi, the clan of the Carmites. 7Those are the clans of the Reubenites. The men enrolled came to 43,730.

8Born to Pallu: Eliab. 9The sons of Eliab were Nemuel, and Dathan and Abiram. These are the same Dathan and Abiram, chosen in the assembly, who agitated against Moses and Aaron as part of Korah's band when they agitated against יהוה. 10Whereupon the earth opened its mouth and swallowed them up with Korah—when that band died, when the fire consumed the two hundred and fifty notables—and they became an example. 11The sons of Korah, however, did not die.

12Descendants of Simeon by their clans: Of Nemuel, the clan of the Nemuelites; of Jamin, the clan of the Jaminites; of Jachin, the clan of the Jachinites; 13of Zerah, the clan of the Zerahites; of Saul, the clan of the Saulites. 14Those are the clans of the Simeonites; [men enrolled:] 22,200.

15Descendants of Gad by their clans: Of Zephon, the clan of the Zephonites; of Haggi, the clan of the Haggites; of Shuni, the clan of the Shunites; 16of Ozni, the clan of the Oznites; of Eri, the clan of the Erites; 17of Arod, the clan of the Arodites; of Areli, the clan of the Arelites. 18Those are the clans of Gad's descendants; men enrolled: 40,500.

19Born to Judah: Er and Onan. Er and Onan died in the land of Canaan.

20Descendants of Judah by their clans: Of Shelah, the clan of the Shelanites; of Perez, the clan of the Perezites; of Zerah, the clan of the Zerahites. 21Descendants of Perez: of Hezron, the clan of the Hezronites; of Hamul, the clan of the Hamulites. 22Those are the clans of Judah; men enrolled: 76,500.

23Descendants of Issachar by their clans: [Of] Tola, the clan of the Tolaites; of Puvah, the clan of the Punites; 24of Jashub, the clan of the Jashubites; of Shimron, the clan of the Shimronites. 25Those are the clans of Issachar; men enrolled: 64,300.

26Descendants of Zebulun by their clans: Of Sered, the clan of the Seredites; of Elon, the clan of the Elonites; of Jahleel, the clan of the Jahleelites. 27Those are the clans of the Zebulunites; men enrolled: 60,500.

28The sons of Joseph were Manasseh and Ephraim—by their clans. 29Descendants of Manasseh: Of Machir, the clan of the Machirites.—Machir begot Gilead.—Of Gilead, the clan of the Gileadites. 30These were the descendants of Gilead: [Of] Iezer, the clan of the Iezerites; of Helek, the clan of the Helekites; 31[of] Asriel, the clan of the Asrielites; [of] Shechem, the clan of the Shechemites; 32[of] Shemida, the clan of the Shemidaites; [of] Hepher, the clan of the Hepherites.—33Now Zelophehad son of Hepher had no sons, only daughters. The names of Zelophehad's daughters were Mahlah, Noah, Hoglah, Milcah, and Tirzah.—34Those are the clans of Manasseh; men enrolled: 52,700.

35These are the descendants of Ephraim by their clans: Of Shuthelah, the clan of the Shuthelahites; of Becher, the clan of the Becherites; of Tahan, the clan of the Tahanites. 36These are the descendants of Shuthelah: Of Eran, the clan of the Eranites. 37Those are the clans of Ephraim's descendants; men enrolled: 32,500. Those are the descendants of Joseph by their clans.

38The descendants of Benjamin by their clans: Of Bela, the clan of the Belaites; of Ashbel, the clan of the Ashbelites; of Ahiram, the clan of the Ahiramites; 39of Shephupham, the clan of the Shuphamites; of Hupham, the clan of the Huphamites. 40The sons of Bela were Ard and Naaman: [Of Ard,] the clan of the Ardites; of Naaman, the clan of the Naamanites. 41Those are the descendants of Benjamin by their clans; men enrolled: 45,600.

42These are the descendants of Dan by their clans: Of Shuham, the clan of the Shuhamites. Those are the clans of Dan, by their clans. 43All the clans of the Shuhamites; men enrolled: 64,400.

44Descendants of Asher by their clans: Of Imnah, the clan of the Imnites; of Ishvi, the clan of the Ishvites; of Beriah, the clan of the Beriites. 45Of the descendants of Beriah: Of Heber, the clan of the Heberites; of Malchiel, the clan of the Malchielites.—46The name of Asher's daughter was Serah.—47These are the clans of Asher's descendants; men enrolled: 53,400.

⁴⁸Descendants of Naphtali by their clans: Of Jahzeel, the clan of the Jahzeelites; of Guni, the clan of the Gunites; ⁴⁹of Jezer, the clan of the Jezerites; of Shillem, the clan of the Shillemites. ⁵⁰Those are the clans of the Naphtalites, clan by clan; men enrolled: 45,400.

⁵¹This is the enrollment of the Israelite men: 601,730.

⁵²יהוה spoke to Moses, saying, ⁵³"Among these shall the land be apportioned as shares, according to the listed names: ⁵⁴with larger groups increase the share, with smaller groups reduce the share. Each is to be assigned its share according to its enrollment. ⁵⁵The land, moreover, is to be apportioned by lot; and the allotment shall be made according to the listings of their ancestral tribes. ⁵⁶Each portion shall be assigned by lot, whether for larger or smaller groups."

⁵⁷This is the enrollment of the Levites by their clans: Of Gershon, the clan of the Gershonites; of Kohath, the clan of the Kohathites; of Merari, the clan of the Merarites. ⁵⁸These are the clans of Levi: The clan of the Libnites, the clan of the Hebronites, the clan of the Mahlites, the clan of the Mushites, the clan of the Korahites.—Kohath begot Amram. ⁵⁹The name of Amram's wife was Jochebed daughter of Levi, who was born to Levi in Egypt; she bore to Amram Aaron and Moses and their sister Miriam. ⁶⁰To Aaron were born Nadab and Abihu, Eleazar and Ithamar. ⁶¹Nadab and Abihu died when they offered alien fire before יהוה.—⁶²Their enrollment of 23,000 comprised all males from a month up. They were not part of the regular enrollment of the Israelites, since no share was assigned to them among the Israelites.

⁶³These are the males enrolled by Moses and Eleazar the priest who registered the Israelites on the steppes of Moab, at the Jordan near Jericho. ⁶⁴Among these there was not one of those enrolled by Moses and Aaron the priest when they recorded the Israelites in the wilderness of Sinai. ⁶⁵For יהוה had said of them, "They shall die in the wilderness." Not one of them survived, except Caleb son of Jephunneh and Joshua son of Nun.

27 ¹The daughters of Zelophehad, of Manassite family—son of Hepher son of Gilead son of Machir son of Manasseh son of Joseph—came forward. The names of the daughters were Mahlah, Noah, Hoglah, Milcah, and Tirzah. ²They stood before Moses, Eleazar the priest, the chieftains, and the whole assembly, at the entrance of the Tent of Meeting, and they said, ³"Our father died in the wilderness. He was not one of the faction, Korah's faction, which banded together against יהוה, but died for his own sin; and he has left no sons. ⁴Let not our father's name be lost to his clan just because he had no son! Give us a holding among our father's kinsmen!"

⁵Moses brought their case before יהוה.

⁶And יהוה said to Moses, ⁷"The plea of Zelophehad's daughters is just: you should give them a hereditary holding among their father's kinsmen; transfer their father's share to them.

⁸"Further, speak to the Israelite people as follows: 'If a householder dies without leaving a son, you shall transfer his property to his daughter. ⁹If he has no daughter, you shall assign his property to his brothers. ¹⁰If he has no brothers, you shall assign his property to his father's brothers. ¹¹If his father had no brothers, you shall assign his property to his nearest relative in his own clan, who shall inherit it.' This shall be the law of procedure for the Israelites, in accordance with יהוה's command to Moses."

¹²יהוה said to Moses, "Ascend these heights of Abarim and view the land that I have given to the Israelite people. ¹³When you have seen it, you too shall be gathered to your kin, just as your brother Aaron was. ¹⁴For, in the wilderness of Zin, when the community was contentious, you disobeyed My command to uphold My sanctity in their sight by means of the water." Those are the Waters of Meribath-kadesh, in the wilderness of Zin.

¹⁵Moses spoke to יהוה, saying, ¹⁶"Let יהוה, Source of the breath of all flesh, appoint a leader for the community ¹⁷who shall go out before them and come in before them, and who shall take them out and bring them in, so that יהוה's community may not be like sheep that have no shepherd." ¹⁸And יהוה answered Moses, Single out Joshua son of Nun, an inspired leader, and lay your hand upon him. ¹⁹Have him stand before Eleazar the priest and before the whole community, and commission him in their sight. ²⁰Invest him with some of your authority, so that the whole Israelite community may obey. ²¹But he shall present himself to Eleazar the priest, who shall on his behalf seek the decision of the Urim before יהוה. By such instruction they shall go out and by such instruction they shall come in, he and all the Israelite [militia], and the whole community."

²²Moses did as יהוה commanded him. He took Joshua and had him stand before Eleazar the priest and before the whole community. ²³He laid his hands upon him and commissioned him—as יהוה had spoken through Moses.

28 ¹יהוה spoke to Moses, saying: ²Command the Israelite people and say to them: Be punctilious in presenting to Me at stated times the offerings of food due Me, as offerings by fire of pleasing odor to Me.

³Say to them: These are the offerings by fire that you are to present to יהוה:

As a regular burnt offering every day, two yearling lambs without blemish. ⁴You shall offer one lamb in the morning, and the other lamb you shall offer at twilight. ⁵And as a meal offering, there shall be a tenth of an *ephah* of choice flour with a quarter of a *hin* of beaten oil mixed in—⁶the regular burnt offering instituted at Mount Sinai—an offering by fire of pleasing odor to יהוה.

⁷The libation with it shall be a quarter of a *hin* for each lamb, to be poured in the sacred precinct as an offering of fermented drink to יהוה. ⁸The other lamb you shall offer at twilight, preparing the same meal offering and libation as in the morning—an offering by fire of pleasing odor to יהוה.

⁹On the sabbath day: two yearling lambs without blemish, together with two-tenths of a measure of choice flour with oil mixed in as a meal offering, and with the proper libation—¹⁰a burnt offering for every sabbath, in addition to the regular burnt offering and its libation.

¹¹On your new moons you shall present a burnt offering to יהוה: two bulls of the herd, one ram, and seven yearling lambs, without blemish. ¹²As meal offering for each bull: three-tenths of a measure of choice flour with oil mixed in. As meal offering for each ram: two-tenths of a measure of choice flour with oil mixed in. ¹³As meal offering for each lamb: a tenth of a measure of fine flour with oil mixed in. Such shall be the burnt offering of pleasing odor, an offering by fire to יהוה. ¹⁴Their libations shall be: half a *hin* of wine for a bull, a third of a *hin* for a ram, and a quarter of a *hin* for a lamb. That shall be the monthly burnt offering for each new moon of the year. ¹⁵And there shall be one goat as a sin offering to יהוה, to be offered in addition to the regular burnt offering and its libation.

¹⁶In the first month, on the fourteenth day of the month, there shall be a passover sacrifice to יהוה, ¹⁷and on the fifteenth day of that month a festival. Unleavened bread shall be eaten for seven days. ¹⁸The first day shall be a sacred occasion: you shall not work at your occupations. ¹⁹You shall present an offering by fire, a burnt offering, to יהוה: two bulls of the

herd, one ram, and seven yearling lambs—see that they are without blemish. [20]The meal offering with them shall be of choice flour with oil mixed in: prepare three-tenths of a measure for a bull, two-tenths for a ram; [21]and for each of the seven lambs prepare one-tenth of a measure. [22]And there shall be one goat for a sin offering, to make expiation in your behalf. [23]You shall present these in addition to the morning portion of the regular burnt offering. [24]You shall offer the like daily for seven days as food, an offering by fire of pleasing odor to יהוה; they shall be offered, with their libations, in addition to the regular burnt offering. [25]And the seventh day shall be a sacred occasion for you: you shall not work at your occupations.

[26]On the day of the first fruits, your Feast of Weeks, when you bring an offering of new grain to יהוה, you shall observe a sacred occasion: you shall not work at your occupations. [27]You shall present a burnt offering of pleasing odor to יהוה: two bulls of the herd, one ram, seven yearling lambs. [28]The meal offering with them shall be of choice flour with oil mixed in, three-tenths of a measure for a bull, two-tenths for a ram, [29]and one-tenth for each of the seven lambs. [30]And there shall be one goat for expiation in your behalf. [31]You shall present them—see that they are without blemish—with their libations, in addition to the regular burnt offering and its meal offering.

29 [1]In the seventh month, on the first day of the month, you shall observe a sacred occasion: you shall not work at your occupations. You shall observe it as a day when the horn is sounded. [2]You shall present a burnt offering of pleasing odor to יהוה: one bull of the herd, one ram, and seven yearling lambs, without blemish. [3]The meal offering with them—choice flour with oil mixed in—shall be: three-tenths of a measure for a bull, two-tenths for a ram, [4]and one-tenth for each of the seven lambs. [5]And there shall be one goat for a sin offering, to make expiation in your behalf—[6]in addition to the burnt offering of the new moon with its meal offering and the regular burnt offering with its meal offering, each with its libation as prescribed, offerings by fire of pleasing odor to יהוה.

[7]On the tenth day of the same seventh month you shall observe a sacred occasion when you shall practice self-denial. You shall do no work. [8]You shall present to יהוה a burnt offering of pleasing odor: one bull of the herd, one ram, seven yearling lambs; see that they are without blemish. [9]The meal offering with them—of choice flour with oil mixed in—shall be: three-tenths of a measure for a bull, two-tenths for the one ram, [10]one-tenth for each of the seven lambs. [11]And there shall be one goat for a sin offering, in addition to the sin offering of expiation and the regular burnt offering with its meal offering, each with its libation.

[12]On the fifteenth day of the seventh month, you shall observe a sacred occasion: you shall not work at your occupations.—Seven days you shall observe a festival of יהוה.—[13]You shall present a burnt offering, an offering by fire of pleasing odor to יהוה: Thirteen bulls of the herd, two rams, fourteen yearling lambs; they shall be without blemish. [14]The meal offerings with them—of choice flour with oil mixed in—shall be: three-tenths of a measure for each of the thirteen bulls, two-tenths for each of the two rams, [15]and one-tenth for each of the fourteen lambs. [16]And there shall be one goat for a sin offering—in addition to the regular burnt offering, its meal offering and libation.

[17]Second day: Twelve bulls of the herd, two rams, fourteen yearling lambs, without blemish; [18]the meal offerings and libations for the bulls, rams, and lambs, in the quantities prescribed; [19]and one goat for a sin offering—in addition to the regular burnt offering, its meal offering and libations.

[20]Third day: Eleven bulls, two rams, fourteen yearling lambs, without blemish; [21]the meal offerings and libations for the bulls, rams, and lambs, in the quantities prescribed; [22]and one goat for a sin offering—in addition to the regular burnt offering, its meal offering and libation.

[23]Fourth day: Ten bulls, two rams, fourteen yearling lambs, without blemish; [24]the meal offerings and libations for the bulls, rams, and lambs, in the quantities prescribed; [25]and one goat for a sin offering—in addition to the regular burnt offering, its meal offering and libation.

[26]Fifth day: Nine bulls, two rams, fourteen yearling lambs, without blemish; [27]the meal offerings and libations for the bulls, rams, and lambs, in the quantities prescribed; [28]and one goat for a sin offering—in addition to the regular burnt offering, its meal offering and libation. [29]Sixth day: Eight bulls, two rams, fourteen yearling lambs, without blemish; [30]the meal offerings and libations for the bulls, rams, and lambs, in the quantities prescribed; [31]and one goat for a sin offering—in addition to the regular burnt offering, its meal offering and libations.

[32]Seventh day: Seven bulls, two rams, fourteen yearling lambs, without blemish; [33]the meal offerings and libations for the bulls, rams, and lambs, in the quantities prescribed; [34]and one goat for a sin offering—in addition to the regular burnt offering, its meal offering and libation.

[35]On the eighth day you shall hold a solemn gathering; you shall not work at your occupations. [36]You shall present a burnt offering, an offering by fire of pleasing odor to יהוה; one bull, one ram, seven yearling lambs, without blemish; [37]the meal offerings and libations for the bull, the ram, and the lambs, in the quantities prescribed; [38]and one goat for a sin offering—in addition to the regular burnt offering, its meal offering and libation.

[39]All these you shall offer to יהוה at the stated times, in addition to your votive and freewill offerings, be they burnt offerings, meal offerings, libations, or offerings of wellbeing.

30 [1]So Moses spoke to the Israelites just as יהוה had commanded Moses.

[2]Moses spoke to the heads of the Israelite tribes, saying: This is what יהוה has commanded:

[3]If a householder makes a vow to יהוה or takes an oath imposing an obligation on himself, he shall not break his pledge; he must carry out all that has crossed his lips.

[4]If a woman makes a vow to יהוה or assumes an obligation while still in her father's household by reason of her youth, [5]and her father learns of her vow or her self-imposed obligation and offers no objection, all her vows shall stand and every self-imposed obligation shall stand. [6]But if her father restrains her on the day he finds out, none of her vows or self-imposed obligations shall stand; and יהוה will forgive her, since her father restrained her.

[7]If she should become someone's [wife] while her vow or the commitment to which she bound herself is still in force, [8]and her husband learns of it and offers no objection on the day he finds out, her vows shall stand and her self-imposed obligations shall stand. [9]But if her husband restrains her on the day that he learns of it, he thereby annuls her vow which was in force or the commitment to which she bound herself; and יהוה will forgive her.—[10]The vow of a widow or of a divorced woman, however, whatever she has imposed on herself, shall be binding upon her.—[11]So, too, if, while in her husband's household, she makes a vow or imposes an obligation on herself by oath, [12]and her husband learns of it, yet offers no objection—thus failing to restrain her—all her vows shall stand and all her self-imposed obligations shall stand. [13]But if her husband does annul them on the day he

finds out, then nothing that has crossed her lips shall stand, whether vows or self-imposed obligations. Her husband has annulled them, and יהוה will forgive her. [14]Every vow and every sworn obligation of self-denial may be upheld by her husband or annulled by her husband. [15]If her husband offers no objection from that day to the next, he has upheld all the vows or obligations she has assumed: he has upheld them by offering no objection on the day he found out. [16]But if he annuls them after [the day] he finds out, he shall bear her guilt.

[17]Those are the laws that יהוה enjoined upon Moses between a husband and his wife, and as between a father and his daughter while in her father's household by reason of her youth.

31 [1]יהוה spoke to Moses, saying, [2]"Avenge the Israelite people on the Midianites; then you shall be gathered to your kin." [3]Moses spoke to the militia, saying, "Let troops be picked out from among you for a campaign, and let them fall upon Midian to wreak יהוה's vengeance on Midian. [4]You shall dispatch on the campaign a thousand from every one of the tribes of Israel."

[5]So a thousand from each tribe were furnished from the divisions of Israel, twelve thousand picked for the campaign. [6]Moses dispatched them on the campaign, a thousand from each tribe, with Phinehas son of Eleazar serving as a priest on the campaign, equipped with the sacred utensils and the trumpets for sounding the blasts. [7]They took the field against Midian, as יהוה had commanded Moses, and slew every male. [8]Along with their other victims, they slew the kings of Midian: Evi, Rekem, Zur, Hur, and Reba, the five kings of Midian. They also put Balaam son of Beor to the sword.

[9]The Israelites took the women and other dependents of the Midianites captive, and seized as booty all their beasts, all their herds, and all their wealth. [10]And they destroyed by fire all the towns in which they were settled, and their encampments. [11]They gathered all the spoil and all the booty, human and beast, [12]and they brought the captives, the booty, and the spoil to Moses, Eleazar the priest, and the Israelite community leadership, at the camp in the steppes of Moab, at the Jordan near Jericho.

[13]Moses, Eleazar the priest, and all the chieftains of the community came out to meet them outside the camp. [14]Moses became angry with the commanders of the army, the officers of thousands and the officers of hundreds, who had come back from the military campaign. [15]Moses said to them, "You have spared every female! [16]Yet they are the very ones who, at the bidding of Balaam, induced the Israelites to trespass against יהוה in the matter of Peor, so that יהוה's community was struck by the plague. [17]Now, therefore, slay every male among the dependents, and slay also every woman who has known a man carnally; [18]but spare every female dependent who has not had carnal relations with a man.

[19]"You shall then stay outside the camp seven days; every one among you or among your captives who has slain a person or touched a corpse shall purify himself on the third and seventh days. [20]You shall also purify every cloth, every article of skin, everything made of goats' hair, and every object of wood."

[21]Eleazar the priest said to the troops who had taken part in the fighting, "This is the ritual law that יהוה has enjoined upon Moses: [22]Gold and silver, copper, iron, tin, and lead— [23]any article that can withstand fire—these you shall pass through fire and they shall be pure, except that they must be purified with water of lustration; and anything that cannot withstand fire you must pass through water. [24]On the seventh day you shall wash your clothes and be pure, and after that you may enter the camp."

[25]יהוה said to Moses: [26]"You and Eleazar the priest and the family heads of the community take an inventory of the booty that was captured, human and beast, [27]and divide the booty equally between the combatants who engaged in the campaign and the rest of the community. [28]You shall exact a levy for יהוה: in the case of the warriors who engaged in the campaign, one item in five hundred, of persons, oxen, asses, and sheep, [29]shall be taken from their half-share and given to Eleazar the priest as a contribution to יהוה; [30]and from the half-share of the other Israelites you shall withhold one in every fifty human beings as well as cattle, asses, and sheep—all the animals—and give them to the Levites, who attend to the duties of יהוה's Tabernacle."

[31]Moses and Eleazar the priest did as יהוה commanded Moses. [32]The amount of booty, other than the spoil that the troops had plundered, came to 675,000 sheep, [33]72,000 head of cattle, [34]61,000 asses, [35]and a total of 32,000 human beings, namely, the females who had not had carnal relations.

[36]Thus, the half-share of those who had engaged in the campaign [was as follows]: The number of sheep was 337,500, [37]and יהוה's levy from the sheep was 675; [38]the cattle came to 36,000, from which יהוה's levy was 72; [39]the asses came to 30,500, from which יהוה's levy was 61. [40]And the number of human beings was 16,000, from which יהוה's levy was 32. [41]Moses gave the contributions levied for יהוה to Eleazar the priest, as יהוה had commanded Moses.

[42]As for the half-share of the other Israelites, which Moses withdrew from the troops who had taken the field, [43]that half-share of the community consisted of 337,500 sheep, [44]36,000 head of cattle, [45]30,500 asses, [46]and 16,000 human beings. [47]From this half-share of the Israelites, Moses withheld one in every fifty humans and animals; and he gave them to the Levites, who attended to the duties of יהוה's Tabernacle, as יהוה had commanded Moses.

[48]The commanders of the troop divisions, the officers of thousands and the officers of hundreds, approached Moses. [49]They said to Moses, "Your servants have made a check of the warriors in our charge, and not one of us is missing. [50]So we have brought as an offering to יהוה such articles of gold as each of us came upon: armlets, bracelets, signet rings, earrings, and pendants, that expiation may be made for our persons before יהוה." [51]Moses and Eleazar the priest accepted the gold from them, all kinds of wrought articles. [52]All the gold that was offered by the officers of thousands and the officers of hundreds as a contribution to יהוה came to 16,750 shekels.—[53]But in the ranks, everyone kept his booty for himself.—[54]So Moses and Eleazar the priest accepted the gold from the officers of thousands and the officers of hundreds and brought it to the Tent of Meeting, as a reminder in behalf of the Israelites before יהוה.

32 [1]The Reubenites and the Gadites owned cattle in very great numbers. Noting that the lands of Jazer and Gilead were a region suitable for cattle, [2]the Gadite and Reubenite [leaders] came to Moses, Eleazar the priest, and the chieftains of the community, and said, [3]"Ataroth, Dibon, Jazer, Nimrah, Heshbon, Elealeh, Sebam, Nebo, and Beon—[4]the land that יהוה has conquered for the community of Israel—is cattle country, and your servants have cattle. [5]It would be a favor to us," they continued, "if this land were given to your servants as a holding; do not move us across the Jordan."

[6]Moses replied to the Gadites and the Reubenites, "Are your brothers to go to war while you stay here? [7]Why will you turn the minds of the Israelites from crossing into the land that יהוה has given them? [8]That is what your fathers did when I sent them from Kadesh-barnea to survey the land. [9]After going up to the wadi Eshcol and surveying the

land, they turned the minds of the Israelites from invading the land that יהוה had given them. ¹⁰Thereupon יהוה was incensed and swore, ¹¹'None of the men from twenty years up who came out of Egypt shall see the land that I promised on oath to Abraham, Isaac, and Jacob, for they did not remain loyal to Me—¹²none except Caleb son of Jephunneh the Kenizzite and Joshua son of Nun, for they remained loyal to יהוה.' ¹³יהוה, incensed at Israel, made them wander in the wilderness for forty years, until the whole generation that had provoked יהוה's displeasure was gone. ¹⁴And now you, a breed of sinful fellows, have replaced your fathers, to add still further to יהוה's wrath against Israel. ¹⁵If you turn away from [God], who then abandons them once more in the wilderness, you will bring calamity upon all this people."

¹⁶Then they stepped up to him and said, "We will build here sheepfolds for our flocks and towns for our children. ¹⁷And we will hasten as shock-troops in the van of the Israelites until we have established them in their home, while our children stay in the fortified towns because of the inhabitants of the land. ¹⁸We will not return to our homes until the Israelites—every one of them—are in possession of their portion. ¹⁹But we will not have a share with them in the territory beyond the Jordan, for we have received our share on the east side of the Jordan."

²⁰Moses said to them, "If you do this, if you go to battle as Shock-troops, at the instance of יהוה, ²¹and every shock-fighter among you crosses the Jordan, at the instance of יהוה, until [God] has personally dispossessed the enemies, ²²and the land has been subdued, at the instance of יהוה, and then you return—you shall be clear before יהוה and before Israel; and this land shall be your holding under יהוה. ²³But if you do not do so, you will have sinned against יהוה; and know that your sin will overtake you. ²⁴Build towns for your children and sheepfolds for your flocks, but do what you have promised."

²⁵The Gadites and the Reubenites answered Moses, "Your servants will do as my lord commands. ²⁶Our children, our wives, our flocks, and all our other livestock will stay behind in the towns of Gilead; ²⁷while your servants, all those recruited for war, cross over, at the instance of יהוה, to engage in battle—as my lord orders."

²⁸Then Moses gave instructions concerning them to Eleazar the priest, Joshua son of Nun, and the family heads of the Israelite tribes. ²⁹Moses said to them, "If every shock-fighter among the Gadites and the Reubenites crosses the Jordan with you to do battle, at the instance of יהוה, and the land is subdued before you, you shall give them the land of Gilead as a holding. ³⁰But if they do not cross over with you as shock-troops, they shall receive holdings among you in the land of Canaan."

³¹The Gadites and the Reubenites said in reply, "Whatever יהוה has spoken concerning your servants, that we will do. ³²We ourselves will cross over as shock-troops, at the instance of יהוה, into the land of Canaan; and we shall keep our hereditary holding across the Jordan."

³³So Moses assigned to them—to the Gadites, the Reubenites, and the halftribe of Manasseh son of Joseph—the kingdom of Sihon king of the Amorites and the kingdom of King Og of Bashan, the land with its various cities and the territories of their surrounding towns. ³⁴The Gadites rebuilt Dibon, Ataroth, Aroer, ³⁵Atrothshophan, Jazer, Jogbehah, ³⁶Bethnimrah, and Bethharan as fortified towns or as enclosures for flocks. ³⁷The Reubenites rebuilt Heshbon, Elealeh, Kiriathaim, ³⁸Nebo, Baalmeon—some names being changed—and Sibmah; they gave [their own] names to towns that they rebuilt. ³⁹The descendants of Machir son of Manasseh went to Gilead and captured it, dispossessing the Amorites who were there;

⁴⁰so Moses gave Gilead to Machir son of Manasseh, and he settled there. ⁴¹Jair son of Manasseh went and captured their villages, which he renamed Havvoth-jair. ⁴²And Nobah went and captured Kenath and its dependencies, renaming it Nobah after himself.

33 ¹These were the marches of the Israelites who started out from the land of Egypt, troop by troop, in the charge of Moses and Aaron. ²Moses recorded the starting points of their various marches as directed by יהוה. Their marches, by starting points, were as follows:

³They set out from Rameses in the first month, on the fifteenth day of the first month. It was on the morrow of the Passover offering that the Israelites started out defiantly, in plain view of all the Egyptians. ⁴The Egyptians meanwhile were burying those among them whom יהוה had struck down, every [male] firstborn—whereby יהוה executed judgment on their gods.

⁵The Israelites set out from Rameses and encamped at Succoth. ⁶They set out from Succoth and encamped at Etham, which is on the edge of the wilderness. ⁷They set out from Etham and turned about toward Pihahiroth, which faces Baalzephon, and they encamped before Migdol. ⁸They set out from Penehahiroth and passed through the sea into the wilderness; and they made a threedays' journey in the wilderness of Etham and encamped at Marah. ⁹They set out from Marah and came to Elim. There were twelve springs in Elim and seventy palm trees, so they encamped there. ¹⁰They set out from Elim and encamped by the Sea of Reeds. ¹¹They set out from the Sea of Reeds and encamped in the wilderness of Sin. ¹²They set out from the wilderness of Sin and encamped at Dophkah. ¹³They set out from Dophkah and encamped at Alush. ¹⁴They set out from Alush and encamped at Rephidim; it was there that the people had no water to drink. ¹⁵They set out from Rephidim and encamped in the wilderness of Sinai. ¹⁶They set out from the wilderness of Sinai and encamped at Kibroth-hattaavah. ¹⁷They set out from Kibrothhattaavah and encamped at Hazeroth. ¹⁸They set out from Hazeroth and encamped at Rithmah. ¹⁹They set out from Rithmah and encamped at Rimmonperez. ²⁰They set out from Rimmon-perez and encamped at Libnah. ²¹They set out from Libnah and encamped at Rissah. ²²They set out from Rissah and encamped at Kehelath. ²³They set out from Kehelath and encamped at Mount Shepher. ²⁴They set out from Mount Shepher and encamped at Haradah. ²⁵They set out from Haradah and encamped at Makheloth. ²⁶They set out from Makheloth and encamped at Tahath. ²⁷They set out from Tahath and encamped at Terah. ²⁸They set out from Terah and encamped at Mithkah. ²⁹They set out from Mithkah and encamped at Hashmonah. ³⁰They set out from Hashmonah and encamped at Moseroth. ³¹They set out from Moseroth and encamped at Benejaakan. ³²They set out from Bene-jaakan and encamped at Hor-haggidgad. ³³They set out from Hor-haggidgad and encamped at Jotbath. ³⁴They set out from Jotbath and encamped at Abronah. ³⁵They set out from Abronah and encamped at Ezion-geber. ³⁶They set out from Ezion-geber and encamped in the wilderness of Zin, that is, Kadesh. ³⁷They set out from Kadesh and encamped at Mount Hor, on the edge of the land of Edom.

³⁸Aaron the priest ascended Mount Hor at the command of יהוה and died there, in the fortieth year after the Israelites had left the land of Egypt, on the first day of the fifth month. ³⁹Aaron was a hundred and twenty-three years old when he died on Mount Hor. ⁴⁰And the Canaanite, king of Arad, who dwelt in the Negeb, in the land of Canaan, learned of the coming of the Israelites.

⁴¹They set out from Mount Hor and encamped at Zalmonah. ⁴²They set out from Zalmonah and encamped at Punon.

43They set out from Punon and encamped at Oboth. 44They set out from Oboth and encamped at Iyeabarim, in the territory of Moab. 45They set out from Iyim and encamped at Dibongad. 46They set out from Dibongad and encamped at Almondiblathaim. 47They set out from Almondiblathaim and encamped in the hills of Abarim, before Nebo. 48They set out from the hills of Abarim and encamped in the steppes of Moab, at the Jordan near Jericho; 49they encamped by the Jordan from Bethjeshimoth as far as Abelshittim, in the steppes of Moab.

50In the steppes of Moab, at the Jordan near Jericho, יהוה spoke to Moses, saying: 51Speak to the Israelite people and say to them: When you cross the Jordan into the land of Canaan, 52you shall dispossess all the inhabitants of the land; you shall destroy all their figured objects; you shall destroy all their molten images, and you shall demolish all their cult places. 53And you shall take possession of the land and settle in it, for I have assigned the land to you to possess. 54You shall apportion the land among yourselves by lot, clan by clan: with larger groups increase the share, with smaller groups reduce the share. Wherever the lot falls for it, that shall be its location. You shall have your portions according to your ancestral tribes. 55But if you do not dispossess the inhabitants of the land, those whom you allow to remain shall be stings in your eyes and thorns in your sides, and they shall harass you in the land in which you live; 56so that I will do to you what I planned to do to them.

34 יהוה spoke to Moses, saying: 2Instruct the Israelite people and say to them: When you enter the land of Canaan, this is the land that shall fall to you as your portion, the land of Canaan with its various boundaries:

3Your southern sector shall extend from the wilderness of Zin alongside Edom. Your southern boundary shall start on the east from the tip of the Dead Sea. 4Your boundary shall then turn to pass south of the ascent of Akrabbim and continue to Zin, and its limits shall be south of Kadesh-barnea, reaching Hazar-addar and continuing to Azmon. 5From Azmon the boundary shall turn toward the Wadi of Egypt and terminate at the Sea.

6For the western boundary you shall have the coast of the Great Sea; that shall serve as your western boundary.

7This shall be your northern boundary: Draw a line from the Great Sea to Mount Hor; 8from Mount Hor draw a line to Lebo-hamath, and let the boundary reach Zedad. 9The boundary shall then run to Ziphron and terminate at Hazar-enan. That shall be your northern boundary.

10For your eastern boundary you shall draw a line from Hazar-enan to Shepham. 11From Shepham the boundary shall descend to Riblah on the east side of Ain; from there the boundary shall continue downward and abut on the eastern slopes of the Sea of Chinnereth. 12The boundary shall then descend along the Jordan and terminate at the Dead Sea.

That shall be your land as defined by its boundaries on all sides.

13Moses instructed the Israelites, saying: This is the land you are to receive by lot as your hereditary portion, which יהוה has commanded to be given to the nine and a half tribes. 14For the Reubenite tribe by its ancestral houses, the Gadite tribe by its ancestral houses, and the half-tribe of Manasseh have already received their portions: 15those two and a half tribes have received their portions across the Jordan, opposite Jericho, on the east, the orient side.

16יהוה spoke to Moses, saying: 17These are the names of the commissioners through whom the land shall be apportioned for you: Eleazar the priest and Joshua son of Nun. 18And you shall also take a chieftain from each tribe through whom the land shall be apportioned. 19These are the names of those commissioners: from the tribe of Judah: Caleb son of Jephunneh. 20From the Simeonite tribe: Samuel son of Ammihud. 21From the tribe of Benjamin: Elidad son of Chislon. 22From the Danite tribe: a chieftain, Bukki son of Jogli. 23For the descendants of Joseph: from the Manassite tribe: a chieftain, Hanniel son of Ephod; 24and from the Ephraimite tribe: a chieftain, Kemuel son of Shiphtan. 25From the Zebulunite tribe: a chieftain, Elizaphan son of Parnach. 26From the Issacharite tribe: a chieftain, Paltiel son of Azzan. 27From the Asherite tribe: a chieftain, Ahihud son of Shelomi. 28From the Naphtalite tribe: a chieftain, Pedahel son of Ammihud. 29It was these whom יהוה designated to allot portions to the Israelites in the land of Canaan.

35 יהוה spoke to Moses in the steppes of Moab at the Jordan near Jericho, saying: 2Instruct the Israelite people to assign, out of the holdings apportioned to them, towns for the Levites to dwell in; you shall also assign to the Levites pasture land around their towns. 3The towns shall be theirs to dwell in, and the pasture shall be for the cattle they own and all their other beasts. 4The town pasture that you are to assign to the Levites shall extend a thousand cubits outside the town wall all around. 5You shall measure off two thousand cubits outside the town on the east side, two thousand on the south side, two thousand on the west side, and two thousand on the north side, with the town in the center. That shall be the pasture for their towns.

6The towns that you assign to the Levites shall comprise the six cities of refuge that you are to designate for a [male] killer to flee to, to which you shall add forty-two towns. 7Thus the total of the towns that you assign to the Levites shall be forty-eight towns, with their pasture. 8In assigning towns from the holdings of the Israelites, take more from the larger groups and less from the smaller, so that each assigns towns to the Levites in proportion to the share it receives.

9יהוה spoke further to Moses: 10Speak to the Israelite people and say to them: When you cross the Jordan into the land of Canaan, 11you shall provide yourselves with places to serve you as cities of refuge to which a [male] killer who has slain a person unintentionally may flee. 12The cities shall serve you as a refuge from the avenger, so that the killer may not die unless he has stood trial before the assembly.

13The towns that you thus assign shall be six cities of refuge in all. 14Three cities shall be designated beyond the Jordan, and the other three shall be designated in the land of Canaan: they shall serve as cities of refuge. 15These six cities shall serve the Israelites and the resident aliens among them for refuge, so that any man who slays a person unintentionally may flee there.

16Anyone, however, who strikes another with an iron object so that death results is a murderer; the murderer must be put to death. 17If one struck another with a stone tool that could cause death, and death resulted, that person is a murderer; the murderer must be put to death. 18Similarly, if one struck another with a wooden tool that could cause death, and death resulted, that person is a murderer; the murderer must be put to death. 19The blood-avenger himself shall put the murderer to death; it is he who shall put that person to death upon encounter. 20So, too, if one pushed another in hate or hurled something at [the victim] on purpose and death resulted, 21or if one struck another with the hand in enmity and death resulted, the assailant shall be put to death; that person is a murderer. The blood-avenger shall put the murderer to death upon encounter.

22But if [a man] pushed without malice aforethought or hurled any object at [the victim] unintentionally, 23or inadvertently dropped upon [the victim] any deadly object of stone, and death resulted—though not being an enemy and not seeking to harm—24in such cases the assembly shall decide between the slayer and the blood-avenger. 25The assembly shall protect the killer from the blood-avenger, and the assembly shall restore him to the city of refuge to which he fled, and there he shall remain until the death of the high priest who was anointed with the sacred oil. 26But if the killer ever goes outside the limits of the city of refuge to which he has fled, 27and the blood-avenger comes upon him outside the limits of his city of refuge, and the blood-avenger kills the killer, there is no bloodguilt on his account. 28For he must remain inside his city of refuge until the death of the high priest; after the death of the high priest, the killer may return to his land holding.

29Such shall be your law of procedure throughout the ages in all your settlements.

30If anyone slays a person, the killer may be executed only on the evidence of witnesses; the testimony of a single witness against a person shall not suffice for a sentence of death. 31You may not accept a ransom for the life of a murderer who is guilty of a capital crime; [a murderer] must be put to death. 32Nor may you accept ransom in lieu of flight to a city of refuge, enabling a man to return to live on his land before the death of the priest. 33You shall not pollute the land in which you live; for blood pollutes the land, and the land can have no expiation for blood that is shed on it, except by the blood of the one who shed it. 34You shall not defile the land in which you live, in which I Myself abide, for I יהוה abide among the Israelite people.

36 1The family heads in the clan of the descendants of Gilead son of Machir son of Manasseh, one of the Josephite clans, came forward and appealed to Moses and the chieftains, family heads of the Israelites. 2They said, "יהוה commanded my lord to assign the land to the Israelites as shares by lot, and my lord was further commanded by יהוה to assign the share of our kinsman Zelophehad to his daughters. 3Now, if they become the wives of persons from another Israelite tribe, their share will be cut off from our ancestral portion and be added to the portion of the tribe into which they become [wives]; thus our allotted portion will be diminished. 4And even when the Israelites observe the jubilee, their share will be added to that of the tribe into which they become [wives], and their share will be cut off from the ancestral portion of our tribe."

5So Moses, at יהוה's bidding, instructed the Israelites, saying: "The plea of the Josephite tribe is just. 6This is what יהוה has commanded concerning the daughters of Zelophehad: They may become the wives of anyone they wish, provided they become wives within a clan of their father's tribe. 7No inheritance of the Israelites may pass over from one tribe to another, but the Israelite [heirs]—each of them—must remain bound to the ancestral portion of their tribe. 8Every daughter among the Israelite tribes who inherits a share must become the wife of someone from a clan of her father's tribe, in order that every Israelite [heir] may keep an ancestral share. 9Thus no inheritance shall pass over from one tribe to another, but the Israelite tribes shall remain bound each to its portion."

10The daughters of Zelophehad did as יהוה had commanded Moses: 11Mahlah, Tirzah, Hoglah, Milcah, and Noah, Zelophehad's daughters, became the wives of their uncles' sons; 12becoming wives within clans of descendants of Manasseh son of Joseph; and so their share remained in the tribe of their father's clan.

13These are the commandments and regulations that יהוה enjoined upon the Israelites, through Moses, on the steppes of Moab, at the Jordan near Jericho.

deuteronomy

1 1These are the words that Moses addressed to all Israel on the other side of the Jordan.—Through the wilderness, in the Arabah near Suph, between Paran and Tophel, Laban, Hazeroth, and Dizahab, 2it is eleven days from Horeb to Kadesh-barnea by the Mount Seir route.—3It was in the fortieth year, on the first day of the eleventh month, that Moses addressed the Israelites in accordance with the instructions that יהוה had given him for them, 4after he had defeated Sihon king of the Amorites, who dwelt in Heshbon, and King Og of Bashan, who dwelt at Ashtaroth [and] Edrei. 5On the other side of the Jordan, in the land of Moab, Moses undertook to expound this Teaching. He said:

6יהוה our God spoke to us at Horeb, saying: You have stayed long enough at this mountain. 7Start out and make your way to the hill country of the Amorites and to all their neighbors in the Arabah, the hill country, the Shephelah, the Negeb, the seacoast, the land of the Canaanites, and the Lebanon, as far as the Great River, the river Euphrates. 8See, I place the land at your disposal. Go, take possession of the land that יהוה swore to your fathers Abraham, Isaac, and Jacob, to assign to them and to their heirs after them.

9Thereupon I said to you, "I cannot bear the burden of you by myself. 10יהוה your God has multiplied you until you are today as numerous as the stars in the sky.—11May יהוה, the God of your ancestors, increase your numbers a thousandfold, and bless you as promised.—12How can I bear unaided the trouble of you, and the burden, and the bickering! 13Pick from each of your tribes representatives who are wise, discerning, and experienced, and I will appoint them as your heads." 14You answered me and said, "What you propose to do is good." 15So I took your tribal leaders as representatives who are wise and experienced, and appointed them heads over you: chiefs of thousands, chiefs of hundreds, chiefs of fifties, and chiefs of tens, and officials for your tribes. 16I charged your magistrates at that time as follows, "Hear out your fellow Israelites, and decide justly between anyone and a fellow Israelite or a stranger. 17You shall not be partial in judgment: hear out low and high alike. Fear no one, for judgment is God's. And any matter that is too difficult for you, you shall bring to me and I will hear it." 18Thus I instructed you, at that time, about the various things that you should do.

19We set out from Horeb and traveled the great and terrible wilderness that you saw, along the road to the hill country of the Amorites, as our God יהוה had commanded us. When we reached Kadesh-barnea, 20I said to you, "You have come to the hill country of the Amorites which our God יהוה is giving to us. 21See, your God יהוה has placed the land at your disposal. Go up, take possession, as יהוה, the God of your fathers, promised you. Fear not and be not dismayed."

22Then all of you came to me and said, "Let us send emissaries ahead to reconnoiter the land for us and bring back word on the route we shall follow and the cities we shall come to." 23I approved of the plan, and so I selected from among you twelve representatives, one from each tribe. ²⁴They made for the hill country, came to the wadi Eshcol, and spied it out. ²⁵They took some of the fruit of the land with them and brought it down to us. And they gave us this report: "It is a good land that our God יהוה is giving to us."

²⁶Yet you refused to go up, and flouted the command of your God יהוה. ²⁷You sulked in your tents and said, "It is out of hatred for us that יהוה brought us out of the land of Egypt, to hand us over to the Amorites to wipe us out. ²⁸What kind of place are we going to? Our brothers have taken the heart out of us, saying, 'We saw there a people stronger and taller than we, large cities with walls sky-high, and even Anakites.'"

²⁹I said to you, "Have no dread or fear of them. ³⁰None other than your God יהוה, who goes before you, will fight for you, just as [God] did for you in Egypt before your very eyes, ³¹and in the wilderness, where you saw how your God יהוה carried you, as a householder carries his son, all the way that you traveled until you came to this place. ³²Yet for all that, you have no faith in your God יהוה, ³³who goes before you on your journeys—to scout the place where you are to encamp—in fire by night and in cloud by day, in order to guide you on the route you are to follow."

³⁴יהוה heard your loud complaint and, becoming angry, vowed: ³⁵Not one of the men [counted in the census], this evil generation, shall see the good land that I swore to give to your fathers—³⁶none except Caleb son of Jephunneh; he shall see it, and to him and his descendants will I give the land on which he set foot, because he remained loyal to יהוה.— ³⁷Because of you יהוה was incensed with me too, saying: You shall not enter it either. ³⁸Joshua son of Nun, who attends you, he shall enter it. Imbue him with strength, for he shall allot it to Israel. ³⁹Moreover, your little ones who you said would be carried off, your children who do not yet know good from bad, they shall enter it; to them will I give it and they shall possess it. ⁴⁰As for you, turn about and march into the wilderness by the way of the Sea of Reeds.

⁴¹You replied to me, saying, "We stand guilty before יהוה. We will go up now and fight, just as our God יהוה commanded us." And [the men among] you each girded yourselves with war gear and recklessly started for the hill country. ⁴²But יהוה said to me, "Warn them: Do not go up and do not fight, since I am not in your midst; else you will be routed by your enemies." ⁴³I spoke to you, but you would not listen; you flouted יהוה's command and willfully marched into the hill country. ⁴⁴Then the Amorites who lived in those hills came out against you like so many bees and chased you, and they crushed you at Hormah in Seir. ⁴⁵Again you wept before יהוה; but יהוה would not heed your cry or give ear to you.

⁴⁶Thus, after you had remained at Kadesh all that long time,

2 ¹we marched back into the wilderness by the way of the Sea of Reeds, as יהוה had spoken to me, and skirted the hill country of Seir a long time.

²Then יהוה said to me: ³You have been skirting this hill country long enough; now turn north. ⁴And charge the people as follows: You will be passing through the territory of your kin, the descendants of Esau, who live in Seir. Though they will be afraid of you, be very careful ⁵not to provoke them. For I will not give you of their land so much as a foot can tread on; I have given the hill country of Seir as a possession to Esau. ⁶What food you eat you shall obtain from them for money; even the water you drink you shall procure from them for money. ⁷Indeed, your God יהוה has blessed you in all your undertakings. [God] has watched over your wanderings through this great wilderness; your God יהוה has been with you these past forty years: you have lacked nothing.

⁸We then moved on, away from our kin, the descendants of Esau, who live in Seir, away from the road of the Arabah, away from Elath and Ezion-geber; and we marched on in the direction of the wilderness of Moab. ⁹And יהוה said to me: Do not harass the Moabites or provoke them to war. For I will not give you any of their land as a possession; I have assigned Ar as a possession to the descendants of Lot.—

¹⁰It was formerly inhabited by the Emim, a people great and numerous, and as tall as the Anakites. ¹¹Like the Anakites, they are counted as Rephaim; but the Moabites call them Emim. ¹²Similarly, Seir was formerly inhabited by the Horites; but the descendants of Esau dispossessed them, wiping them out and settling in their place, just as Israel did in the land they were to possess, which יהוה had given to them.—

¹³Up now! Cross the wadi Zered!

So we crossed the wadi Zered. ¹⁴The time that we spent in travel from Kadesh-barnea until we crossed the wadi Zered was thirty-eight years, until that whole generation of warriors had perished from the camp, as יהוה had sworn concerning them. ¹⁵Indeed, the hand of יהוה struck them, to root them out from the camp until they were finished off.

¹⁶When all the warriors among the people had died off, ¹⁷יהוה spoke to me, saying: ¹⁸You are now passing through the territory of Moab, through Ar. ¹⁹You will then be close to the Ammonites; do not harass them or start a fight with them. For I will not give any part of the land of the Ammonites to you as a possession; I have assigned it as a possession to the descendants of Lot.—

²⁰It, too, is counted as Rephaim country. It was formerly inhabited by Rephaim, whom the Ammonites call Zam-Zummim, ²¹a people great and numerous and as tall as the Anakites. יהוה wiped them out, so that [the Ammonites] dispossessed them and settled in their place, ²²as [God] did for the descendants of Esau who live in Seir, by wiping out the Horites before them, so that they dispossessed them and settled in their place, as is still the case. ²³So, too, with the Avvim who dwelt in villages in the vicinity of Gaza: the Caphtorim, who came from Crete, wiped the out and settled in their place.—

²⁴Up! Set out across the wadi Arnon! See, I give into your power Sihon the Amorite, king of Heshbon, and his land. Begin the occupation: engage him in battle. ²⁵This day I begin to put the dread and fear of you upon the peoples everywhere under heaven, so that they shall tremble and quake because of you whenever they hear you mentioned.

²⁶Then I sent messengers from the wilderness of Kedemoth to King Sihon of Heshbon with an offer of peace, as follows, ²⁷"Let me pass through your country. I will keep strictly to the highway, turning off neither to the right nor to the left. ²⁸What food I eat you will supply for money, and what water I drink you will furnish for money; just let me pass through—²⁹as the descendants of Esau who dwell in Seir did for me, and the Moabites who dwell in Ar—that I may cross the Jordan into the land that our God יהוה is giving us."

³⁰But King Sihon of Heshbon refused to let us pass through, because יהוה had stiffened his will and hardened his heart in order to deliver him into your power—as is now the case. ³¹And יהוה said to me: See, I begin by placing Sihon and his land at your disposal. Begin the occupation; take possession of his land.

³²Sihon with all his troops took the field against us at Jahaz, ³³and our God יהוה delivered him to us and we defeated him and his sons and all his troops. ³⁴At that time we captured all his towns, and we doomed every town—men, women, and children—leaving no survivor. ³⁵We retained as booty only

the cattle and the spoil of the cities that we captured. ³⁶From Aroer on the edge of the Arnon valley, including the town in the valley itself, to Gilead, not a city was too mighty for us; our God יהוה delivered everything to us. ³⁷But you did not encroach upon the land of the Ammonites, all along the wadi Jabbok and the towns of the hill country, just as our God יהוה had commanded.

3 ¹We made our way up the road toward Bashan, and King Og of Bashan with all his troops took the field against us at Edrei. ²But יהוה said to me: Do not fear him, for I am delivering him and all his troops and his country into your power, and you will do to him as you did to Sihon king of the Amorites, who lived in Heshbon.

³So our God יהוה also delivered into our power King Og of Bashan, with all his troops, and we dealt them such a blow that no survivor was left. ⁴At that time we captured all his towns; there was not a town that we did not take from them: sixty towns, the whole district of Argob, the kingdom of Og in Bashan—⁵all those towns were fortified with high walls, gates, and bars—apart from a great number of unwalled towns. ⁶We doomed them as we had done in the case of King Sihon of Heshbon; we doomed every town—men, women, and children—⁷and retained as booty all the cattle and the spoil of the towns.

⁸Thus we seized, at that time, from the two Amorite kings, the country beyond the Jordan, from the wadi Arnon to Mount Hermon—⁹Sidonians called Hermon Sirion, and the Amorites call it Senir—¹⁰all the towns of the Tableland and the whole of Gilead and Bashan as far as Salcah and Edrei, the towns of Og's kingdom in Bashan. ¹¹Only King Og of Bashan was left of the remaining Rephaim. His bedstead, an iron bedstead, is now in Rabbah of the Ammonites; it is nine cubits long and four cubits wide, by the standard cubit!

¹²And this is the land which we apportioned at that time: The part from Aroer along the wadi Arnon, with part of the hill country of Gilead and its towns, I assigned to the Reubenites and the Gadites. ¹³The rest of Gilead, and all of Bashan under Og's rule—the whole Argob district, all that part of Bashan which is called Rephaim country—I assigned to the half-tribe of Manasseh. ¹⁴Jair son of Manasseh received the whole Argob district (that is, Bashan) as far as the boundary of the Geshurites and the Maacathites, and named it after himself: Havvothjair—as is still the case. ¹⁵To Machir I assigned Gilead. ¹⁶And to the Reubenites and the Gadites I assigned the part from Gilead down to the wadi Arnon, the middle of the wadi being the boundary, and up to the wadi Jabbok, the boundary of the Ammonites.

¹⁷[We also seized] the Arabah, from the foot of the slopes of Pisgah on the east, to the edge of the Jordan, and from Chinnereth down to the sea of the Arabah, the Dead Sea.

¹⁸At that time I charged you [men of Reuben, Gad, and Manasseh], saying, "Your God יהוה has given you this country to possess. You must go as shock-troops, warriors all, at the head of your Israelite kin. ¹⁹Only your wives, children, and livestock—I know that you have much livestock—shall be left in the towns I have assigned to you, ²⁰until יהוה has granted your kin a haven such as you have, and they too have taken possession of the land that your God יהוה is assigning them, beyond the Jordan. Then you may return each to the homestead that I have assigned to him."

²¹I also charged Joshua at that time, saying, "You have seen with your own eyes all that your God יהוה has done to these two kings; so shall יהוה do to all the kingdoms into which you shall cross over. ²²Do not fear them, for it is your God יהוה who will battle for you."

²³I pleaded with יהוה at that time, saying, ²⁴"O lord יהוה, You who let Your servant see the first works of Your greatness and Your mighty hand, You whose powerful deeds no god in heaven or on earth can equal! ²⁵Let me, I pray, cross over and see the good land on the other side of the Jordan, that good hill country, and the Lebanon." ²⁶But יהוה was wrathful with me on your account and would not listen to me. יהוה said to me, "Enough! Never speak to Me of this matter again! ²⁷Go up to the summit of Pisgah and gaze about, to the west, the north, the south, and the east. Look at it well, for you shall not go across yonder Jordan. ²⁸Give Joshua his instructions, and imbue him with strength and courage, for he shall go across at the head of this people, and he shall allot to them the land that you may only see." ²⁹Meanwhile we stayed on in the valley near Bethpeor.

4 ¹And now, O Israel, give heed to the laws and rules that I am instructing you to observe, so that you may live to enter and occupy the land that יהוה, the God of your fathers, is giving you. ²You shall not add anything to what I command you or take anything away from it, but keep the commandments of your God יהוה that I enjoin upon you. ³You saw with your own eyes what יהוה did in the matter of Baalpeor, that your God יהוה wiped out from among you every person who followed Baalpeor; ⁴while you, who held fast to your God יהוה, are all alive today.

⁵See, I have imparted to you laws and rules, as my God יהוה has commanded me, for you to abide by in the land that you are about to enter and occupy. ⁶Observe them faithfully, for that will be proof of your wisdom and discernment to other peoples, who on hearing of all these laws will say, "Surely, that great nation is a wise and discerning people." ⁷For what great nation is there that has a god so close at hand as is our God יהוה whenever we call? ⁸Or what great nation has laws and rules as perfect as all this Teaching that I set before you this day?

⁹But take utmost care and watch yourselves scrupulously, so that you do not forget the things that you saw with your own eyes and so that they do not fade from your mind as long as you live. And make them known to your children and to your children's children: ¹⁰The day you stood before your God יהוה at Horeb, when יהוה said to Me, "Gather the people to Me that I may let them hear My words, in order that they may learn to revere Me as long as they live on earth, and may so teach their children." ¹¹You came forward and stood at the foot of the mountain. The mountain was ablaze with flames to the very skies, dark with densest clouds. ¹²יהוה spoke to you out of the fire; you heard the sound of words but perceived no shape—nothing but a voice. ¹³[God] declared to you the covenant that you were commanded to observe, the Ten Commandments, inscribing them on two tablets of stone. ¹⁴At the same time יהוה commanded me to impart to you laws and rules for you to observe in the land that you are about to cross into and occupy.

¹⁵For your own sake, therefore, be most careful—since you saw no shape when your God יהוה spoke to you at Horeb out of the fire—¹⁶not to act wickedly and make for yourselves a sculptured image in any likeness whatever: the form of a man or a woman, ¹⁷the form of any beast on earth, the form of any winged bird that flies in the sky, ¹⁸the form of anything that creeps on the ground, the form of any fish that is in the waters below the earth. ¹⁹And when you look up to the sky and behold the sun and the moon and the stars, the whole heavenly host, you must not be lured into bowing down to them or serving them. These your God יהוה allotted to other peoples everywhere under heaven; ²⁰but you יהוה took and

brought out of Egypt, that iron blast furnace, to be God's very own people, as is now the case.

²¹Now יהוה was angry with me on your account and swore that I should not cross the Jordan and enter the good land that your God יהוה is assigning you as a heritage. ²²For I must die in this land; I shall not cross the Jordan. But you will cross and take possession of that good land. ²³Take care, then, not to forget the covenant that your God יהוה concluded with you, and not to make for yourselves a sculptured image in any likeness, against which your God יהוה has enjoined you. ²⁴For your God יהוה is a consuming fire, an impassioned God.

²⁵When you have begotten children and children's children and are long established in the land, should you act wickedly and make for yourselves a sculptured image in any likeness, causing your God יהוה displeasure and vexation, ²⁶I call heaven and earth this day to witness against you that you shall soon perish from the land that you are crossing the Jordan to possess; you shall not long endure in it, but shall be utterly wiped out. ²⁷יהוה will scatter you among the peoples, and only a scant few of you shall be left among the nations to which יהוה will drive you. ²⁸There you will serve gods of wood and stone, made by human hands, that cannot see or hear or eat or smell.

²⁹But if you search there, you will find your God יהוה, if only you seek with all your heart and soul—³⁰when you are in distress because all these things have befallen you and, in the end, return to and obey your God יהוה. ³¹For your God יהוה is a compassionate God, who will not fail you nor let you perish; [God] will not forget the covenant made on oath with your fathers.

³²You have but to inquire about bygone ages that came before you, ever since God created humankind on earth, from one end of heaven to the other: has anything as grand as this ever happened, or has its like ever been known? ³³Has any people heard the voice of a god speaking out of a fire, as you have, and survived? ³⁴Or has any deity ventured to go and take one nation from the midst of another by prodigious acts, by signs and portents, by war, by a mighty and an outstretched arm and awesome power, as your God יהוה did for you in Egypt before your very eyes? ³⁵It has been clearly demonstrated to you that יהוה alone is God; there is none else. ³⁶From the heavens [God] let you hear the divine voice to discipline you; on earth [God] let you see the great divine fire; and from amidst that fire you heard God's words. ³⁷And having loved your ancestors, [God] chose their heirs after them; [God] personally—in great, divine might—led you out of Egypt, ³⁸to drive from your path nations greater and more populous than you, to take you into their land and assign it to you as a heritage, as is still the case. ³⁹Know therefore this day and keep in mind that יהוה alone is God in heaven above and on earth below; there is no other. ⁴⁰Observe God's laws and commandments, which I enjoin upon you this day, that it may go well with you and your children after you, and that you may long remain in the land that your God יהוה is assigning to you for all time.

⁴¹Then Moses set aside three cities on the east side of the Jordan ⁴²to which a [male] killer could escape, one who unwittingly slew another without having been an enemy in the past; he could flee to one of these cities and live: ⁴³Bezer, in the wilderness in the Tableland, belonging to the Reubenites; Ramoth, in Gilead, belonging to the Gadites; and Golan, in Bashan, belonging to the Manassites.

⁴⁴This is the Teaching that Moses set before the Israelites: ⁴⁵these are the decrees, laws, and rules that Moses addressed to the people of Israel, after they had left Egypt, ⁴⁶beyond the Jordan, in the valley at Bethpeor, in the land of King Sihon of the Amorites, who dwelt in Heshbon, whom Moses and the Israelites defeated after they had left Egypt. ⁴⁷They had taken possession of his country and that of King Og of Bashan—the two kings of the Amorites—which were on the east side of the Jordan ⁴⁸from Aroer on the banks of the wadi Arnon, as far as Mount Sion, that is, Hermon; ⁴⁹also the whole Arabah on the east side of the Jordan, as far as the Sea of the Arabah, at the foot of the slopes of Pisgah.

5 ¹Moses summoned all the Israelites and said to them: Hear, O Israel, the laws and rules that I proclaim to you this day! Study them and observe them faithfully!

²יהוה our God made a covenant with us at Horeb. ³It was not with our ancestors that יהוה made this covenant, but with us, the living, every one of us who is here today. ⁴Face to face יהוה spoke to you on the mountain out of the fire—⁵I stood between יהוה and you at that time to convey יהוה's words to you, for you were afraid of the fire and did not go up the mountain—saying:

⁶I יהוה am your God who brought you out of the land of Egypt, the house of bondage: ⁷You shall have no other gods beside Me.

⁸You shall not make for yourself a sculptured image, any likeness of what is in the heavens above, or on the earth below, or in the waters below the earth. ⁹You shall not bow down to them or serve them. For I your God יהוה am an impassioned God, visiting the guilt of the parents upon the children, upon the third and upon the fourth generations of those who reject Me, ¹⁰but showing kindness to the thousandth generation of those who love Me and keep My commandments.

¹¹You shall not swear falsely by the name of your God יהוה; for יהוה will not clear one who swears falsely by God's name.

¹²Observe the sabbath day and keep it holy, as your God יהוה has commanded you. ¹³Six days you shall labor and do all your work, ¹⁴but the seventh day is a sabbath of your God יהוה; you shall not do any work—you, your son or your daughter, your male or female slave, your ox or your ass, or any of your cattle, or the stranger in your settlements, so that your male and female slave may rest as you do. ¹⁵Remember that you were a slave in the land of Egypt and your God יהוה freed you from there with a mighty hand and an outstretched arm; therefore your God יהוה has commanded you to observe the sabbath day.

¹⁶Honor your father and your mother, as your God יהוה has commanded you, that you may long endure, and that you may fare well, in the land that your God יהוה is assigning to you.

¹⁷You shall not murder. You shall not commit adultery. You shall not steal. You shall not bear false witness against your neighbor.

¹⁸You [men] shall not covet your neighbor's wife. Likewise, none of you shall crave your neighbor's house, or field, or male or female slave, or ox, or ass, or anything that is your neighbor's.

¹⁹יהוה spoke those words—those and no more—to your whole congregation at the mountain, with a mighty voice out of the fire and the dense clouds. [God] inscribed them on two tablets of stone and gave them to me. ²⁰When you heard the voice out of the darkness, while the mountain was ablaze with fire, you came up to me, all your tribal heads and elders, ²¹and said, "Our God יהוה has just shown us a majestic Presence, and we have heard God's voice out of the fire; we have seen this day that humankind may live though addressed by God. ²²Let us not die, then, for this fearsome fire will consume us; if we hear the voice of our God יהוה any longer, we shall die. ²³For what mortal ever heard the voice of the living God speak out of the fire, as we did, and lived? ²⁴You go closer and hear all that our God יהוה says,

and then you tell us everything that our God יהוה tells you, and we will willingly do it."

[25]יהוה heard the plea that you made to me, and יהוה said to me, "I have heard the plea that this people made to you; they did well to speak thus. [26]May they always be of such mind, to revere Me and follow all My commandments, that it may go well with them and with their children forever! [27]Go, say to them, 'Return to your tents.' [28]But you remain here with Me, and I will give you the whole Instruction—the laws and the rules—that you shall impart to them, for them to observe in the land that I am giving them to possess."

[29]Be careful, then, to do as your God יהוה has commanded you. Do not turn aside to the right or to the left: [30]follow only the path that your God יהוה has enjoined upon you, so that you may thrive and that it may go well with you, and that you may long endure in the land you are to possess.

6 [1]And this is the Instruction—the laws and the rules—that your God יהוה has commanded [me] to impart to you, to be observed in the land that you are about to cross into and occupy, [2]so that you, your children, and your children's children may revere your God יהוה and follow, as long as you live, all the divine laws and commandments that I enjoin upon you, to the end that you may long endure. [3]Obey, O Israel, willingly and faithfully, that it may go well with you and that you may increase greatly [in] a land flowing with milk and honey, as יהוה, the God of your ancestors, spoke to you.

[4]Hear, O Israel! יהוה is our God, יהוה alone. [5]You shall love your God יהוה with all your heart, with all your soul, and with all your might. [6]Take to heart these instructions with which I charge you this day. [7]Impress them upon your children. Recite them when you stay at home and when you are away, when you lie down and when you get up. [8]Bind them as a sign on your hand and let them serve as a symbol on your forehead; [9]inscribe them on the doorposts of your house and on your gates.

[10]When your God יהוה brings you into the land that was sworn to your fathers Abraham, Isaac, and Jacob, to be assigned to you—great and flourishing cities that you did not build, [11]houses full of all good things that you did not fill, hewn cisterns that you did not hew, vineyards and olive groves that you did not plant—and you eat your fill, [12]take heed that you do not forget יהוה who freed you from the land of Egypt, the house of bondage. [13]Revere only your God יהוה and worship [God] alone, and swear only by God's name. [14]Do not follow other gods, any gods of the peoples about you—[15]for your God יהוה in your midst is an impassioned God—lest the anger of your God יהוה blaze forth against you, wiping you off the face of the earth.

[16]Do not try your God יהוה, as you did at Massah. [17]Be sure to keep the commandments, decrees, and laws that your God יהוה has enjoined upon you. [18]Do what is right and good in the sight of יהוה, that it may go well with you and that you may be able to possess the good land that your God יהוה promised on oath to your fathers, [19]and that all your enemies may be driven out before you, as יהוה has spoken.

[20]When, in time to come, your children ask you, "What mean the decrees, laws, and rules that our God יהוה has enjoined upon you?" [21]you shall say to your children, "We were slaves to Pharaoh in Egypt and יהוה freed us from Egypt with a mighty hand. [22]יהוה wrought before our eyes marvelous and destructive signs and portents in Egypt, against Pharaoh and all his household; [23]and us [God] freed from there, in order to take us and give us the land promised on oath to our fathers. [24]Then יהוה commanded us to observe all these laws, to revere our God יהוה, for our lasting good and for

our survival, as is now the case. [25]It will be therefore to our merit before our God יהוה to observe faithfully this whole Instruction, as [God] has commanded us."

7 [1]When your God יהוה brings you to the land that you are about to enter and possess, and [God] dislodges many nations before you—the Hittites, Girgashites, Amorites, Canaanites, Perizzites, Hivites, and Jebusites, seven nations much larger than you—[2]and your God יהוה delivers them to you and you defeat them, you must doom them to destruction: grant them no terms and give them no quarter. [3]You shall not intermarry with them: do not give your daughters to their sons or take their daughters for your sons. [4]For they will turn your children away from Me to worship other gods, and יהוה's anger will blaze forth against you, promptly wiping you out. [5]Instead, this is what you shall do to them: you shall tear down their altars, smash their pillars, cut down their sacred posts, and consign their images to the fire.

[6]For you are a people consecrated to your God יהוה: of all the peoples on earth your God יהוה chose you to be God's treasured people. [7]It is not because you are the most numerous of peoples that יהוה grew attached to you and chose you—indeed, you are the smallest of peoples; [8]but it was because יהוה favored you and kept the oath made to your fathers that יהוה freed you with a mighty hand and rescued you from the house of bondage, from the power of Pharaoh king of Egypt.

[9]Know, therefore, that only your God יהוה is God, the steadfast God who keeps the divine covenant faithfully to the thousandth generation of those who love [God] and keep the divine commandments, [10]but who instantly requites with destruction those who reject [God]—never slow with those who reject, but requiting them instantly. [11]Therefore, observe faithfully the Instruction—the laws and the rules—with which I charge you today.

[12]And if you do obey these rules and observe them carefully, your God יהוה will maintain faithfully for you the covenant made on oath with your fathers: [13][God] will favor you and bless you and multiply you—blessing the issue of your womb and the produce of your soil, your new grain and wine and oil, the calving of your herd and the lambing of your flock, in the land sworn to your fathers to be assigned to you. [14]You shall be blessed above all other peoples: there shall be no sterile male or female among you or among your livestock. [15]יהוה will ward off from you all sickness; [God] will not bring upon you any of the dreadful diseases of Egypt, about which you know, but will inflict them upon all your enemies.

[16]You shall destroy all the peoples that your God יהוה delivers to you, showing them no pity. And you shall not worship their gods, for that would be a snare to you. [17]Should you say to yourselves, "These nations are more numerous than we; how can we dispossess them?" [18]You need have no fear of them. You have but to bear in mind what your God יהוה did to Pharaoh and all the Egyptians: [19]the wondrous acts that you saw with your own eyes, the signs and the portents, the mighty hand, and the outstretched arm by which your God יהוה liberated you. Thus will your God יהוה do to all the peoples you now fear. [20]יהוה your God will also send a plague against them, until those who are left in hiding perish before you. [21]Do not stand in dread of them, for your God יהוה is in your midst, a great and awesome God.

[22]יהוה your God will dislodge those peoples before you little by little; you will not be able to put an end to them at once, else the wild beasts would multiply to your hurt. [23]יהוה your God will deliver them up to you, throwing them into utter panic until they are wiped out. [24][God] will deliver their kings into your hand, and you shall obliterate their name

from under the heavens; no one shall stand up to you, until you have wiped them out. ²⁵You shall consign the images of their gods to the fire; you shall not covet the silver and gold on them and keep it for yourselves, lest you be ensnared thereby; for that is abhorrent to your God יהוה. ²⁶You must not bring an abhorrent thing into your house, or you will be proscribed like it; you must reject it as abominable and abhorrent, for it is proscribed.

8 ¹You shall faithfully observe all the Instruction that I enjoin upon you today, that you may thrive and increase and be able to possess the land that יהוה promised on oath to your fathers.

²Remember the long way that your God יהוה has made you travel in the wilderness these past forty years, in order to test you by hardships to learn what was in your hearts: whether you would keep the divine commandments or not. ³[God] subjected you to the hardship of hunger and then gave you manna to eat, which neither you nor your ancestors had ever known, in order to teach you that a human being does not live on bread alone, but that one may live on anything that יהוה decrees. ⁴The clothes upon you did not wear out, nor did your feet swell these forty years. ⁵Bear in mind that your God יהוה disciplines you just as a householder disciplines his son. ⁶Therefore keep the commandments of your God יהוה: walk in God's ways and show reverence.

⁷For your God יהוה is bringing you into a good land, a land with streams and springs and fountains issuing from plain and hill; ⁸a land of wheat and barley, of vines, figs, and pomegranates, a land of olive trees and honey; ⁹a land where you may eat food without stint, where you will lack nothing; a land whose rocks are iron and from whose hills you can mine copper. ¹⁰When you have eaten your fill, give thanks to your God יהוה for the good land given to you.

¹¹Take care lest you forget your God יהוה and fail to keep the divine commandments, rules, and laws which I enjoin upon you today. ¹²When you have eaten your fill, and have built fine houses to live in, ¹³and your herds and flocks have multiplied, and your silver and gold have increased, and everything you own has prospered, ¹⁴[beware] lest your heart grow haughty and you forget your God יהוה—who freed you from the land of Egypt, the house of bondage; ¹⁵who led you through the great and terrible wilderness with its *seraph* serpents and scorpions, a parched land with no water in it, who brought forth water for you from the flinty rock; ¹⁶who fed you in the wilderness with manna, which your ancestors had never known, in order to test you by hardships only to benefit you in the end—¹⁷and you say to yourselves, "My own power and the might of my own hand have won this wealth for me." ¹⁸Remember that it is your God יהוה who gives you the power to get wealth, in fulfillment of the covenant made on oath with your fathers, as is still the case.

¹⁹If you do forget your God יהוה and follow other gods to serve them or bow down to them, I warn you this day that you shall certainly perish; ²⁰like the nations that יהוה will cause to perish before you, so shall you perish—because you did not heed your God יהוה.

9 ¹Hear, O Israel! You are about to cross the Jordan to go in and dispossess nations greater and more populous than you: great cities with walls sky-high; ²a people great and tall, the Anakites, of whom you have knowledge; for you have heard it said, "Who can stand up to the children of Anak?" ³Know then this day that none other than your God יהוה is crossing at your head, a devouring fire; it is [God] who will wipe them out—subduing them before you, that you may quickly dispossess and destroy them, as יהוה promised you.

⁴And when your God יהוה has thrust them from your path, say not to yourselves, "יהוה has enabled us to possess this land because of our virtues"; it is rather because of the wickedness of those nations that יהוה is dispossessing them before you. ⁵It is not because of your virtues and your rectitude that you will be able to possess their country; but it is because of their wickedness that your God יהוה is dispossessing those nations before you, and in order to fulfill the oath that יהוה made to your fathers Abraham, Isaac, and Jacob.

⁶Know, then, that it is not for any virtue of yours that your God יהוה is giving you this good land to possess; for you are a stiff-necked people. ⁷Remember, never forget, how you provoked your God יהוה to anger in the wilderness: from the day that you left the land of Egypt until you reached this place, you have continued defiant toward יהוה.

⁸At Horeb you so provoked יהוה that יהוה was angry enough with you to have destroyed you. ⁹I had ascended the mountain to receive the tablets of stone, the Tablets of the Covenant that יהוה had made with you, and I stayed on the mountain forty days and forty nights, eating no bread and drinking no water. ¹⁰And יהוה gave me the two tablets of stone inscribed by the finger of God, with the exact words that יהוה had addressed to you on the mountain out of the fire on the day of the Assembly.

¹¹At the end of those forty days and forty nights, יהוה gave me the two tablets of stone, the Tablets of the Covenant. ¹²And יהוה said to me, "Hurry, go down from here at once, for the people whom you brought out of Egypt have acted wickedly; they have been quick to stray from the path that I enjoined upon them; they have made themselves a molten image." ¹³יהוה further said to me, "I see that this is a stiff-necked people. ¹⁴Let Me alone and I will destroy them and blot out their name from under heaven, and I will make you a nation far more numerous than they."

¹⁵I started down the mountain, a mountain ablaze with fire, the two Tablets of the Covenant in my two hands. ¹⁶I saw how you had sinned against your God יהוה: you had made yourselves a molten calf; you had been quick to stray from the path that יהוה had enjoined upon you. ¹⁷Thereupon I gripped the two tablets and flung them away with both my hands, smashing them before your eyes. ¹⁸I threw myself down before יהוה—eating no bread and drinking no water forty days and forty nights, as before—because of the great wrong you had committed, doing what displeased and vexed יהוה. ¹⁹For I was in dread of the fierce anger against you which moved יהוה to wipe you out. And that time, too, יהוה gave heed to me.—²⁰Moreover, יהוה was angry enough with Aaron to have destroyed him; so I also interceded for Aaron at that time.—²¹As for that sinful thing you had made, the calf, I took it and put it to the fire; I broke it to bits and ground it thoroughly until it was fine as dust, and I threw its dust into the brook that comes down from the mountain.

²²Again you provoked יהוה at Taberah, and at Massah, and at Kibroth-hattaavah.

²³And when יהוה sent you on from Kadesh-barnea, saying, "Go up and take possession of the land that I am giving you," you flouted the command of your God יהוה—whom you did not put your trust in nor obey.

²⁴As long as I have known you, you have been defiant toward יהוה.

²⁵When I lay prostrate before יהוה those forty days and forty nights, because יהוה was determined to destroy you, ²⁶I prayed to יהוה and said, "O lord יהוה, do not annihilate Your very own people, whom You redeemed in Your majesty and whom You freed from Egypt with a mighty hand. ²⁷Give thought to Your servants Abraham, Isaac, and Jacob, and pay no heed to the stubbornness of this people, its wicked-

ness, and its sinfulness. 28Else the country from which You freed us will say, 'It was because יהוה was powerless to bring them into the land promised to them, and because of having rejected them, that [their god] brought them out to have them die in the wilderness.' 29Yet they are Your very own people, whom You freed with Your great might and Your outstretched arm."

10 1Thereupon יהוה said to me, "Carve out two tablets of stone like the first, and come up to Me on the mountain; and make an ark of wood. 2I will inscribe on the tablets the commandments that were on the first tablets that you smashed, and you shall deposit them in the ark."

3I made an ark of acacia wood and carved out two tablets of stone like the first; I took the two tablets with me and went up the mountain. 4After inscribing on the tablets the same text as on the first—the Ten Commandments that יהוה addressed to you on the mountain out of the fire on the day of the Assembly—יהוה gave them to me. 5Then I left and went down from the mountain, andI deposited the tablets in the ark that I had made, where they still are, as יהוה had commanded me.

6From Beeroth-bene-jaakan the Israelites marched to Moserah. Aaron died there and was buried there; and his son Eleazar became priest in his stead. 7From there they marched to Gudgod, and from Gudgod to Jotbath, a region of running brooks.

8At that time יהוה set apart the tribe of Levi to carry the Ark of יהוה's Covenant, to stand in attendance upon יהוה, and to bless in God's name, as is still the case. 9That is why Levi has received no hereditary portion along with its kin: יהוה is its portion, as your God יהוה spoke concerning it.

10I had stayed on the mountain, as I did the first time, forty days and forty nights; and יהוה heeded me once again: יהוה agreed not to destroy you. 11And יהוה said to me, "Up, resume the march at the head of the people, that they may go in and possess the land that I swore to their fathers to give them."

12And now, O Israel, what does your God יהוה demand of you? Only this: to revere your God יהוה, to walk only in divine paths, to love and to serve your God יהוה with all your heart and soul, 13keeping יהוה's commandments and laws, which I enjoin upon you today, for your good. 14Mark, the heavens to their uttermost reaches belong to your God יהוה, the earth and all that is on it! 15Yet it was to your ancestors that יהוה was drawn out of love for them, so that you, their lineal descendants, were chosen from among all peoples—as is now the case. 16Cut away, therefore, the thickening about your hearts and stiffen your necks no more. 17For your God יהוה is God supreme and Lord supreme, the great, the mighty, and the awesome God, who shows no favor and takes no bribe, 18but upholds the cause of the fatherless and the widow, and befriends the stranger, providing food and clothing.—19You too must befriend the stranger, for you were strangers in the land of Egypt.

20You must revere יהוה: only your God shall you worship, to [God] shall you hold fast, and by God's name shall you swear. 21[יהוה] is your glory and your God, who wrought for you those marvelous, awesome deeds that you saw with your own eyes. 22Your ancestors went down to Egypt seventy persons; and now your God יהוה has made you as numerous as the stars of heaven.

11 1Love, therefore, your God יהוה, and always keep God's charge, God's laws, God's rules, and God's commandments. 2Take thought this day that it was not your children, who neither experienced nor witnessed the lesson of your God יהוה—

God's majesty, mighty hand, and outstretched arm; 3the signs and the deeds that [God] performed in Egypt against Pharaoh king of Egypt and all his land; 4what [God] did to Egypt's army, its horses and chariots; how יהוה rolled back upon them the waters of the Sea of Reeds when they were pursuing you, thus destroying them once and for all; 5what [God] did for you in the wilderness before you arrived in this place; 6and what [God] did to Dathan and Abiram, sons of Eliab son of Reuben, when the earth opened her mouth and swallowed them, along with their households, their tents, and every living thing in their train, from amidst all Israel—7but that it was you who saw with your own eyes all the marvelous deeds that יהוה performed.

8Keep, therefore, all the Instruction that I enjoin upon you today, so that you may have the strength to enter and take possession of the land that you are about to cross into and possess, 9and that you may long endure upon the soil that יהוה swore to your fathers to assign to them and to their heirs, a land flowing with milk and honey.

10For the land that you are about to enter and possess is not like the land of Egypt from which you have come. There the grain you sowed had to be watered by your own labors, like a vegetable garden; 11but the land you are about to cross into and possess, a land of hills and valleys, soaks up its water from the rains of heaven. 12It is a land which your God יהוה looks after, on which your God יהוה always keeps an eye, from year's beginning to year's end.

13If, then, you obey the commandments that I enjoin upon you this day, loving your God יהוה and serving [God] with all your heart and soul, 14I will grant the rain for your land in season, the early rain and the late. You shall gather in your new grain and wine and oil—15I will also provide grass in the fields for your cattle—and thus you shall eat your fill. 16Take care not to be lured away to serve other gods and bow to them. 17For יהוה's anger will flare up against you, shutting up the skies so that there will be no rain and the ground will not yield its produce; and you will soon perish from the good land that יהוה is assigning to you.

18Therefore impress these My words upon your very heart: bind them as a sign on your hand and let them serve as a symbol on your forehead, 19and teach them to your children—reciting them when you stay at home and when you are away, when you lie down and when you get up; 20and inscribe them on the doorposts of your house and on your gates—21to the end that you and your children may endure, in the land that יהוה swore to your fathers to assign to them, as long as there is a heaven over the earth.

22If, then, you faithfully keep all this Instruction that I command you, loving your God יהוה, walking in all God's ways, and holding fast to [God], 23יהוה will dislodge before you all these nations: you will dispossess nations greater and more numerous than you. 24Every spot on which your foot treads shall be yours; your territory shall extend from the wilderness to the Lebanon and from the River—the Euphrates—to the Western Sea. 25No one shall stand up to you: your God יהוה will put the dread and the fear of you over the whole land in which you set foot, as promised.

26See, this day I set before you blessing and curse: 27blessing, if you obey the commandments of your God יהוה that I enjoin upon you this day; 28and curse, if you do not obey the commandments of your God יהוה, but turn away from the path that I enjoin upon you this day and follow other gods, whom you have not experienced. 29When your God יהוה brings you into the land that you are about to enter and possess, you shall pronounce the blessing at Mount Gerizim and the curse at Mount Ebal.—30Both are on the other side of the Jordan, beyond the west road that is in the land of the

Canaanites who dwell in the Arabah—near Gilgal, by the terebinths of Moreh. [31]For you are about to cross the Jordan to enter and possess the land that your God יהוה is assigning to you. When you have occupied it and are settled in it, [32]take care to observe all the laws and rules that I have set before you this day.

12 [1]These are the laws and rules that you must carefully observe in the land that יהוה, God of your ancestors, is giving you to possess, as long as you live on earth.

[2]You must destroy all the sites at which the nations you are to dispossess worshiped their gods, whether on lofty mountains and on hills or under any luxuriant tree. [3]Tear down their altars, smash their pillars, put their sacred posts to the fire, and cut down the images of their gods, obliterating their name from that site.

[4]Do not worship your God יהוה in like manner, [5]but look only to the site that your God יהוה will choose amidst all your tribes as God's habitation, to establish the divine name there. There you are to go, [6]and there you are to bring your burnt offerings and other sacrifices, your tithes and contributions, your votive and freewill offerings, and the firstlings of your herds and flocks. [7]Together with your households, you shall feast there before your God יהוה, happy in all the undertakings in which your God יהוה has blessed you.

[8]You shall not act at all as we now act here, each [householder] as he pleases, [9]because you have not yet come to the allotted haven that your God יהוה is giving you. [10]When you cross the Jordan and settle in the land that your God יהוה is allotting to you, and [God] grants you safety from all your enemies around you and you live in security, [11]then you must bring everything that I command you to the site where your God יהוה will choose to establish the divine name: your burnt offerings and other sacrifices, your tithes and contributions, and all the choice votive offerings that you vow to יהוה. [12]And you shall rejoice before your God יהוה with your sons and daughters and with your male and female slaves, along with the [family of the] Levite in your settlements, for he has no territorial allotment among you.

[13]Take care not to sacrifice your burnt offerings in any place you like, [14]but only in the place that יהוה will choose in one of your tribal territories. There you shall sacrifice your burnt offerings and there you shall observe all that I enjoin upon you. [15]But whenever you desire, you may slaughter and eat meat in any of your settlements, according to the blessing that your God יהוה has granted you. The impure and the pure alike may partake of it, as of the gazelle and the deer. [16]But you must not partake of the blood; you shall pour it out on the ground like water.

[17]You may not partake in your settlements of the tithes of your new grain or wine or oil, or of the firstlings of your herds and flocks, or of any of the votive offerings that you vow, or of your freewill offerings, or of your contributions. [18]These you must consume before your God יהוה in the place that your God יהוה will choose—you and your sons and your daughters, your male and female slaves, and the [family of the] Levite in your settlements—happy before your God יהוה in all your undertakings. [19]Be sure not to neglect the [family of the] Levite as long as you live in your land.

[20]When יהוה enlarges your territory, as promised, and you say, "I shall eat some meat," for you have the urge to eat meat, you may eat meat whenever you wish. [21]If the place where יהוה has chosen to establish the divine name is too far from you, you may slaughter any of the cattle or sheep that יהוה gives you, as I have instructed you; and you may eat to your heart's content in your settlements. [22]Eat it, however, as the gazelle and the deer are eaten: the impure may eat

it together with the pure. [23]But make sure that you do not partake of the blood; for the blood is the life, and you must not consume the life with the flesh. [24]You must not partake of it; you must pour it out on the ground like water: [25]you must not partake of it, in order that it may go well with you and with your descendants to come, for you will be doing what is right in the sight of יהוה.

[26]But such sacred and votive donations as you may have shall be taken by you to the site that יהוה will choose. [27]You shall offer your burnt offerings, both the flesh and the blood, on the altar of your God יהוה; and of your other sacrifices, the blood shall be poured out on the altar of your God יהוה, and you shall eat the flesh.

[28]Be careful to heed all these commandments that I enjoin upon you; thus it will go well with you and with your descendants after you forever, for you will be doing what is good and right in the sight of your God יהוה.

[29]When your God יהוה has cut down before you the nations that you are about to enter and dispossess, and you have dispossessed them and settled in their land, [30]beware of being lured into their ways after they have been wiped out before you! Do not inquire about their gods, saying, "How did those nations worship their gods? I too will follow those practices." [31]You shall not act thus toward your God יהוה, for they perform for their gods every abhorrent act that יהוה detests; they even offer up their sons and daughters in fire to their gods.

13 [1]Be careful to observe only neither add to it nor take that which I enjoin upon you: away from it.

[2]If there appears among you a prophet or a dream-diviner, who gives you a sign or a portent, [3]saying, "Let us follow and worship another god"—whom you have not experienced—even if the sign or portent named to you comes true, [4]do not heed the words of that prophet or that dream-diviner. For your God יהוה is testing you to see whether you really love your God יהוה with all your heart and soul. [5]It is your God יהוה alone whom you should follow, whom you should revere, whose commandments you should observe, whose orders you should heed, whom you should worship, and to whom you should hold fast. [6]As for that prophet or dream-diviner, such a one shall be put to death for having urged disloyalty to your God יהוה—who freed you from the land of Egypt and who redeemed you from the house of bondage—to make you stray from the path that your God יהוה commanded you to follow. Thus you will sweep out evil from your midst.

[7]If your brother, your own mother's son, or your son or daughter, or the wife of your bosom, or your closest friend entices you in secret, saying, "Come let us worship other gods"—whom neither you nor your ancestors have experienced—[8]from among the gods of the peoples around you, either near to you or distant, anywhere from one end of the earth to the other: [9]do not assent or give heed to any of them. Show no pity or compassion, and do not cover up the matter; [10]but take that person's life. Let your hand be the first to put that person to death, followed by the hand of the rest of the people. [11]Stone that person to death for having sought to make you stray from your God יהוה, who brought you out of the land of Egypt, out of the house of bondage. [12]Thus all Israel will hear and be afraid, and such evil things will not be done again in your midst.

[13]If you hear it said, of one of the towns that your God יהוה is giving you to dwell in, [14]that some scoundrels from among you have gone and subverted the inhabitants of their town, saying, "Come let us worship other gods"—whom you have not experienced—[15]you shall investigate and inquire and interrogate thoroughly. If it is true, the fact is

established—that abhorrent thing was perpetrated in your midst—¹⁶put the inhabitants of that town to the sword and put its cattle to the sword. Doom it and all that is in it to destruction: ¹⁷gather all its spoil into the open square, and burn the town and all its spoil as a holocaust to your God יהוה. And it shall remain an everlasting ruin, never to be rebuilt. ¹⁸Let nothing that has been doomed stick to your hand, in order that יהוה may turn from a blazing anger and show you compassion, and in compassion increase you as promised on oath to your fathers—¹⁹for you will be heeding your God יהוה, obeying all the divine commandments that I enjoin upon you this day, doing what is right in the sight of your God יהוה.

14 ¹You are children of your God יהוה. You shall not gash yourselves or shave the front of your heads because of the dead. ²For you are a people consecrated to your God יהוה: your God יהוה chose you from among all other peoples on earth to be a treasured people.

³You shall not eat anything abhorrent. ⁴These are the animals that you may eat: the ox, the sheep, and the goat; ⁵the deer, the gazelle, the roebuck, the wild goat, the ibex, the antelope, the mountain sheep, ⁶and any other animal that has true hoofs which are cleft in two and brings up the cud—such you may eat. ⁷But the following, which do bring up the cud or have true hoofs which are cleft through, you may not eat: the camel, the hare, and the daman—for although they bring up the cud, they have no true hoofs—they are impure for you; ⁸also the swine—for although it has true hoofs, it does not bring up the cud—is impure for you. You shall not eat of their flesh or touch their carcasses.

⁹These you may eat of all that live in water: you may eat anything that has fins and scales. ¹⁰But you may not eat anything that has no fins and scales: it is impure for you.

¹¹You may eat any pure bird. ¹²The following you may not eat: the eagle, the vulture, and the black vulture; ¹³the kite, the falcon, and the buzzard of any variety; ¹⁴every variety of raven; ¹⁵the ostrich, the nighthawk, the sea gull, and the hawk of any variety; ¹⁶the little owl, the great owl, and the white owl; ¹⁷the pelican, the bustard, and the cormorant; ¹⁸the stork, any variety of heron, the hoopoe, and the bat.

¹⁹All winged swarming things are impure for you: they may not be eaten. ²⁰You may eat only pure winged creatures.

²¹You shall not eat anything that has died a natural death; give it to the stranger in your community to eat, or you may sell it to a foreigner. For you are a people consecrated to God יהוה.

You shall not boil a kid in its mother's milk.

²²You shall set aside every year a tenth part of all the yield of your sowing that is brought from the field. ²³You shall consume the tithes of your new grain and wine and oil, and the firstlings of your herds and flocks, in the presence of your God יהוה, in the place where [God] will choose to establish the divine name, so that you may learn to revere your God יהוה forever. ²⁴Should the distance be too great for you, should you be unable to transport them, because the place where your God יהוה has chosen to establish the divine name is far from you and because your God יהוה has blessed you, ²⁵you may convert them into money. Wrap up the money and take it with you to the place that your God יהוה has chosen, ²⁶and spend the money on anything you want—cattle, sheep, wine, or other intoxicant, or anything you may desire. And you shall feast there, in the presence of your God יהוה, and rejoice with your household.

²⁷But do not neglect the [family of the] Levite in your community, for he has no hereditary portion as you have.

²⁸Every third year you shall bring out the full tithe of your yield of that year, but leave it within your settlements. ²⁹Then the [family of the] Levite, who has no hereditary portion as you have, and the stranger, the fatherless, and the widow in your settlements shall come and eat their fill, so that your God יהוה may bless you in all the enterprises you undertake.

15 ¹Every seventh year you shall practice remission of debts. ²This shall be the nature of the remission: all creditors shall remit the due that they claim from their fellow [Israelites]; they shall not dun their fellow [Israelites] or kin, for the remission proclaimed is of יהוה. ³You may dun the foreigner; but you must remit whatever is due you from your kin.

⁴There shall be no needy among you—since your God יהוה will bless you in the land that your God יהוה is giving you as a hereditary portion—⁵if only you heed your God יהוה and take care to keep all this Instruction that I enjoin upon you this day. ⁶For your God יהוה will bless you as promised: you will extend loans to many nations, but require none yourself; you will dominate many nations, but they will not dominate you.

⁷If, however, there is a needy person among you, one of your kin in any of your settlements in the land that your God יהוה is giving you, do not harden your heart and shut your hand against your needy kin. ⁸Rather, you must open your hand and lend whatever is sufficient to meet the need. ⁹Beware lest you harbor the base thought, "The seventh year, the year of remission, is approaching," so that you are mean and give nothing to your needy kin—who will cry out to יהוה against you, and you will incur guilt. ¹⁰Give readily and have no regrets when you do so, for in return your God יהוה will bless you in all your efforts and in all your undertakings. ¹¹For there will never cease to be needy ones in your land, which is why I command you: open your hand to the poor and needy kin in your land.

¹²If a fellow Hebrew man—or woman—is sold to you, he shall serve you six years, and in the seventh year you shall set him free. ¹³When you set him free, do not let him go empty-handed: ¹⁴Furnish him out of the flock, threshing floor, and vat, with which your God יהוה has blessed you. ¹⁵Bear in mind that you were slaves in the land of Egypt and your God יהוה redeemed you; therefore I enjoin this commandment upon you today.

¹⁶But should he say to you, "I do not want to leave you"—for he loves you and your household and is happy with you—¹⁷you shall take an awl and put it through his ear into the door, and he shall become your slave in perpetuity. Do the same with your female slave. ¹⁸When you do set either one free, do not feel aggrieved; for in the six years you have been given double the service of a hired worker. Moreover, your God יהוה will bless you in all you do.

¹⁹You shall consecrate to your God יהוה all male firstlings that are born in your herd and in your flock: you must not work your firstling ox or shear your firstling sheep. ²⁰You and your household shall eat it annually before your God יהוה in the place that יהוה will choose. ²¹But if it has a defect, lameness or blindness, any serious defect, you shall not sacrifice it to your God יהוה. ²²Eat it in your settlements, the impure among you no less than the pure, just like the gazelle and the deer. ²³Only you must not partake of its blood; you shall pour it out on the ground like water.

16 ¹Observe the month of Abib and offer a passover sacrifice to your God יהוה, for it was in the month of Abib, at night, that your God יהוה freed you from Egypt. ²You shall slaughter the passover sacrifice for your God יהוה, from the flock and the herd, in the place where יהוה will choose to establish the divine name. ³You shall not eat anything leavened with it; for seven days thereafter you shall eat unleavened bread, bread of distress—for you departed from the land of Egypt hurriedly—so that you may remember the day of your departure from the land of Egypt as long as you live. ⁴For seven days no leaven shall be found with you in all your territory, and none of the flesh of what you slaughter on the evening of the first day shall be left until morning.

⁵You are not permitted to slaughter the passover sacrifice in any of the settlements that your God יהוה is giving you; ⁶but at the place where your God יהוה will choose to establish the divine name, there alone shall you slaughter the passover sacrifice, in the evening, at sundown, the time of day when you departed from Egypt. ⁷You shall cook and eat it at the place that your God יהוה will choose; and in the morning you may start back on your journey home. ⁸After eating unleavened bread six days, you shall hold a solemn gathering for your God יהוה on the seventh day: you shall do no work.

⁹You shall count off seven weeks; start to count the seven weeks when the sickle is first put to the standing grain. ¹⁰Then you shall observe the Feast of Weeks for your God יהוה, offering your freewill contribution according as your God יהוה has blessed you. ¹¹You shall rejoice before your God יהוה with your son and daughter, your male and female slave, the [family of the] Levite in your communities, and the stranger, the fatherless, and the widow in your midst, at the place where your God יהוה will choose to establish the divine name. ¹²Bear in mind that you were slaves in Egypt, and take care to obey these laws.

¹³After the ingathering from your threshing floor and your vat, you shall hold the Feast of Booths for seven days. ¹⁴You shall rejoice in your festival, with your son and daughter, your male and female slave, the [family of the] Levite, the stranger, the fatherless, and the widow in your communities. ¹⁵You shall hold a festival for your God יהוה seven days, in the place that יהוה will choose; for your God יהוה will bless all your crops and all your undertakings, and you shall have nothing but joy.

¹⁶Three times a year—on the Feast of Unleavened Bread, on the Feast of Weeks, and on the Feast of Booths—all your males shall appear before your God יהוה in the place that [God] will choose. They shall not appear before יהוה empty-handed, ¹⁷but each with his own gift, according to the blessing that your God יהוה has bestowed upon you.

¹⁸You shall appoint magistrates and officials for your tribes, in all the settlements that your God יהוה is giving you, and they shall govern the people with due justice. ¹⁹You shall not judge unfairly: you shall show no partiality; you shall not take bribes, for bribes blind the eyes of the discerning and upset the plea of the just. ²⁰Justice, justice shall you pursue, that you may thrive and occupy the land that your God יהוה is giving you.

²¹You shall not set up a sacred post—any kind of pole beside the altar of your God יהוה that you may make—²²or erect a stone pillar; for such your God יהוה detests.

17 ¹You shall not sacrifice to your God יהוה an ox or a sheep that has any defect of a serious kind, for that is abhorrent to your God יהוה.

²If there is found among you, in one of the settlements that your God יהוה is giving you, a man or woman who has affronted your God יהוה and transgressed the Covenant—³turning to the worship of other gods and bowing down to them, to the sun or the moon or any of the heavenly host,

something I never commanded—⁴and you have been informed or have learned of it, then you shall make a thorough inquiry. If it is true, the fact is established, that abhorrent thing was perpetrated in Israel, ⁵you shall take the man or the woman who did that wicked thing out to the public place, and you shall stone that man or woman to death.—⁶A person shall be put to death only on the testimony of two or more witnesses; no one shall be put to death on the testimony of a single witness.—⁷Let the hands of the witnesses be the first to put [the condemned] to death, followed by the hands of the rest of the people. Thus you will sweep out evil from your midst.

⁸If a case is too baffling for you to decide, be it a controversy over homicide, civil law, or assault—matters of dispute in your courts—you shall promptly repair to the place that your God יהוה will have chosen, ⁹and appear before the levitical priests, or the magistrate in charge at the time, and present your problem. When they have announced to you the verdict in the case, ¹⁰you shall carry out the verdict that is announced to you from that place that יהוה chose, observing scrupulously all their instructions to you. ¹¹You shall act in accordance with the instructions given you and the ruling handed down to you; you must not deviate from the verdict that they announce to you either to the right or to the left. ¹²Should either party act presumptuously and disregard the priest charged with serving there your God יהוה, or the magistrate, that party shall die. Thus you will sweep out evil from Israel: ¹³all the people will hear and be afraid and will not act presumptuously again.

¹⁴If, after you have entered the land that your God יהוה has assigned to you, and taken possession of it and settled in it, you decide, "I will set a king over me, as do all the nations about me," ¹⁵you shall be free to set a king over yourself, one chosen by your God יהוה. Be sure to set as king over yourself one of your own people; you must not set a foreigner over you, one who is not your kin. ¹⁶Moreover, he shall not keep many horses or send people back to Egypt to add to his horses, since יהוה has warned you, "You must not go back that way again." ¹⁷And he shall not have many wives, lest his heart go astray; nor shall he amass silver and gold to excess.

¹⁸When he is seated on his royal throne, he shall have a copy of this Teaching written for him on a scroll by the levitical priests. ¹⁹Let it remain with him and let him read in it all his life, so that he may learn to revere his God יהוה, to observe faithfully every word of this Teaching as well as these laws. ²⁰Thus he will not act haughtily toward his fellows or deviate from the Instruction to the right or to the left, to the end that he and his descendants may reign long in the midst of Israel.

18 ¹The levitical priests, the whole tribe of Levi, shall have no territorial portion with Israel. They shall live only off יהוה's offerings by fire as their portion, ²and shall have no portion among their brother tribes: יהוה is their portion, as promised.

³This then shall be the priests' due from the people: Everyone who offers a sacrifice, whether an ox or a sheep, must give the shoulder, the cheeks, and the stomach to the priest. ⁴You shall also give him the first fruits of your new grain and wine and oil, and the first shearing of your sheep. ⁵For your God יהוה has chosen him and his descendants, out of all your tribes, to be in attendance for service in the name of יהוה for all time.

⁶If a Levite would go, from any of the settlements throughout Israel where he has been residing, to the place that יהוה has chosen, he may do so whenever he pleases. ⁷He may serve in the name of his God יהוה like all his fellow Levites who are there in attendance before יהוה. ⁸They shall receive

equal shares of the dues, without regard to personal gifts or patrimonies.

⁹When you enter the land that your God יהוה is giving you, you shall not learn to imitate the abhorrent practices of those nations. ¹⁰Let no one be found among you who consigns a son or daughter to the fire, or who is an augur, a soothsayer, a diviner, a sorcerer, ¹¹one who casts spells, or one who consults ghosts or familiar spirits, or one who inquires of the dead. ¹²For anyone who does such things is abhorrent to יהוה, and it is because of these abhorrent things that your God יהוה is dispossessing them before you. ¹³You must be wholehearted with your God יהוה. ¹⁴Those nations that you are about to dispossess do indeed resort to soothsayers and augurs; to you, however, your God יהוה has not assigned the like.

¹⁵From among your own people, your God יהוה will raise up for you a prophet like myself; that is whom you shall heed. ¹⁶This is just what you asked of your God יהוה at Horeb, on the day of the Assembly, saying, "Let me not hear the voice of my God יהוה any longer or see this wondrous fire any more, lest I die." ¹⁷Whereupon יהוה said to me, "They have done well in speaking thus. ¹⁸I will raise up for them from among their own people a prophet like yourself, in whose mouth I will put My words and who will speak to them all that I command; ¹⁹and anybody who fails to heed the words [the prophet] speaks in My name, I Myself will call to account. ²⁰But any prophet who presumes to speak in My name an oracle that I did not command to be uttered, or who speaks in the name of other gods—that prophet shall die." ²¹And should you ask yourselves, "How can we know that the oracle was not spoken by יהוה?"—²²if the prophet speaks in the name of יהוה and the oracle does not come true, that oracle was not spoken by יהוה; the prophet has uttered it presumptuously: do not stand I dread of that person.

19 ¹When your God יהוה has cut down the nations whose land your God יהוה is assigning to you, and you have dispossessed them and settled in their towns and houses, ²you shall set aside three cities in the land that your God יהוה is giving you to possess. ³You shall survey the distances, and divide into three parts the territory of the country that your God יהוה has allotted to you, so that any [male] killer may have a place to flee to.—⁴Now this is the case of the killer who may flee there and live: one who has slain another unwittingly, without having been an enemy in the past. ⁵For instance, a man goes with another fellow into a grove to cut wood; as his hand swings the ax to cut down a tree, the ax-head flies off the handle and strikes the other so that he dies. That man shall flee to one of these cities and live.—⁶Otherwise, when the distance is great, the blood-avenger, pursuing the killer in hot anger, may overtake him and strike him down; yet he did not incur the death penalty, since he had never been the other's enemy. ⁷That is why I command you: set aside three cities.

⁸And when your God יהוה enlarges your territory, as was sworn to your fathers, and gives you all the land that was promised to be given to your fathers—⁹if you faithfully observe all this Instruction that I enjoin upon you this day, to love your God יהוה and to walk in God's ways at all times—then you shall add three more towns to those three. ¹⁰Thus blood of the innocent will not be shed, bringing bloodguilt upon you in the land that your God יהוה is allotting to you.

¹¹If, however, a man who is the enemy of another lies in wait and sets upon [the victim] and strikes a fatal blow and then flees to one of these towns, ¹²the elders of his town shall have him brought back from there and shall hand him over to the blood-avenger to be put to death; ¹³you must show

him no pity. Thus you will purge Israel of the blood of the innocent, and it will go well with you.

¹⁴You shall not move your neighbor's landmarks, set up by previous generations, in the property that will be allotted to you in the land that your God יהוה is giving you to possess.

¹⁵A single witness may not validate against a person any guilt or blame for any offense that may be committed; a case can be valid only on the testimony of two witnesses or more. ¹⁶If someone appears against another to testify maliciously and gives incriminating yet false testimony, ¹⁷the two parties to the dispute shall appear before יהוה, before the priests or magistrates in authority at the time, ¹⁸and the magistrates shall make a thorough investigation. If the one who testified is a false witness, having testified falsely against a fellow Israelite, ¹⁹you shall do to the one as the one schemed to do to the other. Thus you will sweep out evil from your midst; ²⁰others will hear and be afraid, and such evil things will not again be done in your midst. ²¹Nor must you show pity: life for life, eye for eye, tooth for tooth, hand for hand, foot for foot.

20 ¹When you [an Israelite warrior] take the field against your enemies, and see horses and chariots—forces larger than yours—have no fear of them, for your God יהוה, who brought you from the land of Egypt, is with you. ²Before you join battle, the priest shall come forward and address the troops. ³He shall say to them, "Hear, O Israel! You are about to join battle with your enemy. Let not your courage falter. Do not be in fear, or in panic, or in dread of them. ⁴For it is your God יהוה who marches with you to do battle for you against your enemy, to bring you victory."

⁵Then the officials shall address the troops, as follows: "Is there anyone who has built a new house but has not dedicated it? Let him go back to his home, lest he die in battle and another dedicate it. ⁶Is there anyone who has planted a vineyard but has never harvested it? Let him go back to his home, lest he die in battle and another harvest it. ⁷Is there anyone who has paid the bride-price for a wife, but who has not yet taken her [into his household]? Let him go back to his home, lest he die in battle and another take her [into his household as his wife]." ⁸The officials shall go on addressing the troops and say, "Is there anyone afraid and disheartened? Let him go back to his home, lest the courage of his comrades flag like his." ⁹When the officials have finished addressing the troops, army commanders shall assume command of the troops.

¹⁰When you approach a town to attack it, you shall offer it terms of peace. ¹¹If it responds peaceably and lets you in, all the people present there shall serve you at forced labor. ¹²If it does not surrender to you, but would join battle with you, you shall lay siege to it; ¹³and when your God יהוה delivers it into your hand, you shall put all its males to the sword. ¹⁴You may, however, take as your booty the women, the children, the livestock, and everything in the town—all its spoil—and enjoy the use of the spoil of your enemy, which your God יהוה gives you.

¹⁵Thus you shall deal with all towns that lie very far from you, towns that do not belong to nations hereabout. ¹⁶In the towns of the latter peoples, however, which your God יהוה is giving you as a heritage, you shall not let a soul remain alive. ¹⁷No, you must proscribe them—the Hittites and the Amorites, the Canaanites and the Perizzites, the Hivites and the Jebusites—as your God יהוה has commanded you, ¹⁸lest they lead you into doing all the abhorrent things that they have done for their gods and you stand guilty before your God יהוה.

¹⁹When in your war against a city you have to besiege it a long time in order to capture it, you must not destroy its trees, wielding the ax against them. You may eat of them, but

you must not cut them down. Are trees of the field human to withdraw before you into the besieged city? ²⁰Only trees that you know do not yield food may be destroyed; you may cut them down for constructing siege-works against the city that is waging war on you, until it has been reduced.

21 ¹If, in the land that your God יהוה is assigning you to possess, someone slain is found lying in the open, the identity of the slayer not being known, ²your elders and magistrates shall go out and measure the distances from the corpse to the nearby towns. ³The elders of the town nearest to the corpse shall then take a heifer which has never been worked, which has never pulled in a yoke; ⁴and the elders of that town shall bring the heifer down to an ever-flowing wadi, which is not tilled or sown. There, in the wadi, they shall break the heifer's neck. ⁵The priests, sons of Levi, shall come forward; for your God יהוה has chosen them for divine service and to pronounce blessing in the name of יהוה, and every lawsuit and case of assault is subject to their ruling. ⁶Then all the elders of the town nearest to the corpse shall wash their hands over the heifer whose neck was broken in the wadi. ⁷And they shall make this declaration: "Our hands did not shed this blood, nor did our eyes see it done. ⁸Absolve, יהוה, Your people Israel whom You redeemed, and do not let guilt for the blood of the innocent remain among Your people Israel." And they will be absolved of bloodguilt. ⁹Thus you will remove from your midst guilt for the blood of the innocent, for you will be doing what is right in the sight of יהוה.

¹⁰When you [an Israelite warrior] take the field against your enemies, and your God יהוה delivers them into your power and you take some of them captive, ¹¹and you see among the captives a beautiful woman and you desire her and would take her [into your household] as your wife, ¹²you shall bring her into your household, and she shall trim her hair, pare her nails, ¹³and discard her captive's garb. She shall spend a month's time in your house lamenting her father and mother; after that you may come to her and thus become her husband, and she shall be your wife. ¹⁴Then, should you no longer want her, you must release her outright. You must not sell her for money: since you had your will of her, you must not enslave her.

¹⁵If a householder has two wives, one loved and the other unloved, and both the loved and the unloved have borne him sons, but the firstborn is the son of the unloved one— ¹⁶when he wills his property to his sons, he may not treat as firstborn the son of the loved one in disregard of the son of the unloved one who is older. ¹⁷Instead, he must accept the firstborn, the son of the unloved one, and allot to him a double portion of all he possesses; since he is the first fruit of his vigor, the birthright is his due.

¹⁸If a householder has a wayward and defiant son, who does not heed his father or mother and does not obey them even after they discipline him, ¹⁹his father and mother shall take hold of him and bring him out to the elders of his town at the public place of his community. ²⁰They shall say to the elders of his town, "This son of ours is disloyal and defiant; he does not heed us. He is a glutton and a drunkard." ²¹Thereupon his town's council shall stone him to death. Thus you will sweep out evil from your midst: all Israel will hear and be afraid.

²²If someone is guilty of a capital offense and is put to death, and you impale the body on a stake, ²³you must not let the corpse remain on the stake overnight, but must bury it the same day. For an impaled body is an affront to God: you shall not defile the land that your God יהוה is giving you to possess.

22 ¹If you see your fellow Israelite's ox or sheep gone astray, do not ignore it; you must take it back to your peer. ²If your fellow Israelite does not live near you or you do not know who [the owner] is, you shall bring it home and it shall remain with you until your peer claims it; then you shall give it back. ³You shall do the same with that person's ass; you shall do the same with that person's garment; and so too shall you do with anything that your fellow Israelite loses and you find: you must not remain indifferent.

⁴If you see your fellow Israelite's ass or ox fallen on the road, do not ignore it; you must raise it together.

⁵A woman must not put on man's apparel, nor shall a man wear woman's clothing; for whoever does these things is abhorrent to your God יהוה.

⁶If, along the road, you chance upon a bird's nest, in any tree or on the ground, with fledglings or eggs and the mother sitting over the fledglings or on the eggs, do not take the mother together with her young. ⁷Let the mother go, and take only the young, in order that you may fare well and have a long life.

⁸When you build a new house, you shall make a parapet for your roof, so that you do not bring bloodguilt on your house if anyone should fall from it.

⁹You shall not sow your vineyard with a second kind of seed, else the crop—from the seed you have sown—and the yield of the vineyard may not be used. ¹⁰You shall not plow with an ox and an ass together. ¹¹You shall not wear cloth combining wool and linen.

¹²You shall make tassels on the four corners of the garment with which you cover yourself.

¹³A householder takes a woman [as his wife] and cohabits with her. Then he takes an aversion to her ¹⁴and makes up charges against her and defames her, saying, "I took this woman; but when I approached her, I found that she was not a virgin." ¹⁵In such a case, the girl's father and mother shall produce the evidence of the girl's virginity before the elders of the town at the gate. ¹⁶And the girl's father shall say to the elders, "I gave this householder my daughter to wife, but he has taken an aversion to her; ¹⁷so he has made up charges, saying, 'I did not find your daughter a virgin.' But here is the evidence of my daughter's virginity!" And they shall spread out the cloth before the elders of the town. ¹⁸The elders of that town shall then take that householder and flog him, ¹⁹and they shall fine him a hundred [shekels of] silver and give it to the girl's father; for [that householder] has defamed a virgin in Israel. Moreover, she shall remain his wife; he shall never have the right to divorce her.

²⁰But if the charge proves true, the girl was found not to have been a virgin, ²¹then the girl shall be brought out to the entrance of her father's house, and her town's council shall stone her to death; for she did a shameful thing in Israel, committing fornication while under her father's authority. Thus you will sweep away evil from your midst.

²²If a man is found lying with another man's wife, both of them—the man and the woman with whom he lay—shall die. Thus you will sweep away evil from Israel.

²³In the case of a virgin who is engaged to a man—if a man comes upon her in town and lies with her, ²⁴you shall take the two of them out to the gate of that town and stone them to death: the girl because she did not cry for help in the town, and the man because he violated another man's wife. Thus you will sweep away evil from your midst. ²⁵But if the man comes upon the engaged girl in the open country, and the man lies with her by force, only the man who lay with her shall die, ²⁶but you shall do nothing to the girl. The girl did not incur the death penalty, for this case is like that of one person attacking and murdering another. ²⁷He came upon

her in the open; though the engaged girl cried for help, there was no one to save her.

²⁸If a man comes upon a virgin who is not engaged and he seizes her and lies with her, and they are discovered, ²⁹the man who lay with her shall pay the girl's father fifty [shekels of] silver, and she shall be his wife. Because he has violated her, he can never have the right to divorce her.

23 ¹No householder shall take his father's former wife [as his own wife], so as to remove his father's garment. ²No man whose testes are crushed or whose member is cut off shall be admitted into the congregation of יהוה. ³No one misbegotten shall be admitted into the congregation of יהוה; no descendant of such, even in the tenth generation, shall be admitted into the congregation of יהוה. ⁴No Ammonite or Moabite shall be admitted into the congregation of יהוה; no descendants of such, even in the tenth generation, shall ever be admitted into the congregation of יהוה, ⁵because they did not meet you with food and water on your journey after you left Egypt, and because they hired Balaam son of Beor, from Pethor of Aram-naharaim, to curse you.—⁶But your God יהוה refused to heed Balaam; instead, your God יהוה turned the curse into a blessing for you, for your God יהוה loves you.—⁷You shall never concern yourself with their welfare or benefit as long as you live.

⁸You shall not abhor an Edomite, for such is your kin. You shall not abhor an Egyptian, for you were a stranger in that land. ⁹Children born to them may be admitted into the congregation of יהוה in the third generation.

¹⁰When you [men] go out as a troop against your enemies, be on your guard against anything untoward. ¹¹If anyone among you has been rendered impure by a nocturnal emission, he must leave the camp, and he must not reenter the camp. ¹²Toward evening he shall bathe in water, and at sundown he may reenter the camp. ¹³Further, there shall be an area for you outside the camp, where you may relieve yourself. ¹⁴With your gear you shall have a spike, and when you have squatted you shall dig a hole with it and cover up your excrement. ¹⁵Since your God יהוה moves about in your camp to protect you and to deliver your enemies to you, let your camp be holy; let [God] not find anything unseemly among you and turn away from you.

¹⁶You shall not turn over to the master a slave who seeks refuge with you from that master. ¹⁷Such individuals shall live with you in any place they may choose among the settlements in your midst, wherever they please; you must not illtreat them.

¹⁸No Israelite woman shall be a prostitute, nor shall any Israelite man be a prostitute. ¹⁹You shall not bring the fee of a whore or the pay of a dog into the house of your God יהוה in fulfillment of any vow, for both are abhorrent to your God יהוה.

²⁰You shall not deduct interest from loans to your fellow Israelites, whether in money or food or anything else that can be deducted as interest; ²¹but you may deduct interest from loans to foreigners. Do not deduct interest from loans to your fellow Israelites, so that your God יהוה may bless you in all your undertakings in the land that you are about to enter and possess.

²²When you make a vow to your God יהוה, do not put off fulfilling it, for your God יהוה will require it of you, and you will have incurred guilt; ²³whereas you incur no guilt if you refrain from vowing. ²⁴You must fulfill what has crossed your lips and perform what you have voluntarily vowed to your God יהוה, having made the promise with your own mouth.

²⁵When you enter a fellow [Israelite]'s vineyard, you may eat as many grapes as you want, until you are full, but you must not put any in your vessel. ²⁶When you enter a fellow [Israelite]'s field of standing grain, you may pluck ears with your hand; but you must not put a sickle to your neighbor's grain.

24 ¹A householder takes a woman [as his wife] and becomes her husband. She fails to please him because he finds something obnoxious about her, and he writes her a bill of divorcement, hands it to her, and sends her away from his house; ²she leaves his household and becomes [the wife] of another householder; ³then this latter householder rejects her, writes her a bill of divorcement, hands it to her, and sends her away from his house; or the householder dies who had last taken her as his wife. ⁴Then the first husband who divorced her shall not take her [into his household] to become his wife again, since she has been defiled—for that would be abhorrent to יהוה. You must not bring sin upon the land that your God יהוה is giving you as a heritage.

⁵When a man has newly taken a woman [into his household as his wife], he shall not go out with the army or be assigned to it for any purpose; he shall be exempt one year for the sake of his household, to give happiness to the woman he has taken.

⁶A handmill or an upper millstone shall not be taken in pawn, for that would be taking someone's life in pawn.

⁷If one is found to have kidnapped—and then enslaved or sold—a fellow Israelite, that kidnapper shall die; thus you will sweep out evil from your midst.

⁸In cases of a skin affection be most careful to do exactly as the levitical priests instruct you. Take care to do as I have commanded them. ⁹Remember what your God יהוה did to Miriam on the journey after you left Egypt.

¹⁰When you make a loan of any sort to your compatriot, you must not enter the house to seize the pledge. ¹¹You must remain outside, while the householder to whom you made the loan brings the pledge out to you. ¹²If the person is needy, you shall not go to sleep in that pledge; ¹³you must return the pledge at sundown, that its owner may sleep in the cloth and bless you; and it will be to your merit before your God יהוה.

¹⁴You shall not abuse a needy and destitute laborer, whether a fellow Israelite or a stranger in one of the communities of your land. ¹⁵You must pay out the wages due on the same day, before the sun sets, for the worker is needy and urgently depends on it; else a cry to יהוה will be issued against you and you will incur guilt.

¹⁶Parents shall not be put to death for children, nor children be put to death for parents: one shall be put to death only for one's own crime.

¹⁷You shall not subvert the rights of the stranger or the fatherless; you shall not take a widow's garment in pawn. ¹⁸Remember that you were a slave in Egypt and that your God יהוה redeemed you from there; therefore do I enjoin you to observe this commandment.

¹⁹When you reap the harvest in your field and overlook a sheaf in the field, do not turn back to get it; it shall go to the stranger, the fatherless, and the widow—in order that your God יהוה may bless you in all your undertakings.

²⁰When you beat down the fruit of your olive trees, do not go over them again; that shall go to the stranger, the fatherless, and the widow. ²¹When you gather the grapes of your vineyard, do not pick it over again; that shall go to the stranger, the fatherless, and the widow. ²²Always remember that you were a slave in the land of Egypt; therefore do I enjoin you to observe this commandment.

25 ¹When there is a dispute between parties and they go to law, and a decision is rendered declaring the one in the right and the other in the wrong—²if the guilty one is to be flogged, the magistrate shall have the person lie down and shall supervise the giving of lashes, by count, as warranted by the offense. ³The guilty one may be given up to forty lashes, but not more, lest being flogged further, to excess, your peer be degraded before your eyes.

⁴You shall not muzzle an ox while it is threshing.

⁵When brothers dwell together and one of them dies and leaves no offspring, the wife of the deceased shall not become another householder's [wife], outside the family. Her husband's brother shall unite with her: he shall take her as his wife and perform the levir's duty. ⁶The first child that she bears shall be accounted to the dead brother, that his name may not be blotted out in Israel. ⁷But if the [family] representative does not want to take his brother's widow [to wife], his brother's widow shall appear before the elders in the gate and declare, "My husband's brother refuses to establish a name in Israel for his brother; he will not perform the duty of a levir." ⁸The elders of his town shall then summon him and talk to him. If he insists, saying, "I do not want to take her," ⁹his brother's widow shall go up to him in the presence of the elders, pull the sandal off his foot, spit in his face, and make this declaration: Thus shall be done to the [family] representative who will not build up his brother's house! ¹⁰And he shall go in Israel by the name of "the family of the unsandaled one."

¹¹If two men get into a fight with each other, and the wife of one comes up to save her husband from his antagonist and puts out her hand and seizes him by his genitals, ¹²you shall cut off her hand; show no pity.

¹³You shall not have in your pouch alternate weights, larger and smaller. ¹⁴You shall not have in your house alternate measures, a larger and a smaller. ¹⁵You must have completely honest weights and completely honest measures, if you are to endure long on the soil that your God יהוה is giving you. ¹⁶For everyone who does those things, everyone who deals dishonestly, is abhorrent to your God יהוה.

¹⁷Remember what Amalek did to you on your journey, after you left Egypt—¹⁸how, undeterred by fear of God, he surprised you on the march, when you were famished and weary, and cut down all the stragglers in your rear. ¹⁹Therefore, when your God יהוה grants you safety from all your enemies around you, in the land that your God יהוה is giving you as a hereditary portion, you shall blot out the memory of Amalek from under heaven. Do not forget!

26 ¹When you enter the land that your God יהוה is giving you as a heritage, and you possess it and settle in it, ²you shall take some of every first fruit of the soil, which you harvest from the land that your God יהוה is giving you, put it in a basket and go to the place where your God יהוה will choose to establish the divine name. ³You shall go to the priest in charge at that time and say to him, "I acknowledge this day before your God יהוה that I have entered the land that יהוה swore to our fathers to assign us."

⁴The priest shall take the basket from your hand and set it down in front of the altar of your God יהוה.

⁵You shall then recite as follows before your God יהוה: "My father was a fugitive Aramean. He went down to Egypt with meager numbers and sojourned there; but there he became a great and very populous nation. ⁶The Egyptians dealt harshly with us and oppressed us; they imposed heavy labor upon us. ⁷We cried to יהוה, the God of our ancestors, and יהוה heard our plea and saw our plight, our misery, and our oppression. ⁸יהוה freed us from Egypt by a mighty hand, by an outstretched arm and awesome power, and by signs and portents, ⁹bringing us to this place and giving us this land, a land flowing with milk and honey. ¹⁰Wherefore I now bring the first fruits of the soil which You, יהוה, have given me."

You shall leave it before your God יהוה and bow low before your God יהוה. ¹¹And you shall enjoy, together with the [family of the] Levite and the stranger in your midst, all the bounty that your God יהוה has bestowed upon you and your household.

¹²When you have set aside in full the tenth part of your yield—in the third year, the year of the tithe—and have given it to the [family of the] Levite, the stranger, the fatherless, and the widow, that they may eat their fill in your settlements, ¹³you shall declare before your God יהוה: "I have cleared out the consecrated portion from the house; and I have given it to the [family of the] Levite, the stranger, the fatherless, and the widow, just as You commanded me; I have neither transgressed nor neglected any of Your commandments: ¹⁴I have not eaten of it while in mourning, I have not cleared out any of it while I was impure, and I have not deposited any of it with the dead. I have obeyed my God יהוה; I have done just as You commanded me. ¹⁵Look down from Your holy abode, from heaven, and bless Your people Israel and the soil You have given us, a land flowing with milk and honey, as You swore to our fathers."

¹⁶יהוה your God commands you this day to observe these laws and rules; observe them faithfully with all your heart and soul. ¹⁷You have affirmed this day that יהוה is your God, in whose ways you will walk, whose laws and commandments and rules you will observe, and whom you will obey. ¹⁸And יהוה has affirmed this day that you are, as promised, God's treasured people who shall observe all the divine commandments, ¹⁹and that [God] will set you, in fame and renown and glory, high above all the nations that [God] has made; and that you shall be, as promised, a holy people to your God יהוה.

27 ¹Moses and the elders of Israel charged the people, saying: Observe all the Instruction that I enjoin upon you this day. ²As soon as you have crossed the Jordan into the land that your God יהוה is giving you, you shall set up large stones. Coat them with plaster ³and inscribe upon them all the words of this Teaching. When you cross over to enter the land that your God יהוה is giving you, a land flowing with milk and honey, as יהוה, the God of your ancestors, promised you—⁴upon crossing the Jordan, you shall set up these stones, about which I charge you this day, on Mount Ebal, and coat them with plaster. ⁵There, too, you shall build an altar to your God יהוה, an altar of stones.

Do not wield an iron tool over them; ⁶you must build the altar of your God יהוה of unhewn stones. You shall offer on it burnt offerings to your God יהוה, ⁷and you shall sacrifice there offerings of wellbeing and eat them, rejoicing before your God יהוה. ⁸And on those stones you shall inscribe every word of this Teaching most distinctly.

⁹Moses and the levitical priests spoke to all Israel, saying: Silence! Hear, O Israel! Today you have become the people of your God יהוה: ¹⁰Heed your God יהוה and observe the divine commandments and laws, which I enjoin upon you this day.

¹¹Thereupon Moses charged the people, saying: ¹²After you have crossed the Jordan, the following shall stand on Mount Gerizim when the blessing for the people is spoken: Simeon, Levi, Judah, Issachar, Joseph, and Benjamin.

¹³And for the curse, the following shall stand on Mount Ebal: Reuben, Gad, Asher, Zebulun, Dan, and Naphtali.

¹⁴The Levites shall then proclaim in a loud voice to all the people of Israel:

[15]Cursed be anyone who makes a sculptured or molten image, abhorred by יהוה, a craftsman's handiwork, and sets it up in secret.—And all the people shall respond, Amen.

[16]Cursed be the one who insults father or mother.—And all the people shall say, Amen.

[17]Cursed be the one who moves a neighbor's landmark.—And all the people shall say, Amen.

[18]Cursed be the one who misdirects a blind person on the way.—And all the people shall say, Amen.

[19]Cursed be the one who subverts the rights of the stranger, the fatherless, and the widow.—And all the people shall say, Amen.

[20]Cursed be the [man] who lies with his father's wife, for he has removed his father's garment.—And all the people shall say, Amen.

[21]Cursed be the one who lies with any beast.—And all the people shall say, Amen.

[22]Cursed be the [man] who lies with his sister, whether daughter of his father or of his mother.—And all the people shall say, Amen.

[23]Cursed be the [man] who lies with his mother-in-law.—And all the people shall say, Amen.

[24]Cursed be the one who strikes down a fellow [Israelite] in secret.—And all the people shall say, Amen.

[25]Cursed be the one who accepts a bribe in the case of the murder of an innocent person.—And all the people shall say, Amen.

[26]Cursed be whoever will not uphold the terms of this Teaching and observe them.—And all the people shall say, Amen.

28 [1]Now, if you obey your God יהוה, to observe faithfully all the divine commandments which I enjoin upon you this day, your God יהוה will set you high above all the nations of the earth. [2]All these blessings shall come upon you and take effect, if you will but heed the word of your God יהוה:

[3]Blessed shall you be in the city and blessed shall you be in the country.

[4]Blessed shall be the issue of your womb, the produce of your soil, and the offspring of your cattle, the calving of your herd and the lambing of your flock.

[5]Blessed shall be your basket and your kneading bowl.

[6]Blessed shall you be in your comings and blessed shall you be in your goings.

[7]יהוה will put to rout before [your army] the enemies who attack you; they will march out against you by a single road, but flee from you by many roads. [8]יהוה will ordain blessings for you upon your barns and upon all your undertakings: you will be blessed in the land that your God יהוה is giving you. [9]יהוה will establish you as God's holy people, as was sworn to you, if you keep the commandments of your God יהוה and walk in God's ways. [10]And all the peoples of the earth shall see that יהוה's name is proclaimed over you, and they shall stand in fear of you. [11]יהוה will give you abounding prosperity in the issue of your womb, the offspring of your cattle, and the produce of your soil in the land that יהוה swore to your fathers to assign to you. [12]יהוה will open for you that bounteous store, the heavens, to provide rain for your land in season and to bless all your undertakings. You will be creditor to many nations, but debtor to none.

[13]יהוה will make you the head, not the tail; you will always be at the top and never at the bottom—if only you obey and faithfully observe the commandments of your God יהוה that I enjoin upon you this day, [14]and do not deviate to the right or to the left from any of the commandments that I enjoin upon you this day and turn to the worship of other gods.

[15]But if you do not obey your God יהוה to observe faithfully all the commandments and laws which I enjoin upon you this day, all these curses shall come upon you and take effect:

[16]Cursed shall you be in the city and cursed shall you be in the country.

[17]Cursed shall be your basket and your kneading bowl.

[18]Cursed shall be the issue of your womb and the produce of your soil, the calving of your herd and the lambing of your flock.

[19]Cursed shall you be in your comings and cursed shall you be in your goings.

[20]יהוה will let loose against you calamity, panic, and frustration in all the enterprises you undertake, so that you shall soon be utterly wiped out because of your evildoing in forsaking Me. [21]יהוה will make pestilence cling to you, until putting an end to you in the land that you are entering to possess. [22]יהוה will strike you with consumption, fever, and inflammation, with scorching heat and drought, with blight and mildew; they shall hound you until you perish. [23]The skies above your head shall be copper and the earth under you iron. [24]יהוה will make the rain of your land dust, and sand shall drop on you from the sky, until you are wiped out. [25]יהוה will put you to rout before your enemies; you shall march out against them by a single road, but flee from them by many roads; and you shall become a horror to all the kingdoms of the earth. [26]Your carcasses shall become food for all the birds of the sky and all the beasts of the earth, with none to frighten them off. [27]יהוה will strike you with the Egyptian inflammation, with hemorrhoids, boil-scars, and itch, from which you shall never recover.

[28]יהוה will strike you with madness, blindness, and dismay. [29]You shall grope at noon as the blind grope in the dark; you shall not prosper in your ventures, but shall be constantly abused and robbed, with none to give help.

[30]If you [a man] pay the bride-price for a wife, another man shall enjoy her. If you build a house, you shall not live in it. If you plant a vineyard, you shall not harvest it. [31]Your ox shall be slaughtered before your eyes, but you shall not eat of it; your ass shall be seized in front of you, and it shall not be returned to you; your flock shall be delivered to your enemies, with none to help you. [32]Your sons and daughters shall be delivered to another people, while you look on; and your eyes shall strain for them constantly, but you shall be helpless. [33]A people you do not know shall eat up the produce of your soil and all your gains; you shall be abused and downtrodden continually, [34]until you are driven mad by what your eyes behold. [35]יהוה will afflict you at the knees and thighs with a severe inflammation, from which you shall never recover—from the sole of your foot to the crown of your head.

[36]יהוה will drive you, and the king you have set over you, to a nation unknown to you or your ancestors, where you shall serve other gods, of wood and stone. [37]You shall be a consternation, a proverb, and a byword among all the peoples to which יהוה will drive you.

[38]Though you take much seed out to the field, you shall gather in little, for the locust shall consume it. [39]Though you plant vineyards and till them, you shall have no wine to drink or store, for the worm shall devour them. [40]Though you have olive trees throughout your territory, you shall have no oil for anointment, for your olives shall drop off. [41]Though you beget sons and daughters, they shall not remain with you, for they shall go into captivity. [42]The cricket shall take over all the trees and produce of your land.

[43]The strangers in your midst shall rise above you higher and higher, while you sink lower and lower: [44]they shall be

your creditors, but you shall not be theirs; they shall be the head and you the tail.

⁴⁵All these curses shall befall you; they shall pursue you an overtake you, until you are wiped out, because you did not heed your God יהוה and keep the commandments and laws that were enjoined upon you. ⁴⁶They shall serve as signs and proofs against you and your offspring for all time. ⁴⁷Because you would not serve your God יהוה in joy and gladness over the abundance of everything, ⁴⁸you shall have to serve—in hunger and thirst, naked and lacking everything—the enemies whom יהוה will let loose against you. [God] will put an iron yoke upon your neck until you are wiped out.

⁴⁹יהוה will bring a nation against you from afar, from the end of the earth, which will swoop down like the eagle—a nation whose language you do not understand, ⁵⁰a ruthless nation, that will show the influential no regard and the vulnerable no mercy. ⁵¹It shall devour the offspring of your cattle and the produce of your soil, until you have been wiped out, leaving you nothing of new grain, wine, or oil, of the calving of your herds and the lambing of your flocks, until it has brought you to ruin. ⁵²It shall shut you up in all your towns throughout your land until every mighty, towering wall in which you trust has come down. And when you are shut up in all your towns throughout your land that your God יהוה has assigned to you, ⁵³you shall eat your own issue, the flesh of your sons and daughters that your God יהוה has assigned to you, because of the desperate straits to which your enemy shall reduce you. ⁵⁴The householder who is most tender and fastidious among you shall be too mean to his brother and the wife of his bosom and the children he has spared ⁵⁵to share with any of them the flesh of the children that he eats, because he has nothing else left as a result of the desperate straits to which your enemy shall reduce you in all your towns. ⁵⁶And she who is most tender and dainty among you, so tender and dainty that she would never venture to set a foot on the ground, shall begrudge the husband of her bosom, and her son and her daughter, ⁵⁷the afterbirth that issues from between her legs and the babies she bears; she shall eat them secretly, because of utter want, in the desperate straits to which your enemy shall reduce you in your towns.

⁵⁸If you fail to observe faithfully all the terms of this Teaching that are written in this book, to reverence this honored and awesome Name, your God יהוה, ⁵⁹יהוה will inflict extraordinary plagues upon you and your offspring, strange and lasting plagues, malignant and chronic diseases—⁶⁰bringing back upon you all the sicknesses of Egypt that you dreaded so, and they shall cling to you. ⁶¹Moreover, יהוה will bring upon you all the other diseases and plagues that are not mentioned in this book of Teaching, until you are wiped out. ⁶²You shall be left a scant few, after having been as numerous as the stars in the skies, because you did not heed the command of your God יהוה. ⁶³And as יהוה once delighted in making you prosperous and many, so will יהוה now delight in causing you to perish and in wiping you out; you shall be torn from the land that you are about to enter and possess. ⁶⁴יהוה will scatter you among all the peoples from one end of the earth to the other, and there you shall serve other gods, wood and stone, whom neither you nor your ancestors have experienced. ⁶⁵Yet even among those nations you shall find no peace, nor shall your foot find a place to rest. יהוה will give you there an anguished heart and eyes that pine and a despondent spirit. ⁶⁶The life you face shall be precarious; you shall be in terror, night and day, with no assurance of survival. ⁶⁷In the morning you shall say, "If only it were evening!" and in the evening you shall say, "If only it were morning!"—because of what your heart shall dread and your eyes shall see. ⁶⁸יהוה will send you back to Egypt in galleys, by a route which I told you you should

not see again. There you shall offer yourselves for sale to your enemies as male and female slaves, but none will buy.

⁶⁹These are the terms of the covenant which יהוה commanded Moses to conclude with the Israelites in the land of Moab, in addition to the covenant which was made with them at Horeb.

29 ¹Moses summoned all Israel and said to them: You have seen all that יהוה did before your very eyes in the land of Egypt, to Pharaoh and to all his courtiers and to his whole country: ²the wondrous feats that you saw with your own eyes, those prodigious signs and marvels. ³Yet to this day יהוה has not given you a mind to understand or eyes to see or ears to hear.

⁴I led you through the wilderness forty years; the clothes on your back did not wear out, nor did the sandals on your feet; ⁵you had no bread to eat and no wine or other intoxicant to drink—that you might know that I יהוה am your God. ⁶When you reached this place, King Sihon of Heshbon and King Og of Bashan came out to engage us in battle, but we defeated them. ⁷We took their land and gave it to the Reubenites, the Gadites, and the half-tribe of Manasseh as their heritage. ⁸Therefore observe faithfully all the terms of this covenant, that you may succeed in all that you undertake.

⁹You stand this day, all of you, before your God יהוה—you tribal heads, you elders, and you officials, all the men of Israel, ¹⁰you children, you women, even the stranger within your camp, from woodchopper to water drawer—¹¹to enter into the covenant of your God יהוה, which your God יהוה is concluding with you this day, with its sanctions; ¹²in order to establish you this day as God's people and in order to be your God, as promised you and as sworn to your fathers Abraham, Isaac, and Jacob. ¹³I make this covenant, with its sanctions, not with you alone, ¹⁴but both with those who are standing here with us this day before our God יהוה and with those who are not with us here this day.

¹⁵Well you know that we dwelt in the land of Egypt and that we passed through the midst of various other nations through which you passed; ¹⁶and you have seen the detestable things and the fetishes of wood and stone, silver and gold, that they keep. ¹⁷Perchance there is among you some man or woman, or some clan or tribe, whose heart is even now turning away from our God יהוה to go and worship the gods of those nations—perchance there is among you a stock sprouting poison weed and wormwood. ¹⁸When hearing the words of these sanctions, such a one may imagine a special immunity, thinking, "I shall be safe, though I follow my own willful heart"—to the utter ruin of moist and dry alike. ¹⁹יהוה will never forgive such individuals. Rather, יהוה's anger and passion will rage against them, till every sanction recorded in this book comes down upon them, and יהוה blots out their name from under heaven.

²⁰[As for such a clan or tribe,] יהוה will single it out from all the tribes of Israel for misfortune, in accordance with all the sanctions of the covenant recorded in this book of Teaching. ²¹And later generations will ask—the children who succeed you, and foreigners who come from distant lands and see the plagues and diseases that יהוה has inflicted upon that land, ²²all its soil devastated by sulfur and salt, beyond sowing and producing, no grass growing in it, just like the upheaval of Sodom and Gomorrah, Admah and Zeboiim, which יהוה overthrew in fierce anger—²³all nations will ask, "Why did יהוה do thus to this land? Wherefore that awful wrath?" ²⁴They will be told, "Because they forsook the covenant that יהוה, God of their ancestors, made with them upon freeing them from the land of Egypt; ²⁵they turned to the service

of other gods and worshiped them, gods whom they had not experienced and whom [God] had not allotted to them. 26So יהוה was incensed at that land and brought upon it all the curses recorded in this book. 27יהוה uprooted them from their soil in anger, fury, and great wrath, and cast them into another land, as is still the case."

28Concealed acts concern our God יהוה; but with overt acts, it is for us and our children ever to apply all the provisions of this Teaching.

30

1When all these things befall you—the blessing and the curse that I have set before you—and you take them to heart amidst the various nations to which your God יהוה has banished you, 2and you return to your God יהוה, and you and your children heed God's command with all your heart and soul, just as I enjoin upon you this day, 3then your God יהוה will restore your fortunes and take you back in love. [God] will bring you together again from all the peoples where your God יהוה has scattered you. 4Even if your outcasts are at the ends of the world, from there your God יהוה will gather you, from there [God] will fetch you. 5And your God יהוה will bring you to the land that your fathers possessed, and you shall possess it; and [God] will make you more prosperous and more numerous than your ancestors.

6Then your God יהוה will open up your heart and the hearts of your offspring—to love your God יהוה with all your heart and soul, in order that you may live. 7יהוה your God will inflict all those curses upon the enemies and foes who persecuted you. 8You, however, will again heed יהוה and obey all the divine commandments that I enjoin upon you this day. 9And your God יהוה will grant you abounding prosperity in all your undertakings, in the issue of your womb, the offspring of your cattle, and the produce of your soil. For יהוה will again delight in your wellbeing as in that of your ancestors, 10since you will be heeding your God יהוה and keeping the divine commandments and laws that are recorded in this book of the Teaching—once you return to your God יהוה with all your heart and soul.

11Surely, this Instruction which I enjoin upon you this day is not too baffling for you, nor is it beyond reach. 12It is not in the heavens, that you should say, "Who among us can go up to the heavens and get it for us and impart it to us, that we may observe it?" 13Neither is it beyond the sea, that you should say, "Who among us can cross to the other side of the sea and get it for us and impart it to us, that we may observe it?" 14No, the thing is very close to you, in your mouth and in your heart, to observe it.

15See, I set before you this day life and prosperity, death and adversity. 16For I command you this day, to love your God יהוה, to walk in God's ways, and to keep God's commandments, God's laws, and God's rules, that you may thrive and increase, and that your God יהוה may bless you in the land that you are about to enter and possess. 17But if your heart turns away and you give no heed, and are lured into the worship and service of other gods, 18I declare to you this day that you shall certainly perish; you shall not long endure on the soil that you are crossing the Jordan to enter and possess. 19I call heaven and earth to witness against you this day: I have put before you life and death, blessing and curse. Choose life—if you and your offspring would live— 20by loving your God יהוה, heeding God's commands, and holding fast to [God]. For thereby you shall have life and shall long endure upon the soil that יהוה swore to your fathers Abraham, Isaac, and Jacob, to give to them.

31

1Moses went and spoke these things to all Israel. 2He said to them:

I am now one hundred and twenty years old, I can no longer be active. Moreover, יהוה has said to me, "You shall not go across yonder Jordan." 3It is indeed your God יהוה who will cross over before you, and who will wipe out those nations from your path; and you shall dispossess them.—Joshua is the one who shall cross before you, as יהוה has spoken.— 4יהוה will do to them as was done to Sihon and Og, kings of the Amorites, and to their countries, when [God] wiped them out. 5יהוה will deliver them up to you, and you shall deal with them in full accordance with the Instruction that I have enjoined upon you. 6Be strong and resolute, be not in fear or in dread of them; for it is indeed your God יהוה who marches with you: [God] will not fail you or forsake you.

7Then Moses called Joshua and said to him in the sight of all Israel: "Be strong and resolute, for it is you who shall go with this people into the land that יהוה swore to their fathers to give them, and it is you who shall apportion it to them. 8And it is indeed יהוה who will go before you. [God] will be with you—and will not fail you or forsake you. Fear not and be not dismayed!"

9Moses wrote down this Teaching and gave it to the priests, sons of Levi, who carried the Ark of יהוה's Covenant, and to all the elders of Israel.

10And Moses instructed them as follows: Every seventh year, the year set for remission, at the Feast of Booths, 11when all Israel comes to appear before your God יהוה in the place that [God] will choose, you shall read this Teaching aloud in the presence of all Israel. 12Gather the people—men, women, children, and the strangers in your communities—that they may hear and so learn to revere your God יהוה and to observe faithfully every word of this Teaching. 13Their children, too, who have not had the experience, shall hear and learn to revere your God יהוה as long as they live in the land that you are about to cross the Jordan to possess.

14יהוה said to Moses: The time is drawing near for you to die. Call Joshua and present yourselves in the Tent of Meeting, that I may instruct him. Moses and Joshua went and presented themselves in the Tent of Meeting. 15יהוה appeared in the Tent, in a pillar of cloud, the pillar of cloud having come to rest at the entrance of the tent.

16יהוה said to Moses: You are soon to lie with your ancestors. This people will thereupon go astray after the alien gods in their midst, in the land that they are about to enter; they will forsake Me and break My covenant that I made with them. 17Then My anger will flare up against them, and I will abandon them and hide My countenance from them. They shall be ready prey; and many evils and troubles shall befall them. And they shall say on that day, "Surely it is because our God is not in our midst that these evils have befallen us." 18Yet I will keep My countenance hidden on that day, because of all the evil they have done in turning to other gods. 19Therefore, write down this poem and teach it to the people of Israel; put it in their mouths, in order that this poem may be My witness against the people of Israel. 20When I bring them into the land flowing with milk and honey that I promised on oath to their fathers, and they eat their fill and grow fat and turn to other gods and serve them, spurning Me and breaking My covenant, 21and the many evils and troubles befall them—then this poem shall confront them as a witness, since it will never be lost from the mouth of their offspring. For I know what plans they are devising even now, before I bring them into the land that I promised on oath.

22That day, Moses wrote down this poem and taught it to the Israelites.

23And [God] charged Joshua son of Nun: "Be strong and resolute: for you shall bring the Israelites into the land that I promised them on oath, and I will be with you."

²⁴When Moses had put down in writing the words of this Teaching to the very end, ²⁵Moses charged the Levites who carried the Ark of the Covenant of יהוה, saying: ²⁶Take this book of Teaching and place it beside the Ark of the Covenant of your God יהוה, and let it remain there as a witness against you. ²⁷Well I know how defiant and stiff-necked you are: even now, while I am still alive in your midst, you have been defiant toward יהוה; how much more, then, when I am dead! ²⁸Gather to me all the elders of your tribes and your officials, that I may speak all these words to them and that I may call heaven and earth to witness against them. ²⁹For I know that, when I am dead, you will act wickedly and turn away from the path that I enjoined upon you, and that in time to come misfortune will befall you for having done evil in the sight of יהוה, whom you vexed by your deeds.

³⁰Then Moses recited the words of the following poem to the very end, in the hearing of the whole congregation of Israel.

32 ¹Give ear, O heavens, let me speak;
Let the earth hear the words I utter!
² May my discourse come down as the rain,
My speech distill as the dew,
Like showers on young growth,
Like droplets on the grass.
³ For the name of יהוה I proclaim;
Give glory to our God!
⁴ The Rock!—whose deeds are perfect,
Yea, all God's ways are just;
A faithful God, never false,
True and upright indeed.
⁵ Unworthy children—
That crooked, perverse generation—
Their baseness has played God false.
⁶ Do you thus requite יהוה,
O dull and witless people?
Is not this the Father who created you—
Fashioned you and made you endure!
⁷ Remember the days of old,
Consider the years of ages past;
Ask your parent, who will inform you,
Your elders, who will tell you:
⁸ When the Most High gave nations their homes
And set the divisions of humanity,
[God] fixed the boundaries of peoples
In relation to Israel's numbers.
⁹ For יהוה's portion is this people;
Jacob, God's own allotment.
¹⁰ [God] found them in a desert region,
In an empty howling waste.
[God] engirded them, watched over them,
Guarded them as the pupil of God's eye.
¹¹ Like an eagle who rouses its nestlings,
Gliding down to its young,
So did [God] spread wings and take them,
Bear them along on pinions;
¹² יהוה alone did guide them,
No alien god alongside.
¹³ [God] set them atop the highlands,
To feast on the yield of the earth;
Nursing them with honey from the crag,
And oil from the flinty rock,
¹⁴ Curd of kine and milk of flocks;
With the best of lambs,
And rams of Bashan, and he-goats;
With the very finest wheat—
And foaming grape-blood was your drink.

¹⁵ So Jeshurun grew fat and kicked—
You grew fat and gross and coarse—
They forsook the God who made them
And spurned the Rock of their support.
¹⁶ They incensed [God] with alien things,
Vexed [God] with abominations.
¹⁷ They sacrificed to demons, no-gods,
Gods they had never known,
New ones, who came but lately,
Who stirred not your forebears' fears.
¹⁸ You neglected the Rock who begot you,
Forgot the God who labored to bring you forth.
¹⁹ יהוה saw and was vexed
And spurned these sons and daughters.
²⁰ [God] said: I will hide My countenance from them,
And see how they fare in the end.
For they are a treacherous breed,
Children with no loyalty in them.
²¹ They incensed Me with no-gods,
Vexed Me with their futilities;
I'll incense them with a no-folk,
Vex them with a nation of fools.
²² For a fire has flared in My wrath
And burned to the bottom of Sheol,
Has consumed the earth and its increase,
Eaten down to the base of the hills.
²³ I will sweep misfortunes on them,
Use up My arrows on them:
²⁴ Wasting famine, ravaging plague,
Deadly pestilence, and fanged beasts
Will I let loose against them,
With venomous creepers in dust.
²⁵ The sword shall deal death without,
As shall the terror within,
To youth and maiden alike,
The suckling as well as the aged.
²⁶ I might have reduced them to naught,
Made their memory cease among humankind,
²⁷ But for fear of the taunts of the foe,
Their enemies who might misjudge
And say, "Our own hand has prevailed;
None of this was wrought by יהוה!"
²⁸ For they are a folk void of sense,
Lacking in all discernment.
²⁹ Were they wise, they would think upon this,
Gain insight into their future:
³⁰ "How could one have routed a thousand,
Or two put ten thousand to flight,
Unless their Rock had sold them,
יהוה had given them up?"
³¹ For their rock is not like our Rock,
In our enemies' own estimation.
³² Ah! The vine for them is from Sodom,
From the vineyards of Gomorrah;
The grapes for them are poison,
A bitter growth their clusters.
³³ Their wine is the venom of asps,
The pitiless poison of vipers.
³⁴ Lo, I have it all put away,
Sealed up in My storehouses,
³⁵ To be My vengeance and recompense,
At the time that their foot falters.
Yea, their day of disaster is near,
And destiny rushes upon them.
³⁶ For יהוה will vindicate God's people
And take revenge for God's servants,
Upon seeing that their might is gone,

And neither bond nor free is left.

37 [God] will say: Where are their gods,
The rock in whom they sought refuge,

38 Who ate the fat of their offerings
And drank their libation wine?
Let them rise up to your help,
And let them be a shield unto you!

39 See, then, that I, I am the One;
There is no god beside Me.
I deal death and give life;
I wounded and I will heal:
None can deliver from My hand.

40 Lo, I raise My hand to heaven
And say: As I live forever,

41 When I whet My flashing blade
And My hand lays hold on judgment,
Vengeance will I wreak on My foes,
Will I deal to those who reject Me.

42 I will make My arrows drunk with blood—
As My sword devours flesh—
Blood of the slain and the captive
From the longhaired enemy chiefs.

43 O nations, acclaim God's people!
For He'll avenge the blood of His servants,
Wreak vengeance on His foes,
And cleanse His people's land.

44Moses came, together with Hosea son of Nun, and recited all the words of this poem in the hearing of the people.

45And when Moses finished reciting all these words to all Israel, 46he said to them: Take to heart all the words with which I have warned you this day. Enjoin them upon your children, that they may observe faithfully all the terms of this Teaching. 47For this is not a trifling thing for you: it is your very life; through it you shall long endure on the land that you are to possess upon crossing the Jordan.

48That very day יהוה spoke to Moses: 49Ascend these heights of Abarim to Mount Nebo, which is in the land of Moab facing Jericho, and view the land of Canaan, which I am giving the Israelites as their holding. 50You shall die on the mountain that you are about to ascend, and shall be gathered to your kin, as your brother Aaron died on Mount Hor and was gathered to his kin; 51for you both broke faith with Me among the Israelite people, at the waters of Meribath-kadesh in the wilderness of Zin, by failing to uphold My sanctity among the Israelite people. 52You may view the land from a distance, but you shall not enter it—the land that I am giving to the Israelite people.

33 1This is the blessing with which Moses, God's envoy, bade the Israelites farewell before he died. 2He said:

יהוה came from Sinai,
And shone upon them from Seir;
[God] appeared from Mount Paran,
And approached from Ribeboth-kodesh,
Lightning flashing at them from [God's] right.

3 Lover, indeed, of the people,
Their hallowed are all in Your hand.
They followed in Your steps,
Accepting Your pronouncements,

4 When Moses charged us with the Teaching
As the heritage of the congregation of Jacob.

5 Then [God] became King in Jeshurun,
When the heads of the people assembled,
The tribes of Israel together.

6 May Reuben live and not die,

Though few be his numbers.

7 And this he said of Judah:
Hear, יהוה, the voice of Judah
And restore him to his people.
Though his own hands strive for him,
Help him against his foes.

8 And of Levi he said:
Let Your Thummim and Urim
Be with Your faithful one,
Whom You tested at Massah,
Challenged at the waters of Meribah;

9 Who said of his father and mother,
"I consider them not."
His brothers he disregarded,
Ignored his own children.
Your precepts alone they observed,
And kept Your covenant.

10 They shall teach Your laws to Jacob
And Your instructions to Israel.
They shall offer You incense to savor
And whole-offerings on Your altar.

11 Bless, יהוה, his substance,
And favor his undertakings.
Smite the loins of his foes;
Let his enemies rise no more.

12 Of Benjamin he said:
Beloved of יהוה,
He rests securely beside [God],
Who protects him always,
As he rests between God's shoulders.

13 And of Joseph he said:
Blessed of יהוה be his land
With the bounty of dew from heaven,
And of the deep that couches below;

14 With the bounteous yield of the sun,
And the bounteous crop of the moons;

15 With the best from the ancient mountains,
And the bounty of hills immemorial;

16 With the bounty of earth and its fullness,
And the favor of the Presence in the Bush.
May these rest on the head of Joseph,
On the crown of the elect of his brothers.

17 Like a firstling bull in his majesty,
He has horns like the horns of the wildox;
With them he gores the peoples,
The ends of the earth one and all.
These are the myriads of Ephraim,
Those are the thousands of Manasseh.

18 And of Zebulun he said:
Rejoice, O Zebulun, on your journeys,
And Issachar, in your tents.

19 They invite their kin to the mountain,
Where they offer sacrifices of success.
For they draw from the riches of the sea
And the hidden hoards of the sand.

20 And of Gad he said:
Blessed be the One who enlarges Gad!
Poised is he like a lion
To tear off arm and scalp.

21 He chose for himself the best,
For there is the portion of the revered chieftain,
Where the heads of the people come.
He executed יהוה's judgments
And God's decisions for Israel.

22 And of Dan he said:
Dan is a lion's whelp

That leaps forth from Bashan.

23 And of Naphtali he said:
O Naphtali, sated with favor
And full of יהוה's blessing,
Take possession on the west and south.

24 And of Asher he said:
Most blessed of sons be Asher;
May he be the favorite of his brothers,
May he dip his foot in oil.

25 May your doorbolts be iron and copper,
And your security last all your days.

26 O Jeshurun, there is none like God,
Riding through the heavens to help you,
Through the skies in His majesty.

27 The ancient God is a refuge,
A support are the arms everlasting.
He drove out the enemy before you
By His command: Destroy!

28 Thus Israel dwells in safety,
Untroubled is Jacob's abode,
In a land of grain and wine,
Under heavens dripping dew.

29 O happy Israel! Who is like you,
A people delivered by יהוה,
Your protecting Shield, your Sword triumphant!
Your enemies shall come cringing before you,
And you shall tread on their backs.

34 [1]Moses went up from the steppes of Moab to Mount Nebo, to the summit of Pisgah, opposite Jericho, and יהוה showed him the whole land: Gilead as far as Dan; [2]all Naphtali; the land of Ephraim and Manasseh; the whole land of Judah as far as the Western Sea; [3]the Negeb; and the Plain—the Valley of Jericho, the city of palm trees—as far as Zoar. [4]And יהוה said to him, "This is the land of which I swore to Abraham, Isaac, and Jacob, 'I will assign it to your offspring.' I have let you see it with your own eyes, but you shall not cross there."

[5]So Moses the servant of יהוה died there, in the land of Moab, at the command of יהוה. [6][God] buried him in the valley in the land of Moab, near Bethpeor; and no one knows his burial place to this day. [7]Moses was a hundred and twenty years old when he died; his eyes were undimmed and his vigor unabated. [8]And the Israelites bewailed Moses in the steppes of Moab for thirty days.

The period of wailing and mourning for Moses came to an end. [9]Now Joshua son of Nun was filled with the spirit of wisdom because Moses had laid his hands upon him; and the Israelites heeded him, doing as יהוה had commanded Moses.

[10]Never again did there arise in Israel a prophet like Moses—whom יהוה singled out, face to face, [11]for the various signs and portents that יהוה sent him to display in the land of Egypt, against Pharaoh and all his courtiers and his whole country, [12]and for all the great might and awesome power that Moses displayed before all Israel.

book two

GOSPEL

The Zoroastrian Magi (Shown in Caravan En Route to Bethlehem)

preface to the gospel

Henry L. Carrigan Jr.

The Flight into Egypt in a Sixteenth-Century Woodcut

EVERY SUNDAY, MILLIONS OF CHRISTIANS around the world—gathered in tiny house churches, rural white clapboard churches, glorious cathedrals and huge megachurches—raise their voices in an age-old plea captured so eloquently in William H. Parker's 1885 hymn, "Tell Me the Stories of Jesus." Parker's hymn, written for his Sunday School students in England, lyrically recalls at least three of the major events that define the life and work of Jesus: his entrance into Jerusalem (on what is now observed as Palm Sunday), his time alone in the last hours of his life in the garden of Gethsemane and his crucifixion. More important, though, Parker's hymn eloquently reveals that the crazy quilt of Christianity is woven from the cloth of storytelling.

Much like the famous hollow-eyed sailor of Samuel Taylor Coleridge's poem, "The Rime of the Ancient Mariner," who tells a compelling story that so transfixes his listener that the hearer is glued to every word of the sailor's story, Jesus captures his followers' attention with stories. Being an observant Jew, Jesus naturally draws upon the stories from the Torah and prophets with which he is intimately familiar, retelling these stories in light of his own understanding of what it means to be a Jew. Although Jesus draws the details of his stories from the everyday lives of his hearers, he often ends his tales with an unexpected twist, surprising (and sometimes frightening) his listeners.

During his life, Jesus was given many titles—prophet, king, messiah, healer—but above all, Jesus was a great storyteller. Crowds gathered around him not only because they had heard stories about him and his work. They came to hear him tell the cracking good tale of the man set upon by thieves on the road from Jericho to Jerusalem and of the man's unlikely rescue by a non-Jewish "neighbor," the Samaritan,[1] or the fast-paced family drama of the younger son who, after wasting his inheritance, followed by a few years of living without much to eat, decides to return home in hope of a warm meal and a cozy bed.[2] Like any good storyteller, Jesus has a million stories to tell.

Indeed, Jesus was one among hundreds of peripatetic bards wandering the rural roads and the dusty paths outside of Jerusalem. In the streets of Jerusalem, sophists—wisecracking philosophers always ready to tell young men a story about the nature of wisdom in order to make a fast buck—plied their trade on street corners. In Jerusalem, Antioch and other larger cities in Palestine, the plays of Aristophanes, Euripides and Sophocles provided entertainment for the masses, while Homer's epic tales of war and conquest, quest and discovery, blindness and recognition were taught to schoolchildren, many of whom learned how to write by imitating (rewriting) these stories. Jesus enters a culture already familiar with the power of storytelling and encounters listeners ready to hang on his every word about a new way of life. But what is it that compels his hearers to listen to Jesus and then to follow him around rather than embracing the other stories in the air at the time? Just as important, how is it that these stories have the power to entrance and transform millions of people still today?

As far as we know, Jesus himself never recorded any of his stories in written form. Jesus' stories were unique because they craftily presented a new way of thinking about the world. All of Jesus' hearers, most of whom were Jews, found themselves subject to the Roman occupation of their territory. In such a situation, Jews—whom the Romans treated as colonial subjects and second-class citizens, even in the Jews' holy city of Jerusalem—had two radically opposed options: assimilate or rebel. In the first case, many Jews took offices in the Roman Empire—such as tax collecting—that provided them some protection and some buffer from the cruelties and the harsh demands of the Roman government. Some religious leaders, notably the Sadducees, worked closely with the Roman government as a strategy to protect their own interests, not to mention their own lives. Other Jews openly, and not so openly, rebelled against the Romans. The Zealots participated in random assassinations of Roman officials, and their final war against the Romans, around 70 CE in a fortress outside of Jerusalem, ended in wholesale defeat. Other Jewish groups sought to preserve the traditions of their religions in various ways, by interpreting the Torah in light of the new situation (Pharisees), by moving away from Jerusalem and establishing a distinct community in which traditions were preserved (Essenes) or by living in and around Jerusalem and reinterpreting the Tanakh in an apocalyptic vein (the followers of Jesus).

Living amid the harsh realities of the Roman Empire—being required by law to worship the emperor instead of God and facing torture, and sometimes death, for not complying—many Jews started looking forward to a day when the Golden Age of David's kingdom would come again (as promised in the Hebrew Scriptures[3]), an age ushered in by a king like David (and in David's lineage) who would oust the hated Roman Empire. Thus, when Jesus showed up telling riveting stories about division and reconciliation, or stories in which hated religious and political leaders got their just desserts, people began coming out in droves to listen to him weave his colorful tales. His listeners also began to take his stories seriously, and some of them began following him on a regular basis. Many of them quit their regular jobs quite dramatically—retelling Jesus' stories to others and enacting his advice. Eventually, some of his followers collected many of the stories in written documents that started to circulate among gatherings of his followers, around forty years after Jesus' death.

As David Bruce points out so well in his introduction to the Gospel, the Gospels are unique documents among the literature of the ancient East. On the one hand, they each purport to tell the story of Jesus—that is, to provide a biography of Jesus—and each is arranged in broadly chronological fashion, from birth to death (though not every Gospel contains a birth narrative). On the other hand, each text opens with a phrase that appears only here among the many savior stories of the ancient world: "This is the good news[4] of Jesus Christ." The final contributing editors of the canonical Gospels, perhaps none of whom were with Jesus when he was alive, shape their texts to particular audiences living in particular places that have particular concerns in mind. Each of these writers thus picks and chooses from the stories that Jesus told in order to suit the writer's desire to tell a good story and to make an important point. In most theories of Gospel composition Matthew and Luke share a common source of oral material, Q, as well as the written account of Mark, while the other Gospel, John, builds its narrative on a "Signs Gospel," another oral source. It is probable that other written Gospels were also circulating both before and after the canonical Gospels, or even at the same time.

These Gospels often filled in the missing information from the canonical texts; for example, in the "Infancy Narrative of Thomas," Jesus is a precocious child who fashions doves from clay and commands them to come to life and fly away merely by clapping his hands. Since the canonical stories contain no records of Jesus as a child, this narrative attempts to demonstrate with its stories that even as a child Jesus could perform miracles. Brian Brown will show how Muslims receive this particular story as retold in the Quran as a verification of messiahship, since God revealed its truth to Muhammad in divine intonation. For various reasons, the early Christian community did not consider such additional Gospels as authoritative for faith and practice. By the fourth century in the Common Era, Matthew, Mark, Luke and John were canonized by the church councils and regarded thereafter as setting the rule (*kanon*) for Christian faith and practice.

David Bruce's introduction to the Gospel sets the Gospels in their larger historical and literary context, and he provides a valuable overview of the role the Gospels play in the larger set of texts called the New Testament. He raises important questions with which Christian communities grapple even today. How accurately do these Gospels portray the words and actions of Jesus? Are the Gospels reliable historical documents? Which are the words of Jesus, and which are the words of the early Church, or the words of the writers of the Gospels? Do these Gospel texts reveal the whole truth about Jesus (a question germane to the conjectures of Brian Brown)? In the case of Matthew and Luke, do we have a group of writers putting together these documents? Since no extant copies of the original texts exist, how much can we trust the texts that we have? Even more important, because most Christians do not read the languages in which the Gospels were originally written and must depend on translations of the Greek texts, the question remains: How reliable are these translations?

While these are significant questions that Christians must continue to ask as they grapple with the New Testament in general and the Gospels in particular, the Gospels remain as compelling as they do simply because they are powerful stories of the life and work of one man and the differences that he made in his community and the world. Because they rang true then as they do today, they became recognized as the core of the Scriptures and, for Christians, normative as the Word of God. In the other texts gathered in this collection—the Torah and the Quran—are other stories transmitted by believers that eventually passed down through generations as central stories important for guiding the faith and practice of communities. Brian Brown's work, in this volume and elsewhere, provides the background for understanding the way that story, as a literary genre, and key stories in particular link the great traditions of Judaism, Christianity and Islam, forming a literary family of faiths. As an inspired story in Zoroastrianism advances into our consciousness, we may be assured that God has spoken a word of story in other traditions as well. For Christians, the stories of Jesus have particular significance as the very core medium of divine expression.

Some stories of our extended family were likely left out, and some stories have multiple versions; the first book of the whole Bible, for example, contains two different versions of the story of creation,[5] each told and written down at different times in history to meet the needs of the listeners. In the same way, the Gospels are powerful stories that Christians recite every Sunday in their churches and that they read and study every day in their homes, offices, colleges and seminaries. A proof of the power of these stories is that, not only that they are read and reread in churches and other places but also that they form the basis of much of the Western world's greatest literature: Goethe's *The Sorrows of Young Werther*, Fyodor Dostoevsky's *The Brothers Karamazov* and *The Idiot*, Thomas Mann's *The Magic Mountain*, Herman Melville's *Billy Budd* and Nikos Kazantzakis's *The Last Temptation of Christ*, among others.

Why do Christians continue to sing "Tell Me the Stories of Jesus"? The Gospel stories provide records of faith to people of faith who gather to remind themselves of the power of these stories that present the "good news" of what God has done for them and for the world in Jesus. These are also the stories that inform the theology of the church, and stories that pervade the world's literature and film because of their deep moral qualities. As the great Jewish writer Elie Wiesel once said (in telling a story about the power of stories), "God made man because He loves stories."

The Good Samaritan in a Seventeenth-Century Engraving

5
gospel and torah

THE MOST OBVIOUS LINKAGE BETWEEN THE GOSPEL AND THE HEBREW SCRIPTURES WAS specifically designed by both the authors of Matthew in that Gospel and by the later church leaders, who edited and arranged the order of the canon of the Christian Scriptures, placing the Gospel according to Matthew as the first book in their "New Testament" for a certain reason. For the sake of the majority of church members, who were Jewish, and to engage other Jewish readers, it was the deliberate agenda of the authors of Matthew's Gospel to link the events of the life of Jesus with prophecies concerning the Messiah in the Hebrew Scriptures as understood and experienced by Jewish Christians, thus presenting Jesus as the Messiah (a word translated as "Christ" in Greek, "Anointed" in English and "Masih" in Arabic). This theme extends through the work of the several contributors to the book of Matthew, and it is pointedly elaborated through the efforts of a final editor.

Matthew is, of course, one of the named disciples/apostles and also the corporate persona of the several writers, editors and sources who compiled the Gospel that bears his name. Speculation continues as to which part or parts, if any, were actually penned by Matthew himself and about the reason for the appellation of this Gospel, since Matthew's name appears nowhere in it. It could well be that at least the opening chapter, with the story of the Magi,[1] was from Matthew's hand, since it is known that much of his postresurrection mission activity took place in Persia.

There are at least three hundred quotations from the Hebrew Scriptures contained in the Christian Scriptures, including some from every book except Esther, Ecclesiastes and Song of Songs. The quotations are most often from the Greek Septuagint version of the Hebrew Bible, usually abbreviated as LXX, denoting the seventy translators said to be employed in that translation. At the time when the "New Testament" was being written, the LXX was in common usage among Greek-speaking Jews all around the Mediterranean world. Occasionally the original Hebrew text is also quoted in the Christian Scriptures. In some ninety instances the LXX is quoted word for word, and in eighty more, the LXX is quoted loosely. The LXX and the Hebrew text are used together in a freestyle blend found in about one hundred quotations, and the Hebrew text is used alone in about thirty instances,[2] where the Hebrew is used for emphasis.

Suggestions that the Christian Scriptures have only a peripheral relation to the Hebrew Scriptures are therefore patently absurd and usually based on an agenda seeking to support a theory of dominant Egyptian, Greek, Gnostic or some other influence. In this study, Zoroastrianism will be offered no textual preeminence to rival the Hebrew Scriptures in the words of the Gospel, although we will investigate significant parallels and connections with the Avesta, both as derivative through the Hebrew Scriptures and in freestanding independent connections. Certainly Christianity was influenced by Greek philosophy, Gnostic beliefs and other contemporary elements, some of which it deliberately addressed. The same can be said of Zoroastrian influence in Christianity that possibly even outranks some of the other influences often considered, but it is the Hebrew Scriptures that form the context of the Christian Scriptures, as will be clearly seen.

After the first generation of church growth, exclusively among Jews, Gentiles were not converted to a Zoroastrian church but to a form of Judaism that had been affected by and expanded into a Zoroastrian worldview acquired in the final phase of the Exile in Babylon. Christians also received this worldview directly from Zoroastrianism in ways we have yet to explore and indirectly through a Judaism that itself had a more dynamically robust worldview than the preexilic tribal religion. Jews wrote every word in the Christian Scripture, and all aspects of the whole story in Hebrew Scriptures are also precious to Christians, even to Christian children in Sunday School. They feel that they "own" the stories of Abraham, Sarah, Jacob, Joseph, Moses, Ruth, David and Esther as surely as if they were born Jewish.

The Jewish community took a balanced approach to the task of maintaining the relationship between their national experience of the faith and its universality. Christians have their own history in this regard, but it, too, is based on an earlier Jewish model. Jesus and the church adopted as a model the twelve tribes of Israel, or the twelve sons of Israel in the function of the twelve disciples. They became the twelve apostles who were sent out into the world from Jerusalem to establish "tribes" of Christians, as referred to by Josephus,[3] Eusebius and others. The tribal system established by Jacob served Israel well for over a thousand years, and it left its stamp on both the Torah and on the Christian church. The apostles and their successors never did establish exactly twelve national churches among the nations, but something like that became the basis of the Christian "denominations," which serve an important tribal function of community bonding.

Saint James was the bishop of Jerusalem, and his "Jacobite" Church became the Syrian Orthodox Church, stretching all the way to southern India under the leadership of Saint Thomas after the death of James. Saint Matthew ministered in Persia, where the church established a beautiful liturgy between eras of Zoroastrian and Muslim dominance. Saint Andrew launched the Greek Orthodox Church, followed by Saints Cyril and Methodius, who started the Bulgarian, Romanian, Serbian and what became the Ukrainian and Russian Orthodox churches. Saint Peter in Rome, Saint John in Asia Minor (Turkey), Saint Mark in Egypt, the Church of Antioch built up by Saint Paul and others on the same model illustrate the way in which national, ethnic or "tribal" branches of Christianity began. Most of these continue in vitality to this day.

The emperor Charlemagne "established" the church in France, more on the model of Constantine, who did not found the Byzantine Greek church but rather established it. The earlier model continued as Saint Augustine of Canterbury began the Church of England and as Saints Columba and Giles founded the church in Scotland, Saint Patrick in Ireland and Saint Boniface in the countries of Northern Europe. The Protestant reformation solidified the trend toward national churches in Europe with Reformed churches in Holland, Switzerland and Hungary and Lutheran churches in Germany and the Scandinavian countries. A shift came in North America as these tribes vied with each other, turning into something more like related but competing clans, a pattern that moved with Protestant missions to Africa and parts of Asia. The Roman Catholic Church, as the largest single tribe, also has its clans in which the liberation orientation in the churches of Holland and Brazil presents somewhat contrasting church cultures compared to the traditionalist Philippine and Polish churches.

Church unions set out to reverse the trend toward tribalism in Canada, India, Australia and elsewhere, but the homogenized brand was not always distinctive enough to hold allegiances, except in China, where Protestants and Catholics are both evolving into robust, new union churches. These distinctive Chinese churches (both Protestant and Catholic) have begun to challenge the fast-growing Orthodox churches of Eastern Europe and both Anglican and evangelical churches in Africa as the dominant tribes of Christianity in the twenty-first century, while Roman Catholic and "mainstream" Protestant denominations are in a period of retrenchment, depending on the strength of their own tribal allegiances.

The reason this is germane to our study is not just that the Christian Church began by twelve apostles, on the Jewish model of twelve tribes. A more significant observation is that despite great differences in worship and other practices, all of these tribes are united by the adherence to the same Christian Scriptures, approved in early centuries by the then "undivided" church. Just as amazing is the fact that all of them equally cherish the Hebrew Scriptures, with the one minor caveat previously described in reference to the extra "Apocryphal" books, which are also Jewish. (These are considered canonical Scriptures by Catholic and Orthodox Christians, although read by Protestants in much the same spirit as they are studied by Jews.)

The deliberate prooftext references to the messiah in every chapter of Matthew are part of a general assumption throughout the Christian Scriptures, that the core meaning of the Hebrew Scriptures was the pointing to Jesus and the preparation for his coming. According to this view, it was always the intention of the Divine to enter human history at a critical juncture "in the fullness of time," and that the salvation of the universe would unfold from that central event. The Hebrew Scripture was therefore considered to be divinely inspired, equal with and intimately connected to the Christian Scripture, although its meaning only makes sense to Christians in the light of the Gospel. The importance of the Zoroastrian connection will become clear, but the Hebrew Scriptures remain the framework of the Christian Scriptures.

In the early church, Marcion was the leading detractor in regard to this understanding. He was a Christian priest who shared the views of the Gnostic element within the church, and he was declared a heretic in 144 CE. To Marcion, the Hebrew Scriptures present a God who was different than the God worshipped by Christians. This Hebrew God created the world and was preoccupied with the Law, while the Christian God redeemed the world, giving prominence to grace and love. Marcion made the first organized collection of Christian writings, truly a "new testament," which completely excluded the Hebrew Scriptures, then in common use in both churches and synagogues around the Mediterranean. His version of the Christian Bible was therefore short, emphasizing salvation as a free gift from God to believers and editing out references to good works or fulfilling the Laws of God in an applied gospel. This meant that even Christian books like the Epistle of Saint James would never be considered, but the anti-Jewish bias was particularly pronounced.

The upshot of Marcion's endeavor was a concerted effort on the part of the church to bring out a list, or "canon" of Scriptures,[4] that was more inclusive, deliberately appreciative of the position of the Jewish people and using the entire canon of the LXX version of the Hebrew Scriptures. The shorter Hebrew canon was adopted later, but only by Protestants. While Marcion's anti-Semitic approach was firmly rejected, his erroneous view that the Hebrew Scriptures are focused narrowly on law without mercy lingered in certain circles and remains a key component in the doctrines of Christian fundamentalism and the misunderstanding of groups like Jews for Jesus.

Jesus himself was thoroughly acquainted with the Hebrew Scriptures. When questioned as to which of God's requirements was most important, he summed up the entire Law by reciting two commandments,[5] quoting one about loving God[6] and another about loving one's neighbor.[7] When tempted by the devil to improve the desert economy by turning stones into bread, he answered, again quoting the Hebrew Scripture, that "man shall not live by bread alone, but by prophecy as well."[8] For that matter, in his teachings, storytelling and conversations as recorded in the Gospel, Jesus himself recited, quoted and referred to chapters and verses in at least half of the books of the Hebrew Scriptures. The following is a very partial list merely to illustrate the point.

Genesis 2:24 (Matthew 19:5; Mark 10:7, 8) re: marriage
Exodus 3:6 (Matthew 22:32; Luke 20:37) re: patriarchs
Leviticus 14:2 (Matthew 8:4) re: ritual cleansing
Numbers 30:2 (Matthew 5:33) re: oaths
Deuteronomy 5:16 (Matthew 15:4; Mark 7:10) re: commandment to honor one's parents
First Samuel 21:4–6 (Matthew 12:3–4) re: Sabbath observance
First Kings 17:9 (Luke 4:25–26) re: widows in Israel
Job 42:2 (Matthew 19:26) re: all things are possible with God
Psalms 8:2; 110:1 (Matthew 21:16; 22:44) re: infants praising and God's vindication
Proverbs 24:12 (Matthew 16:27) re: recompense
Isaiah 6:9, 10 (Matthew 13:14–15; John 12:40) re: rejection
Jeremiah 7:11 (Matthew 21:13; Mark 11:17; Luke 19:45–46) re: a den of robbers

Lamentations 2:1 (Matthew 5:35) re: God's footstool
Daniel 9:27 (Matthew 24:15) re: an abomination in the sanctuary
Hosea 6:6 (Matthew 9:13) re: steadfast love rather than sacrifice
Jonah 1:17 (Matthew 12:40) re: three days and nights in the belly of the sea monster
Micah 7:6 (Matthew 10:21 and 35–36) re: enemies within the household
Zechariah 13:7 (Matthew 26:31) re: scattered sheep
Malachi 3:1 (Matthew 11:10) re: preparing the way

Far from being anti-Semitic, both Jesus and the Christian Scriptures are completely contextualized by their primary Semitic source in a positive manner. To suggest that the disciples and apostles who wrote these Scriptures hated Jews is to say that they hated themselves. It is the use to which later Christians have applied their Scriptures, erroneously, sinfully and in ignorance of their source and meaning, that has been anti-Semitic at various times and places.

The Christian Bible opens in a garden[9] and closes in a city.[10] The journey from the Garden of Eden in Genesis to the New Jerusalem, the City of God in Revelation, takes humanity from its rural roots and isolation to the urban environment and community. Mythically speaking, it is the same place because in both instances "a river runs through it" and "the tree of life" stands at its center. There were people in the garden and there is a garden in the city, but both the people and the environment have changed. Possibly the idealized country living of our grandparents was actually less than perfectly idyllic, and the Bible is not oblivious to the crime, pollution and frantic desperation in our cities either. But humans were meant to live in community, and the environment is meant to be restored to its pristine state. The Bible tells the whole story of the movement from the Garden of Eden to the City of God, a journey we all must share. This is one way to summarize the Bible, but the Christian component makes no sense without the Jewish foundation.

This "type" of understanding was elucidated by Northrop Frye in the last half of the twentieth century, and we will examine a few examples of his "typology." Frye turned literary criticism from an art into a science. His studies were wide ranging, but he suggests that the Judeo-Christian Bible is indeed a literary masterpiece that served as the cornerstone of Eurocentric Western civilization for many centuries. The Bible is now increasingly regarded in a similar way in much of the "developing world," especially in places where the religious energy of the planet appears to be surging as much as robust economic and other sectors, giving Frye's work a universal significance that may eventually extend to the Quran and other Scriptures.

Northrop Frye entered the University of Toronto in 1929 and spent sixty of the next sixty-two years there, teaching at Victoria University and Emmanuel College until his death in 1991. He was absent for part of a year obtaining an MA from Oxford, part of a year in ministry for the United Church of Canada, and part of a year as the visiting Norton Professor at Harvard. The famous mentor of literary giants such as Margaret Atwood and Harold Bloom was described by the latter in 1957 as "the foremost living student of Western literature," and Frye's reputation has only grown since then.

His collected works in thirty-one volumes from the University of Toronto Press begin with his *Fearful Symmetry* of 1947, which transformed the world's understanding of William Blake's poetry and art. It is followed by *Anatomy of Criticism*, which appeared in 1957, proving to be one of the most important works of literary theory of the twentieth century. These credentials are important for the credibility they bring to his later work on the Bible as a masterpiece of world literature. Those needing an introduction to Northrop Frye should begin with his *Double Vision*, written in 1990 and published just after his death in 1991. In it he succinctly and effectively distinguishes between physical and spiritual realities, the latter being the literary basis of the Bible, when not hijacked by literalists attempting to turn its truth into descriptions on the mere physical plane.

The example of Frye's analysis of the garden and the city cited above, connecting the opening chapters of Genesis with the closing chapters of Revelation, appears first in *The Great Code* of 1982, Frye's seminal work on the Bible as literature and Scripture as a unique archetype of literature. Quite apart, for the moment, from his religious beliefs, Frye shows how the Christian Scripture is archetypically rooted in the Hebrew Scripture and how the universal meaning of the Hebrew

Scripture is elucidated by the Christian Scripture. He illustrates this "double mirror" insight in the instances of the identification between John the Baptist and Elijah,[11] between Mary and Miriam (a connection confirmed in the Quran),[12] and between the Magnificat manifesto[13] and the Song of Hannah[14] (also echoed in Psalm 113[15]), all examined as part of his discipline, now increasingly referred to as "archetypal criticism."

The Great Code was followed by *Words with Power* in 1990, which is equally dramatic as Frye engages our understanding of the way the Tower of Babel story[16] is mirrored backward in the story of the Pentecost.[17] Because of its arrogance, humanity lost its ability to communicate with each other at Babel, but at Pentecost a band of discouraged disciples is blessed with the ability to communicate their vision, even with strangers. This is not a comparison of Jewish and Christian religious expressions, since Babel is pre-Jewish and Pentecost involved Jewish people from all over the world. Rather, it shows the integrity of the whole Scriptural enterprise from the perspective of literary criticism.

Frye presents the Gospel by ushering us into the presence of the archetypes of Hebrew Scripture. Those archetypes are rooted in the Torah and are illuminated by the Prophets, in the Writings and in the Christian Scriptures from which the meaning of the Gospel can be derived. Even Jesus and Joshua, whose names are the same (Greek and Hebrew) and who bring the people into a new reality, can be understood in this way, forming the basis of a new discussion between Jewish and Christian believers.

The Christian Scriptures traditionally open with five books of historical narrative—Matthew, Mark, Luke, John and the Acts of the Apostles. The arrangement of these books by the early church is a direct emulation of the Torah and is followed by the "Prophetic" Pauline Epistles and the "Writings" of the Catholic Epistles and Revelation. In this sense, the whole of the Christian Scriptures is dependent on and derivative of the archetype of the entire Hebrew Scriptures.

The Entry Into Jerusalem from a Sixteenth-Century Woodcut

6
gospel and wisdom

*T*HE *DA VINCI CODE* WAS PUBLISHED IN 2003, A BOOK BY DAN BROWN THAT LED TO A 2006 MOVIE of the same title. Despite a cultlike following, according to the author both are fiction. However, many serious observers believe it is time for the Church and others to reassess their position on the role of Mary Magdalene and the importance of information contained in the Gnostic Gospels, upon which Brown's story is based. The idea in the book has been around for some time—that Jesus and Mary Magdalene were married before the crucifixion, which he escaped, avoided or from which he recovered. They supposedly traveled by boat to Provence, in the south of France, where they had children and lived normal lives. Their descendants became the Merovingian dynasty who ruled France and Germany, as well as their modern descendants: the House of Hapsburg, Luxembourg's Grand Ducal Family and other claimants, humble and secret, or mighty and hopeful of assuming power someday.

The legend is recounted in one form or another in various works of fiction and pseudo-history, such as *The Jesus Scroll* by Donovan Joyce in 1973; *The Holy Blood and the Holy Grail*, a compendium by several authors published in 1982; *The Woman with the Alabaster Jar* by Margaret Starbird in 1993; and other books before and after Dan Brown's *Da Vinci Code*. The problems are historical improbability, lack of evidence and the challenge to orthodox Christian theology that is thoroughly grounded in the crucifixion and resurrection motif. Such speculations, based on legends from early centuries, continue to vie for space on the front covers of the Easter editions of *Time* and *Newsweek* magazines today. People know these stories are fiction, but many hope and actually believe that they represent the tip of the iceberg concerning things the Church and traditional scholarship cannot or will not tell them.

An equally fascinating idea, heard of but not known as well in the West, is that as a young man, Jesus went to India. In this case the historical improbabilities are diminished; the evidence, while slight, remains available for investigation; the theological problems are nonexistent; and the payoffs would be immense in terms of resolving Scriptural and related conundrums. Given the impact of Dan Brown's fiction and the history of the canard about Jesus' life in France, it might be interesting to take a look at how our understanding of things could be affected by the myth, or even the possibility that Jesus did make a pilgrimage along the Silk Road to India. He could have done this as a young adult sometime during the fifteen to eighteen years that he disappears from the Gospel record of his activities. Such a journey might have been undertaken in the spirit of young people today who take a year off after high school or university to see the world and "find themselves." Or it might have been embarked upon by a young man already conscious of his messianic destiny, either on a mission or on a journey of discovery of Judaism's wider history, asking questions and entering into discussion in holy places there as he had done in Jerusalem at the beginning of his teenage years. As for objections to the distance, we might begin by noting that Jews had traveled to India for centuries and Saint Thomas traveled to the very southern tip of India about a dozen years after the resurrection of Christ, claims for which there is an abundance of reasonable evidence.

What follows on the next several pages may require a suspension of critical judgment and previous academic assumptions for a few minutes, but we may begin what appears as a fantasy at first with a reminder of the author's final words in the Gospel of John: "There are also many other things that Jesus did; if every one of them were written down, I suppose that the world itself could not contain the books that would be written."[1]

So Christian readers should be open to speculation, others might have no objection and perhaps even Western rationalism could learn some things from the "Jesus in India" legends. No less a figure than Jawaharlal Nehru, the first prime minister of independent India, in a 1932 letter to his daughter, Indira (Gandhi), wrote, "All over Central Asia, in Kashmir, Ladakh and Tibet and even farther north, there is a strong belief that Jesus or Isa traveled about there. People believe that he visited down into India also."[2]

Jesus celebrated his bar mitzvah[3] or visited Jerusalem with his parents at twelve years of age, well before the start of his ministry at age thirty. In a beloved traditional version, the Bible says of the intervening years that "Jesus increased in wisdom and stature and in favor with God and man."[4] In the present context those cherished words of Christian tradition might well be reassessed to elucidate a specific meaning beyond the almost trite charm usually ascribed to them by Christians.

Firstly, with no Western tradition to cloud one's vision, a neutral investigator would react instantly to that reference to "wisdom" in the Eastern context as meaning something related specifically to the Wisdom tradition. Is this our first small step toward a link between Jesus and the Lord of Wisdom?

Jesus as a Precocious Youth with Teachers in the Temple, "Hearing Them and Asking Them Questions"

Secondly, the Greek word *helikia* is traditionally translated as "stature," giving a picture of his parents recording his growth in height with marks on the wall. But, as any scholarly exegete knows, the word *helikia* more correctly means "age," as we read in more accurate contemporary translations,[5] indicating that things were happening in Jesus' life as the years passed.

Finally, in connection with this text, the presumption that the favor of "God and man" is limited to God and local males flies in the face of an obvious reference to mankind or "humanity," as it is usually translated today.[6] So simply taking the words at face value, rather than as a traditional confirmation greeting card verse, we could perhaps read that text as "Jesus studied Wisdom as he grew older, and he developed his relationship with God and with the people of the world."

Modern Western investigations of the myths or stories about Jesus in India began with Louis Jacolliot in 1869 in *La Bible dans L'Indie: Vie de iezeus Christna*. His somewhat flawed investigations of Upanishads, Dharmashastras and other Sanskrit material at least attracted the attention of Friedrich Nietzsche and the Theosophists, and got the ball rolling. Since then a plethora of Western books, articles and other materials have circulated in esoteric circles, from highly speculative theories, easily discarded, to more plausible considerations perhaps deserving further consideration. The speculative 1908 *Aquarian Gospel of Jesus the Christ* on the subject, by Levi Dowling, has been revived and adopted of late by young adults and old boomers who believe the Age of Aquarius is upon us.

More serious attempts at Western-style investigations have yet to be completed, although several related studies are now underway, as referenced in our bibliography.

Ten years ago there was not a university, college or seminary in the world that had credit courses in the Gnostic Gospels, and now they are everywhere. While at present there are none, in the next ten years we may find such courses being presented on Jesus in India, offering to the campus some of the benefits we hope to derive from this present book. We submit the following from Hindu, Buddhist, Muslim and other Eastern and Oriental sources in that spirit.

Before examining the traditions, one caution in particular is to be observed. Most of this information is about reports that Jesus spent a year or several years as a young man traveling and "growing in wisdom." But a few others suggest that his time in the East was postresurrection, or after he was "resuscitated" following the crucifixion. These accounts also fit with Muslim belief that in the confusion, Jesus escaped and someone else may have been crucified. In both such accounts there may be references to the place in Kashmir where some people believe Jesus was buried. In reproducing the traditions of Jesus in India here, we will not attempt to segregate the postresurrection reports from the greater possibility that Jesus did travel as a young man, a motif that requires no theological adjustments or changes to the creeds of the church. If they have any validity from an orthodox Christian perspective, the various "burial sites" can perhaps be regarded as memorial markers commemorating the pilgrimage of one who was later regarded as a significant person.

hindu evidence

The Bhavishyat Maha Purana, the ninth of eighteen medieval narratives of the Hindus known as the Puranas, witnesses to the fact that Jews had both traded and settled in India since before the beginning of the Common Era. It also purportedly describes the arrival of Jesus thus:[7]

> One day, Shalivahana, the chief of the Shakas, came to a snowy mountain. There, in the Land of the Ladakh,[8] a powerful king saw a handsome man sitting on the mountain, who seemed to promise auspiciousness. His skin was like copper and he wore white garments. The king asked the holy man who he was. The other replied: "I am called Isa Putra,[9] born of a virgin, minister of the non-believers, relentlessly in search of the truth."
>
> "O king, lend your ear to the religion that I brought unto the non-believers. Through justice, truth, meditation, and unity of spirit, man will find his way to Isa[10] who dwells in the centre of Light, who remains as constant as the sun, and who dissolves all transient things forever. The blissful image of Isa, the giver of happiness, was revealed in the heart; and I was called Isa-Masih."[11]

This Purana is dated with some confidence to the year 115 CE and is widely ascribed, on unrelated bases, to the well-documented reign of King Shalivahana in the state or kingdom of Gujarat. On its face, it appears as a direct reference to the visit of Jesus, and there is a wealth of other Hindu references, based upon this Purana, speculating on what such a "supreme human" might be like and how such an "avatar" or manifestation of the Divine would operate.

We will see in a subsequent chapter how the turn of the twenty-first century witnessed a flurry of credible research into the remarkable parallels between the sayings of Jesus and those of Buddha, pointing to a visit to India, Buddhist influence in the Middle East or a common Zoroastrian source somewhere in between. Surprisingly, there has been less interest to date in certain Vedic passages that could be seen as virtually an Indian "Old Testament" of prophecies concerning Christ in a wealth of references to sacrifice and the incarnation of God in human form.

Did Jesus learn of such concepts in questioning the teachers, or was he the teacher in references that are difficult to date? The Bhagavad Gita, for example, is traditionally dated as an original part of the Mahabharata between 700 and 400 BCE, marking those elements that appear similar to Christian teaching as either previous to or contemporaneous with Zoroaster. But current speculation, based on poetic style, that the Gita was added to the Mahabharata around 150 CE opens up the possibility that it reflects the teachings of Jesus to some extent. No such claim is made here, but opportunities for research beckon, and it should not be left merely to those with a speculative agenda to find a prooftext for the appearance of Jesus behind every burning bush.

buddhist evidence

In 1887 a Russian war correspondent, Nicolas Notovitch, visited India and Tibet. At the Buddhist Lamasery (monastery) of Hemis in Ladakh, he claimed to have learned of the *Life of Saint Issa, Best of the Sons of Men, Issa* being an alternate spelling for *Isa*, Jesus. His book, including a translated text of the *Life of Saint Issa*, was published in French in 1894 as *La vie inconnue de Jesus Christ*. It was subsequently translated into German, Spanish and Italian and is available in English as *The Unknown Life of Jesus Christ*. Various passages elaborate on Jesus' travels in India, his teachings, his acceptance of the *Shudras* and other untouchables, and his conflicts with the Brahmans and the Zoroastrian priests in Persia of his time.

Notovitch's writings were immediately sensationalized in the media. He was stridently opposed by Anglican, Catholic and Lutheran officials, and popular press debunking followed. Edgar J. Goodspeed in his book *Famous Biblical Hoaxes* claimed that the Buddhist "abbot" of the Hemis community signed a document that denounced Notovitch as an outright liar,[12] a claim that itself has been exposed as a hoax. In India itself there was something of an outcry, and the matter attracted the attention of the school of the late respected Sri Ramakrishna, whose associate, Swami Abhedananda, undertook to investigate the matter, initially from a highly skeptical perspective. Journeying to Tibet, he eventually located the document and made the translation into English that was later published by Notovitch, with permission.[13] Subsequent Indian investigation of this Buddhist source, under the direction of Swami Satyasangananda, of the same reputable school, came to the conclusion that from Ladakh, Jesus spent time at a learning center that later became the University of Nalanda.[14]

Other Buddhist legends purport to have evidence that Jesus traveled as far as Shingo in the Aomori Prefecture of Northern Japan, where it is claimed that he died and was buried in a prominent and still existing earth mound grave, which has had limited attention over the centuries. Other such sources have become available in English only in the last generation. Meanwhile, despite contradictory evidence, a number of authors have taken this information and incorporated it into their own works. For example, in her book *The Lost Years of Jesus: Documentary Evidence of Jesus' 17-Year Journey to the East*, the Christian visionary, Elizabeth Clare Prophet, wrote that Buddhist manuscripts provide evidence that Jesus traveled to India, Nepal, Ladakh and Tibet.[15] Just as the existence of Gnostic documents was only grudgingly acknowledged by a reticent church for centuries but recently investigated rigorously and mined for possible treasure, so also the sketchy evidence for Jesus in India needs scholarly attention at last, despite the seemingly speculative nature of the material.

muslim evidence

Ahmadiyya is a religious movement of one hundred million adherents or more, originating with the life and teachings of Mirza Ghulam Ahmad (1835–1908). It is a messianic movement that considers itself to be Islamic, and its founding leader is considered to have been both the Second Coming of Christ and the appearance of the Madhi, the "Hidden Imam" awaited by Sufi and Shia Muslims in particular. Many mainstream Muslims do not consider Ahmadis to be Muslims, in a manner analogous to the rejection of Jews for Jesus by most Jews, or the rejection of Mormons and Jehovah's Witnesses by many Christians. However, the Ahmadiyya movement holds the doctrine of Jesus in India as a tenet of faith, based on older traditions, and they are not the only Muslims who subscribe to this belief. Many orthodox Muslims believe Jesus came to India after the crucifixion debacle and that his burial site is the Roza Bal Tomb in Kashmir. Two other Muslim holy men are also buried there, one a Sufi who was purported to be a descendant of Jesus. The Ahmadis are by no means

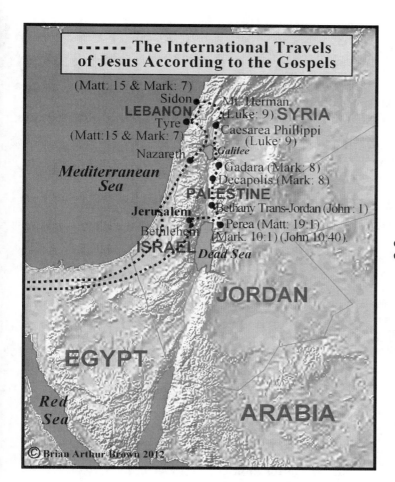

Countries Visited by Jesus according to the Gospels Identified by Their Modern Names

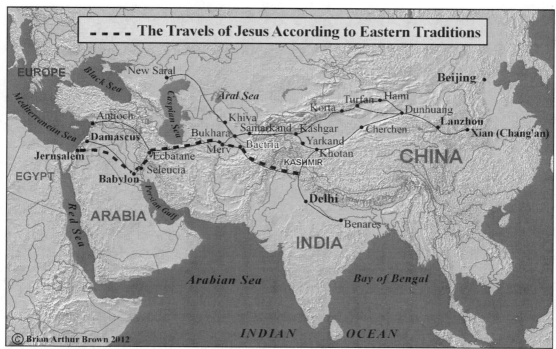

The Silk Route to India and China, Including Possible Route of Jesus as Far as Kashmir

the only group who acknowledge the Roza Bal Tomb, and in fact it is maintained and governed by a Sunni Board of Trustees. The Ahmadis have done the most research regarding Jesus in India in the last hundred years, based on both historical records and local traditions of communities along the ancient Silk Road. Their inquiries have been used as the basis for many maps by others who believe Jesus came to India as a teenager or as a young man, including those who may regard the Roza Bal as simply a monument to his visit.

christian speculation

An entire subcategory of Christian writings in this genre centers around the so-called missing years, often also referred to as the lost years of Jesus. Some of these books and articles are content to acknowledge that he may have spent much or most of those years in Nazareth and traveled to India once, perhaps for a year or a few years just prior to his public ministry in Israel. Others suggest pointedly that the only obvious reason for the complete absence of Jewish/Christian documents covering his years from the age of twelve to the age of thirty is that Jesus himself was absent for at least ten or twelve years during that time.

The Roza Bal site is perhaps of special interest because, unlike other supposed "tombs" of Jesus, there apparently never was an actual body in this casket. In a related way, in 2007 the Discovery Channel and Vision TV, both with studios in Canada, coproduced a documentary, *The Lost Tomb of Jesus*, with James Cameron of *Titanic* and *Avatar* fame as executive producer. It featured the 1996 discovery of a family tomb in Jerusalem in which one of the bone ossuaries was inscribed *Yeshua bar Yehosef'*.[16] It was the Easter sensation for another year, at least in Canada, and it was subsequently rebroadcast in much of the English-speaking world.

Rosa Bal is not a tomb for Jesus in the Western sense, although the tombs for two Muslim holy men buried at this site may be authentic burial chambers. There is an ancient "casket" associated with Jesus, but, as mentioned above, nobody was ever interred in it, because, of course, Muslims believe that Jesus was assumed bodily into heaven at some point, and *casket* is a word sometimes used for a storage chest of precious items. This casket has been moved to the Muslim "Temple of Solomon" standing behind the Roza Bal "Shrine," as the tomb could be called. The casket contains artifacts such as an inscription of ancient provenance, as yet undated. It is said to be contemporaneous with the construction of the shrine itself, and it briefly describes the physical appearance of Yus Asaph,[17] and the special white gown he wore.

The bare bones of the story, that young Jesus could have walked or caravanned to India, ought not to be quite dismissed out of hand. We know from unrelated independent sources that Cochin Jewish traders from Israel settled in Kerala in the south of India in 562 BCE, as possibly Northern Exiles, a community that was augmented following displacements in both 70 and 1492 CE. "Bene Israel" Jewish traders also suffered a shipwreck near Mumbai about a century before the birth of Jesus, leading to a migration by their families to that area. With a permanent population over the centuries, this Jewish community is frequently in the news in India still today due to their prominence and good works in the community. At least two distinct groups of Jews have also migrated to India more recently, but the Jewish presence there in the time of Jesus was similar to the Jewish presence in Egypt, in which he took refuge with his family.

From the North American perspective, the distance from the Galilee region to Kashmir seems great, but European backpackers find the trek over the same distance from Amsterdam to Athens quite within the ability of any healthy young person, and they find a similar Jewish presence in the cities of Europe. The size and shape of the Asian area of the Silk Route under discussion is equal and similar to Chile, some 285,133 square miles (600,000 square kilometers) or 2,640 miles long (4,000 kilometers) by 110 miles wide (160 kilometers).

Jesus showed a burning interest in religious issues by questioning and impressing the teachers in the Temple, even at the age of twelve. Are we to believe that, inquisitive about the world, its people and their beliefs, and both unmarried and healthy, Jesus simply sat at home through the next eighteen years? We are traditionally given to understand that after the death of Joseph he managed the carpenter shop, tended to the needs of his mother and cared for his siblings. But the latter also eventually grew up, and the Scripture shows them caring for their mother during Jesus' ministry. Did the young Jesus never take a vacation? Had he lost the interest in the religious affairs of the world that so "amazed"[18] those who heard him and "astonished"[19] his parents? Had he changed from the youngster who knew his calling even as a youth, almost curtly telling his mother, anxious about him being missing for three days, "Why were you searching for me? Did you not know that I must be in my father's house?,"[20] a reference to God's temple, not Joseph's home.

We have already seen how the Scriptural verse describing his teen and young adult life is freighted with more potential meaning than traditionally assumed, even to suggesting a connection going forward to "Wisdom" as the years unfolded, and an approval from both God and humanity. It is usually suggested that this is all we find in Scripture, but actually there is more.

When Jesus emerged from his secluded, absent, missing or "lost" years, as the case may be, again the people were "amazed"[21] at the way he talked, especially those in his old hometown on his first preaching visit there. It was as if they had not seen him in years, asking, "Where did this man get all this? What is this *wisdom* that has been given to him?"[22] Again we note a repeated reference to Wisdom in the Scriptures about Jesus. "Is this not the carpenter's son? Is not his mother called Mary? And are not his brothers James and Joseph and Simon and Judas? And are not all his sisters with us?"[23] The inference is becoming clear. They know the family and thought they remembered him, but he is talking in a new way and about new things, all somehow associated with Wisdom.

We do not yet know if Jesus ever got all the way to India, although that is within the realm of possibility, but to assume he never went anywhere seems almost absurd. Hints from Hindu, Buddhist and Muslim sources are not enough to trigger the research that would be required to give substance to the hypothesis of Jesus in India. What would be needed is some solid evidence from a Christian source documenting the fact that he traveled abroad in addition to his travels to Egypt as a baby and around Palestine as an adult. There could be no more authoritative Christian source than the Gospel record itself. Before examining the Scripture in this regard, without overstating or understating the case, and without strained speculation or anything incompatible with orthodox Christian doctrine, here is what may have happened.

The young Jesus returned from Jerusalem to Nazareth with his parents, and he was "obedient to them."[24] He lived a normal life, which could have included assisting Joseph in the carpentry shop and doing his duty to the family. According to Christian tradition, Joseph was an older man who died while Jesus was a young man. In that context, Jesus would have become head of the household and taken charge of the shop. In his early twenties, we can assume that he supported his mother and employed his brothers. Olive wood is good for little except souvenirs for tourists, so he would have gone over into nearby Syria to get cedar and other woods in the area now known as Lebanon.

This is about a day's journey, and even closer than Jerusalem in terms of accessibility. He spoke Aramaic, as did the Syrians. They were adherents of the Sabaean religion, but the later story of Jesus with the Samaritan woman at the well shows his interest in "interfaith" dialogue.[25] The Syrians kept the familiar Sabaean name of their religion, as did the Magi, though, like the latter, the Sabaeans had become Zoroastrian in all but name. At some point they had also adopted the dualistic heresy, which may have also been more compatible with their previous outlook.

By the time he was twenty-five, Jesus may have been to Egypt as a baby, to Jerusalem as a child, probably to "Lebanon" several times on business and possibly to other parts of Syria—Damascus itself being only a day away in another direction.[26] Everybody went there, and Jesus was no recluse; indeed, his interest in religious matters had already been recognized. Questions occurred to him, and the Zoroastrian faith had insights to offer, but he would have realized that there was something off-kilter in some of what he was hearing. With his brothers chafing to have more responsibility and Jesus already preparing for what he knew to be his destiny and mission, he might have quite naturally decided to take a trip, arranged the finances for himself and the family, and set out. There are indications in the beginning of his ministry that he is just back from a long trip somewhere, since the people in his village are not quite sure they recognize him.

If he had wanted to make straight for India for some reason, he might have taken the Via Maris, a highway that went north along the Mediterranean coast and farther north inland to join the Silk

Road. But Jesus would possibly want to begin his study tour in Babylon, where there was still a sizable Jewish community and where important religious developments in Jewish history had taken place. In Babylon, where everyone spoke Aramaic as he did, his interest in Zoroastrianism would be heightened immensely, and he would be encouraged to spend time visiting the Zoroastrian heartland in northern Persia, the old Bactrian province where pristine Zoroastrianism still held sway.

It is no great stretch to imagine him traveling and staying there for some months or more. At this time he could have easily made a trip into India, or at least the northern areas of Ladaka, now known as Kashmir, as recalled by Nehru 1,900 years later. There Buddhist monks would have shared their teachings, which apparently coincided with his interpretation of Jewish religious norms. Both were compatible with Zoroastrian theology and practice, a "common source" for both Buddhism and Judaism. (There were Jewish communities in every Silk Road city except Benares, Delhi and Beijing.)

It could be that just as he conversed in the Temple at Jerusalem as a youth years before, asking questions and amazing all who heard him speak, there was again a give and take. Was the revelation of the Saoshyant doctrine in Zoroastrianism part of God's plan for Jesus? One might surmise that Jesus already believed himself to be the Messiah of Israel before he went abroad. He came back to begin his ministry realizing that he was to be the Savior of the world. In any case, when he returned he saw himself primarily in the Redeemer role, which defined his ministry in a manner not particularly Jewish. We have already seen in some detail how the concept of the Messiah as Redeemer appeared in Judaism, but only in conjunction with Zoroastrianism during the Exile, and it was never featured again until Jesus presented himself in that light, possibly after similar contact with the Saoshyant doctrine. We just do not know exactly where he went or how long he stayed, but it is clear that there is a whole side to Jesus that Christians hardly know. There is nothing strained or unorthodox about any of this from a Christian perspective, but it does answer some questions if there is Scriptural evidence that he traveled east.

According to the Christian Scriptures, if we look carefully, he is so at home in Syria, especially the region known today as Lebanon, across the border from northern Israel, that when pressures mount in his ministry, he retreats there to visit privately among friends.[27] This is after a period of intensity and controversy, but he knows somebody in Tyre who has a house where he might take refuge. "He did not want anyone to know he was there."[28] He obviously knows his way around, rather than timidly venturing over the border as if he had never been there. Has no one noticed how clear it is that Jesus has been here before? We might now conclude from this that trips north and east were among the many things Jesus did that were just too numerous to write up in Gospel accounts that focused almost exclusively on his three-year ministry. Tyre is a day's walk from Nazareth, but on at least one occasion, according to the Scriptures, he also reached Sidon, another day's walk beyond Tyre toward present-day Beirut, both cities subscribing to the Zoroastrian state religion, under the Sabaean label.

Somewhere along the way he encountered a woman described as a Syrophoenician. This means that she was ethnically Syrian, so she was some kind of Zoroastrian in religion, as virtually all Syrians were, although the names of the sects and groups differed and changed from age to age. She was living in the part of Syria formerly known as Phoenicia, now Lebanon, where Greek was spoken. She asks him for a favor, of the kind he frequently granted, but he says, "Why should I help you? Don't you know my mission is first to the Jews?"[29] For centuries, Christian preachers have struggled with his seemingly narrow focus and blatant pro-Jewish bias, but Jesus may have had an insight as he tests her for just a brief moment, hoping or knowing she might reply appropriately from the broader perspective he has encountered in her culture and religion. She does not disappoint him, and indeed takes him to task, teaching him and liberating Jesus from the narrow confines of his mission. This may be just what he expected, or at least hoped for in the circumstances, and a happily chastened Jesus responded accordingly. He then returned to the Galilee region, by way of the East Bank through the Decapolis, a separate region known today as Jordan.

Interesting, and of considerable significance, is the fact that this encounter, traditionally regarded as among the most puzzling in the whole of the Gospel, suddenly makes complete sense in the twenty-first century with our new orientation. Jesus is in Zoroastrian territory, and it is unlikely that he would be ignorant of the Saoshyant image of the Redeemer of humanity. Whether or not he has been there before, or even farther east, it is clear that the question of his role beyond Judaism is on his mind. His travels beyond the borders of Israel have impacted his understanding of his purpose and destiny as much as his brief visits to the Temple in Jerusalem. His conversations with people like this Syrophonecian woman are at least as important as the discussions with his Jewish followers. If there is any new insight for Christians in this book, this is it.

This was early in his ministry, and we might suppose that Jesus had taken the Via Maris on his way home from Bactria a few months or a year earlier, through territory where he may have had business associates and friends. He obviously knows these people, and later in that year he refers to them as examples again and again. It is amazing that this tradition has been almost completely ignored by ordinary Christians studying their Scriptures. Every Christian knows that Jesus visited Egypt as an infant, but his adult visits to Lebanon, Syria, Jordan and possibly beyond, though reported in Scripture, are simply not recognized in the consciousness of the Christian community at large. Mark 7:24–30 is of enormous significance in this regard, as is part of chapter 15 of Matthew.

But Jesus was also in Lebanon and Syria when he visited Mount Hermon and Caesarea Philippi, where he asked his disciples, "Who do the people say that I am?"[30] From them personally he got the more Judeo-centric answer to this question that seems to come up whenever he is in Zoroastrian territory. Peter and others affirm that he is the Messiah of Israel, the one expected to reestablish the throne of the Davidic monarchy. He accepts his identification as the Messiah, but he reinterprets it radically in the direction of the Saoshyant Redeemer role, as the Savior of the World. He traveled again to the Gentile East Bank in Jordan in "the country of the Gerasenes,"[31] and when he "returned,"[32] it may have been to Syria, so often was he there.

This region is also considered by many scholars as the area in which the Transfiguration took place six or eight days later,[33] an identification of Jesus with Moses and Elijah, lawgiver and prophet of Israel, but happening outside Israel, where the question of his role and identity was perhaps at issue in the minds of the disciples. Certainly there were minority Jewish groups in Lebanon, Syria and Jordan, but the majority was Zoroastrian, and Jesus was obviously at home among them, even if his disciples were not. All this time traveling, resting, healing and teaching in the areas outside Israel comes as a surprise to many modern Christians, otherwise familiar with the stories of Jesus' life. It is merely the use of modern country names that occasions a startled reaction. We do not know whether Jesus had traveled farther at an earlier time or if he had simply become familiar with the Zoroastrian doctrine of the Saoshyant and other such matters in Zoroastrian territory closer to home on these and probably previous occasions.

Given the impact of Dan Brown's fictional dabbling in stories associated with the Gnostic Gospels, it was perhaps merely a question of time before someone presented a fictional account of Jesus in India. In adding *Jesus: A Story of Enlightenment*[34] to his series of spiritual bestsellers, Deepak Chopra has managed to do this in a manner that comfortably fits the criteria laid out above, none of which actually challenges what is already reported in the canonical Gospels. That point may not be significant to all Western readers, but while Chopra never claims historical accuracy, this non-Church member who loves Jesus finds it easy to relate to the Jesus in India legend in a manner compatible with Orthodox belief. This phenomenon may become noteworthy for Christians in the twenty-first century as their appreciation of the Jesus in India phenomenon increases. Writing in the surrealistic style of Indian movies, introduced to the West in the Bollywood genre, a new art form for many, Chopra presents the story of Jesus in phantasmagorical layers of imagery. This is an art form used by the Gospel writers, themselves all Asian with the exception of Luke, but a literary genre only now about to be recognized and understood as such by churches, East and West, with their rational scholastic perceptions.

With Cecil B. De Mille, Charleton Heston and others, the content of the Torah provides ideal material for production by Hollywood. The Quran is more in the Oriental style, with as much emphasis on engagement with divine rhythm and the evocative power of cadence as on content. The Gospel is where East meets West in Bollywood style, almost accomplished in Handel's *Messiah* and more fully anticipated for the twenty-first century by Andrew Lloyd Webber in *Jesus Christ Superstar*. The nonrationality of crowds breaking into song, the non sequitur narratives, the dancing chorus lines, suspended animation and surrealistic imagery of Bollywood has more in common with the

Gospel style itself than either has with Western narratives that are entirely rational in both format and content. While he is no theologian, and not a Christian, Chopra caught something of the Gospel style that relates naturally to the Bollywood genre that, by coincidence, comes to the West via an Indian film industry operated primarily by Tata Communications, owned by Zoroastrian Parsees. The genre may be coming full circle in the twenty-first century.

On his first visit back to the synagogue of his hometown, Nazareth, the folks did have difficulty in recognizing him, although they had heard he had been preaching in Capernaum. He had been away for perhaps a couple of years or more; he dressed differently and he had strange things to say. The invitation for him to read the Scripture in the village synagogue indicates that he was either a guest or at least someone they have not seen for some time. He has obviously just returned to Nazareth from somewhere, but from where? Sensing their diffidence, he challenges them by reminding them that people outside Israel were favored by God in the past.[35]

He says, "Truly I tell you, no prophet is accepted in the prophet's hometown. But the truth is, there were many widows in Israel in the time of Elijah, when the heaven was shut up three years and six months, and there was a severe famine over all the land; yet Elijah was sent to none of them except to a widow at Zarephath in Sidon."[36] He continues: "There were also many lepers in Israel in the time of the prophet Elisha, and none of them was cleansed, except Naaman the Syrian."[37] Again later, in speaking about those who reject "wisdom" in the various Jewish towns where he preached, he says, "Woe to you, Chorazin! Woe to you, Bethsaida! For if the deeds of power done in you had been done in Tyre and Sidon, they would have repented long ago in sackcloth and ashes."[38]

It is thus apparent that Jesus is quite familiar with what goes on in the non-Jewish communities outside Israel, especially in the Syrian Zoroastrian area to the north and east. He even uses examples close enough to home to which the local populace can relate, and yet the Church and its scholars have been almost blind to these Scriptures when the possibilities of Jesus having traveled are under consideration. To make this point, lest Jesus' penchant for perambulation seem exaggerated, if we overlay just his travels as described in Scripture on a map of the region today (page 195), we see that according to the Bible Jesus visited Egypt, Lebanon (then part of the Roman province of Syria), Syria itself, Jordan (Decapolis), up and down Israel (Judah) and what we could call Palestine—some five or six countries that we know about. Where else this traveler might have journeyed during his "missing years" is indeed conjecture, although there are hints and clues, and the Bible says he did more things than it could possibly record.

With respect to resurrection, judgment, reward and punishment, apocalyptic expressions and the ultimate destruction of the forces of evil, it can be concluded that both Jewish and Christian eschatologies, for example, are largely Zoroastrian. As a Messiah, Jesus functioned almost entirely along Zoroastrian lines. While purportedly of the Davidic line, he showed little passion for restoration of the Davidic monarchy, except in powerfully symbolic ways. He offered redemption from sin, rather than restoration of the Jewish throne. He was a World Savior, rather than simply a Jewish Messiah, and yet the intertwining of these influences is indicative of the balance needed between universal and particular.

There may be Zoroastrian Avestas buried in Jesus' teaching from a source we will examine more fully in the next chapter, but there is at least one that illustrates the point in this context, a teaching that Zoroaster himself derived from the neighboring Hebrew tradition at the earliest stage of his life and training. We have seen where the Little Avesta takes up the Mosaic theme of God's self-revelation as the I AM, and elaborates upon it:

I AM the Keeper,
I AM the Creator,
I AM the Maintainer,
I AM the Discerner,
I AM the Beneficent.

Jesus would have noted this distinct collection of Little Avesta "I AM" sayings in his travels among the Zoroastrians, and he is inspired to do the same thing and to make it a feature of his ministry. The Mosaic burning bush expression, as used by Zoroaster, is applied by Jesus to his role as Saoshyant Messiah, and it should be written in bold as related to the Z motif.

There are actually seven I AM sayings by Jesus (that just happens to be the sacred number for Jews, derived from the Zoroastrians who adopted it from the Vedic source). The seven I AM sayings are scattered, as something to which he kept referring, but they are all reported in the Gospel according to St. John by an author who obviously picked up on a favorite theme of Jesus:

1. "I AM the bread of life."[39]
2. "I AM the light of the world."[40]
3. "I AM the door of the sheep."[41]
4. "I AM the good shepherd."[42]
5. "I AM the resurrection, and the life."[43]
6. "I AM the way, the truth, and the life."[44]
7. "I AM the true vine."[45]

Early in this series of aphorisms, Jesus says something else that is missed by many Christians, leading to a false understanding of their own relationships with believers in other branches of what is clearly a world religion. In chapter 8 of John's Gospel, the Pharisees question Jesus about his credentials and they are distressed that he questions their status as true children of Abraham. The conversation gets heated, but it is instructive regarding the specific use of the phrase *I AM* by Jesus—a deliberate emphasis, as we shall see.

Jesus says, "Very truly, I tell you, whoever keeps my word will never see death."[46] The religious authorities say to him, "Now we know that you have a demon. Abraham died, and so did the prophets; yet you say, 'Whoever keeps my word will never taste death.' Are you greater than our father Abraham, who died? The prophets also died. Who do you claim to be?"[47] Jesus answers, "If I glorify myself, my glory is nothing. It is my Father who glorifies me, he of whom you say, 'He is our God,' though you do not know him. But I know him; if I would say that I do not know him, I would be a liar like you. But I do know him and I keep his word. Your ancestor Abraham rejoiced that he would see my day; he saw it and was glad."[48] Then the Jews said to him, "You are not yet fifty years old, and have you seen Abraham?"[49]

At this point, Jesus made what might be described as one of the greatest claims of his identity. He said to them, "Very truly, I tell you, before Abraham was, I AM."[50] His unique use of the strained syntax of that last sentence tells us that Jesus consciously used the phrase *I am* in a special way, recognizing all the freight it carries. In normal speech, to indicate his eternal life as the Messiah, he might have said, "Before Abraham was, I was." Instead, he makes it clear that he is speaking with the voice that came to Moses from the burning bush. He thus connects himself not only with the God of Abraham but also with both the God of Moses in the Hebrew Scriptures and the God of the Little Avesta in the Zoroastrian Scriptures.

It also explains who is speaking later in John's Gospel when we read, "I AM the way, the truth and the life. No one comes to the father except through me."[51] For centuries Christians have used this passage to assert that nobody can come to God except through Jesus, the man of Galilee. In fact Jesus is here and everywhere using the phrase *I AM* to indicate that he is speaking with the voice of the One who spoke from the burning bush, the universal Savior of Zoroastrianism and the Redeemer of Israel, who is sovereign long previous to the birth of Jesus of Nazareth. Christians of the twenty-first century may see in this understanding a mandate to recognize the fullness of God in the lives of those who have heard this voice and responded in any desert, on any road, or in any cave. Given the antipathy to aggressive evangelism in many parts of the world, Christians who wish to make their Savior known in an age of interfaith respect may now find it appropriate to do so more in "modeling Christ" in their lives and actions than in argumentative presentations. This change in tone has been effective in modern China, for example, and it might be almost welcome in other parts of the world where both actions and assertive claims by Christians have sometimes seemed questionable to others.

In the Little Avesta I AM passages, Jesus must have recognized that Zoroaster knew of Moses and the revelation at the burning bush. We speculated earlier that this may be where Zoroaster first heard the idea of monotheism, early in his training for the priesthood, possibly even under the influence of the Prophet Jeremiah—though strong evidence for that is lacking as yet. Jesus picked up the Mosiac theme, that God addresses people in this I AM motif, and he uses it again and again in a Zoroastrian style. To Jesus, whoever hears the voice from the bush (so to speak) and responds is a person who hears the voice that comes from God and responds to the Divine One. This is a broader interpretation of who gets "saved" than certain Christians may be prepared to accept, but the Scriptural I AM texts, when taken together, are clear on this point.

We do not know, and we may possibly never know, if anything placing Jesus in India is true, or if he only went to Persia, or perhaps just to Syria—trips for which the biblical record is univocal and which suggests that the trips there recorded were subsequent to previous travels. For that matter, if Jesus and his parents made it all the way to Egypt soon after his birth (a trip some regard as apocryphal), the likelihood that a visit by Jesus to at least Zoroastrian Syria is actually immense, even without the biblical record. The young man from Nazareth would have often crossed the Galilee from where Syria is only a few hours' walk. He may well have gone farther, but our minimal projection takes this speculation out of the sphere of the bizarre and into the realm of the perfectly reasonable. If a young Muhammad was exposed to Zoroastrianism, for better and for worse, in caravan trips to Syria, and if Jesus' family found refuge in Egypt to be within reach, we should almost certainly conclude that Jesus traveled at least short distances as a single young man, unless he was totally devoid of interest in even the nearer reaches of the wider world. If such travels did take place, we should expect that they would be reflected in the stories of his life, his teaching and ministry, and we now see that they are.

That connection with Zoroastrianism looms ever larger these days, as another link to literary undercurrents and spiritual imagery in both Hebrew and Christian Scriptures. Indeed, with perhaps some hyperbole, John Dominic Crossan of the Jesus Seminar has hailed the recent English translation of a document on the subject that had languished for centuries in the Vatican Library: "Of the many earliest Christian documents recently discovered inside sealed earthen pots or on forgotten library shelves, *Revelation of the Magi* is by far the most fascinating."[52]

There is a certain irony in the conventional understanding of Matthew's gospel as a deliberate link with Hebrew messianic prophecies. In addressing Jews along the Silk Route, among others, this gospel penned by (or at least named for) Matthew, "the Apostle to the Persians," appears to make an equally deliberate point in connecting Jesus to Zoroastrian prophecies of a Saoshyant messiah through the appearance of Persian Magi in his nativity story, in which these Zoroastrian priests acknowledge Jesus with both gifts and worship.

We have indicated that at the beginning of his ministry Jesus appears to be returning from somewhere farther east, but the very first episode in launching that ministry is especially intriguing. As he seeks the occasion on which to begin a messianic ministry that he believes is from God, Jesus hears that his cousin, John, the son of Zechariah, the Jewish priest, is baptizing people in the River Jordan as a sign of repentance and to prepare them for a new understanding of religion. He recalls the story of Zoroaster at the river, recorded several times in the Avesta and perhaps recounted to him often as the core of the story. He feels compelled to wade into the river to be baptized. As he comes up out of the water, he and perhaps others hear God speak to him, and a dove descends upon him in one of the very few stories recorded in all four Gospels.[53] John is mystified by Jesus seeking to be baptized by him, but Jesus appears to have welcomed the opportunity to deliberately emulate Zoroaster's experience at the river. In this public manifestation and recognition by John, the messianic ministry of Jesus is dramatically confirmed in the connections to both Zoroaster and John, Zoroastrianism and Judaism, the universal and the particular.

In the Book of Job, the last friend to visit is Elihu, whose name actually means "God in Person," one who may be seen by Christians as a Christ figure or a prophecy of Christ. This is yet another hint of the Zoroastrian origins of the Book of Job, since Zoroaster was the first to prophesy a Redeeming Messiah who will appear in person at the climax of time. Elihu assures Job that God has promised to deliver him and, most remarkably from a Christian perspective, this deliverance is because God has provided a "ransom,"[54] a familiar Zoroastrian motif. Twice in the gospels it is emphasized that Jesus came "as a ransom for many,"[55] a theology echoed by Saint Paul, "There is one God and one mediator between God and men, the man, Jesus Christ; who gave himself as a ransom for all."[56] This spiritual insight is a response to Job's earlier assertion, "I know that my Redeemer liveth and he shall stand at the latter day upon the earth."[57] This Zoroastrian theme is echoed in both the Hebrew and the Christian Scriptures.

At the end or climax of his life Jesus concluded his ministry in the Zoroastrian motif during the events leading up to and during the crucifixion and resurrection. At his preliminary trial, when the high priest, Caiphas, asked him, "Are you the Messiah, the Son of the Blessed One?," the earliest Gospel has Jesus answer specifically, "I AM."[58] He then goes directly to Zoroastrian imagery, speaking again to Caiphas, "You will see the Son of Man . . . coming with the clouds of heaven,"[59] a saying of the prophet Daniel, whether apocryphal or set historically in Babylon. The non-Jewish tradition of Jesus' three days in the grave is clearly identifiably the three-day pause as practiced in Zoroastrian funerary rites even still today. The entire Easter motif is more Zoroastrian than Jewish, despite contextual elements reflected in Hebrew prophecy.

Our speculation about the possibility of Jesus traveling the Silk Route is strengthened immeasurably by the realization that there were substantial Jewish communities along that ancient diaspora highway. The Bukharian Jews are one such group, believing themselves to be the descendants of the tribes of Naphtali and Issachar, exiled during the Assyrian conquest of Israel in the seventh century BCE. The Bukharian Jews of today's Uzbekistan and Tajikistan were largely cut off from the rest of the Jewish world until recently. The largest concentrations were in Tashkent, Samarkand, Khokand and especially Bukhara, the ancient Zoroastrian heartland shown on our map on page 195. In the 1950s some Jewish ossuaries from shortly after the time of Christ were discovered at Merv, also shown on our map. In the fourth century CE, the Talmud recounts how Rabbi Shmuel bar Bisna traveled to the region now known as Turkmenistan, visited Bukharian Jews there and protested that their wine was not kosher. In 1793, Rabbi Yosef Maimon, a Sephardic Jew originally from Morocco, traveled from Safed in the Galilee region to Bukhara, finding the Jews living in deplorable conditions. In the middle of the nineteenth century, Bukharian Jews began to relocate to Palestine under Zionist sponsorship. When Bukhara fell under Soviet control in 1917, and through the 1920s and 1930s, thousands of Bukharian Jews fled to pre-state Israel. World War II, the Holocaust and Eastern European pogroms sent many Ashkenazi Jewish refugees from the Soviet Union and Eastern Europe to Uzbekistan, strengthening the Bukharian community prior to 1972. This led to the largest Bukharian Jewish emigrations in history, and today there are about one hundred thousand Bukharian Jews living in Israel, fifty thousand living in the United States and approximately one thousand in Canada. None remain in Tajikistan and less than one thousand remain in Bukhara, the remnant community of Jews possibly visited by Jesus. He would have connected with Judaism, as he did in Syria and elsewhere, but he was also exposed to Zoroastrianism in his travels, as Muhammad would be at a similar age.

It would appear that Jesus had traveled east, perhaps already aware that he was to be the Messiah of Israel, at least according to a certain understanding. How far east he traveled we do not now know, but he returned to Israel believing himself to be the Savior of the World. The Roman holiday on December 25 was dedicated to Mithras, the Vedic deva of light who had been reformed by Zoroaster as an "Immortal" or angel and worshipped as "the Unconquered Sun" on the then winter solstice, when the light began its annual comeback. Was it mere coincidence that Christians took that as the appropriate date to celebrate the birth of Christ, or were the traditions surrounding his birth, seen also in the visit of the Magi, as Zoroastrian as those connected with his death and resurrection? It was Jesus himself who said, "I AM the light of the world,"[60] perhaps speaking as much as Saoshyant as Messiah. The river baptism that launched his vocation and the I AM motif used throughout his ministry are all related to the connection in which we now see a clear Zoroastrian imprint. On the cross Jesus is the *Redeemer* who forgave the criminal beside him who appealed to him. When this *Savior* says to the penitent thief, "Truly I tell you, today you will be with me in *Paradise*,"[61] Jesus is operating in full Zoroastrian mode.

7

gospel and avesta

"Your lamb shall be without blemish."[1]

"Here is the lamb of God who takes away the sin of the world."[2]

"You know that you were ransomed from the futile ways inherited from your ancestors, not with perishable things like silver or gold, but with the precious blood of Christ, like that of a lamb without defect or blemish."[3]

THE VEDIC SCRIPTURE OF INDIA, THE RIG VEDA AS KNOWN TO ZOROASTER, CONTAINS A PROPHECY regarding "a lamb without blemish, which must be sacrificed for the sins of humanity."[4] The Rig Veda itself is dated between 3,000 BCE and 1,200 BCE, and it is readily appreciated that this revelation was part of a common heritage shared between India and Mesopotamia well before Zoroaster. This prophecy and this language in both the written Vedas and the oral Torah of Israel surfaces at about the same time. The piece with the title *Sathpath-brahmana* (or *Sathpath Brahmana*) is from a section known as the "Brahmana of One Hundred Paths," often abbreviated among Hindus as SB. It refers to the Supreme Sacrifice for the sins of humanity by a perfect man who was also the Creator of the universe, a theme more fully developed by the Zoroastrian texts regarding the Saoshyant. Rather than being reincarnated, this "Purush Prajapati" would return to life after the sacrifice, giving worshippers the promise of eternal life in heaven[5] as opposed to eternal punishment in hell.[6] He is the unchangeable path to salvation (*mukti*) as the One Supreme Guru (*Gurugeet*),[7] to use the Hindu terms as reformed by Zoroaster and also adopted by the Buddha.

This imagery was fed into the Zoroastrian articulation of the Saoshyant, and it is similar to a particular understanding about certain verses in the Gospel concerning Jesus as the Lamb of God. Upon learning about it, Christians might well see it as part of the universal prophetic anticipation of Jesus, the Lamb of God in Hebrew prophecy and Christian fulfillment of messianic theology. The Catholic lay theologian, humorist and literary critic G. K. Chesterton is particularly articulate in showing how prophetic instincts in many cultures may be regarded as pointing to Christ, a motif based on the writings of Origen,[8] an early Christian apologist, and a theme that was also used by C. S. Lewis.

The veracity of the Gospel accounts are not diminished just because the myths of virgin births, sacrificial lambs and resurrections are common to the area from the Nile to the Ganges. If, as suggested, this whole section of the world is only about the size and shape of Chile, it should come as no great surprise that these spiritual dynamics overlap, especially when we get to the Axial Age of spiritual fermentation. The claim that these dynamics are to have their fulfillment in a Saoshyant or Redeemer who is identified by Christians as Jesus is a remarkable claim, but it is consistent with an understanding that it and other non-Hebrew prophetic myths point to a coming Messiah.

If Jesus did not go to India, then perhaps "India" went to Judea in the guise of Buddhist missionaries, a possibility worthy of investigation. Jesus might have encountered the influences of Zoroastrianism close to home, since Buddhism developed from Zoroastrianism in the East and migrated, much as Judaism did in the West. Zoroastrianism flourished in India as the Indian Buddhist reformation of Hinduism at the beginning of the Axial Age, within a hundred years of Zoroaster, and down to the time of Jesus. Only later did Buddhism evolve into the Oriental form in which we know it today farther east.

This raises the possibility that Jesus came under Zoroastrian influence in any or all of three ways: through Judaism's Babylonian heritage, by travels into pristine Zoroastrian territories and from Buddhism, in either the Middle East or farther east. The possibilities deserve examination, and any of these three could support the growing sense that while the context of Christianity is certainly Jewish, its subtext may be more Zoroastrian than Gnostic, Essene, Greek or any of the other alternatives that were the subject of speculation in the twentieth century.

The story of Buddha's birth, biography and spiritual awakening are well known and need not be recounted here any more than is necessary for the lives of Moses, Jesus or Muhammad, except for one salient point. The traditional dates for the life of Siddhartha Gautama, the historical Buddha, are 566–486 BCE. The dates for Cyrus the Great are 576–530, and the dates for Second Isaiah are approximately 590–540 BCE. All three reached the apex of their careers around the midpoint of the sixth century BCE, within a hundred years of the birth of Zoroaster. They were all young men at the time the fireworks of Zoroaster's spectacular ministry exploded between 588 and 551 BCE, or in its churning wake.

It is not suggested that either Second Isaiah or the Buddha ever actually met the prophetic initiator of the Axial Age before Zoroaster died, although we may be reasonably certain that Cyrus moved in Zoroaster's circle. In fact, he named his daughter, Atossa, after the wife of Vishtaspa, Zoroaster's royal patron. For that matter, the later rival of Darius for the Persian throne was a certain Gaumata,[9] who may have been the youngest son of Cyrus, bearing a name that some observers have taken to be a Persian rendering of Gautama, the Sanskrit name of Buddha. Clearly we are just beginning to connect the dots in a puzzle of some importance to the world.

The Buddha's awakening took place in Benares, India, about nine hundred miles from Bactria (see map on page 195), the center of Zoroastrian influence that was rippling out in every direction during Siddhartha's youth, challenging the accepted religious norms in a manner that was attractive to the young seeker of wisdom. Since we know it today from an Oriental context farther east, we tend not to think of Buddhism in its original Indian context, but it was no more than an Indian phenomenon in Buddha's own lifetime. It was the Hindu Vedic traditions that he challenged in India. He did so at the very time and in the manner that the Zoroastrian reforms were sweeping through all the areas that had experienced Aryan immigration, from Greece to India, and Buddha was certainly contemporary with the major prophets of Israel.

When the Brahmins eventually accepted the Buddhist reforms and Hinduism renewed itself, India was largely reclaimed for Hinduism, while evolving Buddhist influence continued to flourish from Sri Lanka to China and Japan. When Islam swept into India through Afghanistan in the eleventh century CE, the last vestiges of Buddhism disappeared from the area, except for remnants like the giant statues of Bamyan that were dynamited by the Taliban in 2001. While Cyrus spread Zoroastrian reforms by diplomacy throughout the Persian Empire, Buddha did the same by equally peaceful means through India and the Orient; both developments as part of the Axial Age were launched by the prophetic ministry of Zoroaster. If Jesus ever did visit Persia or India, it would have been local expressions of Zoroastrianism that he would have encountered, almost certainly including the Indian embodiment of Buddhism.

But such Eastern influences could also have come west to Egypt, Israel, Syria or elsewhere many years before the life of Jesus, and there is ample evidence that they did so. In Egyptian graves from as far back as the Eighteenth Dynasty (which fell in 1476 BCE) archaeologists have found Chinese porcelain pottery. From the reign of King David, around 1,000 BCE, to the prophetic ministry of Isaiah we see references to Israel's trade with Ophir, whose Oriental location is still uncertain.

Non-Jewish political and cultural influences eventually permeated Judea, which was an important shipping center for trade between India and the West and the military gateway for invasions of Egypt via land. By the time of Jesus, both land and sea trade routes had run through the area for centuries, leaving it dotted with ruins from Egyptian, Greek, Roman and other outposts.

The central core of the ancient Silk Road trading route connecting the Middle East and the Orient is a corridor of something over half a million square kilometers. As mentioned, it is almost exactly the size of Chile, which is often walked through on a hiking trail known as the Sendero de Chile. The example of Chile has been offered as an illustration of how easily people and ideas traversed such spaces, because that country is about as long and as wide and is much the same shape as the entire Silk Route with its various branches. Indeed, current research has established beyond doubt that even in primitive times the natives of North, Central and South America carried on commerce, exchanged ideas and intermingled populations from Alaska to the tip of Patagonia. The western extension of the Silk Road into Greece and Arabia and the eastern wings into China and India certainly carried goods, people and ideas to particular destinations at various times. Overland routes extending to Persia and western India were especially active after Alexander's invasion of western India 360 years before Christ. Most of the routes, whether connecting to wealthy cities in Egypt or in Greece and Rome, came through Jerusalem, from whence goods for Greece and Rome were shipped via the Mediterranean Sea.

Sea routes from Mumbai and the mouth of the Indus River also went through the Persian Gulf and the Red Sea, and since the distance between the mouths of the Indus and Tigris and Euphrates rivers was only about three hundred miles, much of that trade came up the Gulf of Aquaba and overland to Jerusalem and its nearby port at Joppa, as the Mediterranean trans-shipment point. During Jesus' time, Judea was part of a Roman province, and most of the trade was Roman. Being the wealthiest empire of the time, Rome sent tons of gold-minted *sesterce* coins eastward for goods from India and other places. Much of this trade came over the Mediterranean and through Judea to the Silk Road or south to the sea routes, making Jerusalem a cosmopolitan center.

Because of trade alone, Zoroastrianism and Indian Buddhism were known to the people in Judea, both through visitors and by their own observations in travel. To get on the Silk Road, Jesus probably would have gone east through Syria to Babylon, then northeast to what is now Tehran and on to the Zoroastrian heartland of Bactria. One possible way to explain the parallels between his teachings and Buddhist sayings is to conjecture that he spent some time there in the Buddhist temples "sitting among the teachers, listening to them and asking them questions,"[10] as was his wont since youth. No doubt he would increase in Wisdom, if this were the case, but that is not the only possible explanation for the "parallel sayings," as they are now called.

The Silk Route road runs in both directions, and Philo, a Jewish contemporary of Jesus, noted the presence of a colony of Therapeutae in Alexandria, Egypt.[11] Their name is widely assumed to be a Hellenization of Theravada, the most ancient sect of Indian Buddhism. Although Philo tends to confuse them with Essenes, also located in Alexandria, they are likely Indian Buddhists from an earlier mission. Information about such missions is available from several sources, summarized by Will Durant's popular history account of the great Indian king Ashoka (304–232 BCE), who "sent Buddhist missionaries to all parts of India and Ceylon, even to Syria, Egypt and Greece, where, perhaps, they helped prepare for the ethics of Christ."[12]

Max Muller at Oxford had already shown that some missionaries were actually sent more than thirty years prior to Ashoka's reign. He writes, "That remarkable missionary movement, beginning in 300 BCE, sent forth a succession of devoted men who spent their lives in spreading the faith of the Buddha over all parts of Asia."[13] These are remarkable observations in light of what is now being proposed concerning a link with Jesus. Nothing discovered in the twentieth century has done anything other than to strengthen awareness of the spiritual exchange that accompanied the trade exchange. Interest has been growing quietly over the last hundred years.

The actual analysis of parallels between Jesus and Buddha, and between their teachings, got off to several false starts by British civil servants in India, untrained in such disciplines but fascinated by what they discovered in the course of their work in India and farther east. They did manage to gain the attention of Albert J. Edmunds, an American scholar whose 1902 *Buddhist and Christian Gospels* was the first professional treatment of the parallel texts, a valued resource still in use today. In 1925, Oxford's famous New Testament scholar, B. H. Streeter, observed that "the moral teaching of Buddha has a remarkable resemblance to the Sermon on the Mount of Jesus,"[14] and the interest continued to grow, although without focus.

In the last decade of the twentieth century, as "new age" religious trends found focus in Buddhism, a plethora of creditable studies on the parallels between the sayings of Buddha and Jesus emerged from both Buddhist and Christian sources, practically simultaneously. In 1995 the Buddhist scholar and monk, Thich Nhat Hanh, wrote *Living Buddha, Living Christ*, in which he described them as his two spiritual ancestors, based on the compatibility of their teaching. In the same year Elmar R. Gruber and Holger Kersten presented a brilliant analysis of textual parallels in *The Original Jesus*, published simultaneously in German and English to popular acclaim.

The next year the Dalai Lama himself addressed the subject of the parallel texts in his book, *The Good Heart: A Buddhist Perspective on the Teachings of Jesus*. In the year following that, Marcus Borg, a highly respected scholar of Christian Scriptures, addressed the matter in some depth in *Jesus and Buddha: The Parallel Sayings*, an exhaustive survey to which we will refer. With these scholarly assessments, crowned by the work of the Dalai Lama and Marcus Borg, the subject has moved from fringe speculation to serious study, though a central focus was still lacking, a weakness we hope to address.

The 1995 publication, *The Original Jesus* by Gruber and Kersten, is a veritable *tour de force*. By reputable and articulate scholars, it stands head and shoulders above some of the more speculative works on the subject, although it also raises questions. Put succinctly, Gruber and Kersten believe that the parallels are too many and too close to dismiss, so Jesus must have somehow come into contact with Philo's Essene Buddhists, either by visiting Egypt again as a young adult or in an encounter with Buddhists in one of the Gentile cities in Israel. This could have taken place in either Scythopolis or Sebaste, both on the west side of the Jordan River, not far from his home in Nazareth. This is a bold idea, and the fact that these Indian Buddhists and Jesus both probably spoke Aramaic is a corroborative addition to the theory.

Gruber and Kersten make little of the Zoroastrian Magi connection in Matthew since they are on the trail of an Essene/Gnostic Buddhism. However, the current doyenne of Gnostic studies, Elaine Pagels, alludes to the possibility that Gnosticism itself was derived from Zoroastrianism, building on the research of Christian Gospel scholar Wilhelm Bousset[15] and Jewish philologist Richard Reitzenstein,[16] two leading figures of the History of Religions School[17] who saw Zoroastrianism as the connecting link in all these movements.

While parallel sayings are the main basis of their belief that Jesus must have met and known some Buddhists very well, Gruber and Kersten also open their argument with a birth story event—not the visit of the Magi but the story of Simeon as it appears in the Gospel.[18] More than even the most remarkable parallels among the sayings of Jesus and Buddha, this story of an old man blessing the baby Jesus in the Jerusalem temple so closely mirrors the story of Asita,[19] an old man who blesses the Buddha as an infant, that the similarities are impossible to ignore. It was noticed first in 1914 by Richard Garbe, an Indianologist who famously debunked the extravagant claims of the civil servant amateurs who were beginning these studies, but then even Garbe declared this parallel event to be "beyond chance."[20]

In both cases an elderly man who had devoted his life to religion has been told by heavenly beings that before he dies a child will be born who will bring salvation to the people. Each man takes the baby in his arms, blesses him and prepares to depart this life in peace. Simeon proclaims the infant to be the promised Messiah on the basis of inspiration by the Holy Spirit, and Asita announces that the infant is the Buddha who was to come, inspired by a vision.

The Asita story is found in all ancient biographies of the Buddha, including the most ancient and revered Pali text,[21] centuries before the Common Era. How the story got into the collection of sources of information about Jesus collected by Saint Luke is not hard to imagine. It is Luke's version of a messianic prooftext, eagerly included when, as a folktale, someone reported it as pertaining to Jesus. There is an attempt to justify its conclusion by reporting that the parents of Jesus brought him to the Temple to fulfill the requirements of the law. That purported requirement was that every firstborn male child shall be designated as holy to the Lord, quoting a Scripture[22] that actually excuses people from this duty, thanks to the sacrifice of the Levites. There is no such Jewish requirement that we know of, and no temple, synagogue or home ceremony corresponds to the Gospel account, despite the attempt to imagine appropriate sacrificial offerings to go with the supposed event. In India, however, it was and remains customary to bring a child to the temple for such a dedication.

The parallel sayings provide more than a hundred examples of close similarities between the teachings of Jesus and Buddha. Marcus Borg is perhaps best described as a wise and experienced "editor" rather than the author of *Jesus and Buddha: The Parallel Sayings*, easily the best resource in directly comparing such materials. He groups the parallel sayings into subject areas—Compassion, Wisdom, Materialism, Inner Life, Temptation, Salvation, The Future, Miracles, Discipleship, Attributes and Life Stories—and he provides his own insightful commentary. We will examine about a tenth of the total in Borg's excellent presentation by way of illustrating that they may be too similar to be by chance, and too numerous to ignore.

Buddha: "Consider others as yourself."[23]

Jesus: "Do to others as you would have them do to you."[24]

Buddha: "If anyone should give you a blow with his hand, with a stick, or with a knife, you should abandon any desires and utter no evil words."[25]

Jesus: "If anyone strikes you on the cheek, offer the other also."[26]

Buddha: "The faults of others are easier to see than one's own."[27]

Jesus: "Why do you see the speck in your neighbor's eye, but do not notice the log in your own eye?"[28]

Re: Buddha: "During six years that the Bodhisattva practiced austerities, the demon followed behind him step by step seeking an opportunity to harm him. But he found no opportunity whatsoever and went away discouraged and discontent."[29]

Re: Jesus: "When the devil had finished every test, he departed from him until an opportune time."[30]

Buddha: "Those who have sufficient faith in me, sufficient love for me, are all headed for heaven or beyond."[31]

Jesus: "Everyone who lives and believes in me will never die."[32]

Buddha: "This great earth will be burnt up, will utterly perish and be no more."[33]

Jesus: "Heaven and Earth will pass away."[34]

Buddha: "A monk who is skilled in concentration can cut the Himalayas in two."[35]

Jesus: "If you have faith the size of a mustard seed, you will say to this mountain, 'Move from here to there,' and it will move."[36]

Buddha: "The avaricious do not go to heaven, the foolish do not extol charity. The wise one, however, rejoicing in charity, becomes thereby happy in the beyond."[37]

Jesus: "If you wish to be perfect, go, sell your possessions, and give the money to the poor, and you will have treasure in heaven."[38]

Buddha: "Let us live most happily, possessing nothing; let us feed on joy, like radiant gods."[39]

Jesus: "Blessed are you who are poor, for yours is the kingdom of God."[40]

Buddha: "Let your thoughts of boundless love pervade the whole world."[41]

Jesus: "This is my commandment, that you love one another as I have loved you."[42]

Buddha: "Those who have no accumulation, who eat with perfect knowledge, whose sphere is emptiness, singleness and liberation, are hard to track, like birds in the sky."[43]

Jesus: "Therefore I tell you, do not worry about your life, what you will eat or what you will drink, or about your body, what you will wear. Is not life more than food and the body more than clothing? Look at the birds of the air; they neither sow nor reap, nor gather into barns, and yet your heavenly Father feeds them."[44]

Buddha: "The great cloud rains down on all whether their nature is superior or inferior. The light of the sun and the moon illuminates the whole world, both him who does well and him who does ill, both him who stands high and him who stands low."[45]

Jesus: "Your Father in heaven makes his sun rise on the evil and on the good, and sends rain on the righteous and on the unrighteous."[46]

Buddha: "Let the wise man do righteousness: a treasure that others cannot share, which no thief can steal; a treasure which does not pass away."[47]

Jesus: "Do not store up for yourselves treasures on earth, where moth and rust consume and thieves break in and steal; but store up for yourselves treasures in heaven, where neither moth nor rust consumes and where thieves do not break in and steal."[48]

Buddha: "When Brahmins teach a path that they do not know or see, saying 'This is the only path,' this cannot be right. A file of blind men go on, and the first one sees nothing, the middle one sees nothing, and the last one sees nothing—so it is with the Brahmins."[49]

Jesus: "Can a blind person guide a blind person? Will not both fall into a pit?"[50]

As we begin the analysis of the parallel sayings, it may be helpful to observe that while some parallels are scattered throughout the Gospel, they are concentrated in the Sermon on the Mount and other sayings of Jesus that appear in the document or source known as Q, which forms part of the Gospels by both Matthew and Luke. If we may presume to regard Buddhism as the main Axial Age derivative from Zoroastrianism in the east, the Buddhist parallels in Q may be said to represent Avesta material as buried within the Christian Scriptures.

Q is increasingly regarded by many as possibly the earliest or first "Gospel" in use by the Christian Church, preceding Mark by an undetermined number of years. Both Marcus Borg and Gruber and Kersten note the concentration of parallels with Buddha sayings in Q, but the Gruber-Kersten team goes further in adopting a theory that Q itself comes from three sources, or consists of three sections, one of which is previous to Jesus and may itself be Buddhist.

While Q research continues as one of the most exciting elements of twenty-first century research into the Christian Scriptures, this is perhaps the first instance of where it appears that Gruber and Kersten overextend themselves. They appear to move into speculation beyond evidence that is sufficiently convincing to illustrate a direct personal connection between Jesus and the Buddhists in Israel. For reasons that will become apparent, it may be suggested that Borg, on the other hand, possibly errs on the side of too much caution in his judgment that the Wisdom taught by Jesus and by Buddha is similar merely because they experienced religious phenomena common to humanity. There is an attractive and convincing middle ground that suggests a genuine connec-

The Port City of Tyre in Approximately 1750 CE, Perhaps Little Different from When Jesus Visited

tion between Buddha and Jesus, not tight enough to believe that one copied from the other, but strong enough to suggest the sharing of a common source. We might note that our map of the Silk Route on page 195 shows the birthplace of the Buddha in Banares and the childhood home of Jesus in Nazareth to be equidistant from Bactria, the ancient heartland of Zoroastrianism. The distance is substantial but manageable at just over nine hundred miles (1,500 kilometers) in each instance.

In fact, there are no specific reports of Buddhist monks visiting Israel itself, which would be more noticeable than one person like Jesus visiting Bactria or India, though at least putative reports exist even regarding that particular solitary visit. The original Buddhist religious mission to Egypt was three hundred years earlier and had made little noticeable impact, leading to the assumption that a "colony" left behind did not see itself as a mission to anybody, and Philo's description, while laudatory, confirms that impression.

On the other hand, Borg says, "The primary purpose of this collection of essays and sayings was not to make a scholarly case for similarity. Rather, the purpose of this collection is to provide opportunity for reflection and meditation. The sayings can illuminate each other."[51] While we are indebted to him for an accessible work of considerable scholarship, we may contend that he understates the case for some kind of actual connection between Jesus and Buddha, given his own convincing presentation of parallels that even lay readers find impossible to regard as merely coincidental. Noting the parallels is interesting, but, having let the genie out of the bottle, that is not enough for most of us. The book raises questions such as the following: How could Jesus, living five hundred years after Buddha and almost two thousand miles away, present teachings so similar in nature to the sayings attributed to Buddha in ancient Buddhist Scriptures?

Did Jesus clumsily replicate the sayings of Buddha, or is it not more probable that they had a common source that they each appropriated in their own way? If so, what could it have been?

Sidon in the Then Province of Syria, Visited by Jesus as Mentioned in Mark 7:24, 31 and Parallels (from an engraving by an unknown artist, published in London in 1850 CE)

Borg refers to certain rumors concerning a possible visit to India by Jesus, but he thinks a better explanation of the parallels is that Buddha and Jesus were both merely teaching universal truths. Thus, just as Gruber and Kersten appear to be overreaching in making their case for Jesus meeting Buddhists in Israel, Borg may be said to understate the possibility of any actual connection between Buddhism and Jesus. In both cases they fail to connect Buddhism with Zoroastrianism, despite the fact that the Axial Age affiliation is now almost universally accepted. We are still connecting the dots, noting that while Buddha and Jesus were born some two thousand miles apart, the Zoroastrian heartland, as the midpoint, was accessible to both of them. Zoroastrian influence certainly extended to the Persian Empire of Cyrus, connecting the Indian Empire of Ashoka and the Judaism in which Jesus was raised. We postulate Zoroastrianism as the common source, and while the connections between the Buddha and Jesus do not finally indicate that Jesus ever met Buddhists in or near Palestine, the Z factor does further strengthen the hypothesis that he traveled to the east.

We do not have the original words of Zoroaster, but Buddha's saying, "Anyone who withdraws into meditation can see Brahma with his own eyes,"[52] becomes "Blessed are the pure in heart, for they will see God"[53] when Jesus is speaking to a Jewish audience. His parallels with Buddhist Scriptures, which were themselves derived from the spiritual dynamics of the Zoroastrian Axial Age phenomena, no doubt contained Avesta material otherwise now lost to us.

Finally, we examine another parallel, not between Jesus and Buddha themselves, but, like the adopted story of Simeon, between the first Christian writers and the historical legends from Buddhist sources. In Revelation, Saint John weeps because he sees no one worthy to open the book and to break its seven seals. This can only be done by the Lamb, slaughtered in sacrifice.[54] In the Buddhist Scriptural legend, The Perfection of Wisdom, the book was also sealed with seven seals, and no one could be found who was worthy to open it, inducing the tearful Bodhisattva (Buddha) to sacrifice himself to become worthy.[55] This, too, simply must come from the common source in Zoroastrianism.

Zoroastrianism was also the umbrella over Gnosticism, Essenism, Cabalism, Wisdom traditions and Jewish groups like the one at Qumran, among others. Those others would have included the Sabaeans in Syria, who, like the Magians, had become thoroughly Zoroastrianized by the time of Jesus, though in the context of dualistic heresy. Buddhism was one of the more spectacular reform movements to come out of Zoroastrianism early on, but it was one that had little exposure in Israel until possibly introduced by Jesus. Those Christians who are aghast at the suggestion that Jesus may have borrowed or adapted Buddhist themes should regard his use of those or any other Zoroastrian motifs in the same way they regard his use of the Jewish Scriptures. Jesus was thoroughly grounded in the Jewish context, as we have seen earlier, but Christians consider him the "Savior of the World," and the ideas introduced here are not incompatible with that view.

8
gospel and quran

T HE QURAN IS NOT ABOUT MUHAMMAD, WHO IS SCARCELY MENTIONED IN THE TEXT, BECAUSE the focus of the Quran is not Muhammad's message but God's message to Muslims. Likewise, though the core speeches in Deuteronomy may be from him, the Torah is not about Moses as much as it is about the Hebrew people and their interface with the Divine. The Gospel is different from both in this respect since it is about Jesus, considered by Christians to be the living word of God in a way that the Quran is regarded as the written words of God, and Israel is seen as the living people of God. Thus any appreciation of the Christian Scriptures requires a particular understanding of Jesus in a dynamic tension between metaphor and history. Pope Benedict XVI insists that "being Christian is not the result of an ethical choice or a lofty idea, but the encounter with an event, a person, which gives life a new horizon and a decisive direction."[1]

The Quran does contain much about Jesus, not as future prophecy the way Christians regard the Hebrew Scriptures, but as later prophetic reaction and insight, so we now turn to an examination of the Christian Scriptures in relation to the perspective found in the Quran. As obtuse as theological dogma may seem, we will attempt to engage it in reference to three Christian doctrines that grow out of Scripture but which make little or no sense without the prerequisite of knowing Jesus personally and then letting the Scriptures speak. The doctrine of the Divinity of Christ, the doctrine of the Trinity and the doctrine of the Cross are profound metaphors that took centuries to find universally agreed-upon articulation among Christians. They reflect the Christian experience of God in Christ, and while Scripture is an amplification of that personal experience, doctrine is a reflection upon it that possibly can never make complete sense on its own. This accords with a view of the Christian Scriptures that likewise do not make sense without a personal acquaintance with Jesus.

We will limit the discussion of the Divinity of Christ to the Christian belief that Jesus is the "Son of God." The Quran has at least twelve specific condemnations or rejections of the concept that Jesus was the Son of God. The following are sufficient to illustrate the disagreement:

"He (God) is The Originator of the heavens and the earth; how would he have a son when he has had no companion?"[2]

"Indeed you have brought about a disastrous thing whereby the heavens are almost split asunder and the earth is split, and the mountains fall crashing down—that they attribute a son to The Merciful when it is not fit and proper for The Merciful that He should take a son to Himself."[3]

Did Jesus regard himself as the Son of God? Jesus' own preferred phrase to describe Himself was "Son of Man," and he used that phrase as a Messianic title derived from Hebrew Scriptures of the

Babylonian era almost a hundred times in the four canonical gospels.[4] He did also refer to God as his Father often enough that both his friends and his critics took this as a reference to his sonship, but it can be argued that Jesus spoke metaphorically in these cases and that he never used the term *Son of God* as a title. There are a few possible exceptions to this observation in the Gospel of John, the last Gospel to be written, in which the preference and practice of the Church may have crept back into the mouth of Jesus. In the first three Gospels Jesus never even once describes himself as the Son of God.

But even if Jesus never, or rarely, used "Son of God" as a title, the phrase appears in all four Gospels in the mouths of others, and it is used consistently throughout the rest of the Christian Scriptures, to the complete exclusion of the "Son of Man." The description of Jesus as the Son of God is unrivalled as the heartfelt expression of how his followers experienced Jesus, thought of him and spoke of him. The point is that these Scriptures only "make sense" from the perspective of knowing Jesus in a certain way. In this case, Muslims might begin by recognizing that for many Christians the sonship of Jesus is spiritual and metaphorical, and not necessarily carnal and physical.

Not even many Christian literalists would subscribe to a theory that God personally impregnated Mary with physical sperm, and so the matter is absolutely spiritual; indeed, it is "from the Holy Spirit."[5] Saying what that means in ordinary language is impossible, so the church has resorted to creedal metaphors, despite the attempts by a few to force a literal understanding. Certain Christians may also need to deepen their understanding of the metaphorical power of these doctrines, a manner of communication used in expressing realities that are too deep for ordinary words. This understanding of dogma does not downgrade or denigrate the historical realities on which they are founded but upgrades and enhances their spiritual meaning and authority.

To go even one step further, the Gospel says that "to all who received him, who believe in his name, he gave power to become the sons of God,"[6] giving his use of the phrase an even wider metaphoric meaning not found in the way Jesus used the title, "Son of Man." It is also interesting to note that the term *son of God* is used in other parts of the Bible to refer to Adam,[7] Israel[8] and David[9] as well. In passing we may also note that the Hebrew Scriptures use "Son of Man" as a title for the Messiah, while Christians have largely adopted the messianic phrase "Son of God," and Muslims describe the Messiah as "Son of Mary." None of these distinctions are wrong, but in properly understanding each, they are all instructive.

A second area of both misunderstanding and disagreement is the Trinity, a theological construct actually discussed in the Quran, although it is a word not once mentioned in the Bible. In one Gospel we find Jesus giving "the great commission" to his disciples: "Go therefore and make disciples of all nations, baptizing them in the name of the Father and of the Son and of the Holy Spirit."[10] In one epistle also we find Paul writing, "The grace of the Lord Jesus Christ, the love of God and the communion of the Holy Spirit be with all of you."[11] In neither case are these entities or attributes of God called a trinity, and it was left to the church to flesh out the idea of how these experiences of God should be described. The discussion took centuries, and the first person to use the term *Trinity* to describe the relationship between God the Father, Jesus the Son and the Holy Spirit was the theologian Tertullian in the third century. He was the same scholar who gave the church the phrases *Vetus Testamentum* ("Old Testament") and *Novum Testamentum* ("New Testament"), increasingly falling into disuse today in favor of Hebrew Scriptures and Christian Scriptures, though the Trinity is likely to remain as an expression of the ways Christians have experienced God—even if it is a metaphor not found in the Bible.

There are two clear references to the Trinity in the Quran, and many other verses that reject any kind of divine partnership for God. Those references specifically focused on the Trinity are also related to the foregoing discussion about Jesus as the Son of God:

> Christ Jesus, the son of Mary, was no more than an apostle of God, and his Word, which He bestowed on Mary, and a Spirit proceeding from him. So believe in God and His apostles. Say not "Trinity": desist; it will be better for you: For God is One God: Glory be to Him.[12]

> They do blaspheme who say: God is one of three in a Trinity: for there is no God except One God.[13]

There is also one other verse that involves some considerable misunderstanding by both Muslims and Christians. It is frequently used to illustrate that Muslims believe Christians have a Trinity of Father, Son and Mother, a canard that has led to unnecessary heated discussions.

And behold! God will say: "O Jesus, the son of Mary, didst thou say unto men, 'Worship me and my mother as gods, in derogation of God?' He will say, 'Never could I say what I have no right to say.'"[14]

In spite of the appearance at first glance, the Quran does not actually suggest here or anywhere that Christians believe in a Trinity that consists of God, Jesus and Mary. Over the centuries many Muslims have thought it says so, but the Trinity per se is not even mentioned in this verse, which is actually about something else. To this day one constantly meets Muslim scholars of high rank who protest regarding the Trinity with comments like, "Christians believe that Mary is part of the Trinity with Jesus and God." Muslims need to understand that there has never been a single Christian person, believer or scholar, alive or dead, nor any pronouncement by any Christian body, to suggest such a Trinity of Father, Son and Mother exists. Christians have used this misunderstanding to deride both Muslims and Islam for their "ignorance," but Christians have been equally ignorant in their assumption that this is the meaning of the verse in the Quran.

The English Catholic ecumenist Edward Hulmes has explained the matter well. He writes, "The Qur'anic interpretation of trinitarian orthodoxy as belief in the Father, the Son, and the Virgin Mary, may owe less to a misunderstanding of the New Testament itself than to a recognition of the role accorded by local Arabs to Mary as divine in a special sense."[15] Hulmes is referring to the Chollyridians, a pagan sect from Thrace and Scythia that migrated to Arabia, where it was in vogue many years before Muhammad, worshipping both Mary and Jesus. The verse in question should not be considered as a Quranic teaching on the Christian Trinity, but rather, giving examples of *shirk* (claiming divinity for beings other than God). David Thomas, also at Oxford, describes this verse as a "warning against excessive devotion to Jesus and extravagant veneration of Mary, a reminder linked to the central theme of the Quran that there is only one God and he alone is to be worshipped."[16] These recent comments may be taken as illustrative of a new spirit of more positive attempts at understanding by Christians and Muslims in the twenty-first century.

The fact of the matter is that the Quran, Islam as a religion and Muslim believers in general are united in their concern that the dualism[17] that pervaded and perverted Zoroastrianism not be somehow compounded by Christian belief in a Trinity that could be seen as three separate entities. In reply, it can never be said often enough that Christians believe in only one God but that they have experienced this God in three ways in particular.

Many such areas of seeming contention are based not on Scripture, but on elaborations of Scriptural themes as experienced by Christians in order to make sense of Scripture in light of their experience. Again, it was Tertullian, the first of the "Latin Fathers," who gave the church the terminology. He wrote of "*tres Personae, una Substantia*," which is usually translated into English as "three persons of one substance." *Persons* has come to mean people in English and in many other languages, but in fact the Latin word *persona* means "mask, face or appearance." Perhaps it is more appropriate for Christians to speak of God having three personas.

To offer a shallow illustration, the author of this book is one person with three main personas. He is called "father" by a young woman who lives near Toronto, "son" by an older woman who has lived most of her life in Halifax, and "husband" by a woman who lives with him in Niagara Falls. He is not three persons, although in three very different contexts he has three personas. This is like Christians saying they have experienced three personas of God, rather than saying that God is three persons in one. Christians have experienced God as a Father (Parent or Creator), and have experienced God through Jesus (friend and Savior), and have experienced God as the Holy Spirit (wind and breath of life).[18] Literary critic Northrop Frye might insist that all words are metaphorical, standing for something. The difficulties surrounding the Trinity might be better articulated by acknowledging that "earthly" terms of time and space are inadequate to describe the God who dwells in multidimensional eternity, were it not for the conundrum of Christians who have experienced the transcendent Deity as also an immanent Deity.

There may be other experiences of God, but the three—Creator, Christ and Spirit—are primary for Christians, who note God's own use of the first-person plural ("We") to describe divinity in both the Quran and the Torah. Christians could accuse Muslims who speak of "ninety-nine names of God" as confusing God's identity or having ninety-nine Gods, but this could only be done in a spirit of pernicious petulance, or by deliberately misunderstanding the Muslim dedication to monotheism. In a similar manner, Christians now ask Muslims to stop misreading the Quran itself to the effect that both Mary and Jesus are part of the Trinity, as separate gods. Hindus speak of God having one hundred faces, and if Muslims can find ninety-nine names identifying God in the Quran, the discussion might proceed from the sense that Christians attribute only three "masks" or personas to God. Muslims may object to the word "Trinity," and this powerful metaphor may still be a source of disagreement, but the Quran's stricture is aimed at the Church, rather than at the Christian Scriptures.

Finally, according to many, the Quran appears to deny the crucifixion of Jesus, and with it, one of the most sacred beliefs of Christianity. However, the crucifixion is only mentioned in one verse in the whole Quran, and the precise interpretation of that verse has been the subject of considerable debate between Christians and Muslims, and even among Muslims themselves.

It is commonly held in Islam that the crucifixion of Jesus Christ simply did not occur. Muslims dispute the fact of Jesus' crucifixion, arguing that God would never have dishonored His prophet by allowing Him to undergo such a death. Muslims believe that Jesus was miraculously transported into Paradise and that either Judas Iscariot or someone else got crucified in the melee and confusion surrounding the cross. For that matter, the Gospel accounts are partly based on sketchy evidence and hearsay since, regarding the apostles themselves, the Gospel says that at the most critical juncture in the life of Jesus, "All of them deserted him and fled,"[19] but this explanation is not found in the Quran.

What the Quran says in that one verse is interpreted as

[They said]: "We have killed the Messiah, Jesus, son of Mary, the Messenger of God: yet they killed him not, nor they crucified him; but a likeness was shown to them; and truly those who were at variance about him are in uncertainty about him; they have no knowledge about him, but are pursuing an opinion; and certainly they killed him not. Rather, God exalted him to Himself, and God has been Almighty and Wise."[20]

Most Muslims believe this to mean that Jesus Christ never died and was never resurrected, but simply ascended up to heaven. Yet the Quran itself quotes Jesus earlier as saying, "Peace be on me, the day on which I was given birth, and the day I die, and the day I shall be raised up, living."[21] The Quran does not specifically deny the resurrection, and Christians can agree that they (Roman officers and Jewish authorities) "killed him not," since Jesus himself says, "No one takes my life from me, but I lay it down of my own accord."[22] The Quran confirms that Jesus was not "murdered" against his will, but the fancy lace of its written text leaves more room for the Christian view than is usually sanctioned by Muslims. In the Quran as recited, "They did not *crucify* him" might become "*They* did not crucify him" in Christian ears, a topic for discussion.

This is not an attempt to harmonize the texts of the Quran and the Gospel, which are distinct and different, but rather to more correctly see what each is actually saying in relation to the other. The point of this whole chapter is that Christians believe these things because of their own experience of God, who in Jesus does share in their indignities. He "feels our pain and shares our shame."[23] Traditional orthodox Christian belief is that Jesus was God, who came to earth and was crucified in order to totally identify with humans in their pain and shame. Jesus was then raised by God's own divine power as an assurance that none who identify with Him can be overcome by life's challenges, no matter how horrific. This classical Christian doctrine is, for believers, at a minimum, the most powerfully sophisticated metaphor in the history of the world, its literature and its religion. For Jews, this is a view of the messiah that is unacceptable, for the most part. For Muslims, it is a totally inappropriate view of God. For Christians it is the fundamental measure of how completely God loves each human being. It is at this point that the metaphor "Son of God" becomes less helpful, with the concept of sacrifice needing to be rescued by the Scriptures that assert that God gives himself for us on the cross—a concept expressed by and seen in gospel songs, the sacrifice of the mass, seeing "through" icons, selfless service and any or all of a myriad of other helpful metaphors. One of the more common modern misunderstandings of the doctrine of the cross is the suggestion that it represents appeasement to an angry God who sent his son in order to kill him as an atonement for the sins of believers, a caricature adopted even by some Christians. At this point it is necessary to emphasize the Christian experience of God's love as a Deity who draws near to people to identify with their life and death struggles. But putting absolute trust in God (faith), they are enabled to become one with God in his victory over sin, share in God's resurrection and receive the gift of God's spirit.

Muslims were not the first to question the way these doctrines have been expressed by the church. Alternative forms of Christianity in ancient times did not survive, except for remnants here and there, but of late there has been interest in the Gnostic Gospels, both those preserved in libraries by the church and a trove of others recently discovered in the Nag Hammadi Library, uncovered in the Egyptian desert in 1945. To illustrate alternative answers to the questions at hand, we turn to the Gospel of Barnabas, sometimes erroneously considered to be one of the lesser-known Gnostic Gospels. While, like John's Gospel, it is tinged with Gnostic influence, its core is likely previous to any other Christian/Gnostic documents and its bulk consists of an elaboration from the late Middle Ages. It is one document that liberal Christians have difficulty taking at face value and to which conservatives react with indignation, but it illustrates an important point, albeit in hyperbole.

The Gospel of Barnabas is an apocryphal Gospel, a life of Jesus purportedly written by a first-hand observer that is at variance with the presentation in the Bible. However, it is unique among apocryphal writings in that it is a Gospel widely quoted by Muslims. That is because this document of Christian origin describes Jesus as a human prophet, not the Son of God, and it also presents him as a forerunner of Muhammad. According to both Christian and Muslim scholarship, the Gospel of Barnabas as we have it now is a fourteenth-century collage, based on ancient material and medieval speculation. Original copies produced in that era are extant now only in Spanish and Italian manuscripts. Some of the speculations may have come out of the vortex of the golden age of ecumenism in Spain between the tenth and twelfth centuries when Jews, Christians and Muslims attempted to state their beliefs in terms that might be appreciated by the others. Yet there is little doubt that some of the material contained in the book is from an original Gospel of Barnabas, circulating in the ancient church.

The early church apologist, Irenaeus (130–200 CE), was said to have quoted from the Gospel of Barnabas in support of his views on pure monotheism, as opposed to certain of the more elaborate expressions of trinitarianism.[24] The now lost original Gospel of Barnabas was accepted as a canonical Gospel in the churches of Alexandria until 325 CE. Its value was debated at the council of Nicaea, and there are records of a copy in the papal library from 383 CE until it went missing sometime after the Gospel of Barnabas was listed and condemned in a decree by Pope Gelasius I (492–495 CE). Regardless of the spurious additions to the copies in our possession, we know that this material existed in some form at an early stage of Christianity.

Given its extreme antiquity, this ancient Gospel was quite possibly written by Barnabas, an early companion of Paul on his missionary journeys around the Mediterranean. It is not to be confused with Gnostic documents known as the Epistle of Barnabas and the Acts of Barnabas, both written sometime later in his name. According to the Scriptures, Barnabas eventually fell out with Paul on issues of personnel to be entrusted with the mission and possibly on matters of theology, so he went his own way.[25] Judging by the enduring tone of the Gospel of Barnabas, the matter on which they most sharply disagreed may have related to metaphors articulating the divinity of Jesus, which has always been a stumbling block for Jews and Muslims.

Many Muslim publishing houses have published their own versions of this Gospel, most of them in English, based on the widely accepted 1909 version by Lonsdale and Laura Ragg. Some modern Muslims treat it as an authentic and ancient record of events, though practically all of the more highly respected Muslim scholars recognize its checkered provenance, including Abbas Mahmoud el-Akkad, the esteemed Egyptian specialist in Christian texts.[26] Few deny that the Spanish text contains medieval speculation, and the Italian text in particular includes substantial elements of even more recent addition, such as phrases from Dante's *Inferno*, including "false and lying gods," "raging hunger" and "the seven circles of hell."

So why is the Gospel of Barnabas quoted and studied? It is the Muslim view that the *Injil* (Gospel), delivered through the prophet Isa (Jesus), has itself been corrupted and seriously distorted in the course of Christian copying and accommodation to evolving church doctrine. Consequently, according to Muslim teaching, no absolute confidence should be placed in any text in the Christian Bible, including the four canonical Gospels, as actually representing the teachings of Jesus. From an orthodox Islamic perspective, the Gospel of Barnabas is clearly a document of Christian origin, not Muslim, as is demonstrated by its many points of difference from the Quran, but a document that testifies to divergent doctrine and use of metaphors in the early church.

Despite its corruptions and distortions, Muslim scholars are also pleased to note the many elements of the Gospel of Barnabas that agree with Quranic teaching, such as the denial of Jesus being the Son of God and the prophetic prediction by Jesus of a coming representative of God, whom they believe to be Muhammad. Consequently, many Muslims are inclined to regard the Gospel of Barnabas as representing the survival of suppressed early traditions about Jesus that are compatible with Islam. Their point may have some limited legitimacy in this regard, just as Christians now acknowledge at least peripheral validity to certain Gnostic writings, like the Gospel of Thomas, which, along with spurious material, may well contain sayings of Jesus recorded nowhere else.

To give an example of elements that Christians traditionally regard as heterodox, the Gospel of Barnabas says clearly that Jesus himself said he was *not* the Messiah. The italics are mine, indicating that just as he suggested all believers might become the "sons" or "children of God," he also made it clear that everything his followers saw him do could be done by them, and more as well.[27] The Hebrew Scriptures attach the title of Messiah to several figures, but the Christian and Muslim Scriptures both associate it with Jesus alone, although their meanings are slightly different. Barnabas quotes Jesus as also giving this term a wider connotation. This could not be possible if Jesus actually did see himself as the Zoroastrian Saoshyant, a savior for each one and for all, for time and for eternity.

The church simply rejected what Barnabas reported because it was not in accord with what Christians were experiencing personally in reference to Jesus. The Gospel of Barnabas was not, therefore, included in the canon of Christian Scriptures. There may have been Christians for whom such views resonated for a time, but not for the bishops, priests, elders and members of the church whose personal experience of Jesus dictated what went into Scripture and how it is normally interpreted by those who know Jesus. This point must be understood in any attempt to understand the Gospel Scriptures.

The questions of provenance concerning the Gospel of Barnabas are not very different from issues about the reliability related to the four Gospels of Matthew, Mark, Luke and John, which are actually included in the Christian Scriptures. Their dates are uncertain, their authorship is disputed and their purposes appear in different lights to succeeding generations. These questions have been examined exhaustively by the Jesus Seminar, among many others, and there is little objective proof of their authenticity. The difference is that the canonical Gospels are accepted not because there is proof of their authenticity but because they resonate with the picture of Jesus as he is known or claimed to be known by Christians. This relates to the subjective aspect of Christian Scriptures to which we have alluded previously, and to which we must now return.

This is where a testimony to a Christian's personal relationship with God as revealed in Jesus Christ may correlate with an academic assessment of the Christian Scriptures. These personal observations are offered here to explain to others and to remind Christians of the basis for a correct understanding of the Gospel, including those aspects that appear "hard to believe."

In my childhood I met Jesus in my parents and especially in my grandparents, who knew little theology but did know Him. I also met Jesus in my Sunday School teachers and church camp leaders who, I have since discovered, sometimes gave me wrong information about the Bible but loved me and modeled Christ as they knew Him. One shopkeeper, several school teachers and a policeman gave me to understand that they walked and talked with Jesus. I have also seen Him in the faces of some people who are not in the church but who have known God in a way I can only describe as Christlike, given my own experiences with Jesus, as I have known Him.

In 1966 I was ordained to the ministry in the Maritime Conference of the United Church of Canada, a broad Canadian union of mainly Scottish Presbyterians, English and Irish Methodists, New

England Congregationalists (the Puritan Pilgrims) and some others. I had trained for the ministry in an ecumenical faculty at McGill University in Montreal, which I chose to attend at a time when the United Church was preparing for an ultimately stillborn union with the Anglican Church. In that context I met Jesus again, in the Divine Liturgy of the Anglican tradition. I recognized that He is personally known in that context in a transcendent beauty not experienced as often in the more mundane, prosaic and rational United Church.

After ordination, my first appointment was to a cluster of several small country churches in Alberta, where mature Ukrainian Orthodox priests adopted their junior colleague and introduced me to the mystique of seeing Jesus through icons, as also experienced by the old Russian monks still there from the Alaskan mission and by the professional children of the Ukrainian peasants who populated the prairies and brought those practices into the congregations I was serving. They knew Jesus in a tradition that ultimately outlasted even the Communist Party in their former homeland, and this convinced me of the durability of the church that knows Jesus, even when it experiences great challenges or temporarily loses popular appeal.

As a country, Canada is statistically 75 percent Christian in religious affiliation, and 75 percent of the Christians identify themselves with just three denominations: Anglican, Catholic and United (members, adherents, children and affiliates). The 25 percent classified as "other" often appear more focused and exhibit even greater vitality, while the big three may be in transition to culturally based as opposed to "active member"–based Christianity, similar to Jewish and Islamic traditions where both core participants and cultural affiliates are cherished. The Roman Catholic tradition to which 22 percent of Americans adhere is represented historically as 44 percent in Canada, so most Canadians find themselves in the Catholic environment on occasion, where they encounter Jesus in the sacrament of the mass. The word *palpable* is often overused of late, but the "real presence of Christ" in the bread and wine of Catholic communion can perhaps be best described in that manner in a particular spiritual ethos that remains the single most pervasive religious entity in America, in Canada and also in Mexico, where 88 percent of the population is at least nominally Catholic (and moving north).

The point is that not only do these Christian traditions all use the same Scriptures but the basis of understanding these Scriptures is also identical, specifically in first knowing Jesus and then having that knowledge amplified by Scriptures, which ring true to the experience of His presence in their lives, whether in the mass, the evangelical rally, divine liturgy, the practice of praying through icons, prophetic social activism, the sacrament of the mass, hymns or even just gospel music.

People associated with my own Scottish and Irish Protestant cultural ethnicity have been somewhat dominant through English Canadian history, in which the United Church is the largest Protestant denomination. Its members do not dominate but do permeate community life and enjoy a high level of success, prosperity and influence. This is changing with the welcome influx of Muslim, Hindu and other ethnocultural religious communities, whose members are highly educated and increasingly vigorous as participants in community life.

The presence of Christ in the lives of United Church members is frequently intellectual and oriented toward community service and the promotion of social justice, which is where members of this church seemingly meet and experience the presence of the risen Christ most identifiably. This "theology of the cross" seems almost counterintuitive for congregations of privileged people, but they seem to live up to their understanding of the Gospel when their members effectively identify with the dispossessed, whether abused women, marginalized minority sexual orientations, the working poor, those with various handicaps, immigrants or the eco-realm of creation itself. Like the icons and the mass, this social-justice emphasis in the United Church is clearly focused on experiencing Jesus as he is presented in the Gospel.

This Scottish and Irish Protestant population has not always fared as well in the eastern seaboard and southern states of the United States. There we have lost wars, been subjugated by outside political and economic forces, and we are sometimes regarded as socially regressive. In this context, and in the words used at political rallies, "Are we bitter? Hell, yes!" and "Do we cling to our guns and cling to religion?" Again, "Hell, yes!" We are a people who have tried everything, and only Jesus seems able to "redeem" our impossible situations. There is a special poignancy to the way the poor and less-educated people of my tribe in America know Jesus personally. This way of knowing

Jesus is dramatic, emotional and profoundly effective. It is shared also by those in this demographic who have become "successful" and know that this happened only by grace.

Along with the testimonies of the singers, the gospel music of quartets that still fill the southern auditoriums of this Scottish-Irish homogenous community is ironically echoed across town by black quartets singing "Steal Away" in a emotional backup to a "whooping" style of preaching that I recently learned from African American colleagues at Harvard Divinity School. The manner in which these two symbiotic Christian communities mirror and echo each other is remarkable.

Knowing Jesus personally, rather than knowing about Jesus, is clearly demonstrated by certain fundamentalist and evangelical groups, including some of the very people we accused earlier of being uninformed and emotional. Their redeeming quality is in the sense of knowing Jesus personally and even intimately, attributes that they would cherish above any erudition or sophistication. If they sometimes appear shrill, it is because they have discovered what the Bible calls "a balm in Gilead"[28] as an antidote to their pain and the "pearl of great value"[29] as a trade-off for their economic struggles, and they wish to "shout it from the housetops."[30]

From a somewhat more progressive perspective, Billy Graham knew Jesus personally and introduced Him from the pulpit. Jimmy Carter knew Jesus personally and presented Him in Sunday School classes. More recently in the evangelical community, Jim Wallis has been introducing the Jesus he knows personally in the peace-oriented *Sojourners Magazine*. Reverend Richard Cizik, of the New Evangelical Partnership for the Common Good, gives leadership in the area of the environment, and superchurch evangelist Rick Warren presents Jesus to consumers in his book, *The Purpose Driven Life*, which opens with the profound observation, "It's not about you." These trends are bringing progressive elements of the evangelical community into a new American religious mainstream, where they demonstrate how the Christian Scriptures are to be properly understood in an emerging consensus of love toward their neighbors, including those of other faiths.

At one point in history, the Protestant Reformation thumbed its nose at the established order in a new zeal for pure Christianity, but the Protestants eventually became as established as the old order, and rather than disappear, the Roman Catholic Church experienced a Counter-Reformation of its own. Two hundred years later the fervent Methodist movement challenged the Anglican-established church in much the same way, although again it became transformed into the church image as it took on greater responsibility, and again, the Church of England, chastened and renewed, instead of disappearing, spread its wings worldwide. Christians are living through this same phenomenon in our time as many so-called right-wing evangelicals enter the arena of social responsibility as churches with a mature understanding of Christian doctrine and established "mainstream" Protestants discover that they, too, are able to survive and flourish in new ways. The point is that in each of these "reformations," there has been a recovery of the central emphasis on the person of Jesus as the core identifier of Christian religion and the key to understanding Christian Scriptures.

In 1969, having moved from the Ukrainian heartland in the north of Alberta to a southern city in the same province, I was surprised to be asked by United Church leaders to conduct a "preaching mission" in a nearby village close to the U.S. border, where the only congregation appeared to be dying. These people of my own ethno-religious community had gone through hard times, floods, drought and political neglect, and they were bitter. They were clinging to their guns, as I could see in the rear cab windows of the pickup trucks, but they were seemingly deserting their religion in droves. The once thriving church was practically empty. The music playing in the café was now more country and western than gospel, despite the expressed preference of the owners.

To set the religious scene, it might be acknowledged that fifty years ago there were no Muslims within five hundred kilometers of Medicine Hat, my own new city of less than a hundred thousand people. That city itself then included no Muslims that I ever met, but there were one hundred Jewish families from pioneer days. While I was there I witnessed the movement of the professional children of those Jewish merchants to Calgary, a city of over a million, and the retirement of many seniors to Israel. This reduction of the Jewish presence means that fifty years later the Sons of Abraham Synagogue has difficulty in mustering a minyan of ten men to read the Torah.

Meanwhile the immigrant Muslim population in Medicine Hat has become more than one hundred families, largely centered around the growing Muslim medical fraternity. However, in the nearby village of Irvine, where the preaching mission was to take place, there were no Jews and no Muslims then in a population of one thousand people. There are none of either of those religions today in that village, where the population is half of what it was. The grain elevators are all gone, the several garages have closed, the school burned down and only one general store remains, but the church continues to be the vibrant heart of a farming and ranching community. There would not have been anyone professing atheism forty years ago either, and there appear to be none today. Such was the socio-religious context of my preaching mission as a visitor in a homogeneous Christian community.

For music, church leaders had engaged the Fabulous Switzer Brothers for a week. Taking time away from the family-owned garage and car dealership near Ottawa, this popular gospel quartet from Trinity United Church in Smiths Falls was expected to draw a crowd. The evangelist from Georgia, who had been engaged in hopes of reviving the congregation, had canceled at the last minute, so the local minister and board turned to me, the new minister of a United Church in the nearby city. This came as a surprise to me because my McGill training was rather cerebral, and my ministry was trending toward liturgical development rather than evangelism.

The Switzer Brothers entertained at noon each day in the cafeteria of the school in the village, as was still permitted in those days, and flyers advertising evening services at the church had gone out to every household. By Tuesday or Wednesday evening the church was packed with some three hundred and fifty people, and it remained full until nearly five hundred people appeared for the climactic weekend. The Switzer Brothers warmed up the crowd each evening, and local elders seemed successful in engaging the people's interest in the upcoming programs of the church. I preached with passion, but, as I recall, it was mostly about Jesus, not really introducing Him as present in the room with us.

I did try to relate the love of God as expressed in Jesus to their situation, but it was the gospel music that gave the people a vision and an experience of meeting Jesus personally. It was that factor, in my opinion, that subsequently brought the people back to church, not only to worship but also to Bible study programs that became the key to the congregation's revival and to "Mission and Service" enterprises that were then the hallmark of our denomination.

In acquired Tennessee accents, the skilled but almost tortured harmony of our quartet left little doubt that these men had known pain and personal struggle themselves before getting to know Jesus. I did my best to present Jesus' identity with the poor, the oppressed, or those overdrawn at the bank, any who were sick, downtrodden or otherwise in the grip of circumstances beyond their control. As I concluded, the lights would dim and the quartet would sing a line from a gospel theme song:

Standing somewhere in the shadows you'll find Jesus.[31]

The shadows were lengthening at that hour of the evening, and there was a gentle spirit of loving concern for each other in the beautiful little church. It was then that Scriptural phrases from the Gospel began to make sense, and I used them increasingly. I prayed for God to make Himself known to us in the way Jesus had shown loving care to fishers and farmers in Galilee, to the business people and others oppressed by the Roman government of the day, tax collectors, women in various difficult circumstances and even little children, of whom a number were present in our little church and attentive each evening.

Standing somewhere in the shadows you'll find Jesus.
He's the only one who cares and understands.

We meditated on the fact that while God is always present, He does not coerce us or force us to acknowledge His presence. He is available, and powerfully able to help, but we need to recognize Him.

Standing somewhere in the shadows you'll find Jesus.
He's the only one who cares and understands.
Standing somewhere in the shadows you will find Him.

Of course God cares and understands, and he showed His unity with us by sharing in the most degrading treatment: his arrest, humiliation, whipping, mocking and finally the ignominy of crucifixion, paralleling and exceeding the disgrace and shame experienced even by these people.

While other religions perhaps rightly recognize that this is horrendously inappropriate for the God who is the Sovereign Lord of the Universe, this is the way in which Christians have experienced God. Whether through divine liturgy, icons, the "real presence of Christ" in the communion mass, social justice, or singing gospel songs, it is at the point where Jesus is recognized as present and among them that their Scriptures become authoritative for Christians. The last line of the song drove the point home in a way that is personal and makes sense of the Christian Scriptures in the way that needs to be recognized, even academically.

Standing somewhere in the shadows you'll find Jesus
He's the only one who cares and understands.
Standing somewhere in the shadows you will find Him
And you'll know Him by the nail prints in his hand.

Times have changed and both church structures and social conventions of fifty years ago no longer prevail as Christians seek to articulate their faith to themselves and others. However, through all the ages Christians have adhered to the same set of Scriptures, and just as universal among Christians is the understanding that these Scriptures are comprehended through experience with Jesus, whether in icons, the sacrament of communion, the Divine Liturgy, social justice or music, whether classical or gospel. This explains some differences between Christian denominations, and even differences within denominations, but for Christians it is Jesus who still stands somewhere in the shadows as the authentication of their faith experience and as their key to understanding the otherwise nonsensical Scriptures.

This is the *sine qua non* or the single principle that guides and explains the Christian understanding of Scripture and makes sense of many things that are impossible to understand otherwise, including doctrines like the Trinity and the Cross. Exceptions to this appear to exist only among two groups, on the conservative and the liberal extremes of the Christian spectrum. Conservative fundamentalists interpret Scripture literally, rather than by experience with Jesus, while liberal rationalists interpret Scripture by contemporary standards of rationality and science, again without reference to the experience of Jesus. Both exceptions are peripheral and ephemeral phenomena, rising and passing on at the fringes of Christianity in every age. For purposes of this study, it need only be emphasized that all Christians accept and use the same Scriptures, and virtually all Christians interpret and understand their Scriptures in the light of their experience of Jesus, even though the modes of such experience may vary greatly.

The Last Supper: "A Table Spread for Us"

introduction to the gospel

David Bruce

MOST CHRISTIANS REFER TO THE NEW TESTAMENT AS THE CHRISTIAN SCRIPTURES, ALTHOUGH they are sometimes collectively spoken of as the Gospel, as explained in the prologue to this book. Muslims also follow that practice, based on references to what is called the *Injil*, Arabic word for "Gospel" in the Quran.

the christian writings in the first century

A diverse set of writings from the first century CE, the Christian Scriptures include four biographies, a short history, twenty-one letters and one extended apocalyptic vision. They were all written in popular *koine* Greek, the most universal language of the first century CE. Some of them were written for public reading, others as private correspondence; some were written as treatises, others as counsel offered in specific circumstances; some were written very plainly, others thick with symbolism.

None of their authors, with the exception of the apocalyptic Revelation to John, thought that they were directly channeling "the word of the Lord," as we find so often in the Torah and the Hebrew prophetic writings, or in the Quran. Yet even the earliest letters presume and often name the apostolic authority of their authors, and the four biographies understand themselves as *proclaiming the truth* rather than simply offering opinions or food for thought. On one notable occasion, in a writing datable to about the middle of the first century, one author stops in mid-argument to differentiate his own opinion from his authoritative teaching, as if the authority of his writing has already been presumed.[1] By the time we reach the end of the first century and the writing of the Gospel of John or the Book of Revelation, the use of Christian writings in Christian life and worship has developed in a way that paralleled the Jews' use of the Jewish Scriptures. Several factors contributed to this development.

First, the most authoritative witnesses to Jesus and his mission, the college of the Apostles (*apostle* means "one who is sent," usually referring to the disciples of Jesus) were dying off—mostly through martyrdom—and this presented the need to sort out the various accounts of Jesus' words and deeds. Second, the growing persecution of Christians as members of an illegal religious sect made convening all Christian leaders both difficult and dangerous; being able to quote apostolic authority without the apostle in question present, while sometimes problematic, may have appeared eminently practical. Third, Gentile Christians had begun to outnumber Jewish Christians in many cities of the Empire, and fewer and fewer of the established synagogues would recognize even the

Jewish Christians as members; the destruction of the Temple in 70 CE may have signaled a final break from organized Judaism, requiring sources for a more fixed and formal identification of the new Christian faith. And fourth, both religious and political culture in the first century would have called for documentation of mighty, noble acts: if something important had happened through the life of Jesus and the creation of the Church, it *deserved* to have an authoritative record.

the christian writings in the second century

It wasn't until the second century CE, when rival interpretations of Jesus and his significance gained a significant number of adherents, that lists of authoritative Christian writings began to appear, presumably with the purpose of including some and excluding others. The last half of the second century CE saw a proliferation of writings attributed to the apostles and other important figures, but for the most part these were far different in tone and conceptual content from the previously accepted writings. Especially important in this regard are the writings that promoted two emphases, in contrast with the writings eventually deemed "canonical" and normative.

The first, called *docetism*, already condemned by prominent leaders in the Church, consisted of the specific contention that since spirit is pure and matter is impure, Jesus only *seemed* to have a human body. This denial of Jesus' full participation in humanity led to all sorts of counterassertions, including a reattachment to the historical dimensions of the Jewish Scriptures and a defense of Jesus' bodily resurrection from the dead. In rejecting docetism, the Church insisted that God wasn't saving some people *from* history, but rather saving history itself, and us along with it. Rather than lapse into pietism, the Church renewed its commitment to a vision of salvation as being social and political as well as merely "spiritual."

The second, called *Gnosticism*, was a wider and more diffuse set of religious movements that provided an altogether alternative theology. Most Gnostics believed that they possessed a secret *gnosis*, a knowledge not revealed earlier, that the Creator of our material sphere was not the one true God but a demiurge that had emanated from God, a god who in creating matter created evil—shades of then current dualistic Zoroastrian influence. Some members of the Christian community embraced Gnostic theology and emphasized the demiurge's identification with YHWH, the God of Israel, while others emphasized this lesser god's identification with sin and rebellion. The sheer multiplicity of options within Gnosticism threatened the earlier claim of the Church, found in its older Christian Scriptures, of possessing a message for public proclamation.

Brian Arthur Brown traces some of the developments in ancient Middle Eastern theology, including the monotheistic reforms of Zoroaster, which may have been propelled by his exposure to Jewish monotheism in the seventh century BCE. In turn, Zoroastrianism certainly seems to have made an impact on the theology of those Jews who were exiled to Babylon in the sixth century BCE. Although this is too simply put, there seems to have been in Jewish thinking a postexilic fusion of Israel's ancient claim that YHWH was the ranking "King over all the gods," with the Zoroastrian understanding that in reality there is only *one* true God, with all other "gods" being merely divinities, angels, false gods or idols. Brown further argues cogently that Jesus may have been directly influenced by Zoroastrian theology expressed in the Avestas, which he could have encountered either in India or through contact with Zoroastrians in Syria.

Whether or not the early Christians were aware of Zoroastrianism through direct contact—something likely in itself—they had certainly absorbed it through developing Jewish theology reflected within the Jewish Scriptures. Once docetism had been rejected, with its essentially unhistorical understanding of Jesus, Gnosticism was never an option for a Church looking to a Savior who sought to claim and embrace his historical roots in Jewish faith and practice. Even though Christians of the first and second century were relatively powerless and subject to waves of imperial persecution, they clung to the idea that God had acted *in* history, and that this was the foundation of a new age, a "kingdom" or reign of God that had been inaugurated by Jesus. Sorting through the various Christian (and semi-Christian) writings in circulation, and establishing which were to be considered canonical, would be a means of ensuring the loyalty of the Church in future generations to the apostolic understanding of Jesus as Lord and Christ.

the christian writings in the third and fourth century

Gospel is an old English word used to translate *euangelion*, which literally means "good news." For the first Christians, the proclamation that God had intervened in human history and that Jesus, the teacher, the healer, the self-giving, crucified-but-resurrected one, and not Caesar, the cruel, oppressive, self-serving and self-divinizing one, was the true Lord and King was very good news. It meant that there was hope for the downtrodden, because God had radically taken their side. Mark's account of this opens with the words, "The beginning of the Good News of Jesus Christ, the Son of God."[2] Because of this, all four recognized accounts of Jesus' life, death and resurrection—Matthew, Mark, Luke and John—became known as "Gospels."

Although they were not always listed in this order, apart from Marcion's mid–second century attempt to canonize Luke and exclude the other three, there is no record of any listing having any other Gospel included with these four. Tatian's *Diatesseron* (literally, "out of four") was a second-century harmonization of the four Gospels into a single, chronologically ordered text, perhaps originally written in Syriac. It was used liturgically as Scripture in at least the Syrian Church of the third and fourth centuries, and it may have even been the form of "the Gospel" that Muhammad knew. Its existence signifies an early and abiding interest in the historicity of the Gospel accounts and the elevated status of Matthew, Mark, Luke and John. While certain canonical Gospels may have been read and studied in some locations more than the others, there seems to have been widespread agreement that no single Gospel could capture everything that needed to be said about Jesus: listening for God's voice through the Gospels required quadraphonic sound.

None of these four are ever, at least in the records we have, called by any other names, suggesting that the tradition recorded about the turn of the fourth century may have been established very early—namely, that the Gospels bearing the names of Matthew and John were the recollections of those apostles, in part or in whole, respectively; that the Gospel of Mark contains the recollections of Peter; and that Luke contains recollections gathered from the ministry of Paul, who had not accompanied Jesus as the other apostles had. This is significant in that it may have reinforced or even given rise to the later-expressed norm that every writing to be considered as Christian Scripture must have been widely circulated, recognized by its readership as promoting the "apostolic" faith, and itself have some direct historical connection to one of the apostles.[3]

As for the rest of the Christian Scriptures, various lists circulated throughout the third century, with minor variations. The letters attributed to the apostle Paul were all included. Some wondered aloud about the authenticity of the letter of Jude and the second letter of Peter, and there was widespread concern that the letter of James, which is focused more on ethics than on God's self-revelation in Jesus, was somehow out of place in the collection. The last writing to be included was the Revelation to John because of its distinction in genre and its thinly disguised anti-Roman invective. By the beginning of the fourth century the tradition of the canon as we have it now had taken shape, although it took another century before questions largely ceased and the body of writings as we know it became a settled quantity.

the christian writings as christian scripture

There is no evidence that the earliest Christians thought they were composing and compiling an alternative to the Torah, or to the collection of the Jewish Scriptures: overall, the Christian Scriptures were meant to recollect and expound on what God had done in Jesus, which they interpreted as an extension or "fulfillment" of God's covenant with Israel. According to the Gospels, Jesus had, on the night of his betrayal into the hands of those who would have him crucified, took a cup of wine and declared, "This is the blood of the new covenant, which is poured out for many."[4]

Most Christians have understood Jesus' words as a reference to the "new covenant" spoken of by Jeremiah, that would be written on human hearts rather than stone, now made "new" in the sense of having been fulfilled in the death and resurrection of Jesus. It was as if God had been waiting for humanity to ratify the everlasting covenant with total obedience, and this had finally happened through Jesus. Christians interpreted this as good news for Jew and Gentile alike: God had accepted the self-offering of Jesus on all our behalf and signaled this by raising Jesus from the dead. In the collective consideration of the Apostles, this did not require the erasing of Jewish identity on the one hand, nor did it require the Judaization of the Gentiles on the other. Faithful living, founded on trust in God's grace, would be enough for all. Taken together, the Christian Scriptures came to be known by the name of what they testified to: the new "covenant," or "testament."

Over the centuries, the term *New Testament* has acquired some unfortunate connotations. The assimilation of its Jewish membership in the growing Church, coupled with widespread Jewish rejection of Christian interpretations of Jesus' messianic role, led to a decreasing appreciation of Jewish faith, a caricaturizing of Jews as trusting their salvation to their own relative obedience rather than to God's character and love, and ultimately to hostility, persecution and even some degree of indifference to attempted genocide. Christians have spoken of their "New Testament" as if it were conceptually separable from, inherently superior to and ultimately superseding of the "Old Testament," rather than borne of it. While it is unlikely that Christians will soon forsake using the term *New Testament*, there are encouraging signs that largely Gentile Christians are recognizing and reaffirming the Jewish identity of Jesus, perhaps lessening the derogatory connotations of calling the Jewish Scriptures the "Old" (as if outmoded) Testament.[5]

For Christians, each of their sacred writings is properly interpreted in light of the other Christian Scriptures, and their collective interpretations of the Jewish Scriptures. While the question of what Mark, for instance, might have been thinking as he composed his Gospel is an interesting *historical* question, any Christian reading of Mark's Gospel *as Scripture* must take into account what the reader knows of Paul's letter to the Romans (written at least a decade before Mark) and the Book of Acts (written at least a decade after Mark), even if we suppose that Mark never read Romans and was unfamiliar with the episodes narrated in Acts. While no reader can ignore the variety of theological perspectives, hermeneutical strategies and literary genres in the Christian Scriptures, a Christian reads these writings with the conviction that they share a common faith, a faith understood and shared by himself or herself. Many Christians would go so far as to say that when the Scriptures are read with active faith, the voice of the Scriptures is none other than the voice of the risen Christ.[6]

the christian scriptures as historical records

Attempts in the last couple of centuries to either defend or attack the objectivity of the Christian Scriptures have been sorely misguided. To evaluate the Christian Scriptures as if they were being written with modern criteria of objectivity in mind is to project our cultural assumptions about historicity onto writings that took shape under very different cultural assumptions. For example, the Christian Scriptures repeatedly refer to the authority of the Jewish Scriptures, assume a particular understanding of God's character and power, and suppose that even their most skeptical readers would at least entertain the idea of a miraculous occurrence—all of which the modern historian might dismiss as irrelevant for "unbiased," "scientific" historical research.

It is highly unlikely that any of the events of Jesus' life and ministry were written down in descriptive prose by a disinterested observer as they happened. There was no money to be made in "unbiased" reporting; virtually all historical writing was subsidized by interested parties. It is just as unlikely, though, that a perfectly ordinary first-century rabbi, doing perfectly ordinary things—including dying and staying dead—would have given rise in a few short decades, well within living memory of those who saw and heard him, to exaggerations of mythical proportions. Most historians and anthropologists would agree that this is far too short a time frame for such a development.[7]

What *is* quite likely is, as was the case with other noted first-century rabbis, that Jesus' teachings, along with actions that might illustrate his teachings or his character or his piety, would have been committed both to memory and to parchment by his disciples. It is also quite likely that the Gospel writers selected and "rounded the edges" of the accounts they had received about events during Jesus' ministry and his teachings according to their own theological musings and their projected readership. This accounts for most of the variations in detail among the first three Gospel writers, Matthew, Mark and Luke, when they appear to be relating the same story. In the case of the Acts of the Apostles, Luke's "sequel" to his Gospel, while the stories are selected and arranged for dramatic effect, the interaction with imperial figures offers a reality check: we cannot ignore that historical claims are being made, whether or not we believe them.

In fairness, it should be said that while the authors of the various Christian Scriptures believed what they were saying to be true, they did not necessarily think that what they were saying was perfectly verifiable. While Paul, Peter, John, James and Jude can be found making reasoned arguments in their letters, they all declare that the truth of what they were saying could only be ascertained by having "faith." At a minimum, this faith involves the assent to unproven propositions; at its normative maximum, it is based on readers knowing Jesus personally, if not physically in the flesh, then metaphysically in the spirit. Matthew, Mark, Luke and John can often be found making the historical case for their accounts, whether it be by referencing secular history or well-known religious currents, but they all show evidence of understanding just how much they are asking their readers to believe.

the christian scriptures as testimony

Matthew, Mark, Luke and John wrote the Gospels under the influence of Graeco-Roman biographies, with that genre's stylistic parameters: a description of the subject's birth; narration of a mission-forming challenge; depiction of actions sequenced to reveal the subject's character rather than reproduce chronological order; speeches that were reconstructed so as to both record what was said and draw out the greater significance of the original saying; and a description of the subject's death in such a way as to declare that the subject's character was revealed in his or her destiny. While first-century biography did have to pay attention to facts in order to be credible, it was always understood by the reader that the author considered the subject worthy of praise, and therefore worthy of remembrance: factuality and bias were not considered antithetical in ancient biography, but complementary.

Recently scholars have made use of the category of *testimony* to refer to the Gospels.[8] Like a modern-day infomercial, the Gospels and the Acts of the Apostles, while accountable for the factuality of their claims, are trying to "sell" the reader on their understanding of Jesus and his significance. Testimony, for all its bias, may reveal more, not less, of the truth of its subject. To make another modern analogy, in a court of law, "expert" testimony is that which purports to understand not only *what* happened but *why* it happened and what *its effects* are likely to be. The Gospel writers act like ancient expert witnesses, selecting and arranging their stories to draw out the significance of Jesus' words and actions in the hope that their readers will join the ranks of Jesus' admirers. Every speech, every episode is pressed into the service of the significance of Jesus.

The early Christian letter writers use a similarly unabashed interest in promoting their faith in Jesus. Presumably the teachings and deeds of Jesus were known through oral tradition—it is difficult for those of us in modern, literate societies to understand how sound oral transmission was in ancient times, especially among the lower classes—and fragmentary accounts prior to the composition of the Gospels.[9] Especially significant for them is the death and resurrection of Jesus because of the widely held belief that the meaning of one's life could be seen in one's death. How could a crucified man be worthy of respect, let alone reverence? The letters among the Christian

Scriptures testify that by raising Jesus from the dead, God had declared Jesus' ministry as a fore-taste of God's kingdom and his death as atonement for the sins of humanity. Jesus' end was not a tragedy, but the penultimate episode in *the* divine comedy. Muslims and others might find the resurrection to be a helpful counterbalance to their understandable objection to God being seen by Christians as permitting his messiah to come to an end as ignominious as a crucifixion.

Revelation, the book accepted last, and usually placed last, in the collection of the Christian Scriptures, makes the category of testimony explicit. The author, most likely a different John from the apostle John, describes how he is asked to testify to what he is seeing in his apocalyptic vision. However, there is some intentional "slippage" involved here, as in reality what John testifies to is *Jesus'* testimony: "It is I, Jesus, who sent my angel to you with this testimony for the Churches."[10] In a higher sense, John seems to be saying, true testimony *about* Jesus is the true testimony *of* Jesus.

the christian scriptures in literary formation

For the most part, the letters contained within the Christian Scriptures are intact. There is some disjointedness in Paul's letters to the Corinthians, causing scholars to wonder if at least three letters might have been subsequently molded into two, but this is not certain. In most of the letters there are changes of subject, some more abrupt than others; in the lengthier letters this may be due to the conditions of writing (for example, imprisonment) or the time taken (for example, dictation stretching out over more than one session).

Some of the letters are considered pseudonymous—that is, written under a false name. The difference in tone, style and vocabulary among some of the letters attributed to Paul, or between the two letters attributed to Peter, suggests that others may have written "in the name of Paul" or "in the name of Peter," with or without the named apostle's permission. Of course, it is also completely possible that Paul or Peter used different scribes for different letters, permitted others to assemble their notes in letter form, or simply used different authorial "voices" for different occasions. The Letter to the Hebrews is intriguingly anonymous, its attribution to Paul only arising centuries after its writing. Brian Brown follows Adolph von Harnack in claiming it was written by Priscilla—and left anonymous because of the scandal of its feminine authorship.[11] While Paul mentions only male scribes by name, probably out of respect for the then current standards of legal corroboration, the prominence of women in the early Christian community as leaders, prophetesses and missionaries may suggest that they had a greater hand in authoring or editing documents of the Christian Scriptures, a subject under ongoing investigation.[12]

Without Hebrews, there are thirteen letters attributed to Paul, perhaps a numerical tribute to his being the "thirteenth" disciple of Jesus—the only acknowledged apostle who did not personally accompany Jesus during his ministry. Again, without Hebrews, there are seven "catholic" letters—that is, letters intended for universal distribution rather than written for specific persons or congregations. Altogether, there are twenty-one letters in the Christian Scriptures; while we have no record of such a rationale in settling the canon of the Christian Scriptures, it is difficult to believe that it is a complete coincidence that this number is a multiple of three and seven, each being a significant numeral in Christian thinking.

The Acts of the Apostles was written by the author of Luke's Gospel: they are written in a similar style, with a similar theology, both having Jerusalem as their focal points and both having the same addressee, "Theophilus," which means lover of God, for whom the author had written "a first book."[13] Whether Theophilus was a single individual, perhaps a patron of Luke's, or whether Luke was simply addressing in the singular *any* lover of God, is impossible to say. In Acts, the author switches three times from the third person to the first-person plural, saying that "We . . ." (meaning Paul, the author, and others) went here or there and were involved in this or that. Most scholars have concluded that Luke was, at least at times, a traveling companion of Paul on Paul's missionary journeys, compiling the rest of his history from what he considered to be reliable historical sources.

The sources of John's Gospel are far more obscure and evoke a wide range of opinions. There is little evidence, for instance, of John being dependent on either Mark or the document known as Q. The stories in John are for the most part simply frameworks for lengthy, subtle, metaphysical speeches of Jesus, and few of Jesus' sayings in John correlate with those in the synoptic Gospels. And yet the figure that John presents does not seem, to most readers, to be a different person: Jesus still heals people, Jesus still confronts and challenges people, Jesus still inspires people to have faith in God.[14] However, in John's Gospel Jesus is far more explicit about his relationship to God, and he speaks in language that enormously amplifies what Jesus says in Matthew's Gospel about the disciples being sent out "in the name of the Father, and of the Son, and of the Holy Spirit."

In John, speaking of a mysterious "Beloved Disciple," the author says, "This is the disciple who is testifying to these things and has written them, and we know that his testimony is true."[15] Is this Beloved Disciple in fact John the apostle? Do his recollections reflect private conversations with Jesus, or perhaps discussions among the inner circle of disciples, that Peter did not reveal to Mark? Is John's Jesus the same historical figure as the Jesus we find in Matthew, Mark and Luke? It is at this point that honest readers will admit that they have been affected, more or less, positively or negatively, by the "high" Christology of John's Gospel and its Trinitarian implications: if we embrace the possibility of Jesus' divinity, we likely conclude that John is presenting a more stylized, insightful "biography" of Jesus, but if we have difficulty with the divinity of Jesus, we may conclude that John is presenting the later theological reflections of the Church, with little or no connection to the Jesus who came from Nazareth or his original disciples.

Revelation refers to its author as Jesus' "servant John, who testified to the Word of God,"[16] making it very tempting for one already familiar with John's Gospel, which begins with the prologue, "In the beginning was the Word . . .," to conclude that they were both written by the same author. However, the portrait of Jesus in Revelation, despite taking up images of Jesus as the Word, the Truth, the Lamb and so on, is combative rather than serene, and seemingly vengeful rather than pastoral, such that it is harder to believe that Revelation is from the same pen as the Gospel. It is likely safest to say that Revelation was at least written by someone who considered himself a follower of the writer of the Gospel.

the synoptic gospels: a specific "problem"

Matthew, Mark and Luke are often called the "synoptic" Gospels, because in most respects, especially in contrast with John's Gospel, they share a common view of Jesus. They use, for instance, roughly the same chronology for Jesus' ministry: Jesus is baptized by John the Baptist, endures a time of temptation, heals and teaches, enjoys a short-lived time of public acclaim in Jerusalem and is betrayed and crucified before God raises him from the dead. Nevertheless, scholars have long been intrigued by the large amount of material, especially involving the teaching of Jesus, that is common to Matthew and Luke but not present in Mark. This has been called "the synoptic problem."[17]

The similarity in wording and even, at times, in the order of presentation of this common material make it likely that Matthew and Luke had access to the same or very similar written sources. The majority of scholars studying the Gospels in seminaries today agree that the simplest solution is the two-document hypothesis, which says that Matthew and Luke composed their Gospels using two sources: the Gospel of Mark, from which they borrowed their basic chronology and repertoire of episodes, and a second source that scholars have simply called Q, short for the German word *quelle*, meaning "source," from which they borrowed many recorded sayings and teachings of Jesus.

While some have suggested that Q may have been an oral source, many scholars contend that Q can be completely reconstructed from that which Matthew and Luke share but isn't found in Mark, and that Q is a single, deliberately composed document, perhaps itself having undergone one or two significant edits.[18] Given the almost unprecedented prominence of women in the community of Jesus' disciples, it may well be that women featured more prominently among the story keepers, orally or literarily, than recognized heretofore. There may be some evidence of this in Q.

Why did Matthew and Luke avail themselves of Q? Why did they think this material would "improve" Mark's presentation? Mark's Gospel focuses on the actions of Jesus—his healings, his miracles and his self-offering of his life. By contrast, most of the material in Q is ethical in nature (similar to the Letter of James in this regard), consisting of Jesus' practical teachings on how to live under the reign of God. It may well be that Matthew and Luke, each in their own ways, were seeking to bring Mark's emphasis on God's acting to save us together with Q's emphasis on our social and ethical imitation of God. It is as if the emphasis on what Jesus called the first great commandment, "Love the Lord your God with all of your heart, and with all your soul, and with all your strength," was being effectively complemented with an emphasis on what Jesus called the second great commandment, "You shall love your neighbor as yourself."[19]

In any case, the presence of material that is *only* in Matthew and *only* in Luke means that there were more sources available to them than Mark and Q, both written and oral. This hypothesis shatters the innocent image of Peter dictating his reminiscences to Mark, Matthew dictating his recollections to a scribe, and Paul telling Luke what he remembers the apostles telling him about Jesus, all acting independently and all just happening to narrate much the same things in much the same words. That being said, it doesn't exclude the involvement of the apostles either. It could well be that (1) Mark transcribed Peter's reminiscences, and that (2) Matthew expanded on Mark's work, using Q material for the purpose, and finally (3) Luke, feeling a historian's sense of responsibility but with all of Paul's courageous freedom, followed the lines of Matthew's project while reworking things to produce a different but complementary portrait of Jesus.

There are other possible scenarios, of course, but the fact that most scholars, both biblical and theological, can freely speak of the Gospels having literary sources clearly indicates that the vast majority of Christians subscribe to an understanding that the Christian Scriptures were "inspired" in a way that includes normal writing practices such as research, documentation, memory and creativity. For most Christians, considerations like these can offer us a fuller sense of how the Spirit of God was working in the Church in the first decades after Jesus; it was just as divine, but no more magical, than how God works in the Church today. These considerations do not pose any threat to Christian faith but can actually promote the belief that what survived this historical process, the Gospels as we have them, give us reliable access to the historical and theological reality of Jesus' life and ministry.

the christian scriptures: an overview

THE GOSPELS

Matthew's Gospel[20]

Matthew begins with a stylized genealogy of Jesus, traced from Abraham through King David to Jesus' legal father, Joseph. Matthew reports the scandal of Jesus' "illegitimate" birth, the mysterious visit of the Magi, the murderous jealousy of Herod and Jesus' eventual settlement in Nazareth. Jesus is baptized by the prophet John the Baptist and is prepared for ministry through an extended time of temptation in the wilderness. Jesus then begins his ministry in Galilee, announcing the imminence of God's reign through teaching and healing, calling his first disciples and delivering the Sermon on the Mount. He continues his ministry and extends it by sending his disciples to minister for a time. Opposition to Jesus' ministry grows among the Pharisees and Sadducees, and the disciples are forced to think more deeply about Jesus and his ministry, which leads to a special revelation of Jesus' relationship to God experienced by Peter, James and John. Jesus ceremonially enters Jerusalem and speaks daily to the Passover festival crowds. Jesus, predicting that he will be arrested, shares a last meal with his disciples and leads them to a garden to pray, where Judas betrays him to soldiers who arrest him. He endures a hearing before the high priest and then is taken before the Roman governor, Pilate, who condemns him. Jesus is crucified and placed in a private tomb, where he lies that night and the entire next day. Early on the third day, the women among his followers find the tomb open, and an angel tells them that Jesus is risen and that they should inform the disciples. The frightened women report the news, and Jesus appears to his disciples in Galilee, sending them to share the news with "all nations."[21]

Mark's Gospel[22]

Mark covers much the same ground as Matthew, although it reads like a mystery, with the operative question being, "Who will acknowledge who Jesus really is?" As was fashionable in Greek theater, the "secret" is revealed to the reader in a one-sentence prologue: "The beginning of the good news of Jesus Christ, the Son of God."[23] Quite early in Mark's account, Jesus has to silence an "unclean spirit" who claims to know who Jesus really is, "the Holy One of God," as if Jesus is waiting for those he has come to save to discover the truth, not simply parrot demons. After Jesus forgives the sins of a paralyzed man, those watching are offended, and they ask among themselves, "Who can forgive sins but God alone?" (Mark 2:7) Again, this time in a less pious part of Judea, Jesus is recognized by demons as the "Son of the Most High God," but he soon faces rejection in his own hometown. He feeds five thousand people with a couple of fishes and a few loaves of bread, he even walks on water, but his opponents ask for a sign from heaven as to who he is! Finally, for the inner circle of disciples, Peter and James and John, Jesus' appearance is "transfigured," and none other than God finally speaks from a cloud: "This is my Son, the Beloved."[24] This mountaintop experience is soon followed by the lengthening shadow of Jesus' knowledge that he will be betrayed and crucified. He shares this information with his disciples, but they remain uncomprehending. Leading them into Jerusalem for the Passover—the feast in which a lamb was slain to mark God's deliverance of the Hebrews from the angel of death (Exodus 12:1–32), Jesus is in fact betrayed, and the high priest asks Jesus at his trial, "Are you the Messiah, the Son of the Blessed One?" (Mark 14:61) Only the outsider, the Roman centurion who observes Jesus expire on the cross, deigns to say, "Truly this man was God's Son!" (Mark 15:39) In the oldest copies of Mark's Gospel, after being told that Jesus is risen, the women flee the tomb—and here the Gospel ends abruptly, as if to pose the question to the reader, the audience: "Now that you know who Jesus is, will you have the courage to say so?"

Luke's Gospel[25]

Luke begins with detailed descriptions of the nativity of John the Baptist and Jesus, gives us a glimpse of Jesus as a youth, provides a brief sketch of the Baptist's ministry and offers a (stylized) genealogy for Jesus. As in Matthew, Jesus is tempted by the devil before he begins his ministry. His declaration of his mission is rejected in his hometown, but the demonic forces he is confronting know who he is. He heals and teaches, announcing the imminence of the kingdom of God, calling for others to join him and become his disciples. He faces further opposition as his ministry overflows its ethnic container, and several times Jesus predicts that he will be put to death by the religious authorities. At times popular, Jesus often speaks of the difficulty of following his path. More than Matthew or Mark, Luke emphasizes the role of the Holy Spirit in recreating the human race in Jesus. This means a radically new place for women, Gentiles, the poor and those on the margins of society. Taking up the words of the prophet Isaiah, Jesus says of himself, "The Spirit of the Lord is upon me, because he has anointed me to bring good news to the poor. He has sent me to proclaim release to the captives and recovery of sight to the blind, to let the oppressed go free, to proclaim the year of the Lord's favor."[26] Luke folds into his account the wonderful story of the Good Samaritan and the parables of the Lost Sheep, the Lost Coin and the Prodigal Son.[27] As in Matthew, Jesus, having entered Jerusalem triumphantly, is soon betrayed, arrested, tried and convicted of treason against Judea and Rome. He is crucified, but on the third day he appears alive to his disciples, notably in Jerusalem. In Luke, Jesus is adamant that the new mission of the disciples is just about to begin, and it will be when the Holy Spirit comes and empowers them. In the end, Jesus is carried into heaven.

John's Gospel[28]

John begins by offering us a mystical preface in which Jesus is identified as God's eternal Word: "And the Word became flesh and lived among us."[29] He is hailed as the Lamb of God by John the Baptist, and he begins his ministry by calling disciples, including two of the Baptist's disciples. He turns water into wine at a wedding at the request of his mother, and at the time of the Passover conducts a violent protest in the Temple. He discusses his divine mission in private conversations with a Pharisee, disciples of John the Baptist and a Samaritan woman. He heals an unnamed royal official's son, a lame man and a man born blind, and he feeds a huge crowd with a few loaves and fishes. In each of these episodes, Jesus uses the miracle as an opportunity to speak at length about the spiritual import of these signs: even if his own family members do not believe him, Jesus proclaims himself the Bread of Life, the Living Water, the Light of the World, the Good Shepherd and the Resurrection and the Life. All of this rouses opposition. As he sees his end approaching, Jesus dons the garment of a servant, and he washes his disciples' feet. He promises them that, once he's gone, God will send the Holy Spirit to inspire them and give them eternal life. Jesus is arrested, questioned by Pilate and put to death, but he firmly remains in control of his own destiny: "You would have no power over me unless it had been given you from above."[30] He rises on the third day and appears to his fearful and doubting disciples, including Thomas, to whom he extends the invitation to touch him. Thomas declares his doubts to be vanquished by exclaiming to Jesus, "My Lord and my God!" (John 20:28). In an addendum to John's Gospel, the risen Jesus tells Peter of his impending martyrdom and the extended ministry of "the Beloved disciple," whom tradition has identified with the apostle John. In what was probably the original ending, John's Gospel closes with what seems to be a fitting postscript to the collection of Gospels: "Now Jesus did many other signs in the presence of his disciples, which are not written in this book. But these are written so that you may come to believe that Jesus is the Messiah, the Son of God, and that through believing you may have life in his name."[31]

It is worth noting that in each Gospel, the personal resurrection of Jesus is both indirectly foreshadowed and directly predicted by Jesus, making it not simply the end but rather the climax of the Gospel narratives. This resurrection was not merely a revival of his message but his personal return to life in the fashion anticipated by many Jews of Jesus' day to belong to the Last Day.[32] The centrality of the testimony of the women among Jesus' disciples to the resurrection—an embarrassing reality in a male-dominated society—is, for some scholars, a confirmation of the historicity of their reports.[33]

THE ACTS OF THE APOSTLES[34]

Acts of the Apostles

Acts begins with a brief prologue identifying this work as the sequel to the Gospel of Luke, and the risen Jesus tells them explicitly that their mission is now to every nation, as they are empowered by the Holy Spirit. Jesus is then "lifted up" out of the sight of the disciples and, as at the resurrection, two angels explain what has happened to the bewildered disciples. A little more than a week after that, at a meeting of a hundred and twenty "believers," the disciples are "filled with the Holy Spirit"[35] and given the ability to proclaim the good news in foreign languages. A crowd gathers at the commotion, and Peter preaches to them—and three thousand people are welcomed into the disciples' fellowship that very day. The disciples share the Gospel, often under difficult circumstances and active persecution. Saul, a zealous persecutor of the disciples, is confronted by the risen Jesus, becomes a believer and begins "speaking boldly in the name of Jesus."[36] Prepared by God in a grand vision, Peter begins to preach the Gospel to Gentiles, and at Cornelius's house the Holy Spirit comes upon those who accept his message. Meanwhile, the disciples in the city of Antioch commission Saul and Barnabas to begin preaching in Cyprus and Asia Minor, and they experience the Gentiles accepting their message as well. The question arises as to whether or not Gentiles had to undergo circumcision—that is, become Jews—before they could become followers of Jesus; in a crucial meeting in Jerusalem, the Gentiles are welcomed as they are,[37] so long as they are sincere in doing what they can to keep the interethnic peace.[38] Saul, now called by his Greek name, "Paul," heads to Macedonia and Greece, preaching the Gospel to both Jews and Gentiles. He returns to Antioch, but he sets out again for Greece. He returns to Jerusalem to report to James but is arrested in the Temple on false charges of profaning it by bringing Gentiles with him. Paul is arrested, defends himself, is released and arrested again, and finally appeals to the emperor, which was Paul's right as a Roman citizen. Paul, traveling to Rome for his hearing, is shipwrecked but survives, and eventually he arrives in the capital, preaching the Gospel and living under house arrest awaiting trial.

PAUL'S LETTERS[39]

Romans

In Romans Paul argues that God's righteousness offers us salvation based on Jesus' obedience to God rather than our own obedience to the Law—which, according to Paul, was never the foundation of salvation: our salvation comes through faith in God.

1 and 2 Corinthians

In 1 and 2 Corinthians Paul lays out the parameters for followers of Jesus in the community of the Church, including respect for the ministry of the apostles and the practical support of other churches.

Galatians

In Galatians Paul argues that faith in Jesus and reliance on the Holy Spirit should provide the norms for followers of Jesus, rather than obedience to the Law.

Ephesians

In Ephesians Paul describes the theological foundations and ethical implications of the new community that includes both Jew and Gentile.

Philippians and Colossians

In Philippians Paul offers encouragement in living as followers of Jesus. In Colossians Paul warns against mixing God's revelation in Jesus with elements from other worldviews.

1 and 2 Thessalonians

In 1 and 2 Thessalonians Paul gives instruction and reassurance around the Second Coming of Jesus.

1 and 2 Timothy and Titus

In 1 and 2 Timothy and Titus, the "pastoral letters," Paul outlines the personal and public responsibilities of being a leader in the Church.

Philemon

In Philemon Paul personally appeals to the owner of a runaway slave who has become a believer to set the slave free.

THE CATHOLIC LETTERS[40]

Hebrews

In Hebrews the anonymous writer explains how God's self-revelation in Jesus is superior to any previous revelation. Jesus is superior to angels, to Moses, to the Levitical priesthood and to the sacrifices prescribed in the Old Testament. Therefore we should persevere in faith, like the heroes of the Jewish Scriptures did, and all the more since we have the example of Jesus' suffering for us.

James

In James the head of the Church in Jerusalem argues that true wisdom is love in action, such as having regard for the poor, remaining humble and persevering through times of suffering.

1 and 2 Peter

In 1 and 2 Peter the leading apostle reminds us that because Jesus is risen from the dead, our hope is a living hope. We should therefore live as a holy priesthood, and as servants of God. In imitations of Jesus, who suffered on our behalf, we should be patient in difficult circumstances as good stewards of God's grace, especially those serving as elders. We should live worthy of our calling and trust that God will deal with false teachers, assured that "the day of the Lord" will come.

1, 2 and 3 John

In 1, 2 and 3 John the apostle John urges us to consider God's nature as light (truth) and love, and its implications for our treatment of one another. We are God's children, and we should share God's love that dwells in us. Paramount to understanding God's love is to understand God's incarnation in Jesus. Anyone who teaches anything else is not to be received as a true brother or sister.

Jude

In Jude the brother of James asks us to hold onto the faith and not be deceived by false teachers, whom God will judge severely, and to try to rescue those who are tempted by them.

THE BOOK OF REVELATION[41]

Revelation

Revelation describes a series of visions revealing the future. Included are specific messages to congregations of John's day, a series of apocalyptic judgments, the final defeat of evil and the glorious consummation of the age to come. Revelation is presented in the apocalyptic style introduced to the world in the avestan Gathas by Zoroaster, a style employed at various points in the Hebrew Scriptures and featured throughout much of the Quran. The Quran opens with seven verses taken by Muslims to reflect the seven scrolls in the Book of Revelation, the seventh seal of which is unlocked for the world in the seven thunders of Al-Fatiha, the opening of the Quran, to which we will turn following the presentation of the New Testament in its entirety.

It is interesting to note that in the canonical order of the Christian Scriptures, Matthew opens the collection with a genealogy acknowledging Christian faith as an outgrowth of the journey of the Jewish people, complete with a Zoroastrian "visitation" (represented by the Magi), while Revelation closes the collection with a call to faithfulness amid warnings of judgment, which evokes the later language of the Quran. Whether intentionally or not, the "bookends" of the Christian Scriptures provide literary links with what came before and after the establishment of Christianity among the Western monotheistic traditions.[42]

As presented in the Christian Scriptures, God's ultimate self-revelation consists of the singular life of Jesus, the Jew of Nazareth, regarded by his followers as the Son of God, who inaugurated God's reign by dying and rising on behalf of the whole human race and inviting everyone without distinction into everlasting communion with God. Given the evidence presented in this volume, we are asked to consider whether or not it was that same unifying vision that was described by Zoroaster, long experienced by Jews in community and finally articulated in the revelation of the Quran to Muhammad.

Under a Crescent Moon, "The Seven Thunders of Al-Fatiha" (The Opening of the Scroll in Revelation 10)

gospel text:
the inclusive bible

translator's notes

"Sticks and stones may break my bones, but names can never hurt me," says the old proverb. We now know that this is a lie. Words can wound, alienate, and degrade people. Language can also affirm and express love. Care for language is a show of concern for people and a revelation of the attitudes of the speaker.

The Second Vatican Council recognized the importance of language when it decreed that the liturgy be celebrated in the vernacular and adapted to various cultures so that members of the community might participate more fully (Constitution on the Liturgy, 1963).

In the United States in the 1950s and the 1960s, the racial struggle brought new appreciation of the role of language. Epithets, racist images, and stereotypes were recognized as revelations of and expressions that support racially biased attitudes. Efforts toward more balanced usage were the first stage in consciousness raising and a sign of efforts to lessen racial prejudice.

The rising consciousness of women and men in the United States is likewise confronting us all with the need to be sensitive to language. Church language is predominantly masculine. Male terms, images, and stereotypes, so-called sexist language, dominate church expression.

Such usage is no longer adequate. It is time to build gender equality into the very fabric of church life. The effort to build new gender-balanced ways of speaking helps to educate us toward greater equality for women and men.

—Summary from the introduction to *Liturgy for All People* (1975), initiating *The Inclusive Bible* project by six hundred Jesuits and other Priests for Equality at the Quixote Center in Brentwood, Maryland, with women and men around the world

I F THERE IS ONE WORD TO DESCRIBE THE PROCESS OF DEVELOPING INCLUSIVE LANGUAGE READINGS, it is *transformational*. The transformation we have experienced in our work on these readings challenged us to confront the limits of our language and to ask what baggage is attached to our proclamation scripture. We have been challenged to consider how we think and speak about God and how our concepts influence the way we treat other people. We also have had to consider whether modern renderings of sacred scriptures present modern sexist biases, in addition to biases of the ancient Near East and Mediterranean cultures. In the course of our work, we developed new ideas about the role of sacred scripture in liturgy.

We challenge the traditional ways of speaking about God. Traditional Western religious language calls God "Father" and Jesus "Lord." Our intention is to recover the sense of the text and express that sense in a manner that facilitates immediate application of the Word to the experience of the listener. To that end, we correct our own interpretations by referring them to what scripture scholars have to say about the texts.

This process begins with looking through the standard translations of scripture for sexist and classist forms and attitudes. We compare translations, consult commentaries and, when necessary, go back to the Hebrew and Greek to uncover meanings. Realizing that any translation is an interpretation, we do not limit ourselves to the standard translations, but also look at other inclusive language texts and style forms to understand how others have worked through the problems of sexism in scripture. We go over each text line by line in order to ensure a faithful yet nonsexist rendering in both content and style.

The most difficult problem we address is what can be done about the sexism in scripture without destroying the actual text. Several guiding principles have emerged from our work on this problem. One principle is to determine whether it is the linguistic convention used that expresses a sexist bias or whether the text itself is sexist in its meaning. In all circumstances, we seek to recover the expression's meaning within the context in which it is written without perpetuating the sexism. To accomplish this, we rely on the Greek text as well as commentaries. An example of the way we recover meaning from a sexist phrase is our rendering of "Whore of Babylon" or "Great Prostitute" in the book of Revelation (Rev. 17:1–18). In the standard translations, the word "prostitute" is used to translate a word that, to the culture of the Mediterranean world of the time, was closely related to idolatrous defilement. In our culture, the term implies sex for sale and is usually associated with women. The sense of the term in scripture has more to do with the idolatry of emperor worship and cultic practices than with prostitution. We believe "Great Idolater" comes closer to the actual sense of the text.

Another principle we use is to distinguish between passages that exclude women and passages that actively villainize them. Each of these instances has been handled on its own terms. The role of women in the economy of salvation has long been relegated to the sacristies of salvation history. By attending to recent feminist scripture scholarship, we attempt to recover women's active participation in salvation history. In genealogies, for example, we include both spouses to emphasize that ancestral lineage is not merely passed on by the male. Thus, we speak of Sarah and Abraham instead of Abraham alone; we pair Rebecca and Isaac; and we recognize Leah and Rachel as well as Jacob. When this cannot be done, we stress the actual lineage instead of the male role in the lineage. We also emphasize those times when scripture employs feminine imagery for divine or spiritual beings. In Wisdom literature, we retain the ancient feminine images.

Scriptural language specifically referring to God presents a major problem. Our approach is to try to maintain a personal form. Personal references in common speech have constant recourse to gender-specific words—necessarily so, and for the most part, inoffensively. In the case of scripture, we make our choices as the occasion warrants.

Where the usage is descriptive, we use "Most High," "Most High God," "Almighty" and "Sovereign One" in place of the sexist and classist form "Lord." Where "Lord" is a form of address, we use "Adonai" in Hebrew scripture readings and either "Rabbi" or "Teacher" in Christian scripture readings about Jesus' public ministry. We use "Abba" for "Father," where it expresses a close, familial relationship. We also used the phrase "Loving God" as a substitute for "Father." There are several other options that we discussed but did not use. In the text of the "Our Father," "Imma God," "Our Mother," "Our Father" or "Loving God" can be used as substitutes for our rendering of "Abba God."

In referring to Jesus, we use "Only Begotten," "God's Own" and "Eternally Begotten" in place of "Son of God." "Son of Man" is a difficult problem because it has so many different shades of meaning. We try to capture the prophetic or apocalyptic connotations of the phrase. We use "Chosen One" when it seems to refer to Jesus' self-understanding of his prophetic mission, and "Promised One" when Jesus appears to be speaking about his self-identity as an apocalyptic figure. Another instance of "son of man" is found in the book of Ezekiel. In this book, God is addressing humankind, so we use "mere mortal."

The title "Lord," especially when it refers to Jesus, is hard to replace because it is confessional—that is, to call Jesus Lord is to both recognize in him a divinity and make a commitment to him. To confess that Jesus is Lord is to confess, for example, that Caesar is not Lord. To avoid sexist and classist connotations, we use substitutes for Lord that are meaningful in our own confessing of Jesus, such as Sovereign, Savior and Jesus Reigns.·

Throughout the readings, we have changed "kingdom," which has classist connotations, to refer simply to government and its rulers. In the case of kingdom of God, however, there is more than one meaning; thus, several translations are needed. In the Gospel of Matthew, "kingdom of God" means an active state of being, and we use "reign of God" or "reign of Heaven." Other than its use in Matthew, "kingdom of God" is a state of relationship, so we use "kingdom of God."

Thank you for using these texts and for all your efforts to make the church a community that welcomes diversity while witnessing that in Christ, all are one. We recognize that any rendering of scripture should be undertaken with the utmost discretion and humility. Beyond that, our only defense for our errors or arbitrary decisions—whether detectable or hidden—is that the texts to which our labors are addressed speak of mysteries beyond the reach of any translator. We hope that we are respectful of these mysteries, which will outlast any attempt to capture them in word.

Joe Dearborn

---

*By the time we began translating *The Prophets*, we realized that our audience's sensibilities (and our own as well) had changed in the intervening years with regard to the use of the fourfold name of God, spelled with the letters *y* (Yod), *h* (Heh), *w* (Waw or Vav) and *h* (Heh). This name, sometimes called the Tetragrammaton, is the most sacred Name of God and was only pronounced once a year by the high priest; at other times, the devout would employ circumlocutions to avoid saying the Name, substituting other words such as Adonai ("sir" or "Lord") or Ha-Shem ("the Name") whenever they encountered the Tetragrammaton in the text. English translations most often use "Lord" as a stand-in for the Name; a few use "Yahweh," even though scholars are uncertain as to how the Tetragrammaton was actually pronounced, or "Jehovah," which is a peculiar amalgam, the German form of Yhwh (Jhvh) interspersed with the Hebrew vowel pointings for the word "Adonai." We have chosen to retain the Name in its form of four letters, transliterated from the Hebrew, and with this volume we have extended its use throughout the Hebrew Scriptures.

the new testament

This is the family record of Jesus the Christ, descendant of David, descendant of Abraham:* ² Abraham begot Isaac; Isaac begot Jacob; Jacob begot Judah and his sisters and brothers; ³ Tamar and Judah begot Perez and Zerah; Perez begot Hezron; Hezron begot Ram; ⁴ Ram begot Amminadab; Amminadab begot Nahshon; Nahshon begot Salmon; ⁵ Rahab and Salmon begot Boaz; Ruth and Boaz begot Obed; Obed begot Jesse; ⁶ and Jesse begot David, the ruler.

Bathsheba—who had been the wife of Uriah—and David begot Solomon; ⁷ Solomon begot Rehoboam; Rehoboam begot Abijah; Abijah begot Asa; ⁸ Asa begot Jehoshaphat; Jehoshaphat begot Joram; Joram begot Uzziah; ⁹ Uzziah begot Jotham; Jotham begot Ahaz; Ahaz begot Hezekiah; ¹⁰ Hezekiah begot Manasseh; Manasseh begot Amon; Amon begot Josiah; ¹¹ Josiah begot Jeconiah and his sisters and brothers at the time of the Babylonian captivity.

¹² After the Babylonian captivity, Jeconiah begot Shealtiel; Shealtiel begot Zerubbabel; ¹³ Zerubbabel begot Abiud; Abiud begot Eliakim; Eliakim begot Azor; ¹⁴ Azor begot Zadok; Zadok begot Achim; Achim begot Eliud; ¹⁵ Eliud begot Eleazar; Eleazar begot Matthan; Matthan begot Jacob; ¹⁶ Jacob begot Joseph, the husband of Mary. And from her Jesus was born.

¹⁷ Thus there were fourteen generations from Abraham to David, fourteen generations from David to the Babylonian captivity, and fourteen generations from the Babylonian captivity to the Messiah.

¹⁸ This is how the birth of Jesus came about.

When Jesus' mother, Mary, was engaged to Joseph, but before they lived together, she was found to be pregnant through the Holy Spirit. ¹⁹ Joseph, her husband, an upright person unwilling to disgrace her, decided to divorce her quietly.†

²⁰ This was Joseph's intention when suddenly the angel of God appeared in a dream and said, "Joseph, heir to the House of David, don't be afraid to wed Mary; it is by the Holy Spirit that she has conceived this child. ²¹ She is to have a son, and you are to name him Jesus—'Salvation'— because he will save the people from their sins." ²² All this happened to fulfill what God has said through the prophet:

> ²³ "The virgin will be with child
> and give birth,
> and the child will be named
> Immanuel"

—a name that means "God is with us."

²⁴ When Joseph awoke, he did as the angel of God had directed, and they went ahead with the marriage. ²⁵ He did not have intercourse with her until she had given birth; she had a son, and they named him Jesus.

---

* Matthew's genealogy is a theological construct to demonstrate that Jesus is the Messiah and to show that the course of the history of Israel was leading up to the birth of Jesus. It is deliberately compiled into three sets of fourteen, following the line of the rulers of Judah. In order to maintain the numbering, many names are left out.

† It is important to note that Joseph is the recipient of the revelation from the angel in Matthew's infancy narrative, while Mary is the recipient of the angel's revelation in Luke's narrative.

2 ¹ After Jesus' birth—which happened in Bethlehem of Judea, during the reign of Herod—astrologers from the East arrived in Jerusalem ² and asked, "Where is the newborn ruler of the Jews? We observed his star at its rising and have come to pay homage." ³ At this news Herod became greatly disturbed, as did all of Jerusalem. ⁴ Summoning all the chief priests and religious scholars of the people, he asked them where the Messiah was to be born.

⁵ "In Bethlehem of Judea," they informed him. "Here is what the prophet has written:

> ⁶ 'And you, Bethlehem, land of Judah,
> are by no means least among the leaders of Judah,
> since from you will come a ruler
> who is to shepherd my people Israel.'"

⁷ Herod called the astrologers aside and found out from them the exact time of the star's appearance. ⁸ Then he sent them to Bethlehem, after having instructed them, "Go and get detailed information about the child. When you have found him, report back to me—so that I may go and offer homage, too."

⁹ After their audience with the ruler, they set out. The star which they had observed at its rising went ahead of them until it came to a standstill over the place where the child lay. ¹⁰ They were overjoyed at seeing the star and, ¹¹ upon entering the house, found the child with Mary, his mother. They prostrated themselves and paid homage. Then they opened their coffers and presented the child with gifts of gold, frankincense and myrrh.

¹² They were warned in a dream not to return to Herod, so they went back to their own country by another route.

¹³ After the astrologers had left, the angel of God suddenly appeared in a dream to Joseph with the command, "Get up, take the child and his mother and flee to Egypt. Stay there until I tell you otherwise. Herod is searching for the child to destroy him." ¹⁴ Joseph got up, awakened Jesus and Mary, and they left that night for Egypt. ¹⁵ They stayed there until the death of Herod, to fulfill what God had said through the prophet: "Out of Egypt I have called my Own."

¹⁶ Herod became furious when he realized that the astrologers had outwitted him. He gave orders to kill all male children that were two years old and younger living in and around Bethlehem. The age of the children was based on the date Herod had learned from the astrologers. ¹⁷ Then what was spoken through the prophet Jeremiah was fulfilled:

> ¹⁸ "A voice was heard in Ramah
> sobbing and lamenting loudly:
> it was Rachel weeping for her children;
> she refused to be consoled,
> for they were no more."

¹⁹ After Herod's death, the angel of God appeared in a dream to Joseph in Egypt ²⁰ with the command, "Get up, take the child and his mother, and set out for the land of Israel. Those who had designs on the life of the child are dead."

²¹ Joseph got up, awakened Jesus and Mary, and they returned to the land of Israel. ²² Joseph heard, however, that Archelaus had succeeded Herod as ruler of Judea, and Joseph was afraid to go back there. Instead, because of a warning received by Joseph in a dream, the family went to the region of Galilee. ²³ There they settled in a town called Nazareth. In

this way, what was said through the prophets was fulfilled: "He will be called a Nazarene."

3:1–7:29

At this time John the Baptizer appeared in the desert of Judea, proclaiming, ² "Change your hearts and minds, for the reign of heaven is about to break in upon you!"

³ It was John that the prophet Isaiah described when he said,

"A herald's voice cries in the desert:
'Prepare the way of our God,
    make straight the paths of God!'"

⁴ John was clothed in a garment of camel's hair and wore a leather belt around his waist. Grasshoppers and wild honey were his food. ⁵ At that time, Jerusalem, all Judea and the whole region around the Jordan were going out to him. ⁶ John baptized them in the Jordan River as they confessed their sins.

⁷ When he saw that many of the Pharisees and Sadducees were coming to be baptized, John said to them, "You pack of snakes! Who told you to flee from the coming wrath? ⁸ Give some evidence that you mean to reform! ⁹ And don't pride yourselves on the claim, 'Sarah and Abraham are our parents.' I tell you, God can raise children for Sarah and Abraham from these very stones!

¹⁰ "Even now the ax is laid to the root of the tree. Every tree that is not fruitful will be cut down and thrown into the fire. ¹¹ I will baptize you in water if you have a change of heart, but the One who will follow me is more powerful than I. I'm not fit even to untie the sandals of the Coming One! That One will baptize you in the Holy Spirit and fire, ¹² whose winnowing-fan will clear the threshing floor. The grain will be gathered into the barn, but the chaff will be burned in unquenchable fire."

¹³ Then Jesus came from Galilee to the Jordan to be baptized by John. ¹⁴ John tried to dissuade Jesus, saying, "I should be baptized by you, and yet you come to me!" ¹⁵ But Jesus replied, "Leave it this way for now. We must do this to completely fulfill God's justice." So John reluctantly agreed.

¹⁶ Immediately after Jesus had been baptized and was coming up out of the water, the sky suddenly opened up and Jesus saw the Spirit of God descending as a dove and hovering over him. ¹⁷ With that, a voice from the heavens said, "This is my Own, my Beloved, on whom my favor rests."

4:¹ Then Jesus was led into the desert by the Spirit, to be tempted by the Devil. ² After fasting for forty days and forty nights, Jesus was hungry. ³ Then the tempter approached and said, "If you are the Only Begotten, command these stones to turn into bread."

⁴ Jesus replied, "Scripture has it,

'We live not on bread alone
but on every utterance that comes
    from the mouth of God.'"

⁵ Next the Devil took Jesus to the Holy City, set him on the parapet of the Temple ⁶ and said, "If you are the Only Begotten, throw yourself down. Scripture has it,

'God will tell the angels to take care of you;
with their hands they will support you
that you may never stumble on a stone.'"

⁷ Jesus answered, "Scripture also says, 'Do not put God to the test.'"

⁸ The Devil then took Jesus up a very high mountain and displayed all the dominions of the world in their magnificence, ⁹ promising, "All these I will give you if you fall down and worship me."

¹⁰ At this, Jesus said to the Devil, "Away with you, Satan! Scripture says, 'You will worship the Most High God; God alone will you adore.'"

¹¹ At that the Devil left, and angels came and attended Jesus.

¹² When Jesus heard that John had been arrested, he went back to Galilee. ¹³ He left Nazareth and settled in Capernaum, a lakeside town near the territory of Zebulun and Naphtali. ¹⁴ In this way the prophecy of Isaiah was fulfilled:

¹⁵ "Land of Zebulun, land of Naphtali,
    the way to the sea on the far side of the Jordan,
    Galilee of the Gentiles:
¹⁶ the people who lived in darkness
    have seen a great light;
    on those living in the land of the shadow of death
    a light has dawned."

¹⁷ From that time on, Jesus began proclaiming the message, "Change your hearts and minds, for the kindom of heaven is at hand!"

¹⁸ As Jesus was walking along the Sea of Galilee, he watched two brothers—Simon, who was called Peter, and Andrew—casting a net into the sea. They fished by trade. ¹⁹ Jesus said to them, "Come follow me, and I will make you fishers of humankind." ²⁰ They immediately abandoned their nets and began to follow Jesus.

²¹ Jesus walked along further and caught sight of a second pair of brothers—James and John, ben-Zebedee. They too were in their boat, mending their nets with their father. Jesus called them, ²² and immediately they abandoned both boat and father to follow him.

²³ Jesus traveled throughout Galilee, teaching in the synagogues, proclaiming the Good News of the kindom of heaven and healing all kinds of diseases and sicknesses among the people. ²⁴ His fame spread throughout Syria, and people suffering from illnesses and painful ailments of all kinds—those who were demon-possessed, those who were epileptic, those who were paralyzed—were brought to Jesus, and he healed them. ²⁵ Large crowds followed Jesus, coming from Galilee, the Decapolis, Jerusalem, Judea and Transjordania.

5:¹ When Jesus saw the crowds, he went up on the mountainside, and after he sat down and the disciples had gathered around, ² Jesus began to teach them:

³ "Blessed are those who are poor in spirit:
    the kindom of heaven is theirs.
⁴ Blessed are those who are mourning:
    they will be consoled.
⁵ Blessed are those who are gentle:
    they will inherit the land.
⁶ Blessed are those who hunger and thirst for justice:

they will have their fill.

7 Blessed are those who show mercy to others:
they will be shown mercy.

8 Blessed are those whose hearts are clean:
they will see God.

9 Blessed are those who work for peace:
they will be called children of God.

10 Blessed are those who are persecuted
because of their struggle for justice:
the kindom of heaven is theirs.

11 "You are fortunate when others insult you and persecute you, and utter every kind of slander against you because of me. 12 Be glad and rejoice, for your reward in heaven is great; they persecuted the prophets before you in the very same way.

13 "You are the salt of the earth. But what if salt were to lose its flavor? How could you restore it? It would be fit for nothing but to be thrown out and trampled underfoot.

14 "You are the light of the world. You don't build a city on a hill, then try to hide it, do you? 15 You don't light a lamp, then put it under a bushel basket, do you? No, you set it on a stand where it gives light to all in the house. 16 In the same way, your light must shine before others so that they may see your good acts and give praise to your Abba God in heaven.

17 "Don't think I've come to abolish the Law and the Prophets. I have come not to abolish them, but to fulfill them. 18 The truth is, until heaven and earth pass away, not the smallest letter of the Law, not even the smallest part of a letter, will be done away with until it is all fulfilled. 19 That's why whoever breaks the least significant of these commands and teaches others to do the same will be called the least in the kindom of heaven. Whoever fulfills and teaches these commands will be called great in the kindom of heaven.

20 "I tell you, unless your sense of justice surpasses that of the religious scholars and the Pharisees, you will not enter the kindom of heaven.

21 "You've heard that our ancestors were told, 'No killing' and, 'Every murderer will be subject to judgment.' 22 But I tell you that everyone who is angry with sister or brother is subject to judgment; anyone who says to sister or brother, 'I spit in your face!' will be subject to the Sanhedrin; and anyone who vilifies them with name-calling will be subject to the fires of Gehenna.

23 "If you bring your gift to the altar and there remember that your sister or brother has a grudge against you, 24 leave your gift there at the altar. Go to be reconciled to them, and then come and offer your gift.

25 "Lose no time in settling with your opponents—do so while still on the way to the courthouse with them. Otherwise your opponents may hand you over to the judge, and the judge hand you over to the bailiff, who will throw you into prison. 26 I warn you, you won't get out until you have paid the last penny.

27 "You've heard the commandment, 'No committing adultery.' 28 But I tell you that those who look lustfully at others have already committed adultery with them in their hearts. 29 If your right eye causes you to sin, pluck it out and throw it away. It's better to lose part of your body than to have it all cast into Gehenna. 30 And if your right hand causes you to sin, cut it off and throw it away! It's better to lose part of your body than to have it all cast into Gehenna.

31 "It was also said, 'Whenever a couple divorces, each partner must get a decree of divorce.' 32 But I tell you that everyone who divorces—except because of adultery—forces the spouse to commit adultery. Those who marry the divorced also commit adultery.

33 "Again, you have heard that our ancestors were told, 'Don't break your vow; fulfill all oaths made to our God.' 34 But I tell you not to swear oaths at all. Don't swear by heaven, for it is God's throne; 35 don't swear by the earth, for it is God's footstool. Don't swear by Jerusalem, for it is the city of the great Ruler. 36 And don't swear by your own head, for you can't make a single hair white or black. 37 Say 'Yes' when you mean 'Yes' and 'No' when you mean 'No.' Anything beyond that is from the Evil One.

38 "You've heard the commandment, 'An eye for an eye and a tooth for a tooth.' 39 But I tell you, offer no resistance whatsoever when you're confronted with violence. When someone strikes you on the right cheek, turn and offer the other. 40 If anyone wants to sue you for your shirt, hand over your coat as well. 41 Should anyone press you into service for one mile, go two miles. 42 Give to those who beg from you. And don't turn your back on those who want to borrow from you.

43 "You have heard it said, 'Love your neighbor—but hate your enemy.' 44 But I tell you, love your enemies and pray for your persecutors. 45 This will prove that you are children of God. For God makes the sun rise on bad and good alike; God's rain falls on the just and the unjust. 46 If you love those who love you, what merit is there in that? Don't tax collectors do as much? 47 And if you greet only your sisters and brothers, what is so praiseworthy about that? Don't Gentiles do as much? 48 Therefore be perfect, as Abba God in heaven is perfect.

6:1 "Beware of practicing your piety before others to attract their attention; if you do this, you will have no reward from your Abba God in heaven.

2 "When you do acts of charity, for example, don't have it trumpeted before you; that is what hypocrites do in the synagogues and the streets, that they may be praised by others. The truth is, they've already received their reward in full. 3 But when you do acts of charity, don't let your left hand know what your right hand is doing; 4 your good deeds must be done in secret, and your Abba God—who sees all that is done in secret—will repay you.

5 "And when you pray, don't behave like the hypocrites; they love to pray standing up in the synagogues and on street corners for people to see them. The truth is, they have received their reward in full. 6 But when you pray, go to your room, shut the door, and pray to God who is in that secret place, and your Abba God—who sees all that is done in secret—will reward you.

7 "And when you pray, don't babble like the Gentiles. They think God will hear them if they use a lot of words. 8 Don't imitate them. Your God knows what you need before you ask it. 9 This is how you are to pray:

'Abba God in heaven,
hallowed be your name!
10 May your reign come;
may your will be done on earth as it is in heaven:
11 give us today
the bread of Tomorrow.
12 And forgive us our debts,
as we hereby forgive those
who are indebted to us.
13 Don't put us to the test,
but free us from evil.'

¹⁴ "If you forgive the faults of others, Abba God will forgive you yours. ¹⁵ If you don't forgive others, neither will Abba God forgive you.

¹⁶ "And when you fast, don't look depressed like the hypocrites. They deliberately neglect their appearance to let everyone know that they are fasting. The truth is, they have already received their reward. ¹⁷ But when you fast, brush your hair and wash your face. ¹⁸ Don't let anyone know you're fasting except your Abba God, who sees all that is done in secret. And Abba God—who sees everything that is done in secret—will reward you.

¹⁹ "Don't store up earthly treasures for yourselves, which moths and rust destroy and thieves can break in and steal. ²⁰ But store up treasures for yourselves in heaven, where neither moth nor rust can destroy them and thieves cannot break in and steal them. ²¹ For where your treasure is, there will your heart be as well.

²² "The lamp of the body is the eye. If your eye is sound, your whole body will be filled with light; ²³ but if your eye is diseased, your whole body will be in darkness. And if the light inside you is darkness, how great that darkness will be!

²⁴ "No one can serve two superiors. You will either hate one and love the other, or be attentive to one and despise the other. You cannot give yourself to God and Money. ²⁵ That's why I tell you not to worry about your livelihood, what you are to eat or drink or use for clothing. Isn't life more than just food? Isn't the body more than just clothes?

²⁶ "Look at the birds in the sky. They don't sow or reap, they gather nothing into barns, yet our God in heaven feeds them. Aren't you more important than they? ²⁷ Which of you by worrying can add a moment to your lifespan? ²⁸ And why be anxious about clothing? Learn a lesson from the way the wildflowers grow. They don't work; they don't spin. ²⁹ Yet I tell you, not even Solomon in full splendor was arrayed like one of these. ³⁰ If God can clothe in such splendor the grasses of the field, which bloom today and are thrown on the fire tomorrow, won't God do so much more for you—you who have so little faith?

³¹ "Stop worrying, then, over questions such as, 'What are we to eat,' or 'what are we to drink,' or 'what are we to wear?' ³² Those without faith are always running after these things. God knows everything you need. ³³ Seek first God's reign, and God's justice, and all these things will be given to you besides. ³⁴ Enough of worrying about tomorrow! Let tomorrow take care of itself. Today has troubles enough of its own.

7 ¹ "Don't judge, or you yourself will be judged. ² Your judgment on others will be the judgment you receive. The measure you use will be used to measure you. ³ Why do you look at the splinter in your neighbor's eye and never see the board in your own eye? ⁴ How can you say to your neighbor, 'Let me remove the splinter in your eye,' when the whole time there's a two-by-four in your own? ⁵ Hypocrite! Remove the board from your own eye first; then you'll be able to see clearly to remove the splinter from your neighbor's eye.

⁶ "Don't give dogs what is sacred; don't throw your pearls to pigs. If you do, they'll just trample them underfoot—then turn and tear you to pieces.

⁷ "Ask and keep asking, and you will receive. Seek and keep seeking, and you will find. Knock and keep knocking, and the door will be opened to you. ⁸ For the one who keeps asking, receives. The one who keeps seeking, finds. And the one who keeps knocking, enters.

⁹ "Is there any among you who would hand your daughter a stone when she asked for bread? ¹⁰ Would one of you hand your son a snake when he asked for a fish? ¹¹ If you, with all your faults, know how to give your children what is good, how much more will your Abba God in heaven give good things to those who ask!

¹² "Therefore treat others as you would have them treat you. This is the whole meaning of the Law and the prophets.

¹³ "Enter by the narrow gate. The wide gate puts you on the spacious road to damnation, and many take it. ¹⁴ But it's a small gate, a narrow road that leads to Life, and only a few find it.

¹⁵ "Be on your guard against false prophets who come to you disguised as sheep, but underneath are ravenous wolves. ¹⁶ You will be able to tell them by their fruit. Can people pick grapes from thorns, or figs from thistles? ¹⁷ In the same way, a sound tree produces good fruit and a rotten tree produces bad fruit. ¹⁸ A sound tree cannot produce rotten fruit, and a rotten tree cannot produce good fruit. ¹⁹ Any tree that does not produce good fruit is cut down and thrown in the fire. ²⁰ I repeat, you'll be able to tell them by their fruit.

²¹ "It isn't those who cry out, 'My Savior! My Savior!' who will enter the kindom of heaven; rather, it is those who do the will of Abba God in heaven. ²² When that day comes, many will plead with me, 'Savior! Savior! Have we not prophesied in your name? Have we not exorcised demons in your name? Didn't we do many miracles in your name as well?' ²³ Then I will declare to them, 'I never knew you. Out of my sight, you evildoers!'

²⁴ "Anyone who hears my words and puts them into practice is like the sage who built a house on rock. ²⁵ When the rainy season set in, the torrents came and the winds blew and buffeted the house. It didn't collapse because it had been set solidly on rock. ²⁶ Anyone who hears my words but does not put them into practice is like the fool who built a house on sandy ground. ²⁷ The rains fell; the torrents came; the winds blew and lashed against the house. And it collapsed and was completely ruined."

²⁸ Jesus finished speaking and left the crowds spellbound at his teaching, ²⁹ because he taught with an authority that was unlike their religious scholars.

8:1–11:1

When Jesus came down from the mountain, large crowds followed. ² Suddenly a person with leprosy came forward, knelt down and said, "Rabbi, if you are willing, you can make me clean."

³ Jesus reached out and touched the person. "I am willing. Be clean!" Immediately the leprosy disappeared. ⁴ Jesus then said, "See to it that you tell no one. Go and show yourself to the priest and offer the gift Moses commanded. That should be the proof they need."

⁵ As Jesus entered Capernaum, a centurion approached him and said, ⁶ "Rabbi, my young attendant is at home in bed paralyzed, suffering in great pain."

⁷ Jesus said, "I will come and heal your attendant."

⁸ The centurion replied, "Teacher, I am not worthy to have you under my roof, but just say the word and my boy will be cured. ⁹ I, too, am a person subject to authority and have soldiers subject to me. I say to some, 'Go!' and off they go; to others, 'Come here!' and they come; to my attendants, 'Do this!' and they do it."

¹⁰ When Jesus heard this, he was amazed and said to those nearby, "The truth is, I've found no one in Israel with such great faith. ¹¹ I tell you, many will come from the East and

the West and will take their places at the feast with Sarah and Abraham, Rebecca and Isaac, and Leah and Rachel and Jacob in the kindom of heaven, ¹² while the natural heirs of the kindom will be thrown outside, into the darkness, where there will be weeping and gnashing of teeth." ¹³ Then Jesus said to the centurion, "Go home, it will be done just as you believed it would." And the attendant was healed that very hour.

¹⁴ Entering Peter's house, Jesus found Peter's mother-in-law in bed with a fever. ¹⁵ Jesus touched her hand and the fever left, and she got up and went about her work.

¹⁶ As evening drew near, they brought many to Jesus who were possessed. He expelled the spirits with a word and healed all who were ill, ¹⁷ thereby fulfilling what had been said through Isaiah the prophet: "You took on our infirmities and endured our sufferings."

¹⁸ Jesus, seeing a crowd gathering, gave orders to cross the lake to the other shore.

¹⁹ Then a religious scholar approached and said, "Rabbi, I will follow you wherever you go."

²⁰ Jesus replied, "The foxes have holes, the birds in the sky have their nests, but the Chosen One has nowhere to lie down."

²¹ Another, a disciple, said to him, "Teacher, let me go and bury my mother first."

²² Jesus said, "Follow me, and let the dead bury their own dead."

²³ Then Jesus got into a boat and the disciples followed. ²⁴ Without warning, a violent storm broke over the lake, and the boat began to take on water. But Jesus was sleeping, ²⁵ so they shook him awake, exclaiming, "Save us! We are lost!"

²⁶ Jesus replied, "Why are you afraid? You have so little faith!" Then Jesus stood up and rebuked the winds and the sea, and there was a great calm. ²⁷ The others, dumbfounded, said, "Who is this, whom even the winds and the sea obey?"

²⁸ When Jesus landed at the Gadarene boundary, he encountered two demon-possessed people coming out of the tombs. They were so violent that no one could pass by there. ²⁹ "What do you want from us, Only Begotten of God," they shouted. "Have you come to torture us before the appointed time?" ³⁰ Some distance away a large herd of pigs was feeding. ³¹ The demons pleaded with Jesus and said, "If you expel us, send us into the herd of pigs."

³² Jesus answered, "Out with you!" With that they came forth and entered the pigs. The whole herd charged down the cliff into the lake and drowned in the water.

³³ The swineherds fled and, upon arriving in the town, told everything that had happened, including the story of the pair possessed by demons. ³⁴ Then the entire town came out to meet Jesus and implored him to leave the neighborhood.

9 ¹ Jesus got back into the boat, crossed the lake and returned to his own town. ² Then some people appeared, bringing a person who was paralyzed, stretched out on a pallet. Seeing their faith, Jesus said to the paralyzed person, "Courage, my child, your sins are forgiven."

³ At that, some of the religious scholars said to themselves, "This is blasphemy!"

⁴ Jesus was aware of their thoughts and said, "Why do you harbor evil thoughts? ⁵ Which is easier to say, 'Your sins are forgiven,' or 'stand up and walk'? ⁶ But to prove to you that the Chosen One has authority on earth to forgive sins—" Jesus then turned to the paralyzed person—"Stand up! Take up your mat, and go home." ⁷ With that, the afflicted one got up and went home. ⁸ The crowd was filled with awe

when they saw this, and they praised God for giving such authority to mortals.

⁹ As Jesus walked on, he saw Matthew, a tax collector, at his post. Jesus approached and said, "Follow me," and Matthew got up and followed.

¹⁰ Now it happened that, while Jesus was at table in Matthew's house, many tax collectors and notorious "sinners" came to join Jesus and the disciples at dinner. ¹¹ The Pharisees saw this and complained to the disciples, saying, "What reason can the Teacher have for eating with tax collectors and sinners?"

¹² Overhearing the remark, Jesus said, "People who are in good health don't need a doctor; sick people do. ¹³ Go and learn the meaning of the words, 'I desire compassion, not sacrifices.' I have come to call not the righteous but sinners."

¹⁴ The disciples of John the Baptizer came to Jesus and said, "Why is it that while we and the Pharisees fast, your disciples don't?" ¹⁵ Jesus replied, "How can the guests at a wedding feast mourn while they are still all together? The time will come when the guests will be left alone; then they will fast.

¹⁶ "No one sews a piece of unshrunken cloth onto an old cloak, because the patch will pull away from the cloak and the tear will get worse. ¹⁷ Nor do people put new wine into old wineskins—if they do, the skins will burst, the wine will run out, and the skins will be ruined. No, they put new wine into new wineskins, and both are preserved."

¹⁸ As Jesus was speaking, a synagogue official came up, knelt down and said, "My daughter has just died. But if you come and lay hands on her, she will live." ¹⁹ Jesus got up and went with the official, and so did the disciples.

²⁰ As they were going along, a woman who had suffered from hemorrhages for twelve years came up behind him and touched the hem of his cloak; ²¹ she was saying to herself, "If only I can touch his cloak, I will be healed."

²² Jesus turned around and saw her. "Courage, daughter," he said, "your faith has healed you." That very moment the woman was healed.

²³ When Jesus arrived at the house of the synagogue official, a noisy crowd had gathered, and the flute players who served as mourners had already arrived. ²⁴ When he saw them he said, "Get out! The child is not dead—only asleep." They all laughed at him.

²⁵ After the crowd had been put out, he entered and took the girl by the hand, and she got up. ²⁶ And the news spread throughout the countryside.

²⁷ As Jesus moved on from Capernaum, two blind people followed and cried out, "Heir to the House of David, have pity on us!"

²⁸ When Jesus reached his lodgings, they caught up with him. Jesus said to them, "Do you believe I can do this?"

They said, "Yes, Rabbi."

²⁹ Then he touched their eyes and said, "Because of your faith, it will be done to you." ³⁰ And their sight returned.

Then Jesus sternly warned them, "See that no one learns of this." ³¹ But they went off and talked about him all over the countryside.

³² As they were leaving, some people brought Jesus a person who was possessed by a demon and unable to speak. ³³ Once the demon was expelled, the individual began to speak—to

the great surprise of the crowd. "Nothing like this has ever been seen in Israel!" they said.

³⁴ But the Pharisees said, "He casts out demons through the power of demons."

³⁵ Jesus continued touring all the towns and villages, teaching in their synagogues, proclaiming the Good News of God's reign and curing all kinds of diseases and sicknesses.

³⁶ At the sight of the crowds, Jesus' heart was moved with pity because they were distressed and dejected, like sheep without a shepherd. ³⁷ Jesus said to the disciples, "The harvest is bountiful but the laborers are few. ³⁸ Beg the overseer of the harvest to send laborers out to bring in the crops."

10 ¹ Jesus summoned the Twelve, and gave them authority to expel unclean spirits and heal sickness and diseases of all kinds.

² These are the names of the twelve apostles: the first were Simon, nicknamed Peter—that is, "Rock"—and his brother Andrew; then James, ben-Zebedee, and his brother John; ³ Philip and Bartholomew; Thomas; Matthew, the tax collector; James, ben-Alphaeus; Thaddaeus; ⁴ Simon the Zealot; and Judas Iscariot, who betrayed Jesus.

⁵ These twelve Jesus sent out after giving them the following instructions:

"Don't visit Gentile regions, and don't enter a Samaritan town. ⁶ Go instead to the lost sheep of the house of Israel. ⁷ As you go, make this proclamation: 'The reign of heaven has drawn near.'

⁸ "Heal those who are sick, raise the dead, cure leprosy, expel demons. You received freely—now freely give.

⁹ "Take neither gold nor silver nor copper for your money belts— ¹⁰ no traveling bag, no change of clothes, no sandals, no walking staff—for workers deserve their keep.

¹¹ "Look for worthy people in whatever town or village you come to, and stay with them until you leave. ¹² As you enter a house, bless it. ¹³ If the home is deserving, your peace will descend on it. If it isn't, your peace will return to you.

¹⁴ "If anyone does not receive you or listen to what you have to say, leave that house or town and, once outside it, shake its dust from your feet. ¹⁵ The truth is, on Judgment Day it will go easier for the towns of Sodom and Gomorrah than it will for that town.

¹⁶ "I am sending you out like sheep among wolves. So you must be as clever as snakes, but as innocent as doves. ¹⁷ Be on your guard. People will haul you into court, they will flog you in the synagogues. ¹⁸ For my sake you will be dragged before rulers and governors as witnesses to them and to the Gentiles.

¹⁹ "When they hand you over, don't worry about how to speak or what to say. You'll be given what you should say when the time comes, ²⁰ because it is not you speaking but the Spirit of your Abba God speaking through you.

²¹ "Sibling will betray sibling to death, and parents their children; children will rise up against their parents and have them executed. ²² Everyone will hate you because of me. But whoever stands firm until the end will be saved. ²³ When you are persecuted in one place, flee to another. The truth is, you will not have visited all the towns of Israel before the Chosen One comes.

²⁴ "A student is not superior to the teacher; the follower is not above the leader. ²⁵ The student should be glad simply to become like the teacher, the follower like the leader.

"If the head of the house has been called Beelzebul, how much more the members of the household!

²⁶ "Don't let people intimidate you. Nothing is concealed that will not be revealed, and nothing is hidden that will not be made known. ²⁷ What I tell you in darkness, speak in the light. What you hear in private, proclaim from the housetops.

²⁸ "Don't fear those who can deprive the body of life but can't destroy the soul. Rather, fear the one who can destroy both body and soul in Gehenna.

²⁹ "Are not the sparrows sold for pennies? Yet not a single sparrow falls to the ground without your Abba God's knowledge. ³⁰ As for you, every hair of your head has been counted. ³¹ So don't be afraid of anything—you are worth more than an entire flock of sparrows.

³² "Whoever acknowledges me before others, I will acknowledge before Abba God in heaven. ³³ Whoever disowns me before others, I will disown before Abba God in heaven.

³⁴ "Don't suppose that I came to bring peace on earth. I came not to bring peace, but a sword. ³⁵ I have come to turn

'A son against his father,
a daughter against her mother,
in-law against in-law.
³⁶ One's enemies will be
the members of one's own household.'

³⁷ "Those who love mother or father, daughter or son more than me are not worthy of me. ³⁸ Those who will not carry with them the instrument of their own death—following in my footsteps—are not worthy of me.

³⁹ "You who have found your life will lose it, and you who lose your life for my sake will find it.

⁴⁰ "Those who welcome you also welcome me, and those who welcome me welcome the One who sent me.

⁴¹ "Those who welcome prophets just because they are prophets will receive the reward reserved for the prophets themselves; those who welcome holy people just because they are holy will receive the reward of the holy ones.

⁴² "The truth is, whoever gives a cup of cold water to one of these lowly ones just for being a disciple will not lack a reward."

11 ¹ When Jesus had finished instructing the Twelve, he left the area to teach and preach in the outlying towns of the region.

11:2–13:58

While John was in prison, he heard about the works the Messiah was performing, and sent a message by way of his disciples ³ to ask Jesus, "Are you 'The One who is to come' or do we look for another?"

⁴ In reply, Jesus said to them, "Go back and report to John what you hear and see:
⁵ 'Those who are blind recover their sight;
those who cannot walk are able to walk;
those with leprosy are cured;
those who are deaf hear;
the dead are raised to life;
and the *anawim*—the "have-nots"—
have the Good News preached to them.'

⁶ "Blessed is the one who finds no stumbling block in me."

⁷ As the messengers set off, Jesus began to speak to the crowds about John: "What did you go out to the wasteland to see—a reed swaying in the wind? ⁸ Tell me, what did you go out to see—someone luxuriously dressed? No, those who dress luxuriously are to be found in royal palaces. ⁹ So what did you go out to see—a prophet? Yes, a prophet—and more than a prophet! ¹⁰ It is about John that scripture says,

'I send my messenger ahead of you
to prepare your way before you.'

¹¹ "The truth is, history has not known a person born of woman who is greater than John the Baptizer. Yet the least born into the kindom of heaven is greater than he.

¹² "From the time of John the Baptizer until now, the kindom of heaven has been advancing with power, and powerful people take hold of it. ¹³ The Law and the Prophets prophesied until John came. ¹⁴ And he, if you will believe me, is the Elijah who was to return. ¹⁵ Let those who have ears to hear, hear this!

¹⁶ "What comparison can I make with this generation? They are like children shouting to others as they sit in the marketplace, ¹⁷ 'We piped you a tune, but you wouldn't dance. We sang you a dirge, but you wouldn't mourn.' ¹⁸ For John came neither eating nor drinking, and they say, 'He is possessed.' ¹⁹ The Chosen One comes, eating and drinking, and they say, 'This one is a glutton and a drunkard, a friend of tax collectors and sinners.' Wisdom will be vindicated by her own actions."

²⁰ Then Jesus began to denounce the cities where most of the miracles had been performed, because they did not repent. ²¹ "Woe to you, Chorazin! Woe to you, Bethsaida! For if the miracles worked in you had been worked in Tyre and Sidon, they would have repented long ago in sackcloth and ashes! ²² But the truth is, it will go easier for Tyre and Sidon than for you on the Judgment Day.

²³ "As for you, Capernaum, do you intend to ascend to the heavens? No, you will go down to the underworld! If the miracles worked for you had taken place in Sodom, it would be standing today. ²⁴ But the truth is, it will go easier for Sodom than for you on the Judgment Day."

²⁵ Then Jesus prayed, "Abba God, Creator of heaven and earth, to you I offer praise; for what you have hidden from the learned and the clever, you have revealed to the youngest children. ²⁶ Yes, Abba, everything is as you want it to be."

²⁷ Jesus continued,

"Everything has been handed over to me
by Abba God.
No one knows the Only Begotten
except Abba God,
and no one knows Abba God
except the Only Begotten—
and those to whom the Only Begotten
wants to give that revelation.
²⁸ Come to me,
all you who labor and carry heavy burdens,
and I will give you rest.
²⁹ Take my yoke upon your shoulders
and learn from me,
for I am gentle and humble of heart.
Here you will find rest for your souls,
³⁰ for my yoke is easy
and my burden is light."

12¹ One Sabbath, Jesus walked through the standing grain. The disciples were hungry and began to pick some heads of grain and eat them. ² When the Pharisees saw this, they said to Jesus, "Look! Your disciples are doing something that is forbidden on the Sabbath."

³ Jesus replied, "Have you not read what David did when he and his followers were hungry, ⁴ how he entered God's house and ate the holy bread—something forbidden to him and his followers or anyone other than the priests? ⁵ Have you not read in the Law how priests, when they are serving in the Temple, can break the Sabbath rest without incurring guilt? ⁶ I tell you, something greater than the Temple is here. ⁷ If you understood the meaning of the text, 'I desire compassion, not sacrifices,' you wouldn't have condemned the innocent. ⁸ For the Chosen One is ruler of the Sabbath."

⁹ He left there and went into their synagogue. ¹⁰ A person with a withered hand was also in the synagogue. The Pharisees tried to trap Jesus with a trick question: "Is it lawful to heal on the Sabbath?"

¹¹ But Jesus replied, "Which one of you, if your sheep were to fall in a ditch on the Sabbath, would not grab it and lift it out? ¹² Certainly a person is more valuable than a sheep! So then, yes, it is lawful to do good on the Sabbath."

¹³ Then he said to the person with the withered hand, "Stretch it out." And immediately it was healed and as sound as the other hand.

¹⁴ At this, the Pharisees went outside and began to plot against Jesus to find a way to destroy him. ¹⁵ Jesus knew this and withdrew from the district.

Many followed Jesus and he healed them all, ¹⁶ but he warned them not to make public what he had done. ¹⁷ This silence was to fulfill what the prophet Isaiah said:

¹⁸ "You are my Faithful One, whom I have chosen;
my Beloved, the One in whom I delight:
on you I will put my Spirit,
and you will proclaim justice to the nations.
¹⁹ You will not quarrel or cry out,
and your voice will not be heard in the streets;
²⁰ you will not break the bruised reed
or snuff out the smoldering wick
until justice is led to victory.
²¹ In your name the nations will find their hope."

²² Then they brought someone to Jesus who was demon-possessed, blind and mute; Jesus healed the person and restored both sight and speech. ²³ All the people were astonished, and said, "Could this be the promised Heir to the House of David?"

²⁴ When the Pharisees heard this, they muttered, "The only way he drives out demons is by Beelzebul, the ruler of demons."

²⁵ But Jesus knew what they were thinking and said to them, "Any realm divided against itself will be ruined, and any town or household divided against itself cannot stand. ²⁶ If Satan drives out Satan, the Devil's domain is divided against itself. How then can it stand?

²⁷ "And if I drive out demons by Beelzebul, by whom do your authorities drive them out? Your own people will stand in judgment of you! ²⁸ But if I drive out demons through the Spirit of God, then the reign of God has come upon you!

²⁹ "Again, how can burglars break into a house and carry off its property unless they first tie up the people inside? Only then can they ransack the house.

30 "Those who are not with me are against me. Those who don't gather with me scatter. 31 Therefore, I tell you, every sin and blasphemy will be forgiven, except for blasphemy against the Holy Spirit. 32 Anyone who says a word against the Promised One will be forgiven, but anyone who speaks against the Holy Spirit will not be forgiven, either in this age or in the next.

33 "Make the tree healthy and its fruit will be healthy; neglect the tree and its fruit will be rotten. A tree is known by its fruit.

34 "You brood of vipers! How can what you say be good when you are full of evil? Our words flow from the fullness of our heart: 35 a good person brings good things out of a good storehouse; a bad person brings bad things out of a bad storehouse.

36 "I tell you, on Judgment Day all will give an account of every careless word they ever spoke. 37 Your own words will either acquit you or condemn you."

38 Then some of the religious scholars and Pharisees spoke up: "Teacher, we want to see a miraculous sign from you."

39 Jesus answered, "It is an evil and unfaithful generation that asks for a sign! The only sign to be given is the sign of Jonah the prophet. 40 For as Jonah was in the whale's belly for three days and three nights, so will the Chosen One be three days and three nights in the bowels of the earth.

41 "On Judgment Day the citizens of Nineveh will stand up against this generation and condemn it, because they repented when Jonah preached—but now one greater than Jonah is here. 42 On Judgment Day the Queen of Sheba will rise up against this generation and condemn it, because she came from the ends of the earth to hear Solomon—but now one greater than Solomon is here.

43 "When an unclean spirit goes out of a person it wanders through arid places searching for rest. When it finds none, 44 it says, 'I will return to the home I left.' And upon returning, it finds its old house empty and swept clean. 45 Then it goes and brings back seven other spirits more evil than itself, and they enter and set up housekeeping; the person ends up far worse than before. And that is how it will be with this evil generation!"

46 While Jesus was still speaking to the crowd, his family stood outside, wanting to speak to him. 47 Someone said to Jesus, "Your mother and kin are standing outside, and they are anxious to speak with you." 48 Jesus replied, "Who is my mother? Who are my kin?" 49 Pointing to the disciples, Jesus said, "This is my family. 50 Whoever does the will of Abba God in heaven is my sister and brother and mother."

13 1 Later that day, Jesus left the house and sat down by the lake shore. 2 Such great crowds gathered that he went and took a seat in a boat, while the crowd stood along the shore. 3 He addressed them at length in parables:

"One day, a farmer went out sowing seed. 4 Some of the seed landed on a footpath, where birds came and ate it up. 5 Some of the seed fell on rocky ground, where there was little soil. This seed sprouted at once since the soil had no depth, 6 but when the sun rose and scorched it, it withered away for lack of roots. 7 Again, some of the seed fell among thorns, and the thorns grew up and choked it. 8 And some of it landed on good soil, and yielded a crop thirty, sixty, even

a hundred times what was sown. 9 Let those who have ears to hear, hear this!"

10 When the disciples came to Jesus, they asked, "Why do you speak to the people in parables?" 11 Jesus answered, "The secrets of the kindom of heaven are for you to know, but not for them. 12 To those who have, more will be given until they have an abundance; those who have not will lose what little they have.

13 "I use parables when I speak to the people because they look but don't see, they listen but don't hear or understand. 14 Isaiah's prophecy is being fulfilled in them, which says,

'You will be ever listening, but never understanding;
   you will be ever looking, but never perceiving.
15 For this people's heart
   has become calloused;
they hardly hear with their ears,
   and they have closed their eyes.
Otherwise they might see with their eyes,
   and hear with their ears,
   and understand with their hearts
   and turn back to me,
   and I would heal them.'

16 "But blessed are your eyes because they see, and your ears because they hear. 17 The truth is, many prophets and holy people longed to see what you see but never saw it, to hear what you hear but never heard it.

18 "Now listen to the parable of the sower. 19 When people hear the message about the kindom of God without understanding it, the Evil One comes along and snatches away what was sown in their hearts. This is the seed sown along the path. 20 Those who received the seed that fell on rocky ground are the ones who hear the word and at first welcome it with joy. 21 But they have no roots, so they last only for a while. When some setback or persecution comes because of the message, they quickly fall away. 22 Those who receive the message that fell among the thorns are the ones who hear the word, but then worldly anxieties and the lure of wealth choke it off, and the message produces no fruit. 23 But those who receive the seed that fell on rich soil are those who hear the message and understand it. They produce a crop that yields a hundred, or sixty or thirty times what was sown."

24 Jesus presented another parable to those gathered: "The kindom of heaven is like a farmer who sowed good seed in a field. 25 While everyone was asleep, an enemy came and sowed weeds among the wheat and then made off. 26 When the crop began to mature and yield grain, the weeds became evident as well.

27 "The farmer's workers came and asked, 'Did you not sow good seed in your field? Where are the weeds coming from?'

28 "The farmer replied, 'I see an enemy's hand in this.'

"They in turn asked, 'Do you want us to go out and pull them up?'

29 "'No,' replied the farmer, 'if you pull up the weeds, you might take the wheat along with them. 30 Let them grow together until the harvest, then at harvest time I will order the harvesters first to collect the weeds and bundle them up to burn, then to gather the wheat into my barn.'"

31 Jesus presented another parable to the crowds: "The kindom of heaven is like the mustard seed which a farmer sowed in a field. 32 It is the smallest of all seeds, but when it has grown it is the biggest shrub of all—it becomes a tree so that the birds of the air come to perch in its branches."

33 Jesus offered them still another parable: "The kindom of heaven is like the yeast a baker took and mixed in with three measures of flour until it was leavened all through."

34 Jesus spoke all these things to the crowd in parables. He spoke to them in parables only, 35 to fulfill what had been said through the prophet:

"I will open my mouth in parables,
I will announce things hidden
since the creation of the world."

36 Then Jesus left the crowd and went into the house. The disciples also came in and said, "Explain the parable about the weeds in the field."

37 Jesus answered, "The farmer sowing the good seed is the Chosen One, 38 the field is the world, and the good seed, the citizens of the kindom. The weeds are the followers of the Evil One, 39 and the enemy who sowed them is the Devil. The harvest is the end of the world, while the harvesters are the angels. 40 Just as weeds are collected and burned, so it will be at the end of the age. 41 The Chosen One will send the angels who will weed out the kindom of everything that causes sin and all who act lawlessly. 42 The angels will throw them into the fiery furnace, where there will be weeping and gnashing of teeth. 43 But those who are just will shine like the sun in the kindom of their Abba God. Let those who have ears to hear, hear this!

44 "The kindom of heaven is like a buried treasure found in a field. The ones who discovered it hid it again, and, re-joicing at the discovery, went and sold all their possessions and bought that field.

45 "Or again, the kindom of heaven is like a merchant's search for fine pearls. 46 When one pearl of great value was found, the merchant went back and sold everything else and bought it.

47 "Or again, the kindom of heaven is like a net thrown into the sea, which collected all kinds of fish. 48 When it was full, the fishers hauled it ashore. Then, sitting down, they collected the good ones in a basket and threw away those that were of no use. 49 This is how it will be at the end of time. The angels will come and separate the wicked from the just 50 and throw the wicked into the blazing furnace, where there will be weeping and the gnashing of teeth.

51 "Have you understood all this?"

"Yes," they answered.

52 To this Jesus replied, "Every religious scholar who has become a student of the kindom of heaven is like the head of a household who can bring from the storeroom both the new and the old."

53 When Jesus had finished these parables, he left the area 54 and came to his hometown and began teaching the people in the synagogue, and the people were amazed. They said to one another, "Where did he get this wisdom and these miraculous powers? 55 Isn't this the carpenter's child? Isn't his mother's name Mary, and his brothers James and Joseph and Simon and Judah? 56 His sisters, too, aren't they all here with us? But where did such gifts come from?" 57 And they found him altogether too much for them.

Jesus said to them, "Prophets are only despised in their own home town and in their own households." 58 And Jesus did not work many miracles there because of their lack of faith.

14:1–19:2

At this time, Herod the tetrarch heard about the reputation of Jesus, 2 and he said to his attendants, "This is John the Baptizer, who has risen from the dead. That is why miraculous powers are at work in him."

3 For Herod had arrested John, bound him and thrown him in prison because of Herodias, his brother Philip's wife. 4 For John had told Herod, "It is against the Law for you to have her." 5 He had wanted to kill John but was afraid of the people, who regarded John as a prophet.

6 Then, during the celebration of Herod's birthday, the daughter of Herodias danced for them and pleased Herod 7 so much that he promised on oath to give her whatever she asked. 8 Prompted by her mother, she said, "Give me the head of John the Baptizer on a platter."

9 Herod was distressed, but because his dinner guests had heard the oath, he ordered that her request be granted 10 and had John beheaded in the prison. 11 The head was brought in on a platter and given to the young woman, who carried it to her mother. 12 John's disciples came and took the body and buried it, then went and told Jesus.

13 When Jesus heard about the beheading, he left Naza-reth by boat and went to a deserted place to be alone. The crowds heard of this and followed him from their towns on foot. 14 When Jesus disembarked and saw the vast throng, his heart was moved with pity, and he healed their sick.

15 As evening drew on, the disciples approached Jesus and said, "This is a deserted place and it is already late. Dismiss the crowds so they can go to the villages and buy some food for themselves."

16 Jesus said to them: "There is no need for them to dis-perse. Give them something to eat yourselves."

17 "We have nothing here," they replied, "but five loaves and a couple of fish."

18 "Bring them here," Jesus said. 19 Then he ordered the crowds to sit on the grass. Taking the five loaves and two fish, Jesus looked up to heaven, blessed the food, broke it, and gave it to the disciples, who in turn gave it to the people. 20 All those present ate their fill. The fragments remaining, when gathered up, filled twelve baskets. 21 About five thou-sand families were fed.

22 Jesus insisted that the disciples get into the boat and pre-cede him to the other side. 23 Having sent the crowds away, he went up on the mountain by himself to pray, remaining there alone as night fell. 24 Meanwhile the boat, already a thousand yards from shore, was being tossed about in the waves which had been raised by the fierce winds.

25 At about three in the morning, Jesus came walking toward them on the lake. 26 When the disciples saw Jesus walking on the water, they were terrified. "It is a ghost!" they said, and in their fear they began to cry out.

27 Jesus hastened to reassure them: "Don't worry, it's me! Don't be afraid!"

28 Peter spoke up and said, "If it is really you, tell me to come to you across the water."

29 "Come!" Jesus said.

So Peter got out of the boat and began to walk on the wa-ter toward Jesus. 30 But when he saw how strong the wind was, he became frightened. He began to sink, and cried out, "Save me!"

31 Jesus immediately stretched out his hand and caught Peter. "You have so little faith!" Jesus said to him. "Why did you doubt?"

32 Once they had climbed into the boat, the wind died down. 33 Those who were in the boat showed great reverence, declaring to Jesus, "You are indeed God's Own!"

34 After making the crossing, they landed at Gennesaret. 35 When the people of that place recognized Jesus, they sent word to all the surrounding villages. They brought to Jesus all those who were sick, 36 who begged him to let

them just touch the hem of his cloak, and all who touched it were healed.

15 [1] Some Pharisees and teachers of the Law from Jerusalem then came to Jesus and said, [2] "Why do your disciples violate the tradition of the elders? They don't perform a ritual hand-washing before they eat."

[3] Jesus replied, "And why do you violate the commandments of God for the sake of your tradition? [4] For God said, 'Honor your mother and your father,' and 'Those who curse their mother or father must be put to death.' [5] But you say, 'Whoever says to their parents, "Any support you might have had from me is dedicated to God," is no longer obligated to support them.' [6] You therefore nullify the word of God for the sake of your tradition! [7] You hypocrites! Isaiah prophesied well when he said of you:

[8]   'These people honor me with their lips,
      while their hearts are far from me.
[9]   Their worship of me is worthless,
      and their doctrines are mere human rules.'"

[10] Jesus called the crowd together and said to them, "Hear this and understand: [11] it's not what enters your mouth that defiles you—it's what comes out of your mouth that defiles you."

[12] Then the disciples approached him and said, "Do you realize that the Pharisees were offended by what you said?"

[13] Jesus replied, "Every plant that my Abba God in heaven has not planted will be pulled up by the roots. [14] Ignore them—they are blind people leading other blind people. And when the blind lead the blind, they all will fall into a ditch."

[15] Then Peter said to him, "Explain this parable to us."

[16] Jesus replied, "Do you still not understand? [17] Don't you realize that everything that goes into the mouth passes into the stomach and eventually finds its way into the sewer and is gone? [18] But what comes out of the mouth comes from the heart. This is what makes a person 'unclean.' [19] For from the heart come all sorts of evil intentions—murder, sexual infidelity, promiscuity, stealing, lying, even foul language. [20] These things make a person unclean—not eating with unwashed hands!"

[21] Jesus left there and departed for the district of Tyre and Sidon. [22] It happened that a Canaanite woman living in that area came and cried out to Jesus, "Heir to the House of David, have pity on me! My daughter is horribly demon-possessed."

[23] Jesus gave her no word of response. The disciples came up and repeatedly said to him, "Please get rid of her! She keeps calling after us."

[24] Finally Jesus turned to the woman and said, "My mission is only to the lost sheep of the House of Israel."

[25] She then prostrated herself before him with the plea, "Help me, Rabbi!"

[26] He answered, "But it isn't right to take the children's food and throw it to the dogs."

[27] "True, Rabbi," she replied, "but even the dogs get to eat the scraps that fall from the table."

[28] Jesus then said in reply, "Woman, you have great faith! Your wish will come to pass." At that very moment her daughter was healed.

[29] Going on from there, Jesus came to the shore of the Sea of Galilee, then went up into the hills. He sat there, [30] and large crowds gathered, bringing with them people who had physical deformities, or couldn't walk, or were blind or deaf, and many others; these they put down at Jesus' feet, and he healed them. [31] The crowds were astonished as they saw people who had been mute speaking, people who had been deformed whole again, people who had been lame walking about, and people who had been blind seeing. And they gave glory to the God of Israel.

[32] Jesus called together the disciples and said, "My heart goes out to all the people. By now they have been with us three days and have nothing to eat. I don't want to send them away hungry—they might collapse on the way home."

[33] The disciples said to Jesus, "Where could we get enough food in this deserted place to feed such a crowd?"

[34] Jesus asked, "How many loaves of bread do you have?"

"Seven," they replied, "and a few small fish."

[35] Then he directed the crowd to sit down on the ground. [36] He took the seven loaves and the fish and gave thanks, then broke them and gave them to the disciples, who gave them to the crowds. [37] All ate until they were full. When they gathered up the leftover fragments, they filled seven baskets. [38] Four thousand families were fed.

[39] After Jesus had dismissed the crowd, he got into the boat and sailed to the region of Magadan.

16 [1] The Pharisees and the Sadducees came and asked Jesus for a sign from heaven in order to test him.

[2] He replied, "In the evening you say, 'Tomorrow will be fair, for the sky is red.' [3] In the morning you say, 'It will storm today because the sky is red and overcast.' How is it that you can read the signs in the sky, but don't know how to read the signs of the times?

[4] "It is an evil and unfaithful generation that asks for a sign, and you will get no sign from me—except the sign of Jonah." Then he left them and went away.

[5] Once they had crossed to the far shore of the lake, the disciples realized that they had forgotten to bring bread. [6] Jesus said to them, "Be alert; stay on your guard against the yeast of the Pharisees and the Sadducees."

[7] They discussed this among themselves and concluded, "It is because we didn't bring bread."

[8] Jesus was aware of their discussion and said, "You have so little faith! Why do you talk among yourselves about having no bread? [9] Don't you understand yet? Don't you remember the five loaves for the five thousand, and how many baskets of leftovers you collected? [10] Or the seven loaves for the four thousand, and how many baskets you collected? [11] How could you fail to comprehend that I wasn't talking about bread? I said to be on your guard against the yeast of the Pharisees and Sadducees." [12] Then they realized that he was warning them about the teaching of the Pharisees and Sadducees, not the yeast in bread.

[13] When Jesus came to the neighborhood of Caesarea Philippi, he asked the disciples this question: "What do people say about who the Chosen One is?" [14] They replied, "Some say John the Baptizer, others say Elijah, still others Jeremiah or one of the prophets."

[15] "And you," he said, "who do you say that I am?"

[16] "You are the Messiah," Simon Peter answered, "the Firstborn of the Living God!"

[17] Jesus replied, "Blessed are you, Simon ben-Jonah! No mere mortal has revealed this to you, but my Abba God in

heaven. 18 I also tell you this: your name now is 'Rock,' and on bedrock like this I will build my community, and the jaws of death will not prevail against it.

19 "Here—I'll give you the keys to the reign of heaven:

whatever you declare bound on earth
will be bound in heaven,
and whatever you declare loosed on earth
will be loosed in heaven."

20 Then Jesus strictly ordered the disciples not to tell anyone that he was the Messiah.

21 From that time on, Jesus began to explain to the disciples that he must go to Jerusalem, to suffer many things at the hands of the elders, chief priests and religious scholars, and that he must be killed, and on the third day raised to life.

22 Peter took him aside and began to rebuke him. "Never, Rabbi!" he said. "This will never happen to you!"

23 Jesus turned to Peter and said, "Get yourself behind me, you Satan! You are trying to make me stumble and fall. You're setting your mind not on the things of God, but of mortals."

24 Then Jesus said to the disciples, "If you wish to come after me, you must deny your very selves, take up the instrument of your own death and begin to follow in my footsteps.

25 "If you would save your life, you will lose it; but if you would lose your life for my sake, you will find it. 26 What profit would you show if you gained the whole world but lost yourself? What can you offer in exchange for your very self?

27 "The Promised One will come in the glory of Abba God accompanied by the angels, and will repay all according to their conduct. 28 The truth is, some of you standing here will not taste death before you see the coming of the Promised One's reign."

17 1 Six days later, Jesus took Peter, James and John up on a high mountain to be alone with them.

2 And before their eyes, Jesus was transfigured—his face becoming as dazzling as the sun and his clothes as radiant as light.

3 Suddenly Moses and Elijah appeared to them, conversing with Jesus. 4 Then Peter said, "Rabbi, how good that we are here! With your permission I will erect three shelters here— one for you, one for Moses and one for Elijah!"

5 Peter was still speaking when suddenly a bright cloud overshadowed them. Out of the cloud came a voice which said, "This is my Own, my Beloved, on whom my favor rests. Listen to him!"

6 When they heard this, the disciples fell forward on the ground, overcome with fear. 7 Jesus came toward them and touched them, saying, "Get up! Don't be afraid." 8 When they looked up, they did not see anyone but Jesus.

9 As they were coming down the mountainside, Jesus commanded them, "Don't tell anyone about this until the Chosen One has risen from the dead."

10 The disciples asked, "Why do the religious scholars claim that Elijah must come first?"

11 Jesus replied, "Elijah is indeed coming and will restore all things. 12 But the truth is, Elijah has already come; they didn't recognize him, but treated him as they pleased. The Chosen One will suffer at their hands in the same way." 13 Then the disciples realized that Jesus had been speaking to them about John the Baptizer.

14 One of the crowd came up to Jesus, knelt before him and said, 15 "Teacher, have pity on my child, who has seizures and is very ill. The child will often fall into the fire or the water. 16 Even your disciples have failed to effect a cure."

17 In reply Jesus said, "What an unbelieving and perverse generation you are! How long must I endure you? Bring the child to me." 18 Then Jesus rebuked the demon and it came out, and the child was healed from that moment.

19 The disciples then came to Jesus and asked, "Why couldn't we expel the demon?"

20 Jesus answered, "Because you have so little faith. The truth is, if you have even as much faith as the tiny mustard seed, you can be able to say to this mountain, 'Move from here to there,' and it will move. Nothing will be impossible for you."*

22 When Jesus and the disciples gathered again in Galilee, he said to them, "The Chosen One is going to be put into the hands of others 23 and be killed, but will be raised again on the third day." And the disciples were filled with grief.

24 When they entered Capernaum, the collectors of the Temple tax approached Peter and asked, "Doesn't your Teacher pay the Temple tax?"

25 Peter responded, "Of course he does."

When Peter came into the house, Jesus spoke to him first: "Simon, what is your opinion? Do the rulers of the world collect taxes or levies from their own children, or from foreigners?"

26 Simon replied, "From foreigners."

Jesus observed, "Then their children are exempt. 27 But so we don't offend these people, go to the lake and cast a line, and catch the first fish that bites. Open its mouth and you will find a coin worth twice the Temple tax. Take it and give it to them for both you and me."

18 1 The disciples came up to Jesus with the question, "Who is the greatest in the kindom of heaven?"

2 Jesus called for a little child to come and stand among them. 3 Then Jesus said, "The truth is, unless you change and become like little children, you will not enter the kindom of heaven. 4 Those who make themselves as humble as this child are the greatest in the kindom of heaven.

5 "Whoever welcomes a little child like this in my name welcomes me. 6 But those who would cause any of these little ones who believe in me to stumble would be better off thrown into the sea with millstones around their necks.

7 "Woe to the world because of its stumbling blocks! Stumbling blocks are inevitable, but woe to those through whom they come!

8 "If your hand or foot causes you to sin, cut it off and throw it away. It is better to enter Life without your limbs than to have two hands or two feet and be hurled into the eternal fire. 9 And if your eye causes you to sin, pluck it out and throw it away. It is better to enter Life without sight, than to have two eyes and be hurled into the eternal fire.

10 "See to it that you never despise one of these little ones, for I swear that their angels in heaven are continually in the presence of my Abba God.†

---

* Verse 21 is a later addition: "But this kind of demon doesn't leave except by prayer and fasting."

† Some manuscripts add verse 11: "The Promised One has come to save what was lost."

¹² "What do you think? Suppose a shepherd has a hundred sheep and one of them strays away—won't the shepherd leave the ninety-nine on the hillside and go in search of the stray? ¹³ If the shepherd finds it, the truth is, there is more joy over the one found than over the ninety-nine that didn't stray. ¹⁴ In the same way, it is never the will of your Abba God in heaven that one of these little ones should be lost.

¹⁵ "If your sister or brother should commit some wrong against you, go and point out the error, but keep it between the two of you. If she or he listens to you, you have won a loved one back; ¹⁶ if not, try again, but take one or two others with you, so that every case may stand on the word of two or three witnesses. ¹⁷ If your sister or brother refuses to listen to them, refer the matter to the church. If she or he ignores even the church, then treat that sister or brother as you would a Gentile or a tax collector.

¹⁸ "The truth is, whatever you declare bound on earth will be bound in heaven, and whatever you declare loosed on earth will be loosed in heaven.

¹⁹ "Again I tell you, if two of you on earth join in agreement to pray for anything whatsoever, it will be granted you by my Abba God in heaven. ²⁰ Where two or three are gathered in my name, I am there in their midst."

²¹ Peter came up and asked Jesus, "When a sister or brother wrongs me, how many times must I forgive? Seven times?"

²² "No," Jesus replied, "not seven times; I tell you seventy times seven. ²³ And here's why.

"The kindom of heaven is like a ruler who decided to settle accounts with the royal officials. ²⁴ When the audit was begun, one was brought in who owed tens of millions of dollars. ²⁵ As the debtor had no way of paying, the ruler ordered this official to be sold, along with family and property, in payment of the debt.

²⁶ "At this, the official bowed down in homage and said, 'I beg you, your highness, be patient with me and I will pay you back in full!' ²⁷ Moved with pity, the ruler let the official go and wrote off the debt.

²⁸ "Then that same official went out and met a colleague who owed the official twenty dollars. The official seized and throttled this debtor with the demand, 'Pay back what you owe me!'

²⁹ "The debtor dropped to the ground and began to plead, 'Just give me time and I will pay you back in full!' ³⁰ But the official would hear none of it, and instead had the colleague put in debtor's prison until the money was paid.

³¹ "When the other officials saw what had happened, they were deeply grieved and went to the ruler, reporting the entire incident. ³² The ruler sent for the official and said, 'You worthless wretch! I cancelled your entire debt when you pleaded with me. ³³ Should you not have dealt mercifully with your colleague, as I dealt with you?' ³⁴ Then in anger, the ruler handed the official over to be tortured until the debt had been paid in full.

³⁵ "My Abba in heaven will treat you exactly the same way unless you truly forgive your sisters and brothers from your hearts."

19

¹ When Jesus finished teaching there, he left Galilee and moved on to the area of Judea across the Jordan River. ² Large crowds followed him, and Jesus healed them there.

Some Pharisees approached Jesus to test him. They said, "May we get divorced for any reason whatsoever?"

⁴ Jesus replied, "Haven't you read that in the beginning, the Creator 'made them male and female' ⁵ and declared, 'This is why one person leaves home and cleaves to another, and the two become one flesh'? ⁶ Consequently they are no longer two, but one flesh—and what God has joined together, let no one separate."

⁷ The Pharisees said to Jesus, "Then why did Moses command that a formal decree be written when we divorce?"

⁸ "Because of your stubbornness, Moses let you divorce," he replied, "but at the beginning it was not that way. ⁹ I say to you now that whoever divorces and marries another—except when the other partner has committed adultery—commits adultery themselves."

¹⁰ The disciples said to Jesus, "If that's the case between husband and wife, it's better not to marry!"

¹¹ Jesus replied, "Not everyone can accept this teaching—only those to whom it is given to do so. ¹² Some people are incapable of sexual activity from birth. Some have been made this way by human beings. And there are some who have renounced sexual relations for the sake of the kindom of heaven. Let anyone who can accept this teaching do so."

¹³ Then small children were brought to Jesus so he could lay hands on them and pray for them. The disciples began to scold the parents, ¹⁴ but Jesus said, "Let the children alone—let them come to me. The kindom of heaven belongs to such as these." ¹⁵ And after laying his hands on them, Jesus left that town.

¹⁶ Someone came up to Jesus and asked, "Teacher, what good must I do to possess eternal life?"

¹⁷ Jesus replied, "Why do you ask me about what is good? There is only One who is good. But if you wish to enter into Life, keep the commandments."

¹⁸ "Which ones?" the youth asked.

Jesus replied, "No killing. No committing adultery. No stealing. No bearing false witness. ¹⁹ Honor your parents. Love your neighbor as yourself."

²⁰ The youth said to Jesus, "I have kept all these. What more do I need to do?"

²¹ Jesus said, "If you want to be perfect, go and sell what you own and give the money to poor people, and you will have treasure in heaven. Then come and follow me." ²² Upon hearing this the youth, whose possessions were many, went away sadly.

²³ Jesus said to the disciples, "The truth is, it is difficult for a rich person to enter the kindom of heaven. ²⁴ I'll say it again—it is easier for a camel to pass through the Needle's Eye gate than for the wealthy to enter the kindom of heaven."

²⁵ When the disciples heard this, they were astonished. "Then who can be saved?" they said.

²⁶ Jesus looked at them and said, "For mortals it is impossible, but for God everything is possible."

²⁷ Then Peter spoke: "We have left everything and followed you. What then will there be for us?"

²⁸ Jesus said, "The truth is, when all is made new and the Promised One sits on the throne of glory, you who

have followed me will sit on twelve thrones, judging the twelve tribes of Israel. ²⁹ And everyone who has left home, sisters, brothers, mother, father, children or land for my sake will be repaid a hundredfold, and will also inherit eternal life.

³⁰ "Many who are first will be last and the last will be first.

20 ¹ "The kindom of heaven is like the owner of an estate who went out at dawn to hire workers for the vineyard. ² After reaching an agreement with them for the usual daily wage, the owner sent them out to the vineyard.

³ "About mid-morning, the owner came out and saw others standing around the marketplace without work, ⁴ and said to them, 'You go along to my vineyard and I will pay you whatever is fair.' ⁵ At that they left.

"Around noon and again in the mid-afternoon, the owner came out and did the same. ⁶ Finally, going out late in the afternoon, the owner found still others standing around and said to them, 'Why have you been standing here idle all day?'

⁷ "'No one has hired us,' they replied.

"The owner said, 'You go to my vineyard, too.'

⁸ "When evening came, the owner said to the overseer, 'Call the workers and give them their pay, but begin with the last group and end with the first.' ⁹ When those hired late in the afternoon came up, they received a full day's pay, ¹⁰ and when the first group appeared they assumed they would get more. Yet they all received the same daily wage.

¹¹ "Thereupon they complained to the owner, ¹² 'This last group did only an hour's work, but you've put them on the same basis as those who worked a full day in the scorching heat.'

¹³ "'My friends,' said the owner to those who voiced this complaint, 'I do you no injustice. You agreed on the usual wage, didn't you? ¹⁴ Take your pay and go home. I intend to give this worker who was hired last the same pay as you. ¹⁵ I'm free to do as I please with my money, aren't I? Or are you envious because I am generous?'

¹⁶ "Thus the last will be first and the first will be last."

¹⁷ Jesus was on his way to Jerusalem when he took the Twelve aside and said to them, ¹⁸ "We're going up to Jerusalem now. There the Chosen One will be handed over to the chief priests and religious scholars and will be condemned to death. ¹⁹ They will turn the Chosen One over to the Gentiles to be mocked, scourged and crucified. But on the third day, the Chosen One will rise again."

²⁰ Then the mother of Zebedee's children brought James and John to Jesus, and knelt down beg to a favor of him.

²¹ "What do you want?" Jesus asked.

She answered, "Promise me that in your kindom these children of mine will sit, one at your right hand and the other at your left."

²² Jesus replied, "Do you know what you are asking? Can you drink the cup that I am going to drink?"

"We can," they said.

²³ "Very well," said Jesus, "you will drink my cup. But as for seats at my right hand and my left, these are not mine to give. They belong to those for whom they've been prepared by my Abba God."

²⁴ The other ten, on hearing this, were indignant with the two brothers. ²⁵ But Jesus said to them, "You know how the leaders of the Gentiles push their people around. ²⁶ This is not to happen among you. Anyone among you who aspires to greatness must serve the rest. ²⁷ And anyone among you who wishes to be first must serve the needs of all, as if enslaved— ²⁸ just as the Chosen One came not to be served but to serve, and to die in ransom for many."

²⁹ Jesus and the disciples left Jericho with a large crowd trailing behind. ³⁰ Two blind people sat by the roadside and when they heard that it was Jesus passing by, they began to shout, "Jesus, Heir to the House of David, take pity on us!"

³¹ The crowd shushed them, but they cried out all the louder, "Rabbi, Heir to the House of David, take pity on us!"

³² Jesus stopped and called them over and said, "What do you want me to do for you?"

³³ They answered, "Rabbi, we want our eyes to be opened."

³⁴ Jesus, moved with pity, touched their eyes. Their sight returned immediately, and they followed him.

21 ¹ As they approached Jerusalem, entering Beth-Phage at the Mount of Olives, Jesus sent off two disciples ² with the instructions, "Go into the village straight ahead of you, and immediately you will find a tethered donkey with her colt standing beside her. Untie them and lead them back to me. ³ If anyone questions you, say, 'The Rabbi needs them.' Then they will let them go at once."

⁴ This came about to fulfill what was said through the prophet:

⁵ "Tell the daughter of Zion,

'Your Sovereign comes to you without display,
riding on a donkey, on a colt—
the foal of a beast of burden.'"

⁶ So the disciples went off and did what Jesus had ordered. ⁷ They brought the donkey and her colt, and after they laid their cloaks on the animals, Jesus mounted and rode toward the city.

⁸ Great crowds of people spread their cloaks on the road, while some began to cut branches from the trees and lay them along the path. ⁹ The crowds—those who went in front of Jesus and those who followed—were all shouting,

"Hosanna to the Heir to the House of David!
Blessed is the One who comes
in the name of the Most High!
Hosanna in the highest!"

¹⁰ As Jesus entered Jerusalem, the whole city was stirred to its depths, demanding, "Who is this?"

¹¹ And the crowd kept answering, "This is the prophet Jesus, from Nazareth in Galilee!"

¹² When Jesus entered the Temple, he drove out all those who were selling and buying there. He overturned the tables of the money changers and the seats of those selling doves. ¹³ He said to them, "Scripture says, 'My house is called a house of prayer,' but you make it a den of thieves!"

¹⁴ Those who were blind or couldn't walk came to him in the Temple, and he healed them. ¹⁵ When the chief priests

and teachers of the Law saw the wonderful things Jesus did, and heard the children shouting "Hosanna to the Heir to the House of David!" throughout the Temple area, they became indignant.

¹⁶ "Do you hear what the children are shouting?" they asked him.

"Yes," Jesus replied. "Have you never read, 'From the mouths of children and nursing babies, you have brought forth praise'?" ¹⁷ After leaving them, he went out to Bethany to spend the night.

¹⁸ When he returned to the city early in the morning, Jesus grew hungry. ¹⁹ Seeing a fig tree by the road, he walked over to it but found only leaves. So he said to it, "You will never bear fruit again." And immediately the tree withered.

²⁰ The disciples were amazed when they saw this. "How was it," they asked, "that the tree withered on the spot like that?"

²¹ Jesus answered, "The truth is, if you have faith and don't doubt, not only can you do what I did to the fig tree, but you can even say to this mountain, 'Get up and throw yourself into the sea!' and it will happen. ²² Everything you pray for in faith, you will receive."

²³ Jesus entered the Temple precincts and began teaching. The chief priests and the elders of the people came to him and said, "By what authority are you doing what you do? Who gave you this authority?"

²⁴ "And I," replied Jesus, "will ask you a single question; if you give me the answer, I will tell you my authority for these actions. ²⁵ What was the origin of John's right to baptize? Was it divine or was it human?"

They discussed it among themselves and said, "If we say, 'divine,' he will respond, 'Then why did you refuse to believe him?' ²⁶ But if we say 'human,' we have the people to fear, for they regard John as a prophet." ²⁷ So they replied to Jesus, "We don't know."

Jesus said in reply, "Neither will I tell you by what authority I am doing these things."

²⁸ Jesus continued, "What do you think? There was a landowner who had two children. The landowner approached the elder and said, 'My child, go out and work in the vineyard today.' ²⁹ This first child replied, 'No, I won't,' but afterwards regretted it and went. ³⁰ The landowner then came to the second child and said the same thing. The second child said in reply, 'I'm on my way,' but never went. ³¹ Which of the two did what was wanted?"

They said, "The first."

Jesus said to them, "The truth is, tax collectors and prostitutes are entering the kindom of God before you. ³² When John came walking on the road of justice, you didn't believe him, but the tax collectors and the prostitutes did. Yet even when you saw that, you didn't repent and believe.

³³ "Listen to another parable. There was a property owner who planted a vineyard, put a hedge around it, installed a winepress and erected a tower. Then the owner leased it out to tenant farmers and went on a journey.

³⁴ "When vintage time arrived, the owner sent aides to the tenants to divide the shares of the grapes. ³⁵ The tenants responded by seizing the aides. They beat one, killed another and stoned a third. ³⁶ A second time the owner sent even more aides than before, but they treated them the same way.

³⁷ Finally, the owner sent the family heir to them, thinking, 'They will respect my heir.'

³⁸ "When the vine growers saw the heir, they said to one another, 'Here's the one who stands in the way of our having everything. With a single act of murder we could seize the inheritance.' ³⁹ With that, they grabbed and killed the heir outside the vineyard. ⁴⁰ What do you suppose the owner of the vineyard will do to those tenants?"

⁴¹ They replied, "The owner will bring that wicked crowd to a horrible death and lease the vineyard out to others, who will see to it that there are grapes for the proprietor at vintage time."

⁴² Jesus said to them, "Did you ever read in the scriptures,

'The stone which the builders rejected
has become the chief cornerstone;
it was our God's doing
and we find it marvelous to behold'?

⁴³ "That's why I tell you that the kindom of God will be taken from you and given to people who will bear its fruit.

⁴⁴ "Those who fall on this stone will be dashed to pieces, and those on whom it falls will be smashed."

⁴⁵ When the chief priests and the Pharisees heard these parables, they realized that Jesus was speaking about them. ⁴⁶ Although they sought to arrest him, they feared the crowds, who regarded Jesus as a prophet.

22 ¹ Then Jesus spoke to them again in parables. He said, ² "The kindom of heaven is like this: there was a ruler who prepared a feast for the wedding of the family's heir; ³ but when the ruler sent out workers to summon the invited guests, they wouldn't come. ⁴ The ruler sent other workers, telling them to say to the guests, 'I have prepared this feast for you. My oxen and fattened cattle have been slaughtered, and everything is ready; come to the wedding.' ⁵ But they took no notice; one went off to his farm, another to her business, ⁶ and the rest seized the workers, attacked them brutally and killed them. ⁷ The ruler was furious and dispatched troops who destroyed those murderers and burned their town.

⁸ "Then the ruler said to the workers, 'The wedding feast is ready, but the guests I invited don't deserve the honor. ⁹ Go out to the crossroads in the town and invite everyone you can find.' ¹⁰ The workers went out into the streets and collected everyone they met, good and bad alike, until the hall was filled with guests.

¹¹ "The ruler, however, came in to see the company at table, and noticed one guest who was not dressed for a wedding. ¹² 'My friend,' said the ruler, 'why are you here without a wedding garment?' But the guest was silent. ¹³ Then the ruler said to the attendants, 'Bind this guest hand and foot, and throw the individual out into the darkness, where there will be weeping and gnashing of teeth.'

¹⁴ "Many are called, but few are chosen."

¹⁵ Then the Pharisees went off and began to plot how they might trap Jesus by his speech. ¹⁶ They sent their disciples to Jesus, accompanied by sympathizers of Herod, who said, "Teacher, we know you're honest and teach God's way sincerely. You court no one's favor and don't act out of respect for important people. ¹⁷ Give us your opinion, then, in this case. Is it lawful to pay tax to the Roman emperor, or not?"

¹⁸ Jesus recognized their bad faith and said to them, "Why are you trying to trick me, you hypocrites? ¹⁹ Show me the coin which is used to pay the tax." When they handed Je-

sus a small Roman coin, ²⁰ Jesus asked them, "Whose head is this, and whose inscription?"

²¹ "Caesar's," they replied.

At that, Jesus said to them, "Then give to Caesar what is Caesar's, but give to God what is God's."

²² When they heard this, they were astonished and went away.

²³ Later that day, some Sadducees—who teach that there is no resurrection—came to Jesus and questioned him: ²⁴ "Teacher, Moses said that if a man dies without producing children, his brother must marry his widow and raise up children so that the family name will continue. ²⁵Now, let's say there were seven brothers: the first marries and dies childless, so his brother marries his widow; ²⁶ then the second brother dies childless, then the third, and so forth down to the seventh. ²⁷ Last of all, the woman dies. ²⁸ In this 'resurrection,' whose wife will she be? They had all been married to her!"

²⁹ Jesus replied, "The reason you are mistaken is because you understand neither the scriptures nor the power of God. ³⁰ In the resurrection, people don't marry at all—they are like God's angels. ³¹ But on the subject of the resurrection, haven't you read what God told you? ³² 'I am the God of Abraham and Sarah, the God of Isaac and Rebecca, the God of Jacob and Rachel and Leah!' God is not the God of the dead, but of the living."

³³ When the crowds heard this, they were astonished at Jesus' teaching.

³⁴ When the Pharisees heard that Jesus had left the Sadducees speechless, they gathered together, ³⁵ and one of them, an expert on the Law, attempted to trick Jesus with this question: ³⁶ "Teacher, which commandment of the Law is the greatest?"

³⁷ Jesus answered:

> "'You must love the Most High God
> with all your heart,
> with all your soul and
> with all your mind.'

³⁸ "That is the greatest and first commandment. ³⁹ The second is like it: 'You must love your neighbor as yourself.' ⁴⁰ On these two commandments the whole Law is based—and the Prophets as well."

⁴¹ While the Pharisees were gathered around him, Jesus asked them this question: ⁴² "What do you think about the Messiah? Whose descendant is the Messiah?"

They said, "David's."

⁴³ Then Jesus asked, "Then how is it that David, inspired by the Spirit, calls the Messiah 'Sovereign'? For he says,

⁴⁴ 'The Most High said to my Sovereign,

> "Sit at my right hand
> until I place your enemies under your foot."'

⁴⁵ "If David calls the Messiah 'Sovereign,' how can the Messiah be a descendant of David?"

⁴⁶ No one could reply, and from that day on no one dared ask him any more questions.

23 :¹ Jesus told the crowds and the disciples, ² "The religious scholars and the Pharisees have succeeded Moses as teachers; ³ therefore, perform every observance they tell you to. But don't follow their example; even they don't do what they say. ⁴ They tie up heavy loads and lay them on others' shoulders, while they themselves will not lift a finger to help alleviate the burden.

⁵ "All their works are performed to be seen. They widen their phylacteries and wear huge tassels. ⁶ They are fond of places of honor at banquets and the front seats in synagogues. ⁷ They love respectful greetings in public and being called 'Rabbi.'

⁸ "But as for you, avoid the title 'Rabbi.' For you have only one Teacher, and you are all sisters and brothers. ⁹ And don't call anyone on earth your 'Mother' or 'Father.' You have only one Parent—our loving God in heaven. ¹⁰ Avoid being called leaders. You have only one leader—the Messiah.

¹¹ "The greatest among you will be the one who serves the rest. ¹² Those who exalt themselves will be humbled, but those who humble themselves will be exalted.

¹³ "Woe to you religious scholars and Pharisees, you frauds! You shut the doors of heaven's kindom in people's faces, neither entering yourselves, nor allowing others to enter who want to.

¹⁴ "Woe to you religious scholars and Pharisees, you frauds! You go on and on with prayer for show, all the while devouring the only security that widows have—their houses; you, therefore, will be given the greater punishment.

¹⁵ "Woe to you religious scholars and Pharisees, you frauds! You travel over land and over sea to make a single convert, and once that person is converted, you create a proselyte twice as wicked as yourselves.

¹⁶ "Woe to you, blind guides! You say, 'If anyone swears by the Temple, it means nothing. But if anyone swears by the gold of the Temple, that person is bound by the oath.' ¹⁷ You blind fools! For which is of greater worth—the gold, or the Temple that makes the gold sacred? ¹⁸ You also say, 'If anyone swears by the altar, it means nothing; but those who swear by the gift on the altar are bound by their oath.' ¹⁹ Hypocrites! Which is greater—the offering, or the altar which makes the offering sacred? ²⁰ Those who swear by the altar are swearing by it and by everything on it. ²¹ Those who swear by the Temple are swearing by it and by the One who dwells there. ²² Those who swear by heaven are swearing by God's throne and by the One who is seated on it.

²³ "Woe to you religious scholars and you Pharisees, you frauds! You pay your tithes on mint, dill and cumin while neglecting the weightier matters of the Law—justice, mercy and faithfulness! These you should have practiced, without neglecting the others. ²⁴ You blind guides! You strain out gnats, but swallow camels in the process!

²⁵ "Woe to you religious scholars and Pharisees, you frauds! You clean the outside of the cup and the dish, leaving the inside filled with plunder and lust. ²⁶ Blind Pharisees! First clean the inside of the cup so that the outside may become clean as well.

²⁷ "Woe to you religious scholars and Pharisees, you frauds! You are like whitewashed tombs, beautiful to look at on the outside, but on the inside full of filth and the bones of the dead. ²⁸ In the same way you present a holy exterior to others, but on the inside you are full of hypocrisy and wickedness.

²⁹ "Woe to you religious scholars and Pharisees, you frauds! You build tombs for the prophets and decorate monuments of holy people, ³⁰ saying, 'We never would have joined in shedding the blood of the prophets, had we lived in our ancestors' days.' ³¹ Ha! Your own evidence testifies against you! You are the descendants of those who murdered the prophets! ³² Now it's your turn: finish what your ancestors started.

³³ "You snakes! You brood of vipers! How can you escape eternal damnation? ³⁴ Look, then: I'm sending you prophets, sages and religious scholars—some of whom you'll murder

and crucify, some you'll whip in your synagogues, some you'll hunt down from town to town. 35 And thus you will call down upon yourselves the guilt of all the righteous blood shed on earth, beginning with the blood of Abel the righteous, up to the blood of Zechariah ben-Berekiah—the one you murdered between the Temple and the altar. 36 The truth is, all of this will happen to this generation.

37 "Oh Jerusalem, Jerusalem—you murder the prophets, and you stone those sent to you! Oh, how often have I yearned to gather you together, like a hen gathering her chicks under her wings! But you would have none of it. 38 Therefore your house is being left to you—abandoned.

39 "I tell you, you will not see me again until you say, 'Blessed is the one who comes in the name of our God!'"

24 1 Jesus left the Temple. As he was leaving, the disciples approached and called his attention to the Temple buildings.

2 He replied to them, "Do you see all these buildings? The truth is, not a single stone will be left upon another. All of it will be destroyed."

3 As Jesus sat on the Mount of Olives, the disciples approached him privately and asked, "Tell us, when will this happen? What will be the sign of your Coming and the end of the age?"

4 Jesus replied to them, "Make sure that no one deceives you. 5 For many will come in my name, saying, 'I am the Messiah,' and they will deceive many. 6 You will hear of wars, and rumors of more wars. Don't be alarmed, for these things must happen; but that does not mean it's the end. 7 For nation will war against nation, and empire against empire; there will be famines and earthquakes all over the world, 8 yet all these are only the beginning of the labor pains.

9 "Then they will hand you over to be tortured and executed. And you will be despised by all nations because of my name. 10 At that time many will lose their faith, and they will betray and hate one another. 11 Many false prophets will rise up to deceive you. 12 Lawlessness will increase, and people's love will grow cold. 13 But those who persevere to the end will be saved.

14 "The Good News of the kindom will be proclaimed to the whole world as a witness to all the nations. Then the end will come.

15 "So when you see 'the abomination that causes desolation' that Daniel the prophet speaks of, standing in the holy place"—let the reader understand—16 "then those in Judea must flee to the mountains. 17 People on a housetop must not go downstairs to collect their belongings. 18 Those in the field must not go back to fetch their cloaks. 19 How terrible it will be at that time for pregnant women and nursing mothers! 20 Pray that your escape will not happen in winter or on the Sabbath. 21 At that time there will be terrible turmoil, unmatched from the beginning of time until now, never to be matched again. 22 And if those days were not been shortened, no one would survive. That time will be shortened for the sake of the chosen.

23 "If anyone says to you, 'Look, here's the Messiah!' or, 'There's the Messiah!' don't believe it. 24 False messiahs and false prophets will arise, performing impressive signs and wonders in order to deceive, if it were possible, even the chosen. 25 Look: I have told you everything ahead of time.

26 "So if anyone says to you, 'The Messiah is in the desert,' don't go. If they say, 'The Messiah is in hiding,' don't believe them. 27 For just as the lightning flashes in the East and is visible in the West, so it will be at the coming of the Promised One. 28 It will be as obvious as vultures circling a corpse.

29 "Immediately after the distress of those days,

'The sun will grow dark,
the moon will lose its light,
the stars will fall from the sky
and the powers of heaven will be shaken.'

30 "Then the sign of the Promised One will appear in the sky, and all the tribes of the earth will mourn; they will see the Promised One coming on the clouds of heaven with great power and glory. 31 The Promised One will send forth the angels with a loud trumpet blast to gather the chosen from the four winds, and from one end of heaven to the other.

32 "Take a lesson from the fig tree. When its branches are tender and its leaves sprout, you know that summer is near. 33 In the same manner, when you see all these things, know that the Promised One is near, at the very door.

34 "The truth is, this generation will not pass away until all these things have taken place. 35 Heaven and earth will pass away, but my words never will.

36 "No one knows that day and that hour—not the angels of heaven, nor even the Only Begotten—only Abba God. 37 "The coming of the Promised One will be just like Noah's time. 38 In the days before the flood, people were eating and drinking, having relationships and getting married, right up to the day Noah entered the ark. 39 They were totally unconcerned until the flood came and destroyed them. So it will be at the coming of the Promised One. 40 Two people will be out in the field; one will be taken and one will be left. 41 Two people will be grinding meal; one will be taken and one will be left. 42 Therefore be vigilant! For you don't know the day your Savior is coming.

43 "Be sure of this: if the owner of the house had known when the thief was coming, the owner would have kept a watchful eye and not allowed the house to be broken into. 44 You must be prepared in the same way. The Promised One is coming at the time you least expect.

45 "Who is the faithful, farsighted worker whom the owner of the house puts in charge of the household to provide for their needs at the appropriate times? 46 Happy are the workers whom the owners find at their work upon their return. 47 The truth is, they will be given more responsibility. 48 But if the worker is worthless and thinks, 'The owners will be away a long time,' 49 and browbeats the other workers, eating and drinking to excess, 50 the owners will return on a day when least expected, at the unknown hour. 51 They will scourge the lout, assigning the hypocrite to that place where there is wailing and the grinding of teeth.

25 1 "Then again, the kindom of heaven could be likened to ten attendants who took their lamps and went to meet the bridal party. 2 Five of them were wise; five were foolish. 3 When the foolish ones took their lamps, they didn't take any oil with them, 4 but the wise ones took enough oil to keep their lamps burning. 5 The bridal party was delayed, so they all fell asleep.

6 "At midnight there was a cry: 'Here comes the bridal party! Let's go out to meet them!' 7 Then all the attendants rose and trimmed their lamps. 8 The foolish ones said to the wise, 'Give us some of your oil, for our lamps are go-

ing out.' ⁹ But the wise replied, 'Perhaps there won't be enough for us; run to the dealers and get some more for yourselves.'

¹⁰ "While the foolish ones went to buy more oil, the bridal party arrived; and those who were ready went to the marriage feast with them, and the door was shut. ¹¹ When the foolish attendants returned, they pleaded to be let in. ¹² The doorkeeper replied, 'The truth is, I don't know you.'

¹³ "So stay awake, for you don't know the day or the hour.

¹⁴ "Again, it's like a wealthy landowner who was going on a journey and called in three workers, entrusting some funds to them. ¹⁵ The first was given five thousand dollars, the second two thousand, and the third one thousand, according to each one's ability. Then the landowner went away. ¹⁶ Immediately the worker who received the five thousand went and invested it and made another five. ¹⁷ In the same way, the worker who received the two thousand doubled that figure. ¹⁸ But the worker who received the one thousand instead went off and dug a hole in the ground and buried the money.

¹⁹ "After a long absence, the traveler returned home and settled accounts with them. ²⁰ The one who had received the five thousand came forward bringing the additional five, saying, 'You entrusted me with five thousand; here are five thousand more.'

²¹ "The landowner said, 'Well done! You are a good and faithful worker. Since you were dependable in a small matter, I will put you in charge of larger affairs. Come, share my joy!'

²² "The one who had received the two thousand then stepped forward with the additional two, saying, 'You entrusted me with two thousand; here are two thousand more.'

²³ "The landowner said to this one, 'Cleverly done! You too are a good and faithful worker. Since you were dependable in a small matter, I will put you in charge of larger affairs. Come, share my joy!'

²⁴ "Finally the one who had received the one thousand stepped forward and said to the landowner, 'Knowing your ruthlessness—you who reap where you did not sow and gather where you did not scatter—²⁵ and fearing your wrath, I went off and buried your thousand dollars in the ground. Here is your money back.'

²⁶ "The landowner exclaimed, 'You worthless, lazy lout! So you know that I reap where I don't sow and gather where I don't scatter, do you? ²⁷ All the more reason to deposit my money with the bankers, so that on my return I could have had it back with interest! ²⁸ You, there! Take the thousand away from this bum and give it to the one with the ten thousand.

²⁹ "'Those who have will get more until they grow rich, while those who have not will lose even the little they have. ³⁰ Throw this worthless one outside into the darkness, where there is wailing and grinding of teeth.'

³¹ "At the appointed time the Promised One will come in glory, escorted by all the angels of heaven, and will sit upon the royal throne, ³² with all the nations assembled below. Then the Promised One will separate them from one another, as a shepherd divides the sheep from the goats. ³³ The sheep will be placed on the right hand, the goats on the left.

³⁴ "The ruler will say to those on the right, 'Come, you blessed of my Abba God! Inherit the kindom prepared for you from the creation of the world! ³⁵ For I was hungry and you fed me; I was thirsty and you gave me drink. I was a stranger and you welcomed me; ³⁶ naked and you clothed me. I was ill and you comforted me; in prison and you came to visit me.' ³⁷ Then these just will ask, 'When did we see you hungry and feed you, or see you thirsty and give you drink?

³⁸ When did we see you as a stranger and invite you in, or clothe you in your nakedness? ³⁹ When did we see you ill or in prison and come to visit you?' ⁴⁰ The ruler will answer them, 'The truth is, every time you did this for the least of my sisters or brothers, you did it for me.'

⁴¹ "Then the ruler will say to those on the left, 'Out of my sight, you accursed ones! Into that everlasting fire prepared for the Devil and the fallen angels! ⁴² I was hungry and you gave me no food; I was thirsty and you gave me nothing to drink. ⁴³ I was a stranger and you gave me no welcome; naked and you gave me no clothing. I was ill and in prison and you did not come to visit me.' ⁴⁴ Then they in turn will ask, 'When did we see you hungry or thirsty, or homeless or naked, or ill or in prison, and not take care of you?' ⁴⁵ The answer will come, 'The truth is, as often as you neglected to do this to one of the least of these, you neglected to do it to me.' ⁴⁶ They will go off to eternal punishment, and the just will go off to eternal life."

26:1–28:20

Jesus now finished all he had to say, and he told the disciples, ² "Passover starts in two days, and the Chosen One will be handed over to be crucified."

³ Then the chief priests and the elders of the people gathered in the palace of the high priest, Caiaphas. ⁴ They planned to arrest Jesus under some pretext and execute him—⁵ "But not during the Festival," they agreed, "or we might have a riot on our hands."

⁶ Now when Jesus was in Bethany, at the house of Simon, who had leprosy, ⁷ a woman approached Jesus with an alabaster jar of very expensive ointment. She poured it on his head while he reclined at the table. ⁸ The disciples, witnessing this, were indignant. "What a waste!" they said. ⁹ "This could have been sold at a high price, and the money given to needier people."

¹⁰ Jesus, aware of their concern, said, "Why do you upset the woman? She has done me a good deed. ¹¹ You'll always have poor people with you, but you won't always have me. ¹² When she poured the oil on my body, she was preparing me for burial. ¹³ The truth is, wherever the Good News is proclaimed in the world, she will be remembered for what she has done for me."

¹⁴ One of the Twelve, the one named Judas Iscariot, went off to the chief priests ¹⁵ and said, "What are you willing to give me if I hand Jesus over to you?"

They paid him thirty pieces of silver. ¹⁶ And from that moment he looked for an opportunity to betray Jesus.

¹⁷ On the first day of the Feast of Unleavened Bread, the disciples came up to Jesus and said, "Where do you want us to prepare the Passover for you?"

¹⁸ Jesus told them to go to a certain person in the city and say, "The Teacher says, 'My appointed time draws near. I am to celebrate the Passover in your house.'" ¹⁹ The disciples did as Jesus ordered and prepared the Passover supper.

²⁰ When it grew dark, he reclined at table with the Twelve. ²¹ And while they were eating he said, "The truth is, one of you is about to betray me."

22 They were greatly distressed and started asking him in turn, "Surely, it is not I, Teacher?"

23 Jesus replied, "The one who has dipped his hand into the dish with me is the one who will hand me over. 24 The Chosen One will go as the scriptures foretold—but woe to the one by whom the Chosen One is betrayed! It would be better for that one never to have been born at all."

25 Then Judas, who was betraying Jesus, said, "Surely it is not I, Rabbi?"

Jesus answered, "You have said it yourself."

26 During the meal Jesus took bread, blessed it, broke it and gave it to the disciples. "Take this and eat it," Jesus said. "This is my body." 27 Then he took a cup, gave thanks, and gave it to them. "Drink from it, all of you," he said. 28 "This is my blood, the blood of the Covenant, which will be poured out on behalf of many for the forgiveness of sins. 29 The truth is, I will not drink this fruit of the vine again until the day when I drink it anew with you in my Abba's kindom."

30 Then, after singing the Hallel, they walked out to the Mount of Olives.

31 Jesus then said to them, "Tonight you will all fall away because of me, for scripture says, 'I will strike the shepherd, and the sheep will be scattered.' 32 But after I have been raised, I will go to Galilee ahead of you."

33 Peter responded, "Though all may fall away because of you, I never will!"

34 Jesus replied, "The truth is, before the cock crows tonight, you will deny me three times."

35 Peter said, "Even if I must die with you, I will never disown you." And all the other disciples said the same.

36 Then Jesus went with them to a place called Gethsemane and said to the disciples, "Stay here while I go over there and pray." 37 Jesus took along Peter, James and John and started to feel grief and anguish. 38 Then he said to them, "My soul is deeply grieved, to the point of death. Please, stay here, and stay awake with me."

39 Jesus went on a little further and fell prostrate in prayer: "Abba, if it is possible, let this cup pass me by. But not what I want—what you want."

40 When Jesus returned to the disciples, he found them asleep. He said to Peter, "Couldn't you stay awake with me for even an hour? 41 Be on guard, and pray that you may not undergo trial. The spirit is willing, but the body is weak."

42 Withdrawing a second time, Jesus prayed, "Abba, if this cup cannot pass me by without my drinking it, your will be done!"

43 Once more Jesus returned and found the disciples asleep; they could not keep their eyes open. 44 Jesus left them again, withdrew somewhat and prayed for a third time, saying the same words as before. 45 Finally Jesus returned to the disciples and said to them, "Are you still sleeping? Still taking your rest? The hour is upon us—the Chosen One is being betrayed into the hands of sinners. 46 Get up! Let us be on our way! Look, my betrayer is here."

47 While Jesus was still speaking, Judas, one of the Twelve, arrived—accompanied by a great crowd with swords and clubs. They had been sent by the chief priests and elders of the people. 48 Judas had arranged to give them a signal. "Whomever I embrace is the one," he had said; "take hold of him." 49 He immediately went over to Jesus and said, "Shalom, Rabbi!" and embraced him.

50 Jesus said to Judas, "Friend, just do what you're here to do!" At that moment, the crowd surrounded them, laid hands on Jesus and arrested him.

51 Suddenly, one of those who accompanied Jesus drew a sword and slashed at the high priest's attendant, cutting off an ear. 52 Jesus said, "Put your sword back where it belongs. Those who live by the sword die by the sword. 53 Don't you think I can call on my Abba God to provide over twelve legions of angels at a moment's notice? 54 But then how would the scriptures be fulfilled, which say it must happen this way?"

55 Then Jesus said to the crowd, "Am I a robber, that you have come armed with swords and clubs to arrest me? Every day I sat teaching in the Temple precincts, yet you never arrested me." 56 All this happened in fulfillment of the writings of the prophets. Then all the disciples deserted Jesus and fled.

57 Those who had seized Jesus led him off to Caiaphas, the high priest, where the religious scholars and elders had convened. 58 Peter followed at a distance as far as the high priest's residence. Going inside, Peter sat down with the guards to await the outcome. 59 The chief priests, with the whole Sanhedrin, were busy trying to obtain false testimony against Jesus, so that they might put him to death. 60 They discovered none, despite the many false witnesses who took the stand.

Finally two came forward 61 who stated, "This man has declared, 'I can destroy God's sanctuary and rebuild it in three days.'"

62 The high priest rose and addressed Jesus, "Have you no answer? What about this testimony leveled against you?" 63 But Jesus remained silent. The high priest then said to him, "I order you to tell us under oath, before the living God, whether or not you are the Messiah, the Firstborn of God?"

64 "You have said it yourself," Jesus replied. "But I tell you: soon you will see the Chosen One seated at the right hand of the Power, and coming on the clouds of heaven."

65 At this, the high priest tore his robes and said, "Blasphemy! What further need do we have of witnesses? You yourselves have heard the blasphemy. 66 What is your verdict?"

They responded, "He deserves death!" 67 Then they spat at his face and struck him with their fists. Others slapped Jesus, 68 saying, "Play the prophet for us, Messiah! Who struck you?"

69 While this was happening, Peter was sitting in the courtyard. One of the attendants came over and said, "You were with Jesus the Galilean too, weren't you?"

70 But Peter denied it in front of everyone. He said, "I don't know what you're talking about!"

71 When Peter went out to the gate, another attendant saw him and said to those nearby, "This one was with Jesus of Nazareth."

72 Again he cursed and denied it: "I don't know him!"

73 A little while later, some bystanders came over to Peter and said, "You certainly are one of them! Even your accent gives you away!"

74 At that, Peter began cursing and swore, "I don't know the man!"

Just then a rooster began to crow, 75 and Peter remembered the prediction Jesus had made: "Before the rooster crows, you will disown me three times." Peter went out and cried bitterly.

27 1 At daybreak, all the chief priests and the elders of the people took formal action against Jesus to put him to death. [2] They bound him and led him away to be handed over to Pilate, the governor.

[3] When he saw that Jesus had been condemned, Judas, who had betrayed Jesus, felt remorse. He took the thirty pieces of silver back to the chief priests and elders, [4] and said, "I have sinned! I have betrayed innocent blood!"

"What's that to us?" they answered. "That's your affair!" [5] So Judas flung the money into the sanctuary and left. Then he went off and hanged himself.

[6] The chief priests picked up the silver, observing, "It's against the Law to deposit this in the Temple treasury, since it is blood money." [7] After some discussion, they used the money to buy Potter's Field as a cemetery for foreigners. [8] That is why that field, even today, is called Blood Field. [9] On that occasion, what was said through Jeremiah the prophet was fulfilled:

"They took thirty pieces of silver,
the price for the One
whose price was set
by the children of Israel,
[10] and they paid it out for Potter's Field
just as the Most High commanded me."

[11] Then Jesus was arraigned before Pontius Pilate, the governor, who questioned him. "Are you the King of the Jews?"

Jesus replied, "You say that I am."

[12] Yet when Jesus was accused by the chief priests and elders, he made no reply. [13] Pilate said to Jesus, "Surely you hear how many charges they bring against you?" [14] But Jesus did not answer Pilate on a single count, much to the governor's surprise.

[15] Now, on the occasion of a festival, the governor was accustomed to release one prisoner, whomever the crowd would designate. [16] At the time they were holding a notorious prisoner named Barabbas. [17] So when the crowd gathered, Pilate asked them, "Which one do you wish me to release for you? Barabbas? Or Jesus, the so-called Messiah?" [18] Pilate knew, of course, that it was out of jealousy that they had handed Jesus over.

[19] While Pilate was still presiding on the bench, his wife sent him a message: "Have nothing to do with that innocent man. I had a dream about him last night which has been troubling me all day long."

[20] But the chief priests and elders convinced the crowds that they should ask for Barabbas, and have Jesus put to death. [21] So when the governor asked them, "Which one do you wish me to release for you?" they all cried, "Barabbas!"

[22] Pilate said to them, "Then what am I to do with Jesus, the so-called Messiah?"

"Crucify him!" they all said.

[23] "Why? What crime has he committed?" Pilate asked.

But they only shouted louder, "Crucify him!"

[24] Pilate finally realized that he was getting nowhere with this—in fact, a riot was breaking out. Pilate called for water and washed his hands in front of the crowd, declaring as he did so, "I am innocent of this man's blood. The responsibility is yours." [25] The whole crowd said in reply, "Let his blood be on us and on our children." [26] At that, Pilate released Barabbas to them. But he had Jesus whipped with a cat-o'-nine-tails, then handed him over to be crucified.

[27] The governor's soldiers took Jesus inside the Praetorium and assembled the whole cohort around him. [28] They stripped off his clothes and wrapped him in a scarlet military cloak. [29] Weaving a crown out of thorns, they pressed it onto his head and stuck a reed in his right hand. Then they began to mock Jesus by dropping to their knees, saying, "All hail, King of the Jews!" [30] They also spat at him. Afterward they took hold of the reed and struck Jesus on the head. [31] Finally, when they had finished mocking him, they stripped him of the cloak, dressed him in his own clothes and led him off to crucifixion.

[32] On their way out, they met a Cyrenian named Simon, whom they pressed into service to carry the cross. [33] Upon arriving at a site called Golgotha—which means Skull Place— [34] they gave Jesus a drink of wine mixed with a narcotic herb, which Jesus tasted but refused to drink.

[35] Once they had nailed Jesus to the cross, they divided his clothes among them by rolling dice; [36] then they sat down and kept watch over him. [37] Above his head, they put the charge against him in writing: "This is Jesus, King of the Jews." [38] Two robbers were crucified along with Jesus, one at his right and one at his left.

[39] People going by insulted Jesus, shaking their heads [40] and saying, "So you are the one who was going to destroy the Temple and rebuild it in three days! Save yourself, why don't you? Come down off that cross if you are God's Own!"

[41] The chief priests, the religious scholars and the elders also joined in the jeering: [42] "He saved others but he cannot save himself! So he's the King of Israel! Let's see him come down from that cross, and then we will believe in him. [43] He trusts in God; let God rescue him now, if God is happy with him! After all, he claimed to be God's Own!" [44] The robbers who had been crucified with Jesus jeered at him in the same way.

[45] At noon, a darkness fell over the whole land until about three in the afternoon. [46] At that hour Jesus cried out with a loud voice, "*Eli, Eli, lama sabachthani*?" which means, "My God, My God, why have you forsaken me?" [47] This made some of the bystanders who heard it remark, "He is calling for Elijah!" [48] One of them hurried off and got a sponge. He soaked the sponge in cheap wine and, sticking it on a reed, tried to make Jesus drink. [49] The others said, "Leave him alone. Let's see whether Elijah comes to his rescue."

[50] Once again, Jesus cried out in a loud voice, then he gave up his spirit. [51] Suddenly, the curtain in front of the Holy of Holies was ripped in half from top to bottom. The earth quaked, boulders were split [52] and tombs were opened. Many bodies of holy ones who had fallen asleep were raised. [53] After Jesus' resurrection, they came out of their tombs and entered the holy city, and appeared to many.

[54] The centurion and his cohort, who were standing guard over Jesus' body, were terror-stricken at seeing the earthquake and all that was happening, and said, "Clearly, this was God's Own!"

[55] A group of women were present, looking on from a distance. These were the same women who had followed Jesus from Galilee as ministers to him. [56] Among them were Mary of Magdala; Mary, the mother of James and Joseph; and the mother of Zebedee's children.

57 When evening fell, a wealthy man from Arimathea named Joseph, who had become a disciple of Jesus, 58 came to request the body of Jesus; Pilate issued an order for its release. 59 Taking the body, Joseph wrapped it in fresh linen 60 and laid it in his own tomb, which had been hewn out of rock. Then Joseph rolled a huge stone across the entrance of the tomb and went away. 61 But Mary of Magdala and the other Mary remained sitting there, facing the tomb.

62 The next day—the one following the Day of Preparation—the chief priests and the Pharisees called at Pilate's residence 63 and said, "We recall that, while he was still alive, the impostor made the claim, 'After three days I will rise again.' 64 Therefore, please issue an order to keep the tomb under surveillance until the third day. Otherwise, Jesus' disciples might go and steal his body and tell the people, 'Jesus has been raised from the dead!' This final deception would be worse than the first."

65 Pilate said to them, "You have a guard. Go and secure the tomb as best you can." 66 So they went to seal the tomb and post a guard.

28 1 After the Sabbath, as the first day of the week was dawning, Mary of Magdala came with Mary to inspect the tomb.

2 Suddenly, there was a severe earthquake, and an angel of God descended from heaven, rolled back the stone, and sat on it. 3 The angel's appearance was like lightning, with garments white as snow. 4 The guards shook with fear and fell down as though they were dead.

5 Then the angel spoke, addressing the women: "Don't be afraid. I know you are looking for Jesus the crucified, 6 who is no longer here. Jesus has been raised, exactly as it was foretold. Come and see the burial place. 7 Then go quickly and tell the disciples that Jesus has risen from the dead and now goes ahead of you to Galilee. You will see Jesus there. That is the message I have for you."

8 The women hurried away from the tomb with awe and great joy and ran to carry the good news to the disciples.

9 Suddenly Jesus stood before them and said, "Shalom!" The women came up, embraced Jesus' feet and worshiped. 10 At this, Jesus said to them, "Don't be afraid! Go tell the disciples to go to Galilee, where they will see me."

11 While the women were on their way, some of the guards went into the city and reported to the chief priests what had happened. 12 The chief priests in turn held a meeting with the elders and, after working out their strategy, gave a considerable amount of money to the soldiers, 13 with these instructions: "You are to say, 'His disciples came during the night and stole him away while we were asleep.' 14 And if any word of this gets to the governor, we will straighten it out with him and keep you out of trouble." 15 The soldiers took the money and carried out their instructions. This is the story that circulates among Judeans to this very day.

16 The Eleven made their way to Galilee, to the mountain where Jesus had summoned them. 17 At the sight of the risen Christ they fell down in homage, though some doubted what they were seeing. 18 Jesus came forward and addressed them in these words:

> "All authority has been given me
> both in heaven and on earth;
> 19 go, therefore, and make disciples of all the nations.
> Baptize them in the name
> of Abba God,
> and of the Only Begotten,
> and of the Holy Spirit.
> 20 Teach them to carry out
> everything I have commanded you.
> And know that I am with you always,
> even until the end of the world!"

mark

Here begins the gospel* of Jesus Christ, the Son of God: 2 as it was written in Isaiah the prophet:

> "I send my messenger before you
> to prepare your way,
> 3 a herald's voice in the desert, crying,
> 'Make ready the way of our God.
> Clear a straight path.'"

4 And so John the Baptizer appeared in the desert, proclaiming a baptism of repentance for the forgiveness of sins. 5 The whole Judean countryside and all the people of Jerusalem went out to John and were baptized by him in the Jordan River as they confessed their sins. 6 John was clothed in camel's hair and wore a leather belt around his waist, and he ate nothing but grasshoppers and wild honey. 7 In the course of his preaching, John said, "One more powerful than I is to come after me. I am not fit to stoop and untie his sandal straps. 8 I have baptized you in water, but the One to come will baptize you in the Holy Spirit."

9 It was then that Jesus came from Nazareth in Galilee and was baptized in the Jordan River by John. 10 Immediately upon coming out of the water, Jesus saw the heavens opening and the Spirit descending on him like a dove. 11 Then a voice came from the heavens: "You are my Beloved, my Own. On you my favor rests."

12 Immediately the Spirit drove Jesus out into the wilderness, 13 and he remained there for forty days, and was tempted by Satan. He was with the wild beasts, and the angels looked after him.

14 After John's arrest, Jesus appeared in Galilee proclaiming the Good News of God:

15 "This is the time of fulfillment. The reign of God is at hand! Change your hearts and minds, and believe this Good News!"

---

* The words *to euaggelion*, meaning good news or gospel, have a two-fold meaning here. The first meaning is a proclamation of the risen Christ; the second, Jesus' original message that the reign of God is, as verse 15 puts it, "at hand"—in Greek, *engizo*, which might be translated "on the verge of breaking in upon you."

16 While walking by the Sea of Galilee, Jesus saw the brothers Simon and Andrew casting their nets into the sea, since they fished by trade. 17 Jesus said to them, "Follow me; I will make you fishers of humankind." 18 They immediately abandoned their nets and followed Jesus.

19 Proceeding a little further along, Jesus saw the brothers James and John Bar-Zebedee. They too were in their boat, putting their nets in order. 20 Immediately Jesus called them, and they left their father Zebedee standing in the boat with the hired help, and went off in the company of Jesus.

21 They came to Capernaum, and on the Sabbath Jesus entered the synagogue and began to teach. 22 The people were spellbound by the teaching, because Jesus taught with an authority that was unlike their religious scholars.

23 Suddenly a person with an unclean spirit appeared in their synagogue. It shrieked, 24 "What do you want from us, Jesus of Nazareth? Have you come to destroy us? I know who you are—the Holy One of God!"

25 Jesus rebuked the spirit sharply: "Be quiet! Come out of that person!" 26 At that the unclean spirit convulsed the possessed one violently, and with a loud shriek it came out.

27 All who looked on were amazed. They began to ask one another, "What is this? A new teaching, and with such authority! This person even gives orders to unclean spirits and they obey!" 28 Immediately news of Jesus spread throughout the surrounding region of Galilee.

29 Upon leaving the synagogue, Jesus entered Simon's and Andrew's house with James and John. 30 Simon's mother-in-law lay ill with a fever, and immediately they told Jesus about her.

31 Jesus went over to her, took her by the hand and helped her up, and the fever left her. Then she went about her work.

32 After sunset, as evening drew on, they brought to Jesus all who were ill and possessed by demons. 33 Everyone in the town crowded around the door. 34 Jesus healed many who were sick with different diseases, and cast out many demons. But Jesus would not permit the demons to speak, because they knew who he was.

35 Rising early the next morning, Jesus went off to a lonely place in the desert and prayed there. 36 Simon and some companions managed to find Jesus 37 and said to him, "Everybody is looking for you!"

38 Jesus said to them, "Let us move on to the neighboring villages so that I may proclaim the Good News there also. That is what I have come to do." 39 So Jesus went into their synagogues proclaiming the Good News and expelling demons throughout the whole of Galilee.

40 A person with leprosy approached Jesus, knelt down and begged, "If you are willing, you can heal me."

41 Moved with pity, Jesus stretched out a hand, touched the person with leprosy and said, "I am willing. Be cleansed."

42 Immediately the leprosy disappeared, and the person with the disease was cured. 43 Jesus gave a stern warning and sent the person off. 44 "Not a word to anyone," Jesus said. "Go off and present yourself to the priest and make an offering for your healing as Moses commanded, as a testimony to the religious authorities."

45 But the person who had been healed went off and began to proclaim the whole matter freely, making the story public. As a result it was no longer possible for Jesus to enter a town openly, and Jesus stayed in lonely places. Even so, people kept coming to him from all directions.

2 :1 Jesus came back to Capernaum after several days, and word spread that he was home. 2 People began to gather in such great numbers that there was no longer any room for them, even around the door.

While Jesus was delivering God's word to them, 3 some people arrived bringing a paralyzed person. The four who carried the invalid 4 were unable to reach Jesus because of the crowd, so they began to open up the roof directly above Jesus. When they had made a hole, they lowered the mat on which the paralyzed one was lying. 5 When Jesus saw their faith, he said to the sufferer, "My child, your sins are forgiven."

6 Now some of the religious scholars were sitting there asking themselves, 7 "Why does Jesus talk in that way? He commits blasphemy! Who can forgive sins but God alone?"

8 Jesus immediately perceived in his spirit that they reasoned this way among themselves and said to them, "Why do you harbor such thoughts? 9 Which is easier, to say to this paralyzed person, 'Your sins are forgiven,' or to say, 'Stand up, pick up your mat and walk'? 10 But so you all may know that the Promised One has authority on earth to forgive sins—" Jesus then turned to the paralyzed person— 11 "I tell you, stand up! Pick up your mat and go home."

12 The paralyzed person stood up, picked up the mat and walked outside in the sight of everyone. They were awestruck, and they all gave praise to God and said, "We have never seen anything like this!"

13 Jesus went out again and walked along the lake shore, but people kept coming to him in crowds to listen to his teachings. 14 As he passed by, Jesus saw Levi, ben-Alphaeus, sitting in the tax office. Jesus said, "Follow me," and Levi got up and followed him.

15 While Jesus was reclining to eat in Levi's house, many other tax collectors and notorious "sinners" joined him and the disciples at dinner. There were many people following Jesus. 16 When the religious scholars who belonged to the Pharisee sect saw that he was eating with tax collectors and sinners, they complained to the disciples, "Why does the Teacher eat with these people?"

17 Overhearing the remark, Jesus said to them, "People who are healthy don't need a doctor; sick ones do. I have come to call sinners, not the righteous."

18 Now John's disciples and the Pharisees fasted regularly. Some people came to Jesus with the objection, "Why do John's disciples and those of the Pharisees fast, while yours don't?"

19 Jesus replied, "How can wedding guests fast while the bridegroom is still among them? So long as the bridegroom stays with them, they cannot fast. 20 The day will come, however, when the bridegroom will be taken away; on that day they will fast.

21 "No one sews a patch of unshrunken cloth on an old cloak. Otherwise, the patch pulls away from it—the new from the old—and the tear gets worse. 22 Similarly, no one pours new wine into old wineskins. If one does, the wine will burst the skins, and both wine and skins will be lost. No, new wine is poured into new wineskins."

23 One Sabbath day Jesus took a walk through the grain fields, and the disciples began to pick ears of grain as they

went along. ²⁴ The Pharisees said to Jesus, "Look, why are they doing something on the Sabbath day that is forbidden?"

²⁵ And Jesus replied, "Did you never read what David did in his time of need when he and his followers were hungry— ²⁶ how David went into the house of God when Abiathar was high priest and ate the loaves of offering, which only the priests are allowed to eat, and how he also gave some to those with him?"

²⁷ Then Jesus said to them, "The Sabbath was made for people, not people for the Sabbath. ²⁸ That is why the Chosen One is ruler even of the Sabbath."

3 ¹ Returning to the synagogue, Jesus met someone who had a withered hand. ² Now the religious authorities were watching to see if Jesus would heal the individual on the Sabbath day, as they were hoping for some evidence to use against Jesus. ³ He said to the afflicted one, "Stand and come up front!"

⁴ Then he turned to them and said, "Is it permitted to do a good deed on the Sabbath—or an evil one? To preserve life or to destroy it?"

At this they remained silent. ⁵ Jesus looked around at them with anger, for he was deeply grieved that they had closed their hearts so. Then Jesus said to the person, "Stretch out your hand." The other did so, and the hand was perfectly restored.

⁶ The Pharisees went out and at once began to plot with the Herodians, discussing how to destroy Jesus.

3:7–6:6

Jesus withdrew with the disciples to the lakeside. A great crowd followed him from Galilee, ⁸ and an equally great multitude came from Judea, Jerusalem, Idumea, Trans-jordan and the neighborhood of Tyre and Sidon, because they had heard what he had done.

⁹ In view of their numbers, Jesus told the disciples to have a fishing boat ready so that he could avoid the pushing of the crowd. ¹⁰ Because he had healed many, all who had afflictions kept pressing forward to touch him. ¹¹ Unclean spirits would catch sight of him, fling themselves down at his feet and shout, "You are God's Own," ¹² while he kept ordering them sternly not to reveal who he was.

¹³ Jesus went up the mountain and summoned those followers he wanted, who came and joined him. ¹⁴ He named twelve as his companions whom he would send to preach ¹⁵ and to have authority to expel the demons.

¹⁶ He appointed the twelve as follows: Simon, to whom he gave the name Peter; ¹⁷ James Bar-Zebedee, and John, his brother, to whom he gave the name Boanerges, or "children of thunder"; ¹⁸ Andrew; Philip; Bartholomew; Matthew; Thomas; James Bar-Alphaeus; Thaddaeus; Simon, the Zealot; ¹⁹ and Judas Iscariot, who betrayed Jesus.

²⁰ Then Jesus went home, and again such a crowd gathered that he and the disciples were unable even to eat a meal. ²¹ When Jesus' relatives heard of this, they went out to take charge of him, thinking that he had lost his mind.

²² The religious scholars who had come down from Jerusalem said of Jesus, "He is possessed by Beelzebul," and, "He casts out demons through the ruler of demons."

²³ Summoning them, Jesus spoke in parables: "How can Satan cast out Satan? ²⁴ If a realm is torn by civil strife, it cannot last. ²⁵ If a household is divided according to loyalties, it will not survive. ²⁶ Similarly, if Satan has suffered mutiny in the ranks and is torn by dissension, the Devil is finished and cannot endure. ²⁷ No attacker can enter a stronghold unless the defender is first put under restraint. Only then can the attacker plunder the stronghold.

²⁸ "The truth is, every sin and all the blasphemy the people utter will be forgiven, ²⁹ but those who blaspheme against the Holy Spirit will never have forgiveness. They are guilty of an eternal sin." ³⁰ Jesus spoke all this because they said, "He is possessed by an unclean spirit."

³¹ Jesus' mother and brothers arrived and sent in a message asking for him. ³² A crowd was sitting around Jesus, and they said to him, "Your mother and brothers are outside looking for you." ³³ Jesus replied, "Who is my mother? Who is my family?" ³⁴ And looking around at everyone there, Jesus said, "This is my family! ³⁵ Anyone who does the will of God, that person is my sister, my brother, my mother."

4 ¹ Again Jesus began to preach beside the lake. But such a huge crowd gathered around that he got into a boat and sat there, while the crowd remained on the shore.

² Jesus taught them many things in the form of parables and, in the course of his teaching, said, ³ "Listen carefully. Imagine a sower going out to sow, scattering the seed widely. ⁴ Some of the seed fell on the edge of the path, and the birds came and ate it. ⁵ Some seed fell on rocky ground where it found a little soil, and sprang up immediately because the soil had little depth— ⁶ but then, when the sun came up and scorched it, it withered for lack of roots. ⁷ Some seed fell into thorns, and the thorns grew up and choked it, and it produced no crop. ⁸ And some seed fell into rich soil and grew tall and strong, producing a crop thirty, sixty, even a hundredfold." ⁹ Jesus ended by saying, "If you have ears to hear, then listen."

¹⁰ Now when Jesus was away from the crowd, the Twelve, and others who formed the community, asked what the parable meant. ¹¹ Jesus said, "The secret of the kindom of God is given to you, but to those who are outside, it comes in parables, ¹² so that 'they may look and look again, but not perceive; they may listen and listen again, but not understand.' Otherwise they might be converted and be forgiven."

¹³ Jesus continued, "Don't you understand this parable? Then how will you understand any of the parables? ¹⁴ The sower is sowing the message. ¹⁵ Those on the edge of the path where the message is sown are people who have no sooner heard it, than Satan comes and carries away the message that was sown in them. ¹⁶ Similarly, those who receive the seed on patches of rock are people who, when first they hear the message, immediately welcome it with joy. ¹⁷ But they have no root in themselves, they do not last; when trials or persecutions rise because of my message, they immediately fall away. ¹⁸ Then there are others who receive the seed in thorns. These have heard the message, ¹⁹ but the worries of this world, the lure of riches and all the other passions come in and choke the message, so it produces nothing. ²⁰ And there are those who have received the seed in rich soil. They hear the message and accept it, and they bear fruit, thirty, sixty, and a hundredfold."

²¹ He also said to the crowd, "Would you bring in a lamp and put it under a bushel basket or hide it under the bed? Surely you'd put in on a lampstand! ²² Things are hidden only to be revealed at a later time. They are made secret only to be brought out into the open. ²³ If you have ears to hear, then listen!"

²⁴ He continued, "Listen carefully to what you hear. The amount you measure out is the amount you will receive—and more besides. ²⁵ To those who have, more will be given; from those who have not, what little they have will be taken away."

²⁶ Jesus said further, "The reign of God is like this: a sower scatters seed on the ground, ²⁷ then goes to bed at night and gets up day after day. Through it all the seed sprouts and grows without the sower knowing how it happens. ²⁸ The soil produces a crop by itself—first the blade, then the ear, and finally the ripe wheat in the ear. ²⁹ When the crop is ready, the sower wields the sickle, for the time is ripe for harvest."

³⁰ Jesus went on to say, "What comparison can we use for the reign of God? What image will help to present it? ³¹ It is like a mustard seed which people plant in the soil: it is the smallest of all the earth's seeds, ³² yet once it is sown, it springs up to become the largest of shrubs, with branches big enough for the birds of the sky to build nests in its shade."

³³ Using many parables like these, Jesus spoke the message to them, as much as they could understand. ³⁴ Everything was spoken in parables, but Jesus explained everything to the disciples later when they were alone.

³⁵ With the coming of evening that same day, Jesus said to the disciples, "Let's cross over to the other shore." ³⁶ Leaving the crowd behind, they took Jesus in the boat in which he was sitting. There were other boats with them.

³⁷ Then a fierce gale arose, and the waves were breaking into the boat so much that it was almost swamped. ³⁸ But Jesus was in the stern through it all, sound asleep on a cushion. They woke him and said, "Teacher, doesn't it matter to you that we're going to drown?"

³⁹ Jesus awoke, rebuked the wind and said to the sea, "Quiet! Be calm!" And the wind dropped and everything was perfectly calm. ⁴⁰ Jesus then said to the disciples, "Why were you so frightened? Have you no faith?"

⁴¹ But they became filled with fear and said to one another, "Who is this, whom even the wind and sea obey?"

5 ¹ They came to the region near Gerasa, on the other side of the lake. ² And when he had disembarked, immediately a person with an unclean spirit met them. ³ The possessed one lived among the tombs and could no longer be restrained, even with a chain. ⁴ In fact, shackles and fetters had been used as restraints to no avail. No one had proved strong enough to subdue the demoniac. ⁵ The sufferer would use stones to gash the flesh, howling day and night among the tombs and the mountain crags without interruption.

⁶ Catching sight of Jesus, the bedeviled one ran up and bowed down to Jesus, ⁷ but then started shrieking in a loud voice, "What do you want with me, Jesus, Firstborn of the Most High God? Swear by God that you won't torture me!" ⁸ For Jesus had been saying, "Come out of this person, unclean spirit!"

⁹ "What is your name?" Jesus asked.

"My name is Legion, for there are many of us," was the reply. ¹⁰ And the possessed one begged Jesus not to send them all out of the area.

¹¹ Now there was a large herd of pigs feeding on the mountainside, ¹² and the unclean spirits begged Jesus, "Send us to the pigs so we can enter them." ¹³ Jesus gave them permission. And with that, the unclean spirits came out and entered the pigs, and the herd of about two thousand went rushing down the cliff into the lake, and there they were drowned.

¹⁴ The swineherds ran off and reported this in the town and in the countryside, and the people came to see what really had happened. ¹⁵ As they approached Jesus, they caught sight of the one who had been possessed sitting fully clothed and perfectly sane. And they were filled with fear. ¹⁶ The spectators explained what had happened to the possessed person, and told the townspeople about the pigs. ¹⁷ Then the crowd began to implore Jesus to leave their district.

¹⁸ As Jesus was getting into the boat, the one who had been healed came up and begged to be allowed to go with him. ¹⁹ Jesus answered, "Go home to your people and tell them what our God has done for you." ²⁰ So the former demoniac went off and proceeded to proclaim throughout the Ten Cities what Jesus had done. Everyone was amazed at what they heard.

²¹ When Jesus had crossed again to the other shore in the boat, a large crowd gathered, and he stayed by the lakeside. ²² Then one of the synagogue officials—Jairus by name—came up and, seeing Jesus, fell down ²³ and pleaded earnestly, saying, "My little daughter is desperately sick. Come and lay your hands on her to make her better and save her life." ²⁴ Jesus went with him and a large crowd followed, pressing in from all sides.

²⁵ Now there was a woman who had suffered from hemorrhages for twelve years; ²⁶ after long and painful treatment from various doctors, she had spent all she had without getting better—in fact, she was getting worse. ²⁷ She had heard about Jesus, and she came up behind him in the crowd and touched his cloak. ²⁸ "If I can touch even the hem," she had told herself, "I will be well again." ²⁹ Immediately the flow of blood dried up, and she felt in her body that she was healed of her affliction.

³⁰ Immediately aware that healing power had gone out from him, Jesus turned to the crowd and said, "Who touched my clothes?"

³¹ The disciples said, "You see how the crowd is pressing you and yet you say, 'Who touched me?'"

³² But Jesus continued to look around to see who had done it. ³³ Then the woman came forward, frightened and trembling because she knew what had happened to her, and she fell at Jesus' feet and told him the whole truth.

³⁴ "My daughter," Jesus said, "your faith has saved you; go in peace and be free of your affliction."

³⁵ While Jesus was still speaking, some people arrived from the house of the synagogue official to say, "Your daughter is dead. Why put the Teacher to any further trouble?"

³⁶ But Jesus overheard the remark and said to the official: "Don't be afraid. Just believe." ³⁷ Jesus allowed no one to follow him except Peter and James and James' brother John.

³⁸ They came to the official's house and Jesus noticed all the commotion, with people weeping and wailing unrestrainedly. ³⁹ Jesus went in and said to them, "Why all this commotion and crying? The child is not dead, but asleep." ⁴⁰ At this, they began to ridicule him, and he told everyone to leave.

Jesus took the child's mother and father and his own companions and entered the room where the child lay. ⁴¹ Taking her hand, he said to her, *"Talitha, koum!"* which means, "Little girl, get up!" ⁴² Immediately the girl, who was twelve years old, got up and began to walk about.

At this they were overcome with astonishment. ⁴³ Jesus gave the family strict orders not to let anyone know about it, and told them to give the little girl something to eat.

6 ¹ After leaving there, Jesus came into his own town, followed by the disciples.

² When the Sabbath came, he began to teach in the synagogue, and the many listeners were astonished and said, "Where did he learn all this? What is this wisdom that has been granted, and these miracles that are performed by his hands? ³ Isn't this the carpenter, the son of Mary, the brother of James and Joses and Judah and Simon? Are not his sisters here with us?" They found these things to be stumbling blocks.

⁴ Jesus said to them, "Prophets are not without honor, except in their hometowns and among their own relatives and in their own households." ⁵ And he could work no miracles there, apart from laying his hands upon a few sick people and healing them; ⁶ their lack of faith astounded him. He made the rounds of the neighboring villages instead, and spent the time teaching.

6:7–8:30

Then Jesus summoned the Twelve and began to send them out in pairs, giving them authority over unclean spirits. ⁸ He instructed them that they should take nothing for their journey, except a mere staff—no bread, no bag, no money in their belts. ⁹ They were to wear sandals but, he added, "Do not take a spare tunic."

¹⁰ And Jesus said to them, "Whenever you enter a house, stay there until you leave town. ¹¹ Any place that does not receive you or listen to you, as you leave it, shake off the dust from the soles of your feet as a testimony against them."

¹² And so they set off, proclaiming repentance as they went. ¹³ They cast out many demons and anointed many sick people with oil and healed them.

¹⁴ Meanwhile Herod, the ruler of Judea, had heard about Jesus, whose reputation had become widespread. Some people were saying, "John the Baptizer has been raised from the dead, and that is why such miraculous powers are at work in him." ¹⁵ Others said, "He is Elijah"; still others, "He is a prophet, like one of the prophets of old." ¹⁶ When Herod heard of Jesus, he exclaimed, "John, whom I beheaded, has risen from the dead!"

¹⁷ Now it was Herod who had ordered John arrested, chained and imprisoned on account of Herodias, the wife of his brother Philip, whom Herod had married. ¹⁸ For John had told Herod, "It is against the Law for you to have your brother's wife." ¹⁹ As for Herodias, she was furious with John and wanted to kill him but was unable to do so. ²⁰ Herod feared John, knowing him to be good and holy, and kept him in custody. When Herod heard John speak he was very much disturbed; yet he was moved by John's words.

²¹ Herodias had her chance one day when Herod on his birthday held a dinner for the court circle, military officers and leaders of Galilee. ²² When the daughter of Herodias came in and danced, this delighted Herod and the guests so much that he told the young woman, "Ask me anything you like

and I will give it to you." ²³ And Herod swore an oath, "I will give you anything you ask, even half of my entire realm!"

²⁴ She went out and said to her mother, "What should I ask for?"

Herodias replied, "The head of John the Baptizer."

²⁵ The woman hurried back to Herod and made her request: "I want you to give me the head of John the Baptizer on a platter."

²⁶ Herod was deeply distressed by this request, but remembering the oath he swore before the guests, he was reluctant to break his oath to her. ²⁷ So Herod immediately sent one of the bodyguards with orders to bring John's head. The guard beheaded John in prison, ²⁸ then brought the head in on a platter and gave it to the young woman, who gave it to her mother.

²⁹ When John's disciples heard about this, they came and took the body away and laid it in a tomb.

³⁰ The apostles came back to Jesus and reported all that they had done and taught. ³¹ Jesus said to them, "Come away by yourselves to someplace more remote, and rest awhile." For there were many people coming and going, and the apostles hadn't had time to eat. ³² So they went away in a boat to a deserted area.

³³ The people saw them leaving and many recognized them, so they ran together on foot from all the cities and got there ahead of the apostles. ³⁴ When Jesus went ashore, there was a large crowd waiting for him, and he felt compassion for them because they were like sheep without a shepherd. So he began to teach them many things.

³⁵ By now it was getting very late, and his disciples came up to him and said, "This is a deserted place and it's very late. ³⁶ Why not dismiss them so they can go to the nearby farms and villages and buy something to eat?"

³⁷ Jesus replied, "Give them something to eat yourselves."

They answered, "You want us to spend half a year's wages on bread for them to eat?"

³⁸ "How many loaves do you have?" Jesus asked. "Go look."

When they found out they reported back, "Five, and two fish."

³⁹ Jesus told them to have the people sit down on the grass ⁴⁰ in groups of hundreds and fifties. ⁴¹ Then Jesus took the five loaves and two fish, raised his eyes to heaven and said the blessing. Jesus broke the loaves and handed them to the disciples to distribute among the people. He also passed out the two fish among them.

⁴² They all ate until they had their fill. ⁴³ The disciples gathered up the leftovers and filled twelve baskets of broken bread and fish. ⁴⁴ In all, five thousand families ate that day.

⁴⁵ Immediately Jesus made the disciples get in the boat and go on ahead to Bethsaida, while he dismissed the crowd. ⁴⁶ After leaving them, he went up the hillside to pray.

⁴⁷ When evening came, the boat was far out on the lake, and Jesus was alone on land. ⁴⁸ He saw that the disciples were worn out with rowing, because the wind was against them. About three in the morning, Jesus went out to them, walking on the water. He was about to pass them by ⁴⁹ when they saw him and—thinking it was a ghost—cried out. ⁵⁰ For they had all seen him and were terrified.

Jesus hastened to reassure them: "Calm yourselves! It's me. Don't be afraid." ⁵¹ Jesus got into the boat with them, and the wind died down. They were completely amazed by what had happened, ⁵² for they hadn't understood about the loaves. Their minds were closed.

⁵³ After crossing the lake, Jesus and the disciples came ashore at Gennesaret and tied up their boat there. ⁵⁴ No sooner had they stepped out of the boat than people recognized Jesus. ⁵⁵ The crowds started hurrying about the countryside and brought the sick on stretchers wherever Jesus went. ⁵⁶ Wherever he appeared—in villages, in towns or in the countryside—they laid down the sick in the open places, begging him to let them touch just the fringe of his cloak, and all who touched Jesus got well.

7 ¹ The Pharisees and some of the religious scholars who had come from Jerusalem gathered around Jesus. ² They had noticed that some of the disciples were eating with unclean hands—that is, without ritually washing them. ³ For the Pharisees, and Jewish people in general, follow the tradition of their ancestors and never eat without washing their arms as far as the elbow. ⁴ Moreover, they never eat anything from the market without first sprinkling it. There are many other traditions which have been handed down to them, such as the washing of cups and pots and dishes.

⁵ So these Pharisees and religious scholars asked Jesus, "Why do your disciples not respect the tradition of our ancestors, but eat their food with unclean hands?"

⁶ Jesus answered, "How accurately Isaiah prophesied about you hypocrites when he wrote,

'These people honor me with their lips,
    while their hearts are far from me.
⁷ The worship they offer me is worthless;
    the doctrines they teach are only human precepts.'

⁸ You disregard God's commandments and cling to human traditions."

⁹ Jesus went on to say, "How ingeniously you evade the commandment of God in order to preserve your own tradition! ¹⁰ For Moses said, 'Honor your mother and your father' and, 'Anyone who curses mother or father must be put to death.' ¹¹ But you say that if someone says to their mother or father, 'Any support you might have had from me is *korban*'"—that is, dedicated to God— ¹² "then they're allowed to do nothing more for their parents. ¹³ In this way you nullify God's word in favor of the traditions you have handed down. And you do many other things like this."

¹⁴ Jesus summoned the crowd again and said to them, "Listen to me, all of you, and try to understand. ¹⁵ Nothing that enters us from the outside makes us impure; it is what comes out of us that makes us impure. ¹⁶ If you have ears to hear, then listen."

¹⁷ When Jesus got home, away from the crowd, the disciples questioned him about the parable. ¹⁸ He said to them, "Are you also incapable of understanding? Don't you see that whatever enters us from outside cannot make us impure? ¹⁹ It doesn't enter our heart, just our stomach—then passes out into the sewer." In this way, Jesus pronounced all food clean.

²⁰ He went on, "It is what comes out of us that makes us unclean. ²¹ For it is from within—from our hearts—that evil intentions emerge: promiscuity, theft, murder, adultery, ²² greed, malice, deceit, obscenity, envy, slander, pride, foolishness. ²³ All these evils come from within and make us impure."

²⁴ Jesus left Gennesaret and went to the territory of Tyre and Sidon. There he went into a certain house and wanted no one to recognize him, but he could not pass unrecognized. ²⁵ A woman whose young daughter had an unclean spirit heard about him. She approached Jesus and fell at his feet. ²⁶ The woman, who was Greek, a Syro-Phoenician by birth, begged Jesus to expel the demon from her daughter. ²⁷ He told her, "Let the children of the household satisfy themselves at table first. It is not right to take the food of the children and throw it to the dogs."

²⁸ She replied, "Yes, Rabbi, but even the dogs under the table eat the family's scraps."

²⁹ Then Jesus said to her, "For saying this, you may go home happy; the demon has left your daughter." ³⁰ When she got home, she found her daughter in bed and the demon gone.

³¹ Jesus left the region of Tyre and returned by way of Sidon to the Sea of Galilee, into the district of the Ten Cities. ³² Some people brought an individual who was deaf and had a speech impediment, and begged Jesus to lay hands on that person. ³³ Jesus took the afflicted one aside, away from the crowd, put his fingers into the deaf ears and, spitting, touched the mute tongue with his saliva. ³⁴ Then Jesus looked up to heaven and, with a deep sigh, said, "*Ephphatha!*"—that is, "Be opened!" ³⁵ At once the deaf ears were opened and the impediment cured; the one who had been healed began to speak plainly.

³⁶ Then Jesus warned them not to tell anyone; but the more he ordered them not to, the more they proclaimed it. ³⁷ Their amazement went beyond all bounds: "He has done everything well! He even makes the deaf hear and the mute speak!"

8 ¹ Once again a large crowd assembled, and they had nothing to eat. Jesus called over the disciples and said, ² "My heart goes out to these people. By now they have been with us for three days and have nothing to eat. ³ If I send them away hungry, they will collapse on the way, for some have come a long distance."

⁴ The disciples replied, "How can anyone give these people enough bread in this desolate place?"

⁵ Jesus asked them, "How many loaves do you have?"

"Seven," they replied.

⁶ Then Jesus directed the crowd to sit down. Taking the seven loaves, he gave thanks, broke them, and gave them to the disciples to distribute, and they handed them out to the crowd. ⁷ They also had a few small fish; asking a blessing on the fish, Jesus told them to distribute these also.

⁸ The people in the crowd ate until they were filled—yet they gathered seven wicker baskets of leftovers. ⁹ Those who had eaten numbered about four thousand.

Jesus dismissed them ¹⁰ and then got into the boat with the disciples to go to the region of Dalmanutha.

¹¹ The Pharisees came forward and began to argue with Jesus. They demanded a sign from heaven—as a test. ¹² With a sigh that came straight from his heart, Jesus said, "Why does this generation demand a sign? The truth is, no sign will be given to this generation." ¹³ And leaving them again and getting back into the boat, he went away to the opposite shore.

¹⁴ The disciples had forgotten to bring bread along, and they had only one loaf with them in the boat. ¹⁵ Then Jesus gave them this warning: "Keep your eyes open. Be on guard against the yeast of the Pharisees and the yeast of Herod."

¹⁶ And they said to one another, "It's because we forgot the bread."

¹⁷ Aware of this, Jesus reprimanded them: "Why are you talking about having no bread? Don't you see or understand yet? Are your minds closed? ¹⁸ Have you 'eyes that don't see, ears that don't hear'? Don't you remember ¹⁹ when I broke the five loaves for the five thousand? How many baskets of fragments did you collect?"

They answered, "Twelve."

²⁰ "And when I broke the seven loaves for the four thousand, how many baskets of scraps did you collect?"

"Seven," they replied.

²¹ Then he said to them, "And you still don't understand?"

²² When they arrived at Bethsaida, some people brought a blind villager and begged Jesus for a healing. ²³ Jesus led the blind person by the hand to the outskirts of the village. When he had spat on the person's eyes and laid hands on them, Jesus asked, "Do you see anything?"

²⁴ The blind one answered, "I see people, but they look like trees walking around."

²⁵ Then Jesus laid hands on the eyes a second time, and the villager was restored to clear and distinct sight. ²⁶ Jesus sent the healed person home, warning, "Don't even go into the village."

²⁷ Then he and the disciples set out for the villages around Caesarea Philippi. On the way, Jesus asked the disciples this question: "Who do people say that I am?"

²⁸ They replied, "Some say John the Baptizer; others, Elijah; still others, one of the prophets."

²⁹ "And you," he went on to ask, "who do you say that I am?"

Peter answered, "You are the Messiah!" ³⁰ But Jesus gave them strict orders not to tell anyone about him.

8:31–10:52

Then Jesus began to teach them that the Promised One had to suffer much, be rejected by the elders, chief priests, and religious scholars, be put to death, and rise again three days later. ³² Jesus said these things quite openly.

Peter then took him aside and began to take issue with him. ³³ At this, Jesus turned around and, eyeing the disciples, reprimanded Peter: "Get out of my sight, you Satan! You are judging by human standards rather than by God's!"

³⁴ Jesus summoned the crowd and the disciples and said, "If you wish to come after me, you must deny your very self, take up your cross and follow in my footsteps. ³⁵ If you would save your life, you'll lose it, but if you lose your life for my sake, you'll save it. ³⁶ What would you gain if you were to win the whole world but lose your self in the process? ³⁷ What can you offer in exchange for your soul? ³⁸ Whoever in this faithless and corrupt generation is ashamed of me and my words will find, in turn, that the Promised One and the holy angels will be ashamed of that person, when all stand before our God in glory."

9 ¹ Jesus also said to them, "The truth is, some of you standing here won't taste death before you see God's reign established in power."

² Six days after that, Jesus took Peter and James and John and led them up a high mountain where they could be alone.

And there Jesus was transfigured before their eyes; ³ the clothes Jesus wore became dazzlingly white—whiter than any earthly bleach could make them.

⁴ Elijah appeared to them, as did Moses, and the two were talking with Jesus. ⁵ Then Peter spoke to Jesus. "Rabbi," he said, "how wonderful it is for us to be here! Let us make three shelters—one for you, one for Moses and one for Elijah!" ⁶ Peter did not know what he was saying, so overcome were they all with awe.

⁷ Then a cloud formed, overshadowing them; and there came a voice from out of the cloud: "This is my Beloved, my Own; listen to this One." ⁸ Then suddenly, when they looked around, they saw no one with them anymore—only Jesus.

⁹ As they were coming down from the mountain, Jesus gave them orders not to tell anyone what they had seen until after the Promised One had risen from the dead. ¹⁰ They agreed to this, though they discussed among themselves what "rising from the dead" could mean.

¹¹ And they put the question to Jesus, "Why do the religious scholars say that Elijah must come first?"

¹² He said, "Because Elijah does indeed come first, to restore all things. Yet why does it say in scripture that the Promised One must suffer much and be rejected? ¹³ But I tell you, Elijah has already come, and they have done to him everything they wished, just as it is written."

¹⁴ As they approached the other disciples, they saw a large crowd standing around and some religious scholars arguing with them. ¹⁵ As soon as the crowd caught sight of Jesus, they were awestruck and ran up to greet him.

¹⁶ He asked them, "What are you all discussing?"

¹⁷ "Teacher," someone in the crowd replied, "I have brought to you my child, who is possessed by a mute spirit. ¹⁸ Whenever it comes, it seizes my child and throws the little one into convulsions. My child foams at the mouth and becomes rigid. Just now I asked your disciples to expel the spirit, but they were unable to do so."

¹⁹ Jesus said to the crowd, "What an unbelieving lot you are! How long must I remain with you? How long can I endure you? Bring the child to me."

²⁰ When they did, the spirit caught sight of Jesus and immediately threw the child into convulsions. The child fell to the ground, rolling around and foaming at the mouth.

²¹ Then Jesus questioned the parent, "How long has this been happening?"

"From infancy," was the reply. ²² "Often it throws our little one into the fire and into the water. But if you can do anything, have pity on us and help us!"

²³ "'If you can'?" replied Jesus. "Everything is possible to those who believe!"

²⁴ The child's parent answered, "I do believe. Help my unbelief!"

²⁵ Jesus, on seeing the crowd rapidly gathering, reprimanded the unclean spirit and said, "Mute and deaf spirit, I command you: come out of this child and never again return!"

²⁶ It screamed and threw the child into convulsions, then it came out. The child became like a corpse, and many said, "The little one is dead." ²⁷ But with assistance from Jesus, the child stood up.

²⁸ When Jesus arrived at the house, the disciples asked him privately, "Why is it that we could not expel it?" ²⁹ Jesus replied, "This kind can't be driven out at all—except through prayer."

30 They left that district and began a journey through Galilee, but Jesus did not want anyone to know about it. 31 He was teaching the disciples along these lines: "The Promised One is going to be delivered into the hands of others and will be put to death, but three days later this One will rise again." 32 Though they failed to understand these words, they were afraid to question him.

33 They returned home to Capernaum. Once they were inside the house, Jesus began to ask them, "What were you discussing on the way home?" 34 At this they fell silent, for on the way they had been arguing about who among them was the most important. 35 So Jesus sat down and called the Twelve over and said, "If any of you wants to be first, you must be the last one of all and at the service of all."

36 Then Jesus brought a little child into their midst and, putting his arm around the child, said to them, 37 "Whoever welcomes a child such as this for my sake welcomes me. And whoever welcomes me welcomes not me but the One who sent me."

38 John said to Jesus, "Teacher, we saw someone using your name to expel demons, and we tried to stop it since this person was not part of our group."

39 Jesus said in reply, "Don't try to stop it. No one who performs a miracle using my name can speak ill of me soon thereafter! 40 Anyone who is not against us is with us. 41 The truth is, anyone who gives you a cup of water in my name because you belong to the Messiah will certainly not go without a reward.

42 "Rather than make one of these little ones who believe in me stumble, it would be better to be thrown into the sea with a large millstone hung around your neck.

43 "If your hand causes you to sin, cut it off. It would be better to enter Life crippled than to have hands and go into Gehenna, where the fire never goes out.* 45 If your foot causes you to sin, cut it off. It is better to enter Life crippled than to have two feet and be thrown into Gehenna. 47 And if your eye causes you to sin, pluck it out. It would be better to enter the kingdom of God with one eye than to have two eyes and be drawn into Gehenna, 48 where 'the worm never dies and the fire never goes out.'

49 "Everyone will be salted with fire.

50 "Salt is good. But if salt loses its flavor, how can you make it salty again?

"Have salt in yourselves, and live in peace with one another."

10 1 Jesus left there and came to the districts of Judea and the other side of the Jordan. Once more the crowds gathered around and as usual Jesus began to teach them.

2 Some Pharisees approached Jesus and, as a test, asked, "Is it permissible for husbands to divorce wives?"

3 In reply Jesus asked, "What command did Moses give?"

4 They answered, "Moses permitted a husband to write a decree of divorce and to put her away."

5 But Jesus told them, "Moses wrote the commandment because of your hardness of heart. 6 From the beginning of creation,

'God made them male and female.
7 This is why one person leaves home
   and cleaves to another,
8 and the two become one flesh.'

They are no longer two, but one flesh. 9 What God has united, therefore, let no one divide."

10 Back in the house again, the disciples questioned Jesus once more about this. 11 He told them, "If a man divorces his wife and marries another, he commits adultery against her; 12 and if a woman divorces her husband and marries another, she commits adultery."

13 People were bringing their children to Jesus to have him touch them, but the disciples scolded them for this.

14 When Jesus saw this he was indignant and said to them, "Let the children come to me; do not stop them. It is to just such as these that the kindom of God belongs. 15 The truth is, whoever doesn't welcome the kindom of God as a little child won't enter it."

16 And Jesus took the children in his arms and blessed them, laying his hands on them.

17 As he was setting out on a journey, someone came running up and asked, "Good Teacher, what must I do to share in everlasting life?" 18 Jesus answered, "Why do you call me good? No one is good but God alone. 19 You know the commandments: No killing. No committing adultery. No stealing. No bearing false witness. No defrauding. Honor your mother and your father."

20 The other replied, "Teacher, I have kept all these since my childhood."

21 Then Jesus looked at the person with love and said, "There is one thing more that you must do. Go and sell what you have and give it to those in need; you will then have treasure in heaven. After that, come and follow me."

22 At these words, the inquirer, who owned much property, became crestfallen and went away sadly.

23 Jesus looked around and said to the disciples, "How hard it is for rich people to enter the kindom of God!"

24 The disciples could only marvel at these words. So Jesus repeated what he had said: "My children, how hard it is to enter the realm of God! 25 It is easier for a camel to pass through the Needle's Eye gate than for a rich person to enter the kindom of God!"

26 The disciples were amazed at this and said to one another, "Then who can be saved?"

27 Jesus looked at them and said, "For mortals it is impossible—but not for God. With God all things are possible."

28 Peter was moved to say to Jesus, "We have left everything to follow you!"

29 Jesus answered, "The truth is, there is no one who has left home, sisters or brothers, mother or father, children or fields for me and for the sake of the Gospel 30 who won't receive a hundred times as much in this present age—as many homes, brothers, sisters, mothers, fathers, children and property, though not without persecution—and, in the age to come, everlasting life.

31 "Many who are first will be last, and the last will be first."

32 They were on their way up to Jerusalem, with Jesus leading the way. The disciples were baffled by this move, while the other followers were afraid. Taking the Twelve aside once more, Jesus began to tell them what was going to happen.

33 "We are on our way up to Jerusalem where the Promised One will be handed over to the chief priests and the religious scholars. Then the Promised One will be condemned to death and handed over to the Gentiles 34 to be mocked, spat upon, flogged and finally killed. Three days later the Promised One will rise."

---

* Most manuscripts omit verses 44 and 46, which are identical to verse 48.

35 Zebedee's children James and John approached Jesus. "Teacher," they said, "we want you to grant our request."
36 "What is it?" Jesus asked.
37 They replied, "See to it that we sit next to you, one at your right and one at your left, when you come into your glory."
38 Jesus told them, "You do not know what you are asking. Can you drink the cup I will drink or be baptized in the same baptism as I?"
39 "We can," they replied. Jesus said in response, "From the cup I drink of, you will drink; the baptism I am immersed in, you will share. 40 But as for sitting at my right or my left, that is not mine to give; it is for those to whom it has been reserved."
41 The other ten, on hearing this, became indignant at James and John.
42 Jesus called them together and said, "You know how among the Gentiles those who exercise authority are domineering and arrogant; those 'great ones' know how to make their own importance felt. 43 But it can't be like that with you. Anyone among you who aspires to greatness must serve the rest; 44 whoever wants to rank first among you must serve the needs of all. 45 The Promised One has come not to be served, but to serve—to give one life in ransom for the many."

46 They came to Jericho. As Jesus was leaving Jericho with the disciples and a large crowd, a blind beggar named Bartimaeus ben-Timaeus, was sitting at the side of the road. 47 When he heard that it was Jesus of Nazareth, he began to shout and to say, "Heir of David, Jesus, have pity on me!"
48 Many people scolded him and told him to be quiet, but he shouted all the louder, "Heir of David, have pity on me!"
49 Jesus stopped and said, "Call him here."
So they called the blind man. "Don't be afraid," they said. "Get up; Jesus is calling you." 50 So throwing off his cloak, Bartimaeus jumped up and went to Jesus.
51 Then Jesus said, "What do you want me to do for you?"
"Rabbuni," the blind man said, "I want to see."
52 Jesus replied, "Go, your faith has saved you." And immediately Bartimaeus received the gift of sight and began to follow Jesus along the road.

11:1–13:37

As they approached Jerusalem and came to Bethphage and Bethany at the Mount of Olives, Jesus sent off two of the disciples 2 with this instruction: "Go to the village straight ahead of you, and as soon as you enter it you will find tethered there a colt on which no one has ridden. Untie it and bring it back. 3 If anyone says to you, 'Why are you doing that?' say, 'The Rabbi needs it, but will send it back very soon.'"
4 So they went off, and finding a colt tethered out on the street near a gate, they untied it. 5 Some of the bystanders said to them, "What do you mean by untying that colt?" 6 They answered as Jesus had told them to, and the people let them take it.
7 They brought the colt to Jesus and threw their cloaks across its back, and he sat on it. 8 Many people spread their cloaks on the road, while others spread leafy branches which they had cut from the fields. 9 And everyone around Jesus, in front or in back of him, cried out,

"Hosanna!
Blessed is the One who comes in the name of our
God!

10 Blessed is the coming reign of our ancestor David!
Hosanna in the highest!"

11 Jesus entered Jerusalem and went into the Temple precincts. He inspected everything there, but since it was already late in the afternoon, he went out to Bethany accompanied by the Twelve.

12 The next day when they were leaving Bethany, Jesus felt hungry. 13 Observing a fig tree covered with foliage some distance off, he went over to see if the tree contained any fruit, but upon inspecting it found only leaves—it was not the season for figs. 14 Jesus addressed the fig tree and said, "No one will ever eat fruit from you again." And the disciples witnessed this.

15 Then they went on to Jerusalem. Jesus entered the Temple and began driving out those engaged in selling and buying. He overturned the money changers' tables and the stalls of those selling doves; 16 moreover, he would not permit anyone to carry goods through the Temple area.
17 Then he began to teach them: "Doesn't scripture say, 'My house will be called a house of prayer for all the peoples'? But you have turned it into a den of thieves!"
18 The chief priests and the religious scholars heard about this and began looking for a way to destroy him. At the same time, they were fearful because the whole crowd was under the spell of his teaching.

19 When evening came, Jesus and the disciples went out of the city. 20 Early the next morning, as they were walking along, they saw the fig tree withered to its roots. 21 Peter remembered and said, "Rabbi, look! The fig tree you cursed has withered up."
22 In reply Jesus said, "Put your trust in God. 23 The truth is, if any of you say to this mountain, 'Get up and throw yourself into the sea,' and you don't doubt in your heart, but believe that what you say will happen, it will happen. 24 That's why I tell you that whatever you ask for in prayer, believe that you have already received it, and it will be done for you.
25 "And when you stand praying, forgive anyone against whom you have a grievance, so that your loving God in heaven may in turn forgive you your faults."*

27 They came to Jerusalem again, and as Jesus was walking through the Temple, the chief priests, the religious scholars and the elders asked, 28 "On what authority are you doing these things? Who has given you the power to do them?"
29 "I will ask you a question—only one," Jesus replied. "If you give me an answer, I will tell you on what authority I do the things I do. 30 Tell me, was John's baptism of divine origin, or merely human?"
31 They thought to themselves, "If we say, 'divine,' he will ask, 'Then why did you not put faith in it?' 32 But can we say 'merely human'?"—for they had reason to fear the people, who regarded John as a true prophet. 33 So their answer to Jesus was, "We do not know."
In turn, Jesus said to them, "Then neither will I tell you on what authority I do the things I do."

---

* Verse 26 is a later addition: "If you don't forgive, your loving God in heaven won't forgive your faults either."

12

¹ Once more Jesus began to address them in parables: "A farmer planted a vineyard, put a hedge around it, dug out a vat and erected a tower. Then the farmer leased it to tenants and went on a journey.

² "In due time the farmer sent a subordinate to the tenants to obtain from them the owner's share of the produce from the vineyard. ³ But they seized the subordinate, who, after a beating, was sent off empty-handed. ⁴ Then the owner sent them a second subordinate; this one they treated shamefully too; ⁵ and they killed a third subordinate. So too with many others: some they beat, others they killed.

⁶ "There was one more to send—the farmer's own beloved child. 'They will respect my heir,' thought the farmer. ⁷ But the tenants said to one another, 'Here is the one who will inherit everything. Come, let us kill the heir, and the inheritance will be ours.' ⁸ Then they seized and killed the heir and dragged the body outside the vineyard.

⁹ "What do you suppose will happen? The farmer will come and destroy those tenants and turn the vineyard over to others! ¹⁰ Are you not familiar with this passage of scripture:

'The stone rejected by the builders
has become the cornerstone of the building.
¹¹ This is our God's doing,
and it is marvelous in our eyes.'"

¹² At these words they wanted to arrest Jesus, but they had reason to fear the crowd. They knew well enough that the parable was directed at them. Finally they went away.

¹³ Some Pharisees and Herodians were sent after Jesus to catch him in his speech. ¹⁴ The two groups approached Jesus and said, "Teacher, we know you are truthful and unconcerned about the opinion of others. It is evident you aren't swayed by another's rank, but teach God's way of life sincerely. So: is it lawful to pay tax to the emperor or not? ¹⁵ Are we to pay or not to pay?"

Knowing their hypocrisy, he said to them, "Why are you trying to trick me? Let me see a coin." ¹⁶ When they handed him one, he said to them, "Whose image and inscription do you see here?"

"Caesar's," they answered.

¹⁷ Then Jesus said, "Give to Caesar what is Caesar's, and give to God what is God's." This reply took them completely by surprise.

¹⁸ Then some Sadducees, who hold that there is no resurrection, came to Jesus with a question: ¹⁹ "Teacher, Moses wrote that if anyone dies leaving a wife but no child, his brother must marry the wife and produce offspring. ²⁰ So let's say there were seven brothers. The eldest married a woman and died leaving no children. ²¹ The second married her, and he too died childless. The same happened to the third; ²² in fact, none of the seven left any children behind. Last of all, the woman also died. ²³ At the resurrection, when they all come back to life, whose wife will she be? All seven married her."

²⁴ Jesus said, "You just don't see, because you fail to understand the scriptures or the power of God. ²⁵ When people rise from the dead, they neither marry nor are given in marriage, but live like the angels of heaven. ²⁶ As to the raising of the dead, have you not read in the book of Moses, in the passage about the burning bush, how God told him, 'I am the God of Sarah and Abraham, the God of Rebecca and Isaac, the God of Leah and Rachel and Jacob'? ²⁷ God is the God of the living, not of the dead. You are very much mistaken."

²⁸ One of the religious scholars who had listened to them debating and had observed how well Jesus had answered them, now came up and put a question to him: "Which is the foremost of all the commandments?"

²⁹ Jesus replied, "This is the foremost: 'Hear, O Israel, God, our God, is one. ³⁰ You must love the Most High God with all your heart, with all your soul, with all your mind and with all your strength.' ³¹ The second is this: 'You must love your neighbor as yourself.' There is no commandment greater than these."

³² The scholar said to Jesus, "Well spoken, Teacher! What you have said is true: the Most High is one and there is no other. ³³ To love God with all your heart, with all your understanding and strength, and to love your neighbor as yourself—this is far more important than any burnt offering or sacrifice."

³⁴ Jesus, seeing how wisely this scholar had spoken, said, "You are not far from the kindom of God." And after that no one dared to question Jesus any more.

³⁵ Later, as Jesus was teaching in the Temple, he went on to say, "How can the religious scholars claim, 'The Messiah is David's heir'? ³⁶ David himself, inspired by the Holy Spirit, said,

'God said to my Sovereign:
"Sit at my right hand
until I place your enemies under your foot."'

³⁷ If David addresses this one as 'Sovereign,' how can the Sovereign be David's heir?" The large crowd listened to this with delight.

³⁸ In his teaching, Jesus said, "Beware of the religious scholars who like to walk about in long robes, be greeted obsequiously in the market squares, ³⁹ and take the front seats in the synagogues and the places of honor at banquets. ⁴⁰ These are the ones who swallow the property of widows and offer lengthy prayers for the sake of appearance. They will be judged all the more severely."

⁴¹ Jesus sat down opposite the collection box and watched the people putting money in it, and many of the rich put in a great deal. ⁴² A poor widow came and put in two small coins, the equivalent of a penny.

⁴³ Then Jesus called out to the disciples and said to them, "The truth is, this woman has put in more than all who have contributed to the treasury; ⁴⁴ for they have put in money from their surplus, but she has put in everything she possessed from the little she had—all she had to live on."

13

¹ As Jesus was leaving the Temple, one of the disciples commented in passing, "Look, Teacher! What huge stones these are! What wonderful buildings!"

² Jesus replied, "See these great buildings? Not a single stone will be left on another. Everything will be torn down."

³ As Jesus was sitting on the Mount of Olives facing the Temple, Peter, James, John and Andrew asked him privately, ⁴ "Tell us, when will all this happen? What will be the sign that all this is about to take place?"

⁵ Jesus began by saying, "Be on your guard that no one deceives you. ⁶ Many will come in my name saying, 'I am the One,' and they will deceive many. ⁷ When you hear of wars and rumors of war, do not be alarmed. Things like this must happen, but the end is still to come. ⁸ Nation will rise against nation and empire against empire; there will be earthquakes throughout the world and famines—yet this is only the beginning of the labor pains.

9 "Be on your guard. They will hand you over to the courts, and they will flog you in the synagogues. You will stand before governors and rulers because of me, as a witness before them, 10 for the Good News must first be proclaimed to all. 11 Whenever you are arrested and put on trial, do not fret about what you are going to say. Say whatever is given to you at the time, for it will not be you speaking, but the Holy Spirit.

12 "Sisters and brothers will betray each other to the point of death, and parents will betray their children. Children will rebel against parents and have them put to death. 13 You will be hated by all because of my name. Yet the one who perseveres to the end will be saved.

14 "When you see 'the abomination that causes desolation' set up where it should not be"—let the reader understand—"then those in Judea must escape to the mountains. 15 Those on the housetop must not come down into the house to collect their belongings. 16 Those in the fields must not take time to pick up their cloaks. 17 Woe to the pregnant women and the nursing mothers in those days! 18 Pray that this doesn't happen in winter. 19 For the distress at that time will be unequalled from the beginning of time when God created the world, until now and for all time to come. 20 If the Sovereign One were not to shorten those days, no one would be saved. Because of the chosen ones, God has cut short those days.

21 "And if anyone says to you at that time, 'Look, there is the Messiah!' or, 'Look, here is the Messiah!,' don't believe it. 22 For false Messiahs and false prophets will appear, and will work signs and wonders in order to deceive even the chosen, if that were possible. 23 So be on your guard. I have told you everything beforehand.

24 "But in those days, after that time of distress, the sun will be darkened, the moon will lose its brightness, 25 the stars will fall from the sky and the powers in the heavens will be shaken. 26 Then they will see the Promised One coming in the clouds with great power and glory; 27 then the angels will be sent to gather the chosen from the four winds, from the ends of the earth to the ends of heaven.

28 "Take the fig tree as a parable: as soon as its twigs grow supple and its leaves come out, you know that summer is near. 29 In the same way, when you see these things happening, know that the Promised One is near, right at the door. 30 The truth is, before this generation has passed away, all these things will have taken place. 31 Heaven and earth will pass away, but my words will not pass away.

32 "But as for that day or hour, nobody knows it—neither the angels of heaven, nor the Only Begotten—no one but Abba God. 33 Be constantly on the watch! Stay awake! You do not know when the appointed time will come.

34 "It is like people traveling abroad. They leave their home and put the workers in charge, each with a certain task, and those who watch at the front gate are ordered to stay on the alert. 35 So stay alert! You do not know when the owner of the house is coming, whether at dusk, at midnight, when the cock crows or at early dawn. 36 Do not let the owner come suddenly and catch you asleep. 37 What I say to you, I say to all: stay alert!"

14:1–15:47

Passover and the Feast of Unleavened Bread were to be observed in two days' time. The chief priests and religious scholars were looking for some excuse to arrest Jesus and kill him. 2 But they said, "Not during the festival, or the people may riot."

3 While Jesus was in Bethany reclining at table in the house of Simon, who was afflicted with leprosy, a woman entered carrying an alabaster jar of perfume made from expensive aromatic nard. After breaking the jar, she began to pour the perfume on his head.

4 Some said to themselves indignantly, "What is the point of this extravagant waste of perfume? 5 It could have been sold for over three hundred silver pieces, and the money given to those in need!" They were infuriated with her.

6 But Jesus said, "Let her alone. Why do you criticize her? She has done me a kindness. 7 You will always have poor people among you, and you can do them good whenever you want, but you will not always have me. 8 She has done what she could. She has anointed my body and is preparing it for burial. 9 The truth is, wherever the Good News is proclaimed throughout the world, what she has done will be told in her memory."

10 Then Judas Iscariot, one of the Twelve, went off to the chief priests to hand Jesus over to them. 11 Hearing what he had to say, they were jubilant and promised to give him money. Then Judas started looking for an opportune moment to betray Jesus.

12 On the first day of the Feast of Unleavened Bread, when it was customary to sacrifice the paschal lamb, the disciples said to Jesus, "Where do you want us to prepare the Passover supper for you?"

13 He directed two of the disciples and said to them, "Go into the city, and you will come upon a man carrying a water jar. Follow him 14 into a house he enters and say to the owner, 'The Teacher asks, "Where is my guestroom? I want to eat the Passover meal there with my disciples."' 15 Then you will be shown an upstairs room, spacious, furnished, with everything in order. That is the place you are to get ready for us."

16 Then the disciples went off. When they reached the city, they found it just as Jesus had told them, and they prepared the Passover supper.

17 As it grew dark, Jesus arrived with the Twelve. 18 They reclined at table, and in the course of the meal Jesus said, "The truth is, one of you is about to betray me—one who is eating with me."

19 They were very upset at these words, and one by one they said to him, "Surely it's not me!"

20 Jesus replied, "It is one of you Twelve—one who dips into the dish with me. 21 The Chosen One is going the way the scriptures foretell. But woe to the one by whom the Chosen One is betrayed! It were better had that person never been born."

22 During the meal Jesus took bread, blessed and broke it, and gave it to them saying, "Take this and eat. This is my body." 23 He likewise took a cup, gave thanks and passed it to them, and they all drank from it. 24 Jesus said to them, "This is my blood, the blood of the Covenant, which will be poured out on behalf of many. 25 The truth is, I will never again drink of the fruit of the vine until the day I drink it anew in the kindom of God."

26 After singing songs of praise, they walked out to the Mount of Olives.

As they were walking 27 Jesus said to them, "You will all fall away, for scripture says, 'I will strike the shepherd and the sheep will be scattered.' 28 But after I have been raised, I will go to Galilee ahead of you."

29 Peter said to Jesus, "Even though everyone may fall away, I will not."

30 Jesus said to him, "The truth is, this very night before the cock crows twice, you will deny me three times."

31 But Peter said vehemently, "Even if I have to die with you, I will not disown you!" All the other disciples said the same thing.

32 Then they came to a place named Gethsemane. Jesus said to them, "Sit down here while I pray." 33 Jesus took along with him Peter, James and John. Then he began to be very distressed and troubled, 34 and said to them, "My heart is filled with sorrow to the point of death. Stay here and keep watch."

35 Jesus went a little further off and fell to the ground, praying that if it were possible this hour might pass him by. 36 He said, "Abba, you have the power to do all things. Take this cup away from me. But let it be not my will, but your will."

37 When Jesus returned he found them asleep. He said to Peter, "Asleep, Simon? Could you not stay awake for even an hour? 38 Be on guard and pray that you not be put to the test. The spirit is willing, but the flesh is weak."

39 Going back again, Jesus began to pray in the same words. 40 Upon returning Jesus found them asleep once again. They could not keep their eyes open, nor did they know what to say to him.

41 He returned a third time and said, "Still sleeping? Still taking your rest? It will have to do. The hour is upon us—the Chosen One is being handed into the clutches of evildoers. 42 Get up, let's go. Look! Here comes my betrayer."

43 While Jesus was still speaking, Judas, one of the Twelve, came up accompanied by a crowd carrying swords and clubs; they had been sent by the chief priests, the religious scholars and the elders. 44 The betrayer had arranged this signal for them:"Whomever I embrace is the one; arrest him and take him away under guard." 45 Judas went directly to Jesus, embraced him and said, "Rabbi!" 46 At this, they laid hands on Jesus and arrested him.

47 One of the bystanders drew a sword and struck the high priest's attendant, cutting off an ear. 48 Jesus then said, "Why have you come to arrest me with swords and clubs, as though I were a robber? 49 I was within your reach daily, teaching in the Temple precincts, yet you never arrested me. But let the scriptures be fulfilled."

50 With that, all the disciples deserted Jesus and fled. 51 Following Jesus was a youth wearing nothing but a linen cloth, whom they also tried to arrest 52 but who fled naked, leaving the cloth behind.

53 Then they led Jesus off to the high priest, and all the chief priests, elders and religious scholars gathered together. 54 Peter followed at a distance right into the high priest's courtyard, where he found a seat with the Temple guard and began to warm himself at the fire.

55 The chief priests with the whole Sanhedrin were busy soliciting testimony against Jesus that might lead to his death, but they could not find any. 56 Many gave false testimony against Jesus, but their stories did not agree. 57 Some, for instance, on taking the stand, testified falsely by saying, 58 "We heard him declare, 'I will destroy this Temple made by human hands, and in three days I will build another made without hands!'" 59 But even in this, their testimony did not agree.

60 The high priest stood up before the court and began to interrogate Jesus: "Have you no answer to what these people are testifying against you?" 61 But Jesus remained silent and made no reply. Once again the high priest interrogated him: "Are you the Messiah, the Only Begotten of the Blessed One?"

62 Jesus replied, "I am! And you will see the Chosen One seated at the right hand of the Power and coming with the clouds of heaven."

63 At that, the high priest tore his robes and said, "What further need do we have of witnesses? 64 You have heard the blasphemy. What is your verdict?" They all said Jesus was guilty and condemned him to death.

65 Some of them began to spit on Jesus. They blindfolded and hit him, saying, "Prophesy!" The guards beat him too.

66 While Peter was down in the courtyard, one of the attendants of the high priest came along. 67 When she noticed Peter seated near the fire, she looked more closely at him and said, "You too were with Jesus of Nazareth." 68 Peter said, "I don't know what you're talking about! What do you mean?" Then Peter went out into the gateway. At that moment a rooster crowed.

69 The woman, keeping an eye on him, started again to tell the bystanders, "He's one of them." 70 Once again Peter denied it. A little later the bystanders said to him once more, "You are certainly one of them! You're a Galilean, aren't you?" 71 Peter began to curse, and swore, "I don't even know who you're talking about!" 72 The cock crowed a second time. And Peter recalled the prediction Jesus had made: "Before the cock crows twice, you will deny me three times." He rushed away, weeping.

15:1 As soon as it was daybreak the chief priests, the elders and religious scholars and the whole Sanhedrin reached a decision. They bound Jesus and led him away, and handed him over to Pilate, 2 who interrogated him. "Are you the King of the Jews?" he asked.

Jesus responded, "You are the one who is saying it."

3 The chief priests then brought many accusations against him. 4 Pilate interrogated Jesus again: "Surely you have some answer? See how many accusations they are leveling against you!" 5 But to Pilate's astonishment, Jesus made no further response.

6 Now whenever there was a festival, Pilate would release for them one prisoner—anyone they asked for. 7 There was a prisoner named Barabbas who was jailed along with the rioters who had committed murder in the uprising. 8 When the crowd came to ask that Pilate honor the custom, 9 Pilate rejoined, "Do you want me to release for you the King of the Jews?" 10 Pilate was aware, of course, that it was out of jealousy that the chief priests had handed Jesus over. 11 But the chief priests incited the crowd to have him release Barabbas instead. 12 Pilate again asked them, "What am I to do with the one you call the King of the Jews?"

13 The people shouted back, "Crucify him!"

14 "Why?" Pilate asked. "What crime has he committed?" But they shouted all the louder, "Crucify him!"

15 So Pilate, wishing to satisfy the crowd, released Barabbas to them, and, after having Jesus scourged, handed him over to be crucified.

16 The soldiers led Jesus away into the hall known as the Praetorium; then they assembled the whole battalion. 17 They dressed Jesus in royal purple, then wove a crown of thorns and put it on him. 18 They began to salute him: "All hail! King of the Jews!" 19 They kept striking Jesus on the head with a reed, spitting at him and kneeling in front of him pretending to pay homage. 20 When they had finished mocking him,

they stripped him of the purple and dressed him in his own clothes. Then they led him out to be crucified.

²¹ A passerby named Simon of Cyrene, the father of Alexander and Rufus, was coming in from the fields. The soldiers pressed him into service to carry Jesus' cross. ²² Then they brought Jesus to the site of Golgotha—which means "Skull Place."

²³ They tried to give him wine drugged with myrrh, but he would not take it. ²⁴ Then they nailed him to the cross and divided up his garments by rolling dice for them to see what each should take. ²⁵ It was about nine in the morning when they crucified him.

²⁶ The inscription listing the charge read, "The King of the Jews." ²⁷ With Jesus they crucified two robbers, one at his right and one at his left.*

²⁹ People going by insulted Jesus, shaking their heads and saying, "So you were going to destroy the Temple and rebuild it in three days! ³⁰ Save yourself now by coming down from that cross!" ³¹ The chief priests and the religious scholars also joined in and jeered, "He saved others, but he can't save himself! ³² Let 'the Messiah, the King of Israel' come down from that cross right now so that we can see it and believe in him!" Those who had been crucified with him hurled the same insult.

³³ When noon came, darkness fell on the whole countryside and lasted until about three in the afternoon. ³⁴ At three, Jesus cried out in a loud voice, "Eloi, eloi, lama sabachthani?" which means, "My God, My God, why have you forsaken me?" ³⁵ A few of the bystanders who heard it remarked, "Listen! He is calling on Elijah!" ³⁶ Someone ran and soaked a sponge in sour wine and stuck it on a reed to try to make Jesus drink, saying, "Let's see if Elijah comes to take him down."

³⁷ Then Jesus uttered a loud cry and breathed his last. ³⁸ At that moment the curtain in the sanctuary was torn in two from top to bottom. ³⁹ The centurion who stood guard over Jesus, seeing how he died, declared, "Clearly, this was God's Own!"

⁴⁰ There were also some women present looking on from a distance. Among them were Mary of Magdala; Mary, the mother of James the younger and Joses; and Salome. ⁴¹ These women had followed Jesus when he was in Galilee and attended to his needs. There were also many others who had come up with him to Jerusalem.

⁴² As it grew dark—it was Preparation Day, that is, the eve of the Sabbath— ⁴³ a distinguished member of the Sanhedrin, Joseph from Arimathea, arrived. He was waiting for the reign of God, and he gathered up courage and sought an audience with Pilate, and asked for the body of Jesus.

⁴⁴ Pilate was surprised that Jesus should have died so soon. He summoned the centurion and inquired whether Jesus was already dead. ⁴⁵ Upon learning that this was so, Pilate released the body to Joseph. ⁴⁶ Then, having bought a linen shroud, Joseph took the body of Jesus down, wrapped him in the linen and laid him in a tomb which had been cut out of rock. Finally, he rolled a large stone across the entrance of the tomb. ⁴⁷ Meanwhile, Mary of Magdala and Mary, the mother of Joses, were looking on and observed where Jesus had been laid.

When the Sabbath was over, Mary of Magdala, Mary the mother of James, and Salome bought perfumed oils so that they could anoint Jesus. ² Very early, just after sunrise on the first day of the week, they came to the tomb.

³ They were saying to one another, "Who will roll back the stone for us from the entrance to the tomb?" ⁴ When they looked, they found that the huge stone had been rolled back.

⁵ On entering the tomb, they saw a young person sitting at the right, dressed in a white robe. They were very frightened, ⁶ but the youth reassured them: "Do not be amazed! You are looking for Jesus of Nazareth, the One who was crucified. He has risen; he is not here. See the place where they laid him. ⁷ Now go and tell the disciples and Peter, 'Jesus is going ahead of you to Galilee, where you will see him just as he told you.'"

⁸ They made their way out and fled from the tomb bewildered and trembling; but they said nothing to anyone, because they were so afraid.

The gospel ends here.
Two different endings were added
by later writers.

The "Shorter Ending"

⁹ And immediately they reported all these instructions to Peter and his companions. After this, through them, Jesus sent forth the holy and imperishable proclamation of eternal salvation.

The "Longer Ending"

⁹ Jesus rose from the dead early on the first day of the week, appearing first to Mary of Magdala, out of whom the savior had cast seven devils. ¹⁰ She went and reported it to Jesus' companions, who were grieving and weeping. ¹¹ But when they heard that Jesus was alive and had been seen by her, they refused to believe it.

¹² Later on, as two of them were walking along on their way to the country, Jesus appeared to them in a different form. ¹³ These two went back and told the others, who did not believe them either.

¹⁴ Finally, the risen Christ appeared to the Eleven themselves while they were at table, and scolded them for their disbelief and their stubbornness, since they had put no faith in those who had seen Jesus after the resurrection.

¹⁵ Then Jesus told them, "Go into the whole world and proclaim the Good News to all creation.

¹⁶ "The one who believes it and is baptized will be saved; the one who refuses to believe it will be condemned. ¹⁷ Signs such as these will accompany those who have professed their faith: in my name they will expel demons; they will speak in new tongues; ¹⁸ they will be able to handle poisonous snakes; if they drink anything deadly, it will not harm them; and the sick upon whom they lay their hands will recover."

¹⁹ Then, after speaking to them, the savior was taken up into heaven and was seated at God's right hand. ²⁰ The disciples went forth and preached everywhere. Christ worked with them and confirmed their message through the signs which accompanied them.

---

* Some manuscripts add verse 28: "This fulfilled the scripture, 'He let himself be counted among sinners.'"

luke

Many others have undertaken to compile a narrative of the events which have been fulfilled among us, ² exactly as those happenings were passed on to us by the original eyewitnesses and ministers of the Word. ³ I too have investigated everything carefully from the beginning and have decided to set it down in writing for you, noble Theophilus, ⁴ so that you may see how reliable the instruction was that you received.

⁵ In the days of the ruler Herod, there was a priest named Zechariah, of the priestly class of Abijah. His wife Elizabeth was a descendant of Aaron. ⁶ Both were worthy in the sight of God and scrupulously observed all the commandments and observances of our God. ⁷ They were childless—unable to conceive—and they were both advanced in years.

⁸ Now it was the turn of Zechariah's priestly class to serve. And as he was fulfilling his priestly office before God, ⁹ it fell to him by lot, according to priestly usage, to enter the sanctuary of our God and offer incense. ¹⁰ While the full assembly of people was praying outside at the time of day when the incense was offered, ¹¹ an angel of our God appeared to him, standing to the right of the altar of incense. ¹² Zechariah was deeply disturbed upon seeing the angel, and was overcome with fear.

¹³ The angel said to him, "Don't be frightened, Zechariah. Your prayer has been heard. Your wife Elizabeth will bear a son, whom you'll name John. ¹⁴ He will be your joy and delight and many will rejoice at his birth, ¹⁵ for he will be great in the sight of our God. He must never drink wine or liquor, and he will be filled with the Holy Spirit from his mother's womb. ¹⁶ And he will bring many of the children of Israel back to their God Most High. ¹⁷ He will go before God as a forerunner, in the spirit and power of Elijah, to turn the hearts of parents to their children, and the rebellious to the wisdom of the just—to make ready a people prepared for our God."

¹⁸ Zechariah said to the angel, "How can I be sure of this? I am an old man, and my wife too is advanced in age."

¹⁹ The angel replied, "I am Gabriel, who stands before God. I was sent to speak to you and bring you this good news. ²⁰ But because you have not trusted my words, you'll be mute—unable to speak—until the day these things take place. They'll all come true in due season."

²¹ Meanwhile, the people were waiting for Zechariah and wondered about his delay in the sanctuary. ²² When he finally came out he was unable to speak to them, and they realized that he had seen a vision inside. But he could only make signs to them and remained mute. ²³ Then, when his time of priestly service was over, he went home.

²⁴ Some time later, Elizabeth conceived. She went into seclusion for five months, ²⁵ saying, "our God has done this for me. In these days, God has shown favor to us and taken away the disgrace of our having no children."

²⁶ Six months later, the angel Gabriel was sent from God to a town in Galilee called Nazareth, ²⁷ to a young woman named Mary; she was engaged to a man named Joseph, of the house of David. ²⁸ Upon arriving, the angel said to Mary, "Rejoice, highly favored one! God is with you! Blessed are you among women!"

²⁹ Mary was deeply troubled by these words and wondered what the angel's greeting meant. ³⁰ The angel went on to say to her, "Don't be afraid, Mary. You have found favor with God. ³¹ You'll conceive and bear a son, and give him the name Jesus—'Deliverance.' ³² His dignity will be great, and he will be called the Only Begotten of God. God will give Jesus the judgment seat of David, his ancestor, ³³ to rule over the house of Jacob forever, and his reign will never end."

³⁴ Mary said to the angel, "How can this be, since I have never been with a man?"

³⁵ The angel answered her, "The Holy Spirit will come upon you, and the power of the Most High will overshadow you—hence the offspring to be born will be called the Holy One of God. ³⁶ Know too that Elizabeth, your kinswoman, has conceived a child in her old age; she who was thought to be infertile is now in her sixth month. ³⁷ Nothing is impossible with God."

³⁸ Mary said, "I am the servant of God. Let it be done to me as you say."

With that, the angel left her.

³⁹ Within a few days Mary set out and hurried to the hill country to a town of Judah, ⁴⁰ where she entered Zechariah's house and greeted Elizabeth.

⁴¹ As soon as Elizabeth heard Mary's greeting, the child leaped in her womb and Elizabeth was filled with the Holy Spirit. ⁴² In a loud voice she exclaimed, "Blessed are you among women, and blessed is the fruit of your womb! ⁴³ But why am I so favored, that the mother of the Messiah should come to me? ⁴⁴ The moment your greeting reached my ears, the child in my womb leaped for joy. ⁴⁵ Blessed is she who believed that what our God said to her would be accomplished!"

⁴⁶ Mary said:

"My soul proclaims your greatness, O God,
⁴⁷ and my spirit rejoices in you, my Savior.
⁴⁸ For you have looked with favor
upon your lowly servant,
and from this day forward
all generations will call me blessed.
⁴⁹ For you, the Almighty, have done great things for me,
and holy is your Name.
⁵⁰ Your mercy reaches from age to age
for those who fear you.
⁵¹ You have shown strength with your arm;
you have scattered the proud in their conceit;
⁵² you have deposed the mighty from their thrones
and raised the lowly to high places.
⁵³ You have filled the hungry with good things,
while you have sent the rich away empty.
⁵⁴ You have come to the aid of Israel your servant,
mindful of your mercy—
⁵⁵ the promise you made to our ancestors—
to Sarah and Abraham
and their descendants forever."

⁵⁶ Mary stayed with Elizabeth about three months and then returned home.

57 When the time came for Elizabeth to deliver, she gave birth to a son. 58 When her neighbors and relatives heard that God had been merciful to her, they shared her joy. 59 When all had assembled for the circumcision on the eighth day, they intended to name the baby after his father Zechariah. 60 But his mother spoke up, "No, he is to be called John."

61 They pointed out to her, "But no one in your family has this name." 62 Then they made signs to the father to find out what he wanted the child to be named. 63 The father asked for a writing tablet and wrote, "His name is John." They were all astonished.

64 Immediately Zechariah's mouth was opened and his tongue was loosed, and he began to speak in praise of God. 65 Their neighbors were all filled with awe, and throughout the hill country of Judea, people were talking about these events. 66 All who heard the news stored it in their hearts and said, "What will this child turn out to be?" For God's hand was with him.

67 Zechariah, John's father, was filled with the Holy Spirit and prophesied:

68   "Blessed are you, the Most High God of Israel—
     for you have visited and redeemed your people.
69   You have raised up a mighty savior for us
     of the house of David,
70   as you promised through the mouths of your holy ones,
     the prophets of ancient times:
71   salvation from our enemies
     and from the hands of all our foes.
72   You have shown mercy to our ancestors
     by remembering the holy Covenant
     you made with them,
73   the oath you swore to Sarah and Abraham,
74   granting that we,
     delivered from the hands of our enemies,
     might serve you without fear,
75   in holiness and justice,
     in your presence all our days.
76   And you, my child, will be called
     the prophet of the Most High,
     for you'll go before our God
     to prepare the way for the Promised One,
77   giving the people the knowledge of salvation
     through forgiveness of their sins.
78   Such is the tender mercy of our God,
     who from on high
     will bring the Rising Sun to visit us,
79   to give light to those who live
     in darkness and the shadow of death
     and to guide our feet
     into the way of peace."

80 In the meantime, the child grew up and became strong in spirit. He lived out in the desert until the day he appeared openly in Israel.

2 1 In those days, Caesar Augustus published a decree ordering a census of the whole Roman world. 2 This first census took place while Quirinius was governor of Syria. 3 All the people were instructed to go back to the towns of their birth to register. 4 And so Joseph went from the town of Nazareth in Galilee to "the city of David"—Bethlehem, in Judea, because Joseph was of the house and lineage of David; 5 he went to register with Mary, his espoused wife, who was pregnant.

6 While they were there, the time came for her delivery. 7 She gave birth to her firstborn, a son; she put him in a simple cloth wrapped like a receiving blanket, and laid him in a feeding trough for cattle, because there was no room for them at the inn.

8 There were shepherds in the area living in the fields and keeping night watch by turns over their flock. 9 The angel of God appeared to them, and the glory of God shone around them; they were very much afraid.

10 The angel said to them, "You have nothing to fear! I come to proclaim good news to you—news of a great joy to be shared by the whole people. 11 Today in David's city, a savior—the Messiah—has been born to you. 12 Let this be a sign to you: you'll find an infant wrapped in a simple cloth, lying in a manger."

13 Suddenly, there was a multitude of the heavenly host with the angel, praising God and saying,

14 "Glory to God in high heaven!
And on earth, peace to those on whom God's favor rests."

15 When the angels had returned to heaven, the shepherds said to one another, "Let's go straight to Bethlehem and see this event that God has made known to us." 16 They hurried and found Mary and Joseph, and the baby lying in the manger; 17 once they saw this, they reported what they had been told concerning the child. 18 All who heard about it were astonished at the report given by the shepherds.

19 Mary treasured all these things and reflected on them in her heart. 20 The shepherds went away glorifying and praising God for all they had heard and seen, just as they had been told.

21 When the eighth day arrived for the child's circumcision, he was named Jesus, the name the angel had given him before he was conceived.

22 When the day came for them to be purified, as laid down by the Law of Moses, the couple took Jesus up to Jerusalem and presented him to God. 23 For it's written in the Law of our God, "Every firstborn heir is to be consecrated to God." 24 They likewise came to offer in sacrifice "a pair of turtledoves or two young pigeons," in accord with the dictate of the Law of our God.

25 Now there lived in Jerusalem a man named Simeon. He was devout and just, anticipating the consolation of Israel, and he was filled with the Holy Spirit. 26 She had revealed to Simeon that he wouldn't see death until he had seen the Messiah of God. 27 Prompted by her, Simeon came to the Temple; and when the parents brought in the child to perform the customary rituals of the Law, 28 he took the child in his arms and praised God, saying,

29 "Now, O God, you can dismiss your servant in peace,
    just as you promised;
30 because my eyes have seen the salvation
31 which you have prepared for all the peoples to see—
32 a light of revelation to the Gentiles
    and the glory of your people Israel."

33 As the child's mother and father stood there marveling at the things that were being said, 34 Simeon blessed them and said to Mary, the mother, "This child is destined to be the downfall and the rise of many in Israel, and to be a sign that is rejected, 35 so that the secret thoughts of many may be laid bare. And a sword will pierce your heart as well."

36 There was a woman named Anna, the daughter of Phanuel, of the tribe of Asher, who was also a prophet. She had lived a long life, seven years with her husband, 37 and then as a widow to the age of eighty-four. She never left the Temple, worshipping day and night, fasting and praying. 38 Coming up at that moment, she gave thanks to God and talked about the child to all who anticipated the deliverance of Jerusalem.

39 When the couple had fulfilled all the prescriptions of the Law of God, they returned to Galilee and their own town of Nazareth. 40 The child grew in size and strength. He was filled with wisdom, and the grace of God was with him.

41 The parents of Jesus used to go every year to Jerusalem for the feast of Passover, 42 and when Jesus was twelve, they went up for the celebration as was their custom. 43 As they were returning at the end of the feast, the child Jesus remained behind in Jerusalem, unbeknownst to Mary and Joseph. 44 Thinking Jesus was in their caravan, they continued their journey for the day, looking for him among their relatives and acquaintances.

45 Not finding Jesus, they returned to Jerusalem in search of him. 46 On the third day, they came upon Jesus in the Temple, sitting in the midst of the teachers, listening to them and asking them questions. 47 All who heard Jesus were amazed at his understanding and his answers.

48 When Mary and Joseph saw Jesus, they were astonished, and Mary said, "Son, why have you done this to us? You see that your father and I have been so worried, looking for you." 49 Jesus said to them, "Why were you looking for me? Did you not know I had to be in my Abba's house?"

50 But they didn't understand what he told them. 51 Then Jesus went down with them to Nazareth and was obedient to them. Mary stored these things in her heart, 52 and Jesus grew in wisdom, in years and in favor with God and people alike.

3:1–4:13

In the fifteenth year of Tiberius Caesar, Pontius Pilate was governor of Judea, Herod tetrarch of Galilee, Philip his brother tetrarch of the region of Ituraea and Trachonitis, and Lysanias tetrarch of Abilene. 2 In those days, during the high-priesthood of Annas and Caiaphas, the Word of God came to John, ben-Zechariah, in the desert. 3 John went through the entire region of the Jordan proclaiming a baptism of repentance for the forgiveness of sins, 4 as is written in the words of Isaiah, the prophet:

"A herald's voice in the desert, crying,
'Make ready the way of our God;
clear a straight path.
5 Every valley will be filled,
and every mountain and hill will be leveled.
The twisted paths will be made straight,
and the rough road smooth—
6 and all humankind will see the salvation of God.'"

7 John said to the crowds who came out to be baptized by him, "You pack of snakes! Who warned you to escape the wrath to come? 8 Produce good fruit as a sign of your repentance. And don't presume to say to yourselves, 'We have Sarah and Abraham as our mother and father,' for I tell you that God can raise children for Sarah and Abraham from these very stones. 9 The ax is already laid at the root of the tree; every tree that doesn't produce good fruit will be cut down and tossed into the fire."

10 When the people asked him, "What should we do?" 11 John replied, "Let the one with two coats share with the one who has none. Let those who have food do the same."

12 Tax collectors also came to be baptized, and they said to John, "Teacher, what are we to do?" 13 John answered them, "Exact nothing over and above your fixed amount."

14 Soldiers likewise asked, "What about us?" John told them, "Don't bully anyone. Don't accuse anyone falsely. Be content with your pay."

15 The people were full of anticipation, wondering in their hearts whether John might be the Messiah. 16 John answered them all by saying, "I am baptizing you in water, but someone is coming who is mightier than I, whose sandals I am not fit to untie! This One will baptize you in the Holy Spirit and in fire. 17 A winnowing-fan is in his hand to clear the threshing floor and gather the wheat into the granary, but the chaff will be burnt in unquenchable fire." 18 Using exhortations like this, John proclaimed the Good News to the people.

19 But Herod the tetrarch—whom John rebuked for his wickedness, including his relationship with his sister-in-law, Herodias— 20 committed another crime by throwing John into prison.

21 When all the people were baptized, Jesus also came to be baptized. And while Jesus was praying, the skies opened 22 and the Holy Spirit descended on the Anointed One in visible form, like a dove. A voice from heaven said, "You are my Own, my Beloved. On you my favor rests."

23 When Jesus began to teach, he was about thirty years old. He was begot, as it was thought, of Joseph, who was begot of Heli, 24 begot of Matthat, begot of Levi, begot of Melchi, begot of Jannai, begot of Joseph, 25 begot of Mattathias, begot of Amos, begot of Nahum, begot of Esli, begot of Naggai, 26 begot of Maath, begot of Mattathias, begot of Semein, begot of Josech, begot of Joda, 27 begot of Joanan, begot of Rhesa, begot of Zerubbabel, begot of Shealtiel, begot of Neri, 28 begot of Melchi, begot of Addi, begot of Cosam, begot of Elmadam, begot of Er, 29 begot of Joshua, begot of Eliezer, begot of Jorim, begot of Matthat, begot of Levi, 30 begot of Simeon, begot of Judah, begot of Joseph, begot of Jonam, begot of Eliakim, 31 begot of Melea, begot of Menna, begot of Mattatha, begot of Nathan, begot of David, 32 begot of Jesse, begot of Obed, begot of Boaz, begot of Sala, begot of Nahshon, 33 begot of Amminadab, begot of Admin, begot of Arni, begot of Hezron, begot of Perez, begot of Judah, 34 begot of Jacob, begot of Issac, begot of Abraham, begot of Terah, begot of Nahor, 35 begot of Serug, begot of Reu, begot of Peleg, begot of Eber, begot of Shelah, 36 begot of Cainan, begot of Arphaxad, begot of Shem, begot of Noah, begot of Lamech, 37 begot of Methuselah, begot of Enoch, begot of Jared, begot of Mahalaleel, begot of Cainan, 38 begot of Enosh, begot of Seth, begot of Eve and Adam, begot of God.

4 1 Jesus returned from the Jordan filled with the Holy Spirit, and she led him into the desert 2 for forty days, where he was tempted by the Devil. Jesus ate nothing during that time, at the end of which he was famished.

3 The Devil said to Jesus, "If you are God's Own, command this stone to turn into bread." 4 Jesus answered, "Scripture has it, 'We don't live on bread alone.'"

5 Then the Devil took Jesus up higher and showed him all the nations of the world in a single instant. 6 The Devil said, "I'll give you all the power and the glory of these nations; the power has been given to me and I can give it to whomever I wish. 7 Prostrate yourself in homage before me, and it will all be yours."

8 In reply, Jesus said, "Scripture has it:

'You will worship the Most High God;
God alone will you adore.'"

9 Then the Devil led Jesus to Jerusalem, set him up on the parapet of the Temple and said, "If you are God's Own, throw yourself down from here, 10 for scripture has it,

'God will tell the angels to take care of you;
11 with their hands they'll support you,
that you may never stumble on a stone.'"

12 Jesus said to the Devil in reply, "It also says, 'Do not put God to the test.'"

13 When the Devil had finished all this tempting, Jesus was left alone. The Devil awaited another opportunity.

4:14–9:50

Jesus returned in the power of the Spirit to Galilee, and his reputation spread throughout the region. 15 He was teaching in the Galilean synagogues, and all were loud in their praise.

16 Jesus came to Nazareth, where he had been brought up. Entering the synagogue on the Sabbath, as was his habit, Jesus stood up to do the reading. 17 When the book of the prophet Isaiah was handed him, he unrolled the scroll and found the passage where it was written:

18 "The Spirit of our God is upon me:
because the Most High has anointed me
to bring Good News to those who are poor.
God has sent me to proclaim liberty to those held
captive,
recovery of sight to those who are blind,
and release to those in prison—

19 to proclaim the year of our God's favor."

20 Rolling up the scroll, Jesus gave it back to the attendant and sat down. The eyes of all in the synagogue were fixed on him. 21 Then he said to them, "Today, in your hearing, this scripture passage is fulfilled."

22 All who were present spoke favorably of him; they marveled at the eloquence of the words on Jesus' lips. They said, "Surely this isn't Mary and Joseph's son!"

23 Jesus said to them, "Undoubtedly you'll quote me the proverb, 'Physician, heal yourself,' and say, 'Do here in your own country the things we heard you did in Capernaum.' 24 But the truth is, prophets never gain acceptance in their hometowns.

25 "The truth is, there were many women who were widowed in Israel in the days of Elijah, when the heavens remained closed for three and a half years and a great famine spread over the land. 26 It was to none of these that Elijah was sent, but to a woman who had been widowed in Zarephath, near Sidon. 27 Recall, too, that many had leprosy in Israel in the time of Elisha the prophet, yet not one was cured except Naaman the Syrian."

28 At these words, the whole audience in the synagogue was filled with indignation. 29 They rose up and dragged Jesus out of town, leading him to the brow of the hill on which the city was built, with the intention of hurling him over the edge. 30 But he moved straight through the crowd and walked away.

31 Jesus went down to Capernaum, a town in Galilee. He would teach there on the Sabbath. 32 And the teaching made a great impression on them, because he spoke with authority.

33 In the synagogue one day, there was a person possessed by the spirit of an unclean demon, which shouted in a loud voice, 34 "Leave us alone! What do you want with us, Jesus of Nazareth? Have you come to destroy us? I know who you are: the Holy One of God!"

35 But Jesus said sharply, "Be quiet! Come out!" And the demon threw the person down in front of everyone, then went out without doing any harm.

36 Everyone was struck with astonishment, and they said to one another, "What is this teaching? He commands the unclean spirits with authority and power, and they leave!" 37 And reports of him spread throughout the surrounding countryside.

38 On leaving the synagogue, Jesus entered the house of Simon and his family. Simon's mother-in-law was in the grip of a high fever, and they asked him to help her. 39 Jesus stood over her and rebuked the fever, and it left. She got up immediately and went about her work.

40 At sunset, all who had people sick with a variety of diseases brought them to Jesus, and he laid hands on each and cured them. 41 Demons departed from many, crying out as they did so, "You are the Firstborn of God!" Jesus rebuked them and forbade them to speak, for they knew who the Messiah was.

42 The next morning, Jesus left the house and went to a lonely place. The crowds followed and, when they found Jesus, they tried to keep him from leaving them. 43 But Jesus said, "I must proclaim the Good News of God's reign to the other towns too, because that is what I was sent to do." 44 And he continued preaching in the synagogues of Judea.

5 1 One day, Jesus was standing by Lake Gennesaret, and the crowd pressed in on him to hear the word of God. 2 He saw two boats moored by the side of the lake; the fishers had disembarked and were washing their nets. 3 Jesus stepped into one of the boats, the one belonging to Simon, and asked him to pull out a short distance from the shore; then, remaining seated, he continued to teach the crowds from the boat.

4 When he had finished speaking, he said to Simon, "Pull out into deep water and lower your nets for a catch."

5 Simon answered, "Rabbi, we've been working hard all night long and have caught nothing; but if you say so, I'll lower the nets."

6 Upon doing so, they caught such a great number of fish that their nets were at the breaking point. 7 They signaled to their mates in the other boat to come and help them, and together they filled the two boats until they both nearly sank.

8 After Simon saw what happened, he was filled with awe and fell down before Jesus, saying, "Leave me, Rabbi, for I'm a sinner." 9 For Simon and his shipmates were astonished

at the size of the catch they had made, 10 as were James and John, Zebedee's sons, who were Simon's partners.

Jesus said to Simon, "Don't be afraid; from now on you'll fish among humankind." 11 And when they brought their boats to shore, they left everything and followed him.

12 In one town Jesus was in, there was a person with leprosy. Seeing Jesus, the sufferer fell to the ground and implored him, "Teacher, if you are willing, you can heal me."

13 Jesus stretched out his hand, touched the person and said, "I am willing: be cleansed." Immediately the leprosy disappeared.

14 Jesus then gave this stern warning: "Tell no one, but go and show yourself to the priest and make the offering for your healing that Moses prescribed, as a testimony to them."

15 The reputation of Jesus continued to grow. Large crowds gathered to hear him and to be healed of their sicknesses. 16 But Jesus often withdrew to some place where he could be alone and pray.

17 One day, as Jesus was teaching, there were Pharisees and experts on the Law sitting there, who had come from every village of Galilee and from Judea and Jerusalem. And the power of God was present for Jesus to heal the sick.

18 Then some people appeared, carrying a paralyzed person on a mat; they tried to carry the individual into the house, to set in front of Jesus. 19 But the crowd made it impossible to get in, so they went up on the roof, made an opening in the tiles and lowered the paralyzed one into the middle of the gathering, in front of Jesus.

20 Seeing their faith, Jesus said, "My friend, your sins are forgiven you."

21 The religious scholars and the Pharisees began to murmur among themselves, "Who is this person talking blasphemy? Who can forgive sins but God alone?"

22 But Jesus, aware of their thoughts, responded to them and said, "Why do you harbor such thoughts in your hearts? 23 Is it easier to say, 'Your sins are forgiven you,' or to say, 'Get up and walk'? 24 But to prove to you that the Chosen One has authority on earth to forgive sins—" then he turned to the paralyzed person—"I tell you, get up, take up your mat and go home."

25 Immediately the individual stood up in front of them, picked up the mat and went home, praising God. 26 They were all filled with awe and praised God, saying, "We have seen remarkable things today!"

27 When Jesus went out after this, he saw a tax collector named Levi sitting at his tax booth. "Follow me," Jesus said, 28 and Levi got up, left everything and followed him.

29 Levi gave a big reception at his house for Jesus, and there was a large crowd of tax collectors and others at dinner with them. 30 The Pharisees and the religious scholars complained to Jesus' disciples, "Why do you eat and drink with tax collectors and 'sinners'?"

31 Jesus answered them, "It's not the healthy who need a doctor, but the sick. 32 I have come to call not the virtuous, but sinners to repentance."

33 Then they said to him, "John's disciples fast frequently and offer prayers; the disciples of the Pharisees do the same. Yours, on the contrary, go on eating and drinking."

34 Jesus replied, "Can you make the wedding guests fast while the bridal party is still with them? 35 The day will come when the bridal party will be taken from them; then they'll fast."

36 Jesus then told them this parable: "People never tear a piece from a new garment and sew it on an old one. If they do, not only will they have torn the new garment, but the piece taken from the new will not match the old. 37 And people never put new wine in an old wineskin. If they do, the new wine will burst the skin; the wine will spill out and the skin will be ruined. 38 No, new wine must be put into fresh wineskins.

39 "People never want new wine after they've been drinking the old. They say, 'We like the old better.'"

6 1 One Sabbath, Jesus was walking through the grain fields. The disciples were picking heads of grain, rubbing them with their hands and eating them. 2 Some of the Pharisees asked, "Why are you doing what is prohibited on the Sabbath?"

3 Jesus said, "Haven't you read what David did when he and the troops were hungry— 4 how he entered the House of God and took the consecrated bread and ate it and gave the rest to the others, loaves which only the priests are allowed to eat?"

5 Then Jesus said to them, "The Chosen One is ruler over the Sabbath."

6 On a different Sabbath, Jesus came to teach in a synagogue where there was a person with a withered right hand. 7 The religious scholars and Pharisees were looking for a reason to accuse Jesus, so they watched him closely to see if he would heal on the Sabbath.

8 But Jesus knew their thoughts and said to the person with the withered hand, "Get up and stand here in front." So the afflicted one got up and stood in front of everyone. 9 Jesus said to the others, "I ask you, is it lawful on the Sabbath to do good—or evil? To preserve life—or destroy it?" 10 He looked around at them all, then said to the one with the infirmity, "Stretch out your hand." The other did so, and the hand was perfectly restored.

11 At this they were furious and began to discuss with one another what they could do to Jesus.

12 It was about this time that Jesus went out to the mountains to pray, spending the night in communion with God. 13 At daybreak, he summoned the disciples and picked out twelve of them, whom he named as apostles: 14 Simon—to whom he gave the name Peter—and his brother Andrew; James and John; Philip and Bartholomew; 15 Matthew and Thomas; James, ben-Alphaeus, and Simon, who was called the Zealot; 16 Judas ben-James, and Judas Iscariot, who became a traitor.

17 Coming down the mountain with them, Jesus stopped in a level area where there were a great number of disciples. A large crowd of people was with them from Jerusalem and all over Judea, to as far north as the coastal region of Tyre and Sidon— 18 people who had come to hear Jesus and be healed of their diseases, and even to be freed from unclean spirits. 19 Indeed, the whole crowd was trying to touch Jesus, because power was coming out of him and healing them all.

20 Looking at the disciples, Jesus said:

"You who are poor are blessed,
for the reign of God is yours.

²¹ You who hunger now are blessed,
for you'll be filled.
You who weep now are blessed,
for you'll laugh.
²² You are blessed when people hate you,
when they scorn and insult you
and spurn your name as evil
because of the Chosen One.
²³ On the day they do so,
rejoice and be glad:
your reward will be great in heaven,
for their ancestors treated the prophets the same
way.
²⁴ But woe to you rich,
for you are now receiving your comfort in full.
²⁵ Woe to you who are full,
for you'll go hungry.
Woe to you who laugh now,
for you'll weep in your grief.
²⁶ Woe to you when all speak well of you,
for their ancestors treated the false prophets
in the same way.

²⁷ "To you who hear me, I say: love your enemies. Do good to those who hate you, ²⁸ bless those who curse you, and pray for those who mistreat you. ²⁹ When they slap you on one cheek, turn and give them the other; when they take your coat, let them have your shirt as well. ³⁰ Give to all who beg from you. When someone takes what is yours, don't demand it back.

³¹ "Do to others what you would have them do to you. ³² If you love those who love you, what credit does that do you? Even 'sinners' love those who love them. ³³ If you do good only to those who do good to you, what credit does that do you? Even 'sinners' do as much. ³⁴ If you lend to those you expect to repay you, what credit does that do you? Even 'sinners' lend to other 'sinners,' expecting to be repaid in full. ³⁵ Love your enemies and do good to them. Lend without expecting repayment, and your reward will be great. You'll rightly be called children of the Most High, since God is good even to the ungrateful and the wicked.

³⁶ "Be compassionate, as your loving God is compassionate. ³⁷ Don't judge, and you won't be judged. Don't condemn, and you won't be condemned. Pardon, and you'll be pardoned. ³⁸ Give, and it will be given to you: a full measure—packed down, shaken together and running over—will be poured into your lap. For the amount you measure out is the amount you'll be given back."

³⁹ He also told them a parable: "Can a blind person act as guide to another who is blind? Won't they both fall into a ditch? ⁴⁰ "The student is not above the teacher. But all students will, once they are fully trained, be on a par with their teacher.

⁴¹ "How can you look at the splinter in another's eye, yet miss the plank in your own? ⁴² How can you say to another, 'Let me remove the splinter from your eye,' but fail to see the board lodged in your own? Hypocrite, remove the board from your own eye first; then you'll see clearly enough to remove the splinter from the eye of another.

⁴³ "A tree doesn't produce bad fruit any more than a bad tree produces good fruit. ⁴⁴ Each tree is known by its yield. Figs are not taken from thorn bushes, or grapes picked from briars. ⁴⁵ Good people produce goodness from the good they've stored up in their hearts; evil people produce evil from the evil stored up in their hearts. People speak from the fullness of their hearts.

⁴⁶ "Why do you call out, 'Rabbi, Rabbi,' but don't put into practice what I teach you? ⁴⁷ Those who come to me and hear my words and put them into practice—I'll show you who they're like: ⁴⁸ they are like the person who, in building a house, dug deeply and laid the foundation on a rock. When a flood arose, the torrent rushed against the house, but failed to shake it because of its solid foundation. ⁴⁹ On the other hand, anyone who has heard my words, but has not put them into practice, is like the person who built a house on sand, without any foundation. When the torrent rushed upon it, the house immediately collapsed and was completely destroyed."

7 ¹ After having finished this discourse in the hearing of the people, Jesus entered Capernaum. ² A centurion had a favorite attendant who was, at that moment, sick to the point of death. ³ Hearing about Jesus, the centurion sent some Jewish elders to ask him to come and save the attendant's life. ⁴ The elders approached Jesus and petitioned earnestly. "This centurion deserves this favor from you," they said; ⁵ "he loves our nation and was the one who built our synagogue."

⁶ Jesus set out with them. When he was only a short distance from the house, the centurion sent out friends to convey this message: "Rabbi, don't trouble yourself, for I am not worthy to have you enter my house. ⁷ That's why I didn't presume to come to you myself. Just give the order and my attendant will be cured. ⁸ I, too, know the meaning of an order, having soldiers under my command. I give orders, and they obey."

⁹ On hearing this, Jesus was amazed, and turned to the crowd that was following and said, "I tell you, I've never found this much faith among the Israelites."

¹⁰ When the messengers returned to the house, they found the attendant in perfect health.

¹¹ Soon afterward, Jesus went to a town called Nain, and the disciples and a large crowd accompanied him. ¹² As Jesus approached the gate of the town, a dead body was being carried out—the only son of a widowed mother. A considerable crowd of townspeople were with her.

¹³ Jesus was moved with pity upon seeing her and said, "Don't cry." ¹⁴ Then Jesus stepped forward and touched the coffin; at this, the bearers halted. Jesus said, "Young man, get up."

¹⁵ The dead youth sat up and began to speak, and Jesus gave him back to his mother.

¹⁶ Fear seized them all, and they began to praise God. "A great prophet has risen among us," they said, and, "God has truly visited us." ¹⁷ This was the report that spread about Jesus throughout Judea and the surrounding country.

¹⁸ John's disciples reported these things to him. John summoned two of them ¹⁹ and sent them to Jesus with the question, "Are you the One who is to come, or must we wait for someone else?"

²⁰ When the couriers came to Jesus, they said, "John the Baptizer has sent us to you to ask, 'Are you the One who is to come, or must we wait for someone else?'"

²¹ Immediately Jesus went and healed many people of diseases, sicknesses and evil spirits, and gave sight to many who were blind. ²² Then he gave the couriers this answer: "Go and report to John what you have seen and heard. Those who are blind recover their sight, those who are crippled walk, those with leprosy are cured, those who are deaf hear, the dead are raised to life, and those who are poor have the Good News preached to them. ²³ Happy is the one who doesn't lose faith in me."

²⁴ When John's messengers had left, Jesus began to talk about John to the crowds: "What did you go out into the wilderness to see? A reed swaying in the breeze? ²⁵ What, really, did you go out to see? Someone dressed in fine clothes? No—those who dress in fine clothes and live luxuriously are to be found in mansions. ²⁶ But what did you go out to see? A prophet? Yes, I tell you, and much more than a prophet.

²⁷ "This is the one about whom scripture says, 'I send my messenger ahead of you, to prepare your way before you.' ²⁸ I tell you, there is no one born of woman who is greater than John. But the least in the kindom of God is greater than he is."

²⁹ All the people who heard him, even tax collectors, acknowledged God's goodness, because they had received baptism from John. ³⁰ The Pharisees and the experts on the Law, on the other hand, thwarted God's plan for themselves because they had refused John's baptism.

³¹ Jesus continued, "To what can I compare the people of this generation? What are they like? ³² They are like children sitting in the marketplace and calling out to one another, 'We piped you a tune but you wouldn't dance, we sang you a dirge but you wouldn't weep.' ³³ What I mean is that John the Baptizer came neither eating bread nor drinking wine, and you said, 'He is demon-possessed!' ³⁴ The Chosen One came and both ate and drank, and you say, 'Here is a glutton and a drunkard, a friend of tax collectors and sinners!' ³⁵ Wisdom, however, is vindicated by all her children."

³⁶ One of the Pharisees invited Jesus to dinner. Jesus went to his house and reclined at table. ³⁷ A woman who had a low reputation in that town came to the house. She had learned that Jesus was dining with the Pharisee, so she brought with her an alabaster jar of perfumed oil. ³⁸ She stood behind Jesus, crying, and her tears fell on his feet. Then she dried his feet with her hair, kissed them, and anointed them with the oil.

³⁹ When the Pharisee saw this, he said to himself, "If this fellow were the Prophet, he'd know who this woman is that is touching him, and what a low reputation she has."

⁴⁰ In answer to the Pharisee's thoughts Jesus said, "Simon, I have something to tell you."

"Tell me, Teacher," he said.

⁴¹ "Two people owed money to a creditor. One owed the creditor the equivalent of two years' wages; the other, two months' wages. ⁴² Both were unable to pay, so the creditor wrote off both debts. Which of them was more grateful to the moneylender?"

⁴³ Simon answered, "I suppose the one who owed more." Jesus said, "You are right."

⁴⁴ Turning to the woman, he said to Simon, "See this woman? I came into your house and you gave me no water to wash my feet, but she has washed them with her tears and dried them with her hair. ⁴⁵ You gave me no kiss of greeting, but she covered my feet with kisses. ⁴⁶ You didn't anoint my head with oil, but she anointed my feet with oil. ⁴⁷ For this reason, I tell you, her sins, which are many, have been forgiven—see how much she loves! But the one who is forgiven little, loves little."

⁴⁸ Then Jesus said to the woman, "Your sins are forgiven."

⁴⁹ Those also sitting at the table began to ask among themselves, "Who is this who even forgives sins?"

⁵⁰ Meanwhile Jesus said to her, "Your faith has saved you. Go in peace."

8:1 Now soon after this, Jesus journeyed through the towns and villages proclaiming the Good News of God's reign. With Jesus went the Twelve, ² as well as some women he had healed of evil spirits and sicknesses; Mary of Magdala, from whom he had cast out seven demons; ³ Joanna, the wife of Herod's steward Chuza; Suzanna; and many others who were contributing to the support of Jesus and the Twelve with their own funds.

⁴ With a large crowd gathering, and people from every town finding their way to him, Jesus used this parable: ⁵ "A farmer went out to sow some seed. In the sowing, some seed fell on the footpath where it was walked on, and the birds of the air ate it up. ⁶ Some fell on rocky ground, sprouted up, then withered through lack of moisture. ⁷ Some fell among thorns, and the thorns growing up with it stifled it. ⁸ But some seed fell on good ground, grew up and yielded grain a hundredfold."

Whenever Jesus would say something like this, he would exclaim, "Whoever has ears to hear, hear this!"

⁹ The disciples began asking Jesus what the meaning of this parable might be.

¹⁰ He replied, "To you the mysteries of the kindom of God have been confided, but the rest have only parables—so that 'they may look but never see, listen but never understand.'

¹¹ "This is the meaning of the parable. The seed is the word of God. ¹² Those on the footpath are people who hear, but the Devil comes and takes the word out of their hearts, lest they believe and be saved. ¹³ Those on the rocky ground are the ones who, when they hear the word, receive it with joy. But they have no roots; they believe for a while, but fall away in time of testing. ¹⁴ The seed that fell among thorns are those who hear, but their progress is choked by the cares, riches and pleasures of life, so they don't mature and produce fruit. ¹⁵ The seed on good ground are those who hear the word in a spirit of openness, hold it close, and bear fruit through perseverance.

¹⁶ "People never light a lamp only to put it under a basket or under a bed; they put it on a lampstand so that whoever comes in may see the light. ¹⁷ There is nothing hidden that will not be exposed, nothing concealed that will not be known and brought to light. ¹⁸ Take care, therefore, how you listen: to those who have, more will be given; those without will lose even the little bit they thought they had."

¹⁹ Now Jesus' mother and kin came to see him, but they couldn't get near him because of the crowd. ²⁰ Someone told Jesus, "Your mother and kin are outside, waiting to see you."

²¹ Jesus replied, "My mother and my kin are those who hear the word of God and put it into practice."

²² One day Jesus boarded a boat with the disciples and said, "Let's cross to the other side of the lake." So they cast off. ²³ As they were sailing, Jesus took a nap.

Soon a squall came down on the lake, and they began to take on water to a dangerous degree. ²⁴ They woke him and said, "Rabbi, Rabbi! We're sinking!"

Jesus got up, and reprimanded the wind and the waves. Immediately the storm subsided and all was calm again. ²⁵ "Where is your faith?" he asked them.

But they were both afraid and amazed, and they said to one another, "Who is this, who gives orders to the wind and the waves, and they obey him?"

²⁶ They came to the region of the Gerasenes, which is opposite Galilee. ²⁷ Jesus was stepping from the boat when he was met by a person from the town who was possessed by demons. The demoniac had not worn clothes for a long time, and was homeless, living among the tombs instead.

²⁸ Seeing Jesus, the individual cried out and fell at his feet, shouting loudly, "What do you want with me, Jesus, Only Begotten of the Most High God? I beg you, don't torture me!" ²⁹ —for Jesus was ordering the unclean spirit to come out of the person. This spirit had seized the demoniac many times in the past, who then needed to be restrained with chains and shackles and kept under guard—yet every time, the possessed person would break the bonds and be driven by the demon into deserted places.

³⁰ "What is your name?" Jesus asked.

"Legion," it replied, because many demons had entered the person. ³¹ And they pleaded with Jesus not to order them to depart into the abyss.

³² A large herd of pigs was feeding nearby on the hillside. The demons pleaded with Jesus to allow them to enter the swine, and he gave them permission. ³³ The demons left the person and entered the pigs, and the herd rushed down the hillside into the lake and drowned.

³⁴ When the swineherds saw what had happened, they ran away to tell the story in town and throughout the countryside. ³⁵ The local residents came out to see what happened. And as they approached Jesus, they also saw the exorcised person sitting at Jesus' feet, clothed and of a right mind. And they were afraid. ³⁶ Those who had witnessed it told the others how the possessed one had been made whole. ³⁷ Panic overcame the whole population of the region of the Gerasenes, and they asked Jesus to leave them.

When Jesus had gotten into the boat to leave,³⁸ the person who had been healed asked to go with him. But Jesus said, "No, ³⁹ go back home and tell everyone what God has done for you." So the one who had been made whole went off and proclaimed throughout the region what Jesus had accomplished.

⁴⁰ When Jesus returned, a crowd of people was waiting for him and welcomed him. ⁴¹ A man named Jairus, an official of the synagogue, stepped forward and fell at Jesus' feet. He begged Jesus to come to his house, ⁴² for his only daughter—who was twelve years old—was dying.

As Jesus moved along, the crowd almost crushed him. ⁴³ In the crowd was a woman who had suffered from hemorrhages for twelve years, and had found no one who could heal her. ⁴⁴ She came up behind Jesus and touched the fringe of his cloak, and immediately the bleeding stopped.

⁴⁵ "Who touched me?" Jesus asked.

When no one nearby responded, Peter said, "Rabbi, it's the crowd pressing around you."

⁴⁶ But Jesus said, "Someone touched me. I felt power leave me."

⁴⁷ When the woman realized that she had been noticed, she approached in fear and knelt before him. She explained in front of the crowd why she had touched him and how she had been instantly healed.

⁴⁸ Jesus said to her, "Daughter, your faith has healed you. Go in peace."

⁴⁹ While Jesus was still talking, someone from the house of Jairus, the synagogue official, arrived and said, "Your daughter died. Don't trouble the Teacher anymore."

⁵⁰ But when Jesus heard this, he said to the messenger, "Don't be afraid. Have faith, and she will be made well."

⁵¹ When he arrived at the house, Jesus ordered no one to enter with him except Peter, John, James and the girl's parents. ⁵² Everyone was weeping and wailing for the child, but Jesus said, "Stop crying. She is not dead, just sleeping." ⁵³ But they ridiculed him, for they knew she was dead.

⁵⁴ Jesus took her hand and said softly, "Get up, child." ⁵⁵ Her breath returned to her and she got up immediately. And he told them to give her something to eat. ⁵⁶ The parents were astonished, but he ordered them to tell no one what had happened.

9 ¹ Jesus called the Twelve together and gave them power and authority to overcome all demons and to cure diseases. ² He sent them forth to proclaim the kindom of God and to heal the afflicted.

³ Jesus told them, "Take nothing for the journey, neither walking staff, nor travelling bag, nor bread, nor money. Don't even take a change of clothes. ⁴ Stay at whatever house you enter, and proceed from there. ⁵ As for those who don't receive you, leave that town and shake its dust from your feet as a testimony against them."

⁶ So they set out and went from village to village, spreading the Good News everywhere and healing people.

⁷ Now Herod the tetrarch heard of all that Jesus was doing, and was perplexed, for some were saying, "John has been raised from the dead"; ⁸ others, "Elijah has appeared"; and still others, "One of the prophets of old has risen."

⁹ But Herod said, "I myself had John beheaded. Who is this about whom I hear all these reports?" And Herod kept trying to see Jesus.

¹⁰ When the apostles returned, they reported to Jesus what they had done. Taking them with him, he retreated to the town of Bethsaida where they could be by themselves. ¹¹ But when the crowd found out, they followed him. Jesus welcomed the crowd and spoke to them about the reign of God, and healed all who were in need of healing.

¹² As sunset approached, the Twelve came and said to Jesus, "Dismiss the crowd, so they can go into the surrounding villages and countryside and find lodging and food, for this is a remote and isolated area."

¹³ Jesus answered them, "Give them something to eat yourselves!" The disciples replied, "We have nothing but five loaves and two fish. Or do you want us to go and buy food for all these people?" ¹⁴ There were about five thousand gathered.

Jesus said to the disciples, "Have them sit down in groups of fifty or so." ¹⁵ They did so and got them all seated. ¹⁶ Then, taking the five loaves and two fishes, Jesus raised his eyes to heaven, said a blessing over them, broke them and gave them to the disciples for distribution to the crowd.

¹⁷ They all ate until they were satisfied and, when the leftovers were collected, there were twelve baskets full.

¹⁸ One day when Jesus was praying in seclusion and the disciples were with him, he put the question to them, "Who do the crowds say that I am?"

¹⁹ "John the Baptizer," they replied, "and some say Elijah, while others claim that one of the prophets of old has returned from the dead."

²⁰ "But you—who do you say that I am?" Jesus asked them. Peter replied, "God's Messiah."

²¹ Jesus strictly forbade them to tell this to anyone.

²² "The Chosen One," Jesus said, "must suffer grievously, be rejected by the elders, the chief priests, and the religious scholars, be put to death, and then be raised up on the third day."

²³ Then Jesus said to all of them, "You who wish to be my followers must deny your very self, take up your cross—the instrument of your own death—every day, and follow in my steps. ²⁴ If you would save your life, you'll lose it, and if you would lose your life for my sake, you'll save it. ²⁵ What profit is there in gaining the whole world if you lose or forfeit yourselves in the process?

²⁶ "Those who are ashamed of me and of my words, of them will the Chosen One be ashamed in that coming, in the glory of Abba God and of the holy angels. ²⁷ The truth is, there are some standing here right now who will not taste death before they see the kindom of God."

²⁸ About eight days after saying this, Jesus took Peter, John and James and went up onto a mountain to pray. ²⁹ While Jesus was praying, his face changed in appearance and the clothes he wore became dazzlingly white. ³⁰ Suddenly two people were there talking with Jesus—Moses and Elijah. ³¹ They appeared in glory and spoke of the prophecy that Jesus was about to fulfill in Jerusalem.

³² Peter and the others had already fallen into a deep sleep, but awakening, they saw Jesus' glory—and the two people who were standing next to him. ³³ When the two were leaving, Peter said to Jesus, "Rabbi, how good it is for us to be here! Let's set up three tents, one for you, one for Moses and one for Elijah!" Peter didn't really know what he was saying.

³⁴ While Peter was speaking, a cloud came and overshadowed them, and the disciples grew fearful as the others entered it. ³⁵ Then from the cloud came a voice which said, "This is my Own, my Chosen One. Listen to him!" ³⁶ When the voice finished speaking, they saw no one but Jesus standing there. The disciples kept quiet, telling nothing of what they had seen at that time to anyone.

³⁷ The following day, when they came down the mountain, a large crowd awaited him. ³⁸ A man stepped out of the crowd and said, "Teacher, please come and look at my son, my only child. ³⁹ A demon seizes him and he screams, and it throws him into convulsions until he foams at the mouth. It releases the boy only with difficulty, and when it does, he is exhausted. ⁴⁰ I begged your disciples to cast it out, but they couldn't."

⁴¹ Jesus said in reply, "You unbelieving and perverse generation! How much longer must I be among you and put up with you? Bring the child to me." ⁴² As the boy approached, the demon dashed the child to the ground and threw him into a violent convulsion. But Jesus reprimanded the unclean spirit, healed the child and returned him to his father. ⁴³ All present were awestruck at the greatness of God.

In the midst of all the crowd's amazement at these things, Jesus said to the disciples, ⁴⁴ "Let these words sink in: the Chosen One must be delivered into the hands of others." ⁴⁵ But they failed to understand this statement; its meaning was so concealed from them that they didn't grasp it at all, and they were afraid to question Jesus about the matter.

⁴⁶ A dispute arose among the disciples as to which of them was the greatest.

⁴⁷ Jesus, who knew their thoughts, took a little child and had it stand next to him. ⁴⁸ Then he said to them, "Whoever welcomes this child in my name welcomes me. And anyone who welcomes me, welcomes the One who sent me. For the lowliest among you is the greatest."

⁴⁹ John said, "Rabbi, we saw someone casting out devils in your name, and—because the individual doesn't follow along with us—we tried to put a halt to it."

⁵⁰ Jesus replied, "Don't stop it, for anyone who is not against you is for you."

9:51–19:27

As the time approached when he was to be taken from this world, Jesus firmly resolved to proceed toward Jerusalem ⁵² and sent messengers on ahead. They entered a Samaritan town to make preparations for him, ⁵³ but the Samaritans wouldn't welcome Jesus because his destination was Jerusalem.

⁵⁴ When the disciples James and John saw this, they said, "Rabbi, do you want us to call down fire from heaven and destroy them?" ⁵⁵ But Jesus turned and reprimanded them.* ⁵⁶ Then they set off for another town.

⁵⁷ As they were making their way along, they met a fellow traveler who said to Jesus, "I'll follow you wherever you go."

⁵⁸ Jesus replied, "Foxes have lairs, the birds of the sky have nests, but the Chosen One has nowhere to rest."

⁵⁹ To another traveler Jesus said, "Follow me."

The traveler replied, "Let me bury my father first."

⁶⁰ Jesus said in return, "Let the dead bury their dead; you go and proclaim the reign of God everywhere."

⁶¹ Yet another traveler approached Jesus in this way: "I'll be your follower, Rabbi, but first let me say goodbye to my people at home."

⁶² Jesus answered, "Whoever puts a hand to the plow but keeps looking back is unfit for the reign of God."

10 ⁱ After this, Jesus appointed seventy-two others, and sent them on ahead in pairs to every town and place he intended to visit. ² He said to them, "The harvest is rich, but the workers are few; therefore, ask the overseer to send workers to the harvest.

³ "Be on your way, and remember: I am sending you as lambs in the midst of wolves. ⁴ Don't carry a walking stick or knapsack; wear no sandals and greet no one along the way. ⁵ And whatever house you enter, first say, 'Peace be upon this house!' ⁶ If the people live peaceably there, your peace will rest on them; if not, it will come back to you. ⁷ Stay in that house, eating and drinking what they give you, for the laborer is worth a wage. Don't keep moving from house to house.

⁸ "And whatever city you enter, after they welcome you, eat what they set before you ⁹ and heal those who are sick in that town. Say to them, 'The reign of God has drawn near to you.' ¹⁰ If the people of any town you enter don't welcome you, go into its streets and say, ¹¹ 'We shake the dust of this town from our feet as testimony against you. But know that the reign of God has drawn near.' ¹² I tell you, on that day the fate of Sodom will be less severe than that of such a town.

¹³ "Woe to you, Chorazin! And woe to you, Bethsaida! If the miracles worked in your midst had occurred in Tyre and Sidon, they would long ago have repented in sackcloth and ashes! ¹⁴ It will go easier on the day of judgment for Tyre and Sidon than for you. ¹⁵ And as for you, Capernaum, will

---

* Later manuscripts read: ". . . them: 'You don't know what kind of spirit this is coming from. The Chosen One came not to destroy people's lives, but to save them.' Then they . . . "

you exalt yourself to the skies? No, you'll be hurled down to Hades!

¹⁶ "Anyone who listens to you, listens to me. Anyone who rejects you, rejects me; and those who reject me, reject the One who sent me."

¹⁷ The seventy-two disciples returned with joy, saying, "Rabbi, even the demons obey us in your name!"

¹⁸ Jesus replied, "I watched Satan fall from the sky like lightning. ¹⁹ Look: I've given you the power to tread on snakes and scorpions—even all the forces of the enemy—and nothing will ever injure you. ²⁰ Nevertheless, don't rejoice in the fact that the spirits obey you so much as that your names are inscribed in heaven."

²¹ At that moment Jesus rejoiced in the Holy Spirit and said, "I offer you praise, Abba, ruler of heaven and earth, because what you have hidden from the learned and the clever you have revealed to mere children. Yes, Abba, you have graciously willed it so. ²² Everything has been entrusted to me by you. No one knows me except through you, and no one knows you except through me—and those to whom I choose to reveal you."

²³ Turning to the disciples, Jesus spoke to them privately: "Blessed are the eyes that see what you see. ²⁴ For I tell you, many prophets and rulers wanted to see what you see but never saw it, to hear what you hear but never heard it."

²⁵ An expert on the Law stood up to put Jesus to the test and said, "Teacher, what must I do to inherit everlasting life?"

²⁶ Jesus answered, "What is written in the law? How do you read it?"

²⁷ The expert on the Law replied:

"You must love the Most High God
with all your heart,
with all your soul,
with all your strength
and with all your mind,
and your neighbor as yourself."

²⁸ Jesus said, "You have answered correctly. Do this and you'll live."

²⁹ But the expert on the Law, seeking self-justification, pressed Jesus further: "And just who is my neighbor?"

³⁰ Jesus replied, "There was a traveler going down from Jerusalem to Jericho, who fell prey to robbers. The traveler was beaten, stripped naked, and left half-dead. ³¹ A priest happened to be going down the same road; the priest saw the traveler lying beside the road, but passed by on the other side. ³² Likewise there was a Levite who came the same way; this one, too, saw the afflicted traveler and passed by on the other side.

³³ "But a Samaritan, who was taking the same road, also came upon the traveler and, filled with compassion, ³⁴ approached the traveler and dressed the wounds, pouring on oil and wine. Then the Samaritan put the wounded person on a donkey, went straight to an inn and there took care of the injured one. ³⁵ The next day the Samaritan took out two silver pieces and gave them to the innkeeper with the request, 'Look after this person, and if there is any further expense, I'll repay you on the way back.'

³⁶ "Which of these three, in your opinion, was the neighbor to the traveler who fell in with the robbers?"

³⁷ The answer came, "The one who showed compassion." Jesus replied, "Then go and do the same."

³⁸ As they traveled, Jesus entered a village where a woman named Martha welcomed him to her home. ³⁹ She had a sister named Mary, who seated herself at Jesus' feet and listened to his words.

⁴⁰ Martha, who was busy with all the details of hospitality, came to Jesus and said, "Rabbi, don't you care that my sister has left me all alone to do the household tasks? Tell her to help me!"

⁴¹ Jesus replied, "Martha, Martha! You're anxious and upset about so many things, ⁴² but only a few things are necessary—really only one. Mary has chosen the better part, and she won't be deprived of it."

11 ¹ One day Jesus was praying, and when he had finished, one of the disciples asked, "Rabbi, teach us to pray, just as John taught his disciples."

² Jesus said to them, "When you pray, say,

'Abba God,
hallowed be your Name!
May your reign come.
³ Give us today
Tomorrow's bread.
⁴ Forgive us our sins,
for we too forgive everyone who sins against us;
and don't let us be subjected to the Test.'"

⁵ Jesus said to them, "Suppose one of you has a friend, a neighbor, and you go to your neighbor at midnight and say, 'Lend me three loaves of bread, ⁶ because friends of mine on a journey have come to me, and I have nothing to set before them.'

⁷ "Then your neighbor says, 'Leave me alone. The door is already locked and the children and I are in bed. I can't get up to look after your needs.' ⁸ I tell you, though your neighbor will not get up to give you the bread out of friendship, your persistence will make your neighbor get up and give you as much as you need.

⁹ "That's why I tell you, keep asking and you'll receive; keep looking and you'll find; keep knocking and the door will be opened to you. ¹⁰ For whoever asks, receives; whoever seeks, finds; whoever knocks, is admitted. ¹¹ What parents among you will give a snake to their child when the child asks for a fish, ¹² or a scorpion when the child asks for an egg? ¹³ If you, with all your sins, know how to give your children good things, how much more will our heavenly Abba give the Holy Spirit to those who ask?"

¹⁴ Jesus was casting out a demon that made its host unable to talk. When the demon left, the mute person spoke, to the crowd's amazement. ¹⁵ Some said, "It's by Beelzebul, the prince of demons, that he casts out demons." ¹⁶ Still others, to test Jesus, were demanding a sign from heaven.

¹⁷ Jesus knew what they were really thinking and said to them, "Every nation divided against itself will be ruined, and a house divided against itself will fall. ¹⁸ If the realm of Satan is divided against itself, how can it stand?—since you say it's by Beelzebul that I cast out demons. ¹⁹ If I cast out demons by Beelzebul, by whom do your people cast them out? In that case, let them act as your judges. ²⁰ But if it is by

the finger of God that I cast out demons, then the reign of God has come upon you.

²¹ "When strong, fully armed guards protect the courtyard, its possessions go undisturbed. ²² But when a stronger force comes and overpowers the guards, the victors carry off and divide the spoils.

²³ "Those who are not with me are against me, and those who don't gather with me, scatter.

²⁴ "When an unclean spirit has gone out of a person, it wanders through arid wastes, searching for a resting place; failing to find one, it says, 'I'll go back to where I came from.' ²⁵ It then returns, to find the house swept and tidied. ²⁶ Next it goes out and returns with seven other spirits far worse than itself, who enter in and dwell there—with the result that the person is then far worse off than at the outset."

²⁷ While Jesus was speaking, a woman from the crowd called out, "Blessed is the womb that bore you and the breasts that nursed you!"

²⁸ "Rather," Jesus replied, "blessed are those who hear the word of God and obey it!"

²⁹ When the crowds pressed around Jesus, he began to speak to them in these words: "This is a wicked generation! It asks for a sign, but none will be given except the sign of Jonah. ³⁰ For just as Jonah was a sign for the Ninevites, so will the Promised One be a sign for this generation. ³¹ Sheba, the ruler of the South, will rise at the Judgment along with the members of this generation, and she will condemn them. For she came from the ends of the earth to listen to Solomon's wisdom, but now One greater than Solomon is here. ³² The people of Nineveh will stand up at the Judgment with this generation and condemn it. For they repented at the preaching of Jonah, and now One greater than Jonah is here.

³³ "You don't light a lamp only to hide it in the cellar or to put it under a bucket. You put it on a stand where people see it when they come in.

³⁴ "The lamp of your body is your eye. If your eye is sound, the whole body is filled with light. But if your eye is diseased, your body is filled with darkness. ³⁵ See to it then that the light in you doesn't fade into darkness. ³⁶ If your whole body is full of light, however, with no darkness in it, it will be completely lit—the way it is when the light of a lantern shines on you."

³⁷ After Jesus finished talking, a Pharisee invited him home to dine. Jesus entered and reclined at the table for the meal. ³⁸ Seeing this, the Pharisee was surprised that Jesus had not performed the ritual washings prescribed before eating.

³⁹ Jesus said, "You Pharisees! You cleanse the outside of cup and dish, but within, you are filled with thievery and wickedness. ⁴⁰ Fools! Didn't the One who made the outside make the inside too? ⁴¹ But if you give to those poorer than you, all things will be clean for you.

⁴² "Woe to you Pharisees! You pay tithes on mint, rue and all the garden plants, while neglecting justice and the love of God. These are the things you should practice, without omitting the others.

⁴³ "Woe to you Pharisees! You love the front seats in synagogues and the marks of respect in public.

⁴⁴ "Woe to you! You are like hidden tombs over which people walk unaware."

⁴⁵ In reply, one of the experts in the Law said, "Teacher, in speaking this way you insult us too."

⁴⁶ Jesus replied, "Woe to you lawyers as well! You lay impossible burdens on the people, but won't lift a finger to lighten them.

⁴⁷ "Woe to you! You build monuments to the prophets, but it was your ancestors who murdered them. ⁴⁸ You show that you stand behind the deeds of your ancestors: they did the murdering and you build the monuments! ⁴⁹ That's why the wisdom of God has said, 'I'll send them prophets and apostles, some of whom they'll persecute and others they'll kill, ⁵⁰ so that this generation will have to account for the blood of all the prophets shed since the foundation of the world.' ⁵¹ Their guilt stretches from the blood of Abel to the blood of Zechariah, who met his death between the altar and the sanctuary! Yes, I tell you, this generation will have to account for it.

⁵² "Woe to you experts on the Law! You have taken away the key to knowledge. And not only haven't you gained access, you have stopped others who were trying to enter!"

⁵³ When Jesus was leaving this gathering, the religious scholars and Pharisees began to be extremely hostile to him and question him closely on a multitude of subjects, ⁵⁴ setting traps to catch Jesus with something he might say.

12 ¹ Meanwhile thousands of people had gathered, a crowd so dense that they were trampling each other. Jesus spoke first to the disciples:

"Be on your guard against the yeast of the Pharisees, which is hypocrisy.

² "There is nothing concealed that will not be revealed, nothing hidden that will not be made known. ³ Everything you have said in the dark will be heard in the daylight; what you have whispered in locked rooms will be proclaimed from the rooftops.

⁴ "I tell you, my friends: don't be afraid of those who kill the body and then can do no more. ⁵ I'll tell you whom you ought to fear: fear the one who has the power to kill you and then cast you into Gehenna. Yes, I tell you, this is the one to fear. ⁶ Aren't five sparrows sold for a few pennies? Yet not one of them is neglected by God. ⁷ In fact, even the hairs on your head are counted! Don't be afraid: you are worth more than a whole flock of sparrows.

⁸ "I tell you, if you acknowledge me in front of other people, the Chosen One will acknowledge you before the angels of God. ⁹ But those who disown me in the presence of mortals will be disowned in the presence of the angels of God.

¹⁰ "Those who speak against the Chosen One will be forgiven, but those who blaspheme the Holy Spirit will never be forgiven.

¹¹ "When they bring you before synagogues, rulers and authorities, don't worry about how to defend yourselves or what to say. ¹² The Holy Spirit will teach you at that moment all that should be said."

¹³ Someone in the crowd said to Jesus, "Teacher, tell my brother to give me my share of our inheritance."

¹⁴ Jesus replied, "Friend, who has set me up as your judge or arbiter?" ¹⁵ Then he told the crowd, "Avoid greed in all its forms. Your life isn't made more secure by what you own—even when you have more than you need."

¹⁶ Jesus then told them a parable in these words: "There was a rich farmer who had a good harvest.

¹⁷ "'What will I do?' the farmer mused. 'I have no place to store my harvest. ¹⁸ I know! I'll pull down my grain bins and build larger ones. All my grain and goods will go there. ¹⁹ Then I'll say to myself: You have blessings in reserve for many years to come. Relax! Eat, drink and be merry!'

²⁰ "But God said to the farmer, 'You fool! This very night your life will be required of you. To whom will all your accumulated wealth go?'

²¹ "This is the way it works with people who accumulate riches for themselves, but are not rich in God."

²² Then he said to the disciples, "That's why I tell you, don't worry about your life and what you are to eat. Don't worry about your body and what you are to wear. ²³ For life is more than food, and the body is more than clothing. ²⁴ Take a lesson from the ravens. They don't sow or reap. They have neither a food cellar nor a barn, yet God feeds them. And how much more valuable are you than birds? ²⁵ Can any of you, for all your worrying, add a single hour to your life? ²⁶ If even the smallest things are beyond your control, why worry about all the rest?

²⁷ "Notice how the flowers grow. They neither labor nor weave, yet I tell you, not even Solomon in all his splendor was robed like one of these! ²⁸ If that is how God clothes the grass in the field—which is here today and thrown into the fire tomorrow—how much more will God look after you! You have so little faith!

²⁹ "As for you, don't set your hearts on what you'll eat or what you'll drink. Stop worrying! ³⁰ All the nations of the world seek these things, yet your Abba God well knows what you need. ³¹ Set your sights on the kindom of God, and all these other things will be given to you as well.

³² "Fear not, little flock, for it has pleased your Abba to give you the kindom.

³³ "Sell what you own and give the money to poorer people. Make purses for yourselves that don't wear out—treasures that won't fail you, in heaven that thieves can't steal and moths can't destroy. ³⁴ For wherever your treasure is, that's where your heart will be.

³⁵ "Be dressed and ready, and keep your lamps lit. ³⁶ Be like the household staff awaiting the owner's return from a wedding, so that when the owner arrives and knocks, you'll open the door without delay. ³⁷ It will go well with those staff members whom the owner finds wide awake upon returning. I tell you the absolute truth, the owner will put on an apron, seat them at table and proceed to wait on them. ³⁸ Should the owner happen to come at midnight, or before sunrise, and find them prepared, it will go well with them.

³⁹ "Understand this: no homeowner who knew when a thief was coming would have let the thief break in! ⁴⁰ So be on guard—the Promised One will come when least expected."

⁴¹ Peter said, "Do you intend this parable just for us, Teacher, or do you mean it for everyone?"

⁴² Jesus said, "It's the faithful and farsighted steward that the owner leaves to supervise the staff and give them their rations at the proper time. ⁴³ Happy the steward whom the owner, upon returning, finds busy! ⁴⁴ The truth is, the owner will put the steward in charge of the entire estate. ⁴⁵ But let's say the steward thinks, 'The owner is slow in returning' and begins to abuse the other staff members, eating and drinking and getting drunk. ⁴⁶ When the owner returns unexpectedly, the steward will be punished severely and ranked among those undeserving of trust.

⁴⁷ "The staff members who knew the owner's wishes but didn't work to fulfill them will get a severe punishment, ⁴⁸ whereas the one who didn't know them—even though deserving of a severe punishment—will get off with a milder correction. From those who have been given much, much will be required; from those who have been entrusted much, much more will be asked.

⁴⁹ "I've come to light a fire on the earth. How I wish the blaze were ignited already! ⁵⁰ There is a baptism I must still receive, and how great is my distress until it is accomplished!

⁵¹ "Do you think I'm here to bring peace on earth? I tell you, the opposite is true: I've come to bring division. ⁵² From now on a household of five will be divided—three against two and two against three, ⁵³ father against son, son against father, mother against daughter, daughter against mother, mother-in-law against daughter-in-law, daughter-in-law against mother-in-law."

⁵⁴ Jesus said again to the crowds, "When you see a cloud rising in the west, you immediately say that rain is coming—and so it does. ⁵⁵ When the wind blows from the south, you say it's going to be hot—and so it is. ⁵⁶ You hypocrites! If you can interpret the portents of earth and sky, why can't you interpret the present time?

⁵⁷ "Tell me, why don't you judge for yourselves what is just? ⁵⁸ When you're going with your opponent to appear before a magistrate, try to settle with your antagonist on the way, lest you be turned over to the judge, and the judge deliver you to the bailiff, and the bailiff throw you into prison. ⁵⁹ I tell you, you won't be released until you've paid your opponent in full—to the last penny."

13 ¹ On the same occasion, there were people present who told Jesus about some Galileans whose blood Pilate had mixed with their own sacrifices.

² Jesus replied, "Do you think these Galileans were the greatest sinners in Galilee just because they suffered this? ³ Not at all! I tell you, you'll all come to the same end unless you change your ways. ⁴ Or take those eighteen who were killed by a falling tower in Siloam. Do you think they were more guilty than anyone else who has lived in Jerusalem? ⁵ Certainly not! I tell you, you'll all come to the same end unless you change your ways."

⁶ Jesus told this parable: "There was a fig tree growing in a vineyard. ⁷ The owner came out looking for fruit on it, but didn't find any. The owner said to the vine dresser, 'Look here! For three years now I've come out in search of fruit on this fig tree and have found none. Cut it down. Why should it clutter up the ground?'

⁸ "In reply, the vine dresser said, 'Please leave it one more year while I hoe around it and fertilize it. ⁹ If it bears fruit next year, fine; if not, then let it be cut down.'"

¹⁰ One Sabbath, Jesus was teaching in one of the synagogues. ¹¹ There was a woman there who for eighteen years had a sickness caused by a spirit. She was bent double, quite incapable of standing up straight.

¹² When Jesus saw her, he called her over and said, "Woman, you are free of your infirmity." ¹³ He laid his hands on her, and immediately she stood up straight and began thanking God.

¹⁴ The head of the synagogue, indignant that Jesus had healed on the Sabbath, said to the congregation, "There are six days for working. Come on those days to be healed, not on the Sabbath."

¹⁵ Jesus said in reply, "You hypocrites! Which of you doesn't let your ox or your donkey out of the stall on the Sabbath to water it? ¹⁶ This daughter of Sarah and Abraham has been in the bondage of Satan for eighteen years. Shouldn't she have been released from her shackles on the Sabbath?" ¹⁷ At these words, Jesus' opponents were humili-

ated; meanwhile, everyone else rejoiced at the marvels Jesus was accomplishing.

¹⁸ Jesus continued, "What does the kindom of God resemble? To what will I liken it? ¹⁹ It's like a mustard seed which a gardener took and planted in the garden. It grew and became a large shrub, and the birds of the air nested in its branches."

²⁰ Then he went on, "To what will I compare the kindom of God? ²¹ It's like the yeast which a baker added to three measures of flour and kneaded until the whole ball of dough began to rise."

²² Jesus went through cities and towns teaching, all the while making his way to Jerusalem.

²³ Someone asked, "Will only a few people be saved?"

Jesus replied: ²⁴ "Try to come in through the narrow door. Many, I tell you, will try to enter and won't succeed. ²⁵ Once the head of the household gets up and locks the door, you may find yourselves standing outside, knocking and saying, 'Please open the door! It's us!' but the answer will come, 'I don't know you or where you come from.' ²⁶ Then you'll begin to say, 'But we ate and drank in your company. You taught in our streets.' ²⁷ But you'll hear, 'I tell you, I don't know where you come from. Get away from me, you evildoers!'

²⁸ "There will be wailing and the grinding of teeth when you see Sarah and Abraham, Rebecca and Isaac, Leah and Rachel and Jacob and all the prophets, safe in the kindom of God, and you yourselves rejected. ²⁹ People will come from the East and the West, from the North and the South, and will take their places at the feast in the kindom of God. ³⁰ Some who are last will be first, and some who are first will be last."

³¹ Just then, some Pharisees came to Jesus and said, "You need to get out of town, and fast. Herod is trying to kill you."

³² Jesus replied, "Go tell that fox, 'Today and tomorrow, I'll be casting out devils and healing people, and on the third day I'll reach my goal.' ³³ Even with all that, I'll need to continue on my journey today, tomorrow and the day after that, since no prophet can be allowed to die anywhere except in Jerusalem.

³⁴ "O Jerusalem, Jerusalem! You kill the prophets and stone those who are sent to you! How often have I wanted to gather your children together as a mother bird collects her babies under her wings—yet you refuse me! ³⁵ So take note: your house will be left to you desolate. I tell you, you will not see me again until you say, 'Blessed is the One who comes in the name of our God!'"

14 ¹ One Sabbath, when Jesus came to eat a meal in the house of one of the leading Pharisees, the guests watched him closely. ² Directly in front of Jesus was a person who suffered from edema.

³ Jesus asked the experts on the Law and the Pharisees, "Is it lawful to heal on the Sabbath or not?" ⁴ But they kept silent. With that, Jesus laid hands on the individual and healed the swelling, then sent the person away.

⁵ Jesus said to the guests, "If one of you has a child—or even an ox—and it falls into a pit, won't you rescue it immediately, even on the Sabbath day?" ⁶ They had no answer to this.

⁷ Jesus went on to address a parable to the guests, noticing how they were trying to get a place of honor at the table.

⁸ "When you're invited to a wedding party, don't sit in the place of honor, in case someone more distinguished has been invited. ⁹ Otherwise the hosts might come and say to you, 'Make room for this person,' and you would have to proceed shamefacedly to the lowest place. ¹⁰ What you should do is go and sit in the lowest place, so that when your hosts approach you they'll say, 'My friend, come up higher.' This will win you the esteem of the other guests. ¹¹ For all who exalt themselves will be humbled, and those who humble themselves will be exalted."

¹² Then Jesus said to the host, "Whenever you give a lunch or dinner, don't invite your friends or colleagues or relatives or wealthy neighbors. They might invite you in return and thus repay you. ¹³ No, when you have a reception, invite those who are poor or have physical infirmities or are blind. ¹⁴ You should be pleased that they can't repay you, for you'll be repaid at the resurrection of the just."

¹⁵ One of the guests heard this and said to Jesus, "Happy are those who eat bread in the kindom of God!"

¹⁶ Jesus responded, "A landowner was giving a large dinner and sent out many invitations. ¹⁷ At dinnertime, the landowner instructed an aide to say to those invited, 'Come to the feast, everything is ready.' ¹⁸ But they began to excuse themselves, each and every one. The first one said to the aide, 'I've just bought some land, and I need to go out and inspect it. Please send my regrets.' ¹⁹ Another said, 'I've just bought five yoke of oxen, and I need to go out and test them. Please excuse me.' ²⁰ A third said, 'I've just gotten married, so of course I can't come.'

²¹ "The aide returned and reported all this to the landowner. The landowner became angry and said to the aide, 'Go into town, into the streets and alleys, and bring in those who are poor or crippled, and those who are blind or lame.' ²² After doing so, the aide reported, 'Your orders have been carried out, and there's still room.' ²³ The landowner then said to the aide, 'Go out and scour the side roads and the back roads and make them come in. I want my house to be full! ²⁴ But I tell you, not one of those I had initially invited will taste a bite of my dinner.'"

²⁵ Large crowds followed Jesus. He turned to them and said, ²⁶ "If any of you come to me without turning your back on your mother and your father, your loved ones, your sisters and brothers, indeed your very self, you can't be my follower. ²⁷ Anyone who doesn't take up the cross and follow me can't be my disciple.

²⁸ "If one of you were going to build a tower, wouldn't you first sit down and calculate the outlay to see if you have enough money to complete the project? ²⁹ You'd do that for fear of laying the foundation and then not being able to complete the work—because anyone who saw it would jeer at you ³⁰ and say, 'You started a building and couldn't finish it.' ³¹ Or if the leaders of one country were going to declare war on another country, wouldn't they first sit down and consider whether, with an army of ten thousand, they could win against an enemy coming against them with twenty thousand? ³² If they couldn't, they'd send a delegation while the enemy is still at a distance, asking for terms of peace.

³³ "So count the cost. You can't be my disciple if you don't say goodbye to all of your possessions.

³⁴ "Salt is useful, but if it loses its taste, how can it be resalted again? ³⁵ It's fit neither for the soil nor for the compost pile, so it's thrown away. Whoever has ears to hear, hear this."

15 ²¹ Meanwhile, the tax collectors and the "sinners" were all gathering around Jesus to listen to his teaching, ² at which the Pharisees and the religious scholars murmured, "This person welcomes sinners and eats with them!"

³ Jesus then addressed this parable to them: ⁴ "Who among you, having a hundred sheep and losing one of them, doesn't leave the ninety-nine in the open pasture and search for the lost one until it's found? ⁵ And finding it, you put the sheep on your shoulders in jubilation. ⁶ Once home, you invite friends and neighbors in and say to them, 'Rejoice with me! I've found my lost sheep!' ⁷ I tell you, in the same way there will be more joy in heaven over one repentant sinner than over ninety-nine righteous people who have no need to repent.

⁸ "What householder, who has ten silver pieces and loses one, doesn't light a lamp and sweep the house in a diligent search until she finds what she had lost? ⁹ And when it is found, the householder calls in her friends and neighbors and says, 'Rejoice with me! I've found the silver piece I lost!' ¹⁰ I tell you, there will be the same kind of joy before the angels of God over one repentant sinner."

¹¹ He added, "A man had two sons. ¹² The younger of them said to their father, 'Give me the share of the estate that is coming to me.' So the father divided up the property between them. ¹³ Some days later, the younger son gathered up his belongings and went off to a distant land. Here he squandered all his money on loose living.

¹⁴ "After everything was spent, a great famine broke out in the land, and the son was in great need. ¹⁵ So he went to a landowner, who sent him to a farm to take care of the pigs. ¹⁶ The son was so hungry that he could have eaten the husks that were fodder for the pigs, but no one made a move to give him anything. ¹⁷ Coming to his senses at last, he said, 'How many hired hands at my father's house have more than enough to eat, while here I am starving! ¹⁸ I'll quit and go back home and say, "I've sinned against God and against you; ¹⁹ I no longer deserve to be called one of your children. Treat me like one of your hired hands."' ²⁰ With that, the younger son set off for home.

"While still a long way off, the father caught sight of the returning child and was deeply moved. The father ran out to meet him, threw his arms around him and kissed him. ²¹ The son said to him, 'I've sinned against God and against you; I no longer deserve to be called one of your children.' ²² But his father said to one of the workers, 'Quick! Bring out the finest robe and put it on him; put a ring on his finger and shoes on his feet. ²³ Take the calf we've been fattening and butcher it. Let's eat and celebrate! ²⁴ This son of mine was dead and has come back to life. He was lost and now he's found!' And the celebration began.

²⁵ "Meanwhile the elder son had been out in the field. As he neared the house, he heard the sound of music and dancing. ²⁶ He called one of the workers and asked what was happening. ²⁷ The worker answered, 'Your brother is home, and the fatted calf has been killed because your father has him back safe and sound.'

²⁸ "The son got angry at this and refused to go in to the party, but his father came out and pleaded with him. ²⁹ The older son replied, 'Look! For years now I've done every single thing you asked me to do. I never disobeyed even one of your orders, yet you never gave me so much as a kid goat to celebrate with my friends. ³⁰ But then this son of yours comes home after going through your money with prostitutes, and you kill the fatted calf for him!'

³¹ "'But my child!' the father said. 'You're with me always, and everything I have is yours. ³² But we have to celebrate and rejoice! This brother of yours was dead and has come back to life. He was lost and now he's found.'"

16 ²¹ Jesus said to the disciples, "There was a wealthy landowner who, having received reports of a steward mismanaging the property, ² summoned the steward and said, 'What's this I hear about you? Give me an account of your service, for it's about to come to an end.' ³ The steward thought, 'What will I do next? My employer is going to fire me. I can't dig ditches. I'm ashamed to go begging. ⁴ I have it! Here's a way to make sure that people will take me into their homes when I'm let go.'

⁵ "So the steward called in each of the landowner's debtors. The steward said to the first, 'How much do you owe my employer?' ⁶ The debtor replied, 'A hundred jars of oil.' The steward said, 'Take your invoice, sit down quickly and make it fifty.' ⁷ To another the steward said, 'How much do you owe?' The answer came, 'A hundred measures of wheat,' and the steward said, 'Take your invoice and make it eighty.'

⁸ "Upon hearing this, the owner gave this devious worker credit for being enterprising! Why? Because the children of this world are more astute in dealing with their own kind than are the children of light. ⁹ So I tell you: make friends for yourselves through your use of this world's goods, so that when they fail you, you'll be welcomed into an eternal home. ¹⁰ If you can trust others in little things, you can also trust them in greater, and anyone unjust in a slight matter will also be unjust in a greater. ¹¹ If you can't be trusted with filthy lucre, who will trust you with true riches? ¹² And if you haven't been trustworthy with someone else's money, who will give you your own?

¹³ "Subordinates can't have two superiors. Either they'll hate the one and love the other, or be attentive to the one and despise the other. You can't worship both God and Money."

¹⁴ The Pharisees, who were greedy, heard all this and began to deride Jesus. ¹⁵ He said to them, "You justify yourselves in the eyes of mortals, but God reads your hearts. What people think is important, God holds in contempt.

¹⁶ "Up until the time of John, the Law and the prophets were proclaimed; but since then, the Good News of the kindom of God is taught, and everyone is trying to push their way into it. ¹⁷ Yet it's easier for heaven and earth to pass away than for the tiniest part of a letter to drop out of the Law.

¹⁸ "If you divorce your spouse and marry someone else, you're committing adultery. And if you marry someone who is divorced, you're committing adultery.

¹⁹ "Once there was a rich person who dressed in purple and linen and feasted splendidly every day. ²⁰ At the gate of this person's estate lay a beggar named Lazarus, who was covered with sores. ²¹ Lazarus longed to eat the scraps that fell from the rich person's table, and even the dogs came and licked Lazarus' sores. ²² One day poor Lazarus died and was carried by the angels to the arms of Sarah and Abraham. The rich person likewise died and was buried.

²³ In Hades, in torment, the rich person looked up and saw Sarah and Abraham in the distance, and Lazarus resting in their company.

²⁴ "'Sarah and Abraham,' the rich person cried, 'have pity on me! Send Lazarus to dip the tip of his finger in water and cool off my tongue, for I am tortured by these flames!' ²⁵ But they said, 'My child, remember that you were well off in your lifetime, while Lazarus was in misery. Now Lazarus has found consolation here, and you have found torment. ²⁶ But that's not all. Between you and us there is a fixed chasm, so that those who might wish to come to you from here can't do so, nor can anyone cross from your side to us.'

²⁷ The rich person said, 'I beg you, then, to send Lazarus to my own house ²⁸ where I have five siblings. Let Lazarus be a warning to them, so that they may not end in this place of torment.' ²⁹ But Sarah and Abraham replied, 'They have Moses and the prophets. Let your siblings hear them.' ³⁰ 'Please, I beg you,' the rich person said, 'if someone would only go to them from the dead, then they would repent.' ³¹ 'If they don't listen to Moses and the prophets,' Sarah and Abraham replied, 'they won't be convinced even if someone should rise from the dead!'"

17 ¹ Jesus said to the disciples, "Stumbling blocks will inevitably arise, but woe to those through whom stumbling blocks come! ² Those people would be better off thrown into the sea with millstones around their necks, than to make one of these little ones stumble.

³ "Be on your guard. If your sisters or brothers do wrong, correct them; if they repent, forgive them. ⁴ If they sin against you seven times a day, and seven times a day turn back to you saying, 'I'm sorry,' forgive them."

⁵ The apostles said to Jesus, "Increase our faith!"

⁶ Jesus answered, "If you had faith the size of a mustard seed, you could say to this mulberry tree, 'Uproot yourself and plant yourself in the sea,' and it would obey you.

⁷ "If one of you had hired help plowing a field or herding sheep, and they came in from the fields, would you say to them, 'Come and sit at my table?' ⁸ Wouldn't you say instead, 'Prepare my supper. Put on your apron and wait on me while I eat and drink. You can eat and drink afterward'? ⁹ Would you be grateful to the workers who were just doing their job? ¹⁰ It's the same with you who hear me. When you have done all you have been commanded to do, say, 'We are simple workers. We have done no more than our duty.'"

¹¹ On the journey to Jerusalem, Jesus passed along the borders of Samaria and Galilee. ¹² As Jesus was entering a village, ten people with leprosy met him. Keeping their distance, ¹³ they raised their voices and said, "Jesus, Rabbi, have pity on us!"

¹⁴ When Jesus saw them, he responded, "Go and show yourselves to the priests."

As they were going, they were healed. ¹⁵ One of them, realizing what had happened, came back praising God in a loud voice, ¹⁶ then fell down at the feet of Jesus and spoke his praises. The individual was a Samaritan.

¹⁷ Jesus replied, "Weren't all ten made whole? Where are the other nine? ¹⁸ Was there no one to return and give thanks except this foreigner?" ¹⁹ Then Jesus said to the Samaritan, "Stand up and go your way; your faith has saved you."

²⁰ The Pharisees asked Jesus when the reign of God would come.

Jesus replied, "The reign of God doesn't come in a visible way. ²¹ You can't say, 'See, here it is!' or 'There it is!' No—look: the reign of God is already in your midst."

²² Jesus said to the disciples, "The time will come when you'll long to see one of the days of the Promised One, but you won't see it. ²³ People will say, 'You can find the Promised One over here,' or 'Look over there!' But don't leave, and don't follow them. ²⁴ No, it will be like the lightning that flashes from one end of the sky to the other, on the day of the Promised One. ²⁵ First, however, the Promised One must suffer many things and be rejected by this generation.

²⁶ "As it was in the days of Noah, so will it be in the days of the Promised One. ²⁷ They ate and drank, they took husbands and wives, right up to the day Noah entered the ark—and when the flood came, it destroyed them all. ²⁸ It was the same in the days of Lot: they ate and drank, they bought and sold, built and planted. ²⁹ But on the day Lot left Sodom, fire and brimstone rained down from heaven and destroyed them all.

³⁰ "It will be like that on the day the Promised One is revealed. ³¹ On that day, if people are on the rooftop and their belongings are in the house, they shouldn't go down to get them, nor should the farmer in the field turn back— ³² remember Lot's wife! ³³ Those who try to save their lives will lose them, and those who lose their lives will save them. ³⁴ I tell you, there will be two people in one bed; one will be taken and the other left. ³⁵ Two millers will be grinding grain together; one will be taken and the other left. ³⁶ Two farmers will be in the field; one will taken and the other left."

³⁷ The disciples interrupted him. "Where, Teacher?" they asked.

Jesus answered, "Wherever the carcass is, there will the vultures gather."

18 ¹ Jesus told the disciples a parable on the necessity of praying always and not losing heart: ² "Once there was a judge in a certain city who feared no one—not even God. ³ A woman in that city who had been widowed kept coming to the judge and saying, 'Give me legal protection from my opponent.' ⁴ For a time the judge refused, but finally the judge thought, 'I care little for God or people, ⁵ but this woman won't leave me alone. I'd better give her the protection she seeks, or she'll keep coming and wear me out!'"

⁶ Jesus said, "Listen to what this corrupt judge is saying. ⁷ Won't God then do justice to the chosen who call out day and night? Will God delay long over them? ⁸ I tell you, God will give them swift justice.

"But when the Promised One comes, will faith be found anywhere on earth?"

⁹ Jesus spoke this parable addressed to those who believed in their own self-righteousness while holding everyone else in contempt: ¹⁰ "Two people went up to the Temple to pray; one was a Pharisee, the other a tax collector. ¹¹ The Pharisee stood and prayed like this: 'I give you thanks, O God, that I'm not like others—greedy, crooked, adulterous—or even like this tax collector. ¹² I fast twice a week. I pay tithes on everything I earn.'

¹³ "The other one, however, kept a distance, not even daring to look up to heaven. In real humility, all the tax collector said was, 'O God, be merciful to me, a sinner.' ¹⁴ Believe me, the tax collector went home from the Temple right with God, while the Pharisee didn't. For those who exalt themselves will be humbled, while those who humble themselves will be exalted."

¹⁵ People even brought their infants forward for Jesus to touch. When the disciples saw this, they scolded the parents. ¹⁶ However, Jesus intervened by calling the children to himself. He said, "Let the children come to me. Don't stop them, for the kindom of heaven belongs to such as these. ¹⁷ The truth is, whoever doesn't welcome the kindom of God like a child will never enter it."

¹⁸ A young ruler asked him, "Good Teacher, what must I do to inherit eternal life?"

¹⁹ Jesus responded, "Why do you call me good? Only God is good! ²⁰ You know the commandments: 'No adultery. No killing. No stealing. No false testimony. Honor your mother and father.'"

²¹ The wealthy person replied, "I've observed all of these from my youth."

²² When Jesus heard this he said, "There is one thing left for you to do. Sell everything you own and give the money to those poorer than you—and you'll have treasure in heaven. Then come and follow me."

²³ This news was received with a heavy heart, because the ruler was extremely wealthy.

²⁴ Jesus looked at the ruler and said, "How hard it is for those who are wealthy to enter the kindom of God! ²⁵ It's easier for a camel to crawl through the Needle's Eye gate than for the wealthy to enter the kindom of God."

²⁶ Those who heard this said, "Then who can be saved?"

²⁷ Jesus replied, "What is impossible for mortals is possible for God."

²⁸ Then Peter said, "What about us? We have given up everything we own to follow you!"

²⁹ Jesus said, "The truth is, whoever gives up home or spouse or sisters or brothers or parents or children for the kindom of God ³⁰ will receive many times as much in this age, and eternal life in the age to come."

³¹ Then Jesus took the Twelve aside and said to them, "Listen: we are going up to Jerusalem, and everything written by the prophets about the Chosen One will come to pass. ³² The Chosen One will be handed over to the Gentiles to be mocked, insulted, spat upon, ³³ beaten and finally killed— but on the third day, the Chosen One will rise again." ³⁴ But the Twelve couldn't make anything of this. The meaning of Jesus' words was hidden from them, and they didn't understand what he was telling them.

³⁵ As Jesus neared Jericho, a blind person sat at the side of the road, begging. ³⁶ Hearing a crowd go by, the beggar asked, "What's that?" ³⁷ They said that Jesus of Nazareth was passing by.

³⁸ The beggar shouted, "Jesus, Heir of David, have pity on me!" ³⁹ Those in the lead sternly ordered the blind beggar to be quiet, but the sufferer shouted all the more, "Heir of David, have pity on me!"

⁴⁰ Jesus stopped and had the blind beggar brought to him. ⁴¹ "What do you want me to do for you?" he asked.

"Rabbi, I want to see."

⁴² Jesus said to the beggar, "Receive your sight. Your faith has healed you."

⁴³ At that very moment, sight was restored to the beggar, who joined the crowd, giving praise to God. All the people witnessed it and they too gave praise to God.

19:¹ Entering Jericho, Jesus passed through the city. ² There was a wealthy person there named Zacchaeus, the chief tax collector. ³ Zacchaeus was trying to see who Jesus was, but he couldn't do so because of the crowd, since he was short.

⁴ In order to see Jesus, Zacchaeus ran on ahead, then climbed a sycamore tree that was along the route. ⁵ When Jesus came to the spot, he looked up and said, "Zacchaeus, hurry up and come on down. I'm going to stay at your house today." ⁶ Zacchaeus quickly climbed down and welcomed Jesus with delight.

⁷ When everyone saw this, they began to grumble, "Jesus has gone to a sinner's house as a guest."

⁸ Zacchaeus stood his ground and said to Jesus, "Here and now I give half my belongings to poor people. If I've defrauded anyone in the least, I'll pay them back fourfold."

⁹ Jesus said to the tax collector, "Today salvation has come to this house, for this is what it means to be a descendant of Sarah and Abraham. ¹⁰ The Promised One has come to search out and save what was lost."

¹¹ While the crowd was listening, Jesus went on to tell a parable, because he was near Jerusalem where they thought the reign of God was about to appear. ¹² Jesus said:

"A member of the nobility went to a faraway country to become its ruler for a time. ¹³ Before leaving, the noble summoned ten overseers and gave them each ten minas—about three years' wages—and said to them, 'Invest this until I return.' ¹⁴ But the noble's new subjects rebelled and immediately sent a delegation with the message, 'We won't have you ruling over us!' ¹⁵ So the noble returned home, even though fully authorized to rule.

"The noble sent for the overseers to whom the money had been given, to learn what profit each had made. ¹⁶ The first came and said, 'The sum you gave me was doubled for you.' ¹⁷ 'Well done,' the noble replied. 'You showed yourself capable in a small matter. For that you can govern ten cities.' ¹⁸ The second came and said, 'Your investment has netted half again as much.' ¹⁹ The noble said, 'Then you'll govern five cities.' ²⁰ The third came in and said, 'Here's your money; I hid it for safekeeping. ²¹ You see, I was afraid of you because you are notoriously exacting. You withdraw what you never deposited. You reap what you never sowed.'

²² "The noble replied, 'You worthless lout! I intend to judge you on your own evidence. So, you knew I was exacting, withdrawing what I never deposited, reaping what I never sowed? ²³ Why, then, didn't you put the money on deposit with the moneylenders, so that upon my return I could get it back with interest?' ²⁴ The noble said to those standing around, 'Take the money from this one and give it to the one who had the ten minas.' ²⁵ 'Yes, but that overseer already has ten,' they replied. ²⁶ The noble responded, 'I tell you, whoever has will be given more, but those who don't have will lose the little they have. ²⁷ Now, about those enemies of mine who didn't want me to be their ruler: bring them in, and kill them in my presence.'"

19:28–22:6

Having said this, Jesus went ahead with the ascent to Jerusalem.

²⁹ Approaching Bethphage and Bethany, near what is called the Mount of Olives, Jesus sent two of the disciples with these instructions: ³⁰ "Go into the village ahead of you. Upon entering it, you'll find a tethered colt that no one has yet ridden. Untie it and lead it back. ³¹ If anyone should ask you, 'Why are you untying it?' say, 'The Rabbi needs it.'"

³² They departed on their errand and found things just as Jesus had said. ³³ As they untied the colt, its owners said to them, "Why are you doing that?"

³⁴ They explained that the Rabbi needed it. ³⁵ Then the disciples led the animal to Jesus and, laying their cloaks on it, helped him mount.

³⁶ People spread their cloaks on the roadway as Jesus rode along. ³⁷ As they reached the descent from the Mount of Olives, the entire crowd of disciples joined them and began to rejoice and praise God loudly for the display of power they had seen, saying,

³⁸ "Blessed is the One who comes in the name of our God!
Peace in heaven, and glory in the highest!"

³⁹ Some of the Pharisees in the crowd said to Jesus, "Teacher, rebuke your disciples!"

⁴⁰ Jesus replied, "I tell you, if they were to keep silent, the very stones would cry out!"

⁴¹ Coming within sight of Jerusalem, Jesus wept over it ⁴² and said, "If only you had known the path to peace today! But now it has been hidden from your eyes. ⁴³ Days will come upon you when your enemies will encircle you with a rampart, hem you in and press you hard from every side. ⁴⁴ They'll wipe you out, you and your children within your walls, and won't leave one stone on top of another within you, because you failed to recognize the time of your visit from God."

⁴⁵ Then Jesus entered the Temple and began throwing out the vendors, ⁴⁶ saying, "Scripture says, 'My Temple will be a house of prayer'—but you have made it a den of thieves!"

⁴⁷ Jesus was teaching in the Temple area every day. Meanwhile, the chief priests and religious scholars were looking for a way to destroy him, as were the leaders of the people, ⁴⁸ but they had no idea how to achieve it—the entire population was listening and hanging onto his every word.

20 ¹ One day as Jesus was teaching the people in the Temple and proclaiming the Good News, the chief priests and the religious scholars, together with the elders, approached him ² and said, "Tell us by what authority you are doing these things. Who authorized you?"

³ Jesus replied, "And I'll ask you a question. ⁴ John's baptism—did it come from heaven, or from mortals?"

⁵ They discussed the question among themselves and concluded, "If we answer 'from heaven,' he'll ask, 'Then why didn't you believe him?' ⁶ But if we answer 'from mortals,' all the people will stone us, for they believe that John was a prophet." ⁷ So they said they didn't know where it came from.

⁸ Jesus said, "Then I won't tell you by what authority I do these things."

⁹ Then Jesus went on to tell the people this parable: "A landowner planted a vineyard, leased it to several farmers and left for a long journey. ¹⁰ When the time came, a worker was sent to the farmers to collect the landowner's share of the harvest. The farmers drove the worker off with a beating. ¹¹ So the landowner sent a second worker, who likewise was beaten and driven off empty-handed. ¹² A third was beaten, and sent packing with none of the harvest.

¹³ "The owner of the vineyard said, 'What will I do? I'll send my firstborn, whom I love; maybe that will get their respect.'

¹⁴ But when the tenants learned of this, they conspired to kill the heir in order to gain control of the inheritance. ¹⁵ So they murdered the firstborn outside the vineyard.

"What will the landowner do to them? ¹⁶ The owner will come and execute those tenants and turn the vineyard over to others."

When the people heard this, they said, "God forbid!"

¹⁷ But Jesus stared at them and said, "Then tell me what the scripture means when it says,

'The stone which the builders rejected
became the cornerstone.'

¹⁸ "All who fall on that stone will be dashed to pieces, and all those upon whom it falls will be scattered like powder."

¹⁹ The religious scholars and the chief priests tried to lay hands on him that very hour, for they understood the parable to be about them. But they feared the people. ²⁰ So they bided their time by sending spies, who pretended to be righteous in order to entrap Jesus by something he said. Then they would turn him over to the power and authority of the governor.

²¹ So the spies asked him, "Rabbi, we know that what you say and teach is right. You show no partiality; you teach the way of God truthfully. ²² Is it proper for us to pay tribute to Caesar or not?"

²³ Jesus saw through their deceitfulness and said, ²⁴ "Show me a denarius. Whose picture and name are on it?"

They said, "Caesar's."

²⁵ He said, "Then give to Caesar what belongs to Caesar. Give to God what is God's."

²⁶ They were unable to find fault with his public statements. And they were so in awe of his answer that they fell silent.

²⁷ Some Sadducees—the ones who claim there is no resurrection—came forward to pose this question: ²⁸ "Teacher, Moses wrote that if a man's brother dies leaving a wife and no child, the brother should marry the woman now widowed, to raise up children with her. ²⁹ Let's say that there were seven brothers. The first one married and died childless. ³⁰ The second brother then married the woman, ³¹ then the third, and so on. All seven died without leaving her any children. ³² Finally the woman herself died. ³³ At the resurrection, who will be her husband? Remember, seven married her."

³⁴ Jesus said to them, "The children of this age marry each other, ³⁵ but those judged worthy of a place in the age to come and of the resurrection from the dead don't take husbands or wives. ³⁶ They can no longer die, like the angels—they are children of God, since they are children of the resurrection. ³⁷ That the dead rise again was even demonstrated by Moses when, in the passage about the bush, he called the Most High 'the God of Sarah and Abraham, and the God of Rebecca and Isaac, and the God of Leah and Rachel and Jacob.' ³⁸ God is not the God of the dead, but of the living. All are alive to God."

³⁹ Some of the religious scholars responded, "Well said, Teacher." ⁴⁰ They didn't dare ask Jesus anything else.

⁴¹ Then he said to them, "How can they say that the Messiah is the descendant of David? ⁴² For David himself says in the Book of Psalms,

'The Most High said to my Sovereign,
"Sit at my right hand
⁴³ until I place your enemies
under your foot."'

⁴⁴ "Now, if David calls the Messiah 'Sovereign,' how can the Messiah also be David's descendant?"

⁴⁵ While all the people were listening, Jesus said to the disciples, ⁴⁶ "Beware of the religious scholars, who love to

go about in long robes and be greeted deferentially in the marketplace. They take the front seats in the synagogue and places of honor at banquets. ⁴⁷ They swallow up the property of women who are widowed and make a show of offering lengthy prayers. People like them will be severely punished."

21 ¹ Jesus looked up and saw rich people putting their offerings into the Temple treasury, ² and then he noticed an impoverished woman, a widow, putting in two copper coins. ³ At that he said, "The truth is, this woman has put in more than all the rest. ⁴ They made contributions out of their surplus, but she from her want has given what she couldn't afford—every penny she had to live on."

⁵ Some disciples were speaking of how the Temple was adorned with precious stones and votive offerings. Jesus said, ⁶ "You see all these things? The day will come when one stone won't be left on top of another—everything will be torn down."

⁷ They asked, "When will this happen, Rabbi? And what will be the sign that it's about to happen?"

⁸ Jesus said, "Take care not to be misled. Many will come in my name, saying, 'I am the One' and 'The time is at hand.' Don't follow them. ⁹ And don't be perturbed when you hear of wars and insurrections. These things must happen first, but the end doesn't follow immediately."

¹⁰ Then he said to them, "Nation will rise against nation, and empire against empire. ¹¹ There will be great earthquakes, plagues and famines in various places—and in the sky there will be frightening omens and great signs. ¹² But before any of this, they'll arrest you and persecute you, bringing you before synagogues and sending you to prison, bringing you to trial before rulers and governors. And it will all be because of my name— ¹³ this will be your opportunity to give your testimony. ¹⁴ So make up your minds not to worry about your defense beforehand, ¹⁵ for I'll give you the words, and a wisdom that none of your adversaries can take exception to or contradict. ¹⁶ You'll be betrayed even by your parents, brothers, sisters, relatives and friends, and some of you will be put to death. ¹⁷ Everyone will hate you because of me, ¹⁸ yet not a hair of your head will be harmed. ¹⁹ By patient endurance, you'll save your lives.

²⁰ "When you see Jerusalem encircled by soldiers, know that its devastation is near. ²¹ If you're in Judea at that time, flee to the mountains; if you're in the heart of the city, escape it; if you're in the country, don't go back to the city. ²² These indeed will be the days of retribution, when all that is written must be fulfilled.

²³ "Women who are pregnant or nursing will fare badly in those days! The distress in the land and the wrath against this people will be great. ²⁴ The people will fall to the sword; they'll be led captive into the lands of the Gentiles. Jerusalem will be trampled by the Gentiles, until the times of the Gentiles are fulfilled.

²⁵ "Signs will appear in the sun, the moon and the stars. On the earth, nations will be in anguish, distraught at the roaring of the sea and the waves. ²⁶ People will die of fright in anticipation of what is coming upon the earth. The powers in the heavens will be shaken. ²⁷ After that, people will see the Chosen One coming on a cloud with great power and glory. ²⁸ When these things begin to happen, stand up straight and raise your heads, because your ransom is near at hand."

²⁹ And he told them a parable: "Look at the fig tree, or any other tree. ³⁰ You see when they're budding and know that summer is near. ³¹ In the same way, when you see all these things happening, know that the reign of God is near. ³² The truth is, this generation will not pass away until all this takes

place. ³³ The heavens and the earth will pass away, but my words will not pass away.

³⁴ "Be on your guard lest your spirits become bloated with indulgence, drunkenness and worldly cares. That day will suddenly close in on you like a trap. ³⁵ It will come upon all who dwell on the face of the earth, so be on your watch. ³⁶ Pray constantly for the strength to escape whatever comes, and to stand secure before the Chosen One."

³⁷ Jesus taught in the Temple during the days, and he spent the nights on the hill called the Mount of Olives. ³⁸ And all the people came to the Temple early each morning to hear him.

22 ¹ Now the Feast of the Unleavened Bread, also known as Passover, drew near, ² and the chief priests and the religious scholars sought a way to kill Jesus, for they feared the people.

³ Then Satan took possession of Judas, who was called Iscariot, one of the Twelve. ⁴ He went to the chief priests and the Temple guards to discuss with them how he might betray Jesus. ⁵ They were delighted and agreed to give him money. ⁶ Judas accepted, then began to look for the opportune moment to hand Jesus over to them—when people were not present.

22:7–23:56

When the day of the Feast of the Unleavened Bread arrived, when the Passover lamb was to be sacrificed, ⁸ Jesus sent Peter and John out with the instructions, "Go and make the preparations for us to eat the Passover."

⁹ They asked, "Where do you want us to prepare the seder?"

¹⁰ Jesus answered, "When you enter the city, a man will meet you carrying a jar of water. Follow him into the house he enters. ¹¹ Say to the owner of the house, 'The Rabbi asks, "Where is the guest room where I can eat the Passover seder with my disciples?"' ¹² The owner will show you a large furnished upper room. Make the preparations there."

¹³ They went out and found everything as Jesus had told them. And they prepared the Passover.

¹⁴ When the hour had come, Jesus took a place at the table with the apostles. ¹⁵ Jesus said to them, "I've longed to eat this Passover with you before I suffer. ¹⁶ I tell you, I will not eat it again until everything is fulfilled in the reign of God." ¹⁷ Then taking a cup of wine, Jesus gave thanks and said, "Take this and share it among you. ¹⁸ I tell you, I will not drink wine from now on, until the reign of God comes." ¹⁹ Then Jesus took bread and gave thanks for it, broke it, and gave it to them, saying, "This is my body, which will be given for you. Do this in remembrance of me." ²⁰ Jesus did the same with the cup after supper and said, "This cup is the New Covenant in my blood, which will be poured out for you.

²¹ "Look! The hand of my betrayer is at this table with me. ²² The Chosen One is following the appointed course. But woe to the person by whom that One is betrayed!" ²³ Then they began to argue among themselves as to which of them would do such a deed.

²⁴ Another dispute arose among them about who would be regarded as the greatest. ²⁵ But Jesus said to them, "Earthly rulers domineer over their people. Those who exercise authority over them are called their 'benefactors.' ²⁶ This must not happen with you. Let the greatest among you be like the

youngest. Let the leader among you become the follower. ²⁷ For who is the greater? The one who reclines at a meal, or the one who serves it? Isn't it the one reclining at table? Yet here I am among you as the one who serves you.

²⁸ "You are the ones who have stood by me faithfully in trials. ²⁹ Just as God has given me dominion, so I give it to you. ³⁰ In my reign, you will eat and drink at my table, and you'll sit on thrones judging the twelve tribes of Israel.

³¹ "Simon, Simon! Satan has demanded that you be sifted like wheat. ³² But I've prayed for you, that your faith may not fail. You, in turn, must give strength to your sisters and brothers."

³³ "Rabbi," Peter answered, "with you I'm prepared to face imprisonment and even death!"

³⁴ Jesus responded, "I tell you, Peter, before the rooster crows today you'll have denied three times that you know me."

³⁵ Jesus said to them, "When I sent you off without purse, traveling bag or sandals, were you in need of anything?"

"No, nothing!" they replied.

³⁶ He said, "Now, however, the one who has a purse had better carry it; the same with a travelling bag. And if they don't have a sword, they should sell their cloaks and buy one! ³⁷ For I tell you, what was written in scripture must be fulfilled in me: 'The suffering servant was counted among criminals'—for whatever refers to me must be fulfilled."

³⁸ And they said, "Look, Rabbi, here are two swords!"

Jesus answered, "That is enough."

³⁹ Then Jesus went out and made his way as usual to the Mount of Olives; the disciples accompanied him. ⁴⁰ When they reached the place, Jesus said to them, "Pray that you not be put to the test."

⁴¹ Then Jesus withdrew about a stone's throw from them, knelt down and prayed, ⁴² "Abba, if it's your will, take this cup from me; yet not my will but yours be done."*

⁴⁵ When Jesus rose from prayer, he came to the disciples and found them sleeping, exhausted with grief. ⁴⁶ He said to them, "Why do you sleep? Wake up, and pray that you not be subjected to the trial."

⁴⁷ While Jesus was still speaking, a crowd suddenly appeared with Judas, one of the Twelve, at their head. Judas came over to Jesus to embrace him, ⁴⁸ but Jesus said, "Judas, are you betraying the Chosen One with a kiss?"

⁴⁹ Those who were around Jesus, realizing what was going to happen, said, "Rabbi, should we strike them with our swords?" ⁵⁰ One of them struck the attendant of the high priest, cutting off an ear.

⁵¹ But Jesus said, "Stop! No more of this!" Then Jesus touched the attendant's ear and healed it.

⁵² But to those who had come out against him—the chief priests, the chiefs of the Temple Guard and the elders—Jesus said, "Why do you come out with swords and clubs as if I were a robber? ⁵³ I was with you in the Temple every day, and you could have laid hands on me any time you wanted. But this is your hour—the triumph of darkness!"

⁵⁴ They arrested Jesus and led him away, arriving at the house of the high priest. Peter followed at a distance ⁵⁵ and

sat down in the midst of those who had kindled a fire in the courtyard and were sitting around it. ⁵⁶ One of the high priest's attendants saw him sitting there at the fire, and she stared at him and said, "This one was with Jesus, too."

⁵⁷ But Peter denied it. "I don't know him!" he said.

⁵⁸ A little later, someone else noticed Peter and remarked, "You're one of them too!"

But Peter said, "No, I'm not."

⁵⁹ About an hour later, someone else insisted, "Surely this fellow was with them, too. He even talks like a Galilean."

⁶⁰ "I don't even know what you are talking about!" Peter said.

Just then, as Peter was still speaking, a rooster crowed. ⁶¹ Jesus turned and looked at Peter. Then Peter remembered Jesus saying, "Before a rooster crows today, you'll deny me three times." ⁶² Peter went out and wept bitterly.

⁶³ Meanwhile, those who held Jesus in custody were amusing themselves at his expense. ⁶⁴ They blindfolded and slapped him, and then taunted him. "Play the prophet! Which one struck you?" they mocked. ⁶⁵ And they hurled many other insults at him.

⁶⁶ At daybreak the Sanhedrin—which was made up of the elders of the people, the chief priests and the religious scholars—assembled again. Once they had brought Jesus before the council, ⁶⁷ they said, "Tell us, are you the Messiah?"

Jesus replied, "If I tell you, you'll not believe me. ⁶⁸ And if I question you, you won't answer! ⁶⁹ But from now on, the Chosen One will have a seat at the right hand of the Power of God."

⁷⁰ Then all of them said, "So you are God's Own?"

Jesus answered, "Your own words have said it!"

⁷¹ "What need do we have of witnesses?" they said. "We have heard it from his own mouth!"

23 ¹ Then the whole assembly arose and led Jesus to Pilate. ² They began to accuse Jesus by saying, "We found this one subverting our nation, opposing the payment of taxes to Caesar and even claiming to be Messiah, a king."

³ Then Pilate questioned Jesus: "Are you the King of the Jews?"

"You have said it." Jesus answered.

⁴ Then Pilate reported to the chief priests and the crowds: "I find no guilt in him!"

⁵ But they insisted, "He stirs up the people wherever he teaches, through the whole of Judea, from Galilee to Jerusalem."

⁶ On hearing this, Pilate asked whether Jesus was a Galilean, ⁷ and learning that Jesus was from Herod's jurisdiction, sent Jesus off to Herod, who was also in Jerusalem at this time.

⁸ Now, at the sight of Jesus, Herod was very pleased. From the reports he had heard about Jesus, he had wanted for a long time to see him. Herod hoped to see Jesus perform some miracle.

⁹ Herod questioned him at great length, but Jesus wouldn't answer. ¹⁰ The chief priests and religious scholars stood there, accusing Jesus vehemently. ¹¹ So Herod and the soldiers treated Jesus with contempt and ridicule, put a magnificent robe upon him and sent him back to Pilate. ¹² Herod and Pilate, who had previously been set against each other, became friends that day.

¹³ Pilate then called together the chief priests, the ruling class and the people, ¹⁴ and said to them, "You have brought this person before me as someone who incites people to rebellion. I have examined him in your presence and have found no basis for any charge against him arising from your allegations. ¹⁵ Neither has Herod, for Jesus has been sent back to us. Obviously, he has done nothing to deserve death. ¹⁶ Therefore, I will punish Jesus, but then I will release him."

---

* Later manuscripts add verses 43 and 44: "An angel then appeared to Jesus from heaven to strengthen him. In anguish, Jesus prayed all the more fervently, and sweat, like drops of blood, fell to the ground."

17 Pilate was obligated to release one prisoner to the people at festival time. 18 The whole crowd cried out as one, "Take him away! We want Barabbas!" 19 Barabbas had been imprisoned for starting a riot in the city, and for murder.

20 Pilate wanted to release Jesus, so he addressed them again. 21 But they shouted back, "Crucify him, crucify him!"

22 Yet a third time, Pilate spoke to the crowd, "What wrong has this Jesus done? I've found nothing that calls for death! Therefore, I'll have him flogged, and then I'll release him."

23 But they demanded that Jesus be crucified, and their shouts increased in volume. 24 Pilate decided that their demands should be met. 25 So he released Barabbas, the one who had been imprisoned for rioting and murder, and Jesus was handed over to the crowd.

26 As they led Jesus away, they seized Simon—a Cyrenean who was just coming in from the fields—and forced him to carry the cross behind Jesus.

27 A large crowd was following, many of them women who were beating their breasts and wailing for him. 28 At one point, Jesus turned to these women and said, "Daughters of Jerusalem, don't weep for me! Weep rather for yourselves and for your children! 29 The time is coming when it will be said, 'Blessed are the childless, the wombs that have never given birth and the breasts that have never nursed.' 30 Then people will say to the mountains, 'Fall on us!' and to the hills, 'Cover us up!' 31 For if they do these things when the wood is green, what will happen when it is dry?"

32 Two others were also led off with Jesus, criminals who were to be put to death. 33 When they had reached the place called The Skull, they crucified Jesus there—together with the criminals, one on his right and one on his left. 34 And Jesus said, "Abba forgive them. They don't know what they are doing." Then they divided his garments, rolling dice for them.

35 The people stood there watching. The rulers, however, jeered him and said, "He saved others, let him save himself—if he really is the Messiah of God, the Chosen One!" 36 The soldiers also mocked him. They served Jesus sour wine 37 and said, "If you are really the King of the Jews, save yourself!" 38 There was an inscription above Jesus that read, "This is the King of the Jews."

39 One of the criminals who hung there beside him insulted Jesus, too, saying, "Are you really the Messiah? Then save yourself—and us!"

40 But the other answered the first with a rebuke: "Don't you even fear God? 41 We are only paying the price for what we have done, but this one has done nothing wrong!"

42 Then he said, "Jesus, remember me when you come into your glory."

43 Jesus replied, "The truth is, today you'll be with me in paradise!"

44 It was about noon, and darkness fell on the whole land until three in the afternoon, 45 because of an eclipse of the sun. Then the curtain in the sanctuary was torn in two, 46 and Jesus uttered a loud cry and said, "Abba, into your hands I commit my spirit."

Saying this, Jesus breathed for the last time.

47 The centurion who saw this glorified God, saying, "Surely this one was innocent." 48 When the crowds that had gathered for the spectacle saw what had happened, they returned home beating their breasts and weeping. 49 All the acquaintances of Jesus and the women who had come with him from Galilee stood at a distance, looking on.

50 There was a member of the Sanhedrin named Joseph, 51 who had not consented to their action. Joseph was from Arimathea and lived in anticipation of the reign of God. 52 He approached Pilate and asked for the body of Jesus. 53 Joseph took the body down, wrapped it in fine linen and laid it in a tomb cut out of rock, where no one had yet been laid. 54 It was Preparation Day, and the Sabbath was about to begin.

55 The women who accompanied Jesus from Galilee followed Joseph, saw the tomb and watched as the body was placed in it. 56 Then they went home to prepare the spices and ointments. But they rested on the Sabbath, according to the Law.

24:1–53

On the first day of the week, at the first sign of dawn, the women came to the tomb bringing the spices they had prepared. 2 They found the stone rolled back from the tomb; 3 but when they entered the tomb, they didn't find the body of Jesus.

4 While they were still at a loss over what to think of this, two figures in dazzling garments stood beside them. 5 Terrified, the women bowed to the ground. The two said to them, "Why do you search for the Living One among the dead? 6 Jesus is not here; Christ has risen. Remember what Jesus said to you while still in Galilee— 7 that the Chosen One must be delivered into the hands of sinners and be crucified, and on the third day would rise again." 8 With this reminder, the words of Jesus came back to them.

9 When they had returned from the tomb, they told all these things to the Eleven and the others. 10 The women were Mary of Magdala, Joanna, and Mary the mother of James. The other women with them also told the apostles, 11 but the story seemed like nonsense and they refused to believe them. 12 Peter, however, got up and ran to the tomb. He stooped down, but he could see nothing but the wrappings. So he went away, full of amazement at what had occurred.

13 That same day, two of the disciples were making their way to a village called Emmaus—which was about seven miles from Jerusalem—14 discussing all that had happened as they went.

15 While they were discussing these things, Jesus approached and began to walk along with them, 16 though they were kept from recognizing Jesus, 17 who asked them, "What are you two discussing as you go your way?"

They stopped and looked sad. 18 One of them, Cleopas by name, asked him, "Are you the only one visiting Jerusalem who doesn't know the things that have happened these past few days?"

19 Jesus said to them, "What things?"

They said, "About Jesus of Nazareth, a prophet powerful in word and deed in the eyes of God and all the people—20 how our chief priests and leaders delivered him up to be condemned to death and crucified him. 21 We were hoping that he was the One who would set Israel free. Besides all this, today—the third day since these things happened—22 some women of our group have just brought us some astonishing news. They were at the tomb before dawn 23 and didn't find the body; they returned and informed us that they had seen a vision of angels, who declared that Jesus was alive. 24 Some of our number went to the tomb and found it to be just as the women said, but they didn't find Jesus."

²⁵ Then Jesus said to them, "What little sense you have! How slow you are to believe all that the prophets have announced! ²⁶ Didn't the Messiah have to undergo all this to enter into glory?" ²⁷ Then beginning with Moses and all the prophets, Jesus interpreted for them every passage of scripture which referred to the Messiah. ²⁸ By now they were near the village they were going to, and Jesus appeared to be going further. ²⁹ But they said eagerly, "Stay with us. It's nearly evening—the day is practically over." So the savior went in and stayed with them.

³⁰ After sitting down with them to eat, Jesus took bread, said the blessing, then broke the bread and began to distribute it to them. ³¹ With that their eyes were opened and they recognized Jesus, who immediately vanished from their sight.

³² They said to one another, "Weren't our hearts burning inside us as this one talked to us on the road and explained the scriptures to us?" ³³ They got up immediately and returned to Jerusalem, where they found the Eleven and the rest of the company assembled. ³⁴ They were greeted with, "Christ has risen! It's true! Jesus has appeared to Simon!" ³⁵ Then the travelers recounted what had happened on the road, and how they had come to know Jesus in the breaking of the bread.

³⁶ While they were still talking about this, Jesus actually stood in their midst and said to them, "Peace be with you."

³⁷ In their panic and fright, they thought they were seeing a ghost. ³⁸ Jesus said to them, "Why are you disturbed? Why do such ideas cross your mind? ³⁹ Look at my hands and my feet; it is I, really. Touch me and see—a ghost doesn't have flesh and bones as I do." ⁴⁰ After saying this, Jesus showed them the wounds.

⁴¹ They were still incredulous for sheer joy and wonder, so Jesus said to them, "Do you have anything here to eat?" ⁴² After being given a piece of cooked fish, ⁴³ the savior ate in their presence.

⁴⁴ Then Jesus said to them, "Remember the words I spoke when I was still with you: everything written about me in the Law of Moses and the Prophets and the psalms had to be fulfilled."

⁴⁵ Then Jesus opened their minds to the understanding of the scriptures, ⁴⁶ saying, "That is why the scriptures say that the Messiah must suffer and rise from the dead on the third day. ⁴⁷ In the Messiah's name, repentance for the forgiveness of sins will be preached to all nations, beginning at Jerusalem. ⁴⁸ You are witnesses of all this.

⁴⁹ "Take note: I am sending forth what Abba God has promised to you. Remain here in the city until you are clothed with the power from on high."

⁵⁰ Then Jesus took them to the outskirts of Bethany, and with upraised hands blessed the disciples. ⁵¹ While blessing them, the savior left them and was carried up to heaven. ⁵² The disciples worshiped the risen Christ and returned to Jerusalem full of joy. ⁵³ They were found in the Temple constantly, speaking the praises of God.

john

1:1–2:12

In the beginning
  there was the Word;
  the Word was in God's presence,
  and the Word was God.
² The Word was present to God
    from the beginning.
³ Through the Word
    all things came into being,
    and apart from the Word
    nothing came into being
    that has come into being.
⁴ In the Word was life,
    and that life was humanity's light—
⁵ a Light that shines in the darkness,
    a Light that the darkness has never overtaken.

⁶ Then came one named John, sent as an envoy from God, ⁷ who came as a witness to testify about the Light, so that through his testimony everyone might believe.⁸ He himself wasn't the Light; he only came to testify about the Light—the true Light that illumines all humankind.

⁹ The Word was coming into the world—
¹⁰ was in the world—
    and though the world
    was made through the Word,
    the world didn't recognize it.
¹¹ Though the Word came to its own realm,
    the Word's own people didn't accept it.
¹² Yet any who did accept the Word,
    who believed in that Name,
    were empowered to become children of God—
¹³ children born not of natural descent,
    nor urge of flesh
    nor human will—
    but born of God.
¹⁴ And the Word became flesh
    and stayed for a little while among us;
    we saw the Word's glory—
    the favor and position a parent gives an only child—
    filled with grace,
    filled with truth.

¹⁵ John testified by proclaiming, "This is the one I was talking about when I said, 'The one who comes after me ranks ahead of me, for this One existed before I did.'"

¹⁶ Of this One's fullness
    we've all had a share—
    gift on top of gift.
¹⁷ For while the Law was given through Moses,
    the Gift—and the Truth—came through Jesus Christ.
¹⁸ No one has ever seen God;
    it is the Only Begotten,
    ever at Abba's side,
    who has revealed God to us.

¹⁹ Now the Temple authorities sent emissaries from Jerusalem—priests and Levites—to talk to John. "Who are you?" they asked.

This is John's testimony: ²⁰ he didn't refuse to answer, but freely admitted, "I am not the Messiah."

²¹ "Who are you, then?" they asked. "Elijah?"

"No, I am not," he answered.

"Are you the Prophet?"

"No," he replied.

22 Finally they said to him, "Who are you? Give us an answer to take back to those who sent us. What do you have to say for yourself?"

23 John said, "I am, as Isaiah prophesied, the voice of someone crying out in the wilderness, 'Make straight our God's road!'"

24 The emissaries were members of the Pharisee sect. 25 They questioned him further: "If you're not the Messiah or Elijah or the Prophet, then why are you baptizing people?"

26 John said, "I baptize with water because among you stands someone whom you don't recognize—27 the One who is to come after me—the strap of whose sandal I am not worthy even to untie."

28 This occurred in Bethany, across the Jordan River, where John was baptizing.

29 The next day, catching sight of Jesus approaching, John exclaimed, "Look, there's God's sacrificial lamb, who takes away the world's sin! 30 This is the one I was talking about when I said, 'The one who comes after me ranks ahead of me, for this One existed before I did.' 31 I didn't recognize him, but it was so that he would be revealed to Israel that I came baptizing with water."

32 John also gave this testimony: "I saw the Spirit descend from heaven like a dove, and she came to rest on him. 33 I didn't recognize him, but the One who sent me to baptize with water told me, 'When you see the Spirit descend and rest on someone, that is the One who will baptize with the Holy Spirit.' 34 Now I have seen for myself and have testified that this is the Only Begotten of God."

35 The next day, John was by the Jordan again with two of his disciples. 36 Seeing Jesus walk by, John said, "Look! There's the Lamb of God!" 37 The two disciples heard what John said and followed Jesus.

38 When Jesus turned around and noticed them following, he asked them, "What are you looking for?"

They replied, "Rabbi,"—which means "Teacher"—"where are you staying?"

39 "Come and see," Jesus answered.

So they went to see where he was staying, and they spent the rest of the day with him. It was about four in the afternoon.

40 One of the two who had followed Jesus after hearing John was Andrew, Simon Peter's brother. 41 The first thing Andrew did was to find Simon Peter and say, "We've found the Messiah!"—which means "the Anointed One."

42 Andrew brought Simon to Jesus, who looked hard at him and said, "You are Simon ben-Jonah; I will call you 'Rock'"—that is, "Peter."

43 The next day, after Jesus had decided to leave for Galilee, he met Philip and said, "Follow me." 44 Philip came from Bethsaida, the same town as Andrew and Peter.

45 Philip sought out Nathanael and said to him, "We've found the One that Moses spoke of in the Law, the One about whom the prophets wrote: Jesus of Nazareth, son of Mary and Joseph."

46 "From Nazareth?" said Nathanael. "Can anything good come from Nazareth?"

"Come and see," replied Philip.

47 When Jesus saw Nathanael coming toward him, he remarked, "This one is a real Israelite. There is no guile in him."

48 "How do you know me?" Nathanael asked him.

Jesus answered, "Before Philip even went to call you, while you were sitting under the fig tree, I saw you."

49 "Rabbi," said Nathanael, "you're God's Own; you're the ruler of Israel!"

50 Jesus said, "Do you believe just because I told you I saw you under the fig tree? You'll see much greater things than that."

51 Jesus went on to tell them, "The truth of the matter is, you will see heaven opened, and the angels of God ascending and descending upon the Chosen One."

2 1 Three days later, there was a wedding at Cana in Galilee, and Mary, the mother of Jesus, was there. 2 Jesus and his disciples had likewise been invited to the celebration.

3 At a certain point, the wine ran out, and Jesus' mother told him, "They have no wine."

4 Jesus replied, "Mother, what does that have to do with me? My hour has not yet come."

5 She instructed those waiting on tables, "Do whatever he tells you."

6 As prescribed for Jewish ceremonial washings, there were six stone water jars on hand, each one holding between fifteen and twenty-five gallons. 7 "Fill those jars with water," Jesus said, and the servers filled them to the brim.

8 "Now," said Jesus, "draw some out and take it to the caterer." They did as they were instructed.

9 The caterer tasted the water—which had been turned into wine—without knowing where it had come from; the only ones who knew were those who were waiting on tables, since they had drawn the water. The caterer called the bride and groom over 10 and remarked, "People usually serve the best wine first; then, when the guests have been drinking a while, a lesser vintage is served. What you've done is to keep the best wine until now!"

11 Jesus performed this first of his signs at Cana in Galilee; in this way he revealed his glory, and the disciples believed in him.

12 After this Jesus went down to Capernaum with his mother, brothers and sisters, and disciples. They stayed there a few days.

2:13–3:21

Since it was almost the Jewish Passover, Jesus went up to Jerusalem.

14 In the Temple, he found people selling cattle, sheep and pigeons, while moneychangers sat at their counters. 15 Making a whip out of cords, Jesus drove them all out of the Temple—even the cattle and sheep—and overturned the tables of the money changers, scattering their coins. 16 Then he faced the pigeon sellers: "Take all this out of here! Stop turning God's house into a market!" 17 The disciples remembered the words of scripture: "Zeal for your house consumes me."

18 The Temple authorities intervened and said, "What sign can you show us to justify what you've done?"

19 Jesus answered, "Destroy this temple, and in three days I will raise it up."

20 They retorted, "It has taken forty-six years to build this Temple, and you're going to raise it up in three days?" 21 But the temple he was speaking of was his body. 22 It was only after Jesus had been raised from the dead that the disciples remembered this statement and believed the scripture—and the words that Jesus had spoken.

23 While Jesus was in Jerusalem for the Passover festival, many people believed in him, for they could see the signs he was performing. 24 But Jesus knew all people, and didn't entrust himself to them. 25 Jesus never needed evidence about people's motives; he was well aware of what was in everyone's heart.

come out into the light,
so that it may be plainly seen
that what they do is done in God."

3:22—4:54

After this, Jesus and the disciples went into Judea; Jesus spent some time with them there and performed baptisms. ²³ John also was baptizing—in Aenon, near Salim, where water was plentiful—and people were constantly coming to be baptized. ²⁴ This was, of course, before John had been put in prison.

²⁵ A controversy about purification arose between some of John's disciples and a certain Temple authority. ²⁶ They came to John and said, "Rabbi, that person who was with you across the Jordan—the One about whom you've been testifying—is baptizing now, and everyone is going to him."

²⁷ John replied, "None can lay claim to anything unless it is given to them from heaven. ²⁸ You yourselves are witnesses to the fact that I said, 'I am not the Messiah; I am the Messiah's forerunner.' ²⁹ The bride and the groom are for each other. The bridal party just waits there listening for them and is overjoyed to hear their voices. This is my joy, and it is complete. ³⁰ Now the Messiah must increase, and I must decrease.

³¹ The one who comes from above
is above all;
the one who is of the earth
belongs to the earth
and speaks of earthly things.
The one who comes from above
³² testifies about things seen and heard above,
yet no one accepts this testimony.
³³ But those who do accept this testimony
attest to God's truthfulness.
³⁴ For the one whom God has sent
speaks the words of God,
for God gives the Spirit without reserve.
³⁵ Abba God loves the Only Begotten,
to whom all things have been entrusted.
³⁶ Everyone who believes in the Only Begotten
has eternal life.
But everyone who rejects the Only Begotten
won't see life,
for God's wrath stays on them."

4 ¹ When Jesus learned that the Pharisees had heard he was attracting and baptizing more disciples than John ² —though it was really not Jesus baptizing, but his disciples— ³ he left Judea and returned to Galilee. ⁴ This meant that he had to pass through Samaria.

⁵ He stopped at Sychar, a town in Samaria, near the tract of land Jacob had given to his son Joseph, ⁶ and Jacob's Well was there. Jesus, weary from the journey, came and sat by the well. It was around noon.

⁷ When a Samaritan woman came to draw water, Jesus said to her, "Give me a drink." ⁸ The disciples had gone off to the town to buy provisions.

⁹ The Samaritan woman replied, "You're a Jew. How can you ask me, a Samaritan, for a drink?"—since Jews had nothing to do with Samaritans.

¹⁰ Jesus answered, "If only you recognized God's gift, and who it is that is asking you for a drink, you would have

3 ¹ A certain Pharisee named Nicodemus, a member of the Sanhedrin, ² came to Jesus at night. "Rabbi," he said, "we know you're a teacher come from God, for no one can perform the signs and wonders you do, unless by the power of God."

³ Jesus gave Nicodemus this answer:

"The truth of the matter is,
unless one is born from above,
one cannot see the kindom of God."

⁴ Nicodemus said, "How can an adult be born a second time? I can't go back into my mother's womb to be born again!"

⁵ Jesus replied:

"The truth of the matter is,
no one can enter God's kindom
without being born of water and the Spirit.
⁶ What is born of the flesh is flesh;
what is born of the Spirit is Spirit.
⁷ So don't be surprised when I tell you that
you must be born from above.
⁸ The wind blows where it will.
You hear the sound it makes,
but you don't know where it comes from
or where it goes.
So it is with everyone
who is born of the Spirit."

⁹ "How can this be possible?" asked Nicodemus.

¹⁰ Jesus replied, "You're a teacher of Israel, and you still don't understand these matters?

¹¹ "The truth of the matter is,
we're talking about what we know;
we're testifying about what we've seen—
yet you don't accept our testimony.
¹² If you don't believe
when I tell you about earthly things,
how will you believe
when I tell you about heavenly things?
¹³ No one has gone up to heaven
except the One who came down from heaven—
the Chosen One.
¹⁴ As Moses lifted up the serpent in the desert,
so the Chosen One must be lifted up,
¹⁵ so that everyone who believes in the Chosen One
might have eternal life.
¹⁶ Yes, God so loved the world
as to give the Only Begotten One,
that whoever believes may not die,
but have eternal life.
¹⁷ God sent the Only Begotten into the world
not to condemn the world,
but that through the Only Begotten
the world might be saved.
¹⁸ Whoever believes in the Only Begotten avoids
judgment,
but whoever doesn't believe is judged already
for not believing in the name
of the Only Begotten of God.
¹⁹ On these grounds is sentence pronounced:
that though the light came into the world,
people showed they preferred darkness to the light
because their deeds were evil.
²⁰ Indeed, people who do wrong hate the light and
avoid it,
for fear their actions will be exposed;
²¹ but people who live by the truth

asked him for a drink instead, and he would have given you living water."

¹¹ "If you please," she challenged Jesus, "you don't have a bucket and this well is deep. Where do you expect to get this 'living water'? ¹² Surely you don't pretend to be greater than our ancestors Leah and Rachel and Jacob, who gave us this well and drank from it with their descendants and flocks?"

¹³ Jesus replied, "Everyone who drinks this water will be thirsty again. ¹⁴ But those who drink the water I give them will never be thirsty; no, the water I give will become fountains within them, springing up to provide eternal life."

¹⁵ The woman said to Jesus, "Give me this water, so that I won't grow thirsty and have to keep coming all the way here to draw water."

¹⁶ Jesus said to her, "Go, call your husband and then come back here."

¹⁷ "I don't have a husband," replied the woman.

"You're right—you don't have a husband!" Jesus exclaimed. ¹⁸ "The fact is, you've had five, and the man you're living with now is not your husband. So what you've said is quite true."

¹⁹ "I can see you're a prophet," answered the woman. ²⁰ "Our ancestors worshiped on this mountain, but you people claim that Jerusalem is the place where God ought to be worshiped."

²¹ Jesus told her, "Believe me, the hour is coming when you'll worship Abba God neither on this mountain nor in Jerusalem. ²² You people worship what you don't understand; we worship what we do understand—after all, salvation is from the Jewish people. ²³ Yet the hour is coming—and is already here—when real worshippers will worship Abba God in Spirit and truth. Indeed, it is just such worshippers whom Abba God seeks. ²⁴ God is Spirit, and those who worship God must worship in spirit and truth."

²⁵ The woman said to Jesus, "I know that the Messiah—the Anointed One—is coming and will tell us everything."

²⁶ Jesus replied, "I who speak to you am the Messiah."

²⁷ The disciples, returning at this point, were shocked to find Jesus having a private conversation with a woman. But no one dared to ask, "What do you want of him?" or "Why are you talking with her?"

²⁸ The woman then left her water jar and went off into the town. She said to the people, ²⁹ "Come and see someone who told me everything I have ever done! Could this be the Messiah?" ³⁰ At that, everyone set out from town to meet Jesus.

³¹ Meanwhile, the disciples were urging Jesus, "Rabbi, eat something."

³² But Jesus told them, "I have food to eat that you know nothing about."

³³ At this, the disciples said to one another, "Do you think someone has brought him something to eat?"

³⁴ Jesus explained to them,

"Doing the will of the One who sent me
and bringing this work to completion
is my food.
³⁵ Don't you have a saying,
'Four months more
and it will be harvest time'?
I tell you,
open your eyes and look at the fields—
they're ripe and ready for harvest!
³⁶ Reapers are already collecting their wages;
they're gathering fruit for eternal life,
and sower and reaper will rejoice together.
³⁷ So the saying is true:
'One person sows; another reaps.'
³⁸ I have sent you to reap
what you haven't worked for.
Others have done the work,
and you've come upon the fruits of their labor."

³⁹ Many Samaritans from that town believed in Jesus on the strength of the woman's testimony—that "he told me everything I ever did." ⁴⁰ The result was that, when these Samaritans came to Jesus, they begged him to stay with them awhile. So Jesus stayed there two days, ⁴¹ and through his own spoken word many more came to faith. ⁴² They told the woman, "No longer does our faith depend on your story. We've heard for ourselves, and we know that this really is the savior of the world."

⁴³ On the third day, Jesus left Samaria for Galilee. ⁴⁴ Now Jesus had pointed out that a prophet is not esteemed in the prophet's own country. ⁴⁵ So when he arrived in Galilee, it was the Galileans who welcomed him, because they themselves had been at the feast and had seen all that he had done in Jerusalem on that occasion. ⁴⁶ That's why Jesus returned to Cana in Galilee, where he had turned the water into wine.

At Capernaum there lived a royal official whose child was ill. ⁴⁷ Upon hearing that Jesus had returned to Galilee from Judea, the official went and begged Jesus to come down and restore health to the child, who was near death.

⁴⁸ Jesus replied, "Unless you people see signs and wonders, you won't believe!"

⁴⁹ "Rabbi," the official pleaded, "come down before my child dies."

⁵⁰ Jesus said, "Return home; your child lives."

The official believed what Jesus said and started for home. ⁵¹ On the way, the official was met by members of the household with the news that the child was going to live. ⁵² When the official asked at what time the fever broke, they said, "About one o'clock yesterday afternoon." ⁵³ The official realized that this was the very hour that Jesus had said, "Your child lives." The whole household then became believers.

⁵⁴ This was the second sign that Jesus performed, after he had left Judea for Galilee.

5:1–47

Some time after this, there was a Jewish festival and Jesus went up to Jerusalem. ² Now in Jerusalem, near the Sheep Gate, there is a pool with five porticoes; its Hebrew name is Bethesda. ³ The place was crowded with sick people—those who were blind, lame or paralyzed—lying there waiting for the water to move. ⁴ An angel of God would come down to the pool from time to time, to stir up the water; the first one to step into the water after it had been stirred up would be completely healed.*

⁵ One person there had been sick for thirty-eight years. ⁶ Jesus, who knew this person had been sick for a long time, said, "Do you want to be healed?"

⁷ "Rabbi," the sick one answered, "I don't have anyone to put me into the pool once the water has been stirred up. By the time I get there, someone else has gone in ahead of me."

⁸ Jesus replied, "Stand up! Pick up your mat and walk."

---

* Many of the manuscripts end verse 3 at "or paralyzed," and delete verse 4 altogether.

⁹ The individual was immediately healed, and picked up the mat and walked away.

This happened on a Sabbath. ¹⁰ Consequently, some of the Temple authorities said to the one who had been healed, "It's the Sabbath! You're not allowed to carry that mat around!"

¹¹ The healed one explained, "But the person who healed me told me, 'Pick up your mat and walk.'"

¹² They asked, "Who is this who told you to pick up your mat and walk?"

¹³ The healed person had no idea who it was, since Jesus had disappeared into the crowd that filled the place.

¹⁴ Later on, Jesus met the individual in the Temple and said, "Remember, now, you've been healed. Give up your sins so that something worse won't overtake you." ¹⁵ The healed one went off and informed the Temple authorities that Jesus was the one who had performed the healing.

¹⁶ It was because Jesus did things like this on the Sabbath that the Temple authorities began to persecute him. ¹⁷ Jesus said to them, "Abba God is working right now, and I am at work as well." ¹⁸ Because of this, the Temple authorities were even more determined to kill him. Not only was he breaking the Sabbath but, worse still, he was speaking of God as "Abba"—that is, "Papa"—thereby making their relationship one of intimacy and equality.

¹⁹ This was Jesus' answer:

"The truth of the matter is,
the Only Begotten can do nothing alone,
but can only follow Abba God's example.
For whatever Abba does,
the Only Begotten does—
and does in the same way.
²⁰ For Abba God loves the Only Begotten,
and teaches the Only Begotten by example.
And God will show the Only Begotten
even greater works than you've seen—
works that will astonish you.
²¹ Indeed, just as Abba God raises the dead and gives
     them life,
so the Only Begotten gives life to anyone at will.
²² For Abba God judges no one,
having entrusted all judgment to the Only Begotten,
²³ so that all may honor the Only Begotten
as they honor Abba God.
Whoever doesn't honor the Only Begotten
dishonors the One who sent the Only Begotten—
Abba God.
²⁴ The truth of the matter is,
whoever listens to my words
and believes in the One who sent me
has eternal life
and isn't brought to judgment,
having passed from death to life.
²⁵ The truth of the matter is,
the hour will come—
in fact is here already—
when the dead will hear
the voice of God's Only Begotten,
and all who hear it will live.
²⁶ For just as Abba God is the source of life,
God has ordained that the Only Begotten
also be the source of life—
²⁷ and be given authority to execute judgment
as the Chosen One of God.
²⁸ Don't be surprised at this,
because the hour is coming
when those in the grave
will hear the Chosen One's voice
²⁹ and come forth:
those who did good will rise to life
and those who did evil will rise to condemnation.
³⁰ I can do nothing by myself;
I can only judge as I am told to judge.
And my judging is just,
because my aim is to do not my own will,
but the will of the One who sent me.
³¹ If I testify on my own behalf,
my testimony is not valid;
³² but someone else is testifying on my behalf,
and I know that this one's testimony is true.
³³ You've sent messengers to John,
who has testified to the truth—
³⁴ not that I depend on human testimony;
it's only for your salvation
that I explain things this way.
³⁵ John was the lamp, set aflame and burning bright,
and for a while you rejoiced willingly in his light.
³⁶ Yet I have testimony that is greater than John's:
the works that Abba God has given me to do.
These very works that I do
testify on my behalf that Abba God has sent me.
³⁷ Moreover the One who sent me
has also testified on my behalf.
You've never heard God's voice;
you've never seen God's form—
³⁸ nor have you ever had God's words
abiding in your hearts,
because you don't believe
the one whom God has sent!
³⁹ Search the scriptures—
the ones you think give you eternal life:
those very scriptures testify about me.
⁴⁰ Yet you're unwilling to come to me
to receive that life.
⁴¹ It's not that I accept human praise—
⁴² it is simply that I know you,
and you don't have the love of God in your hearts.
⁴³ I have come in the name of Abba God,
yet you don't accept me.
But let others come in their own name
and you'll accept them!
⁴⁴ How can you believe,
when you accept praise from one another,
yet don't seek the praise
that comes from the One God?
⁴⁵ Don't imagine that I will be your accuser before
     Abba God;
it is Moses who accuses you—
the one in whom you've put your hope.
⁴⁶ For if you really believed Moses,
you would believe me,
for it was about me that Moses wrote.
⁴⁷ But if you don't believe what Moses wrote,
how can you believe what I say?"

6:1–71

Some time later, Jesus crossed over to the other side of the Sea of Galilee—that is, Lake Tiberius— ² and a huge crowd followed him, impressed by the signs he gave by healing sick people. 3 Jesus climbed the hillside and sat down there with the disciples. 4 It was shortly before the Jewish feast of Passover.

5 Looking up, Jesus saw the crowd approaching and said to Philip, "Where can we buy some bread for these people to eat?" 6 Jesus knew very well what he was going to do, but asked this to test Philip's response.

7 Philip answered, "Not even with two hundred days' wages could we buy loaves enough to give each of them a mouthful!"

8 One of the disciples, Simon Peter's brother Andrew, said, 9 "There's a small boy here with five barley loaves and two dried fish. But what good is that for so many people?"

10 Jesus said to them, "Make the people sit down." There was plenty of grass there, and as many as five thousand families sat down. 11 Then Jesus took the loaves, gave thanks, and gave them out to all who were sitting there; he did the same with the fish, giving out as much as they could eat.

12 When the people had eaten their fill, Jesus said to the disciples, "Gather up the leftover pieces so that nothing gets wasted." 13 So they picked them up and filled twelve baskets with the scraps left over from the five barley loaves.

14 The people, seeing this sign that Jesus had performed, said, "Surely this is the Prophet who was to come into the world." 15 Seeing that they were about to come and carry him off to crown him as ruler, Jesus escaped into the hills alone.

16 As evening approached, the disciples went down to the lake. 17 They got into their boat, intending to cross to Capernaum, which was on the other side of the lake. By this time it was dark, and Jesus had still not joined them; 18 moreover, a stiff wind was blowing and the sea was becoming rough.

19 When they had rowed three or four miles, they caught sight of Jesus approaching the boat, walking on the water. They were frightened, 20 but he told them, "It's me. Don't be afraid." 21 They were about to take him into the boat, but suddenly the boat was ashore at their destination.

22 The next day, the crowd that had stayed on the other side of the lake saw that only one boat had been there; and they knew that Jesus had not gotten into the boat with the disciples—that the disciples had set off by themselves. 23 Other boats, however, had put in from Tiberias, near the place where the bread had been eaten after the Rabbi had given thanks. 24 When the people saw that neither Jesus nor the disciples were there, they got into those boats and crossed to Capernaum looking for Jesus.

25 When they found Jesus on the other side of the lake, they said, "Rabbi, when did you get here?"

26 Jesus answered them,

"The truth of the matter is,
you're not looking for me because you've seen signs,
but because you've eaten your fill of the bread.
27 You shouldn't be working for perishable food,
but for life-giving food that lasts for all eternity;
this the Chosen One can give you,
for the Chosen One bears the seal of Abba God."

28 At this they said, "What must we do to perform the works of God?"

29 Jesus replied,

"This is the work of God:
to believe in the one whom God has sent."

30 So they asked Jesus, "What sign are you going to give to show us that we should believe in you? What will you do? 31 Our ancestors had manna to eat in the desert; as scripture says, 'God gave them bread from heaven to eat.'"

32 Jesus said to them,

"The truth of the matter is,
Moses hasn't given you bread from heaven;
yet my Abba gives you the true bread from heaven.
33 For the bread of God
is the one who comes down from heaven
and gives life to the world."

34 "Teacher," they said, "give us this bread from now on."
35 Jesus explained to them,

"I am the bread of life.
No one who comes to me will ever be hungry;
no one who believes in me will be thirsty.
36 But as I told you,
you see me and still don't believe.
37 Everyone Abba God gives me will come to me,
and whoever comes to me I won't turn away.
38 For I have come from heaven, not to do my own will,
but the will of the One who sent me.
39 It is the will of the One who sent me
that I lose none of those given to me,
but rather raise them up on the last day.
40 Indeed, this is the will of my Abba:
that everyone who sees and believes in
the Only Begotten will have eternal life.
These are the ones I will raise up on the last day."

41 The Temple authorities started to grumble in protest because Jesus claimed, "I am the bread that came down from heaven." 42 They kept saying, "Isn't this Jesus, son of Mary and Joseph? Don't we know his mother and father? How can he claim to have come down from heaven?"

43 "Stop your grumbling," Jesus told them.
44 "No one can come to me
unless drawn by Abba God, who sent me—
and those I will raise up on the last day.
45 It is written in the prophets:
'They will all be taught by God.'
Everyone who has heard God's word
and has learned from it
comes to me.
46 Not that anyone has seen Abba God—
only the one who is from God has seen Abba God.
47 The truth of the matter is,
those who believe have eternal life.
48 I am the bread of life.
49 Your ancestors ate manna in the desert,
but they died.
50 This is the bread that comes down from heaven,
and if you eat it you'll never die.
51 I myself am the living bread
come down from heaven.
If any eat this bread,
they will live forever;
the bread I will give
for the life of the world
is my flesh."

52 The Temple authorities then began to argue with one another. "How can he give us his flesh to eat?"
53 Jesus replied,

"The truth of the matter is,
if you don't eat the flesh
and drink the blood of the Chosen One,
you won't have life in you.
54 Those who do eat my flesh and drink my blood
have eternal life,

and I will raise them up on the last day.
⁵⁵ For my flesh is real food
and my blood is real drink.
⁵⁶ Everyone who eats my flesh and drinks my blood
lives in me, and I live in them.
⁵⁷ Just as the living Abba God sent me
and I have life because of Abba God,
so those who feed on me
will have life because of me.
⁵⁸ This is the bread that came down from heaven.
It's not the kind of bread your ancestors ate,
for they died;
whoever eats this kind of bread
will live forever."

⁵⁹ Jesus spoke these words while teaching in the synagogue in Capernaum.

⁶⁰ Many of his disciples remarked, "We can't put up with this kind of talk! How can anyone take it seriously?"

⁶¹ Jesus was fully aware that the disciples were murmuring in protest at what he had said. "Is this a stumbling block for you?" he asked them.

⁶² "What, then, if you were to see the Chosen One
ascend to where the Chosen One came from?
⁶³ It is the spirit that gives life;
the flesh in itself is useless.
The words I have spoken to you
are spirit and life.
⁶⁴ Yet among you there are some
who don't believe."

Jesus knew from the start, of course, those who would refuse to believe and the one who would betray him. ⁶⁵ He went on to say:

"This is why I have told you
that no one can come to me
unless it is granted by Abba God."

⁶⁶ From this time on, many of the disciples broke away and wouldn't remain in the company of Jesus. ⁶⁷ Jesus then said to the Twelve, "Are you going to leave me, too?"

⁶⁸ Simon Peter answered, "Rabbi, where would we go? You have the words of eternal life. ⁶⁹ We have come to believe; we're convinced that you are the Holy One of God."

⁷⁰ Then Jesus replied, "Haven't I chosen you Twelve? Yet one of you is a devil." ⁷¹ Jesus meant that one of the Twelve, Judas, son of Simon Iscariot, was going to betray him.

7:1–10:39

After this, Jesus walked through Galilee. He had decided not to travel to Judea, because the Temple authorities were trying to kill him.

² As the Jewish Feast of Tabernacles approached, ³ Jesus' sisters and brothers said to him, "Why not leave here and go to Judea so that your disciples there can also see the works you do. ⁴ Those destined for public life don't do things in secret. Since you're working these miracles, let the whole world know!" ⁵ For even his own siblings didn't believe in him.

⁶ Jesus answered, "Now is not the right time for me. But for you, any time is right. ⁷ The world can't hate you. But it hates me because I testify that its ways are evil. ⁸ Go up to the feast yourselves. I am not going to this feast because my time is yet to come." ⁹ Having said this, he stayed in Galilee.

❀ ❀ ❀

¹⁰ Once Jesus' sisters and brothers had gone up to the festival, he too went up—not publicly, but in secret, as it were.

¹¹ At the festival the Temple authorities were looking for Jesus and asking, "Where is he?" ¹² The crowd stood around whispering about him. Some said, "He's a good teacher." Others, however, said, "No, he is leading us astray." ¹³ Yet no one spoke about Jesus openly for fear of the Temple authorities.

¹⁴ When the Feast was half over, Jesus went to the Temple and began to teach. ¹⁵ The crowd was amazed and said, "He certainly knows his letters! But how is that possible when he's never had any formal education?"

¹⁶ Jesus answered,

"My teaching is not my own.
It comes from the One who sent me.
¹⁷ All who are prepared to do the will of God
will know whether my teaching comes from God
or whether I speak on my own.
¹⁸ Those who speak on their own
seek their own glory.
Those who seek the glory of the One who sends them
are truthful and do nothing unjust.
¹⁹ Didn't Moses give you the Law?
Yet not one of you keeps the Law!
Why are you trying to kill me?"

²⁰ The crowd answered, "You're possessed! Who is trying to kill you?"

²¹ Jesus replied, "I worked one miracle, and you're all amazed by it. ²² Moses gave you circumcision as a sign of the Covenant—actually, it came from our ancestors and not from Moses—and you perform it on the Sabbath. ²³ If a baby can receive the sign of the Covenant on the Sabbath in order to keep the Law of Moses, why are you angry with me for making a person whole on the Sabbath? ²⁴ Stop judging for the sake of appearances! Start judging justly!"

²⁵ Meanwhile some of the people of Jerusalem were saying, "Isn't this the one they want to kill? ²⁶ And here he is, speaking freely, and they have nothing to say to him! Can it be true that the authorities have made up their minds that this is the Messiah? ²⁷ Yet we all know where this fellow comes from, but when the Messiah comes, no one will know that one's origins."

²⁸ At this, Jesus, still teaching in the Temple area, cried out,

"So, you think you know me and my origins!
Yet I haven't come of my own accord—
I was sent by One who is true,
whom you don't even know.
²⁹ But I do know this One,
because those are my origins,
and by this One I was sent."

³⁰ They would have arrested Jesus then, but no one laid a hand on him because his time had not yet come.

³¹ There were many in the crowd, however, who believed in Jesus. They said, "Will the coming Messiah perform more miracles than this person?" ³² The Pharisees heard the crowd murmuring to this effect; so the Pharisees and the chief priests sent the Temple guards to arrest him.

³³ Jesus said, "I will be with you only a little longer, then I will go to the One who sent me. ³⁴ You'll look for me and won't find me. For where I am, you cannot come."

³⁵ Those gathered there said to one another, "Where is he going that we won't find him? Will he go abroad to our people scattered among the Greek Diaspora, and will he teach the Greeks? ³⁶ What is the meaning of the statement, 'You'll look for me and won't find me. For where I am, you cannot come'?"

37 On the last and greatest day of the festival, Jesus stood up and shouted,

> "Any who are thirsty,
> let them come to me and drink!
> 38 Those who believe in me, as the scripture says,
> 'From their innermost being
> will flow rivers of living water.'"

39 Here Jesus was referring to the Spirit, which those who came to believe were to receive—though she had not yet been given, since Jesus had not been glorified. 40 Several people in the crowd who had heard the words of Jesus began to say, "This must be the Prophet." 41 But others were saying, "He's the Messiah." Still others said, "Surely the Messiah is not to come from Galilee? 42 Doesn't scripture say that the Messiah, being of David's lineage, is to come from Bethlehem, the village where David lived?" 43 So the people were sharply divided over this. 44 Some of them even wanted to arrest Jesus. However, no one laid hands on him.

45 The Temple guards went back to the chief priests and Pharisees, who said to them, "Why haven't you brought him in?"

46 "No one ever spoke like that before," the guards responded.

47 "So, you too have been taken in!" the Pharisees replied. 48 "Do any of the Sanhedrin believe in him? Any of the Pharisees? 49 This rabble knows nothing about the Law—and they are damned anyway!"

50 One of their own, Nicodemus—the same person who had come to Jesus earlier—said to them, 51 "Since when does our Law condemn anyone without first hearing the accused and knowing all the facts?"

52 "Don't tell us you're a Galilean, too!" they taunted him. "Look it up. You'll see that no prophet comes from Galilee."

53 *After that, everyone went home, **8** 1 and Jesus went out to the Mount of Olives.

2 At daybreak, he reappeared in the Temple area, and when the people started coming to him, Jesus sat down and began to teach them.

3 A couple had been caught in the act of adultery, though the scribes and Pharisees brought only the woman, and they made her stand there in front of everyone. 4 "Teacher," they said, "this woman has been caught in the act of adultery. 5 In the Law of Moses, the punishment for this act is stoning. What do you say about it?" 6 They were posing this question to trap Jesus so that they could charge him with something.

Jesus simply bent down and started tracing on the ground with his finger. 7 When they persisted in their questioning, Jesus straightened up and said to them, "Let the person among you who is without sin throw the first stone at her." 8 Then he bent down again and wrote on the ground.

9 The audience drifted away one by one, beginning with the elder. This left Jesus alone with the woman, who continued to stand there. 10 Jesus finally straightened up again and said, "Where did they go? Has no one condemned you?"

11 "No one, Teacher," came the reply.

"I don't condemn you either. Go on your way—but from now on, don't sin any more."

---

* John 7:53—8:11 is not found in most of the manuscripts.

12 The next time Jesus spoke to them, he said,

> "I am the light of the world.
> Whoever follows me won't walk in darkness,
> but will have the light of life."

13 The Pharisees said to him, "You're testifying about yourself, so your testimony isn't valid."

14 Jesus replied,

> "Even if I do testify about myself,
> my testimony is valid,
> because I know where I came from
> and where I am going.
> But you know neither where I come from
> nor where I am going.
> 15 You people judge by external things;
> I don't judge anyone at all.
> 16 But even if I were to judge,
> my judgment would be true
> because I am not alone in it—
> the One who sent me
> joins me in that judgment.
> 17 Even in the Law it is written
> that it takes two witnesses for testimony to be
> admissible.
> 18 Well, I bear witness about myself,
> and my Abba, who sent me,
> bears witness about me as well."

19 They asked Jesus, "Where is this 'Abba' of yours?" Jesus replied,

> "You don't know me,
> nor do you know my Abba;
> if you knew me,
> you would know my Abba as well."

20 Jesus spoke these words in front of the Temple treasury, while he was teaching. No one seized him, because his hour had not yet come.

21 Again he said to them:

> "I am going away.
> You'll look for me,
> but you'll die in your sins.
> Where I am going
> you cannot come."

22 At this, some of the Temple authorities said to one another, "Is he going to kill himself? Is this what he means by saying, 'Where I am going, you cannot come'?"

23 Jesus went on,

> "You belong to what is below;
> I am from above.
> You're of this world;
> I am not of this world.
> 24 I have told you already,
> you'll die in your sins.
> Yes, you will surely die in your sins
> unless you believe that I AM."

25 So they said to Jesus, "Who are you?" Jesus answered,

> "What have I told you from the beginning?
> 26 About you I have much to say
> and much to condemn;
> But the One who sent me is truthful
> and what I have learned
> I now declare to the world."

[27] They didn't grasp that Jesus was speaking about Abba God. [28] Jesus continued,

> "When you have lifted up the Chosen One,
> then you'll know that I AM
> and that I do nothing of myself;
> I say only what Abba God has taught me.
> [29] The One who sent me is with me
> and has not deserted me,
> because I always do God's will."

[30] While he spoke, many became believers. [31] Jesus said to those who believed in him,

> "If you live according to my teaching,
> you really are my disciples;
> [32] then you'll know the truth,
> and the truth will set you free."

[33] "We're descendants of Sarah and Abraham," they replied. "Never have we been the slaves of anyone. What do you mean by saying, 'You'll be free'?"

[34] Jesus answered them,

> "The truth of the matter is,
> everyone who lives in sin
> is the slave of sin.
> [35] Now a slave doesn't always remain part of a
>   household;
> an heir, however, is a member of that house forever.
> [36] So if the heir—the Only Begotten—makes you free,
> you will be free indeed.
> [37] I know that you're descended from Sarah and
>   Abraham;
> but in spite of that you want to kill me
> because my message has found no room in you.
> [38] I speak of what I have seen with Abba God,
> and you do what you learned from your parents."

[39] They repeated, "Our parents are Sarah and Abraham." Jesus said to them,

> "If you *were* the children of Sarah and Abraham,
> you would do as they did.
> [40] As it is, you want to kill me
> when I tell you the truth, which I heard from God.
> That is not what Sarah and Abraham did;
> [41] you're doing what your parents did."

They cried, "We're no illegitimate breed! We're born of God alone."

[42] Jesus answered,

> "If you were born of God,
> you would love me;
> for I came forth from God,
> and I was sent from God.
> I didn't come of my own will:
> it was God who sent me.
> [43] Why don't you understand what I am saying to
>   you?
> It's because you cannot bear to hear what I say.
> [44] You're children of the Devil,
> and children want to do their parents' will.
> The Devil was a murderer from the beginning
> and is not grounded in truth,
> because there is no truth in it.
> When the Devil lies,
> it speaks its native tongue.
> The Devil is a liar—
> the source of all lies.
> [45] But I speak the truth,
> yet you don't believe me.

> [46] Can any of you convict me of sin?
> If I do speak the truth,
> why don't you believe me?
> [47] Whoever belongs to God
> hears the words of God.
> And that's precisely why you don't hear them—
> because you're not of God."

[48] The Temple authorities replied, "Aren't we right to say that you're a Samaritan—a heretic—and that you're possessed by a devil?"

[49] Jesus answered, "I am not possessed. I honor God, my Abba, and you dishonor me. [50] I don't seek my own glory. There is One who seeks it and judges it.

> [51] "The truth of the matter is,
> anyone who keeps my word
> will never see death."

[52] They retorted, "Now we're sure you're possessed! Sarah and Abraham are dead; the prophets are dead; yet you claim, 'Anyone who keeps my word will never know death.' [53] Surely you don't pretend to be greater than our ancestors, Sarah and Abraham, who died! Or the prophets, who died! Who do you make yourself out to be?"

[54] Jesus answered,

> "If I glorify myself,
> that glory comes to nothing.
> But the One who glorifies me is Abba God,
> of whom you say, 'This is our God.'
> [55] You haven't come to know God,
> but I do,
> and if I were to say, 'I don't know God,'
> I would be a liar, like you!
> But I do know God,
> and I faithfully keep God's word.
> [56] Your ancestors Sarah and Abraham rejoiced
> to think that they would see my day—
> and they did see it, and were glad."

[57] Then the authorities objected, "You're not yet fifty years old, and you say you've seen Sarah and Abraham?"

[58] Jesus answered them,

> "The truth of the matter is,
> before Sarah and Abraham ever were,
> I AM."

[59] At this, they picked up rocks to throw at Jesus. But he hid himself and slipped out of the Temple.

9 [1] As Jesus walked along, he saw someone who had been blind from birth. [2] The disciples asked Jesus, "Rabbi, was it this individual's sin that caused the blindness, or that of the parents?"

[3] "Neither," answered Jesus,

> "It wasn't because of anyone's sin—
> not this person's, nor the parents'.
> Rather, it was to let God's works shine forth
> in this person.
> [4] We must do the deeds of the One who sent me
> while it is still day—
> for night is coming,
> when no one can work.
> [5] While I am in the world,
> I am the light of the world."

⁶ With that, Jesus spat on the ground, made mud with his saliva and smeared the blind one's eyes with the mud. ⁷ Then Jesus said, "Go, wash in the pool of Siloam"—"Siloam" means "sent." So the person went off to wash, and came back able to see.

⁸ Neighbors and those who had been accustomed to seeing the blind beggar began to ask, "Isn't this the one who used to sit and beg?" ⁹ Some said yes; others said no—the one who had been healed simply looked like the beggar.

But the individual in question said, "No—it was me."

¹⁰ The people then asked, "Then how were your eyes opened?"

¹¹ The answer came, "The one they call Jesus made mud and smeared it on my eyes, and told me to go to Siloam and wash. When I went and washed, I was able to see."

¹² "Where is Jesus?" they asked.

The person replied, "I have no idea."

¹³ They took the one who had been born blind to the Pharisees. ¹⁴ It had been on a Sabbath that Jesus had made the mud paste and opened this one's eyes. ¹⁵ The Pharisees asked how the individual could see. They were told, "Jesus put mud on my eyes. I washed it off, and now I can see."

¹⁶ This prompted some Pharisees to say, "This Jesus cannot be from God, because he doesn't keep the Sabbath." Others argued, "But how could a sinner perform signs like these?" They were sharply divided.

¹⁷ Then they addressed the blind person again: "Since it was your eyes he opened, what do you have to say about this Jesus?"

"He's a prophet," came the reply.

¹⁸ The Temple authorities refused to believe that this one had been blind and had begun to see, until they summoned the parents. ¹⁹ "Is this your child?" they asked, "and if so, do you attest that your child was blind at birth? How do you account for the fact that now your child can see?"

²⁰ The parents answered, "We know this is our child, blind from birth. ²¹ But how our child can see now, or who opened those blind eyes, we have no idea. But don't ask us—our child is old enough to speak without us!" ²² The parents answered this way because they were afraid of the Temple authorities, who had already agreed among themselves that anyone who acknowledged Jesus as the Messiah would be put out of the synagogue. ²³ That was why they said, "Our child is of age and should be asked directly."

²⁴ A second time they summoned the one who had been born blind and said, "Give God the glory instead; we know that this Jesus is a sinner."

²⁵ "I don't know whether he is a sinner or not," the individual answered. "All I know is that I used to be blind, and now I can see."

²⁶ They persisted, "Just what did he do to you? How did he open your eyes?"

²⁷ "I already told you, but you won't listen to me," came the answer. "Why do you want to hear it all over again? Don't tell me you want to become disciples of Jesus too!"

²⁸ They retorted scornfully, "You're the one who is Jesus' disciple. We're disciples of Moses. ²⁹ We know that God spoke to Moses, but we have no idea where this Jesus comes from."

³⁰ The other retorted: "Well, this is news! You don't know where he comes from, yet he opened my eyes! ³¹ We know that God doesn't hear sinners, but that if people are devout and obey God's will, God listens to them. ³² It is unheard of that anyone ever gave sight to a person blind from birth. ³³ If this one were not from God, he could never have done such a thing!"

³⁴ "What!" they exclaimed. "You're steeped in sin from birth, and you're giving us lectures?" With that they threw the person out.

³⁵ When Jesus heard of the expulsion, he sought out the healed one and asked, "Do you believe in the Chosen One?"

³⁶ The other answered, "Who is this One, that I may believe?"

³⁷ "You're looking at him," Jesus replied. "The Chosen One is speaking to you now."

³⁸ The healed one said, "Yes, I believe," and worshiped Jesus.

³⁹ And Jesus said, "I came into this world to execute justice—to make the sightless see and the seeing blind."

⁴⁰ Some of the Pharisees who were nearby heard this and said, "You're not calling us blind, are you?"

⁴¹ To which Jesus replied, "If you were blind, there would be no sin in that. But since you say, 'We see,' your sin remains.

10

¹ "The truth of the matter is,
whoever doesn't enter the sheepfold
through the gate
but climbs in some other way
is a thief and a robber.

² The one who enters through the gate
is the shepherd of the sheep,

³ the one for whom the keeper opens the gate.
The sheep know the shepherd's voice;
the shepherd calls them by name
and leads them out.

⁴ Having led them all out of the fold,
the shepherd walks in front of them
and they follow
because they recognize the shepherd's voice.

⁵ They simply won't follow strangers—
they'll flee from them
because they don't recognize the voice of strangers."

⁶ Even though Jesus used this metaphor with them, they didn't grasp what he was trying to tell them. ⁷ He therefore said to them again:

"The truth of the matter is,
I am the sheep gate.

⁸ All who came before me
were thieves and marauders
whom the sheep didn't heed.

⁹ I am the gate.
Whoever enters through me will be safe—
you'll go in and out and find pasture.

¹⁰ The thief comes only to steal
and slaughter and destroy.
I came that you might have life
and have it to the full.

¹¹ I am the good shepherd.
A good shepherd would die for the sheep.

¹² The hired hand, who is neither shepherd
nor owner of the sheep,
catches sight of the wolf coming
and runs away,
leaving the sheep to be scattered
or snatched by the wolf.

¹³ That's because the hired hand works only for pay
and has no concern for the sheep.

¹⁴ I am the good shepherd.
I know my sheep
and my sheep know me,

¹⁵ in the same way Abba God knows me
and I know God—

and for these sheep
I will lay down my life.

¹⁶ I have other sheep
that don't belong to this fold—
I must lead them too,
and they will hear my voice.
And then there will be one flock,
one shepherd.

¹⁷ This is why Abba God loves me—
because I lay down my life,
only to take it up again.

¹⁸ No one takes my life from me;
I lay it down freely.
I have the power to lay it down,
and I have the power to take it up again.
This command I received from my Abba."

¹⁹ These words once more divided the Temple authorities.
²⁰ Many said, "He is possessed, he's raving mad! Why do you listen to him?"

²¹ Others said, "These are not the words of a person possessed by a demon. Could a demon open the eyes of a blind person?"

²² The time came for Hanukkah, the Feast of the Dedication, in Jerusalem. ²³ It was winter, and Jesus was walking in the Temple area, in Solomon's Porch, ²⁴ when the Temple authorities surrounded him and said, "How long are you going to keep us in suspense? If you really are the Messiah, tell us plainly."

²⁵ Jesus replied,

"I did tell you,
but you don't believe.
The work I do in my Abba's name
gives witness in my favor,

²⁶ but you don't believe
because you're not my sheep.

²⁷ My sheep hear my voice.
I know them, and they follow me.

²⁸ I give them eternal life,
and they will never be lost.
No one will ever
snatch them from my hand.

²⁹ Abba God, who gave them to me, is greater than anyone,
and no one can steal them from Abba God.

³⁰ For Abba and I are One."

³¹ With that, the Temple authorities reached again for rocks to stone him.

³² Jesus protested and said, "I have shown you many good works from Abba God. For which of these do you stone me?"

³³ "It's not for any 'good works' that we're stoning you," they replied, "but for blaspheming. You're human, yet you make yourself out to be God."

³⁴ Jesus answered,

"Isn't it written in your Law,
'I said, You are gods?'

³⁵ So the Law uses the word 'gods'
of those to whom the word of God was addressed—
and scripture can't be broken.

³⁶ Yet you say—to someone whom Abba God has consecrated
and sent into the world—
'You're blaspheming,'
because I say, 'I am God's Only Begotten.'

³⁷ If I am not doing Abba God's work,
there is no need to believe me;

³⁸ but if I am doing God's work—
even if you don't believe me—
at least believe in the work I do.
Then you'll know for certain
that Abba God is in me
and I am in Abba God."

³⁹ At these words, they again attempted to arrest Jesus, but he eluded their grasp.

10:40–11:54

Jesus went back again across the Jordan River to the place where John had been baptizing earlier, and while he stayed there, ⁴¹ many people came to him. "John may never have performed a sign," they said, "but everything John said about this person was true." ⁴² And many of them believed in Jesus.

11 ¹ There was a certain man named Lazarus, who was sick. He and his sisters, Mary and Martha, were from the village of Bethany. ² Mary was the one who had anointed the feet of Jesus with perfume and dried his feet with her hair, and it was her brother Lazarus who was sick. ³ The sisters sent this message to Jesus: "Rabbi, the one you love is sick."

⁴ When Jesus heard this, he said, "This sickness will not end in death; it is happening for God's glory, so that God's Only Begotten may be glorified because of it."

⁵ Jesus loved these three very much. ⁶ Yet even after hearing that Lazarus was sick, he remained where he was staying for two more days. ⁷ Finally he said to the disciples, "Let's go back to Judea."

⁸ They protested, "Rabbi, it was only recently that they tried to stone you—and you want to go back there again?"

⁹ Jesus replied,

"Aren't there twelve hours of daylight?
Those who walk by day don't stumble,
because they see the world bathed in light;

¹⁰ those who go walking by night will stumble
because there is no light in them."

¹¹ After Jesus said this, he said to the disciples, "Our beloved Lazarus has fallen asleep. I am going to Judea to wake him."

¹² The disciples objected, "But Rabbi, if he's only asleep, he'll be fine."

¹³ Jesus had been speaking about Lazarus' death, but they thought he was talking about actual sleep. ¹⁴ So he said very plainly, "Lazarus is dead! ¹⁵ For your sakes I am glad that I wasn't there, that you might come to believe. In any event, let us go to him."

¹⁶ Then Thomas, "the Twin," said to the rest, "Let's go with Jesus, so that we can die with him."

¹⁷ When Jesus arrived in Bethany, he found that Lazarus had already been in the tomb for four days. ¹⁸ Since Bethany was only about two miles from Jerusalem, ¹⁹ many people had come out to console Martha and Mary about their brother.

²⁰ When Martha heard that Jesus was coming, she went to meet him, while Mary stayed at home with the mourners.

²¹ When she got to Jesus, Martha said, "If you had been here, my brother would never have died! ²² Yet even now, I am sure that God will give you whatever you ask."

²³ "Your brother will rise again!" Jesus assured her. ²⁴ Martha replied, "I know he will rise again in the resurrection on the last day."

²⁵ Jesus told her,

"I am the Resurrection,
and I am Life:
those who believe in me
will live, even if they die;
²⁶ and those who are alive and believe in me
will never die.

"Do you believe this?"

²⁷ "Yes!" Martha replied. "I have come to believe that you are the Messiah, God's Only Begotten, the One who is coming into the world."

²⁸ When she had said this, Martha went back and called her sister Mary. "The Teacher is here, asking for you," she whispered.

²⁹ As soon as Mary heard this, she got up and went to him. ³⁰ Jesus hadn't gotten to the village yet. He was at the place where Martha had met him. ³¹ Those who were there consoling her saw her get up quickly and followed Mary, thinking she was going to the tomb to mourn. ³² When Mary got to Jesus, she fell at his feet and said, "If you had been here, Lazarus never would have died."

³³ When Jesus saw her weeping, and the other mourners as well, he was troubled in spirit, moved by the deepest emotions. ³⁴ "Where have you laid him?" Jesus asked.

"Come and see," they said. ³⁵ And Jesus wept.

³⁶ The people in the crowd began to remark, "See how much he loved him!" ³⁷ Others said, "He made the blind person see; why couldn't he have done something to prevent Lazarus' death?"

³⁸ Jesus was again deeply moved. They approached the tomb, which was a cave with a stone in front of it. ³⁹ "Take away the stone," Jesus directed.

Martha said, "Rabbi, it has been four days now. By this time there will be a stench."

⁴⁰ Jesus replied, "Didn't I assure you that if you believed you would see the glory of God?" ⁴¹ So they took the stone away.

Jesus raised his eyes to heaven and said, "Abba, thank you for having heard me. ⁴² I know that you always hear me, but I have said this for the sake of the crowd, that they might believe that you sent me!"

⁴³ Then Jesus called out in a loud voice, "Lazarus, come out!" ⁴⁴ And Lazarus came out of the tomb, still bound hand and foot with linen strips, his face wrapped in a cloth. Jesus told the crowd, "Untie him and let him go free."

⁴⁵ Many of those who had come to console Martha and Mary, and saw what Jesus did, put their faith in him.

⁴⁶ Some others, however, went to the Pharisees and reported what Jesus had done. ⁴⁷ As a result, the chief priests and the Pharisees called a meeting of the Sanhedrin. "What are we to do," they said, "with this one who is performing all these miracles? ⁴⁸ If we let him go on like this, everybody will believe in him, and then the Romans will come and destroy both our Temple and our nation."

⁴⁹ One of them, Caiaphas, who was high priest that year, said, "You don't seem to have grasped the situation at all; ⁵⁰ you fail to see that it is better for one person to die for the people, than for the whole nation to be destroyed." ⁵¹ He didn't say this of his own accord; as high priest that year, he was prophesying that Jesus was to die for the nation— ⁵² and not for the nation only, but to gather together into one body the scattered children of God.

⁵³ From that day they were determined to kill him. ⁵⁴ So Jesus no longer went about openly in Judea, but left the area for a town called Ephraim, in the region bordering on a desert, and stayed there with the disciples.

11:55–12:50

The Jewish Passover was near, and many of the country folk who had gone up to Jerusalem to purify themselves ⁵⁶ were looking for Jesus, saying to one another as they stood in the Temple, "What do you think? Will he come to the festival or not?"

⁵⁷ By now, the chief priests and the Pharisees had given their orders that anyone who knew where Jesus was should report it, so that they could arrest him.

12 ¹ Six days before Passover, Jesus went to Bethany, the village of Lazarus, whom Jesus had raised from the dead. ² There they gave a banquet in Jesus' honor, at which Martha served. Lazarus was one of those at the table. ³ Mary brought a pound of costly ointment, pure nard, and anointed the feet of Jesus, wiping them with her hair. The house was full of the scent of the ointment.

⁴ Judas Iscariot, one of the disciples—the one who was to betray Jesus—protested, ⁵ "Why wasn't this ointment sold? It could have brought nearly a year's wages, and the money been given to poor people!" ⁶ Judas didn't say this because he was concerned for poor people, but because he was a thief. He was in charge of the common fund and would help himself to it.

⁷ So Jesus replied, "Leave her alone. She did this in preparation for my burial. ⁸ You have poor people with you always. But you won't always have me."

⁹ Meanwhile a large crowd heard that Jesus was there and came to see not only Jesus, but also Lazarus, whom he raised from the dead. ¹⁰ So the chief priests planned to kill Lazarus as well, ¹¹ since it was because of him that many of the people were leaving them and believing in Jesus.

¹² The next day, the great crowd that had come for the Passover feast heard that Jesus was coming to Jerusalem, ¹³ so they got palm branches and went out to meet him. They shouted joyfully,

"Hosanna!
Blessed is the One who comes
in the name of our God—
the ruler of Israel!"

¹⁴ Jesus rode in sitting upon a donkey, in accord with scripture:

¹⁵ "Fear not, O people of Zion!
Your ruler comes to you
sitting on a donkey's colt."

¹⁶ At the time, the disciples didn't understand all this, but after Jesus was glorified they recalled that the people had done to him precisely what had been written about him.

¹⁷ Those who had been present when Jesus called Lazarus from the tomb and raised him from the dead continued to

spread the word. [18] A crowd gathered, and they went out to meet Jesus because they had heard he had performed this miraculous sign.

[19] Then the Pharisees said to one another, "See, this is getting us nowhere. Look—the whole world is running after him."

[20] Among those who had come up to worship at the Passover festival were some Greeks. [21] They approached Philip, who was from Bethsaida in Galilee, and put forth this request: "Please, we would like to see Jesus." [22] Philip went to tell Andrew, and together the two went to tell Jesus.

[23] Jesus replied,

"Now the hour has come
for the Chosen One to be glorified.
[24] The truth of the matter is,
unless a grain of wheat
falls on the ground and dies,
it remains only a single grain;
but if it dies,
it yields a rich harvest.
[25] If you love your life
you'll lose it;
if you hate your life in this world
you'll keep it for eternal life.
[26] Anyone who wants to work for me
must follow in my footsteps,
and wherever I am,
my worker will be there too.
Anyone who works for me
will be honored by Abba God.
[27] Now my soul is troubled.
What will I say:
'Abba, save me from this hour?'
But it was for this very reason
that I have come to this hour.
[28] Abba, glorify your name!"

A voice came from heaven: "I have glorified it, and I will glorify it again."

[29] The crowds that stood nearby heard this and said it was a clap of thunder; others said, "It was an angel speaking."

[30] Jesus answered, "It was not for my sake that this voice came, but for yours.

[31] "Sentence is now being passed on this world;
now the ruler of this world will be overthrown.
[32] And when I am lifted up from this earth,
I will draw all people to myself."

[33] By these words Jesus indicated the kind of death he would die.

[34] The crowd answered, "We've heard from the Law that the Messiah will remain forever. So how can you say, 'The Chosen One must be lifted up.' Who is this Chosen One?"

[35] Jesus said to them,

"The light will be with you
only a little while longer.
Walk while you have the light,
before darkness overtakes you.
Those who walk in the dark
don't know what they're doing.
[36] Believe in the light
while you still have the light.
Only then will you become
children of light."

After he said this, Jesus left and went into seclusion.

❋ ❋ ❋

[37] Even after Jesus worked so many miracles in their presence, they still didn't believe in him. [38] This fact fulfilled the words of the prophet Isaiah:

"O God, who has believed what we've heard?
To whom has the authority of our God been
revealed?"

[39] This is why they could not believe—as Isaiah said again,

[40] "God has blinded their eyes
and hardened their hearts,
lest they see with their eyes
and understand with their hearts
and be converted,
and I would have to heal them."

[41] Isaiah said this because he saw Jesus glorified and spoke about him.

[42] And yet many, even among the leaders, believed in Jesus. They refused to state their belief openly because they were afraid of the Pharisees and of being expelled from the synagogue. [43] For they cared more about what people thought of them than about the glory of God.

[44] Jesus proclaimed publicly:

"Whoever believes in me
believes not so much in me
as in the One who sent me;
[45] and whoever sees me
sees the One who sent me.
[46] I have come as light into the world,
so that whoever believes in me
need not remain in the dark anymore.
[47] Anyone who hears my words
and doesn't keep them faithfully
won't be condemned by me,
since I've come not to condemn the world
but to save it.
[48] Those who reject me and don't accept my words
already have their judge:
the message I have spoken
will be their judge on the last day.
[49] For I haven't spoken on my own;
no, what I was to say—how I was to speak—
was commanded by Abba God who sent me.
[50] Since I know that God's commandment is eternal
life,
I say whatever Abba God has told me to say."

13:1–17:26

It was before the Feast of Passover, and Jesus realized that the hour had come for him to pass from this world to Abba God. He had always loved his own in this world, but now he showed how perfect this love was.

[2] The Devil had already convinced Judas Iscariot, son of Simon, to betray Jesus. So during supper, [3] Jesus—knowing that God had put all things into his own hands, and that he had come from God and was returning to God—[4] rose from the table, took off his clothes and wrapped a towel around his waist. [5] He then poured water into a basin, and began to wash the disciples' feet, and dry them with the towel that was around his waist.

[6] When Jesus came to Simon Peter, Peter said, "Rabbi, you're not going to wash my feet, are you?"

[7] Jesus answered, "You don't realize what I am doing right now, but later you'll understand."

8 Peter replied, "You'll never wash my feet!"

Jesus answered, "If I don't wash you, you have no part with me."

9 Simon Peter said to Jesus, "Then, Rabbi, not only my feet, but my hands and my head as well!"

10 Jesus said, "Any who have taken a bath are clean all over and only need to wash their feet—and you're clean, though not every one of you." 11 For Jesus knew who was to betray him. That is why he said, "Not all of you are clean."

12 After washing their feet, Jesus put his clothes back on and returned to the table. He said to them, "Do you understand what I have done for you? 13 You call me "Teacher," and "Sovereign"—and rightly, for so I am. 14 If I, then—your Teacher and Sovereign—have washed your feet, you should wash each other's feet. 15 I have given you an example, that you should do as I have done to you.

16 "The truth of the matter is,
no subordinate is greater than the superior;
no messenger outranks the sender.
17 Once you know all these things,
you'll be blessed if you put them into practice.
18 What I say is not said about you all—
for I know the ones I chose—
but so that scripture can be fulfilled:
'One who partook of bread with me
has raised a heel against me.'
19 I tell you this now, before it takes place,
so that when it takes place you may believe that I
AM.
20 The truth of the matter is,
whoever accepts the one I send
accepts me,
and whoever welcomes me
welcomes the One who sent me."

21 Having said this, Jesus became troubled in spirit and said, "The truth of the matter is, one of you will betray me."

22 The disciples looked at each other, puzzled as to whom he could mean. 23 One of them, the disciple whom Jesus loved, was next to Jesus. 24 Simon Peter signaled him to ask Jesus whom he meant. 25 He leaned back against Jesus' chest and asked, "Rabbi, who is it?"

26 Jesus answered, "The one to whom I give the piece of bread I dip in the dish." He dipped the piece of bread and gave it to Judas, son of Simon Iscariot.

27 After Judas took the bread, Satan entered his heart. Jesus said to him, "Be quick about what you're going to do." 28 None of the others at the table understood the reason Jesus said this. 29 Since Judas had charge of the common fund, some of them thought Jesus was telling him to buy what was needed for the festival, or to give something to the poor. 30 As soon as Judas took the piece of bread, he went out into the night.

31 Once Judas left, Jesus said,
"Now is the Chosen One glorified
and God is glorified as well.
32 If God has been glorified,
God will in turn glorify the Chosen One
and will do so very soon.
33 My little children,
I won't be with you much longer.
You'll look for me,
but what I said to the Temple authorities, I say to
you:
where I am going,
you cannot come.

34 I give you a new commandment:
Love one another.
And you're to love one another
the way I have loved you.
35 This is how all will know that you're my disciples:
that you truly love one another."

36 Simon Peter said, "Rabbi, where are you going?" Jesus replied,

"Where I am going,
you cannot follow me now,
though you'll follow me later."

37 "Rabbi," Peter said, "Why can't I follow you now? I will lay down my life for you!"

38 "Lay down your life for me?" exclaimed Jesus. "The truth of the matter is, before the cock crows you'll have disowned me three times!

14 1 "Don't let your hearts be troubled.
You have faith in God;
have faith in me as well.
2 In God's house there are many dwelling places;
otherwise, how could I have told you
that I was going to prepare a place for you?
3 I am indeed going to prepare a place for you,
and then I will come back to take you with me,
that where I am
there you may be as well.
4 You know the way that leads to where I am going."
5 Thomas replied, "But we don't know where you're
going. How can we know the way?"
6 Jesus told him,
"I myself am the Way—
I am Truth,
and I am Life.
No one comes to Abba God
but through me.
7 If you really knew me,
you would know Abba God also.
From this point on,
you know Abba God
and you have seen God."

8 "Rabbi," Philip said, "show us Abba God, and that will be enough for us."

9 Jesus replied, "Have I been with you all this time, Philip, and still you don't know me?

Whoever has seen me has seen Abba God.
How can you say, 'Show us your Abba'?
10 Don't you believe that I am in Abba God
and God is in me?
The words I speak are not spoken of myself;
it is Abba God, living in me,
who is accomplishing the works of God.
11 Believe me that I am in God and God is in me,
or else believe because of the works I do.
12 The truth of the matter is,
anyone who has faith in me
will do the works I do—
and greater works besides.
Why? Because I go to Abba God,
13 and whatever you ask in my name I will do,
so that God may be glorified in me.
14 Anything you ask in my name
I will do.
15 If you love me
and obey the command I give you,

16 I will ask the One who sent me
to give you another Paraclete, another Helper
to be with you always—

17 the Spirit of truth,
whom the world cannot accept
since the world neither sees her nor recognizes her;
but you can recognize the Spirit
because she remains with you
and will be within you.

18 I won't leave you orphaned;
I will come back to you.

19 A little while now and the world will see me no
more;
but you'll see me;
because I live,
and you will live as well.

20 On that day you'll know
that I am in God,
and you are in me,
and I am in you.

21 Those who obey the commandments
are the ones who love me,
and those who love me
will be loved by Abba God.
I, too, will love them
and will reveal myself to them."

22 Judas—not Judas Iscariot—said, "Rabbi, why is it that
you'll reveal yourself to us, and not to the whole world?"

23 Jesus answered,

"Those who love me will be true to my word,
and Abba God will love them;
and we will come to them
and make our dwelling place with them.

24 Those who don't love me
don't keep my words.
Yet the message you hear is not mine;
it comes from Abba God who sent me.

25 This much have I said to you while still with you;

26 but the Paraclete, the Holy Spirit
whom Abba God will send in my name,
will instruct you in everything
and she will remind you of all that I told you.

27 Peace I leave with you;
my peace I give to you;
but the kind of peace I give you
is not like the world's peace.
Don't let your hearts be distressed;
don't be fearful.

28 You've heard me say,
'I am going away but I will return.'
If you really loved me,
you would rejoice because I am going to Abba God,
for Abba is greater than I.

29 I tell you this now, before it happens,
so that when it happens you will believe.

30 I won't speak much more with you,
because the ruler of this world,
who has no hold on me,
is at hand;

31 but I do this so that the world may know
that I love Abba God
and do as my Abba has commanded.

"Let's get up now, and be on our way.

15:1 "I am the true vine,
and my Abba is the vine grower

2 who cuts off every branch in me that doesn't bear
fruit,
but prunes the fruitful ones
to increase their yield.

3 You've been pruned already,
thanks to the word that I have spoken to you.

4 Live on in me,
as I do in you.
Just as a branch cannot bear fruit of itself
apart from the vine,
neither can you bear fruit
apart from me.

5 I am the vine;
you are the branches.
Those who live in me and I in them
will bear abundant fruit,
for apart from me you can do nothing.

6 Those who don't live in me
are like withered, rejected branches,
to be picked up and thrown on the fire and burned.

7 If you live on in me,
and my words live on in you,
ask whatever you want
and it will be done for you.

8 My Abba will be glorified
if you bear much fruit
and thus prove to be my disciples.

9 As my Abba has loved me,
so have I loved you.
Live on in my love.

10 And you will live on in my love
if you keep my commandments,
just as I live on in Abba God's love
and have kept God's commandments.

11 I tell you all this that my joy may be yours,
and your joy may be complete.

12 This is my commandment:
love one another as I have loved you.

13 There is no greater love
than to lay down one's life for one's friends.

14 And you are my friends,
if you do what I command you.

15 I no longer speak of you as subordinates,
because a subordinate doesn't know a superior's
business.
Instead I call you friends,
because I have made known to you
everything I have learned from Abba God.

16 It was not you who chose me;
it was I who chose you
to go forth and bear fruit.
Your fruit must endure,
so that whatever you ask of Abba God in my name
God will give you.

17 This command I give you:
that you love one another.

18 If you find that the world hates you,
remember that it hated me before you.

19 If you belonged to the world,
the world would love you as its own;
but the reason it hates you
is that you don't belong to the world—
because I chose you out of the world.

20 Remember what I told you:
a subordinate is never greater than a superior—
so know that they will persecute you
as they persecuted me,

they will respect your words
as much as they respected mine.
21 They'll do all this to you because of my Name,
for they know nothing of Abba God who sent me.
22 If I hadn't come and spoken to them,
they would have been blameless.
But as it is,
they have no excuse for their sin.
23 All those who hate me
also hate my Abba.
24 If I had not done among them
the works that no one else has ever done,
they would be blameless.
But as it is, they have seen and hated
both me and my Abba.
25 Yet all this was only to fulfill
what is written in the Law:
'They hated me without cause.'
26 When the Paraclete comes—
the Spirit of Truth who comes from Abba God,
whom I myself will send from my Abba—
she will bear witness on my behalf.
27 You too must bear witness,
for you've been with me from the beginning.

16 1 I have told you all this
to keep your faith from being shaken.
2 They will expel you from synagogues—
and indeed, the hour is coming when anyone
who kills you will claim to be serving God.
3 They will do these things
because they know neither Abba God nor me.
4 But I have told you these things
so that when the time comes,
you'll remember that I told you ahead of time.
I didn't tell you this at first
because I was with you.
5 Now I am going to the One who sent me—
yet not one of you has asked, 'Where are you going?'
6 You're sad of heart
because I tell you this.
7 Still, I must tell you the truth:
it is much better for you that I go.
If I fail to go,
the Paraclete will never come to you,
whereas if I go,
I will send her to you.
8 When she comes,
she will prove the world wrong
about sin, about justice
and about judgment.
9 About sin—
in that they refuse to believe in me;
10 about justice—
because I go to Abba God
and you will see me no more;
11 about judgment—
for the ruler of this world has been condemned.
12 I have much more to tell you,
but you can't bear to hear it now.
13 When the Spirit of truth comes,
she will guide you into all truth.
She won't speak on her own initiative;
rather, she'll speak only what she hears,
and she'll announce to you
things that are yet to come.

14 In doing this, the Spirit will give glory to me,
for she will take what is mine
and reveal it to you.
15 Everything that Abba God has
belongs to me.
This is why I said that
the Spirit will take what is mine
and reveal it to you.
16 Within a short time you won't see me,
but soon after that you'll see me again."

17 At that, some of the disciples asked one another, "What
can he mean, 'Within a short time you won't see me, but
soon after that you'll see me'? And didn't he say he is going
back to Abba God?"
18 They kept asking, "What is the 'short time'? We don't
know what he means."
19 Since Jesus was aware that they wanted to question
him, he said, "You're asking one another about my saying,
'In a short time you'll lose sight of me, but soon after that
you'll see me again.'

20 "The truth of the matter is,
you'll weep and mourn
while the world rejoices;
you'll grieve for a time,
but your grief will turn to joy.
21 When a woman is in labor
she cries out, because her time has come.
When she has borne her baby
she no longer remembers her pain,
because of her joy that a child
has been born into the world.
22 In the same way,
you are now grieving;
but I will see you again
and then you'll rejoice,
and no one will take away your joy.
23 On that day you'll no longer
question me about anything.
The truth of the matter is,
if you ask Abba God for anything in my name,
it will be given to you.
24 Until now you haven't asked
for anything in my name.
Ask, and you will receive
so that your joy will be complete.
25 I have spoken these things to you
in veiled language.
A time is coming when I will no longer do so—
I will tell you about Abba God in plain speech.
26 On that day you will ask
in my name.
Now, I am not saying that I'll petition Abba God for
you—
27 God already loves you,
because you have loved me
and have believed that I came from God.
28 I came from Abba God
and have come into the world,
and now I leave the world
to go to Abba God."

29 His disciples said, "At last you're speaking plainly and
not using metaphors! 30 We're convinced that you know everything. There is no need for anyone to ask you questions.
We do indeed believe you came from God."

³¹ Jesus answered them,
    "Do you really believe?
³² An hour is coming—in fact, it has already come—
    when you will all be scattered
    and go your own ways,
    leaving me alone;
    yet I can never be alone,
    for Abba God is with me.
³³ I have told you all this
    that in me you may find peace.
    You will suffer in the world.
    But take courage!
    I have overcome the world."

17 ¹ After Jesus said this, he looked up to heaven and said,
    "Abba, the hour has come!
    Glorify your Only Begotten
    that I may glorify you,
² through the authority you've given me over all
    humankind,
    by bestowing eternal life on all those you gave me.
³ And this is eternal life:
    to know you, the only true God,
    and the one you have sent,
    Jesus, the Messiah.
⁴ I have given you glory on earth
    by finishing the work you gave me to do.
⁵ Now, Abba, glorify me with your own glory,
    the glory I had with you before the world began.
⁶ I have manifested your Name
    to those you gave me from the world.
    They were yours, and you gave them to me;
    and now they have kept your word.
⁷ Now they know that everything you've entrusted to
    me
    does indeed come from you.
⁸ I entrusted to them
    the message you entrusted to me,
    and they received it.
    They know that I really came from you;
    they believe it was you who sent me.
⁹ And it's for them that I pray—
    not for the world,
    but for these you've given me—
    for they are really yours,
¹⁰ just as all that belongs to me is yours,
    and all that belongs to you is mine.
    It is in them
    that I have been glorified.
¹¹ I am in the world no more,
    but while I am coming to you,
    they are still in the world.
    Abba, holy God,
    protect those whom you have given me
    with your Name—
    the Name that you gave me—
    that they may be one,
    even as we are one.
¹² As long as I was with them,
    I guarded them with your Name
    which you gave me.
    I kept careful watch,
    and not one of them was lost,
    except for the one who was destined to be lost
    in fulfillment of scripture.

¹³ Now I am coming to you;
    I say all this while I am still in the world
    that they may have my joy
    fulfilled in themselves.
¹⁴ I gave them your word,
    and the world has hated them for it
    because they don't belong to the world
    any more than I belong to the world.
¹⁵ I don't ask you to take them out of the world,
    but to guard them from the Evil One.
¹⁶ They are not of the world,
    any more than I am of the world.
¹⁷ Consecrate them—
    make them holy through the truth—
    for your word is truth.
¹⁸ As you have sent me into the world,
    so I have sent them into the world;
¹⁹ I consecrate myself now for their sakes,
    that they may be made holy in truth.
²⁰ I don't pray for them alone.
    I pray also for those
    who will believe in me through their message,
²¹ that all may be one,
    as you, Abba, are in me and I in you;
    I pray that they may be one in us,
    so that the world may believe that you sent me.
²² I have given them the glory you gave me
    that they may be one, as we are one—
²³ I in them, you in me—
    that they may be made perfect in unity.
    Then the world will know that you sent me,
    and that you loved them as you loved me.
²⁴ Abba, I ask that those you gave me
    may be here with me,
    so they can see this glory of mine
    which is your gift to me,
    because of the love you had for me
    before the foundation of the world.
²⁵ Righteous One, the world hasn't known you,
    but I have;
    and these people know
    that you sent me.
²⁶ To them I have revealed your Name,
    and I will continue to reveal it
    so that the love you have for me
    may live in them,
    just as I may live in them."

18:1–19:42

After Jesus had said all this, he left with the disciples and crossed the Kidron Valley. There was a garden there, and Jesus and the disciples entered it.

² Judas, the traitor, knew the place well, because Jesus often met there with his disciples. ³ Judas led the Roman cohort to the place, along with some Temple guards sent by the chief priests and Pharisees. All were armed and carried lanterns and torches.

⁴ Then Jesus, aware of everything that was going to take place, stepped forward and said to them, "Who are you looking for?"

⁵ "Are you Jesus of Nazareth?" they asked.

Jesus said, "I am." Now Judas, the traitor, was with them. ⁶ When Jesus said, "I am," they all drew back and fell to the ground.

⁷ Again, Jesus asked them, "Who are you looking for?"

They replied, "Jesus of Nazareth."

⁸ Jesus said, "I have already told you that I am the one you want. If I am the one you're looking for, let the others go." ⁹ This was to fulfill what he had spoken: "Of those you gave me, I have not lost a single one."

¹⁰ Simon Peter, who had a sword, drew it and struck the high priest's attendant, cutting off his right ear. The name of the attendant was Malchus.

¹¹ Jesus said to Peter, "Put your sword back in its sheath. Am I not to drink the cup Abba God has given me?"

¹² Then the cohort and its captain and the Temple guards seized and bound Jesus. ¹³ They took him first to Annas. Annas was the father-in-law of Caiaphas, who was high priest that year. ¹⁴ It was Caiaphas who had advised the Temple authorities that it was better to have one person die on behalf of the people.

¹⁵ Simon Peter and another disciple followed Jesus. This disciple, who was known to the high priest, entered his courtyard with Jesus, ¹⁶ while Peter hung back at the gate. So the disciple known to the high priest went back and spoke to the doorkeeper, and brought Peter inside.

¹⁷ The doorkeeper said, "Aren't you one of this guy's followers?"

But Peter answered, "No, I'm not."

¹⁸ Now the night was cold, so the attendants and guards had lit a charcoal fire and were warming themselves. Peter was with them as well, keeping warm.

¹⁹ The high priest questioned Jesus about his disciples and his teachings. ²⁰ Jesus answered, "I have spoken publicly to everyone; I have always taught in synagogues and in the Temple area where the whole Jewish people congregates. I have said nothing in secret. ²¹ So why do you question me? Ask those who have heard me. Ask them what I said to them—they know what I said."

²² When Jesus said this, one of the guards standing by slapped him and said, "Is this how you answer the high priest?"

²³ "If I've said anything wrong," Jesus replied, "point it out; but if I'm right in what I said, why do you strike me?"

²⁴ Then Annas sent him, still shackled, to Caiaphas the high priest.

²⁵ Meanwhile, Simon Peter was still standing there warming himself. Others asked him, "Aren't you one of his disciples?"

But Peter denied it, saying, "I am not!"

²⁶ One of the attendants of the high priest, a relative of the attendant whose ear Peter had severed, spoke up: "Didn't I see you in the garden with him?"

²⁷ Again Peter denied it. At that moment a rooster crowed.

²⁸ At daybreak, they led Jesus from the house of Caiaphas to the Praetorium. The Temple authorities didn't enter the Praetorium, for they would have become ritually unclean and unable to eat the Passover seder. ²⁹ So Pilate went out to them and asked, "What charges do you bring against this person?"

³⁰ They responded, "We wouldn't have brought him to you if he weren't a criminal."

³¹ Pilate told them, "Take him yourselves, and judge him by your own Law."

The Temple authorities replied, "We don't have the power to put anyone to death." ³² This was to fulfill what Jesus had said about the way he was going to die.

³³ So Pilate reentered the Praetorium and summoned Jesus. "Are you the King of the Jews?" asked Pilate.

³⁴ Jesus answered, "Do you say this of your own accord, or have others told you about me?"

³⁵ Pilate replied, "Am I Jewish? It is your own people and the chief priests who hand you over to me. What have you done?"

³⁶ Jesus answered, "My realm is not of this world; if it belonged to this world, my people would have fought to keep me out of the hands of the Temple authorities. No, my realm is not of this world."

³⁷ Pilate said, "So you're a King?"

Jesus replied, "You say I'm a King. I was born and came into the world for one purpose—to bear witness to the truth. Everyone who seeks the truth hears my voice."

³⁸ "Truth? What is truth?" asked Pilate.

With that, Pilate went outside and spoke to the people. "I find no guilt in him," he said. ³⁹ "But according to your custom, I always release a prisoner at the Passover. Do you want me to release 'the King of the Jews'?"

⁴⁰ They shouted, "Not him! We want Barabbas!" Barabbas was a robber.

19 ¹ So Pilate ordered that Jesus be flogged. ² Then the soldiers wove a crown out of thorns and put it on his head, and dressed him in a purple robe. ³ They went up to him repeatedly and said, "All hail the King of the Jews!" And they struck him in the face.

⁴ Pilate came outside once more and said to the crowd, "Look, I'll bring him out here to make you understand that I find no guilt in him." ⁵ So Jesus came out wearing the purple robe and the crown of thorns, and Pilate said, "Look upon the one you accuse!"

⁶ When the chief priests and the Temple guards saw Jesus, they shouted, "Crucify him! Crucify him!"

Pilate told them, "Do it yourself. I find no reason to condemn him."

⁷ "We have a law," the Temple authorities replied, "that says he ought to die because he claimed to be the Only Begotten of God."

⁸ When Pilate heard this, he was even more afraid. ⁹ He went back into the Praetorium and asked Jesus, "Where do you come from?"

Jesus didn't answer.

¹⁰ Then Pilate said to Jesus, "You refuse to speak? Bear in mind that I have the power to release you—and the power to crucify you."

¹¹ "You would have no authority over me," Jesus replied, "unless it had been given to you by God. Therefore the person who handed me over to you has the greater sin."

¹² Upon hearing this, Pilate attempted to set Jesus free. But the crowd shouted, "If you set him free, you're no 'friend of Caesar.' Anyone who claims to be a king defies Caesar!"

¹³ Hearing these words, Pilate took Jesus outside and seated himself on the judge's seat at the place called the Pavement—"Gabbatha," in Hebrew.

¹⁴ Now it was almost noon on Preparation Day for the Passover. Pilate said to the people, "Here is your king!"

¹⁵ "Take him away!" they shouted. "Take him away! Crucify him!"

Pilate asked, "Do you want me to crucify your king?"

The chief priests said, "We have no king but Caesar!" ¹⁶ Then Pilate handed Jesus over to them to be crucified.

So they took Jesus, ¹⁷ carrying his own cross, to what is called the Place of the Skull—in Hebrew, "Golgotha." ¹⁸ There they crucified him, along with two others, one on either side of Jesus.

¹⁹ Pilate wrote a notice and had it put on the cross. It read, "Jesus of Nazareth, King of the Jews." ²⁰ The notice, in Hebrew, Greek and Latin, was read by many people, because the place where Jesus was crucified was near the city. ²¹ The chief priests said to Pilate, "Don't write 'King of the Jews,' but, 'This one said, I am King of the Jews.'"

²² Pilate replied, "I have written what I have written."

²³ After the soldiers had crucified Jesus, they took his clothing and divided it into four pieces, one piece for each soldier. They also took the seamless robe. ²⁴ The soldiers said to one another, "Let's not tear it. We can throw dice to see who will get it."

This happened in order to fulfill the scripture, "They divided my garments among them and, for my clothing, they cast lots." And this is what they did.

²⁵ Standing close to Jesus' cross were his mother; his mother's sister, Mary, the wife of Clopas; and Mary of Magdala. ²⁶ When Jesus saw his mother and the disciple whom he loved standing there, he said to his mother, "Here is your son." ²⁷ Then he said to his disciple, "Here is your mother." From that moment, the disciple took her into his household.

²⁸ After this, Jesus knew that now all was completed, and to fulfill scripture perfectly, he said, "I am thirsty." ²⁹ There was a jar of cheap wine nearby, so they put a sponge soaked in the wine on a hyssop stick and raised it to his lips.

³⁰ Jesus took the wine and said, "It is finished." Then he bowed his head and gave up his spirit.

³¹ Since it was Preparation Day, the Temple authorities asked Pilate to let them break the legs of those crucified, and take their bodies from the crosses. They requested this to prevent the bodies remaining on the cross during the Sabbath, since that particular Sabbath was a solemn feast day. ³² So the soldiers came and broke the legs of first one and then the other who had been crucified with Jesus. ³³ But when they came to Jesus, they found that he was already dead, so they didn't break his legs. ³⁴ One of the soldiers, however, pierced Jesus' side with a lance, and immediately blood and water poured out. ³⁵ This testimony has been given by an eyewitness whose word is reliable; the witness knows that this testimony is the truth, so that you will believe. ³⁶ These things were done to fulfill the scripture, "Not one of his bones will be broken." ³⁷ And again, another scripture says, "They will look on the one whom they have pierced."

³⁸ After this, Joseph of Arimathea, a disciple of Jesus—but a secret one, for fear of the Temple authorities—asked Pilate for permission to remove the body of Jesus, and Pilate granted it. So Joseph came and took it away. ³⁹ Nicodemus came as well—the same one who had first come to Jesus by night—and he brought about one hundred pounds of spices, a mixture of myrrh and aloes. ⁴⁰ They took the body of Jesus and wrapped it with the spices in linen cloths, according to the Jewish burial custom.

⁴¹ There was a garden in the place where Jesus had been crucified, and in the garden was a new tomb where no one had ever been buried. ⁴² Since it was the day before the Sabbath and the tomb was nearby, they buried Jesus there.

20:1–21:25

Early in the morning on the first day of the week, while it was still dark, Mary of Magdala came to the tomb. She saw that the stone had been rolled away from the entrance, ² so she ran off to Simon Peter and the other disciple—the one Jesus loved—and told them, "The Rabbi has been taken from the tomb! We don't know where they have put Jesus!"

³ At that, Peter and the other disciple started out toward the tomb. ⁴ They were running side by side, but then the other disciple outran Peter and reached the tomb first. ⁵ He didn't enter, but bent down to peer in and saw the linen wrappings lying on the ground. ⁶ Then Simon Peter arrived and entered the tomb. He observed the linen wrappings on the ground, ⁷ and saw the piece of cloth that had covered Jesus' head lying not with the wrappings, but rolled up in a place by itself. ⁸ Then the disciple who had arrived first at the tomb went in. He saw and believed. ⁹ As yet, they didn't understand the scripture that Jesus was to rise from the dead. ¹⁰ Then the disciples went back to their homes.

¹¹ Meanwhile, Mary stood weeping beside the tomb. Even as she wept, she stooped to peer inside, ¹² and there she saw two angels in dazzling robes. One was seated at the head and the other at the foot of the place where Jesus' body had lain.

¹³ They asked her, "Why are you weeping?"

She answered them, "Because they have taken away my Rabbi, and I don't know where they have put the body."

¹⁴ No sooner had she said this than she turned around and caught sight of Jesus standing there, but she didn't know it was Jesus. ¹⁵ He asked her, "Why are you weeping? For whom are you looking?"

She supposed it was the gardener, so she said, "Please, if you're the one who carried Jesus away, tell me where you've laid the body and I will take it away."

¹⁶ Jesus said to her, "Mary!"

She turned to him and said, "Rabboni!"—which means "Teacher."

¹⁷ Jesus then said, "Don't hold on to me, for I have not yet ascended to Abba God. Rather, go to the sisters and brothers and tell them, 'I'm ascending to my Abba and to your Abba, my God and your God!'"

¹⁸ Mary of Magdala went to the disciples. "I have seen the Teacher!" she announced. Then she reported what the savior had said to her.

¹⁹ In the evening of that same day, the first day of the week, the doors were locked in the room where the disciples were, for fear of the Temple authorities.

Jesus came and stood among them and said, "Peace be with you." ²⁰ Having said this, the savior showed them the marks of crucifixion.

The disciples were filled with joy when they saw Jesus, ²¹ who said to them again, "Peace be with you. As Abba God sent me, so I'm sending you."

²² After saying this, Jesus breathed on them and said,

"Receive the Holy Spirit.
²³ If you forgive anyone's sins, they are forgiven.
If you retain anyone's sins, they are retained."

²⁴ It happened that one of the Twelve, Thomas—nicknamed Didymus, or "Twin"—was absent when Jesus came. ²⁵ The other disciples kept telling him, "We've seen Jesus!"

Thomas' answer was, "I'll never believe it without putting my finger in the nail marks and my hand into the spear wound."

²⁶ On the eighth day, the disciples were once more in the room, and this time Thomas was with them. Despite the locked doors, Jesus came and stood before them, saying, "Peace be with you."

²⁷ Then, to Thomas, Jesus said, "Take your finger and examine my hands. Put your hand into my side. Don't persist in your unbelief, but believe!"

²⁸ Thomas said in response, "My Savior and my God!"

²⁹ Jesus then said,

"You've become a believer
because you saw me.
Blessed are those who have not seen
and yet have believed."

³⁰ Jesus performed many other signs as well—signs not recorded here—in the presence of the disciples. ³¹ But these have been recorded to help you believe that Jesus is the Messiah, the Only Begotten, so that by believing you may have life in Jesus' Name.

21 ¹ Later Jesus again was manifested to the disciples at Lake Tiberias. This is how the appearance took place.

² Assembled were Simon Peter, Thomas "the Twin," Nathanael of Cana in Galilee, Zebedee's children, and two other disciples. ³ Simon Peter said to them, "I'm going out to fish."

"We'll join you," they replied, and went off to get into their boat.

All through the night they caught nothing. ⁴ Just after daybreak, Jesus was standing on the shore, though none of the disciples knew it was Jesus. ⁵ He said to them, "Have you caught anything, friends?"

"Not a thing," they answered.

⁶ "Cast your net off to the starboard side," Jesus suggested, "and you'll find something."

So they made a cast and caught so many fish that they couldn't haul the net in. ⁷ Then the disciple whom Jesus loved cried out to Peter, "It's the Teacher!"

Upon hearing this, Simon Peter threw on his cloak—he was naked—and jumped into the water.

⁸ Meanwhile the other disciples brought the boat to shore, towing the net full of fish. They were not far from land—no more than a hundred yards. ⁹ When they landed, they saw that a charcoal fire had been prepared, with fish and some bread already being grilled. ¹⁰ "Bring some of the fish you just caught," Jesus told them. ¹¹ Simon Peter went aboard and hauled ashore the net, which was loaded with huge fish—one hundred fifty-three of them. In spite of the great number, the net was not torn.

¹² "Come and eat your meal," Jesus told them.

None of the disciples dared to ask, "Who are you?"—they knew it was the savior.

¹³ Jesus came over, took the bread and gave it to them, and did the same with the fish. ¹⁴ This marked the third time that Jesus had appeared to the disciples after being raised from the dead.

¹⁵ When they had eaten their meal, Jesus said to Simon Peter, "Simon ben-John, do you love me more than these?"

Peter said, "Yes, Rabbi, you know that I'm your friend."

Jesus said, "Feed my lambs."

¹⁶ A second time Jesus put the question, "Simon ben-John, do you love me?"

Peter said, "Yes, Rabbi, you know that I'm your friend."

Jesus replied, "Tend my sheep."

¹⁷ A third time Jesus asked him, "Simon ben-John, do you love me as a friend would?"

Peter was hurt because Jesus asked, "Do you love me?" a third time. So he said, "You know everything, Rabbi. You know that I am your friend."

Jesus said, "Feed my sheep.

¹⁸   The truth of the matter is,
when you were young,
you put on your own belt
and walked where you liked;
but when you get old,
you will stretch out your hands
and someone else will put a belt around you
and take you where you don't want to go."

¹⁹ With these words, Jesus indicated the kind of death by which Peter would glorify God.

Then the savior said, "Follow me."

²⁰ Peter turned around and noticed that the disciple whom Jesus loved was following them—the one who had leaned over during the supper and asked, "Rabbi, which one will hand you over?" ²¹ Seeing him, Peter was prompted to ask, "But what about him, Rabbi?"

²² Jesus replied, "If I want him to stay behind until I come, what does it matter to you? You're to follow me." ²³ This is how the rumor spread among the sisters and brothers that this disciple would not die. Yet Jesus had not said to Peter, "He won't die," but rather, "If I want him to stay behind until I come, what does it matter to you?"

²⁴ This disciple is the one who was an eyewitness to these things and wrote them down, and we know that his testimony is true.

²⁵ There are many other things that Jesus did—yet if they were written down in detail, the world itself, I suppose, couldn't hold all the books that would have to be written.

acts of the apostles

1:1–2:47

In my earlier account, Theophilus, I dealt with everything that Jesus had done and taught, ² from the beginning until the day he was taken up, after he had given instructions through the Holy Spirit to the apostles he had chosen. ³ After the Passion, Jesus appeared alive to the apostles—confirmed through many convincing proofs—over the course of forty days, and spoke to them about the reign of God.

⁴ On one occasion, Jesus told them not to leave Jerusalem. "Wait, rather, for what God has promised, of which you have heard me speak," Jesus said. ⁵ "John baptized with water, but within a few days you will be baptized with the Holy Spirit."

⁶ While meeting together they asked, "Has the time come, Rabbi? Are you going to restore sovereignty to Israel?"

⁷ Jesus replied, "It's not for you to know times or dates that Abba God has decided. ⁸ You will receive power when the Holy Spirit comes upon you; then you will be my witnesses in Jerusalem, throughout Judea and Samaria, and even to the ends of the earth."

⁹ Having said this, Jesus was lifted up in a cloud before their eyes and taken from their sight. ¹⁰ They were still gazing up into the heavens when two messengers dressed in white stood beside them. ¹¹ "You Galileans—why are you standing here looking up at the skies?" they asked. "Jesus, who has been taken from you—this same Jesus will return, in the same way you watched him go into heaven."

¹² The apostles returned to Jerusalem from the Mount of Olives, a mere Sabbath's walk away. ¹³ Entering the city, they went to the upstairs room where they were staying—Peter, John, James and Andrew; Philip, Thomas, Bartholomew and Matthew; James ben-Alphaeus; Simon, a member of the Zealot sect; and Judah ben-Jacob. ¹⁴ Also in their company were some of the women who followed Jesus, his mother Mary, and some of Jesus' sisters and brothers. With one mind, they devoted themselves to constant prayer.

¹⁵ One day Peter stood up in the midst of the believers, a gathering of perhaps a hundred and twenty. ¹⁶ "Sisters and brothers," he said, "the saying in scripture, uttered long ago by the Holy Spirit through the mouth of David, was destined to be fulfilled in Judas, the one who guided those who arrested Jesus. ¹⁷ He was one of our number and had been given a share in this ministry. ¹⁸ He bought a field with the money he received for his injustice. He collapsed there, his body burst open, and his guts poured out. ¹⁹ Everyone in Jerusalem heard about it, and the field became known as 'Akeldama,' the Field of Blood.

²⁰ "But David wrote in the book of Psalms,

'Let his encampment be desolate;
may no one dwell on it.'

And,

'Let another take his office.'

²¹ "It is necessary, therefore, that one of those who accompanied us all the time that Jesus moved among us, ²² from the baptism of John until the day Jesus was taken up from us, should be named as witness with us to the Resurrection."

²³ At that, they nominated two—Joseph, called Barsabbas or Justus, and Matthias. ²⁴ Then they prayed, "O God, you can read the hearts of people. Show us which of these two you have chosen ²⁵ to occupy this apostolic ministry, replacing Judas, who turned away and went his own way." ²⁶ They then drew lots between the two. The choice fell to Matthias, who was added to the eleven apostles.

2 ¹ When the day of Pentecost arrived, they all met in one room. ² Suddenly they heard what sounded like a violent, rushing wind from heaven; the noise filled the entire house in which they were sitting. ³ Something appeared to them that seemed like tongues of fire; these separated and came to rest on the head of each one. ⁴ They were all filled with the Holy Spirit and began to speak in other languages as she enabled them.

⁵ Now there were devout people living in Jerusalem from every nation under heaven, ⁶ and at this sound they all assembled. But they were bewildered to hear their native languages being spoken. ⁷ They were amazed and astonished: "Surely all of these people speaking are Galileans! ⁸ How does it happen that each of us hears these words in our native tongue? ⁹ We are Parthians, Medes and Elamites, people from Mesopotamia, Judea and Cappadocia, Pontus and Asia, ¹⁰ Phrygia and Pamphylia, Egypt and the parts of Libya around Cyrene, as well as visitors from Rome— ¹¹ all Jews, or converts to Judaism—Cretans and Arabs, too; we hear them preaching, each in our own language, about the marvels of God!"

¹² All were amazed and disturbed. They asked each other, "What does this mean?" ¹³ But others said mockingly, "They've drunk too much new wine."

¹⁴ Then Peter stood up with the Eleven and addressed the crowd: "Women and men of Judea, and all you who live in Jerusalem! Listen to what I have to say! ¹⁵ These people are not drunk as you think—it's only nine o'clock in the morning! ¹⁶ No, it's what Joel the prophet spoke of:

¹⁷   'In the days to come—
        it is our God who speaks—
        I will pour out my Spirit
        on all humankind.
        Your daughters and sons will prophesy,
        your young people will see visions,
        and your elders will dream dreams.
¹⁸   Even on the most insignificant of my people,
        both women and men,
        I will pour out my Spirit in those days,
        and they will prophesy.
¹⁹   And I will display wonders
        in the heavens above
        and signs on the earth below:
        blood, fire and billowing smoke.
²⁰   The sun will be turned into darkness
        and the moon will become blood
        before the coming of the
        great and sublime day of our God.
²¹   And all who call upon the name
        of our God will be saved.'

²² "People of Israel, hear this: Jesus of Nazareth was sent to you with miracles, portents and signs as his credentials—which God performed through him in your midst, as you well know. ²³ Jesus was delivered up by the set purpose and plan of God; you even made use of godless people to crucify and kill him. ²⁴ God freed him from death's bitter pangs,

however, and raised him up again, for it was impossible that death could keep its hold on him. 25 David says,

'I have set our God ever before me;
God is at my right hand, and I will not be disturbed.
26 My heart has been glad, my tongue has rejoiced,
my body will live on in hope,
27 for you will not abandon my soul to Hades,
nor will you let your faithful one undergo decay.
28 You have shown me the paths of Life;
you will fill me with joy in your presence.'

29 "Sisters and brothers, I can speak confidently to you about our ancestor David. He died and was buried, and his grave is with us to this day. 30 But he was a prophet, and he knew that God had promised him with an oath that one of his descendants would sit upon his throne. 31 So what he was foreseeing and talking about was the resurrection of the Messiah: the one not abandoned to the underworld, whose body didn't decay. 32 God raised Jesus to life, and we are all witnesses to that.

33 "Exalted to the right hand of God, Jesus received the promise of the Holy Spirit from Abba God, and what you now hear and see is the outpouring of that promise. 34 For David, who didn't ascend into the heavens, said,

'God said to my Sovereign:
"Sit at my right hand
35 until I place your enemies under your foot."'

36 "Therefore, let the whole House of Israel know beyond any doubt that God made this Jesus—whom you crucified—both Messiah and Sovereign."

37 When they heard this, they were deeply shaken. They asked Peter and the other disciples, "What are we to do?"

38 Peter replied, "You must repent and be baptized, each one of you, in the name of Jesus the Messiah, that your sins may be forgiven; then you will receive the gift of the Holy Spirit. 39 It was to you and your children that the promise was made, and to all those still far off whom our God calls."

40 In support of his testimony, Peter used many other arguments and kept saying, "Save yourselves from this corrupt generation!" 41 They were convinced by his arguments, and they accepted what he said and were baptized. That very day about three thousand were added to the number of those converted.

42 They devoted themselves to the apostles' instructions and the communal life, to the breaking of bread and the prayers. 43 A reverent fear overtook them all, for many wonders and signs were being performed by the apostles. 44 Those who believed lived together, shared all things in common; 45 they would sell their property and goods, sharing the proceeds with one another as each had need. 46 They met in the Temple and they broke bread together in their homes every day. With joyful and sincere hearts they took their meals in common, 47 praising God and winning the approval of all the people. Day by day, God added to their number those who were being saved.

3:1–5:42

One day, when Peter and John were going up to the Temple for prayer at about three in the afternoon, 2 a person who from birth was unable to walk was being carried in. Every day the individual was brought to the Temple gate called "the Beautiful," to beg from people as they came in.

3 Seeing Peter and John on their way in, the person being carried begged them for alms. 4 Peter fixed his gaze on the individual, as did John. "Look at us!" Peter said. 5 The person looked at them intently, hoping to get something.

6 Then Peter said, "I have neither silver nor gold, but what I have I give you! In the name of Jesus Christ of Nazareth, walk!"

7 Peter pulled the person up by the right hand. Immediately the beggar's ankles and feet became strong; 8 the individual jumped up, stood for a moment, began to walk around, then went into the Temple with them—walking, jumping about, and praising God. 9 When the people saw the beggar walking and giving praise to God, 10 they recognized the one who used to sit and beg at the Beautiful Gate of the Temple. They were struck with astonishment—utterly stupefied at what had happened.

11 As the person who had been healed stood clinging to Peter and John, the whole crowd rushed over to them excitedly in Solomon's Porch. 12 When Peter saw this, he addressed the people as follows:

"Why does this surprise you? Why do you stare at us as if we had made this person walk by our own power or holiness? You are Israelites, 13 and it is the God of Sarah and Abraham, Rebecca and Isaac, Leah and Rachel and Jacob, the God of our ancestors, who has glorified Jesus—the same Jesus you handed over and then disowned in the presence of Pilate, after Pilate had decided to release him. 14 You disowned the Holy and Just One and asked instead for the release of a murderer. 15 You put to death the Author of life, whom God raised from the dead—a fact to which we are witnesses. 16 It is the name of Jesus, and faith in it, that has strengthened the limbs of this one whom you see and know well. Such faith has given this beggar perfect health, as all of you can see.

17 "Yet I know, my sisters and brothers, that you acted out of ignorance, just as your leaders did. 18 God has brought to fulfillment by this means what was announced long ago by the prophets: that the Messiah would suffer. 19 Therefore, reform your lives! Turn to God, that your sins may be wiped away, 20 and that God may send a season of refreshment. Then our God will send you Jesus, the preordained Messiah, 21 whom heaven must keep until the restoration of all things comes, which God promised through the holy prophets in ancient times. 22 Moses, for example, said, 'our God will raise up a prophet like me for you, from among your own kinfolk. You must listen to everything this prophet tells you. 23 Anyone who doesn't listen is to be cut off ruthlessly from the people.' 24 In fact, all the prophets who have ever spoken, from Samuel onward, have predicted these days.

25 "You are the heirs of the prophets, the heirs of the Covenant the Most High made with our ancestors when God told Sarah and Abraham, 'In your offspring all the families of the earth will be blessed.' 26 It was for you that God raised up and sent this Jesus, to bless you by turning every one of you from your wicked ways."

4 :1 While the apostles were still addressing the crowd, the priests, the captain of the Temple guard and the Sadducees came up to them, 2 angry because they were teaching the people and proclaiming the resurrection of the dead in the person of Jesus. 3 It was evening by now, so the authorities arrested the apostles and put them in jail for the night. 4 Despite this, many of those who had heard the speech believed—the total number had now risen to something like five thousand.

5 When the leaders, the elders and the scribes met the next day in Jerusalem, 6 Annas the high priest, Caiaphas, Jochanan,

Alexander and all who were of the high priestly class were there. 7 They brought Peter and John before them and began to interrogate them: "By what power and in whose name have you done this?"

8 Then Peter, filled with the Holy Spirit, spoke up: "Leaders of the people! Elders! 9 If we must answer today for a good deed done to a person who was unable to walk, and explain how this person has been made whole, 10 then you and all the people of Israel must realize that it was done in the name of Jesus Christ of Nazareth, whom you crucified and whom God raised from the dead. In the power of that Name, this person stands before you perfectly sound. 11 This Jesus is 'the stone rejected by the builders which has become the cornerstone.' 12 There is no salvation in anyone else, for there is no other name under heaven given to the human race by which we must be saved."

13 They were amazed as they observed the self-assurance of Peter and John, and they realized that the speakers were uneducated and of no standing. Then they recognized them as having been with Jesus.

14 When they saw the person who had been healed standing there with them, they could think of nothing to say, 15 so they ordered them out of the court while they consulted. 16 "What will we do with these two? Everyone who lives in Jerusalem knows what a remarkable show of power took place through them. We can't deny it. 17 To stop this from spreading further among the people, we must give them a stern warning never to mention the Galilean's name to anyone again." 18 So the priests and elders called the apostles back and made it clear that under no circumstances were they to speak the name of Jesus or teach anything about Jesus.

19 Peter and John answered, "Judge for yourselves whether it's right in God's sight for us to obey you rather than God. 20 Surely we cannot help speaking of what we have heard and seen."

21 At that point, they were dismissed with further warnings. The court could find no way to punish them, because all the people were praising God for what they had seen and heard. 22 The person who had been miraculously healed was over forty years old.

23 After being released, they went back to their own people and told them what the priests and elders had said. 24 On hearing the story, they all raised their voices in prayer to the Most High and said, "O Sovereign God, 'who made heaven and earth, the seas and all that is in them,' 25 you have said by the Holy Spirit through the lips of David, your servant,

> 'Why this arrogance among the nations,
> these futile plots among the peoples?
> 26 Rulers of the earth are setting out to war,
> and leaders are making alliances
> against the Most High
> and against God's Anointed One.'

27 "This is what has come true: in this very city, Herod and Pontius Pilate made an alliance with the Gentiles and the peoples of Israel, against your holy child Jesus whom you anointed, 28 but only to bring about the very thing that you in your strength and wisdom had predetermined should happen.

29 "And now, O God, take note of their threats and help your faithful ones to proclaim your message with all boldness: 30 stretch out your hand to heal and to work miracles and marvels through the name of your holy child Jesus." 31 As they prayed, the house where they were assembled was shaken; they were all filled with the Holy Spirit and began to proclaim the word of God boldly.

32 The community of believers was of one mind and one heart. None of them claimed anything as their own; rather, everything was held in common. 33 The apostles continued to testify with great power to the resurrection of Jesus Christ, and they were all given great respect; 34 nor was anyone needy among them, for those who owned property or houses would sell them 35 and give the money to the apostles. It was then distributed to any members who might be in need.

36 There was a certain Levite from Cyprus named Joseph— to whom the apostles gave the name Barnabas, which means "encourager." 37 He sold a farm that he owned and made a donation of the money, presenting it to the apostles.

5 :1 Now a couple, Ananias and Sapphira, sold a piece of their property too, 2 but they conspired to keep part of the proceeds for themselves. Ananias brought the remainder and presented it to the apostles.

3 Peter said, "Ananias, has Satan so possessed you that you lie to the Holy Spirit by secretly withholding part of the proceeds of the property? 4 It belonged to you and Sapphira before you sold it, didn't it? And when you sold it, didn't you still have control of the money? How could you have conceived such a thing in your heart? You have not lied to people. You have lied to God!"

5 When Ananias heard this, he dropped dead on the spot. Great fear came upon all those present. 6 Young people in the crowd came up, wrapped up the body and took it away for burial.

7 About three hours later, Sapphira entered. She was unaware of what had happened. 8 Peter said to her, "Did you sell the property for such-and-such a price?"

"Yes," she replied, "that was the price."

9 Peter said to her, "Why did you conspire to test the Spirit of our God? Listen! The feet of those who buried your husband are at the door, and they will carry you out as well!"

10 She immediately dropped dead at his feet. The young people entered and found her dead, so they carried her out and buried her next to her husband.

11 Great fear overcame the whole church and all who heard about this incident.

12 Through the hands of the apostles, many signs and wonders occurred among the people. By mutual agreement, they used to meet in Solomon's Porch. 13 But none of the others dared to join them, despite the fact that the people held the apostles in great esteem.

14 Even so, more and more believers, women and men in great numbers, were continually added to their community— 15 to the extent that people even carried their sick relatives and friends into the street and laid them on cots and mattresses, in the hope that when Peter passed by, his shadow might fall on one or another of them. 16 Crowds from the towns around Jerusalem would gather, too, bringing their sick people and those who were troubled by unclean spirits, and they were all being healed.

17 Then the high priest and all his supporters, who were members of the Sadducee party, were filled with jealousy; 18 they arrested the apostles and threw them into jail.

19 During the night, however, an angel of God opened the gates of the jail, led them out and said, 20 "Go and stand in the Temple and tell the people all about this Life." 21 When they heard this, they went into the Temple at dawn and resumed their preaching.

When the high priest and his supporters arrived, they convened the Sanhedrin—the full senate of Israel—and sent word to the jail that the prisoners were to be brought in. ²² But when the Temple guard got to the jail, they couldn't find them, and they hurried back to report, ²³ "We found the jail securely locked and the guards at their posts outside, but when we opened the cell, we found no one inside."

²⁴ On hearing this report, the captain of the Temple guard and the high priests didn't know what to make of it. ²⁵ Then a courier arrived with fresh news: "At this very moment those you put in jail are in the Temple. They're standing there in the Temple, teaching the people." ²⁶ At that, the captain went off with the guard and arrested them once again, but without a show of force, for fear of being stoned by the crowd.

²⁷ The apostles were taken before the Sanhedrin, and the high priest began to interrogate them: ²⁸ "We gave you strict orders not to teach about that name, yet you have filled Jerusalem with your teaching—and you're determined to make us responsible for this Jesus' blood."

²⁹ To this, Peter and the apostles replied, "Better for us to obey God than people! ³⁰ The God of our ancestors has raised Jesus, whom you put to death by hanging him on a tree. ³¹ This One, who has been exalted to God's right hand as Ruler and Savior, is to bring repentance and the forgiveness of sins to Israel. ³² We are eyewitnesses to this. And so is the Holy Spirit, who has been given to those who obey God."

³³ When the Sanhedrin heard this, they were furious and intended to kill the apostles. ³⁴ However, a member of the Sanhedrin—a Pharisee named Gamaliel, an authority on the Law and respected by the people—stood up and asked that the apostles be removed from the room. ³⁵ Then he addressed the Sanhedrin:

"Israelites, think twice about what you are going to do with these people. ³⁶ Not long ago, a certain Theudas came around and tried to pass himself off as someone important. About four hundred joined him. But when he was killed, all his followers scattered, and that was the end of it. ³⁷ Then there was Judah the Galilean, at the time of the census. He attracted supporters too, but when he was killed, his support dissipated. ³⁸ The present case is similar. My advice is that you leave these people alone and let them be. If this movement, this activity, is of human origin, it will destroy itself. ³⁹ If, on the other hand, it comes from God, not only will you be unable to destroy them, but you might find yourselves fighting against God."

⁴⁰ They took Gamaliel's advice, and called in the apostles and flogged them. After ordering them not to speak again in the name of Jesus, they dismissed them. ⁴¹ The apostles left the Sanhedrin full of joy that they had been judged worthy to suffer shame for the sake of the Name. ⁴² Every day they preached in the Temple and in people's homes, continually proclaiming Jesus as the Messiah.

6:1–8:3

In those days, as the number of disciples grew, a dispute arose between the Hellenistic Jews and those who spoke Hebrew, that the Greek-speaking widows were being neglected in the daily distribution of food. ² The Twelve assembled the community of disciples and said, "It's not right for us to neglect the word of God in order to wait on tables. ³ Look around among your numbers for seven people who are acknowledged to be deeply spiritual and prudent, and we will appoint them to this task. ⁴ This will permit us to concentrate on prayer and the ministry of the word."

⁵ The proposal was unanimously accepted by the community. They selected Stephen, full of faith and the Holy Spirit; Philip; Prochorus; Nicanor; Timon; Parmenas; and Nicolaus of Antioch, who had been a convert to Judaism. ⁶ They were presented to the apostles, who prayed over them and laid hands on them.

⁷ The word of God continued to spread, while at the same time the number of disciples in Jerusalem increased enormously, and a large group of priests became obedient to the faith.

⁸ Stephen was filled with grace and power to work miracles and great signs among the people. ⁹ But then certain individuals came forward who were members of what was called the Synagogue of Freedom, and argued with Stephen; some were from Cyrene and Alexandria, others from Cilicia and Asia Minor. ¹⁰ They found they were no match for Stephen's wisdom, because Stephen was speaking through the Spirit.

¹¹ So they procured some false witnesses to say, "We heard him using blasphemous language against Moses and against God." ¹² They incited the people, the elders and the scribes, and together they seized Stephen and dragged him away, bringing him before the Sanhedrin.

¹³ Again they put up the false witnesses, who said, "This person is always making speeches against the Holy Place and the Law. ¹⁴ We've heard him say that Jesus of Nazareth is going to destroy the sanctuary and alter the traditions Moses handed down to us." ¹⁵ The members of the Sanhedrin looked intently at Stephen, whose face appeared to them like the face of an angel.

7 ¹ The high priest asked, "Is this true?"

² Stephen replied, "Sisters and brothers, mothers and fathers, members of the Sanhedrin, hear what I have to say! The God of Glory appeared to Sarah and Abraham, our ancestors, before they left Mesopotamia and before they settled in Haran. ³ God said to them, 'Leave this place—your land and your relatives—for the place I will show you.' ⁴ So they left Chaldaea and settled in Haran. After their parents died, they migrated to the place where you now live—⁵ without an inheritance and without a single square foot of land.

"But God promised this place to them and their descendants, even though they were childless. ⁶ God said, 'Your descendants will be aliens in a foreign land, where they will be enslaved and oppressed for four hundred years. ⁷ But I will pass judgment on the people who enslaved them. After that they will come out of bondage and worship me here.' ⁸ Then God gave them the sign of the Covenant—they became the parents of Isaac, circumcising him on the eighth day. Isaac passed the Covenant on to Jacob and Rachel and Leah, and they passed it on to their twelve children.

⁹ "These twelve grew jealous of Joseph, and sold him into slavery in Egypt. But God, who was with Joseph, ¹⁰ rescued him from his troubles and gave him such wisdom that he caught the eye of Pharaoh, the ruler of Egypt, who made him governor of the country and ruler of the entire household.

¹¹ "Then a famine struck Egypt and Canaan. It wrought such suffering that our ancestors couldn't find food to eat. ¹² But when Jacob heard that there was grain in Egypt, he sent our forebears there on a first visit. ¹³ On their second visit, Joseph told his brothers who he was. He explained the same to Pharaoh about his family. ¹⁴ Then he sent for Jacob, Rachel and Leah, along with all their relatives—about seventy-five families in all— ¹⁵ and they all went down into Egypt. When Jacob and our ancestors died, they were bur-

ied in Egypt, [16] to be brought back eventually to Shechem and placed in the tomb that Sarah and Abraham purchased from the children of Hamor in Shechem.

[17] "When the time grew near for the fulfillment of the promise God made to Sarah and Abraham, the number of our people had grown very large. [18] Then another ruler, who knew nothing about Joseph, came to power. [19] He exploited our people and tyrannized them, forcing them to abandon their babies and let them die from exposure.

[20] "It was at this time that Moses was born. Lovely in God's sight, Moses was nursed in his parents' house for three months. [21] Then Moses too was abandoned to the elements, but was discovered by Pharaoh's daughter, who adopted and raised him as her own child. [22] He was educated in all the wisdom of the Egyptians and grew powerful in speech and deeds.

[23] "When Moses was forty years old he decided to visit his kinfolk, the Israelites. [24] When he saw one of them being abused by an Egyptian, he rescued the Israelite by killing the Egyptian. [25] Moses assumed that his kin would realize that God was offering them liberation through himself, but they didn't understand. [26] The next day, Moses came across two Israelites fighting; he tried to reconcile them by saying, 'Friends, you're related by blood—why are you hurting each other?' [27] One of them pushed Moses aside, saying, 'Who appointed you our ruler and judge? [28] Are you planning to kill me as you did the Egyptian yesterday?' [29] Moses fled when he heard this, and settled in the land of Midian. While there he had two children with his wife Zipporah.

[30] "Forty years later, in the wilderness near Mount Sinai, an angel appeared to Moses in the fire of a burning thorn bush. [31] Moses was amazed when he saw it. As he approached the bush, the voice of our God came out of it: [32] 'I am the God of your ancestors—the God of Sarah and Abraham, of Rachel and Leah and Jacob, of Rebecca and Isaac.' Moses, shaking with fear, dared not look at it anymore. [33] But our God said to him, 'Take off your shoes, for the place where you stand is holy ground. [34] I have witnessed the oppression of my people in Egypt. I have heard their groaning, and I have come down to set them free. Come now, and I will send you back to Egypt.'

[35] "This is the same Moses they rejected by saying, 'Who made you our ruler and judge?' Now, it was Moses who was being sent by God as both liberator and ruler, with the help of the angel who appeared to him in the burning bush. [36] It was Moses who led them out of Egypt, and worked wonders and signs in Egypt, at the Red Sea and in the desert for forty years. [37] It was Moses who said to the Israelites, 'God will send you a prophet like me from your own people.' [38] It was Moses who, in the assembly in the desert, spoke with the angel on Mount Sinai and with our ancestors. It was Moses who was entrusted with the words of life to hand on to us.

[39] "But our ancestors refused to listen to him. Instead, they pushed him aside and turned their hearts back to Egypt. [40] They said to Aaron, 'Make gods for us so they can lead us. We don't know what has happened to this Moses, who led us out of Egypt.' [41] So they made an idol shaped like a calf and offered sacrifices to it, rejoicing in what they had made with their hands. [42] But God turned away from them and abandoned them to the worship of the heavenly bodies. For it is written in the book of the prophets,

'Did you bring me sacrifices and offerings
    for forty years in the desert, O house of Israel?
[43] No, you carried the shrine of Moloch
    and the star of your God Rephan—
    those idols you made to adore—
So now I will exile you even further than Babylon.'

[44] "Our ancestors had the Tabernacle of Testimony with them in the desert. It had been constructed by Moses as God had directed, according to the pattern Moses was shown. [45] It was handed down to the next generation, who brought it along with Joshua when they dispossessed the nations that God drove out as they advanced. It stayed here until the time of David, [46] who so enjoyed God's favor that he asked God if he could build a dwelling place for the God of Jacob—[47] though it was Solomon who actually built the Temple.

[48] "Yet the Most High doesn't dwell in houses made by human hands, as it says in scripture:

[49] 'Heaven is my judgment seat,
    and the earth is my footstool.
What kind of house can you build for me?' says
    Your God;
    'or what is to be my resting place?
[50] Didn't my hand make all these things?'

[51] "You stubborn people! Your hearts and ears are completely covered! You're always resisting the Holy Spirit, just as your ancestors did before you. [52] Was there ever any prophet whom your ancestors didn't persecute? In their day, they put to death those who foretold the coming of the Just One. And now it has been your turn as the Just One's betrayers and murderers. [53] You who received the Law by the hands of angels are the very ones who haven't kept it!"

[54] They were infuriated when they heard this, and ground their teeth at him. [55] Stephen, meanwhile, filled with the Holy Spirit, looked to the sky and saw the glory of God, and Jesus standing at the right side of God. [56] "Look!" he exclaimed. "I see the heavens opened, and the Chosen One standing at God's right hand!"

[57] The onlookers were standing there, shouting and holding their hands over their ears as they did so. They rushed at him as one, [58] and dragged him out of the city. The witnesses then stoned him, having laid their robes at the feet of a young man named Saul.

[59] As they were stoning him, Stephen prayed, "O Jesus, receive my spirit." [60] He fell to his knees and cried out in a loud voice, "Please, don't hold this sin against them!" And with that, he died.

8 [1] Saul completely approved of the killing. On that day a great persecution broke out against the church at Jerusalem, and all except the apostles were scattered throughout Judea and Samaria. [2] Godly women and men buried Stephen and mourned deeply for him. [3] During this time, Saul worked for the total collapse of the church. Going from house to house, he dragged off women and men and put them in prison.

8:4–12:25

Those who had been scattered began to proclaim the Good News wherever they went. [5] Philip went down to the town of Samaria and there proclaimed the Messiah to them. [6] Without exception, the crowds paid close attention to Philip, listening to his message and taking note of the miracles he performed. [7] Many people were freed from unclean spirits, which came out of them shrieking loudly. Many people who couldn't move or couldn't walk were healed. [8] The rejoicing in the town rose to a fever pitch.

[9] A man named Simon had been practicing magic in the city, astonishing the people of Samaria. He claimed to be someone great, [10] and everyone, from prominent citizens to the lowly born, were paying attention to him and saying, "He is what is known as the Great Power of God." [11] They paid attention to

him because he had astonished them with magic for so long. 12 But they came to believe Philip as he preached the Good News of the kindom of God and the name of Jesus Christ, and both women and men were baptized. 13 Even Simon became a believer. He followed Philip everywhere, constantly amazed when he saw the miracles and great signs that took place.

14 When the apostles in Jerusalem heard that Samaria had accepted the word of God, they sent Peter and John to them. 15 The two went down to these people and prayed that they would receive the Holy Spirit. 16 She had not yet come down upon any of them, since they had only been baptized in the name of Jesus. 17 Upon arriving, the pair laid hands on the Samaritans and they received the Holy Spirit.

18 When Simon saw that the Spirit was given through the laying on of hands by the apostles, he offered them money, 19 saying, "Give me this power, too, so that anyone I lay hands on will receive the Holy Spirit."

20 Peter replied, "May your money perish with you, for thinking that you can buy what God has given for nothing! 21 You have no part or share in this ministry, for your heart isn't right before God. 22 Repent of your wickedness and pray to our God, that you may still be forgiven for thinking as you did. 23 I can see that you are caught in the gall of bitterness and the bondage of iniquity."

24 Simon replied, "Pray to our God for me yourselves, so that what you said may not happen to me."

25 After they gave their testimony and proclaimed the word of Christ, they returned to Jerusalem and preached the Good News to many Samaritan villages.

26 An angel of God spoke to Philip and said, "Be ready to set out at noon along the road that goes to Gaza, the desert road." 27 So Philip began his journey.

It happened that an Ethiopian eunuch, a court official in charge of the entire treasury of Candace, the ruler of Ethiopia, had come to Jerusalem on a pilgrimage 28 and was returning home. He was sitting in his carriage and reading the prophet Isaiah.

29 The Spirit said to Philip, "Go up and meet that carriage." 30 When Philip ran up, he heard the eunuch reading Isaiah the prophet and asked, "Do you understand what you are reading?"

31 "How can I," the eunuch replied, "unless someone explains it to me?" With that, he invited Philip to get in the carriage with him. 32 This was the passage of scripture being read:

"You are like a sheep being led to slaughter,
you are like a lamb that is mute in front of its
shearers:
like them, you never open your mouth.
33 You have been humiliated
and have no one to defend you.
Who will ever talk about your descendants,
since your life on earth has been cut short?"

34 The eunuch said to Philip, "Tell me, if you will, about whom the prophet is talking—himself or someone else?"

35 So Philip proceeded to explain the Good News about Jesus to him.

36 Further along the road they came to some water, and the eunuch said, "Look, there is some water right there. Is there anything to keep me from being baptized?"*

---

* Later manuscripts add verse 37: "And Philip said, 'If you believe with all your heart, you may.' And the eunuch said, 'I believe that Jesus Christ is the Only Begotten of God.'"

38 He ordered the carriage to stop; then Philip and the eunuch both went down into the water, and Philip baptized him. 39 When they came out of the water, the Spirit of God snatched Philip away; the eunuch didn't see him anymore, and went on his way rejoicing.

40 Philip found himself at Ashdod next, and he went about proclaiming the Good News in all the towns, until he came to Caesarea.

9 1 Meanwhile Saul continued to breathe murderous threats against the disciples of Jesus. He had gone up to the high priest 2 and asked for letters, addressed to the synagogues in Damascus, that would authorize him to arrest and take to Jerusalem any followers of the Way that he could find, both women and men.

3 As he traveled along and was approaching Damascus, a light from the sky suddenly flashed about him. 4 He fell to the ground and heard a voice saying, "Saul, Saul, why are you persecuting me?"

5 "Who are you?" Saul asked.

The voice answered, "I am Jesus, and you are persecuting me. 6 Get up now and go into the city, where you will be told what to do." 7 Those traveling with him were speechless. They heard the voice, but could see no one. 8 Saul got up from the ground unable to see, even though his eyes were open. They had to take him by the hand and lead him into Damascus. 9 For three days he continued to be blind, during which time he ate and drank nothing.

10 There was a disciple in Damascus named Ananias. Christ appeared to him in a vision, saying, "Ananias."

Ananias said, "Here I am."

11 Then Christ said to him, "Go at once to Straight Street, and at the house of Judah ask for a certain Saul of Tarsus. He is there praying. 12 Saul had a vision that a man named Ananias will come and lay hands on him so that he would recover his sight."

13 But Ananias protested, "I have heard from many sources about Saul and all the harm he has done to your holy people in Jerusalem. 14 He is here now with authorization from the chief priests to arrest everybody who calls on your name."

15 Christ said to Ananias, "Go anyway. Saul is the instrument I have chosen to bring my Name to Gentiles, to rulers, and to the people of Israel. 16 I myself will show him how much he will have to suffer for my name."

17 With that Ananias left. When he entered the house, he laid his hands on Saul, saying, "Saul, my brother, I have been sent by Jesus Christ, who appeared to you on the way here, to help you recover your sight and be filled with the Holy Spirit."

18 Immediately, something like scales fell from Saul's eyes, and he regained his sight. He got up and was baptized, 19 and his strength returned after he had eaten some food.

Saul stayed with the believers in Damascus for a few days, 20 and soon began proclaiming in the synagogues that Jesus was the Only Begotten of God.

21 Everyone who heard Saul was amazed. They said, "Isn't this the one who wiped out those in Jerusalem who called on the name of Jesus? Didn't Saul come here just so he could bring them in chains before the chief priests?"

22 But Saul kept growing in strength and confounding the Jewish authorities in Damascus by proving that Jesus is the Messiah.

23 After many days had gone by, the Jewish authorities plotted together to do away with him, 24 but Saul learned of their plot. They were watching the city gates day and night trying to put him to death, 25 but one night his students came and got him, and had him escape through an opening in the wall, lowering him to the ground in a basket.

26 When Saul arrived back in Jerusalem, he tried to join the disciples there, but they were all afraid of him, not believing that he was a disciple. 27 Then Barnabas took charge of him and introduced him to the apostles. He explained to them how, on his journey, Saul had seen and conversed with Jesus, and how ever since that encounter, Saul had been speaking out fearlessly in the name of Jesus at Damascus.

28 Saul stayed on with them, moving freely about Jerusalem and expressing himself quite openly in the name of Christ. 29 He even addressed the Greek-speaking Jews and debated with them. They responded, however, by trying to kill him. 30 When the sisters and brothers learned of this, some of them took Saul down to Caesarea and sent him off to Tarsus.

31 Throughout all Judea, Galilee and Samaria, the church was at peace, building itself up, living in reverence of God and growing in numbers with the consolation of the Holy Spirit. 32 While Peter was traveling throughout the region, he also went to the saints living in Lydda. 33 There he found a person named Aeneas, who was paralyzed and had been bedridden for eight years. 34 Peter said to him, "Aeneas, Jesus Christ heals you. Get up and make your bed." Aenaeus got up at once. 35 All the inhabitants of Lydda and Sharon, upon seeing him, were converted to Jesus.

36 Now in Joppa there was a disciple, a woman named Tabitha—"Dorcas," in Greek—who never tired of doing kind things or giving to charity. 37 About this time she grew ill and died. They washed her body and laid her out in an upstairs room.

38 Since Lydda was near Joppa, the disciples sent two couriers to Peter with the urgent request, "Please come over to us without delay." 39 Peter set out with them as they asked.

Upon his arrival, they took him upstairs to the room. All the townswomen who had been widowed stood beside him weeping, and showed him the various garments Dorcas had made when she was still with them.

40 Peter first made everyone go outside, then knelt down and prayed. Turning to the body, he said, "Tabitha, stand up." She opened her eyes, then looked at Peter and sat up. 41 He gave her his hand and helped her to her feet. The next thing he did was to call in those who were believers—including the widows—to show them that she was alive.

42 This became known all over Joppa and, because of it, many came to believe in Jesus Christ. 43 Peter remained awhile in Joppa, staying with Simon, a leather tanner.

10 1 There was a centurion named Cornelius in the Italian cohort stationed in Caesarea. 2 The household of Cornelius was full of God-fearing people; they prayed to God constantly and gave many charitable gifts to needy Jewish people.

3 One day at about three in the afternoon Cornelius had a vision. He distinctly saw an angel of God enter the house and call out, "Cornelius!"

4 Cornelius stared at the angel, completely terrified, and replied, "I'm at your service."

The angel said, "Your prayers and offerings to the poor are pleasing to God. 5 Send a deputation to Joppa and ask for a person named Simon who is called Peter. 6 He is staying with a tanner also named Simon, whose house is by the sea."

7 After the angel had departed, Cornelius called together three members of the household, 8 explained everything to them and sent them off to Joppa.

9 About noon the next day, shortly before they were to arrive in Joppa, Peter went up to the roof terrace to pray. 10 He was hungry and asked for something to eat. While the meal was being prepared, he fell into a trance. 11 Peter saw heaven standing open, and something like a large sheet being lowered to earth by its four corners. 12 It contained all kinds of animals, birds and reptiles.

13 A voice said, "Stand up, Peter. Make your sacrifice, and eat."

14 But Peter said, "I can't, my God. I have never eaten anything profane or unclean."

15 The voice spoke a second time and said, "Don't call anything profane that God has made clean."

16 This happened three times, then the sheet disappeared into the heavens.

17 Peter was still pondering the vision when Cornelius' deputation arrived. They had asked directions to Simon's house and were now standing at the door. 18 They called out to ask if Simon, known as Peter, was there. 19 While Peter reflected on the vision, the Spirit said, "A deputation is here to see you. 20 Hurry down, and don't hesitate to go with them. I sent them here."

21 He went down and said to the deputation, "I'm the one you are looking for. What do you want?"

22 They answered, "Cornelius, a centurion—an upright and God-fearing person, respected by the Jewish people— was directed by a holy angel to send for you. We are to bring you to the household of Cornelius to hear what you have to say." 23 Peter invited them in and gave them hospitality.

Peter left the next day, accompanied by some of the co-workers from Joppa. 24 They reached Caesarea the day after. Cornelius was waiting for them, along with his household and many close friends.

25 As Peter entered the house, Cornelius met him, dropped to his knees and bowed low. 26 As he helped Cornelius to his feet, Peter said, "Get up! I'm a human being, just like you!"

27 While talking with Cornelius, Peter went in and found many people gathered there. 28 He said to them, "You know it's unlawful for a Jew to associate with Gentiles or visit them. But God made it clear to me not to call anyone unclean or impure. 29 That's why I made no objection when I was summoned. Why have you sent for me?"

30 Cornelius answered, "Four days ago, I was here praying at this hour—three in the afternoon. Suddenly a figure in shining robes stood before me 31 and said, 'Cornelius, your prayers have been heard and your charity has been accepted as a sacrifice before God. 32 Send to Joppa and invite Simon, known as Peter, who is staying in the house of Simon the tanner, who lives by the sea.' 33 I sent for you immediately, and you were kind enough to come. Now we are all gathered here before you to hear the message God has given you for us."

34 So Peter said to them, "I begin to see how true it is that God shows no partiality—35 rather, that any person of any nationality who fears God and does what is right is acceptable to God. 36 This is the message God has sent to the people of Israel, the Good News of peace proclaimed through Jesus Christ, who is Savior of all.

37 "You yourselves know what took place throughout Judea, beginning in Galilee with the baptism John proclaimed. 38 You know how God anointed Jesus of Nazareth with the Holy Spirit and with power, and how Jesus went about doing good works and healing all who were in the grip of the Devil, because God was with him. 39 We are eyewitnesses to all that Jesus did in the countryside and in Jerusalem. Finally, Jesus was killed and hung on a tree, 40 only to be raised by God on the third day. God allowed him to be seen, 41 not by everyone, but only by the witnesses who had been chosen beforehand by God—that is, by us, who ate and drank with Christ after the resurrection from the dead. 42 And Christ commissioned us to preach to the people and to bear witness that this is the one set apart by God as judge of the living and the dead. 43 To Christ Jesus all the prophets testify, that everyone who believes has forgiveness of sins through this Name."

44 Peter had not finished speaking these words when the Holy Spirit descended upon all who were listening to the message. 45 The Jewish believers who had accompanied Peter were surprised that the gift of the Holy Spirit had been poured out on the Gentiles also, 46 whom they could hear speaking in tongues and glorifying God.

Then Peter asked, 47 "What can stop these people who have received the Holy Spirit, even as we have, from being baptized with water?" 48 So he gave orders that they be baptized in the name of Jesus Christ. After this was done, they asked him to stay on with them for a few days.

11 1 The apostles and the community in Judea heard that Gentiles, too, had accepted the word of God. 2 As a result, when Peter went up to Jerusalem, some of the Jewish believers took issue with him. 3 "So you have been visiting the Gentiles and eating with them, have you?" they said.

4 Peter then explained the whole affair to them step by step from the beginning: 5 "One day when I was in the town of Joppa, I fell into a trance while at prayer and had a vision of something like a big sheet being let down from heaven by its four corners. This sheet came quite close to me. 6 I watched it intently and saw in it all sorts of animals and wild beasts—everything possible that could walk, crawl or fly. 7 Then I heard a voice that said to me, 'Now, Peter, make your sacrifice and eat.' 8 I replied, 'I can't, my God. Nothing profane or unclean has ever entered my mouth!' 9 And a second time the voice spoke from heaven, 'Don't call profane what God has made clean.' 10 This happened three times, then the sheet and what was in it was drawn up to heaven again.

11 "Just at that moment, three couriers stopped outside the house where we were staying; they had been sent from Caesarea to fetch me, 12 and the Spirit told me to have no hesitation about returning with them. These six believers came with me as well, and we entered Cornelius' house. 13 He told us he had seen an angel standing in the house who had said, 'Send messengers to Joppa and bring back Simon, known as Peter; 14 he has a message for you that will save you and your entire household.'

15 "I had hardly begun to speak when the Holy Spirit came down on them in the same way she came on us in the beginning, 16 and I remembered what Christ had said: 'John baptized with water, but you will be baptized with the Holy Spirit.' 17 I realized then that God was giving them the same gift that had been given to us when we came to believe in our Savior Jesus Christ. And who am I to stand in God's way?"

18 This account satisfied them, and they gave glory to God, saying, "God has granted the repentance that leads to life—even to Gentiles!"

19 Those scattered by the persecution that arose because of Stephen made their way as far as Phoenicia, Cyprus and Antioch, but they usually proclaimed the message only to Jews. 20 Some of them, however, who came from Cyprus and Cyrene, went to Antioch where they started preaching to the Greeks, proclaiming the Good News of Jesus Christ to them as well. 21 Christ honored their efforts, and a large number of Greeks became believers.

22 The church in Jerusalem heard about this, so they sent Barnabas to Antioch. 23 Upon arriving, he rejoiced to see the evidence of God's favor. And he urged them to remain faithful to Christ with heartfelt devotion, 24 for he was good and faithful and filled with the Holy Spirit. And a large number of people was brought to Christ.

25 Barnabas then left for Tarsus to look for Saul, 26 and when he found him he brought him to Antioch. For a whole year they remained there, meeting with the church and instructing a large number of people. It was at Antioch that the disciples were first called Christians.

27 At this time, some prophets came down from Jerusalem to Antioch. 28 One of them, whose name was Agabus, stood up and—in the power of the Spirit—prophesied that a famine would spread throughout the entire Roman Empire. The same thing had happened before, during the reign of Claudius. 29 The disciples agreed that everyone, according to ability, should send relief to the sisters and brothers in Judea. 30 They did this and sent their contributions to the elders in care of Barnabas and Paul.

12 1 It was about this time that Herod, the ruler of Judea, began to persecute some members of the church. 2 He put John's brother, James, to death with the sword. 3 And when he noticed that this pleased the Jewish leaders, he decided to arrest Peter as well—which he did during the Feast of Unleavened Bread.

4 Peter was taken into custody and put into prison. Herod assigned four squads of four soldiers each to guard him. He intended to put him up on public trial after the end of Passover week. 5 So Peter was kept in prison, but the church prayed to God continually on his behalf.

6 On the night before Herod was to open the trial, Peter slept, bound with double chains, between two guards—while more guards kept watch outside the door. 7 Suddenly the angel of God stood before him and the cell was filled with light.

The angel nudged Peter in the side to awaken him. "Get up, and hurry," the angel said, and the chains fell from Peter's wrists. 8 The angel continued, "And put on your belt and your sandals." Peter did so. Then the angel said, "Wrap your cloak around yourself and follow me." 9 So he followed the angel out, unsure whether what he was experiencing was really happening, or whether he was having a vision.

10 They passed by one guard post and then another, and came to the iron gate leading to the city, which opened for them by itself. They went through it and walked the length of one street, when suddenly the angel disappeared. 11 It was only then that Peter recovered his senses. "Now I know," he said, "that all of this is true—that our God really did send

an angel to rescue me from the hand of Herod and from all that the Jewish people were so certain would happen to me."

¹² When Peter realized this, he went to the house of Mary, the mother of John Mark. A number of people were gathered there praying. ¹³ Peter knocked at the gateway door and an attendant named Rhoda came to answer. ¹⁴ When she recognized Peter's voice, she was so overjoyed that she raced back without opening it and announced that Peter was at the gate.

¹⁵ "You're out of your mind," they said.

But she kept insisting it was so.

"Then it must be his angel," they said.

¹⁶ Meanwhile, Peter continued to knock. When they opened the door and saw that it was really him, they were amazed. ¹⁷ Peter motioned with his hand for quiet and explained to them how God led him out of prison. He added, "Tell James and the sisters and brothers." Then he left for another place.

¹⁸ At daybreak there was a huge commotion among the soldiers over what had become of Peter. ¹⁹ Herod ordered a search, and when they didn't find Peter, Herod cross-examined the guards and then had them executed. Then he left Judea for a stay in Caesarea.

²⁰ For some time, Herod had been on bad terms with the people of Tyre and Sidon. Now they joined forces and sent a delegation to Blastus, Herod's chamberlain, and enlisted his support. With that in place, they negotiated a peace treaty, because they depended on Herod's territory for their food supply.

²¹ On the appointed day, Herod—in royal robes and seated on the rostrum—addressed them. ²² The people proclaimed, "This is the voice of a god, not a man!" ²³ Immediately, an angel of God struck Herod down because he didn't give God the glory. Herod was eaten away with worms and died.

²⁴ The word of God continued to spread and increase. ²⁵ Barnabas and Saul completed their mission and returned to Jerusalem, bringing John Mark with them.

13:1–15:35

The church at Antioch had a number of prophets and teachers: Barnabas; Simeon, also known as Niger; Lucius of Cyrene; Manaen, who had been raised with Herod the tetrarch; and Saul.

² One day while they were worshipping God and fasting, the Holy Spirit said, "I want Barnabas and Saul set apart for the work to which I have called them." ³ After the church members had fasted and prayed, they laid hands on the pair and sent them along.

⁴ So the two of them, sent out by the Holy Spirit, went down to Seleucia and sailed from there to Cyprus. ⁵ They arrived at Salamis and immediately went about proclaiming the word of God in the Jewish synagogues. John was with them as their assistant.

⁶ They traveled the full length of the island. At Paphos they met a Jewish magician and false prophet named Bar-Jesus. ⁷ He was one of the attendants of the proconsul Sergius Paulus, who was a person of great intelligence.

Sergius Paulus summoned Barnabas and Paul and asked to hear the word of God. ⁸ But Elymas, as the magician's name is translated, opposed them to keep the proconsul from converting to the faith.

⁹ At that moment, Saul, who had changed his name to Paul, was filled with the Holy Spirit. He looked Elymas full in the face and said, ¹⁰ "You charlatan, you fraud, you child of the Devil, you enemy of all that is just! Stop distorting the right ways of the Most High! ¹¹ Look now at how the hand

of our God is upon you. You will be blind and for a while unable to see the sun." Immediately, everything went dark and misty for him. He groped about asking for someone to take him by the hand. ¹² The proconsul—observing all that had happened, and astonished by the teaching about Christ—became a believer.

¹³ Paul and his companions went by sea from Paphos to Perga in Pamphylia, where John left them and returned to Jerusalem. ¹⁴ They continued to travel on from Perga and came to Antioch in Pisidia.

On the Sabbath, they entered the synagogue and sat down. ¹⁵ After the readings from the Law and the Prophets, the leaders of the synagogue sent this message to them: "Friends, if you have any exhortation for the people, please speak up."

¹⁶ Paul stood up, raised his hand for silence and began to speak. "Fellow Israelites," he said, "and you others who revere our God, listen to what I have to say! ¹⁷ The God of this nation Israel chose our ancestors, made our people great when they were living as foreigners in Egypt, then through divine power led them out, ¹⁸ and for about forty years took care of them in the desert. ¹⁹ After destroying seven nations in the land of Canaan, God gave them the inheritance of their land, ²⁰ after about four hundred and fifty years.

"After this God gave them judges, down to the prophet Samuel. ²¹ But then they demanded a ruler, and God gave them Saul ben-Kish, a member of the tribe of Benjamin. ²² After forty years, God deposed him and made David their ruler, with these approving words: 'I have selected David ben-Jesse, a person after my own heart, who will carry out my whole purpose.' ²³ To keep this promise, God has given to Israel a savior, one of David's descendants—Jesus, ²⁴ whose coming was heralded by John when he proclaimed a baptism of repentance for the whole people of Israel. ²⁵ Before John ended his ministry, he said, 'I am not the one you think I am; the one who is coming after me, I'm not fit to undo the sandals on his feet.'

²⁶ "Friends—children of the family of Sarah and Abraham, and you others who worship our God—this message of salvation is meant for you. ²⁷ What the people of Jerusalem and their rulers did, though they didn't realize it, was in fact to fulfill the prophecies which are read on every Sabbath. ²⁸ Though they found no grounds for putting Jesus to death, they begged Pilate to carry out the execution. ²⁹ When they carried out everything that had been foretold, they crucified and then buried him in a tomb. ³⁰ But God raised Jesus from the dead, ³¹ and for many days he appeared to those who had accompanied him from Galilee to Jerusalem. And it's these same companions of Jesus who are now his witnesses before our people.

³² "We ourselves announce to you the Good News. It was to our ancestors that God made the promise. ³³ But it's to us, their children, that God fulfilled the promise, by raising Jesus from the dead. As scripture says in the second psalm, 'You are my Own; today I have begotten you.'

³⁴ "The fact that God raised Jesus from the dead, never to return to corruption, is affirmed in these words: 'I will give you the sure and holy blessings promised to David.' ³⁵ This is explained in another text: 'You will not allow your Holy One to suffer corruption.' ³⁶ Now, David died when he had served God's will in his lifetime. He was buried with his ancestors and underwent corruption. ³⁷ But the One whom God raised from the dead did not undergo corruption.

[38] "Sisters and brothers, let it be known that through Jesus the forgiveness of sins is proclaimed to you—and freedom from everything that kept you from being right with God, which the Law of Moses could not do. [39] It is through Jesus that all who believe are made right with God. [40] Take care that what the prophets said doesn't happen to you:

[41] 'Observe, you scoffer, and marvel—
and perish!
For I am accomplishing a work in your days,
a work that you will never believe
even if someone would describe it to you.'"

[42] As Paul and Barnabas were leaving, they were invited to speak on this same theme the following Sabbath.

[43] When the synagogue service had broken up, many Jewish worshippers and God-fearing converts to Judaism joined Paul and Barnabas. In their talks, Paul and Barnabas urged them to continue in the grace of God.

[44] On the next Sabbath, almost the whole city gathered to hear the word of God. [45] When the leaders of the synagogue saw the crowds, they were filled with jealousy and began to contradict everything Paul said and to revile him.

[46] Paul and Barnabas spoke out fearlessly nonetheless: "We had to proclaim the word of God to you first, but since you have rejected it—since you don't think yourselves worthy of eternal life—we now turn to the Gentiles. [47] For this is what Christ instructed us to do:

'I have made you a light for the nations,
so that my salvation may reach the ends of the
earth.'"

[48] It made the Gentiles very happy to hear this, and they thanked God for the message. All who were destined for eternal life became believers. [49] Thus the word of God was carried throughout that area.

[50] But the leaders of the synagogue worked on some of the notable, God-fearing members of the community and convinced them to turn against Paul and Barnabas. They finally expelled them from the territory.

[51] So Paul and Barnabas shook the dust from their feet in protest and went on to Iconium. [52] But the disciples were filled with joy and with the Holy Spirit.

14 [1] At Iconium Paul and Barnabas went to the Jewish synagogue. They spoke so effectively that a great number of Jews and Greeks came to believe. [2] Some of the disbelieving Jews, however, stirred up and poisoned the minds of the Gentiles against the sisters and brothers. [3] So they stayed on for some time, speaking fearlessly about Christ, who then confirmed what they said about divine grace by granting that signs and wonders occur through them. [4] The people of the city, however, were divided—some supported the disbelievers, some supported the apostles.

[5] Eventually a move was made by a group of Gentiles, Jews, and synagogue leaders to abuse Paul and Barnabas and have them stoned. [6] When they learned of this, the apostles fled to the safety of Lycaonia where, in the towns of Lystra and Derbe and in the surrounding countryside, [7] they preached the Good News.

[8] At Lystra there was an individual who had never walked a step, afflicted from birth with no strength in the feet. [9] On one occasion this person was listening to Paul preaching, and they looked directly into each other's eyes. When Paul saw that the person had enough faith to be made whole, [10] he called out in a loud voice, "Stand up! On your feet!" And the person jumped up and began to walk around.

[11] When the crowds saw what Paul had done, they cried out in the Lycaonian language, "These two are gods who have come to us in the form of humans!" [12] They addressed Barnabas as Zeus; Paul they called Hermes, since he was doing most of the talking. [13] Even the priest of the temple of Zeus, which stood outside the town, brought oxen and garlands to the gates, to offer sacrifice with the crowds.

[14] When the apostles Barnabas and Paul heard this, they tore their garments and rushed out into the crowd. [15] "Friends, why are you doing this?" they shouted. "We are mortals like you. We have come with Good News to make you turn from these empty idols to the living God, who made heaven and earth and the sea and all that these hold. [16] In the past, God allowed each nation to go its own way. [17] But even then, God didn't leave you without personal evidence of the good things being done for you. God sends you rain from heaven, makes the crops grow when they should, and fills your hearts with food and gladness."

[18] Yet even with a speech such as this, they could hardly stop the crowds from offering sacrifice to them.

[19] Some members of the Jewish party from Antioch and Iconium arrived and won the people over. They stoned Paul and dragged him out of the town, leaving him there for dead. [20] His students quickly formed a circle about him, and before long he got up and went back into the town.

The next day, he left with Barnabas for Derbe. [21] After they had proclaimed the Good News in that town and made numerous disciples, they retraced their steps to Lystra and Iconium first, then to Antioch.

[22] They put fresh heart in the disciples there, encouraging them to persevere in their faith. "We all have to experience many hardships," they said, "before we enter the kindom of God." [23] In each church they appointed elders and, with prayer and fasting, commended them to God, in whom they had put their faith.

[24] Then they passed through Pisidia and came to Pamphylia. [25] After proclaiming the word in Perga, they went down to Attalia. [26] From there they sailed back to Antioch, where they had first been commended to the grace of God for the work they had now completed. [27] On their arrival, they assembled the church and gave an account of all that God had done with them, and of how they had opened the door of faith to the Gentiles. [28] Then they spent some time there with the disciples.

15 [1] Then some Jewish Christians came down to Antioch and began to teach the believers, "Unless you follow exactly the traditions of Moses, you cannot be saved." [2] Paul and Barnabas strongly disagreed with them and hotly debated their position. Finally, it was decided that Paul, Barnabas and some others should go up to see the apostles and elders in Jerusalem about this question.

[3] All the members of the church saw them off, and as they made their way through Phoenicia and Samaria, Paul and Barnabas told how the Gentiles had been converted. Their story was received with great joy among the sisters and brothers. [4] When Paul's group arrived in Jerusalem, they were welcomed by that church, and by the apostles and the elders, to whom they gave an account of all that God had accomplished through them. [5] Some of the converted Pharisees got up and demanded that such Gentiles be forced to

convert to Judaism first, before being baptized, and be told to follow the Law of Moses. ⁶ Accordingly, the apostles and the elders convened to look into the matter.

⁷ After much discussion, Peter said to them, "Friends, you know that God chose me from your midst a long time ago—so that the Gentiles would hear the message of the Gospel from my lips and believe. ⁸ God, who can read everyone's heart, bore witness to this by granting the Holy Spirit to them as the Spirit has been granted to us. ⁹ God made no distinction, but purified their hearts as well by means of faith.

¹⁰ "Why, then, do you put God to the test by trying to place on the shoulders of these converts a yoke which neither we nor our ancestors were able to bear? ¹¹ But just as we believe we are saved through the grace of Jesus Christ, so are they." ¹² At this, the whole assembly fell silent.

They listened to Barnabas and Paul as the two described all the signs and wonders God had worked among the Gentiles through them. ¹³ When they finished their presentation, James spoke up. "Sisters and brothers, listen to me," he said. ¹⁴ "Simon has told you how God initially became concerned about taking from among the Gentiles a people for God's name. ¹⁵ The words of the prophets agree with this, since the scriptures say,

¹⁶ '"After that I will return
and rebuild the fallen house of David;
I will rebuild it from its ruins
and restore it.
¹⁷ Then the rest of humankind,
all the Gentiles who are called by my Name,
will look for God,"
¹⁸ says the Most High,
who makes these things
which were known so long ago.'

¹⁹ "It is my judgment, therefore, that we shouldn't make it more difficult for Gentiles who are turning to God. ²⁰ We should merely write to them to abstain from anything polluted by idols, from sexual immorality and from eating meat of unbled or strangled animals. ²¹ After all, for generations now Moses has been proclaimed in every town and has been read aloud in the synagogues on every Sabbath."

²² Then the apostles and elders decided, in agreement with the whole Jerusalem church, to choose delegates to send to Antioch with Paul and Barnabas. They chose Judas known as Barsabbas and Silas, both leading members of the community. ²³ They were to deliver this letter:

"From the apostles and elders,

"To our Gentile sisters and brothers in Antioch, Syria and Cilicia:

"Greetings! ²⁴ We hear that some of our number, without any instructions from us, have upset you with their discussions and disturbed your peace of mind. ²⁵ Therefore, we have unanimously resolved to choose representatives and send them to you, along with our beloved Barnabas and Paul, ²⁶ who have risked their lives for the name of Jesus Christ. ²⁷ So we are sending you Judas and Silas, who will convey this message by word of mouth: ²⁸ it is the decision of the Holy Spirit, and ours as well, not to lay on you any burden beyond that which is strictly necessary— ²⁹ namely, to abstain from meat sacrificed to idols, from meat of unbled or strangled animals and from fornication. You will be well advised to avoid these things. Farewell."

³⁰ The party left and went down to Antioch, where they called together the whole community and delivered the letter. ³¹ When it was read, there was great delight at the encouragement it gave them.

³² Judas and Silas, themselves prophets, spoke for a long time, giving encouragement and strength to the sisters and brothers. ³³ The two spent some time there, and then returned home bearing greetings of peace from the sisters and brothers to the apostles and elders who sent them. ³⁴ But Silas decided to remain there. ³⁵ Paul and Barnabas stayed in Antioch and, with many others, taught and proclaimed the Good News, the word of God.

15:36–19:20

After some time Paul said to Barnabas, "Let's return to all the cities where we preached the word of God and see how they're doing." ³⁷ Barnabas suggested taking John Mark along with them as well. ³⁸ But Paul said no, because he had deserted them in Pamphylia and had not continued to work with them. ³⁹ The disagreement between Paul and Barnabas grew so sharp that they parted company. Barnabas took Mark and sailed to Cyprus. ⁴⁰ Paul chose Silas and left—after being commended by the sisters and brothers to the grace of God. ⁴¹ Paul traveled through Syria and Cilicia, consolidating the churches along the way.

16:¹ Paul went to Derbe and from there to Lystra. There was a disciple there named Timothy, whose mother was Jewish and a believer, and whose father was Greek. ² Since the sisters and brothers in Lystra and Iconium spoke highly of Timothy, ³ Paul was eager to have him come along on the journey. But because of the Jews who were in that region, Paul had Timothy circumcised, for everyone knew that his father was Greek. ⁴ As they made their way from town to town, they passed on the decisions reached by the apostles and elders in Jerusalem. ⁵ And the churches grew stronger in faith and daily increased in number.

⁶ They next traveled through Phrygia and Galatian territory, because they had been prevented by the Holy Spirit from preaching the word in the province of Asia. ⁷ When they reached the frontier of Mysia, they thought to cross through it into Bithynia, but the Spirit of Jesus would not allow them to cross, ⁸ so they went through Mysia and came down to Troas.

⁹ Then one night Paul had a vision. A Macedonian stood before him and said, "Come over to Macedonia and help us." ¹⁰ After this vision, we* immediately made efforts to get across to Macedonia, convinced that God had called us to bring them the Good News.

¹¹ We put out to sea from Troas and set a course straight for Samothrace, and the next day on to Neapolis; ¹² from there we went to Philippi, which is one of the bigger cities in Macedonia and a Roman colony, and spent a few days there.

¹³ On the Sabbath we went along the river outside the gates, thinking we might find a place of prayer. We sat down and preached to the women who had come to the gathering. ¹⁴ One of them was named Lydia, a devout woman from the town of Thyatira who was in the purple-dye trade. As she listened to us, Christ opened her heart to accept what Paul was saying. ¹⁵ After she and her household were baptized, she extended us an invitation: "If you are convinced that I am a believer in Christ, please come and stay with us." We accepted.

---

* Luke, a physician and the author of Acts, apparently joins Paul's group at Troas.

¹⁶ Once when we were going to prayer, we met a household worker who was possessed by a spirit of divination, and who made a great deal of money for her employers through its fortune telling. ¹⁷ She began to follow Paul and the rest of us, shouting, "These are faithful followers of the Most High God, who proclaim to you the way of salvation!" ¹⁸ She did this for many days.

Finally one day Paul lost his temper, and turned around and said to the spirit, "In the name of Jesus Christ I command you to leave this woman!" It left her that moment.

¹⁹ When her employers saw that their profitable operation was now hopelessly dead, they seized Paul and Silas and dragged them before the authorities in the public square. ²⁰ They brought them to the chief magistrates and said, "These people are Jews and are disturbing the peace ²¹ by advocating practices which are unlawful for us Romans to accept or practice."

²² The crowd joined in the attack on them, and the magistrates stripped them and ordered them to be flogged. ²³ They were whipped many times and thrown into prison, and the jailer was told to keep a close watch on them. ²⁴ So, following these instructions, the warden threw them into the innermost cell of the prison and chained their feet to a stake.

²⁵ About midnight, Paul and Silas were praying and singing hymns to God as the other prisoners listened. ²⁶ Suddenly a severe earthquake shook the place, rocking the prison to its foundation. Immediately all the doors flew open, and everyone's chains were pulled loose. ²⁷ When the jailer woke up and found the doors wide open, he drew a sword and was about to commit suicide, presuming that the prisoners had escaped.

²⁸ But Paul shouted, "Don't harm yourself! We're all still here."

²⁹ The jailer called for a light, then rushed in and fell trembling at the feet of Paul and Silas, and, ³⁰ after a brief interval, led them out and asked them, "What must I do to be saved?"

³¹ They answered, "Believe in Jesus the Savior, and you will be saved—you and everyone in your household."

³² They proceeded to preach the word of God to the jailer and his whole household. ³³ At that late hour of the night he took them in and bathed their wounds; then he and the whole household were baptized. ³⁴ He led them up into his house, spread a table before them, and the whole family joyfully celebrated their newfound faith in God.

³⁵ In the morning the magistrates sent officers with the order, "Release them both."

³⁶ The jailer reported to Paul, "The magistrates have ordered your release. Go in peace."

³⁷ "What's this?" replied Paul. "They beat us publicly and throw us, Roman citizens, into prison without a trial. And now they want to release us quietly? No! They'll have to come and escort us out themselves!"

³⁸ The officers brought this news to the magistrates, who were horrified to learn that Paul and Silas were Roman citizens. ³⁹ So the magistrates came to assuage them, led them out of prison and begged them to leave the city.

⁴⁰ From prison Paul and Silas returned to Lydia's house, where they met with the sisters and brothers to give them encouragement. Then they left.

17 ¹ When Paul and Silas had traveled through Amphipolis and Apollonia, they came to Thessalonica, where there was a Jewish synagogue. ² As was his custom, Paul visited the congregation; on three consecutive Sabbaths he debated with them from the scriptures— ³ explaining and proving that the Messiah had to suffer and rise from the dead. "This Messiah," he said, "is the Jesus I am proclaiming to you." ⁴ Some of them were convinced and joined Paul and Silas, along with a large number of God-fearing Greeks, and quite a few prominent women as well.

⁵ However, the Jews became jealous and, recruiting some reprobates from the marketplace, formed a mob and soon had the whole city in an uproar. They made for Jason's house, intending to find Paul and Silas there and bring them before the assembled people. ⁶ They weren't there, however, so they dragged Jason and some of the faithful off to the city council, shouting, "The people who have been turning the world upside down are now here. ⁷ Jason has been housing them. They all defy Caesar's edicts and claim that there is another ruler—Jesus." ⁸ The mob stirred up the crowd and city magistrates who, upon hearing the charges, ⁹ made Jason and the others post bond before releasing them.

¹⁰ When night fell, the sisters and brothers sent Paul and Silas to Berea. Once there, they went to the Jewish synagogue. ¹¹ These worshippers were more open-minded than those in Thessalonica. They heard the message willingly and studied the scriptures daily to determine whether it was true. ¹² Many of them became believers, as did many prominent Greek women and men.

¹³ But when the Jews of Thessalonica learned that the word of God was now being taught in Berea, they came there to make trouble and stir up the people. ¹⁴ The sisters and brothers immediately sent Paul to the seacoast, but Silas and Timothy stayed behind. ¹⁵ Paul was taken as far as Athens by an escort, who then returned with instructions for Silas and Timothy to join Paul as soon as possible.

¹⁶ As Paul waited for them in Athens, his spirit was revolted at the sight of the city given over to idols. ¹⁷ So he debated in the Jewish synagogue with both the Jews and the God-fearing Greeks who worshiped there, and every day spoke in the marketplace to whomever came along. ¹⁸ Even some Epicurean and Stoic philosophers argued with him. Some said, "What is this chatterbox trying to say?" Others said, "He seems to be a promoter of foreign gods," because he was preaching about "Jesus" and "the Resurrection."

¹⁹ They invited Paul to accompany them to the Council of the Areopagus and said, "Let us learn of this new teaching you describe. ²⁰ You bring some strange notions to our ears, and we would like to know the meaning of all this." ²¹ The Athenians and the foreigners living there loved talking about and listening to the latest ideas whenever they could.

²² Then Paul stood up before the council of the Areopagus and delivered this address: "Citizens of Athens, I note that in every respect you are scrupulously religious. ²³ As I walked about looking at your shrines, I even discovered an altar inscribed, 'To an Unknown God.' Now, what you are worshipping in ignorance I intend to make known to you.

²⁴ "For the God who made the world and all that is in it, the Sovereign of heaven and earth, doesn't live in sanctuaries made by human hands, ²⁵ and isn't served by humans, as if in need of anything. No! God is the One who gives everyone life, breath—everything. ²⁶ From one person God created all of humankind to inhabit the entire earth, and set the time for each nation to exist and the exact place where each nation should dwell. ²⁷ God did this so that human beings would seek, reach out for, and perhaps find the One who is not really far from any of us— ²⁸ the One in whom we live and

move and have our being. As one of your poets has put it, 'We too are God's children.'

²⁹ "If we are in fact children of God, then it's inexcusable to think that the Divine Nature is like an image of gold, silver or stone—an image formed by the art and thought of mortals. ³⁰ God, who overlooked such ignorance in the past, now commands all people everywhere to reform their lives. ³¹ For a day has been set when the whole world will be judged with justice. And this judge, who is a human being, has already been appointed. God has given proof of all of this by raising this judge from the dead."

³² When they heard about the resurrection of the dead, some sneered, while others said, "We must hear you on this topic some other time." ³³ At that, Paul left the council. ³⁴ A few women and men joined Paul and believed. Among them was Dionysius, a member of the Areopagus, a woman named Damaris and a few others.

18²¹ After this, Paul left Athens and went to Corinth. ² There he met a Jew named Aquila, whose family came from Pontus. Aquila and his wife Priscilla had recently left Rome because an edict of Claudius had expelled all the Jews from Rome. Paul went to visit them, ³ and when he discovered that they were tentmakers—of the same trade as himself—he lodged with them, and they worked together. ⁴ Every Sabbath, in the synagogue, Paul led discussions in which he tried to persuade Greeks and Jews alike.

⁵ When Silas and Timothy came down from Macedonia, Paul was absorbed in preaching and giving evidence to the Jewish people that Jesus was the Messiah. ⁶ When they turned against him and started to insult him, he took his cloak and shook it out in front of them, saying, "Your blood is on your own heads; from now on I can go to the Gentiles with a clear conscience."

⁷ Then he left the synagogue and moved to a house next door, which belonged to a worshipper of God named Justus. ⁸ The president of the synagogue, Crispus, and his household became believers in Christ. Many Corinthians who heard Paul also believed and were baptized. ⁹ One night God said to him in a vision, "Don't be afraid. Go on speaking and don't be silent, ¹⁰ for I am with you. No one will attack you or harm you, because I have many people in this city." ¹¹ So Paul stayed for a year and a half, teaching them the word of God.

¹² While Gallio was proconsul of Achaia, the members of the local synagogue rose up in one accord against Paul, and brought him into court. ¹³ "This one," they charged, "is persuading the people to worship God in ways that are against the Law."

¹⁴ Paul was about to speak in self-defense when Gallio said to Paul's accusers, "If it were a serious crime or a serious fraud, I would give you a patient and reasonable hearing. ¹⁵ But since this is a dispute about terminology and titles and your own law, you must see to it yourselves. I refuse to judge such matters." ¹⁶ With that, he dismissed them from court.

¹⁷ Then they all pounced on Sosthenes, a leader of the synagogue, and beat him in full view of the bench. But Gallio paid no attention to the incident.

¹⁸ Paul stayed on in Corinth for some time. Eventually he left the sisters and brothers and sailed for Syria, in the company of Priscilla and Aquila. At the port of Cenchrea, he shaved his head because of a vow he had made.

¹⁹ When they reached Ephesus, Paul left them and went alone to the Jewish synagogue to debate with the worshippers. ²⁰ They asked him to stay longer, but he declined. ²¹ Yet when he did leave, he said, "I will return if God wills it." After that he set sail from Ephesus. ²² When he landed at Caesarea, he went up to greet the church.

Then he came down to Antioch. ²³ After spending some time there, Paul set out again, traveling systematically through Galatian territory and Phrygia to reassure all the disciples.

²⁴ A Jew named Apollos, a native of Alexandria with a reputation for eloquence, arrived by ship at Ephesus. He was both well-versed in scripture and instructed in the Way of Christ. ²⁵ Fervent in spirit, Apollos taught and spoke accurately about Jesus, although he knew firsthand only about John's baptism. ²⁶ He too began to express himself fearlessly in the synagogue. When Priscilla and Aquila heard Apollos, they took him home and explained the Way of Christ in greater detail. ²⁷ Apollos wanted to go to Achaia, and so the sisters and brothers encouraged him by writing the disciples there to meet him.

When Apollos arrived, he greatly strengthened those who through God's favor had become believers. ²⁸ He was vigorous in his public refutation of the Jewish party, as he went about establishing from the scriptures that Jesus was the Messiah.

19²¹ While Apollos was in Corinth, Paul passed through the interior of the country and came to Ephesus. There Paul found disciples, ² to whom he put the question, "Did you receive the Holy Spirit when you became believers?"

They replied, "No, we were never even told there was such a thing as a Holy Spirit."

³ "Then how were you baptized?" he asked.

"With John's baptism," they responded.

⁴ Paul then explained, "John's baptism was a baptism of repentance; he insisted that the people believe in the one who was to come after him—in other words, Jesus."

⁵ When they heard this, they were baptized in the name of Jesus Christ. ⁶ And the moment Paul laid his hands on them, the Holy Spirit came down on them, and they began to speak in tongues and prophesy. ⁷ There were about twelve of them.

⁸ Paul entered the synagogue and, over a period of about three months, debated fearlessly, with persuasive arguments, about the reign of God.

⁹ But some among the congregation dissented, refused to believe and publicly disparaged the Way. Paul left them, along with his disciples, and held his daily debates in the lecture hall of Tyrannus. ¹⁰ This continued for two years, and all the Jews and Greeks throughout Asia heard the word of God.

¹¹ God worked such remarkable miracles through Paul ¹² that even handkerchiefs or aprons which touched him, when applied to sick people, healed them and drove evil spirits from them.

¹³ Then some roving Jewish exorcists tried invoking the name of Jesus Christ over those who had evil spirits, by saying, "I command you to come out—by Jesus, whom Paul preaches!"

¹⁴ Among the exorcists trying this were the seven children of Sceva, a Jewish high priest. ¹⁵ The evil spirit they were trying to exorcise came at them with, "Jesus I know, and Paul I know, but who are you?" ¹⁶ Then the person possessed by the demon sprang on them and overpowered them one

by one. They were mauled so badly that they fled from the house naked and bleeding.

¹⁷ When the news of this incident reached the ears of Jews and Greeks living in Ephesus, they grew fearful, and the name of Jesus Christ became greatly esteemed. ¹⁸ Many believers came forward and confessed to practicing sorcery. ¹⁹ And a number of these brought their books of magic and made a public bonfire out of them. It was estimated that the value of the documents came to fifty thousand silver pieces—almost a hundred fifty years' wages. ²⁰ In this way the word of God spread widely and successfully.

19:21–28:31

When all this had come to pass, Paul decided to return to Jerusalem by way of Macedonia and Achaia. "And after that," he said, "I must visit Rome as well." ²² Then he sent Timothy and Erastus, two of his coworkers, ahead to Macedonia. He remained in the province of Asia a little longer.

²³ It was about this time that a controversy broke out concerning the Way. ²⁴ A silversmith named Demetrius, who employed a large number of workers crafting silver shrines to Diana, ²⁵ called together his workers and others in related crafts. "As you all know," he said, "we make a good living from this craft. ²⁶ Undoubtedly you have heard about this fellow Paul—who, not only in Ephesus but throughout most of Asia, has led astray a vast number of people by teaching that gods made by hand are not gods at all. ²⁷ This teaching threatens not only our very livelihood, but also the prestige of the temple of the Great Goddess—Diana. She who is worshiped throughout Asia and the whole world may even be stripped of her divine majesty."

²⁸ When the workers heard this, they became enraged and started shouting, "Great is Diana of the Ephesians!" ²⁹ Their rage spread throughout the city, and the populace came together in the amphitheater, bringing with them two of Paul's Macedonian traveling companions, Gaius and Aristarchus. ³⁰ Paul intended to go in among the crowd, but was dissuaded by his disciples. ³¹ As a matter of fact, some friendly provincial officials sent word to Paul advising him not to venture into the theater.

³² By now mass confusion reigned in the gathering, and most of them didn't even know why they had assembled. Some shouted one thing, while others shouted another. ³³ Members of the Jewish community there hustled Alexander to the front, who motioned with his hand for order. He intended to explain things to the gathering. ³⁴ But when they realized he was Jewish, they shouted in unison, "Great is Diana of the Ephesians!"

They were at it for two hours ³⁵ when the town clerk finally stilled the crowd and said, "Women and men of Ephesus, who among the living doesn't know that the city of the Ephesians is the guardian of the temple of the great Diana, and of her statue that fell from the heavens? ³⁶ No one can contradict these facts! So there is no need for you to get so worked up and do something foolhardy. ³⁷ The two you brought here have neither committed sacrileges against our Goddess nor blasphemed her. ³⁸ If Demetrius and the silversmiths want to take action against anyone, the courts are in session and the proconsuls are available; let them press charges. ³⁹ If you have anything more to bring up, let it be settled in the regular assembly. ⁴⁰ As matters stand, we are already in danger of being accused of rioting for today's activities, since there's no real cause for it, and we don't have an explanation." ⁴¹ With this, the town clerk dismissed the crowd.

20 ²¹ Once the uproar was over, Paul sent for the disciples and encouraged them, said goodbye and left for Macedonia. ² As he passed through those places he gave the believers much encouragement, and eventually came to Greece, ³ where he stayed for three months.

As Paul prepared to set sail for Syria, he learned that the members of the local synagogue were plotting against him. So he changed his itinerary and returned by way of Macedonia. ⁴ Traveling with him were Sopater, son of Pyrrhus, from Beroea; Aristarchus and Secundus from Thessalonica; Gaius from Derbe; Timothy; and Tychicus and Trophimus from the province of Asia. ⁵ They went on ahead and waited for us at Troas. ⁶ We sailed from Philippi after the Feast of Unleavened Bread and caught up with them in five days. We spent a week in Troas.

⁷ On the first day of the week, we gathered to break bread. Paul spoke to them, and as he planned to leave the next day, he went on until midnight. ⁸ There were a number of lamps in the upstairs room where they were gathered. ⁹ And as Paul went on and on, a youth named Eutychus grew drowsy as he sat on a window sill; he fell asleep, tumbled out the window of the three-story building, and died. ¹⁰ But Paul went down and flung himself on the youth and, cradling him in his arms, said, "Don't worry, he's still alive." ¹¹ Paul then returned to the upper room, broke bread and ate. He continued to talk until dawn; then he left. ¹² They took the youth away alive, to their great joy.

¹³ The plan was that we would now go ahead by sea. So we set sail for Assos, where we would meet up with Paul. He planned it this way, for he wanted to go by land. ¹⁴ When he met us at Assos, we took him aboard and went on to Mitylene. ¹⁵ The next day we left there and came to a point off Chios; the day after that we crossed over to Samos, and we made Miletas on the third day. ¹⁶ Paul had decided to sail past Ephesus and avoid Asia all together, since he was anxious to get to Jerusalem, if possible, in time for Pentecost.

¹⁷ Paul sent word from Miletus to Ephesus, summoning the elders of that church. ¹⁸ When they came he addressed these words to them: "You know how I lived among you from the first day I set foot in the province of Asia—¹⁹ how I served Christ in humility through the sorrows and trials that came my way from the plotting of certain Jewish individuals and groups. ²⁰ I have not hesitated to do anything that might be helpful to you. I have taught you in public and in private, ²¹ urging both Jews and Greeks alike to turn to God and to believe in our Savior Jesus Christ.

²² "But now, as you see, I'm on my way to Jerusalem, compelled by the Spirit and not knowing what will happen to me there—²³ except that the Holy Spirit has been warning me from city to city that chains and hardships await me. ²⁴ However, I don't count my life of any value to myself. All I want is to finish my race and complete the task assigned to me by Jesus Christ—bearing witness to the Good News of God's grace. ²⁵ I know as I speak these words that none of you among whom I went about preaching the kindom will ever see my face again. ²⁶ Therefore, I solemnly declare today that I take the blame for no one's conscience, ²⁷ for I have never shrunk from announcing to you God's design in its entirety.

²⁸ "Keep watch over yourselves and over the whole flock the Holy Spirit has given you to guard. Shepherd the church of God, which was purchased with a high price—Christ's blood. ²⁹ I know quite well that when I am gone, savage

wolves will invade you and will have no mercy on the flock. ³⁰ Even from your own ranks, there will be those coming forward with a travesty of the truth, to lead away any who will follow them.

³¹ "So be on your guard. Don't forget that for three years, night and day, I never ceased warning you individually, even to the point of tears. ³² I now commend you to God, and to the word of God's grace, which has the power to build you up and give you your inheritance among all the holy ones. ³³ Never did I set my heart on anyone's silver or gold or fine clothes. ³⁴ You yourselves know that these hands of mine have served both my needs and those of my companions. ³⁵ I have always pointed out to you that it's by such hard work that you must help the weak. You need to recall the words of Jesus, who said, 'It is more blessed to give than to receive.'"

³⁶ After this discourse, Paul knelt down with them all and prayed. ³⁷ They began to weep without restraint, throwing their arms around him and kissing him, ³⁸ for they were deeply saddened to hear that they would never see his face again. Then they escorted him to the ship.

21 ¹ Tearing ourselves away from them, we put to sea and sailed to Cos, and on the next day to Rhodes and from there to Patara. ² There we found a ship bound for Phoenicia, so we boarded and set sail. ³ When we came to Cyprus we passed it on the port side and headed for Syria, landing at Tyre. Here the ship unloaded its cargo. ⁴ Finding disciples there, we stayed with them for a week. Moved by the Spirit, they repeatedly counseled Paul not to go to Jerusalem. ⁵ But when our week was ended, we continued our journey. All the disciples and their families escorted us out of the city, and there on the beach we knelt to pray. ⁶ Then we made our goodbyes and boarded the ship, and they returned to their homes.

⁷ The voyage from Tyre ended when we came to Ptolemais, where we greeted our sisters and brothers and visited them for one day. ⁸ The next day we went to Caesarea. There we stayed with Philip the evangelist, one of the Seven. ⁹ He had four unmarried daughters who were prophets.

¹⁰ We had been there for several days when a prophet named Agabus came down from Judea. ¹¹ When he came to see us, he took Paul's belt, bound his own hands and feet with it and said, "The Holy Spirit says, 'The one who owns this belt will be bound this way in Jerusalem by the Temple authorities, and they will hand this person over to the Gentiles.'"

¹² When we heard this, all of us present begged Paul not to go up to Jerusalem. ¹³ Paul replied, "Are you trying to diminish my resolve by your crying? I am prepared not only to be bound but even to die for the name of Jesus Christ." ¹⁴ When it became obvious his mind was set, we fell silent, saying, "God's will be done."

¹⁵ After this, we made the necessary preparations for the journey and left for Jerusalem. ¹⁶ Some of the disciples from Caesarea accompanied us and led us to the house of our host, Mnason of Cyprus, who had been one of the earliest disciples.

¹⁷ When we arrived in Jerusalem, the sisters and brothers welcomed us warmly. ¹⁸ The next day Paul accompanied us to visit James; all the elders were present. ¹⁹ Paul greeted them and gave a detailed report of what God had accomplished among the Gentiles through Paul's ministry.

²⁰ They all gave praise to God when they heard the report. But they said to Paul, "You see, brother, how many thousands of our Jewish sisters and brothers are now believers—all of them resolute keepers of the Law! ²¹ They have heard that you teach people of the diaspora to abandon Moses, to stop circumcising their male children and to stop observing the various customs. ²² What are we to do? Certainly they will learn that you have arrived!

²³ "This is what we recommend: we have four believers here who have taken a Nazirite vow. ²⁴ Take them and purify yourself along with them; pay their expenses so that they may have their heads shaved. In this way, everyone will know that the reports they have heard about you are false, and that you still regularly live by the Law. ²⁵ Regarding our Gentile sisters and brothers, we sent them our decision that they are to abstain from food sacrificed to idols, from meat of unbled or strangled animals, and from sexual immorality."

²⁶ So the next day Paul took the four and was purified with them. Then he went to the Temple and gave notice when the day of purification would be completed and when the offering would be presented on their behalf.

²⁷ When the seven days were almost over, some Jews from Asia Minor saw Paul in the Temple. They stirred up the crowd and seized him, ²⁸ shouting, "Children of Israel, help us! This is the person who preaches against our people, against our Law and against this place everywhere he goes, to anyone who will listen! Not only that, he has brought Greeks into the Temple and has defiled this holy place!" ²⁹ As it happened, they had previously seen Trophimus the Ephesian in the city with him, and presumed that Paul had brought him into the Temple.

³⁰ The whole city was in an uproar, with people scurrying about. They seized Paul and dragged him out of the Temple, and immediately the gates were closed behind them. ³¹ They were on the verge of killing him when news reached the commander of the cohort that all Jerusalem was breaking out in riot. ³² He immediately took soldiers and centurions and charged down to the crowd. When the crowd saw the commander and the troops, they stopped beating Paul.

³³ The commander approached, arrested Paul and had him bound with two chains. Then he attempted to find out who he was and what he had done. ³⁴ Different people in the crowd called out different charges. This resulted in such an uproar that it became impossible for the commander to gather the facts he needed. So he ordered Paul into the barracks. ³⁵ By the time Paul came to the steps, the soldiers had to carry him because of the violence of the crowd. ³⁶ The mob kept following from behind and shouting, "Away with him!"

³⁷ As Paul was about to be taken into the barracks, he asked the commander if he could have a word with him. The commander said, "So, you speak Greek! ³⁸ Aren't you the Egyptian who started the recent revolt and led the four thousand assassins into the desert?"

³⁹ Paul replied, "I am Jewish, a citizen of the well-known city of Tarsus in Cilicia. Give me your permission to speak to the people."

⁴⁰ The officer gave permission, and Paul, standing on the top step, motioned to the people to be quiet. When they grew silent he addressed them in Aramaic:

22

[1] "Sisters and brothers, mothers and fathers, listen to my defense, which I now offer to you."

[2] When they realized he was speaking to them in Aramaic, they became utterly silent. He continued, [3] "I am Jewish, born at Tarsus in Cilicia. I was raised in this city and studied at the feet of Gamaliel. I was educated in the exact observance of the Law of our ancestors. I was as full of zeal for God as you are here. [4] I persecuted the followers of the Way to their death. I captured women and men and sent them to prison in chains. [5] The high priest and the elders will bear witness to this, for they sent me with letters of introduction to their peers in Damascus. I went there to deliver prisoners back here for punishment.

[6] "As I neared Damascus, at about noon a bright light from heaven suddenly shone all around me. [7] I fell to the ground and heard a voice say to me, 'Saul, Saul, why are you persecuting me?' [8] 'Who are you?' I asked. The voice said to me, 'I am Jesus of Nazareth, and you are persecuting me.' [9] My traveling companions saw the light, but didn't hear the voice of the one speaking to me. [10] I asked, 'What must I do?' Jesus answered, 'Get up and go into Damascus. Once there, you will be told what to do.' [11] Because I was blinded by the brightness of the light, my companions led me by hand into Damascus.

[12] "A person named Ananias, a devout observer of the Law and one highly regarded by the Jewish community in Damascus, came to see me. [13] He stood beside me and said, 'Saul, my brother, receive your sight.' My sight returned at that instant and I was able to see him. [14] He said to me, 'The God of our ancestors has chosen you to know the divine will, and to see the Just One and to hear the Messiah's voice. [15] You are to be the Messiah's witness to all humankind, bearing testimony about all you have seen and heard. [16] Now why do you delay? Go and get yourself baptized, wash away your sins and call on the name of Jesus.'

[17] "When I returned to Jerusalem and was praying in the Temple, I fell into a trance [18] and saw Jesus. 'Hurry,' Jesus said, 'leave Jerusalem at once; for they refuse to accept your testimony about me.' [19] 'But my Sovereign,' I replied, 'it's because they know that I formerly moved from synagogue to synagogue, beating and imprisoning those who believe in you. [20] They know that when the blood of your witness Stephen was shed, I stood by in full agreement, and even held the cloaks of the murderers while they stoned him.' [21] Then Jesus said to me, 'Go! I will send you far away to the Gentiles.'"

[22] The crowd listened attentively up until he said this, then they began to shout, "Rid the earth of this one! He's not fit to live!" [23] As they screamed, waved their cloaks over their heads and flung dust into the air, [24] the commander had Paul taken into the barracks and interrogated with the whip, to figure out why the people were vilifying him like this.

[25] As they prepared him for the flogging, Paul said to the centurion on duty, "Is it lawful to scourge a person who is a Roman citizen and has not been brought to trial?"

[26] When he heard this, the centurion went to the commander and said, "Do you realize what you're about to do? This person is a Roman citizen!"

[27] The commander came to Paul and asked, "Are you a Roman citizen?"

"I am," he answered.

[28] The commander commented, "I bought my citizenship for a large sum of money."

Paul replied, "Actually, I was born a citizen."

[29] At this, those who were preparing to interrogate him withdrew, and the commander became frightened when he realized he had put a Roman citizen in chains.

[30] The next day, the commander released Paul from prison, intending to look carefully into the charge which the Temple authorities were bringing against him. He summoned the chief priests and the whole Sanhedrin to a meeting; then he brought Paul down and made him stand before them.

23

[1] Paul looked intently at the Sanhedrin and said, "Friends, I have conducted myself before God in all good conscience to this day."

[2] At this the high priest Ananias commanded the attendants to strike Paul on the mouth. [3] Paul replied to this, "God is going to strike you, you whitewashed wall! How dare you sit there to judge me according to the Law, and then break the Law by ordering me to be struck?"

[4] Those nearby said, "You are insulting God's high priest!"

[5] Paul answered, "I didn't realize he was the high priest, for scripture says, 'You will not curse a ruler of your people.'"

[6] Now Paul was aware that some of them were Sadducees and some Pharisees. Consequently, he began his speech before the Sanhedrin this way: "I am a Pharisee, the descendant of Pharisees. I find myself on trial now because of my hope in the resurrection of the dead." [7] At these words, a dispute broke out between Pharisees and Sadducees, which divided the whole assembly. [8] The Sadducees, of course, maintain that there is no resurrection and deny the existence of angels and spirits, while the Pharisees believe in all these things.

[9] A loud uproar ensued. Finally, some of the religious scholars who were Pharisees stood up and declared emphatically, "We don't find this man guilty of any crime. Perhaps a spirit or an angel has spoken to him." [10] At this, the commander feared they would tear Paul to pieces. He therefore ordered his troops to go down and rescue Paul from their midst and take him back to headquarters. [11] That night God appeared at Paul's side and said, "Courage! Just as you have borne witness to me here in Jerusalem, so must you do the same in Rome as well."

[12] At daybreak, the Temple officials hatched a plot and bound themselves by oath that they would neither eat nor drink until they had killed Paul. [13] More than forty joined in the conspiracy. [14] They went to the chief priest and the elders and said, "We have made a solemn vow to eat nothing until we have killed Paul. [15] You and the Sanhedrin must now request the commander to bring him before you on the pretext that you need to examine his case more closely. For our part, we are prepared to kill him before he reaches you."

[16] Now Paul's nephew heard of the plot and reported it to Paul in the barracks. [17] Paul called one of the centurions and said, "Take this youth to the commander. He has something to report."

[18] The centurion took the youth to the commander and explained, "The prisoner Paul asked me to bring this youth to you, for he has something to report."

[19] The tribune took him by the hand, pulled him aside and asked, "Now, what is it you want to tell me?"

[20] The youth said, "The Temple authorities have hatched a plot to ask you to bring Paul before the Sanhedrin tomorrow, as though they were going to inquire more thoroughly into his case. [21] Don't do it. For more than forty of them plan to ambush him. They have vowed not to eat or drink until they have killed him. They are ready and await your order."

[22] The commander dismissed the youth with the counsel, "Don't tell anyone what you have told me."

[23] Then he called for two of his centurions and said, "Call out two hundred soldiers, seventy cavalry and two hun-

dred archers for a nine o'clock movement tonight. ²⁴ Provide horses for Paul and deliver him to Felix the governor. Deliver him unharmed."

²⁵ He also wrote the following letter:

²⁶ "From Claudius Lysias,

"To His Excellency, Governor Felix:

"Greetings. ²⁷ This person was seized by a Jewish mob with murder on its mind. But I, along with my troops, intervened and rescued him, for I learned that he was a Roman citizen. ²⁸ With the intent to determine what charge to lay before him, I took him before their Sanhedrin. ²⁹ I was able to ascertain that the accusations concerned questions about their Law, but that there was no charge worthy of imprisonment or the death penalty. ³⁰ When I was informed that there was a conspiracy against him, I sent him to you immediately and ordered the accusers to state their case against him in your presence."

³¹ So the soldiers, following orders, took Paul and escorted him to Antipatris after dark. ³² The next day, they returned to the barracks and left it up to the cavalry to complete the journey. ³³ When the cavalry arrived in Caesarea, they delivered the letter and Paul to the governor. ³⁴ The governor read the letter and asked Paul what province he was from. When he heard that Paul was Cilician, ³⁵ the governor replied, "I will hear your case when your accusers arrive."

Then he ordered Paul to be held in Herod's Praetorium, the governor's official residence.

24 ¹ Five days later, the high priest Ananias, accompanied by some elders and a lawyer named Tertullus, came down and filed formal charges against Paul before the governor.

² Paul was called, and Tertullus presented the case for the prosecution: "Your Excellency, Felix, we enjoy a longstanding peace and beneficial reforms because of your responsible stewardship. ³ And we are grateful for this. ⁴ So, rather than take up too much of your time, in your kindness grant us a brief hearing.

⁵ "This person is a troublemaker. He stirs up our Jewish sisters and brothers everywhere. He is a ringleader of the Nazarene sect, ⁶ and he even attempted to desecrate the Temple. So we arrested him with the intent of judging him according to our Law, ⁷ but the commander Lysias intervened and violently took him out of our jurisdiction. He then ordered us to appear before you. ⁸ We invite you to learn for yourself the truth of our accusations against him." ⁹ The high priest and the elders spoke up and agreed with the charge.

¹⁰ Then the governor motioned Paul to speak. Paul said, "I know that you have administered justice over this nation for many years, so I will confidently make my defense. ¹¹ As you can readily ascertain, it's no more than twelve days since I went up to Jerusalem on pilgrimage. ¹² But it's a lie that they found me arguing with anyone or stirring up a mob, either in the Temple or the synagogue or the city. ¹³ Neither can they prove these charges they make against me. ¹⁴ But I can admit that I worship the God of our ancestors in accordance with the Way, which they call a sect. I hold to my beliefs in accordance with the Law and with what the prophets have written. ¹⁵ I trust in the same God that they do, that there will be a resurrection of the just and unjust alike. ¹⁶ In view of this, I strive to keep a clear conscience before God and before all people.

¹⁷ "After many years of absence, I came to Jerusalem to give alms for needy people and to make offerings. ¹⁸ It was while I was doing this that they found me, after having been purified, in the Temple. There was no crowd and no disturbance. ¹⁹ However, some Jewish authorities came down from Asia Minor—they should be here, if they have any reason to accuse me. ²⁰ At least let those who are here say what crime I committed when I spoke before the Sanhedrin—²¹ unless it's the one thing that I shouted out to them: 'It's over the issue of the resurrection of the dead that I am on trial before you today.'"

²² At this point Felix, who had accurate information about the Way, ordered a continuance of the case. "When Lysias the commander comes down," he said, "I will decide your case." ²³ He then ordered the centurion to keep Paul in custody, but free from restrictions, and to allow his friends to care for his needs.

²⁴ Several days later, Felix and his wife Drusilla—who was Jewish—came and sent for Paul, who told them about faith in Christ Jesus. ²⁵ But when Paul touched on the subjects of justice, self-control and the coming judgment, Felix grew alarmed and said, "You are dismissed for now! I will send for you later at a more convenient time." ²⁶ At the same time Felix had hopes of being offered a bribe, so he sent for Paul quite often and had discussions with him.

²⁷ After a period of two years, Felix was replaced by Porcius Festus. And since Felix was determined to win favor with the Jewish community, he left Paul in prison.

25 ¹ After Festus had been in the province for three days, he went up to Jerusalem from Caesarea. ² The chief priests and leaders of the Jewish community met with him and presented their charges against Paul. ³ They requested a concession: to have Paul be sent to Jerusalem. They were plotting to kill him along the way. ⁴ However, Festus replied that Paul would remain in custody in Caesarea, and that he himself would be going there before too long. ⁵ He added, "Let some of your authorities come down with me, and if he has done anything wrong they can file charges."

⁶ After spending eight or ten days there, Festus went down to Caesarea. The very next day, he took his seat on the tribunal and called for Paul to be brought before him. ⁷ Once Paul appeared, the Temple authorities who had come down from Jerusalem formed a circle around Paul and pelted him with unfounded accusations.

⁸ Paul said in his defense, "I have committed no crime against Jewish Law, against the Temple or against Caesar."

⁹ Festus, who wanted to be seen in a favorable light among Jewish people, said, "Are you willing to go up to Jerusalem and be tried before me there?"

¹⁰ Paul replied, "I am standing before the tribunal of Caesar, where I belong. I have not committed a crime against the Jewish people, as you very well know. ¹¹ If I am convicted of a capital crime, I don't refuse to die. But if their charges are specious, no one has the right to hand me over to them. I appeal to Caesar."

¹² Festus interrupted the proceedings to confer with his advisers. Then he said to Paul, "You have appealed to Caesar, you will go to Caesar."

¹³ After a few days, Agrippa the ruler and Bernice, his sister, arrived in Caesarea and paid Festus a courtesy call. ¹⁴ Since

they were to spend several days there, Festus referred Paul's case to the ruler. "There is a prisoner here," he said, "whom Felix left behind in custody. ¹⁵ While I was in Jerusalem, the chief priests and the elders presented their case against this man and demanded condemnation. ¹⁶ I replied that it was not a Roman practice to hand accused persons over before they have been confronted by their accusers and given a chance to defend themselves against their charges. ¹⁷ When they came here, I didn't delay the matter. The very next day, I took my seat on the bench and ordered the accused brought in. ¹⁸ His accusers confronted him, but they didn't charge him with any of the crimes I suspected.

¹⁹ "Instead they differed with him over issues in their own religion, and about a certain Jesus who had died, but who Paul claimed is alive. ²⁰ Not knowing how to decide the case, I asked whether the prisoner was willing to go to Jerusalem and stand trial there on these charges. ²¹ Paul appealed to be kept here until there could be an imperial investigation of his case, so I issued orders that he be kept in custody until I could send him to Caesar."

²² Then Agrippa said to Festus, "I would like to hear this person, too."

"You will hear him tomorrow," Festus replied.

²³ The next day Bernice and Agrippa arrived with great pomp and ceremony, entering the auditorium attended by the commanders of the cohort and the notables of the city. Then Festus ordered Paul into the auditorium.

²⁴ Festus said, "Honored guests, Agrippa and Bernice, and notables of our city, look at this man! He is the one the whole Jewish community—both in Jerusalem and here—loudly declares doesn't deserve to live. ²⁵ But I have not found a capital offense. And as he has appealed to the emperor, I have decided to send him to Rome. ²⁶ But I find myself lacking something to write our sovereign about this case. So I have brought him here before all of you, and especially you, Agrippa, so that our hearing may result in material for my report. ²⁷ It seems absurd to send up the prisoner without indicating the charges against him!"

26 ¹ Agrippa then said to Paul, "You may speak on your own behalf."

² So Paul held up his hand and initiated his defense:

"I consider myself fortunate, your highness, that I am given the opportunity to state my case before you, and to address all the charges against me by the Jewish authorities. ³ This is especially so because you are an expert in issues pertaining to Jewish customs and controversies. Please, I beg you, be patient as you listen to me.

⁴ "The way in which I was raised as a child, beginning among my own people and later in Jerusalem, is well known among the Jewish community. ⁵ They have known from the beginning and could testify, if they were willing, that I have lived the life of a Pharisee—the strictest party of our religion.

⁶ "And now I am on trial because of my hope in the promise of God to our ancestors. ⁷ This is the promise our twelve tribes hope to attain as they zealously worship God night and day. Your highness, this hope is the reason I am put on trial by my Jewish sisters and brothers. ⁸ Tell me why any of you consider it incredible that God should raise the dead?

⁹ "Personally, I too once thought myself obligated to work fervently to oppose the name of the Nazarene known as Jesus. ¹⁰ I did this in Jerusalem. I was authorized by the chief priests to imprison many of the believers. And I cast my vote against them when they were sentenced to death. ¹¹ I moved from synagogue to synagogue punishing them and

charging them with blasphemy. I even persecuted them in foreign cities.

¹² "I was on such a journey to Damascus, fortified with the authority and commission of the high priests. ¹³ That day—around noon, your highness—I saw a light brighter than the sun come down from heaven. Its brilliance enveloped me and my travelers. ¹⁴ We all fell to the ground, and I heard a voice saying to me in Aramaic, 'Saul, Saul, why are you persecuting me? It only hurts you to resist my prodding.' ¹⁵ 'Who are you?' I asked. And the reply came, 'I am Jesus, and you are persecuting me. ¹⁶ Get up now on your two feet. I am appearing to you to appoint you as my servant, to bear testimony about what you have seen of me, and what you will be shown soon. ¹⁷ I will deliver you from your own people, and from the Gentiles to whom I will send you. ¹⁸ You will open their eyes, so that they will turn from darkness to light, from the control of Satan to God—that they may receive forgiveness of sins, and an inheritance among those who have been sanctified through faith in me.'

¹⁹ "Consequently, your highness, I couldn't be disobedient to the heavenly vision. ²⁰ So I proclaimed it originally to the citizens of Damascus, then to those in Jerusalem and all the inhabitants of Judea, and finally to the Gentiles. I preached repentance and turning to God, with good works as a sign of their repentance. ²¹ It was because of this that the citizens of Jerusalem seized me in the Temple and tried to murder me. ²² But I have been blessed with God's help. That is why I stand to this very day, testifying to the great and lowly alike. I say nothing more than what the prophets and Moses predicted: ²³ that the Messiah must suffer and, being the first to rise from the dead, would proclaim—both to our people and to the Gentiles as well—that the Light has come."

²⁴ At this point in his defense, Festus loudly interrupted Paul: "Paul, you are deranged! Your immense learning is driving you to madness."

²⁵ "Most excellent Festus," Paul replied, "I am not deranged. I speak nothing that isn't true and reasonable. ²⁶ The ruler knows these issues, and I speak to him with assurance, since I'm confident that nothing spoken here has escaped his notice—it was not done in a corner. ²⁷ Agrippa—do you believe the Prophets, your highness? I know that you do."

²⁸ Agrippa said to Paul, "In a short time you will have persuaded me to become a Christian!"

²⁹ "A short time or a long time!" Paul replied, "I pray to God that both you and all present who hear my words would come to be as I am—with the exception of these chains!"

³⁰ At this point the ruler arose, along with the governor, Bernice, and those sitting with them. ³¹ Once they had left the room, they compared notes and came to a consensus. "What this person is doing doesn't deserve the death penalty—or even imprisonment."

³² Then Agrippa said to Festus, "He might have been set free by now if he had not appealed to Caesar!"

27 ¹ Once it was decided that we should sail for Italy, Paul and some other prisoners were put into the custody of a centurion named Julius, of the Augustan cohort. ² We embarked in a ship from Adramyttium, bound for ports along the province of Asia Minor. Accompanying us was Aristarchus, a Macedonian from Thessalonica. ³ The next day, we landed at Sidon, and Julius was considerate enough to allow Paul to go to his friends for provisions.

⁴ We embarked from there and sailed to the leeward side of Cyprus because of headwinds. ⁵ Then we sailed in open

water along the coast of Cilicia and Pamphylia, and in two weeks arrived at Myra in Lycia. 6 There the centurion found a ship from Alexandria bound for Italy, and put us aboard. 7 For the next several days we made little headway and arrived off Cnidus only after much difficulty. The wind made it impossible to land there, so we sailed to the leeward side of Crete, off Cape Salmone. 8 We coasted along with difficulty until we reached a place called Fair Havens, near the town of Lasea.

9 All of this had consumed a huge amount of time, and sailing was now dangerous since it was so late in the year—even the Day of Atonement had come and gone. Paul warned everyone, 10 "Friends, I perceive that this voyage now faces dangerous weather; we run the risk of losing our cargo, our ship and even our lives." 11 But the centurion gave more heed to the captain and the ship's owner than to Paul. 12 Because the harbor was unsuitable for wintering, the majority agreed to set sail with the hope of reaching Phoenix, a harbor in Crete facing both southwest and northwest, to spend the winter there.

13 A mild breeze out of the south came up and, sensing this as a good omen, they weighed anchor and sailed close to the shore of Crete. 14 Before long, a hurricane force wind called a "northeaster" struck down on them from across the island. 15 The ship was enveloped by the storm and couldn't be turned into the wind, so we had to give way to the wind and allow ourselves to be driven along by its force.

16 As we ran along the leeward side of an island known as Clauda, we managed with difficulty to gain control of the ship's dinghy. 17 Next they passed cables under the ship itself. Then, for fear of running aground on the shallows of Syrtis, they lowered the sea anchor and let themselves be driven along. 18 We were being buffeted by the storm so violently that on the next day they tossed some of the cargo overboard. 19 On the third day, they tossed the ship's gear overboard with their own hands. 20 For several days neither the sun nor the stars were visible, while the storm was assailing us. At last we gave up all hope of surviving.

21 Then, when they had been without food for a long time, Paul stood up among them. "Friends," he said, "had you heeded my advice and not set out from Crete, you would not have suffered all this loss, all this damage. 22 But now I ask you to hold on to your courage. For none of you will be lost, only the ship. 23 Last night an angel of the God to whom I belong and whom I serve stood beside me 24 and said, 'Don't be afraid, Paul. You are to stand trial before Caesar, so God has granted you the safety of all who sail with you.' 25 So, take heart, friends, for I believe that events will take place just as I have been told. 26 We are to run aground on an island."

27 After another two weeks—we were still drifting and in the Adriatic Sea by now—the crew sensed that we were near land. 28 They took soundings and measured twenty fathoms. A little later they measured fifteen fathoms. 29 So, for fear of running aground on a reef, they let out four anchors from the stern and prayed for the sun to rise. 30 The crew then tried to abandon ship. They lowered the dinghy into the water with the pretext that they were going to lay out anchors from the bow. 31 But Paul said to the centurion and his soldiers, "If the crew doesn't stay aboard, you won't be saved." 32 So the soldiers scuttled the dinghy by cutting its ropes.

33 A little before daybreak Paul urged them all to eat something. "For the last two weeks," he said, "you have been under constant tension and have eaten nothing. 34 I urge you to have something to eat; there is no doubt about your safety. Not a hair of your head will be lost." 35 With this, he took some bread and gave thanks to God while standing before them all. Then he broke the bread and began to eat.

36 They were all encouraged by this and began to eat as well. 37 In all, there were two hundred seventy-six aboard. 38 After they all had their fill, they lightened the load by tossing the wheat overboard.

39 At daybreak, even though they didn't recognize the land, they spied a bay with a beach. Intending to run the ship aground at this point, 40 they cut loose the anchors to abandon them to the sea, loosened the lines of the rudder, and hoisted the foresail to the wind and tried for the beach. 41 But the current carried the ship into a sandbar and grounded it. The bow was so wedged that it couldn't be moved, and the pounding surf began to break up the stern.

42 Initially, the soldiers intended to kill the prisoners to keep them from escaping by swimming away, 43 but the centurion intervened and thwarted their plan, because he wanted to spare Paul's life. He ordered those who could swim to jump overboard and make for shore. 44 He ordered the others to follow on planks or pieces of debris from the ship. All came ashore safe and sound.

28

1 Once safely ashore, we learned that the island was Malta. 2 The inhabitants were especially friendly. They built a huge fire and bade us welcome, for it had started to rain and was cold. 3 Paul had collected an armful of firewood and was putting it onto the fire when a snake, escaping from the heat, fastened itself onto his hand. 4 When the locals saw the snake hanging from his hand, they said to one another, "He must be a murderer. For divine justice would not let him live, even though he escaped the sea." 5 Paul, meanwhile, shook the snake into the fire with no ill effects. 6 They waited, expecting him to swell up and suddenly drop dead. After a long wait, and unable to detect anything unusual happening, they changed their minds and decided he was a god.

7 Nearby there were estates belonging to Publius, the chief official of the island. He welcomed us with open arms and entertained us cordially for three days. 8 It so happened that Publius' father was ill, suffering from dysentery and a fever. Paul went in to see him, and after praying, healed him by the laying on of hands. 9 Once this happened, others suffering from illnesses came and were healed. 10 They honored us with many gifts. When it came time to sail, they supplied the provisions.

11 After three months, we set sail on a ship which had wintered at the island. It was an Alexandrian ship with the figurehead of the twin gods Castor and Pollux. 12 We put in at Syracuse and spent three days there, 13 and then moved along the coast to Rhegium. After a day there, a south wind sprang up, and two days later we made Puteoli. 14 Here we found some sisters and brothers, who invited us to spend a week with them.

At last we came to Rome. 15 When the sisters and brothers there learned of our arrival, they came from as far as the Forum of Appius and Three Taverns—thirty and forty miles away—to meet us. Paul took courage when he saw them and gave thanks to God.

16 Upon arriving in Rome, Paul was allowed to take a lodging of his own, although a soldier was assigned as a guard.

17 Three days later, Paul invited the prominent members of the Jewish community for a visit. When they had gathered he said, "Friends, I have done nothing against our people or against our ancient customs. Yet in Jerusalem I was handed over to the Romans as a prisoner. 18 The Romans tried my case and wanted to release me because they found nothing against me deserving death. 19 When the Temple authorities

objected, I was forced to appeal to Caesar, though I had no cause to make accusations against my own people. [20] This is the reason, then, that I have asked to see you and to speak with you. I wear these chains solely because I share the hope of Israel."

[21] They replied, "We received no correspondence from Judea about you, and none of the sisters and brothers arriving from there have reported any rumors or anything negative about you. [22] For our part, we want to hear what you think, for we understand that this sect is generally denounced everywhere."

[23] So they set a date to come to his lodgings. When the day arrived, people came in great numbers. From early morning until evening Paul set forth his position. He declared to them the kindom of God and tried to convince them about Jesus—arguing from the Law of Moses and from the prophets.

[24] Some were convinced by what he said, though most were skeptical; [25] they argued among themselves and didn't come to any agreement. But before they left, Paul made one last effort. He said, "The Holy Spirit was right when she spoke to your ancestors through the prophet Isaiah:

[26] 'Go to this people and say,

You will keep on listening but won't understand,
you will keep on looking but won't perceive.
[27] For the heart of this people has become hardened;
they hardly hear with their ears, and their eyes are shut.
Otherwise they might see with their eyes,
hear with their ears,
understand with their heart
and turn and be healed.'

[28] "Know, therefore, that this salvation of God has been sent to the Gentiles. They will listen to it."

[29] When Paul finished, his Jewish listeners left, arguing seriously over what had been said.

[30] For two full years, Paul stayed on in his rented lodgings, welcoming all who came to visit. [31] With full assurance, and without any hindrance whatever, Paul preached the kindom of God and taught about our Savior Jesus Christ.

ROMANS

1:1–2:11

From Paul, a servant of Christ Jesus, called to be an apostle and set apart to proclaim [2] the Good News, which God promised long ago through the prophets, as the holy scriptures record—the Good News [3] concerning God's Only Begotten, who was descended from David according to the flesh, [4] but was made the Only Begotten of God in power, according to the spirit of holiness, by the resurrection from the dead: Jesus Christ our Savior. [5] We have been favored with apostleship, that we may bring to obedient faith all the nations, [6] among whom are you who have been called to belong to Jesus Christ;

[7] To all in Rome, beloved of God and called to be holy people: Grace and peace from our Abba God and our Savior Jesus Christ.

[8] First, I thank my God through Jesus Christ for all of you and for the way your faith is proclaimed throughout the world. [9] As God is my witness—the God I worship with my spirit by preaching the Good News of God's Only Begotten—I pray for you constantly. [10] And I pray that, God willing, I will be able to find the way to visit you.

[11] I long to see you, either to share with you some spiritual gift [12] or to find encouragement from you through our common faith. I want you to know, sisters and brothers, that I have often planned to visit you, but until now I have been prevented from doing so. [13] I want to work as fruitfully among you as I have done among the other Gentiles. [14] I owe a duty to both Greeks and non-Greeks, to the wise and the foolish alike. [15] That is why I am so eager to bring the Good News to you in Rome as well.

[16] For I am not ashamed of the Good News: it is itself the very power of God, effecting the deliverance of everyone who believes the Good News—to the Jew first, but also to the Greek. [17] For in that Gospel, God's justice is revealed—a justice which arises from faith and has faith as its result. As it is written, "By being faithful, those who are upright will find life."

[18] At the same time, however, God's passionate and just anger is also being revealed; it rages from heaven against all of humankind's willful impiety and refusal to honor God, against the injustices committed by people who actively suppress the truth through their injustice.

[19] For what is knowable about God is plain and obvious to everyone; indeed, it is God who has made it obvious to them. [20] Though invisible to the eye, God's eternal power and divinity have been seen since the creation of the universe, understood and clearly visible in all of nature. Humankind is, therefore, without excuse.

[21] For although they knew God, they didn't give God honor or praise and never even said, "Thank you"; instead, their reasoning became increasingly empty and inept, and their undiscerning hearts were darkened. [22] Professing to be wise, they became fools: [23] they exchanged the glory of the immortal and incorruptible God for mere images—images of mortal, corruptible humans, and birds, animals and reptiles. [24] So God gave them over to their hearts' desire—to promiscuous immorality, to the devaluing of their bodies with each other. [25] They exchanged the reality of God for a lie, and worshiped and served what was created rather than the Creator, who is forever praised. Amen.

[26] That is why God turned them over to their demeaning passions. Their women went from having sexual relations that were natural for them to relations that were contrary to their own natures. [27] And their men who would have naturally had sexual relations with women abandoned those ways and became consumed with burning passions for one another. Thus both sexes acted against their nature and received in their own personalities the consequences of their error.

[28] Furthermore, since they didn't think it worthwhile to retain the knowledge of God, God abandoned them to their own depraved minds. They were driven to do things that shouldn't be done [29] and were filled with every kind of injustice, evil, greed and malice. They became full of envy, murder, bickering, treachery and deceit. They became gossips, [30] slanderers, God-haters; they were insolent, arrogant and boastful, inventors of evil, and rebellious to their parents. [31] They were senseless, faithless, heartless and ruthless.

³² And even though they knew God's just mandate—that everyone who does such things deserves death—they not only continued to do these things, but encouraged others to do the same.

2:1 Yet every one of you who passes judgment has no excuse: by your judgment you convict yourself, since you do the very same things! ² We know that God's judgment rightly falls on people who do such things— ³ so how do you expect to escape God's judgment, since you who condemn these things in others do them yourselves? ⁴ Or do you think lightly of God's rich kindness and forbearance? Don't you know that God's kindness is an invitation for you to repent?

⁵ In spite of this, your hard and impenitent hearts are storing up retribution for that day of wrath when the just judgment of God will be revealed, ⁶ when every person will be repaid for what they have done: ⁷ eternal life to those who strive for glory, honor and immortality by patiently doing right; ⁸ wrath and fury to those who selfishly disobey the truth and obey wickedness. ⁹ Yes, affliction and anguish will come upon all who have done evil—the Jew first, then the Greek. ¹⁰ But there will be glory, honor and peace for everyone who has done good—to the Jew first, then the Greek. ¹¹ With God there is no favoritism.

2:12–3:26

All who sin independently of the Law will also perish independently of the Law; and all who sin under the Law will be judged by the Law. ¹³ It is not those who hear the Law who are just before God, but those who keep the Law who will be justified. ¹⁴ For instance, when Gentiles do naturally things required by the Law, they are a Law unto themselves, even though they don't have the Law. ¹⁵ They demonstrate that the demands of the Law are written on their hearts—they have a witness, their own conscience—and their conflicting thoughts accuse or even defend them. ¹⁶ All this will occur—according to the Good News I preach—on the day when God judges the secrets of humankind through Jesus Christ.

¹⁷ Now if you describe yourself as Jewish, if you rely on the Law, if you are proud of your relationship with the Most High, ¹⁸ if you know God's will and can tell right from wrong since you have been instructed in the Law, ¹⁹ if you are confident that you are a guide for the blind and a beacon for those in the dark, ²⁰ if you teach the ignorant and instruct the immature—because you have in the Law the very embodiment of knowledge and truth— ²¹ then why don't you teach yourself as well as others? ²² You who preach against stealing, do you steal? You who condemn adultery, do you commit adultery? You who despise idols, do you rob temples? ²³ You who boast of the Law, do you dishonor God by breaking the Law? ²⁴ It says in scripture, "It is because of you that the name of God is reviled among the Gentiles."

²⁵ The sign of the Covenant—circumcision—has value if you keep the Law. But if you break the Law, you might as well become a Gentile! ²⁶ If those who are not members of the Covenant keep the spirit of the Law, won't they be judged as though they kept the Law? ²⁷ Moreover, those who keep the Law but are not actual members of the Covenant will judge you as a lawbreaker, even though you have the written code and the sign of the Covenant.

²⁸ Being Jewish is more than following the letter of the Law; the sign of the Covenant is more than a visible sign. ²⁹ You are really Jewish if you are inwardly Jewish, and the real sign of the Covenant is on your heart. It is a matter of following the spirit, not the letter, of the Law. A person like this seeks praise not from humankind, but from God.

3:1 Then what benefit is there in being Jewish? What benefit is there in having the sign of the Covenant? ² Much, in every respect. First of all, the Jewish people were entrusted with the message of God. ³ What if some of them were unfaithful? Will their unfaithfulness nullify God's faithfulness? ⁴ Not at all! God will still be true, though all humankind lies—as scripture says, "That you may be right when you speak and prevail when you are judged."

⁵ But if our lack of holiness provides proof of God's justice, what can we say? That God is unjust—I am using a human analogy—in being angry with us? ⁶ Certainly not! That would imply that God could not judge the world. ⁷ One might as well say, "If my lie makes God's truth all the more glorious by comparison, why am I being condemned as a sinner?" ⁸ Why not say, "Do evil so that good may come of it!" Some slanderers have even accused us of teaching this; they are getting just what they deserve.

⁹ What, then? Are Jews better than Gentiles? Not at all! We have already declared that Jews and Greeks alike are all subjects of sin. ¹⁰ As it is written:

"There are no just, not even one;
¹¹ there is not one who understands,
not one who seeks God.
¹² All have turned away,
all alike have become worthless;
there is no one who does good,
not a single one."
¹³ "Their throats are open graves;
their tongues are full of deceit."
"Viper's venom is on their lips."
¹⁴ "Their mouths are full of bitter curses."
¹⁵ "Their feet are swift to shed blood;
¹⁶ they leave ruin and misery in their wake,
and ¹⁷ they do not know the way of peace."
¹⁸ "There is no fear of God before their eyes."

¹⁹ Now we know that what the Law says is said to those under the Law. Therefore, let every mouth be silenced, and let all of humankind be open to God's judgment. ²⁰ This is because we are not justified in the sight of God by keeping the Law: law only makes us aware of sin.

²¹ But now the justice of God has been manifested apart from the Law, even though both Law and prophets bear witness to it; ²² the justice of God works through faith in Jesus Christ for all who believe. There are no exceptions: ²³ everyone has sinned; everyone falls short of the glory of God. ²⁴ Yet everyone has also been undeservedly justified by the gift of God, through the redemption wrought in Christ Jesus. ²⁵ God presented Christ as a propitiatory sacrifice, for the atonement of all who have faith in Christ's blood. And God did so to manifest divine justice—because God showed forbearance by remitting sins committed in the past, ²⁶ in order to demonstrate divine justice in the present—so that the Most High might be both a just judge and the One who justifies those who believe in Jesus.

3:27–4:25

What room is there then for boasting? It is ruled out. In what law do we boast—the law of works? No: only the law of faith. ²⁸ We maintain that one is justified by faith—apart from keeping the Law. ²⁹ Does God belong to the Jews alone?

Isn't God also the God of the Gentiles? Yes, of the Gentiles too. ³⁰ And because there is only one God, it is the same God who will justify Jew and Gentile through the same faith. ³¹ Do we then render the Law null and void? Not at all—we give the Law its true value!

4 ¹ What will we say about Sarah and Abraham, our ancestors according to the flesh? ² Certainly if they were justified by their deeds they had grounds for boasting—but not in God's view. ³ For what does scripture say? "Sarah and Abraham believed God, and it was credited to them as righteousness."

⁴ Now, when a person works, the wages are regarded not as a favor, but as what is due. ⁵ But when people do nothing except believe in the One who justifies the ungodly, their faith is credited as righteousness. ⁶ Thus David congratulates those to whom God credits righteousness without action on their part:

⁷ "Blessed are they whose iniquities are forgiven,
whose sins are covered over.

⁸ Blessed is the person
to whom God imputes no guilt."

⁹ Is this blessedness only for Jewish people, or is it meant for others as well? Call Sarah and Abraham to mind: we have been saying that their faith justified them. ¹⁰ When did this justification occur? Was it before or after Abraham had received the sign of the Covenant? It was before, not after. ¹¹ In fact, this sign of the Covenant—circumcision—was given after he believed, as a sign and a guarantee that his earlier faith had justified him. In this way Sarah and Abraham became the ancestors of all Gentile believers, who could then be considered justified as well. ¹² These too are the ancestors of those under the Covenant—provided they follow the path of faith that Sarah and Abraham walked before they received the sign of the Covenant.

¹³ The promise made to Sarah and Abraham and their descendants—that they would inherit the world—did not depend on the Law; it was made in view of the righteousness that comes from faith. ¹⁴ For if those who live by the Law are heirs, then faith is pointless and the promise is worthless. ¹⁵ The Law forever holds the potential for punishment. Only when there is no Law can there be no violation.

¹⁶ Hence everything depends on faith; everything is grace. Thus the promise holds true for all of Sarah's and Abraham's descendants, not only for those who have the Law, but for all who have their faith. They are the mother and the father of us all, ¹⁷ which is why scripture says, "I will make you the parents of many nations"—all of which is done in the sight of the God in whom they believed, the God who restores the dead to life and calls into being things that don't exist.

¹⁸ Hoping against hope, Sarah and Abraham believed, and so became the mother and father of many nations, just as it was once promised them: "Numerous as this will your descendants be." ¹⁹ Sarah and Abraham, without growing weak in faith, thought about their bodies, which were very old—he was about one hundred, and she was well beyond childbearing age. ²⁰ Still they never questioned or doubted God's promise; rather, they grew strong in faith and gave glory to God, ²¹ fully persuaded that God could do whatever was promised. ²² Thus, Sarah's and Abraham's faith "was credited to them as righteousness."

²³ The words, "was credited to them," were not written with Sarah and Abraham alone in mind; ²⁴ they were intended for us, too. For our faith will be credited to us if we believe in the One who raised Jesus our Savior from the dead, ²⁵ the Jesus who was handed over to death for our sins and raised up for our justification.

5 ¹ Now since we have been made right in God's sight by our faith, we are at peace with God through our Savior Jesus Christ. ² Because of our faith, Christ has brought us to the grace in which we now stand, and we confidently and joyfully look forward to the day on which we will become all that God has intended. ³ But not only that—we even rejoice in our afflictions! We know that affliction produces perseverance; ⁴ and perseverance, proven character; and character, hope. ⁵ And such a hope does not disappoint, because the love of God has been poured out in our hearts through the Holy Spirit, who has been given to us.

⁶ At the appointed time, when we were still powerless, Christ died for us godless people. ⁷ It is not easy to die even for a good person—though of course for someone really worthy, there might be someone prepared to die—⁸ but the proof of God's love is that Christ died for us even while we were sinners.

⁹ Now that we have been justified by Christ's blood, it is all the more certain that we will be saved by Christ from God's wrath. ¹⁰ For if we were reconciled to God by Christ's death while we were God's enemies, how much more certain that we who have been reconciled will be saved by Christ's life! ¹¹ Not only that, we go so far as to make God our boast through our Savior Jesus Christ, through whom we have now received reconciliation.

¹² Therefore, sin entered the world through the first humans, and through sin, death—and in this way death has spread through the whole human race, because all have sinned. ¹³ Sin existed in the world long before the Law was given, even though it's not called "sin" when there is no law. ¹⁴ Even so, death reigned over all who lived from our first parents until Moses, even though their sin—unlike that of our first parents—was not a matter of breaking a law.

¹⁵ But the gift is not like the offense. For if by the offense of one couple all died, how much more did the grace of God—and the gracious gift of the One Jesus Christ—abound for all! ¹⁶ The gift that came to us is not at all like what came through the ones who sinned. In the one case, the sentence followed upon one offense and brought condemnation; in the other, the free gift came after many offenses and brought complete acquittal. ¹⁷ If death began its reign through one person because of an offense, so much more will those who receive the overflowing grace and the gift of justice live and reign through the One Jesus Christ.

¹⁸ To sum up, then: just as a single offense brought condemnation to all, a single righteous act brought all acquittal and life. ¹⁹ Just as through one person's disobedience, all became sinners, so through one person's obedience, all will become just.

²⁰ When the Law came, the inability to obey the Law came all the more. But where sin increased, grace abounded all the more, ²¹ so that where sin had reigned in death, grace might reign through the justice that leads to eternal life, through Jesus Christ our Savior.

6 ¹ What can we say, then? Should we go on sinning so that grace might abound? ² Of course not! We're dead to sin, so how can we continue to live in it?

³ Don't you know that when we were baptized into Christ Jesus, we were baptized into Christ's death? ⁴ We've been buried with Jesus through baptism, and we joined with Je-

sus in death, so that as Christ was raised from the dead by God's glory, we too might live a new life.

⁵ For if we have been united with Christ in the likeness of Christ's death, we will also be united with Christ in the likeness of Christ's resurrection. ⁶ We must realize that our former selves have been crucified with Christ to make the body of sin and failure completely powerless, to free us from slavery to sin: ⁷ for when people die, they have finished with sin.

⁸ But we believe that, having died with Christ, we will also live with Christ—⁹ knowing that Christ, having been raised from the dead, will never die again: death is now powerless over our Savior. ¹⁰ When Christ died, Christ died to sin, once for all, so that the life Christ lives is now life in God. ¹¹ In this way, you too must consider yourselves to be dead to sin—but alive to God in Christ Jesus.

¹² So don't let sin rule your mortal body and make you obey its lusts; ¹³ don't offer the members of your body to sin as weapons of injustice any more. Rather, offer yourselves to God as people alive from the dead, and your bodies to God as weapons for justice. ¹⁴ Sin no longer has power over you, for you are now under grace, not under the Law.

¹⁵ Where does all this lead? Just because we are not under the Law but under grace, are we free to sin? By no means! ¹⁶ You must realize that when you offer yourselves to someone else in obedience, you are bound to obey that person, whether you subject yourself to sin, which leads to death, or to obedience, which leads to justice. ¹⁷ Thanks be to God, that though once you were slaves of sin, you became obedient from the heart to that rule of teaching imparted to you; ¹⁸ freed from your sin, you became forever committed to justice.

¹⁹ I use the following example from human affairs because of your weak human nature. Just as you used to enslave your bodies to impurity and licentiousness for their degradation, now make them stewards of justice for their sanctification. ²⁰ When you were slaves to sin, you felt no need to work for justice. ²¹ What benefit did you enjoy from these things that you are now ashamed of, all of which lead to death? ²² But now that you are freed from sin and have offered yourselves to God in obedience, your benefit is that you are being made holy; your outcome is eternal life. ²³ The wages of sin is death, but the gift of God is eternal life in Christ Jesus our Savior.

7:1–8:13

Sisters and brothers, those of you who have studied law know that laws have power over us only during our lifetime. ² For example, married people are bound to each other only so long as they are alive, but all these obligations end when one of them dies. ³ If one partner commits to someone else during the life of the marriage, that partner is legally an adulterer. But if one spouse dies, the other can marry again without becoming an adulterer.

⁴ That is why you, my sisters and brothers, are now dead to the Law through the body of Christ. You are now able to belong to another—the One who rose from the dead—so that we might bear fruit for God. ⁵ Before we were converted, our sinful passions were not controlled by the Law. Consequently, these passions, which were aroused by the Law, went to work in our bodies to bear fruit for death. ⁶ But now we are freed from the Law, dead to what once bound us. Now we are free in the new way of the Spirit, not in the old way of a written Law.

⁷ Does it follow that the Law is sin? Of course not! Yet I wouldn't have known what sin was except for the Law.

And I didn't know what "to covet" meant until I read, "No coveting." ⁸ But sin, seizing the opportunity afforded by the commandment, produced in me every kind of covetousness. For apart from Law, sin is dead; ⁹ and I once lived outside the Law. But when the commandment came, sin sprang to life, and I died. ¹⁰ I found that the very commandment intended to bring life actually brought death. ¹¹ For sin, seizing the opportunity afforded by the commandment, deceived me—and through the commandment put me to death.

¹² The Law is holy, and what it commands is holy, just, and good. ¹³ Does that mean that something good killed me? No. But sin, to show itself in its true colors, used that good thing to kill me. Thus sin, thanks to the commandments, exercised all its sinful power over me.

¹⁴ We know that the Law is spiritual. But I am carnal. I have been sold to sin as a slave. ¹⁵ I don't understand what I do—for I don't do the things I want to do, but rather the things I hate. ¹⁶ And if I do the very thing I don't want to do, I am agreeing that the Law is good. ¹⁷ Consequently, what is happening in me is not really me, but sin living in me.

¹⁸ I know that no good dwells in me, that is, in my human nature; the desire to do right is there, but not the power. ¹⁹ What happens is that I don't do the good I intend to do, but the evil I do not intend. ²⁰ But if I do what is against my will, it is not I who do it, but sin that dwells in me. ²¹ This means that even though I want to do what is right, a law that leads to wrongdoing is always at hand. ²² My inner self joyfully agrees with the law of God, ²³ but I see in my body's members another law, in opposition to the law of my mind; this makes me the prisoner of the law of sin in my members.

²⁴ How wretched I am! Who can free me from this body under the power of death? ²⁵ Thanks be to God—it is Jesus Christ our Savior! This, then, is the problem: I serve the law of God with my mind, but I serve the law of sin with my flesh.

8 ²¹ There is no longer any condemnation, however, for those who are in Christ Jesus. ² The law of the Spirit—the Spirit of life in Christ Jesus—has freed you from the law of sin and death. ³ What the Law was powerless to do because human nature made it so weak, God did—by sending the Only Begotten in the likeness of sinful flesh as a sin offering, thereby condemning sin in the flesh. ⁴ In this way, the just demands of the Law could be fulfilled in us, who live not according to the flesh but according to the Spirit. ⁵ Those who live according to the flesh have their mind set on the things of the flesh; those who live by the Spirit, on things of the Spirit.

⁶ The mind of the flesh is death, but that of the Spirit is life and peace. ⁷ The mind of the flesh stands in opposition to God; it is not subject to God's law—indeed, it cannot be, ⁸ since those who are in the flesh cannot please God. ⁹ But you are not in the flesh; you are in the Spirit, since the Spirit of God dwells in you. Those who do not have the Spirit of Christ do not belong to Christ. ¹⁰ But if Christ is in you, then though the body is dead because of sin, the spirit lives because of righteousness. ¹¹ If the Spirit of the One who raised Jesus from the dead dwells in you, then the One who raised Christ from the dead will also bring your mortal bodies to life through the Spirit dwelling in you.

¹² Therefore, we are under an obligation, my sisters and brothers—but not to the flesh or to live according to the flesh. ¹³ If you live according to the flesh, you will die, but if you live by the Spirit, you will put to death the evil deeds of the body and you will live.

Those who are led by the Spirit of God are the children of God. [15] For the Spirit that God has given you does not enslave you and trap you in fear; instead, through the Spirit God has adopted you as children, and by that Spirit we cry out, "Abba!" [16] God's Spirit joins with our spirit to declare that we are God's children. [17] And if we are children, we are heirs as well: heirs of God and coheirs with Christ, sharing in Christ's suffering and sharing in Christ's glory.

[18] Indeed, I consider the sufferings of the present to be nothing compared with the glory that will be revealed in us. [19] All creation eagerly awaits the revelation of the children of God. [20] Creation was subjected to transience and futility, not of its own accord, but because of the One who subjected it—in the hope [21] that creation itself would be freed from its slavery to corruption and would come to share in the glorious freedom of the children of God. [22] We know that from the beginning until now, all of creation has been groaning in one great act of giving birth. [23] And not only creation, but all of us who possess the firstfruits of the Spirit—we too groan inwardly as we wait for our bodies to be set free.

[24] In hope we were saved. But hope is not hope if its object is seen; why does one hope for what one sees? [25] And hoping for what we cannot see means awaiting it with patient endurance.

[26] The Spirit, too, comes to help us in our weakness. For we don't know how to pray as we should, but the Spirit expresses our plea with groanings too deep for words. [27] And God, who knows everything in our hearts, knows perfectly well what the Spirit is saying, because her intercessions for God's holy people are made according to the mind of God.

[28] We know that God makes everything work together for the good of those who love God and have been called according to God's purpose. [29] They are the ones God chose long ago, predestined to share the image of the Only Begotten, in order that Christ might be the firstborn of many. [30] Those God predestined have likewise been called; those God called have also been justified; and those God justified have, in turn, been glorified.

[31] What should be our response? Simply this: "If God is for us, who can be against us?" [32] Since God did not spare the Only Begotten, but gave Christ up for the sake of us all, we may be certain, after such a gift, that God will freely give us everything. [33] Who will bring a charge against God's chosen ones? Since God is the One who justifies, [34] who has the power to condemn? Only Christ Jesus, who died—or rather, was raised—and sits at the right hand of God, and who now intercedes for us!

[35] What will separate us from the love of Christ? Trouble? Calamity? Persecution? Hunger? Nakedness? Danger? Violence? [36] As scripture says, "For your sake, we're being killed all day long; we're looked upon as sheep to be slaughtered." [37] Yet in all this we are more than conquerors because of God who has loved us. [38] For I am certain that neither death nor life, neither angels nor demons, neither the present nor the future, [39] neither heights nor depths—nor anything else in all creation—will be able to separate us from the love of God that comes to us in Christ Jesus, our Savior.

9:1–11:12

I speak the truth in Christ; I am not lying—my conscience bears me witness in the Holy Spirit [2] that there is great grief and constant pain in my heart. [3] Indeed, I would cut myself off from Christ if that would save my sisters and brothers, my kinfolk—[4] the Israelites. Theirs were the adoption as God's children, the glory, the covenants, the Law-giving, the worship and the promises; [5] theirs was the ancestry, and from them came the Messiah—at least, according to human ancestry. Blessed forever be God who is over all! Amen.

[6] It's not that the word of God has failed. It's just that not all who have descended from Israel are Israelites. [7] Nor are they all children of Sarah and Abraham simply because they are descended from them, because "it is through Isaac—not Esau—that your name will be carried on." [8] In other words, physical descent doesn't determine who are children of God, but rather belief in the promise. [9] For this is the wording of the promise: "This time next year I will return and Sarah will have a child."

[10] Even more relevant is what Rebecca was told while she was pregnant by our ancestor Isaac—[11] well before her twins were born, and long before either child had done anything good or bad. In order to emphasize that God's choice is free—[12] for it depends on the One who calls, not on human deeds—Rebecca was told, "The older will serve the younger," [13] or as scripture says elsewhere, "Jacob I loved, but Esau I hated."

[14] Does it follow that God is unjust? Certainly not. [15] Consider what God says to Moses, "I will have mercy on whom I have mercy, and I will have compassion on whom I will have compassion." [16] In other words, it doesn't depend on one's will or efforts, but on our merciful God. [17] For the scripture says to Pharaoh, "I raised you up for this purpose, that I might show my power in you and that your name might be proclaimed in all the earth." [18] Therefore, God has mercy and hardens hearts at will.

[19] You'll ask me, "If that's the case, how can God ever blame anyone, since no one can oppose the divine will?" [20] But what right have you, mere mortal, to question God? The pot has no right to say to the potter, "Why did you shape me this way?" [21] Surely a potter can do what she wants with the clay! It is clearly for her to decide what lump of clay or what kind of pot, ordinary or special, is to be thrown.

[22] Imagine that the Almighty is ready to show wrath and display divine power, yet patiently endures those people who test the divine mercy, however much those lumps of clay deserve to be destroyed. [23] The Most High puts up with them, all for the sake of those to whom God wants to mercifully reveal the wealth of divine glory—they are vessels prepared for this glory. [24] Well, we are those vessels. Whether we are Jews or Gentiles, we are the ones God has called. [25] As it says in Hosea:

> "Those who are not my people
> I will call 'my people,'
> and those who are not my loved ones,
> 'my loved ones.'"

[26] and,

> "In the very place where it was said to them,
> 'You are not my people,'
> they will be called
> 'daughters and sons of the living God.'"

[27] Isaiah cried out concerning Israel:
> "Though the number of the Israelites
> be like the sand of the sea,
> only the remnant will be saved.
[28] For our God will execute sentence
> on the earth decisively and quickly."
[29] As Isaiah said earlier,
> "Unless the Most High
> had left us descendants,

we would have become like Sodom;
we would have been like Gomorrah."

³⁰ What then will we say? That the Gentiles, who were not looking for righteousness, found it all the same: a righteousness that comes from faith— ³¹ while Israel, looking for a righteousness that comes from the Law, failed to do what the Law required. ³² Why? Because Israel sought righteousness based not on faith, but on works. They stumbled over the "stumbling stone" ³³ mentioned in scriptures:

"Look: I lay in Zion a stone to make people stumble
and a rock to trip them up,
but whoever believes in God
will not be disappointed."

10 ¹ My sisters and brothers, my heart's desire and prayer to God for the Israelites is that they attain salvation. ² For I can testify that they have zeal for God. But their zeal is not based on knowledge. ³ Not recognizing the righteousness that comes from God, they sought to establish their own instead of submitting to God.

⁴ The Messiah, however, is the goal and fulfillment of the Law, and everyone who has faith will be made righteous.

⁵ Moses writes about the righteousness that comes from the Law: "Those who do these things will live by them." ⁶ But the righteousness that comes from faith says, "Don't say in your heart, 'Who will ascend to heaven?'"—that is, to bring Christ down—⁷ "or 'Who will descend into the underworld?'"—that is, to bring Christ up from the dead. ⁸ But what does it say? "The word is near you, on your lips and in your heart." This is the Word of faith. ⁹ For if you confess with your lips that Jesus is Sovereign and believe in your heart that God raised Jesus from the dead, you will be saved. ¹⁰ Faith in the heart leads to being put right with God, confession on the lips to our deliverance.

¹¹ Scripture says, "No one who believes in God will be put to shame." ¹² Here there is no difference between Jew and Greek; all have the same Creator, rich in mercy toward those who call: ¹³ "Everyone who calls on the name of the Most High will be saved."

¹⁴ How then can they call on the One in whom they have not believed? And how can they believe in the One about whom they have not heard? And how can they hear if no one preaches to them? ¹⁵ And how can they preach unless they are sent? As scripture says, "How beautiful are the feet of those who bring the Good News!"

¹⁶ But not everyone has heeded the Good News. For Isaiah says, "O God, who has believed what we proclaimed?" ¹⁷ So you see that faith comes from hearing, and hearing from the word of Christ. ¹⁸ But I ask, didn't they hear? Of course they did: "Their voice has gone out into all the world, their words to the ends of the earth." ¹⁹ So I ask another question: Is it possible that Israel didn't understand? Moses answered this long ago:

"I will make you envious of those
who aren't even a nation;
I will make you angry
because of the Gentiles,
who have no understanding."

²⁰ Isaiah said it even more clearly: "I was found by those who did not seek me; I revealed myself to those who did not ask for me." ²¹ But concerning Israel, Isaiah says, "All day long I stretched out my hand to a disobedient and obstinate people."

11 ¹ I ask, then, has God rejected the chosen people? Of course not! I myself am an Israelite, descended from Sarah and Abraham, of the tribe of Benjamin. ² No, God has not rejected the chosen people, who were foreknown long ago.

Don't you know what the scriptures say about Elijah—how he complained to God about Israel's behavior? ³ "O God, they have killed your prophets and torn down your altars. I am the only one left, and they are trying to kill me." ⁴ What did God say to him? "I have reserved for myself seven thousand who have not bent the knee to Baal." ⁵ In the same way, today there's also a remnant—one chosen by grace. ⁶ And if it is by grace, then it is no longer by works—for if it were, grace would no longer be grace.

⁷ What follows? That what Israel sought so earnestly it did not achieve—but those who were chosen did. The rest were hardened, ⁸ as it says in scripture:

"God gave them a sluggish spirit,
eyes that could not see
and ears that could not hear,
down to this very day."
⁹ And David says:
"May their own table become a trap and a snare,
a stumbling block and a punishment.
¹⁰ Let their eyes grow dim so they cannot see,
and bend their backs forever."

¹¹ I ask further, does their stumbling mean that they are forever fallen? Not at all! Rather, by their transgressions salvation has come to the Gentiles, to stir Israel to envy. ¹² But if their transgression and their diminishment have meant riches for the Gentile world, how much more will their fulfillment be!

11:13–36

I say this now to you Gentiles: inasmuch as I am the apostle of the Gentiles, I glory in my ministry, ¹⁴ trying to rouse my own people to jealousy and save some of them. ¹⁵ For if their rejection has meant reconciliation for the world, what will their acceptance mean? Nothing less than life from the dead!

¹⁶ If the first part of the dough offered as firstfruits is holy, the whole batch is holy. If the root is holy, the branches are holy as well. ¹⁷ But if some of the branches have broken off, and you, a wild olive shoot, have been grafted in their place and share in the rich sap of the olive tree, ¹⁸ don't be arrogant toward those branches. If you find yourself feeling arrogant, remember that you don't support the root—the root supports you! ¹⁹ You might say, "Branches were broken off so that I could be grafted in." ²⁰ That is so. But they were broken off for lack of faith. You stand there only through your faith. So don't become arrogant, but stand in awe. ²¹ For if God didn't spare the natural branches, neither will you be spared.

²² Witness, then, both the kindness and severity of God: severity toward those who fell, and kindness to you—provided you remain in God's kindness, otherwise you too will be cut off. ²³ And those who did not accept the Messiah—if they come to believe—will be regrafted: God is able to graft them in again. ²⁴ After all, if you were cut from what is by nature a wild olive tree, and grafted, contrary to nature, into a cultivated tree, how much more readily will they, the natural branches, be grafted into their own olive tree!

²⁵ Sisters and brothers, I don't want you to be ignorant of this mystery, lest you be conceited: blindness has come upon part of Israel only until the full number of Gentiles enter in, ²⁶ and then all Israel will be saved. As scripture says,

"Out of Zion will come the Deliverer
who will remove all impiety from Jacob;
²⁷ this is the Covenant I will make with them
when I take away their sins."

²⁸ With respect to the Good News, they are enemies of God because of you; with respect to their call, however, they are beloved by the Most High because of their ancestors. ²⁹ For God's gift and call are irrevocable.

³⁰ Just as you were once disobedient to God and now have received mercy through Israel's disobedience, ³¹ now they have become disobedient—since God wished to show you mercy—that they too may receive mercy. ³² God has imprisoned everyone in disobedience in order to have mercy on everyone.

³³ Oh, how deep are the riches and the wisdom and the knowledge, how inscrutable the judgments, how unsearchable the ways of God! ³⁴ For, "Who has known the mind of God or been God's counselor? ³⁵ Who has given God anything to deserve something in return?" ³⁶ For all things are from God and through God and for God. To God be glory forever! Amen.

12:1–13:14

Sisters and brothers, I beg you through the mercy of God to offer your bodies as a living sacrifice, holy and acceptable to God—this is your spiritual act of worship. ² Don't conform yourselves to this age, but be transformed by the renewal of your minds, so that you can judge what God's will is—what is good, pleasing and perfect.

³ In light of the grace I have from God, I urge each of you not to exaggerate your own importance. Each of you must judge yourself soberly by the standard of faith God has given you. ⁴ Just as each of us has one body with many members—and these members don't have the same function—⁵ so all of us, in union with Christ, form one body. And as members of that one body, we belong to each other.

⁶ We have gifts that differ according to the grace given to each of us. If your gift is prophecy, use it in proportion to your faith. ⁷ If your gift is ministry, use it for service. If you are a teacher, use your gift for teaching. ⁸ If you are good at preaching, then preach boldly. If you give to charity, do so generously; if you are a leader, exercise your authority with care; if you help others, do so cheerfully.

⁹ Your love must be sincere. Hate what is evil and cling to what is good.

¹⁰ Love one another with the affection of sisters and brothers. Try to outdo one another in showing respect.

¹¹ Don't grow slack, but be fervent in spirit: the One you serve is Christ.

¹² Rejoice in hope; be patient under trial; persevere in prayer.

¹³ Look on the needs of God's holy people as your own; be generous in offering hospitality.

¹⁴ Bless your persecutors—bless and don't curse them.

¹⁵ Rejoice with those who rejoice, weep with those who weep. ¹⁶ Have the same attitude toward everyone.

Don't be condescending to those who aren't as well off as you; don't be conceited.

¹⁷ Don't repay evil with evil.

Be concerned with the highest ideal in the eyes of all people.

¹⁸ Do all you can to be at peace with everyone.

¹⁹ Don't take revenge; leave room, my friends, for God's wrath. To quote scripture, "'Vengeance is mine, I will pay them back,' says our God." ²⁰ But there is more:

"If your enemies are hungry, feed them;
if they are thirsty, give them drink.
For in doing so, you will heap burning coals
upon their heads."

²¹ Don't be overcome by evil, but overcome evil by doing good.

13¹ Obey governing authorities. All government comes from God, so civil authorities are appointed by God. ² Therefore, those of you who rebel against authority are rebelling against God's decision. For this you are liable to be punished. ³ Good behavior is not afraid of authorities, only bad behavior. If you want to live without fear of authority, do what is right and authority will even honor you. ⁴ The state carries out God's will in order to serve you. However, if you do wrong, be afraid. For the state doesn't carry the sword for nothing: it does as God directs and is an agent of God's wrath, bringing punishment on wrongdoers. ⁵ That's why it's necessary to obey—not only out of fear of being punished, but for the sake of conscience as well. ⁶ That is also why you pay taxes, for the authorities carry out God's will, devoting themselves to this very cause. ⁷ Pay to all what is their due: taxes to tax collectors, tolls to toll collectors, respect to whom respect is due and honor to whom honor is due.

⁸ Owe no debt to anyone—except the debt that binds us to love one another. If you love your neighbor, you have fulfilled the Law. ⁹ The commandments—no committing adultery, no killing, no stealing, no coveting, and all the others—are all summed up in this one: "Love your neighbor as yourself." ¹⁰ Love never wrongs anyone—hence love is the fulfillment of the Law.

¹¹ Besides, you know the time in which we are living. It is now the hour for you to wake from sleep, for our salvation is closer than when we first accepted the faith. ¹² The night is far spent; the day draws near. So let us cast off deeds of darkness and put on the armor of light. ¹³ Let us live honorably as in daylight, not in carousing and drunkenness, not in sexual excess and lust, not in quarreling and jealousy. ¹⁴ Rather, clothe yourselves with our Savior Jesus Christ, and make no provision for the desires of the night.

14:1–15:13

Welcome those whose faith is weak, and don't argue with them. ² The opinions of people range from those who believe they may eat any sort of meat, to those whose faith is so weak they eat only vegetables. ³ Those who eat everything must not despise those who abstain. The ones who abstain must not pass judgment on those who eat, for God has welcomed them. ⁴ Who are you to judge someone else's worker? It's for the employer to decide if the worker has succeeded or failed—and the worker will succeed, for our God has the power to make it so. ⁵ One person considers one day more sacred than another, another considers all days equally sacred—and both are equally certain of their own opinions. ⁶ The person who observes special days does it for our God. Whoever eats meat does it for our God and gives thanks to God. Whoever abstains does it for our God and gives thanks to God.

⁷ We don't live for ourselves, nor do we die for ourselves. ⁸ While we live, we live for Christ Jesus, and when we die, we die for Christ Jesus. Both in life and in death we belong to Christ. ⁹ That's why Christ died and came to life again—in order to reign supreme over both the living and the dead.

¹⁰ But you, how can you sit in judgment of your sisters or brothers? Or you, how can you look down on your sisters or brothers? We will all have to appear before the judgment seat of God. ¹¹ Scripture says, "'As surely as I live'—it is our God who speaks—'every knee will bend before me and every tongue will give praise to God.'" ¹² We will all have to give an account of ourselves before God.

¹³ So stop passing judgment on one another. Rather, we must resolve not to be stumbling blocks or obstructions to each other. ¹⁴ I know—and am convinced in our Savior Jesus—that no food is unclean in itself. But it is unclean for someone who is convinced it is unclean. ¹⁵ If your sister or brother is upset by what you eat, you are no longer acting in love. Don't cause their downfall, for whom Christ died, by your eating. ¹⁶ At the same time, don't let what is for you a good thing be spoken of as being evil. ¹⁷ For the kindom of God is a matter not of eating and drinking, but of justice, peace and joy in the Holy Spirit. ¹⁸ If we all serve Christ this way, we will be pleasing to God and respected by our sisters and brothers.

¹⁹ Therefore, let us conduct ourselves in ways that lead to peace and mutual growth. ²⁰ Don't destroy the work of God over a question of food. All food really is clean, but it's wrong for us to eat anything that is a stumbling block to another. ²¹ It's best not to eat meat or drink wine, or do anything else, if it will make somebody fall away. ²² On the other hand, be confident in your personal belief before God, and don't condemn yourself for doing something you really believe is all right to do. ²³ If you have doubts about eating but you eat anyway, you are judged because your eating doesn't come from faith— ²⁴ and whatever is not from faith is sin.

15 ¹ We who are strong have a duty to endure the failings of the weak, without trying to please ourselves. ² We should be attentive to our neighbors and encourage them to become stronger. ³ For Christ was not self-serving, as it says in scripture: "The insults of those who insult you have fallen on me."

⁴ Everything written before our time was written for our instruction, that we might derive hope from the lessons of patience and the words of encouragement in the scriptures. ⁵ May God, the source of all strength and encouragement, enable you to live in perfect harmony with one another according to the Spirit of Christ Jesus, ⁶ so that with one heart and one voice, you may praise the God of our Savior Jesus Christ.

⁷ Accept one another as Christ accepted us, for the glory of God. ⁸ Christ became a servant of the chosen people to live out the truth of God's promise to them, ⁹ and at the same time to give the Gentiles cause to glorify God for showing mercy. As scripture has it,

"Therefore I will praise you among the nations
and I will sing to Your Name."

¹⁰ Again, it says,

"Rejoice, all you nations, with God's people."

¹¹ And again:

"Praise our God, all you nations,
and let all the peoples praise the Most High."

¹² And Isaiah too says,

"The root of Jesse is coming
and will arise to rule over the nations,

and they will place their trust in the Coming One."

¹³ May the God of hope fill you with such peace and joy in your faith, that you may be filled with hope by the power of the Holy Spirit.

I am convinced, my sisters and brothers, that you are filled with goodness, that you have complete knowledge and that you are able to give good advice to one another. ¹⁵ Even so, I have written to you rather boldly in parts of this letter, by way of reminder. I take this liberty because God has given me the grace ¹⁶ to be a minister of Christ Jesus among the Gentiles, with the priestly duty of preaching the Good News of God, so that the Gentiles may be offered up as a pleasing sacrifice, consecrated by the Holy Spirit. ¹⁷ This means I can take glory in Christ Jesus for the work I have done for God.

¹⁸ I will not dare to speak of anything except what Christ has done through me to win the Gentiles to obedience—by word and deed, ¹⁹ with mighty signs and marvels, by the power of God's Spirit. As a result, I have completed preaching the Good News of Christ, from Jerusalem all the way around to Illyria. ²⁰ It has been a point of honor with me never to preach in places where Christ's name was already known, for I did not want to build on a foundation laid by another, ²¹ but rather to fulfill the words of scripture: "Those who received no word of God will see God, and those who have never heard of God will understand."

²² That's why I have been kept from visiting you for so long. ²³ But now, since I have no more work in these regions, ²⁴ I hope to visit you on my way to Spain. I will spend some time with you and hope that you will help me on my journey. ²⁵ For now, I must travel to Jerusalem to take a gift of money to the holy ones— ²⁶ Macedonia and Achaia have made a generous contribution for those who are needy among them. ²⁷ They were pleased to do so; actually, it pays a debt to Jerusalem. For if the Gentiles have come to share in their spiritual bounty, they owe it to our Jewish sisters and brothers to share with them their material bounty. ²⁸ So when I have completed this task and officially handed over this contribution to them, I am off to Spain and will visit with you on the way. ²⁹ I know that when I come to you I will bring rich blessings from Christ.

³⁰ I beg you, sisters and brothers, by our Savior Jesus Christ and by the love of the Holy Spirit, to join me in my struggle by praying to God for me. ³¹ Pray that I may be rescued from the unbelievers in Judea, and that my work in Jerusalem may be acceptable to the holy ones. ³² Then, God willing, I will come to you with joy, and together we will be refreshed. The God of peace be with you all. Amen.

16 ¹ I commend to you our sister Phoebe, a deacon of the church at Cenchrea. ² Welcome her, in the name of our God, in a way worthy of the holy ones, and help her with her needs. She has looked after a great many people, including me.

³ Give my greetings to Prisca and Aquila; they were my coworkers in the service of Christ Jesus, ⁴ and even risked their lives for my sake. Not only I but all the churches of the Gentiles are grateful to them. ⁵ Remember me also to the congregation that meets in their house.

Greetings to my beloved Epaenetus; he is the first convert to Christ from Asia.

⁶ My greetings to Mary, who has worked hard for you, ⁷ and to Andronicus and Junia, my kin and fellow prisoners; they are outstanding apostles, and they were in Christ even before I was. ⁸ Greetings to Ampliatus, who is dear to me in Christ; ⁹ to Urbanus, our coworker in the service of Christ; and to my beloved Stachys. ¹⁰ Greetings to Apelles, who has endured such trials for Christ. Greetings to those who belong to the household of Aristobulus; ¹¹ greetings to my relative Herodian. Greetings to those in the household of Narcissus who are Christians. ¹² Greetings to the sisters Tryphaena and Tryphosa, who work hard for our God; greetings to my friend Persis who has done so much for our God. ¹³ Greetings to Rufus, chosen in our God, and to his mother, who has been a mother to me as well. ¹⁴ Greetings to Asyncritus, Phlegon, Hermes, Patrobas, Hermas and all the others with them. Greetings to ¹⁵ Philologus, Julia, Nereus and his sister, and Olympas, and all the holy ones with them.

¹⁶ Greet one another with a holy kiss. All the churches of Christ send you greetings.

¹⁷ I urge you, sisters and brothers, to be on your guard against those who foment trouble and put obstacles in your way, contrary to the teaching you learned. Steer clear of them. ¹⁸ For such people don't serve Jesus Christ, but rather their own appetites. By smooth talk and flattering speech they deceive the hearts of the unsuspecting. ¹⁹ While your obedience is famous everywhere—which fills me with joy over you—my counsel is that you are to be wise about what is good, and innocent of what is evil.

²⁰ The God of peace will soon crush Satan under your feet. The grace of Our Savior Jesus Christ be with you.

²¹ My coworker, Timothy, sends greetings, as do my relatives, Lucius, Jason and Sosipater.

²² I, Tertius, who have written down this letter, send you my greetings in Christ. ²³ Greetings also from Gaius, who is host to me and to the whole church. Erastus, the city treasurer, and our brother Quartus wish to be remembered to you.

²⁴ The grace of our Savior Jesus Christ be with you all. Amen.

²⁵ To God—who is able to strengthen you in the Good News that I proclaim when I proclaim Jesus Christ, the Good News that reveals the mystery hidden for many ages, ²⁶ but has now been manifested through the writings of the prophets, and at the command of the eternal God made known to all the Gentiles, that they may believe and obey—to God ²⁷ who alone is wise, may glory be given through Jesus Christ to endless ages. Amen!

1 corinthians

1:1–9

From Paul, called by God's will to be an apostle of Jesus Christ, together with Sosthenes our brother,

² To the church of God in Corinth, you who have been consecrated in Christ Jesus and called to be a holy people, as well as to all who, wherever they may be, call on the name of Jesus Christ, their Redeemer and ours:

³ Grace and peace from our Loving God and our Savior Jesus Christ.

⁴ I continually thank my God for you because of the gift bestowed on you in Christ Jesus, ⁵ in whom you have been richly endowed with every gift of speech and knowledge. ⁶ In the same way, the testimony about Christ has been so confirmed among you ⁷ that you lack no spiritual gift, as you wait for the revelation of our Savior Jesus Christ. ⁸ God will strengthen you to the end, so that you will be blameless on the day of our Savior Jesus Christ. ⁹ God, through whom you have been called into intimacy with Jesus our Savior, is faithful.

1:10–3:23

I beg you, sisters and brothers, in the name of our Savior Jesus Christ, to agree in your message. Let there be no factions; rather, be united in mind and judgment. ¹¹ I have been informed, my sisters and brothers, by certain members of Chloe's household, that you are quarreling among yourselves. ¹² What I mean is, one of you is saying, "I belong to Paul," another, "I belong to Apollos," still another, "I belong to Cephas," still another, "I belong to Christ." ¹³ What—has Christ been divided into parts? Was it Paul who was crucified for you? Was it in Paul's name that you were baptized?

¹⁴ Frankly, I'm thankful I didn't baptize any of you, except Crispus and Gaius, ¹⁵ so that none of you can say you were baptized in my name! ¹⁶ Oh yes, I did baptize the household of Stephanas, but no one else as far as I can remember.

¹⁷ The point is, Christ didn't send me to baptize but to preach the Gospel—not with human rhetoric, however, lest the cross of Christ be rendered void of its meaning! ¹⁸ For the message of the cross is complete absurdity to those who are headed for ruin, but to us who are experiencing salvation, it is the power of God. ¹⁹ Scripture says, "I will destroy the wisdom of the wise and thwart the learning of the learned." ²⁰ Where are the wise? Where are the scholars? Where are the philosophers of this age? Has not God turned the wisdom of this world into folly? ²¹ If it was God's wisdom that the world in its wisdom would not know God, it was because God wanted to save those who have faith through the foolishness of the message we preach.

²² For while the Jews call for miracles and the Greeks look for wisdom, ²³ here we are preaching a Messiah nailed to a cross. To the Jews this is an obstacle they cannot get over, and to the Greeks it is madness— ²⁴ but to those who have been called, whether they are Jews or Greeks, Christ is the power and the wisdom of God. ²⁵ For God's foolishness is wiser than human wisdom, and God's weakness is stronger than human strength.

²⁶ Consider your calling, sisters and brothers. Not many of you were wise by human standards, not many were influential, and surely not many were well-born. ²⁷ God chose those whom the world considers foolish to shame the wise, and singled out the weak of this world to shame the strong. ²⁸ The world's lowborn and despised, those who count for nothing, were chosen by God to reduce to nothing those who were something. ²⁹ In this way no one should boast before God. ³⁰ God has given you life in Christ Jesus and has made Jesus our wisdom, our justice, our sanctification and our

redemption. 31 This is just as it is written, "Let the one who would boast, boast in our God."

2 :1 As for myself, sisters and brothers, when I came to you I did not come proclaiming God's testimony with any particular eloquence or wisdom. 2 No, I determined that while I was with you I would know nothing but Jesus Christ—Christ crucified. 3 When I came among you, it was in weakness and fear, and with much trepidation. 4 My message and my preaching did not rest on philosophical arguments, but on the convincing power of the Spirit. 5 As a consequence, your faith rests not on human wisdom, but on the power of God.

6 Still, there is a certain wisdom which we express among the spiritually mature. It is not a wisdom of this age, however, nor of the rulers of this age, who are headed for destruction. 7 No, what we utter is God's wisdom: a mysterious, hidden wisdom. God planned it before all ages for our glory. 8 None of the rulers of this age knew the mystery; if they had known it, they would never have crucified the Sovereign of Glory. 9 Of this wisdom it is written,

"Eye has not seen, ear has not heard,
nor has it so much as dawned on anyone
what God has prepared
for those who love God."

10 Yet God has revealed this wisdom to us through the Holy Spirit. She searches out all things, even the deep things of God. 11 After all, no one knows one's thoughts except one's own inner spirit; by the same token, no one knows God's thoughts except God's Spirit. 12 We haven't received the spirit of the world but the Spirit of God, so that we can understand what God has freely given us. 13 And this is precisely what we talk about, not using words taught us by human wisdom, but words taught by the Spirit, expressing spiritual thoughts in spiritual words.

14 People without the Spirit do not accept what the Spirit of God teaches. Such teachings seem like foolishness to them because they can't understand them; such things must be spiritually discerned. 15 Spiritual people, on the other hand, can discern all things, though they themselves can be discerned by no one— 16 for, "Who understands the mind of the Most High? Who would give instruction to God?" We, however, have the mind of Christ.

3 :1 Unfortunately, sisters and brothers, I was unable to speak to you as spiritual people. I had to treat you as sensual people, still infants in Christ. 2 I fed you with milk, not solid food, since you weren't ready for it. Indeed, you still aren't ready for it, 3 since you're still far too carnal—a fact that should be obvious from all the jealousy and wrangling that there is among you, from the way that you go on behaving like ordinary people! 4 What could be more nonspiritual than your slogans, "I belong to Paul," and "I belong to Apollos"?

5 After all, who is Apollos? And who is Paul? They are ministers through whom you came to believe. Even the different ways in which they brought the Gospel were assigned to them by God. 6 I did the planting, Apollos did the watering, but God caused the growth. 7 Neither the planter nor the waterer matters—only God, who makes things grow. 8 It is all one who does the planting and who does the watering; and all will be duly paid according to their share in the work. 9 We are coworkers with God; you are God's farm, God's building.

10 By the grace God gave me, I acted as a wise architect and laid the foundation. Someone else is doing the building. But each of you doing the building must do it carefully.

11 For no one can lay a foundation other than the one already in place—Jesus Christ. 12 You may build on this foundation using gold, silver, precious stones, wood, grass or straw. 13 Regardless of the material, the Day will come when your work will be revealed for what it is. It will be revealed in fire, and that fire will test the quality of your work. 14 If your building survives, you will receive your reward. 15 If it burns down, you will be the loser. You will survive, but only as one who goes through fire.

16 Aren't you aware that you are the temple of God, and that the Spirit of God dwells in you? 17 If you destroy God's temple, God will destroy you—for the temple of God is holy, and you are that temple.

18 Don't delude yourselves. Any who think themselves wise in a worldly way had better become fools. 19 In that way you will really be wise, for the wisdom of this world is absurdity with God—as scripture says, "God knows how empty are the thoughts of the wise," 20 and again, "God is not convinced by the arguments of the wise." 21 So there is nothing to boast about in anything human, 22 whether it be Paul or Apollos or Cephas or the world or life or death or the present or the future—all these are yours, 23 and you belong to Christ, and Christ belongs to God.

4:1–21

Therefore, we should be regarded as people in service to Christ, as people entrusted with the mysteries of God. 2 The first requirement of those who have been given a trust is faithfulness. 3 It matters little to me whether you or any human court pass judgment on me. I do not even pass judgment on myself. 4 Mind you, I have nothing on my conscience. But that does not mean I am declaring myself innocent. Christ is the One to judge me— 5 so stop passing judgment prematurely. Christ will bring to light what is hidden in darkness and manifest the intentions of hearts. At that time, all will receive from God the praise they deserve.

6 Now, sisters and brothers, everything I have just said I have applied to Apollos and myself as examples to benefit you. Take a lesson from the saying, "Do not go beyond what is written." None of you should take pride in one person over another. 7 What makes you superior to someone else? What do you have that was not given to you? And if it was a gift, how can you boast as if you had worked for it?

8 You act as if you have all you need now—as if you were wealthy now, or had become rulers without us! Oh, how I wish you had become rulers—then we could share ruling with you!

9 Rather, it seems to me God has put us apostles at the end of the parade, like those doomed to die in the arena. We have been made a spectacle to the whole universe, to angels and humans alike. 10 Here we are fools for Christ's sake, but you are so wise in Christ! We are weak, but you are strong! You are honored, while they sneer at us! 11 At this very hour we go hungry and thirsty, we are in rags, we are roughly treated, we are homeless. 12 We work hard at manual labor. When we are insulted, we give a blessing. When we are persecuted, we endure it. 13 When we are slandered, we answer politely. We have become the scum of the earth, the dregs of humanity, to this very day.

14 I am writing you this way not to shame you but to admonish you, my dear children. 15 You may have ten thousand tutors in Christ, but you have only me as your parent. It was I who begot you in Christ Jesus through my preaching of the Gospel.

¹⁶ Therefore, I beg you to imitate me. ¹⁷ For this reason I send you Timothy, my beloved and faithful child in our God. Timothy will remind you of the way I live in Christ, as I teach everywhere in all the churches.

¹⁸ When it seemed that I was not coming to you, some of you assumed a role of self-importance. ¹⁹ But I will be visiting you soon, God willing, and then I will see what you can really do—not what you boastfully say you can do. ²⁰ For the kindom of God is not just words but power. ²¹ What is your preference? Should I come to you with a paddle, or with a loving and gentle spirit?

5:1–6:20

I have been told that there is sexual immorality among you, and of a kind that does not occur even among the Gentiles—a man living with his father's wife. ² How can you be so proud of yourselves? You should be in mourning! Those who do such a thing ought to be expelled from the community. ³ Though I am far away in body, I am with you in spirit and have already passed judgment ⁴ in the name of our Savior Jesus Christ on the ones who did this deed. United in spirit with you and empowered by our Savior Jesus Christ, ⁵ I hereby hand them over to Satan for the destruction of their flesh, so that their spirits may be saved on the day of our Savior.

⁶ This boasting of yours is an ugly thing. Don't you know that a little yeast has its effect all through the dough? ⁷ Get rid of the old yeast to make for yourselves fresh dough, unleavened bread, as it were; Christ our Passover has been sacrificed. ⁸ So let us celebrate the feast—not with the old yeast, the yeast of corruption and wickedness, but with the unleavened bread of sincerity and truth.

⁹ Remember when I wrote to you to dissociate yourselves from immoral people? ¹⁰ I did not mean to include all in the world who are sexually immoral, or all the greedy and the swindlers, or the idolators. To do this, you would have to leave the world! ¹¹ What I wrote is that you must dissociate yourselves from any so-called Christians who are leading immoral lives, or are greedy or idolatrous, are slanderers or drunkards, or are dishonest. You shouldn't even eat with these people.

¹² It's not my business to judge outsiders. As for insiders, however, you be the judge. ¹³ Let God judge the outsiders—you just get rid of the evildoers among you.

6 ¹ But what do you do instead? You take your neighbor to court to be judged by the unjust instead of by God's holy people! How dare you! ² Don't you know that the holy ones will judge the world? And if you are to judge the world, why are you unfit to judge trifling matters? ³ Since we are also to judge angels, it follows that we can judge matters of everyday life. ⁴ But when you have had cases like that, you appoint as your judges people who are not respected members of the church! ⁵ I say this to your shame: is there no one among you wise enough to judge a dispute among believers? ⁶ Instead, sisters and brothers are taking each other to court—and having their cases heard by unbelievers! ⁷ The very fact that you have lawsuits among you means that you're completely defeated already. Why not put up with injustice instead? Why not let yourselves be cheated? ⁸ Instead, you yourselves injure and cheat your very own.

⁹ Don't you realize that the unholy will not inherit the kindom of God? Do not deceive yourselves: no fornicators, idolaters, adulterers, hustlers, pederasts, ¹⁰ thieves, misers,

drunkards, slanderers or extortionists will inherit God's kindom. ¹¹ And such were some of you! But you have been washed, consecrated and justified in the name of our Savior Jesus Christ and in the Spirit of our God.

¹² "Everything is allowed"—but not everything is beneficial for me. "Everything is allowed"—but I will not be dominated by anything.

¹³ "Food is for the stomach and the stomach for food, and God will do away with them both in the end"—but the body is not for immorality; it is for God, and God is for the body. ¹⁴ God, who raised Jesus from the dead, will raise us also by the same power.

¹⁵ Don't you see that your bodies are members of Christ? Would you have me take Christ's members and make them members of someone promiscuous? God forbid! ¹⁶ Don't you know that when you sleep with someone, you're sleeping with all of their partners as well? For it is said, "The two will become one flesh." ¹⁷ But whoever is joined to Christ becomes one spirit with Christ.

¹⁸ Shun lewd conduct. Every other sin a person commits is outside that person's body, but sexual sins are sins against one's own body. ¹⁹ You must know that your body is a temple of the Holy Spirit, who is within you—the Spirit you have received from God. You are not your own. ²⁰ You have been bought with a price. So glorify God in your body.

7:1–40

Now for the matters about which you wrote.

Yes, it is a good thing for a woman or a man not to marry. ² But since there is so much immorality, each woman should have her own husband and each husband should have his own wife. ³ The wife and husband should mutually fulfill their marital duties to each other. ⁴ The husband's body belongs not to him alone, but also to the wife, and the wife's body belongs not to her alone, but also to the husband. ⁵ Do not deprive each other except by mutual consent and within a time frame so that you can devote yourselves to prayer. But come together again lest you invite Satan to tempt you through your weakness. ⁶ Let me make a suggestion—it is not a decree: ⁷ I would hope that everyone could be like me. But we all have our own particular gifts from God. One has the gift for one thing and another has the gift for another thing.

⁸ To the single, widows and widowers, I say: it is good for you to stay unmarried, as I am. ⁹ But if you cannot control yourselves, then you should marry, for it is better to be married than to burn with passion.

¹⁰ I have this to say to you who are in relationships—and this is not from me but from God: you are not to leave your partners. ¹¹ But if you do separate, you must either remain single or be reconciled to each other; you are not to divorce each other.

¹² To the rest of you, I say—this is not from God but from me: ¹³ if one of you has a mate who is not a believer, and if the believer is willing to live with the unbeliever, then there must not be a divorce. ¹⁴ For the unbelieving member of the relationship is sanctified through the believing member. If this were not so, any children of the relationship would be unclean; as it is, they are holy.

¹⁵ Now if the unbeliever leaves, let it be. For the believing partner is not bound to the relationship in such circumstances. God has called us to live in peace. ¹⁶ For how do you know, wife, whether you will save your husband or not? And how do you know, husband, whether you will save your wife or not?

17 The point is, whatever lot God has assigned you, whatever God has called you to do, continue in it. This is the direction I give to all the churches. 18 Anyone who was Jewish at the time of the call need not disguise it. 19 Anyone who was a Gentile at the time of the call, need not convert to Judaism. Jew or Gentile, the only thing that matters is to keep the commandments of God. 20 Let everyone remain in the condition they were in at the time of their call.

21 Were you a slave at the time of your call? Don't let it bother you. However, if you have a chance to gain your freedom, by all means do so. 22 For a slave, when called to be in Christ, is a free person. And a free person called to be in Christ becomes Christ's slave. 23 You have all been bought and paid for, so do not become a slave to a human being. 24 Sisters and brothers, continue in the state which you were in when God called you.

25 I have not received any commandment from God with respect to remaining celibate, but I give my opinion as one who is trustworthy, thanks to the mercy of God. 26 Because of the present crisis, it seems good to me for you to remain as you are. 27 Are you married? Do not seek a divorce. Are you single? Do not go looking for a mate. 28 But if you do marry—whether you are male or female, old or young—it is not a sin. However, those who do get married will face many problems in this life, and I want to spare you that.

29 I tell you, sisters and brothers, the time is short. From now on, those with spouses should live as though they had none. 30 Those who mourn should live as though they had nothing to mourn for, and those who rejoice should live as though they had nothing to laugh about. Buyers should conduct themselves as though they owned nothing, 31 and those who have to deal with the world should live as if all their dealings meant nothing—for the world as we know it is passing away.

32 I would like you to be free of all worries. Unmarried people are busy with God's affairs and are concerned with pleasing God, 33 but married people are busy with this world's demands and occupied with pleasing their spouses. 34 This means they are divided. Single women and men concern themselves with our God's doings. Their aim is to be devoted to God in body and spirit. But married couples are troubled with the world's affairs, and they devote themselves to their spouses.

35 I tell you this for your own good. I have no desire to place restrictions on you, but I do want to promote what is good, what will help you to devote yourselves entirely to God.

36 If you feel that it is wrong to discourage your children from marrying as they grow older, and that you should do something about it, you are free to do as you like. You are not sinning if they marry. 37 But those who—while standing firm in their resolve, while not feeling forced, while in control of their own wills—have resolved not to discourage them from marrying are doing the right thing. 38 In other words, to marry is a good thing; not to marry is a better thing.

39 One mate is bound to the other throughout life. But if one dies, the other is free to enter into a new relationship—if the new intended belongs to Christ. 40 However, in my opinion, one is happier if one remains single, and I think I have the Spirit of God in this matter.

8:1–13

Now, concerning food sacrificed to idols.

We all possess knowledge. But knowledge puffs up, whereas love builds up. 2 You may think you know something, but you still won't know it the way you ought. 3 But anyone who loves God is known—completely—by God.

4 Well then, what about eating food sacrificed to idols? We know that idols have no real existence, that there is no God but the One. 5 Even though there are so-called gods in the heavens—and on the earth as well, where there seem to be many gods and sovereigns— 6 for us there is only One God, Abba God, from whom all things come and for whom we live; there is one Sovereign, Jesus Christ, through whom everything was made and through whom we live.

7 Some people, accustomed to idol worship until recently, are consumed with guilt every time they eat meat they buy in the market, because they know that the meat had been sacrificed to idols—and their conscience, because it is weak, gets defiled every time they eat. 8 But food cannot bring us closer to God. We lose nothing if we refuse to eat. We gain nothing if we choose to eat.

9 Be on your guard, however, that this liberty of yours does not become a pitfall for the weak. 10 Suppose someone who has this knowledge sees you eating in some idol's temple, won't this person be tempted to eat meat offered to idols? 11 Realize that your knowledge—that idols are nothing and thus it is all right to eat this meat freely—might be the ruination of a weak sister or brother, for whose sake Christ died. 12 By sinning against your sisters and brothers in this way and injuring their weak consciences, you are sinning against Christ. 13 Therefore, if meat causes my sister or brother to stumble, I will never eat it again—I don't want to be an occasion for sin to them.

9:1–27

Am I not free? Am I not an apostle? Didn't I see our Savior Jesus, and aren't you yourselves my work in Christ? 2 Even if I were not an apostle to others, I would still be an apostle to you, for you are the seal of my apostleship in Christ! 3 So my answer to those who would sit in judgment of me is this: 4 don't we have the right to eat and drink? 5 Don't we have the right to have Christian spouses with us on our travels—as do all the other apostles, and Jesus' own family members, and Cephas? 6 Or is it only Barnabas and I who must work for a living? 7 Who has ever served in the army at one's own expense? Who plants a vineyard and refuses to eat its grapes? Who shepherds a flock and does not drink the milk from the flock?

8 Sure, these are only human comparisons, but doesn't the Law say the same thing? 9 It is written in the Law of Moses: "Do not muzzle the ox while it is treading out the corn." Is God concerned about oxen? 10 Or is God really concerned about us? Yes, this was written for our sake to show that the plower plows and the thresher threshes in hope of receiving a share of the harvest. 11 If we have sown a spiritual harvest among you, can we not expect a material harvest from you? 12 Others have the right of support from you. Surely our right to support is even greater.

In point of fact, we have never exercised any of these rights. On the contrary, we have put up with everything in order not to obstruct the Good News of Christ. 13 Do you not know that those ministering in the Temple get their food from the Temple and those serving at the altar share in the sacrificial offerings? 14 In the same way, Christ directed that those who preach the Gospel should get their living from the Gospel. 15 Yet I have not claimed any of these rights. Nor do I write this to secure this treatment for myself. I would rather die than have anyone take away this boast.

¹⁶ Not that I do boast about preaching the Gospel; I am under compulsion and have no choice. I am ruined if I do not preach the Gospel! ¹⁷ If I do it willingly, I have my reward; if unwillingly, I am nonetheless entrusted with a charge. ¹⁸ What then is my reward? It is simply this: that when preaching, I offer the Gospel free of charge and do not assert the authority the Gospel gives me. ¹⁹ Although I am not bound to anyone, I put myself into the service of all so as to win over as many as possible.

²⁰ To the Jews I became even more Jewish, to win over the Jewish people; even though I am not subject to the Law, I made myself subject to the Law, to win those who are subject to the Law. ²¹ To those who have no law, I was free of the Law, too—though not free from God's Law, being subject to the Law of Christ—to win those who have no law. ²² To the weak I became weak to win the weak. I have become all things to all people, that I might save at least some of them. ²³ In fact, I do all that I do for the sake of the Gospel in the hope of having a share in its blessings.

²⁴ You know that in a race everyone runs, but only one wins the prize. So run in such a way as to win! ²⁵ Athletes deny themselves all sorts of things. They do this to win a laurel wreath, even though it withers. We, on the other hand, do so to win an imperishable crown.

²⁶ I don't run like one who loses sight of the finish line. I don't fight as if I were beating the air. ²⁷ What I do is discipline my body and keep it under control, for fear that, after having preached to others, I myself should be disqualified.

10:1–33

I want you to remember this: our ancestors were all under the cloud and all passed through the sea; ² by the cloud and the sea all of them were baptized into Moses. ³ All ate the same spiritual food. ⁴ All drank the same spiritual drink—they drank from the spiritual rock that was following them, and the rock was Christ, ⁵ yet we know that God was not pleased with most of them, for "they were struck down in the desert." ⁶ These things happened as an example to keep us from evil desires such as theirs.

⁷ Do not become idolators, as some of them were, for scripture says, "The people sat down to eat and drink and got up to indulge in revelry." ⁸ We must not take part in sexual immorality, as some of them did; twenty-three thousand of them died in one day. ⁹ We must not test our God, as some of them did; they were killed by snakes.

¹⁰ Nor are you to grumble as some of them did, for which they were killed by the destroying angel. ¹¹ The things that happened to them serve as an example and have been written as a warning to us, upon whom the end of the ages has come. ¹² For all these reasons, let those who think they are standing upright watch out lest they fall!

¹³ No test has overtaken you but what is common to all people. You can be confident that God is faithful and will not let you be tested beyond your means. And with any trial God will provide you with a way out of it, as well as the strength to bear the trial.

¹⁴ I tell you, my dear friends, shun idolatry. ¹⁵ I address you as sensible people; you may judge for yourselves what I am saying. ¹⁶ The cup of blessing which we bless—is it not a sharing in the blood of Christ? The bread we break—is it not a sharing in the body of Christ? ¹⁷ Because the loaf of bread is one, we who are many are one body, for we all partake of the one loaf. ¹⁸ Or look at the people of Israel: those who eat the sacrifices are in communion with the altar.

¹⁹ Now, I don't mean to imply that a sacrifice offered to an idol is anything, or that the idol itself is anything; ²⁰ it's just that pagans make sacrifices to demons, not to God, and I do not want you to be in communion with demons. ²¹ You cannot drink the cup of our Savior and the cup of demons too; you cannot partake of our Savior's table and the table of demons. ²² Do we want to provoke our Savior to jealous anger? Surely we are not that strong!

²³ "Everything is allowed"—but not everything is good for you. "Everything is allowed"—but not everything is helpful. ²⁴ So don't do things out of self-interest; always seek the good of others.

²⁵ Feel free to eat anything that is sold in the meat market, without raising questions of conscience. ²⁶ After all, "The earth is our God's, and everything in it." ²⁷ By the same token, if some nonbelievers invite you to a meal, feel free to go and eat whatever they put on the table with a clear conscience. ²⁸ However, if someone says to you, "This food was offered in sacrifice to idols before it was sold," don't eat it, out of consideration for those who call it to your attention, and for conscience's sake—²⁹ that is, for their conscience, not yours, since our freedom shouldn't be judged by someone else's conscience! ³⁰ If I eat the meal with thankfulness, why should I be reviled over something for which I thank God?

³¹ But whatever you eat or drink—whatever you do—do it all for the glory of God. ³² Give no offense, whether to Jew or to Greek or to the church of God, ³³ just as I try to please everyone in any way I can. I do this by seeking not my own advantage, but that of the many, that they may be saved.

11:1–16

Imitate me as I imitate Christ.

² You are to be praised for remembering me so constantly, and for maintaining the teachings just as I handed them down to you.

³ You say in your letter, however, that since God is the head of Christ, then Christ is the head of man, and man is the head of woman. ⁴ And that if a man prays or prophesies with his head covered, it is a sign of disrespect for his "head," that is, Christ; ⁵ but that if a woman prays or prophesies with her head uncovered, it's a sign of disrespect for her "head," that is, man—and that this is just as disreputable as going around with her head shaved.

⁶ If a woman won't cover her head, your argument goes, she really should have her hair cut off—but if she's too ashamed to do so, she should wear a head covering. ⁷ A man shouldn't cover his head, since he's the image and glory of God; woman, on the other hand, is the glory of man. ⁸ "Man did not come from woman," you say, "didn't the woman come from man? ⁹ And man was not created for the sake of woman—wasn't woman created for the sake of man?"

¹⁰ The point I was trying to make was that women are to have an outward sign of prophetic authority—the covering of their "head"—because angels are always present when you worship. ¹¹ You need to learn, however, that in Christ, woman is not different from man, and man is not different from woman. ¹² Woman may come from man, but man is born of woman. And both come from God.

¹³ So you be the judge. "Is it appropriate for a woman to pray to God with a bare head?" ¹⁴ Let nature herself be your teacher. Men generally feel it's not respectable to have long hair, ¹⁵ while women treat long hair as their glory—and besides, that way their head is always "covered"! ¹⁶ But if

people still want to argue the matter, let's just say we have no other custom, nor do the churches of God.

11:17–34

What I now have to say is not said in praise.

Your meetings do more harm than good. 18 In the first place, I hear that when you gather for a meeting there are divisions among you, and I'm inclined to believe it. 19 No doubt there have to be factions among you, to distinguish those who are to be trusted from those who aren't. 20 The point is, when you hold your agape meals, it is not the Eucharist you've been commemorating, 21 for as you eat, each of you goes ahead without waiting for anyone else. One remains hungry, while another gets drunk. 22 Don't you have homes where you can eat and drink? Surely you have enough respect for the community of God not to embarrass poor people! What can I say to you? You'll get no praise from me in this matter!

23 What I have passed on to you, I received from Christ—that on the night he was betrayed, our Savior Jesus took bread, 24 gave thanks and broke it, saying, "This is my body, which is broken for you. Do this in remembrance of me." 25 In the same way, after supper, he took the cup and said, "This cup is the New Covenant in my blood. Whenever you drink it, do it in remembrance of me." 26 For every time you eat this bread and drink this cup, you proclaim Jesus' death until Christ comes.

27 Any unfit person who eats the bread or drinks from the cup sins against the body and blood of Christ. 28 Everyone, therefore, should examine themselves before they eat of the bread and drink of the cup, 29 because those who eat and drink without discerning the Body of Christ eat and drink condemnation on themselves. 30 This is why many of you are weak and ill, and some of you are dying.

31 If only we judged ourselves rightly, we wouldn't be judged in this way. 32 But when God punishes us like this, we are being disciplined so that we will not be condemned along with the world. 33 Therefore, my sisters and brothers, when you assemble for a meal, wait for one another. 34 All who are hungry should eat at home, so that your meetings will not be the cause of your condemnation.

The other matters I will straighten out when I come.

12:1–14:40

Now dear sisters and brothers, I want to instruct you on the matter of spiritual gifts. 2 Remember how, when you were still nonbelievers, you were drawn to mute idols and led astray by them?

3 It is for this reason that I want you to understand that no one can be speaking under the influence of the Holy Spirit and say, "Curse Jesus"; by the same token, no one can say, "Jesus Christ reigns supreme," unless under the influence of the Holy Spirit.

4 There is a variety of gifts, but always the same Spirit. 5 There is a variety of ministries, but we serve the same One. 6 There is a variety of outcomes, but the same God is working in all of them. 7 To each person is given the manifestation of the Spirit for the common good.

8 To one, the Spirit gives wisdom in discourse, to another, the word of knowledge through the same Spirit. 9 Through the Spirit, one person receives faith; through the same Spirit, another is given the gift of healing; 10 and still another, miraculous powers. Prophecy is given to one; to another, power to distinguish one spirit from another. One receives the gift of tongues; another, that of interpreting tongues. 11 But it is one and the same Spirit who produces all these gifts and distributes them as she wills.

12 The body is one, even though it has many parts; all the parts—many though they are—comprise a single body. And so it is with Christ. 13 It was by one Spirit that all of us, whether we are Jews or Greeks, slaves or citizens, were baptized into one body. All of us have been given to drink of the one Spirit. 14 And that Body is not one part; it is many.

15 If the foot should say, "Because I am not a hand, I do not belong to the body," does that make it any less a part of the body? 16 If the ear should say, "Because I am not an eye, I do not belong to the body," would that make it any less a part of the body? 17 If the body were all eye, what would happen to our hearing? If it were all ear, what would happen to our sense of smell? 18 Instead of that, God put all the different parts into one body on purpose. 19 If all the parts were alike, where would the body be?

20 They are, indeed, many different members but one body. 21 The eye cannot say to the hand, "I do not need you," any more than the head can say to the feet, "I do not need you." 22 And even those members of the body which seem less important are in fact indispensable. 23 We honor the members we consider less honorable by clothing them with greater care, thus bestowing on the less presentable a propriety 24 which the more presentable do not need. God has so constructed the body as to give greater honor to the lowly members, 25 that there may be no dissension in the body, but that all the members may be concerned for one another. 26 If one member suffers, all the members suffer with it; if one member is honored, all the members share its joy.

27 You, then, are the body of Christ, and each of you is a member of it. 28 Furthermore, God has set up in the church, first, apostles; second, prophets; third, teachers; then miracle workers, healers, assistants, administrators and those who speak in tongues. 29 Are all apostles? Are all prophets? Are all teachers? Do all work miracles 30 or have the gift of healing? Do all speak in tongues, or do all have the gift of interpretation of tongues?

31 Set your hearts on the greater gifts. But now I will show you the way which surpasses all the others.

13 1 Even if I can speak in all the tongues of earth—and those of the angels too—but do not have love, I am just a noisy gong, a clanging cymbal. 2 If I have the gift of prophecy such that I can comprehend all mysteries and all knowledge, or if I have faith great enough to move mountains, but do not have love, I am nothing. 3 If I give away everything I own to feed those poorer than I, then hand over my body to be burned, but do not have love, I gain nothing.

4 Love is patient; love is kind. Love is not jealous, it does not put on airs, and it is not snobbish; 5 it is never rude or self-seeking; it is not prone to anger, nor does it brood over injuries. 6 Love doesn't rejoice in what is wrong, but rejoices in the truth. 7 There is no limit to love's forbearance, to its trust, its hope, its power to endure.

8 Love never fails. Prophecies will cease; tongues will be silent; knowledge will pass away. 9 Our knowledge is imperfect and our prophesying is imperfect. 10 When the perfect comes, the imperfect will pass away. 11 When I was a child, I used to speak like a child, think like a child, reason like a child. But when I became an adult, I put childish ways aside. 12 Now we see indistinctly, as in a mirror; then we will see face to face. My knowledge is imperfect now; then I will know even as I am known.

13 There are, in the end, three things that last: faith, hope, and love. But the greatest of these is love.

14

¹ So pursue the way of love, but earnestly desire spiritual gifts as well, especially the gift of prophecy. ² Those who speak in tongues do not speak to us but to God—for no one understands them when they talk in the Spirit about mysterious things. ³ On the other hand, those who prophesy do talk to us—and they do so for our edification, encouragement and comfort. ⁴ Those who speak in tongues benefit only themselves, but those who prophesy benefit all the church. ⁵ While I would like all of you to speak in tongues, I would much rather that you prophesy. Because those who prophesy are more important than those who speak in tongues—unless they also interpret, in which case the church benefits, too.

⁶ Now, my sisters and brothers, if I were to come to you speaking in tongues, what good would it be if I didn't also give some revelation or knowledge or a prophecy or a teaching? ⁷ Think of a musical instument, a flute or a harp—how can you tell what tune is being played if all the notes sound alike? ⁸ Or if the trumpet gives an indistinct sound, who will be prepared for the attack? ⁹ So it is with you. If you don't produce intelligible speech, how will anyone know what you are saying? You will just be talking to the air. ¹⁰ There are endless numbers of languages in the world, and all of them have meaning. ¹¹ But if I don't know the meaning of a language, I am a foreigner to the person speaking, and the person speaking is a foreigner to me. ¹² So it is with you. As long as you eagerly desire spiritual gifts, desire those that benefit the entire community.

¹³ It is for this reason that all of you who have the gift of tongues must pray for the gift to interpret them. ¹⁴ For if I use the gift of tongues in my prayer, my spirit may be praying but my mind is not. ¹⁵ What can we do about this? I will pray with my spirit, and I will pray with my mind also. And I will sing praises with my spirit, and with my mind as well. ¹⁶ Otherwise, if you are praising God with the spirit only, how can the uninitiated say the "Amen" to your thanksgiving—they don't know what you are saying! ¹⁷ You may be giving thanks well enough, but the other person is not edified.

¹⁸ I thank God that I speak in tongues more than any of you. ¹⁹ But when I am among the community, I would rather speak five intelligible words than ten thousand words in tongues.

²⁰ Sisters and brothers, stop thinking like children. With respect to evil, be like children, but in your thinking, be like adults. ²¹ It is written in the Law:

"'Through people speaking strange languages
and through the lips of foreigners
I will speak to these people,
and still they will not listen to me,'
says our God."

²² Tongues, therefore, are a sign for believers, but not for unbelievers. Prophecy, however, is for unbelievers, not believers.* ²³ If inquirers or unbelievers were to come into the gathering of the whole church where everybody was speaking in tongues, wouldn't they decide that you were all mad? ²⁴ But if you were all prophesying when inquirers or unbelievers entered—they'd find themselves convicted and called to repentance by everyone speaking. ²⁵ When they find their secret thoughts laid bare, they'll fall on their faces, worship God, and exclaim, "God is really with you!"

²⁶ So, my dear sisters and brothers, what is to be done? When you gather, let everybody be ready with a hymn or a sermon or a revelation, or ready to use the gift of tongues or to give an interpretation. It must always be for the common good. ²⁷ If there are present those who speak in tongues, let two or three—no more—be allowed to do it. They should speak one at a time, and someone must be available to interpret. ²⁸ If no interpreter is present, the speakers should not speak in church and should speak only to themselves and to God. ²⁹ Let two or three of the prophets speak, with the others discerning if the message is true. ³⁰ If one of the discerners should receive a revelation, then the speaker should stop. ³¹ For you should all prophesy in turn, so that everybody will learn something and be encouraged. ³² Prophets can always control their spirit of prophecy. ³³ God is a God of peace, not disorder.

As in all the churches of the holy ones, ³⁴ only one spouse has permission to speak. The other is to remain silent, to keep in the background, as it says in the Law. ³⁵ If the silent one has questions to ask, ask them at home. It is disgraceful for a spouse to speak improperly in church.

³⁶ Did the word of God originate with you? Are you the only people it has reached? ³⁷ If any of you think you are a prophet or spiritually gifted, acknowledge that what I am writing to you is Christ's command. ³⁸ If you ignore this, you yourself will be ignored.

³⁹ Therefore, sisters and brothers, be eager to prophesy and do not forbid speaking in tongues. ⁴⁰ Let everything be done with propriety and order.

15:1–58

Sisters and brothers, I want to remind you of the Gospel I preached to you, which you received and in which you stand firm. ² You are being saved by it at this very moment, if you hold fast to it as I preached it to you. Otherwise you have believed in vain.

³ I handed on to you, first of all, what I myself received: that Christ died for our sins in accordance with the scriptures; ⁴ that he was buried and, in accordance with the scriptures, rose on the third day; ⁵ that he was seen by Peter, then by the Twelve. ⁶ After that, he was seen by more than five hundred sisters and brothers at once, most of whom are still alive, although some have fallen asleep. ⁷ Next he was seen by James, then by all the apostles. ⁸ Last of all he was seen by me, as one yanked from the womb.

⁹ I am the least of the apostles; in fact, because I persecuted the church of God, I do not even deserve the name. ¹⁰ But by God's favor I am what I am. This favor that God has given to me has not proven fruitless. Indeed, I have worked harder than all the others, not on my own but through the grace of God. ¹¹ In any case, whether it be I or they, this is what we preach and this is what you believed.

¹² Tell me, if we proclaim that Christ was raised from the dead, how is it that some of you say there is no resurrection of the dead? ¹³ If there is no resurrection of the dead, then not even Christ has been raised. ¹⁴ And if Christ has not been raised, then all of our preaching has been meaningless—and everything you've believed has been just as meaningless. ¹⁵ Indeed, we are shown to be false witnesses of God, for we solemnly swore that God raised Christ from the dead—which did not happen if in fact the dead are not raised. ¹⁶ Because

---

* Our rendering, following the lead of famed translator J. B. Phillips, inverts the actual Greek text, which reads, "Tongues, therefore, are a sign for unbelievers, but not for believers. Prophecy, however, is for believers, not unbelievers." Phillips explained in his commentary that he "felt bound to conclude, from the sense of the next three verses, that we have here either a slip of the pen on the part of Paul, or, more probably, a copyist's error."

if the dead are not raised, then Christ is not raised, ¹⁷ and if Christ is not raised, your faith is worthless. You are still in your sins, ¹⁸ and those who have fallen asleep in Christ are the deadest of the dead. ¹⁹ If our hopes in Christ are limited to this life only, we are the most pitiable of the human race.

²⁰ But as it is, Christ has in fact been raised from the dead, the firstfruits of those who have fallen asleep.

²¹ For since death came through one human being, in the same way the resurrection of the dead has come through one human being. ²² Just as in the first human all die, so in Christ all will come to life again, ²³ but all of them in their proper order: Christ as the firstfruits, and then the faithful when Christ comes again. ²⁴ After that will come the end, when Christ hands over the kindom to God the Creator, having done away with every sovereignty, authority and power. ²⁵ Christ must reign until God has put all enemies under Christ's foot, ²⁶ and the last enemy to be destroyed is death, ²⁷ for everything is "put under" Christ's foot. But when it says that everything has been subjected, it is clear that this does not include God, who subjected everything to Christ. ²⁸ When, finally, everything has been subjected to Christ, Christ will in turn be subjected to the God who had subjected everything to Christ—and so God will be all in all.

²⁹ Now, if there is no resurrection, what do people hope to gain by being baptized for the dead? If the dead are not raised at all, why be baptized on their behalf? ³⁰ What about ourselves? Why do we constantly endanger ourselves? ³¹ I face death daily—I mean that, sisters and brothers—just as surely as I glory over you in Christ Jesus our Savior. ³² If at Ephesus I fought wild animals, so to speak, for personal gain, what have I gained? You are saying, "Let us eat and drink, for tomorrow we die." ³³ Stop being led astray: "Bad company corrupts the noblest people." ³⁴ Come to your senses. Behave properly and stop sinning! There are some of you who seem not to know God at all! Shame on you!

³⁵ Perhaps someone will ask, "How are the dead to be raised up? What kind of body will they have?" ³⁶ What a stupid question! The seed you sow does not germinate unless it dies. ³⁷ When you sow, you do not sow the full-blown plant but a kernel of wheat or some other grain. ³⁸ Then it is given the body God designed for it—with each kind of seed getting its own kind of body.

³⁹ Not all flesh is the same. Human beings have one kind, animals have another, birds another, and fish another. ⁴⁰ Then there are heavenly bodies and earthly bodies. Heavenly bodies have a beauty of their own, and earthly bodies have a beauty of their own. ⁴¹ The sun has one kind of brightness, the moon another, and the stars another. And star differs from star in brightness.

⁴² So it is with the resurrection of the dead. What is sown is a perishable body, what is raised is incorruptible. ⁴³ What is sown is ignoble, what is raised is glorious. Weakness is sown, strength is raised up. ⁴⁴ A natural body is sown, and a spiritual body is raised up. If there is a natural body, then there is also a spiritual body.

⁴⁵ The first Adam, as scripture says, "became a living soul," but the last Adam has become a life-giving spirit. ⁴⁶ That is, the natural comes first, not the spiritual; after that comes the spiritual. ⁴⁷ The first, being from the earth, is earthly by nature; the second is from heaven. ⁴⁸ As this earthly one was, so are we of the earth; and as the One from heaven is, so are we in heaven. ⁴⁹ And we, who have been modeled on the earthly, likewise will be modeled on the One from heaven.

⁵⁰ Put another way, sisters and brothers, I declare to you that flesh and blood cannot inherit the kindom of God. Neither can the perishable inherit what is imperishable. ⁵¹ I will share with you a mystery: we are not all going to die, but we will be changed. ⁵² It will be instantaneous, in the twinkling of an eye—when the last trumpet sounds. It will sound, and the dead will be raised, imperishable, and we will be changed, too. ⁵³ For our present perishable nature must put on imperishability, and our mortal nature must put on immortality.

⁵⁴ When this perishable nature has put on imperishability, and when this mortal body has put on immortality, then the words of scripture will come true: ⁵⁵ "Death is swallowed up in victory. Death, where is your victory? Death, where is your sting?" ⁵⁶ Now the sting of death is sin, and sin gets its power from the Law—⁵⁷ but thank God for giving us the victory through our Savior Jesus Christ!

⁵⁸ Be steadfast and persevering, my beloved sisters and brothers, fully engaged in the work of Jesus. You know that your toil is not in vain when it is done in Christ.

16:1–24

Now about the collection for the holy ones. Do what I told the Galatian churches to do: ² on the first day of the week, put aside what you can afford in order to avoid the collection being made after I come. ³ Then, while I am there, I will send those whom you designate with letters of recommendation and your gifts to Jerusalem. ⁴ If it is advisable for me to go, too, they may travel with me.

⁵ I will come to you after I pass through Macedonia, for I intend to pass through Macedonia. ⁶ And I may be staying with you for awhile, perhaps for the winter. That way you can help me on my journey, wherever that will be. ⁷ I don't mean this to be just a passing visit. I hope to spend some time with you, if our God allows.

⁸ In any case, I will stay at Ephesus until Pentecost, ⁹ for a huge door of opportunity has opened itself for me. Many people oppose me there.

¹⁰ If Timothy comes, see that you don't scare him off, for he is doing God's work, as I am. ¹¹ No one is to despise him simply because he is young. Send him on his way in peace that he may come to us. I am expecting him, as are the rest of us.

¹² Now about our brother Apollos: I begged him to come to you with the others. He was adamant not to go now, but he will come to you as soon as he can.

¹³ Be on your guard. Stand firm in the faith; be courageous; be strong. ¹⁴ Let all that you do be done in love.

¹⁵ There is one more thing. You know how the Stephanas family—the first converts in Achaia—have worked very hard in the service of the holy ones. ¹⁶ Well, now you should put yourselves at the service of people like them, and of everyone who helps in that work. ¹⁷ I am delighted that Stephanas, Fortunatus and Achaicus have arrived, because they make up for your absence. ¹⁸ They refresh my spirit as well as yours. I hope you appreciate workers like these.

¹⁹ The churches of Asia send you greetings. Aquila and Prisca, along with the community that meets in their house, send you their warmest greetings in Christ. ²⁰ All the sisters and brothers greet you. Greet one another with a holy kiss.

²¹ I, Paul, write this greeting in my own hand.

²² Whoever does not love our God is cursed. "Marana tha!"

²³ The grace of our Savior Jesus be with you. ²⁴ My love to all of you in Christ Jesus. Amen.

2 corinthians

1:1–7

From Paul, an apostle of Jesus Christ by the will of God, and Timothy our colleague,

To the church of God in Corinth, together with all the holy ones throughout Achaia:

[2] Grace and peace to you from God our Creator and our Savior Jesus Christ.

[3] Blessed be Abba God, the God of our Savior Jesus Christ, the Source of all mercies and the God of all consoling, [4] who comforts us in all our troubles so that we can comfort those in any trouble with the same comforting God has given us. [5] For while the sufferings of Christ are abundantly ours, our comforting is just as abundant through Christ.

[6] If we are troubled, it is for your comfort and salvation; if we are comforted, it too is for your comfort, which helps you patiently endure the same sufferings we suffer. [7] And our hope for you is firmly grounded, because we know that though you share in our sufferings, you share in our consolation as well.

1:8–3:3

We want you to know, sisters and brothers, about the hardships we suffered in the province of Asia. We underwent severe stress, well beyond our ability to cope, to the point of despairing of life itself. [9] In our hearts we felt we were doomed, which taught us not to rely on ourselves but on God, who raises the dead to life. [10] God rescued us from so great a peril as death, and we will continue to be rescued by God, on whom we have set our hope. [11] Please continue to help us through your prayers, though. The more you pray for us, the more others will give thanks for the blessings granted in answer to our prayers.

[12] Allow us to boast—and my conscience tells me this is true—that we have conducted ourselves in the world, and especially treated you, with a reverence and sincerity that comes only from God. We further attest, by God's grace, that it has been without ulterior motives. [13] For we don't write anything you can't read and understand. And we hope that you will understand completely— [14] as you have come to understand partially—so that you can boast of us just as we will boast of you in the day of our Savior Jesus.

[15] Because I was so sure of this, I had meant to come to you first so that you might benefit twice— [16] I planned to visit you both on my way to Macedonia and on my return trip, then to have you send me on my way to Judea. [17] And don't think I acted lightly, unsure of my intentions, when I planned this. Don't think I make my plans with ordinary human motives—so that I say "Yes, yes," then in the same breath, "No, no"! [18] As sure as God is faithful, I declare that my word to you is not "yes" one minute and "no" the next.

[19] Jesus Christ, whom Sivanus, Timothy and I preached to you as the Only Begotten of God, was not alternately "yes" and "no"; Jesus is never anything but "yes." [20] No matter how many promises God has made, they are "yes" in Christ. Therefore it is through Jesus that we address our Amen to God when we worship together. [21] God is the One who firmly establishes us along with you in Christ; it is God who anointed us [22] and sealed us, putting the Spirit in our hearts as our bond and guarantee.

[23] As God is my witness, I swear that, in an attempt to spare your feelings, I did not return to Corinth. [24] I'm not a tyrant over your faith. Rather, I am a coworker with you for your happiness. By faith you stand firm.

2 [1] So I made up my mind not to pay you a second painful visit. [2] I may have hurt you, but if so I have hurt the only ones who could give me any comfort. [3] I wrote what I did to make sure that when I came I would not be vexed by those same people who, under normal circumstances, would make me happy! Surely you know that my happiness relies on you all being happy. [4] For I wrote to you with a heavy and anguished heart and many tears. I wrote not to grieve you, but that you might know how much I love you.

[5] One individual has been the cause of a great deal of pain, not just to me but, to a degree—not to exaggerate—to all of you. [6] The punishment imposed by the majority on the person in question is sufficient. [7] The appropriate next step is to forgive and encourage the offender, to avoid a breakdown because of so much misery. [8] I urge you to reaffirm your love for this individual. [9] For I really wrote to test your character, to see if you were obedient in everything. [10] Whoever you forgive, I forgive. And what I have forgiven—if there has been anything to be forgiven—I have done so for your sake, in the presence of Christ. [11] And so we will not be outwitted by Satan, for we are aware of the Devil's intentions.

[12] Now, when I went to Troas to preach the Good News of Christ, I discovered a door open for me to minister. [13] But I was particularly anxious over not meeting my brother Titus there, so I said goodbye to them and moved on to Macedonia.

[14] But thanks be to the Most High who makes us, in Christ, sharers in the divine triumph, and everywhere we go manifests through us the sweet aroma of the knowledge of God. [15] For we are the incense of Christ that ascends to God on behalf of those being saved—and of those who are perishing. [16] We are the stench of death to one, and the fragrance of life to the other.

Now I ask, who is qualified for work like this? [17] At least we don't go around peddling the word of God for profit. Many others do, you know. We speak before God with sincerity—in Christ—as envoys of God.

3 [1] Am I beginning to brag again? Or do I need letters of recommendation to you or from you, as others might? [2] You are my letter, known and read by all, written on your hearts. [3] Clearly you are a letter of Christ which I have delivered, a letter written not with ink, but with the Spirit of the living God; not on tablets of stone, but on tablets of flesh in the heart.

3:4–4:6

The great confidence we have before God, we have because of Christ. [5] It is not that we are entitled of ourselves to take credit for anything. Our sole credit is from God, [6] who made us qualified ministers of a new Covenant, a covenant not of a written Law but of Spirit. The written Law kills, but the Spirit gives life.

[7] Now if the ministry that brought death, carved in writing on stone, was inaugurated with such glory that the Israelites could not look on Moses' face because of the radiance that shone on it, fading though it was— [8] how much

greater will be the glory of the ministry of the Spirit? ⁹ If the ministry of the Covenant that condemned had splendor, greater by far is the splendor of the ministry that justifies! ¹⁰ Indeed, when you compare that limited glory with this surpassing glory, the former is no glory at all. ¹¹ If what was destined to pass away was given in glory, greater by far is the glory that endures.

¹² With such hope we are very bold in what we say. ¹³ And we are not like Moses, who covered his face with a veil to keep the Israelites from gazing at the radiance as it faded away. ¹⁴ But their minds had been dulled, and to this day the same veil remains whenever the old Covenant is read—it has not been taken away, for only in Christ can it be removed. ¹⁵ To this day, whenever Moses is read, a veil covers their understanding.

¹⁶ But whenever anyone turns to our God, the veil is removed. ¹⁷ Now our God is the Spirit, and where the Spirit of our God is, there is freedom. ¹⁸ And we, who with unveiled faces reflect our God's glory, grow brighter and brighter as we are being transformed into the image we reflect. This is the work of our God, who is Spirit.

4 ¹ Therefore, because we have this ministry through God's mercy, we do not give in to discouragement. ² On the contrary, we renounce the shameful deeds that were kept hidden. We are not deceitful, nor do we adulterate the word of God. But by speaking the truth plainly, we commend ourselves to every person's conscience in the sight of God.

³ If our Gospel can be called veiled in any sense, it is only for those who are headed toward destruction. ⁴ Their unbelieving minds have been blinded by the god of the present age, so that they do not see the splendor of the Gospel showing forth the glory of Christ, the image of God. ⁵ It is not ourselves we preach, but Christ Jesus as Sovereign, and ourselves as your workers for Jesus' sake. ⁶ For God, who said, "Let light shine out of darkness," has shone in our hearts, so that we in turn might make known the glory of God shining on the face of Christ.

4:7–6:2

But this treasure we possess is in earthen vessels, to make it clear that its surpassing power comes from God and not from us. ⁸ We are afflicted in every way possible, but we are not crushed; we are full of doubts, but we never despair. ⁹ We are persecuted, but never abandoned; we are struck down, but never destroyed. ¹⁰ Continually we carry about in our bodies the death of Jesus, so that in our bodies the life of Jesus may also be revealed. ¹¹ While we live, we are constantly being delivered to death for Jesus' sake, so that the life of Jesus may also be revealed in our bodies. ¹² So then, death is at work in us, but life is at work in you.

¹³ But as we have the same spirit of faith that is mentioned in scripture—"I believed and therefore I spoke"—we too believe and therefore speak, ¹⁴ knowing that the One who raised Jesus to life will in turn raise us with Jesus, and place you with us in God's presence. ¹⁵ You see, all of this is for your benefit, so that the grace that is reaching more and more people may cause thanksgiving to overflow, to the glory of God.

¹⁶ That is why we don't lose heart. And though this physical self of ours may be falling into decay, the inner self is renewed day by day. ¹⁷ These light and momentary troubles train us to carry the weight of an eternal glory which will make these troubles insignificant by comparison. ¹⁸ And we have no eyes for things that are visible, but only for things that are invisible; visible things last only for a time, but the invisible are eternal.

5 ¹ For we know that when our earthly tent is folded up, there is waiting for us a house built by God, an everlasting home in the heavens, not made by human hands. ² And while in this tent, we lament—longing to be clothed with our heavenly home—³ because when we are dressed we will not be found naked. ⁴ While we are in this tent we groan and find it a burden, because we don't want to be naked, but to be clothed, so that what is mortal is swallowed up by life. ⁵ God made us for this very purpose and gave us the pledge of the Spirit to safeguard our future.

⁶ And so we are always full of confidence, even though we realize that to live in the body means to be absent from Jesus Christ. ⁷ We walk by faith, not by sight. ⁸ We are full of confidence, I repeat, and would actually prefer to be absent from the body and make our home with Christ. ⁹ Whether we are living in the body or absent from it, we are intent on pleasing Christ. ¹⁰ For we must all appear before the judgment seat of Christ, and each of us will get what we deserve for the things we do while in the body, good or bad.

¹¹ It is because we know "the fear of God" that we try to persuade others. What we really are is plain to God, and I hope it is also plain to your conscience. ¹² No, we are not attempting to commend ourselves to you once again. We are just giving you a reason to be proud of us. In that way you will have an answer for those who boast of what is seen, rather than what is in the heart. ¹³ If we are beside ourselves, it is for the sake of God. If we are in our right minds, it is for you.

¹⁴ The love of Christ overwhelms us whenever we reflect on this: that if one person has died for all, then all have died. ¹⁵ The reason Christ died for all was so that the living should live no longer for themselves but for Christ, who died and was raised to life for them.

¹⁶ And so from now on, we don't look on anyone in terms of mere human judgment. Even if we did once regard Christ in these terms, that is not how we know Christ now. ¹⁷ And for anyone who is in Christ, there is a new creation. The old order has passed away; now everything is new! ¹⁸ All of this is from God, who ransomed us through Christ—and made us ministers of that reconciliation. ¹⁹ This means that through Christ, the world was fully reconciled again to God, who didn't hold our transgressions against us, but instead entrusted us with this message of reconciliation. ²⁰ This makes us Christ's ambassadors, as though God were making the appeal directly through us. Therefore we implore you in Christ's name: be reconciled to God. ²¹ For our sake, God made the One who was without sin to be sin, so that by this means we might become the very holiness of God.

6 ¹ As Christ's coworkers we beg you not to receive the grace of God in vain. ² For God says through Isaiah, "At the acceptable time I heard you, and on the day of salvation I helped you." Now is the acceptable time! Now is the day of salvation!

6:3–7:1

We take pains to avoid giving offense to anyone, for we don't want our ministry to be blamed. ⁴ Instead, in all that we do we try to present ourselves as ministers of God, acting with patient endurance amid trials, difficulties, distresses, ⁵ beatings, imprisonments and riots; in hard work, sleepless nights and hunger. ⁶ We conduct ourselves with innocence, knowledge, patience and kindness in the Holy Spirit, in sincere love,

7 with the message of truth and the power of God, wielding the weapons of justice with both right hand and left— 8 regardless of whether we are honored or dishonored, spoken of favorably or unfavorably. We are called impostors, yet we are truthful; 9 we are called unknowns, yet we are famous; we are said to be dying, yet we are alive; punished, but not put to death; 10 sorrowful, though we are always rejoicing; poor, yet we enrich many. We seem to have nothing, yet we possess everything!

11 We have spoken frankly to you, Corinthians; we've opened our hearts wide to you. 12 We're not holding anything back; you, on the other hand, are holding back your affection from us. 13 It would be a fair exchange—I speak as to my children—if you'd open your hearts as widely to us as we do to you.

14 Don't be harnessed in an uneven team with nonbelievers. Justice and inequity are not companions; light and darkness have nothing in common. 15 Christ is not allied with Belial, and a believer has nothing in common with a nonbeliever. 16 The Temple of God has nothing in common with idols, for we are the Temple of the living God. As God has said:

"I will live with them
and move among them,
and I will be their God,
and they will be my people."

17 "'Therefore, come away from them,
and be separate,'
says Your God.
'Touch nothing that is unclean,
and I will welcome you.'"

18 "'I will be a Parent to you,
and you will be daughters
and sons to me,'
says Your God Almighty."

7 1 Since we have these promises, dear sisters and brothers, let us wash off everything that contaminates body and spirit, working to make our holiness perfect out of reverence for God.

7:2–16

Make room for us in your hearts. We have not wronged anyone or ruined anyone or exploited anyone. 3 I do not say this to put any blame on you. As I have already said, you are in our hearts—that we may live together or die together. 4 I have the greatest confidence in you. I take great pride in you. I am greatly encouraged and filled with joy all the more because of our troubles.

5 Even after we came to Macedonia, this body of ours found no rest. We were harrassed on all sides—quarrels on the outside, fear on the inside. 6 But God, who comforts the afflicted, comforted us with the arrival of Titus—7 and not only by his arrival, but also by the comfort you gave to him. He told us all about your yearning for me, how sorry you were and how concerned for me. I am happier now than I was before.

8 For even if I caused you sorrow by my letter, I don't regret it. I did regret it before—I see that the letter saddened you, at least for a while—9 but now I am happy. I rejoice not that you were made to suffer, but that your suffering led to your repentance. Your suffering is the kind of which God approves. And so you did not endure any kind of loss because of us. 10 Godly sorrow means changing for the better and having no regrets. To suffer as the world suffers brings death. 11 See

what salutary effects godly suffering has produced in you: what keenness, what earnestness, what indignation, what fear, what yearning, what concern, what zeal to see justice done! At every point you have shown yourselves blameless in this matter. 12 So then, though I wrote the letter to you, it was not for the sake of the offender or the one offended. It was written so that you could see for yourselves how devoted to us you are in the sight of God. 13 We are encouraged by this.

Besides this encouragement, we are especially delighted to see Titus so happy. Thanks to you, he has no more worries. 14 I had boasted to him about you, and you have not embarrassed me. In fact, our boasting to Titus proved to be as true as anything we have said. 15 His heart goes out to you all the more when he recalls how willing you all have been, and with what deep respect you welcomed him. 16 I am very happy because I have complete confidence in you.

8:1–9:15

Now, sisters and brothers, we want to tell you how God's grace has been given to the churches in Macedonia. 2 In the midst of severe trial, their overflowing joy and deep poverty have produced an abundant generosity. 3 I can swear that they gave not only what they could afford but much more, spontaneously, 4 begging and begging us for the favor of sharing in this service to God's holy ones and—5 quite unexpectedly—they offered themselves first to God, and then to us, in keeping with God's will. 6 This is why I have asked Titus, who has already begun this work of charity among you, to bring it to a successful completion: 7 that just as you are rich in every respect, in faith and discourse, in knowledge, in total concern, and in the love we inspired in you, you may also abound in this work of grace.

8 It is not an order I am giving you, but the opportunity to test your generous love against the earnestness which others show. 9 You are well acquainted with the favor shown by our Savior Jesus Christ, who, though rich, became poor for your sake, so that you might become rich by Christ's poverty.

10 As I say, this is only a suggestion—it's my counsel about what is best for you in this matter. A year ago, you were not only the first to act, but you did so willingly. 11 Finish that work, so that your eagerness to begin can be matched by your eagerness to finish, according to your means. 12 For so long as the heart is willing, it's what you have that is acceptable, not what you don't have.

13 This doesn't mean that by giving relief to others, you ought to make things difficult for yourselves! It's just a question of balancing 14 what happens to be your surplus now against their present need; one day they may have something to spare that will supply your own need. That is how we strike a balance, 15 as scripture says: "The one who gathered much had no excess, and the one who gathered little did not go short."

16 I thank God for putting into the heart of Titus the same concern for you that I have myself. 17 He did what he was asked, and because he is concerned, he is coming to you now on his own initiative. 18 And we are sending, along with Titus, someone who is praised in all the churches for being a brilliant preacher of the Gospel. 19 What's more, this individual has also been appointed as our traveling companion by the churches on this errand of mercy. We do it for the glory of God, and to show our eagerness to help. 20 By doing so, we hope to avoid any criticism of the way we administer such a large fund. 21 For we are trying to do what is right in the sight of both God and people.

²² In addition, we're sending along another coworker, who has proven diligent in earlier testings, but who is even more diligent now because of a tremendous faith in you. ²³ As for Titus, he is my colleague and coworker among you. As for the other two coworkers, they are delegates of the churches and an honor to Christ. ²⁴ Therefore, before all the churches, give them a proof of your love, and prove to them that we are justified to be proud of you.

9 ¹ There's really no need for me to write to you about offering your services to the holy ones. ² For I know how anxious you are to help, and I've boasted about you to the Macedonians: "Achaia has been ready since last year." In fact, your zeal has stirred up most of them! ³ Even so, I'm sending the coworkers so that our boasting about you in this matter won't prove to have been empty—and to show that you are indeed ready, as I said you would be. ⁴ If any of the Macedonians should accompany me and find you unprepared, we—not to mention you!—would be humiliated after being so confident. ⁵ It's for this reason that I thought it necessary for the coworkers to precede us, and to arrange in advance for this generous gift you promised. In this way we will dispel all doubts that it comes as a bountiful and free gift, not an extorted one.

⁶ Keep this in mind: if you plant sparingly, you will reap sparingly, and if you plant bountifully, you will reap bountifully. ⁷ You must give according to what you have inwardly decided—not sadly, not reluctantly, for God loves a giver who gives cheerfully. ⁸ There are no limits to the grace of God, who will make sure you will always have enough of everything and even a surplus for good works, ⁹ as scripture says:

> "God scattered abroad
> and gave to poor people;
> God's justice endures forever."

¹⁰ The One who provides seed for the planter and bread for food will also supply and enlarge your store of seed and increase your harvest of justice. ¹¹ You will be made rich in every way for your generosity, for which we give thanks to God.

¹² For the administration of this service not only supplies fully the needs of the holy ones, but also overflows in thanksgivings to God. ¹³ By offering this service, you prove yourselves. And that makes them give glory to God for the way you obey and profess the Gospel of Christ, and for your generosity to them and to everyone. ¹⁴ And their prayers also show how they are drawn to you because of the exceeding grace of God in you. ¹⁵ Thanks be to God for such an indescribable gift!

10:1–11:15

I myself appeal to you by the gentleness and meekness of Christ—I who am so humble when face to face with you, but who bullies you when away! ² I only ask that I do not have to bully you when I come—for I'll be bold if I need to be—to confront some among you I could name, who think we live by worldly standards.

³ Though we live in the world, we don't fight in a worldly way. ⁴ Our weapons, however, have the power of God to destroy fortresses. ⁵ We demolish every argument and pretension that resists the knowledge of God, and we take every thought captive and make it obedient to Christ. ⁶ We're ready to punish every disobedience, once your obedience is complete.

⁷ Look at what confronts you. Those who are convinced that they belong to Christ need to realize that we belong to Christ just as much as they do. ⁸ And even if I should boast a little too much about our authority—which Christ gave for building up and not for tearing down—I will not be ashamed of it. ⁹ I don't want you to think of me as someone who frightens you only by letter. ¹⁰ Someone said, "His letters are weighty and forceful, but in person he is unremarkable and not even a preacher." ¹¹ Such people must understand that what we are in words when absent, we are in actions when present.

¹² We do not dare to classify or compare ourselves with some who recommend themselves. They are foolish because they measure and compare themselves only with themselves. ¹³ We, on the other hand, won't boast without a measurable standard. Our standard is the measuring stick God gave us, which is long enough to reach you. ¹⁴ We are not overreaching ourselves. Otherwise we would not have reached you—and we were the first to come all the way to you with the Gospel of Christ. ¹⁵ Nor do we exceed our limits by boasting about the work of others. Yet our hope is that as your faith increases, our influence among you will increase accordingly—within proper limits— ¹⁶ so that we may carry the Gospel to places far beyond you. We won't boast of work completed in another person's territory. ¹⁷ As scripture says, "Let those who boast, boast in our God," ¹⁸ for it is not those who commend themselves who are approved, but those who are commended by our God.

11 ¹ Will you endure a little of my foolishness? Humor me, please. ² You see, the jealousy that I feel for you is God's own jealousy: I stood as witness to your marriage with Christ to testify about your purity before Christ. ³ My fear is that you—just as our first parents were deceived by the cunning of the serpent—will let your ideas get corrupted and turned away from simple and pure devotion to Christ. ⁴ I say this because when someone comes preaching a Jesus other than the one we preached, or telling you to receive a different spirit than the Spirit you received, or to accept a gospel other than the Gospel you accepted, you seem to endure it quite well.

⁵ I consider myself not the least bit inferior to the "super apostles." ⁶ I may be unskilled in speech, but I'm certainly not lacking in knowledge. We have made this evident to you in every conceivable way. ⁷ I lowered myself to elevate you—I proclaimed the Gospel of God to you without cost. Was that a sin? ⁸ I robbed other churches by receiving financial support from them while serving you. ⁹ And while I was with you, I was careful not to be a burden to anyone—any time I needed something, my Macedonian coworkers supplied what I needed. I've kept myself from being a burden to you in any way, and I will continue to do so. ¹⁰ As surely as the truth of Christ is in me, nobody in all of Achaia will prevent me from boasting. ¹¹ And you think I don't love you? God knows I do!

¹² And what I am doing I intend to continue to do. I will leave no opportunity for those who want to boast that they are our equals. ¹³ No—these people are false apostles and deceitful workers who pose as apostles of Christ. ¹⁴ And no wonder: even Satan pretends to be an angel of light. ¹⁵ One need not be surprised that the Devil's minions impersonate agents of righteousness. They will come to the end that their actions deserve.

I repeat, let no one take me for a fool. But if you must, treat me like a fool, and let me do a little boasting of my own. ¹⁷ What I am saying I say not as Christ would, but as a fool, in this overconfident boasting of mine.

¹⁸ Since many are boasting of their worldly accomplishments, I too will boast. ¹⁹ You gladly tolerate fools, since you yourselves are so wise. ²⁰ You've been patient with someone who enslaves you, devours you, takes advantage of you, puts on airs and hits you in the face. ²¹ I'm ashamed to say that we have a weakness for doing these very things!

But what anyone else dares to boast about—I speak with absolute foolishness now—I also dare to boast. ²² Are they Hebrews? So am I! Are they Israelites? So am I! Are they the seed of Sarah and Abraham? So am I! ²³ Are they ministers of Christ? Now I'm really talking like a fool—I am more of one! I have worked much harder, been in prison far more often, been flogged more severely, and been exposed to death time and again. ²⁴ Five times I was given thirty-nine lashes by the Temple authorities. ²⁵ Three times I was beaten with sticks. They stoned me once. I was shipwrecked three times, once spending a night and a day in the open sea. ²⁶ And I have been constantly on the move—in danger from raging rivers, in danger from highway robbers, in danger from Jews, in danger from Gentiles, in danger in the city, in danger in the country, in danger at sea and in danger from false sisters and brothers. ²⁷ I have labored long and hard, often going without sleep; I've known hunger and thirst, often going without food; I've been cold and naked. ²⁸ And on top of everything, there is the daily stress of my anxiety for all the churches. ²⁹ Who is weak, that I don't feel that weakness? Who is led into sin, that I am not tortured by it? ³⁰ But if I must boast, I will boast of my shortcomings.

³¹ The God and Creator of our Savior Jesus, who is blessed forever, knows that I do not lie. ³² When I was at Damascus, the governor under the ruler Aretas stationed guards around the city to take me into custody. ³³ But I was lowered in a basket through a window in the wall and escaped.

12 ¹ I must go on boasting, however useless it may be, and speak of visions and revelations from God. ² I know someone who fourteen years ago was caught up in the third heaven. Whether it was in the body or out of the body I do not know—only God knows. ³ And I know that this person—whether it was in the body or out of the body I do not know, only God knows— ⁴ was caught up to paradise to hear words that cannot be uttered, words that no one may speak. ⁵ About this person I will boast, but I will do no boasting about myself, unless it be about my weaknesses. ⁶ And even if I were to boast, it wouldn't be foolish of me, because I am speaking the truth.

But I refrain, so that no one will think more of me than is justified by what I do or say. ⁷ Because of the surpassing greatness of the revelations, in order to keep me from becoming conceited, I was given a thorn in my flesh—a messenger of Satan to beat me—to keep me from exalting myself! ⁸ Three times I begged God that it might leave me. ⁹ And God said to me, "My grace is sufficient for you, for power is perfected in weakness." Most gladly, therefore, I would rather boast about my weaknesses, that the power of Christ may dwell in me. ¹⁰ So I am content with weakness, with mistreatment, with distress, with persecutions and difficulties for the sake of Christ; when I am powerless, it is then that I am strong.

I've been a fool, but you forced me to it. I ought to have been commended by you. Even though I am nothing, I am in no way inferior to these "super apostles." ¹² The things that mark a true apostle—signs, wonders, miracles—were unfailingly produced among you. ¹³ How were you less privileged than the other churches—with the exception that I wasn't a burden to you? Forgive me this wrong!

¹⁴ Now I'm ready to come to you a third time. I won't be a burden, for I want not what is yours, but you. After all, children are not expected to save money for their parents; rather, parents save for their children. ¹⁵ And I am perfectly willing to spend—and to be expended as well—for the sake of your souls. But if I love you more, am I to be loved less in return? ¹⁶ At least I wasn't a burden to you; but cunning as I am, I caught you by deceit. ¹⁷ Did I exploit you through any of those I sent to you? ¹⁸ I urged Titus to go and send our coworker. Did Titus exploit you? It goes without saying that Titus and I have always been guided by the same Spirit and walk in the same path.

¹⁹ Do you get the impression that we've been defending ourselves to you all along? We've been speaking in Christ, and in the sight of God. And it is all for your benefit, dearly beloved. ²⁰ For I fear that when I come, I may find you not as I want you to be. And you may find me not as you want me to be. And there may be rivalry, jealousy, outbursts of anger, disputes, slander, gossip, deceit and disorder. ²¹ I am afraid that when I come again, my God may humiliate me before you. And I fear I will be grieving over many who have sinned earlier and have not repented of the impurity, immorality and debauchery they committed.

13 ¹ This will be the third time I come to you: "Every charge must be established by the testimony of two or three witnesses." ² I already gave you a warning when I was with you the second time. And I warn you now, before I come: I will have no mercy on those of you who sinned earlier, or on any of the others. ³ You want proof, you say, that Christ is speaking through me—me, whom you have known not as a weakling but as a power among you? ⁴ But our Savior was crucified through weakness and now lives through the power of God. Likewise, we are weak in Christ, yet we live in Christ by the power of God, to serve you.

⁵ Test yourselves to see if you're really walking in the faith. Examine yourselves! Don't you realize that Jesus Christ is in you? —That is, unless you fail the test! ⁶ I hope you come to see that we haven't failed it. ⁷ We pray to God that you won't commit any wrongdoing—not that we should appear to be in the right, but that you should do right, even if we appear to be in the wrong. ⁸ For we can't do anything against the truth—only for it. ⁹ And we rejoice when you are strong and we are weak. We pray that you will be made complete.

¹⁰ I write this while I am away from you, so that when I come, I need not be severe in my use of authority, which God gave me for building up, not for tearing down.

¹¹ And now, sisters and brothers, I must say goodbye. Mend your ways. Encourage one another. Live in harmony and peace, and the God of love and peace will be with you. ¹² Greet one another with a holy kiss. ¹³ All the holy ones send greetings to you.

¹⁴ The grace of our Savior Jesus Christ and the love of God and the friendship of the Holy Spirit be with you all!

galatians

1:1–12

From Paul, appointed to be an apostle, not through human agency but through Jesus Christ, and through Abba God, who raised Christ from the dead— [2] and from all the sisters and brothers who are here with us,*

To the churches of Galatia:

[3] Grace and peace to you from God our Creator and our Savior Jesus Christ, [4] whose self-sacrifice for our sins rescued us from this present wicked world, in accordance with the will of our God and Creator, [5] to whom be the glory forever and ever!

[6] I am astonished that you have so soon turned away from the One who called you by the grace of Christ, and have turned to a different gospel—[7] one which is really not "good news" at all. Some who wish to alter the Good News of Christ must have confused you. [8] For if we—or even angels from heaven—should preach to you a different gospel, one not in accord with the gospel we delivered to you, let us—or them—be cursed! [9] We've said it before and I'll say it again: if any preach a gospel to you that is contrary to the one you received, let them be cursed!†

[10] Whom am I trying to please now—people or God? Is it human approval I am seeking? If I still wanted that, I wouldn't be what I am—a servant of Christ! [11] I assure you, my sisters and brothers: the gospel I proclaim to you is no mere human invention. [12] I didn't receive it from any person, nor was I schooled in it. It came by revelation from Jesus Christ.‡

1:13–2:21

You have heard, I know, the story of my former way of life in Judaism. You know that I went to extremes in persecuting the church of God and tried to destroy it; [14] I went far beyond most of my contemporaries regarding Jewish observances because of my great zeal to live out all the traditions of my ancestors.

[15] But the time came when God, who had set me apart before I was born, called me by divine grace, choosing [16] to reveal Christ through me, that I might spread Christ among the Gentiles. Immediately, without seeking human advisors [17] or even going to Jerusalem to see those who were apostles before me, I went off to Arabia; later I returned to Damascus. [18] Three years after that, I went up to Jerusalem to get information from Peter, with whom I stayed for fifteen days.§ [19] I didn't meet any other apostle except James, the brother of Jesus. [20] I declare before God that what I have just written is true.

---

* Paul opens this letter by establishing his authority, explicitly claiming the title of apostle and declaring that his claim to the title is of divine origins.

† Paul is probably referring to those who preach that acceptance of the Mosaic Law is necessary for salvation. Paul's theology is that there is only one gospel, which he preached to them, which is salvation through Jesus Christ.

‡ Paul was being accused of preaching a message derived from others and watering the message down for Gentiles. Paul explicitly denies this, asserting once again the divine origin of his apostolic mission.

§ The Greek infinitive *historesai* literally means, "to get information from," as it has been translated here. Its meaning, though, is ambiguous. It has been interpreted to mean "to see" or "to visit." Paul's visit seems to be to learn from Peter about the life and ministry of Jesus.

[21] After that I visited the regions of Syria and Cilicia. [22] The communities of Christ in Judea had no idea what I looked like; [23] they had only heard that "the one who was formerly persecuting us is now preaching the faith he tried to destroy," [24] and they gave glory to God because of me.

2 [1] After fourteen years, I went up to Jerusalem again with Barnabas, this time taking Titus with me; [2] my going there was prompted by a revelation. Once there, I laid out for them the Gospel as I present it to the Gentiles. All of this took place in private conference with the leaders, to make sure that the course I was pursuing, or had pursued, was not useless.¶

[3] They even tried—unsuccessfully—to compel Titus, who had accompanied me, to be circumcised, since he was Greek. [4] The question came up because some of the community infiltrated our ranks to spy on the freedom we have in Christ Jesus in order to enslave us. [5] We didn't capitulate to them for one moment; we wanted to ensure that the truth of the Good News would remain intact for you. [6] Consequently, the acknowledged "leaders" there—importance is of no concern to me; we are all equal before God—had nothing to add to the Good News I preach.

[7] On the contrary, they recognized that I had been entrusted with the Good News for the Gentiles, just as Peter had for the Jewish people.** [8] The same One who appointed Peter as apostle to the Jewish people gave me a similar mission to the Gentiles. [9] Recognizing the grace that had been given to me, James, Peter and John—these leaders, these pillars—shook hands with Barnabas and me as a sign of partnership: we were to go to the Gentiles and they to the Jews. [10] The only thing they insisted on was that we should remember to help those poorer than we—the very thing I was eager to do.

[11] When Peter came to Antioch, however, I opposed him to his face, since he was manifestly in the wrong. [12] His custom had been to eat with the Gentiles but, after certain friends of James arrived, he stopped doing this and kept away from them altogether, for fear of the group that insists Gentiles must convert to Judaism first. [13] The other Jews joined him in this hypocrisy, and even Barnabas felt obliged to copy this behavior.

[14] When I saw they weren't respecting the true meaning of the Good News, I said to Peter in front of everyone, "You are a Jew, yet you live like a Gentile and not a Jew. So why do you want to make the Gentiles adopt Jewish ways? [15] Though we're Jewish by nature and not Gentile 'sinners,' [16] we know that people aren't justified by following the Law, but by believing in Jesus Christ. That is why we too have believed in Christ—so that we can be justified by faith in Christ, not by obeying the Law. No one will be justified by keeping the Law!"

[17] But if it becomes evident that we ourselves are sinners while we seek justification in Christ, does this imply that Christ has induced us to sin? Absolutely not! [18] If I rebuild what I had destroyed, then I prove that I am in fact a destroyer!

[19] It was through the Law that I died to the Law, to live for God. [20] I have been crucified with Christ, and it's no longer I who live, but Christ who lives in me. I still live my own life, but it's a life of faith in Jesus our Savior, who loves me and who gave himself for me. [21] I will not nullify God's grace—for if justification is available only through the Law, then Christ died needlessly.

¶ The correlation of this event with the account in Acts 15 is one of the most difficult problems of the Christian Scriptures.

** Paul is asserting equality with Peter, though their fields of mission are different.

You foolish Galatians! Who has cast a spell over you, in spite of the clear and public portrayal you have had of the crucifixion of Jesus Christ? 2 Let me ask one question: was it because you practiced the Law that you received the Holy Spirit, or because you believed what was preached to you? 3 Are you so foolish that, having begun by the Spirit, you would now try to finish through human effort? 4 Was everything you suffered in vain? If this is how you are ending up, it has all been in vain indeed! 5 Does God give you the Spirit so freely and work miracles among you because you practice the Law, or because you believe what was preached to you?

6 Recall that Abraham "believed God, and it was credited to him as righteousness." 7 Realize, then, that those who believe are the children of Abraham. 8 Because scripture saw in advance that God would justify the Gentiles through faith, it foretold this Good News to Abraham: "All nations will be blessed in you." 9 So then all who believe are blessed along with Abraham, who believed first.

10 All who depend on observances of the Law, on the other hand, are under a curse. Scripture says, "Everyone who doesn't abide by everything written in the book of the Law and carry it out is cursed." 11 It should be obvious that no one is justified in God's sight by the Law, for "the just will live by faith." 12 But the Law doesn't depend on faith—its terms are that "those who keep the Law will live because of it."

13 Christ, however, has redeemed us from the Law's curse by becoming a curse for us, as scripture says: "Anyone who is hanged on a tree is cursed." 14 This happened so that the blessing bestowed on Abraham might come to the Gentiles in Christ Jesus, thereby making it possible for us to receive the promised Spirit through faith.

Sisters and brothers, take an example from daily life: no one can annul or amend a human contract once it is ratified. 16 Consider the promises that were addressed to Abraham and his offspring. The scripture doesn't use "to your offspring" in the sense of many descendants, but "to your offspring" in the sense of a single individual—Christ. 17 What I mean is this: the Law, which came four hundred and thirty years later, doesn't annul the Covenant previously established by God, or it would cancel the promise. 18 For if you receive something through a legal inheritance, it doesn't come from a promise—yet it's precisely as a promise that God gave the gift to Abraham.

19 Why, then, was the Law added? It was added to teach people right from wrong until the "descendant" to whom the promise had been made would come. The Law was promulgated by angels through a mediator. 20 Now, there can be a mediator only when there are two parties, whereas God is only one. 21 Does this mean that the Law is opposed to the promises of God? Certainly not! On the other hand, we could have been justified by the Law only if it had the power to give life.

22 Scripture has locked everything under the constraint of sin. Why? So that the promise might be fulfilled in those who believe because of their faith in Jesus Christ.

23 Before faith came, we were under the constraint of the Law, locked in until the faith that was coming would be revealed. 24 In other words, the Law was our monitor until Christ came to bring about our justification through faith. 25 But now that faith is here, we are no longer in the monitor's charge.

26 Each one of you is a child of God because of your faith in Christ Jesus. 27 All of you who have been baptized into Christ have clothed yourselves with Christ. 28 In Christ there is no Jew or Greek, slave or citizen, male or female. All are one in Christ Jesus.*

29 Furthermore, if you belong to Christ, you are the offspring of Abraham, which means you inherit all that was promised. 4:1 What I am saying is that as long as the heir remains a child, it's no different from being a slave—even if the child owns everything— 2 since the child is under the supervision of guardians and trustees until the time set by the parents. 3 In the same way, before we came of age, we were enslaved to the elemental principles of the world. 4 When the designated time had come, God sent forth the Christ—born of a woman, born under the Law—to deliver from the Law those who were subjected to it, 5 so that we might receive our status as adopted heirs. 6 The proof that you are children of God is the fact that God has sent forth into our hearts the Spirit of the Child who calls out "Abba!" 7 You are no longer slaves, but daughters and sons! And if you are daughters and sons, you are also heirs, by God's design.

8 Once you were ignorant of God and enslaved to "gods" who are not really gods at all. 9 Now that you have come to know God—or rather, now that God knows you—how can you turn back to weak and worthless elemental powers? Do you want to be enslaved by them all over again? 10 You and your special days and months and seasons and years! 11 You make me feel I have wasted all my time with you!

I beg you, sisters and brothers, become like me—for I have become like you. You have never treated me so coolly before. 13 Call to mind that an illness originally gave me the opportunity to preach the Good News to you. 14 You never gave the slightest indication of being revolted or disgusted because of my disease, which was such a trial to you. Rather, you treated me as if I were a messenger from God—or even as if I were Christ Jesus. 15 Where has all that joy of yours gone? I swear that, had it been possible, you would have plucked out your eyes and given them to me! 16 Has my telling you the truth made me your enemy?

17 The blame lies in those people who feign interest in you—their interest is self-serving. They intend to isolate you from us, so that you will be zealous for them instead. 18 To be zealous is admirable, if it's for a good purpose. But it must be this way always, and not just when I am with you. 19 My dear children, I must go through the pangs of giving birth to you once more, until Christ is formed in you. 20 How I wish I were with you now! How I wish I could change my tone! How I wish I weren't so perplexed about you!

21 I ask you, you who strive to be subject to the Law—do you understand what the Law asks of you? 22 For scripture says that Abraham had two children—one by Hagar, who was a slave, and the other by Sarah, who was freeborn. 23 The child of the slave had been begotten in the course of nature, but the child of the free woman was the fruit of the promise. 24 All this is clearly an allegory: the two women stand for the

---

* This passage is the climax of Paul's letter, establishing the equality of all those united in Christ through the Spirit.

two Covenants. One is from Mt. Sinai, and she gave birth to children in slavery: this is Hagar. ²⁵ Hagar represents Mt. Sinai in Arabia—which corresponds to the present Jerusalem, which is in slavery like Hagar's children.

²⁶ But the Jerusalem on high is freeborn, and it's she who is our mother. ²⁷ That is why scripture says,

> "Rejoice, you who are infertile,
> who has borne no children;
> break into song,
> you stranger to the pains of childbirth!
> For there are more born of the forsaken one
> than born of the wedded wife!"

²⁸ Now you, sisters and brothers, are children of the promise, like Rebecca and Isaac. ²⁹ At that time, the child born because of the urge of the flesh persecuted the child born through the urge of the Spirit. It's the same way now. ³⁰ For scripture says, "Drive away the slave woman and her child, for the child born of the slave woman will not share in the inheritance with the free woman's child." ³¹ Therefore, my sisters and brothers, we are children not of a slave, but of a mother who is free.

5 ²¹ When Christ freed us, we were meant to remain free. Stand firm, therefore, and don't submit to the yoke of slavery a second time! ² Pay close attention to me—Paul—when I tell you that if you let yourself be subjected to the Law, Christ will be of no use to you! ³ I point out once more to all who subject themselves to even one part of the Law that they are bound to keep the Law in its entirety. ⁴ Any of you who seek your justification in the Law have severed yourselves from Christ and fallen from God's favor.

⁵ It is in the Spirit that we eagerly await the justification we hope for, and only faith can yield it. ⁶ In Christ Jesus, neither adherence to the Law nor disregard of it counts for anything—only faith, which expresses itself through love.

⁷ You were running a good race. Who cut you off and made you cautious about obeying the truth? ⁸ This persuasion doesn't come from the One who called you. ⁹ The yeast seems to be spreading through the whole batch of you. ¹⁰ I am confident in our God that you will agree with me. I am equally confident that whoever is upsetting you in this matter will receive the appropriate judgment.

¹¹ As for me, if I were still preaching the need to fulfill the Law's requirements, then I wouldn't continue to be persecuted the way I am—and my preaching about the cross would not be the stumbling block that it is. ¹² And as for those who keep harrassing Gentile Christians to submit to the Law and become circumcised: may their knives slip!

5:13–6:18

My sisters and brothers, you were called to freedom; but be careful, or this freedom will provide an opening for self-indulgence. Rather, serve one another in works of love, ¹⁴ since the whole of the Law is summarized in a single command: "Love your neighbor as yourself." ¹⁵ If you go on snapping at one another and tearing each other to pieces, be careful, or you may end up destroying the whole community.

¹⁶ Let me put it this way: if you are guided by the Spirit, you will be in no danger of yielding to self-indulgence. ¹⁷ Since our flesh is at odds with the Spirit—and the Spirit with our flesh—the two are so opposed that you cannot do whatever you feel like doing. ¹⁸ If you are guided by the Spirit, you are not under the Law.

¹⁹ It's obvious what proceeds from the flesh: lewd conduct, impurity, licentiousness, ²⁰ idolatry, sorcery, hostility, arguments, jealousy, outbursts of anger, selfish rivalries, dissensions, factions, ²¹ envy, drunkenness, orgies and so forth. I warn you as I have warned you before: those who do these sorts of things won't inherit the kindom of God!

²² By contrast, the fruit of the Spirit is love, joy, peace, patient endurance, kindness, generosity, faithfulness, ²³ gentleness and self-control. Against these sorts of things there is no law! ²⁴ Those who belong to Christ Jesus have crucified their ego, with its passions and desires. ²⁵ So since we live by the Spirit, let us follow her lead. ²⁶ We must stop being conceited, contentious and envious.

6 ²¹ Sisters and brothers, if one of you is caught in any sin, the more spiritual among you should correct the offender in a spirit of gentleness—remembering that you may be tempted yourselves. ² Bear one another's burdens, and thus fulfill the law of Christ.

³ But if you think you are important when you are not, you are deceiving yourself. ⁴ Examine your own work, each of you. If you find something to boast about, at least it's something of your own and not just empty comparison with your neighbor. ⁵ Carry your own load!

⁶ Those under instruction in the word should always contribute to the support of the instructor.

⁷ Don't be deceived—God cannot be cheated: where you sow, there you will reap. ⁸ If you sow in the field of self-indulgence, you will reap corruption. If you sow in the field of the Spirit, you will reap the harvest of eternal life. ⁹ Never grow tired of doing good. We will reap a harvest at the proper time—if we don't grow weary. ¹⁰ So, while we still have time, do good to all and especially to those of the household of faith.

¹¹ Look how big these letters are when I write to you in my own hand!

¹² Those who are pressuring the men among you to be circumcised are only trying to win favor with others, so they won't be persecuted for the cross of Christ. ¹³ They themselves are circumcised but don't even keep the Law. They want you to accept circumcision just so they can boast about it.

¹⁴ May I never boast of anything but the cross of our Savior Jesus Christ! Through it the world has been crucified to me and I to the world. ¹⁵ It means nothing whether one bothers with the externals of religion or not. All that matters is that one is created anew.

¹⁶ Peace and mercy on all who follow this rule of life and on the Israel of God. ¹⁷ Henceforth, let no one trouble me, for my body bears the marks of Jesus.

¹⁸ Sisters and brothers, may the grace of our Savior Jesus Christ be with your spirit. Amen.

ephesians

1:1–23

From Paul, an apostle of Christ Jesus by the will of God,
To the holy ones in Ephesus who are faithful in Christ Jesus:
² Grace and peace to you from God our Creator and from our Savior Jesus Christ.

³ Praised be the Maker of our Savior Jesus Christ, who has bestowed on us in Christ every spiritual blessing in the heavens! ⁴ Before the world began, God chose us in Christ to be holy and blameless and to be full of love; ⁵ God likewise predestined us through Christ Jesus to be adopted children—such was God's pleasure and will—⁶ that everyone might praise the glory of God's grace which was freely bestowed on us in God's beloved, Jesus Christ.

⁷ It is in Christ and through the blood of Christ that we have been redeemed and our sins forgiven, so immeasurably generous is God's favor ⁸ given to us with perfect wisdom and understanding. ⁹ God has taken pleasure in revealing the mystery of the plan through Christ, ¹⁰ to be carried out in the fullness of time; namely, to bring all things—in heaven and on earth—together in Christ.

¹¹ In Christ we were willed an inheritance; for in the decree of God—and everything is administered according to the divine will and counsel—we were predestined ¹² to praise the glory of the Most High by being the first to hope in Christ. ¹³ In Christ you too were chosen. When you heard the Good News of salvation, the word of truth, and believed in it, you were sealed with the promised Holy Spirit, ¹⁴ who is the pledge of our inheritance, the deposit paid against the full redemption of a people who are God's own—to the praise of God's glory.

¹⁵ From the time I first heard of your faith in Christ Jesus and your love for all of the holy ones, ¹⁶ I have never stopped thanking God for you and remembering you in my prayers. ¹⁷ I pray that the God of our Savior Jesus Christ, the God of glory, will give you a spirit of wisdom and of revelation, to bring you to a rich knowledge of the Creator.

¹⁸ I pray that God will enlighten the eyes of your mind so that you can see the hope this call holds for you—the promised glories that God's holy ones will inherit, ¹⁹ and the infinitely great power that is exercised for us who believe. You can tell this from the strength of God's power at work in Jesus, ²⁰ the power used to raise Christ from the dead and to seat Christ in heaven at God's right hand, ²¹ far above every sovereignty, authority, power or dominion, and above any other name that can be named—not only in this age, but also in the age to come. ²² God has put all things under Christ's feet and made Christ, as the ruler of everything, the head of the church, ²³ and the church is Christ's body; it's the fullness of the One who fills all of creation.

2:1–3:21

You were dead because of your sins and offenses, ² which you commited in your allegiance both to the present age and to the ruler of the power of the air—that spirit who is even now at work among "the children of rebellion." ³ And all of us were among them; we lived at the level of the flesh, following every whim of the flesh, every fancy of this age, and so by nature deserved God's wrath like the rest.

⁴ But God, rich in mercy and loving us so much, ⁵ brought us to life in Christ, even when we were dead in our sins. It is through this grace that we have been saved. ⁶ God raised us up and, in union with Christ Jesus, gave us a place in the heavenly realm, ⁷ to display in ages to come how immense are the resources of God's grace and kindness in Christ Jesus. ⁸ And it is by grace that you have been saved, through faith—and even that is not of yourselves, but the gift of God. ⁹ Nor is it a reward for anything that you have done, so nobody can claim the credit. ¹⁰ We are God's work of art, created in Christ Jesus to do the good things God created us to do from the beginning.

¹¹ Bear in mind that at one time the men among you who were Gentiles physically—called "the Uncircumcised" by those who call themselves "the Circumcised," all because of a minor operation—¹² had no part in Christ and were excluded from the community of Israel. You were strangers to the Covenant and its promise; you were without hope and without God in the world.

¹³ But now in Christ Jesus, you who once were far off have been brought near by the blood of Christ. ¹⁴ For Christ is our peace, who made both groups into one and broke down the barrier of hostility that kept us apart. ¹⁵ In his own flesh, Christ abolished the Law, with its commands and ordinances, in order to make the two into one new person, thus establishing peace ¹⁶ and reconciling us all to God in one body through the cross, which put to death the enmity between us. ¹⁷ Christ came and "announced the Good News of peace to you who were far away, and to those who were near"; ¹⁸ for through Christ, we all have access in one Spirit to our God.

¹⁹ This means that you are strangers and aliens no longer. No, you are included in God's holy people and are members of the household of God, ²⁰ which is built on the foundation of the apostles and the prophets, with Christ Jesus as the capstone. ²¹ In Christ the whole building is joined together and rises to become a holy temple in our God; ²² in Christ you are being built into this temple, to become a dwelling place of God in the Spirit.

3 ¹ For I, Paul—a prisoner of Christ Jesus for the sake of you Gentiles— ² am sure that you have heard of God's grace, of which I was made a steward on your behalf; ³ this mystery, as I have briefly described it, was given to me by revelation. ⁴ When you read this, you can understand my insight into the mystery of Christ, ⁵ which was unknown to the people of former ages, but is now revealed by the Spirit to the holy apostles and prophets. ⁶ That mystery is that the Gentiles are heirs, as are we; members of the Body, as are we; and partakers of the promise of Jesus the Messiah through the Good News, as are we.

⁷ I became a minister of the Good News by the gift of divine grace given me through the working of God's power. ⁸ To me, the least of all believers, was given the grace to preach to the Gentiles the unfathomable riches of Christ ⁹ and to enlighten all people on the mysterious design which for ages was hidden in God, the Creator of all.

¹⁰ Now, therefore, through the church, God's manifold wisdom is made known to the rulers and powers of heaven, ¹¹ in accord with the age-old design, carried out in Christ Jesus our Savior, ¹² in whom we have boldness and confident access to God through our faith in Christ. ¹³ So, I beg you,

never be discouraged because of my sufferings for you. They are your glory.

[14] That is why I kneel before Abba God, [15] from whom every family in heaven and on earth takes its name. [16] And I pray that God, out of the riches of divine glory, will strengthen you inwardly with power through the working of the Spirit. [17] May Christ dwell in your hearts through faith, so that you, being rooted and grounded in love, [18] will be able to grasp fully the breadth, length, height and depth of Christ's love and, with all God's holy ones, [19] experience this love that surpasses all understanding, so that you may be filled with all the fullness of God. [20] To God—whose power now at work in us can do immeasurably more than we ask or imagine—[21] to God be glory in the Church and in Christ Jesus through all generations, world without end! Amen.

4:1–5:20

I plead with you, then, in the name of our Redeemer, to lead a life worthy of your calling. [2] Treat one another charitably, in complete selflessness, gentleness and patience. [3] Do all you can to preserve the unity of the Spirit through the peace that binds you together. [4] There is one body and one Spirit—just as you were called into one hope when you were called. [5] There is one Savior, one faith, one baptism, [6] one God and Creator of all, who is over all, who works through all and is within all.

[7] Each of us has received God's grace in the measure in which Christ has bestowed it. [8] Thus you find scripture saying,

> "You ascended on high,
> leading captives in your train,
> and giving gifts to people."

[9] "You ascended"—what does this mean but that Christ first descended into the lower regions of the earth? [10] The One who descended is the very One who ascended high above the heavens in order to fill the whole universe.

[11] And to some, the gift they were given is that they should be apostles; to some, prophets; to some, evangelists; to some, pastors and teachers. [12] These gifts were given to equip fully the holy ones for the work of service, and to build up the body of Christ—[13] until we all attain unity in our faith and in our knowledge of the Only Begotten of God, until we become mature, attaining to the whole measure of the fullness of Christ.

[14] Let us then be children no longer, tossed here and there, carried about by every wind of doctrine, or by human trickery or crafty, deceitful schemes. [15] Rather, let us speak the truth in love, and grow to the full maturity of Christ, the head. [16] Through Christ, the whole body grows. With the proper functioning of each member, firmly joined together by each supporting ligament, the body builds itself up in love.

[17] So I declare and testify together with Christ that you must stop living the kind of life the world lives. Their minds are empty, [18] they have no understanding, they are alienated from the life of God—all because they have hardened their hearts. [19] They've dulled their sense of right and wrong, for they have abandoned themselves to sensuality in order to indulge in every form of licentiousness and greed.

[20] That is hardly the way you have learned from Christ, [21] unless you failed to hear properly, when you were taught what the truth is in Jesus. [22] You must give up your old way of life; you must put aside your old self, which is being corrupted by following illusory desires. [23] Your mind must be renewed by a spiritual revolution, [24] so that you can put on the new self that has been created in God's likeness, in the justice and holiness of the truth.

[25] Therefore, let's have no more lies. Speak truthfully to each other, for we are all members of one body.

[26] When you get angry, don't let it become a sin. Don't let the sun set on your anger, [27] or you will give an opening to the Devil.

[28] You who have been stealing, stop stealing. Go to work. Do something useful with your hands, so you can have something to share with the needy.

[29] Be on your guard against foul talk. Say only what will build others up at that moment. Say only what will give grace to your listeners.

[30] Don't grieve the Holy Spirit of God, with whom you were sealed for the day of redemption. [31] Get rid of all bitterness, all rage and anger, all harsh words, slander and malice of every kind. [32] In place of these, be kind to one another, compassionate and mutually forgiving, just as God has forgiven you in Christ.

[5:1] Try, then, to imitate God as beloved children. [2] Walk in love as Christ loved us, and offered himself in sacrifice to God for us, a gift of pleasing fragrance.

[3] As for lewd conduct or promiscuousness or lust of any sort, let these things not even be mentioned among you, as befitting God's holy people. [4] Nor should there be any obscene, silly or suggestive talk; all that is out of place. Instead, give thanks. [5] Make no mistake about this: no promiscuous, unclean or lustful person—in effect an idolator—has any inheritance in the kindom of Christ and of God. [6] Let no one deceive you with worthless arguments: these are sins that bring God's wrath down on the disobedient; [7] therefore, have nothing to do with them. [8] There was a time when you were darkness, but now you are light in Christ. Live as children of the light.

[9] Light produces every kind of goodness, justice and truth. [10] Be correct in your judgment of what pleases our Savior. [11] Take no part in deeds done in darkness, which bear no fruit; rather, expose them. [12] It's shameful even to mention the things these people do in secret; [13] but when such deeds are exposed and seen in the light of day, everything that becomes visible is light. [14] That's why we read,

> "Awake, O sleeper, arise from the dead,
> and Christ will give you light."

[15] Keep careful watch over your conduct. Don't act like fools, but like wise and thoughtful people. [16] Make the most of your time, for these are evil days. [17] Don't continue in ignorance, but try to discern the will of God. [18] Avoid getting drunk on wine—that is debauchery! Instead be filled with the Spirit, [19] meditating on psalms and hymns and spiritual songs, singing and making music to God in your hearts. [20] Always give thanks to Abba God for everything, in the name of Jesus our Messiah.

5:21–6:9

Defer to one another out of reverence for Christ. [22] Those of you who are in committed relationships should yield to each other as if to Christ, [23] because you are inseparable from each other, just as Christ is inseparable from the body—the church—as well as being its Savior. [24] As the church yields to Christ, so you should yield to your partner in everything.

[25] Love one another as Christ loved the church. He gave himself up for it [26] to make it holy, purifying it by washing it with the Gospel's message, [27] so that Christ might have a

glorious church, holy and immaculate, without mark or blemish or anything of that sort. [28] Love one another as you love your own bodies. Those who love their partners love themselves. [29] No one ever hates one's own flesh; one nourishes it and takes care of it as Christ cares for the church—[30] for we are members of Christ's body.

[31] "This is why one person leaves home
and clings to another,
and the two become one flesh."

[32] This is a great foreshadowing; I mean, it refers to Christ and the church. [33] In any case, each of you should love your partner as yourself, with each showing respect for the other.

6 [1] Children, obey your parents in Christ, for that is right. [2] "Honor your mother and your father" is the first commandment to carry a promise with it: [3] "that it may go well with you, and that you may have long life on earth." [4] Mothers and fathers, don't anger your children. Bring them up with the training and instruction befitting Christ.

[5] Workers, work diligently and support one another with the respect and sincere loyalty that you owe to Christ. [6] Don't render service just for appearance's sake, or only to please others, but do God's will with your whole heart as Christ's own workers. [7] Give your service willingly, doing it for Christ rather than for mortals. [8] You know that everyone, whether on the bottom rung or on the top, will be repaid by God for whatever they do. [9] When you are in a position of authority, act responsibly toward those in your charge. Stop threatening them. Remember that we all have a greater Authority over us in heaven who plays no favorites.

Finally, draw your strength from Christ and from the strength of that mighty power. [11] Put on the full armor of God so that you can stand firm against the tactics of the Devil. [12] Our battle ultimately is not against human forces, but against the sovereignties and powers, the rulers of the world of darkness, and the evil spirits of the heavenly realms. [13] You must put on the armor of God if you are to resist on the evil day and, having done everything you can, to hold your ground. [14] Stand fast then, with truth as the belt around your waist, justice as your breastplate, [15] and zeal to spread the Good News of peace as your footgear. [16] In all circumstances, hold faith up before you as your shield; it will help you extinguish the fiery darts of the Evil One. [17] Put on the helmet of salvation, and carry the sword of the Spirit, which is the word of God.

[18] Always pray in the Spirit, with all your prayers and petitions. Pray constantly and attentively for all God's holy people. [19] Pray also for me, that God will open my mouth and put words on my lips, that I may boldly make known the mystery of the Good News—that mystery [20] for which I am an ambassador in chains. Pray that I may have courage to proclaim it as I ought.

[21] I would like you to have news of me and of what I am doing. My dear coworker, Tychicus, a loyal minister in Christ, will tell you everything. [22] I am sending him to you precisely for this purpose—to reassure you and give you news of us.

[23] May God our Creator and our Savior Jesus Christ bring peace, love and faith to all our sisters and brothers. [24] May grace and eternal life be with all who love our Savior Jesus Christ.

philippians

From Paul and Timothy, who serve Christ Jesus,

To all the holy ones in Christ Jesus at Philippi, together with their bishops and deacons:

[2] Grace and peace be yours from our Abba God and from Jesus Christ, our Savior.

[3] I thank my God every time I think of you. [4] In every prayer I utter, as I plead on your behalf, I rejoice [5] at the way you have all continually helped promote the Good News from the very first day. [6] And I am sure of this much: that God, who has begun the good work in you, will carry it through to completion, right up to the day of Christ Jesus. [7] It's only right that I should entertain such expectations about you, since I hold all of you dear—you who are all partakers of grace with me, even when I lie in prison or am summoned to defend the solid ground on which the Good News rests.

[8] God knows how much I long for each of you with all the affection of Christ Jesus! [9] My prayer is that your love may abound more and more, both in understanding and in wealth of experience, [10] so that with a clear conscience and blameless conduct you may learn to value the things that really matter, up to the very day of Christ. [11] It's my wish that you be found rich in the harvest of justice which Jesus Christ has ripened in you, to the glory and praise of God.

I'm glad to announce to you, sisters and brothers, that what has happened to me has actually served to advance the Good News. [13] Consequently it has become clear throughout the Praetorium and everywhere else that I am in chains for Christ. [14] Because of my chains, most of our sisters and brothers in Christ have been encouraged to speak the word of God more fearlessly.

[15] It's true that some preach Christ out of envy and rivalry, but others do so with the right intention. [16] These latter act out of love, aware that I am here in the defense of the Good News. [17] The others, who proclaim Christ for selfish or jealous motives, don't care if they make my chains heavier to bear.

[18] All that matters is that in any and every way, whether from specious or genuine motives, Christ is being proclaimed! That is what brings me joy. [19] Indeed, I will continue to rejoice in the conviction that this will result in my salvation, thanks to your prayers and the support I receive from the Spirit of Jesus Christ. [20] I firmly trust and anticipate that I will never be put to shame for my hopes; I have full confidence that, now as always, Christ will be exalted through me, whether I live or die.

[21] For to me, "life" means Christ; hence, dying is only so much gain. [22] If, on the other hand, I am to continue living on earth, that means productive toil for me—and I honestly don't know which I prefer. [23] I'm strongly attracted to both: I

long to be freed from this life and to be with Christ, for that is the far better thing; 24 yet it's more urgent that I remain alive for your sakes. 25 This fills me with the confidence that I will stay with you and persevere with you all, for the sake of your joy and your progress in the faith. 26 My being with you once again should make you even prouder of me in Christ.

27 Conduct yourselves, then, in a way worthy of the Gospel of Christ. If you do, whether I come and see you myself or hear about your behavior from a distance, it will be clear that you're standing firm in unity of spirit, and exerting yourselves with one accord for the faith of the Gospel, 28 without being intimidated by your enemies. Standing together without fear is an indication that they will be destroyed and you will be saved. It's a divine signal that God— 29 on behalf of our Savior—has given you the privilege of believing in and suffering for Christ. 30 You're now experiencing the same struggle that you saw in me—and now hear that I still have.

2 1 If our life in Christ means anything to you—if love, or the Spirit that we have in common, or any tenderness or sympathy can persuade you at all— 2 then be united in your convictions and united in your love, with a common purpose and a common mind. That is the one thing that would make me completely happy. 3 There must be no competition among you, no conceit, but everybody is to be humble: value others over yourselves, 4 each of you thinking of the interests of others before your own. 5 Your attitude must be the same as that of Christ Jesus:

6   Christ, though in the image of God,
     didn't deem equality with God
     something to be clung to—
7   but instead became completely empty
     and took on the image of oppressed humankind:
     born into the human condition,
     found in the likeness of a human being.
8   Jesus was thus humbled—
     obediently accepting death, even death on a cross!
9   Because of this, God highly exalted Christ
     and gave to Jesus the name above every other name,
10   so that at the name of Jesus every knee must bend
     in the heavens, on the earth and under the earth,
11   and every tongue proclaim to the glory of God:
     Jesus Christ reigns supreme!

12 Therefore, my dear friends, you who are always obedient to my urging, work out your salvation with fear and trembling, not only when I happen to be with you, but all the more now that I'm absent. 13 It is God at work in you that creates the desire to do God's will.

14 In everything you do, act without grumbling or arguing; 15 prove yourselves innocent and straightforward, children of God beyond reproach, in the midst of a twisted and depraved generation—among which you shine like stars in the sky, 16 while holding fast to the word of life. As I look to the day of Christ, you give me cause to boast, proving that I didn't run the race in vain or work to no purpose. 17 Even if my life is to be poured out like a libation upon the sacrificial offering of your faith, I'm glad of it and rejoice with all of you. 18 May you be glad for the same reason, and rejoice with me!

2:19–3:16

I hope in our Savior Jesus to send Timothy to you soon. And I will be cheered when I hear news of you. 20 I have no one else here like him, and he's genuinely concerned about you. 21 All the others seem more interested in their own welfare than in Christ Jesus. 22 But you know how Timothy proved himself—as a child helping a parent—by working with me to further the Good News. 23 So I intend to send him as soon as I see how things go with me. 24 And I am confident in Christ that I, too, will be coming soon.

25 I feel I need to send back to you Epaphroditus—brother, coworker, spiritual warrior—who is also your messenger to me, the one you sent to be my companion in work and in battle. 26 But he misses you all and was distressed when he learned that you had heard of his illness. 27 Yes, he was sick; he almost died. But God had mercy on him—and on me as well, so that I wouldn't have one grief on top of another. 28 I'll be sending him back as soon as I can. I know you'll be happy to see him again, and that will make me less worried about you. 29 Welcome him heartily in Christ—people like him should be held in the highest regard. 30 Know that he came so close to death in doing the work of Christ. He risked his life to give me the help that you were unable to provide.

3 1 Finally, my sisters and brothers, rejoice in Christ. To write the same things again is no burden for me, but I do it for your safety.

2 Beware of the dogs! Beware of the troublemakers! Beware of the mutilators, who insist that Gentile Christians must become circumcised! 3 We are the true circumcision—we are ourselves the sign of the Covenant—each and every one of us who worships in the Spirit of God and glories in Christ Jesus, rather than trusts in external signs.

4 Yet I can be confident even there! If they think they have the right to put their trust in external evidence, I have even more right! 5 I was circumcised on the eighth day, being of the stock of Israel and the tribe of Benjamin, a Hebrew of Hebrew origins; in legal observance I was a Pharisee, 6 and so zealous that I persecuted the church. I was above reproach when it came to justice based on the Law.

7 But those things I used to consider gain, I now count as loss for the sake of Christ. 8 What is more, I consider everything a loss in light of the surpassing knowledge of my Savior Jesus Christ, for whose sake I have forfeited everything. I count everything else as garbage, so that Christ may be my wealth— 9 indeed, that I may be found in Christ, not having any justice of my own based on observance of the Law. The justice I possess is that which comes through faith in Christ. It has its origin in God and is based on faith. 10 All I want is to know Christ, and the power of the resurrection, and how to share in Christ's sufferings by being formed into the pattern of Jesus' death— 11 perhaps even to arrive at the resurrection from the dead.

12 It's not that I have reached it yet, or have already finished my course; but I'm running the race in order to grab hold of the prize if possible, since Christ Jesus has grabbed hold of me. 13 Sisters and brothers, I don't think of myself as having reached the finish line. I give no thought to what lies behind, but I push on to what is ahead. 14 My entire attention is on the finish line as I run toward the prize—the high calling of God in Christ Jesus.

15 We who are mature should adopt this attitude. And if you have a different opinion on any matter, God will make that clear to you as well. 16 Just resolve to live up to what we have already attained.

3:17–4:23

Join in following my example, my sisters and brothers. Take as your guide those who follow the example that we set. 18 Unfortunately, many go about in a way which shows them to be enemies of the cross of Christ. I have often said this to you before; this time I say it with tears: ¹⁹ their end is destruction, their god is their belly, and their glory is in their shame. I'm talking about those whose minds are set on the things of this world.

²⁰ But we have our citizenship in heaven; it's from there that we eagerly await the coming of our Savior Jesus Christ, ²¹ who will give a new form to this lowly body of ours and remake it according to the pattern of the glorified body, by Christ's power to bring everything under subjection.

4 ¹ For these reasons, my sisters and brothers—you whom I so love and long for, you who are my joy and my crown—continue, my dear ones, to stand firm in Christ Jesus.

² I implore Euodia and Syntyche to come to an agreement with each other in Christ. ³ And I ask you, Syzygus, to be a true comrade and help these coworkers. These two women struggled at my side in defending the Good News, along with Clement and the others who worked with me. Their names are written in the Book of Life.

⁴ Rejoice in the Savior always! I say it again: Rejoice! ⁵ Let everyone see your forbearing spirit. Our Savior is near. ⁶ Dismiss all anxiety from your minds; instead, present your needs to God through prayer and petition, giving thanks for all circumstances. ⁷ Then God's own peace, which is beyond all understanding, will stand guard over your hearts and minds in Christ Jesus.

⁸ Finally, my sisters and brothers, your thoughts should be wholly directed to all that is true, all that deserves respect, all that is honest, pure, decent, admirable, virtuous or worthy of praise. ⁹ Live according to what you have learned and accepted, what you have heard me say and seen me do. Then will the God of peace be with you.

¹⁰ It gave me great joy in our God that your concern for me bore fruit once more. You had been concerned all along, of course, but lacked the opportunity to show it. ¹¹ I don't say this because I am in need, for whatever the situation I find myself in, I have learned to be self-sufficient. ¹² I know what it is to be brought low, and I know what it is to have plenty. I have learned the secret: whether on a full stomach or an empty one, in poverty or plenty, ¹³ I can do all things through the One who gives me strength.

¹⁴ Still, it was kind of you to want to share in my hardships. ¹⁵ You yourselves know, my dear Philippians, that at the start of my evangelizing, when I left Macedonia, not a single congregation except yours shared with me by giving me something for what it had received. ¹⁶ Even when I was at Thessalonica, you sent something for my needs, not once but twice. ¹⁷ It's not that I am eager for the gift; rather, my concern is for the ever-growing balance in your account. ¹⁸ Here's my receipt—it says I've been fully paid, and more. I am well supplied because of what I received from you through Epaphroditus—a fragrant offering—a sacrifice acceptable and pleasing to God.

¹⁹ In return, our God will fulfill all your needs in Christ Jesus, as lavishly as only God can. ²⁰ All glory to our God and Creator for unending ages! Amen.

²¹ Give my greetings to all the holy ones in Christ Jesus. The sisters and brothers who are with me send their greetings. ²² All the holy ones send their greetings, especially those who belong to Caesar's household.

²³ The grace of our Savior Jesus Christ be with your spirit.

colossíans

1:1–20

From Paul, an apostle of Christ Jesus by the will of God, and our brother Timothy,

² To the holy and faithful sisters and brothers in Christ at Colossae:

Grace and peace to you from our Loving God.

³ We always give thanks to the Abba God of our Savior Jesus Christ whenever we pray for you, ⁴ ever since we heard about your faith in Christ Jesus and the love you show toward all the holy ones, ⁵ because of the hope stored up for you in heaven. It is only recently that you heard of this, when it was announced in the message of the truth. The Good News ⁶ which has reached you is spreading all over the world; it is producing the same fruit there as it did among you, ever since you heard about God's grace and understood what it really is. ⁷ Epaphras, who taught you, is one of our closest coworkers and a faithful laborer of Christ on our behalf, ⁸ and it was he who told us all about your love in the Spirit.

⁹ Therefore, since the day we heard about you, we've been praying for you unceasingly and asking that you attain the full knowledge of God's will, in perfect wisdom and spiritual understanding. ¹⁰ Then you'll lead a life worthy and pleasing to our God in every way. You'll multiply good works of every sort and grow in the knowledge of God. ¹¹ And by the might of God's glory you'll be endowed with the strength needed to stand fast and endure joyfully whatever may happen.

¹² Thanks be to God for having made you worthy to share in the inheritance of the holy ones in light! ¹³ God rescued us from the authority of darkness and brought us into the reign of Jesus, God's Only Begotten. ¹⁴ And it is through Jesus that we have redemption, the forgiveness of sins.

¹⁵ Christ is the image of the unseen God
and the firstborn of all creation,
¹⁶ for in Christ were created
all things in heaven and on earth:
everything visible and invisible,
Thrones, Dominations, Sovereignties, Powers—
all things were created through Christ and for Christ.
¹⁷ Before anything was created, Christ existed,
and all things hold together in Christ.
¹⁸ The church is the body;
Christ is its head.
Christ is the Beginning,
the firstborn from the dead,
and so Christ is first in every way.
¹⁹ God wanted all perfection to be found in Christ,
²⁰ and all things to be reconciled to God through
Christ—
everything in heaven and everything on earth—
when Christ made peace
by dying on the cross.

1:21–2:8

At one time, you were alienated from God by the way you thought and the evil things you did. ²² But now you are reconciled in Christ's mortal body through death, so that you can now stand before God holy, pure and blameless—²³ provided you persevere and stand firm on the solid base of your faith. Never let yourselves drift away from the hope promised by the Good News that you have heard, which even now is being preached to the whole human race, and for which I, Paul, was made a minister.

²⁴ Even now I find my joy in the suffering I endure for you. In my own body I fill up what is lacking in the sufferings of Jesus, for the sake of Christ's body, the church. ²⁵ I became a minister of this church through the commission God gave me, to preach among you the word in its fullness— ²⁶ that mystery hidden from ages and generations past, but now revealed to God's holy ones. ²⁷ God's will was to make known to them the priceless glory which this mystery brings to the nations—the mystery of Christ in you, the hope of glory. ²⁸ This is the Christ we proclaim while we admonish everyone and teach them in the full measure of wisdom, hoping to make everyone complete in our Savior. ²⁹ For this I work and struggle, impelled by Christ's own working, which is so powerful a force in me.

2 ¹ I want you to know how hard I am struggling for you and for the Laodiceans, and for the many others who have never seen me personally. ² I work so that their hearts will be strengthened, so that they will be knit together in love, enriched with full assurance by their knowledge of the mystery of God—namely Christ—³ in whom every treasure of wisdom and knowledge is hidden.

⁴ I say this so that no one deceives you with persuasive arguments. ⁵ I may be absent in body, but I'm with you in spirit. I rejoice in seeing your good discipline and your firm faith in Christ.

⁶ Since you have received Christ Jesus, live your whole life in our Savior. ⁷ Send your roots deep and grow strong in Christ—firmly established in the faith you've been taught, and full of thanksgiving. ⁸ Make sure that no one traps you and deprives you of your freedom by some secondhand, empty and deceptive philosophy that is based on the principles of the world instead of Christ.

2:9–3:17

In Christ the fullness of divinity lives in bodily form, ¹⁰ and in Christ you find your own fulfillment—in the One who is the head of every Sovereignty and Power. ¹¹ In Christ you have been given the Covenant through a transformation performed not by human hands, but by the complete stripping away of your body of flesh. This is what "circumcision" in Christ means. ¹² In baptism you were not only buried with Christ but also raised to life, because you believed in the power of God who raised Christ from the dead. ¹³ And though you were dead in sin and did not have the Covenant, God gave you new life in company with Christ, pardoning all our sins. ¹⁴ God has canceled the massive debt that stood against us with all its hostile claims, taking it out of the way and nailing it to the cross. ¹⁵ In this way God disarmed the Principalities and the Powers and made a public display of them after having triumphed over them at the cross.

¹⁶ From now on, don't let anyone pass judgment on you because of what you eat or drink, or whether you observe festivals, new moons or Sabbaths. ¹⁷ These are mere shadows of the reality that is to come; the substance is Christ. ¹⁸ Don't let those who worship angels and enjoy self-abasement judge you. These people go into great detail about their visions, and their worldly minds keep puffing up their already inflated egos. ¹⁹ These people are cut off from the head that, with the ligaments and sinews, holds the whole body together, in order to attain its fullness of being in God.

²⁰ So if, in Christ, you've really died to the elemental principles of this world, why do you let regulations dictate to you, as though you were still living in the world? ²¹ "Don't handle this!" "Don't taste that!" "Don't touch those!" ²² These prohibitions concern things that perish with use. They are concerned with human values and regulations. ²³ These values and rules—through self-abasement, self-imposed religious practices and false humility—give the impression of true wisdom, but they have no value in restraining licentiousness.

3 ¹ Since you've been resurrected with Christ, set your heart on what pertains to higher realms, where Christ is seated at God's right hand. ² Let your thoughts be on heavenly things, not on the things of earth. ³ After all, you died, and now your life is hidden with Christ in God. ⁴ But when Christ—who is your life—is revealed, you too will be revealed with Christ in glory.

⁵ So put to death everything in you that belongs to your old nature: promiscuity, impurity, guilty passion, evil desires and especially greed, which is the same thing as idolatry. ⁶ These are the sins which provoke God's wrath. ⁷ Your own conduct was once like this, when these things were your very life. ⁸ But now you must rid yourselves of them all: anger, rage, malice, slander and abusive language. ⁹ Stop lying to one another.

What you have done is put aside your old self with its past deeds ¹⁰ and put on a new self, one that grows in knowledge as it is formed anew in the image of its Creator. ¹¹ And in that image, there is no Greek or Hebrew; no Jew or Gentile; no barbarian or Scythian; no slave or citizen. There is only Christ, who is all in all.

¹² Because you are God's chosen ones, holy and beloved, clothe yourselves with heartfelt compassion, with kindness, humility, gentleness and patience. ¹³ Bear with one another; forgive whatever grievances you have against one another—forgive in the same way God has forgiven you. ¹⁴ Above all else, put on love, which binds the rest together and makes them perfect.

¹⁵ Let Christ's peace reign in your hearts since, as members of one body, you have been called to that peace. Dedicate yourselves to thankfulness. ¹⁶ Let the Word of Christ, rich as it is, dwell in you. Instruct and admonish one another wisely. Sing gratefully to God from your hearts in psalms, hymns and songs of the Spirit. ¹⁷ And whatever you do, whether in speech or in action, do it in the name of Jesus our Savior, giving thanks to God through Christ.

3:18–4:6

You who are in committed relationships, be submissive to each other. This is your duty in Christ Jesus. ¹⁹ Partners joined by God, love each other. Avoid any bitterness between you. ²⁰ Children, obey those responsible for you in everything, for this is what pleases God the most. 21 And if you are responsible for children, don't nag them, lest they lose heart.

22 Workers, work diligently in everything you do—not only to win favor, but wholeheartedly and reverently, out of respect for Christ. 23 Do whatever you do from the heart. You are working for Christ, not for people. 24 You know you'll be rewarded by God with an inheritance. You serve our Savior Jesus Christ. 25 Anyone who does wrong will be paid in kind, without partiality. 4:1 When you are in a position of authority, treat your people with justice and fairness. We all have an Authority over us in heaven.

2 Devote yourself to prayer and thanksgiving, but keep alert as well. 3 Pray for us, too, that God will open a door for proclaiming the mystery of Christ, for which I am in prison. 4 Pray that I may proclaim it as clearly as I should. 5 Be wise in your ways toward non-Christians. Make the most of every opportunity you have with them. 6 Talk to them tactfully, seasoned with salt as it were, and know how to respond to the needs of each one.

4:7–18

Tychicus will tell you all the news about me. He is a beloved brother, a loyal coworker and companion in the service of Christ. 8 I send him to you for the express purpose of reassuring you with news about us—and to encourage your hearts. 9 Onesimus, who is one with you and a faithful and dear brother to me, will be accompanying Tychicus. They will tell you everything that is happening here.

10 Aristarchus, who is here in prison with me, sends greetings, as does Barnabas' cousin Mark, about whom you have received these instructions: if he comes to you, greet him warmly. 11 Joshua, who is called Justus, sends greetings as well. Of those working with me for God's kindom, these three are the only Jewish believers. They are a great comfort to me. 12 Epaphras, who is one of your number and who serves Jesus Christ, sends greetings. He never stops laboring in prayer for you, so that you'll stand firm and hold securely to the will of God. 13 I can speak for him that he works hard for you and for those at Laodicea and Hierapolis. 14 My dear friend Luke, the doctor, sends greetings, as does Demas.

15 Pass on my greetings to the sisters and brothers at Laodicea, to Nympha, and to the church in her house. 16 After this letter has been read among you, send it to be read in the church of the Laodiceans, and get the letter I'm sending to Laodicea and read it to your church. 17 Tell Archippus, "See to it that you carry out the work that our God wants you to do."

18 I, Paul, write this greeting in my own hand. Remember my chains. Grace be with you.

1 thessalonians

1:1–10

From Paul, Silas and Timothy,
To the people of the church in Thessalonica, who belong to Abba God and our Savior Jesus Christ:
May grace and peace be yours.

2 We always thank God for all of you and remember you in our prayers. 3 We call to mind before our God and Creator how you are proving your faith by your actions, laboring in love, and showing constancy of hope in our Savior Jesus Christ.

4 We know, sisters and brothers beloved of God, that you have been chosen. 5 Our preaching of the Gospel was not a mere matter of words. It was done in the power of the Holy Spirit and with complete conviction. You know very well the sort of life we led when we were with you, which was for your sake.

6 You, in turn, followed the example set by us and by Jesus—receiving the word, despite great trials, with the joy that comes from the Holy Spirit. 7 In this way, you've become a model for all the believers in Macedonia and Achaia.

8 The word of Christ has been resounding from you—and not only in Macedonia and Achaia: the news of your faith in God is celebrated everywhere, which makes it unnecessary for us to say anything more. 9 They themselves report to us what kind of reception we had among you, how you turned from idols to God, to be faithful witnesses of the living and true God, 10 and to await the appearance from heaven of Jesus, the Only Begotten, whom God raised from the dead and who will deliver us from the wrath to come.

2:1–3:8

And you yourselves know, sisters and brothers, that our coming among you was not without effect. 2 We had, as you know, been given rough treatment at Philippi, and it was our God who gave us the courage to proclaim the Good News to you in the face of stiff opposition. 3 We don't preach because of impure motives or deceit or any sort of trickery; 4 rather, it was God who decided that we are fit to be entrusted with the Good News, and when we are speaking, we're trying to please not mortals, but God, who can read our inmost thoughts.

5 You know very well—and we can swear it before God—that never at any time has our speech been simple flattery or a cover for trying to get money; 6 nor have we ever looked for any special honor from you or from anyone else—even though we could have imposed ourselves on you as apostles of Christ. 7 On the contrary, while we were with you we were as gentle as any nursing mother caring for her little ones. 8 So well disposed were we toward you, in fact, that we were willing to share with you not only the Good News, but our very lives as well—you had become that dear to us.

9 Let us remind you, sisters and brothers, of our toil and hardship; we worked night and day in order not to be a burden to anyone while we preached the Good News of God to you. 10 You are witnesses, and so is God, that our treatment of you since you have become believers has been just, upright and impeccable. 11 You likewise know how we treated every one of you, as parents do their children—encouraging, comforting and urging you 12 to live lives worthy of God, who calls you into glory and the kindom. 13 And we constantly thank God for the way you received the words we preached to you, not as our word but as the word of God, which it really was. And it changed your lives when you believed it.

14 For you, sisters and brothers, have become imitators of the churches of God in Christ Jesus that are in Judea. You suffered the same things from your own compatriots as they, in turn, did from the Judeans— 15 who killed our Savior Jesus and the prophets and drove us out of the country. They don't please God and are hostile to everyone else, 16 because they hinder us from preaching to the Gentiles—which fills the measuring cup of their sins to overflowing. But the wrath of God has finally started to overtake them.

¹⁷ However, sisters and brothers, soon after we were separated from you—in body but never in heart—we were all the more desirous of seeing you face to face. ¹⁸ We wanted to come to you—I, Paul, tried more than once—but Satan prevented it. ¹⁹ For what is our hope, or joy, or the crown in which we glory in our Savior Jesus at the Coming? It's you: ²⁰ you are our glory and joy.

3 ¹ When we could bear it no longer, we decided to be left behind in Athens, ² and instead sent Timothy, our companion and God's coworker in spreading the Good News of Christ. His assignment was to encourage you and keep you strong in your faith, ³ so that none of you would become unsettled by the present troubles. You knew very well that we were destined to encounter them; ⁴ even when we were with you, we warned you to expect persecution. And that is exactly what you've found. ⁵ I couldn't stand it any more, so I sent someone to check on your faith; I was afraid the Tempter might have tried to test you, and our efforts might have been in vain.

⁶ Now Timothy is back from visiting you, and he has told us good things about your faith and love, that you have fond memories of us and want to see us just as much as we want to see you. ⁷ We have been much consoled by your faith throughout our distress and persecution—⁸ so much so that we will continue to flourish only if you stand firm in our Savior.

How can we thank God enough for you, for all the joy we feel before God on your account? ¹⁰ We earnestly pray night and day to be able to see you again and make up for any shortcomings in your faith. ¹¹ May our loving Abba God and Jesus, our Savior, direct our steps back to you. ¹² May Christ increase to overflowing your love for one another and for all people, even as our love does for you; ¹³ may Christ strengthen your hearts, making them blameless and holy before our Abba God at the coming of our Savior Jesus with all the holy ones.

4 ¹ Now, my sisters and brothers, we urge you and appeal to you in our Savior Jesus, to make more and more progress in the kind of life that you are meant to live—the life that God wants, as you learned from us, and as you are already living it. ² You haven't forgotten the instructions we gave you by the authority of our Savior Jesus. ³ What God wants is for you all to be holy. God wants each of you to keep away from sexual immorality ⁴ and learn to control your own body in a manner that is holy and honorable, ⁵ and not be mired in passionate lust like the Gentiles who do not know God; ⁶ and in this matter no one should wrong their neighbors or take advantage of them. The Almighty will punish us for all such sins, as we have already told you and warned you. ⁷ God calls us not to immorality but to holiness. ⁸ Therefore, whoever rejects these instructions rejects not mortals but God, who gives you the Holy Spirit.

⁹ As regards love for other believers, there is no need for me to write you. God already has taught you to love one another, ¹⁰ and this you are doing toward all the sisters and brothers throughout Macedonia. Yet we exhort you to even greater progress. ¹¹ Make it a point of honor to lead a quiet life and attend to your own affairs. Work with your hands as we directed you to do, ¹² so that you'll be a good example to outsiders and not be dependent on anybody.

Sisters and brothers, we want you to be clear about those who sleep in death; otherwise you might yield to grief and lose all hope. ¹⁴ For if we believe that Jesus died and rose again, in the same way God will bring with Jesus all who have fallen asleep believing in Jesus. ¹⁵ We are speaking to you now just as if Jesus were speaking to you: we who live, who survive until Jesus returns, will have no advantage over those who have fallen asleep. ¹⁶ No, Jesus will personally come down from heaven with a shout, at the sound of the archangel's voice and the trumpet of God, and those who have died in Christ will rise first. ¹⁷ Then we the living, the survivors, will be caught up with them in the clouds to meet Jesus in the air—and thenceforth we will be with Jesus unceasingly. ¹⁸ Therefore console one another with these words.

5 ¹ But as to specific times and eras, sisters and brothers, you don't need me to tell you anything— ² you know very well that the Day of God is coming like a thief in the night. ³ Just when people are saying, "At last we have peace and security," then destruction will fall on them with the suddenness of labor pains, and there will be no escape.

⁴ But you, sisters and brothers, are not in the dark. The Day of God will not catch you like a thief. ⁵ No, you are all children of light and children of the day. We don't belong to the darkness or the night. ⁶ So let's not be asleep as others are—let's be awake and sober! ⁷ Those who sleep do so at night, and those who get drunk do so at night. ⁸ But we belong to the day, so let us be sober. Let us put on the breastplate of faith and love, and the helmet of the hope of salvation.

⁹ God has destined us not to suffer wrath, but to receive salvation through our Savior Jesus Christ, ¹⁰ who died for us so that, whether awake or asleep, we might live together with Christ. ¹¹ So encourage each other and build each other up, just as you're already doing.

We ask you, sisters and brothers, to respect those who labor among you, who have charge over you in Christ as your teachers. ¹³ Esteem them highly, with a special love because of their work.

Live in peace with each other.

¹⁴ We urge you, sisters and brothers, to warn the idlers, cheer up the fainthearted, support the weak, and be patient with everyone. ¹⁵ Make sure that no one repays one evil with another. Always seek what is good for each other—and for all people.

¹⁶ Rejoice always, ¹⁷ pray constantly, ¹⁸ and give thanks for everything—for this is God's will for you in Christ Jesus.

¹⁹ Don't stifle the Spirit; ²⁰ don't despise the prophetic gift. ²¹ But test everything and accept only what is good. ²² Avoid any semblance of evil.

²³ May the God of peace make you perfect in holiness. May you be preserved whole and complete—spirit, soul, and body—irreproachable at the coming of our Savior Jesus Christ. ²⁴ The One who calls us is trustworthy: God will make sure it comes to pass.

²⁵ Sisters and brothers, pray for us.

²⁶ Greet all the sisters and brothers with a holy kiss. ²⁷ My orders, in the name of Christ, are that this letter is to be read to all the sisters and brothers.

²⁸ The grace of our Savior Jesus Christ be with you.

2 thessalonians

1:1–12

From Paul, Silas and Timothy,

To the church of the Thessalonians, who belong to our Abba God and our Savior Jesus Christ:

² Grace and peace be yours from our Abba God and our Savior Jesus Christ.

³ It's only right that we thank God unceasingly for you, sisters and brothers, because your faith grows more and more, and your love for each other increases—⁴ so much so that in God's churches we boast about your perseverance and faith in the midst of all the persecutions and trials you are enduring. ⁵ All this is evidence that God's judgment is right, and as a result you'll be counted worthy of the dominion of God, for which you are suffering.

⁶ Know that God is just, and will repay with affliction those who afflict you. ⁷ God will give relief to you who are suffering now, and to us as well, when our Savior Jesus will be revealed in blazing fire from heaven with the mighty angels. ⁸ Jesus will punish those who don't acknowledge God—and those who don't obey the Good News of our Savior Jesus. ⁹ Their punishment will be eternal destruction—separation from the presence of Christ and the majesty of Christ's power—¹⁰ on the day Christ comes to be glorified in the saints and to be marveled at by the faithful. You are included because you believed our testimony to you.

¹¹ Knowing all this, we pray continually that God will make you worthy of the call, fulfill all your desires for goodness, and empower all your works of faith. ¹² In this way, the name of our Savior Jesus Christ will be glorified in you, and you in Christ, by the grace of our God and of our Savior Jesus Christ.

2:1–17

Concerning the coming of Jesus Christ and our being gathered to meet our Savior, we beg you, sisters and brothers, ² don't become easily agitated or disturbed by some prophecy, report or letter falsely attributed to us, which says that the day of our Savior has come. ³ Let no one deceive you, in any way. It cannot happen until the Great Falling Away occurs, and the rebel, the Lost One, has appeared.

⁴ This is the Enemy, the one who claims to be so much greater than all that people call "God," greater than every object of worship—so much so that it enthrones itself in God's sanctuary and claims to be God. ⁵ Surely you remember me telling you these things when I was with you?

⁶ And now you also know what is holding the Lost One back now, only to appear at the proper time. ⁷ Rebellion is already at work, but secretly, and the one who holds it back must be removed first. ⁸ Then the Rebel will appear openly, whom Christ will destroy with nothing more than a breath, bringing that rebellion to an end with the revelation of Christ's presence.

⁹ Christ's coming, however, will coincide with the activity of Satan. There will be all kinds of fake miracles, signs and wonders. ¹⁰ There will be every form of evil to deceive those already bound for destruction, because they would not grasp the love of the truth that could have saved them. ¹¹ The reason God sends them such a delusive influence—and therefore makes them believe a lie— ¹² is to condemn all who have not believed the truth, but chose evil instead.

¹³ But we ought to thank God always for you, sisters and brothers loved by Christ, because God chose you from the beginning—to be saved by the sanctifying Spirit and by believing in the truth.

¹⁴ God called you through our preaching of the Good News, so that you might gain the glory of our Savior Jesus Christ. ¹⁵ Therefore, sisters and brothers, stand firm. Hold fast to the traditions you received from us, either by word of mouth or by letter. ¹⁶ May our Savior Jesus Christ and our Abba God—who loved us and in mercy gave us eternal consolation and hope— ¹⁷ console your hearts and strengthen them for every good work and word.

3:1–18

Finally, sisters and brothers, pray for us that the message of Christ may spread rapidly and be honored, as it was with you. ² Pray that we may be denied the interference of bigoted and wicked people. Faith is not given to everyone. ³ But our God, who is faithful, will strengthen you and guard you from the Evil One. ⁴ We have confidence in our God that what we taught you, you are now doing and will continue to do. ⁵ May our God direct your hearts to the love of the Most High and the fortitude of Christ.

⁶ In the name of our Savior Jesus Christ, we urge you, sisters and brothers, to keep away from anyone who refuses to work and live according to the teachings we passed on to you. ⁷ You know how you ought to imitate us. We didn't live undisciplined lives when we were among you, ⁸ nor did we depend on anyone for food. Rather, we worked night and day, laboring to the point of exhaustion so as not to impose on any of you—⁹ not that we had no claim on you, but that we might present ourselves as an example for you to imitate. ¹⁰ Indeed, when we were with you we used to lay down the rule that anyone who didn't work didn't eat.

¹¹ We hear that some of you are undisciplined, doing no work at all, but acting like busybodies. ¹² We command all such people and urge you strongly in our Savior Jesus Christ, to earn the food you eat by working hard and keeping quiet.

¹³ My sisters and brothers, never tire of doing what is right. ¹⁴ Take special note of those who don't obey our teachings in this letter. Shame them by refusing to associate with them. ¹⁵ Even so, regard them not as enemies, but as sisters or brothers.

¹⁶ Now may the God of peace give you peace at all times and in every circumstance. God be with you all!

¹⁷ I, Paul, write this greeting in my own handwriting—the mark of authenticity in every letter—it is my own writing.

¹⁸ May the grace of our Savior Jesus Christ be with you all.

1 timothy

From Paul, apostle of Christ Jesus by the command of God our Savior and Christ Jesus our hope,

² To Timothy, my true child in the faith:

May grace, mercy and peace be yours from Abba God and from Jesus Christ our Savior.

³ I repeat the request I made when I was leaving for Macedonia: stay on at Ephesus, and insist that certain people stop teaching false doctrines ⁴ and cease devoting themselves to myths and endless genealogies. These things promote endless speculations rather than God's providential work—which is revealed by faith. ⁵ The purpose of this instruction is love from a pure heart, a clear conscience, and a sincere faith. ⁶ Some people, however, have strayed from these and have turned to empty discussion. ⁷ They want to be teachers of the Law, but they don't know what they're asserting so confidently.

⁸ We know that the Law is good, but only if it is treated like any law. ⁹ Law is not meant for people who are just, but for the lawless and rebellious, for the irreligious and the wicked, for those who kill their parents, for murderers, ¹⁰ for men and women who traffic in human flesh, for kidnappers, liars and perjurers. It is for everything else that is contrary to sound teaching— ¹¹ that is, whatever conforms to the Good News of the blessed God, which was entrusted to me.

¹² I thank Christ Jesus our Savior, who has strengthened me, given me this work, and judged me faithful. ¹³ I used to be a blasphemer, a persecutor, a violent man; but because in my unbelief I didn't know what I was doing, I have been treated mercifully, ¹⁴ and the grace of our God has been granted to me in overflowing measure, as was the faith and love which are in Christ Jesus.

¹⁵ Here's a saying that can be trusted and is worthy of your complete acceptance: "Christ Jesus came into the world to save sinners." Of these I myself am the worst. ¹⁶ But I was dealt with mercifully for this reason: so that in me—the worst case of all—Jesus Christ might demonstrate perfect patience; and so that I might become an example to those who would later have faith in Christ and gain everlasting life. ¹⁷ To the Ruler of ages, the immortal, the invisible, the only God, be honor and glory forever and ever! Amen.

I want to give you some instructions, Timothy, my child, in keeping with the prophecies that were made about you. Through them may you fight the good fight, ¹⁹ with faith and a good conscience as your weapons. Others have put conscience aside and wrecked their faith—²⁰ people like Hymenaeus and Alexander, whom I have handed over to Satan to be taught not to blaspheme.

2 ¹ First of all, I urge that prayers be offered for everyone—petitions, intercessions and thanksgivings—² and especially for rulers and those in authority, so that we may be able to live godly and reverent lives in peace and quiet. ³ To do this is right, and will please God our Savior, ⁴ who wants everyone to be saved and to reach full knowledge of the truth. ⁵ For there is only one God, and there is only one mediator between God and humankind—Christ Jesus, who

was one of us, ⁶ and who at the proper time sacrificed himself as a ransom and a testimony for all.

⁷ Because of this I have been appointed to be a preacher, an apostle, and—this is the truth, now, I'm not lying—a faithful and honest teacher to the Gentiles.

⁸ Therefore, I want people everywhere to lift their hands up reverently in prayer, without anger or dissension.

⁹ I also want women to dress modestly and decently, not with braided hair or gold or pearls or expensive clothes. ¹⁰ Their adornment should be the good works that are proper for women who profess to be religious. ¹¹ Women are to be quiet and completely submissive during religious instruction. ¹² I don't permit a woman to teach or to have authority over a man. She must remain silent. ¹³ After all, Adam was formed first, then Eve. ¹⁴ And Adam was not the one deceived—it was the woman who was deceived and became a sinner. ¹⁵ But women will be saved through childbearing—provided they continue in faith, love and holiness, with propriety.

3 ¹ You can depend on this: whoever wants to be a bishop aspires to a noble task. ² Bishops must be irreproachable, married only once, even-tempered, self-controlled, modest and hospitable. They should be good teachers. ³ They must not be addicted to drink. They shouldn't be contentious; instead, they should be gentle and peaceful. They must be free from the love of money. ⁴ They must be good managers of their own households, keeping their children under control without sacrificing their dignity. ⁵ For if bishops don't know how to manage their own households, how can they take care of the church of God? ⁶ They shouldn't be new converts, lest they become conceited and thus incur the punishment once meted out to the Devil. ⁷ They must also be well thought of by those outside the church, to ensure that they don't fall into disgrace, which is the Devil's trap.

⁸ In the same way, deacons must be dignified and straightforward. They may not overindulge in drink or give in to greed. ⁹ They must hold fast to the mystery of the faith with a clear conscience. ¹⁰ They should be put on probation first, and then—if there is nothing against them—they may serve as deacons. ¹¹ Their spouses, similarly, should be serious, mature, temperate and entirely trustworthy. ¹² Deacons must have been married only once and must be good managers of their children and their households. ¹³ Those who serve well as deacons gain a worthy place for themselves and acquire much assurance in their faith in Christ Jesus.

¹⁴ Although I hope to visit you soon, I am writing you these instructions ¹⁵ so that if I should be delayed, you will know what kind of conduct befits a member of God's household—which is the church of the living God, the pillar and foundation of the truth. ¹⁶ Wonderful indeed is the mystery of our faith, as we say in our profession of faith:

"Christ appeared in the flesh,
was vindicated in the Spirit,
was seen by angels,
was proclaimed among the nations,
is believed in throughout the world
and was taken up into glory."

Now, the Spirit has explicitly said that during the last times some of us will desert the faith and listen to deceitful spirits and demonic teachings. [2] These teachings come from hypocritical liars, whose consciences have been seared as with a red-hot iron. [3] They forbid people to marry. They also forbid certain foods, which God created to be accepted with thanksgiving by all who believe and know the truth. [4] For everything God created is good, and nothing is to be rejected provided thanksgiving is given for it; [5] it is made holy by the word of God and prayer.

[6] If you will explain these instructions to the sisters and brothers, you will be a good minister of Christ Jesus, nourished on the truths of the faith and on the sound teachings you have followed. [7] Have nothing to do with godless myths and empty old fables.

Train yourself for godliness. [8] "Physical exercises have limited use, but spiritual exercises have unlimited value—they're a benefit both here and now and for all eternity." [9] —There's another saying that can be trusted and is worthy of your complete acceptance! [10] The focus of all our efforts is the trust we put in the living God, the Savior of the whole human race—particularly of those who believe.

[11] This is what you are to enforce in your teachings.

[12] Let no one look down on you because you are young, but be a consistent example for other believers in speech, in love, in life, in faith and in purity. [13] Until I arrive, give attention to the public reading of scripture, to preaching and to teaching. [14] Don't neglect the spiritual gift you received through the prophetic word when the presbyters laid their hands on you. [15] Attend to your duties with great devotion, so that everyone can see your progress. [16] Watch yourself and watch your teaching; persevere in both tasks. By doing so, you will bring salvation to yourself and to all who hear you.

5 [1] Don't speak harshly to an older man, but appeal to him as a father. Treat younger men as brothers. [2] Treat older women as you would your mother, and younger women with propriety, as you would your sisters.

[3] Give proper recognition to women who have been widowed and are truly in need. [4] For women who have been widowed while they still have children or grandchildren, their first duty is to practice godliness with their own families, and to try not to be a drain on their parents' finances. This is what pleases God. [5] Those who are truly widowed, those who are really alone, should put their hope in God and continue in prayer and supplication night and day. [6] But those who give themselves to willful pleasure are dead while they live. [7] Remind the people of this, so that their lives may be irreproachable. [8] People who don't provide for their relatives, especially those in the immediate household, have denied the faith and are worse than unbelievers.

[9] Let a widow be put on the list of widows to receive support if she is at least sixty years old and married only once. [10] This woman must be known for her good deeds, such as the way she has raised her family, showed hospitality, washed the feet of the holy ones, helped those in need, and involved herself in all kinds of good work.

[11] Don't put young women who are widows on the list. Their sensual desires tend to get stronger than their dedication to Christ, and they want to remarry— [12] which invites others to judge them for being unfaithful to their original promise. [13] Furthermore, they learn to become idlers, going from house to house. Not only that, they become gossips and busybodies, talking about things they ought not to. [14] So I think it is better for young women who have been widowed to remarry, to have children, to manage a home, and not to give the enemy an opportunity for slander. [15] There are already some who have turned away to follow Satan.

[16] If a Christian woman has relatives who are widowed, she must assist them and not let the church be burdened with them. Then the church can help those who are truly alone.

[17] Presbyters who do their work well are to be doubly honored, especially those who preach and teach. [18] For scripture says, "Don't muzzle the ox while it is threshing the grain," and, "Workers deserve their wages." [19] Don't accept an accusation against a presbyter if it doesn't have two or three witnesses. [20] If any are found to be at fault, reprimand them publicly, to warn the rest.

[21] Before God and before Jesus Christ and the chosen angels, enforce these rules without partiality. Show no favoritism. [22] Don't be too quick to ordain people—otherwise you'll share responsibility for the sins of others. Keep yourself pure.

[23] Stop drinking only water. Have a little wine because of your stomach and your frequent illnesses.

[24] The faults of some people are obvious long before anyone complains about them. Others have faults that are not discovered until afterwards. [25] So it is with our work: good deeds are obvious. But even when they are not, they cannot be hidden forever.

6 [1] Those who are under the yoke of domination should consider their superiors as worthy of full respect, so that the Name of God and our teachings may not be brought into disrepute. [2] If their overseers are believers, those who are in subjection should show their overseers even greater respect, for they are members of the same family. Indeed, they should be even more diligent in their work, because those who benefit from the work are believers, and they are beloved.

These are the things you are to teach and preach. [3] All those who advocate any other teaching, who don't hold to the sound doctrine of our Savior Jesus Christ and the teaching proper to true religion, [4] should be recognized as both conceited and ignorant. They have an unhealthy interest in controversies and debates. From these come envy, dissension, slander, evil suspicions— [5] in other words, the bickering of those with twisted minds who have lost sense of the truth. Such people value religion only as a means of personal gain.

There is, of course, great benefit in religion, but only for those who are content with what they have.

[7] We brought nothing into the world, nor have we the power to take anything out. [8] If we have food and clothing, we have all that we need. [9] Those who want to be rich are falling into temptation and a trap. They are letting themselves be captured by foolish and harmful desires which draw us down to ruin and destruction. [10] The love of money is the root of all evil. Some people, in their passion for it, have strayed from the faith and have come to grief amid great pain.

[11] But you are to flee from these things. As one dedicated to God, strive to be a person of integrity and piety, filled with faith and love, patience and gentleness. [12] Run the great race of faith. Take firm hold of the everlasting life to which you were called when, in the presence of many witnesses, you made your good profession of faith.

[13] Before God, who gives life to all, and before Christ Jesus, who spoke up as a witness for the truth in front of Pontius Pilate, I charge you [14] to keep God's command without fault or reproach until our Savior Jesus Christ appears. [15] This appearance God will bring to pass at a chosen time. God alone

is the Sovereign over all, the blessed and only ruler above all earthly rulers, ¹⁶ who alone possesses immortality, and who dwells in unapproachable light, whom no human being has ever seen or can see. To God be the honor and the everlasting kindom! Amen.

¹⁷ Warn those who are blessed with this world's goods not to look down on other people. They are not to put their hope in wealth, for it is uncertain. Instead, they are to put their hope in God, who richly provides us with all that we need for our enjoyment. ¹⁸ Tell them they are to do good and be wealthy in good works. They are to be generous and willing to share. ¹⁹ In this way, they'll create a treasure for the future, and guarantee the only life that is real.

²⁰ Dear Timothy, guard what has been entrusted to you. Avoid the blasphemous philosophical discussions and absurdities of what is falsely called knowledge. ²¹ Some have adopted it and have lost the faith.

Grace be with you.

2 timothy

1:1–2:26

From Paul, by the will of God an apostle of Christ Jesus, sent to proclaim the promise of life in Christ Jesus,

² To Timothy, my dear child:

May grace, mercy and peace from God the Creator and from Christ Jesus our Savior be with you.

³ I thank God, the God of my ancestors—whom I worship with a clear conscience—whenever I remember you in my prayers, as indeed I do constantly, night and day.

⁴ When I recall your tears, I long to see you again, which would fill me with joy. ⁵ I'm reminded of your sincere faith, which first lived in your grandmother Lois, then in your mother Eunice, and now, I'm certain, in you as well.

⁶ That's why I want to remind you to fan into flame the gift of God, which is in you through the laying on of my hands. ⁷ For God didn't give us a spirit of timidity, but a spirit of power, of love, of self-discipline.

⁸ So don't be ashamed to give your testimony about Christ, and don't be ashamed of me, Christ's prisoner. But join with me in suffering for the Gospel by the power of God, ⁹ who has saved us and called us to a holy life—not because of anything we have done, but because of God's own purpose and grace. This grace was given to us in Christ Jesus before the beginning of time, ¹⁰ but it has now been revealed through the appearing of our Savior Jesus Christ, who has destroyed death, and brought life and immortality to light through the Gospel.

¹¹ And it was for this Gospel that I was appointed a herald and an apostle and a teacher. ¹² That's why I'm suffering as I am. Yet I'm not ashamed, because I know whom I have believed, and I'm convinced that Jesus Christ is able to guard what has been entrusted to me until that final Day.

¹³ Take what you have heard me say as a model of sound teaching, in faith and love in Christ Jesus. ¹⁴ Guard the rich deposit of faith with the help of the Holy Spirit, who dwells within us.

¹⁵ As you know, Phygelus, Hermogenes and all the others from the province of Asia Minor have deserted me. ¹⁶ But our God will have mercy on the household of Onesiphorus. He was often a comfort to me and wasn't ashamed of my chains. ¹⁷ On the contrary, when he came to Rome, he searched me out and found me. ¹⁸ May God grant him divine mercy on that Day, for you know very well how much he helped me in Ephesus.

2 ²¹ Be strong, my child, in the grace that is in Christ Jesus. ² Everything that you've heard me teach in the presence of many witnesses—pass it on to trustworthy people, so that they, in turn, will teach others. ³ Bear up under hardship, as I do: stay single-minded, in Christ Jesus. ⁴ After all, those serving in national service don't get involved in business affairs—not if they want to keep their superiors happy. ⁵ Or take athletes—they can't accept the winner's crown unless they play by the rules. ⁶ And it is the hardworking farmer who has the first share of the crops. ⁷ Reflect on what I'm saying and our God will give you complete understanding in this matter.

⁸ Remember that Jesus Christ, a descendant of David, was raised from the dead. This is the Gospel I preach; ⁹ in preaching it I suffer as a criminal—even to the point of being thrown into chains—but there is no chaining the word of God! ¹⁰ Therefore I bear with all of this for the sake of those whom God has chosen, in order that they may obtain salvation in Christ Jesus, and with it, eternal glory.

¹¹ You can depend on this:

If we have died with Christ,
we will also live with Christ;
¹² if we hold out to the end,
we will also reign with Christ.
If we deny Christ,
Christ will deny us.
¹³ If we are unfaithful,
Christ will remain faithful,
for Christ can never be unfaithful.

¹⁴ Keep reminding people of these things. Warn them before God against quarrelling about words, which is of no value and only ruins those who listen. ¹⁵ Do your best to present yourself to God as one approved, a worker who doesn't need to be ashamed and who correctly handles the word of truth.

¹⁶ Avoid profane, idle talk, for people who engage in it move further and further away from true religion. ¹⁷ This kind of talk spreads like gangrene. Among these talkers are Hymenaeus and Philetus, ¹⁸ who have deviated from the truth. They claim that the resurrection has already taken place—and they have destroyed the faith of some. ¹⁹ Nevertheless, God's foundation stands firmly, bearing this inscription: "Christ knows those who belong to God," and, "All who call on the Name of our God must avoid wickedness."

²⁰ Not all the dishes in a large household are made of silver and gold. Some are made of wood, others are earthenware. Some are made for special occasions and some for everyday use. ²¹ Those who cleanse themselves from wickedness will become a vessel "for special occasions," useful to Christ and ready for any good work. ²² Run from youthful lusts; pursue justice, faith, love and peace, in union with all those who call on our God with a pure heart. ²³ Avoid futile and silly debates, for they breed quarrels. ²⁴ And as a servant of Christ, you must not engage in quarrels; instead, be gentle with everyone—a good teacher, patient and tolerant. ²⁵ Be gentle when you correct those who argue with you—perhaps God will grant them

repentance, the grace to recognize the truth, ²⁶ and they will come to their senses. Thus they may be freed of Satan's snare, where they have been captives to the Devil's will.

3:1–4:22

Realize that there are going to be terrible times in the last days. ² People will be self-centered and money-grubbing, boastful, arrogant and abusive, disobedient to their parents, ungrateful, irreligious, ³ callous and implacable. They will be slanderers, profligates, lovers of violence and haters of everything good. ⁴ They will be treacherous, reckless, and conceited; they'll be lovers of pleasure rather than lovers of God. ⁵ They will maintain the external form of religion, but will deny its power. Have nothing to do with these people.

⁶ They are the type who worm their way into families and gain control over the weak-willed—those oppressed by sin and driven by sinful desires. ⁷ These types are always learning, but are never able to come to the knowledge of the truth. ⁸ People like this defy the truth, just as Jannes and Jambres opposed Moses. Their minds are corrupt and their faith is a mockery. ⁹ But they won't continue much longer. Their foolishness, like that of those other two, will be obvious to all.

¹⁰ You have followed closely my teaching and my conduct. You have observed my purpose, faith, patience, love and endurance, ¹¹ and my persecutions and sufferings—like what happened to me in Antioch, Iconium and Lystra. What persecutions I endured—yet our God rescued me from all of them! ¹² In fact, anyone who wants to live a godly life in Christ Jesus can expect to be persecuted. ¹³ But all the while, impostors and charlatans will go from bad to worse, deceiving others and deceiving themselves.

¹⁴ You, for your part, must remain faithful to what you have learned and believed, because you know who your teachers were. ¹⁵ Likewise, from your infancy you have known the sacred scriptures, the source of wisdom which through faith in Christ Jesus leads to salvation. ¹⁶ All scripture is inspired of God, and is useful for teaching—for reprimanding, correcting, and training in justice— ¹⁷ so that the people of God may be fully competent and equipped for every good work.

4 ¹ In the presence of God and of Jesus Christ, who will judge the living and the dead, and in view of the appearance and reign of Christ, I charge you ² to preach the word; to be prepared in season and out of season; to correct, reprimand and encourage with great patience and careful instruction. ³ For the time is coming when people won't put up with sound doctrine. Instead, to suit their own desires, they will gather around them a great number of teachers who say what their fickle ears want to hear. ⁴ They will turn their ears away from truth and turn aside to myths. ⁵ But you, keep your head in all situations; endure hardship, perform your work as an evangelist and fulfill your ministry.

⁶ As for me, my life is already being poured out like a libation. The time of my dissolution is near. ⁷ I have fought the good fight; I have finished the race; I have kept the faith. ⁸ Now a laurel wreath awaits me; on that day our God, the just Judge, will award it to me—and not only to me, but to all who have longed for Christ's appearing.

⁹ Do your best to come to me as soon as you can. ¹⁰ Demas, enamored of worldly things, left me and went to Thessalonica; Crescens has gone to Galatia, and Titus to Dalmatia. ¹¹ Luke is the only one with me. Get Mark and bring him with you, for he is helpful to me in my work. ¹² I have sent Tychicus to Ephesus. ¹³ When you come, bring the cloak I left with Carpus in Troas, and the scrolls—especially the parchment ones.

¹⁴ Alexander the coppersmith caused me great harm. Our God will compensate him according to his actions. ¹⁵ Be on your guard against him, for he has strongly opposed our preaching. ¹⁶ I found myself alone and without a single witness at my first defense. Pray that they not be punished for it.

¹⁷ Christ stood by my side and gave me strength, so that through me the proclamation might be completed and all the nations might hear the Gospel. That's how I was saved from the lion's jaws. ¹⁸ Christ will continue to rescue me from all attempts to do me harm, and will bring me safe to the higher realm. To Jesus Christ be glory forever and ever! Amen.

¹⁹ Greet Prisca, Aquila and the family of Onesiphorus. ²⁰ Erastus remained in Corinth, and I left Trophimus behind at Miletus because he was ill. ²¹ Do your best to get here before winter.

Greetings to you from Eubulus, Pudens, Linus, Claudia and all the sisters and brothers.

²² May Christ be with your spirit. Grace be with you.

títus

1:1–16

From Paul, God's servant and an apostle of Jesus Christ, sent to strengthen the faith of those whom God has chosen, and to promote their knowledge of the truth which godliness embodies, ² all in the hope of that eternal life which God promised before the ages began—and God cannot lie. ³ This is the appointed time, manifested in the preaching entrusted to me by the command of God our Savior.

⁴ To Titus, my own true child in our common faith:

May grace and peace be yours from Abba God and Christ Jesus our Savior.

⁵ The reason I left you in Crete was so that you might accomplish what had been left undone, especially the appointment of presbyters in every town.

As I instructed you, ⁶ presbyters must be irreproachable, married only once, and the parents of children who are believers and are known not to be wild and insubordinate.

⁷ Bishops, as God's stewards, must be blameless. They must not be self-willed or arrogant, addicted to drink, violent or greedy. ⁸ On the contrary, they should be hospitable, and love goodness, and be steady, just, holy and self-controlled. ⁹ In their teachings, they must hold fast to the authentic message, so that they'll be able both to encourage the faithful to follow sound doctrine, and to refute those who contradict it.

¹⁰ This is necessary, frankly, because there are many rebellious types out there—idle talkers and deceivers, especially those who demand conversion to Judaism before becoming a Christian. ¹¹ They must be silenced, for they're upsetting entire households by teaching things they shouldn't teach, and doing it for financial gain. ¹² One of their own prophets once said, "Cretans have always been liars, evil animals and lazy gluttons." ¹³ This is a true statement.

Therefore, rebuke them sharply, so that they'll be sound in the faith. ¹⁴ That should keep them from listening to empty myths and from heeding the commands of those who are no longer interested in the truth. ¹⁵ To the pure all things are pure, but to those who are corrupted and lack faith, nothing can be pure. The corruption is both in their minds and in their consciences. [16] They claim to know God, while denying it with their actions. They're vile, disobedient, and quite incapable of doing good.

2:1–3:9

2 [1] As for yourself, let your speech be consistent with sound doctrine. [2] Tell your older people that they must be temperate, reserved and moderate; [3] they should be sound in faith, loving and steadfast; they must behave in ways that befit those who belong to God. They must not be slanderers or drunkards.

[4] By their good example, they must teach younger couples to love each other and their children, [5] to be sensible, live pure lives, work hard, and be kind and submissive in their love relationships. In this way the message of God will not fall into disgrace. [6] Tell young people to keep themselves completely under control— [7] and be sure that you yourself set them a good example. Your teaching must have the integrity of serious, [8] sound words to which no one can take exception. That way no opponent will be able to find anything bad to say about us, and hostility will yield to shame.

[9] Tell workers that they're to obey their superiors and always do what they're told without arguing. [10] And there must be no petty thieving. They must show complete honesty at all times. In this way they'll be a credit to the teaching of God our Savior.

[11] The grace of God has appeared, offering salvation to all. [12] It trains us to reject godless ways and worldly desires, and to live temperately, justly and devoutly in this age [13] as we await our blessed hope—the appearing of the glory of our great God and our Savior Jesus Christ. [14] It was Christ who was sacrificed for us, to redeem us from all unrighteousness and to cleanse a people to be Christ's own, eager to do what is right.

[15] Teach these things, whether you are giving instructions or correcting errors. Act with full authority, and let no one despise you.

3 [1] Remind people to be loyally subject to the government and its officials, to obey the laws, and to be ready to do whatever is good. [2] Tell them not to speak evil of anyone or to be quarrelsome. They must be forebearing and display perfect courtesy to all.

[3] We ourselves were once foolish, disobedient and far from the true faith; we were addicted to our passions and to pleasures of various kinds. We went our way in malice and envy, filled with self-hatred and hating one another. [4] But when the kindness and love of God our Savior appeared, [5] we were saved, not because of any righteous deeds we had done, but because of God's own mercy. We were saved through the baptism of new birth and renewal by the Holy Spirit. [6] This Spirit God lavished on us through Jesus Christ, our Savior, [7] that we might be justified through grace and become heirs to the hope of eternal life. [8] This is doctrine you can rely on.

I want you to be quite uncompromising in teaching this. Then those who now believe in God will keep their minds occupied doing good works. These things are excellent and beneficial to everyone. [9] But avoid pointless speculation, genealogies, rivalries and quarrels about the Law. They're useless and futile.

3:10–15

If people dispute what you teach, give them a first and even a second warning. After that, have no more to do with them. [11] Be assured that such people are twisted, sinful and self-condemned.

[12] As soon as I have sent Artemus or Tychicus to you, do your best to join me at Nicopolis. I have decided to spend the winter there. [13] Send Zenas the lawyer and Apollos on their journey, and see that they have everything they need.

[14] All our people are to learn to do what is good for their practical lives as well. They'll then be able to provide for their daily needs and not be unproductive.

[15] All who are with me send greetings. Grace be with you all.

philemon

1–25

From Paul, a prisoner for Christ Jesus, and Timothy, our brother,

To Philemon, our dear friend and coworker, [2] to Apphia, our sister, to Archippus, our companion in the struggle, and to the church that meets in your house:

[3] Grace and peace from Abba God and Our Savior Jesus Christ.

[4] I always mention you in my prayers and thank God for you [5] because I hear of the love and faith you have for our Savior Jesus and for all the saints. [6] I pray that you'll be active in sharing your faith, so that you'll fully understand all the good things we're able to do for the sake of Christ.

[7] I find great joy and comfort in your love, because through you the hearts of the holy ones have been refreshed. [8] Therefore, though I feel I have every right in Christ to command you to do what ought to be done, [9] I prefer to appeal in the name of love.

Yes, I, Paul, an ambassador and now a prisoner for Christ, [10] appeal to you for my child, of whom I have become the parent during my imprisonment. He has truly become Onesimus—"Useful"—[11] for he who was formerly useless to you is now useful indeed both to you and to me. [12] It is he that I am sending to you—and that means I'm sending my heart!

[13] I had wanted to keep him with me, that he might help me in your place while I'm in prison for the Good News; [14] but I didn't want to do anything without your consent, so that kindness might not be forced on you, but be freely bestowed. [15] Perhaps he was separated from you for a while for this reason—that you might have him back forever, [16] no longer as a subordinate, but as more—a beloved brother, especially dear to me. And how much dearer he'll be to you, since now you'll know him both in the flesh and in Christ!

[17] If you regard me as a partner, then, welcome Onesimus as you would me. [18] If he has done you any injury or owes you anything, charge it to me. [19] I, Paul, write this in my own hand: I agree to pay. And I won't even mention that you owe me your very self!

²⁰ You see, my friend, I want to make you "useful" to me in Christ. Refresh this heart of mine in Christ. ²¹ I write with complete confidence in your obedience, since I am sure you will do even more than I ask.

²² There is one more thing. Prepare a guest room for me. I hope to be restored to you through your prayers.

²³ Epaphras, a prisoner with me in Christ Jesus, sends greetings. ²⁴ And so do my colleagues Mark, Aristarchus, Demas and Luke.

²⁵ May the grace of our Savior Jesus Christ be with your spirit.

hebrews

1:1–14

In times past, God spoke in fragmentary and varied ways to our ancestors through the prophets; ² in these final days, God has spoken to us through the Only Begotten, who has been made heir of all things and through whom the universe was first created. ³ Christ is the reflection of God's glory, the exact representation of God's being; all things are sustained by God's powerful Word. Having cleansed us from our sins, Jesus Christ sat down at the right hand of the Glory of heaven— ⁴ as far superior to the angels as the name Christ has inherited is superior to theirs.

⁵ For to which of the angels did God ever say,

"You are my Own;
today I have begotten you,"

or,

"I will be your parent,
and you will be my child,"

⁶ or, as when God said upon bringing the Firstborn into the world,

"Let all the angels of God worship you"?

⁷ Of the angels God says,

"I make the angels winds,
my servants flames of fire."

⁸ But to the Only Begotten, God says,

"Your throne, O God,
will last forever and ever,
and justice is the scepter
of your reign.
⁹ You love justice as much
as you hate wickedness;
therefore, God, your God,
has set you above your companions
and anointed you
with the oil of gladness";

¹⁰ and,

"In the beginning, O God,
you laid the foundations of the earth,
and the heavens
are the work of your hands.
¹¹ They will perish,
but you will remain;
they will all wear out like a garment.
¹² You will roll them up like a cloak,
and like a garment they will be changed.
But you are the same,
and your years never end."

¹³ But to which of the angels did God ever say,

"Sit at my right hand
and I will place your enemies
under your foot"?

¹⁴ The truth is, all angels are ministering spirits, sent out to serve those who will inherit salvation.

2:1–4:11

Therefore, we must be more attentive to what we've been taught, so that we don't drift away. ² For if the promise made through angels was binding, and every infringement and disobedience received its just punishment, ³ how will we escape if we ignore so great a salvation? This salvation, which was first announced by Christ, was confirmed for us by those who heard the message. ⁴ God also confirmed their witness to it with signs, wonders, miracles of all kinds—and by freely distributing the gifts of the Holy Spirit.

⁵ God didn't create the inhabited earth of which we speak to have it be ruled by angels. ⁶ Somewhere this testimony is found:

"Who are we that you should be mindful of us?
We are mere mortals, and yet you care for us!
⁷ You have made us little less than the angels
and crowned us with glory and honor.
⁸ You have put all things under our feet."

In subjecting all things to us, God left nothing unsubjected. At present, we don't see all things thus subject; ⁹ but we do see Jesus, who was made "little less than the angels, crowned with glory and honor" by dying on the cross—so that, through the gracious will of God, Jesus might taste death for us all.

¹⁰ Indeed, it was fitting that, when bringing many to glory, God, for whom and through whom all things exist, should make the author of their salvation perfect through suffering. ¹¹ The one who makes holy and those who are made holy are all from the One God. And because of this, Jesus is not ashamed to call us sisters and brothers, ¹² as it is written:

"I will proclaim your Name
to my sisters and brothers,
I will sing your praise
in the midst of the assembly."
¹³ And again,
"I will put my trust in God."

And again, Jesus says,

"Here I am,
with the children God has given me."

¹⁴ Since the children of God are flesh and blood, Jesus likewise partook of that flesh and blood, that by dying he might render powerless the one who has the power of death—that is, the Devil— ¹⁵ and free those whose fear of death had enslaved them all their lives. ¹⁶ Surely Jesus came to help not angels but rather the children of Sarah and Abraham! ¹⁷ Therefore, Jesus had to become like his sisters and brothers in every way, in order to be a merciful and faithful high priest on our behalf, to make atonement for the sins of the people. ¹⁸ And since Jesus suffered while being tempted, he is able to help others who are being tempted.

3 ¹ Therefore, holy sisters and brothers—and you all have the same heavenly call—fix your thoughts on Jesus, the

apostle and high priest of our confession. ² He was faithful to the One who appointed him, just as Moses stayed faithful, alone of all God's house. ³ But Jesus has been found worthy of greater honor than Moses, just as the builder of a house receives more honor than the house itself. ⁴ Of course, every house is built by someone, but the builder of all things is God. ⁵ Moses was faithful as a servant in all of God's house, serving as a witness to the things that were to be revealed later. ⁶ Christ, on the other hand, is faithful over God's house as the heir.

And we are God's house—if we persevere to the end, firmly holding on to our confidence and the hope of which we boast. ⁷ As the Holy Spirit says,

"Today,
if you hear my voice,
⁸   don't harden your hearts
as they did at the rebellion,
in the day of testing in the desert,
⁹   when your ancestors tested and tried me
and saw my works for forty years.
¹⁰   Because of this I was angry with that generation
and I said, 'They have always been of erring heart
and have never known my ways.'
¹¹   So I swore in my anger,
'They will never enter my place of rest.'"

¹² Take care, my sisters and brothers, lest any of you have an evil and unfaithful spirit and fall away from the living God. ¹³ Encourage one another daily while it is still "today," so that no one grows hardened by the deceit of sin. ¹⁴ We have become partners in Christ, provided we maintain to the end that confidence with which we began.

¹⁵ For it is said,

"Today,
if you hear my voice,
don't harden your hearts
as they did at the rebellion."

¹⁶ Who were those who heard and rebelled? Wasn't it all those who came out of Egypt with Moses? ¹⁷ And with whom was God angry for forty years? Wasn't it with those who sinned, whose bodies fell in the desert? ¹⁸ And to whom did God swear that they wouldn't enter into God's rest, if not those who disobeyed? ¹⁹ Thus we see that they couldn't enter because they lacked faith.

4 ¹ Although the promise that all may enter God's rest still stands, you must be careful of falling short of it. ² We've had the Good News proclaimed to us—and so did our ancestors. But the message they heard didn't profit them, for they didn't combine it with faith. ³ It is we who have believed who will enter into that rest, just as God said,

"So I swore in my anger,
'They will never enter my rest.'"

Yet God's work was finished with the creation of the world, ⁴ for in reference to the seventh day one passage says, "And God rested from work on the seventh day," ⁵ and again in that passage, God says, "They will never enter my rest." ⁶ Then we have established that some will reach it, and that those who formerly had the Good News proclaimed to them didn't enter because of their disobedience. ⁷ Therefore God has set a particular day—"Today"—when God spoke through David long ago, as we said earlier:

"Today,
if you hear my voice,
don't harden your hearts."

⁸ For if Joshua had led them into this rest, God wouldn't have spoken about another day to come. ⁹ Therefore, there must still be a rest reserved for God's people—the Sabbath rest. ¹⁰ For all those who enter God's rest also rest from their own work, just as God did.

¹¹ Therefore, let us strive to enter into that rest, so that no one may fall by imitating the example of our ancestors' disobedience.

4:12–8:6

God's word is living and active, sharper than any double-edged sword. It pierces so deeply that it divides even soul and spirit, bone and marrow, and is able to judge the thoughts and intentions of the heart. ¹³ Nothing is concealed from God; all lies bare and exposed before the eyes of the One to whom we have to render an account.

¹⁴ Since, then, we have a great high priest who has passed through the heavens—Jesus, the Firstborn of God—let us hold fast to our profession of faith. ¹⁵ For we don't have a high priest who is unable to sympathize with our weaknesses, but one who was tempted in every way that we are, yet never sinned. ¹⁶ So let us confidently approach the throne of grace to receive mercy and favor, and find help in time of need.

5 ¹ Every high priest taken from among the faithful is appointed on their behalf to deal with the things of God, to offer gifts and sacrifices for sins. ² The high priest is able to deal patiently with erring sinners, being likewise beset by weakness— ³ and so must make personal sin offerings as well as those for the people. ⁴ One doesn't take on this honor by one's own initiative, but only when called by God, as Aaron was. ⁵ Even Christ didn't presume to take on the office of high priest. Christ was appointed high priest by the One who said,

"You are my Own;
today I have begotten you";
⁶   and in another place,
"You are a priest forever,
according to the order of Melchizedek."

⁷ In the days when he was in the flesh, Jesus offered prayers and supplications with loud cries and tears to God, who was able to save him from death, and Jesus was heard because of his reverence. ⁸ Firstborn though he was, Jesus learned to obey through suffering. ⁹ But having been made perfect, Jesus became, for all who obey, the source of eternal salvation, ¹⁰ and he was designated by God to be a high priest according to the order of Melchizedek.

¹¹ We have many things to say about this, but explaining is difficult because you have grown slow to understand. ¹² Really, even though you ought to be teachers by this time, you need someone to teach you anew the basic elements of God's word. You need milk, not solid food. ¹³ All those who are still living on milk cannot digest the doctrine of righteousness because they are still babies. ¹⁴ Solid food is for the mature, for those whose minds are trained to distinguish right from wrong.

6 ¹ So let's leave behind the elementary teachings about Christ and move on to maturity, without laying the same foundation—repentance from dead works and faith in God,

2 and teachings about baptism, the laying on of hands, the resurrection of the dead and eternal judgment. 3 And this, God willing, is what we will do.

4 As for those people who were once brought into enlightenment, who tasted the heavenly gift, who have shared in the Holy Spirit 5 and who have tasted the good word of God and the powers of the age to come— 6 if they still fall away, it is impossible for them to come to repentance and renewal a second time. They are crucifying—and publicly disgracing—the Only Begotten of God all over again. 7 A field that is well watered by frequent rain and yields a good crop useful to the farmer receives a blessing from God. 8 A field that grows thorns and thistles is abandoned as if it were cursed, and it will end up being burned.

9 Even though we speak like this, beloved, we are confident of better results in your case, results related to salvation. 10 God is not unjust and will not forget your work and the love you have demonstrated by your past and present service to God's holy people. 11 Our one desire is that each of you show the same zeal to the end, to the perfect fulfillment of our hopes. 12 Don't grow careless, but imitate those who, through faith and perseverance, are inheriting the promises.

13 When God made the promise to Sarah and Abraham, it was made alone, for there was no one greater to swear by. 14 And God said to them, "I will indeed bless you and multiply you." 15 Because of that, Sarah and Abraham persevered and saw the promise fulfilled.

16 People, of course, swear an oath by someone greater than themselves; an oath gives firmness to the promise and puts an end to all argument. 17 In the same way, God, wanting to make the heirs to the promise thoroughly realize that the divine promise was unalterable, guaranteed it by an oath. 18 Now, therefore, there are two unalterable things— the promise and the oath—in which it was impossible for God to be lying. We should now, having found safety, take a firm grip on the hope that is held out to us. 19 Like a sure and firm anchor of our lives, that hope extends beyond the veil 20 through which Jesus, our forerunner, has passed on our behalf, being made high priest forever according to the order of Melchizedek.

7 :1 Recall that Melchizedek, ruler of Salem, priest of the Most High God, went to meet Abraham, who was on his way back after the slaughter of the rulers, and blessed him; 2 and also that it was to Melchizedek that Abraham gave a tenth of all that he had. Melchizedek—which means "ruler of righteousness"—was also ruler of Salem—that is, "ruler of peace." 3 With no mother, no father, no genealogy, no beginning of days or end of life, Melchizedek is like God's Only Begotten and remains a priest forever.

4 Try to fathom how great this person was. After all, the patriarch Abraham gave him a tenth of the treasure he had captured. 5 The descendants of Levi who receive the office of priesthood are, according to the Law, commanded to exact tithes from the people, their sisters and brothers, even though they also descended from Abraham. 6 But this person, not a descendant of Levi, still exacted tithes from Abraham, and then blessed the partriarch—the one who had received the promises. 7 Now, it's obvious that a lesser person is blessed by a greater person. 8 Further, in the one case, the tithe is collected by mortals, who die; in the other case, by the one who, the testimony says, lives on. 9 It could also be said that even Levi, who received tithes, actually paid them in the person

of Abraham. 10 For Levi was still in the loins of his ancestor Abraham when Melchizedek came to meet him.

11 Now if perfection came through the levitical priesthood—since because of this priesthood the Law was given to the people—why was a new priesthood necessary? And why one according to the order of Melchizedek, and not the order of Aaron? 12 Because any change in the priesthood means a change in the Law as well.

13 The one about whom these things were said came from a different tribe, and the members of that tribe never did service at the altar. 14 Everyone knows that Christ came from Judah, a tribe that Moses didn't even mention when dealing with priests.

15 The matter becomes even clearer when there appears a second Melchizedek, 16 who is a priest not by virtue of a law about physical descent, but by the power of an indestructible life. 17 Scripture testifies, "You are a priest forever, according to the order of Melchizedek."

18 On the one hand, the former commandment is annulled because it is ineffective and useless: 19 the Law wasn't able to make anything perfect. On the other hand, this commandment is replaced by a better hope—one that brings us nearer to God.

20 What's more, this didn't happen without the taking of an oath. 21 The others became priests without an oath. But Jesus became a priest with an oath, when God said to him,

"Our God has sworn,
and will not renege on it:
you are a priest forever."

22 Through this oath Jesus became the guarantee of a better covenant.

23 There's another difference: there were so many priests in the old Covenant because death prevented them from continuing their work. 24 But Christ lives on forever, and Christ's work as priest doesn't pass on to someone else. 25 And so Christ is able, now and always, to save those who come to God through Christ, because Christ lives forever to plead to God for them.

26 God ordained that we should have such a high priest— one who is holy, who has no fault or sin, who has been set apart from sinners and raised above the heavens. 27 Jesus is not like other high priests and doesn't need to offer sacrifices every day, first for personal sins and then for the sins of the people. Christ's self-sacrifice was offered once and for all. 28 For the Law appoints as high priests people who are weak; but God's sworn promise, which came later than the Law, appoints the Only Begotten, who has been made perfect forever.

8 :1 The key to what we are saying is this: we have such a high priest, who sits at the right hand of the throne of Majesty in heaven, 2 a minister of the sanctuary and of that true tabernacle set up by God and not by mortals. 3 Now every high priest is appointed to offer gifts and sacrifices— hence the necessity of this priest to have something to offer.

4 If this high priest were on earth, it would not be as a priest, for there are priests already offering the gifts which the Law prescribes. 5 They offer worship in a sanctuary which is only a copy and shadow of the heavenly one—for Moses, when about to erect the tabernacle, was warned, "See that you make everything according to the pattern shown you on the mountain."

6 But now Jesus, our high priest, has obtained a more excellent ministry as mediator of a better covenant, founded on better promises.

If that first Covenant had been faultless, there would have been no reason to have a second one. 8 But God, finding fault with them, says,

> "Days are coming—it is Your God who speaks—
> when I will establish a new Covenant
> with the house of Israel and the house of Judah,
> 9 but not a covenant like the one I made with their ancestors
> on the day I took them out of the land of Egypt.
> They abandoned that Covenant of mine,
> and so I deserted them—
> it is Your God who speaks.
> 10 No, this is the Covenant I will make
> with the house of Israel
> when those days arrive—
> it is Your God who speaks.
> I will put my laws into their minds
> and write them on their hearts.
> Then I will be their God
> and they will be my people.
> 11 There will be no need
> for neighbor to try to teach neighbor,
> or sister and brother to say to each other,
> 'Learn to know our God.'
> No, they will all know me,
> the least no less than the greatest,
> 12 since I will forgive their iniquities
> and never again remember their sins."

13 In saying "a new covenant," God declares the first one obsolete. And what has grown old and become obsolete is ready to disappear.

9 :1 Now the first Covenant had regulations governing worship and a sanctuary, a sanctuary on this earth. 2 Two tabernacles were constructed: the outer one, called the sanctuary, which held the lampstand, the table, and the showbread; 3 and the inner tabernacle, behind the second veil, called the Holy of Holies, 4 which held the gold altar of incense, and the gold-plated Ark of the Covenant. In it were the gold jar containing the manna, the staff of Aaron that had budded, and the stone tablets of the Covenant. 5 Above the Ark was the throne of glory, with the glorious cherubim outspread over it. But we cannot go into further details now.

6 Once these elements were in place, priests regularly entered the outer sanctuary to carry out their acts of worship. 7 But only the high priest entered the inner sanctuary, once a year, and always with blood, which was both a self-offering and an offering for the sins of the people. 8 In this way, the Holy Spirit is showing that the way into the inner sanctuary had not yet been revealed while the outer sanctuary was still standing. 9 This is a symbol for the present time. Gifts and offerings made under these regulations cannot clear the conscience of the worshipper. 10 They are rules about the outward life, relating to food and drink and ablutions at various times. They were intended to be in force only until the time of the new order.

11 But Christ, who came as high priest of the good things which came to be, entered once and for all into the greater and more perfect tabernacle, the one made not by human hands, that is, not belonging to this creation. 12 It wasn't with the blood of goats and calves, but with our Savior's own blood that Christ entered the holy place, and once and for all obtained eternal redemption. 13 For if the sprinkling of the blood of goats and bulls and a heifer's ashes can sanctify those who are defiled so that their flesh is cleansed, 14 how much more will the blood of Christ, a perfect self-sacrifice to God through the eternal Spirit, cleanse our consciences from dead works, to worship the living God!

15 Christ is the mediator of a new Covenant, so that the people who were called by God may receive the eternal inheritance that was promised. This happens because a death has taken place which cancels the sins committed under the first Covenant.

16 In the case of a will, the death of the testator must be established, 17 for a will becomes valid only at death—it has no force while the testator is alive. 18 This is why even the first Covenant wasn't inaugurated without something being killed. 19 When Moses had given all the commandments of the Law to the people, he took the blood of calves and goats, together with some water, scarlet wool and branches of hyssop, and sprinkled both the book and the people. 20 He said, "This is the blood of the Covenant that God has laid down for you." 21 In the same way, he sprinkled the tabernacle and the ceremonial vessels of worship. 22 In fact, according to the Law, almost everything has to be purified with blood. If there is no shedding of blood, there is no forgiveness.

23 So if it was necessary for the copies of heavenly things to be purified this way, then the heavenly things have to be purified by a higher form of sacrifice than this. 24 For Christ didn't go into a holy place made by human hands, a copy of the real one. Christ went into heaven itself and now appears on our behalf in the presence of God. 25 High priests of old went into the Most Holy Place every year with the blood of an animal. But Christ didn't make a self-offering more than that one time; 26 otherwise, Christ would have had to suffer many times ever since the creation of the world. But now that the Consummation is upon us, Christ has appeared once and for all, to remove sin through self-sacrifice. 27 It is appointed that everyone must die once and then be judged by God. 28 In the same way, Christ was offered once to bear the sins of many, and then will appear a second time—not to deal with sin, but to save those who are waiting for Christ's appearing.

10 :1 Since the Law was only a reflection of the good things to come and not their true reality, it was quite incapable of perfecting the worshippers by the same sacrifices offered continually year after year. 2 Otherwise, wouldn't the priests have stopped offering them because the worshippers, once cleansed, would no longer have had consciousness of sin? 3 But through these sacrifices there came only a yearly reminder of sins, 4 because it is impossible for the blood of bulls and goats to take away sins.

5 And this is what Jesus said, on coming into the world:

> "You who wanted no sacrifice or oblation
> prepared a body for me.
> 6 In burnt offerings or sacrifices for sin
> you took no pleasure.
> 7 Then I said, just as it was written of me
> in the scroll of the book,
> 'God, here I am!
> I have come to do your will.'"

8 In saying that God doesn't want burnt offerings and sacrifices—which are offered according to the Law—9 and then saying, "I have come to do your will," Jesus abolishes the first Covenant in order to establish the second. 10 By God's will, we have been sanctified through the offering of the body of Jesus Christ once and for all.

11 Every other priest performs services every day and offers the same sacrifices many times; but these sacrifices can

never take away sins. ¹² Christ, however, offered one sacrifice for sins, an offering that is effective forever. Then Christ sat down at the right hand of God, ¹³ and now waits there until God puts all enemies in their rightful place. ¹⁴ With one sacrifice then, Jesus has made perfect forever those who are being sanctified.

¹⁵ The Holy Spirit also attests to this, first saying,

¹⁶ "'This is the Covenant I will make with them
when those days arrive,' says our God:
'I will put my laws into their hearts
and write them on their minds.'"

¹⁷ Then she adds,
"I will never again remember
their sins or offenses."

¹⁸ So when sins and evil deeds have been forgiven, an offering to take away sins is no longer needed.

¹⁹ Therefore, sisters and brothers, since the blood of Jesus makes us confident to enter the holy place ²⁰ by the new and living path opened for us through the veil—that is to say, the body of Jesus— ²¹ and since we have the supreme high priest presiding over the house of God, ²² let us enter it filled with faith and with sincerity in our hearts, our hearts sprinkled and cleared from any trace of bad conscience and our bodies washed with pure water. ²³ Let us keep firm in the hope we profess, because the One who made the promise is faithful.

²⁴ Let us always think how we can stimulate each other to love and good works. ²⁵ Don't stay away from the meetings of the community, as some do, but encourage one another; and do this all the more as you see the Day drawing near.

²⁶ For if we sin deliberately after we have received knowledge of the truth, there no longer remains any sacrifice for sins. ²⁷ There only remains the fearful prospect of judgment and of the raging fire that will consume the enemies of God. ²⁸ Anyone who rejects the Law of Moses is put to death without mercy on the testimony of two or three witnesses. ²⁹ So if you trample God's Only Begotten underfoot and treat the blood of the Covenant, which sanctified you, as if it were something unclean, insulting the Spirit of grace, how much more severely do you think you deserve to be punished? ³⁰ We know the One who said, "Vengeance is mine, I will repay!" and, "our God will judge the people." ³¹ It is a terrifying thing to fall into the hands of the living God.

³² Call to mind those earlier days, after you had been enlightened, when you stood your ground in a great struggle of suffering. ³³ Sometimes you were exposed to insults and violence. Sometimes you stood by associates who received such treatment. ³⁴ You joined in the suffering of those in prison. You gladly accepted the confiscation of your property, for you knew that you possessed something better and lasting.

³⁵ So don't throw away your confidence. It will provide you with a great reward. ³⁶ You'll need endurance to carry out God's will and receive what has been promised.

³⁷ "In just a little while,
the One who is coming will come
and will not delay.

³⁸ The just will live by their faith,
but if they hesitate,
I will take no pleasure in them."

³⁹ You and I are not the sort to "hesitate" and be lost by it. We are the sort who have faith and are saved.

Faith is the reality of all that is hoped for; faith is the proof of all that is unseen. ² Because of faith, our ancestors were approved by God.

³ By faith, we understand that the world was created by the word from God, and that what is visible came into being through the invisible.

⁴ By faith, Abel offered a better sacrifice to God than Cain, and for that was declared to be just; God spoke well of his offerings. And by faith Abel still speaks, even though he is dead.

⁵ By faith, Enoch was taken up and didn't have to experience death—"he was seen no more because God took him." Even before he was taken, he was commended as one who pleased God. ⁶ And without faith it is impossible to please God, because anyone who comes to God must believe that God exists, rewarding those who earnestly seek the divine glory.

⁷ By faith, Noah—warned about things not yet seen—revered God and built an ark in order to save his household. By faith, Noah condemned the world and inherited the justice which comes through faith.

⁸ By faith, Sarah and Abraham obeyed when they were called, and went off to the place they were to receive as a heritage; they went forth, moreover, not knowing where they were going.

⁹ By faith, Sarah and Abraham lived in the promised land as resident aliens, dwelling in tents with their children and grandchildren, who were heirs of the same promise—¹⁰ for they were looking forward to the city with foundations, whose designer and maker is God.

¹¹ By faith, Sarah received the ability to conceive, even though she was past childbearing age, for she thought that the One who had made the promise was worthy of trust. ¹² As a result of this faith, there came forth from one woman and one man, themselves as good as dead, descendants as numerous as the stars in the sky and the sands of the seashore.

¹³ All of them died in faith. They didn't obtain what had been promised, but saw and welcomed it from afar. By acknowledging themselves to be strangers and exiles on the earth, ¹⁴ they showed that they were looking for a country of their own. ¹⁵ If they had been thinking of the country from which they had come, they'd have been able to return to it. ¹⁶ But they were searching for a better country, a heavenly one. So God isn't ashamed of them, or ashamed to be called their God. That's why God has prepared a city for them.

¹⁷ By faith, Abraham, when put to the test, offered up Isaac. Abraham, who had received the promises, was ready to sacrifice his only son, ¹⁸ of whom it was said, "Through Isaac will your descendants be called." ¹⁹ He reasoned that God was able to raise Isaac from the dead, and so he received Isaac back as a symbol.

²⁰ By faith, Isaac blessed Jacob and Esau concerning their future.

²¹ By faith, Jacob, near death, blessed each of Joseph's sons, leaning on the top of his staff as though bowing in worship.

²² By faith, Joseph, near the end of his life, recalled the Exodus of the Israelites and made arrangements for his own burial.

²³ By faith, Moses was hidden by his parents for three months after his birth. They defied the royal edict because they saw he was such a fine child.

²⁴ By faith, Moses, now an adult, refused to be identified as the son of the Pharaoh's daughter. ²⁵ He chose to endure ill-treatment along with the people of God rather than enjoy the fleeting pleasures of sin. ²⁶ He considered disgrace for the sake of the Messiah something more precious than the treasures of Egypt. He was looking forward to his reward.

²⁷ By faith, he left Egypt, not fearing Pharaoh's rage. He persevered because he saw the Invisible One.

²⁸ By faith, he kept the Passover and the sprinkling of the blood, so that the Destroyer wouldn't touch the firstborn children of Israel.

²⁹ By faith, the people passed through the Sea of Reeds as though on dry land. When the Egyptians tried the same, they drowned.

³⁰ By faith, the walls of Jericho fell after being encircled for seven days.

³¹ By faith, Rahab the prostitute didn't perish with those who were disobedient, after she welcomed the spies in peace.

³² What more can I say? There is no time for me to give an account of Gideon, Barak, Samson, Jephthah, or David, Samuel and the prophets. ³³ These were those who through faith conquered nations, did what was just and earned the promises. They shut the jaws of lions, ³⁴ put out raging fires and emerged unscathed from battle. They were weak people who were given strength, became brave in battle and put foreign invaders to flight. ³⁵ Some came back from the dead to their spouses by resurrection. Others submitted to torture, refusing release so that they could rise again to a better life. ³⁶ Still others endured mockery, scourgings—even chains and imprisonment. ³⁷ They were stoned, sawed in half, even beheaded. They were homeless, dressed in the skins of sheep and goats; they were penniless and given nothing but ill treatment— ³⁸ the world wasn't worthy of them!— and they wandered in deserts and slept on mountains and in caves and ravines. ³⁹ These are all heroes of our faith, but none of them received what was promised, ⁴⁰ since God had provided something better for us, so that they would not be made perfect apart from us.

12 ¹ Therefore, since we are surrounded by such a great cloud of witnesses, let us lay aside everything that impedes us and the sin that so easily entangles us. Let us run with perseverance the race laid out for us. ² Let us not lose sight of Jesus, who leads us in our faith and brings it to perfection.

For the sake of the joy to come, Jesus endured the cross, heedless of its shame, and now sits at the right of God's throne. ³ Think of Jesus—who endured such opposition from sinners—so that you will not grow weary and lose heart. ⁴ In your struggles against sin, you still haven't resisted to the point of shedding your blood.

⁵ Moreover, you have forgotten the encouraging words addressed to you as daughters and sons,

> "My children, when our God corrects you,
> don't treat it lightly;
> and don't get discouraged
> when you are reprimanded.
> ⁶ For God disciplines the ones God loves
> and punishes all whom God acknowledges
> as daughters and sons."

⁷ Endure your trials as the discipline of God, who deals with you as daughters and sons. Have there ever been any children whose parents didn't discipline them? ⁸ If you aren't disciplined—and everyone receives discipline—then you are illegitimate children and not heirs.

⁹ Moreover, we had our human parents to discipline us, and we respected them for it. Wouldn't we much rather submit ourselves to our spiritual Parent, and live? ¹⁰ Our parents applied discipline for the short term—doing what they thought best. But God does it for our own good—that we may share in the divine holiness.

¹¹ At the time it is administered, any discipline seems a cause for grief, not joy, but later it bears fruit in peace and justice for those formed by it. ¹² So hold up your drooping hands and steady your trembling knees. ¹³ Make straight the path you tread, that your halting limbs will not be dislocated, but healed.

¹⁴ Always strive for peace with everyone and for the holiness without which no one can see our God. ¹⁵ See to it that no one falls short of God's grace, and that no bitter root starts growing, causing trouble and spreading defilement as it grows.

¹⁶ Take care that there be no immoral or godless person like Esau, who sold his own birthright for a single meal. ¹⁷ You know that later, when he wanted to inherit the blessing, he was rejected. Even though he sought it with tears, he couldn't bring about a change of heart.

¹⁸ What you have come to is nothing known to the senses: not a blazing fire, or a gloom turning to total darkness, or a storm, ¹⁹ or trumpeting thunder, or the great voice speaking such that those hearing it begged that no more be said to them. ²⁰ They couldn't bear to hear the command, "If even an animal touches the mountain, it must be stoned." ²¹ Indeed, so fearful was the spectacle that even Moses said, "I am terrified and trembling."

²² What you have drawn near to is Mount Zion and the city of the living God, the heavenly Jerusalem, where myriad angels have gathered for the festival with the whole church—²³ in which everyone is a "firstborn" and a citizen of heaven. You have come to God, the supreme Judge, and have been placed with the spirits of the holy ones who have been made perfect. ²⁴ You have come to Jesus—the mediator who brings a new Covenant—and to the sprinkled blood which pleads even more insistently than that of Abel.

²⁵ Make sure that you never refuse to listen to the One who speaks. If the people who refused to listen to the warning while on earth didn't escape, how much less will we escape if we refuse to listen to the voice of warning that comes from heaven? ²⁶ God's voice shook the earth then, but now God promises, "Once more I will shake not only the earth but also the heavens." ²⁷ That promise means that the things being shaken are created things, so that only those things that cannot be shaken will remain. ²⁸ Therefore, since we have inherited an unshakeable kindom, let us thankfully worship God in a way that is acceptable—in reverence and in awe. ²⁹ For our God is a consuming fire.

13:1–25

Continue to love each other as sisters and brothers.

² Don't neglect to show hospitality to strangers, for by doing so some people have entertained angels without knowing it.

³ Keep in mind those who are in prison, as though you were in prison with them. And be mindful of those who are being treated badly, since you know what they are enduring.

⁴ Let marriage be honored by everyone, and let the marriage bed be kept undefiled, for God will judge covenant breakers and adulterers.

⁵ Put the love of money out of your lives and be content with what you have, for God has said, "I will never leave you or forsake you." ⁶ Thus we may say with confidence,

"God is my Helper,
and I will not be afraid;
what can mere humans do to me?"

⁷ Remember your leaders, who preached the Word of God to you, and as you reflect on the outcome of their lives, imitate their faith. ⁸ Jesus is the same yesterday, today and forever.

⁹ Don't be led astray by all kinds of strange teachings. It is better to rely on grace for inner strength than on dietary laws, which don't give spiritual benefits to those who live by them. ¹⁰ We have our own altar, from which even those who serve in the tabernacle have no right to eat. ¹¹ The bodies of animals whose blood the high priest brings into the sanctuary as a sin offering are burned outside the camp. ¹² In the same way, Jesus suffered outside the city gate to sanctify the people with his own blood. ¹³ Let us, then, go to him outside the camp and share his degradation. ¹⁴ For there is no eternal city for us in this life—we seek the one which is to come.

¹⁵ Through Jesus let us continually offer God a sacrifice of praise—that is, the fruit of lips that acknowledge God's Name.

¹⁶ Keep doing good works and sharing your resources. These are the sacrifices that please God.

¹⁷ Obey your leaders, acknowledge their authority, because they must give an account of how they look after your souls. Make this a joy for them to do, and not a burden, for that would be of no advantage to you.

¹⁸ Pray for us. We are sure that we have a clear conscience, since we desire to live honorably in every way. ¹⁹ I ask you particularly to pray for my early return to you.

²⁰ May the God of peace, who brought back from the dead the great Shepherd of the sheep in the blood of the eternal Covenant, Jesus our Savior, ²¹ furnish you with all that is good, so you may do all that is pleasing to God. To Christ be glory forever! Amen.

²² Sisters and brothers, I ask that you take these words of advice kindly, for I have written you only a brief letter.

²³ I want you to know that our brother Timothy has been released from prison. If he arrives in time, he will be with me when I see you. ²⁴ Greetings to all your leaders and to all the saints. Those in Italy send you greetings.

²⁵ Grace be with you all. Amen.

james

1:1–27

From James, a servant of God and our Savior Jesus Christ,
To the twelve tribes of the diaspora:
Greetings.

² Think of it as pure joy, my sisters and brothers, whenever you face trials of any sort. ³ You understand that your faith is put to the test only to make you patient, ⁴ but patience too has its practical results—it's to make you fully mature and lacking in nothing.

⁵ If you lack wisdom, ask for it from God, who gives generously and ungrudgingly to all, and it will be given to you. ⁶ But you must ask in faith, never doubting, for the doubter is like the surf tossed and driven by the wind. ⁷ People like this must not expect to receive anything from God, ⁸ for they are devious and erratic in all they do.

⁹ Let sisters and brothers who are in humble circumstances take pride in their high position, ¹⁰ and let rich people take pride in their lowliness, for they will disappear "like the flowers of the field." ¹¹ When the sun comes up with its scorching heat and parches the meadow, the flowers wither and the meadow's loveliness disappears. Just so will the rich people wither away amid their many concerns.

¹² Blessed are those who persevere under trial! Once their worth has been proven, they will receive the crown of life that God has promised to the faithful. ¹³ No one who is tempted is free to say, "I am being tempted by God." God, who is not touched by evil, tempts no one. ¹⁴ Those who are tempted are attracted and seduced by their own wrong desires. ¹⁵ Then the desires conceive and give birth to sin, and when that sin is fully grown, it too has a child—death.

¹⁶ Make no mistake about this, my dear sisters and brothers: ¹⁷ every worthwhile gift, every genuine benefit comes from above, descending from the Creator of the heavenly luminaries, who cannot change and is never in shadow. ¹⁸ God willingly gave birth to us with a word spoken in truth, so that we may be, as it were, the firstfruits of God's creatures.

¹⁹ Remember this, my dear sisters and brothers: be quick to listen, but slow to speak and slow to anger; ²⁰ for God's justice is never served by our anger. ²¹ So do away with all your filth and the last vestiges of wickedness in you. Humbly welcome the word which has been planted in you, because it has power to save you.

²² But act on this word—because if all you do is listen to it, you're deceiving yourselves. ²³ Those who listen to God's word but don't put it into practice are like those who look into mirrors at their own faces; ²⁴ they look at themselves, then go off and promptly forget what they looked like. ²⁵ But those who look steadily at the perfect law of freedom and make it their habit—not listening and then forgetting, but actively putting it into practice—will be blessed in all that they do.

²⁶ If those who don't control their tongues imagine that they are devout, they're deceiving themselves and their worship is pointless. ²⁷ Pure, unspoiled religion, in the eyes of our Abba God, is this: coming to the aid of widows and orphans when they are in need, and keeping oneself uncontaminated by this world.

2:1–26

My sisters and brothers, your faith in our glorious Savior Jesus Christ must not allow favoritism. ² Suppose there should come into your assembly a person wearing gold rings and fine clothes and, at the same time, a poor person dressed in shabby clothes. ³ Suppose further you were to take notice of the well-dressed one and say, "Sit right here, in the seat of honor"; and say to the poor one, "You can stand!" or "Sit over there by my footrest." ⁴ Haven't you in such a case discriminated in your hearts? Haven't you set yourselves up like judges who hand down corrupt decisions?

⁵ Listen, dear sisters and brothers: didn't God choose those who are poor in the eyes of the world to be rich in faith, and heirs of the kindom promised to those who love God? ⁶ Yet you've treated poor people shamefully! Aren't rich people exploiting you? Aren't they the ones who haul you into the

courts, 7 and who blaspheme that noble Name by which you've been called?

8 You're acting rightly, however, if you fulfill the venerable law of the scriptures: "Love your neighbor as yourself." 9 But if you show favoritism, you commit sin, and that same law convicts you as transgressors. 10 Those who keep the whole Law except for one small point are still guilty of breaking all of it. 11 The One who said, "No adultery," also said, "No killing." So even if you don't commit adultery, if you do commit murder, you still break the Law.

12 Talk and behave as people who will be judged by the law of freedom, 13 because judgment without mercy will be the lot of those who are not merciful. Mercy triumphs over judgment.

14 My sisters and brothers, what good is it to profess faith without practicing it? Such faith has no power to save. 15 If any are in need of clothes and have no food to live on, 16 and one of you says to them, "Goodbye and good luck. Stay warm and well-fed," without giving them the bare necessities of life, then what good is this? 17 So it is with faith. If good deeds don't go with it, faith is dead.

18 Some of you will say that you have faith, while I have deeds. Fine: I'll prove to you that I have faith by showing you my good deeds. Now you prove to me that you have faith without any good deeds to show. 19 You believe in the One God. Fine. But even the demons have the same belief, and they tremble with fear. 20 Don't you realize, you idiots, that faith without good deeds is useless?

21 Wasn't our ancestor Abraham justified by his actions when he offered his child Isaac on the altar? 22 There you see proof that faith and deeds were working together and that faith was made complete by the deeds. 23 You also see that the scripture was fulfilled which says, "Abraham believed God, and it was credited to him as justice." This is why he is called "the friend of God." 24 So you see, people are justified by their works and not by faith alone.

25 And in the same way, wasn't even Rahab the prostitute justified by works when she welcomed the messengers and showed them a different way to leave?

26 Be assured, then, that faith without works is as dead as a body without a spirit.

3:1–5:20

Only a few of you, my sisters and brothers, should be teachers. You should realize that those of us who are teachers will be called to a stricter account. 2 After all, each of us falls from time to time.

However, those who never say anything wrong are truly close to perfection, because they can then control every part of themselves. 3 Once we put bits into the mouths of horses to make them obey us, we control the rest of their bodies. 4 The same with ships—no matter how large they are, and even if they are driven by fierce winds, they are directed by a very small rudder to wherever the captain wants to go.

5 The tongue is like that. It's a small part of the body, yet it makes great boasts. See how tiny the spark is that sets a huge forest ablaze! 6 The tongue is such a flame. Among all the parts of the body, the tongue is a whole wicked world in itself. It infects the entire body. Its flames encircle our course from birth, and its fire is kindled by hell. 7 All kinds of animals—birds, reptiles and creatures of the sea—can be tamed by us, 8 but no one can tame the tongue. It's a restless evil, full of deadly poison. 9 We use it to say, "Praised be our God and Creator"; then we use it to curse each other—we who are created in the image of God. 10 Blessing and curse come

out of the same mouth. This shouldn't be, my sisters and brothers! 11 Does a spring emit both pure water and brackish water? 12 My sisters and brothers, can a fig tree produce olives, or can a grapevine produce figs? No—and neither can a fountain produce both salt water and fresh water.

13 If there are any wise and learned among you, let them show it by good living—with humility, and with wisdom in their actions. 14 But if you have the bitterness of jealousy or self-seeking ambition in your hearts, be careful or you'll find yourself becoming arrogant and covering up the truth with lies. 15 This kind of "wisdom" doesn't come from above. It's earthbound, animal-like and demonic. 16 Where there is jealousy and ambition, there is also disharmony and wickedness of every kind. 17 The wisdom from above, however, has purity as its essence. It works for peace; it's kind and considerate. It's full of compassion and shows itself by doing good. Nor is there any trace of partiality or hypocrisy in it. 18 Peacemakers, when they work for peace, sow the seeds which will bear fruit in holiness.

4 :1 Where do these conflicts and battles among you first start? Isn't it that they come from the desires that battle within you? 2 You want something but don't get it, so you're prepared to kill to get it. You have ambitions that you can't satisfy, so you fight to get your way by force. The reason you don't have what you want is that you don't ask for it in prayer. 3 And when you do ask and don't get it, it's because you haven't prayed properly. You have prayed in order to indulge your own pleasures.

4 You faithless people, don't you know that making the world your friend is making God your enemy? Those who want to befriend the world make themselves enemies of God. 5 Do you think scripture says for no good reason that "the Spirit planted in us is passionate to the point of jealousy"? 6 She bestows a greater gift, which is why scripture says, "God resists the proud and favors the humble."

7 Submit yourselves, then, to God. Resist the Devil, and it will flee from you. 8 Draw near to God, and God will draw near to you.

Clean your hands, you sinners; purify your hearts, you double-dealers! 9 Look at your wretched condition and weep for it in misery. Be miserable rather than laughing, gloomy instead of happy. 10 Humble yourselves before our God, who will then raise you on high.

11 Sisters and brothers, don't slander one another. Whoever speaks evil of a sister or judges a brother, speaks against the Law and judges it. When you judge the Law, you cease keeping it and become a judge of it. 12 But there is only one Lawgiver, one Judge—only one who is able to save or destroy. Who then are you to judge your neighbor?

13 Come now, you who say, "Today or tomorrow we'll go to such-and-such a city, spend a year there, open a business and get rich." 14 You can never tell what your life will be like or what will happen tomorrow. You're no more than a vapor that appears briefly and then disappears. 15 Instead, you ought to say, "If it's our God's will, we will live to do such-and-such." 16 As it is, you boast and brag; all such boasting is evil. 17 Anyone who knows the right thing to do and doesn't do so—to that person it is sin.

5 :1 Now an answer for the rich: weep and howl for the miseries that are coming to you. 2 Your wealth is all rotting; your clothes are eaten up by moths. 3 Your gold and silver are corroding, and the same corrosion will be your own sentence: it will consume your flesh like fire. This is what you've stored up for yourselves to receive on the last day. 4 Laborers mowed your fields, and you cheated them! Listen to the wages that you kept back: they call out against you; realize that the cries of the reapers have reached the ears of our God Most High. 5 On earth you've had a life of comfort and luxury; you've been fattening yourselves for the day of slaughter. 6 It was you who condemned the innocent and killed them; they offered you no resistance.

7 Be patient, my sisters and brothers, until the appearance of Christ. See how the farmer awaits the precious yield of the soil, looking forward to it patiently while the soil receives the winter and spring rains. 8 You, too, must be patient. Steady your hearts, because the coming of Christ is at hand.

9 Don't grumble against one another, my sisters and brothers, or you will be judged. The Judge is standing at the door! 10 To learn how to persevere patiently under hardship, sisters and brothers, take as your models the prophets who spoke in the name of the Most High. 11 The ones we call "blessed" are the ones who persevered. You've heard of the patience of Job—do you remember what God, who is compassionate and merciful, did for him at the end of the story?

12 Above all, my sisters and brothers, don't swear any oath by heaven or by earth or by anything else. Let your "yes" be yes and your "no" be no. In this way you're not liable to judgment.

13 Are any of you in trouble? Then pray. Are any of you in good spirits? Then sing a hymn of praise. 14 Are any of you sick? Then call for the elders of the church, and have them pray over those who are sick and anoint them with oil in the name of Christ. 15 And this prayer offered in faith will make them well, and Christ will raise them up. If they have sinned, they will be forgiven. 16 So confess your sins to one another, and pray for one another, that you may be healed.

The prayers of the just are powerful and effective. 17 Elijah was human just like us, yet he prayed that it wouldn't rain, and it didn't rain for three and a half years. 18 Then he prayed again, and the heavens gave rain and the earth produced its crop.

19 My sisters and brothers, if you should wander from the truth and another should bring you back, 20 remember that whoever turns sinners from the error of their ways saves them from death and cancels a multitude of sins.

1 peter

1:1–12

1:13–2:10

From Peter, an apostle of Jesus Christ,

To those who live as resident aliens dispersed throughout Pontus, Galatia, Cappadocia, Asia and Bithynia—2 who have been chosen according to the foreknowledge of God the Creator, through the sanctifying work of the Spirit, that you may obey Jesus Christ and be sprinkled with Christ's blood:

May grace and peace be yours in abundance.

3 Praised be the Abba God of our Savior Jesus Christ, who with great mercy gave us new birth: a birth into hope, which draws its life from the resurrection of Jesus Christ from the dead; 4 a birth to an imperishable inheritance incapable of fading or defilement, which is kept in heaven for you 5 who are guarded with God's power through faith; a birth to a salvation which stands ready to be revealed in the last days.

6 There is cause for rejoicing here. You may, for a time, have to suffer the distress of many trials. 7 But this is so that your faith, which is more precious than the passing splendor of fire-tried gold, may by its genuineness lead to praise, glory and honor when Jesus Christ appears. 8 Although you have never seen Christ, you love Christ; and without seeing, you still believe, and you rejoice with inexpressible joy touched with glory, 9 because you are achieving faith's goal—your salvation.

10 This is the salvation the prophets were looking for and searching for so carefully; their prophecies were about the grace which has come to you. 11 The Spirit of Christ which was in them foretold the sufferings of Christ, and the glories that would come after those sufferings. They tried to find out at what time and in what circumstances all this was to happen. 12 However, it was revealed to them that the news they brought—regarding all the things that have now been announced to you by those who proclaimed the Good News, through the Holy Spirit who was sent from heaven—was for you and not for themselves. Even the angels long to catch a glimpse of such things.

So make your minds ready for action, and be sober. Put your hope in nothing but the grace that will be given you when Jesus Christ is revealed. 14 Be children of obedience. Don't behave the way you did when, in your ignorance, your desires were all you knew. 15 Be holy in everything you do, since it is the Holy One who has called you— 16 as scripture says, "You will be holy, for I am holy."

17 When you pray, you call on Abba God, who judges everyone impartially on the basis of their actions. Since this is so, conduct yourselves reverently during your sojourn in a foreign land. 18 Realize that you were delivered from the futile way of life your ancestors handed on to you, not by any diminishable sum of gold or silver 19 but by Christ's blood, which is beyond all price: the blood of a spotless, unblemished lamb 20 foreknown before the world's foundation and revealed for your sake in these last days. 21 It is through Christ that you are believers in God, the God who raised Christ from the dead into glory. Your faith and hope, then, are centered in God.

22 By obedience to the truth you have purified yourselves for a genuine love of your sisters and brothers. Therefore love one another constantly, from the heart. 23 Your rebirth has come not from a perishable seed but from an imperishable one— the living and enduring word of God. 24 For, as Isaiah says,

"All people are grass,
and the glory of mortals is like the flower of the field.
The grass withers, the flower wilts,
25 but the word of our God endures forever."

Now this "word" is the Good News which was proclaimed to you.

2 1 Therefore, never be spiteful, deceitful, hypocritical, envious or critical of each other.

2 Like newborn babies, be hungry for nothing but milk— the pure milk of the word that will make you grow into salvation, 3 now that you have "tasted that our God is good."

⁴ Come to Christ—a living stone, rejected by mortals but approved nonetheless, chosen and precious in God's eyes. ⁵ And you are living stones as well: you are being built as an edifice of spirit, to become a holy priesthood, offering spiritual sacrifices to God through Jesus Christ. ⁶ For scripture has it,

"See, I am laying a cornerstone in Zion;
an approved stone, and precious.
Those who put their faith in it
will not be shaken."

⁷ The stone is precious for you who have faith. But for those without faith,

"The stone which the builders rejected
has become the cornerstone,"

and, at the same time,

⁸ "an obstacle and a stumbling block."

Those who stumble and fall are the disbelievers in God's word; it is their destiny to do so.

⁹ You, however, are a "chosen people, a royal priesthood, a consecrated nation, a people set apart" to sing the praises of the One who called you out of the darkness into the wonderful, divine light. ¹⁰ Once you were "not a people," but now you are the people of God; once there was "no mercy for you," but now you have found mercy.

2:11–4:19

Dear friends, I urge you, as strangers and aliens in this world, to abstain from sinful passions which attack the soul. ¹² Live such good lives among the Gentiles that, though they accuse you of doing wrong, they may see your good deeds and glorify God on the day of visitation.

¹³ Accept the authority of every human institution for the sake of Christ, whether it be the ruler as the supreme authority, ¹⁴ or the governors who are sent by the ruler to punish wrongdoers and to commend those who are good citizens. ¹⁵ For it is the will of God that by doing right you may silence those who are foolish in their ignorance. ¹⁶ Live as free women and men. Don't use your freedom to cloak evil, but to serve God.

¹⁷ Respect all people. Love the family of believers. Stand in awe before God. Honor the ruler.

¹⁸ You who are in bondage, show respect to your overseers—both to those who are good and considerate and to those who are cruel. ¹⁹ For grace is given if you endure unjust punishment for your conscience in the name of God.

²⁰ What credit is there if you patiently endure harsh punishment as a result of your sin? But if you put up with suffering for doing what is right, this is acceptable in God's eyes. ²¹ It was for this that you were called, since Christ suffered for you in just this way and left you an example. You must follow in the footsteps of Christ, ²² who did no wrong, who spoke no deceit, ²³ who did not return insults when insulted, who, when made to suffer, did not counter with threats. Instead, Christ trusted the One who judges justly. ²⁴ It was Christ's own body that brought our sins to the cross, so that all of us, dead to sin, could live in accord with God's will. By Christ's wounds you are healed. ²⁵ At one time you were straying like sheep, but now you have returned to the Shepherd, the Guardian of your souls.

3 ¹ Those of you in relationships, be submissive to one another—so that spouses who have not yet submitted to the Word may be won over ² when they witness the example and respectful attitude of their partners. ³ Dress modestly,

and not for show—without fancy hairstyles, gold jewelry or fine apparel. ⁴ Your attractiveness should reside inside, in the heart, with the imperishable quality of a gentle and calm disposition, which is precious in the sight of God. ⁵ We have the example of holy people of ages past who hoped in God and were attractive because of their humility. ⁶ Didn't Sarah confirm their destiny when she called Abraham "Sovereign One?" You are children of Sarah and Abraham when you fearlessly do what is good.

⁷ Husbands have a special obligation to be understanding and nurturing. Men, though physically stronger than women, must nonetheless acknowledge their equal status—that women are joint heirs of the gift of life. Doing so will ensure that your prayers are not hindered.

⁸ All of you must be of one mind. Be sympathetic, loving, compassionate, humble. ⁹ Never return evil for evil, or insult for insult, but give a blessing instead. You were called to do this, to inherit a blessing yourself. ¹⁰ For,

"Whoever would love life
and see good days
must keep the tongue from evil
and the lips from deceitful talk.
¹¹ They must turn from evil to good,
they must seek peace and pursue it.
¹² For the eyes of our God
are on the just,
and the ears of our God
attend to their prayers.
But the face of our God
is turned against evildoers."

¹³ Who is going to harm you if your goal is to do what is right? ¹⁴ But even if you do suffer for what is right, count it a blessing. Don't fear what they fear. Don't be afraid, and don't worry.

¹⁵ In your hearts, set Jesus apart as holy and sovereign. Should anyone ask you the reason for this hope of yours, be ever ready to reply, but speak gently and respectfully. ¹⁶ Keep your conscience clear so that, whenever you are defamed, those who slander your way of life in Christ may be shamed. ¹⁷ If it should be God's will that you suffer, it is better to do so for good deeds than for evil ones.

¹⁸ The reason Christ died for sins once for everyone—the just for the sake of the unjust—was in order to lead you to God. Jesus was put to death in the flesh but was given life in the Spirit. ¹⁹ And in the Spirit, Jesus went and preached to the imprisoned spirits. ²⁰ They had refused obedience long ago, while God waited patiently in the days of Noah and the building of the ark, in which a few persons, eight in all, were brought to safety through the water. ²¹ That water prefigured the water of baptism through which you are now brought to safety. Baptism is not the washing away of physical dirt, but the appeal made to God by a good conscience: it brings salvation through the resurrection of Jesus Christ, ²² who entered heaven and is now at the right hand of God, having dominion over angelic authorities and powers.

4 ¹ Accordingly, remind yourselves of what Christ suffered while among us, and equip yourselves with a similar attitude. For if you suffer in the body, you have broken with sin and, ² as a result, you won't spend the rest of your life on human desires, but on the will of God. ³ You dallied long enough in the past, living the kind of life some Gentiles choose: licentious living, lust, drunkenness, orgies, carousing and following false gods. 4 In all this, they consider it odd when you don't leap into the same flood of dissipation, and they slander you. 5 But they will eventually answer for it before the One who stands ready to judge the living and the dead. 6 This explains why the Gospel was preached also to the dead—that though judged in the flesh like the rest of humankind, they might live for God in the Spirit.

7 The end of all things is near. Therefore be clear-minded and self-controlled so that you can pray. 8 Above all, let your love for one another be constant, for love covers a multitude of sins. 9 Be mutually hospitable without complaining.

10 As generous distributors of God's manifold grace, put your gifts at the service of one another, each in the measure you have received. 11 The one who speaks should deliver God's message. The one who serves should do so with the strength provided by God, so that in all things God may be glorified through Jesus Christ, who has been given all glory and dominion throughout the ages. Amen.

12 Don't be surprised, my dear friends, that a trial by fire is occurring in your midst. It is a test for you, but it shouldn't catch you off guard. 13 Rejoice, instead, insofar as you share the Savior's sufferings, so that when the glory of Christ is revealed, you will rejoice exceedingly. 14 Happy are you when you are insulted for the sake of Christ, for then God's Spirit in her glory has come to rest on you.

15 See to it, however, that none of you suffers for being a murderer, a thief, an evildoer, or a destroyer of another's rights. 16 If anyone suffers for being a follower of Christ, however, that one ought not be ashamed, but rather should glorify God in virtue of that Name.

17 It is time for the judgment to begin with the family of God. And if we are only the beginning, what will happen by the time those who disobey the Good News of God are judged? 18 If it is hard for a good person to be saved, where will the wicked and the sinners be? 19 Therefore those who suffer according to God's will do the right thing, and commit themselves to their faithful Creator.

I send a word of advice to the elders among you. I, too, am an elder, as well as a witness to the sufferings of Christ and a partaker of the glory that will be revealed.

2 Shepherd the flock entrusted to you. Shepherd it, not just out of duty, but eagerly, as God would have it. Don't do it for money, but do it freely.

3 Don't be pompous or domineering, but set an example for the whole community to follow. 4 Then when the chief Shepherd comes, you will receive a crown of unfading glory. 5 Let the young among you respect the leadership of the elders. Let all of you clothe yourselves in humility toward each other, for "God opposes the proud and gives grace to the humble." 6 Therefore, humble yourselves before God's mighty power, that you may be exalted by God on the appointed day.

7 Cast all your cares on God, who cares for you. 8 Be sober. Be watchful. For your adversary the Devil roams about like a roaring lion seeking someone to devour. 9 Stand up to the Devil as one strong in faith, fortified with the knowledge that your sisters and brothers throughout the world share the same afflictions.

10 But the God of all grace, who called you to eternal glory through Jesus Christ, will fulfill, restore, strengthen and establish you after you have suffered a little while. 11 To God be glory and dominion forever and ever! Amen.

12 This letter was dictated to Silas, a faithful coworker I know and can trust. I have written this note to exhort you, and to testify that this is the true grace of God. Stand steadfast in it.

13 The church in "Babylon," chosen just as you are, sends greetings, as does my son Mark. 14 Greet one another with a holy kiss. Peace to all who are in Christ.

2 peter

From Simon Peter, servant and apostle of Jesus Christ,

To those who received a faith equal to ours through the justice of our God and Savior Jesus Christ:

2 May grace and peace be yours in abundance through your knowledge of our God and of Jesus our Sovereign.

3 Divine power has given us everything we need for life and godliness through our knowledge of God, who called us to share in the divine glory and goodness. 4 In bestowing these gifts, God has given us the guarantee of something very great and wonderful to come. Through them you'll be able to share the divine nature, and escape corruption from a world sunk in vice.

5 For this very reason, make every effort to add to your faith, goodness; and to goodness, knowledge; 6 and to knowledge, self-control; and to self-control, perseverance; and to perseverance, godliness; 7 and to godliness, familial love; and to familial love, truly unselfish love.

8 For if these qualities are yours and they are growing in you, they will protect you from becoming ineffective and unfruitful; and they will bring you to a true knowledge of our Savior Jesus Christ. 9 But those who lack these qualities are blind and nearsighted and have forgotten that they are

cleansed of their past sins. 10 Sisters and brothers, you have been called and chosen. Strive that much harder to be up to your calling. In this way you will avoid stumbling 11 and will ultimately receive a warm welcome into the eternal kindom of our Sovereign and Savior Jesus Christ.

My goal is to remind you constantly of these truths, even though you already know them and firmly possess them. 13 I consider it right, so long as I am in this tent that is my body, to motivate you with reminders. 14 For I know that I will soon be laying aside this earthly tent, as our Savior Jesus Christ has foretold to me. 15 I will be diligent in my teaching, so that even after I'm gone you will be able to recall these truths.

16 We did not cleverly devise fables when we taught you of the power and coming of our Savior Jesus Christ; we ourselves saw the majesty of our Savior. 17 For Jesus was honored and glorified by our Creator God when the voice of the Majestic Glory spoke out, "This is my Own, whom I love, and with whom I am well pleased." 18 We heard this ourselves—this voice from heaven—when we were with Jesus on the holy mountain. 19 Moreover, we have the prophetic word, which

is even more certain. Depend on it for your own good as a light shining in the dark, until first light breaks and the morning star rises in your hearts.

[20] At the same time, you need to know that no prophecy of scripture ever occurred by one's own interpretation. [21] Prophecy never comes through an act of human will, but comes as people have spoken for God under the power of the Holy Spirit.

2 [1] Even so, there were false prophets in the past among our people, and you will have your share of false prophets in the future. They will subtly introduce false heresies among you, to the point of denying the One who paid the price for their freedom. They will quickly fall to ruin, [2] but many will follow their licentious practices, and the Way of Truth will fall under a cloud of doubt because of them. [3] They will use lies to exploit you through greed.

But since the very beginning, their sentence has perpetually hung over them, and their damnation never sleeps. [4] When the angels sinned, God did not spare them, but condemned them to the dungeons of the underworld to await the final judgment. [5] Nor did the Most High spare the ancient world. God spared Noah, the paragon of justice, along with seven others, but flooded the ungodly world; [6] God turned the cities of Sodom and Gomorrah into a pile of ashes as a warning to the ungodly about the future; [7] God rescued the just Lot, who was oppressed by the filthy conduct of wicked people [8] that he both witnessed and heard about as he lived among them; he suffered daily torment to his soul because of their lawlessness. [9] But God knows how to rescue the godly from torment, and to incarcerate the unjust until the day of judgment.

[10] This pertains especially to those who succumb to the desires of the flesh, and to those who rebel against all authority. These bold and willful people are not afraid to revile the glorious angels— [11] even though the angels, with all their superior strength and power, don't speak a word of judgment against them in the presence of our God. [12] These people—who blaspheme anything they don't understand—are irrational animals, bred to be captured and killed, destroying themselves by their own destructive instincts. [13] They will reap evil in reward for the evil they do. They revel in the daylight just for the fun of it. They are nothing but stains and blemishes. And they make amusement at your expense, even when you sit as a guest at their table. [14] With their adulterous eyes they seduce the unstable because of their infinite capacity for sin. Their profession is greed—an accursed breed! [15] They have abandoned the straight and narrow, straying onto the way of Balaam ben-Beor, who lusted for the wages of injustice. [16] But he was admonished by a mute animal, a donkey speaking with a human voice, which put an end to the prophet's madness. [17] These people are waterless wells and storm-driven mists. Utter darkness is reserved for them. [18] With their hollow, arrogant talk about the pleasures of the flesh, they seduce people who have only just escaped from those who live in error. [19] They promise freedom, while they themselves are slaves to sin—for whatever dominates you makes you a slave.

[20] If you've survived the enticements of the world through knowing our Sovereign and Savior Jesus Christ, you'll be ultimately worse off than at the start if you slip and are overcome a second time. [21] Better not to have known the way of holiness, than to have known it and later reject the holy commandment. [22] What happens to that person shows the truth of the proverbs: "The dog turns back to its vomit," and, "The sow is bathed only to wallow again in the mud."

3:1–18

Beloved, this is the second letter I have written you. I wrote both of them to stir up your honest minds. [2] Call to mind what the holy prophets of old taught us, and the commandments of our Savior Jesus Christ which you received from the apostles.

[3] Keep in mind that in the last days naysayers will show up to deride you, all the while following their own evil desires, [4] and asking, "Where is this promised 'coming'? From the time our ancestors died, life goes on as it has from the creation!" [5] They choose to ignore the fact that by God's word the heavens existed at the beginning, and that the earth was created out of water and through water. [6] By this same word, waters flooded the world then in existence and destroyed it. [7] The present heavens and earth are destined for fire by this same word and are being preserved until the day of judgment when all the ungodly are destroyed.

[8] This point must not be overlooked, dear friends: in the eyes of the Most High, one day is like a thousand years, and a thousand years are like a day. [9] God does not delay in keeping the promise, as some mean "delay." Rather, God shows you generous patience, desiring that no one perish but that all come to repentance.

[10] The day of our God will come like a thief, and on that day the heavens will vanish with a roar; the elements will catch fire and fall apart, and the earth and all its works will be destroyed in the flames. [11] Since everything is to be destroyed in this way, what holy and devoted lives you should lead! [12] Look for the coming of the Day of God, and try to hasten it along. Because of it, the heavens will be destroyed in flames and the elements will melt away in a blaze. [13] But what we await are new heavens and a new earth where, according to the promise, God's justice will reside. [14] So beloved, while waiting for this, make every effort to be found at peace and without stain or defilement in God's sight. [15] Consider our God's patience as your opportunity for salvation.

Our dear brother Paul also wrote you about this, according to the wisdom he had been given. [16] Paul writes this way and speaks of these issues in all of his letters—though he does, admittedly, write some things that are hard to understand, which ignorant and unbalanced people distort to their own undoing, as they do the other scriptures.

[17] But be forewarned, beloved sisters and brothers: do not be carried away by the errors of unprincipled people and thus forfeit the security you enjoy. [18] Instead, grow in the grace and knowledge of our Sovereign and Savior Jesus Christ, who is glorified now and for all eternity. Amen.

1 john

1:1–2:17

That which was from the beginning,
which we have heard,
and seen with our eyes,
and have looked at
and touched with our hands:
the Word, who is Life—
this is the subject of our letter.

2 That life came to be;
we saw it and bear witness to it.
We proclaim to you the eternal life
which was with Abba God
and was manifested to us.

3 What we have seen and heard
we declare to you,
so that you may be one with us—
as we are one with Abba God
and with the Only Begotten, Jesus Christ.

4 We write this to fulfill our joy.

5 This, then, is the message we heard from Jesus
and declare to you:
God is light,
and in God there is no darkness at all.

6 If we say we have intimacy with God
while still living in darkness,
we are liars
and do not live in truth.

7 But if we live in the light,
as God is in the light,
we are one with each other,
and the blood of Jesus, the Only Begotten,
purifies us from all sin.

8 If we say we are without sin,
we lie, and the truth is not in us.

9 But if we admit our sins,
God, the faithful and just One,
will forgive our sins
and cleanse us from all injustice.

10 If we say we have not sinned,
we call God a liar
and show that God's Word is not in us.

2 1 My little ones,
I am writing this to keep you from sin.
But if anyone should sin,
we have an Advocate with God—
Jesus Christ, who is just.

2 Jesus is the full payment for our sins,
and not for our sins only,
but for those of the whole world.

3 We can be sure that we know God
only by keeping the commandments.

4 Anyone who says, "I know God,"
and does not keep the commandments
is a liar and refuses to admit the truth.

5 But when anyone does obey God's word,
God's love comes to perfection in that person.

This is how you know that you are in God: 6 if you say you abide in Christ, you ought to live the same kind of life as

Christ. 7 Dear friends, this is not a new commandment that I am writing to tell you, but an old commandment—one that you were given from the beginning. The old commandment is the message you have heard. 8 On the other hand, what I am writing to you is indeed a new commandment. Its truth is seen in Christ and in you, because the night is passing and the true light is already shining. 9 Those who claim to be in the light but hate their neighbors are still in the dark. 10 But those who love their neighbors are living in the light and need not be afraid of stumbling. 11 Those who hate their neighbors are in the darkness and do not know where they are going, because the darkness has blinded them.

12 I am writing to you, my children,
because your sins have already been forgiven
through the name of Jesus.

13 I am writing to you, mothers and fathers,
who have come to know the One
who has existed from the beginning.
I am writing to you, young women and men,
who have already conquered the Evil One.
I have written to you, children,
because you already know our Creator.

14 I have written to you, mothers and fathers,
who have come to know the One
who has existed from the beginning.
I have written to you, young women and men,
because you are strong,
and the Word of God remains in you,
and you have overcome the Evil One.

15 Do not love this passing world or anything that is in the world. The love of Abba God is not in anyone who loves this world, 16 for anything that this world has to offer—the cravings of the flesh, the cravings of the eye, the boastful pride of life—could never come from Abba God, but only from this world. 17 And this world, with its cravings, is passing away; but anyone who does the will of God will not pass away.

2:18–4:6

Children, it is the final hour; just as you heard that the Antichrist was coming, so now many such antichrists have appeared. This is how we know that these are the last days. 19 These rivals of Christ came from our own numbers, but they never really belonged. If they had belonged, they would have stayed with us. But they left us, which proves that not one of them ever belonged to us.

20 But you have been anointed by the Holy One, so that all knowledge is yours. 21 My reason for writing is not that you don't know the truth, but that you do, and that you already know that no lie can come from the truth.

22 Who is the liar? The person who denies that Jesus is the Christ. Such a person is an antichrist and is denying Abba God as well as the Only Begotten. 23 No one who denies the Only Begotten has Abba God; whoever acknowledges the Only Begotten has Abba God as well.

24 As for you, let what you heard from the beginning remain with you, then you in turn will remain in the Only Begotten and in Abba God. 25 And this is the promise Christ gave us: eternal life. 26 I write these things to you about those who are trying to lead you astray. 27 As for you, the anointing you received from Christ remains in you, and you do not need anyone to teach you. The anointing that Christ gave you

teaches you everything; you are anointed with truth, not with a lie. Remain in Christ, then, as the anointing taught you. [28] Remain in Christ, then, my children, so that when Christ returns we need not hide in shame on the day of that coming. [29] You know that God is righteous; you should know, then, that everyone whose life is righteous is born of God.

3 [1] See what love Abba God has lavished on us
in letting us be called God's children!
Yet that in fact is what we are.
The reason the world does not recognize us
is that it never recognized God.
[2] My dear friends,
now we are God's children,
but it has not been revealed
what we are to become in the future.
We know that when it comes to light
we will be like God,
for we will see God
as God really is.

[3] All who keep this hope keep themselves pure, just as Christ is pure.

[4] Anyone who sins at all breaks the Law, because to sin is to break the Law. [5] Now, you know that Christ, who is sinless, appeared to abolish sin. [6] So everyone who lives in union with Christ does not continue to sin, but whoever continues to sin has never seen or known Christ.

[7] Dear children, do not let anyone lead you astray; to live a holy life is to be holy, just as Christ is holy. [8] To lead a sinful life is to belong to the Devil, since the Devil was a sinner from the beginning. It was to undo everything the Devil has done that the Only Begotten of God appeared. [9] Those who have been born of God do not sin. Because God's seed remains inside them, they cannot sin when they have been born of God. [10] In this way, we distinguish the children of God from the children of the Devil. Any who do not live holy lives and love their sisters and brothers are not children of God.

[11] This, remember, is the message you heard from the beginning: we should love one another. [12] Do not be like Cain, who belonged to the Evil One and killed his brother. Why did Cain kill Abel? Because his own deeds were wicked and Abel's deeds were just.

[13] Do not be surprised, sisters and brothers, if the world hates you. [14] We know that we have passed from death to life because we love our sisters and brothers; if we refuse to love we are still dead. [15] Those who hate their sisters or brothers are murderers. And murderers, you know, do not have eternal life in them.

[16] This is how we know what love is: Jesus Christ died for us. And we, too, ought to lay down our lives for our sisters and brothers. [17] If you have more than enough material possessions and see your neighbors in need yet close your hearts to them, how can the love of God be living in you? [18] My children, our love must not be simply words or mere talk—it must be true love, which shows itself in action and truth. [19] This, then, is how we'll know we belong to the truth; this is how we'll be confident in God's presence, [20] even if our consciences condemn us. We know that God is greater than our consciences and that God knows everything. [21] And if our consciences do not condemn us, my friends, then we have confidence before God, [22] and we will receive whatever we ask from God's hand—because we keep the commandments and do what is pleasing in God's sight. [23] The commandments are these: that

we believe in the name of God's Own, Jesus Christ, and that we love one another as we were told to do. [24] Those who keep these commandments live in God and God lives in them. We know that God lives in us by the Spirit given to us.

4 [1] Dear friends, it is not every spirit that you can trust. Test them to see if they come from God. There are many false prophets in the world. [2] This is how you can recognize the Spirit of God: every spirit that acknowledges that Jesus Christ came in the flesh is from God. [3] And every spirit that does not acknowledge Jesus is not from God. This spirit is the Antichrist, which you have heard about and is already in the world.

[4] Dear friends, you have already overcome these false prophets, because you are from God and have in you the One who is greater than anyone in the world. [5] As for them, they are of the world; they speak the language of the world, and the world listens to them. [6] But we are from God, and those who know God listen to us. Those who are not of God refuse to listen to us. This is how we can tell the spirit of truth from the spirit of falsehood.

4:7–21

Beloved,
let us love one another
because love is of God;
everyone who loves is begotten of God
and has knowledge of God.
[8] Those who do not love have known nothing of God,
for God is love.
[9] God's love was revealed in our midst in this way:
by sending the Only Begotten into the world,
that we might have faith through the Anointed One.
[10] Love, then, consists in this:
not that we have loved God,
but that God has loved us
and has sent the Only Begotten
to be an offering for our sins.
[11] Beloved,
if God has loved us so,
we must have the same love for one another.
[12] No one has ever seen God.
Yet if we love one another,
God dwells in us,
and God's love is brought to perfection in us.
[13] The way we know that we remain in God and God
in us
is that we have been given the Spirit.
[14] We have seen for ourselves and can testify
that God has sent the Only Begotten as Savior of the
world.
[15] When any acknowledge that Jesus is the Only
Begotten,
God dwells in them
and they in God.
[16] We have come to know and to believe
in the love God has for us.
God is love,
and those who abide in love
abide in God,
and God in them.

[17] Love will come to perfection in us when we can face the day of judgment without fear—because our relation to

this world is just like Christ's. ¹⁸ There is no fear in love, for perfect love drives out fear. To fear is to expect punishment, and anyone who is afraid is still imperfect in love.

¹⁹ We love because God first loved us. ²⁰ If you say you love God but hate your sister or brother, you are a liar. For you cannot love God, whom you have not seen, if you hate your neighbor, whom you have seen. ²¹ If we love God, we should love our sisters and brothers as well; we have this commandment from God.

5:1–21

Everyone who believes that Jesus is the Messiah
has been born of God.
Everyone who loves God
loves the One who has come from God.
² We can be sure that we love God's children
when we love God and do what God has
commanded.
³ The love of God consists of this:
that we keep God's commandments.
And these commandments are not burdensome.
⁴ Everyone born of God conquers the world,
and the power that has conquered the world
is our faith.
⁵ Who then can overcome the world?
The one who believes
that Jesus is the Only Begotten of God.
⁶ Jesus Christ came by water and blood—
not by water alone,
but with water and blood.
⁷ It is the Spirit who testifies to this,
and she is truth.

⁸ So there are three witnesses: the Spirit, the water, and the blood, and all three of them are of one accord. ⁹ We accept the testimony of human witnesses, but God's testimony is much greater—and this is God's testimony, given as evidence of the Only Begotten of God. ¹⁰ Those who believe in this One have this evidence within their hearts. Those who don't believe God have made God a liar by refusing to believe in the testimony given on behalf of the Only Begotten of God. ¹¹ The testimony is this: God has given us eternal life, and this life is in the Only Begotten. ¹² Whoever has the Only Begotten has life, and whoever does not have the Only Begotten does not have life.

¹³ I have written all this to you who believe in the Only Begotten of God, so that you may know that you have eternal life.

¹⁴ We are quite confident that if we ask anything of God, and if it is in accord with God's will, it will be heard. ¹⁵ And knowing that whatever we ask, we are heard, we understand that the request is already granted in the asking. ¹⁶ If any of you sees a sister or brother committing a sin that is not a deadly sin, you have only to pray and God will give life to the sinner. This is only for those whose sin is not deadly. There is a sin that leads to death, and I do not say that you must pray about that. ¹⁷ Every kind of wrongdoing is evil, but not all sin is deadly.

¹⁸ We know that everyone begotten of God does not sin, because the Only Begotten of God protects them, and the Evil One does not touch them. ¹⁹ We know that we belong to God, but the whole world lies in the power of the Evil One. ²⁰ We know, too, that the Only Begotten of God has come and has given us knowledge about the One who is true. We are in the One who is true, and we are in our Savior Jesus Christ. This is the true God; this is eternal life.

²¹ Children, watch out for false gods.

2 john

1–13

From the elder,

To the chosen one and her children, whom I love in the truth—and not only I, but also all who have come to know the truth— ² because of the truth that lives in us and is with us forever:

³ May grace, mercy, and peace be with you in truth and love, from God our Creator and from Jesus Christ, God's Only Begotten.

⁴ It has given me great joy to find some of your children walking in the path of truth, just as we were commanded by Abba God. ⁵ Now I would make this request of you—but it is not as if I were writing you some new commandment; rather, it is a commandment we have had from the start: let us love one another. ⁶ And this is love, that we walk according to the commandments; and as you have heard from the beginning, the commandment is the way in which you should walk.

⁷ Many deceitful people have gone out into the world, people who do not acknowledge Jesus Christ as coming in the flesh. They are the spirit of the Deceitful One! They are the Antichrist! ⁸ Look out that you yourselves do not lose what you have worked for; you must receive your reward in full. ⁹ Those who are so progressive that they do not remain rooted in the teaching of Christ do not possess God, while those who remain rooted in the teaching possess both Abba God and the Only Begotten.

¹⁰ Any who come to your house without this doctrine are not to be welcomed. Don't even greet them, ¹¹ for whoever greets them shares in their evil work.

¹² There are many things I have to tell you, but I choose not to use paper and ink. Rather, I choose to visit you and talk to you personally so that our joy may be complete.

¹³ The children of your chosen sister send you their greetings.

3 john

1–15

From the elder,
To Gaius, my dear friend, whom I love in truth:

² My dear friend, I pray that all is well with you, and that you are as healthy physically as your soul is spiritually. ³ It was a source of great joy for me to receive from some of our coworkers word of your faithfulness to the truth, and your continued walk in the truth. ⁴ My greatest source of joy is to hear that my children live by the truth.

⁵ My friend, you demonstrate fidelity by all that you do for the travelling teachers and missionaries, even though they are strangers; ⁶ indeed, they have testified to your love before the church. And you will do a good thing if, in a way that pleases God, you help them to continue their journey. ⁷ It was for the sake of the Name that they set out, and they are accepting nothing from the Gentiles. ⁸ Therefore, we owe it to such people to support them and thus share in the work of truth.

⁹ I wrote a letter for the members of the church, but Diotrephes, who enjoys dominating, refuses to acknowledge us. ¹⁰ So if I do come, I will tell everyone what he is doing, and how he spreads malicious gossip about us. As if that weren't enough, he not only refuses to welcome our coworkers, he also interferes with those who want to do so, and banishes them from the church.

¹¹ But as for you, my dear friend, don't imitate evil. Imitate what is good instead. Those who do what is right are children of God; those who do what is evil have never seen God.

¹² Everyone has good things to say about Demetrius—as does the truth itself. I too vouch for Demetrius, and you know that my word is true.

¹³ There are many other things I want to tell you, but I hesitate to put them to pen and ink. ¹⁴ However, I look forward to seeing you shortly, when we will talk face to face.

¹⁵ Peace be with you. Friends here send their greetings. Greet friends there by name.

jude

1–25

From Jude, a servant of Jesus Christ and a brother of James,
To those among the called who are dear to God the Creator and kept safe for Jesus Christ:

² May mercy, peace and love be yours in abundance.

³ My dear friends, I eagerly anticipated writing to you about the salvation we all share. But now I feel compelled to write and exhort you to contend for the faith which was once and for all time consigned to the holy people of God. ⁴ Certain individuals have infiltrated your ranks. These are the very ones we wrote you about long ago, when we condemned them for ungodliness. They turn the grace of our God into a license for immorality, and reject our Sovereign and Savior Jesus Christ.

⁵ Let me remind you what you already know—that our God liberated a people from Egypt, but later destroyed those who did not believe. ⁶ Let me also remind you of the angels who held positions of supreme authority, which they gave up, abandoning their assigned domain; God now keeps them chained in darkness awaiting the judgment of the great day. ⁷ Likewise, Sodom and Gomorrah and their neighboring towns serve as a warning to us—they received the punishment of eternal fire because of their sexual promiscuity and their pursuit of fleshly vice.

⁸ In the same way, these deluded people defile their bodies, reject authority and malign the glorious angels. ⁹ Not even Michael the archangel, when arguing with the Devil about the body of Moses, dared to use such abusive language. All Michael said was, "May our God rebuke you!" ¹⁰ But these people speak abusively of anything they do not understand. And those things they do understand—instinctively, like mute animals—will eventually be their destruction. ¹¹ Tragically, they will reap what they have sowed, for they have followed the path of Cain. They have rushed headlong into Balaam's mistake, and will receive the same reward. They rebelled—and will perish—as did Korah.

¹² These people are a dangerous element at your agape feasts. They come only for the food, and only for themselves. They are wind-blown, rainless clouds. They are twice-dead autumn trees, without roots or fruit. ¹³ They are wild waves of the sea, foaming with shame. They are shooting stars destined for the darkness of the black hole. ¹⁴ Enoch, in the seventh generation after Adam, had them in mind when he prophesied,
"I tell you,
our God will come with tens of thousands of holy ones
¹⁵ to execute judgment on all of humankind,
to judge guilty the wicked for all their evil deeds
and the ungodly for their defiant words
against the Almighty."

¹⁶ These people are mischief-makers and grumblers whose only goals are their selfish desires. Arrogance pours from their mouths, and they flatter people any time it will help them get their way.

¹⁷ Remember, my friends, what the apostles of our Savior Jesus Christ told you to expect. ¹⁸ "At the end-time," they told you, "there will be those who sneer at religion and follow only their own wicked desires." ¹⁹ These are divisive people who, bereft of the Spirit, have only their natural instincts to rely on.

²⁰ But you, dear friends, strengthen yourselves in your holy faith—pray in the Holy Spirit. ²¹ Stay true to God's love and embrace the mercy of our Savior Jesus Christ, which leads to eternal life. ²² Reassure those who have doubts. ²³ Rescue others by snatching them from the fire. With still others, show them mercy tempered by fear—so much that you'd hate even to touch their clothing, so polluted are they by the flesh.

²⁴ But there is One who can prevent you from falling and make you stand pure and exultant in the presence of eternal glory. ²⁵ To God, the only God, who saves us through Jesus Christ our Sovereign, be glory, majesty, authority and power—who was before all time, is now, and will be forever. Amen.

the Revelation of jesus christ

1:1–8

This is the Revelation of Jesus Christ, given by God to show the faithful what must happen very soon. God made it known by sending an angel to John, the faithful subject, ² who in writing down everything he saw, bears witness to the word of God and the testimony of Jesus Christ. ³ Happy are those people who read this prophetic message, and happy are those who hear it and heed what is written in it, for the time is near!

⁴ From John,
To the seven churches in the province of Asia:
Grace and peace to you, from the One who is, who was, and who is to come, from the seven spirits before the throne ⁵ and from Jesus Christ, the faithful witness, the Firstborn from the dead, sovereign of the rulers of the earth.
To Christ—who loves us, and who has freed us from our sins by the shedding of blood, ⁶ and who has made us to be a kindom of priests to serve our God and Creator—to Jesus Christ be glory and power forever and ever! Amen.

⁷ Look! Christ is coming on the clouds
for every eye to see,
even those who pierced Jesus,
and all the peoples of the earth
will mourn over Christ.
So be it! Amen.

⁸ "I am the Alpha and the Omega," says our God, "who is, who was and who is to come, the Almighty."

1:9–3:22

I, John, your brother, who share with you the trial, the kindom, and the perseverance we have in Jesus, was on the island of Patmos because I proclaimed God's word and bore witness to Jesus. ¹⁰ It was the first day of the week and I was in the Spirit, when suddenly I heard behind me a piercing voice like the sound of a trumpet, ¹¹ which said, "Write on a scroll what you see, and send it to the seven churches: to Ephesus, Smyrna, Pergamum, Thyatira, Sardis, Philadelphia and Laodicea."

¹² I turned around to see who spoke to me, and I saw seven lampstands of gold ¹³ and, among the lampstands, a figure of human appearance wearing an ankle-length robe with a golden sash across its chest. ¹⁴ The figure's head and hair were white as wool or snow, and its eyes were like a blazing flame. ¹⁵ Its feet were like burnished bronze refined in a furnace, and its voice was like the sound of crashing surf. ¹⁶ In its right hand the figure held seven stars, and out of its mouth came a sharp, double-edged sword. Its face shown like the sun at high noon.

¹⁷ When I saw it, I fell down as though dead. It touched me with its right hand and said, "Don't be afraid. I am the First and the Last, ¹⁸ the Living One. Once I was dead, but now I live forever and ever. I hold the keys of death and the underworld. ¹⁹ Write down, therefore, everything you see—things as they are now, and things that will take place in the future. ²⁰ The seven stars you saw in my right hand, and the seven golden lampstands, are symbols: the seven stars are

the angels of the seven churches, and the seven lampstands are the seven churches.

2 ²¹ "To the angel of the church in Ephesus, write this:
The One who holds the seven stars in its right hand and walks among the seven golden lampstands says this: ² I know your deeds, your labors, your patient endurance. I know you cannot tolerate the wicked, that you have tested the impostors who claimed to be apostles and found them false. ³ I know, too, that you have patiently endured hardship for my sake and have not become discouraged. ⁴ I hold this against you, though: you have left your first love. ⁵ Call to mind the heights from which you have fallen. Repent and do the good you did at first. If you don't repent, I will come to you and remove your lampstand from its place. ⁶ But you have this in your favor: you loathe what the Nicolaitans are doing, which I also hate.

⁷ Whoever has ears to hear, listen to what the Spirit says to the churches. To the one who overcomes, I will give the right to eat from the tree of life which stands in the paradise of God.

⁸ "To the angel of the church in Smyrna, write this:
The First and the Last, who died and came to life, says this: ⁹ I know your hardships and your poverty—yet you are rich. I know the slander of those who profess to be Jewish but are not; they are really members of the synagogue of Satan. ¹⁰ Don't be afraid of the sufferings that come. I tell you, the Devil is about to send some of you to prison to test you, and you will undergo an ordeal for ten days. Be faithful until death, and I will give you the crown of life.

¹¹ Whoever has ears to hear, listen to what the Spirit says to the churches. The one who overcomes will not be destroyed by the second death.

¹² "To the angel of the church in Pergamum, write this:
The One with the sharp, two-edged sword says this: ¹³ I know that you live where Satan is enthroned. Yet you remain faithful to my name, and you did not renounce your faith in me—even in the days of Antipas, my faithful witness, who was martyred in your city, where Satan lives.

¹⁴ Nevertheless, I have a few complaints against you. You have among you those who hold to the teachings of Balaam, who instructed Balak to put a stumbling block in front of the Israelites, tempting them to sin by eating food sacrificed to idols and by being sexually promiscuous. ¹⁵ Likewise you also have among you those who hold to the teachings of the Nicolaitans. ¹⁶ You must repent, or I will soon come to you and attack these people with the sword of my mouth.

¹⁷ Whoever has ears to hear, listen to what the Spirit says to the churches. To the one who overcomes I will give the hidden manna and a white stone—a stone with a new name written on it, known only to the person who receives it.

¹⁸ "To the angel of the church in Thyatira, write this:
The Only Begotten of God, who has eyes like a blazing flame, and feet like burnished bronze, says this: ¹⁹ I know your works, your love and faith, your service and endurance, and that you're still making progress.

²⁰ Nevertheless, I have a complaint against you: you tolerate Jezebel, who claims to be a prophet, who leads my

faithful astray so that they become promiscuous and eat food sacrificed to idols. ²¹ I have given her time to repent, but she refuses to give up her idolatry. ²² So I will cast her on a bed of suffering, and I will plunge those who join her into intense suffering, unless they repent of their ways. ²³ I will kill her children with a plague. Then all the churches will realize that I search hearts and minds to give to each of you what your behavior deserves. ²⁴ But I say to the rest of you in Thyatira, to you who have not held to her teachings and know nothing of Satan's so-called deep secrets: on you I will impose no other burden. ²⁵ Just hold on to what you have until I come.

²⁶ To the one who overcomes and keeps my ways until the end, I will give authority over the nations; ²⁷ 'you will rule them with an iron scepter, you will shatter them like pottery,' just as I have received authority from Abba God. ²⁸ And I will give you the morning star. Whoever has ears to hear, listen to what the Spirit says to the churches.

3 ¹ "To the angel of the church in Sardis, write this:

The One who holds the seven spirits of God and the seven stars says this: I know your conduct; I know the reputation you have of being alive, when in fact you are dead! ² Wake up and strengthen what remains before it dies. I find that the sum of your deeds is less than complete in the sight of my God. ³ Call to mind how you accepted what you heard; keep to it, and repent. If you don't rouse yourselves, I will come upon you like a thief, at a time you cannot know. ⁴ I realize you have in Sardis a few people who have not soiled their garments; these will walk with me in white because they are worthy.

⁵ The one who overcomes will go clothed in white. I will never erase your name from the book of life, but will acknowledge you in the presence of our God and the angels. ⁶ Whoever has ears to hear, listen to what the Spirit says to the churches.

⁷ "To the angel of the church in Philadelphia, write this:

The One who is holy and true, who holds the key of David, who opens what no one can close, who closes what no one can open, says this: ⁸ I know all about you. And now I have placed before you an open door, which no one can close. I know that though you have limited strength, you have kept my word and not denied my name. ⁹ Now I will make the synagogue of Satan—those who claim to be Jewish and are not, for they are liars—I will make them come and fall at your feet and acknowledge that I have loved you. ¹⁰ Because you have kept my command to endure all trials, I will also keep you safe in the time of trial that is going to come upon the whole world to test it. ¹¹ I am coming soon. Hold fast to what you have, so that no one will take your crown.

¹² The one who overcomes I will make into a pillar in the Temple of my God, and you will stay there forever. I will inscribe on you the Name of my God and the name of the city of my God, the new Jerusalem which comes down from my God in heaven. On you I will also write my new name. ¹³ Whoever has ears to hear, listen to what the Spirit says to the churches.

¹⁴ "To the angel of the church in Laodicea, write this:

The Amen, the Witness faithful and true, the Source of God's creation, says this: ¹⁵ I know your deeds, I know that you are neither cold nor hot. How I wish you were one or the other—hot or cold! ¹⁶ But because you are lukewarm, neither hot nor cold, I will vomit you out of my mouth! ¹⁷ You keep saying, "I am so rich and secure that I want for nothing."

Little do you realize how wretched you are, how pitiable and poor, how blind and naked! ¹⁸ Take my advice. Buy from me gold refined by fire, if you would be truly rich. Buy white garments to wear, if the shame of your nakedness is to be covered. Buy ointment to smear on your eyes, if you would see once more. ¹⁹ Whoever is dear to me, I will correct and discipline. Be earnest about it, therefore. Repent! ²⁰ Here I stand, knocking at the door. If any hear me calling and open the door, I will enter the house and have supper with them.

²¹ To the one who overcomes I will give the right to sit with me on my throne, as I myself overcame and took my seat beside my Abba God on the heavenly throne. ²² Whoever has ears to hear, listen to what the Spirit says to the churches.

4:1–8:1

After this I saw a door standing open above me in heaven, and I heard the trumpetlike voice which had spoken to me before. It said, "Come up here, and I will show you what must take place in the time to come."

² Immediately I was caught up in the Spirit. A throne was standing there in heaven, and on the throne was seated ³ One who looked like jasper and carnelian. Around the throne was a halo the color of emerald.

⁴ Surrounding the throne were twenty-four other thrones, upon which were seated twenty-four elders; they were clothed in white garments and had gold crowns on their heads. ⁵ From the throne came flashes of lightning and peals of thunder; before it burned seven flaming torches, the seven spirits of God. ⁶ The floor around the throne was like a sea of glass that shone as crystal.

At the very center, around the throne itself, stood four living creatures; they were covered with eyes front and back. ⁷ The first creature resembled a lion, the second an ox, the third had a human face, while the fourth looked like an eagle in flight. ⁸ Each of the four living creatures had six wings and eyes all over, inside and out. Day and night, without pause, they sing,

"Holy, holy, holy, is our God Almighty,
who was, who is, and who is to come!"

⁹ Whenever these creatures give glory and honor and praise to the One seated on the throne, who lives forever and ever, ¹⁰ the twenty-four elders fall down and worship the One seated on the throne, who lives forever and ever. They throw down their crowns before the throne and sing,

¹¹ "O God Most High, you are worthy
to receive glory and honor and power!
For you have created all things;
by your will they came to be and were made!"

5 ¹ In the right hand of the One who sat on the throne, I saw a scroll. It had writing on both sides and was sealed with seven seals.

² Then I saw a mighty angel proclaiming in a loud voice, "Who is worthy to open the scroll and break its seals?" ³ But no one in heaven, on earth or under the earth could be found to open the scroll or examine its contents. ⁴ I wept bitterly because no one could be found to open or examine the scroll.

⁵ One of the elders said to me, "Don't weep. The Lion of the tribe of Judah, the Root of David, has triumphed and will open the scroll with the seven seals."

⁶ Then, between the throne with the four living creatures and the elders, I saw a Lamb standing, a Lamb that had been slain. It had seven horns and seven eyes; these eyes are the

seven spirits of God sent to all parts of the world. ⁷ The Lamb came and received the scroll from the right hand of the One who sat on the throne.

⁸ When it had taken the scroll, the four living creatures and the twenty-four elders fell down before the Lamb. Each of the elders held a harp, and golden bowls filled with incense, which are the prayers of God's holy people. ⁹ This is the new hymn they sang:

> "Worthy are you to receive the scroll
> and break the seven seals,
> for you were slain.
> With your blood you purchased for God
> members of every race and tongue,
> of every people and nation.
> ¹⁰ You made of them a kindom,
> priests to serve our God,
> and they will reign on the earth."

¹¹ Then in my vision, I heard the voices of many angels who surrounded the throne together with the living creatures and the elders. They were numberless, thousands and tens of thousands, ¹² and they all cried out:

> "Worthy is the Lamb that was slain
> to receive power and wealth,
> wisdom and strength,
> honor and glory and praise!"

¹³ Then I heard the voice of every creature in heaven, on the earth, under the earth and in the sea. Everything in all creation cried aloud:

> "To the One seated on the throne and to the Lamb,
> be praise and honor,
> glory and dominion,
> forever and ever!"

¹⁴ The four living creatures said, "Amen!" and the elders fell on their faces and worshiped.

6 ¹ Then I watched as the Lamb broke the first of the seven seals, and I heard one of the four living creatures shout in a voice like thunder, "Come!"

² I looked, and there was a white horse with a rider holding a bow. The rider was given a victor's laurel and rode out as one bent on victory.

³ When the lamb broke the second seal, I heard the second living creature cry out, "Come!"

⁴ And out came another horse, a bright red one. Its rider was given a sword, with the mandate to take away peace from the earth, so that people would slaughter one another.

⁵ When the lamb broke the third seal, I heard the third living creature cry out, "Come!"

I looked, and there was a black horse, and its rider held a pair of scales. ⁶ Then I heard what sounded like a voice from among the four living creatures say, "A ration of wheat for a day's wages, and three rations of barley for a day's wages, and take care not to harm the wine and the oil."

⁷ When the lamb broke the fourth seal, I heard the voice of the fourth living creature cry out, "Come!"

⁸ I looked, and there was a pale, ghastly green horse. Its rider was named Death, and the netherworld followed close behind. They were given authority over a quarter of the world to kill by the sword, by famine, by plague and by wild animals.

⁹ When the lamb broke the fifth seal, underneath the altar I saw the souls of all the people who were killed because they had borne witness to the Word of God. ¹⁰ They shouted in a loud voice, "How much longer, Holy Sovereign One, before you sit in judgment and avenge our blood on the inhabitants of the earth?"

¹¹ Then each of them was given a white robe, and they were told to be patient a while longer, until the full number of the faithful—sisters and brothers who were to be killed just as they had been—was complete.

¹² I watched as the lamb broke the sixth seal. There was a great earthquake, and the sun turned black as coarse sackcloth. The moon turned blood red, ¹³ and the stars of the sky fell to earth like figs falling from the tree in a strong wind. ¹⁴ The sky tore and withdrew like two scrolls rolling up, and every mountain and island was removed from its place.

¹⁵ Then all the rulers of the earth—the governors, the military leaders, rich and influential people—as well as every other person, enslaved or free, took to the mountains and hid in caves and among the rocks. ¹⁶ They cried out to the rocks and the mountains, "Fall on us and hide us from the One who sits on the throne and from the wrath of the Lamb! ¹⁷ The great day of their wrath has come! Who can survive it?"

7 ¹ After this I saw the four angels that stood at the four corners of the earth, holding back the four winds of the world to prevent them from blowing on the land or on the sea or in the trees. ² Then I saw another angel rising from the east, carrying the seal of the living God. It called out in a powerful voice to the four angels who had been given the power to devastate the land and the sea: ³ "Don't harm the land or the sea until we have put our God's seal on the foreheads of the faithful!"

⁴ Then I heard the number of those who were marked with the seal: there were 144,000, out of all the tribes of Israel. ⁵ From the tribe of Judah 12,000 were marked with the seal; from the tribe of Reuben, 12,000; from the tribe of Gad, 12,000; ⁶ from the tribe of Asher, 12,000; from the tribe of Naphtali, 12,000; from the tribe of Manasseh, 12,000; ⁷ from the tribe of Simeon, 12,000; from the tribe of Levi, 12,000; from the tribe of Issachar, 12,000; ⁸ from the tribe of Zebulun, 12,000; from the tribe of Joseph, 12,000; and from the tribe of Benjamin, 12,000.

⁹ After that, I saw before me an immense crowd without number, from every nation, tribe, people and language. They stood in front of the throne and the Lamb, dressed in long white robes and holding palm branches. ¹⁰ And they cried out in a loud voice,

> "Salvation is of our God,
> who sits on the throne,
> and of the Lamb!"

¹¹ All the angels who were encircling the throne, as well as the elders and the four living creatures, prostrated themselves before the throne. They worshiped God ¹² with these words: "Amen! Praise and glory and wisdom and thanksgiving and honor and power and strength be to our God forever and ever! Amen!"

¹³ Then one of the elders asked me, "These people in white robes—who are they, and where do they come from?"

¹⁴ I answered, "You are the one who knows." Then the elder said to me, "These are the ones who survived the great period of testing; they have washed their robes in the blood

of the Lamb and made them white. [15] That's why they stand before God's throne and the One they serve day and night in the Temple; the One who sits on the throne will shelter them forever. [16] Never again will they be hungry or thirsty; the sun and its scorching heat will never beat down on them, [17] for the Lamb, who is at the center of the throne, will be their shepherd and will lead them to springs of living water. And God will wipe every last tear from their eyes."

8 [1] When the Lamb opened the seventh seal, there was silence in heaven for about half an hour.

8:2–11:18

Then I saw the seven angels who stand before God being given seven trumpets.

[3] Another angel, who had a golden censer, came and stood before the altar. It was given a large quantity of incense to offer with the prayers of all the holy ones, on the golden altar that stood before the throne. [4] The smoke of the incense, together with the prayers of the holy ones, went up before God from the angel's hand.

[5] Then the angel took the censer, filled it with fire from the altar, and threw it down onto the earth. Immediately there came peals of thunder, loud noise, flashes of lightning and an earthquake.

[6] The seven angels who had been given the seven trumpets prepared to blow them.

[7] When the first angel blew its trumpet, there came hail and fire mixed with blood, which was hurled down on the earth. A third of the earth was burned up, as was a third of the trees, and all the green grass.

[8] When the second angel blew its trumpet, something like a huge mountain blazing with fire was thrown into the sea. [9] A third of the sea was turned into blood, a third of all the creatures living in the sea died, and a third of the ships were destroyed.

[10] When the third angel blew its trumpet, a great star burning like a torch fell from the sky. The star fell on a third of all the rivers and springs. [11] The name of the star is Wormwood, and a third of the waters were poisoned as if by wormwood. Many people died from the waters which had become poisonous.

[12] When the fourth angel blew its trumpet, a third of the sun, a third of the moon and a third of the stars were struck, so that a third of them grew dark. A third of the day and a third of the night were without light.

[13] As I watched, I heard an eagle flying overhead cry out in a loud voice, "Sorrow! Sorrow! Sorrow to the inhabitants of the earth because of the trumpet blasts about to be sounded by the next three angels!"

9 [1] Then the fifth angel blew its trumpet, and I saw a star that had fallen from the sky to the earth. The star was given the key to the shaft leading down to the Abyss. [2] When it unlocked the shaft to the Abyss, smoke billowed out of the Abyss like smoke from a huge furnace. The smoke from the Abyss darkened the sun and the sky.

[3] Out of the smoke came locusts, and they rained down onto the earth. They were given power like the scorpions of the earth. [4] They were instructed not to harm any of the grass, plants or trees of the earth—only those people who did not have the seal of God on their foreheads. [5] They were instructed not to kill, but only to torment them for five months; their torment was a sting like the scorpion's. [6] When this happens people will seek death, but will not find it; they will long to die, but death will shun them.

[7] The locusts looked like horses ready for battle. They had what looked like gold crowns on their heads, and their faces resembled those of humans. [8] They had long hair on their heads, and their teeth were like those of a lion. [9] They had scales like iron breastplates, and the noise of their wings sounded like many horses and chariots thundering into battle. [10] They had tails like scorpions, complete with stingers, and their tails had the power to torment people for five months. [11] They had as their ruler the angel of the Abyss, whose name is Destroyer—in Hebrew, Abaddon; in Greek, Apollyon.

[12] The first sorrow has passed. Two more are yet to come.

[13] The sixth angel blew its trumpet, and I heard a voice coming from the four horns of the golden altar before God. [14] It said to the sixth angel who had the trumpet, "Release the four angels who are bound at the great river Euphrates."

[15] So the four angels who had been kept ready for this very hour and day and month and year were released to slay a third of humankind. [16] The number of the mounted troops was two hundred million—I heard their number.

[17] As the vision continued I saw horses and their riders: their breastplates were flame red, hyacinth blue and sulphur yellow; the horses had lion's heads, and fire, smoke and sulphur were coming out of their mouths. [18] It was by these three plagues—the fire, the smoke, and the sulphur that came out of their mouths—that a third of humankind was slain. [19] The power of the horses was in their mouths and in their tails; their tails were like snakes, with heads that inflicted injury.

[20] The rest of humankind—those who were not slain by these plagues—refused to repent of the work of their hands. They didn't stop worshipping demons and idols made of gold, silver, bronze, stone and wood—idols that cannot see or hear or walk. [21] Nor did they turn from their murders, their sorcery, their debauchery or their stealing.

10 [1] Then I saw another mighty angel coming down from heaven. It was robed in a cloud with a rainbow over its head. Its face was like the sun and its legs were like pillars of fire. [2] In its hands it held a small scroll, unrolled. It put its right foot in the sea and its left foot on the land.

[3] The angel shouted so loud that it was like a lion roaring. When it shouted, the seven thunders raised their voices, too. [4] And when the seven thunders had spoken, I was about to write it down when I heard a voice from heaven say to me, "Seal up what the seven thunders have spoken. Don't write it down."

[5] Then the angel I saw standing on the sea and on the land raised its right hand to heaven. [6] And it swore, "By the One who lives forever and ever, who made heaven and all that is in it, and the earth and all that it bears, and the sea and all that it holds: the time of waiting is over! [7] When the seventh angel sounds its trumpet, the hidden plan of the Most High will be fulfilled, as was promised in the Good News to God's faithful, the prophets."

⁸ Then the voice that I had heard from heaven spoke to me again and said, "Go, take the scroll from the hand of the angel standing on the land and on the sea."

⁹ I went up to the angel and said, "Give me the little scroll."

The angel said to me, "Here, take it and eat it! It will be sour in your stomach, but in your mouth it will taste as sweet as honey."

¹⁰ I took the little scroll from the angel's hand and ate it. In my mouth it tasted as sweet as honey, but when I swallowed it my stomach turned sour. ¹¹ Then someone said to me, "You must once again prophesy about many peoples, nations, languages and rulers."

11 ¹ Then I was given a reed as a measuring rod, and I was told, "Go and measure the sanctuary of God, and the altar, and count the people worshipping there. ² Exclude the outer court of the sanctuary and don't measure it, for it has been handed over to the Gentiles who will trample the holy city for forty-two months. ³ And I will send my two witnesses, clothed in sackcloth, to prophesy for those 1,260 days."

⁴ These two witnesses are the two olive trees and the two lampstands which stand in the presence of the God of the earth. ⁵ If anyone tries to harm them, fire will come out of the mouths of these witnesses to devour their enemies. Anyone attempting to harm them must be killed in this way.

⁶ These witnesses have power to shut up the sky so that no rain will fall during the time of their mission. They also have power to turn water into blood and to afflict the earth at will with any kind of plague.

⁷ When they have finished giving their testimony, the beast that comes up from the abyss will wage war against them and will conquer and kill them. ⁸ Their corpses will lie in the streets of the great city—the one symbolically called "Sodom," and "Egypt"—where their Sovereign was crucified. ⁹ People from every race and civilization, language and nation, will stare at their corpses for three and a half days but refuse to bury them. ¹⁰ The earth's inhabitants will gloat over them, and in their merriment will exchange gifts, because these two prophets harassed everyone on earth.

¹¹ But after three and a half days, the breath of life returned to them from God. When they stood on their feet, sheer terror gripped those who saw them. ¹² The two prophets heard a loud voice from heaven say to them, "Come up here!" Then they went up to heaven in a cloud as their enemies looked on.

¹³ At that very hour there was a violent earthquake, and a tenth of the city collapsed. Seven thousand people were killed in the earthquake. The survivors were terrified and gave glory to the God of heaven.

¹⁴ The second sorrow has passed. The third is coming soon.

¹⁵ Then the seventh angel blew its trumpet. And loud voices in heaven began calling,

"The kindom of the world
has become the kindom of our God
and of God's Messiah,
who will reign forever and ever!"

¹⁶ And the twenty-four elders, who were seated on their thrones before God, prostrated themselves and worshiped God, ¹⁷ saying,

"We give thanks to you, Sovereign God Almighty,
the One who is and who was,
for using your great power
and establishing your reign.

¹⁸ The nations raged,
but now it is time for your own anger,
and time for judging the dead,
and for rewarding your faithful and your prophets,
and your holy ones and those who revere your
Name—
both great and small—
and for destroying those
who destroy the earth."

11:19–15:4

Then God's sanctuary in heaven was opened, and within it the Ark of the Covenant could be seen. There were flashes of lightning, loud noises, peals of thunder, an earthquake and a violent hailstorm.

12 ¹ Then a great sign appeared in heaven: a woman clothed with the sun, with the moon under her feet, with twelve stars on her head for a crown. ² She was pregnant and in labor, crying out in pain as she was about to give birth.

³ Then another sign appeared in heaven: a huge red dragon, with seven heads and ten horns, and each of the seven heads with a crown. ⁴ Its tail swept a third of the stars from the sky and hurled them down to the earth.

The dragon stood before the woman about to deliver, to devour her child the moment she gave birth. ⁵ The woman gave birth to a male child, a son, who is to rule the world with an iron rod. But the child was snatched straight up to God and God's throne. ⁶ The woman fled into the desert, to a place prepared for her by God, where she will be kept safe for 1,260 days.

⁷ Then war broke out in heaven. Michael and the angels fought against the dragon. The dragon and its angels fought back, ⁸ but they were defeated and driven out of heaven. ⁹ The great dragon, the primeval serpent who is called the Devil or Satan, who had deceived the whole world, was hurled down to the earth, and its angels were banished with it.

¹⁰ Then I heard a loud voice in heaven shout:

"Now have come salvation and power,
and the kindom of God,
and all authority for God's Anointed.
For the accuser of our sisters and brothers,
who accused them before our God night and day,
has been brought down.
¹¹ They triumphed over the accuser
by the blood of the Lamb,
and by the word of their testimony;
their love of life
did not dissuade them from death.
¹² Let the heavens rejoice
and all who dwell in them;
but woe to you,
earth and sea,
for the Devil has come down to you
filled with fury,
for it knows
that its days are numbered."

¹³ When the dragon saw that it had been hurled to the earth, it pursued the woman who gave birth to the male child. ¹⁴ The woman was given the two wings of the great eagle, so she could fly to the place prepared for her in the desert, where she was looked after for three and a half years, out of the

serpent's reach. [15] So the serpent vomited a river of water from its mouth to sweep the woman away in the current. [16] But the earth came to the woman's rescue by opening its mouth and swallowing the river that the dragon had vomited up.

[17] Then the dragon was enraged with the woman, and went off to wage war with the rest of her offspring—those who keep God's commandments and hold to the testimony of Jesus.

Then I stood on the seashore, **13**[:1] and I watched a beast emerge from the sea. It had seven heads and ten horns, with a crown on each horn. Each head was marked with a blasphemous name. [2] The beast looked like a leopard, with paws like a bear and a mouth like a lion. The dragon gave the beast its power and its throne and its worldwide authority.

[3] I noticed that one of its heads seemed to have been fatally wounded, but the wound had healed. The whole world marveled at that, and followed the beast. [4] People worshiped the dragon because it had given authority to the beast; they also worshiped the beast and said, "Who can compare with the beast, and who can challenge it?"

[5] The beast was given a mouth to utter arrogant and blasphemous words, and to exercise authority for forty-two months. [6] The beast opened its mouth to blaspheme God, and to slander the Name and the dwelling place of God and those who live in heaven. [7] It was allowed to make war against the holy ones and to conquer them. And it was granted authority over every tribe, people, tongue and nation. [8] All the inhabitants of the earth will worship the beast—all whose names have not been written in the book of life since the creation of the world, which belongs to the Lamb who was slain.

[9] Whoever has ears to hear, listen!
[10] Whoever is destined for captivity,
into captivity will go.
Whoever is destined to die by the sword,
by the sword will die.

This calls for patient endurance and faithfulness on the part of the holy ones.

[11] Then I saw a second beast come out of the earth. It had two horns like a lamb, but it spoke like a dragon. [12] It exercised all the authority of the first beast on its behalf, and made the earth and its inhabitants worship the first beast, whose fatal wound had healed. [13] And it worked great miracles, even calling fire down from heaven onto the earth while people watched. [14] It deceived the inhabitants of the earth with the miracles it was able to work.

And it ordered them to set up a statue in honor of the beast who had been wounded by the sword and revived. [15] It was given permission to breathe life into the statue, so that the statue could speak and cause all who refused to worship the statue to be killed. [16] It also forced everyone—small and great, rich and poor, free and oppressed—to be branded on the right hand or on the forehead. [17] No one could buy or sell without the mark—that is, the name of the beast, or the number that stood for its name.

[18] Wisdom is required here. Let those who have insight figure out a number for this beast—a "human" number: 666.

14[:1] Then I saw the Lamb in my vision. It was standing on Mount Zion, and with it were the hundred forty-four thousand who had its name and the name of Abba God written on their foreheads.

[2] I heard a sound from heaven which resembled the roaring of the deep, or loud peals of thunder; the sound I heard was like the melody of harpists playing on their harps. [3] They were singing a new hymn before the throne in the presence of the four living creatures and the elders. This hymn no one could learn except the hundred forty-four thousand who had been ransomed from the world. [4] They are the ones who have never defiled themselves sexually: they are pure, and they follow the Lamb wherever it goes. They have been ransomed as the firstfruits of humankind for God and the Lamb. [5] On their lips no deceit has been found; they are indeed without flaw.

[6] Then I saw another angel flying high overhead, sent to announce the Good News of eternity to all who live on the earth—every nation, race, language and tribe. [7] It said in a loud voice, "Give reverence and glory to God, for the hour of divine judgment has come. Worship the One who made the heavens, the earth, the sea and the springs of water."

[8] A second angel followed and said, "Babylon has fallen! Babylon the Great has fallen, who made the whole world drink the wine of its corrupt passions."

[9] A third angel followed them and shouted, "All who worship the beast and its image, or accept its mark on the forehead or the arm, [10] will drink the wine of God's fury, which has been poured, undiluted, into the cup of divine wrath. They will be tormented with burning sulphur in the presence of the holy angels and of the Lamb. [11] The smoke of their torments will rise up forever and ever. There will be no rest, day or night, for those who worshiped the beast and its image, or accepted the mark of its name."

[12] This calls for the endurance of the holy ones, those who keep God's commandments and remain faithful to Jesus.

[13] Then a voice from heaven said, "Write this down: Happy are they who die in our God for all eternity."

"Yes," says the Spirit, "let them rest from their work, for their deeds accompany them."

[14] In my vision a white cloud appeared, and on the cloud sat someone who looked like the Promised One, wearing a crown and holding a sharp sickle. [15] Then an angel came out of the Temple and in a loud voice cried out to the one sitting on the cloud, "Use your sickle and cut down the harvest, for now is the time to reap; the earth's harvest is fully ripe." [16] So the one sitting on the cloud wielded the sickle over all the earth and reaped the earth's harvest.

[17] Then out of the Temple in heaven came another angel, who likewise held a sharp sickle. [18] A second angel, who was in charge of the fire at the altar of incense, cried out in a loud voice to the one who held the sharp sickle, "Use your sharp sickle and gather the grapes from the vines of the earth, for the clusters are ripe." [19] So the angel wielded the sickle over the earth and gathered the grapes of the earth. The angel threw them into the huge winepress of God's wrath. [20] They were crushed in the winepress outside the city, and the blood poured out of the press to the height of a horse's bridle for sixteen hundred furlongs.

15[:1] I saw another sign in heaven, great and awe-inspiring: seven angels holding the seven final plagues which would bring God's wrath to a climax.

[2] I then saw something like a sea of glass commingled with fire. On the sea of glass were standing those who had won the victory over the beast and its image and the number that signified its name. They were playing the harps used in worshipping God, [3] and they sang the song of Moses, servant of God, and the song of the Lamb:

"Mighty and wonderful are your works,
O God Almighty!

Just and true are your ways,
O Ruler of the nations!
4 Who would dare refuse your honor,
or the glory due your Name, O God?
Since you alone are holy,
all nations will come
and worship in your presence.
Your mighty deeds are clearly seen."

15:5–16:21

After this I saw the Temple, the Tent of the Testimony in heaven, opened, 6 and out came seven angels with seven plagues. They were wearing pure white linen, each with a gold sash around its waist. 7 Then one of the four living creatures gave each of the seven angels a bowl filled with the fury of God, who lives forever and ever. 8 Then the Temple filled so completely with the smoke from the glory of God and from God's power, that no one could enter it until the seven plagues of the seven angels were completed.

16 1 Then I heard a loud voice speaking from the temple to the seven angels: "Go, and pour out the seven bowls of God's fury on the earth."

2 The first angel went out and poured its bowl over the earth. Ugly and virulent sores broke out on the people who wore the mark of the beast and worshiped its image.

3 The second angel poured out its bowl onto the sea, which became like the blood of a corpse, and every living creature in the sea died.

4 The third angel poured its bowl onto the rivers and the springs of water. They also turned to blood. 5 Then I heard the angel in charge of the waters say,

"You are just in these judgments,
Sovereign God Almighty,
you who are and who were;
6 for they have shed the blood
of your holy ones and your prophets,
and you have given them blood
to drink as they deserve."

7 Then I heard the altar itself say,

"Truly, Sovereign God Almighty,
the punishments you give
are true and just."

8 The fourth angel poured its bowl on the sun. This angel had the power to burn people with fire. 9 Even though people were scorched by the searing heat, they cursed the Name of God, who had the power to cause such plagues. And they refused to repent or give glory to God.

10 The fifth angel poured its bowl onto the throne of the beast, and its empire was plunged into darkness. People bit their tongues in agony, 11 and cursed the God of heaven because of their pains and sores. But they did not repent of their deeds.

12 The sixth angel emptied its bowl onto the great river Euphrates. Its water dried up so that an entrance was made for the rulers of the East. 13 Then I saw, coming out of the mouths of the dragon, the beast and the false prophet, three foul spirits that looked like frogs—14 demonic spirits who worked miracles. They went out to the rulers of the whole world, to call them together for battle on the great Day of Almighty God.

15 "Behold, I will come like a thief. Blessed are those who stay awake and keep their clothes with them, so they need not go naked and be shamefully exposed."

16 They then gathered the rulers together in the place that is called, in Hebrew, Armageddon.

17 The seventh angel poured its bowl into the air, and out of the Temple came a loud voice that said, "It is finished." 18 Then there were lightning flashes, peals of thunder and a great earthquake—such a violent earthquake that it was unmatched since humankind began on earth. 19 The great city split into three parts, and the cities of the world collapsed. But God remembered Babylon the Great and made it drain the cup filled with the wine of God's fury. 20 Every island fled away and the mountains vanished. 21 Huge, hundred-pound hailstones fell from the sky onto the people. Yet the people still blasphemed God for the plague of hail, because it was the most terrible plague.

17:1–19:10

An angel who had been holding one of the seven bowls came to me and said, "Come here and I will show you the punishment of the famous Idolater who reigns near the place of many waters. 2 The rulers of the earth joined in the Idolater's sin, and the inhabitants of the earth got drunk on the wine of their idolatry."

3 Then the angel carried me away in the Spirit to a desert place, where I saw a figure on a scarlet beast that was covered with blasphemous names. The beast had seven heads and ten horns. 4 The figure was dressed in purple and scarlet, and glittered with gold, precious stones and pearls. It held a gold wine cup filled with the abominable and sordid work of debauchery.

5 This cryptic name was written on its forehead: "Babylon the Great, Source of All Idolatry and of the Abominations of the Earth." 6 I saw that the figure was drunk on the blood of the holy ones and on the blood of the martyrs for Jesus.

When I saw this I was completely mystified. 7 The angel said to me, "Why are you mystified? I will explain to you the mystery of the figure and of the beast it rides, which has the seven heads and the ten horns. 8 The beast you saw once existed but is no more. It will arise from the Abyss, but only to go to its destruction. The inhabitants of the earth whose names have not been written in the book of life from the creation of the world will be amazed when they see the beast, because it once was, now is not, and yet is still to come.

9 "Here is something for a shrewd mind: the seven heads represent seven hills, and the figure is sitting on them. 10 They are also seven rulers. Five have fallen and one still lives. And the seventh has not yet come—but when it does, this ruler will remain only for a short time. 11 The beast that once was, and now is not, is the eighth ruler. It is the eighth, but it belongs to the seven—and it is going to its destruction.

12 "The ten horns you saw are ten rulers; they have not yet received their realms, but for one hour they receive authority as rulers along with the beast. 13 They are all of one mind, and they will put their powers at the beast's disposal. 14 They will go to war against the Lamb, but the Lamb will defeat them. For the Lamb is the Sovereign of Sovereigns

and the Ruler of Rulers, and those who follow the Lamb are the called, the chosen and the faithful."

¹⁵ Then the angel said to me, "The waters you saw, beside which the famous Idolater sat, are peoples and multitudes and nations and languages. ¹⁶ But the time will come when the beast and the ten horns you saw will hate the Idolater. They will bring it to ruin and leave it naked; they will eat its flesh and burn the remains. ¹⁷ For God has influenced their minds to carry out the divine will: to delegate their rulership to the beast, until God's words are fulfilled. ¹⁸ The Idolater you saw is the great city that reigns over the rulers of the earth."

18

¹ After this, I saw another angel coming down from heaven. Its authority was so great that the earth was lit up by its glory. ² The angel cried out in a strong voice,

"Fallen, fallen, is Babylon the great!
It has become the dwelling place for demons.
It is a haunt for every unclean spirit,
a cage for every filthy and disgusting bird.
³ For all the nations have drunk
the maddening wine of idolatry.
The rulers of the earth
joined in the Idolater's sin,
and the the earth's buyers and sellers
grew rich because of their idolatrous greed."

⁴ Then I heard another voice from heaven say,

"Come out of the Idolater, my people,
so that you will not share in its sins,
so that you will not receive any of its plagues,
⁵ for its sins are piled up to the heavens,
and God remembers such crimes.
⁶ Repay the Idolater as it has paid others!
Pay back double for what it has done!
Mix the Idolater a double portion
from its own cup!
⁷ Give back as much torture and grief
as the glory and luxury it wallowed in.
To itself the Idolater boasts,
'I reign above all!
I need no one, nor will I ever mourn anyone.'
⁸ So the Idolater's plagues will come in a single day:
disease, mourning and famine,
and then it will be consumed by fire.
For mighty is the God who judges the Idolater."

⁹ The rulers of the earth who debauched and lived in luxury with the Idolater will mourn and weep. Seeing the smoke as it burns ¹⁰ and terrified at its torment, they will keep their distance and cry out,

"Mourn, mourn for this great city,
Babylon, so powerful a city!
In one hour your doom has come!"

¹¹ The merchants of the earth will weep and mourn for the great city, because nobody is left to buy their cargoes of goods— ¹² cargoes of gold, silver, precious stones and pearls; fine linen, purple silk and scarlet cloth; all the fragrant woods; articles of ivory, bronze, iron and marble; ¹³ cargoes of cinnamon and spices, incense, myrrh and frankincense; wine and olive oil, flour and wheat; cattle and sheep, horses and carriages; and the bodies and souls of women and men.

¹⁴ "All the fruit you craved
is gone from you.
Gone forever, never to return,
is your life of riches and ease."

¹⁵ The merchants who dealt in these things and gained their wealth from the great city will stand far off, terrified at its torment. Weeping and mourning, ¹⁶ they will say,

"Mourn, mourn for this great city;
clothed in fine linen,
purple and scarlet,
for all your finery of gold,
jewels and pearls,
¹⁷ in one hour this great wealth is destroyed."

All the sea captains and sailors, all who travel by sea, and all who earn their living off the sea will keep their distance. ¹⁸ They will cry out, when they see the smoke from its burning, "What city was ever as great as this city?" ¹⁹ And they will pour ashes on their heads, weep, mourn and cry out,

"Mourn, mourn for this great city,
where all who had ships at sea
grew wealthy through its riches.
In one hour it has been destroyed.
²⁰ Rejoice over it, O heaven!
Rejoice, you holy ones, apostles and prophets.
God has judged it for all it did to you."

²¹ Then another angel picked up a stone like a huge mill-stone and hurled it into the sea, and said,

"Babylon the great city
will be cast down like this—
with violence, and never more be found!
²² No tunes of harpists and minstrels,
of flutists and trumpeters,
will ever again be heard in you!
Never again will you contain skilled workers;
never again will the sound of the mill be heard in you!
²³ No light from a burning lamp
will ever again shine out in you!
No voice of bride and groom
will ever again be heard in you!
Because your merchants were the world's nobility,
you led all nations astray by your sorcery.
²⁴ "In the Great Idolater you will find the blood of prophets and holy ones, and all the blood that was ever shed on earth."

19

¹ After this I heard what sounded like the loud song of a great assembly in heaven. They were singing,

"Alleluia!
Salvation, glory, and power belong to our God,
² whose judgment is true and just,
who has condemned the Great Idolater
that corrupted the earth with its idolatry,
who has avenged the blood of its subjects
which was shed by its hand."

³ And again they sang out,

"Alleluia!
The smoke from it
rises forever and ever."

⁴ The twenty-four elders and the four living creatures prostrated themselves and worshiped God, who sat on the throne. And they cried, "Amen! Alleluia!"

⁵ Then a voice came from the throne, saying,

"Praise our God,
all you servants of God,
you who fear the Most High,
both small and great."

6 Then I heard what sounded like a great multitude, like the sound of rushing water, like loud peals of thunder, shouting,

> "Alleluia!
> Our Sovereign God has begun to reign!
7 Let us rejoice and be glad,
> and give praise to God—
> for the wedding day of the Lamb is at hand.
> The betrothed is ready,
8 and wearing a bright, clean linen garment."

The linen represents the righteous acts of the holy ones.

9 The angel then said to me, "Write this down: 'Happy are they who have been invited to the wedding feast of the Lamb.'" And the angel added, "These are the true words of God." 10 At this I fell at the angel's feet to offer worship. But it said, "Don't do that! I am a servant just like you and all your sisters and brothers who bear witness to Jesus. It is God you must worship! For the witness of Jesus is the spirit of prophecy."

19:11–21:8

Then I saw heaven itself standing open, and a white horse appeared. Its rider was called Faithful and True—a warrior for justice, a judge with integrity. 12 This warrior has eyes like a blazing flame, and is crowned with many crowns, inscribed with a name no one else has ever known. 13 The warrior wears a cloak dipped in blood, and is known by the name "The Word of God."

14 The armies of heaven were following the warrior, also riding on white horses. They were dressed in dazzling white linen. 15 Out of the warrior's mouth comes a sharp sword to strike down the nations. They will be ruled with an iron rod, and the warrior will tread out the wine of Almighty God's fierce wrath. 16 This is the name written on the warrior's robe and thigh: "Sovereign of Sovereigns and Ruler of Rulers."

17 And I saw an angel standing in the sun. The angel cried out to all the birds flying overhead, "Come, gather together for God's great banquet! 18 You will eat the flesh of rulers, military officers and those under their command, horse and rider alike—the flesh of all people, oppressor and oppressed, small and great."

19 Then I saw the beast and the rulers of the earth and their armies, gathered together to fight the army which the warrior led. 20 But the beast was captured, as was the false prophet who had worked miracles on the beast's behalf. With these miracles, the false prophet had deceived all those who had been branded with the mark of the beast and who worshiped its statue. The two were thrown alive into the fiery lake of burning sulphur. 21 All the rest were killed by the sword that came out of the warrior's mouth. And all the birds gorged themselves on their flesh.

20:1 Then I saw an angel come down from heaven, holding in its hands the key to the Abyss and a huge chain. 2 It seized the dragon, the ancient serpent—the one called "the Devil" and "Satan"—and chained it up for a thousand years. 3 The angel hurled it into the Abyss, which it closed and sealed over the dragon. It did this so that it might not lead nations astray until the thousand years are over. After this, the dragon is to be released for a short time.

4 Then I saw some thrones. Those who were sitting on them were empowered to pass judgment. I also saw the spirits of those who had been beheaded for their witness to Jesus and the word of God, those who had never worshiped the beast or its image or accepted its mark on their foreheads or their hands. They came to life again and reigned with Christ for a thousand years. 5 The rest of the dead did not come to life until the thousand years were over. This is the first resurrection. 6 Happy and holy are those who share in the first resurrection! The second death has no power over them. They will be priests of God and of Christ and will reign with Christ for a thousand years.

7 When the thousand years are over, Satan will be released from prison, 8 and will go out to deceive the nations in the four quarters of the earth—Gog and Magog—to gather them for battle. In number they are like the sand on the seashore. 9 They will march the breadth of the earth and surround the camp of the holy ones, the beloved city. But fire will come down from heaven and consume them. 10 And Satan, who deceived them, will be thrown into the lake of fire and sulphur, where the beast and the false prophet are. They will be tormented day and night forever and ever.

11 Next I saw a large white throne and the One who sat there. The earth and the sky fled from its presence until they could no longer be seen. 12 I saw the dead, the great and the lowly, standing before the throne. Lastly, among the scrolls, the book of life was opened. The dead were judged according to their conduct as recorded in the scrolls. 13 The sea gave up its dead; then Death and the netherworld gave up their dead. All given up were judged according to their conduct. 14 Then Death and the netherworld were hurled into the pool of fire, which is the second death; 15 anyone whose name was not found inscribed in the book of life was hurled into this pool of fire.

21:1 Then I saw new heavens and a new earth. The former heavens and the former earth had passed away, and the sea existed no longer. 2 I also saw a new Jerusalem, the holy city, coming down out of heaven from God, beautiful as a bride and groom on their wedding day.

3 And I heard a loud voice calling from the throne, "Look! God's Tabernacle is among humankind! God will live with them; they will be God's people, and God will be fully present among them. 4 The Most High will wipe away every tear from their eyes. And death, mourning, crying and pain will be no more, for the old order has fallen."

5 The One who sat on the throne said, "Look! I'm making everything new!" and added, "Write this, for what I am saying is trustworthy and true."

6 And that One continued, "It is finished. I am the Alpha and the Omega, the Beginning and the End. To those who are thirsty I will give drink freely from the spring of the water of life. 7 This is the rightful inheritance of the overcomers. I will be their God and they will be my daughters and sons. 8 But the legacy of cowards, the unfaithful, the depraved, the murderers, the fornicators, sorcerers, idolaters, and all liars is the burning lake of fiery sulphur, which is the second death."

21:9–22:21

Then one of the seven angels that had held the seven bowls of the seven last plagues approached me and said, "Come and let me show you the betrothed of the Lamb."

10 The angel then carried me away in the Spirit to the top of a very high mountain, and showed me the holy city Jerusalem coming down out of heaven from God. 11 It shone with God's glory and gleamed like a precious jewel, like a sparkling diamond. 12 Its wall was huge and very tall, and

it had twelve gates with twelve angels as sentinels. On the twelve gates were written the names of the twelve tribes of Israel; ¹³ three of its gates faced east, three north, three south and three west. ¹⁴ The wall had twelve foundation stones on which were written the names of the Lamb's twelve apostles.

¹⁵ The angel who talked with me carried a gold measuring rod to measure the city, its gates and its wall. ¹⁶ The city was laid out foursquare; it was as long as it was wide. The angel measured the city with the rod and found it to be 12,000 stadia—or 1,500 miles—in length, width and height. ¹⁷ The wall measured 144 cubits—or 2,160 feet—in thickness; the angel was using the standard measure.

¹⁸ The wall was made of jasper, and the city of pure gold, as pure as glass. ¹⁹ The foundation stones of the city wall were decorated with every kind of precious stone. The first one was jasper, the second was sapphire, the third was chalcedony, the fourth was emerald, ²⁰ the fifth was sardonyx, the sixth was carnelian, the seventh was chrysolite, the eighth was beryl, the ninth was topaz, the tenth was chrysoprase, the eleventh was jacinth, and the twelfth foundation was amethyst. ²¹ The twelve gates were twelve pearls, each gate made of a single pearl. The main street of the city was of pure gold, as pure as glass.

²² I saw no Temple in the city, for God Almighty and the Lamb were themselves the Temple. ²³ There was no sun or moon: God's glory was its light, and the Lamb was its lamp. ²⁴ The nations will walk by the city's light, and the rulers of the earth will bring their treasures. ²⁵ The city's gates will never be shut by day, and there will be no night there. ²⁶ The glory and honor of the nations will be brought into it. ²⁷ But nothing unclean will ever enter it, nor will anyone who does loathsome things or tells lies. Only those whose names are written in the book of life of the Lamb will enter.

22 ¹ The angel then showed me the river of life-giving water, clear as crystal, which issued from the throne of God and of the Lamb, ² and flowed down the middle of the streets. On either side of the river grew the trees of life which produce fruit twelve times a year, once each month; their leaves serve as medicine to heal the nations. ³ There will no longer be any curse.

The throne of the Almighty and of the Lamb will be there, and God's subjects will serve faithfully. ⁴ They will see the Most High face to face, and bear God's name on their foreheads. Night will be no more. They will need no light from lamps or the sun, for our God will give them light, and they will reign forever.

⁶ The angel said to me, "These words are trustworthy and true; the Most High, the God of the spirits of the prophets, has sent an angel to show the faithful what must happen very soon."

⁷ "Remember, I am coming very soon!
Happy are you who heed
the prophetic message of this book!"

⁸ I, John, am the one who heard and saw these things.

I prostrated myself in worship before the angel who had shown them to me. ⁹ But the angel said, "Don't do that! I am a servant, just like you and your sisters and brothers, the prophets, and those who treasure what you have written in this book. It is God you must worship."

¹⁰ Then the angel told me, "Don't keep the prophecies in this book a secret, for the appointed time is near. ¹¹ Let those who do wrong continue to do wrong. Let the vile continue to be vile. Let those who are just continue to do justice. Let those who are holy continue to be holy."

¹² "Remember, I am coming soon!
I bring with me the reward
that will be given to all people
according to their conduct.
¹³ I am the Alpha and the Omega,
the First and the Last,
the Beginning and the End.
¹⁴ Happy are they who wash their robes
so as to have free access to the tree of life
and enter the city through its gates.
¹⁵ Outside are the dogs, the sorcerers,
debaucherers, murderers,
idolaters and the deceitful.

¹⁶ "It is I, Jesus, who has sent my angel to give you this testimony about the churches. I am the Root and Offspring of David, the Morning Star shining bright."

¹⁷ The Spirit and the Betrothed say, "Come!"

Let the one who hears it answer, "Come!"

Let the thirsty come forward. Let all who desire it accept the gift of life-giving water.

¹⁸ I warn everyone who hears the prophetic words of this book: if anyone adds anything to them, God will add to that person the plagues described in this book; ¹⁹ if anyone excludes anything from this book of prophecy, God will exclude that person from the tree of life and from the holy city, which are described here.

²⁰ The One who gives this testimony says, "Yes, I am coming soon!" Amen! Come, Jesus!

²¹ The grace of our Savior Jesus Christ be with you all. Amen.

book three

THE QURAN

Islamic word-art has a depth of meaning, new to non-Muslims, as illustrated in the structure of Mohamed Zakariya's calligraphy *harisun aleikum*, "he is ardently anxious over you" (Quran 9:128–29). In this piece, Zakariya creates an axis with the elongated letter *l* in *aleikum* driving upward to anchor the whole piece, with smaller letters leaning leftward and heraldic medallions, providing both a stability and a vulnerability in which the letters themselves depict the meaning of this particular verse.

preface to the sublime quran

Laleh Bakhtiar

OR THE MUSLIM, THE QURAN CONTAINS THE COVENANT BETWEEN THE HUMAN RACE AND GOD. When God asked in the Quran, "Am I not your Lord?," the human beings responded, "Yea. We bore witness."[1] By bearing witness, the human beings became God's vice-regents or agents on earth, the overseers of God's creation, the protectors of both the manifest and the hidden.

The word *Quran* means "recitation." It was received through the ear and not the eye, which, of course, is a different kind of experience. It is through listening to and reciting the Arabic of the Quran that one participates in the Divine Presence. Any and every translation is considered to be just that, a translation, and not the Quran itself.

The Arabic is chanted into a baby's ear at birth; she learns verses by heart as she grows up; she speaks certain of the phases as she learns to speak and later as she begins to perform the five daily formal prayers; verses are recited at her marriage ceremony and at her death where others pray for her soul as she returns to the Source from which she came.

During her lifetime, she may memorize the entire Quran, a great blessing and mercy from God. However, in many Islamic countries, including most in the Middle East, she is prohibited from reciting the Quran in public.[2]

In several verses, the Quran repeats that it is guidance, healing and mercy as it contains the knowledge of how reality is structured and our place as human beings within it. It contains the basis for Islamic Law (*Shariah*), including moral injunctions and legal principles. It speaks of the nature of God and the universe as well as the final end and the hereafter. It describes the meaning of her being, of human life, often through parables from which she learns how to live her life.

As guidance, the message of the Quran also tells the stories of the lives of Mary, Jesus, the prophets, tribes and the pharaoh. These stories of people and the problems that they faced also describe those who chose the way of hypocrisy and division among humankind—those who had gone astray as opposed to those who were sent to guide humanity to the Straight Path. The people described symbolize energies and forces that exist within the human soul of each and every one of us.

Muslims know this because the Quran says that guidance is taught to the believer through signs. Every verse in the Quran is a sign (*ayah*), just as everything in the created universe is a sign of the Presence of God. God says, "We will cause them to see Our signs on the horizons and within themselves until it becomes clear to them that it is The Truth,"[3] showing the correspondence between the verses of the Quran and the creation of nature.

Muslims often refer to the Quran for healing, as it says, "We send down the Quran what is a healing and a mercy for the ones who believe and it increases not the ones who are unjust, but in a loss"[4] and "And when I was sick, it is He Who heals me."[5] In this way, the original Arabic of the Quran is like a talisman that not only protects the human beings but also heals them through the sounds of the Recitation. It brings comfort and a sense of peace filled as it is with *barakah*, or divine blessings.

And the Quran is a mercy, a mercy to all human beings, as God says in the Quran, "My mercy encompassed everything,"[6] including the prophet who was sent as a mercy to humanity: "We sent thee not but as a mercy for the worlds."[7] It is in this capacity that the Quran says, "Obey God and the Messenger so that perhaps you will find mercy."[8]

An important distinction between this translation and other present English translations arises from the fact that this is the first critical English translation of the Quran by a woman. However, that does not necessarily make this a feminist translation. *The Sublime Quran* is the translation of a person who practices spiritual integrity (*futuwwa*), or spiritual chivalry as it is sometimes called. It should also be noted that none of the reasons given as to how this translation differs from all other English translations has anything to do with my being a woman. They are all indications of gender-free intellectual reasoning.

Just as I found a certain lack of internal consistency in previous English translations, I also found that little attention had been given to the woman's point of view. While the absence of a woman's point of view in Quranic translation and commentary for almost 1,500 years since the revelation began clearly needs to change, it must be acknowledged that there are many men who are supportive of the view of women as complements to themselves, as the completion of their human unity. To them, I and other Muslim women are eternally grateful. They relate to women as the Quran and Hadith intended. The criticism women have is toward those men and women who are not open to this understanding, who are exclusive in opposition to the Quran and Sunnah's inclusiveness. Clearly the intention of the Quran is to see man and woman as complements of one another, not as superior-inferior.

Consequently, in the following translation, I address a main criticism of Islam made in regard to a human rights issue—namely, that a husband can beat his wife after two stages of trying to reason with her.[9] At this point I should say that there will be those who see me as a person having a particular Muslim point of view. Let me assure the reader that I am most certainly a Muslim woman. I have been schooled in Sufism, which includes both the Jafari (Shia) and Hanafi, Hanbali, Maliki and Shafii (Sunni) points of view. As an adult, I lived nine years in a Jafari community in Iran and have been living in a Hanafi community in Chicago for the past fifteen years with Maliki and Shafii friends. While I understand the positions of each group, I do not represent any specific one, as I find living in America makes it difficult enough to be a Muslim, much less to choose to follow one sect or another. However, in this translation I have not added any indication of differences in recitation between the sects so that it does represent the majority view.

I grew up in the United States with a single parent, a Christian, American mother. My father, an Iranian, lived in Iran. I was an adult before I came to know him. He was not religious, but spiritual, devoting his life as a physician to help to heal the suffering of people. My mother was not a Catholic, but she sent me to a nearby Catholic school. At the age of eight I wanted to become a Catholic, to which she had no objection. When I was twenty-four, I went to Iran for the first time as an adult, with my husband and our children. I began taking classes in Islamic culture and civilization taught by Seyyed Hossein Nasr. One day he asked me what religion I followed, and I said that I had been brought up as a Christian. He said, "Well, now that you are in Iran and your father is Muslim, everyone will expect you to be Muslim." I said, "I don't know anything about Islam." He replied, "Well, learn!" And that was the beginning of my journey, culminating in this translation.

I have personally been blessed by my contacts with the most understanding and compassionate of men in my lifetime, and I have never found myself in a situation of being physically threatened or beaten. But in reading about and hearing firsthand stories of women who have, I felt the deep sense that I am essentially and spiritually one with them by my very existence. The question I kept asking myself during the years of working on the translation: How could God, the Merciful, the Compassionate, sanction husbands beating their wives?

The need to pay attention to this feeling did not surface until the day I first publicly presented the results of this translation of *The Sublime Quran* at the WISE (Women's Islamic Initiative in Spirituality and Equity) Conference (November 2006), where one hundred and fifty Muslim women from all over the world had gathered to discuss the possibility of forming a Women's Islamic Council. I gave the logic as to why the word *to beat* in 4:34 has been a misinterpretation. At the end of the session, two Muslim women approached me. They said that they work in shelters for battered women and that they and the women in the shelters have been waiting for over 1,400 years for someone to pay attention to this issue through a translation of the Quran. The heavy weight of responsibility suddenly fell upon my shoulders. I had to publish my findings as soon as possible to initiate a dialogue with the exclusivists. Hopefully, the initiating of a dialogue will further open the minds and awaken to consciousness and conscience those men who place their hands on the Word of God, giving themselves permission to beat their wives and those women who believe they deserve to be beaten!

The Quran is the eternal Word of God for those who are Muslims. Prophet Muhammad, peace and the mercy of God be upon him, did not believe that he was bringing a new religion. Rather, as the Last and Final Prophet, he was teaching: the manifesting of humility and sincerity and outward conforming with the law of God and the taking upon oneself to do or to say as the Prophet has done or said. Therefore, for those who follow "sincerity in religion without hypocrisy" or Islam as their way of life, Prophet Muhammad, peace and the mercy of God be upon him, completed the message of a way of life that has existed continuously from ancient times. This way of life is an open system with no beginning and no finite end. It has existed in the past, but it begins again in the present and goes on for an eternity, making it an example of an open history—no beginning and no end—eternal. The message for the present, as it was for prophets such as Abraham, Moses and Jesus, may God bless them all, is this: "There is no god but God," Who alone is to be worshiped. This is the central message of *tawhid* or the Oneness of God. The concept of sincerity in this way of life or subscribing to His way of life connected itself little by little through transition from one prophet to another, culminating in the message of the Quran.

The Quran was revealed to the Prophet in the Arabic language in the early seventh century CE, and it is the Arabic of the Quran that is considered to be the eternal Word of God. It is only the recitation or reading of the Arabic that has spiritual efficacy. Any and every translation is considered to be an interpretation of the Quran and not the Quran itself. The questions that the translation of *The Sublime Quran* poses relate to the way some verses have been interpreted over the centuries, interpretations that oppose the Sunnah of the Prophet.

For the Muslim, the Quran, meaning "Recitation," is the eternal Word of God revealed to the Prophet Muhammad, peace and the mercy of God be upon him, over a period of twenty-two years and five months. This is considered to be the greatest miracle of Prophet Muhammad. He was unlettered, yet he was chosen to receive the Arabic Recitation (Quran), which is considered to be unique in style, possessing a sense of unity of language and level of discourse. One of the greatest acts of worship for a Muslim, then, is to memorize the Arabic Recitation. One who does so is called a *hafiz*. But in order to recite the Quran in Arabic (*tilawah*) one must study the Quranic sciences, which are studied through many sciences, including *tajwid, qirat* and *tafsir*. *Tajwid* teaches how the text is divided together with its rhythm and phonetics. The reciter must understand the meaning of the Signs or verses in order to determine how to recite, where to pause, where to take a breath and so forth so that the meaning of the Quran is preserved. Many concepts do not end when the verse ends but continue on to the next verse or verses. Without understanding the meaning, one cannot place emphasis where it is needed.

While the Quran was revealed in the oral tradition and oral transmission remains important, after it was compiled into the written form we now have, the Quran became the first book-length example of Arabic literature. It is the bridge between the pre-Islamic oral tradition that focused on narrative or poetic traditions and the written language that rapidly produced great works of prose and poetry. It was compiled into the form of a book by the same scribes who had written down the verses as they were revealed to the Prophet; verses written on pieces of parchment, leather, stone tablets, animal shoulder blades, palm leaves and pieces of cloth.

The Quran refers to the Recitation by different names, one of which is *The Sublime Quran* (*al-quran al-azim*, 15:87), the name chosen for this present translation. Being sublime refers to the Quran's spiritual value. In its sublimity it guides and inspires beyond the material world that it transcends. One can only understand the sublimity of the Quran if one begins with some standard that establishes a system based in justice and fairness in order to be able to enter the world of the spiritual and intuition. One has to begin with some criterion. That is another of the names the Quran gives itself, *al-furqan* or the Criterion: the discernment between right and wrong, good and evil, lawful and unlawful, truth and falsehood. Brian Arthur Brown argues cogently that the concept of *furqan* may be in large measure confirmation of the revelation given to Zoroaster as the *Fargan*, but the Quran, as *The* Criterion, is the standard by which to determine the correctness of a judgment or conclusion. It is the measure, the reference point against which other things may be evaluated.

This brings me to the issue that has dominated press reviews of *The Sublime Quran*, from humble masjid newsletters to the *New York Times*, since the release of the first edition of this translation in 2007. I use the Quran itself to support my translation of Quran 4:34, which has become something of a cause celebre among both conservative Muslims who prefer the formal equivalence that I use and progressive Muslims who note the dynamic equivalence based on the Sunnah of the Prophet himself. As a larger issue in translation, I defer at this point to the translator's notes that I am privileged to offer following Dr. Brown's chapters of contextual commentary and the introduction to the Quran by my esteemed colleague, Dr. Nevin Reda.

I have chosen to continuously engage in the greater struggle for self-improvement. This is the beginning stage of the Sufi path (including *murruwa*, or moral reasonableness, leading to *futuwwa*, or spiritual chivalry), and I cannot even claim that I have moved beyond that.

God knows best.

9

zoroastrians in the quran

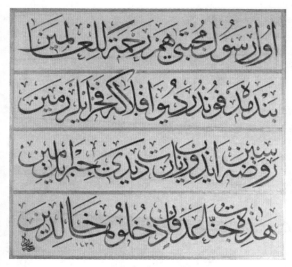

Mercy to the Worlds

I F ZOROASTRIANISM IS A SUBTEXT OF THE THREE MAJOR RELIGIONS ORIGINATING IN WESTERN monotheism, its role, its influence and its impact in Islam is very different than in Judaism and Christianity. As we have seen, Zoroastrianism may owe its monotheistic origins to Moses and Hebrew sources (the sensitivity of modern Zoroastrians on this point notwithstanding), and it offered both theological succor and logistical support to Israel in the final years of the Babylonian Exile and the Return to Jerusalem. Then, long after this pristine Zoroastrianism had been largely transformed from monotheism into a dualism of equal and competing religious forces, Jesus appears to have defined his destiny as Savior of the World and personal Redeemer of all who trust him based on Zoroastrian prophecy as much as anything in the Hebrew Scriptures.

Persia's position as a superpower was just a military, political and cultural memory by the time of Muhammad, but Zoroastrianism was still the state religion of the remnant empire. Its tenets and its Scriptures continued in a dominant role in provinces like Syria, where it appears to have been subsumed under the Sabaean religion. The Sabaeans dated their history to a time even before Zoroaster, but like the Magi earlier and the Manicheans later, they were Zoroastrian in all but name by the time Muhammad visited Syria as a boy, caravanning with his uncle more than once, and as a young man leading business expeditions for the employer he would later marry.

These experiences of dualistic Sabaean Zoroastrianism, and its need for corrective surgery, were augmented later in Muhammad's prophetic ministry by the wise counsel of his companion and friend, Salman El-Farsi (Salman the Persian), who had left Zoroastrianism. Salman had converted to Christianity at first, and his "interfaith" influence in Islam has not yet been fully appreciated. The intimate spiritual relationship between Salman and Muhammad lasted over many years and no doubt exposed the Prophet to the contradiction posed by a dualistic religion that also still used and celebrated the liturgies and Scriptures of pristine Zoroastrian monotheism, dating back to Zoroaster himself, a situation crying out for resolution. Both forms of this ancient religion would have been on Muhammad's mind as God revealed the truth to him.

While material in the Quran that "confirms, critiques and amplifies" Jewish and Christian Scriptures is easily identifiable, there is no reference to Muhammad ever visiting Bethlehem or spending time in Jerusalem (except of course in the Night Journey) the way he visited in the Syrian province of the Persian Empire. While he knew many Jews and Christians, there is no reference to any collegial friendship comparable to his closeness to Salman, a Zoroastrian convert to Islam. We can therefore picture Muhammad reminiscing about what he observed in Syria and in deep discussion with this Persian companion, learning of the Zoroastrian faith, history and practice, and making the case for Islam.

This would perhaps lead into times of meditation and prayer in which the Prophet would receive fresh revelations from God that not only won Salman over but later also Persia/Iran itself. The myth that Persia was simply conquered by the sword is only partially true. Zoroastrianism was finally bankrupt, and the proponents of Islam were eager to fill the vacuum. Both intellectual leaders and the common people of Persia were yearning for something more substantial, and the Quran appeared as if much of it was written for them, which, in certain measure, it was. While Islam was successful in various ways in many non-Arab countries, it was nowhere more successful than in Persia, and we can connect this to Islam's critique of Zoroastrianism; rejecting and condemning its dualism, amplifying and exulting in its monotheism.

With the conversion of most Persians to Islam, Zoroastrianism was reduced to minority status. Muslims have always considered the Zoroastrians, like the Christians and Jews of Arabia, to be preexisting Scriptural monotheists, or "People of the Book." In effect, for all practical purposes, Ahura Mazda was equated with the God of Abraham, the Avesta was sufficiently Scriptural to be placed in a category with the Torah and the Gospel, and Zoroaster came to be regarded as a prophet, despite strict censure of later Avestan writings that appeared to be non-monotheistic.

As mentioned in the prologue, shortly before this book went to press the publisher commissioned four qualified scholars to independently evaluate the text for any inconsistencies or other problems that could diminish its expected impact in the academic community. One of their most valuable recommendations was from a reviewer identified only as a scholar who "specializes in Judaism." This reviewer made the point that the Scriptures of Zoroastrianism are given considerable weight in this book, but the compendium would benefit from specific examples of the ancient Avesta. The response to this helpful suggestion was agreement to include a sample of such verses in the text, an arrangement completed just before the rolling of the presses.

The Zoroastrian Scriptures still extant represent about 10 percent of the original, which would have been somewhat larger than the entire Christian Bible. What remains now comprises a volume somewhat smaller than the Torah, or about half the size of the Christian New Testament. It opens with the Gathas by Zoroaster himself, the poetic psalm-like prayers that set the style for most of the rest of the collection. The first complete modern translation was completed in 1864 by Professor Friedrich von Spiegel (1820–1905), a German translation of "the original manuscripts" now at Harvard University, brought out serially from 1852 to 1863. Under the simple title, *Avesta*, its English translation was completed by Arthur Henry Bleeck in 1864. Frequently reprinted and still available, it uses a strict formal equivalence that has been continued in more recent original translations with improved linguistic research. From within the Parsee community, Piloo Nanavutty offered a charming dynamic equivalent translation of *The Gathas of Zarathustra* in 1999, limited mainly by untranslated phrases unfamiliar to most English readers, although appreciated in the increasingly English-speaking Parsee community.

This has led to the present attempt to offer a paraphrased dynamic equivalent sample, relying on everything we know about Zoroaster's life, passion, impact and theology, but presented in a style believably representing the clarity and dynamism of this prophet whose message so changed the world. The current offering is aided by the *Textual Sources for the Study of Zoroastrianism* by Mary Boyce, and it is inspired by the brilliant synthesis of recent scholarship presented in *The Hymns of Zoroaster* (2010) by M. L. West, emeritus fellow of All Souls College, Oxford, and fellow of the British Academy. While still somewhat hamstrung by formal equivalence to a language and a sometimes opaque text, with which we are all still struggling, West's accompanying commentary is the new gold standard in Zoroastrian scholarship in the new era of greater certainty about the dates of Zoroaster himself.

The paraphrases in this publication are an attempt to appreciate the power and majesty of the Avesta text and the intimacy between its first author and God. They are dependent upon the five sources mentioned above, based primarily on Spiegel and Bleeck for vocabulary, though enriched by the other three, who supply insights to the meaning. This brief selection from the Gatha section of the Avesta illustrates Zoroaster's monotheism, clouded later by the appearance of "divinities" who are first recognized as something akin to angels but who grew in importance to become gods almost equal to their creator. This trend later motivated Muslims in their drive to recover a pure monotheism for themselves, for Jews and Christians, and for Zoroastrians as well. We include here the Gatha that presents Zoroaster's questions that some of us now believe were answered directly by Isaiah, as outlined previously. One of our samples is obviously from the crisis moment early in his ministry when Zoroaster felt impelled to move from his birthplace in Eastern Iran (Scythia/ Assyria/Azerbaijan) to the region of Bactria, where he flourished for the next forty years. Also included are references to Zoroaster's expectation of Saoshyant redeemers or "saviors" (in the plural, described elsewhere as three in number) who might come early to redeem creation, at the climax of history and at the end of time. Finally, while using the flowing syntax of dynamic equivalence in these examples, there has been every effort to stick to the formal equivalent language to illustrate what is apparent in all these translations—that the Avesta is indeed echoed, and its truths are confirmed in the Quran.

Zoroastrianism may have influenced Judaism and Christianity at various levels, described elsewhere in this text, but there is little evidence that the words of that revelation are much reproduced in the Torah or the Gospel. However, a school-aged child can connect the words and phrases of the Avesta (or at least the Gatha portion) with the concepts in the Quran. It can be presumed that Muhammad did not "copy" Avesta material any more than he "copied" directly from the Torah or the Gospel, but just as he received revelations echoing and confirming the earlier revelations of Hebrew and Christian Scriptures, it becomes apparent that some of the revelations in the Quran relate to previous revelations in the Avesta in much the same manner.

In what follows, we witness a turning point in religious development of the world that swept throughout the region of the emerging Persian Empire and beyond, as humanity quite suddenly shifted from a creaturely dependence to active partnership with the Divine.

worship[1]

With hands outstretched in worship, I pray to you and seek your help,
O Lord of Wisdom, placing your bountiful will above everything.
I offer right actions combined with good thoughts,
To connect Wisdom with even souls in nature, like that of the cow.

I approach you, O Lord of Wisdom, as a mortal with good thoughts,
So you can bless me personally, both materially and spiritually.
Such blessings are your appropriate responses to the needs of believers.

I will praise you with right actions and good thoughts.
O Lord of Wisdom, your dominion is unimpaired.
My piety is worthy of an answer, so come to my aid.

I have summoned the spiritual resources to lift my thoughts on high,
Knowing that you, O Lord of Wisdom, reward right actions.
As long as I possess ability and strength I will pursue justice.

O Right One, may I see a vision of you as my thoughts rise to you?
Let our compliance become a path to you, O Lord of Wisdom.
In submission may we impress even predators with our hymns.

Join your good thoughts with ours, and make righteousness your gift.
In honest words, O Lord, give support to this camel herder, and to all.
Lord, give us what we need to overcome the acts of hostility by the foe.

O Right One, reward our good thoughts with your blessing.
Out of your holiness, empower King Vishtaspa and me.
O Lord of Wisdom, provide your authority,
Showing the requirements in which we may receive your care.

Revelation[2]

In accord with the laws of primordial existence,
the Day of Judgment shall come.
The wicked and the righteous together
Shall see their falsehoods and their honesty weighed up.

The person who is honest to others, whether kith or kin, O Lord,
Or even the ones who serve the needs of cattle in the field,
Shall themselves find pasture and peace.

So, God, I worship you and seek to avoid disobedience,
Whether in the challenges of family, or in the life of the clan,
In community service, or with ignorance like beasts in the field.

Reveal to me your purpose and your requirements,
So that I may attain your dominion,
The path of life that is in accord with your will.

As your priest, I call for truth and seek to fulfill my calling.
Assist me to undertake my ministry to the people,
By taking counsel with you, O Lord of Wisdom.

Come to me now, in your manifest essence, O God.
May my faith in you be vindicated among the believers.
Let all your promises to me be seen to be true.

Everything that is good in life comes from you, O Lord of Wisdom,
All that was, everything that is, and all that shall be.
You reward us all according to our faithfulness, and we pray
That we may grow in righteousness in response to your dominion.

O Lord, you are the Mighty One of Wisdom.
Devotion and truth which nurture human life belong to you.
Hear my prayer and have mercy upon me in any reckoning to be made.

Arise within me, O Lord, and fulfill my desire
To serve you perfectly with unfailing devotion.
Accept my self-offering and confer your power for good.

From afar, draw near and reveal yourself to me.
Let me share in your sovereign reign, O Lord,
And instruct your people in devotion and in truth.

As an offering, this camel herder gives body and breath,
So that you may be served in good thoughts and good deeds,
Described in words that correspond to your dominion.

Glory to God[3]

I realized that your very nature is bountiful, O God,
When I recognized you as the originator of life.

You offer both words of revelation and deeds which bear fruit.
Sun, moon and stars of creation reflect your glory, as may we.

As this turning point of realization, Lord, you come and bless.
Your sovereignty and your wisdom lead us on to truth.
Our devotion will allow you to guide us in wisdom.

I realized that your very nature is bountiful, O God,
When your wisdom encircled me and inquired of me,
"Who are you? To what people do you belong?
What will it take for your Lord to engage you?"

Then I answered you, first and foremost, I am a simple Camel Herder.
But I am an enemy of falsehood and lying, as best I know.
My goal in life is to respond to the glory I see in you, Lord,
To worship and praise you with songs of rejoicing.

this i ask[4]

This I ask of you, so tell me truly Lord,
How are you to be worshipped?
O Lord of Wisdom, will you speak to me as a friend?
And may other worshippers gain wisdom from our encounter?

This I ask of you, so tell me truly Lord,
Can life be renewed by salvation during this existence,
And can human beings be blessed through understanding,
With your truth acting as the healer, and you as our friend?

This I ask of you, so tell me truly Lord,
At the beginning of creation, who was the father of order?
Who set the sun and the stars in their orbits and caused the moon to wax and wane?
These things and many more I long to understand, Lord God of Wisdom.

This I ask of you, so tell me truly Lord,
Who holds up the earth and who keeps the sky from falling?
Who brought water into being to nourish the plants?
Who but you, Wise Lord, is the breath of the wind and the spirit of the cloud?

This I ask of you, so tell me truly Lord,
Which worker of wonders called forth the speed of light
Across the expanse of darkness, in rhythms of sleep and waking?
From whom came times of dawn, mid-day and nightfall to regulate our work?

This I ask of you, so tell me truly Lord,
How am I to grow in understanding of
Your revelations enshrined in sublime teachings?
I learned of them first through your wisdom, my greatest joy.

This I ask of you, so tell me truly Lord,
How am I to remain faithful to you in daily living?
Will you teach me, Lord, how to be loyal to your sovereignty?
Or is it only you that can dwell in truth and wisdom?

This I ask of you, so tell me truly Lord,
Is the revelation I received for everyone,
And will it be enough to sustain my livelihood?
Or am I to live a life of devotion apart from the world?

This I ask of you, so tell me truly Lord,
How shall others who see the vision express their devotion?
I was chosen to spread abroad your truth,
But I look upon others with apprehension.

This I ask of you, so tell me truly Lord,
Who is really a disciple of the truth and who lives by lies?
Am I to proclaim your truth to those who are hostile,
Or is salvation intended for those who receive it gladly?

salvation[5]

To which land shall I flee? Where shall I seek refuge?
I am excluded from family and clan.
The community I would serve has rejected me
And the tyrants of the territory are no better.
How can I please you, Lord, where there is no response?

I know I am ineffective here, My Wise Lord.
My cattle are few and my followers are scattered.
I lament my situation to you as my only true friend.
Give me a vision of your strength in Wisdom.

O Lord of Wisdom, when will you send your Redeemers,
To bring in the sparkling light of salvation,
The Redeemers who offer inspiration and guidance?
As for me, here and now, I rely on your Spirit alone.

day of judgment[6]

Protect me as long as this perishable world is dominant, O Lord,
Until wickedness and lies are obliterated in the Day of Judgment.
Mortals and immortals alike, both good and evil, abound,
But your promise of salvation gives your devotees the courage to go on.

Tell me, O Lord of Wisdom, since you know all things,
Will the just overcome the unjust in this life,
Or do we await the Day of Judgment
For the glorious renewal of life that is to come?

Right teaching is available to the one who is able to understand
The truth from you, O Lord of Wisdom, giver of all good.
In your benevolence, you provide the most profound insights,
Those that are integral to your wise understanding.

So in your great wisdom, O Lord,
Welcome those mortals who respond to your invitation.
Those whose thoughts and actions are in accord
With your desires and purposes.

Let good rulers govern us rather than corrupt,
So that surrounded by good governance,
We may live in piety and in harmony with nature,
As symbolized by the contentment of the cow.

For it is our cattle that provide for us,
Even as we provide for them.
And the vegetation so prevalent in creation
Remains as the context for the life we share.

In such a life, why should cruelty and violence prevail?
Let all who would triumph do so with understanding
Of the truth which underlies our existence,
And which draws us together for worship in your house, O God.

Truly I acknowledge your dominion, O Wise Lord,
What will you provide for me in response to my devotion?
Where will I find the resources for the followers you desire
To promote your cause of justice and of truth?

When will I be able to perceive the manifestation of sovereignty
Which will pit your truth against the hostile malice all around us?
Let me see the specific expression of your truth
In the coming Saviour, who brings his reward with him.

O Lord of Wisdom, when will mortals see salvation?
When do we eliminate our intoxication with power,
Which deludes both the rulers and their people
And through which these lands are corrupted?

When, O Wise Lord, can we expect to see devotion and justice combine
To give safety and good pasture beneath your sovereign control?
Who will establish peace and security in the midst of blood-thirsty conflict?
From whom will the penetrating insights come to set us free in truth?

Such will be the Saviours and Redeemers of the lands,
Working through wisdom in harmony with truth.
Your Saoshyants will fulfill your purposes in the universe.
They are destined to prevail against all the forces of doom.

This selection of clustered verses, after the pattern used by Mary Boyce and some others, serves to illustrate the intimacy between Zoroaster and God. It is limited to Gathas widely accepted as being composed by Zoroaster himself, expressed with a spiritual sophistication that is a breakthrough as compared with both the older theological constructs of his Vedic predecessors and the awkward caricatures of his religion represented by previous Western translations. It is not suggested that the above paraphrases represent an advance in linguistic scholarship. If there is any improvement in the presentation, it is derived from a more flowing syntax and the application of our growing knowledge about Zoroaster, his influence and his prophetic passion.

In the cadences presented here we may at last glimpse the turning point in which belief develops into the spiritual power that transformed the people of the ancient world, as stated, "from a creaturely dependence to active partnership with the Divine." Indeed, we see something of that understanding earlier in Israel, along with its monotheism, in Abraham, Moses and the pre-Zoroastrian prophets, but it is Zoroaster who sees and presents this partnership as a universal vision, a partnership with the Divine that is open to all humanity. The impact of that realization, as articulated and implemented by his followers at the apex of Persian rule as the world's first superpower, with reverberations from the Orient to Europe, triggered the spiritual tsunami in what we now call the Axial Age. Israel itself was, of course, among those most dramatically impacted due to its close association with Zoroastrians in Persia during the Exile, but the reforms of Hinduism, the birth of Buddhism and other related developments, both philosophical and religious, have been well documented elsewhere. The connections to Christianity and Islam are presented in this volume.

We see the reflection of Hebrew and Christian Scriptures in the Quran, but the issue of the place of Zoroastrian Scriptures in the Quran falls into the category of what, in conversation, is sometimes called "the elephant in the room"—that is, something clearly obvious but not discussed or acknowledged by anyone. If the Roman Empire and the rule of Alexander the Great are mentioned in the Quran, and if regional religions like Judaism and Christianity are discussed, how could it be possible that the Quran makes no mention of Persia and Zoroastrianism, Arabia's most powerful neighbor and most significant religious influence, respectively? The fact is that these influences are indeed addressed in the Quran, but in such a manner that they are so pervasive as to be almost invisible, forming the context of much of this Scripture. Just as water is invisible to fish and air is invisible to humans, it may be only in an interfaith study like this one that the "water" (Persia) and the "air" (Zoroastrianism) of the Quran can be seen and identified.

The facts about Salman El-Farsi, Muhammad's Persian companion, are well known, though too often mentioned only "in passing." We also recognize Persian "loan words," like *paradise* (heaven) and *houri* (beautiful maiden), that somehow form part of the revelations from God in the Quran. If we were to mark such words in bold in our imagined Z factor edition of the Scriptures, the number of such markers in the Quran itself would grow exponentially as we proceeded. We further suggest the possibilities that Avesta chapters known as *Fargans* (teachings on purity) may be a link to the *Furqan* (Criterion) of the Quran, that scores of Avesta chapters are critiqued in the Quran and that material from dozens of the more recent and corrupt Avesta chapters is specifically condemned in the Quran.

We now propose that Zoroastrianism itself may be identified in the Quran by the name of its nearest exponent—the Sabaean religion in Syria, as adapted to conform with the continuing influence of the state religion of the old Persian Empire. Earlier references to this thesis may have raised eyebrows among knowledgeable Muslim readers who have traditionally identified the Sabaeans with a still-surviving group of followers of John the Baptist in Iraq. In fact, there were three ethnic entities who claimed historical affiliation with the original Sabaeans—the one in Iraq, another in Yemen and a third in Syria, where Muhammad himself was first exposed to them as practitioners of a form of the Zoroastrian religion.

Jews and Christians are not required to agree with the Islamic perspective, but fruitful discussion and mutual growth in understanding requires that in learning about the Quran, they must appreciate the Muslim perspective on the Quran as being as legitimate as the communal perspective of the Torah and the focus on Jesus in the Gospel. Additional truth may lie elsewhere, but let us at least begin by always recognizing what Jews, Christians and Muslims believe about their own Scriptures. The Hebrew Scriptures received a patently positive reception in Book One, even as important questions were raised. The Christian Scriptures received the same treatment in Book Two, a sensitive presentation despite the issue of how these sacred texts are to be understood. Nothing less will be presented in this examination of the Muslim Quran: a sincere desire to appreciate it in the most favorable light, even while recognizing certain challenges.

Muslims may need convincing that the Avesta is as prominent between the lines in the Quran as the Bible is, but they have no objection to this proposition in principle. Muhammad did not believe the revelations he received were of a different essence than the truth from God as it had been revealed to Jews and Christians of old, or to Zoroastrians, Sabaeans and possibly others. It seemed by their corrupt application of God's Word that the Scriptures of the Hebrews and Christians had become jumbled and distorted. While the Quran was "the same story" set in the Arabian context for the first time, it contained little that was new. It clearly critiqued the previous revelations as they were found in Muhammad's time.

In some cases, especially in reference to Zoroastrianism dualism as practiced at the time of Muhammad, the critiquing was negative and the amplification was corrective. At the same time, as we shall discover, whenever the material to be re-presented was of pristine Zoroastrian monotheism, it is embraced as generously in the Quran as are the finer points of Jewish and Christian Scriptural teachings. The Avesta-related passages are not recognized simply because the originals no longer exist, but finding echoes of them in the Quran may be quite possible.

Traditionally recognized as among the "People of the Book" along with Jews and Christians, Zoroastrians appear to be identified in the Quran as Sabaeans. How else can we possibly explain the absence of Zoroastrian Scriptures in the Quran and the lack of adequate references to Persia as Arabia's most influential neighbor, outranking Judaism and Christianity in religion and more significant than Greece and Rome in Arabian history and current events? As the Magi became Zoroastrian under domination, and as Mithraism and all the other religions were subsumed into Zoroastrianism in some manner, it is a reasonable assumption that some Sabaeans went through a similar willing absorption into the religion of the Persian Empire. This was the situation that prevailed in the time period when young Muhammad caravanned into Syria, where he experienced the dualistic Zoroastrianism he later sought to replace by the pure religion given to him by God. What he saw was Zoroastrianism in headlong decline, though he knew it first by the Sabaean identity then current in Syria, since God always spoke to Muhammad in language and terms he understood in the context of his life experiences.

At some point later, most likely under the influence of Salman, Muhammad was also exposed to the more ancient teachings of Zoroastrianism—the portions of Avesta Scripture passed down from Zoroaster himself that make their appearances in Quranic revelations later in Muhammad's life. The splendor and power of the latter (as in the above prayers) would have impressed Muhammad, much as his earlier intuition that he could build directly on the Jewish foundation and Christian community. None of this should be taken as implying that Muhammad used Zoroastrian Avestas as direct sources any more than he used the Hebrew or Christian material as it was given to him by Jews and Christians. In every case it seemed clear to Muhammad that the material was re-presented by God in a fresh revelation, and everyone who has heard the Quran recited has to be impressed by its powerful witness of this assertion.

We note how the Quran applies euphemistic names to both Christians (who are sometimes called Nazareans) and Zoroastrians (called Sabaeans) in the following verse from chapter 2, a section that occurs late in the Quran chronologically. The revelations never give up the Muslim hope for harmonious relations with Jews, Christians, Zoroastrians or anybody else who believes.

Those who believe (in the Quran), and those who follow the Jewish (Scriptures), and the Christians and the Sabaeans,—and any who believe in God and the Last Day, and work righteousness, shall have their reward with their Lord.[7]

And repeating this verse, using *The Sublime Quran* translation:

Truly those who have believed and those who became Jews and the Sabaeans and the Christians and the Zoroastrians[8] and those who ascribe partners[9]—truly God will distinguish between them on the Day of Resurrection.

The breakthrough in understanding occurs when we recognize that along with the Roman Empire and the empire of Alexander the Great (both mentioned in the Quran), the Persian Empire loomed large in Muhammad's own experience. Along with what sometimes appeared to be corrupt Judaism and corrupt Christianity (which they may have been in Muhammad's experience), God also spoke to him of a corrupt Zoroastrianism, but as with Judaism and Christianity, there was also much to be confirmed and amplified in the prophecies of Zoroaster.

Mahmoud Ayoub, considered by many to be an *éminence grise* of Islam in North America, has done the groundwork and laid the foundation for our recognition of Zoroastrians in the Quran being identified by the name *Sabaean*. He first adopts the position, later incorporated into *The Sublime Quran* translation by Laleh Bakhtiar, that references to the Magi are indeed references to Zoroastrians as being one of those groups who kept their old names while becoming subsumed into the Zoroastrian religious ethos. Second, he acknowledges a confusion as to the identities of at least two groups who continued to use the name Sabaean. Third, and most telling of all, he makes the point that while the Sabaeans are traditionally acknowledged as "People of the Book," they had no specific religious "book" of their own,[10] whereas at the beginning of the Islamic era, the reconstituted Zoroastrian Avesta was used by many such groups. This huge collection of writings, including pristine prophetic poems by Zoroaster and more recent works, would be "the Book" of the Sabaeans!

With the help of linguistic markers, we may actually be able to identify more Avesta-related chapters and verses in the Quran than verses that are Torah or Gospel related. We would then suggest a Zoroastrian context for large parts of the Quran, again a context as "invisible" to readers at first as water is to fish and air is to humans.

If we are now able to identify the Avesta-related material, confirmed and critiqued in the Quran, we might see not only a reflection of the Zoroastrianism that needed to be purified but also some aspects of pristine Zoroastrianism as it also affected Judaism and Christianity in earlier periods, although previously unrecognized. Examples would include the most ancient Vedic roots of the creation story in Genesis and the messianic theology related to the Saoshyant as now understood in the Christian Gospel. Such Avestas, the method of their rediscovery and their impact on critical analysis of Hebrew and Christian Scriptures are merely introduced in our presentation of *Three Testaments*. There is detailed work ahead that may occupy scholars for years to come.

The Quran itself insists time and time again that God's gracious revelation has been presented to all people previously, where it has been maintained in various mixtures of purity and corruption. We will present what follows from this according to the Muslim traditional orthodox understanding, recognizing also that Jews and Christians have no difficulty acknowledging that their own Scriptures are frequently "jumbled" in order, as a divine "work in progress" in which both scholarship and readership have roles.

Without making too much of it, nor indeed too little, the diagram that follows represents one respectful and graphic understanding of the Quran at the present stage of interfaith investigation. It is based on the student work at St. Andrew's Theological College in Trinidad in 2009, and while it has been scrutinized and modified by Muslim scholars in our circle, it is still to be regarded as preliminary, tentative and experimental. If validated, it would break new ground in illustrating the principle that clusters of material in the Quran can be identified as relating to God's previous revelations to Zoroaster, shown in white. Those white portions, previously revealed to Zoroaster and recorded in the Avesta, were not "copied" into the Quran any more than the Hebrew Torah or Christian Gospel portions, identified in the diagram as striped and gray, respectively. Such material was revealed afresh to Muhammad, though just as some verses of Hebrew and Christian Scriptures appear almost verbatim from the Bible record, the opening and closing of the Quran, chapter 1 and chapters 113 and 114, may have an almost literal affinity with the Avesta—a matter for Muslim scholars to adjudicate. In a more general sense, anything in the Quran that is related to the Day of Judgment, for example, should be correlated to earlier Zoroastrian revelations, just as references to the law given to Moses are correlated to the Hebrew revelations and allusions to Jesus as the messiah are correlated to the Christian connection. Confirmations of Hanif monotheistic oral traditions and condemnations of Arabian idolatry, superstition and pagan practices are also shown and are as obvious as the revelations rejecting Babylonian polytheism.

In this diagram (also available online), the sections of the Quran corresponding to previous revelations, confirmed or corrected, and false religions, condemned and rejected, are given names for purposes of classroom or book club discussion. Images are limited to black, white and gray colors in this printed text, and passages related to the Zoroastrian Avesta are shown in white, which we call "sunshine" (it is yellow in the online version). Those echoing the Hebrew Torah are shown in a striped design we call "prayershawl" (blue online), and those corresponding to Christian Gospel material are shown in the gray "cloud-of-presence" (sunset pink), recalling the baptism, transfiguration and ascension of Jesus. Babylonian polytheism is shown here in slanting stripes we call "pathways astray" (orange online), while the monotheism of the desert Hanifs is pictured as "arabesque tapestry" (purple online). Arabian idolatry, paganism and superstitions are shown in a design we call "sandstorm" in this book (tan online), and the asides unique to the Quran, parenthetical explanations and applications of the eternal words of God to the particular situation of Arabia in the time of Muhammad are shown here in the black of "Night Journey" (though green online).

This book may trigger PhD thesis projects on the possible relationship between Zoroaster and Jeremiah or Israelite exiles in Scythia, an area from Northern Syria to Azerbaijan. It may promote research on the impact of visits to Zoroastrian territory by Jesus, both his travels as recorded in Scripture and journeys that may be among the many "other things" done by him. We are especially hopeful that such a spirit of scholarly inquiry may extend to vigilant in-depth investigation of the identification of Zoroastrian and other previous revelations as reflected in the 114 revelations of the Quran, verses now identified as Z, or related to the Z factor as previously discussed. Such exercises should obviously be extended to Z passages in the Torah and the Gospel.

In diagrammatic scale, chapters of less than one hundred verses are shown in units or bars four millimeters deep (chapter 1). Those between one hundred and two hundred verses occupy bars eight millimeters deep (chapter 6), and those up to three hundred verses are shown in bars of twelve millimeters in depth (chapter 7). The sizes of the colored blocks are equal to the proportion of that chapter that confirms or critiques specific previous revelations. For example, the box showing chapter 6

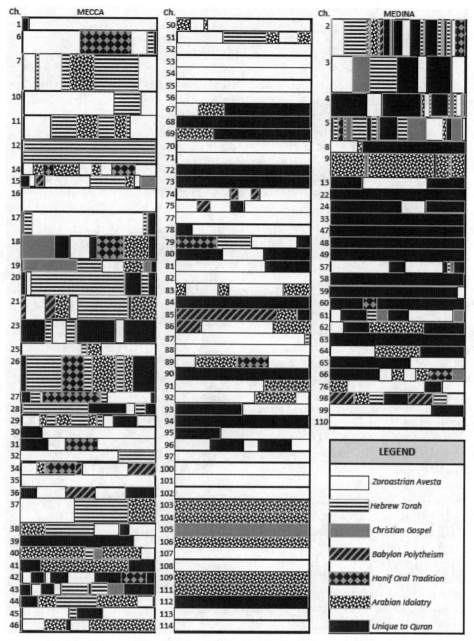

The Diagram of Previous Revelations from God Confirmed in the Quran
(color copies available online for download at www.BrianArthurBrown.com)

illustrates that about 48 percent of its contents may reflect the previous Avesta revelation in two white blocks, some 40 percent appears to be related to previous Hanif oral traditions of revelation as shown in "tapestry," 10 percent of this chapter reflects revelations given previously to Jews and 2 percent is unique to the Quran. In identifying material related to the various previous revelations, according to Islamic understanding, it is too early in this work to claim to be exact in reference to precise chapter and verse, and many sections are indeed replete with mixed images. The diagram may be regarded as impressionistic, pending further research, though "forensic" methods, as described, were applied to each chapter as rigorously as possible at this stage of the investigation.

The most obvious feature of the diagram as presented here is the preponderance of material reflecting what was revealed in the Avesta Scriptures of Zoroastrianism, shown in white, far surpassing even the Jewish and especially the Christian Scriptural echoes. This should not be a surprise, given the predominance of Zoroastrian influence of Arabia's largest, nearest and most significant neighbors, identified in this study by the name of its closest exemplar, the Sabaean religion. The title, *The Diagram of Previous Revelations from God Confirmed in the Quran*, makes a point that Muslims already

understand but that Jews and Christians need to appreciate—namely, that confirmation of previous revelations is by far the dominant motif of the Quran, though critique, putative correction and even condemnation are all important elements.

Theological chapters revealed in Mecca represent approximately two-thirds of the Quran, while the application of God's instruction in Medina is represented in the remaining third. The Quran is regarded by Muslims as uniquely complete within itself, but it is presented largely through the previous revelations that were given afresh by God to Muhammad. He may have heard of many or even most of these revelations in the form of popular culture, Jewish or Christian oral traditions, much of which seemed corrupt, as presented to him. Material from revelations by God in previous times and in other places are not regarded by Muslims as "sources" for the Quran, since they were obviously not simply copied. The truths of these previous revelations are believed to be confirmed by the Quran and preserved in a form appropriate for study and comparison with previous versions. Their value to Christians and Jews in particular is only now being realized, and their facility for disclosure of as yet unrecognized

The Eid Mubarak Stamp from the United States Post Office in the Forever Format

Zoroastrian material has a potential for Bible study that has yet to be fathomed. *The Diagram of Previous Revelations from God Confirmed in the Quran* is also available free of charge at www.BrianArthurBrown .com, where it can be downloaded in dimensions from letter size to posters.

Does the Quran also "confirm" Hindu and Buddhist Scriptures, as is sometimes asserted among Muslims with a popular understanding? It does affirm the sending of prophets from God to all peoples, but it only confirms the written Scriptures of the "People of the Book"—that is, Jews, Christians and Zoroastrians (Sabaeans). However, one important aspect of the recognition of the Zoroastrian connection is the relationship of the Zoroastrian Avesta to the Vedic Scriptures found in reformed Hindu and early Buddhist sources. The Avesta is a transformation of Vedic theology that resulted in a reform of Hinduism and the birth of Buddhism, so that in confirming the Zoroastrian Avesta it may be truly said that in addition to affirming the fact that revelations came to all peoples, the Quran also confirms the truths of many passages of Hindu and Buddhist Scriptures. None of this is shown in the above diagram, except indirectly in the portions shown to relate to the Zoroastrian Avesta Scriptures.

10

torah in the quran

"The best of you is the one who learns the Koran, then teaches it."

EVERY MUSLIM IN THE WORLD KNOWS THE story of Abraham, much as it appears in the Hebrew Scriptures, with additional revelations about Abraham's childhood in the Quran, as God's filter for ancient Middle Eastern lore, and supplemented by discussions between Muhammad and his companions in the Hadith. The core of the story as it relates to Muslim belief has to do with the biblical and Quranic accounts of God's graciousness to Hagar, Abraham's second wife, and her son, Ishmael, from whom all Arabs claim descent. To draw that story out of its Torah cradle is instructive, keeping in mind that these particular essentials of historical legend are as spiritually precious to Muslims as they are to Jews or Christians. The Quran not only confirms the monotheism of the Torah but also insists that this quintessential Jewish belief began with Abraham and was refined and amplified by God through Moses.

According to the Bible, and like Muhammad in a similar polygamous environment, for many years Abraham had only one wife. He loved Sarah and he was faithful, but he was anxious over the question of an heir, lest his entire estate someday should go to his servant, Eliezar of Damascus.[1] As Abraham prayed about his anxiety, he was led out of his tent complex to where God said to him, "Look toward heaven and count the stars, if you are able to count them." Then he said to him, "So shall your offspring be."[2] But Sarah continued childless, and at the age of eighty-four, ten years younger than her husband, she was past the normal childbearing age for someone who had never previously conceived.[3]

Knowing Abraham's anxiety about an heir, she proposed that he take Hagar, a girl from Egypt and her personal handmaiden, as his second wife.[4] When Hagar became pregnant it seemed to Sarah that this slave girl treated her mistress with contempt, and when Sarah responded harshly, Hagar ran away. The angel of the Lord found her in the wilderness and urged her to return with the promise from God, "I will greatly increase your offspring, and they shall be too many to count."[5] The angel announced that she would have a son and that he should be called Ishmael (God Heeds), and he bade her return to Sarah's household. Hagar submitted to God and called him El-roy (God Sees). She returned and presented that son to Abraham when the patriarch was aged eighty-six.

When he was aged ninety-nine, Abraham again heard God speak about their covenant and its succession through a son to be born to Sarah. At different times, both Abraham and Sarah laughed

417

at the prospect, but Abraham said to God, "O that Ishmael might live by your favor!"[6] God assured him it would be so, but that nevertheless the specific covenant would pass through another son, Isaac (Laughter). "As for Ishmael, I have *heeded* you. I hereby bless him. I will make him fertile and exceedingly numerous. He shall be the father of twelve chieftains, and I will make of him a great nation."[7] To mark this covenant with all males of his family, Abraham and his son, Ishmael, aged thirteen, were circumcised on that day, as were all their slaves and every male associated with the household.[8] Isaac was yet to be conceived.

But when Abraham was one hundred, Sarah, at age ninety, presented him with a "crown prince," the recognized progeny of the chief and his primary or principal wife, and Isaac was circumcised on the eighth day.[9] Some years later, as Sarah watched her son playing with his older brother, she again demanded the expulsion of the slave wife, Hagar, and her son with her, lest they become interested in rights of inheritance. The matter distressed Abraham greatly, for it concerned a son of his. But God said to Abraham, "Do not be distressed over the boy or your slave. Whatever Sarah tells you, do as she says, for it is through Isaac that offspring shall be called for you. As for the son of the slave-woman, I will make a nation of him too, for he is your seed."[10]

The next morning Abraham supplied Hagar with what food and water she could carry and sent her on her way with Ishmael. The Torah has them trekking through the desert from Mamre to Beersheba. The Quran extends their travels to Mecca (then known and pronounced as Bacca) where, depleted of resources and weary after a journey by various means over several days, she put the boy under a bush for shade.[11] According to the Quran, she then dashed and scurried between hilltops seeking water or help from any passing caravan.[12] Hagar ran back and forth seven times until she collapsed in tears at the prospect of her son's death.[13]

God heard the cry of the boy, and an angel of the Lord called to Hagar from Heaven and said to her, "What troubles you, Hagar? Fear not, for God has *heeded* the cry of the boy where he is. Come, lift up the boy and hold him by the hand, for I will make a great nation of him." Then God opened her eyes, and she saw a well of water. She went and filled the skin with water and let the boy drink. God was with the boy, and he grew up; he dwelt in the wilderness and became a bowman. He lived in the wilderness of Paran, and his mother got a wife for him from the land of Egypt.[14]

Her frantic dashing is, of course, reenacted every year by millions of Muslims at the place of the spring of water, called *Zamzam*, during the pilgrimage to Mecca known as the Hajj, a reenactment that recalls the vulnerability of all believers and their dependence on God's grace and mercy. Zamzam is located near or adjoining the site where Abraham visited Ishmael and his mother and where they built or rebuilt the ancient shrine known as the Kabbah.[15] The additional details of the stories of Hagar and Ishmael in the Quran are not in any substantial conflict with the account recorded in the Torah, and so it may be seen as merely supplemental, much like the stories of Abraham's childhood that do not appear in the Torah.[16]

On the other hand, more of a correction to the story from a Muslim perspective is the later Quranic teaching that the son offered for sacrifice on Mount Moriah was Ishmael. Muslims believe that Isaac was later inserted into the Torah text as corruption or tampering to reflect his position as principal heir according the Jewish belief. The comparison of the versions of the story is instructive, a popular exercise in cross-referencing the texts.[17]

But the fact of the matter is that the Quran contains only a little of this entire material, whether as supplemental or corrective, in the Muslim view. It is presumed that readers of the Quran know the original stories either from the earlier Hebrew source or through the refined summaries in the Hadith. According to Muslims, the key to understanding these Torah revelations concerning the Arab matriarch and her son is the motif of grace to Hagar and to Ishmael. God is merciful toward the powerless who trust him, as much or more so than to those of influence or prominence. There is reverence for Abraham, and even for Sarah, but there is a special poignancy in God's dealing with the oppressed, a theme that occurs frequently in the Torah as well as the Quran.

After these episodes the Torah rarely mentions Ishmael, except to acknowledge that the two half-brothers, Ishmael and Isaac, together bury their father in Hebron in a harmony not often maintained at that shrine by their descendants today. The connection continued when, some years later, Esau married the daughter of Ishmael, who would be his cousin. Finally, there is indirect praise of

Ishmael in one of the Hebrew Psalms, and reference to him and his mother passing through that valley and finding water: "Happy is the man who finds refuge in You, whose mind is on the pilgrim highways. They pass through the Valley of Bacca, regarding it as a place of springs."[18]

When Muslims say that neither they nor Muhammad had previous knowledge of what is in the Quran, they obviously do not mean that Muhammad was the only person living in Arabia who did not know about Abraham, the other Hebrew prophets, Jesus, Mary and the disciples, not to mention other information to which the Bible alludes and that is found in various forms in ancient Middle Eastern lore. There were both Orthodox and Nestorian Christians in practically every town, and Jews both traveled through and settled in significant numbers, as well as monotheistic Hanif nomads with their oral versions of the stories. There were Babylonian magicians and idolaters native to the region, whose religions were infused with biblical imagery by this time in a manner similar to the ways in which Haitian voodoo uses it today. It was clarity and fresh meaning that Muhammad was given in his revelations, meditations and reveries. As the poets ascribing their inspiration to "muses" will say, "I don't know where that came from," and as musicians so often attribute their melodies to something beyond themselves, the experience of Muhammad was all this, in possibly the most intense form the world has seen, as a gift from God.

How the revelations came to Muhammad, as God's Apostle, is described in the hadiths. Aisha, the youngest of Muhammad's wives and called "the mother of the faithful believers," wrote, "Al-Harith bin Hisham asked God's Apostle 'O God's Apostle! How is the Divine Inspiration revealed to you?' God's Apostle replied, 'Sometimes it is revealed like the ringing of a bell; this form of Inspiration is the hardest of all, and then this state passes off after I have grasped what is inspired. Sometimes the Angel comes in the form of a man and talks to me and I grasp whatever he says.'" Aisha recalled, "Verily I saw the Prophet being inspired Divinely on a very cold day and noticed the sweat dropping from his forehead."[19]

Another Scripture from the Torah that is particularly cherished by Muslims concerns a prophecy by Moses that the Quran regards as primary among several prophecies referring to Muhammad himself in the Bible. Israel's most holy prophet and lawgiver spoke specifically about the surrounding Arab nations at the end of his ministry. Moses had just finished announcing God's promise that He would raise up another leader to replace him as prophet in Israel, taken as a reference to Joshua. Then, almost parenthetically, as it appears in the text of Hebrew Scripture, Moses makes an almost identical prophecy regarding a prophet for the neighboring (Arab) peoples, quoting what the LORD said to him: "I will raise up a Prophet for them from among their own people, like yourself; I will put My words in his mouth, and he will speak unto them all that I command him."[20]

No such prophet of the stature of Moses arose for centuries in Arabia but, when he came forth, Muhammad was recognized by many Jews, Christians and other Arabians as the one foretold by Moses. Muslims believe, as did Muhammad himself, that the Hebrew Scripture referred to him in this prophecy from the lips of Moses. This central dogma in the Muslim religion is verified by several references in the Quran itself, but especially where Allah speaks of those to whom he extends mercy:

> Those who follow the apostle, the unlettered prophet whom they find mentioned in their own Scriptures—in the Law and the Gospel. He commands them what is just and forbids them what is evil: he allows them as lawful what is good and pure and prohibits them from what is bad and impure; He releases them from their heavy burdens and from the yokes that are upon them. So it is those who believe in him who honor him, help him and follow the light which is sent down with him; it is they who will prosper.[21]

Some Christians claim that the prophet to come was a reference to Jesus, who ministered to Jews and to other nations, but he was not from the other nations, and Christians do not regard him as a prophet. There can be no doubt that in the Quran, the "unlettered prophet" is a reference to Muhammad, and of further interest is the comment that he is there mentioned in what the Quran calls *Taurat* and *Injil*, both the Hebrew and the Christian Scriptures, the Law and the Gospel. Muslims everywhere regard these verses in the Hebrew Scriptures as a clear example of prophecy concerning Muhammad, along with Christian Scriptures that also prophesy his coming, as we shall see.

It would appear that at the beginning of the seventh century CE the Jewish community in Arabia was possibly sharing with Jews elsewhere in one of their periodic outbursts of Messianic expectation. This would seem to have taken place at the very time when Christians were going through one of their own recurring outbreaks of fervor related to anticipation of the Second Coming of Christ. Arabs could do no less than speculate about their own destiny as the only people around who lacked such a historic expectation, except for the often quoted prophecy of Moses, to which they now turned in popular anticipation.

A respected twentieth-century historian of Islam documented these movements and related historical vignettes from the earliest histories of Islam. Martin Lings paraphrases the ancient records in the light and language of modern historians. His material is distilled reliably from biographies of the Prophet that, with only traces of folk legend, deserve more attention than has been accorded to them outside Islam. Lings, a Christian who became a Muslim, was a close associate and personal friend of fellow Oxford scholar C. S. Lewis, an agnostic who became a Christian. Of all recent popular biographies of Muhammad, that of Lings is among the most reliable, opening his principal opus[22] with the above references to important Torah passages as addressed in the Quran. A summary of his paraphrase of original sources will suffice for our purpose here, but along with the admirable biographies of Muhammad by Karen Armstrong, Huston Smith and others, Muslims would hope that Jews, Christians and others would include Lings in their studies.

Lings tells of Muhammad's challenging childhood, brought up by his mother after his father's death, and by his grandparents after her death, and in the household of his loving but impoverished uncle, Abu Talib. He then moves on to describe the first recorded instance of the application of Moses's prophecy to Muhammad. "Ahmad," as Muhammad was known in his youth, assisted his uncle as part of a caravan to Syria. They stopped for refreshment at a Christian hermitage near their destination, where a monk named Bahira, knowing the eagerness of Arabs to experience the advent of their own prophet, had been reviewing that passage in Hebrew Scripture. Sensing an aura about this handsome, intelligent, diligent and spiritual teenager, Bahira enthused that if ever there was to be such a prophet, he had never seen a more likely candidate.[23]

Such stories resonate like those of Samuel and Jesus in the temples of their times, though the Islamic provenance is just so much more extensive. Bahira was not the last person to make such an observation about Muhammad, for he did seem remarkable in every way, so much so that as a young caravaner he soon got the top job, impressed the wise and wealthy widow he worked for, and married her.[24] He might have lived "happily ever after," except for the turmoil in his soul over the corruption and idolatry all around him.

With this background, it becomes easier to accept and understand the second recorded reference to the Mosaic prophecy in connection with Muhammad. It was again a Christian, Waraqah, the cousin of Muhammad's wife, who, when recognizing the divine source of Ahmad Muhammad's poetic utterance, immediately and confidently connected it to the fulfillment of the prophecy in Hebrew Scripture. Sketchy details of these stories notwithstanding, the point is that from the very beginning, the earliest histories present a record of the connection between the Islam of the Muslims and its recognition by Christians as being rooted in Hebrew Scripture in the ongoing intertwining of the three traditions.

The "cast of characters" in the Quran fleshes out its relationship to the Torah. Of twenty-five personas in the Quran identified as prophets in Islam, twenty-one are familiar to us from the Hebrew Scriptures.

Arabic[25]	English
Haroon	Aaron
Ibrahim	Abraham
Aadam	Adam
Dawoud	David
Hud	Eber
Ilyas	Elijah
al-Yasa	Elisha
Idris	Enoch
Zul-Kifl	Ezekiel

Arabic[25]	English
Ishaq	Isaac
Ismail	Ishmael
Yaqub	Jacob
Shu'ayb	Jethro
Ayyub	Job
Yunus	Jonah
Yusuf	Joseph
Lut	Lot
Musa	Moses
Nooh	Noah
Saleh	Shelah
Sulaiman	Solomon

Uzair or "Ezra" could perhaps be added to this list (the prophets not in the Torah are Zechariah, John the Baptist, Jesus and Muhammad). Many other Torah personas are also mentioned in the Quran, including Saul, Goliath, Haman, Nimrod and others identified by name, plus men like Cain and Abel and women like Sarah and Hagar, who appear but are identified by name only in the Hadith commentaries. Others from among the Bani Israel, from Samuel to Jeremiah, are also dealt with in a fulsome manner in the Hadith conversations between Muhammad and his companions. But the point must be well taken regarding the extensive and intimate link between the Torah and the Quran, if only based on the "cast of characters" above, of whom it may be noted that Moses is the single person appearing most frequently in the Quran.

Most of the references to figures in the Quran who appear first in Hebrew Scriptures assume prior knowledge about them on the part of the reader or hearer, whether from the Hebrew sources circulating in Arabia at the time of Muhammad or from the Hadith commentaries in summary, with interpretation. There is a parallel in the example of the appearance of characters from the Hebrew Scriptures in the Christian Scriptures when Jonah, Job, David and both major and minor prophets are mentioned, quoted or discussed by Jesus in the Gospels and by the apostles in their epistles. Again, there is rarely any background information, since it was expected that everyone in this extended family knew these stories. Joseph is an exception in the Quran,[26] which presents a slightly expanded version of parts of the basic Torah story.[27] The Quran gives a complete narrative, just as in the Bible, plus such details as the name of Zulaikah, the wife of Potiphar, and her explanation of her attempt to seduce Joseph. Such details are also common in the Hadith version of Bible stories as recounted by Muhammad, who added meaning to information circulating among his many Jewish and Christian companions, without a claim of direct revelation by the Divine. In the case of Joseph, it is believed that when companions asked him for more understanding of the earlier prophet who ruled Egypt and was buried there, God very soon gave Muhammad a new and direct revelation in recitation format. It included details from both Hebrew Scriptures and Middle Eastern lore, plus the evocative connotation of the cherished story as directly from God, another excellent cross-reference exercise for those engaged in the current comparative practice of "Scriptural reasoning."

While the Quran appears to the uninitiated to be jumbled chronologically, it is not more so than many parts of the Bible to which its readers have become accustomed. For example, the editing together of sources has David appearing first as a mature man in Saul's court, before his appearance on the battlefield to face Goliath as a teen unknown to the king. Likewise, once again, the comparison of the Quran with the Book of Psalms is instructive, where laments, thanksgivings and other themes appear in a seemingly random order that goes unnoticed by believers who simply take them as they come.

Unlike unfortunate aspects of the troubles between Christians and Jews, the tense relationship between Muslims and Jews in many parts of the world today is not based on a long or consistent history. While present acrimonies tend to highlight any previous strife, in various centuries, in different countries and diverse circumstances, Jews and Muslims have often lived together in complete or considerable harmony. The rupture in good relations that prevailed early in the twentieth century was largely occasioned by Arab sympathy for the Axis powers in World War II to counterweight British and French influence in the Middle East and as a vehicle for an anticolonial campaign. This policy led them into a conflict relationship with European Jewry, exacerbated by the postwar increase in Jewish emigration to the British protectorate of Palestine, with the intention of establishing a Jewish state. Based on previous history, this might have happened peacefully and cooperatively had it not been for the wider world context of the war and the drive toward independence of these colonies and protectorates. At this point, the world prays for the miracle of a family reconciliation, appropriate to the rights and needs of all parties in these regards, and seeks a dynamically harmonious future for all members of Abraham's family in the ancient land and elsewhere.

Unfortunately, as often happens with Scripture, the Quran can be quoted in support of two contrary positions in relation to Jews and the Children of Israel, in spite of the intertwining of motifs observed first in the Torah. Early in his prophetic ministry, it was revealed to Muhammad that Jews and also Christians might share in the Muslim revival of true religion, and Muhammad never lost sight of that dream. But after the migration of Muslims to Medina, they were faced with more substantial Jewish "tribes" or communal neighborhoods with significant business, religious and cultural interests of their own, particularly those known as the Banu Qaynuqa, the Banu Nadir and the Banu Qurayza.

Most of the Arab inhabitants of this new Muslim center converted to Islam, but among the large Jewish community that lived there, only a few converted. After only two years, Muhammad's initially warm relationship with the Jews began to deteriorate, and the Jewish believers were treated harshly, especially in the context of war, whenever their loyalty was in question. To Jews and Christians, Islam became increasingly identified as a threat, and in spite of Muhammad's earlier hopes for harmony, he felt bitterly betrayed by those who might have been an important source of support. The seeming invective against Jews in Quranic chapters revealed in those years should hardly be seen as against Judaism but as against particular Jews in those particular circumstances.

There are more than sixty verses in the Quran that speak directly about or to the Jews. More than half use the phrase "Children of Israel" (*bani Israil*), others use the terms *Jews* (*yahud*) or *those who are Jewish* (*alladhina hadu*). The Quran also speaks of the People of the Book (*ahl al-kitab*) and "those who have been given the Book" (*alladhina utu al-kitab*). These particular verses often refer to both Christians and Jews as those who received the Scriptures in pre-Islamic times, but the Quran also mentions the Torah specifically more than a dozen times, and it mentions the Psalms of David. Indeed, chapter 17 of the Quran is simply titled "The Children of Israel." In the following examples, God speaks in the plural, as in the opening verses of the Torah and elsewhere, in reference to the gift of the Torah to the Jews.

O children of Israel, indeed We delivered you from your enemy and made a covenant with you on the right side of the mountain, and We sent down for you manna and quails.[28]

We did aforetime give the Book to Moses: Be not then in doubt of its reaching (thee): and We made it a guide to the Children of Israel.[29]

We did aforetime grant the Children of Israel the Book, the power of command and prophethood; the critical judgment and the priesthood.[30]

Elsewhere the Jews are lumped in with Christians as "apes and swine," as the main sources of disappointment to the nascent Islamic religion. Babylonian polytheists and Arabian idolaters were not embraced warmly either, but not as much was expected of them. There is truly no feud as bitter as a family feud. So, in the context of tension and conflict, we find extremely negative revelations about the Jews, from whom so much had been expected. Such passages are frequently blurred and strained, and they are nearly always part of a wider polemic against anyone not accepting the new religion. It is just such passages to which critics appeal when seeking to illustrate Islamic intolerance, especially in reference to "hatred of the Jews," which is beside the point as such in every single example.

Not all of them are alike: Of the People of the Book there is a portion that stands (for what is right); they rehearse the signs of God all night long, and they prostrate themselves in adoration. They believe in God and the Last Day; they enjoin what is right and forbid what is wrong; and they hasten (in emulation) in (all) good works: They are in the ranks of the righteous.[31]

Taking these verses as a whole, whether speaking about Jews, Children of Israel or People of the Book, it is obvious that in the Quran the Jews are not condemned as a people; only those who fail to uphold their covenant with God and to reverence God are condemned. Possibly many Jews need to be assured on this point today, and possibly many Muslims need to review it.

The language of the Arabic Quran is among the most beautiful ever recited, as Christians and Jews are beginning to discover at the increasing number of interfaith activities around the world. Among the few things that compare with the Quran are certain sections of the Bible in beloved translations. Psalm 23, "The Lord Is My Shepherd," in the Hebrew Scripture and the Lord's Prayer in the Christian Scripture make sense in any translation, but for many English speakers, the beauty of such language is found only in the King James Authorized Version, which explains why that version was emulated for so long in both Jewish and Christian translations, both Protestant and Catholic, and how it is so easily memorized.

It is like that also with the creation story, the Ten Commandments, the Christmas story of the one "wrapped in swaddling clothes and lying in a manger"[32] or Saint Paul's Hymn to Love: "Though I speak with the tongues of men and of angels, and have not love, I am become as sounding brass, or a clanging cymbal."[33] Even with the availability of more accurate translations of both the Hebrew and Christian Scriptures, Jewish people prefer to recite together the beloved traditional texts of the *Shema*[34] and the traditional opening of Friday Shabbat Kiddush.[35] Christians recite the Twenty-Third Psalm and the Lord's Prayer with a similar cultural adhesion, and woe betide the young preacher at a funeral who invites mourners to attempt recitation using the more prosaic modern versions that fail to reverberate in the soul.

This may be as close as Jews and Christians can come to understanding the Muslim affection for the very words of the Quran and the determination not to lose that feeling by translating it. Jews and Christians can hardly be expected to realize this, but it would appear that, when recited in Arabic, the whole of the Quran has that combination of evocative rhythm and transcendent power that they associate with only certain special passages of their own Scriptures.

In anyone else, we might ascribe the events surrounding the first revelations of the Quran to something like a "midlife crisis," brought on by the sense of powerlessness an individual sometimes feels in the face of negative circumstances and dwindling opportunities to make changes. As a young man, attractive and winsome, Muhammad had a way with people and a way with figures that made him successful in the commercial caravan business, rough and tumble though it was. Certain aspects of the business may have weighed heavily upon him and, as he reached maturity, the immorality and corruption of Arabian community life was especially painful, particularly in Mecca, and principally around the ancient shrine in the heart of the city.

This *Kabbah* was traditionally believed by many to have been built by "Adam" back in the mists of time and, after deterioration, practically everybody believed it to have been rebuilt by Abraham and his son, Ishmael, at the dawn of the monotheistic age. This Mecca of tourism and pilgrimage, surrounded by 360 altars to various ancient gods and goddesses, experienced physical deterioration in Muhammad's time also, but it was rebuilt again since it was the main industry of the community. But the deterioration of spiritual values around the Kabbah was of intense concern to Muhammad. Some god could be found to forgive any sin for a price, and sadly, in his view, the examples of Jews and Christians in synagogue and church were not much better.

Muhammad was illiterate, but he was a deeply spiritual person who was deeply troubled about the corruption and immorality of his society. At about forty years of age he developed the practice of maintaining his sanity by solitary meditation in his favorite cave retreat. On one such occasion he was practically overcome when God gave him his first psalm-like poem of spiritual truth and judgment, transmitted through none other than the angel Gabriel. It was a verse about the origins of human life and God's communication of his will to humanity, found now as part of chapter 96 of the Quran. He knew he was inspired, that this was not something he made up himself, but something from God.

Still trembling, he remembered the beautiful little verse and recited it to his family when he got home. They realized immediately this was not just their beloved husband and father talking, but that the beauty and power of his words had to be from God. They loved his little verse and kept it. His wife's Christian cousin[36] was the first to assert that this was a gift from the God of the Hebrew prophets, an interesting initial intersection of the three religions.

The Quran is made up of 114 such utterances or "psalms" given by God, usually through the voice of the angel Gabriel. Some are as short as Psalm 23 in the Hebrew Scriptures, and some even longer than Psalm 119, but the look and feel of the Hebrew psalms are helpful for both Christians and Jews to relate to the image and rhythm of these *surahs*, or little "chapters," of the Quran. Such experiences came to Muhammad over a period of twenty-three years, often unexpectedly, sometimes months or even years apart. Each one of the resulting recitations is validated in its authenticity by its own impact on the hearers.

The impact and the influence of this collection of oracular prophecies on both individuals and on whole societies has been immense, even though Muslims often confess that its content sometimes seems secondary to the impact of its aural majesty. The contents are getting more scrutiny these days than ever before in history, by Muslims and others, especially Jews and Christians, both critics and those seeking to understand.

At first, modern Westerners were inclined to treat the Quran as a quaint, even esoteric, rehashing of some of the main stories of the Bible, whitewashing the believing characters and tarring the unbelievers with stern judgment. A more gracious assessment based on the same observations might be that believers are treated with the grace we all need, while unbelievers get "tough love," as a timely warning about the consequences of their actions. Noting that a disproportionate number of Christians and Jews who become Muslim are highly educated might lead to an awareness that there must be a depth of profundity in the Quran that escapes any shallow introduction. With the possible exception of bright young African Americans in prison, exemplified by Malcolm X, it is a common fact of observation that more PhDs than grade school dropouts convert to Islam.

Having suggested how Muhammad *did* receive the Quran, it might be helpful to explode some myths, based on ignorance, prejudice or both, to show how the Quran was *not* received. False assumptions have led to misunderstandings of the origins of the Quran. A clumsy application of Western critical techniques, by persons whose agendas are perhaps tainted by preconceived negative conclusions about Islam, has led to widespread circulation of false information. In an era in which good will and truth must compete with fear and loathing, it is unfortunately necessary to counter this misinformation. The following brief excerpt from a Wiki service, full of false assumptions, illustrates the point. Be forewarned that, while widespread among Christians and Jews in certain quarters, based on informed critical and cultural understandings to be presented below, we may conclude that the spirit of such presentations is often prejudiced and their contents are sometimes false. The following quotation is offensive not only to many Muslims but also to Christians, Jews and others who are well informed in these regards. The opening words are patently false, as "most Quranic experts" then listed in the article apparently include no Muslims, and misinformation grows from there, even if sincerely proffered.

> Most Quranic experts attribute the Qur'an in its form today to post–seventh century alterations. The consensus is, "independent scholars studying the Qur'an and Hadith, have concluded that the Islamic Scripture was not revealed to just one man, but was a compilation of later redactions and editions formulated by a group of men, over the course of a few hundred years. The Qur'an which we read today is not that which was in existence in the mid-seventh century, but is a product of the eighth and ninth centuries. It was not conceived in Mecca or Medina, but in Baghdad." The origins of Islam and the Qur'an are dubious. This is the opinion of renowned scholars and professors of Islam, history, Arabic and many other fields.[37]

Wikipedia, and its offshoots and emulators, are rarely regarded as authoritative on any subject, but they often do reflect popular culture with its frequent misconceptions. The list of "experts" in the above paragraph includes many associated with prominent universities. Some of these persons have little personal connection with the Muslim community, others are not held in high regard in the Islamic world and a few are reputable scholars who simply applied now discredited methods to their research. Though not as blatantly virulent as many assessments of the content of the Quran (calling it "ignorant," "hateful" and "violent") now circulating on the Internet and in books by some of these same "experts," the above unsubstantiated opinions are based on attempts to apply the methods of Western source-criticism to the study of the Quran.

Such an exercise might be compared with the views of some whose exposure to art has been limited to Western-style paintings. Upon being introduced to a work of Oriental art, such persons have been known to exclaim, "But most of the canvas is blank." In Western art every square centimeter does indeed get colored, but in Oriental art it is the spaces that evoke meaning, while the sketched images and lines of paint are but sophisticated hints to guide the imagination. So it is with the Quran, which is a full canvas for believers, despite what seems like empty spaces, missing words and a dependence on the wealth of allusions worthy of scholarly interpretation equal to anything at rabbinical school or seminary. When properly recited, this welter of divine intimations evokes a deep and awe-inspiring appreciation of God's presence, God's will and God's purpose. This direct connection with the Divine is cultivated and prized above anything a prosaic study or "critical analysis" of the printed words could offer.

The production of lace offers another example of this concept. Since the invention of the bobbin in Belgium in 1561, lace has been mass produced in Europe, but without much hands-on appreciation of its particular nature. Originating in Egypt, lace has been a luxury product from there to Afghanistan for millennia. The essence of its delicate beauty is not the string but the holes. The spaces are shaped by the string, to be sure, but the judges in lace competitions do not focus on the string but on the delicate and evocative spaces where the manifestation of beauty is expressed. The application of Western critical techniques to any analysis of the text of the Quran is like an examination of only the string. "Interpretations" of the Quran, such as the classic version by Yusuf Ali, frequently attempt to convey allusion to the deeper meanings by the inclusion of insightful intimations in brackets that are not actually in the text but which may contain something possibly found in the recitation tone and voice inflection, as explicated earlier regarding crucifixion.

The authentic Quran is recited, not written or read, and the actual breath of every reciter is redolent with God's beauty and power. So many oblique inferences are implied in the Quran that it may be said to have an unfathomable depth containing "all truth," as understood by Muslims. It is in this context that seeming conflicts with Christian "truths" or Jewish understandings are capable of resolution by a recognition that such conflicts are about the color, thickness and composition of the string, whether in Torah, Gospel, Quran or even Avesta or other revelations. When critics are unable to see how the Quran could possibly "confirm" all previous Scriptures, it is because they fail to recognize that such confirmation is believed to be as much or more in the breathing space as in the string. Talmudic discussion and Christian meditations offer a related but less intrinsic example of the same approach. Those familiar with the distinction may realize that the traditional study or analysis of the Bible could be described as a "left brain" function, examining the details, while the recitation of the Quran is a "right brain" function, dealing with the whole picture. Failure to appreciate the distinction is a prescription for misunderstanding, especially in reference to what the written Quran alone fails to convey, according to the traditional Muslim understanding.

Islamic critical analysis of the Quran on its own terms, which the West is only beginning to appreciate, continued and flourished again in the fourth Islamic century (tenth century CE). In eras when Islamic culture and society have suffered, as through much of the twentieth century, the Muslim community has sometimes been more inclined to simply take refuge in the delicate but powerful experience of the Quran. During this time, patently ridiculous attempts at discrediting the Quran on the basis of Western critical techniques were undertaken by Christians, Jews and others, as illustrated.

That is not to say that critical methods appropriate to the exegetical task cannot, or have not, been used by Muslim scholars and others of good faith in times past, or that such is not possible today. Islamic sources tell us that Muhammad's followers would argue about the Quran, even in his own lifetime. This is because Muhammad himself provided contradicting versions of the recitations, which only became written "Scriptures" as an aid to memory. A notable example is given by Bukhari, the most respected author of the six canonical Hadith, the writings of which, while not Scriptural, contain the words of the Prophet and his conversations with his companions. This discussion of a chapter of the Quran, Al-Furqan, is attributed to Umar, the second caliph after Muhammad died.

> Umar bin Khattab said, "I heard Hisham bin Hakim bin Hizam reciting Surah Al-Furqan during the lifetime of Allah's Apostle. I listened to his recitation and noticed that he recited it in several ways which Allah's Apostle had not taught me. So I was on the point of attacking him in the prayer, but I waited till he finished, and then I seized him by the collar. 'Who taught you this Surah which I have heard you reciting?' He replied, 'Allah's Apostle taught it to me.' I said, 'You are lying. Allah's Apostle taught me in a different way this very Surah which I have heard you reciting.' So I led him to Muhammad. 'O Allah's Apostle! I heard this person reciting Surah-al-Furqan in a way that you did not teach me.' The Prophet said, 'Hisham, recite!' So he recited in the same way as I heard him recite it before. On that, Allah's Apostle said, 'It was revealed to be recited in this way.' Then the Prophet said, 'Recite, Umar!' So I recited it as he had taught me. Allah's Apostle said, 'It was revealed to be recited in this way, too.' He added, 'The Qur'an has been revealed to be recited in several different ways, [38] so recite of it that which is easier for you.'"[39]

As for the suggestion that the Quran was compiled by "a group of men" and "not in Mecca or Medina, but in Baghdad," the truth is virtually the opposite. It was composed in both Mecca and Medina, compiled piecemeal during the Prophet's lifetime, and informed scholarship now concludes that much of it may have been written down by women. Muhammad entrusted the work to his family and his extended family, those he referred to with affection and respect as "The People of the House."

In that circle, five women of the immediate family are known to have had literary skills, as did four men who were adopted, hired or married into the household. Of those men, one named Zaid was adopted, as yet uneducated and too young to record Quranic verses when the first recitations were revealed in Mecca. Another, coincidentally also named Zaid, joined the family circle as Muhammad's secretary later in the Medina era, after most of the revelations there had been already recorded. Abu Bakr, Muhammad's father-in-law, could write, but not well, and while his house was nearby, he was not actually part of the Prophet's household—although his daughter was.

This daughter was Aisha, Muhammad's youngest wife, whose advanced education the Prophet himself facilitated. She was the widow who later contributed more to the Hadith record than anyone else within the household, and she would certainly have worked on the Quran. The final male person who could have assisted in the compilation was 'Ali ibn Abi Talib, the redoubtable husband of Muhammad's daughter, Fatima, who lived in the compound and had literary interest and skills. He may have contributed to this work, but there is no record of his having done so, though his wife, Fatima, is known to have made or compiled her own *mushof*, or collection of Quranic material, while the Prophet was still living.

In such a household, writing appears to have been "women's work" (an intimation of possibilities in earlier Jewish and Christian aristocratic and leadership households like that of David[40] and James). This Fatima was the influential daughter of Muhammad's first wife, Kadijah, who was literate herself through the Mecca period when nobody else in the household had such skill, except possibly her daughter, leading to the current assumption that all the Mecca chapters are written in a feminine hand.

In addition to Kadijah, Fatima and the aforementioned Aisha, at least two other younger wives were known for their literary abilities and their contributions to such work over the years—namely, Umm Salamah and Hafsah. The latter was indeed so connected to the task of Quranic transcription that Umar, the second caliph to reign after the death of the Prophet, later entrusted her with the household version for safe keeping. This was after both Abu Bakr and Ali took pains to ensure that the entire family collection was preserved, and Zaid, the secretary, had assembled that initial edition. That material would become known as the Medina Codex—entrusted to Hafsah, who verified its contents as one who would at least recognize her own handwriting and probably that of the others.

11

gospel in the quran

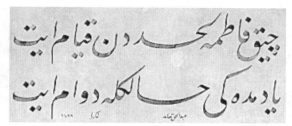

Arise Fatima

THE TORAH IS MORE PROMINENT IN THE Quran than the Gospel, and Moses is quoted or referred to an astounding 124 times while Jesus is referred to by name just twenty-five times. Indeed, both the Quran and the Gospel are steeped in spiritual imagery and powerful metaphors seen first in the Torah, which forms a backdrop for them even greater than the Zoroastrian motifs behind all three. However, the Gospel-related material in the Quran is substantial enough to require examination on its own.

In a previous chapter we recognized that problems between Christians and Muslims have been largely based on gross misinformation and even deliberate misrepresentation of each other's positions on a number of issues. Christian ridicule of the Quran has been comparable in motivation to church-sponsored anti-Semitism, and for Muslims it is an offence of that order of magnitude. We believe ourselves to be well beyond either in this study, moving forward by advancing from traditionally negative assessments and bitter polemics to mutual understanding and respect, even though such understanding may not necessarily imply agreement.

That said, there are delightful vistas of the Gospel in the Quran, not as extensive as the Torah references, but new and different perspectives on what Christians call "the old, old story." Again, it is not expected that Christians should necessarily agree with what they discover in these regards, but to understand Islam, it will be helpful to appreciate how the Gospel looks from a Quranic perspective. For example, the term *Isa-Masih* (the Arabic translation of Yeshua Messiah, or Jesus Christ), as used in the Hindu Purana quoted earlier, is possibly an earlier Aramaic term used to translate the Persian word *Saoshyant*.[1] It is more familiar from its usage in the Quran in reference to Jesus, where he is called by this name six times, leading to the supposition that the phrase is Islamic in origin. There is nothing to support that supposition, but what we may take from this observation is an awareness that Islam possibly resonates as much of the Zoroastrian mode of messianic theology as it does of the Hebrew model. Regardless, the Quran does confirm the revelations concerning Jesus as the Messiah. What this means may be a subject for potentially fruitful discussion. The confirmation relates primarily to the Gospel as we know it, but it also includes Quranic reference to heterodox Christian traditions, also under review in church circles.

According to the Quran, in the Gospel Jesus said to the Children of Israel,

I have come to you, with signs from your Lord, in that I make for you, out of clay, as it were, the figure of a bird by God's leave.[2] And I heal those born blind, and the lepers, and I quicken the dead, by God's leave.[3]

In addition to other sayings of Jesus in the Quran, from his crib as a baby (those echoing the apocryphal material ascribed to Thomas), and items identical to the canonical Gospels in his adult ministry as above, there is a wealth of "sayings" of Jesus in the Hadith and other ancient Muslim sources. For anyone who finds the parallel sayings of Buddha or the aphorisms of the Gnostic Gospels of interest, the sayings of Jesus in early Muslim literature will be a gold mine. They are Middle Eastern oral traditions of the desert in the Arabic language, another cognate of Aramaic, which finally appeared in written form as the Muslim community began to develop an Arabic literature shortly after Muhammad. They are about as distant in time from Jesus as Jesus was from Zoroaster (or Buddha), and they present a useful example of how such traditions were transmitted in that world. The differences between some of them and the Bible verses is noticeable, but often they are not greater than the differences between Matthew and Luke in the wording of the Lord's Prayer or the Sermon on the Mount, for example. Many of the sayings attributed to Jesus are from two Islamic books on asceticism,[4] and the provenance of these things will become important to us as we grow in appreciation of their value.

After awareness of these sayings developed in the eighteenth century, an English translation of some seventy-seven of them appeared in the late nineteenth century.[5] This collection was followed by three collections of the Muslim sayings of Jesus, which were compiled in various languages in the twentieth century,[6] based on over fifty smaller collections in classical Arabic sources. These all have been helpfully collated and translated in the twenty-first century in an absolutely enchanting work, *The Muslim Jesus* by Tarif Khalidi. This insightful resource should now have a place on every scholar's bookshelf next to *Jesus and Buddha: The Parallel Sayings* by Marcus Borg. These sayings of Jesus also resemble the "pithy sayings" of the Gnostic Gospels that contribute to an emerging picture of Jesus as a Jewish storyteller who also frequently used a particular style of "one liners," sometimes tinged with humor or irony. This is not the storytelling Jesus we know from the canonical Gospels, where the writers exercised editorial responsibility for collating the material into a publishing format, but this Jesus of folk memory in the ancient Middle East is not necessarily in conflict with the Jesus known by Christians. As we did with the parallel sayings connected to Buddha, we will limit ourselves to a review of about 10 percent of the sayings offered in *The Muslim Jesus* collection, with notes to delineate the parallels or similarities to the Bible as well as other pieces of information germane to our purposes, simply using the numbering system devised by Khalidi, whose fine volume might be consulted regarding attribution of the ancient sources.

1. Jesus saw a person committing theft. Jesus asked, "Did you commit theft?" The man answered, "Never! I swear by Him than whom there is none worthier of worship." Jesus said, "I believe God and falsify my eye."[7]

4. Jesus said, "If it is a day of fasting for one of you, let him anoint his head and beard and wipe his lips so that people will not know that he is fasting. If he gives with the right hand, let him hide this from his left hand. If he prays, let him pull down the door curtain, for God apportions praise as He apportions livelihood."[8]

36. Jesus used to say, "Charity does not mean doing good to him who does good to you, for this is to return good for good. Charity means that you should do good to him who does you harm."[9]

63. Jesus said, "In truth I say to you, the folds of heaven are empty of the rich. It is easier for a camel to pass through the eye of a needle than for a rich man to enter paradise."[10]

65. Christ said, "If you desire to devote yourselves entirely to God and to be the light to the children of Adam, forgive those who have done you evil, visit the sick who do not visit you, be kind to those who are unkind to you, and lend to those who do not repay you."[11]

68.	Christ said, "Not as I will, but as You will. Not as I desire, but as You desire."[12]
80.	Christ passed by a group of Israelites who insulted him. Every time he spoke a word of evil, Christ answered with good. Simon the pure said to him, "Will you answer them with good each time they speak evil?" Christ said, "Each person spends of what he owns."[13]
98.	"Blessed is he who sees with his heart but whose heart is not in what he sees."[14]
102.	Christ said, "You will not commit adultery as long as you avert your eyes."[15]
127.	Jesus and his disciples passed by a dog's carcass. The disciples said, "How foul is his stench." Jesus said, "How white are his teeth." He said this in order to teach them a lesson—namely, to forbid slander.[16]
128.	A pig passed by Jesus. Jesus said, "Pass in peace." He was asked, "Spirit of God, how can you say this to a pig?" Jesus replied, "I hate to accustom my tongue to evil."[17]
138.	Among the revelations of God to Jesus in the Gospel is the following: "We filled you with yearning but you did not yearn, and we mourned for you but you did not cry."[18]
143.	Jesus said to the Israelites, "Do not reward a wrongdoer with wrongdoing, for this will nullify your virtue in God's sight."[19]
155.	Jesus said, "The merciful in this world is the one who will be shown mercy in the next world."[20]
172.	Jesus said, "The likeness of this world to the next is like a man who has two wives: if he pleases one, he arouses the other's resentment."[21]
190.	Jesus said, "O Israelites, Moses forbade you to commit adultery, and he did well to forbid it. I forbid you to even contemplate it, for he who contemplates it without acting upon it is like an earthenware house in which a fire is lit: even though it does not burn, it becomes charred from the smoke." "O Israelites, Moses forbade you to swear by God falsely, and he did well to forbid it. I forbid you to swear by God at all, be it falsely or truly."[22]
194.	Jesus said, "Beware of glancing at women, and glancing again, for this sows lust in the heart, seduction enough for him who does it."[23]
211.	It is written in the Gospel, "He who prays for those who treat him badly defeats Satan."[24]
214.	Christ said, "Seeds grow in a plain but not among rocks. So, also, wisdom flourishes in the heart of a humble man but not in the heart of the proud. Do you not see how the man who flaunts his head to the ceiling will dash it, while he who lowers his head shelters and protects it?"[25]
216.	Jesus said, "Why do you come to me dressed like monks, though your hearts are the hearts of wolves and predators? Wear the clothes of kings but mortify your hearts with the fear of God."[26]
233.	Jesus said to his disciples, "Pray God that He may make this agony—meaning death—easy for me, for I have come to fear death so much that my fear of death has made me acquainted with death."[27]
254.	Jesus looked down upon the Ghuta of Damascus from a high place and said, "O Ghuta, even if the wealthy man is unable to reap a fortune from you, the poor man will not fail to get his fill of bread from you."[28]
256.	Jesus used to say, "He who prays and fasts but does not abandon sin is inscribed in the Kingdom of God as a liar."[29]
267.	God revealed to Jesus, "Be in gentleness toward people like the earth beneath their feet, in generosity like flowing water, and in mercy like the sun and the moon, for they rise upon both the good and the evil."[30]
269.	Jesus prepared food for his disciples. When they had eaten, he washed their hands and feet. They said to him, "Spirit of God, it is we, rather, that should do this." He replied, "I have done this so that you would do it to those whom you teach."[31]
294.	Jesus said, "What does it profit a man if he sells his soul for all that is in the world, and then leaves all that he sold it for as an inheritance to someone else while he himself has ruined his soul? Blessed is he who saves his soul, preferring it to all that is in the world."[32]

From sources in Iraq, Iran and Syria, mainly Kufa, Baghdad and Damascus, approximately 90 percent of these references are related to verses in the Gospel according to Matthew, the least European of Gospel sources, although Mark, Luke and John are also represented. It is interesting to note how often Jesus is referred to as "Messiah" (*masih*)[33] or Christ in these early references, as well as "Spirit of God."

The titles given to Jesus by God in the Quran are also instructive as to the regard in which he is held in Islam; no ordinary "prophet" (*nabi*)[34] he, but also "Messenger of God" (*rasul*),[35] "Spirit from God" (*ruhun mina' Llah*),[36] "The Righteous" (*as-saalihiin*)[37] and even the "Word of God" (*kalimatu-Llah*),[38] all phrases cherished by Christians. In addition, other distinctively Muslim phrases used to describe Jesus, including Servant of God, Sign, Example, Witness, Mercy, Eminent, Upright and Blessed, are all found sprinkled throughout the Quran.

Despite different meanings attached to some of these names, what we have in the first series listed is a "Christology" that is even higher than that accepted by the small proportion of Christians who tend toward Unitarianism. There is room for fruitful discussion here, because Muslims believe that they are the propagators and protectors of true Christian doctrine. Saying so does not make it so, but it moves the discussion to a plane not anticipated by many Christians. It is agreed between Christians and Muslims that Jesus was not "murdered" on the cross, as mentioned earlier, Christians believing that the matter was in his hands and he allowed these things to happen, while Muslims believe he was never killed but rather assumed bodily into heaven.

What is missing for Christians in the names listed above is the concept of "Savior" and the related Jewish notion of God as "Redeemer," both originating with and derived from the Zoroastrian source, which is rejected in the main by Islam. But again we might consider the mantra of certain "progressive" Christians who say, "Nobody died for my sins," and the counterpart position in the greater self-reliance of Judaism. Regarding titles of Jesus, because the use of Masih is so prominent in the Quran, this might also be an opportune place to reiterate that the Jewish title for the Messiah is "Son of Man," although the title of the church (possibly less favored by Jesus) is "Son of God," while the Quran consistently uses the appellation "Son of Mary."

As for other Gospel characters in the Quran, the occurrence of Mary is especially prominent. Her name appears thirty-four times in the Quran as compared with just nineteen appearances in the Christian Scriptures. Beloved by Muslims, ironically she always appears in Christian art wearing the hijab or headscarf, whether in Catholic statues, Orthodox icons, Protestant Christmas cards or stained-glass windows in all Christian traditions. There may be European countries where she would now be banned if she appeared in person, rather than in their cherished artworks. While never succumbing to the "cult of Mary" abuses that have occasionally plagued certain churches, Muslims hold Mary in greater esteem than any other woman, with the possible exception of Aisha, the Prophet's wife mentioned but unnamed in the Quran as the ideal woman (compared by some to the "Pharaoh's wife" of the same name, who is also the daughter of the previous pharaoh, the princess who adopted Moses). It is Mary alone among women who is mentioned by name in the Quran.

There is a whole chapter of the Quran named in Mary's honor, and another for her father. Indeed, both of Mary's parents are mentioned in the Quran and identified in the Hadith as Anna and Imran, similar to the Christian nonbiblical tradition, which identifies the parents of Mary as Anna and Joachim. The fact that Mary is given a typological identification with Miriam (same name in Arabic), the sister of Moses, is a concept freighted with so many theological and other implications that we cannot consider it here. In reference to her pregnancy and giving birth to Jesus, the Muslim understanding of Mary's virginity would also be a concept larger in scale than we could possibly attempt here.

These matters and the now familiar Quranic versions of the birth of John the Baptist and the Christmas story[39] will all provide grist for the mill of future discussions in the Judeo-X-Islamic family. It is to her parents' prayer for a child they could dedicate to the priesthood that we may allude in this investigation in an attempt to plumb some depth of new understanding.

> Behold! A woman of Imran said: "O my Lord! I do dedicate unto Thee what is in my womb for Thy special service; so accept this of me, for Thou hearest and knowest all things." When she was delivered, she said, "O my Lord, I behold! I am delivered of a female child!" And God knew best what she brought

forth. "And nowise is the male like the female. I have named her Mary, and I commend her and her offspring to Thy protection from the Evil One, the Rejected." Right graciously did her Lord accept her: He made her grow in purity and beauty; To the care of Zakariya was she assigned.[40]

Well-informed Muslims understand the Quran to mean that Zechariah, the priest, took responsibility for her training so that she could fulfill the priestly vocation in an appropriate manner. Any history of this role for Mary has escaped the biblical record in the Gospel, and whether an appreciation of this tradition might someday have a bearing on women assuming the role of imam more often in Islam or, say, the ordination of women in the Roman Catholic Church remains to be seen, but some sense of this is carried forward in Mary's unique relationship to the priesthood as understood in the Roman Catholic tradition. Pope John Paul II described it thus:

> Mother and Son, Mary and the High Priest, were united from the very beginning in the priestly, sacrificial self-offering to the will of the Father. Our Lady pronounced her fiat to all the suffering involved with being Mother of the Redeemer saying, "Be it done unto me according to your word," while Jesus consented to His priestly mission from the Father saying, "Behold I come to do Your will." In this perfect correspondence between Mother and Son a close relationship has been established between Mary's motherhood and Christ's priesthood. Mary stands behind her Son and dedicates herself totally to His priestly mission as Mediator and Redeemer of all. Her dedication, however, did not end with Jesus' death on the cross. This bond continues and is extended throughout the centuries between Mary and every priest who participates in the ministerial priesthood of Christ. As Mother of Christ, Mary is in a special way the Mother of each and every priest. She takes each priest into her care, just as she cared for Jesus.[41]

This discussion between Muslims and Catholics is beyond the purview of Protestants and Jews.

Finally, in this connection, the story of how Muhammad entered the Kabbah in Mecca and cleansed it from idols is told by his early biographer Ibn Ishaq. It has an element that is so extraordinary and almost compromising for Muslims that it has actually been widely suppressed. Muhammad and his triumphant armies came marching in, destroyed the idols and cleansed the Kabbah, but what remained in the Kabbah after its cleansing from idolatry might surprise even many Muslims, much less Christians. The Hadith narrates the story in a manner that typically attributes the information through several reliable sources.

> The Quraysh had put pictures in the Kabah, including two of Jesus, son of Mary, and of Mary (on both of whom be peace!). I. Shihab said how Asma' d. Shaqr narrated that a woman of Ghassan joined in the pilgrimage of the Arabs and when she saw the picture of Mary in the Kabah she said, "My father and my mother be your ransom! You are surely an Arab woman!" The apostle (Muhammad) ordered that all the pictures should be erased, except those of Jesus and Mary.[42]

Aside from his connection with Mary, Zechariah's story in the Quran[43] is so similar to its appearance in the Bible[44] that it is among the favorites of students in classes in Scriptural reasoning who claim to enrich their understandings of their own Scriptures through an appreciation of others. Zechariah prays for a son and heir who will please God with a prophetic ministry and is struck dumb as a sign from God until the birth of Yahya, or John. The tomb of Zechariah is believed by Muslims to lie within the Great Mosque of Aleppo in Syria.

John the Baptist is known in the manner prayed for by his father in both traditions, and his story, as told in the Bible, is fully recounted in Hadith where he is honored as the forerunner of the messiah. The veneration of Yahya (John), as it developed in Islam, was possibly somewhat parallel to both Byzantine Orthodox Christian practice as well as that of the Mandaean sect of John's own followers that survives in Iraq today. Early reports claim that the Umayyad caliph al-Walid I unearthed the head of Yahya in Jerusalem and placed it on a pillar in Damascus. The Oratory (*maqām*) of Yahya, located in the Umayyad Mosque in Damascus, is an important shrine to John the Baptist that has existed through to modern times. On the Christian side of this equation, during the summer of 2010 archaeologists claimed to have unearthed the bone relics belonging to Saint John the Baptist on Saint Ivan Island near the seaside town of Sozopol, an Orthodox retreat center off the Bulgarian coast—notably without the head.

The Christian church and the disciples of Jesus get short shrift as such in the Quran, the former reflected simply in sacramental images and the latter dealt with only as a group, though some Muslims see a reference to Peter, John and finally the apostle Paul, presumably at Antioch,[45] the only city in which all three preached, where they experienced first rejection and finally acceptance of their message:

> When we first sent to them two apostles, they rejected them, but we strengthened them with a third. They said "Truly we have been sent on a mission to you."[46]

Perhaps more impressive is what Muslims see as the reference to Muhammad in the Christian Scriptures. Muslims believe that in the Gospel (*Injil*), Jesus validates the prophecy concerning Muhammad by Moses, and specifically affirms and strengthens it. The Quran itself supports this understanding of the role that Jesus exercised in acknowledging Muhammad, as recorded in a chapter known as Battle Array:

> And remember, Jesus, son of Mary, said: "O Children of Israel! I am the apostle of God [sent] to you, confirming the Law [which came] before me, and giving glad tidings of an Apostle to come after me, whose name shall be Ahmad."[47]

For Muslims, the first part of this verse is a prooftext of the role and ministry of Jesus in fulfilling the prophecy of Moses, which is found in the Quran. It is then coupled with what Muslims take as a sure prophecy about Muhammad from the lips of Jesus, which is recorded in several specific Christian Scriptures, as they read them. It appears to Muslims that Jesus prophesies the coming of Muhammad through the identical words in Greek, Arabic and English when Jesus promised the coming of an "Advocate," as read by Christians, or "Praiseworthy One," as read by Muslims. The Greek word is *Paraclete*, which translates into English as "Advocate" and which in Arabic is spelled *Ahmad*—and also in the original Aramaic spoken by Jesus—meaning "Praiseworthy." Muhammad's name Ahmad, short for Muhammad, was the name used in his childhood and among his intimates. The references to this prophecy in Christian Scripture, as recalled in the Quran, are all found in John's Gospel,[48] where Jesus uses the word four times in promising to send an advocate, or a "praiseworthy" Ahmad. The repeated promise has received more notice in the Muslim world than most Christians have ever realized. The Muslim reading that God would send Ahmad is certainly plausible, though it is news indeed to Christians who have presumed that these prophecies refer to the coming of what they call the Holy Spirit.

This Muslim interpretation is no more esoteric than many Christian or even Jewish traditional understandings of specific verses that support their various theological positions. How do Roman Catholics come to the conclusion that every later bishop of Rome is the successor of Peter in the matter mentioned in the Gospel, where Jesus says of Peter, "Upon this rock I will build my church"?[49] On the face of it, this verse could be taken as a reference to building the church on every later fisherman who sailed the Sea of Galilee in Peter's boat, but the truth is that the apostles and their successors felt that Jesus meant every successor to Peter in his future leadership of the church in the "eternal city," as Rome was known. At least half the Christians in the world today share that intuitive feeling and interpret the Scriptures accordingly. Likewise, on the face of it, the Catholic understanding that women cannot be ordained because Jesus called only males to be his disciples makes no more sense than to suggest that only Jews can be ordained, since Jesus called no Gentiles to be disciples, but the Church felt otherwise. These inferences are all based on traditional understandings of the mind of Christ, not upon Scripture. They may be valid, but they are no more or no less reasonable than the Muslim reading of the references to the coming of Ahmad, although the Muslim understanding is at least Scriptural, in the view of Muslims.

That this understanding comes not from the Hadith or from any later tradition but from the Quran itself, as Muhammad received it, is of profound significance to Muslims. It seals the argument that Islam should be seen as in the succession of lawful Israel and the legitimate church, whose members follow Moses, Jesus and Muhammad and read the Torah, Gospel and Quran. Because Islam is subsequent to Christianity and Judaism, it seems self-evident to the Muslim in the street that it supersedes what came before, though only to whatever extent those previous revelations had become corrupted. This new "supersessionism" is no more acceptable to Christians than their own traditional supersessionism is to Jews. Objections may be futile at this juncture, however; the point is that Islam does not present itself as a new religion but as confirming, critiquing and amplifying what has come before, not based on the desire to present a new word on these things but based on their reading of Christian Scriptures, which is similar to the Christian reading of Hebrew Scriptures, as described earlier.

However, Muhammad's principal identity to Muslims is not as the Advocate or as the Praiseworthy, but as *the* Prophet—in fact, the *final* prophet in the line of prophets identified in the Hebrew and Christian Scriptures. He does not bring new revelations but rather a spiritual summary that completes and corrects the record of previous revelations and presents them, at last, to Arabs and, through them, to the world. For Muslims who hold Jesus and Moses in such reverent regard, it is a painful mystery that Christians and Jews accord Muhammad such little respect as any kind of prophet. Christian assemblies have recently issued statements recognizing the covenant relationship Muslims have with God, in words similar to recent expressions directed toward Jews, but any recognition or acknowledgment of Muhammad as a prophet has not happened, although small steps in that direction have been taken in a few places.

Hans Küng, one of the most beloved and respected Roman Catholic theologians of the twentieth century and beyond, has made some helpful observations in this regard in a compendium of writings on "the new ecumenism" called *Christianity and the World Religions,* published in 1986.[50] Küng suggests that the Christian Scriptures appear open to the expectation of prophets after Jesus, provided that their message is in basic agreement with his. Küng's reading of the Quran highlights some aspects of the teaching of Jesus that the church has neglected since the early Hellenistic period. He proposes that Christians and Jews both look again at Muhammad's prophetic role in reminding the church and the synagogue of certain of their own doctrines. These thoughts by one recently described by the Anglican archbishop of Canterbury[51] as "our greatest living theologian" were developed further in his twenty-first-century writings,[52] as echoed by Karen Armstrong,[53] among others.

To illustrate that possibility from an inaccurate inference often made by Muslims, Muhammad might actually be considered "the seal of the prophets"[54] by Christians and Jews, if by that they were all given to understand that he represents God's "seal of approval" on all the others, rather than that he is necessarily the last prophet. Muhammad may indeed be the last of the classical style of prophets, but that is not the meaning of the phrase in Arabic, regardless of the inference in this regard by many Muslims. The Arabic word for "last" is *akkhir,* whereas the Arabic word for "seal" is *khatam,* as used in this instance. *Khatam* may have a variety of valid meanings, as in "royal seal" or "seal of approval," an emblem or confirmation of that which has happened or that which is to come. This is the specific word used in the Quran to describe Muhammad, and both Jews and Christians might be pleased to accept this "seal of approval" in reference to their own prophets. If he is also the last such prophet, so be it, if we are speaking not merely of ongoing revelation but only of a certain style and ethos of prophecy stretching from before Zoroaster to Muhammad. Indeed, if Jews and Christians are not prepared to accept that Muhammad is the final prophet to be mentioned in their Scriptures, they might more graciously acknowledge that he is the final prophet of Scripture to the extent that we recognize these sacred texts as a family corpus.

The Muslim message to Zoroastrianism was this: "Your monotheism was well and good but your dualism is an abomination." Islam has a similar message for Christianity and for Judaism whenever they appear to become inclusive of anything that deviates from the oneness of God. This is not just quibbling over theological terms: "chosen people vs. all people," "virgin vs. maiden," "resurrection vs. escape." The anger of Islam toward modernity today relates to a perceived loss of focus by Jews and Christians, seen earlier in the treachery of Jews toward Muhammad late in his life (which he overcame with the greatest regret) and in the Crusades of Christians in the Middle Ages (which Muslims believe they won anyway). Right or wrong, these are valid perspectives, applied to what appears as the degeneration of religion in the West in modern times in relation to the oneness of God and single-minded devotion to God.

Finally, in juxtaposing the Gospel and the Quran, there is a connection between the last book of the Christian Scriptures and the very first chapter of the Quran, a relationship that again is common currency among Muslims but unknown among Christians in particular. The first chapter of the Quran is called *Al-Fatiha*, "The Opening," a title that is customarily linked to a specific verse in the Bible that describes a mighty angel "holding a little scroll, which lay *open* in his hand."[55] The Hebrew word for "open" is *fatoah*, and the Arabic is *fatiha*, a link somewhat dependent on the frequent assumption that the Revelation was first written in Hebrew and translated into Greek. This opening of the Quran refers to the opening of the scroll, and it is addressed to God as a prayer. The next verse continues, "When he shouted, the voices of the seven thunders spoke,"[56] and these "seven thunders" in the book of Revelation are taken by Muslims to refer to the seven verses of "The Opening." John continues, "And when the seven thunders spoke, I was about to write; but I heard a voice from heaven say, Seal up what the seven thunders have said and do not write it down."[57] Thus it would not be possible for the meaning of the seven thunders to be understood until the Quran appeared, representing the "opening" of the scroll.

Like claims about Moses prophesying in reference to Muhammad as the divinely appointed prophet to the Arabs, and like Jesus promising that Ahmad would come as the Praiseworthy One to reveal God's message, such matters, including this consideration of "The Opening" of the Quran, are of little consequence and make little sense to Jews and Christians until compared with superficial implausibilities in their own traditions, taken on faith. For Muslims, "The Opening" has the ring of revelation about it, and its sets the stage for dramatic final considerations of the deep and almost subterranean linkages among these religious traditions and Zoroastrianism. The Book of Revelation is seen by Muslims as a prologue to the Quran, and they believe we are living through the unfolding of its prophecies as elaborated in the Quran.

12

avesta in the quran

Salvation Is Sincerity

To Muslims, the Quran is a miracle on par with the created universe itself. It overshadows Islam, Muhammad and the Muslim community. Muslims say that God created the religion through the Quran, in contrast to the Torah and the Gospel Scriptures that God produced through the existing communities. The evocative timbre of the Quran generates a self-authenticating experience of God's own presence as the divine words resonate physically in the chest of the reciter or vibrate in the ears of the believer. The Quran is to Muslims what Christ is to Christians and what the chosen people or Holy Nation is to Jews. (While it seems like a minor matter to others, then, the burning of the Quran is to Muslims, in a certain sense, an equivalent of the crucifixion of Christ or the Holocaust of Jews—a point to be appreciated among those who say that, while they cherish the Bible, they would never react so strongly to its desecration.)

However, with respect to the text, there are three unique features of the Quran that are especially germane to our quest to identify echoes of the Zoroastrian Avesta in it. First, Muhammad neither composed nor personally wrote down any of the Quran; second, the Quran itself attests that what God revealed to the Prophet had been revealed previously to Moses, Jesus and others; and third, that except for asides to Muhammad and certain instructions to his followers, most of what is in the Quran purports to be of universal application.

The Quran is unique, in the Muslim view, only insofar as it is the most complete articulation of the Divine Word that has been accurately preserved. The other such revelations, having once been complete, have now become either extinct or corrupted to a greater or lesser extent by the passage of time, by copying errors, or even by deliberate falsification. These claims may seem extravagant to Jews, Christians and others, though it may be acknowledged that Christian literalists and Jewish ultraorthodox, among others, claim a similar infallibility for their Scriptural texts, and they do so without even the grace to suggest that others have ever received such a word, well preserved or otherwise. In this sense the Muslim claim is the more gracious, and that grace extends further when we consider the implications of the above features and the liberty they bestow on anyone who wishes to study and appropriately critique the Quran.

Babylonian and Returning Jews, who also understood the wider implications, applied the divinely inspired universal vision of Zoroaster locally. They have always encouraged other people to make their own local applications of such universal principles while maintaining their own particularities. The universalism of divine principles was a focus of the Christian Church, but it was still rooted in Jewish culture at first and later embodied in local communities, national cultures and new denominations. In spite of its claims of catholicity, the Church has perhaps always needed to acquire a deeper appreciation of the Zoroastrian universalism inherent in Jesus' own understanding of his messianic role, particularly as regards the grace of God received in other religions—a matter under consideration by many Church bodies at present.

Muhammad was technically illiterate, as was typical for most men in his time, but he was by no means ignorant, and God prepared him to receive the universal revelations in several ways related to his own local circumstances. While his heart may have been completely open to God, his mind was not a blank slate. For example, the Arabic language, in which the Quran was to be couched, was his mother tongue. In a similar way, it is clear that when the Quran speaks directly on historical and cultural issues, it pertains to subjects on which Muhammad was as well informed as anyone else in his community. To illustrate, when the Quran speaks of magic, sorcery, astrology, stars, planets, dreams, witchcraft, moon and gods, we have references to Babylonian polytheism. Muhammad would have already known of such things and their sources, from Arabic community life and Middle Eastern lore, needing only divine revelation to understand them correctly. By this time, Babylonian culture and religion was just a fringe element of minor importance in the remnant Persian Empire. In the Quranic revelations concerning Babylonians, God expressed divine judgment, condemnation and warnings about such things without actually mentioning Babylonians by name, though it is not difficult to identify them and their polytheistic sorcery.[1] Of course, other cultures do speak of "magic," for instance, but when magic appears in close repeated conjunction with sorcery, gods in the plural and astrology, "magic" becomes a linguistic marker for Babylonian references, as do other words in such a context.

The presence of unnamed Babylonian reference points in the Quran, recognized over all the centuries by Islamic scholars, is mentioned here only in anticipation of the similarly unnamed Zoroastrian reference points, the difference being that these have not been as widely acknowledged heretofore. Any Babylonian material is easily recognized because it sticks out like a sore thumb, whereas the Zoroastrian material is so pervasive that it is almost invisible, as referenced in the earlier illustration of water and fish, or air and humans. But water is essential for fish, and humans could not survive without air. In a similar way, Zoroastrian material in the Quran is crying out for acknowledgment and may need to be recognized for Islam to fulfill its destiny in the modern world. It may indeed be an important means whereby we all can access the universal vision and recognize it when we see it in others, to whatever extent.

In a modest manner, initial recognition of Zoroastrian material in the Quran may be the gift of Jews and Christians to Muslims, who themselves almost incidentally located the Dead Sea Scrolls and the Nag Hammadi Library that Jews and Christians could not see. Russians and Americans in the International Space Station can see outlines of ancient Roman encampments in Britain that are invisible to the dedicated farmers who work that land every year. In much the same way, this investigation, with its respectful commitment to the integrity of the Quran, may be able to see things in it that have escaped detection by dedicated scholars of Islam for centuries.

The presence of Zoroastrian Avesta references in the Quran are just as clear as the well-known Babylonian references, although because they are far more pervasive they have been largely unnoticed, inasmuch as they represent almost half the context of the Quran. While we find linguistic markers that are words used elsewhere in many cultures, a large number of clustered key words can be identified in the Quran from their extensive and clustered use in the Avesta material still in our possession. Upon realizing the possibility of identifying the Avesta references in this way during the winter of 2005 to 2006, I contacted Mary Boyce, who, as mentioned, had been mentoring my growing appreciation of the Zoroastrian role in religious history. I found her ecstatic about this prospect of identifying Avesta verses in the Quran.

From her sickbed, which within a few months became her deathbed, she chatted at length, suggesting potential key words that could be linguistic markers from her intimate knowledge of the extant Zoroastrian texts. Unfortunately, her suggestions got blended with my own guesses as we both contributed to the list, so that I cannot give her precise attributions. Nor can I offer uniform authentication or ranking of probability based on her recognized expertise. I do recall my own discovery and suggestion that the Avesta's *Fargan* may be related to the Quran's *Furqan*, as referring to chapters in which the "criterion" for purity is the subject matter, an observation that again had her enthusiastic endorsement as a prospective link. Some of the other key words that we initially agreed might be used as linguistic markers in this exercise, when taken together, were as follows: *adversary, angels, archers, bountiful (or beneficent), cattle, choice, compassion (or compassionate), cow, creation, demons, dominion, fire, firmament, freedom, gardens, horses, immortal, judgment, law, lies, mercy (or merciful), order, pasture, path (or way), resurrection, righteousness, rivers, salvation, seven, sin (deviate or go astray), soul, sun, shining (or radiant), thunder, truth, water, wind, wisdom, world, usury.*

Some experts and other readers may be already identifying additional potential linguistic markers for this exercise, but these are all words that anticipated the Judeo-X-Islamic lexicon at the point of their first specialized appearance in the Zoroastrian Avesta. We then identified a number of tight phrases in this connection, including *light and life, good and evil, light and darkness, right and wrong* and *heaven and hell*, repeated in both the Avesta and the Quran in a connected fashion or an almost dualistic symbiosis not found elsewhere at that time.

Certain nouns in the Avesta are also connected with particular adjectives, and the coupling is repeated again and again in the Quran: *water flowing*, or *water flowing under, straight paths, swift horses* and *six days*, as well as *sun, moon* and *stars*, usually connected, whereas in Babylonian astrology they are habitually separated. All this is in addition to the long recognized Quranic use of the Persian loan words, *houris* (beautiful maiden) and *paradise* (originally from the Persian *pairidaeza*, "pleasure garden"). These were earlier clues that we now see to be intimately connected and used exclusively in the cluster sections identified by all the other factors.

It may still be early in the ascertaining of the full extent of the Zoroastrian subtext in the Quran, and the confirmation of its pristine monotheistic vision in Islamic holy writ, but detailed authentication of this work by Muslims has already begun and will surely continue. To illustrate, chapter 12 of the Quran could be used to reconstruct the story of Joseph, had the Torah been lost. Likewise the birth story of John the Baptist could be reconstructed from chapter 19 of the Quran, had the Gospel been somehow destroyed. In the same way, lost Avesta texts can hopefully now be reconstructed from material in the Quran. The quest to find them may be undertaken by anyone in a spirit of respectful interfaith inquiry.

For centuries, Muslim scholars and students have studied the Torah and the Gospel, *Taurat* and *Injil*, with diligence and respect. At this point Jewish and Christian scholars and students have begun to pore over the Quran, and in a marked change of attitude from previous days of polemics and negativity, they do so with humble sincerity and respect. Nothing in this book should be construed to suggest that it is incumbent upon Jews or Christians to accept the Muslim understanding of these things, or vice versa. The goal is to appreciate each other's Scriptures in the most positive and helpful light, to offer our own insights to each other and to possibly find elements that may relate to an expanded appreciation by each community of their own Scriptures.

In 2009 I was invited to teach a couple of classes in interfaith studies for a semester at Saint Andrew's Theological College, the Presbyterian seminary in Trinidad, West Indies. Eight ordination-track scholars were required to take the more intensive class, and the other class was an elective program for which twenty-eight students registered, representing almost half the student body, and including the eight scholars from my other class plus a few faculty members. Through a Hindi-language orientation of a mission to Indian indentured workers in the nineteenth century, the Presbyterian Church in this country is some 99 percent South Asian in membership, so interest in the Vedic Zoroastrian roots of imagery in the Torah and the Gospel, as well as the Quran, fueled the enthusiasm of many students and some faculty. They were joined for these Saturday morning classes and "laboratory exercises" by part-time laypersons, clergy doing continuing education, teachers in the Presbyterian school system, presiding elders of local congregations, visiting students from other Christian denominations and interfaith visitors from other religions on an island where the Hindu and Muslim populations are very substantial.

This college had taken responsibility for the "global south" launch of my 2007 book, *Noah's Other Son*, which was by then in use there in congregations, the seminary and the public, which had been engaged through a series of media presentations and discussions. There was widespread enthusiasm about this follow-up general course, which was supportively monitored by Muslim leaders in particular. The course was three months long, and I had faculty support in presenting the hypothesis of the Zoroastrian background in a "forensic" study of the Hebrew, Christian and Muslim Scriptures and administrative support in running these Saturday activities to avoid conflict with other classes. Twenty-eight students, in seven teams of four persons each, scrutinized every chapter of the Quran for "linguistic markers" pointing to a Zoroastrian subtext, on the hypothesis as developed with the assistance of Mary Boyce three years earlier. The hypothesis was expanded by the addition of Zoroastrian liturgical and interrogatory markers described below, and the staff of Naparima College, the prominent Presbyterian high school on the same campus, provided valuable computerized research support.

The students produced the first draft of the chart illustrating this hypothesis, already presented in chapter 9 of this text and available to our readers in full color, free of charge, online.[2] The Reverend Joy Abdul-Mohan, principal of the seminary, took a colorful electronic presentation of the students' work to the May 2009 interfaith conference in New York at which this project was commissioned, and the hypothesis of a possible Zoroastrian subtext of the three scriptures received its first hearing by representative scholars.

Much further work needs to be done on this embryonic hypothesis, although its basic principles are now being well received. Other scholars with more professional knowledge of both Islam and Zoroastrianism will refine and develop this general hypothesis in their own ways. The research exercise is currently being replicated and expanded at various Jewish, Catholic, Protestant and Muslim institutions in different parts of the world. This particular piece of detective work should have payoffs as beneficial to Christians and Jews as to Muslims. For Christians, this evidence of the breadth and endurance of Zoroastrian theology might imply its availability to Jesus as part of his messianic self-understanding in a context that has been simply "over the horizon" of the radar screen of Western awareness. For Jews, it may stand as confirmation of the increasing awareness of the dynamics of what happened during the Exile and the Return, together with increased appreciation for both the Zoroastrian monotheism rooted in Israel and the Zoroastrian subtext of later prophecy and Wisdom literature.

In previous chapters it became clear that such an encounter with Zoroastrianism in Babylon presents no theological challenge to Judaism, and the possibility that a young Jesus traveled some distance along the Silk Road poses no challenge to orthodox Christian theology. In both cases these hypotheses simply enrich the traditions and help to answer some questions. In a similar manner now, non-Muslim readers should understand that the identification of Zoroastrian-related material in the Quran is perfectly acceptable in the traditional Islamic view and, in some sense, even more to be expected by Muslims than by Jews or Christians.

The question on everyone's mind is the extent to which we can actually identify specific Zoroastrian Avesta texts in the Quran with confidence at the initial stage of this new discipline. It may be that the largest number of "Z" Factor or Zoroastrian passages in the Quran are condemnations of later Zoroastrian belief that God had a rival in Satan who either equaled or approached divine status in a negative modality. In addition to linguistic markers, in identifying more positive Avesta-reflective material we should also look for whatever is possibly liturgical in the Quran, since 90 percent of extant Avestas are liturgical and it is believed that much the same prevails in large parts of what is lost. Not much in the Quran is specifically liturgical, in the sense of actual prayers addressed to God as opposed to words from God (frequently changed into prayers by Muslims in daily observances), but among linguistic markers, liturgical allusions and Zoroastrian names for God and adjectives describing the Divinity and the destiny of humanity, we can identify some connections with a fair degree of confidence.

A final criterion identifying possible Zoroastrian references is the use of questions of the sort that Second Isaiah was at pains to answer. There are so many instances of questions in the Quran that we may find those originating in Zoroastrian clusters to be emulated in other revelations, or, perhaps most question motifs will fall into linguistically clustered liturgical Zoroastrian material. At this point, the bulk of evidence comes from the linguistic markers as identified, even in this preliminary fashion, but the criteria are expanding. Part of this is simply a "feel" for a Zoroastrian ethos in certain sections of the Quran, once readers become sufficiently familiar with both texts.

From a traditional Muslim perspective, in the Quran God corrected or perhaps "amplified" the Hebrew and Christian Scriptures that had been revealed earlier. In a similar way, if the verses identified as Zoroastrian references are comparable to verses in the Avesta, a Muslim perspective would quite certainly assert that God corrected them and refreshed the wording in presenting them to Muhammad, so that they would conform to the possibly corrupted originals. This is in accord with a traditional Muslim understanding of the nature of the Quran. A number of tentative examples are offered here, beginning and ending with the ones of which we are most confident. In the first and last chapters of the Quran the similarity to the Avesta may be as close in wording as the most comparable verses from the Torah and the Gospel as found in the Quran. Having presented the outlines of what we can see from our great distance in "space," we are aware of how deeply flawed the details of our examples may be and how much work lies ahead for those "farmers on the ground" who love this Scriptural landscape.

The very best example of a recovered Avesta passage is chapter 1 of the Quran, "The Opening," often introduced to Jews and Christians as "The Twenty-Third Psalm of Islam" or "The Lord's Prayer of Islam" to indicate its place of affection and esteem in Islamic culture. It is frequently used at interfaith public services as a Muslim part of the liturgy that can be shared by the wider community with instant rapport. In "The Opening" the key phrases describe God using Zoroastrian linguistic markers like *Merciful*, *Compassionate* and *Lord of the Worlds*, also referring to *Day of Judgment*, *straight path* and those who *go astray*. These are all key Zoroastrian theological concepts, clustered here in a few short verses in liturgical format.

While most of the Quran is the recitation of God's words to humanity, in contrast to Zoroastrian liturgy that is mainly addressed to God, among the clearest exceptions are "The Opening," which is a prayer in Zoroastrian meter, wording, style and theology, and also the Muawizatayn, a concluding pair of chapters, which are also brief prayers and are similarly Zoroastrian in style. Muslims have developed a rich derivative mode of prayers based on passages of Scripture from the Quran. Such prayers or *duas* form an important part of the five daily devotions, but they are mainly revelations *from* God that are turned into prayers *to* God by changes in who is speaking. With "The Opening" (the first chapter) and with the Muawizatayn ("The Closing" chapters), and also with certain others, no such transition is necessary.

In the opinion of certain Islamic scholars, "The Opening" was one of the earliest revelations bestowed upon the Prophet. Ali ibn Abi Talib, the first imam of Islam, a cousin of Muhammad and the Prophet's son-in-law, was even of the opinion that it was the very first revelation. This view is contradicted by authentic Traditions quoted by Bukhari and others, which unmistakably show that the first five verses of chapter 96 ("The Germ-Cell") constituted the beginning of revelation. On this kind of rationale, and from their own recollections, equally ancient and reliable sources like Abu Hurairah, the Yemeni leader of Islam who was with Muhammad in Medina, insist that "The Opening" is late and was revealed in Medina. By this time Muhammad was surrounded and supported by followers from many quarters, including Salman, the Persian. The belief that this is a later revelation, possibly in response to Muhammad's concerns about Zoroastrian corruptions, seems to fit our thesis that, by the grace of God, good things from Zoroaster are also included in the Quran, either reworked or as it was, in a manner similar to snippets from the Taurat and the Injil that appear virtually intact as part of portions representing the previous revelations. The following examples are from sections possibly related to material in the Avesta still available in Muhammad's time, possibly an oral tradition re-presented by God's grace with linguistic and metric echoes of Zoroaster's voice. The first example is "The Opening" itself.

the opening

Praise be to God, the Cherisher and Sustainer of the worlds;
Most Gracious, Most Merciful; Master of the Day of Judgment.
We worship You, and we seek Your aid. Show us the straight way,
The way of those on whom You have bestowed Your Grace,
Those whose portion is not wrath, and who do not go astray.[3]

It is recognized that the resonance of the Quran is only complete in the Arabic language, often reducing "translation" to a mere interpretation of the content, with copious footnotes but without the evocative and melodic experience. While interpretations into various languages are helpful for study, we put Yusuf Ali's emendated paraphrase into poetic scanning at least, to hint at a sense of meter in Avestas that Muhammad must have heard prior to the experiences of direct revelation relating to such Zoroastrian material. The Yusuf Ali interpretation captures the apocalyptic style of the Quran demonstrated in the Book of Revelation in the Christian Scriptures, again presented in the apocalyptic style also associated with Zoroaster. The Yusuf Ali version is also cherished because, by the judicious use of brackets to hint at meanings alluded to in Arabic, it portrays the quality of "lace" associated with the divine voice, evocative holes and all, as anyone familiar with Quranic recitation can attest. In these paraphrases we fuse the Yusuf Ali wording (integrating his bracketed portions and adjusting to current English usage) to Laleh Bakhtiar's use of formal equivalence, enhancing the meaning with occasional phrases from the Muhammad Marmaduke Pickthall version, using the flowing syntax of Thomas Cleary's *Essential Quran*. The Zoroastrian feel of the passages shines through all these resources in a way unlike anything in the Torah or the Gospel.

thunder

It is God Who shows you the lightning, by way both of fear and hope:
It is He Who raises up the clouds, heavy with fertilizing rain!
The thunder repeats His praises, and so do the angels, with awe:

He flings the loud-voiced thunder-bolts,
And therewith He strikes whomsoever He will.
Yet these dare to dispute about God, and the strength of His power![4]

The chapter that bears the title *Furqan*, or "Criterion" in English, may be suspected of having some special connection to the Zoroastrian *Fargan*, since the concept as well as the name is similar. In addition to the following brief excerpt, the whole chapter might be examined for its appearance of Satan and admixtures of gardens and other linguistic markers, blended with echoes of Hebrew, Christian and other images, the way imagery flows and combines in an inspired song or poem. We give the excerpt the Persian title.

fargan

He Who created heaven and earth and all that is between in six days,
And is then firmly established on the Throne of Authority:
He is God Most Gracious:

Ask then about Him of any acquainted with such things.
When it is said to them, "Adore God Most Gracious?,"
They say, "And what is God Most Gracious?
Shall we adore that which you command us?"

Blessed is He Who made constellations in the skies,
And placed in them a lamp and a moon giving light;

It is He Who made the Night and the Day to follow each other.
He gives light to those who celebrate His praises and show their gratitude.
The servants of God Most Gracious walk on the earth in humility,
And when the ignorant address them, they say, "Peace!"[5]

Sweeping in from the northern mountains, Cyrus was first impressed by the public gardens of Nineveh, which survived long enough for later history to often mistake them for the Seventh Wonder of the World slightly south. Then a year later he was so amazed by those very Hanging Gardens of Babylon, built by Nebuchadnezzar only a few years before that, that he named his closest advisors "Companions of the Gardens," where he walked, centuries before Muhammad gave similar titles to his companions. The garden image found its way into Hebrew Scriptures in the Garden of Eden in Genesis, into the Christian Scriptures as the garden at the center of the City of God in Revelation and into the Quran as Paradise, the eternal oasis. In all these cases we are dealing with the Zoroastrian imagery, from the Persian (*pairidaeza*) "pleasure garden," not the Greek heaven (*ouranos*). In addition to all the other clues, in the following passage, *Companions of the Garden* would certainly be in bold to identify it as part of the Z factor.

gardens of paradise

The trumpet shall be sounded, when behold!
From the sepulchres mortals will rush forth to their Lord!
They will say: "Ah! Woe unto us!
Who hath raised us from our beds of repose?"

"This is what God Most Gracious had promised.
And true was the word of the apostles!"
It will be no more than a single blast,
When lo! they will all be brought up before Us!

Then, on that Day, not a soul will be wronged in the least,
And you shall be repaid for your past Deeds.
The Companions of the Garden shall have joy on that Day;
They and their associates will be in groves of shade.

They will be reclining on Thrones of dignity;
Every fruit will be there for their enjoyment;
They shall have whatever they call for, and
"Peace!"—a word from the Lord Most Merciful![6]

Women played perhaps secondary but nonetheless substantial roles in the authoring, writing and editing of the three Scriptures featured in *Three Testaments*, as increasingly recognized and acknowledged by Marc Brettler, David Bruce and Nevin Reda in their introductions to these Scriptures. So far, little has been learned about any such role or any female literary subculture in Zoroastrianism, a negative that may have been part of its legacy to the three religions under consideration, despite an abundance of female literary figures in other surrounding cultures. So it may not be surprising that the Quran, with its debt to Avestan revelations, uses a Persian word to display an image of mere physical beauty as the hallmark of femininity across much of the whole family tradition.

houris

The Righteous will be in a position of Security,
Among the Gardens and Springs of Paradise;
Dressed in fine silk and in rich brocade, they will face each other;

We shall join them to Companions with beautiful and lustrous eyes.
There can they call for every kind of fruit in peace and security;
Nor will they there taste Death, except the first death.

They will be preserved from the penalty of the blazing Fire,
As a Bounty from the Lord!
This will be their crowning triumph![7]

While few of these excerpts have the quality or characteristics of prayer, they carry forward the Zoroastrian ethos of liturgy in a new format given by God that Muslims traditionally transpose into *dua* meditations for use in daily prayer.

praise and glory

Whatever is in the heavens and on earth,—
let it declare the Praises and Glory of God.
for He is the Exalted in Might, the Wise.

To Him belongs the dominion of the heavens and the earth:
It is He Who gives Life and Death;
and He has Power over all things.

He is the First and the Last,
the Evident and the Immanent:
and He has full knowledge of all things.

He it is Who created the heavens and the earth in Six Days,
and is firmly established on the Throne of Authority.
He knows what enters the earth and what comes out of it.

He knows what comes down from heaven and what mounts up to it.
And He is with you wheresoever you may be.
For truly, God sees well all that you do.

To Him belongs the dominion of the heavens and the earth:
And all the affairs of the world are referred back to God.
He merges Night into Day, and He merges Day into Night.

He has full knowledge of the secrets of all hearts.
Your part is to believe in God and His Prophet, and
Give charity out of that which He has bequeathed to you.

Those of you who believe
And those who expend in charity,
For you there is a great Reward.[8]

No Hebrew or Christian points of reference, no Arabian paganism or Babylonian polytheism, no unbelievers or hypocrites—nothing from such other previous revelations appears in what follows, except for the Zoroastrian context, like the fish's water and the human's air, buttressed by a liberal sprinkling of linguistic markers. This portion of the Quran is not a hymn or a prayer, and it is obviously not "copied" from Zoroastrianism. But the style and content of Zoroastrian material would be the raw material confirmed, critiqued and amplified by God in what He gave afresh to the Prophet Muhammad, possibly after a visit of caravans from Syria, or after a long campfire discussion with his friend and colleague, Salman the Persian.

judgment

When the sky is cleft asunder, and when the Stars are scattered;
When the Oceans are suffered to burst forth;

And when the Graves are turned upside down;—
Then shall each soul know what it has done and is left undone.

What has seduced you from your Lord Most Beneficent?
He created you and fashioned you in due proportion.
He gave you a heart for justice and created you to do His will.
But you reject Righteousness and Judgment!

Truly guardian angels are appointed to protect you,
Kind and honourable, writing down your deeds:
They know and understand all that you do.

As for the Righteous, they will be in bliss;
And the Wicked, they will be in the Fire,
Which they will enter on the Day of Judgment,
And they will not be able to keep away therefrom.

What will explain to you what the Day of Judgment is?
What explanation will describe the Day of Judgment?
On that Day no soul shall have power to do anything for anyone:
And the authority, on that Day, will be wholly with God.[9]

It would appear from the Gathas that the concept of the human soul is unique to Zoroaster in its origins, and to Zoroastrianism as a religion. Its appearance in the subsequent development of the three religions is integral to each in its own context. Its association with creation as an integral part of the whole, as in the following excerpt from the Quran, may be part of the common legacy, enduring in the fresh and unique revelations like this one given to Muhammad.

sun, moon and soul

By the Sun and his glorious splendour;
By the Moon as she follows him;
By the Day as it shows the Sun's glory;
By the Night as it conceals it;

By the Firmament and its wonderful structure;
By the Earth and its wide expanse:
By the Soul, and the proportion and order given to it;

By our enlightenment as to what is right and wrong,
True success comes to those who are purified,
And failure to those who are corrupt.[10]

Finally, in this brief series of tentative examples, if a good argument can be made that "The Opening" shows signs of a previous prayer revealed to Zoroaster, the case is nearly that strong with the remarkable decision of the compliers of the Quran to close it with a certain two-part prayer in the last two short chapters, providing "opening" and "closing" bookends from revelations related to Zoroastrianism as the third of the main "previously revealed" Scriptures found in the Quran.

These last are prayerful liturgical pieces much like prayers extant in Zoroastrian liturgy today. Indeed, they are sufficiently different from all but "The Opening" that there is a well-known tradition, reliably transmitted in the Hadith through several chains of transmitters, that Muhammad's respected Companion, Hadrat Abdullah bin Mas'ud, did not regard them as Quranic at all. He refrained from including them in his personal collection of the Quran in the era prior to the establishment of the household version in the possession of Hafsah as the "authorized version," in the official Medina Codex.[11] The fact that the Muawizatayn, as these two chapters are known, does appear in the household edition is enough for later commentators to be sure that Muhammad himself did recite them. For our purposes, we may refer to the Muawizatayn as "The Closing." They do belong in the Quran, although his respected Companion insisted that the command to recite them was merely enjoined upon the Prophet, *sallalahu alayhi wa ala alihi salam*, "for seeking God's refuge." They have a ring of solace about them, and one can easily picture the Prophet turning to God in this way in times of stress, much as did Zoroaster, no matter the manner in which God revealed these gems to Muhammad.

A second testimony delegating "The Closing" to a separate and different tradition comes from the Maliki school of Shari'a, the basis of the legal system of Sunni Islam as practiced today in Morocco, Algeria, Tunisia, Libya, southern Egypt, Sudan and regions of West and Central Africa. Based on the legal instructions developed by Malik bin Anas in the eighth century, its prescriptions are based on the *Kitab al Muwatta'*, the oldest surviving lawbook from the first Islamic century. It is passing strange that followers of this system (called Malikis) do not recite the Muawizatayn in the five obligatory daily prayers at all, but instead recite them in the late evening as part of the optional prayers between Isha prayer (nightfall) and Fajr prayer (dawn). The offsetting of these little chapters in these various ways may indicate an awareness in pristine Islam that they are so significantly different in some way that they are not to be integrated into the prayer rhythms that use the other chapters.

The case that "The Opening" and "The Closing" are also found in the Zoroastrian Scriptures would be open and shut if we had the complete Avesta and found them there, just as we find direct parallels between the Quran and the Bible in passages concerning Joseph and John the Baptist, for example. Short of some implausible theory that these verses were originally written in Persian, compared to the rest of the Quran in Arabic, it is impossible to prove with absolute certainty that these specific verses are representations of material originally found in the Zoroastrian Avesta. The circumstantial evidence would suggest that they were circulating in Muhammad's time and culture, that God revealed to the Prophet that he should recite them for his own comfort, and that he was moved to do so, thus recognizing them as part of the Quran. The uncertainty concerning them in some quarters may have been related to a realization that they were also found elsewhere, but that may take nothing from the fact that God revealed them freshly to the one that many regard as His final prophet with a new rhythm and power in Arabic. Muhammad takes refuge in God from the evil one who is not equal to God, and we are invited to do the same—a fitting conclusion to the Quranic portion of our study.

the closing

I seek refuge with You, Lord of the Dawn,
From the mischief of created things;
From the mischief of Darkness as it overspreads;
From the mischief of those who practice Secret Arts;
And from the mischief of envious practices.

I seek refuge with You, Lord and Cherisher of Mortals,
Sovereign King of Mankind, Godly Judge of Mortals,
From the mischief of those who whisper evil threats.
From the one who whispers in the hearts of mankind,
And who whispers among Immortals and mortals alike.[12]

introduction to the quran

Nevin Reda

text

There Is No Divinity Except God

THE ARABIC TERM *QUR'AN*, "RECITATION," IS derived from the root *q-r-'*, "to read, to read out loud, to recite,"[1] and it occurs seventy times in the Quran as a reference to the Scripture proper or to the act of reciting it. According to the Islamic tradition, the first-known words of this book were an imperative form of the root, commanding the Prophet Muhammad to read/recite the revelation[2]: "Read/recite in the Name of your Lord Who created."[3] The command was delivered in the cave of Hira' on the outskirts of Mecca around 610 CE and was the start of a series of mantic (that is, prophetic, supernatural, divine-related) experiences, which continued in a piecemeal fashion for twenty years or more to eventually form the Scripture as we have it today. Thus, the Quran is the corpus of texts recited by the Prophet Muhammad (c. 570–632 CE) as a divine revelation and which have been received and propagated by the Muslim community as such.

While the term is quite unique in the Arabic language—there is only one Quran—parallel usages do exist in the Syriac and Hebrew traditions. Arabic, Syriac and Hebrew belong to the same family of languages, known as the Semitic languages in reference to Shem, the son of Noah, the eponym and presumed forefather of the people who are native to these languages. The closest parallel to the word *Quran* comes from the Syriac—*qeryana*, or *lectionary*, a term that is still used in Christian Liturgy to refer to the reading out loud of Scriptures. Hebrew does not have such a word as a cognate noun, but it does have the imperative and other verb forms, used in linguistically similar ways to its Arabic counterpart.[4]

setting

The linguistic commonalities are not the only ways in which the Quran connects with the Jewish and Christian heritages. All three look toward an ancient history and a common beginning, centered on the figure of Abraham. The city of Mecca, Muhammad's birthplace, is home to a centuries-old pilgrimage, commemorating the story of the patriarch, his wife Hagar and his son Ishmael. The pilgrim rituals reenact highlights of the family's sojourn in Mecca, where Hagar and Ishmael are also buried. Ritual circumambulations5 around the structure focus on the worship of the one God, Abraham's imageless deity. Every year, pilgrims repeat Hagar's frantic quest for water, running in her footsteps and drinking from the very spring that appeared miraculously for her. The sacrifice of a sheep celebrates the primeval one and the special favor bestowed upon Abraham and Ishmael. Thus, Muhammad's hometown was replete with images of an ancient heritage that have found continuation in Islamic ritual and written expression in the Quran.

Muhammad's early environment contained several groups of people, with whom the Quran is in conversation. They include polytheistic Arab idolaters, monotheistic Arab Hanifs, Jews, Christians and Zoroastrians. Perhaps the most visible of these are the polytheistic Arabs, who traced their descent to Abraham through Ishmael. Known as *mushrikun*, "those who cause to be included," Muhammad's contemporaries worshipped the God of Abraham and prayed to him for forgiveness every year during their circumambulations, but they also included a number of secondary deities in their religious devotions. They prized tribal solidarity (*'asabiyya*) and had a code of chivalry (*murruwa*), but their poetry does not show evidence of a belief in an afterlife.

The Hanifs seem to be Arabs who had retained Abraham's monotheistic practices. Not many were left in Muhammad's day: only four are mentioned by name in the classical sources.6 There is some ambiguity associated with their religion—some of them seem to have also been Christian at some point or other in their lives. Muhammad's pre-Islamic abstention from polytheism and his solitary meditations during the month of Ramadan may be the best examples of their practices. The Quran portrays the emerging Islamic faith as a continuation and a renewal of the Abrahamic Hanif tradition.7

Christianity was a well-known faith among the Arabs, even though its shape may have differed from Pauline Christianity as we know it today. The Quran does not use the Arabic word for Christians, *masihiyyun*, but rather *nasara*, Nazarenes, which may have etymological links to the early Nazarenes, or Ebionites as some of them are known. The word also means "helpers"; hence, Christians are those who helped and supported Jesus Christ. Many Christians lived in the area of Najran to the south of Mecca, and they sent a delegation to visit the Prophet during his stay in the city of Medina. Few Christians lived in Mecca or Medina.

Judaism was also known to the ancient Arabs, since many Jews had settled in Arabia, usually living in tribal groupings, like their Arabian counterparts. Some lived in the city of Medina, where the Prophet spent the later years of his mission. Jews are called by various names in the Quran. They include Children of Israel, Jews (*yahud*) and another derivative, "those that have repented (*hadu*)," which indicates an unusual etymology for *yahud*. The term *Jew* is thereby not simply associated with the ancestral Judah, but also with the highly prized characteristic of repentance. Jews and Christians together are called "People of the Book," a term that can also include other peoples who have recorded Scriptures.

Zoroastrians are termed *majus* in the Quran. Another word, *Sabians* (*sabi'un*), does not as clearly refer to Zoroastrians, even though it can be interpreted as such. In Medina, one of Muhammad's famous companions and early converts, Salman El-Farsi, is of Zoroastrian origin, even though he had become a Christian before converting to Islam.

The majority of Muhammad's Meccan contemporaries did not welcome his message of a return to the worship of God alone. For them, housing the various deities added to their immediate prosperity and prestige. The deities often belonged to tribes and people with whom they had trade agreements, guaranteeing safe passage for the Meccan caravans traveling to Yemen in the south or Syria in the north. The deities were also a major religious attraction, drawing more visitors in the pilgrim season. Consequently Muhammad's message was heavily resisted, and early Muslims met with severe persecution. In the year 622 CE, Muhammad had to flee for his life to the city of Medina, where he had established earlier contact and in which Islam had successfully spread. His journey marks the start of the Islamic calendar and the beginning of the Medinan period. Accordingly, some of the Quran's contents are connected to the Meccan period, whereas others are Medinan.

format and genre

The Quran comes in the form of a short, introductory prayer and a lengthy response. In the opening prayer, God is praised as the compassionate lord and teacher of humankind; his ability to pass judgment is remembered and his sole help and guidance is supplicated.[8] In the subsequent response, the entire book is presented as the divine answer to this prayer: "In the Name of God, The Merciful, The Compassionate. Alif Lam Mim. That is the Book—there is no doubt in it, a guidance for the ones who are Godfearing."[9] While the opening prayer begins by affirming previously established rubrics common to many faith traditions across the globe,[10] the rest of the Quran affects piecemeal change until the outlines of the Islamic faith tradition are complete.

The Quran's verses and passages are organized into suras, which are similar to chapters, since they are the main divisions of the book.[11] All in all, it has 114 chapters of varying length, ranging from 286 verses (chapter 2) to three verses (chapter 108). Suras broadly decrease in length and are not ordered chronologically. Thus, after the brief seven-verse opening prayer comes the longest of the chapters, followed by the second longest, and so on. The first chapter chronologically, which begins with the word *Recite*, is number 96 in the final organization of the Quran. It has nineteen verses.

Chapters have names, which are not considered part of the original revelation but which were used by the early Muslims to refer to the individual units. For example, chapter 2, al-Baqara, means "The Cow" due to a distinctive story of a cow. These suras begin with the *basmala*, "the verse": "In the Name of God, The Merciful, The Compassionate."[12] Thus, when recited in communal prayers, this phrase signals the beginning of a new chapter.

While the first verse is generally uniform, the contents of chapters vary greatly, often even internally within each one. They contain narratives, laws, prayers, doxologies and more, intertwined together in a coherent composition. Individual topics, such as the story of Abraham, are rarely concentrated in one chapter but are dispersed throughout the Quran. Accordingly, one may find Abraham building the sanctuary in chapter 2:124–29 and going through planet, moon and sun worship on his way to monotheism in chapter 6:75–79. Repetitions occur frequently, but they are usually expanded with new material in their new context. For example, prayer is mentioned in 2:3, then expanded with the act of bowing or kneeling in 2:43 and then elaborated further by the prayer in times of fear in 2:238–39. The classical Arabic sources note this feature and have sometimes termed it "concision and elaboration,"[13] since the contents are mentioned in a brief form and then provided with more detail in a later context. Sometimes it is the other way around: earlier contents appear in a summarized form or are briefly referred to in a later context. The repetitions often carry nuances from previous or later passages, thereby layering verses with meanings from other verses. Certain foundational beliefs and practices are found recurrently throughout the Quran: a reader cannot read too many pages without coming across expansions on monotheism or prayer. In English, "progression" may be a better term for this feature than the literal translation "concision and elaboration," since "progression" is broader and can also indicate reaching a goal of some kind.

Progression can also be a feature of chapters as a whole. For example, chapter 2's tripartite structure is progressive. It consists of three panels, each panel longer than the one before it. The first panel deals with humanity as a whole, the second with the Children of Israel and the third with the nascent Muslim community. Here, the panels show a chronological progression in the history of humankind. Each panel also has three parts: a story, an instruction section and a test of some kind. In the first panel, the story is about Adam and Eve and it illustrates the primordial election of humankind to a special position as vicegerents on earth. In the second panel, the story section portrays the Children of Israel in the wilderness with Moses, also showing their election to a privileged position. The final panel depicts the primeval origins of the election of the Muslim community with the story of Abraham and Ishmael, followed by a set of instructions incumbent upon their new status. The chapter covers the basic outlines of the Islamic faith and is tantamount to a first comprehensive lesson in the religion. Subsequent chapters build on the material in chapter 2, developing it further and organizing it into units that become progressively smaller. The Quran ends in a seven-verse prayer, similar to the way it begins, again as noted previously.

The question of genre is one that has puzzled scholars in recent decades. While some of the prayers and shorter chapters recall hymns, others are so long and varied that they no longer seem to fit that description. A recent suggestion is that the genre of the Quran can be described by the term *apocalyptic*, *apocalypse* meaning "revelation."[14] This genre often contains eschatological material dealing with the end of times, a topic that occurs frequently in the Quran. While the suggestion has convincing arguments, the Quran also has hymnic features, since it begins and ends in praise and prayer, in addition to the musical quality of its rhythms and rhymes and its poetic content. These features make it suitable for recitation in the public sphere and in communal prayers.

major themes

The Quran has many themes, which all seem to revolve around the idea of God. Not only does God often appear as the speaker—as can be noted in the Quran's "I" or "we"—but all of the Quran's themes describe God in one way or the other.

Even disparate themes are also sometimes held together by a common idea centered on the deity. For example, in the array of themes in chapter 2, this thread is a dominant aspect of God: God as Guide. The theme is signaled by the leading keyword *guidance*, which occurs in high numbers throughout the chapter and in crucial locations, always with God as the ultimate source of guidance. The various sections of this chapter elaborate this attribute, so that the picture of God that finally emerges is that of a universal, transcendent, systematic guide, a sender of prophets with the particularities of guidance to those whom he elects, who ultimately guides to success or failure.

Eschatology is another theme that recurs throughout the text, sometimes with vivid images of the Day of Judgment, heaven and hell. The descriptions are often tied to certain characteristics of God, such as God's grace, mercy and compassion or God's justice, wisdom and sovereignty. Nature themes also abound, such as deliberations on the moon, sun and stars, fauna and flora, human nature and human development, topography and the constitution of the oceans, the water cycle and more. These themes usually depict God's creative power, his uniqueness and his dominion over his creations. The water cycle and the different stages of human development before and after birth illustrate God's ability to raise the dead and to bring life where there is no life. These themes often occur in context with the idea of resurrection on the Day of Judgment, which posed great problems for pre-Islamic Arabs.

God is also portrayed as the creator of supernatural beings, such as the angels, created from light, and the Jinn, created from fire (of which Satan is one). Divine books that are mentioned by name include Torah (*taurat*), Gospel (*injil*) and the Psalms of David (*zabur*).[15]

Stories of prophets are also profuse, many of them biblical, such as Adam, Noah, Enoch, Abraham, Lot, Ishmael, Isaac, Saul, David, Solomon, Job, Moses, Jesus and Mary,[16] but also nonbiblical, like Hud, Saleh and Shu'ayb. Some of these prophets are mentioned several times, whereas others are referenced only once. The longest sustained narrative is that of Joseph, which covers the bulk of chapter 12. These stories often gave reassurance to Muhammad that he was not alone, that there had been others like him that came before his time and that all other prophets were rejected by their people and were vindicated in the end.

A few important personages who were not prophets also occur in the text, like the Queen of Sheba or Dhu'l-Qarnayn, possibly referring to Alexander the Great. Occasionally, chapters contain historical information including events that happened in Muhammad's time or the names of some of his compatriots, such as his uncle Abu Lahab.[17] They sometimes have prophecies; for example, a Roman victory over the Persians is predicted.[18]

Moral and ethical imperatives are also profuse in the text, teaching kindness, forgiveness and charity, egalitarianism of all human beings irrespective of race or gender, respect for individual privacy, anger management, humility, honesty, truthfulness and more. Usury, theft, robbery, fornication, adultery, intoxicating beverages, slander, backbiting and verbal abuse are discouraged in strong terms, sometimes by delineating specific legal punishments for those convicted of certain crimes. For example, adulterers, whether men or women, who are convicted on the basis of the testimony of four reliable witnesses, receive one hundred lashes, while if they happen to be slaves, this punishment is decreased to fifty lashes.[19]

Relatively few verses deal with rituals and legal imperatives; however, these, too, address a comprehensive number of issues. They include pilgrim rites, ritual prayers, charity and fasting. Laws relate to marriage and divorce, the rights of orphans, inheritance, dietary restrictions, punishments for specific crimes, rules for warfare and more. Some of these rules and regulations are quite detailed; for example, concerning warfare. Verses 2:190–95 outline the basic rules, which are then expanded in subsequent chapters. Permission is granted to fight back against those who initiate war until they desist and turn to peace. Initiating war is prohibited, as is the transgression of certain boundaries during war, such as the violation of sanctuaries. The reason for going to war is given as putting a stop to persecution and to establish freedom of religion. These rules are harmonized with verses that instruct Muslims to repay unkindness with kindness and to forgive harm and abuse[20] by means of a dividing line. This line is delineated as when religious persecution reaches the extent of killing and turning Muslims out of their homes, similar to what we would regard as religious or ethnic cleansing today.[21] While the rules of war delineate a defensive, limited war, there are pedagogical undercurrents to it. Fighting, together with spending, is presented as a kind of test of faith, since it entails putting one's life and wealth on the line for God.

orality

As a recitation, the Quran has a distinct oral dimension as can be noted in the liturgy and elsewhere. For example, the entire Quran is recited during the extra *tarawih* prayers in the month of Ramadan in many mosques around the world. Oral texts tend to differ from the visual ones we are used to seeing today: in order for listeners to be able to discern the structure and compositional schemas of what they are hearing, oral texts require certain organizational tools that diverge from visual structural markers, such as titles, chapter headings, indentation, footnotes and page numbers. Oral structural markers include deviations from established patterns, vocative changes in addressees and, most of all, repetitions.

The above-mentioned basmala is the main tool for distinguishing between chapters: it indicates the beginning of new ones. Repetitions in their various forms also signal internal subunits, highlighting the text and delineating its structure. For example, verbatim repetitions frame the main parts of chapter 2, while topical repetitions define its general structure, thereby helping listeners understand the flow of ideas and the compositional schema. The various types of repetitions not only delineate the various subunits of the text but they also unify it and serve as memory aids.

The act of reciting the Quran often sounds like chanting and has a certain musical quality, due to the various rhythms and rhymes incorporated into its composition. For example, the verses of chapter 54 ("The Moon") all end with a short, closed syllable ending with the *r* consonant and have a distinctive meter. Some verses display parallelism, a feature known from biblical Hebrew poetry. Parallel verses have similar structures and will sometimes say things in similar ways (synonymous parallelism) or in opposite ways (antithetical parallelism) or continue the thoughts of the previous verse (synthetic parallelism). Hence, from a contemporary Western perspective, the Quran sounds very much like poetry: a musical kind of poetry.

However, the Quran clearly states that it is not to be defined as poetry (*shi'r*).[22] In Arabic, formal poetry has strict meters and end rhymes, to which the loose Quranic structures do not adhere. Then again, it does resemble rhymed prose (*saj'*), which is associated with the speech of the priests who ministered to the pre-Islamic secondary deities in Mecca.[23] But just as the Quran states that Muhammad is not a poet, it also states that Muhammad is not a priest[24]—there is no recollection in his known history of him ever functioning as either. Moreover, the association of rhymed prose with the pre-Islamic priesthood is a sensitive topic and has discouraged comparisons in the classical literature. Thus, only a few have pointed out the similarities between the Quran's style and the mantic speech of the pre-Islamic priesthood.

Recent studies acknowledge the similarities, but they also point to the differences between the priestly and the Quranic modes of expression.[25] It is not strange that the Quranic speech should resemble that of the ancient priests, since it was the known mode of mantic expression. People would expect any messages from divine beings to be in rhymed prose. However, there are major differences between the Quran and these previous modes. Priests used to give short, cryptic communications, made up of few lines, which do not compare in length to the Quran. The worldview and contents of the Quran also differ substantially. The utterances of the pre-Islamic priesthood dealt with things like lost camels, raids and paternity issues. They were not generally concerned with salvation, pedagogical, ethical or legal matters, as is evident in the Quran. In addition, the supernatural sources of the mantic communications differ. While Muhammad portrays his immediate source as the angel Gabriel, the priests were believed to receive their sayings from a different kind of supernatural being, the Jinn.

textuality

The Quran also identifies itself as a book (*kitab*), thereby underlining its written dimension. In the very beginning of chapter 2, it specifies that the guidance that was requested in the opening chapter comes in the form of a book: "That is The Book—there is no doubt in it, a guidance for the ones who are Godfearing." However, even though the Quran was conceived of as a book very early in Islamic history, producing it in the form of a written, coherent document posed many challenges.

The text itself posed one such challenge. Scholars are in agreement that it was disseminated in small quantities over a period of twenty years or more and contained variations, so that it needed to be brought together and standardized in order to reach its final form. The Islamic tradition portrays the Prophet telling his followers where to place each verse upon receiving it. However, the tradition is not in agreement on the organization of the chapters; while some scholars attribute the organization to the reign of the third caliph, 'Uthman (644–655 CE), others attribute it to the Prophet himself.[26] In addition, there are discrepancies as to when the text was compiled and transcribed into a book.

Standardizing the text also posed a challenge. The sources record small variations in the early days, such as the dialectal variations. Writing materials were generally primitive and not conducive to producing sophisticated books. In the Prophet's day, they consisted of palm leaves, potsherds, skin and bones. Occasionally, papyrus, parchment and vellum were used; however, these materials were relatively few and expensive. In addition, the script was defective and did not contain all the vowels and ways of distinguishing between consonants that are in use today. According to the Islamic sources, the Quran was not formally transcribed in book form with bound leaves (*mushaf*) until the reign of 'Uthman. The first major fine-tuning of the script is attributed to the time of Abu al-Aswad al-Du'ali (d. 688 CE). Thus, the early written texts were mainly used as a mnemonic device to aid people's memories, and they went hand in hand with a strong tradition of memorization.

In addition to the limitations of the writing materials and script, few people knew how to read and write. The Prophet himself is portrayed as illiterate. According to the Islamic sources, when the angel Gabriel first communicated with Muhammad, telling him to "read/recite in the name of God," the Prophet answered, "I do not read," indicating his inability to read and write. However, the tradition also indicates a strong impetus on writing. For example, the above exchange between the Prophet and Gabriel is followed by these verses: "Read/Recite in the Name of your Lord Who created. . . . Read/Recite: Your Lord is the Most Generous, He Who taught by the pen. He taught the human being what he knew not."[27] Hence, there is a strong focus on writing with a pen, which necessitated using the available scribes and teaching new individuals literacy skills in order to preserve and propagate the Quran.

The Islamic biographical sources have entries for several such individuals who collected and transcribed the Quran. For example, Umm Waraqah, a woman of Medina, stands out, because she had collected the sacred text in the Prophet's lifetime and was commanded by him to lead the people of her area in prayer, an activity that invariably included Quran recitation. As a collector of the Quran and a prayer leader, this role was so important that the Prophet forbade her to participate in the war effort when she asked to join the men and women who took part in the defense of Medina. She was thereby in charge of preserving and disseminating the Quran in the Prophet's absence.[28]

Hafsah (d. 665 CE), wife to the Prophet, was another individual who stands out due to the major role she played in the collection and preservation of the Quran. According to the tradition, the Prophet appointed a tutor to teach her how to read and write, and so she had her own written copy. In addition, the sources associate her with keeping the master document, compiled from various loose materials, which was used in the production of the official copies made during the reign of 'Uthman.[29] Hafsah was not the only one of the Prophet's wives to play a role in the dissemination of the Quran; verse 33:34 specifically asks them to mention the verses that they hear in their homes. In keeping with this responsibility, Hafsah, Umm Salamah (d. 680 CE) and Aisha (d. 678 CE) are accredited with having memorized the entire Quran and were renowned reciters. Thus, members of the Prophet's own household participated in the effort to transcribe and disseminate the Quran.[30]

The biographical and other sources portray Zayd ibn Thabit (d. 665 CE) as another major figure in the documentation process. He was one of the most visible scribes, who wrote portions of the Quran at Muhammad's dictation. He is also accredited with overseeing two major milestones in the final production: the gathering of a complete, official document during the reign of Abu Bakr (632–634 CE), and the making of a standardized master copy and duplicates that were sent to the outlying realms during the reign of 'Uthman. The sources show that the first project was as a result of 'Umar's (d. 644 CE) concern that the death of the memorizers might lead to the loss of some of the Quran, since several had already died in the battle of Yamamah in 633 CE. The second project is attributed to a concern for the reading disparities that appeared in the distant regions of the newly emerging Islamic Empire, which had spread at an alarming rate over a large geographical area. The sources portray 'Uthman ordering the text's collection and the transcribing of a master copy in the form of a bound book. A committee supervised by Zayd oversaw the standardization process, so that any dialectal, spelling or other disparities were removed. This committee did not always agree. In moments of disagreement they followed the dialect of Quraysh. Any manuscripts or other pieces of writing that had errors were burned. Noteworthy about the collection process is the witnessing requirement. According to the sources, two individuals duly witnessed each fragment before it was officially transcribed.[31]

Today the traditional Islamic account of the collection of the Quran has increasingly come under scrutiny. The reliability of some of the most highly regarded sources has come into question, since some of the leading Western scholars found discrepancies among them. A popular approach in the West today is the tradition-critical approach, with scholars carefully examining the Islamic sources in order to determine the nature of their reliability. Most Western scholars accept the second account, which attributes the collection and the making of a standardized text to the reign of 'Uthman, but reject the first account, which places an initial, formal collection of the Quran during the reign of Abu Bakr.[32]

Other Western scholars discredit the early accounts entirely and have therefore come up with vastly different conclusions. Chief among them are John Wansbrough and John Burton. Wansbrough dates the compilation of the Quran to the late second/early third century of Islam, locating this initiative in Mesopotamia, but he has failed to identify historical sources supporting his dating, the individuals involved, and the smaller details of this endeavor.[33] He has used what has been described as a "conjecture and verification" approach,[34] which begins with conjecture and proceeds to see if this conjecture fits the known facts. In Wansbrough's case, there is material evidence disproving it, such as codex San'ā' 20–33.1,[35] which has been published in the interim. In addition, there are other manuscripts in various libraries around the world,[36] which seem to have escaped scholarly attention for some time.[37] Thus, there is material evidence that disproves Wansbrough's theory of late compilation. John Burton, on the other hand, attributes the final compilation of the Quran to the time of Muhammad. He, too, discredits the traditional accounts that place the first compilation later in the time of Abu Bakr, regarding them as a means to bolster the scholarly elite's legal authority. While both these scholars have brought intellectually provocative perspectives to the study of the

Quran, Burton's theory is by far the more convincing, particularly when set against the backdrop of the power struggles between traditionalists and rationalists in the second century or so of Islam.

While 'Uthman's codex did much to standardize the Quranic text, variant readings have still accrued over the years. These readings differ in minor ways, such as vowels or weak consonants, since they are limited by the confines of the skeletal 'Uthmanic text. They do not generally affect the meaning in any significant way. The most noticeable variation is in the *hamzah*, the guttural stop that functions as a consonant in the Arabic language.[38]

In the Islamic tradition, at least fourteen such variant readings have been widely accepted and propagated, each with an authoritative chain of transmission going back to the Prophet.[39] However, the invention of the printing press and the production of the Egyptian Royal edition in 1924 have relegated the bulk of these readings to the background. This edition follows the Hafs 'an 'Asim reading, named after two individuals in its chain of transmission. While this reading is by far the most popular today, the Warsh 'an Nafi' reading also has adherents, particularly in Northwest Africa.

Perhaps the most interesting variation in the Quranic text is one that does not actually occur in the contemporary editions and one for which there is no documented variant reading. Today, minor orthographical changes in the guttural stop of the word *wa'adribuhunna* in verse 4:34 can affect the meaning quite profoundly. A strongly defined guttural stop would have the meaning of "go away from [your wives]," while a weak guttural stop would indicate a range of meanings including "beat [your wives]."[40] In contemporary editions, it is possible to distinguish between these two stops by means of different orthographical symbols—the strongly defined guttural stop looks like an open, underlined circle (*hamzat al-qat'*), while the weak stop looks like a closed, somewhat flattened circle (*hamzat al-wasl*). However, in the Prophet's day, these orthographical symbols were not known, since they developed much later. It was therefore not possible to differentiate between them on the basis of the written text alone. It was also not realistically possible to distinguish between them aurally, particularly in the Qurayshi tribal dialect, where they tended to assimilate their stops. Once these symbols were invented, scribes needed to make a choice as to which symbol they would use, a choice that would incidentally reflect their cultural understanding of the meaning of the word. The symbol we see in today's orthography is the weak stop, which can mean "beat [your wives]." Thus, we can see that the act of writing and the choice of symbols can sometimes involve interpretation.[41] The alternative understanding, "go away from," is reflected in *The Sublime Quran* interpretation by Laleh Bakhtiar.[42]

interpretation

If one were to ask, "What is the one big question that occupies Muslims today?" and "What challenges Muslims the way biblical source criticism has challenged Jews and Christians?," the answer would not be the text of the Quran. The above issues, while important within both classical and contemporary scholarship, have posed no major problems for Muslims, since the text of the Quran has been fixed and generally accepted as the inimitable word of God for centuries.[43] While the text-related questions that arose within Western Quran scholarship have also trickled into Muslim scholarship, they have been mainly noticed by the scholarly elite and have not gained the attention of the masses in any major way. Rather, the biggest question Muslims face today is how to interpret the sacred text. This challenge is one that has occupied previous generations across the ages and still causes deep divides even in the present time.

classical commentaries

As may be inferred from the above, the sources record a great deal of information about the Quran and its history. Much of this information can be found in specific genres of literature, such as collections of reports about the Prophet Muhammad, his biography, commentaries, compilations of the biographies of his companions, histories and more. Within the first two centuries of Islam, concerns were expressed regarding the accuracy of these materials, and safeguards were put in place to ensure some measure of reliability. The sources indicate that these measures differed substantially from what was used for the Quran: instead of two living eyewitnesses testifying to the written record, informants now typically reported on events that happened a century or more before their time and so they were required to name their sources all the way back to the original source.[44] Thus, if the informant was reporting something about the Prophet, they needed to list the names of the persons who had handed down the report one by one in a linear fashion until they received it.[45] The system thereby relied on chains of transmission and oral tradents, who may or may not have used written records.[46] Their reports did not go unchallenged; the first centuries of Islam saw the development of sophisticated techniques to critique and determine their level of authenticity. In turn, the early reports were formally written down and compiled into books and larger collections.

Chains of transmission became a common phenomenon within Muslim intellectual life, and they lie at the heart of the classical exegetical tradition, *tafsir*. By the tenth century, a popular form of commentary was in place, organized in a consecutive manner, where the Quranic verses were listed one after the other with comments beneath each one.[47] The comments consisted largely of a list of explanations attributed to authority figures from the Prophet's family, his companions or their immediate successors. Some of these authority figures were of Jewish or Christian origin and passed on material from biblical and extrabiblical sources.[48] The commentaries thereby allowed room for several different opinions, even while limiting interpretation to a set number of individuals. They generally examined verses or small passages virtually independently of the rest of their literary context. They set the tone for subsequent commentaries.

As the commentary tradition evolved, it incorporated insights from a variety of sources and disciplines, while at the same time repeating the same old material. Thus, the interpretations of the early authority figures continued to be promulgated in subsequent generations, expanded with new add-ons. Once something had made it into the tradition, it became very difficult to ignore. While new composers had the choice of what to include and what to leave out, at any point in time, their work was in conversation with the tradition in its entirety, just by virtue of their choices and the way they organized their material. This eclecticism and sense of continuity and change has come to be described within contemporary scholarship as the genealogical character of the tafsir tradition.[49] It is what makes the Islamic commentary tradition so very distinctive.

The inclusivity and the versatility of the tradition make the task of classifying commentaries into different genres somewhat challenging. It is not unusual for a commentary to possess materials that cut across various different disciplines and contain insights from them all. Nevertheless, scholars have identified mystical, legal, traditionalist, sectarian and other genres, since some commentaries are known for their focus and expertise in a specific area.[50] Another suggested classification is one based on function. Some commentaries tend to be encyclopedic, covering much of the available material. They often run into twenty volumes or more, even up to one hundred volumes. Others have been dubbed *madrasa* (school) style and are more manageable, being limited to the material a teacher sees fit to transmit to the students.[51] They are usually much shorter than the encyclopedic commentaries, sometimes about four volumes or so in size.

the exegetical sciences

In time, scholars collected the traditional Quran-related subjects and synthesized them into what became known as the exegetical sciences (*'Ulum al-Qur'an*). These fields of knowledge include things like Meccan and Medinan revelations, occasions of revelation, the collection and organization of the Quran, famous reciters, rules of recitation, codices, variant readings, language, grammar, poetics, rhetorics, abrogation,[52] hermeneutics and more.

Some of these fields historicize the Quran and explain the text's circumstances, such as the venue or the occasion of revelation. Often, commentaries will begin with this information, citing it before proceeding into the various explanations and analysis. Chapters and verses are usually identified as either Meccan or Medinan, with the occasional contradicting report, placing them at both locations.

Scholars have noted that Meccan and Medinan chapters tend to have different characteristics, which they associated with the changing circumstances of the early Muslim community. For example, in Mecca, when Muslims were few and Islam still in its infancy, chapters tended to address matters of belief, while Medinan chapters are more concerned with community building, relations with other communities and legal issues.

"Occasions" of revelation (*asbab al-nuzul*) are also sometimes translated as "reasons" of revelation and provide the immediate context of the revelation. They are a genre of report that places certain verses or chapters within a narrative framework, illustrating historical events and supplying details. For example, a number of reports depict the occasion of revelation for verse 33:35. They explain that a woman by the name of Asma' bint 'Umays (d. 706 CE), upon coming back from Ethiopia, entered upon the Prophet's wives and asked what had been revealed about women in her absence. Upon learning that there was nothing in particular, she went to the prophet and said, "Women are in a state of failure and loss." He asked, "Why is that?" She answered, "Because they are not mentioned positively in the Quran in the same way men are mentioned."[53] In Umm Salamah's own words, as they are traced back to her through the report's chain of transmission, the following occurred:

> I was in awe one day, when he proceeded to call from the pulpit and recited: "Truly the ones who are males who submit and the ones who are females who submit, and the ones who are males who believe and the ones who are females who believe, and the ones who are morally obligated males and the ones who are morally obligated females, and the ones who are sincere males and the ones who are sincere females, and the ones who are males and remain steadfast and the ones who are females and remain steadfast, and the ones who are humble males and the ones who are humble females, and the ones who are charitable males and the ones who are charitable females, and the ones who are males who fast and the ones who are females who fast, and the males who guard their private parts and the females who guard them, and the ones who are males who remember God frequently and ones who are females who remember, God has prepared for them forgiveness and a sublime compassion."[54]

These reports thereby place the verse within a narrative context, explaining the events leading up to the revelation, the names of the people involved in these events and when and where this verse was revealed. These details are not provided in the Quran but have developed in their own genre of writing, which has enriched the commentary tradition.

These and other exegetical sciences have been summarized and synthesized into significant works that have formed part of the curriculum of various educational institutions in the Muslim world for centuries. One work that stands out in the tradition is that of Suyuti (d. 1505 CE), and it has been more or less definitive for this genre for the past five centuries.[55] This book among others has provided a hermeneutics for the Quran that has proven to be fairly influential even today.[56] It has classified the various types of Quran interpretations into four epistemological categories. The first category is interpreting the Quran intertextually by means of the Quran, while the second, third and fourth categories are tradition based, using reports attributed to the Prophet, his companions and their immediate successors, respectively, to explain the Quran.

Few reports that explain specific verses have chains of transmission that extend all the way back to the Prophet. The bulk of available reports either stop at one of his contemporaries or their immediate successors. Sunnis and Shias do not always agree on which of these individuals can be considered authoritative; thus, reports contained in Sunni and Shia commentaries often differ. Shia commentaries also include reports attributed to the line of Shia imams, who descend from 'Ali (d. 661 CE) and Fatima (d. 632 or 633 CE), the Prophet's daughter. In practice, the various reports have formed the basis for traditional interpretations for centuries. On the other hand, modern reformers have often relied on the first, Quran-based category when producing new methodologies and exegetical works.

modern exegesis

Muslim experience of modernity has been intimately linked to the experience of colonialism and the struggle to regain political independence and sovereignty. Reformers saw the need to rebuild their societies and find Quran interpretations that were in keeping with the needs of their time. Many were highly critical of the traditionalist interpretations that actively confined the Quran to the worldview and understandings of individuals living in the first and early second centuries of Islam, as seen through the eyes of later generations. Consequently, the nineteenth century saw a move away from traditionalist explanations and the search for new interpretations, which would serve their changing circumstances. The work of the pioneers of this movement, like Muhammad 'Abduh in Eygpt (d. 1905) and Sir Sayyid Ahmad Khan in India (d. 1898), has paved the way for subsequent generations.

The twentieth century saw a number of new developments, such as the literary, scientific and feminist trends in Quran exegesis. Pioneers of the literary approach advocated treating the Quran as any literary text and analyzed it as such.[57] A variety of approaches fall under the literary umbrella, such as the thematic approach,[58] which looks at the various themes in the Quran, and the holistic approach, which approaches chapters and even the entire Quran as a literary whole.[59] Some of these trends can be located within the first, Quran-based exegetical method of traditional hermeneutics, since they use the Quran's repetitions and elaborations and other text-connected features in their interpretive endeavors. The scientific trend uses modern science to interpret some of the nature-related and other science-related material in the Quran.[60] For example, the Quran's portrayal of the oceans with their layers of darkness is likened to modern knowledge of the composition of the oceans.[61] Feminist interpretations do not always identify themselves as feminist and include some prominent works by North American scholars, such as Amina Wadud,[62] Asma Barlas,[63] Nimat Hafez Barazangi[64] and others.

While all these new trends have appeared, many of the old works are still in circulation. The most widely read classical book today is that of ibn Kathir (d. 1373 CE), who applied the above-mentioned four-tiered hermeneutics, using the Quran and the reports attributed to the Prophet, his companions and their successors in his interpretations.[65] This work has been published and republished in the Muslim world and abridged by at least three different scholars.[66] An abridgment is also available in English.[67] Its popularity is an indication of how well traditional interpretations are thriving today.

Contemporary Muslims grapple with some of the same questions that their predecessors tackled, primarily the question of authority. Who has the authority to interpret the Quran? To what extent are we bound by tradition? These are pressing questions Muslims have asked and sought to answer in different ways, thereby contributing to a plethora of ideas. Sunnis have come to consider certain individuals from the first and second generations to be authoritative, due to their proximity to the Prophet. Then again, Shias have looked to other individuals, primarily from the Prophet's family, whom they consider to be his heirs in interpretive authority, while the mystically inclined Sufis have looked to certain sages as having a special kind of knowledge. Others within the various Muslim sects and religious orientations have sought a more egalitarian approach where anyone can read and interpret the text for himself or herself. Those having expertise in certain areas have brought insights from linguistic, literary, theological, scientific, feminist and other fields of study. Today, Muslims face the challenges of navigating these various currents in their constant quest to derive meaning and encompass the nuances of the sacred text.

quran text:
the sublime quran

translator's notes

CERTAIN CRITERIA WERE USED IN *THE SUBLIME QURAN* THAT SEPARATE THIS TRANSLATION FROM other English translations of the Quran. I will present four brief examples, and then one in considerable depth, as promised in my "Preface to the Quran."

NO COMMENTARY

Without presenting any footnote commentary for the non-Arabic speaker, *The Sublime Quran* presents an English version of the Quran that can truly be said to be a translation, one that reflects the mercy of the Divine Presence, and not an interpretation. Each reader of the English translation of *The Sublime Quran* is able to actively awaken to the mercy within it, rather than to passively accept the commentary of another's personal view. It gives the reader a chance to see how each and every word reflects the divine intention. It also allows the translation to be free of any transient denominational, political or doctrinal bias. Questions, then, that may arise for the reader could be: What does it mean to me? What does it say to me today since the Quran is eternal? In what way can I identify with it? What do I feel when I read it?

Al-Ghazzali,[*] the great Muslim theologian, has said that the Quran is not a historical document, and each person should read or recite it for himself or herself. If it is treated as a historical document, it loses its eternal quality. Al-Ghazzali asks, "How can one suppose otherwise when the Quran was revealed to the Messenger not only for him particularly, but as a spiritual cure, guidance, mercy and light for all the world?"[†] As the Quran says, "We send down in the Quran what is a healing and a mercy for the ones who believe."[‡]

UNIVERSAL

The Prophet of Islam did not receive the revelation of the Quran from Gabriel to bring a new religion. As a mercy to humanity, he came to confirm the messages brought by the prophets who

---

[*]d. 1111.

[†]See Muhammad al-Ghazzali, *Recitation of the Quran*.

[‡]Quran 16:126.

preceded him in time. As I began work on this translation, which has been the great privilege of my life, I asked myself: How would a translation of the Quran speak to the universality of the original?

The translation of *The Sublime Quran*, in the revised edition employed in this text, is an attempt to show how the Quran is not bound by time or space. In doing so, words chosen for the translation tend to be, where the context allows, of an eternal and a universal rather than a particular nature.

Inclusive Language

Thus broadening the perspective of the Quran, in comparison to many translations, the English became inclusive rather than exclusive, as indeed some other English translations are. It is our hope that in this way a larger audience can understand and relate to the message of the Quran. An inclusive example would be the translation of the derivatives of *k f r*, literally meaning "to hide or cover over something." Most English translations use the verb "to disbelieve" or "to be an infidel," making the active participle "one who disbelieves" or "one who is an infidel." In the present translation a more inclusive viable terminology is used—namely, "to be ungrateful," the active participle being "one who is ungrateful." The Quran itself declares its timelessness and universality. Therefore, its understanding must also be eternal and for all time, inclusive of all of humanity rather than exclusive to one group of people.

Applying the above criteria to the word *aslama*, "he submitted," in the eight times that it appears in the form of *islam*, it is translated according to its universal meaning as "submission," and the forty-two times that its form as *muslim* appears, it is translated according to its universal meaning as "one who submits."

Another example of the use of inclusive language is an attempt to speak to people in their own language, in the use of God instead of Allah. Many English-speaking Muslims, as well as many of the English translations of the Quran to date, use *Allah* when speaking English instead of *God*. The intention on the part of the speaker is to maintain a sense of piety. They feel that using *Allah* in English moves them in that direction.

However well intentioned such persons may be, the use of the word *Allah* instead of *God* when speaking English, first of all, does not follow the Quranic verse that tells the Prophet to speak to people in their own language. In addition, it does not follow the *Sunnah* or practices of the Prophet, who did speak to people in their own language. In addition, it creates a divide between Muslims who use the word and the English-speaking people of various faiths to whom they are speaking. In effect, it creates the illusion that there is more than One God—Allah and God. The response of the English-speaking person of another faith is to say, "I do not understand your religion; you have a different God than I do and you call Him Allah." It needs to be clearly explained to English-speaking Muslims that, unlike what they may feel, they do not have a monopoly on the word *Allah*. Arabic-speaking Christians and Arabic-speaking Jews also refer to God as Allah. The Old Testament and New Testament when translated into Arabic use Allah for God.

Finally, when words in a verse refer directly to a woman or women or wife or wives and the corresponding pronouns such as (they, them, those), I have placed an (f) after the word to indicate the word refers to the feminine gender specifically. In other instances, in the Arabic language (as in Spanish), the masculine pronoun may be used generically to include both male and female human beings.

THOU VS. YOU

Another important difference between this translation and other English translations is in regard to the second-person singular (thou) as opposed to the second-person plural (you) in English, where the Arabic language is very specific. There are fourteen personal pronouns in Arabic, as opposed to six in English usage today. Arabic includes the nominative, "thou"; the objective, "thee"; and the possessive, "thy." In the English translation of *The Sublime Quran*, the pronouns "you" and "your" were used throughout. However, if "you" or "your" appeared in bold, it means the original was "thou, thee or thine." The distinction between using the second-person singular (thou, thee, thy) refers to the Oneness of God, the singular God. When "you" or the second-person plural is used for God, we are indicating that there are plural gods. This is the only sin that the Quran says is unforgivable.

QURAN 4:34

To understand the sublimity of the Quran, one should begin with some standard that establishes a system based in justice and fairness in order to be able to enter the world of the spiritual and intuition. In my preface essay, when I promised to return to the techniques of translation, I suggested that one has to begin with some criterion, which for Muslims is the Quran itself, specifically as understood by the Prophet himself.

As the Quran refers to the Prophet as a mercy to humanity and the model whose example should be followed, it is clear that he would have carried out any and all of the commands in the Quran that related to his life, yet we find an exception in *drb* (to beat) according to the interpreters over the centuries.

It is in this regard, since God's mercy encompasses everything, including obeying the Messenger *"so that perhaps you will find mercy,"* that *The Sublime Quran* translation reverts the misinterpretation of Chapter 4 Verse 34 to the way that that Prophet understood it when it was revealed to him. English translations that pre-date *The Sublime Quran* translate the verse in question as "Husbands who fear disobedience (*nushuz*) on the part of their wives, first admonish them, then leave their sleeping places, then beat them."·

This clearly goes against the command to obey God and His Messenger, as the Prophet never beat women when faced with *nushuz* from his wives. He went away. Therefore, this first critical translation by a woman translates the relevant passage as "Husbands who fear resistance (*nushuz*) on the part of their wives, first admonish them, then abandon their sleeping places, then go away from them."†

In addition to the fact that the Prophet understood the verse to mean "go away," misinterpreting the verse not only goes against the mercy of God, but also creates a contradiction that is not present in the Quran. The importance of addressing this issue correctly in our time cannot be overstated.

The Prophet encouraged marriage and discouraged divorce. We read in Chapter 2 Verse 231 that husbands who want to divorce their wives must do so honorably. They cannot harm their wives. When we reflect on this verse in relation to Chapter 4 Verse 34, we conclude that a Muslim woman who is to be divorced cannot be harmed, but a Muslim woman who wants to remain married does so under the threat of being beaten. This clearly goes against the encouragement of marriage by the Prophet as opposed to divorce, as well as going against God's mercy that encompasses everything.

For the sake of readers who are keenly interested in the matter of translation, I will delve into this contentious matter at a depth that may give broad additional insights to those just becoming accustomed to the intricacies of Quranic study methods. The most conclusive argument in Islamic tradition to prove or disprove something is to use the Quran to prove another point in the Quran. The method is called *tafsir al-quran bi-l-quran*. This I will do. I will show how the present erroneous interpretation of 4:34 and the verb *idribuhu* creates a contradiction not in the Quran itself and denies, at least in two cases, rights that the Quran clearly gives to women.

For the Muslim, the Prophet is the living Quran; that is, he practiced exactly whatever God revealed in the Quran. If it was a command to do good (fasting, daily formal prayer, pilgrimage, purifying alms, charity), he performed these commands. If it was to prevent a wrong like drinking alcohol, gambling or eating pork, he refrained from these things. As the living Quran, the life, behavior and sayings of the Prophet serve as a model for all Muslims.

As the Quran refers to the Prophet as a mercy to humanity and the model whose example should be followed, it is clear that he would have carried out any and all of the commands (imperative forms of the verb) in the Quran that related to his life, yet we find an exception in the word *d r b*, according to the interpreters over the centuries.

---

*Quran 4:34 traditional English wording.

†Quran 4:34 in *The Sublime Quran*.

The meaning of the root letters *d r b* without any special preposition include the following: to encompass; to cast, throw or fling upon the ground; to set a barrier; to engender; to turn about; to make a sign or to point with the hand; to prohibit, prevent or hinder from doing a thing one has begun; to seek glory; to avoid or shun or leave; to turn away oneself; to be with shame; to be in a state of commotion; to be in a state between hope and fear; and to go away. The verb *daraba* appears fifty-eight times in the Quran. In only twenty-two cases does it not appear with a preposition. Of these twenty-two times, eleven times it means "to strike," four times it means "to stamp" and seven times it means something other than "to strike" or "to stamp." In 2:73 and 43:5 it means "to turn something about," in 13:17 it means "to compare," in 18:17 it means "to seal the ears," in 24:31 it means "to draw" and in 57:13 it means "to set up between." In regard to 24:31, the verse relates to the hijab or covering for women. The relevant part states, "And let them (f) draw their head coverings over their bosoms." Clearly one cannot "strike" or "beat" their head coverings over their bosoms! Therefore, in terms of linguistics, the verb *daraba,* as used in the Quran, does not always mean "to strike." It clearly does not mean that in 4:34, as the following arguments will show.

With special prepositions, *daraba fi' l- ard* means to travel; with the preposition *ala* it means to stomp; with the preposition *an* it means to turn something away; with the preposition *bayn* it means to set up between, to separate. As a verbal noun, it means striking; with the preposition *fi* it means traveling or journeying. Of the twelve times it appears as a command in the Quran, two are commands to angels in the same verse—namely, "Mention when thy Lord revealed to the angels: I am truly with you, so make those who have believed firm. I will cast alarm into the hearts of those who were ungrateful. So strike above their necks and strike each of their fingers from them" (8:12); three are followed by the word for "parable" so they become the command, "And propound to them the parable" (18:32), "And propound for them the parable" (18:45) and "And propound a parable for them" (36:13).

Four times the word appears as commands to Moses: "Strike the rock with thy staff" (2:60); "Strike the rock with thy staff" (7:160); "Then strike for them a dry road in the sea" (20:77); "Strike the sea with thy staff" (26:63). The command is given once to the Children of Israel. Here the imperative form is used as it relates to the story of the cow: "So We said: 'Strike him [the dead man] with some of it' [the cow]" (2:73). Muhammad Asad, a Jewish convert to Islam (and therefore familiar with Jewish tradition), rejects this interpretation and declares that the story as told by most interpreters is not true.

The eleventh use of the imperative form of *daraba*—namely, *idribuhu*—relates to the story of Job (Ayub) (38:44). This verse (38:44) is most often translated as "And take in thy hand a bundle of rushes and strike with it and fail not thy oath." It is clearly unspecific as to what aspect of Job's life this verse refers to. Early commentators and interpreters embellished the story from the Old Testament. There Job's faithful and long-suffering wife, Rahmah, at some point in Job's patient bearing of his afflictions, tells him to end his suffering by means of suicide. Quranic commentators said that at one time, out of desperation for money, she sold her hair in order to buy bread for Job. Satan hurried to Job to increase his grief and anguish, saying that his wife had committed adultery, and as a punishment, her hair was cut off. Once Rahmah returned to Job, Job saw her hair was cut. He became angry and swore an oath to beat her with one hundred strokes. His wife was in despair because Job, whom she dearly loved and whom she vowed she would never leave, had accused her unjustly. Once God healed Job and returned his fortune to him, Job became reluctant to carry out his oath. Muslim commentators then say that the angel Gabriel told Job of her innocence but he said that, in spite of her being innocent, Job should honor his oath by striking his wife lightly with a bundle of one hundred rushes. It does not take much for one to see how outside the pale of the Quran this story from commentators and interpreters is that Gabriel would tell Job that it was more important to carry out his oath than to beat an innocent person, even lightly. Rahmah had been the most exemplary wife. Once Job lost all of his material wealth, she did not leave him as his other two wives had done, but instead began earning money as a cleaning woman in order to be able to provide food for her husband. When others in the village found Job's state so disgusting, they were not even prepared to help Rahmah carry him to a garbage heap. Yet she remained faithful throughout his long ordeal and to be punished by a bundle of one hundred rushes for whatever a satanic force may have said that she had said or done goes against so many Quranic verses that listing them would only be tiresome to the reader!

To apply any aspect of this story as rationalization for *idribuhu* in 4:34 being interpreted as "beat" (lightly) goes against the rest of the verse for another reason as well. The first statement in 4:34 is that husbands are supporters of their wives because God has given some of them an advantage over others and because they shared their wealth. In the case of Job, his wife Rahmah was the support of the family, so the rest does not qualify Job to be able to "beat" his wife, even "lightly." That is strong enough in argument to be the basis for some commentators to suggest that Job was supposedly told to strike his wife lightly in order not to fail his oath, whereas 5:89 says that God "will not take you to task for what is unintentional in your oaths," or Job could have chosen the more humane way and paid an expiation for an oath that he could not fulfill. In addition, the root letters of *h n th* in the first form mean not only "fail not in your oath," but also, according to *Taj al-Arus*, "to retract or revoke one's oath." As we have seen, the root letters *d r b* also mean to cast, throw or fling to the ground, so the verse can be translated as "And take in thy hand a bundle of rushes and cast them upon the ground and retract thy oath." Therefore it is a misinterpretation for commentators to use the story of Job and his faithful wife in any sort of justification for a husband to beat his wife, even lightly. In *The Old Testament: An Islamic Perspective*, Jay R. Crook (Muhammad Nur) adds in conclusion to this story, "Nevertheless there will always remain a suspicion that the original oral tradition (of the story of Rahmah and Job) was lost or distorted and the later Muslim commentators, unable to retrieve it, adopted the story of Job's wife from the later Jewish Job cycle to meet their exegetic needs."

The twelfth usage of *d r b* in the imperative form is in 4:34, allowing husbands to "strike, beat, hit, chastise or spank" a *nushuz* wife. Yet in all of the canonical works there is no reference to Prophet Muhammad, peace and the mercy of God be upon him, having ever beaten women. It is the misinterpretation of the word *idribuhu* in 4:34 that this translation challenges, emphasizing that this misinterpretation must revert back to the way the Prophet understood it through his behavior when facing the exact same situation. Therefore, mine is not a personal interpretation but one that calls for the elevation of the Prophet and a return to the Sunnah.

The misinterpretation is not in the Arabic of the Quran, the eternal Word of God revealed to Prophet Muhammad, peace and the mercy of God be upon him, but it is how commentators over the centuries have interpreted the Word of God that is at issue. The issue of beating a wife has not been declared criminal as it should have been. It is clearly a criminal act to beat another person and an expiation is required for having done so. This has not been the interpretation of jurists over the centuries in regard to 4:34 as it should have been.

We have to ask ourselves, why did the Prophet not beat his wives, if it was a command in the Quran? First of all, when the verse was revealed to him, it appears from his behavior in the same type of situation that he did not consider it to mean "beat them" referring to his wives. This might possibly be because the Quran uses three other words for strike or beat—namely, in 28:15, 38:41 and 51:29. In 28:15 Moses struck a young man with his fist. The root letters are not *d r b*, which we know also means "to strike," but *w k z*. In the case of 38:44, the command to Job to stomp his foot, the root letters used are *r k d* and not *d r b*, which can also mean "to stamp" or "to stomp." In 51:29, when Sarah, the wife of Abraham, was told she would have a child, she struck, slapped or smote her face on purpose, the root letters being *s k k* and not *d r b*, which, as has been stated, also means "to strike" or "to smite." Therefore, just as other Arabic words may mean "to strike," so the root letters *d r b* may mean other than "to strike"—that is, "to go away" or "to separate." Based on his character, a model for all of humanity, he knew innately that it was wrong to harm another human being.

Second, he knew that according to 16:126 one is commanded to chastise with the same chastisement that that person has been given. "And if you chastise (*aqaba*) then chastise with the like of that with which you were chastised" (16:126), a verse actually revealed before 4:34 so that the Prophet would have been aware of it when 4:34 was revealed. Therefore, conceivably, if a husband harms his wife by beating her, according to 16:126, his wife would be allowed to chastise her husband in return. The Prophet would have intuitively known that if a husband were to beat his wife, she could reciprocate to her husband. He clearly believed that it was not within his Sunnah to do such a thing. Therefore, he showed by his behavior that 4:34 and the use of the word *daraba* means "go away from them" or "leave them" and let the emotions subside.

Third, the Prophet's respect for the female gender was legendary. This included not only his wives, the mothers of the believers, but his daughters as well. He had a very special relationship with his daughter Fatima, the only one of his daughters to survive him. How could he beat his wives and not consider that someone might beat one of his beloved daughters?

Fourth, the Prophet knew that marriage was based on mutual respect and love. The Quran often tells husbands and wives to consult on issues with each other. It would be unfair and unjust to think that God would have revealed a verse that allowed husbands to beat their wives instead of separating for a short period of time and allowing the anger to subside. Then they would be able to once again consult with one another.

Therefore, anyone who claims to follow the Sunnah of the Prophet must do the same thing, because the Sunnah of the Prophet is not to scourge, beat, hit, hurt, spank or chastise any woman. The word *idribuhu* is a command, an imperative form of the verb, yet a command the Prophet did not carry out if it means "beat them (f)." However, he did carry it out when it means "go away from them (f)."

I have often been asked, "How can you go against the tradition and over 1,400 years of commentary?" My response is, if we study Islamic history after the time of the four Rightly Guided Caliphs, we Muslims have had almost 1,500 years of uninterrupted rule by tyrants and dictators (with the exception of a few years of a pious ruler*). Does that mean that we cannot go against history and demand pious, benevolent rulers? No, of course not, as we see by the positive changes in governance taking place in many Muslim countries in the twenty-first century for the first time. The minute any individual member of the Muslim community or *ummah* gains consciousness of a wrong being done in the name of God, he or she has the responsibility to speak out in the name of Islam. I ask for the forgiveness of the One God for any errors in this translation, at the same time that I ask for His blessings.

God knows best.

Laleh Bakhtiar

---

*Caliph Umar ibn abd al-Aziz, 717–720 CE.

the sublime quran

*In the Name of God, The Merciful, The Compassionate.*¹ᐟ¹

The Praise belongs to God, Lord of the worlds,¹ᐟ²
The Merciful, The Compassionate,¹ᐟ³
One Who is Sovereign of the Day of Judgment.¹ᐟ⁴
Thee alone we worship and to Thee alone we pray
    for help.¹ᐟ⁵
Guide us on the straight path,¹ᐟ⁶
the path of those to whom Thou wert gracious, not
    the ones against whom Thou art angry, nor the
    ones who go astray.¹ᐟ⁷

CHAPTER 2 THE COW

In the Name of God, The Merciful, The Compassionate
*Alif Lām Mīm.*²ᐟ¹

That is the Book—there is no doubt ^in it^, a guidance for the ones who are Godfearing:²ᐟ² Those who believe in the unseen²ᐟ³ and perform the formal prayer, and they spend out of what We provided them, and those who believe in what was caused to descend to thee, and what was caused to descend before thee, and they are certain of the world to come.²ᐟ⁴ Those are on a guidance from their Lord and those, they are the ones who prosper.²ᐟ⁵

Truly, as for those who were ungrateful, it is the same to them whether thou hadst warned them or thou hast warned them not. They believe not.²ᐟ⁶ God sealed over their hearts and over their inner hearing and a blindfold over their inner sight. And there is a tremendous punishment for them.²ᐟ⁷

And among humanity are some who say: We believed in God and in the Last Day, and yet they are not ones who believe.²ᐟ⁸ They seek to trick God and those who believed while they deceive none but themselves, but they are not aware.²ᐟ⁹ In their hearts is a sickness. Then, God increased them in sickness, and for them is a painful punishment because they had been lying against themselves.²ᐟ¹⁰

And when it was said to them not to make corruption in and on the earth, they said: Truly, we are only ones who make things right.²ᐟ¹¹ No doubt they, they are the ones who make corruption except they are not aware.²ᐟ¹²

And when it was said to them: Believe as humanity believed, they said: Will we believe as the fools believed? No! Truly, they, they are the fools, except they know not.²ᐟ¹³

And when they met those who believed, they said: We believed. And when they went privately to their satans, they said: Truly, we are with you. We were only ones who ridicule. ²ᐟ¹⁴

God ridicules them and causes them to increase in their defiance, to wander unwilling to see.²ᐟ¹⁵ Those are those who bought fallacy for guidance, so their trade was not bettered nor had they been ones who are truly guided.²ᐟ¹⁶

Their parable is like a parable of those who started a fire. Then, when it illuminated what was around it, God took away their light and left them in shadows where they perceive not.²ᐟ¹⁷ Unwilling to hear, unwilling to speak, unwilling to see, then, they will not return to the way.²ᐟ¹⁸

Or as a cloudburst from heaven in which there are shadows and thunder and lightning. They lay their fingertips in their ears from the thunderbolt, being fearful of death. And God is One Who Encloses the ones who are ungrateful.²ᐟ¹⁹ The lightning almost snatches their sight. When it illuminated

for them, they walked in the light. And when it grew dark against them, they stood still.

And if God willed, He would have taken away their having the ability to hear and their sight. Truly, God is Powerful over everything.²ᐟ²⁰

O humanity! Worship your Lord Who created you and those who were before you so that perhaps you will be Godfearing.²ᐟ²¹ It is He Who assigned the earth for you as a place of restfulness and the heaven as a canopy. And He caused water to descend from heaven and from it drove out fruit of trees as provision for you. Then, assign not rivals to God while you, you know.²ᐟ²²

And if you had been in doubt about what We sent down to Our servant, then approach with a chapter of the Quran—the like of it—and call to your witnesses other than God if you had been ones who are sincere.²ᐟ²³ And if you accomplish it not—and you will never accomplish it—then be Godfearing of the fire whose fuel is humanity and rocks, prepared for the ones who are ungrateful.²ᐟ²⁴

And give good tidings to those who believed and did as the ones in accord with morality, that for them will be Gardens beneath which rivers run. Whenever they were provided from there of its fruit as provision they would say: This is what we were provided before. And they will be brought it—ones that resemble one another—and in it for them will be purified spouses. And they are ones who will dwell in them forever!²ᐟ²⁵

Truly, God is not ashamed that He propound a parable, even of a gnat or whatever is above it. So as for those who believed, then, they know that it is The Truth from their Lord, but those who were ungrateful, then they will say: What did God mean by this parable?

He causes many to go astray by it and He guides many by it. And He causes none to go astray by it, but the ones who disobey—²ᐟ²⁶ those who break the compact of God after a solemn promise and sever what God commanded that it be joined and make corruption in and on the earth. Those, they are the ones who are losers!²ᐟ²⁷

How is it you are ungrateful to God? You had been lifeless, then, He gave you life. again, He will cause you to die. Again, He will give you life. And, again, you are returned to Him.²ᐟ²⁸

It is He Who created for you all that is in and on the earth. Again, He turned His attention to the heaven. Then, He shaped them into seven heavens. And He is Knowing of everything.²ᐟ²⁹

And when thy Lord said to the angels: Truly, I am assigning on the earth a vicegerent. They said: Wilt Thou be One Who Makes on it someone who makes corruption on it and sheds blood, while we glorify Thy praise and sanctify Thee? He said: Truly, I know what you know not!²ᐟ³⁰

And He taught Adam the names, all of them. Again, He presented them to the angels and said: Communicate to Me the names of these if you had been ones who are sincere.²ᐟ³¹

They said: Glory be to Thee! We have no knowledge but what Thou hadst taught us. Truly, Thou, Thou alone art The Knowing, The Wise.²ᐟ³²

He said: O Adam! Communicate to them their names. So then, when he communicated to them their names, He said: Did I not say to you: Truly, I know the unseen of the heavens and the earth, and I know what you show and what you had been keeping back.²ᐟ³³

And mention when We said to the angels: Prostrate yourselves to Adam! They, then, prostrated themselves but Iblis. He refused and grew arrogant. He had been among the ones who are ungrateful.²·³⁴

And We said: O Adam! Inhabit the Garden, thou and thy spouse: Eat freely from it both of you wherever you both willed, but come not near this, the tree or you both will be among the ones who are unjust.²·³⁵

Then, Satan caused both of them to slide back from there and drove both of them out from that in which they both had been.

And We said: Get down some of you as an enemy to some other. And for you on the earth, a time appointed and sustenance for awhile.²·³⁶

Adam, then, received words from his Lord for He turned to him in forgiveness. Truly, He, He is The Accepter of Repentance, The Compassionate.²·³⁷

We said: Get down altogether from it. And whenever guidance approaches you from Me, then, whoever heeded My guidance, then, there will be neither fear in them nor will they feel remorse.²·³⁸

But those who were ungrateful and denied Our signs, those will be the Companions of the Fire. They are ones who will dwell in it forever!²·³⁹

O Children of Israel! Remember My divine blessing with which I was gracious to you and live up to the compact with Me. I will live up to the compact with you. And have reverence for Me alone.²·⁴⁰

And believe in what I caused to descend, that which establishes as true what is with you. And be not the first one who is ungrateful for it. And exchange not My signs for a little price. And fear Me, God, alone.²·⁴¹

And confuse not The Truth with falsehood nor keep back The Truth while you know.²·⁴²

And perform the formal prayer, and give the purifying alms, and bow down with the ones who bow down.²·⁴³

You command humanity to virtuous conduct and forget yourselves while you relate the Book? Will you not, then, be reasonable?²·⁴⁴

And pray for help with patience and formal prayer. And, truly, it is arduous, but for the ones who are humble,²·⁴⁵ those who bear in mind that, truly, they, they will be ones who encounter their Lord and that to Him they will be ones who return.²·⁴⁶

O Children of Israel! Remember My divine blessing with which I was gracious to you, and that I gave advantage to you over the worlds.²·⁴⁷ And be Godfearing of a Day when no soul will give recompense for another soul at all, nor will intercession be accepted from it nor an equivalent be taken from it nor will they be helped.²·⁴⁸

And mention when We delivered you from the people of Pharaoh who cause an affliction to befall you of a dire punishment. They slaughter your children and save alive your women. And in that there is a tremendous trial from your Lord.²·⁴⁹

And mention when We separated the sea for you, and We rescued you, and We drowned the people of Pharaoh while you look on.²·⁵⁰

And mention when We appointed for Moses forty nights. Again, you took the calf to yourselves after him and you were ones who are unjust.²·⁵¹ Again, We pardoned you after that, so that perhaps you will give thanks.²·⁵²

And mention when We gave Moses the Book, and the Criterion between right and wrong, so that perhaps you will be truly guided.²·⁵³

And mention when Moses said to his folk: O my folk! Truly, you did wrong to yourselves by your taking the calf

to yourselves to worship, so repent to One Who is your Fashioner and kill yourselves. That would be better for you with One Who is your Fashioner. Then He will turn to you in forgiveness. Truly, He, He is The Accepter of Repentance, The Compassionate.²·⁵⁴

And mention when you said: O Moses! We will never believe thee until we see God publicly. So the thunderbolt took you while you look on.²·⁵⁵ Again, We will raise you up after your death so that perhaps you will give thanks. ²·⁵⁶ And We shaded over you cloud shadows. We caused to descend to you the manna and the quails. Eat of what is good that We provided you. And they did not wrong Us. Rather, they had been doing wrong to themselves.²·⁵⁷

And mention when We said: Enter this town, then, eat freely from it whatever you willed, and enter the door as one who prostrates oneself and say: Unburden us of sin! We will forgive you your transgressions. And We will increase the ones who are doers of good.²·⁵⁸

Then, those who did wrong substituted another saying—other than what was said to them—so We caused to descend on those who did wrong wrath from heaven, because they had been disobeying.²·⁵⁹

And mention when Moses asked for water for his folk. Then, We said: Strike the rock with thy staff. Then, twelve springs ran out from it. Every clan knew their drinking place. Eat and drink from the provision of God, and do no mischief in and on the earth as ones who make corruption.²·⁶⁰

And mention when you said: O Moses! We will never endure patiently with one kind of food, so call to thy Lord for us to drive out for us of what the earth is bringing forth of its green herbs and its cucumbers and its garlic and its lentils and its onions.

Moses said: Would you have in exchange what is lesser for what is higher? Get down to a settled country. Then, truly for you is what you asked for.

And stamped on them were abasement and wretchedness. And they drew the burden of anger from God. That was because they had been ungrateful for the signs of God, and kill the Prophets without right. That, because they rebelled, and they had been exceeding the limits.²·⁶¹

Truly, those who believed, and those who became Jews, and the Christians and the Sabeans, whoever believed in God and the Last Day and did as one in accord with morality, then, for them, their compensation is with their Lord. And there will be neither fear in them nor will they feel remorse.²·⁶²

And when We took your solemn promise, and We exalted the mount above you: Take what We gave you with firmness, and remember what is in it, so that perhaps you will be Godfearing. ²·⁶³

Again, after that you turned away, and if it were not for the grace of God on you, and His mercy certainly, you would have been among the ones who are losers.²·⁶⁴

And, certainly, you knew those who exceeded the limits among you on the Sabbath, to whom We said: Be you apes, ones who are driven away.²·⁶⁵ Then, We made this an exemplary punishment for the former of them, and of succeeding generations, and an admonishment for the ones who are Godfearing.²·⁶⁶

And mention when Moses said to his folk: Truly, God commands that you sacrifice a cow.

They said: Hast thou taken us to thyself in mockery?

He said: I take refuge with God that I be among the ones who are ignorant!²·⁶⁷

They said: Call to thy Lord for us to make manifest to us what she is!

Moses said: Truly, He says: She should be a cow that is neither old nor virgin—middle-aged between them—so accomplish what you are commanded.²·⁶⁸ They said: Call to thy Lord for us to make manifest to us what hue she is.

He said: Truly, He says: She is a saffron-colored cow—one that is bright in hue—that makes the ones who look on her joyous.²·⁶⁹

They said: Call to thy Lord for us to make manifest to us what she is. Truly, cows resembled one another to us, and, truly, if God willed we would be ones who are truly guided.²·⁷⁰

He said: Truly, He says she is a cow neither broken to plow the earth, nor to draw water for cultivation, that which is to be handed over without blemish on her.

They said: Now thou hadst brought about The Truth. So they sacrificed her, and they almost accomplish it not.²·⁷¹

And mention when you killed a soul, then, you put up an argument over it. And God was One Who Drives Out what you had been keeping back.²·⁷²

So We said: Turn him away with some of it!

Thus, God gives life to the dead, and He causes you to see His signs, so that perhaps you will be reasonable.²·⁷³

Again, after that, your hearts became hard, so that they were as rocks or harder in hardness. And, truly, from the rocks there are some that the rivers gush forth from it. And, truly, there are some that split open so water goes forth from it. And, truly, some, that from it get down from dreading God. And God is not One Who is Heedless of what you do.²·⁷⁴

Are you desirous that they believe in you? Surely, a group of people among them had been hearing the assertion of God. Yet again, they tamper with it after they were reasonable, and they know?²·⁷⁵

And when they met those who believed, they said: We believed. And when they went privately—some of them with some others—they said: Will you divulge to them what God opened to you, so that they argue with you about it before your Lord? Will you not, then, be reasonable?²·⁷⁶

Know they not that God knows what they keep secret, and what they speak openly.²·⁷⁷

And among them are the unlettered who know nothing of the Book but fantasy. And, truly, they but surmise.²·⁷⁸

And woe to those who write down the Book with their own hands.

Again, they say: This is from God.

Certainly, they exchange it for a little price. Then, woe to them for what their hands wrote down. And woe to them for what they earn!²·⁷⁹

And they said: The fire will never touch us, but for numbered days.

Say: Took you to yourselves a compact from God?

If so, God never breaks His compact; or say you about God what you know not?²·⁸⁰

Yea! Whoever earned an evil deed and is enclosed by his transgression, then those will be the Companions of the Fire. They are ones who will dwell in it forever!²·⁸¹

And those who believed and did as the ones in accord with morality, those will be the Companions of the Garden. They, ones who will dwell in it forever!²·⁸²

And mention when We took a solemn promise from the Children of Israel not to worship other than God, and goodness to the ones who are your parents and to the possessors of kinship and the orphans and the needy. And speak with kindness to humanity. And perform the formal prayer, and give the purifying alms.

Again, you turned away but a few among you. You are ones who turn aside.²·⁸³

And mention when We took your solemn promise: You will not shed your blood, nor drive yourselves out from your abodes.

Again, you were in accord and you, you bear witness.²·⁸⁴

Again, you are these—killing yourselves, and driving out a group of people among you from their abodes, to support one another against them in sin and deep seated dislike. And if they approach you as prisoners of war, you redeem them, although expelling them is that which is forbidden to you. Then, believe you in some of the Book, and are ungrateful for some? Then, what will be the recompense of whoever commits that among you, but degradation in this present life? And on the Day of Resurrection, they will be returned to the hardest punishment. And God is not One Who is Heedless of what you do.²·⁸⁵

Those are those who bought this present life for the world to come, so the punishment on them will not be lightened, nor will they be helped.²·⁸⁶

And, certainly, We gave Moses the Book and We sent Messengers following after him. And We gave Jesus son of Mary the clear portents, and confirmed him with the hallowed Spirit. Is it that whenever a Messenger drew near you with what you yourselves yearn not for, you grew arrogant, and you denied a group of people, and you kill a group of people?²·⁸⁷

And they said: Our hearts are encased! Nay! God cursed them for their ingratitude, so little is what they believe!²·⁸⁸

Mention when a Book from God drew near them, that which establishes as true what was with them—and before that they had been asking for victory over those who were ungrateful—so when drew near them what they recognized, they were ungrateful for it. Then, the curse of God is on the ones who are ungrateful!²·⁸⁹

Miserable was that for which they sold out themselves for it, that they are ungrateful for what God caused to descend, resenting that God sends down of His grace on whom He wills of His servants. They drew the burden of anger on anger. And for the ones who are ungrateful, there is a despised punishment.²·⁹⁰

And when it was said to them to believe in what God caused to descend, they said: We believe in what was caused to descend to us.

And they are ungrateful for what is beyond it, while it is The Truth, that which establishes as true what is with them. Say: Why, then, kill you the Prophets of God before if you had been ones who believe?²·⁹¹

And, certainly, Moses drew near you with the clear portents. Again, you took the calf to yourselves after him. And you are ones who are unjust.²·⁹²

And mention when We took your solemn promise, and We exalted the mount above you: Take what We gave you with firmness and hear. They said: We heard and we rebelled, and they were steeped with love for the calf in their hearts because of their ingratitude.

Say: Miserable was what commands you to it of your belief if you had been ones who believe.²·⁹³

Say: If the Last Abode for you had been with God—that which is exclusively for you—excluding others of humanity—then, covet death if you had been ones who are sincere.²·⁹⁴

And they never covet it ever because of what their hands put forward, and God is Knowing of the ones who are unjust.²·⁹⁵

And, certainly, thou wilt find them to be eager among humanity for this life, even of those who ascribed partners with God. Each one of them wishes that he be given a long life of a thousand years, yet he still would not be one who is drawn away from the punishment, even if he be given a long life, and God is Seeing of what they do.²·⁹⁶

Say: Whoever had been an enemy of Gabriel knows then, truly, it was sent down through him to thy heart with the permission of God, that which establishes as true what was before it, and as a guidance and good tidings for the ones who believe.²·⁹⁷

Whoever had been an enemy of God and His angels, and His Messengers and Gabriel and Michael, then, truly, God is an enemy of the ones who are ungrateful.²⁹⁸

And, certainly, We caused to descend to thee signs, clear portents. And none are ungrateful for them, but the ones who disobey.²⁹⁹

Is it not that whenever they made a contract—a compact—a group of people among them repudiated it? Nay! Most of them believe not.²¹⁰⁰

And when a Messenger drew near them from God—one who establishes as true what was with them—a group of people repudiated among those who were given the Book, the Book of God—behind their backs as if they had not been knowing that it was God's Book.²¹⁰¹

And they followed what the satans recount during the dominion of Solomon. And Solomon was not ungrateful, except the satans were ungrateful. They teach humanity sorcery, and what was caused to descend to the two angels at Babylon—Harut and Marut. But neither of these two teach anyone unless they say: We are only a test, so be not ungrateful. And they learn from these two that by it they separate and divide between a man and his spouse. And they were not ones who injured anyone with it, but by the permission of God. And they learn what hurts them and profits them not. And, certainly, they knew that whoever bought it, for him in the world to come was not any apportionment. And miserable was that for which they sold themselves. Would that they had been knowing!²¹⁰²

And if they believed and were Godfearing, certainly, their place of spiritual reward from God was better. Would that they had been knowing!²¹⁰³

O those who believed! Say not: Look at us, but say: Wait for us patiently and hear. And for the ones who are ungrateful, there is a painful punishment.²¹⁰⁴ Neither wish those who were ungrateful from among the People of the Book, nor the ones who are polytheists that any good be sent down to you from your Lord. And God singles out for His mercy whom He wills. And God is Possessor of the Sublime Grace.²¹⁰⁵

For whatever sign We nullify or cause it to be forgotten, We bring better than it, or similar to it. Hast thou not known that God is Powerful over everything?²¹⁰⁶ Hast thou not known that God, to Him is the dominion of the heavens and the earth, and not for you other than God is there either a protector or a helper?²¹⁰⁷

Or want you that you ask your Messenger as Moses was asked before? And whoever takes disbelief in exchange for belief, then, surely, he went astray from the right way.²¹⁰⁸

Many of the People of the Book wished that after your belief they return you to being one who is ungrateful out of jealousy within themselves even after The Truth became clear to them. So pardon and overlook until God brings His command. Truly, God is Powerful over everything.²¹⁰⁹

And perform the formal prayer and give the purifying alms. And whatever good you put forward for yourselves, you will find it with God. Truly, God is Seeing of what you do.²¹¹⁰

And they said: None will enter the Garden, but ones who had been Jews or Christians. That is their own fantasies. Say: Prepare your proof if you had been ones who are sincere.²¹¹¹ Yea! Whoever submitted his face to God, and he is one who is a doer of good, then, for him his compensation is with his Lord. And there will be neither fear in them, nor will they feel remorse.²²¹²

And the Jews said: The Christians are not based on anything. And the Christians said: The Jews are not based on anything, although they both recount the Book. Thus, said those who know not a thing like their saying. So God will give judgment between them on the Day of Resurrection about what they had been at variance in it.²¹¹³

And who does greater wrong than those who prevented access to the places of prostration to God so that His Name not be remembered in them, and endeavored for their devastation? It had not been for those to enter them, but as ones who are fearful. For them is degradation in the present, and for them is a tremendous punishment in the world to come.²¹¹⁴

And to God belongs the East and the West. So wherever you turn to, then, again, there is the Countenance of God. Truly, God is One Who is Extensive, Knowing.²¹¹⁵

And they said: God took to Himself a son. Glory be to Him! Nay! To Him belongs whatever is in the heavens and the earth. All are ones who are morally obligated to Him,²¹¹⁶ Beginner of the heavens and the earth and when He decreed a command, then, truly, He says to it: Be! Then, it is!²¹¹⁷

And those who know not said: Why does God not speak to us or a sign approach us?

Thus, said those who were before them like their saying. Their hearts resembled one another. Surely, We made manifest the signs for a folk who are certain.²¹¹⁸

Truly, We sent thee with The Truth as a bearer of good tidings and as a warner. And thou wilt not be asked about the Companions of Hellfire.²¹¹⁹

The Jews will never be well-pleased with thee, nor the Christians until thou hast followed their creed. Say: Truly, guidance of God. It is the guidance. And if thou hadst followed their desires after what drew near thee of the knowledge, there is not for thee from God either a protector or a helper.²¹²⁰

Those to whom We gave the Book recount it with a true recounting. Those believe in it, and whoever is ungrateful for it, then, those, they are the ones who are losers.²¹²¹

O Children of Israel! Remember My divine blessing with which I was gracious to you, and that I gave you an advantage over the worlds.²¹²²

And be Godfearing of a Day when no soul will give recompense for another soul at all, nor will the equivalent be accepted from it, nor will intercession profit it, nor will they be helped.²¹²³

And mention when his Lord tested Abraham with words; then, he fulfilled them.

God said: Truly, I am One Who Makes thee a leader for humanity.

He said: And of my offspring?

He said: Attain not My compact the ones who are unjust.²¹²⁴

And mention when We made the House a place of spiritual reward for humanity and a place of sanctuary: And take the Station of Abraham to yourselves as a place of prayer. And We made a compact with Abraham, and Ishmael saying that: Purify My House for the ones who circumambulate it, and the ones who cleave to it, and the ones who bow down, and the ones who prostrate themselves.²¹²⁵

And mention when Abraham said: My Lord! Make this a safe land, and provide its people with fruits, whomever of them believed in God and the Last Day.

God said: And whoever is ungrateful, I will give him enjoyment for awhile. Again, I will compel him to the punishment of the fire. And miserable will be the Homecoming!²¹²⁶

And mention when Abraham elevates the foundations of the House with Ishmael saying: Our Lord! Receive it from us. Truly, Thou, Thou alone art The Hearing, The Knowing.²¹²⁷ Our Lord! And make us ones who submit to Thee, and, of our offspring, a community of ones who submit to Thee. And cause us to see our devotional acts, and turn to us in forgiveness. Truly, Thou, Thou alone art The Accepter of Repentance, The Compassionate.²¹²⁸ Our Lord! And raise Thou up, then, in the midst of them, a Messenger from among them who will recount to them Thy signs and teach them the Book, and wisdom and make them pure. Truly, Thou, Thou alone art The Almighty, The Wise.²:¹²⁹

And who shrinks from the creed of Abraham, but he who fooled himself? And, certainly, We favored him in the present. And, truly, in the world to come he will be among the ones in accord with morality.²:¹³⁰

When his Lord said to him: Submit! He said: I submitted to the Lord of the worlds.²:¹³¹

And Abraham charged his children to it, and Jacob: O my children! Truly, God favored the way of life for you. Then, be not overtaken by death but you be ones who submit to the One God. ²:¹³²

Or had you been witnesses when death attended Jacob when he said to his children: How will you worship after me?

They said: We will worship thy God and the God of thy fathers—Abraham and Ishmael and Isaac—One God. And we are ones who submit to Him.²:¹³³

That was, surely, a community that passed away. For them is what they earned, and for you is what you earned and you will not be asked about what they had been doing.²:¹³⁴

And they said: Be you ones who are Jews or Christians, you will be truly guided.

Say thou: Nay! We follow the creed of Abraham a monotheist. And he had not been of the ones who are polytheists.²:¹³⁵

Say: We believed in God and what was caused to descend to us, and what was caused to descend to Abraham and Ishmael and Isaac and Jacob and the Tribes and whatever was given Moses and Jesus, and whatever was given to the Prophets from their Lord. We separate and divide not between anyone of them. And we are ones who submit to Him.²:¹³⁶

So if they believed the like of what you believed in it, then, surely, they were truly guided. And if they turned away, then, they are not but in breach. So God suffices for you against them. And He is The Hearing, The Knowing.²:¹³⁷

Life's color is from God. And who is fairer at coloring than God? And we are ones who worship Him.²:¹³⁸

Say: Argue you with us about God? And He is our Lord and your Lord. And to us are our actions, and to you are your actions. And we are to Him ones who are sincere and devoted.²:¹³⁹

Or say you about Abraham and Ishmael and Isaac and Jacob and the Tribes had been ones who are Jews or Christians?

Say: Are you greater in knowledge or God?

And who does greater wrong than he who had been keeping back testimony from God that is with him, and God is not One Who is Heedless of what you do.²:¹⁴⁰

That is a community that surely passed away; for it is what it earned and for you is what you earned and you will not be asked about what they had been doing.²:¹⁴¹

The fools among humanity say: What turned them from their direction of formal prayer to which they had been towards?

Say: To God belongs the East and the West. He guides whom He wills to a straight path.²:¹⁴²

And, thus, We made you a middle community that you be witnesses to humanity, and that the Messenger be a witness to you. And We made not the direction of the formal prayer which thou hadst been towards but that We make evident whoever follows the Messenger from him who turns about on his two heels. And, truly, it had been grave, but for those whom God guided. And God had not been wasting your belief. Truly, God is Gentle toward humanity, Compassionate.²:¹⁴³

Surely, We see the going to and fro of thy face toward heaven. Then, We will turn thee to a direction of formal prayer that thou wilt be well-pleased with it. Then, turn thy face to the direction of the Masjid al-Haram. And wherever you had been, turn your faces to its direction. And, truly,

those who were given the Book know that it is The Truth from their Lord, and God is not One Who is Heedless of what they do.²:¹⁴⁴

And even if thou wert to bring to those who were given the Book every sign, they would not heed thy direction of formal prayer. Nor art thou one who heeds their direction of formal prayer. Nor are some of them ones who heed the direction of the other's formal prayer. And if thou hadst followed their desires after the knowledge brought about to thee, then, truly, thou wouldst be among the ones who are unjust.²:¹⁴⁵

Those to whom We gave the Book recognize it as they recognize their children, while, truly, a group of people among them keep back The Truth while they know²:¹⁴⁶ it is The Truth from their Lord. So be thou not among the ones who contest.²:¹⁴⁷

And everyone has a direction to that which he turns. Be forward, then, in good deeds. Wherever you be, God will bring you altogether for the Judgment. Truly, God is Powerful over everything.²:¹⁴⁸ And from wherever thou hadst gone forth, then, turn thy face in the direction of the Masjid al-Haram. And, truly, this is The Truth from thy Lord, and God is not One Who is Heedless of what you do.²:¹⁴⁹ And from wherever thou hadst gone forth, then, turn thy face to the direction of the Masjid al-Haram. And wherever you had been, then, turn your faces to the direction of it so that there be no disputation from humanity against you, but from those of them who did wrong. Dread them not, then, but dread Me.

And I fulfill My divine blessing on you—so that perhaps you will be truly guided—²:¹⁵⁰ as We sent to you a Messenger from among you who recounts Our signs to you, and makes you pure, and teaches you the Book and wisdom, and teaches you what you be knowing not.²:¹⁵¹ So remember Me and I will remember you. And give thanks to Me, and be not ungrateful!²:¹⁵²

O those who believed! Pray for help with patience and formal prayer. Truly, God is with the ones who remain steadfast.²:¹⁵³

And say not about those who are slain in the way of God: They are lifeless. Nay! They are living, except you are not aware ²:¹⁵⁴

We will, certainly, try you with something of fear and hunger and diminution of wealth and lives and fruits, and give good tidings to the ones who remain steadfast,²:¹⁵⁵ those who, when an affliction lit on them, they said: Truly, we belong to God and, truly, we are ones who return to Him.²:¹⁵⁶ Those, blessings will be sent on them from their Lord and mercy. And those, they are the ones who are truly guided.²:¹⁵⁷

Truly, Safa and Marwa are among the Waymarks of God, so whoever made the pilgrimage to Makkah to the House or visited the Kabah, then, there is no blame on him that he circumambulates between the two. And whoever volunteered good, then, truly, God is One Who is Responsive, Knowing.²:¹⁵⁸

Truly, those who keep back what We caused to descend of the clear portents and the guidance, after We made it manifest to humanity in the Book—those, God curses them and the ones who curse, curse them.²:¹⁵⁹

But those who repented, and made things right, and made things manifest, then, those—I will turn to them in forgiveness. And I am The Accepter of Repentance, The Compassionate.²:¹⁶⁰

Truly, those who were ungrateful, and they died and they were ones who are ungrateful, those, on them is a curse of God, and the angels and humanity, one and all.²:¹⁶¹ They are ones who will dwell in it forever. The punishment will not be lightened for them nor will they be given respite.²:¹⁶²

And your God is One God. There is no god but He, The Merciful, The Compassionate.²:¹⁶³

Truly, in the creation of the heavens and the earth and the alteration of the nighttime and the daytime and the boats that run on the sea with what profits humanity, and what God caused to descend from heaven of water, and gave life to the earth after its death, and disseminated on it all moving creatures, and diversified the winds and the clouds, ones caused to be subservient between heaven and earth, are the signs for a folk who are reasonable.²:¹⁶⁴

Yet there are among humanity some who take to themselves rivals besides God. They love them like they should cherish God. And those who believed are stauncher in cherishing God.

And if only those who did wrong would consider when they will see the punishment that all strength belongs to God, and that God is Severe in punishment.²:¹⁶⁵ When they will clear themselves—those who were followed from those who followed them—and they will see the punishment, all cords will be cut asunder from them.²:¹⁶⁶

Those who were followed said: If there be a return again for us, then, we would clear ourselves from them as they cleared themselves from us. Thus, God will cause them to see their actions with regret for them, and they will never be ones who go forth from the fire.²:¹⁶⁷

O humanity! Eat of what is in and on the earth—lawful, wholesome—and follow not the steps of the Satan. Truly, he is a clear enemy to you.²:¹⁶⁸ Truly, he commands you to evil and depravity, and that you say about God what you know not.²:¹⁶⁹

And when it was said to them: Follow what God caused to descend. They said: Nay! We will follow whatever we discovered our fathers were following on it—even though their fathers had been not at all reasonable—nor are they truly guided.²:¹⁷⁰

And the parable of those who were ungrateful is like the parable of those who shout to what hears not, but a crying out and pleading yet those to which they call out to are deaf, dumb and blind, so they are not reasonable.²:¹⁷¹

O those who believed! Eat of what is good that We provided you and give thanks to God if it had been He alone whom you worship.²:¹⁷²

Truly, He forbade carrion for you and blood and the flesh of swine and what was hallowed to any other than God, but whoever was driven by necessity, without being one who is willfully disobedient, and not one who turns away, then, it is not a sin for him. Truly, God is Forgiving, Compassionate.²:¹⁷³

Truly, those who keep back what God caused of the Book to descend, and exchange it for a little price, those, they consume not into their bellies but fire. God will not speak to them on the Day of Resurrection nor will He make them pure. And for them will be a painful punishment.²:¹⁷⁴ Those are those who bought fallacy for guidance and punishment for forgiveness. So how they are ones who remain steadfast for the fire!²:¹⁷⁵

That is because God sent down the Book with The Truth and, truly, those who were at variance regarding the Book are in a wide breach.²:¹⁷⁶

It is not virtuous conduct that you turn your faces towards the East or the West. Rather, virtuous conduct consists of: Whoever believed in God and the Last Day and the angels and the Book and the Prophets. And whoever gave wealth out of cherishing Him to the possessors of kinship and to the orphans and to the needy and to the traveler of the way and to the one who begs and the freeing of a bondsperson, and whoever performed the formal prayer, and gave the purifying alms, and the ones who live up to their compact when they made a contract, and the ones who remain steadfast in desolation and tribulation and at the time of danger, those are those who were sincere and those, they are the ones who are Godfearing!²:¹⁷⁷

O those who believed! Reciprocation was prescribed for you for the slain: the freeman for the freeman and the servant for the servant and the female for the female. But whoever was forgiven a thing by his brother, the pursuing be as one who is honorable, and the remuneration be with kindness. That is a lightening from your Lord, and a mercy. And he who exceeded the limits after that, then, for him is a painful punishment.²:¹⁷⁸

And for you in reciprocation there is the saving of life, O those imbued with intuition, so that perhaps you will be Godfearing.²:¹⁷⁹

It is prescribed for you when death attended anyone of you if one left goods, to bequeath to the ones who are your parents and the nearest kin as the one who is honorable, an obligation for the ones who are Godfearing.²:¹⁸⁰ Then, whoever substituted it after he heard it, truly, the sin of it is only on those who substitute it. Truly, God is Hearing, Knowing.²:¹⁸¹ Then, whoever feared from one who makes a testament, a swerving from the right path or sin, and, then, made things right between them, there is no sin on him. Truly, God is Forgiving, Compassionate.²:¹⁸²

O those who believed! Formal fasting was prescribed for you as it was prescribed for those who were before you so that perhaps you will be Godfearing.²:¹⁸³ Fasting is prescribed for numbered days. Then, whoever among you had been sick or on a journey, then, a period of other days. And for those who cannot fast is a redemption of food for the needy. And whoever volunteered good, it is better for him. And that you formally fast is better for you if you had been knowing.²:¹⁸⁴

The month of Ramadan is that in which the Quran was caused to descend—a guidance for humanity—and clear portents of the guidance, and the Criterion between right and wrong. So whoever of you bore witness to the month, then, formal fasting, and whoever had been sick or on a journey, then, a period of other days. God wants ease for you, and wants not hardship for you, so that you perfect the period and that you magnify God because He guided you so that perhaps you will give thanks.²:¹⁸⁵

And when My servants asked thee about Me, then, truly, I am near. I answer the call of one who calls when he will call to Me. So let them respond to Me and let them believe in Me, so that perhaps they will be on the right way.²:¹⁸⁶

It is permitted for you on the nights of formal fasting to have sexual intercourse with your wives. They (f) are a garment for you and you are a garment for them (f). God knew that you had been dishonest to yourselves so He turned to you in forgiveness and pardoned you. So now lie with them (f) and look for what God prescribed for you. And eat and drink until the white thread becomes clear to you from the black thread at dawn. Again, fulfill the formal fasting until night. And lie not with them (f) when you are ones who cleave to the places of prostration. These are the ordinances of God. Then, come not near them. Thus, God makes His signs manifest to humanity so that perhaps they will be Godfearing.²:¹⁸⁷

And consume not your wealth between yourselves in falsehood, nor let it down in bribes to the ones who judge so that you consume a group of people's wealth among humanity in sin while you know.²:¹⁸⁸

They ask thee about the new moons. Say: They are appointed times for humanity, and the pilgrimage to Makkah.

It is not virtuous conduct that you approach houses from the back. Rather, virtuous conduct was to be Godfearing, and approach houses from their front doors. And be Godfearing of God so that perhaps you will prosper.²:¹⁸⁹

And fight in the Way of God those who fight you, but exceed not the limits. Truly, God loves not the ones who exceed the limits.²:¹⁹⁰

And kill them wherever you came upon them, and drive them out from wherever they drove you out. And persecution is more grave than killing. And fight them not near the Masjid al-Haram unless they fight you in it. But if they fought you, then kill them. Thus, this is the recompense for the ones who are ungrateful. [2:191] Then, if they refrained themselves, then, truly, God is Forgiving, Compassionate.[2:192]

And fight them until there be no persecution, and the way of life be for God. Then, if they refrained themselves, then, there is to be no deep seated dislike, but against the ones who are unjust.

Fight aggression [2:193] committed in the Sacred Month, in the Sacred Month and so reciprocation for all sacred things. So whoever exceeded the limits against you, exceed you the limits against him likewise as he exceeded the limits against you? Be Godfearing of God and know that God is with the ones who are Godfearing.[2:194]

And spend in the way of God, and cast not yourselves by your own hands into deprivation by fighting.

^And do good^. Truly, God loves the ones who are doers of good.[2:195]

And fulfill the pilgrimage to Makkah, and the visit for God. And if you were restrained, then, whatever was feasible of sacrificial gifts. And shave not your heads until the sacrificial gift reaches its place of sacrifice. Then, whoever had been sick among you, or has an injury of his head, then, a redemption of formal fasting, or charity or a ritual sacrifice. And when you were safe, then, whoever took joy in the visit and the pilgrimage to Makkah then whatever was feasible of a sacrificial gift. Then, whoever finds not the means, then, formal fasting for three days during the pilgrimage to Makkah and seven when you returned, that is ten completely. That would be for he whose people are not ones who are present at the Masjid al-Haram. And be Godfearing of God and know that God is Severe in repayment.[2:196]

The pilgrimage to Makkah is in known months. And whoever undertook the duty of pilgrimage to Makkah in them, then, there is no sexual intercourse nor disobedience nor dispute during the pilgrimage to Makkah. And whatever good you accomplish, God knows it. And take provision. Then, truly, the best ration is God-consciousness. So be Godfearing, O those imbued with intuition![2:197]

There is no blame on you that you be looking for grace from your Lord. And when you pressed on from Arafat, then remember God at the Sacred Monument. And remember Him as He guided you, although you had been before this, certainly, of the ones who go astray.[2:198] Again, press on from where humanity pressed on, and ask God for forgiveness. Truly, God is Forgiving, Compassionate.[2:199]

And when you satisfied your devotional acts, then, remember God like your remembrance of your fathers, or a stauncher remembrance. And among humanity are some who say: Our Lord! Give to us in the present! And for him, there is no apportionment in the world to come![2:200]

And among them are some who say: Our Lord! Give us benevolence in the present and benevolence in the world to come and protect us from the punishment of the fire![2:201] Those, for them is a share of what they earned. And God is Swift at reckoning.[2:202]

And remember God during numbered days. So whoever hastened on in two days, then, there is no sin on him. And whoever remained behind, then, there is no sin on him. And for whoever was Godfearing, be Godfearing of God. And know that to Him you will be assembled.[2:203]

And among humanity is one whose sayings impress thee about this present life and he calls to God to witness what is in his heart while he is most stubborn in altercation.[2:204] And when he turned away, he hastened about the earth so that he makes corruption in and on it, and he causes the cultivation and stock to perish, but God loves not corruption.[2:205] And when it was said to him: Be Godfearing of God! Vainglory took him to sin. So hell is enough for him! And, certainly, it will be a miserable Final Place![2:206]

And among humanity is he who sells himself looking for the goodwill of God, and God is Gentle with His servants.[2:207]

O those who believed! Enter into peacefulness collectively and follow not the steps of Satan. Truly, he is a clear enemy to you.[2:208] But if you slipped after drew near you the clear portents, then, know that God is Almighty, Wise.[2:209]

So do they look on but that God approach them in the overshadowing of cloud shadows? And the angels? The command would be decided. And commands are returned to God.[2:210]

Ask the Children of Israel how many a sign, a clear portent, We gave them. And whoever substitutes the divine blessing of God after it drew near him, then, truly, God is Severe in repayment.[2:211]

Made to appear pleasing to those who were ungrateful is this present life, and they deride those who believed. But those who were Godfearing will be above them on the Day of Resurrection. And God provides for whomever He wills without reckoning.[2:212]

Humanity had been of one community. Then, God raised up the Prophets, ones who give good tidings and ones who warn. And with them He caused the Book to descend with The Truth to give judgment among humanity about what they were at variance in it. None were at variance in it but those who were given it after the clear portents drew near them because of their insolence to one another. Then, God guided those who believed to The Truth—about what they were at variance in it—with His permission. And God guides whom He wills to a straight path.[2:213]

Or assumed you that you would enter the Garden while approaches you not the likeness of those who passed away before you? Desolation and tribulation afflicted them. And they are so convulsed that even the Messenger says, and those who believed with him: When will there be help from God? No doubt, truly, the help of God is Near.[2:214]

They ask thee what they should spend. Say: Whatever you spent for good is for the ones who are your parents and the nearest kin and the orphans and the needy and the traveler of the way. And whatever good you accomplish, then, truly, God is Knowing of it.[2:215]

Fighting was prescribed for you although it is disliked by you. And perhaps you dislike a thing and it is good for you. And perhaps you love a thing, and it is worse for you. And God knows and, truly, you know not.[2:216]

They ask thee about the Sacred Month and fighting in it. Say: Fighting in it is deplorable and barring from the way of God and ingratitude to Him. And to bar from the Masjid al-Haram, and expelling people from it are more deplorable with God.

And persecution is more deplorable than killing.

And they cease not to fight you until they repel you from your way of life, if they are able.

And whoever of you goes back on his way of life, then, dies while he is one who is ungrateful, those, their actions were fruitless in the present and in the world to come. And those will be the Companions of the Fire. They are ones who will dwell in it forever.[2:217]

Truly, those who believed and those who emigrated and struggled in the way of God, those hope for the mercy of God. And God is Forgiving, Compassionate.[2:218]

They ask thee about intoxicants and gambling.

Say: In both of them there is deplorable sin and profits for humanity. And their sin is more deplorable than what is profitable.

And they ask thee how much they should spend.

Say: What is extra.

Thus, God makes manifest His signs to you so that perhaps you will reflect ²·²¹⁹ on the present and the world to come.

And they ask thee about orphans.

Say: Making things right for them is better. And if you intermix with them, then they are your brothers/sisters. God knows the one who makes corruption from the one who makes things right. And if God willed, He would have overburdened you. Truly, God is Almighty, Wise.²·²²⁰

Marry not ones who are female polytheists until they believe. The one who is a believing, female bond servant is better than the one who is a female polytheist even if she impressed you and wed not the ones who are male polytheists until they believe.

And one who is a believing, male bond servant is better than the one who is a male polytheist even if he impressed you. Those call you to the fire while God calls you to the Garden and to forgiveness with His permission. And He makes manifest His signs to humanity so that perhaps they will recollect.²·²²¹

They ask thee about menstruation. Say: It is an impurity, so withdraw from your wives during menstruation. Come not near them (f) until they cleanse themselves. And then when they (f) cleansed themselves, approach them (f) as God commanded you. Truly, God loves the contrite and He loves the ones who cleanse themselves.²·²²²

Your wives are a place of cultivation for you, so approach your cultivation whenever you willed and put forward for yourselves. And be Godfearing of God. And know that you will be one who encounters Him. And give thou good tidings to the ones who believe.²·²²³

And make God not an obstacle with your sworn oaths to your being good, and being Godfearing, and making things right among humanity. And God is Hearing, Knowing.²·²²⁴

God will not take you to task for idle talk in your sworn oaths. Rather, He will take you to task for what your hearts earned. And God is Forgiving, Forbearing.²·²²⁵

For those who vow abstinence from their wives, await four months. Then, if they changed their minds, then, truly, God is Forgiving, Compassionate.²·²²⁶ And if they resolved on setting them (f) free, then, truly, God is Hearing, Knowing.²·²²⁷

And the women who are to be divorced will await by themselves three menstrual periods. And it is not lawful for them (f) that they (f) keep back what God created in their (f) wombs, if they (f) had been believing in God, and the Last Day. Their husbands have better right to come back during that period if they (m) wanted to make things right. For the rights of them (f) in regard to their husbands is the like of rights of their (f) husbands in regard to them (f), as one who is honorable.

And men have a degree over them (f). And God is Almighty, Wise.²·²²⁸

Setting free is said two times: Then, hold fast to them (f) as one who is honorable or setting them (f) free with kindness. And it is not lawful for you that you take anything of what you gave them (f) unless they both fear that they both will not perform the ordinances of God. And if you feared that they both will not perform the ordinances of God, then, there is no blame on either of them in what she offered as redemption for that. These are the ordinances of God, so exceed not the limits. And whoever violates the ordinances of God, then, those, they are the ones who are unjust.²·²²⁹

And if he divorced her finally, then, she is not lawful to him after that until she marries a spouse other than him. Then, if that husband divorced her irrevocably, there is no blame on either of them if they return to one another if both of them thought that they will perform within the ordinances of God, and these are the ordinances of God. He makes them manifest for a folk who know.²·²³⁰

And when you divorced wives, and they (f) reached their (f) term, then, hold them (f) back as one who is honorable or set them (f) free as one who is honorable. But hold them (f) not back by injuring them so that you commit aggression. And whoever commits that, then, surely, he did wrong himself.

And take not to yourselves the signs of God in mockery. Remember the divine blessing of God on you, and what He caused to descend to you from the Book and wisdom. He admonishes you with it. And be Godfearing of God and know that God is Knowing of everything.²·²³¹

And when you revocably divorced wives, and they (f) reached their (f) term, then, place not difficulties for them (f) that they (f) re-marry their former spouses when they agreed among themselves as one who is honorable. This is admonished for him—whoever had been among you who believes in God and the Last Day—that is pure and purer for you. And God knows and you know not.²·²³²

And the ones who are mothers will breast feed their (f) children for two years completely for whoever wanted to fulfill breast feeding. And on one to whom a child is born is their (f) provision and their clothing (f) as one who is honorable. No soul is placed with a burden, but to its capacity.

Neither the one who is a mother be pressed for her child, nor the one to whom a child is born for his child. And on one who inherits is the like of that. While if they both wanted weaning by them agreeing together and after consultation, then, there is no blame on either of them.

And if you wanted to seek wet-nursing for your children, then, there is no blame on you when you handed over what you gave as one who is honorable. And be Godfearing of God. And know that God is Seeing of what you do.²·²³³

And those of you whom death will call to itself, forsaking spouses, they (f) will await by themselves (f) four months and ten days. And when they (f) reached their term, then, there is no blame on you in what they (f) accomplished for themselves (f), as one who is honorable. God is Aware of what you do.²·²³⁴

And there is no blame on you in what you offered with it of a proposal to women, or for what you hid in yourselves. God knew that you will remember them (f), except appoint not with them (f) secretly, unless you say a saying as one who is honorable. And resolve not on the knot of marriage until she reaches her prescribed term. And know that God knows what is within yourselves. So be fearful of Him. And know that God is Forgiving, Forbearing.²·²³⁵

There is no blame on you if you divorced wives whom you touch not, nor undertake a duty to them (f) of a dowry portion. And make provision for them (f). For the one who is wealthy—according to his means—and for the one who is needy—according to his means—with a sustenance, one that is honorable, an obligation on the ones who are doers of good²·²³⁶

And if you divorced them (f) before you touch them (f), and you undertook the duty of a dowry portion for them (f), then, half of what you undertook as a duty unless they (f) pardon it or they (m) pardon it in whose hand is the marriage knot. And that they (m) pardon is nearer to God-consciousness. Forget not grace among you. Truly, God is Seeing of what you do.²·²³⁷

Be watchful of the formal prayers and the middle formal prayer. Stand up as ones who are morally obligated to God.²:²³⁸

And if you feared, then, pray on foot or as one who is mounted. And when you were safe, then, remember God, for He taught you what you be not knowing.²:²³⁹

And those whom death will call to itself forsaking spouses, will bequeath for their spouses sustenance for a year without expelling them (f). But if they (f) went forth themselves (f), then, there is no blame on you in what they (f) accomplished for themselves (f) as one who is honorable. And God is Almighty, Wise.²:²⁴⁰

And for ones who are divorced females, sustenance, as one who is honorable. This is an obligation on the ones who are Godfearing.²:²⁴¹ Thus, God makes manifest His signs to you so that perhaps you will be reasonable.²:²⁴²

Hast thou not considered those who went forth from their abodes while they were in the thousands being fearful of death? And God said to them: Die! Again, He gave them life. Truly, God is Possessor of Grace for humanity except most of humanity gives not thanks.²:²⁴³

So fight in the Way of God, and know that God is Hearing, Knowing.²:²⁴⁴

Who is he who will lend God a fairer loan that He will multiply it for him manifold times? And God seizes and extends and you are returned to Him.²:²⁴⁵

Hast thou not considered the Council of the Children of Israel after Moses when they said to a Prophet of theirs: Raise up a king for us, and we will fight in the way of God.

He said: Perhaps if fighting was prescribed for you, you would not fight.

They said: Why should we not fight in the way of God when we were driven out of our abodes with our children.

Then, when fighting was prescribed for them, they turned away, but for a few of them. And God is Knowing of the ones who are unjust.²:²⁴⁶

And their Prophet said to them: Truly, God raised up for you Saul, a king.

They said: How would it be for him to have dominion over us when we have better right to dominion than he, as he is not given plenty of wealth?

He said: Truly, God favored him over you, and increased him greatly in the knowledge and the physique. And God gives His dominion to whom He wills. And God is One Who is Extensive, Knowing.²:²⁴⁷

And their Prophet said to them: Truly, a sign of his dominion is that there would approach you the Ark of the Covenant. In it is tranquility from your Lord, and abiding wisdom of what the people of Moses left, and the people of Aaron. And the angels will carry it. Truly, in that is a sign for you if you had been ones who believe.²:²⁴⁸

So when Saul set forward with his army he said: Truly, God is One Who Tests you with a river. So whoever would drink of it, he is not of me, and whoever tastes it not, truly, he is of me, but he who scoops up with a scooping of his hand.

So they drank of it, but a few of them. Then, when he crossed it, he and those who believed with him, they said: There is no energy for us today against Goliath and his armies.

Said those who think they truly would be ones who encounter God: How often a faction of a few vanquished a faction of many with the permission of God! And God is with the ones who remain steadfast.²:²⁴⁹

And so when they departed against Goliath and his armies they said: Our Lord! Pour out patience on us, and make our feet firm, and help us against the folk—the ones who are ungrateful.²:²⁵⁰ So they put them to flight with the permission of God. And David killed Goliath.

And God gave him the dominion and wisdom, and taught him of what He wills. And if not for God driving humanity back—some by some others—the earth would have, certainly, gone to ruin, except God is Possessor of Grace to the worlds.²:²⁵¹

These are the signs of God. We recount to thee The Truth. And, truly, thou art among the ones who are sent.²:²⁵²

These are the Messengers. We gave advantage, some of them over some others. Of them are those to whom God spoke and some of them He exalted in degree. And We gave Jesus son of Mary the clear portents and confirmed him with the hallowed Spirit. And if God willed, those who were after them have fought one another after the clear portents drew near them, except they were at variance. And some of them believed, while some of them were ones who are ungrateful. And if God willed, they would not have fought one another, except God accomplishes what He wants.²:²⁵³

O those who believed! Spend of what We provided you, before a Day approaches when there is neither trading in it nor friendship nor intercession. And the ones who are ungrateful, they are the ones who are unjust.²:²⁵⁴

God! There is no god but He, The Living, The Eternal. Neither slumber takes Him nor sleep. To Him belongs whatever is in the heavens and whatever is in and on the earth. Who will intercede with Him but with His permission? He knows what is in front of them and what is behind them. And they will not comprehend anything of His knowledge, but what He willed. His Seat encompassed the heavens and the earth, and He is not hampered by their safe-keeping. And He is The Lofty, The Sublime.²:²⁵⁵

There is no compulsion in the way of life. Surely, right judgment became clear from error. So whoever disbelieves in false deities and believes in God, then, surely, he held fast to the most firm handhold. It is not breakable. And God is Hearing, Knowing.²:²⁵⁶

God is The Protector of those who believed. He brings them out from the shadows into the light. And those who were ungrateful, their protectors are false deities. They bring them out from the light into the shadows. Those will be the Companions of the Fire. They are ones who will dwell in it forever.²:²⁵⁷

Hast thou not considered him who argued with Abraham about his Lord because God gave him dominion?

Mention when Abraham said: My Lord is He Who gives life and causes to die.

He said: I give life and cause to die.

Abraham said: Truly, God brings the sun from the East, so bring thou the sun from the West! Then, he who was ungrateful was dumfounded. And God guides not the unjust folk.²:²⁵⁸

Or like the one who passed by a town and it was one that has fallen down into ruins.

He said: How will God give life to this after its death? So God caused him to die for a hundred years. Again, He raised him up.

He said: How long hadst thou lingered in expectation?

He said: I lingered in expectation for a day or some part of a day.

He said: Nay. Thou hadst lingered in expectation a hundred years. Then look on thy food and thy drink. They are not spoiled. And look on thy donkey. We made thee a sign for humanity. And look on the bones, how We set them up. Again, We will clothe them with flesh.

So when it became clear to him, he said: I know that God is Powerful over everything.²:²⁵⁹

And mention when Abraham said: My Lord! Cause me to see how Thou wilt give life to the dead.

He said: Wilt thou not believe?

He said: Yea, but so my heart be at rest.

He said: Again, take four birds, and twist them to thyself. Again, lay a part of them on every mountain. Again, call to them. They will approach thee coming eagerly. And know thou that God is Almighty, Wise.²:²⁶⁰

A parable of those who spend their wealth in the way of God is like a parable of a grain. It puts forth seven ears of wheat. In every ear of wheat, a hundred grains. And God multiplies for whom He wills. And God is One Who is Extensive, Knowing.²:²⁶¹

Those who spend their wealth in the way of God and, again, pursue not what they spent with reproachful reminders nor injury, the compensation for them is with their Lord. And there will be neither fear in them nor will they feel remorse.²:²⁶²

An honorable saying and forgiveness are better than charity succeeded by injury. And God is Sufficient, Forbearing.²:²⁶³ O those who believed! Render not untrue your charities with reproachful reminders nor injury like he who spends of his wealth to show off to humanity, and believes not in God and the Last Day. His parable is like the parable of a smooth rock. Over it is earth dust. A heavy downpour lit on it, and left it bare. They have no power over anything of what they earned and God guides not the ungrateful folk.²:²⁶⁴

And the parable of those who spend their wealth looking for the goodwill of God and for confirming their souls is like the parable of a garden on a hillside. A heavy downpour lit on it. Then, it gave its harvest double. And even if lights not on it a heavy downpour, then a dew. And God is Seeing of what you do.²:²⁶⁵

Would anyone of you wish that he have a garden of date palm trees and grapevines beneath which rivers run with all kinds of fruits in it for him? Then, old age lit on him, and he had weak offspring. Then, a whirlwind lit on it in which there is a fire. Then, it was consumed. Thus, God makes manifest His signs for you so that perhaps you will reflect.²:²⁶⁶

O those who believed! Spend of what is good that you earned, and from what We brought out for you from the earth. And aim not at getting the bad of it to spend while you would not be ones who take it, but you would close an eye to it. And know that God is Sufficient, Worthy of Praise.²:²⁶⁷

Satan threatens you with poverty and commands you to depravity; whereas God promises you His forgiveness from Himself and His grace. And God is One Who is Extensive, Knowing.²:²⁶⁸ He gives wisdom to whom He wills. And whomever is given wisdom, then, surely, was given much good and none recollects no doubt but those imbued with intuition.²:²⁶⁹ And whatever of contributions you spent or vows that you vowed, then, truly, God knows it. And for the ones who are unjust there is no helper.²:²⁷⁰

If you show your charity, then, how bountiful it is while if you conceal it and give it to the poor, that would be better for you. This absolves you of some of your evil deeds. And God is Aware of what you do.²:²⁷¹

Their guidance is not on thee. But God guides whomever He wills. And whatever of good you spend, it is for yourselves. And spend not but looking for the Countenance of God. And whatever of good you spend, your account will be paid to you in full and you will not be wronged.²:²⁷²

Spend for the poor, those who were restrained in the way of God and are not able to travel on the earth. The one who is ignorant assumes them to be rich because of their having reserve. Thou wilt recognize them by their mark. They ask not persistently of humanity. And whatever of good you spend, then, truly, God is Knowing of that.²:²⁷³

Those who spend their wealth by nighttime and daytime, secretly or in public, then, for them, their compensation is with their Lord. And there will be neither fear in them nor will they feel remorse.²:²⁷⁴

Those who consume usury will not arise, but like he who arises whom Satan prostrated by touch. That is because they said: Trading is only like usury and yet God permitted trading and forbade usury. So whoever drew near an admonishment from his Lord and refrained himself, for him is what was past. And his command is with God. While whoever reverted, then, those will be the Companions of the Fire. They, ones who will dwell in it forever!²:²⁷⁵

God eliminates usury, and He causes charity to increase. And God loves not any sinful ingrate. ²:²⁷⁶

Truly, those who believed and did as the ones in accord with morality and performed the formal prayer and gave the purifying alms, for them, their compensation is with their Lord. And there will be neither fear in them nor will they feel remorse. ²:²⁷⁷

O those who believed! Be Godfearing of God. And forsake what remained of usury, if you had been ones who believe.²:²⁷⁸ But if you accomplish it not, then, give ear to war from God and His Messenger. And if you repented, you will have your principal capital, doing no wrong to others nor will you be wronged.²:²⁷⁹

If a debtor had been possessing adversity, a respite until a time of ease and prosperity. And it is better for you that you be charitable, if you had been knowing.²:²⁸⁰ And be Godfearing of a Day on which you are returned to God. Again, every soul will be paid its account in full for what it earned, and they will not be wronged.²:²⁸¹

O those who believed! When you contracted a debt for a term—that which is determined—then, write it down. Let one who is a scribe write it down between you justly. One who is a scribe should not refuse to write it down as God taught him. So let him write down and let the debtor dictate. Let him be Godfearing of God, his Lord, and diminish not anything out of it. But if the debtor had been mentally deficient, or weak, or not able to dictate himself, then, let his protector dictate justly.

And call two witnesses to bear witness from among your men. Or if there are not two men, then a man and two women, with whom you are well-pleased as witnesses, so that if one of them (f) goes astray, then, the other one of the two will remind her. And the witnesses will not refuse when they were called. And grow not weary that you write it down, be it small or great, with its term. That is more equitable with God and more upright for testimony, and likelier not to be in doubt unless it be a trade, that which is transferred at the time—to give and take among yourselves. Then, there is no blame on you if you write it not down. And call witnesses when you have a transaction. Let neither one who is a scribe nor witness be pressed. And if you accomplish that, then, it is, truly, disobedience on your part. So be Godfearing of God. And God teaches you. And God is Knowing of everything.²:²⁸²

And if you had been on a journey and find no one who is a scribe, then, a guarantee of that which is held in hand. But if any of you entrusted to another, then, let who was trusted give back his trust and let him be Godfearing of God, his Lord, and keep not back testimony. And he who keeps back, he, then, truly, his heart is one that is perverted. And God is Knowing of what you do.²:²⁸³

To God belongs what is in the heavens and in and on the earth. Whether you show what is within yourselves, or conceal it, God will make a reckoning with you for it. And He will forgive whom He wills. And He will punish whom He wills. And God is Powerful over everything.²:²⁸⁴ The Messenger believed in what was caused to descend to him from his Lord as do the ones who believe. All believed in God and

His angels and His Books and His Messengers saying: We separate and divide not among anyone of His Messengers. And they said: We heard and we obeyed, so grant Thy forgiveness, Our Lord! And to Thee is the Homecoming.²:²⁸⁵

God places not a burden on a soul beyond its capacity. For it is what it earned and against it is what it deserved. Our Lord! Take us not to task if we forgot or made a mistake. Our Lord! Burden us not with a severe test like that which Thou hadst burdened those who were before us. Our Lord! Load us not such that we have no energy for it and pardon us and forgive us and have mercy on us. Thou art our Defender so help us against the folk, the ones who are ungrateful.²:²⁸⁶

CHAPTER 3
THE FAMILY OF IMRAN

In the Name of God The Merciful, The Compassionate
*Alif Lām Mīm.*³:¹

God! There is no god but He, The Living, The Eternal.³:²

He sent down to thee the Book with The Truth, that which establishes as true what was before it. And He caused to descend the Torah and the Gospel³:³ before this as a guidance for humanity. And He caused to descend the Criterion between right and wrong. Truly, those who were ungrateful for the signs of God, for them is a severe punishment. And God is Almighty, Possessor of Requital.³:⁴

Truly, God, nothing is hidden from Him in or on the earth nor in heaven.³:⁵ It is He Who forms you in the wombs how He wills. There is no god but He, Almighty, Wise.³:⁶

It is He who caused the Book to descend to thee. In it are signs, ones that are definitive. They are the essence of the Book and others, ones that are unspecific. Then, those whose hearts are swerving, they follow what was unspecific in it, looking for dissent and looking for an interpretation, but none knows its interpretation but God. And the ones who are firmly rooted in knowledge say: We believed in it as all is from our Lord. And none recollects, but those imbued with intuition.³:⁷

Our Lord! Cause our hearts not to swerve after Thou hadst guided us. And bestow on us mercy from that which proceeds from Thy Presence. Truly, Thou, Thou alone art The Giver.³:⁸ Our Lord! Truly, Thou art One Who Gathers humanity on a Day in which there is no doubt in it. Truly, God breaks not His solemn declaration.³:⁹

Truly, those who were ungrateful, it will not avail them—neither their wealth nor their children—against God at all. And those, they will be fuel for the fire,³:¹⁰ in like manner of the people of Pharaoh and those who were before them. They denied Our signs so God took them because of their impiety. And God is Severe in repayment.³:¹¹

Say to those who were ungrateful: You will be vanquished and you will be assembled into hell. It will be a miserable Final Place.³:¹²

Surely, there had been a sign for you in the two factions who met one another—one faction fights in the way of God and the other as ones who are ungrateful, whom they see twice the like of visibly in their eyes. And God confirms with His help whom He wills. Truly, in this is a lesson for those imbued with insight.³:¹³

Made to appear pleasing to humanity was the cherishing of lust: From women and children and that which is heaped up heaps of gold and silver and horses, ones that are distinguished, and flocks and cultivation, that is the enjoyment of this present life, while God, with Him is the goodness of the Destination.³:¹⁴

Say: Shall I tell you of better than that? For those who were Godfearing, with their Lord are Gardens beneath which rivers run. They are ones who will dwell in them forever with purified spouses and contentment from God. And God is Seeing His servants,³:¹⁵ those who say: Our Lord! Truly, we believed, so forgive us our impieties and protect us from the punishment of the fire:³:¹⁶

They are the ones who remain steadfast and the ones who are sincere and the ones who are morally obligated and the ones who spend in the way of God and the ones who ask for forgiveness at the breaking of day.³:¹⁷

God bore witness that there is no god but He, as do the angels and those imbued with the knowledge, the ones who uphold equity. There is no god but He, The Almighty, The Wise.³:¹⁸

Truly the way of life with God is submission to the One God. And at variance were those who were given the Book after what drew near them of the knowledge out of insolence among themselves. And whoever is ungrateful for the signs of God, then, truly, God is Swift in reckoning.³:¹⁹

So if they argued with thee, then say: I submitted my face to God as have those who followed me. And say to those who were given the Book and to the unlettered: Have you submitted to God? If they submitted to God, then, surely, they were truly guided. And if they turned away, then, on thee is only delivering the message. And God is Seeing of His servants.³:²⁰

Truly, those who are ungrateful for the signs of God and kill the Prophets without right and kill those who command to equity from among humanity, then, give thou to them the good tidings of a painful punishment.³:²¹ Those, those are they whose actions were fruitless in the present and the world to come. And for them there is no one who helps.³:²²

Hast thou not considered those who were given a share of the Book? They are called to the Book of God to give judgment between them. Again, a group of people among them turn away and they, they are ones who turn aside.³:²³

That is because they said: The fire will not touch us but for numbered days.

And they were deluded in their way of life by what they had been devising.³:²⁴ How then will it be when We gathered them on a Day, there is no doubt in it? The account of every soul will be paid in full for what it earned and they, they will not be wronged?³:²⁵

Say: O God! The One Who is Sovereign of Dominion, Thou hast given dominion to whom Thou hast willed, and Thou hast torn away dominion from whom Thou hast willed. Thou hast rendered powerful whom Thou hast willed, and Thou hast abased whom Thou hast willed. In Thy hand is the good. Truly, Thou art Powerful over everything.³:²⁶ Thou hast caused the nighttime to be interposed into the daytime. And Thou hast caused the daytime to be interposed into the nighttime. And Thou hast brought out the living from the dead. And Thou hast brought out the dead from the living. Thou hast provided to whomever Thou hast willed without stinting.³:²⁷

Let not the ones who believe take to themselves the ones who are ungrateful for protectors instead of the ones who believe. And whoever accomplishes that is not with God in anything, unless it is because you are cautious towards them. And God cautions you of Himself. And to God is the Homecoming.³:²⁸

Say: Whether you conceal what is in your breasts or show it, God knows it and He knows whatever is in the heavens and whatever is in and on the earth. And God is Powerful over everything.³:²⁹

A Day when every soul will find that which is brought forward of good and what it did of evil. It will wish that there be between this and between that a long space of time. God cautions you of Himself. And God is Gentle to the servants.³·³⁰

Say: If you had been loving God, then, follow me. And God will love you and forgive you your impieties. God is Forgiving, Compassionate.³·³¹

Say: Obey God and the Messenger. Then, if they turned away, then, truly, God loves not the ones who are ungrateful.³·³²

Truly, God favored Adam and Noah and the people of Abraham and the people of Imran above all the worlds,³·³³ some of one another's offspring. And God is The Hearing, The Knowing.³·³⁴

Mention when the woman of Imran said: My Lord! I vowed to Thee what is in my womb—that which is dedicated—so receive Thou this from me. Truly, Thou, Thou alone art The Hearing, The Knowing.³·³⁵

Then, when she brought forth she said: My Lord! Truly, I brought her forth, a female. And God is greater in knowledge of what she brought forth. And the male is not like the female. And, truly, I named her Mary. And, truly, I commend her to Thy protection and her offspring from the accursed Satan.³·³⁶

So her Lord received her with the very best acceptance. And her bringing forth caused the very best to develop in her. And Zechariah took charge of her. Whenever Zechariah entered upon her in her sanctuary, he found her with provision. He said: O Mary! From where is this for thee (f)? She said: This is from God. Truly, God provides to whom He wills without reckoning.³·³⁷

There Zechariah called to his Lord. He said: My Lord! Bestow on me good offspring from Thy Presence. Truly, Thou art hearing the supplication.³·³⁸

Then, the angels proclaimed to him while he was one who stands to invoke blessings in the sanctuary that God gives thee good tidings of Yahya—one who establishes the Word of God as true—a chief and concealer of secrets and a Prophet among the ones in accord with morality.³·³⁹

He said: My Lord! How is it I will have a boy while, surely, I reached old age and my woman is a barren woman.

He said: Thus, God accomplishes what He wills.³·⁴⁰

He said: My Lord! Assign a sign for me.

He said: Thy sign is that thou wilt not speak to humanity for three days but by gesture and remember thy Lord frequently, and glorify in the evening and early morning.³·⁴¹

And mention when the angels said: O Mary! Truly, God favored thee (f), and purified thee (f), and favored thee (f) above women of the world.³·⁴² O Mary! Be thou morally obligated to thy Lord and prostrate thyself (f) and bow down (f) with the ones who bow down.³·⁴³ That is tidings from the unseen We reveal to thee.

And thou hadst not been present with them when they cast their pens as to which of them would take control of Mary, nor hadst thou been present with them when they strive against one another.³·⁴⁴

Mention when the angels said: O Mary! Truly, God gives thee (f) good tidings of a Word from Him. His name is the Messiah—Jesus son of Mary—well-esteemed in the present and the world to come and among the ones who are brought near.³·⁴⁵ And he will speak to humanity from the cradle and in manhood and be among the ones in accord with morality.³·⁴⁶

She said: My Lord! How is it I will be with child when no mortal touches me?

He said: Thus, God creates whatever He wills. When He decreed a command, then, He only says to it: Be! Then, it is!³·⁴⁷

And He teaches him the Book and wisdom and the Torah and the Gospel³·⁴⁸ to be a Messenger to the Children of Israel saying that: Surely I drew near you with a sign from your Lord that I will create for you out of clay a likeness of

a bird. Then, I breathe into it and it will become a bird with the permission of God. And I cure one who is blind from birth and the leper and give life to dead mortals with the permission of God. And I tell you what you eat and what you store up in your houses. Truly, in that is a sign for you if you had been ones who believe.³·⁴⁹ And I come with that which establishes as true what was before me of the Torah, and permit you some of what was forbidden to you. And I drew near you with a sign from your Lord. So be Godfearing of God and obey Me.³·⁵⁰ Truly, God is my Lord and your Lord so worship Him. This is a straight path.³·⁵¹

And when Jesus became conscious of their ingratitude, he said: Who are my helpers for God?

The disciples said: We will be helpers for God. We believed in God and bear thee witness that we are ones who submit to God.³·⁵²

Our Lord! We believed in what Thou hadst caused to descend. And we followed the Messenger so write us down with the ones who bear witness.³·⁵³

And they planned and God planned. And God is Best of the ones who plan.³·⁵⁴

Mention when God said: O Jesus! I will be One Who Gathers thee and One Who Elevates thee to Myself and One Who Purifies thee from those who were ungrateful, and One Who Makes those who followed thee above those who were ungrateful until the Day of Resurrection. Again, you will return to Me. Then, I will give judgment between you about what you had been at variance in it.³·⁵⁵

So as for those who were ungrateful, then, I will punish them with a severe punishment in the present and the world to come. And for them there is no one who helps.³·⁵⁶

And to those who believed and did as the ones in accord with morality, We will pay them their account with full compensation. And God loves not the ones who are unjust.³·⁵⁷

These We recount to thee are of the signs and the wise remembrance.³·⁵⁸

Truly the parable of Jesus with God is like the parable of Adam. He created him from earth dust. Again, He said to him: Be! Then, he is!³·⁵⁹ The Truth is from thy Lord, so be not of the ones who contest.³·⁶⁰

Then, to whoever argued with thee about it after what drew near thee of the knowledge, say: Approach now! Let us call to our children and your children and our women and your women and ourselves and yourselves. Again we will humbly supplicate, and we lay the curse of God on the ones who lie.³·⁶¹

This is, truly, a narrative of The Truth. And there is no god but God. And, truly, God, He is The Almighty, The Wise.³·⁶² Then, truly, if they turned away, then, truly, God is Knowing of the ones who make corruption.³·⁶³

Say: O People of the Book! Approach now to a word common between us and between you that we worship none but God and ascribe nothing as partners with Him, that none of us take others to ourselves as lords besides God.

And if they turned away, then, say: Bear witness that we are ones who submit to God.³·⁶⁴

O People of the Book! Why argue with one another about Abraham while neither was the Torah caused to descend nor the Gospel until after him. Will you not, then, be reasonable?³·⁶⁵ Lo, behold! You are these who argued with one another about what you have some knowledge. Why, then, argue with one another about what is with you when you have no knowledge? And God knows and you know not.³·⁶⁶

Abraham had been neither a Jew nor a Christian, but he had been a monotheist, one who submits to God. He had not been of the ones who were polytheists.³·⁶⁷

Truly, of humanity closest to Abraham are those who followed him and this Prophet and those who believed. And God is Protector of the ones who believe.3:68

A section of the People of the Book wished that they cause you to go astray. And they cause none to go astray, but themselves, and they are not aware.3:69

O People of the Book! Why be ungrateful for the signs of God while you bear witness?3:70 O People of the Book! Why confuse you The Truth with falsehood, and keep back The Truth while you know?3:71

And a section of the People of the Book said: Believe in what was caused to descend to those who believed at the beginning of the daytime. Disbelieve at the last of the day so that perhaps they will return to disbelief.3:72 And believe none, but one who heeded your way of life.

Say: Truly guidance is The Guidance from God and believe not that anyone be given the like of what you were given, so that he argue with you before your Lord.

Say: Truly, the grace is in the hand of God. He gives it to whomever He wills. And God is One Who is Extensive, Knowing.3:73 He singles out for His mercy whom He wills. And God is Possessor of Sublime Grace.3:74

And among the People of the Book is he who, if thou hast entrusted him with a hundredweight, he would give it back to thee. And among them is he who, if thou hast entrusted him with a dinar, he would not give it back to thee unless thou hadst continued as one who stands over him.

That is because they said: There is no way of moral duty on us as to the unlettered.

And they are lying against God while they, they know.3:75

Yea! Whoever lived up to his compact and was Godfearing, then, truly, God loves the ones who are Godfearing.3:76

Truly, those who exchange the compact of God and their sworn oaths for a little price, those, there is no apportionment for them in the world to come. And God will neither speak to them, nor look on them on the Day of Resurrection nor will He make them pure. And for them is a painful punishment.3:77

And, truly, among them is a group of people who distort their tongues with the Book so that you assume it is from the Book, although it is not from the Book.

And they say: It is from God, although it is not from God. And they say a lie against God while they know.3:78

It had not been for a mortal that God should give him the Book and critical judgment and the prophethood and, again, he say to humanity: Be you servants of me instead of God! Rather, he would say: Be you masters, because you had been teaching the Book and because you had been studying it.3:79 Nor would He command you to take to yourselves the angels and the Prophets as lords. Would He command you to ingratitude after you are ones who submit to God?3:80

And mention when God took a solemn promise from the Prophets: Whatever I gave you of the Book and wisdom, again, if a Messenger drew near you with that which establishes as true what is with you, you will believe in him and you will help him.

He said: Are you in accord? And will you take on My severe test?

They said: We are in accord.

He said: Then, bear witness and I am with you among the ones who bear witness.3:81

Then, whoever turned away after this, then, those, they are the ones who disobey.3:82

Desire they other than the way of life of God while to Him submitted whatever is in the heavens and the earth willingly or unwillingly and they are returned to Him?3:83

Say: We believed in God and what was caused to descend to us and what was caused to descend to Abraham and Ishmael and Isaac and Jacob and the Tribes and what was given to Moses and Jesus and the Prophets from their Lord. We separate and divide not between anyone of them and we are ones who submit to Him.3:84

And whoever be looking for a way of life other than submission to God, it will never be accepted from him. And he, in the world to come, will be among the ones who are losers.3:85

How will God guide a folk who disbelieved after their belief?

And they bore witness to The Truth of the Messenger after the clear portents drew near them. And God guides not the unjust folk.3:86 Those, their recompense is that the curse of God is on them and of the angels and of humanity, one and all,3:87 ones who will dwell with it forever. Neither will the punishment be lightened from them, nor will they be given respite.3:88

But those who repented after that and made things right, then, truly, God is Forgiving, Compassionate.3:89

Truly, those who disbelieved after their belief, again, added to their disbelief. Their remorse will never be accepted. Those, they are the ones who go astray.3:90

Truly, those who were ungrateful and died when they were ones who are ungrateful, it will not be accepted from anyone of them the earth full of gold, even if he offered it as ransom. Those, for them, is a painful punishment, and for them there is no one who helps.3:91

You will never attain virtuous conduct until you spend of what you love. And whatever thing you spend, truly, God is Knowing of it.3:92

All food had been allowed to the Children of Israel, but what Israel, Jacob, forbade to himself before the Torah was sent down. Say: Then, approach with the Torah and recount it if you had been ones who are sincere.3:93

Then, whoever devised lies against God after that then, those, they are the ones who are unjust.3:94

Say: God was Sincere, so follow the creed of Abraham—a monotheist—and not had he been among the ones who are polytheists.3:95

Truly, the first House set in place for humanity was that which is at Bekka, that which is blessed, and a guidance for the worlds.3:96 In it are clear portents, signs, the Station of Abraham. And whoever entered it had been one who is safe. And to God is a duty on humanity of pilgrimage to the House in Makkah for whoever was able to travel the way to it. And whoever was ungrateful, then truly God is Independent of the worlds.3:97

Say: O People of the Book! Why be ungrateful for the signs of God? And God is Witness over what you do.3:98

Say: O People of the Book! Why bar you from the way of God he who believed, desiring crookedness when you are witnesses? God is not One Who is Heedless of what you do.3:99

O those who believed! If you obey a group of people of those who were given the Book, they will repel you after your belief turning you into ones who are ungrateful.3:100

And how would you be ungrateful when the signs of God are recounted to you, and His Messenger is among you? And whoever cleaves firmly to God was, then, surely guided to a straight path.3:101

O those who believed! Be Godfearing of God as it is His right that He be feared. And die not but that you be ones who submit to the One God.3:102

And cleave firmly to the rope of God altogether and be not split up. And remember the divine blessing of God on you when you had been enemies. Then, He brought your hearts together. You became brothers/sisters by His divine blessing. You had been on the brink of an abyss of the fire and He saved you from it. Thus, God makes manifest to you His signs so that perhaps you will be truly guided.3:103

And let there be a community from among you who calls to good and commands to that which is honorable and prohibits that which is unlawful. And those, they are the ones who prosper.3:104 And be not like those who split up and were at variance after the clear portents drew near them. And those, for them is a tremendous punishment3:105 on a Day when faces will brighten and faces will cloud over.

As for those whose faces cloud over: Disbelieve you after your belief? Then experience the punishment for what you had been ungrateful.3:106

And as for those whose faces brightened, they are in the mercy of God. They, ones who will dwell in it forever.3:107 These are the signs of God. We recount them to thee in Truth. And God wants not injustice in the worlds.3:108

And to God belongs whatever is in the heavens and whatever is in and on the earth. To God all commands are returned.3:109

You had been the best community that was brought out for humanity. You command to that which is honorable and prohibit that which is unlawful and believe in God. And if the People of the Book believed, it would have been better for them. Some of them are the ones who believe, but most of them are the ones who disobey.3:110 They will never injure you but are an annoyance. And if they fight you, they will turn their backs on you. Again, they will not be helped.3:111

Abasement was stamped on them wherever they were come upon—but those with a rope to God and a rope to humanity—and they drew the burden of anger from God and wretchedness was stamped on them. That is because they had been ungrateful for the signs of God and kill the Prophets without right. That is because they rebelled and had been exceeding the limits.3:112

They are not all the same. Among the People of the Book is a community of ones who are upstanding. They recount the signs of God in the night watch of the night and they, they prostrate themselves.3:113 They believe in God and the Last Day and they command that which is honorable and prohibit that which is unlawful and they compete with one another in good deeds. Those are among the ones in accord with morality.3:114 And whatever of good they accomplish will never go unappreciated. And God is Knowing of the ones who are Godfearing.3:115

Truly, those who were ungrateful never will avail them their wealth nor their children against God at all. And those will be the Companions of the Fire. They are ones who will dwell in it forever.3:116

The parable of what they spend in this present life is like the parable of a freezing wind in it that lit on the cultivation of the folk who did wrong themselves and caused it to perish. And God did not wrong them, but they do wrong themselves.3:117

O those who believed! Take not to yourselves as close friends other than yourselves. They stop at nothing to ruin you. They wished that misfortune would fall on you. Surely, their hatred showed itself from their mouths and what their breasts conceal is greater. Surely, We made manifest to you the signs if you had been reasonable.3:118 Lo, behold! You are those imbued with love for them, but they love you not.

And you believed in the Book, all of it. And when they met you, they said: We believe. But when they went privately, they bit the tips of their fingers at you in rage.

Say: Die in your rage. Truly God is Knowing of what is within the breasts.3:119 If benevolence touches you, it raises anger in them, but if an evil deed lights on you, they are glad about it. But if you endure patiently and are Godfearing, their cunning will not injure you at all. Truly, God is One Who Encloses what they do.3:120

And when thou hadst set forth in the early morning from thy family to place the ones who believe at their positions for fighting, God is Hearing, Knowing.3:121

Mention when two sections are about to lose heart among you although God was their Protector. And let the ones who believe put their trust in God.3:122

And, certainly, God helped you at Badr while you were humiliated in spirit. So be Godfearing of God so that perhaps you will give thanks.3:123

Mention when thou hast said to the ones who believe: Suffices you not that your Lord will reinforce you with three thousand among the angels? Ones who are caused to descend,3:124 yea! if you endure patiently and are Godfearing? And if they approach you instantly here, your Lord will reinforce you with five thousand angels—ones who are sweeping on.3:125

And God made it but as good tidings to you so that with it your hearts will be at rest. And there is no help, but from God, The Almighty, The Wise,3:126 for He will sever a selection of those who were ungrateful or suppress them so they turn about as ones who are frustrated.3:127

It is none of thy affair at all if He turns to them in forgiveness or He punishes them, for, truly, they are ones who are unjust.3:128

And to God belongs whatever is in the heavens and whatever is in and on the earth. He forgives whom He wills and punishes whom He wills. And God is Forgiving, Compassionate.3:129

O those who believed! Consume not usury—that which is doubled and redoubled—and be Godfearing of God so that perhaps you will prosper.3:130

And be Godfearing of the fire that was prepared for the ones who are ungrateful.3:131 And obey God and the Messenger so that perhaps you will find mercy.3:132 And compete with one another for forgiveness from your Lord and for a Garden whose depth is as the heavens and the earth that was prepared for the ones who are Godfearing,3:133 those who spend in gladness and tribulation and the ones who choke their rage and the ones who pardon humanity. And God loves the ones who are doers of good.3:134

And those who, when they committed an indecency or did wrong to themselves, they remembered God. Then, they asked for forgiveness for their impieties. And who forgives impieties but God? And persist not in what impiety they committed while they know.3:135 Those, their recompense is forgiveness from their Lord and Gardens beneath which rivers run, ones who will dwell in them forever. And how bountiful is the compensation for the ones who work!3:136

Customs passed away before you. So journey through the earth; then, look on how had been the Ultimate End of the ones who deny.3:137 This is a clear explanation for humanity, a guidance and an admonishment for the ones who are Godfearing.3:138 And be not feeble nor feel remorse. And you will be among the lofty, if you had been ones who believe.3:139

If a wound afflicts you, surely, a wound afflicted the folk similar to that. And these are the days We rotate among humanity so that God knows those who believed and takes witnesses to Himself from among you—and God loves not the ones who are unjust—3:140 and so that God may prove those who believed and eliminate the ones who are ungrateful.3:141

Or assumed you that you would enter the Garden while God knows not those who struggled among you and knows the ones who remain steadfast?3:142 And, certainly, you had been coveting death before you were to meet it. Then, surely, you saw and look on it.3:143

And Muhammad is only a Messenger. Surely, Messengers passed away before him. Then, if he died or be slain, will you turn about on your heels? And he who turns about on his heels will not injure God at all. And God will give recompense to the ones who are thankful.³:¹⁴⁴

It had not been for any soul to die, but with the permission of God. Prescribed is that which is appointed. And whoever wants a reward for good deeds in the present, We will give him that. And whoever wants a reward for good deeds in the world to come We will give him that. And We will give recompense to the ones who are thankful.³:¹⁴⁵

And how many a Prophet whom, along with him, many thousands fought, but none lost confidence with what lit on them in the way of God, nor were they weakened nor were they to give in. And God loves the ones who remain steadfast.³:¹⁴⁶

And their saying had been only that they said: Our Lord! Forgive us our impieties and our excessiveness in our affairs. And make our feet firm and help us against the folk, the ones who are ungrateful.³:¹⁴⁷

So God gave them a reward for good deeds in the present and the goodness of reward for good deeds in the world to come. And God loves the ones who are doers of good.³:¹⁴⁸

O those who believed! If you obey those who were ungrateful, they will repel you back on your heels and you will turn about—ones who are losers.³:¹⁴⁹

Nay! God is your Defender and He is Best of the ones who help.³:¹⁵⁰

We will cast into the hearts of those who were ungrateful, alarm, because they ascribed partners with God. And He sends not down for it authority. And their place of shelter will be the fire. And miserable will be the place of lodging of the ones who are unjust.³:¹⁵¹

And, certainly, God was sincere to you in His promise when you blasted the enemy with His permission until you lost heart and you contended with one another about the command and you rebelled after He caused you to see what you longed for in the spoils of war. Among you are some who want the present and among you are some who want the world to come. Again, He turned you away from them that He test you and, certainly, He pardoned you. And God is Possessor of Grace for the ones who believe.³:¹⁵²

When you mount up, not attentive to anyone and the Messenger calls you from your rear, then, He repaid you, lament for lament, so that you neither feel remorse for what slipped away from you, nor for what lit on you. And God is Aware of what you do.³:¹⁵³

Again, He caused to descend safety for you after lament. Sleepiness overcomes a section of you while a section caused themselves grief thinking of God without right, a thought out of the Age of Ignorance.

They say: Have we any part in the command?

Say: Truly, the command is entirely from God.

They conceal within themselves what they show not to thee. They say: If there had been for us any part in the command, we would not be killed here.

Say: Even if you had been in your houses, those would have departed—whom it was prescribed they be slain—for the Final Place of sleeping, so that God tests what is in your breasts and He proves what is in your hearts. And God is Knowing of what is in the breasts.³:¹⁵⁴

Truly, those of you who turned away on a day two multitudes met one another, only Satan caused them to slip back for some of what they earned. And, certainly, God pardoned them. Truly God is Forgiving, Forbearing.³:¹⁵⁵

O those who believed! Be not like those who were ungrateful and said about their brothers when they traveled through the earth or had been ones who are combatants: If they had been with us, neither would they have died, nor would they have been slain, so that God makes this a cause of regret in their hearts. And God gives life and causes to die. And God is Seeing of what you do.³:¹⁵⁶

And if you were slain in the way of God or died, certainly, forgiveness and mercy from God are better than what they gather in the present.³:¹⁵⁷

And if you died or were slain, it is, certainly, to God you will be assembled.³:¹⁵⁸

And it is by the mercy of God thou wert gentle with them. And if thou hadst been hard, harsh of heart, they would have broken away from around thee. So pardon them and ask for forgiveness for them. And take counsel with them in the affair. But when thou art resolved, then, put thy trust in God. Truly, God loves the ones who put their trust in Him.³:¹⁵⁹

If God helps you, then none will be one who is a victor over you. And if He withdraws His help from you, then, who is there who helps you after Him? And in God put their trust the ones who believe.³:¹⁶⁰

It had not been for a Prophet that he defraud. And whoever defrauds, what he defrauded will approach him on the Day of Resurrection. Again, the account will be paid in full of every soul for what he earned and they will not be wronged.³:¹⁶¹

So, then, is he who followed the contentment of God like he who drew the burden of the displeasure of God and whose place of shelter will be hell? And miserable will be the Homecoming!³:¹⁶² They have degrees with God. And God is Seeing of what they do.³:¹⁶³

Certainly, God showed grace to the ones who believe when he raised up among them a Messenger from themselves who recounts His signs to them and makes them pure and teaches them the Book and wisdom. And, truly, before that they had been, certainly, clearly wandering astray.³:¹⁶⁴

And why, when an affliction lit on you, surely, you lit two times its like on them. Say: Where is this from?

Say: It is from yourselves. Truly, God is Powerful over everything.³:¹⁶⁵

And what lit on you on a day when the two multitudes met one another was with the permission of God that He would know the ones who believe³:¹⁶⁶ and He would know those who were hypocrites. It was said to them: Approach now! Fight in the way of God or drive back.

They said: If we would have known there would be fighting, we would, certainly, have followed you.

They were nearer to disbelief on that day than to belief. They say with their mouths what is not in their hearts. And God is greater in knowledge of what they keep back.³:¹⁶⁷

Those who said to their brothers while they sat back: If they obeyed us, they would not have been slain.

Say: Then, drive off death from yourselves, if you had been ones who are sincere.³:¹⁶⁸

And assume not those who were slain in the way of God to be lifeless. Nay! They are living with their Lord. They are provided for,³:¹⁶⁹ glad for what God gave them of His grace. And rejoice at the good tidings for those who have not yet joined them from behind them. There will be neither fear in them, nor will they feel remorse.³:¹⁷⁰ They rejoice at the good tidings of the divine blessing from God and His grace and that God will not waste the compensation of the ones who believe,³:¹⁷¹ those who responded to God and the Messenger after wounds lit on them. For those of them who did good among them and were Godfearing, there is a sublime compensation.³:¹⁷²

Those to whom humanity said: Truly, humanity has gathered against you, so dread them, but it increased them in belief and they said: God is enough for us. And how excellent is He, The Trustee.3:173

So they turned about with divine blessing from God and grace and evil afflicts them not and they followed the contentment of God and God is Possessor of Sublime Grace.3:174

It is only Satan who frightens you with his protectors. So fear them not, but fear Me if you had been ones who believe.3:175 And let not those who compete with one another in ingratitude dishearten thee. Truly, they will never injure God at all. God wants to assign no allotment for them in the world to come and for them is a tremendous punishment.3:176 Truly, those who bought ingratitude at the price of belief will never injure God at all. And for them will be a painful punishment.3:177

And those who were ungrateful should not assume that the indulgence We grant to them is better for them. We only grant indulgence to them so that they add sin! And for them is a despised punishment.3:178

God will not forsake the ones who believe to what you are in until He differentiates the bad from what is good. And God will not inform about the unseen, but God elects from His Messengers whom He wills. So believe in God and His Messengers. And if you believe and are Godfearing, then, for you there is a sublime compensation.3:179 And assume not those who are misers that what God gave them of His grace is better for them. Nay! It is worse for them. To be hung around their necks will be what they were misers with on the Day of Resurrection. And to God belongs the heritage of the heavens and the earth. And God is Aware of what you do.3:180

Certainly, God heard the saying of those who said: Truly, God is poor and we are rich. We will write down what they said and their killing of the Prophets without right. And We will say: Experience the punishment of the burning!3:181 That is for what your hands put forward and that God is not unjust to His servants.3:182

Those who said: Truly, God made a compact with us that we believe not in a Messenger until He approaches with a sacrifice to be consumed by the fire.

Say: Surely, Messengers brought about to you before me the clear portents and even of what you spoke. Then, why have you killed them if you had been ones who are sincere?3:183

Then if they denied thee, surely, Messengers before were denied who drew near with the clear portents and the Psalms and the illuminating Book.3:184

Every soul is one that experiences death. Your account will be paid with full compensation on the Day of Resurrection. Then, whoever was drawn away from the fire and was caused to enter the Garden, surely, won a triumph. And what is this present life but the delusion of enjoyment?3:185

You will, certainly, be tried with your wealth and yourselves and you will, certainly, hear much annoyance from those who were given the Book before you and from those who ascribed partners with God. And if you endure patiently and are Godfearing, then, truly, that is of the commands to constancy.3:186

And when God took a solemn promise from those who were given the Book: You will make it manifest to humanity and keep it not back. Yet they repudiated it behind their backs and exchange it for a little price. And miserable will be what they buy!3:187

Assume not that those who are glad for what they brought and who love to be praised for what they accomplish not, assume not, then, that they will be kept safe from the punishment. And for them, a painful punishment.3:188

To God belongs the dominion of the heavens and of the earth. And God is Powerful over everything.3:189

Truly, in the creation of the heavens and of the earth and the alteration of nighttime and daytime there are signs for those imbued with intuition,3:190 those who remember God while upright and sitting and on their sides and they reflect on the creation of the heavens and the earth: Our Lord! Thou hadst not created this in vain. Glory be to Thee! Then, protect us from the punishment of the fire.3:191 Our Lord! Whomever Thou hast caused to enter the fire, surely, Thou hadst covered him with shame and there will not be for the ones who are unjust any helpers.3:192 Our Lord! Truly, we heard one who calls out, cries out for belief: Believe in your Lord! So we believed. Our Lord! So forgive Thou our impieties and absolve us of our evil deeds and gather us to Thee with the pious.3:193 Our Lord! Give us what Thou hadst promised us through Thy Messengers and cover us not with shame on the Day of Resurrection. Truly, Thou wilt not break Thy solemn declaration.3:194

And their Lord responded to them: I waste not the actions of ones who work among you from male or female. Each one of you is from the other. So those who emigrated and were driven out from their abodes and were maligned on My way and who fought and were slain, I will, certainly, absolve them of their evil deeds. And I will, certainly, cause them to enter into Gardens beneath which rivers run, a reward for good deeds from God. And God, with Him is the goodness of rewards for good deeds.3:195

Let not the going to and fro delude thee of those who were ungrateful in the land3:196—a little enjoyment—again, their place of shelter will be hell. And it will be a miserable Final Place.3:197

But those who were Godfearing of their Lord, for them will be Gardens beneath which rivers run, ones who will dwell in them forever, a hospitality from God. And what is with God is best for the pious.3:198 And, truly, among the People of the Book are those who believe in God and what was caused to descend to you and what was caused to descend to them, ones who are humble toward God. They exchange not the signs of God for a little price. Those, for them, their compensation is with their Lord. And, truly, God is Swift in reckoning.3:199 O those who believed! Excel in patience and be steadfast. And be Godfearing of God so that perhaps you will prosper.3:200

CHAPTER 4 THE WOMEN

In the Name of God The Merciful, The Compassionate

O humanity! Be Godfearing of your Lord Who created you from a single soul and, from it, created its spouse and from them both disseminated many men and women. And be Godfearing of God through Whom you demand rights of one another and the wombs, the rights of blood relations. Truly, God had been watching over you.4:1

And give the orphans their property and take not in exchange the bad of yours for what is good of theirs. And consume not their property with your own property. Truly, this had been criminal, a hateful sin.4:2

And if you feared that you will not act justly with the orphans, then, marry who seems good to you of the women, by twos, in threes or four. But if you feared you will not be just, then, one or what your right hands possessed. That is likelier that you not commit injustice.4:3

And give wives their marriage portion as a spontaneous gift. Then, truly, if they (f) were pleased to offer to you anything of it on their (f) own, consume it wholesomely with repose.4:4

And give not the mentally deficient your wealth that God assigned to you to maintain for them, but provide for them from it and clothe them. And say honorable sayings to them.4:5

And test the orphans until when they reached the age for marriage. Then, if you observed them to be of right judgment, then, release their property to them and consume it not excessively and hastily, for they will develop. And whoever had been rich, let him have restraint and whoever had been poor, then, let him consume as one who is honorable. And when you released their property to them, call witnesses over them. And God sufficed as a Reckoner.⁴ᐟ⁶

For men is a share of what was left by the ones who are their parents and the nearest kin. And for women is a share of what was left by the ones who are their parents and nearest kin whether it was little or it was much—an apportioned share.⁴ᐟ⁷

And when the division is attended by those imbued with kinship and the orphans and the needy, then, provide for them from it and say honorable sayings to them.⁴ᐟ⁸ And let executors dread like those who, if they left behind weak offspring, would fear for them. Then, let them be Godfearing of God and let them say appropriate sayings.⁴ᐟ⁹ Truly, those who consume the wealth of orphans with injustice, consume only fire into their bellies and they will roast in a blaze.⁴ᐟ¹⁰

God enjoins you concerning your children. For the male, the like allotment of two females. And if there had been women, more than two, then, for them (f) two-thirds of what he left. But if there had been one, then, for her is half. And for one's parents, for each one of them a sixth of what he left, if he would have a child. Then, if he be with no child and his parents inherited, then, a third to his mother. Then, if he had brothers, then a sixth for his mother. This is after any bequest he enjoins or any debt. Your parents or your children, you are not informed which of them is nearer to you in profit. This is a duty to God. Truly, God had been Knowing, Wise.⁴ᐟ¹¹

And for you is a half of what your spouses left if they be with no child. Then, if they (f) had a child, then, for you is a fourth of what they (f) left. This is after any bequest which they bequeath or any debt. And for them (f) a fourth of what you left if you be with no child. And if you had a child, then, for them (f) is an eighth of what you left. This is after any bequest which you bequeath or any debt. And if a man would have no direct heirs, or a woman, but indirect heirs, and has a brother or sister, then, for each one of them (f), a sixth. Then, if there would be more than that, then, they would be ascribed associates in a third. This is after any bequest which is bequeathed or any debt without being one who presses the heirs. This is the enjoinment from God. And God is Knowing, Forbearing.⁴ᐟ¹²

These are the ordinances of God. And whoever obeys God and His Messenger, He will cause to enter Gardens beneath which rivers run, ones who will dwell in them forever. And that is the winning the sublime triumph.⁴ᐟ¹³

And whoever rebels against God and His Messenger and violates His ordinances, He will cause him to enter fire, one who shall dwell in it forever and he will have a despised punishment.⁴ᐟ¹⁴

And those who approach indecency among your wives, call to four among you to bear witness against them (f). Then, if they bore witness to the affair, then, hold them (f) back in their houses until death gathers them (f) to itself or God makes a way for them (f).⁴ᐟ¹⁵

And those two who among you approach that, then penalize them both. Then, if they repented and made things right, then, turn aside from them. Truly, God had been Accepter of Repentance, Compassionate.⁴ᐟ¹⁶

To turn only to God for forgiveness is for those who do evil in ignorance and, again, soon they are remorseful. Then, those are whom God turns to in forgiveness. And God had been Knowing, Wise.⁴ᐟ¹⁷

And there is not remorsefulness for those who do evil deeds until when one of them was attended by death, he would say: I, truly, repented now nor for those who die while they are ones who are ungrateful. Those, We made ready for them a painful punishment.⁴ᐟ¹⁸

O those who believed! It is not lawful for you that you inherit women unwillingly, and place not difficulties for them (f) so that you take away some of what you gave them (f), unless they approach a manifest indecency. And live as one who is honorable with them (f).

Then, if you disliked them (f) perhaps you dislike something in which God makes much good.⁴ᐟ¹⁹ And if you wanted to exchange your spouse in place of another spouse and you gave one of them (f) a hundredweight, so take not anything from it. Would you take it by false charges to harm her reputation and in clear sin?⁴ᐟ²⁰

And how would you take it when one of you had sexual intercourse with the other and they (f) took from you an earnest solemn promise? ⁴ᐟ²¹ And marry not women whom your fathers married unless it was in the past. Truly, it had been an indecency and repugnant and how evil a way!⁴ᐟ²²

Your mothers were forbidden to you and your daughters and your sisters and your paternal and maternal aunts and daughters of your brothers and daughters of your sisters and your foster mothers, those who breast fed you, and your sisters through fosterage and mothers of your wives and your stepdaughters, those who are in your care from wives, those with whom you have lain—but if you have not yet lain with them (f), then there is no blame on you; and wives of your sons who are of your loins; and that you should not gather two sisters together unless it be from the past. Truly, God had been Forgiving, Compassionate.⁴ᐟ²³

Forbidden to you are the ones who are married women, but from females whom your right hands (f) possessed. This is prescribed by God for you. And were permitted to you those who were beyond these so that with your wealth you be looking as males, ones who seek wedlock, not as ones who are licentious males. For what you enjoyed of it from them (f), give them (f) their bridal due as their dowry portion. And there is no blame on you for what you agreed on among yourselves after the duty. Truly, God had been Knowing, Wise.⁴ᐟ²⁴

And whoever of you is not affluent to be able to marry the ones who are free, chaste females, the female believers, then, from females whom your right hands possessed, the ones who are female spiritual warriors, female believers And God is greater in knowledge about your belief. You are of one another. So marry them (f) with the permission of their people, and give them (f) their bridal due as one who is honorable, they being ones who are free, chaste females, without being ones who are licentious females, nor females, ones who take lovers to themselves. And when they (f) are in wedlock, if they (f) approached indecencies, then on them is half of the ones who are free, chaste females of the punishment. That is for those who dreaded fornication among you. And that you endure patiently is better for you. God is Forgiving, Compassionate.⁴ᐟ²⁵

God wants to make manifest to you and to guide you to customs of those who were before you and to turn to you in forgiveness. And God is Knowing, Wise.⁴ᐟ²⁶

God wants that He turn to you in forgiveness while those who follow their lusts want that you turn against God in a serious deviation.⁴ᐟ²⁷ God wants to lighten the burden on you. And the human being was created weak.⁴ᐟ²⁸

O those who believed! Consume not your wealth between you with falsehood, but that it be a transaction of agreeing together among you.

And kill not yourselves. Truly, God had been Compassionate to you.⁴·²⁹

But whoever accomplishes that through deep seated dislike and injustice, We will scorch him in a fire. And that would have been easy for God.⁴·³⁰

If you avoid major sins that you are prohibited, We will absolve you of your minor sins and cause you to enter a generous gate.⁴·³¹

And covet not what God gave as advantage of it to some of you over others. For men is a share of what they deserved and for women is a share of what they (f) deserved. And ask God for His grace. Truly, God had been Knowing of everything.⁴·³²

And to everyone We assigned inheritors to what the ones who are your parents and the nearest kin left. And those with whom you made an agreement with your sworn oaths, then, give them their share. Truly, God had been Witness over everything.⁴·³³

Men are supporters of wives because God gave some of them an advantage over others and because they spent of their wealth. So the females, ones in accord with morality are the females, ones who are morally obligated and the females, ones who guard the unseen of what God kept safe.

And those females whose resistance you fear, then admonish them (f) and abandon them (f) in their sleeping places and go away from them (f). Then if they (f) obeyed you, then look not for any way against them (f). Truly, God had been Lofty, Great.⁴·³⁴

And if you feared a breach between the two, then, raise up an arbiter from his people and an arbiter from her people. If they both want to make things right, God will reconcile it between the two. Truly, God had been Knowing, Aware.⁴·³⁵

And worship God and ascribe nothing as partners with Him. And kindness to the ones who are your parents and to the possessors of kinship and the orphans and the needy, to the neighbor who is as a possessor of strangeness and the neighbor who is kin and to the companion by your side and the traveler of the way and whom your right hands possessed. Truly, God loves not ones who had been proud, boastful,⁴·³⁶ those who are misers and command humanity to miserliness and keep back what God gave them of His grace.

And We made ready for the ones who are ungrateful a despised punishment⁴·³⁷ and for those who spend their wealth to show off to humanity and believe neither in God nor in the Last Day. And to whomever Satan would be a comrade, then how evil a comrade!⁴·³⁸

And what would be for them if they believed in God and the Last Day and spent out of what God provided them? God had been Knowing of them.⁴·³⁹

Truly, God does not wrong even the weight of an atom. And if there be benevolence, He multiplies it and gives that which proceeds from His Presence a sublime compensation.⁴·⁴⁰

Then, how will it be when We brought about from each community a witness and We brought thee about as witness against these?⁴·⁴¹

On a Day those who were ungrateful and rebelled against the Messenger will wish that the earth be shaped over them but they will not keep back God's discourse.⁴·⁴²

O those who believed! Come not near the formal prayer while you are intoxicated until you know what you are saying nor defiled but as one who passes through a way until you wash yourselves. And if you had been sick or on a journey or one of you drew near from the privy or you came into sexual contact with your wives and you find no water, then, aim at getting wholesome, dry earth. Then, wipe your faces and your hands. Truly, God had been Pardoning, Forgiving. Hast thou not considered those who were given a share of the Book? They exchange fallacy and they want you to go astray from the way.⁴·⁴⁴

And God is greater in knowledge of your enemies. And God sufficed as a protector. And God sufficed as a helper.⁴·⁴⁵

Among those who became Jews are those who tamper with words out of context. They say: We heard and we rebelled and: Hear—without being one who is caused to hear and: Look at us—distorting their tongues and discrediting the way of life. And if they said: We heard and we obeyed and: Hear thou and: Wait for us, it would have been better for them and more upright, except God cursed them for their ingratitude. So they believe not but a few.⁴·⁴⁶

O those who were given the Book! Believe in what We sent down, that which establishes as true what was with you, before We obliterate faces, and repel them backward or curse them as We cursed the Companions of the Sabbath. And the command of God had been one that is accomplished.⁴·⁴⁷ Truly, God forgives not to ascribe partners with Him and He forgives other than that whomever He wills. And whoever ascribes partners with God, then, surely, he devised a serious sin.⁴·⁴⁸

Hast thou not considered those who make themselves seem pure? Nay! God makes pure whom He wills and they will not be wronged in the least.⁴·⁴⁹ Look on how they devise a lie against God; and it sufficed as clear sin.⁴·⁵⁰

Hast thou not considered those who were given a share of the Book? They believe in false gods and false deities and they say to those who were ungrateful: These are better guided than those who believed in the way!⁴·⁵¹ Those are those whom God cursed. And for whomever God curses, then, thou wilt not find a helper for him.⁴·⁵²

Or share they in the dominion?

Then, they give not humanity in the least.⁴·⁵³

Are they jealous of humanity for what God gave them of His grace? Then, surely, We gave the people of Abraham the Book and wisdom and We gave them a sublime dominion.⁴·⁵⁴

Then, among them are some who believed in him and among them are some who barred him. And hell sufficed for a blaze.⁴·⁵⁵ Truly, those who were ungrateful for Our signs, We will scorch them in a fire. As often as their skins were wholly burned, We will substitute with other skins so that they will experience the punishment. Truly, God had been Almighty, Wise.⁴·⁵⁶

And those who believed and did as the ones in accord with morality, We will cause them to enter into Gardens beneath which rivers run, ones who will dwell in them forever, eternally. For them in it will be purified spouses. And We will cause them to enter into plenteous shady shadow.⁴·⁵⁷

Truly, God commands you to give back trusts to the people. And when you gave judgment between humanity, give judgment justly. Truly, how excellent God admonishes you of it. Truly, God had been Hearing, Seeing.⁴·⁵⁸

O those who believed! Obey God and obey the Messenger and those imbued with authority among you. Then, if you contended with one another in anything, refer it to God and the Messenger if you had been believing in God and the Last Day. That is better and a fairer interpretation. ⁴·⁵⁹

Hast thou not considered those who claim that they believed in what was caused to descend to thee and what was caused to descend before thee? They want to take their disputes to another for judgment—to false deities—while they were commanded to disbelieve in them, but Satan wants to cause them to go astray—a far wandering astray.⁴·⁶⁰

And when it was said to them: Approach now to what God caused to descend and approach now to the Messenger thou hadst seen the ones who are hypocrites barring thee with hindrances.⁴·⁶¹

How then will it be when they are lit on by an affliction for what their hands put forward?

Again, they drew near thee, swearing by God: Truly, we wanted but kindness and conciliation!⁴⁶² They are those whom God knows what is in their hearts. So turn aside from them and admonish them and say to them concerning themselves penetrating sayings.⁴⁶³

And We never sent a Messenger, but he is obeyed with the permission of God. And if, when they did wrong themselves, they drew near to thee and asked for the forgiveness of God and the Messenger asked for forgiveness for them, they found God Accepter of Repentance, Compassionate.⁴⁶⁴

But no! By thy Lord! They will not believe until they make thee a judge in what they disagreed about between them. Again, they find within themselves no impediment to what thou hadst decided, resigning themselves to submission, full submission.⁴⁶⁵

And if We prescribed for them that you: Kill yourselves, or: Go forth from your abodes, they would not have accomplished it, but a few of them. And had they accomplished what they are admonished by it, it would have been better for them and a stauncher confirming.⁴⁶⁶ And, then, We would have given them from that which proceeds from Our Presence a sublime compensation.⁴⁶⁷ And We would have guided them on a straight path.⁴⁶⁸

And whoever obeys God and the Messenger, those are to whom God was gracious among the Prophets and just persons and the witnesses and the ones in accord with morality. And excellent were those as allies!⁴⁶⁹ That is the grace from God. And God sufficed as Knowing.⁴⁷⁰

O those who believed! Take your precautions. Then, move forward in companies of men or move forward altogether.⁴⁷¹ And, truly, among you is he who lingers behind. Then, if affliction lit on you, he would say: Surely, God was gracious to me that I not be a witness to them.⁴⁷² And if the grace of God lit on you, certainly, he would say, as if there be not any affection between you and between him: Would that I had been with them so that I would have won a triumph, winning a sublime triumph!⁴⁷³ Then, let fight in the way of God those who sell this present life for the world to come. And whoever fights in the way of God, then, is slain or is vanquished, We will give him a sublime compensation.⁴⁷⁴

And why should you not fight in the way of God and for the ones taken advantage of due to weakness among the men and the women and the children, those who say: Our Lord! Bring us out from this town whose people are the ones who are unjust and assign for us a protector from Thy Presence and assign for us a helper from Thy Presence?⁴⁷⁵

Those who believed fight in the way of God. And those who were ungrateful fight in the way of the false deity. So fight the protectors of Satan. Truly the cunning of Satan had been weak.⁴⁷⁶

Hast thou not considered those who when it was said to them: Limit your hands from warfare and perform the formal prayer and give the purifying alms?

Then, when fighting was prescribed for them, there was a group of people among them who dread humanity, even dreading God or with a more severe dreading, and they said: Our Lord! Why hadst Thou prescribed fighting for us? Why hadst Thou not postponed it for another near term for us?

Say: The enjoyment of the present is little and the world to come is better. For whomever was Godfearing, you will not be wronged in the least.⁴⁷⁷

Wherever you be, death will overtake you, even if you had been in imposing towers. And when benevolence lights on them, they say: This is from God. And when an evil deed lights on them, they say: This is from thee.

Say: All is from God. So what is with these folk that they understand almost no discourse?⁴⁷⁸ Whatever of benevolence lit on thee is from God. And whatever evil deeds lit on thee, then, is from thyself. And We sent thee to humanity as a Messenger. And God sufficed as Witness.⁴⁷⁹

Whoever obeys the Messenger, surely, obeyed God and whoever turned away, then We sent thee not as a guardian over them.⁴⁸⁰

And they say: Obedience! Then, when they departed from thee, a section of them spent the night planning on other than what thou hast said. And God records what they spend the night planning. So turn aside from them and put thy trust in God. And God sufficed as Trustee.⁴⁸¹

But no! They meditate not on the Recitation. And if it had been from other than God, certainly, they would have found in it many contradictions.⁴⁸² Whenever drew near them a command of public safety or fear, they broadcasted it. But if they referred it to the Messenger, and to those imbued with authority among them, they would have known it—those who investigate from among them. And if it were not for the grace of God on you and His mercy, certainly, you would have followed Satan, but a few.⁴⁸³

So fight thou in the way of God. Thou art not placed with a burden but for thyself. And encourage the ones who believe. Perhaps God will limit the might of those who were ungrateful. And God is Stauncher in might and Stauncher in making an example.⁴⁸⁴

Whoever intercedes with a benevolent intercession, there will be for himself a share of it. And whoever intercedes with an intercession for bad deeds, there will be for himself a like part of it. And God had been over everything One Who Oversees.⁴⁸⁵

And when you were given greetings with greetings, then, give greetings fairer than that or return the same to them. Truly, God had been over everything a Reckoner.⁴⁸⁶

God, there is no god but He. He will, certainly, gather you on the Day of Resurrection. There is no doubt about it. And who is one who is more sincere in discourse than God?⁴⁸⁷

Then, what is it with you that you be two factions concerning the ones who are hypocrites? And God overthrew them for what they earned? Want you to guide whom God caused to go astray? And whomever God causes to go astray, thou wilt never find for him a way.⁴⁸⁸

They wished for you to be ungrateful as they were ungrateful so you become equals. So take not to yourselves protectors from them until they emigrate in the way of God. Then, if they turned away, then, take them and kill them wherever you found them. And take not to yourselves from them either a protector or a helper,⁴⁸⁹ but those who reach out to a folk who between you and between them is a solemn promise or when they drew near to you, their breasts were reluctant that they fight you or they fight their folk?

And if God willed, He would have given them authority over you and they would have fought you. So if they withdrew from you and fight not against you and gave a proposal of surrender to you, then, God has not assigned any way for you against them.⁴⁹⁰

You will find others who want that they be safe from you and that they be safe from their folk. Whenever they were returned to temptation, they were overthrown in it. So if they withdraw not from you, nor give a proposal of surrender to you and limit not their hands, then, take them and kill them wherever you came upon them. And those, We made for you a clear authority against them.⁴⁹¹

And it had not been for the one who believes to kill one who believes unless by error. And whoever killed one who believes by error the letting go of a believing bondsperson and blood money should be handed over to his family unless that family be charitable. And if he had been from the enemy folk of yours and he be one who believes, then, there should be the letting go of a believing bondsperson.

And if he had been of a folk who between you and between them is a solemn promise, then, blood money should be handed over to the family and the letting go of a believing bondsperson. Then, whoever finds not the means, then, formally fast for two successive months as a penance from God. And God had been Knowing, Wise.[4:92]

And whoever kills one who believes as one who is willful, then, his recompense is hell, one who will dwell in it forever. And God was angry with him and cursed him and He prepared for him a tremendous punishment.[4:93]

O those who believed! When you traveled in the way of God, then be clear and say not to whomever gave you a proposal of peace: Thou art not one who believes, looking for advantage in this present life. With God is much gain. Thus, you had been like that before, then God showed grace to you, so be clear. Truly, God had been Aware of what you do.[4:94]

Not on the same level are the ones who sit at home among the ones who believe—other than those imbued with disability—and the ones who struggle in the way of God with their wealth and their lives. God gave advantage to the ones who struggle with their wealth and their lives by a degree over the ones who sit at home. And to each God promised the fairer. And God gave advantage to the ones who struggle over the ones who sit at home with a sublime compensation[4:95] degrees from Him and forgiveness and mercy. And God had been Forgiving, Compassionate.[4:96]

Truly, those whom the angels gathered to themselves—ones who are unjust to themselves—they will say: In what condition had you been?

They will say: We had been ones taken advantage of due to weakness on the earth.

They will say: Be not the earth of God that which is extensive enough to emigrate in it? Then, for those, their place of shelter will be hell. And how evil a Homecoming![4:97]

But the ones taken advantage of due to weakness of the men and the women and the children who are neither able to access some means, nor are they truly guided to the way[4:98] then those, perhaps God will pardon them. And God had been Pardoning, Forgiving.[4:99]

And whoever emigrates in the way of God will find in and on the earth many places of refuge and plenty. And whoever goes forth from his house as one who emigrates for God and His Messenger, and, again, death overtakes him, then, surely, his compensation will fall on God. And God had been Forgiving, Compassionate.[4:100]

And when you traveled on the earth, there is no blame on you if you shorten the formal prayer if you feared that you would be persecuted by those who were ungrateful. The ones who are ungrateful, they had been for you a clear enemy.[4:101]

And when thou hadst been among them, performing the formal prayer with them, let a section of them stand up with thee and take their weapons. And when they prostrated themselves, then, let them move behind you and let another section approach who has not yet formally prayed. Then, let them formally pray with thee and let them take their precaution and their weapons. Those who were ungrateful wished for you to be heedless of your weapons and your sustenance. They would turn against you with a single turning. And there is no blame on you if you had been annoyed because of rain or you had been sick that you lay down your weapons. And take precaution for yourselves. Truly, God prepared for the ones who are ungrateful a despised punishment.[4:102] Then, when you satisfied the formal prayer, then, remember God when upright and sitting and on your sides. And, then, when you were secured, perform the formal prayer. Truly, the formal prayer had been—for the ones who believe—a timed prescription.[4:103]

And be not feeble in looking for the folk. If you be suffering, they suffer as you suffer, yet you hope for from God what they hope not for, and God had been Knowing, Wise.[4:104]

Truly, We caused to descend to thee the Book with The Truth so that thou wilt give judgment between humanity by what God caused thee to see. And be thou not the pleader for ones who are traitors.[4:105] And ask God for forgiveness. Truly, God had been Forgiving, Compassionate.[4:106]

And dispute not for those who are dishonest to themselves. Truly, God loves not anyone who had been a sinful betrayer.[4:107] They conceal themselves from humanity, but they conceal themselves not from God, as He is with them when they spend the night planning with sayings with which He is not well-pleased. God had been One Who Encloses what they do.[4:108]

Lo, behold! You are these who disputed for them in this present life. Then, who will dispute with God for them on the Day of Resurrection? Or who will be a trustee over them?[4:109] And whoever does evil or does wrong to himself, again, asks for forgiveness from God will, truly, find God Forgiving, Compassionate.[4:110]

And whoever earns a sin, truly, he earns it only against himself. And God had been Knowing, Wise.[4:111]

And whoever earns a transgression or a sin, and, again, accuses an innocent one, surely, laid a burden on himself of false charges that harm another's reputation and a clear sin.[4:112]

And were it not for the grace of God on thee and His mercy, a section of them was about to do something that would cause thee to go astray. And they cause none to go astray but themselves and they injure thee not at all. And God caused the Book to descend to thee and wisdom and taught thee what thou art not knowing. The grace of God had been sublime upon thee.[4:113]

No good is there in most of their conspiring secretly, but for him who commanded charity or one who is honorable or makes things right between humanity. And whoever accomplishes that—looking for the goodwill of God—then, We will give him a sublime compensation.[4:114]

And whoever makes a breach with the Messenger after the guidance became clear to him and follows a way other than that of the ones who believe, We will turn him away from what he turns to and We will scorch him in hell. How evil a Homecoming![4:115]

Truly, God forgives not to ascribe partners with Him. And He forgives other than that whomever He wills. And whoever ascribes partners with God, then, surely, went astray, a wandering far astray.[4:116]

They call to other than Him none but female gods and they call to but the rebellious Satan.[4:117] God cursed him.

And Satan said: Truly, I will take to myself of Thy servants, an apportioned share,[4:118] and I will cause them to go astray. And I will fill them with false desires. And I will command them, then they will slit the ears of the flocks. And I will command them, and they will alter the creation of God. And whoever takes Satan to himself for a protector other than God, then, surely, he lost, a clear loss.[4:119]

Satan promises them and fills them with false desires and Satan promises them nothing but delusion.[4:120]

Those, their place of shelter will be hell and they will find no way to escape from it.[4:121]

But those who believed and did as the ones in accord with morality, We will cause them to enter Gardens beneath which rivers run, ones who will dwell in them forever, eternally. The promise of God is true. And who is One More Sincere in speech than God?⁴·¹²²

Paradise will be neither after your fantasies, nor the fantasies of the People of the Book. Whoever does evil will be given recompense for it and he will not find for himself other than God either a protector or a helper.⁴·¹²³

And whoever does as the ones in accord with morality—whether male or female—and is one who believes then, those will enter the Garden and they will not be wronged, in the least.⁴·¹²⁴

And who is fairer in the way of life than he who submitted his face to God and he is one who is a doer of good and followed the creed of Abraham, a monotheist? And God took Abraham to Himself as a friend.⁴·¹²⁵

And to God is whatever is in the heavens and whatever is in and on the earth. And God had been One Who Encloses everything.⁴·¹²⁶

And they ask thee for advice about women.

Say: God pronounces to you about them (f) and what is recounted to you in the Book about women who have orphans, those to whom (f) you give not what was prescribed for them (f) because you prefer that you marry them (f) and about the ones taken advantage of due to weakness among children and that you stand up for the orphans with equity. And whatever you accomplish of good, then, truly, God had been Knowing of it.⁴·¹²⁷

And if a woman feared resistance or turning aside from her husband no blame on either of them that they make things right between the two, that there be reconciliation. And reconciliation is better.

And persons were prone to stinginess.

And if you do good and are Godfearing, then, truly, God had been Aware of what you do.⁴·¹²⁸

You will never be able to be just between wives, even if you were eager so incline not with total inclination away from her, forsaking her as if she be one who is in suspense. And if you make things right and are Godfearing, then, truly, God had been Forgiving, Compassionate.⁴·¹²⁹

And if the two split up, God will enrich each of them from all His plenty. And God had been One Who is Extensive, Wise.⁴·¹³⁰

And to God is whatever is in the heavens and whatever is in and on the earth and, certainly, We charged those who were given the Book before you, and to you, that you be Godfearing of God alone. And if you are ungrateful, then, truly, to God belongs whatever is in the heavens and whatever is in and on the earth. And God had been Sufficient, Worthy of Praise.⁴·¹³¹

And to God belongs whatever is in the heavens and whatever is in and on the earth. And God sufficed as a Trustee.⁴·¹³² If He wills, He will cause you to be put away—O humanity—and approach with others. And over that God had been Powerful.⁴·¹³³

Whoever had been wanting a reward for good deeds in the present, then with God is The Reward for good deeds in the present and in the world to come. And God had been Hearing, Seeing.⁴·¹³⁴

O those who believed! Be staunch in equity as witnesses to God even against yourselves or the ones who are your parents or the nearest of kin, whether you would be rich or poor, then God is Closer to both than you are. So follow not your desires that you become unbalanced. And if you distort or turn aside, then, truly, God had been Aware of what you do.⁴·¹³⁵

O those who believed! Believe in God and His Messenger and the Book which He sent down to His Messenger and the Book that He caused to descend before. And whoever is ungrateful to God and His angels and His Books and His Messengers and the Last Day, then, surely, went astray, a wandering far astray.⁴·¹³⁶

Truly those who believed, and, again, disbelieved, and, again, believe and, again, disbelieve, and, again, added to disbelief, neither will God be forgiving of them nor guide them to a way.⁴·¹³⁷

Give thou good tidings to the ones who are hypocrites that, truly, for them is a painful punishment,⁴·¹³⁸ those who take to themselves the ones who are ungrateful as their protectors instead of the ones who believe! Are they looking for great glory with them? Truly, then, all great glory belongs to God alone.⁴·¹³⁹

And, surely, He sent down to you in the Book that when you heard the signs of God being unappreciated and being ridiculed, then, and sit not with them until they discuss in conversation about other than that or else, you will be like them. Truly, God is One Who Gathers the ones who are hypocrites and the ones who are ungrateful altogether in hell.⁴·¹⁴⁰

Those who lie in wait for you, if there had been a victory from God for you, they would say: Have we not been with you?

If the ones who are ungrateful had been with a share, they would say: Gain we not mastery over you and secure you from among the ones who believe?

And God will give judgment between you on the Day of Resurrection. God will never assign the ones who are ungrateful any way over the ones who believe.⁴·¹⁴¹

Truly, the ones who are hypocrites seek to trick God. And He is The One Who Deceives them, and when they stood up for formal prayer, they stood up lazily to make display to humanity. And they remember not God but a little,⁴·¹⁴² ones who are wavering between this and that, neither with these, nor with these. And whom God causes to go astray, thou wilt never find a way for him.⁴·¹⁴³

O those who believed! Take not to yourselves the ones who are ungrateful as protectors instead of the ones who believe. Want you to assign to God clear authority against yourselves?⁴·¹⁴⁴

Truly, the ones who are hypocrites will be in the lowest, deepest reaches of the fire. And thou wilt not find for them any helper,⁴·¹⁴⁵ but those who repented and made things right and cleaved firmly to God and made sincere their way of life for God, then, those will be with the ones who believe. And God will give the ones who believe a sublime compensation.⁴·¹⁴⁶

What would God accomplish by your punishment if you gave thanks to Him and believed in Him? God had been One Who is Responsive, Knowing.⁴·¹⁴⁷

God loves not the open publishing of evil sayings, the open publishing of evil sayings, but by him who was wronged. God had been Hearing, Knowing.⁴·¹⁴⁸

If you show good or conceal it or pardon evil, then, truly, God had been Pardoning, Powerful.⁴·¹⁴⁹ Truly, those who are ungrateful to God and His Messengers and they want to separate and divide between God and His Messengers and they say: We believe in some and we disbelieve in others, they want that they take themselves to a way between that.⁴·¹⁵⁰ Those, they are, in truth, the ones who are ungrateful. We made ready for the ones who are ungrateful a despised punishment.⁴·¹⁵¹

And those who believed in God and His Messengers and they separate and divide not between any of them, those, He will give them their compensation. And God had been Forgiving, Compassionate.⁴·¹⁵²

The People of the Book ask thee that thou hast sent down to them a Book from heaven. Surely, they had asked Moses for greater than that. Then, they said: Cause us to see God publicly. So a thunderbolt took them for their injustice. Again, they took the calf to themselves after what drew near to them—the clear portents. Even so We pardoned that. And We gave Moses a clear authority.⁴:¹⁵³

And We exalted the mount above them for their solemn promise. And We said to them: Enter the door as ones who prostrate themselves. And We said to them: Disregard not the Sabbath! And We took from them an earnest solemn promise⁴:¹⁵⁴ for their breaking their solemn promise and their ingratitude for the signs of God and their killing the Prophets without right and their saying: Our hearts are encased. Nay! God set a seal on them for their ingratitude—so they believe not but a few—⁴:¹⁵⁵ and for their ingratitude and their saying against Mary serious, false charges to harm her reputation⁴:¹⁵⁶ and for their saying: We killed the Messiah, Jesus son of Mary, the Messenger of God.

And they killed him not, nor they crucified him. Rather, a likeness to him of another was shown to them. And, truly, those who were at variance in it are in uncertainty about it. There is no knowledge with them about it but they are pursuing an opinion. And they for certain killed him not.⁴:¹⁵⁷ Nay! God exalted him to Himself. And God had been Almighty, Wise.⁴:¹⁵⁸ Yet there is none among the People of the Book but will, surely, believe in Jesus before his death. And on the Day of Resurrection he will be a witness against them.⁴:¹⁵⁹

So for the injustice of those who became Jews, We forbade them what was good that was permitted to them and for their barring many from the way of God⁴:¹⁶⁰ and for their taking usury—although they were prohibited from it—and for their consuming the wealth of humanity with falsehood. We made ready for the ones who are ungrateful among them a painful punishment.⁴:¹⁶¹

But the ones who are firmly rooted in knowledge among them and the ones who believe, they believe in what was caused to descend to thee and what was caused to descend before thee. They are the ones who perform the formal prayer. And they are the ones who give the purifying alms. They are the ones who believe in God and the Last Day. It is those to whom We will give a sublime compensation.⁴:¹⁶²

Truly, We revealed to thee, as We revealed to Noah and the Prophets after him. And We revealed to Abraham and Ishmael and Isaac and Jacob and the Tribes and Jesus and Job and Jonah and Aaron and Solomon. And We gave David the Psalms.⁴:¹⁶³

And Messengers We related to thee before and Messengers We relate to thee not. God spoke directly to Moses, speaking directly.⁴:¹⁶⁴ Messengers are ones who give good tidings and ones who warn so that humanity not be in disputation against God after the Messengers. And God had been Almighty, Wise.⁴:¹⁶⁵

And God bears witness to what He caused to descend to thee. He caused it to descend with His knowledge. And the angels also bear witness. And God sufficed as witness.⁴:¹⁶⁶

Truly, those who were ungrateful and barred others from the way of God, they, surely, went astray, a wandering far astray.⁴:¹⁶⁷ Truly, those who were ungrateful and did wrong, God will never be forgiving of them, nor guide them to a road ⁴:¹⁶⁸ but the road to hell, ones who will dwell in it forever, eternally. And that had been easy for God.⁴:¹⁶⁹

O humanity! Surely, the Messenger drew near you with The Truth from your Lord. So believe, it is better for you. And if you are ungrateful, then, truly, to God is whatever is in the heavens and the earth. And God had been Knowing, Wise.⁴:¹⁷⁰

O People of the Book! Go not beyond the limits in your way of life and say not about God but The Truth: That the Messiah, Jesus son of Mary, was a Messenger of God and His Word that He cast to Mary and a Spirit from Him. So believe in God and His Messengers. And say not: Three. To refrain yourselves from it is better for you. There is only One God. Glory be to Him that He have a son! To Him belongs whatever is in the heavens and whatever is in and on the earth and God sufficed as a Trustee.⁴:¹⁷¹

The Messiah will never disdain that he be a servant of God nor the angels, the ones who are brought near to Him. And whoever disdains His worship and grows arrogant, He will assemble them altogether to Himself.⁴:¹⁷²

Then, as for those who believed and did as the ones in accord with morality, then, He will pay their compensation in full and increase His grace for them. And as for those who disdained and grew arrogant, He will punish them with a painful punishment. They will not find for themselves other than God a protector or a helper.⁴:¹⁷³

O humanity! Surely, there drew near you proof from your Lord. And We caused to descend to you a clear light.⁴:¹⁷⁴

So for those who believed in God and cleaved firmly to Him, then, He will cause them to enter into mercy from Him and grace and guide them to Himself on a straight path.⁴:¹⁷⁵

They ask thee for advice.

Say: God pronounces to you about indirect heirs. If a man perished and he be without children and he has a sister, then, for her is half of what he left. And he inherits from her if she be without children. And if there had been two sisters, then, for them (f), two-thirds of what he left. And if there had been brothers/sisters, men and women, the man will have the like allotment as two females. God makes manifest to you so that you go not astray, and God is Knowing of everything.⁴:¹⁷⁶

CHAPTER 5 THE TABLE SPREAD WITH FOOD

In the Name of God The Merciful, The Compassionate

O those who believed! Live up to your agreements. Flocks of animals were permitted to you, but what is now recounted to you: You are not ones who are permitted hunting while you are in pilgrim sanctity. Truly, God gives judgment how He wants.⁵:¹

O those who believed! Profane not the waymarks of God nor the Sacred Month nor the sacrificial gift nor the garlanded nor ones who are bound for the Sacred House looking for grace from their Lord and contentment. And when you left your pilgrim sanctity, then, hunt.

And let not that you detest a folk who barred you from the Masjid al-Haram drive you into exceeding the limits. And cooperate with one another in virtuous conduct and God-consciousness and cooperate not with one another in sin and deep seated dislike. And be Godfearing of God. Truly, God is Severe in repayment.⁵:²

Carrion was forbidden to you and blood and flesh of swine and what of it was hallowed to other than God and the one that is a strangled beast and the one that is beaten to death and the animal one fallen to its death and the animal gored to death or eaten by a beast of prey—but what you slew lawfully—and what were sacrificed to fetishes and what you partition by divining arrows. That is contrary to moral law. Today, those who were ungrateful gave up hope because of your way of life. So dread them not but dread Me.

Today, I perfected your way of life for you and I fulfilled My divine blessing on you and I was well-pleased with submission to the One God for your way of life.

Whoever was driven by necessity due to emptiness—not one who inclines to sin—then, truly, God is Forgiving, Compassionate.⁵:³

They ask thee what was permitted to them. Say: That which is good was permitted to you and what you taught of hunting creatures, as one who teaches hunting dogs of what God taught you. So eat of what they seized for you and remember the Name of God over it and be Godfearing of God. Truly, God is Swift in reckoning.⁵:⁴

Today, what is good was permitted to you. The food of those to whom We gave the Book is allowed to you and your food is allowed to them. And the ones who are free, chaste females from the females, ones who believe and the ones who are free, chaste females from among those who were given the Book before you when you were to give them their bridal due, as males, ones who seek wedlock, not as ones who are licentious males, nor as males, ones who take lovers to themselves.

And whoever disbelieves after belief, then, surely, his actions will be fruitless. And he in the world to come will be among the ones who are losers.⁵:⁵

O those who believed! When you stood up for the formal prayer, then, wash your faces and your hands up to the elbows and wipe your heads and your feet up to the ankles. If you had been defiled, then, cleanse yourselves. And if you had been sick or on a journey or one of you drew near from the privy or you came into sexual contact with your wives and you find no water, then, aim at getting wholesome, dry earth and wipe your faces and hands with it. God wants not to make any impediment for you and He wants to purify you and to fulfill His divine blessing on you, so that perhaps you will give thanks.⁵:⁶

And remember the divine blessing of God on you and His solemn promise that he made as a covenant with you by it when you said: We heard and we obeyed.

And be Godfearing of God. Truly, God is Knowing of what is in the breasts.⁵:⁷

O those who believed! Be staunch in equity as witnesses to God and let not that you detest a folk drive you into not dealing justly. Be just. That is nearer to God-consciousness. And be Godfearing of God. Truly, God is Aware of what you do.⁵:⁸

And God promised those who believed and did as the ones in accord with morality that for them is forgiveness and a sublime compensation.⁵:⁹

And those who were ungrateful and denied Our signs, those will be the Companions of Hellfire!⁵:¹⁰

O those who believed! Remember the divine blessing of God on you when they, a folk, were about to extend their hands against you, but He limited their hands from you. And be Godfearing of God. And in God let the ones who believe put their trust.⁵:¹¹

And, certainly, God took a solemn promise from the Children of Israel and We raised up among them twelve chieftains. And God said: Truly, I am with you. If you performed the formal prayer and gave the purifying alms and believed in My Messengers and you supported them and you lent God a fairer loan, I would, certainly, absolve you of your evil deeds. And I would, certainly, cause you to enter Gardens beneath which rivers run. Then, whoever among you was ungrateful after this, then, surely, he went astray from the right way.⁵:¹²

Then, for their breaking their solemn promise, We cursed them and We made their hearts ones that harden. They tamper with the words out of context and they forgot an allotment of what they were reminded of in it. Thou wilt not cease to peruse the treachery of them, but a few of them. Then, overlook and pardon them. Truly, God loves the ones who are doers of good.⁵:¹³

And from those who said: We are Christians, We took their solemn promise, but they forgot an allotment of what they were reminded of it so We stirred up enmity and hatred among them until the Day of Resurrection. And God will tell them of what they had been crafting.⁵:¹⁴

O People of the Book! Surely, Our Messenger drew near you. He makes manifest to you much of what you had been concealing of the Book and pardons much. Surely, from God drew near you a light and a clear Book.⁵:¹⁵ God guides with it whoever followed His contentment to ways of peace and He brings them out from the shadows into the light with His permission and He guides them to a straight path.⁵:¹⁶

Certainly, ungrateful were those who said: Truly, God is the Messiah, the son of Mary. Say: Who, then, has any sway over God? If He wanted to He would cause the Messiah son of Mary and his mother to perish and whatever is in and on the earth altogether. To God belongs the dominion of the heavens and the earth and what is between the two. He creates what He wills. And God is Powerful over everything. ⁵:¹⁷

And the Jews and Christians said: We are the children of God and His beloved.

Say: Why, then, does He punish you for your impieties? Nay! You are mortals whom He created. He forgives whom He wills and He punishes whom He wills. And to God belongs the dominion of the heavens and the earth and what is even between the two. And to Him is the Homecoming!⁵:¹⁸

O People of the Book! Surely, Our Messenger drew near you. He makes manifest to you the way of life—after an interval without Messengers—so that you say not: There drew not near us either a bearer of good tidings or a warner. Then, surely, drew near to you a bearer of good tidings and a warner. And God is Powerful over everything.⁵:¹⁹

And mention when Moses said to his folk: O my folk! Remember the divine blessing of God on you when He assigned Prophets among you and assigned kings and gives you what He gave not to anyone of the worlds.⁵:²⁰

O my folk! Enter the region, one that is sanctified, that God prescribed for you and go not back, turning your back, for, then, you will turn about as ones who are losers.⁵:²¹

They said: O Moses! Truly, in it is a haughty folk and we will never enter it until they go forth from it, but if they go forth from it, then, we will, certainly, be ones who enter.⁵:²²

Two men to whom God was gracious said among those who fear to disobey: Enter on them through the door! And when you entered it, you will, certainly, be ones who are victors. And put your trust in God if you had been ones who believe.⁵:²³

They said: O Moses! We will never enter it as long as they continued in it, so thou and thy Lord, you two go and fight. We are here, ones who sit at home.⁵:²⁴

He said: My Lord! I control no one but myself and my brother so separate Thou between us and between the folk, the ones who disobey.⁵:²⁵

He said: Truly, it is that which is forbidden to them ^for forty years.^ They will wander about the earth. So grieve not for the folk, the ones who disobey.⁵:²⁶

And recount thou to them the tiding of the two sons of Adam in Truth when they both brought near a sacrifice and it was received from one of them but there is non-acceptance from the other.

He said: I will, surely, kill thee.

He said: Truly, God receives only from the ones who are Godfearing.⁵:²⁷ If thou wert to extend thy hand against me so that thou wouldst kill me, I would not be one who stretches out my hand towards thee so that I kill thee. I fear God, Lord of the worlds.⁵:²⁸ Truly, I want that thou wilt draw the burden of my sin and thy sin, then, to be among the Companions of the Fire. That is the recompense of the ones who are unjust.⁵:²⁹

Then, his soul prompted him to kill his brother. And he killed him and became among the ones who are losers.⁵:³⁰ Then, God raised up a raven to scratch the earth, to cause him to see how to cover up the naked corpse of his brother.

He says: Woe to me! Was I unable to be like this raven to cover up the naked corpse of my brother? Then, he became among the ones who were remorseful.⁵:³¹

On account of that, We prescribed for the Children of Israel that whoever killed a person, other than in retribution for another person, or because of corruption in and on the earth, it will be as if he had killed all of humanity. And whoever gave life to one, it will be as if he gave life to all of humanity. And, certainly, our Messengers drew near them with the clear portents. Again, truly, many of them after that were ones who were excessive in and on the earth.⁵:³²

The only recompense for those who war against God and His Messenger and hasten about corrupting in and on the earth, is that they be killed or caused to be crucified or their hands and their feet be cut off on opposite sides or they be expelled from the region. That for them is their degradation in the present. And for them in the world to come, there is a tremendous punishment,⁵:³³ but for those who repented before you have power over them. So know you that God is Forgiving, Compassionate.⁵:³⁴

O those who believed! Be Godfearing of God and look for an approach to Him and struggle in His way so that perhaps you will prosper.⁵:³⁵

Truly, those who were ungrateful, if they had whatever is in and on the earth and the like of it with as much again that they offer it as ransom from the punishment on the Day of Resurrection, it would not be received from them and for them is a painful punishment.⁵:³⁶ They will want to go forth from the fire, but they will not be ones who go forth from it. And for them is an abiding punishment.⁵:³⁷

And as for the one who is a male thief and the one who is a female thief, then, sever their hands as recompense for what they earned, an exemplary punishment from God. And God is Almighty, Wise.⁵:³⁸ But whoever repents after his injustice and made things right, then, truly, God will turn to him in forgiveness. Truly, God is Forgiving, Compassionate.⁵:³⁹

Hast thou not known that to God, to Him belongs the dominion of the heavens and the earth? He punishes whom He wills and He forgives whom He wills. And God is Powerful over everything.⁵:⁴⁰ O Messenger! Let them not dishearten thee—those who compete with one another in ingratitude among those who said: We believed with their mouths while their hearts believe not.

And among those who became Jews are ones who hearken to lies, ones who hearken to folk of others who approach not thee. They tamper with the words out of context. They say: If you were given this, then, take it, but if you are not given this, then, beware!

And for whomever God wants to test, thou wilt never have sway over him against God at all. Those are whom God wants not to purify their hearts. For them in the present is degradation. And for them in the world to come is a tremendous punishment.⁵:⁴¹ They are ones who hearken to lies, the ones who devour the wrongful.

Then, if they drew near thee, then, give thou judgment between them or turn aside from them. And if thou hast turned aside from them, then, they will never injure thee at all. And if thou hadst given judgment, then, give judgment between them with equity. Truly, God loves the ones who act justly.⁵:⁴²

And how will they make thee their judge while with them is the Torah wherein is the determination of God? Yet, again, after that, they turn away. Those are the ones who believe not.⁵:⁴³

Truly, We caused the Torah to descend wherein is guidance and light. The Prophets give judgment with it, those who submitted to God, for those who became Jews and the rabbis and learned Jewish scholars who committed to memory the Book of God and they had been witnesses to it. So dread not humanity, but dread Me. And exchange not My signs for a little price. And whoever gives not judgment by what God caused to descend, those, they are the ones who are ungrateful.⁵:⁴⁴

And We prescribed for them in it: A life for a life and an eye for an eye and a nose for a nose and an ear for an ear and a tooth for a tooth and for injuries to the body, reciprocation. Then, whoever was charitable and forgives it, it will be an atonement for him. And whoever gives judgment not by what God caused to descend, then, those, they are the ones who are unjust.⁵:⁴⁵

And We sent following in their footsteps, Jesus son of Mary, one who establishes as true what was before him in the Torah. And We gave him the Gospel in which is guidance and light, and that which establishes as true what was before him in the Torah and a guidance and admonishment for the ones who are Godfearing.⁵:⁴⁶

And let the People of the Gospel give judgment by what God caused to descend in it. And whoever gives not judgment by what God caused to descend, then, those, they are the ones who disobey.⁵:⁴⁷

And We caused the Book to descend to thee with The Truth, that which establishes as true what was before it of the Book and that which preserves it. So give judgment between them by what God caused to descend. And follow not their desires that drew near thee against The Truth.

For each among you We made a divine law and an open road. And if God willed, He would have made you one community to try you with what He gave you so be forward in good deeds. To God is your return altogether. Then, He will tell you about what you had been at variance in it.⁵:⁴⁸

And give judgment between them by what God caused to descend and follow not their desires and beware of them so that they tempt thee not from some of what God caused to descend to thee. And if they turned away, then, know that God only wants that He light on them for some of their impieties. And, truly, many within humanity are ones who disobey.⁵:⁴⁹

Look they for a determination of Age of Ignorance? And who is fairer than God in determination for a folk who are certain?⁵:⁵⁰

O those who believed! Take not to yourselves the Jews and the Christians as protectors. Some of them are protectors of one another. And whoever among you turns away to them, then, he is of them. Truly, God guides not the folk, the ones who are unjust.⁵:⁵¹

And thou hast seen those who in their hearts is a sickness. They compete with one another. They say: We dread that a turn of fortune should light on us. Then, perhaps God brings a victory or a command from Him? Then, they will become—from what they kept secret within themselves—ones who are remorseful.⁵:⁵²

And those who believed will say: Are these they who swore an oath by God—the most earnest of sworn oaths—that they were with you?

Their actions were fruitless. They became ones who are losers.⁵:⁵³

O those who believed! Whoever of you goes back on his way of life, God will bring the folk whom He loves and who love Him, humble-spirited towards the ones who believe, disdainful towards the ones who are ungrateful. They struggle in the way of God and they fear not the reproach of one who is reproached. That is the grace of God. He gives it to whom He wills. And God is One Who is Extensive, Knowing.⁵ᐟ⁵⁴

Your protector is only God and His Messenger and those who believed and those who perform the formal prayer and give the purifying alms and they are ones who bow down.⁵ᐟ⁵⁵

And whoever turns in friendship to God and His Messenger and those who believed, then, behold the Party of God. They are the ones who are victors.⁵ᐟ⁵⁶

O those who believed! Take not to yourselves those who took to themselves your way of life in mockery and as a pastime from among those who were given the Book before you and the ones who are ungrateful, as protectors. And be Godfearing of God if you had been ones who believe.⁵ᐟ⁵⁷

And when you cried out for formal prayer they took it to themselves in mockery and as a pastime. That is because they are a folk who are not reasonable.⁵ᐟ⁵⁸

Say: O People of the Book! Seek you revenge on us because we believed in God and what was caused to descend to us and what was caused to descend before, while, truly, most of you are ones who disobey?⁵ᐟ⁵⁹

Say: Will I tell thee of worse than that as a reward from God? He whom God cursed and with whom He was angry and He made some of them into apes and swine who worshiped the false deities. Those are worse placed and ones who go astray from the right way.⁵ᐟ⁶⁰

And when they drew near you they said: We believed. And, surely, they entered with ingratitude and they, surely, went forth with it. And God is greater in knowledge of what they had been keeping back.⁵ᐟ⁶¹

And thou hast seen many of them competing with one another in sin and deep seated dislike and in consuming the wrongful. What they had been doing was miserable.⁵ᐟ⁶²

Why prohibit not the rabbis and learned Jewish scholars their sayings of sin and their consuming the wrongful? Miserable was what they had been crafting.⁵ᐟ⁶³

And the Jews said: The hand of God is one that is restricted! Restricted were their hands! And they were cursed for what they said.

Nay! His hands are ones that are stretched out: He spends how He wills. And, certainly, many of them increase by what was caused to descend to thee from thy Lord in defiance and in ingratitude. And We cast among them enmity and hatred until the Day of Resurrection. Whenever they kindled a fire of war, God extinguished it. And they hasten about corrupting in and on the earth. And God loves not the ones who make corruption.⁵ᐟ⁶⁴

And if the People of the Book believed and were Godfearing, certainly, We would have absolved them from their evil deeds and caused them to enter into Gardens of Bliss.⁵ᐟ⁶⁵

And if they adhered to the Torah and the Gospel—what was caused to descend to them from their Lord, they would, certainly, have eaten in abundance from above them and from beneath their feet.

Among them is a community of ones who halt between two opinions. But many of them, how evil is what they do!⁵ᐟ⁶⁶

O Messenger! State what was caused to descend to thee from thy Lord, for if thou hast not accomplished it, then, thou wilt not have stated His message. And God will save thee from the harm of humanity. Truly, God guides not the folk, the ones who are ungrateful.⁵ᐟ⁶⁷

Say: O People of the Book! You are not based on anything until you adhere to the Torah and the Gospel and what was caused to descend to you from your Lord. And, certainly, many of them increase by what was caused to descend to

thee from thy Lord in defiance and ingratitude. So grieve not for folk, the ones who are ungrateful.⁵ᐟ⁶⁸

Truly, those who believed, those who became Jews and Sabeans and Christians—whoever believed in God and the Last Day and did as one in accord with morality, then, there will be neither fear in them nor will they feel remorse.⁵ᐟ⁶⁹

Certainly, We took a solemn promise from the Children of Israel and We sent Messengers to them. Whenever a Messenger drew near them with what they themselves yearn not for, a group of people denied them and a group of people kill them.⁵ᐟ⁷⁰

And they assumed there would be no test. They were in darkness and became unhearing. Again, God turned to them in forgiveness. Again, in darkness and became unhearing many of them. And God is Seeing of what they do.⁵ᐟ⁷¹

And, certainly, were ungrateful those who said: Truly, God is He, the Messiah, son of Mary, but the Messiah said: O Children of Israel! Worship God, my Lord and your Lord. Truly, whoever ascribes partners with God, then, surely, God forbade the Garden to him. And his place of shelter will be the fire. And for the ones who are unjust, there are no helpers.⁵ᐟ⁷²

Certainly, ungrateful were those who said: Truly, God is the third of three. There is no god but One God. And if they refrain not themselves from what they say, there will afflict those who were ungrateful among them a painful punishment.⁵ᐟ⁷³

Will they not, then, turn to God for forgiveness and ask for His forgiveness? And God is Forgiving, Compassionate.⁵ᐟ⁷⁴

The Messiah son of Mary was not but a Messenger. Surely, Messengers passed away before him. And his mother was a just person (f). They both had been eating food. Look on how We make manifest the signs to them. Again, look on how they are misled!⁵ᐟ⁷⁵

Say: Worship you other than God what controls neither hurt nor profit for you? And God, He is The Hearing, The Knowing.⁵ᐟ⁷⁶

Say: O People of the Book! Go not beyond limits in your way of life but with The Truth and follow not the desires of the folk who, surely, went astray before. And they caused many to go astray. And they themselves went astray from the right way.⁵ᐟ⁷⁷

Those who were ungrateful were cursed among the Children of Israel by the tongue of David and that of Jesus son of Mary. That was because they would rebel and they had been exceeding the limits.⁵ᐟ⁷⁸ They had not been forbidding one another from that which is unlawful that they committed. Miserable was what they had been committing!⁵ᐟ⁷⁹

Thou hast seen many of them turning away to those who were ungrateful. Miserable was what was put forward for them themselves so that God was displeased with them and in their punishment they are ones who will dwell in it forever.⁵ᐟ⁸⁰

If they had been believing in God and the Prophet and what was caused to descend to him, they would not have taken them to themselves protectors, but many of them are ones who disobey.⁵ᐟ⁸¹

Truly, thou wilt find the hardest of humanity in enmity to those who believed are the Jews and those who have ascribed partners with God. And, certainly, thou wilt find the nearest of them in affection to those who believed are those who said: We are Christians. That is because among them are priests and monks and they grow not arrogant.⁵ᐟ⁸²

And when they heard what was caused to descend to the Messenger, thou hast seen their eyes overflow with tears because they recognized The Truth.

They say: Our Lord! We believed so write us down with the ones who bear witness.⁵ᐟ⁸³

And why believe we not in God and in what drew near us of The Truth?

And we are desirous that Our Lord would cause us to enter the Garden among the folk—the ones in accord with morality.⁵:⁸⁴ Then, God repaid them for what they said—Gardens beneath which rivers run, ones who will dwell in them forever. And that is the recompense of the ones who are doers of good.⁵:⁸⁵

But those who are ungrateful and denied Our signs, those will be the Companions of Hellfire.⁵:⁸⁶

O those who believed! Forbid not what is good that God permitted to you and exceed not the limits. Truly, God loves not the ones who exceed the limits.⁵:⁸⁷ And eat of what God provided you, the lawful, what is good. And be Godfearing of God in Whom you are ones who believe.⁵:⁸⁸

God will not take you to task for what is idle talk in your oaths, but He will take you to task for oaths you made as an agreement. Then, its expiation is the feeding of ten needy people of the average of what you feed your own people or clothing them or letting go of a bondsperson. But whoever finds not the means, then, formal fasting for three days. That is the expiation for your oaths when you swore them. And keep your oaths safe. Thus, God makes manifest His signs to you so that perhaps you will give thanks.⁵:⁸⁹

O those who believed! Truly, intoxicants and gambling and fetishes and divining arrows are of the disgraceful actions of Satan. Then, avoid them so that perhaps you will prosper.⁵:⁹⁰ But Satan only wants that he precipitate enmity and hatred between you through intoxicants and gambling and bar you from the remembrance of God and from formal prayer. Then, will you be ones who desist?⁵:⁹¹

And obey God and obey the Messenger and beware. Then, truly, if you turned away, then, know that only on Our Messenger is the delivering of Our clear message.⁵:⁹²

There is not for those who believed and did as the ones in accord with morality blame for what they tasted when they were Godfearing and believed and did as the ones in accord with morality and, again, they were Godfearing and believed. And, again, they were Godfearing and did good. And God loves the ones who are doers of good.⁵:⁹³

O those who believed! Certainly, God will try you with something of the game that your hands and your lances attain so that God knows who fears Him in the unseen. Then, whoever exceeded the limits after that, for him is a painful punishment.⁵:⁹⁴

O those who believed! Kill not game when you are in pilgrim sanctity. And whoever of you killed as one who is willful, then, the recompense is like what he killed of flocks by two possessors of justice who give judgment.

Among you will be a sacrificial gift—that which reaches the Kabah—or the expiation of food for the needy or the equivalent of that in formal fasting so that he, certainly, experiences the mischief of his conduct. God pardoned what is past. And whoever reverted to it, then, God will requite him. And God is Almighty, Possessor of Requital.⁵:⁹⁵

The game of the sea was permitted to you and the food of it as sustenance for you and for a company of travelers, but the game of dry land was forbidden to you as long as you continued in pilgrim sanctity. And be Godfearing of God to Whom you will be assembled.⁵:⁹⁶

God made the Kabah the Sacred House, maintaining it for humanity and the Sacred Month and the sacrificial gift and the garlanded. That is so that you will know that God knows whatever is in the heavens and whatever is in and on the earth and that God is Knowing of everything.⁵:⁹⁷ Know that God is Severe in repayment and that God is Forgiving, Compassionate.⁵:⁹⁸

What is with the Messenger is not but the delivering of the message. And God knows whatever you show and whatever you keep back.⁵:⁹⁹

Say: Not on the same level are the bad and what is good even if the prevalence of the bad impressed thee. So be Godfearing of God, O those imbued with intuition, so that perhaps you will prosper.⁵:¹⁰⁰

O those who believed! Ask not about things that if they are shown to you would raise anger in you. Yet if you ask about them at the time when the Quran is being sent down, they will be shown to you. God pardoned that which is past. And God is Forgiving, Forbearing.⁵:¹⁰¹

Surely, the folk asked about them before you. Again, they became ones who are ungrateful for it.⁵:¹⁰²

God made not the thing called Bahirah nor Saibah nor Wasilah nor Hami, but those who were ungrateful, they devise lies against God and most of them are not reasonable.⁵:¹⁰³

And when it was said to them: Approach now to what God caused to descend and to the Messenger, they said: Enough is what we found our fathers upon.

Even though their fathers had been knowing nothing nor are they truly guided?⁵:¹⁰⁴

O those who believed! Upon you is the charge of your souls. He who went astray injures you not if you were truly guided. To God is the return of you all. Then, He will tell you what you had been doing.⁵:¹⁰⁵

O those who believed! Have testimony between you when death attended anyone of you. At the time of bequeathing, have two possessors of justice from among yourselves or two others from among others if you traveled through the region and the affliction of death lit on you. You will detain them both after the formal prayer. And they will swear by God.

If you were in doubt about them, have them say: We will not exchange it for a price even if he had been possessing kinship. And we will not keep back testimony of God. Truly, we, then, would be among the ones who are perverted.⁵:¹⁰⁶

Then, if it was ascertained that the two merited an accusation of sin, then, two others will stand up in their station from among those who are the most deserving, nearest in kinship, and they both swear an oath by God saying: Our testimony has a better right than the testimony of the other two. And we exceeded not the limits, for, truly, we, then, would be among the ones who are unjust.⁵:¹⁰⁷

That is likelier that they bring testimony in proper form or they fear that their oaths will be repelled after the others' oaths. So be Godfearing of God and hear. And God guides not the folk, the ones who disobey.⁵:¹⁰⁸

On a Day when God will gather the Messengers and will say: What was your answer?

They will say: We have no knowledge. Truly, Thou, Thou alone art Knower of the unseen.⁵:¹⁰⁹

Mention when God said: O Jesus son of Mary! Remember My divine blessing on thee and on the one who is thy mother, when I confirmed thee, Jesus, with the hallowed Spirit so that thou hast spoken to humanity from the cradle and in manhood and when I taught thee the Book and wisdom and the Torah and the Gospel and when thou hast created from clay the likeness of a bird with My permission and thou hast breathed into it and it becomes a bird with My permission and thou hast cured one blind from birth and the leper with My permission and when thou hast brought out the dead with My permission and when I limited the Children of Israel from thee when thou hadst drawn near them with the clear portents.

And those who were ungrateful among them said: This is nothing but clear sorcery.⁵:¹¹⁰

Mention when I inspired the disciples: Believe in Me and My Messenger.

They said: We believed and bear witness that we are ones who submit to God.⁵:¹¹¹

Mention when the disciples said: O Jesus son of Mary! Is thy Lord able to send down to us a table spread with food from heaven?

Jesus said: Be Godfearing of God, if you had been ones who believe.⁵:¹¹²

They said: We want that we eat of it so that our hearts be at rest and we know that thou, surely, wast sincere to us and that we be the ones who bear witness to that.⁵:¹¹³

Jesus son of Mary said: O God! Our Lord! Cause to descend for us a table spread with food from heaven that it will be a festival for the first of us and the last of us and a sign from Thee. And provide us. And Thou art Best of the ones who provide.⁵:¹¹⁴

God said: Truly, I am One Who Sends Down to you. But whoever is ungrateful after that among you, then, I will punish him with a punishment that I punish not anyone of the worlds.⁵:¹¹⁵

And mention when God said: O Jesus son of Mary! Hadst thou said to humanity: Take me and my mother to yourselves other than God?

He would say: Glory be to Thee! It is not for me that I say what there is no right for me to say. If I had been saying it, then, surely, Thou wouldst have known it. Thou hast known what is in my soul and I know not what is in Thy Soul. Truly, Thou, Thou alone art Knower of the unseen.⁵:¹¹⁶ I said not to them but what Thou hadst commanded me of it: That you worship God, my Lord and your Lord. And I had been witness over them as long as I continued among them. Then, when Thou hadst gathered me to Thyself, Thou hadst been The Watcher over them. Thou art, truly, Witness over everything.⁵:¹¹⁷

If Thou art to punish them, then, they are but Thy servants. And if Thou art to forgive them truly, Thou, Thou alone art The Almighty, The Wise.⁵:¹¹⁸

God would say: This Day the ones who are sincere will profit from their sincerity. For them are Gardens beneath which rivers run, ones who will dwell in them forever, eternally. God was well-pleased with them and they are well-pleased with Him. That is the winning the sublime triumph.⁵:¹¹⁹

To God belongs the dominion of the heavens and the earth and whatever is in and on them. And He is Powerful over everything.⁵:¹²⁰

CHAPTER 6 THE FLOCKS

In the Name of God The Merciful, The Compassionate

The Praise belongs to God Who created the heavens and the earth and made the shadows and the light. Again, those who were ungrateful to their Lord, they equate others to Him.⁶:¹

It was He Who created you from clay, and, again, decided a term, a term, that which was determined by Him. Again, you contest.⁶:²

And He is God in the heavens and in and on the earth. He knows your secret and what you openly publish and He knows whatever you earn.⁶:³

And a sign not approaches for them from the signs of their Lord but they would be ones who turn aside from it.⁶:⁴

Then, surely, they denied The Truth when it drew near to them. Then, tidings approach them of what they had been ridiculing of it.⁶:⁵

Consider they not how many a generation before them We caused to perish? We established them firmly in and on the earth such as We firmly establish not for you. And We sent abundant rain from heaven. And We made rivers run

beneath them. So We caused them to perish for their impieties and We caused to grow after them other generations.⁶:⁶

And if We sent down to thee a Book on parchment, then, they would have stretched towards it with their hands. Those who were ungrateful would have said: This is nothing but clear sorcery.⁶:⁷

And they said: Why was an angel not caused to descend to him?

And, certainly, if We caused to descend an angel, the command would be decided. Again, no respite would be given to them.⁶:⁸

And if We made him an angel, certainly, We would have made him as a man and We would have confused them when they are already confused.⁶:⁹

And, certainly, Messengers were ridiculed before thee. So those who derided them were surrounded by what they had been ridiculing.⁶:¹⁰

Say: Journey through the earth; again, look on how had been the Ultimate End of the ones who deny.⁶:¹¹

Say: To whom is whatever is in the heavens and the earth?

Say: To God. He prescribed mercy for Himself. He will, certainly, gather you on the Day of Resurrection. There is no doubt in it. Those who lost themselves that Day, then, they will not believe.⁶:¹²

And to Him belongs whatever inhabited the nighttime and the daytime. And He is The Hearing, The Knowing.⁶:¹³

Say: Will I take to myself, other than God, a protector, One Who is Originator of the heavens and the earth? And it is He who feeds and He who is never fed.

Say: Truly, I was commanded: that I be the first who submitted to the One God And thou hast not been among the ones who are polytheists.⁶:¹⁴

Say: Truly, I fear if I rebelled against my Lord, the punishment of the tremendous Day!⁶:¹⁵

He who is turned away from it on that Day, then, surely, He had mercy on him. And that is the winning the clear triumph.⁶:¹⁶

And if God touches thee with harm, then, no one will remove it but He. And if He touches thee with good, then, He is Powerful over everything.⁶:¹⁷ He is The One Who is Omniscient over His servants. And He is The Wise, The Aware.⁶:¹⁸

Say: Which thing is greater in testimony?

Say: God is Witness between me and you. And this, the Quran, was revealed to me that I should warn you with it and whomever it reached. Truly, are you bearing witness that there are other gods with God?

Say: I bear not such witness.

Say: He is not but One God and I am, truly, free from partners you ascribe with Him.⁶:¹⁹

Those to whom We gave the Book recognize it as they recognize their own children. But those, they who lost themselves, they believe not.⁶:²⁰

And who does greater wrong than he who devised a lie against God or denied His signs. Truly, the ones who are unjust will not prosper.⁶:²¹

And on a Day We will assemble them altogether. Again, We will say to those who ascribed partners with God: Where are your ascribed associates with God whom you had been claiming?⁶:²²

Again, their dissent will not be but that they would say: By God! Our Lord! We had not been ones who are polytheists.⁶:²³ Look on how they have lied against themselves. Went astray with them that which they had been devising.⁶:²⁴

And among them are those who listen to thee. But We laid sheathes on their hearts so that they not understand it and in their ears is a heaviness. And if they are to see every sign they will not believe in it. So that when they drew near thee, they dispute with thee.

Those who were ungrateful say: This is nothing but fables of the ancient ones.⁶:²⁵

And they prohibit others from it. And they withdraw aside from it. And they cause to perish, no doubt, none but themselves, but they are not aware.⁶:²⁶¹

And if thou wouldst see when they would be stationed by the fire, they will say: Would that we be returned to life. Then, we would not deny the signs of our Lord and we would be among the ones who believe.⁶:²⁷

Nay! Shown to themselves will be what they had been concealing before. And even if they were returned, they would revert to what they were prohibited from there and, truly, they are the ones who lie. ⁶:²⁸

They said: There is nothing but this, our present life and we are not ones who will be raised up.⁶:²⁹

And if thou wouldst see when they would be stationed before their Lord. He would say: Is this not The Truth?

They would say: Yea, by Our Lord.

He would say: Then, experience the punishment for what you had been ungrateful.⁶:³⁰

Surely, those lost who denied the meeting with God until when the Hour drew near them suddenly, they would say: What a regret for us that we neglected in it! And they will carry heavy loads on their backs. How evil is what they bear!⁶:³¹

And this present life is nothing but a pastime and diversion. And the Last Abode is better for those who are Godfearing. Will you not, then, be reasonable?⁶:³²

Surely, We know that what they say disheartens thee. Truly, they deny thee not. Rather the ones who are unjust negate the signs of God.⁶:³³

And, certainly, Messengers before thee were denied yet they endured patiently that they were denied and they were maligned until Our help approached them. And no one will change the Word of God. And, certainly, there drew near thee tidings of the ones who are sent.⁶:³⁴

If their turning aside had been troublesome to thee, then, if thou wert able, be looking for a hole in the earth or a ladder to heaven so that thou wouldst bring them some sign. If God willed, He would have gathered them to The Guidance. Be thou not among the ones who are ignorant.⁶:³⁵ It is only those who hear who respond. As for the dead, God will raise them up. Again, they are returned to Him.⁶:³⁶

And they said: Why was a sign not sent down to him from his Lord?

Say: Truly, God is One Who Has Power over what sign He sends down, except most of them know not.⁶:³⁷

And there is no moving creature in or on the earth, none that is a fowl flying with its two wings, but they are communities like yours. We neglected not anything in the Book. Again, they will be assembled to their Lord.⁶:³⁸

And those who denied Our signs are unwilling to hear and unwilling to speak. They are in the shadows. Whomever God wills, He causes to go astray. And whomever He wills, He lays on a straight path.⁶:³⁹

Say: Considered you that if the punishment of God approached you or the Hour approached you, would you call to any other than God if you had been ones who are sincere?⁶:⁴⁰

Nay! To Him alone you would call and He would remove that for which you call to Him—if He willed—and you will forget whatever partners you ascribe with Him.⁶:⁴¹

And, certainly, We sent to communities that were before thee. Then, We took them with desolation and tribulation so that perhaps they will lower themselves to Us.⁶:⁴² Then, why when drew near them Our might, they lowered not

themselves? Rather, their hearts became hard. And Satan made appear pleasing to them what they had been doing.⁶:⁴³

So when they forgot about what they were reminded in it, We opened to them the doors of everything. Until when they were glad with what they were given, We suddenly took them. That is when they were ones who are seized with despair.⁶:⁴⁴ So cut off were the last remnant of the folk who did wrong. And The Praise belongs to God, Lord of the worlds.⁶:⁴⁵

Say: Considered you that if God took your having the ability to hear and your sight and sealed over your hearts, what god other than God restores them to you?

Look on how We diversify the signs! Again, they still drew aside.⁶:⁴⁶

Say: Considered you that if the punishment of God approached you suddenly or publicly, will anyone be caused to perish but the folk, the ones who are unjust?⁶:⁴⁷

We send not the ones who are sent, but as ones who give good tidings and ones who warn. So whoever believed and made things right, then, there will be neither fear in them nor will they feel remorse.⁶:⁴⁸

But those who denied Our signs, the punishment will afflict them because they had been disobeying.⁶:⁴⁹

Say: I say not to you: With me are treasures of God nor that I know the unseen nor say I to you that I am an angel. I follow only what is revealed to me.

Say: Are they on the same level—the unwilling to see and the seeing? Will you, then, not reflect?⁶:⁵⁰

And warn with the Quran those who fear that they will be assembled before their Lord. Other than He there is neither a protector nor an intercessor, so that perhaps they will be Godfearing.⁶:⁵¹

And drive not away those who call to their Lord in the morning and the evening, wanting His Countenance. Their reckoning is not on thee at all. And thy reckoning is not on them at all. If thou wast to drive them away, then, thou wouldst be among the ones who are unjust.⁶:⁵²

Thus, We tried some of them with others that they should say: Is it these to whom God showed grace from among us? Is not God greater in knowledge of the ones who are thankful?⁶:⁵³

And when drew near thee, those who believe in Our signs, say: Peace be to you. Your Lord prescribed mercy for Himself so that anyone of you who did evil in ignorance—again, repented afterwards and made things right—then, truly, He is Forgiving, Compassionate.⁶:⁵⁴

And, thus, We explain Our signs distinctly so that the way is indicated for the ones who sin.⁶:⁵⁵

Say: I was prohibited that I worship those whom you call to other than God.

Say: I will not follow your desires, for, then, I would have gone astray. I would not be of the ones who are truly guided.⁶:⁵⁶

Say: I am with a clear portent from my Lord and you denied it. I have not of that which you seek to hasten. The determination is with God. He relates The Truth. And He is Best of the ones who distinguish truth from falsehood.⁶:⁵⁷

Say: Truly, if with me was what you seek to hasten, the command would be decided between me and between you. And God is greater in knowledge of the ones who are unjust.⁶:⁵⁸

With Him are the keys of the unseen. None knows them but He. And He knows whatever is on dry land and in the sea. Not a leaf descends but He knows it, nor a grain in the shadows of the earth, nor fresh nor dry thing, but it is in a clear Book.⁶:⁵⁹

It is He Who gathers you to Himself by nighttime and He knows what you were busy with by daytime. Again, He raises you up in it so that the term, that which is determined, is decided. Again, to Him is your return. Again, He will tell you of what you had been doing.⁶:⁶⁰

And He is The One Who Is Omniscient over His servants. And He sends over you recorders until when death drew near one of you. Our messengers gathered him to themselves and they neglect not.[6:61]

Again, they would be returned to God, their Defender, The True. Is not the determination for Him? And He is The Swiftest of the ones who reckon.[6:62]

Say: Who delivers you from the shadows of the dry land and the sea? You call to Him humbly and inwardly: If Thou wert to rescue us from this, we will be of the ones who are thankful.[6:63]

Say: God delivers you from them and from every distress. And, again, you ascribe partners with Him.[6:64]

Say: He is The One Who Has Power to raise up on you a punishment from above you, or from beneath your feet or to confuse you as partisans and to cause you to experience the violence of some of you to one another. Look on how We diversify the signs so that perhaps they will understand![6:65]

And thy folk denied it and it is The Truth.

Say: I am not a trustee over you.[6:66]

For every tiding there is an appointed time. And you will know it.[6:67]

And when thou hadst seen those who engage in idle talk about Our signs, then, turn aside from them until they discuss in conversation other than that. And if Satan should cause thee to forget, then, after a reminder, sit not with the folk, the ones who are unjust.[6:68]

There is not on those who are Godfearing anything of their reckoning, but a reminder so that perhaps they will be Godfearing.[6:69]

Forsake those who took to themselves their way of life as a pastime and as a diversion and whom this present life deluded. But remind with it, the Quran, so that a soul would not be given up to destruction for what it earned.

Other than God there is not for it a protector nor an intercessor.

And even if it be an equitable equivalent, it will not be taken from it. Those are those who were given up to destruction for what they earned. For them is a drink of scalding water and a painful punishment because they had been ungrateful.[6:70]

Say: Will we call to other than God what can neither hurt nor profit us? And are we repelled on our heels after God guided us like one whom the satans lured, bewildered in and on the earth although he has companions who call him to the guidance saying: Approach us?

Say: Truly, the guidance of God is The Guidance. And we were commanded to submit to the Lord of the worlds[6:71] and to perform the formal prayer and be Godfearing of Him. And it is He to Whom you will be assembled.[6:72]

And it is He Who created the heavens and the earth with The Truth.

And on a Day He says: Be! Then, it is! His saying is The Truth. And His is the dominion on a Day when the trumpet will be blown. He is One Who Knows of the unseen and the visible. And He is The Wise, The Aware.[6:73]

And mention when Abraham said to his father Azar: Hast thou taken idols to thyself as gods? Truly, I see thee and thy folk clearly wandering astray.[6:74]

And, thus, We cause Abraham to see the kingdom of the heavens and the earth so that he would be of the ones who are certain in belief.[6:75]

So when night outspread over him, he saw a star. He said: This is my Lord. Then, when it set, he said: I love not that which sets.[6:76]

Then, when he saw the moon, that which rises, he said: This is my Lord. Then, when it set, he said: If my Lord guides me not, certainly, I would have been among the folk, the ones gone astray.[6:77]

Then, when he saw the sun, that which rises, he said: This is my Lord. This is greater. Then, when it set, he said: O my folk! Truly, I am free from the partners you ascribe with Him.[6:78] Truly, I turned my face to He Who Originated the heavens and the earth—as a monotheist and I am not of the ones who are polytheists.[6:79]

And his folk argued with him. He said: You argue with me about God while, surely, He guided me? I fear not whatever partners you ascribe with Him. When my Lord wills a thing, my Lord encompassed everything in His knowledge. Will you not, then, recollect?[6:80]

And how should I fear what you ascribed as partners with Him while you fear not that you ascribe as partners with God? He sends not down to you any authority for it. Then, which of the two groups of people has better right to a place of sanctuary if you had been knowing?[6:81]

Those who believed and confuse not their belief with injustice, those, to them belongs the place of sanctuary. And they are ones who are truly guided.[6:82]

And that was Our disputation that We gave Abraham against his folk. We exalt in degrees whom We will, truly, thy Lord is Wise, Knowing.[6:83]

And We bestowed on him Isaac and Jacob. Each of them We guided. And Noah We guided before and among his offspring are David and Solomon and Job and Joseph and Moses and Aaron. And, thus, We gave recompense to the ones who are doers of good.[6:84]

And Zechariah and Yahya and Jesus and Elijah—all are among the ones in accord with morality.[6:85]

And Ishmael and Elisha and Jonah and Lot. We gave all an advantage over the worlds.[6:86]

And from among their fathers and their offspring and their brothers/sisters, We elected them and We guided them to a straight path.[6:87] That is guidance of God. He guides with it whom He wills of His servants. And if they ascribed partners with Him, what they had been doing was fruitless for them.[6:88]

Those are those to whom We gave the Book and critical judgment and prophethood.

So if these are ungrateful for them, then, surely, We charged a folk with them who is not of the ones who are ungrateful for them.[6:89]

Those are those whom God guided. So imitate their guidance. Say: I ask of you no compensation for it. It is not but a reminder for the worlds.[6:90]

And they measured not God with His true measure when they said: God caused not to descend anything to a mortal.

Say: Who caused the Book to descend that was brought about for Moses as a light and guidance for humanity? You make it into parchments. You show them some of it and conceal much of it. And you were taught what you know not, you nor your fathers.

Say: God revealed it. Again, forsake them playing, engaging in their idle talk.[6:91]

And this is a Book We caused to descend—that which is blessed—and that which establishes as true what was before it and for thee to warn the Mother of Towns and who are around it and those who believe in the world to come believe in it. And they over their formal prayers are watchful.[6:92]

And who does greater wrong than he who devised lies against God or said: It was revealed to me, when nothing is revealed to him.

Or who said: I will cause to descend the like of what God caused to descend.

And if thou wouldst see when the ones who are unjust are in the perplexity of death and the angels—the ones who stretch out their hands will say: Relinquish your souls. Today, you will be given recompense with the humiliating punishment for what you had been saying about God other than The Truth. And you had been growing arrogant to His signs.⁶ᐟ⁹³

And, certainly, you drew near Us one by one as We created you the first time. And you left what We granted you behind your backs. We see not your intercessors with you, those whom you claimed as your ascribed associates. Certainly, the bonds between you were cut asunder. And gone astray from you is what you had been claiming.⁶ᐟ⁹⁴

Truly, it is God who is One Who Causes to Break Forth the grain and the pit of a date. He brings out the living from the dead and is One Who Brings Out the dead from the living. That is God. Then, how you are misled.⁶ᐟ⁹⁵

He is One Who Causes to Break Forth the morning dawn and He made the night as a place of comfort and rest and the sun and the moon to keep count. That is the foreordaining of The Almighty, The Knowing.⁶ᐟ⁹⁶

And it is He Who made the stars for you so that you will be truly guided by them in the shadows of dry land and the sea. Surely, We explained distinctly the signs for a folk who know.⁶ᐟ⁹⁷

And it is He Who caused you to grow from a single soul, then, a temporary stay and a repository. Surely, We explained distinctly the signs for a folk who understand.⁶ᐟ⁹⁸

And it is He Who caused to descend water from heaven. Then, We brought out from it every kind of bringing forth. Then, We brought out herbs from it.

We bring out from it thick-clustered grain and from the date palm tree, from the spathe of it, thick clusters of dates, that which draws near and gardens of the grapevines and the olives and the pomegranates, like each to each and not resembling one another. Look on its fruit when it bore fruit and its ripening. Truly, in this are signs for a folk who believe.⁶ᐟ⁹⁹

And they made as associates with God—the jinn—although He created them. And they falsely attributed to Him sons and daughters without knowledge. Glory be to Him! Exalted is He above what they allege.⁶ᐟ¹⁰⁰

He is Beginner of the heavens and the earth. How would He have a child when He is without a companion and He created everything and He is Knowing of everything?⁶ᐟ¹⁰¹

That is God, your Lord. There is no god but He—the One Who is Creator of everything—so worship Him. For He is Trustee over everything.⁶ᐟ¹⁰²

No sight overtakes Him, but He overtakes sight. And He is The Subtle, The Aware.⁶ᐟ¹⁰³

Surely, clear evidence drew near you from your Lord. So whoever perceived, it will be for his own soul. Whoever was in darkness will be against his own soul.

Say: And I am not a guardian over you.⁶ᐟ¹⁰⁴

And, thus, We diversify the signs and they will say: Thou hadst received instruction and We will make the Quran manifest for a folk who know.⁶ᐟ¹⁰⁵

Follow thou what was revealed to thee from thy Lord. There is no god but He. Turn thou aside from the ones who are polytheists.⁶ᐟ¹⁰⁶ And if God willed, they would not have ascribed partners with Him, We made thee not a guardian over them, nor art thou a trustee for them.⁶ᐟ¹⁰⁷

And offend not those who call to other than God so that they not offend God out of spite without knowledge. Thus, We made to appear pleasing the actions of every community. Again, to their Lord is their return. Then, He will tell them what they had been doing.⁶ᐟ¹⁰⁸

And they swear by God the most earnest sworn oaths that if a sign would draw near them, they would, certainly, believe in it. Say: The signs are only with God. And what

will cause you to realize that even if the signs were to draw near, they would not believe?⁶ᐟ¹⁰⁹

We will turn around and around their minds and their sight as they believe not in it the first time. And We will forsake them in their defiance, wandering unwilling to see.⁶ᐟ¹¹⁰

And even if We sent down the angels to them and the dead spoke to them and we assembled everything against them, face to face, yet they would not believe unless God wills, except many of them are ignorant.⁶ᐟ¹¹¹

And, thus, We made an enemy for every Prophet, satans from among humankind and the jinn. Some of them reveal to some others an ornamented saying, a delusion. And if thy Lord willed, they would not have accomplished it. So forsake them and what they devise,⁶ᐟ¹¹² while minds will bend towards it of those who believe not in the world to come and they will be well-pleased with it. And they will gain what the ones who gain gain.⁶ᐟ¹¹³

Will I be looking for an arbiter other than God while it is He Who caused to descend to you the Book, one that is distinct? And those to whom We gave the Book, they know that it is one that is sent down by thy Lord with The Truth. So thou hast not been among the ones who contest.⁶ᐟ¹¹⁴

Completed was the Word of thy Lord in sincerity and justice. There is no one who changes His Words. And He is The Hearing, The Knowing.⁶ᐟ¹¹⁵

And if thou hast obeyed most of who are on the earth, they will cause thee to go astray from the way of God. They follow nothing but opinion and they only guess.⁶ᐟ¹¹⁶

Truly, thy Lord is He Who is greater in knowledge of who goes astray from His way. And He is greater in knowledge of the ones who are truly guided.⁶ᐟ¹¹⁷

So eat of that over which the Name of God was remembered if you had been ones who believe in His signs.⁶ᐟ¹¹⁸

And why should you not eat of that over which the Name of God was remembered on it?

Surely, He explained distinctly to you what He forbade to you unless you were driven by necessity to it. And, truly, many cause others to go astray by their desires without knowledge. Truly, thy Lord, He is greater in knowledge of the ones who exceed the limits.⁶ᐟ¹¹⁹

And forsake manifest sin and its inward part. Truly, those who earn sin, they will be given recompense for what they had been gaining.⁶ᐟ¹²⁰

Eat not of that over which the Name of God is not remembered on it. Truly, it is contrary to moral law. And, truly, the satans will reveal to their protectors so that they dispute with you and if you obeyed them, truly, you would be of the ones who are polytheists.⁶ᐟ¹²¹

Is he who had been lifeless and We gave him life and We made a light for him by which he walks among humanity like he who is in the shadows and is not one who goes forth from them? Thus, it was made to appear pleasing to ones who are ungrateful what they had been doing.⁶ᐟ¹²²

And, thus, We made in every town greater ones who sin that they plan in it. Yet they plan not but against themselves although they are not aware.⁶ᐟ¹²³

And when a sign drew near them they said: We will not believe until we are given the like of what was given to Messengers of God. God is greater in knowledge where to assign His message. On those who sinned will light contempt from God and a severe punishment for what they had been planning.⁶ᐟ¹²⁴

And whomever God wants, He guides him. He expands his breast for The Submission to One God. And whomever He wants to cause to go astray, He makes his breast tight, troubling, as if he had been climbing up a difficult ascent. Thus, God assigns disgrace on those who believe not.⁶ᐟ¹²⁵

And this is the path of thy Lord, one that is straight. Surely, We explained distinctly the signs for a folk who recollect.[6:126] For them is the abode of peace with their Lord. And He is their protector for what they had been doing.[6:127] And mention on a Day He will assemble them altogether.

O assembly of the jinn! Surely, you acquired much from humankind.

And their protectors among humankind would say: Our Lord! Some of us enjoyed some others and we reached our term that was appointed by Thee for us.

He would say: The fire is your place of lodging, ones who will dwell in it forever, but what God willed. Truly, thy Lord is Wise, Knowing.[6:128]

And, thus, that is how We make some of them friends with some others who are ones who are unjust to one another for what they had been earning.[6:129]

O assembly of jinn and humankind! Approach not Messengers from among yourselves relating to you My signs, and warning you of the meeting of this, your Day?

They said: We bore witness against ourselves. This present life deluded them and they bore witness against themselves that they had been ones who are ungrateful.[6:130] That is because thy Lord would never be One Who Causes to Perish towns unjustly while their people are ones who are heedless.[6:131]

And for everyone there are degrees for what they did. And thy Lord is not One Who is Heedless of what they do.[6:132]

Thy Lord is The Sufficient, Possessor of Mercy. If He wills, He will cause you to be put away and will make a successor after you of whomever He wills, just as He caused you to grow from offspring of other folk.[6:133]

Truly, what you are promised is, certainly, that which arrives and you will not be ones who frustrate it.[6:134]

Say: O my folk! Act according to your ability. Truly, I too am one who acts.

Then, you will know for whom the Ultimate End will be the abode. Truly, the ones who are unjust will not prosper.[6:135]

And they assigned to God of what He made numerous of cultivation and flocks a share.

Then, they said in their claim: This is for God and this is for our ascribed associates.

But what had been ascribed for their associates then, reaches not out to God and what had been ascribed for God then, reaches out to their associates. How evil is the judgment they give![6:136]

And, thus, made to appear pleasing to many of the ones who are polytheists was the killing of their children by those whom they ascribe as associates with Him so that they deal them destruction and so that they confuse their way of life for them. And if God willed, they would not have accomplished it. So forsake them and what they devise.[6:137]

And they said: These flocks and cultivation are banned. None should taste them, but whom we will, so they claim. And there are flocks whose backs were forbidden and flocks that they remember not the Name of God on it, a devising against Him. He will give them recompense for what they had been devising.[6:138]

And they said: What is in the bellies of these flocks is exclusively for our males and is that which is forbidden to our female spouses, but if it would be born dead, then, they are ascribed as associates in it. He will give recompense to them for their allegations. Truly, He is Wise, Knowing.[6:139]

They, surely, lost those who foolishly kill their children without knowledge. They forbade what God provided them in a devising against God. They, surely, went astray and had not been ones who are truly guided.[6:140]

And it is He Who caused gardens to grow, trellised and without being trellised and the date palm trees and a variety of harvest crops and the olives and the pomegranates resembling and not resembling one another. Eat of its fruit when it bore fruit and give its due on the day of its reaping and exceed not all bounds. Truly, He loves not the ones who are excessive.[6:141]

And of the flocks are some as beasts of burden and some for slaughter. Eat of what God provided you and follow not in the steps of Satan. Truly, he is a clear enemy to you.[6:142]

Eight diverse pairs; two of sheep and two of goats. Say: Forbade He the two males or the two females? Or what is contained in the wombs of the two females? Tell me with knowledge if you had been ones who are sincere.[6:143]

And of the camels two and of cows two, say: Forbade He the two males or the two females or what is contained in the wombs of the two females? Had you been witnesses when God charged you with this? Then, who does greater wrong than he who devised a lie against God to cause humanity to go astray without knowledge. Truly, God guides not the folk, the ones who are unjust.[6:144]

Say: I find not in what was revealed to me to taste that which is forbidden to taste, but that it be carrion or blood, that which is shed or the flesh of swine for that, truly, is a disgrace or was hallowed—contrary to moral law—to other than God on it. Then, whoever was driven by necessity other than being one who is willfully disobedient or one who turns away. Then, truly, thy Lord is Forgiving, Compassionate.[6:145]

And to those who became Jews, We forbade every possessor of claws. And of the cows and the herd of sheep, We forbade them their fat, but what their backs carried or entrails or what mingled with bone. Thus, we gave them recompense for their insolence and We are, truly, ones who are sincere.[6:146]

If they denied thee, say: Your Lord is the Possessor of Extensive Mercy. And His might is not repelled from the folk, ones who sin.[6:147]

Those who ascribed partners with God will say: If God willed, neither would we have ascribed partners with God, nor our fathers, nor would we have forbidden anything. Thus, denied those who were before them until they experienced Our might.

Say: Is there any knowledge with you that you bring out to us? You follow not but opinion and, then, you only guess.[6:148]

Say: God has the conclusive disputation. And if He willed, He would have guided you one and all.[6:149]

Say: Come on! Bring your witnesses who bear witness that God forbade this. Then, if they bore witness, bear you not witness with them. And follow thee not the desires of those who denied Our signs and those who believe not in the world to come and they equate others with their Lord.[6:150]

Say: Approach now. I will recount what your Lord forbade you Ascribe nothing as partners with Him. And show kindness to the ones who are your parents. And kill not your children from want. We will provide for you and for them.

And come not near any indecencies whether these were manifest or what was inward. And kill not a soul which God forbade, unless rightfully. He charged you with that so that perhaps you will be reasonable.[6:151]

And come not near the property of the orphan but with what is fairer until one reaches the coming of age. And live up to the full measure and balance with equity. We will not place a burden on any soul, but to its capacity.

And when you said something, be just, even if it had been with possessors of kinship and live up to the compact of God. Thus, He charged you with it so that perhaps you will recollect.[6:152]

And that this is My straight path, so follow it. And follow not the ways that will split you up from His way. He charged you this with it, so that perhaps you will be Godfearing.[6:153]

Again, We gave Moses the Book rendered complete for him who did good, a decisive explanation of all things and as a guidance and mercy, so that perhaps they will believe in the meeting with their Lord.⁶:¹⁵⁴

And this Book We caused to descend is that which is blessed so follow it and be Godfearing so that perhaps you will find mercy, ⁶:¹⁵⁵ so that you not say: The Book was only caused to descend to two sections before us. And, truly, we had been ones who are heedless of their study.⁶:¹⁵⁶

Or so that you not say: If the Book was caused to descend to us, we would have been better guided than they. Surely, there drew near you clear portents from your Lord and a guidance and a mercy. And who, then, does greater wrong than he who denied the signs of God and drew aside from them. We will give recompense to those who draw aside from Our signs with a dire punishment because they had been drawing aside.⁶:¹⁵⁷

Look they on only that the angels approach them? Or thy Lord approach them? Or some signs of thy Lord approach them? On a Day that approach some signs of thy Lord, belief will not profit a person if he believed not before, nor earned good because of his belief. Say: Wait awhile! We too are ones who are waiting awhile!⁶:¹⁵⁸

Truly, those who separated and divided their way of life and had been partisans, be thou not concerned with them at all. Truly, their affair is only with God. Again, He will tell them what they had been accomplishing.⁶:¹⁵⁹

Whoever drew near with benevolence, then, for him, ten times the like of it. And whoever drew near with an evil deed, then, recompense will not be given but with its like and they, they will not be wronged.⁶:¹⁶⁰

Say: Truly, my Lord guided me to a straight path, a truth-loving way of life, the creed of Abraham, the monotheist. And he had not been of the ones who are polytheists.⁶:¹⁶¹

Say: Truly, my formal prayer and my ritual sacrifice and my living and my dying are for God, Lord of all the worlds.⁶:¹⁶²

No associates are to be ascribed with Him and of this was I commanded and I am the first of the ones who submit to God.⁶:¹⁶³

Say: Is it other than God that I should desire as a lord while He is Lord of everything? And each soul will earn only for itself. No burdened soul will bear another's heavy load. Again, to your Lord will you return. Then, He will tell you about what you had been at variance in it.⁶:¹⁶⁴

And it is He who made you as viceregents on the earth and exalted some of you above some others in degree that He try you with what He gave you. Truly, thy Lord is Swift in repayment and He, truly, is Forgiving, Compassionate.⁶:¹⁶⁵

CHAPTER 7
THE ELEVATED PLACES

In the Name of God The Merciful, The Compassionate
*Alif Lām Mīm Sād.*⁷:¹

It is a Book that was caused to descend to thee. So let there be no impediment in thy breast about it so that thou wilt warn with it and as a reminder to the ones who believe.⁷:²

Follow what was caused to descend to you from your Lord and follow not protectors other than He. Little you recollect!⁷:³

And how many towns We caused to perish! And Our might drew near them at night or when they were ones who sleep at noon!⁷:⁴

Then, there had been no calling out when Our might drew near to them, but that they said: Truly, we had been ones who are unjust.⁷:⁵

Then, We will, certainly, ask those to whom were sent Messengers to them and We will, certainly, ask the ones who are sent.⁷:⁶

Then, We will relate to them with knowledge for We had never been of ones who are absent.⁷:⁷

The weighing of deeds on that Day will be The Truth. So ones whose balance was heavy from good deeds, then, those, they are the ones who prosper.⁷:⁸

And ones whose balance was made light from bad deeds those are those who have lost their souls because they had been doing wrong with Our signs.⁷:⁹

And, certainly, We established you firmly on the earth and We made for you in it a livelihood. But little you give thanks!⁷:¹⁰

And, certainly, We created you. Again, We formed you. Again, We said to the angels: Prostrate yourselves before Adam! Then, they prostrated themselves, but Iblis. He would not be of the ones who prostrate themselves.⁷:¹¹

He said: What prevented thee from prostrating thyself when I commanded thee?

Satan said: I am better than he. Thou hadst created me of fire and Thou hadst created him of clay.⁷:¹²

He said: So get thee down from this! It will not be for thee to increase in pride in it. Then, thou go forth. Truly, thou art of the ones who are disgraced.⁷:¹³

Satan said: Give me respite until the Day they are raised up.⁷:¹⁴

He said: Truly, thou art among the ones who are given respite.⁷:¹⁵

Satan said: Because Thou hadst led me into error, certainly, I will sit in ambush for them on Thy path, one that is straight.⁷:¹⁶

Again, I will approach them from between the front of them and from behind them and from their right and from their left. And Thou wilt not find many of them ones who are thankful.⁷:¹⁷

He said: Go thou forth from this—one who is scorned, one who is rejected. Whoever heeded thee among them, I will, certainly, fill hell with you, one and all.⁷:¹⁸

And: O Adam! Inhabit thou and thy spouse the Garden and both eat from where you both willed, but neither of you come near this tree or you both will be of the ones who are unjust.⁷:¹⁹

And Satan whispered evil to them both to show them both what was kept secret from them both—their intimate parts. And he said: The Lord of both of you prohibited you both from this tree so that neither of you be angels nor be ones who will dwell forever.⁷:²⁰

And he swore an oath to them both that I am the one who gives advice to both of you.⁷:²¹ Then, he led both of them on to delusion. Then, when they both experienced of the tree, the intimate parts of both showed to both themselves and both of them took to doing stitching together over both from the leaves of the Garden.

And the Lord of both of them proclaimed to them: Prohibited I not both of you from that tree? And said I not to both of you: Truly, Satan is a clear enemy of you both.⁷:²²

They both said: Our Lord! We did wrong to ourselves. And if Thou wilt not forgive us and have mercy on us, we will, certainly, be among the ones who are losers.⁷:²³

He said: Get you down, some of you an enemy to some other. And for you on the earth an appointed time and enjoyment for awhile.⁷:²⁴ He said: You will live in it and you will die in it and from it you will be brought out.⁷:²⁵

O Children of Adam! Surely, We caused to descend to you garments to cover up your intimate parts and finery, but the garment of God-consciousness, that is better. That is of the signs of God so that perhaps they will recollect!⁷:²⁶

O Children of Adam! Let not Satan tempt you as he drove your parents out of the Garden, tearing off their garments from both of them to cause them to see their intimate parts. Truly, he and his type sees you whereas you see them not. Truly, We made he and the satans protectors of those who believe not.⁷²⁷

And when they committed an indecency, they said: We found our fathers on it and God commanded us in it.

Say: Truly, God commands not depravities. Say you about God what you know not?⁷²⁸

Say: My Lord commanded me to equity.

And set your faces at every place of prostration and call to Him ones who are sincere and devoted in the way of life to Him. As He began you, you will revert to Him.⁷²⁹

He guided a group of people and a group of people realized their fallacy. Truly, they took satans to themselves as protectors instead of God and they assume that they are ones who are truly guided.⁷³⁰

O Children of Adam! Take your adornment at every place of prostration.

And eat and drink, but exceed not all bounds. Truly, He loves not the ones who are excessive.⁷³¹

Say: Who forbade the adornment of God which He brought out for His servants. And what is the good of His provision? Say: They are for those who believed in this present life and, exclusively, on the Day of Resurrection. Thus, We explain distinctly the signs for a folk who know.⁷³²

Say: My Lord forbade not but indecencies—what was manifest or what was inward—and sins and unrightful insolence, to ascribe partners with God when He sends not down for it any authority and that you say about God what you know not.⁷³³

And for every community there is a term. And when their term drew near, they will not delay it by an hour, nor press it forward.⁷³⁴

O Children of Adam! If Messengers from among you approach relating My signs to you, then, whoever was Godfearing and made things right, then, there will be neither fear in them nor will they feel remorse.⁷³⁵

But those who denied Our signs and grew arrogant against them, those are the Companions of the Fire; they are ones who will dwell in it forever.⁷³⁶

Then, who does greater wrong than he who devised a lie against God or denied His signs? Those, they will attain their share from the Book.

Until Our Messengers drew near to gather them to themselves, they will say: Where are who you had been calling on other than God?

They will say: They went astray from us.

And they bore witness against themselves that, truly, they had been ones who are ungrateful.⁷³⁷

He will say: Enter among the communities that passed away before you of jinn and humankind into the fire.

Every time a community entered, it would curse its sister community until when they will come successively in it altogether.

The last of them would say to the first of them: Our Lord! These caused us to go astray so give them a double punishment of the fire.

He will say: For everyone it is double except you know not.⁷³⁸

And the first of them would say to the last of them: You have had no superiority over us so experience the punishment for what you had been earning.⁷³⁹

Truly, those who denied Our signs and grew arrogant among them, the doors of heaven will not be opened up to them nor will they enter the Garden until a he-camel penetrates through the eye of the needle. And, thus, We give recompense to the ones who sin.⁷⁴⁰

For them hell will be their cradling and above them, the overwhelming event. Thus, We give recompense to the ones who are unjust.⁷⁴¹

But for those who believed and did as the ones in accord with morality, We place no burden on any soul beyond its capacity. Those will be the Companions of the Garden. They are ones who will dwell in it forever.⁷⁴²

And We will draw out what was in their breasts of grudges. And rivers will run beneath them. And they will say: The Praise belongs to God Who truly guided us to this! And we would not have been guided if God guided us not. Certainly, the Messengers of our Lord drew near us with The Truth. And it was proclaimed to them that this, the Garden, was given to you as inheritance for what you had been doing.⁷⁴³

And the Companions of the Garden would cry out to the Companions of the Fire: Surely, we found what our Lord promised us to be true. Found you not what your Lord promised to be true?

They would say: Yes.

Then, it will be announced by one who announces among them: May the curse of God be on the ones who are unjust,⁷⁴⁴ those who bar the way of God and who desire it to be crooked.

And in the world to come they will be ones who are ungrateful.⁷⁴⁵

And between them both is a partition. And on the Elevated Places will be men who recognize everyone by their mark. And they will cry out to the Companions of the Garden that: Peace be on you.

They enter it not and they are desirous of it.⁷⁴⁶

And when their sight would be turned away of its own accord to the Companions of the Fire, they will say: Our Lord assign Thou us not with the folk, ones who are unjust!⁷⁴⁷

The Companions of the Elevated Places would cry out to men whom they would recognize by their mark. They would say: Your amassing availed you not, nor that you had been growing arrogant.⁷⁴⁸

Are these, those about whom you swore an oath that God would never impart mercy? Enter the Garden. There will be neither fear in you nor will you feel remorse.⁷⁴⁹

And the Companions of the Fire would cry out to the Companions of the Garden: Pour some water on us, or some of what God provided us.

They would say: Truly, God forbade them both to the ones who are ungrateful,⁷⁵⁰ those who took their way of life to themselves as a diversion and as a pastime.

This present life deluded them. So today We will forget them as they forgot the meeting of this their Day and because they had been negating Our signs.⁷⁵¹

And, surely, We brought about a Book to them in which We explained distinctly, with knowledge, a guidance and a mercy for a folk who believe.⁷⁵²

Did they look on for nothing but its interpretation? The Day its interpretation approaches, those who forgot it before will say: Surely, Messengers of our Lord drew near us with The Truth. Have we any intercessors who will intercede for us? Or will we be returned so we do other than what we had been doing before?

Surely, they lost themselves. Went astray from them what they had been devising.⁷⁵³

Truly, your Lord is God, He Who created the heavens and the earth in six days. Again, He turned His attention to the Throne. He covers the nighttime with the daytime that seeks it out urgently. And the sun and the moon and the stars are ones caused to be subservient to His command. Truly, His is not but the creation and the command. Blessed be God, Lord of the worlds.⁷·⁵⁴

Call to your Lord humbly and inwardly. Truly, He loves not the ones who exceed the limits.⁷·⁵⁵

Make not corruption in the earth after things were made right and call to Him with fear and hope. Truly, the mercy of God is Near to the ones who are doers of good.⁷·⁵⁶

And it is He Who sends the winds, ones that are bearers of good news before His mercy until when they were charged with heavy clouds. We will drive it to a dead land. Then, We caused water to descend from the cloud and with it We bring out by water all kinds of fruits. Thus, We bring out the dead so that perhaps you will recollect.⁷·⁵⁷

As for the good land, its plants go forth with permission of its Lord. While, as for what was bad, it goes forth not but scantily. Thus, We diversify the signs for a folk who give thanks.⁷·⁵⁸

Surely, We sent Noah to his folk. And he said: O my folk! Worship God! You have no god other than He. Truly, I fear for you the punishment of a tremendous Day.⁷·⁵⁹

The Council of his folk said: Truly, we see thee clearly wandering astray.⁷·⁶⁰

He said: O my folk! There is no fallacy in me. I am only a Messenger from the Lord of the worlds.⁷·⁶¹ I state the messages of my Lord to you and advise you and I know from God what you know not.⁷·⁶²

Or marveled you that there drew near you a remembrance from your Lord through a man among you that he warn you and that you be Godfearing so that perhaps you will find mercy?⁷·⁶³

Then, they denied him. Then, We rescued him and those who were with him on the boat and We drowned those who denied Our signs. Truly, they, they had been a folk in the dark.⁷·⁶⁴

And to Ad, God sent their brother Hud. He said: O my folk! Worship God. You have no god but He. Will you not, then, be Godfearing?⁷·⁶⁵

The Council of those who were ungrateful said among his folk: Truly, we see foolishness in thee. And, truly, we think that thou art among the ones who lie.⁷·⁶⁶

He said: O my folk! There is no foolishness in me. I am only a Messenger from the Lord of the worlds.⁷·⁶⁷ I state the messages of my Lord to you and I am one who gives advice to you, trustworthy.⁷·⁶⁸

Or marveled you that there drew near you a remembrance from your Lord through a man from among you that he may warn you?

And remember when He made you viceregents after the folk of Noah and increased you greatly in constitution? Then, remember the benefits of God so that perhaps you will prosper.⁷·⁶⁹

They said: Hast thou brought about to us that we should worship God alone and forsake what our fathers had been worshipping? So approach us with what thou hast promised us if thou hadst been among the ones who are sincere.⁷·⁷⁰

He said: Surely, fell on you disgrace and anger from your Lord. Dispute you with me over names which you named, you and your fathers, for which God sent not down any authority? Then, wait awhile. Truly, I will be with you among the ones who are waiting awhile.⁷·⁷¹

Then, We rescued him and those with him by a mercy from Us.

And We severed the last remnant of those who denied Our signs. And they had not been ones who believe.⁷·⁷²

And to Thamud God sent their brother Salih.

He said: O my folk! Worship God! You have no god but He.

Surely, drew near you clear portents from your Lord. This is the she-camel of God as a sign so allow her to eat on the earth of God and afflict her not with evil so a painful punishment not take you.⁷·⁷³

And remember when He made you viceregents after Ad and placed you on the earth. You take to yourselves palaces on the plains and carve out the mountains as houses. So remember the benefits of God. And do no mischief as ones who make corruption in and on the earth.⁷·⁷⁴

Said the Council of those who grew arrogant among his folk to those who were taken advantage of due to their weakness, to those who believed among them: Know you that Salih is one who is sent from his Lord?

They said: Truly, in what he was sent, we are ones who believe.⁷·⁷⁵

Those who grew arrogant said: Truly, we are in what you believed, ones who disbelieve.⁷·⁷⁶

Then, they crippled the she-camel and defied the command of their Lord and they said: O Salih! Approach us with what thou hast promised us if thou hadst been among the ones who are sent.⁷·⁷⁷

So the quaking of the earth took them. And it came to be in the morning they were in their abodes ones who are fallen prostrate.⁷·⁷⁸

Then, he turned away from them and said: O my folk! Certainly, I expressed to you the message of my Lord and advised you, except you love not the ones who give advice.⁷·⁷⁹

And mention Lot, when he said to his folk: You approach indecency as preceded you not anyone therein in the worlds?⁷·⁸⁰ Truly, you, you approach men with lust instead of women? Nay! You are a folk, ones who are excessive.⁷·⁸¹

And the answer of his folk had not been but that they said: Bring them out from your town. Truly, they are a clan to cleanse themselves.⁷·⁸²

Then, We rescued him and his people, but his woman. She had been among the ones who stay behind.⁷·⁸³ And We rained down a rain on them. So look on how had been the Ultimate End of the ones who sin.⁷·⁸⁴

And to Midian God sent their brother Shuayb.

He said: O my folk! Worship God! You have no god other than He. Surely, a clear portent drew near you from your Lord so live up to the full measure and the balance and diminish not the things of humanity nor make corruption in and on the earth after things were made right. That will be better for you if you had been ones who believe.⁷·⁸⁵ And sit not by every path intimidating and barring from the way of God those who believed in Him and you desire it to be crooked. And remember when you had been few and He augmented you. And look on how had been the Ultimate End of the ones who make corruption.⁷·⁸⁶

And if there had been a section of you who believed in what I was sent with and a section believe not, have patience until God gives judgment between us. And He is Best of the ones who judge.⁷·⁸⁷

Said the Council of those who grew arrogant from among his folk: O Shuayb! We will, certainly, drive thee out—and those who believed with thee—from our town or else you revert to our creed. He said: Even if we had been ones who dislike it?⁷·⁸⁸

Surely, we would have devised a lie against God if we reverted to your creed after God delivered us from it. And it will not be for us that we revert to it unless God, our Lord, wills. Our Lord encompassed everything in knowledge. In God we put our trust. Our Lord! Give victory between us and between our folk in Truth and Thou art Best of the ones who are deliverers.⁷·⁸⁹

But said the Council of those who were ungrateful among his folk: If you followed Shuayb, then, truly, you will be ones who are losers.⁷˸⁹⁰

Then, the quaking of the earth took them and they came to be in the morning ones who are fallen prostrate in their abodes. Those who denied Shuayb had been as if they had not dwelt in them.⁷˸⁹¹ Those who denied Shuayb they, they had been the ones who were losers.⁷˸⁹²

So he turned away from them and said: O my folk! Certainly, I expressed to you the messages of my Lord and I advised you. Then, how should I grieve for a folk, ones who are ungrateful?⁷˸⁹³

And We sent not any Prophet to a town, but We took its people with tribulation and desolation so that perhaps they will lower themselves.⁷˸⁹⁴

Again, We substituted in place of evil deeds, benevolence, until they exceeded in number and they said: Surely, our fathers were touched by tribulation and gladness.

Then, We took them suddenly while they are not aware.⁷˸⁹⁵

And if the people of the towns believed and were God-fearing, We would have opened blessings for them from the heaven and the earth, except they denied. So We took them for what they had been earning.⁷˸⁹⁶

Were, then, the people of the towns safe when Our might approaches them at night while they are ones who sleep?⁷˸⁹⁷

Or were the people of the towns safe when Our might approaches them in the forenoon while they play?⁷˸⁹⁸

Were they safe from the planning of God?

No one deems himself safe from the planning of God but the folk, the ones who are losers!⁷˸⁹⁹

Guides not those who inherit the earth after its previous people that if We will, We would light on them for their impieties, and We set a seal on their hearts so they hear not?⁷˸¹⁰⁰

These are the towns. Their tidings We relate to thee. And, certainly, their Messengers drew near them with the clear portents. But they had not been believing in what they denied before. Thus, God set a seal on the hearts of the ones who are ungrateful.⁷˸¹⁰¹

And We found not in many of them any compact. And, truly, We found many of them are ones who disobey.⁷˸¹⁰²

Again, We raised up Moses after them with Our signs to Pharaoh and his Council, but they did wrong to them. So look on how had been the Ultimate End of the ones who make corruption.⁷˸¹⁰³

And Moses said: O Pharaoh! Truly, I am a Messenger from the Lord of the worlds.⁷˸¹⁰⁴ I am approved on condition that I say nothing but The Truth about God. Surely, I drew near you with a clear portent from your Lord. So send the Children of Israel with me.⁷˸¹⁰⁵

Pharaoh said: If thou hadst been drawing near with a sign, then, approach with it if thou hadst been among the ones who are sincere.⁷˸¹⁰⁶

Then, Moses cast his staff. That is when it became a clear serpent.⁷˸¹⁰⁷ And he drew out his hand. That is when it was shimmering white to the ones who look.⁷˸¹⁰⁸

The Council of the folk of Pharaoh said: Truly, this is a knowing sorcerer.⁷˸¹⁰⁹ He wants to drive you out from your region so what is your command?⁷˸¹¹⁰

They said: Put him and his brother off and send to the cities to the place where ones who assemble are.⁷˸¹¹¹ Let them approach thee with every knowing sorcerer.⁷˸¹¹²

And the ones who are sorcerers drew near to Pharaoh.

They said: Truly, would we have compensation if we had been the ones who are victors?⁷˸¹¹³

Pharaoh said: Yes! And, truly, you will be of the ones who are brought near to me.⁷˸¹¹⁴

They said: O Moses! Either thou cast, or will we be the ones who cast?⁷˸¹¹⁵

He said: You cast. So when they cast, they cast a spell on the eyes of the personages and terrified them. And a tremendous sorcery drew near.⁷˸¹¹⁶

And We revealed to Moses that: Cast thy staff. That is when it swallowed what they faked.⁷˸¹¹⁷ Thus, The Truth came to pass and proved false what they had been doing.⁷˸¹¹⁸

So they were vanquished there and turned about as ones who are disgraced.⁷˸¹¹⁹

The ones who are sorcerers were made to fall down as ones who prostrate themselves.⁷˸¹²⁰

They said: We believed in the Lord of the worlds,⁷˸¹²¹ the Lord of Moses and Aaron.⁷˸¹²²

Pharaoh said: You believed in Him before I give permission to you. Truly, this is a plan you planned in the city that you drive out the people from it but you will know.⁷˸¹²³ I will, certainly, cut off your hands and your feet on opposite sides. Again, I will cause you to be crucified, one and all.⁷˸¹²⁴

They said: Truly, we are ones who are turning to our Lord.⁷˸¹²⁵ Thou hast sought revenge on us only because we believed in the signs of our Lord when they drew near us. Our Lord! Pour out patience on us and call us to Thyself as ones who submit to God.⁷˸¹²⁶

And the Council of the folk of Pharaoh said: Wilt thou forsake Moses and his folk to make corruption in and on the earth while they forsake thee and thy gods?

Pharaoh said: We will slay their children and we will save alive their women. And truly, we are ones who are ascendant over them.⁷˸¹²⁷

Moses said to his folk: Pray for help from God and have patience. Truly, the earth belongs to God. He gives it as inheritance to whom He wills of His servants. And that is the Ultimate End for the ones who are Godfearing.⁷˸¹²⁸

They said: We were maligned before thou hast approached us and after thou hast drawn near to us.

He said: Perhaps your Lord will cause your enemy to perish and make you successors to him on the earth so that He will look on how you do.⁷˸¹²⁹

And, certainly, We took the people of Pharaoh with years of diminution of fruits, so that perhaps they will recollect.⁷˸¹³⁰

And when benevolence drew near them, they would say: This belongs to us.

But if an evil deed lights on them, they augur ill of Moses and who were with him. Certainly, that which are their omens are with God except most of them know not.⁷˸¹³¹

And they said: Whatever sign thou hast brought to us to cast a spell on us with it, we will not be ones who believe in thee.⁷˸¹³²

Then, We sent on them the deluge and the locusts and the lice and the frogs and blood as distinct signs, but they grew arrogant and they had been a folk, ones who sin.⁷˸¹³³

And when the wrath fell on them, they said: O Moses! Call to thy Lord for us because of the compact made with thee. If thou wert to remove the wrath from us, we would, certainly, believe in thee. And we will send the Children of Israel with thee.⁷˸¹³⁴

But when We removed the wrath from them for a term, that which is conclusive, they break their oath.⁷˸¹³⁵ So We requited them and drowned them in the water of the sea because they denied Our signs and they had been ones who are heedless of them.⁷˸¹³⁶

And We gave as inheritance to the folk who had been taken advantage of due to their weakness, the east of the region and its west which We blessed.

And completed was the fairer Word of thy Lord for the Children of Israel because they endured patiently.

And We destroyed what Pharaoh and his folk had been crafting and what they had been constructing.⁷:¹³⁷

And We brought the Children of Israel over the sea. Then, they approached on a folk who give themselves up to their idols. They said: O Moses! Make for us a god like the gods they have.

He said: Truly, you are an ignorant folk!⁷:¹³⁸ Truly, these are the ones who are ruined and falsehood is what they had been doing.⁷:¹³⁹

He said: Should I look for any god other than God for you while He gave you an advantage over the worlds?⁷:¹⁴⁰

Mention when We rescued you from the people of Pharaoh who cause an affliction to befall you of a dire punishment. They slay your children and save alive your women. And in that was a trial for you from your Lord, tremendous.⁷:¹⁴¹

And We appointed thirty nights for Moses. And We completed them with ten more. Thus, fulfilled was the time appointed by his Lord of forty nights. And Moses said to his brother, Aaron: Be my successor among my folk and make things right and follow not the way of the ones who make corruption.⁷:¹⁴²

And when Moses drew near Our time appointed and his Lord spoke to him, he said: O my Lord! Cause me to see that I look on Thee.

He said: Thou wilt never see Me but look on the mountain. Then, if it stayed fast in its place, then, thou wilt see Me. Then, when his Lord Self-disclosed to the mountain, He made it as ground powder and Moses fell down swooning.

And when he recovered he said: Glory be to Thee! I repented to Thee and I am the first of the ones who believe.⁷:¹⁴³

He said: O Moses! Truly, I favored thee above humanity by My messages and by My assertion. So take what I gave thee and be among the ones who are thankful.⁷:¹⁴⁴

And We wrote down for him on the Tablets something of all things and an admonishment and a decisive explanation of all things.

So take these with firmness and command thy folk to take what is fairer. I will cause you to see the abodes of the ones who disobey.⁷:¹⁴⁵ I will turn away from My signs those who increase in pride on the earth without right. And if they see every sign, they believe not in it. And if they see the way of right judgment, yet they will not take that way to themselves. But if they see the way of error, they will take themselves to that way. That is because they denied Our signs and had been ones who are heedless of them.⁷:¹⁴⁶

And as for those who denied Our signs and the meeting in the world to come, their actions were fruitless. Will they be given recompense but for what they had been doing?⁷:¹⁴⁷

And the folk of Moses took to themselves after him from out of their glitter a calf, a lifeless body like one that has the lowing sound of flocks. See they not that it neither speaks to them nor guides them to a Way? Yet they took it to themselves. And they had been the ones who are unjust.⁷:¹⁴⁸

And when they became ones who are remorseful and saw that they, surely, went astray, they said: If our Lord not have mercy on us and forgive us, we will, certainly, be among the ones who are losers.⁷:¹⁴⁹

And when Moses returned to his folk enraged, grieved, he said: Miserable was what you succeeded in after me. Would you hasten the command of your Lord?

And he cast down the Tablets. He took his brother by his head, pulling him to himself.

Aaron said: O son of my mother, truly, the folk took advantage of my weakness and are about to kill me. So let not my enemies gloat over me and assign me not with the folk, the ones who are unjust.⁷:¹⁵⁰

Moses said: Lord! Forgive me and my brother and cause us to enter into Thy mercy for Thou art One Who is Most Merciful of the ones who are merciful.⁷:¹⁵¹

Those who took the calf to themselves attain anger from their Lord and abasement in this present life. And, thus, We give recompense to the ones who devise.⁷:¹⁵²

But those who did evil deeds and repented and, again, believed, truly, thy Lord, after that, will be Forgiving, Compassionate.⁷:¹⁵³

And when the anger subsided in Moses, he took the Tablets. There was guidance and mercy in their inscription for those, they who have reverence for their Lord.⁷:¹⁵⁴

And Moses chose of his folk seventy men for Our time appointed. And when the quaking of the earth took them, he said: Lord! If Thou wilt, Thou wouldst cause them to perish and me before. Wouldst Thou cause us to perish for what the foolish among us accomplished? It is not but Thy test. With it Thou wilt cause to go astray whom Thou wilt and Thou wilt guide whom Thou hadst willed. Thou art our protector, so forgive us and have mercy on us for Thou art Best of the ones who forgive.⁷:¹⁵⁵ And prescribe for us in the present benevolence and in the world to come. Truly we turned back to Thee.

He said: I light My punishment on whom I will and My mercy encompassed everything. Then, I will prescribe it for those who are Godfearing and give the purifying alms and those, they who believe in Our signs,⁷:¹⁵⁶ those who follow the Messenger—the unlettered Prophet—whom they will find with them that which is a writing in the Torah and the Gospel. He commands them to that which is honorable and prohibits them from that which is unlawful. And He permits to them what is good and forbids them from deeds of corruption. And He lays down for them severe tests, and the yokes that had been on them. So those who believed in him and supported him and helped him and followed the light that was caused to descend to him, those, they are the ones who prosper.⁷:¹⁵⁷

Say: O humanity! Truly, I am the Messenger of God to you all of Him to Whom belongs the dominion of the heavens and the earth. There is no god but He. He gives life and He causes to die. So believe in God and His Messenger, the unlettered Prophet, who believes in God and His words and follow him so that perhaps you will be truly guided.⁷:¹⁵⁸

And among the folk of Moses there is a community that guides with The Truth and by it is just.⁷:¹⁵⁹

And We sundered them into twelve tribes as communities. And We revealed to Moses when his folk asked him for water: Strike the rock with thy staff.

Then, burst forth out of it twelve springs: Surely, each clan knew its drinking place. And We shaded them with cloud shadows. We caused to descend manna and the quails for them. Eat of what is good that We provided you!

And they did not wrong Us, but they had been doing wrong to themselves.⁷:¹⁶⁰

And mention when it was said to them: Inhabit this town and eat from it wherever you willed.

Say: Unburden us of sin!

And enter the door as ones who prostrate themselves We will forgive your transgressions. We will increase the ones who are doers of good.⁷:¹⁶¹

But among those who did wrong, they substituted a saying other than what was said to them. Then, We sent wrath from heaven because they had been doing wrong.⁷:¹⁶²

And ask them about the town—that which had been bordering the sea—when they disregarded the Sabbath, when their great fish would approach them on the day of the Sabbath, one that was visible on the shore. And the day they keep not the Sabbath, they approach them not. Thus,

We try them because they had been disobeying.[7:163] And mention when a community of them said: Why admonish a folk whom God is One Who Causes them to Perish or One Who Punishes them with a severe punishment.

They said: To be free from guilt before your Lord and so that perhaps they will be Godfearing.[7:164]

So when they forgot of what they were reminded, We rescued those who prohibited evil and We took those who did wrong with a terrifying punishment because they had been disobeying.[7:165]

Then, when they defied what they were prohibited We said to them: Be you apes, ones who are driven away.[7:166]

And mention when thy Lord caused to be proclaimed that He would, surely, raise up against them until the Day of Resurrection who cause an affliction to befall on them of a dire punishment. Truly, thy Lord is Swift in repayment. And, truly, He is Forgiving, Compassionate.[7:167]

And We sundered them in the region into communities. Some of them were the ones in accord with morality and others were other than that. And We tried them with benevolence and evil deeds so that perhaps they will return to obedience.[7:168]

Then, after that succeeded successors who inherited the Book. They take advantage of this nearer world, and they say: We will be forgiven.

And if an advantage approaches them like it, they will take it. Is not a solemn promise taken from them with the Book that they would say about God only The Truth? And studied they not what is in it, and know that the Last Abode is better for those who are Godfearing? Will you not, then, be reasonable?[7:169]

And those who keep fast to the Book and performed the formal prayer, We will not waste the compensation of the ones who make things right.[7:170]

Mention when We shook up the mountain over them, as if it had been an overshadowing, and they thought it was that which would fall on them: It was said: Take with firmness what We gave you and remember what is in it so that perhaps you will be Godfearing.[7:171]

And mention when thy Lord took from the Children of Adam—from their generative organs—their offspring and called to them to witness of themselves: Am I not your Lord? They said: Yea! ^We bore witness^ so that you say not on the Day of Resurrection: Truly, we had been ones who were heedless of this.[7:172]

Or you not say: Our fathers before us ascribed partners with God. We had been offspring after them. Wilt Thou cause us to perish for what the ones who deal in falsehood accomplished?[7:173]

And, thus, We explain Our signs distinctly so that perhaps they will return.[7:174]

And recount to them the tiding of him to whom We gave Our signs, but he cast himself off from them. So Satan pursued him then, he had been among the ones who are in error.[7:175]

And if We willed, We would have exalted him with them, but he inclined towards the earth, and followed his own desires. And his parable is like the parable of a dog. If thou wilt attack it, it pants. Or if thou wilt leave it, it pants. That is the parable of the folk, those who denied Our signs. Then, relate these narratives so that perhaps they will reflect.[7:176]

How evil is the parable of the folk who denied Our signs! And they had been doing wrong to themselves.[7:177]

Whomever God guides, then, he is one who is truly guided. And whomever He causes to go astray, then, those, they are the ones who are losers.[7:178]

And, certainly, We made numerous for hell many of the jinn and humankind. They have hearts with which they understand not. And they have eyes with which they perceive not. And they have ears with which they hear not. Those are like flocks. Nay! They are ones who go astray. Those, they are the ones who are heedless.[7:179]

To God belongs the Fairer Names, so call to Him by them. And forsake those who blaspheme His Names. They will be given recompense for what they had been doing.[7:180]

And of whom We created there is a community that guides with The Truth, and with it, it is just.[7:181]

And those who denied Our signs, We will draw them on gradually from where they will not know.[7:182] And I will grant them indulgence for awhile. Truly, My strategizing is sure.[7:183]

Reflect they not? There is no madness in their companion. He is but a clear warner.[7:184]

Expect they not in the kingdom of the heavens and the earth and whatever things God created that perhaps their term be near? Then, in which discourse after this will they believe?[7:185]

Whomever God causes to go astray then, there is no one who guides him. And He forsakes them in their defiance, wandering unwilling to see.[7:186]

They ask thee about the Hour, when will it berth? Say: The knowledge of that is only with my Lord. None will display its time but He. It was heavy, hidden in the heavens and the earth. It will approach you not but suddenly. They will ask thee as if thou hadst been one who is well-informed about it. Say: The knowledge of that is only with God, but most of humanity knows not.[7:187]

Say: I rule not over myself either for profit or for hurt, but what God willed. And if the unseen had been known to me, I would have acquired much good and evil would not have afflicted me. I am but a warner and a bearer of good tidings to a folk who believe.[7:188]

It is He Who created you from a single soul. And out of it made its spouse that he rest in her. And when he laid over her, she carried a light burden and moved about with it. But when she was weighed down, they both called to God their Lord saying: If Thou wouldst give us one in accord with morality, we will certainly be among the ones who are thankful.[7:189]

Then, when He gave them both one in accord with morality, they made ascribed associates with Him in what He gave them both. God was Exalted above partners they ascribe![7:190]

Ascribe they partners with God who create nothing and are themselves created?[7:191]

And they are not able to help them nor help themselves?[7:192]

And if you call them to the guidance, they will not follow you.

It is equal whether you called to them or you be ones who remain quiet.[7:193]

Truly, those whom you call to other than God are servants like you. So call to them and let them respond to you if you had been ones who are sincere.[7:194]

Have they feet by which they walk? Or have they hands by which they seize by force? Or have they eyes by which they perceive? Or have they ears by which they hear?

Say: Call you to your ascribed associates.

Again, try to outwit me and give me no respite.[7:195]

Truly, God is my protector, Who sent down the Book. And He takes into His protection the ones in accord with morality.[7:196]

And those whom you call to other than Him, they are not able to help you, nor are they able to help themselves.[7:197] And if you call them to the guidance, they hear not. Thou hast seen them look on thee, but they perceive not.[7:198]

Take the extra and command what is honorable. And turn aside from the ones who are ignorant.[7:199] But if enmity is sown by Satan in thee, sowing enmity, then, seek refuge in God. Truly, He is Hearing, Knowing.[7:200]

Truly, those who were Godfearing when they were touched by a visitation from Satan, they recollected. That is when they were ones who perceive.[7:201] And their brothers/sisters cause them to increase in error, and, again, they never stop short.[7:202]

When thou hast not approached them with a sign, they said: Why hadst thou not improvised one?

Say: I follow only what is revealed to me from my Lord. This is clear evidence from your Lord and guidance and mercy for a folk who believe.[7:203]

And when the Quran was recited, listen and pay heed so that perhaps you will find mercy.[7:204]

And remember thy Lord in thyself humbly and with awe instead of openly publishing the sayings at the first part of the day and the eventide. And be thou not among the ones who are heedless.[7:205]

Truly, those who are with thy Lord grow not arrogant from His worship. And they glorify Him and they prostrate themselves to Him.[7:206]

CHAPTER 8
THE SPOILS OF WAR

In the Name of God The Merciful, The Compassionate

They ask thee about the spoils of war.

Say: The spoils of war belong to God and the Messenger so be Godfearing of God and make things right among you and obey God and his Messenger if you had been ones who believe.[8:1]

The ones who believe are only those whose hearts took notice when God was remembered. When His signs were recounted to them, their belief increased and they put their trust in the Lord—[8:2] those who perform the formal prayer and spend out of what We provided them,[8:3] those, they are the ones who truthfully believe. For them are degrees with their Lord and forgiveness and generous provision.[8:4]

Just as thy Lord brought thee out from thy house with The Truth, and, truly, a group of people among the ones who believe were the ones who dislike it.[8:5] They dispute with thee about The Truth—after it became clear—as if they had been driven to death and they look on at it.[8:6]

And when God promises you, one of the two sections: It will, truly, be for you. And you wish that the one that is unarmed should be yours. And God wants that He verify The Truth by His Words and to sever the last remnant of the ones who are ungrateful[8:7] that He may verify The Truth and render the falsehood untrue even if the ones who sin disliked it.[8:8]

Mention when you cry for help from your Lord and He responded to you: Truly, I am One Who Reinforces you with a thousand angels, ones who come one after another.[8:9]

And did God make this as good tidings for you so that with it your hearts will be at rest in it?

And there is no help but from God alone. Truly, God is Almighty, Wise.[8:10]

Mention when a sleepiness enwraps you as a safety from Him. He sends down water from heaven for you and He purifies you by it and causes to be put away from you the defilement of Satan. He invigorates your hearts and makes your feet firm by it.[8:11]

Mention when thy Lord reveals to the angels: I am, truly, with you, so make those who believed firm. I will cast alarm into the hearts of those who were ungrateful. So strike above their necks and strike each of their fingers from them.[8:12]

That is because they made a breach with God and His Messenger. And to whomever makes a breach with God and His Messenger, then, truly, God is Severe in repayment.[8:13]

That is for you, so experience it, and, truly, for the ones who are ungrateful, the punishment of the fire.[8:14]

O those who believed! When you met those who were ungrateful marching to battle, then, turn not your backs to them in flight.[8:15]

And whoever turns his back that Day—but one who withdraws from fighting for a purpose—or one who moves aside to another faction, he, surely, drew the burden of the anger from God and his place of shelter will be hell. And miserable will be the Homecoming![8:16]

Then, you kill them not, but God killed them. And thou hadst not thrown when thou hadst thrown but God threw. He tries by experiment the ones who believe with a fairer trial from Him. Truly, God is Hearing, Knowing.[8:17]

That is so, and, truly, God is One Who Makes Frail the cunning of the ones who are ungrateful.[8:18]

If you seek a judgment then, surely, drew near to you the victory. And if you refrain yourselves, then, that would be better for you. And if you revert, We will revert. And your factions will not avail you at all even if they were many. And God is with the ones who believe.[8:19]

O those who believed! Obey God and His Messenger and turn not away from him when you hear his command.[8:20] And be not like those who said: We heard, when they hear not.[8:21]

Truly, the worst of moving creatures with God are unwilling to hear and unwilling to speak, those who are not reasonable.[8:22]

If God knew any good in them He would have caused them to be willing to hear. And even if He had caused them to be willing to hear, truly, they would have turned away, and they are ones who turn aside.[8:23]

O those who believed! Respond to God and to the Messenger when He called you to what gives you life. And know, truly, that God comes between a man and his heart and that to Him you will assemble.[8:24] Be Godfearing of a test which will not light on those of you, particularly, who did wrong. And know that God is, truly, Severe in repayment.[8:25]

And remember when you were few, ones taken advantage of due to weakness on the earth. You fear humanity would snatch you away so He gave you refuge and confirmed you with His help and provided you with what is good so that perhaps you will give thanks.[8:26]

O those who believed! Betray not God and the Messenger nor betray your trusts when you know.[8:27] And know that your wealth and your children are a test and that God, with Him is a sublime compensation.[8:28]

O those who believed! If you are Godfearing of God, He will assign you a Criterion between right and wrong and will absolve you of your evil deeds and will forgive you. And God is Possessor of Sublime Grace.[8:29]

And mention when those who were ungrateful plan against thee to bring thee to a standstill or to kill thee or to drive thee out. And they plan and God plans, but God is Best of the ones who plan.[8:30]

And when Our signs are recounted to them, they said: We heard this. If we will, we would say the like of this. Truly, this is only fables of ancient ones.[8:31]

And when they said: O God! Truly, if this had been The Truth from Thee, rain down rocks on us from heaven or bring us a painful punishment.[8:32]

But God had not been punishing them with thee among them. Nor had God been One Who Punishes them while they ask for forgiveness.[8:33]

And what is with them that God should not punish them while they bar worshippers from the Masjid al-Haram and they had not been its protectors? Truly, its protectors are but ones who are Godfearing except most of them know not.[8:34]

Their formal prayer at the House had been nothing but whistling and clapping of hands. So experience the punishment because you had been ungrateful.[8:35]

Truly, those who were ungrateful spend their wealth so that they bar the way of God. They will spend it. Again, it will become a regret for them. Again, they will be vanquished. And those who were ungrateful will be assembled in hell.[8:36]

God will differentiate the bad from what is good. And He will lay the bad, some on some other, and heap them up altogether and lay them into hell. Those, they are the ones who are losers.[8:37]

Say to those who were ungrateful: If they refrain themselves, what is past will be forgiven. And if they repeat then, surely, a custom passed of the ancient ones as a warning.[8:38]

And fight them until there be no persecution and the way of life—all of it—be for God. Then, if they refrained themselves, then, truly, God is Seeing of what they do.[8:39]

And if they turned away, then, know that God is your Defender. How excellent a Defender and how excellent a Helper![8:40]

And know that whatever thing you gain as booty, then, truly one-fifth of it belongs to God and to the Messenger and to the possessors of kinship and the orphans and the needy and the traveler of the way if you had been believing in God and in what We caused to descend to Our servant on the Day of the Criterion between right and wrong, the day when the two multitudes met one another. And God is Powerful over everything.[8:41]

Mention when you were on the nearer bank of the valley and they were on the farther bank of the valley and the cavalcade was below you. Even if you made a promise together, you would be, certainly, at variance as to the solemn declaration because God decrees a command that had been one that is accomplished so that he who perishes would have perished by a clear portent and he who lives would live on by a clear portent. And, truly, God is Hearing, Knowing.[8:42]

Mention when God causes thee to see them as few in thy slumbering. If He caused thee to see them as many, you would have lost heart and contended with one another about the command except God saved you. Truly, He is Knowing of what is in the breasts.[8:43]

And mention when He causes you to see them when you met one another as few in your eyes and He makes you few in their eyes so that God decrees a command that had been one that is accomplished. And commands are returned to God.[8:44]

O those who believed! When you met a faction, then, stand firm and remember God frequently so that perhaps you will prosper.[8:45] And obey God and His Messenger and contend not with one another. Then, you lose heart and your competence go. And have patience. Truly, God is with the ones who remain steadfast.[8:46]

And be not like those who went forth from their abodes recklessly to show off to personages and bar them from the way of God. And God is One Who Encloses what they do.[8:47]

And mention when Satan made to appear pleasing their actions to them and said: No one will be ones who are victors against you this day from among all personages. And, truly, I will be your neighbor.

But when the two factions sighted one another, he receded on his two heels and said: Truly, I am free of you. Truly, I see what you see not. Truly, I fear God. And God is Severe in repayment.[8:48]

Mention when the ones who are hypocrites say and those who, in their hearts, is a sickness: Their way of life deluded these, but whoever puts his trust in God. Then, truly, God is Almighty, Wise.[8:49]

And if thou wouldst see when those who were ungrateful are called to themselves by the angels, they are striking their faces and their backs saying: Experience the punishment of the burning.[8:50]

That is because of what your hands put forward of evil and, truly, God is not unjust to His servants.[8:51]

In like manner of the people of Pharaoh—and of those before them—they were ungrateful for the signs of God so God took them for their impieties. Truly, God is Strong, Severe in repayment.[8:52]

Know that God will never be One Who Causes to Alter a divine blessing when He was gracious to a folk unless they first alter what is within themselves. And, truly, God is Hearing, Knowing.[8:53]

In like manner of the people of Pharaoh, and those before them, they denied the signs of their Lord, so We caused them to perish for their impieties. And We drowned the people of Pharaoh. And they all had been ones who are unjust.[8:54]

Truly, the worst of moving creatures with God are those who were ungrateful, so they will not believe.[8:55]

Those with whom thou hast made a contract, again, they break their compact every time and they are not Godfearing.[8:56] So if thou hast come upon them in war, then, break them up, whoever is behind them, so that perhaps they will recollect.[8:57]

And if thou hast feared treachery from a folk, then, dissolve the relationship with them equally. Truly, God loves not the ones who are traitors.[8:58]

Assume thou not that those who were ungrateful will outdo Me. Truly, they will never weaken Him.[8:59]

And prepare for them whatever you were able of strength, including a string of horses, to put fear in the enemy of God and your enemy and others besides whom you know them not. God knows them. And whatever thing you spend in the way of God, the account will be paid in full to you and you will not be wronged.[8:60]

And if they tended towards peace, then, tend thou towards it and put thy trust in God. Truly, He is The Hearing, The Knowing.[8:61]

And if they want to deceive thee, then, truly, God is Enough. It is He Who confirmed thee with His help and with the ones who believe.[8:62] And He brought their hearts together.

If thou hadst spent all that is in and on the earth, thou wouldst not have brought together their hearts, except God brought them together. Truly, He is Almighty, Wise.[8:63]

O Prophet! God is Enough for thee and for whoever followed thee among the ones who believe.[8:64]

O Prophet! Encourage fighting to the ones who believe. If there be twenty of you, ones who remain steadfast, they will vanquish two hundred. And if there be a hundred of you, they will vanquish a thousand of those who were ungrateful because they are a folk who understand not.[8:65]

Now God lightened your burden from you for He knew that there was a weakness in you. So if there would be a hundred of you, ones who remain steadfast, they will vanquish two hundred. And if there would be a thousand of you, they will vanquish two thousand with the permission of God. And God is with the ones who remain steadfast.[8:66]

It had not been for a Prophet that he would have prisoners of war unless he gives a sound thrashing in the region. You want the advantages of the present, but God wants the world to come. And God is Almighty, Wise.[8:67]

Were it not for a preceding prescription from God, you would, certainly, be afflicted with a tremendous punishment for what you took.8:68

Eat of what you gained as booty, lawful, what is good. And be Godfearing of God. Truly, God is Forgiving, Compassionate.8:69

O Prophet! Say to whom are in your hands of the prisoners of war: If God knows any good in your hearts, He will give you better than what was taken from you and He will forgive you. And God is Forgiving, Compassionate.8:70

But if they want treachery against thee, they, surely, betrayed God before, so He gave thee power over them. And God is Knowing, Wise.8:71

Truly, those who believed and emigrated and struggled with their wealth and their lives in the way of God, and those who gave refuge and helped, those are protectors, some of some others.

And those who believed, but emigrate not, you have no duty of friendship to them at all until they emigrate.

And if they asked you for help in the way of life, then, it would be upon you to help them, but against the folk whom between you and between them there is a solemn promise. And God is Seeing of what you do.8:72

And those who were ungrateful, some are protectors of some others. If you accomplish not allying with other believers there will be persecution on the earth and the hateful sin of corruption.8:73

And those who believed and emigrated and struggled in the way of God and those who gave refuge and helped, those, they are the ones who truthfully believe. For them is forgiveness and generous provision.8:74

And those who believed afterwards, and emigrated and struggled beside you, then, those are of you.

And those imbued through wombs, blood relations, some are more deserving than some others in what is prescribed by God, truly, God is Knowing of everything.8:75

CHAPTER 9 REPENTANCE

God and His Messenger declare disassociation from those with whom you made a contract among the ones who were polytheists who violated it:9:1

Roam about on the earth for four months and know that you will not be ones who frustrate God and that God is One Who Covers with shame the ones who are ungrateful.9:2

And the announcement from God and His Messenger to humanity on the day of the greater pilgrimage to Makkah is that God is free from the ones who are polytheists and so is His Messenger. Then, it will be better for you if you repented. But if you turned away, then, know that you are not ones who frustrate God. And give thou tidings to those who were ungrateful of a painful punishment.9:3

But those with whom you made a contract—among the ones who are polytheists—and again, they reduce you not at all nor do they back anyone against you, then, fulfill their compact with them until their term of contract expires. Truly, God loves the ones who are Godfearing.9:4

When the months of pilgrim sanctity were drawn away, then, kill the ones who are polytheists wherever you found them and take them and besiege them and sit in every place of ambush. Then, if they repented and performed the formal prayer and gave the purifying alms, then, let them go their way. Truly, God is Forgiving, Compassionate.9:5

And if anyone of the ones who are polytheists sought asylum with thee, then, grant him protection so that he hears the assertions of God. Again, convey thou him to a place of safety. That is because they are a folk who know not.9:6

How will there be for the ones who are polytheists a compact with God and with His Messenger but for those with whom you made a contract near the Masjid al-Haram?

If they go straight with you, then, go straight with them. Truly, God loves the ones who are Godfearing.9:7

How?

And if they get the better of you, they regard not ties of relationship with you nor a pact?

They please you with their mouths, but their hearts refuse compliance and many of them are ones who disobey.9:8

They sold out the signs of God for a little price and barred others from His way. Truly, how evil is what they had been doing.9:9

They regard not towards one who believes either ties of relationship or a pact. And those, they are the ones who exceed the limits.9:10

But if they repented and performed the formal prayer and gave the purifying alms, then, they are your brothers/sisters in your way of life, We explain the signs distinctly for a folk who know.9:11

But if they broke their sworn oaths after their compact and discredited your way of life, then, fight the leaders of ingratitude. Truly, they, their sworn oaths are nothing to them, so that perhaps they will refrain themselves.9:12

Will you not fight a folk who broke their sworn oaths and were about to expel the Messenger?

Began they the first time against you?

Will you dread them?

God has a better right that you should dread Him if you had been ones who believe.9:13

Fight them! God will punish them by your hands and cover them with shame and help you against them. And He will heal the breasts of a folk, ones who believe,9:14 and He causes to be put away the rage in their hearts.

And God turns to whom He wills in forgiveness. And God is Knowing, Wise.9:15

Or assumed you that you would be left before God knows those who struggled among you? And take not anyone to yourselves other than God and His Messenger and the ones who believe as intimate friends. And God is Aware of what you do.9:16

It had not been for the ones who are polytheists to frequent the places of prostration to God while they are ones who bear witness against themselves of their ingratitude. Those, their actions were fruitless. They are ones who will dwell in the fire forever!9:17

Only he frequents places of prostration to God who believed in God and the Last Day and performed the formal prayer and gave the purifying alms and dreads none but God. Perhaps those will be among the ones who are truly guided.9:18

Made you the giving of water to drink to the ones who are pilgrims and frequenting the Masjid al-Haram the same as he who believed in God and the Last Day and struggled in the way of God? They are not on the same level with God. And God guides not the folk, ones who are unjust.9:19

Those who believed and emigrated and struggled in the way of God with their wealth and their lives are sublime in their degree with God. And those, they are the ones who are victorious.9:20

Their Lord gives them good tidings of mercy from Him and His contentment and of Gardens for them in which is abiding bliss.9:21 They are ones who will dwell in them forever, eternally. Truly, God, with Him is a sublime compensation.9:22

O those who believed! Take not to yourselves your fathers and brothers/sisters as protectors if they embraced disbelief instead of belief. And whoever of you turns away to them, then, those, they are the ones who are unjust.⁹:²³

Say: If had been your fathers and your children and your brothers/sisters and your spouses and your kinspeople and the wealth you gained and the transactions you dread slacken and the dwellings with which you are well-pleased were more beloved to you than God and His Messenger and struggling in His Way, then, await until God brings His command. And God guides not the folk, ones who disobey.⁹:²⁴

God, certainly, helped you in many battlefields and on the day of Hunayn when you were impressed with your great numbers, but it avails you not at all. And the earth was narrow for you for all its breadth. Again, you turned as ones who draw back.⁹:²⁵

Again, God caused His tranquility to descend on His Messenger and on the ones who believed and caused armies you see not to descend and punished those who were ungrateful. And this is the recompense of the ones who were ungrateful.⁹:²⁶

Again, God will turn to whom He will in forgiveness after that. And God is Forgiving, Compassionate.⁹:²⁷

O those who believed! Truly, the ones who are polytheists are unclean, so let them come not near the Masjid al-Haram after this year.

And if you feared being poverty-stricken, God will enrich you out of His grace if He willed. Truly, God is Knowing, Wise.⁹:²⁸

Fight those who believe not in God nor the Last Day nor forbid what God and His Messenger forbade nor practice the way of life of The Truth among those who were given the Book until they give the tribute out of hand and they be ones who comply.⁹:²⁹

And the Jews said: Ezra is the son of God and the Christians said: The Messiah is the son of God. That is the saying with their mouths. They conform with the sayings of those who were ungrateful before. God took the offensive. How they are misled!⁹:³⁰

They took to themselves their learned Jewish scholars and their monks as lords—other than God—and the Messiah son of Mary. And they were only commanded to worship The One God. There is no god but He! Glory be to Him above the partners they ascribe!⁹:³¹

They want to extinguish the light of God with their mouths, but God refuses so that He fulfill His light even if the ones who are ungrateful disliked it. ⁹:³²

It is He Who sent His Messenger with the guidance and the way of life of The Truth so that He may uplift it over all ways of life, even if the ones who are polytheists disliked it.⁹:³³

O those who believed! Truly, there are many of the learned Jewish scholars and monks who consume the wealth of humanity in falsehood and bar from the way of God and those who treasure up gold and silver and spend it not in the way of God. Give to them tidings of a painful punishment,⁹:³⁴ on a Day it will be hot in the fire of hell. Then, by it are branded their foreheads and their sides and their backs.

It will be said: This is what you treasured up for yourselves so experience what you had been treasuring up.⁹:³⁵

Truly, the period of months with God is twelve lunar months in the Book of God. On the day when He created the heavens and the earth of them. Four are sanctified. That is the truth-loving way of life. So do not wrong yourselves in it.

And fight the ones who are polytheists collectively, as they fight you collectively. And know that God is with the ones who are Godfearing.⁹:³⁶

Truly, the postponing a Sacred Month is an increase in ingratitude. By it are caused to go astray those who were ungrateful, for they permit it a year, and forbid it a year, so that they agree with the period that God forbade, and they permit what God forbade.

Made to appear pleasing to them was the evil of their actions. And God guides not the folk, the ones who are ungrateful.⁹:³⁷

O those who believed! What was it with you when was said to you: Move forward in the way of God, you inclined heavily downwards to the earth?

Were you so well-pleased with this present life instead of the world to come? But the enjoyment of this present life is not but little compared to the world to come.⁹:³⁸

Unless you move forward, He will punish you with a painful punishment and will have in exchange for you a folk other than you. And you will not injure Him at all. And God is Powerful over everything.⁹:³⁹

If you help him not, then, surely, God helped him when those who were ungrateful drove him out.

The second of two, when they were both in the cavern, he says to his companion: Feel no remorse. Truly, God is with us.

Then, God caused His tranquility to descend on him and confirmed him with armies that you see not and made the word of those who were ungrateful the lowest. And the Word of God is Lofty. God is Almighty, Wise.⁹:⁴⁰

Move forward light and heavy and struggle with your wealth and your lives in the way of God. That is better for you if you had been knowing.⁹:⁴¹

If it had been a near advantage and an easy journey, they would have followed thee, except the destination of the journey was distant for them. And they will swear by God: If we were able, we would, certainly, have gone forth with you.

They will cause themselves to perish. And God knows that they are the ones who lie.⁹:⁴²

God pardon thee! Why hadst thou given permission to them before it becomes clear to thee those who were sincere and thou hast known who are the ones who lie?⁹:⁴³

They ask not permission of thee, those who believe in God and the Last Day, that they struggle with their wealth and their lives. And God is Knowing of the ones who are Godfearing.⁹:⁴⁴

It is only those who ask permission of thee who believe not in God and the Last Day and whose hearts were in doubt, so they go this way and that in their doubts.⁹:⁴⁵

And if they wanted to go forth, certainly, they would have prepared for it some preparation, except God disliked arousing them, so He caused them to pause and it was said: Sit along with the ones who sit at home.⁹:⁴⁶

If they went forth with you, they would have increased nothing for you, but ruination. And they would have rushed to and fro in your midst with insolent dissension. And among you are ones who would have harkened to them. And God is Knowing of the ones who are unjust.⁹:⁴⁷

Certainly, they were looking for dissension before. And they turned around and around for thee the commands until The Truth drew near, and the command of God became manifest although they were ones who dislike it.⁹:⁴⁸

Among them is he who says: Give me permission and tempt me not. But they descended into dissension. And, truly, hell is that which encloses the ones who are ungrateful.⁹:⁴⁹

If lights on thee benevolence, they are raised to anger, but if an affliction lights on thee, they say: Surely, we took our commands before. And they turn away and they are glad.⁹:⁵⁰

Say: Nothing will light on us but what God had been prescribing for us. He is our Defender. And in God let the ones who believe put their trust.⁹:⁵¹

Say: Are you watching for something, but one of the two fairer things to befall us? And we watch for you, whether

God will light on you a punishment from Him or from our hands. So watch! We are ones who are waiting with you.⁹:⁵²

Say: Spend willingly or unwillingly. There will be only non-acceptance. Truly, you, you had been a folk, ones who disobey.⁹:⁵³

And nothing prevented their contributions being accepted from them but that they were ungrateful to God and His Messenger and that they not approach formal prayer but while they are lazy and they spend but as ones who dislike to spend.⁹:⁵⁴

So let not their wealth impress thee nor their children. God wants only to punish them in this present life and so that their souls depart while they are ones who are ungrateful.⁹:⁵⁵

And they swear by God that they are, truly, of you while they are not of you. They are but a folk who are in fear.⁹:⁵⁶ If they find a shelter or a place to creep into or a place of retreat, they would turn to it as they rush away.⁹:⁵⁷

And among them there are some who find fault with thee about charities. If they were given a part of it, they were well-pleased, but if they are not given of it, that is when they are displeased.⁹:⁵⁸

Better if they were well-pleased with what God gave them and His Messenger. And they had said: God is Enough for us. God will give to us of His grace and so will His Messenger. Truly, to God we are ones who quest.⁹:⁵⁹

Charities are only for the poor and the needy and the ones who work to collect it and the ones whose hearts are brought together and to free the bondsperson and the ones who are in debt and in the way of God and for the traveler of the way. This is a duty to God. And God is Knowing, Wise.⁹:⁶⁰

And among them are those who malign the Prophet and say: He is unquestioning.

Say: He is unquestioning of what is good for you. He believes in God and believes in ones who believe. And he is a mercy to those of you who believed. And those of you who malign the Messenger of God, for them is a painful punishment.⁹:⁶¹

They swear by God to you to please you, but God and His Messenger have better right that they should please Him if they had been ones who believe.⁹:⁶²

Know they not that whoever opposes God and His Messenger, then, truly, for him will be the fire of hell—one who will dwell in it forever? That is the tremendous degradation.⁹:⁶³

The ones who are hypocrites are fearful that should be sent down against them a chapter of the Quran to tell them what is in their hearts.

Say: Ridicule us, but, truly, God is One Who Drives Out that of which you are fearful.⁹:⁶⁴

And if thou hadst asked them, they would say: Truly, we had only been engaging in idle talk and playing.

Say: Was it God and His signs and His Messenger that you had been ridiculing?⁹:⁶⁵

Make no excuses! Surely, you disbelieved after your belief. If We pardon a section of you, We will punish another section because, truly, they had been ones who sin.⁹:⁶⁶

The ones who are male hypocrites and the ones who are female hypocrites, some are of some other. They command that which is unlawful and prohibit that which is honorable and close their hands. They forgot God so He forgot them. Truly, the ones who are hypocrites, they are the ones who disobey.⁹:⁶⁷

And God promised the males, ones who hypocrites and the females, ones who are hypocrites and the ones who are ungrateful, the fire of hell, ones who will dwell in it forever! It will be enough for them. God cursed them. And for them is an abiding punishment.⁹:⁶⁸

Like those before you who had been with more strength than you and more wealth and children, they enjoyed their apportionment so you enjoyed your apportionment as enjoyed those who were before you their apportionment. And you engaged in idle talk as they engaged in idle talk. As to those, their actions were fruitless in the present and are such in the world to come. And those, they are the ones who are losers.⁹:⁶⁹

Approaches them not the tidings of those before them—the folk of Noah and of Ad and of Thamud, and of a folk of Abraham, and of the Companions of Midian, and that which are cities overthrown? Their Messengers approached them with the clear portents. So it had not been God who did wrong to them, rather, they had been doing wrong to themselves.⁹:⁷⁰

The males, ones who believe and the females, ones who believe, some are protectors of some other. They command to that which is honorable and they prohibit that which is unlawful and they perform the formal prayer and give the purifying alms and obey God and His Messenger. Those, God will have mercy on them. Truly, God is Almighty, Wise.⁹:⁷¹

God promised males, the ones who believe and the females, the ones who believe, Gardens beneath which rivers run, ones who will dwell in them forever and good dwellings in the Gardens of Eden. And the greater contentment is with God. That, it is the winning of the sublime triumph.⁹:⁷²

O Prophet! Struggle with the ones who are ungrateful and the ones who are hypocrites and be thou harsh against them. And their place of shelter will be hell. Miserable will be the Homecoming!⁹:⁷³

They swear by God that they said not against the Prophet but, certainly, they said the word of ingratitude and they were ungrateful after their submission to God.

And they were about to do something that they never attain.

And they sought revenge but that God would enrich them and His Messenger with His grace. And if they repent, it would be better for them. And if they turn away, God will punish them with a painful punishment in the present and in the world to come. And there is not for them on earth either a protector or a helper.⁹:⁷⁴

And of them are some who made a contract with God saying: If He gave us of His grace, we will be charitable and, certainly, we will be among the ones in accord with morality.⁹:⁷⁵

Then, when He gave them of His grace, they were misers with it and turned away and they were ones who turn aside.⁹:⁷⁶

He made the consequence hypocrisy in their hearts until a Day they will meet Him because they broke with God what they promised Him, because they had been lying against Him.⁹:⁷⁷

Know they not that God knows their conspiring secretly and their secret? And that God is The Knower of the unseen.⁹:⁷⁸

Those who find fault with ones who are volunteer donors to charities from among the ones who believe and those who find not but their striving to give, so they derided them. God will deride them. And they will have a painful punishment.⁹:⁷⁹

Ask for forgiveness for them or ask not for forgiveness for them, if thou hast asked for forgiveness for them seventy times, God will never forgive them. That is because they were ungrateful to God and His Messenger. And God guides not the folk, the ones who disobey.⁹:⁸⁰

The ones who are left behind were glad of their positions behind the Messenger of God. And they disliked struggling with their wealth and themselves in the way of God. And they said: Move not forward in the heat.

Say: The fire of hell has more severe heat. Would that they had been understanding!⁹:⁸¹

So let them laugh a little and weep much as a recompense for what they had been earning.⁹:⁸²

Then, God returned thee to a section of them. And they asked thy permission for going forth.

Then, say: You will never ever go forth with me nor fight an enemy with me. You were well-pleased sitting the first time. Then, sit—ones who await with who lagged behind. 9:83

Pray thou not formally for any of them who died, ever, nor stand up at his grave. Truly, they were ungrateful to God and His Messenger and died while they are ones who disobey. 9:84

And let not their wealth impress you nor their children. For God only wants to punish them with these in the present and their souls depart while they were ones who are ungrateful. 9:85

When a chapter of the Quran was caused to descend saying that: Believe in God and struggle along with His Messenger, those imbued with affluence ask permission of thee. And they said: Forsake us. We would be with the ones who sit at home. 9:86

They were well-pleased to be with those who stay behind. And a seal was set on their hearts so they understand not. 9:87

But the Messenger and those who believed with him struggled with their wealth and their lives. Those, for them are good deeds. And those, they are the ones who will prosper. 9:88

God prepared for them Gardens beneath which rivers run, ones who will dwell in them forever. That is the winning of the sublime triumph. 9:89

And the ones who make excuses drew near from among the nomads that permission be given them. And they sat back, those who lied against God and His Messenger. There will light on those who were ungrateful among them a painful punishment. 9:90

Not on the weak nor on the sick nor on those who find nothing to spend is there fault if they were true to God and His Messenger. There is no way against the ones who are doers of good. And God is Forgiving, Compassionate. 9:91

Nor on those who when they approached thee that thou wouldst find mounts to carry them, thou hadst said: I find not what will carry you. So they turned away while their eyes overflow with tears of grief when they find nothing for them to spend in the way of God. 9:92

The way of blame is only against those who ask thee permission to remain behind and they are rich. They were well-pleased to be with those who stay behind. And God set a seal on their hearts so that they know not. 9:93

They will make excuses to you when you returned to them. Say: Make no excuses. We will never believe you. Surely, God told us news about you. God and His Messenger will consider your actions. Again, you will be returned to One Who Knows the unseen and the visible. Then, He will tell you of what you had been doing. 9:94

They will swear to you by God when you turned about to them so that you renounce them. So renounce them. Truly, they are a disgrace. And their place of shelter will be hell, as a recompense for what they had been earning. 9:95

They swear to you so that you will be well-pleased with them. So while you be well-pleased with them, then, truly, God is not well-pleased with the folk, the ones who disobey. 9:96

The nomads are stauncher in ingratitude and hypocrisy and more likely not to know the ordinances that God caused to descend to His Messenger. And God is Knowing, Wise. 9:97

And of the nomads are some who take what they spend to themselves as something owed them and await for some turn of your fortunes. Theirs will be the reprehensible turn of fortune. And God is Hearing, Knowing. 9:98

And of the nomads are some who believe in God and the Last Day and take for himself what he spends—as an offering to God—and blessings of the Messenger that will be sent for them. No doubt these are not but an offering from them. God will cause them to enter into His mercy. Truly, God is Forgiving, Compassionate. 9:99

As for the forerunners, the ones who take the lead among the ones who emigrate and the helpers and those who followed them with kindness, God was well-pleased with them and they were well-pleased with Him. He prepared for them Gardens beneath which rivers run, ones who will dwell in them forever, eternally. That is the winning of the sublime triumph. 9:100

And from around you of the nomads are ones who are hypocrites. And from among the people of the city, some grew bold in hypocrisy. Thou hast not known them but We know them. We will, truly, punish them two times in this world. Again, they will be returned to a tremendous punishment. 9:101

And others acknowledged their impieties. They mixed actions, ones in accord with morality with others that are bad deeds. Perhaps God will turn to them in forgiveness. Truly, God is Forgiving, Compassionate. 9:102

Take charity from their wealth to purify them and make them pure with it. And invoke blessings for them. Truly, thy entreaties will bring a sense of comfort and rest to them. And God is Hearing, Knowing. 9:103

Know they not that God is He Who accepts remorse from His servants and takes charities and that God, He is The Accepter of Repentance, The Compassionate? 9:104

And say: Act!

God will consider your actions and so will His Messenger and the ones who believe. And you will be returned to Him, One Who Knows of the unseen and the visible. Then, He will tell you what you had been doing. 9:105

And there are others, ones who are waiting in suspense for the command of God. Either He will punish them or He will turn to them in forgiveness. And God is Knowing, Wise. 9:106

Mention those who took to themselves places of prostration by injuring and in ingratitude and separating and dividing between the ones who believe and as a stalking place for whoever warred against God and His Messenger before. And they will, certainly, swear that: We wanted nothing but the fairer. And God bears witness that they are, truly, ones who lie. 9:107

And stand not up in it ever! A place of prostration that was founded from the first day on God-consciousness is more rightful that thou hast stood up in it. In it are men who love to cleanse themselves. And God loves the ones who cleanse themselves. 9:108

Is one who founded his structure on the God-consciousness of God and His contentment better than he who founded his structure on the brink of a crumbling, tottering bank of a river so that it tumbled with him into the fire of hell? And God guides not the folk, the ones who are unjust! 9:109

The structure they built will cease not the skepticism in their hearts until their hearts are cut asunder. And God is Knowing, Wise. 9:110

Truly, God bought from the ones who believe themselves and their properties. For them is the Garden! They fight in the way of God so they kill and are slain. It is a promise rightfully on Him in the Torah and the Gospel and the Quran. And who is more true to His compact than God?

Then, rejoice in the good tidings of the bargain that you made in trading with Him. And that, it is the winning the sublime triumph 9:111 for the repentant worshippers, the ones who praise, the ones who are inclined to fasting, the ones who bow down, the ones who prostrate themselves, the ones who command that which is honorable and the ones who prohibit that which is unlawful, and the ones who guard the ordinances of God, and give thou good tidings to the ones who believe! 9:112

It had not been for the Prophet and those who believed to ask for forgiveness for ones who are polytheists—even if they had been imbued with kinship—after it became clear to them that they are the Companions of Hellfire.⁹:¹¹³ And had not been Abraham asking for forgiveness for his father only because of a promise he had promised him? Then, when it became clear to him that, truly, he was an enemy to God, he cleared himself from him. Truly, Abraham was sympathetic and forbearing.⁹:¹¹⁴

God would not have been causing a folk to go astray after He guided them until He makes manifest to them of what they should be Godfearing. Truly, God is Knowing of everything.⁹:¹¹⁵

Truly, God, to Him belongs the dominion of the heavens and the earth. He gives life and He causes to die. And there is not for you other than God, either a protector or a helper.⁹:¹¹⁶

Certainly, God turned towards the Prophet and the ones who emigrate and the helpers who followed him in the hour of adversity after the hearts of a group of people were about to swerve among them. Again, He turned towards them. Truly, He is Gentle, Compassionate.⁹:¹¹⁷

And upon the three who were left behind when the earth became narrow for them—for all its breadth—and their souls became narrow for them and they thought that there was no shelter from God, but in Him, again, He turns to them in forgiveness so that they would turn towards Him. Truly, God, He is The Accepter of Repentance, The Compassionate.⁹:¹¹⁸

O those who believed! Be Godfearing of God and be with the ones who are sincere.⁹:¹¹⁹ It had not been for the people of the city and among the nomads around them to stay behind from the Messenger of God nor prefer themselves more than himself. That is because they were neither lit on by thirst nor fatigue nor emptiness in the way of God nor tread they any treading on any ground—enraging the ones who are ungrateful—nor glean any gleaning of ground against the enemy but as an action in accord with morality written down for them. Truly, God wastes not the compensation of the ones who are doers of good.⁹:¹²⁰

Nor spend they contributions—be they small or great—nor cross they over a valley, but it was written down for them that God will give recompense to them for the fairer of what they had been doing.⁹:¹²¹

And it had not been for the ones who believe to move forward collectively. If every band moved not forward of them but a section of people only, that they become learned in the way of life and that they warn their folk when they returned to them so that perhaps they will beware?⁹:¹²²

O those who have believed! Fight the ones who are close to you of the ones who are ungrateful. And let them find harshness in you. And know that God is with the ones who are Godfearing.⁹:¹²³

And whenever there was caused to descend a chapter of the Quran, some of them say: Which of you had this increased in belief? As for those who believed, it increased them in belief and they rejoice at the good tidings.⁹:¹²⁴

But as for those who, in their hearts, is a sickness, it increased disgrace to their disgrace and they died while they are the ones who are ungrateful.⁹:¹²⁵

Consider they not that they are tried one time or two times a year? Again, they neither repent nor they recollect.⁹:¹²⁶

And whenever there was caused to descend a chapter of the Quran, some looked at some others saying: Is anyone seeing you?

Again, they took flight. God turned away from their hearts because they are a folk who understand not.⁹:¹²⁷

Certainly, there drew near to you a Messenger from among yourselves. It was grievous to him that you fell into misfortune. He is anxious for you and to the ones who believe, gentle, compassionate.⁹:¹²⁸

But if they turned away, say: God is enough for me. There is no god but He. In Him I put my trust. And He is the Lord of the Sublime Throne.⁹:¹²⁹

CHAPTER 10 JONAH

In the Name of God The Merciful, The Compassionate
*Alif Lām Rā.*¹⁰:¹

These are the signs of the wise Book. Had it been for humanity to wonder that We revealed to a man from among them that: Warn humanity and give thou good tidings to those who believed so that they will have a sound footing with their Lord?

The ones who are ungrateful said: Truly, this is one who is a clear sorcerer.¹⁰:²

Truly, your Lord is God Who created the heavens and the earth in six days.

Again, He turned Himself to the Throne managing the command. There is no intercessor but after His permission. That is God, your Lord, so worship Him alone. Will you not, then, recollect?¹⁰:³

To Him is your return, altogether. The promise of God is true. It is He Who begins the creation.

Again, He will cause it to return so that He may give recompense to those who believed and did as the ones in accord with morality with equity. And those who are ungrateful, for them is a drink of scalding water and a painful punishment because they had been ungrateful.¹⁰:⁴

It is He Who made the sun an illumination and the moon as a light and ordained its mansions so that you would know the number of the years and the reckoning. God created that only in Truth. He explains distinctly the signs for a folk who know.¹⁰:⁵

Truly, in the alternation of the nighttime and the daytime and whatever God has created in the heavens and the earth are signs for a folk who are Godfearing.¹⁰:⁶

Truly, those who hope not for their meeting with Us, but were well-pleased with this present life and were secured in it, those are they, ones who are heedless of Our signs.¹⁰:⁷

Those, their place of shelter will be the fire because of what they had been earning.¹⁰:⁸

Truly, those who believed and did as the ones in accord with morality, their Lord will guide them in their belief. Rivers will run beneath them in Gardens of Bliss.¹⁰:⁹

They will be calling out from there: Glory be to Thee, O God! And their greetings in it will be: Peace! And the last of their calling out will be that: The Praise belongs to God the Lord of the worlds!¹⁰:¹⁰

And if God is to quicken the worst for humanity, as they would desire to hasten for the good, their term would be decided. But We forsake those who hope not for the meeting with Us, wandering unwilling to see in their defiance.¹⁰:¹¹

And when harm afflicted the human being, he calls to Us on his side or as one who sits at home or as one who is standing up. But when We removed his harm from him, he passed by as if he had never been calling to Us for harm that afflicted him. Thus, made to appear pleasing to the ones who are excessive is what they had been doing.¹⁰:¹²

And, certainly, We caused to perish generations before you when they did wrong while their Messengers drew near with the clear portents, but they had not been such as to believe. Thus, We give recompense to the folk, the ones who sin.¹⁰:¹³

Again, We made you viceregents on the earth after them that We look on how you would do.¹⁰:¹⁴

And when are recounted to them Our signs, clear portents, those who hope not for their meeting with Us said: Bring us a Recitation other than this or substitute it.

Say: It be not possible for me to substitute it of my own accord. I follow nothing but what is revealed to me. Truly, I fear if I rebelled against my Lord a punishment on the tremendous Day.¹⁰:¹⁵

Say: If God willed, I would not have related it to you nor would He have caused you to recognize it. Surely, I lingered in expectation among you a lifetime before this. Will you not, then, be reasonable?¹⁰:¹⁶

So who did greater wrong than he who devised a lie against God or denied His signs? Truly, the ones who sin will not prosper.¹⁰:¹⁷

And they worship other than God things that injure them not, nor profit them.

And they say: These are our intercessors with God.

Say: Are you telling God of what He knows not in the heavens nor in and on the earth? Glory be to Him and exalted is He above partners they ascribe.¹⁰:¹⁸

And humanity had not been but one community, but, then, they became at variance. And if it were not for a Word that preceded from thy Lord, it would be decided between them immediately about what they are at variance in it.¹⁰:¹⁹

And they say: Why was a sign not caused to descend from his Lord?

Say: Truly, the unseen belongs only to God. So wait awhile. Truly, I am with you of the ones who are waiting awhile.¹⁰:²⁰

And when We caused humanity to experience mercy after tribulation afflicted them, that is when they conspired against Our signs.

Say: God is Swifter in planning. Truly, Our messengers write down what you plan.¹⁰:²¹

He it is Who sets you in motion through dry land and the sea until when you had been in boats and they ran them with the good wind and they were glad in it. A tempest wind drew near them. Waves drew near from every place, and they thought that they were enclosed by it. They called to God, ones who are sincere and devoted in their way of life to Him saying: If Thou wert to rescue us from this, we will, certainly, be of the ones who are thankful.¹⁰:²²

But when He rescued them, that is when they are insolent in and on the earth without right.

O humanity, your insolence is only against yourselves, an enjoyment of this present life. Again, to Us is your return. Then, We will tell you what you had been doing.¹⁰:²³

The parable of this present life is but like water that We caused to descend from heaven. It mingled with the plants of the earth—from which you eat—humanity and flocks—until when the earth took its ornaments and was decorated and its people thought that, truly, they are ones who have power over it! Our command approached it by nighttime or by daytime. Then, We made it stubble as if it flourished not yesterday. Thus, We explain distinctly the signs for a folk who reflect.¹⁰:²⁴

And God calls to the Abode of Peace and He guides whom He wills to a straight path.¹⁰:²⁵

For those who did good is the fairer and increase. Neither will gloom come over their faces nor abasement. Those are the Companions of the Garden. They are ones who will dwell in it forever.¹⁰:²⁶

And for those who earned evil deeds, the recompense of an evil deed will be its like and abasement will come over them. They will have none but God as One Who Saves from Harm. It is as if their faces were covered with a strip of the night, one in darkness. Those are the Companions of the Fire. They are ones who will dwell in it forever.¹⁰:²⁷

And on a Day We will assemble them altogether. Again, We will say to those who ascribed partners with God: Stay in your place, you and your ascribed associates. Then, We will set a space between them. And their ascribed associates would say: It had not been us that you were worshipping.¹⁰:²⁸

And God sufficed as a witness between you and between us. We had been of your worship certainly, ones who are heedless.¹⁰:²⁹

There every soul will be tried for what it has did in the past. And they would be returned to God, their Defender, The Truth. And from them will go astray what they had been devising.¹⁰:³⁰

Say: Who provides for you from the heaven and the earth? Who controls having the ability to hear and sight? And Who brings out the living from the dead and brings out the dead from the living? And who manages the command?

They will, then, say: God!

Say: Will you not be Godfearing?¹⁰:³¹

Such is God, your Lord, The Truth. And what else is there after The Truth but wandering astray. Where, then, turn you away?¹⁰:³²

Thus, was the Word of thy Lord realized against those who disobeyed that they will not believe.¹⁰:³³

Say: Are there among your ascribed associates with God anyone who begins the creation and, then, causes it to return?

Say: God begins the creation. Again, He causes it to return. Then, how you are misled!¹⁰:³⁴

Say: Are there among your ascribed associates with God anyone who guides to The Truth?

Say: God guides to The Truth. Has not He who guides to The Truth a better right to be followed than he who guides not unless he himself be guided? What is the matter with you? How you give judgment!¹⁰:³⁵

And most of them follow nothing but opinion. Truly, opinion avails them not against The Truth at all. Truly, God is Knowing of what they accomplish.¹⁰:³⁶

This Recitation had not been devised by other than God because it establishes as true what was before it and as a decisive explanation of the Book. There is no doubt in it. It is from the Lord of the worlds.¹⁰:³⁷

Or they will say: He devised it. Say: Bring a chapter of the Quran like it and call to whomever you were able—other than God—if you had been ones who are sincere.¹⁰:³⁸

Nay! They denied the knowledge that they comprehend not while approaches them not the interpretation. Thus, those who were before them denied. So look on how had been the Ultimate End of the ones who are unjust!¹⁰:³⁹

And of them are some who believe in it and of them are some who believe not in it. And thy Lord is greater in knowledge of the ones who make corruption.¹⁰:⁴⁰

And if they denied thee, then, thou say: For me are my actions and for you are your actions. You are free of what I do and I am free of what you do.¹⁰:⁴¹

And among them are some who listen to thee. So hast thou caused someone unwilling to hear, to hear if they had not been reasonable?¹⁰:⁴²

And among them are some who look on thee. So hast thou guided the unwilling to see if they had not been perceiving?¹⁰:⁴³

Truly, God does not wrong humanity at all, but humanity does wrong itself.¹⁰:⁴⁴

And on a Day He will assemble them as if they had not been lingering in expectation but an hour of the daytime. They will recognize one another among themselves. Surely, those who denied lost the meeting with God and they had not been ones who are truly guided.¹⁰:⁴⁵

Whether We cause thee to see some of what We promise them or We call thee to Us, then, to Us is their return. Again, God will be witness to what they accomplish.¹⁰:⁴⁶

Every community has its Messenger. So, then, when their Messenger drew near, it would be decided between them with equity. And they, they will not be wronged.¹⁰:⁴⁷

And they say: When is this promise if you had been ones who are sincere?¹⁰:⁴⁸

Say: I control not either hurt or profit for myself, but what God willed.

To every community there is a term. When their term draws near, neither will they delay it an hour nor will they press it forward.¹⁰:⁴⁹

Say: Considered you that if His punishment approached you at nighttime or at daytime, for which portion would the ones who sin be ones who seek to hasten?¹⁰:⁵⁰

Again, when it falls on you, believed you in it? Now? While you had been seeking to hasten it?¹⁰:⁵¹

Again, it would be said to those who did wrong: Experience the infinite punishment! Will you be given recompense but for what you had been earning?¹⁰:⁵²

And they ask thee to be told: Is it true? Say: Yes! By my Lord it is The Truth and you are not ones who frustrate Him.¹⁰:⁵³

And if there would be for every person who did wrong whatever is in or on the earth, he would, certainly, offer it for his ransom. And they would keep secret their self-reproach when they considered the punishment. But it will be decided between them with equity. And they, they will not be wronged.¹⁰:⁵⁴

No doubt to God belongs all that is in the heavens and the earth. No doubt the promise of God is true, but most of them know not.¹⁰:⁵⁵

It is He Who gives life and causes to die and to Him you will return.¹⁰:⁵⁶

O humanity! Surely, an admonishment drew near you from your Lord and a healing for what is in the breasts and a guidance and mercy for ones who believe.¹⁰:⁵⁷

Say: In the grace of God and in His mercy therein let them be glad. That is better than what they gather.¹⁰:⁵⁸

Say: Considered you from what God caused to descend for you of provision and that you made some of it unlawful and some lawful?

Say: Gave God permission to you or devise you against God?¹⁰:⁵⁹

And what is the opinion of those who devise a lie against God on the Day of Resurrection? Truly, God is Possessor of Grace to humanity, but most of them give not thanks.¹⁰:⁶⁰

Neither hast thou been on any matter nor hast thou recounted from the Recitation nor are you doing any action but We had been ones who bear witness over you when you press on it. And nothing escapes from thy Lord of the weight of an atom in or on the earth nor in the heaven nor what is smaller than that nor what is greater than that but it is in a clear Book.¹⁰:⁶¹

No doubt with the faithful friends of God there will be neither fear in them nor will they feel remorse.¹⁰:⁶²

Those who believed and had been Godfearing,¹⁰:⁶³ for them are good tidings in this present life and in the world to come. There is no substitution of the Words of God. That, it is the winning the sublime triumph.¹⁰:⁶⁴

And let not their saying dishearten thee. Truly, all great glory belongs to God. He is The Hearing, The Knowing.¹⁰:⁶⁵

No doubt to God belongs whatever is in the heavens and whatever is in and on the earth. And follow not those who call to ascribed associates other than God. They follow nothing but opinion and they do nothing but guess.¹⁰:⁶⁶

It is He Who made the nighttime for you so that you rest in it and the daytime for one who perceives. Truly, in this are signs for a folk who hear.¹⁰:⁶⁷

They said God took to Himself a son. Glory be to Him. He is Sufficient. To Him is whatever is in the heavens and in and on the earth. With you there is no authority for this. Say you against God what you know not?¹⁰:⁶⁸

Say: Truly, those who devise lies against God, they will not prosper, ¹⁰:⁶⁹ only an enjoyment in the present! Again, to Us will be their return. Again, We will cause them to experience the severe punishment because they had been ungrateful.¹⁰:⁷⁰

And recount to them the tidings of Noah when he said to his folk: O my folk! If my station had been troublesome to you and my reminding you of the signs of God, then, in God I put my trust. So summon up your affair along with your ascribed associates. Again, there be no cause for doubt in your affair. Again, decide against me and give me no respite.¹⁰:⁷¹

Then, if you turned away, I asked you not for any compensation. My compensation is with God. And I was commanded that I be of the ones who submit to God.¹⁰:⁷²

Then, they denied him, so We delivered him and some with him on the boat. And we made them the viceregents while We drowned those who denied Our signs. Then, look on how had been the Ultimate End of the ones who are warned!¹⁰:⁷³

Again, We raised up Messengers after him to their folk. They drew near them with the clear portents. But they had not been believing in what they had denied before of it. Thus, We set a seal on the hearts of the ones who exceed the limits.¹⁰:⁷⁴

Again, We raised up after them Moses and Aaron to Pharaoh and his Council with Our signs. Then, they grew arrogant, and they had been a folk, ones who sin.¹⁰:⁷⁵

So when The Truth drew near them from Us, they said: Truly, this is clear sorcery!¹⁰:⁷⁶

Moses said: Say you this about The Truth when it drew near you? Is this sorcery? And the ones who are sorcerers will not prosper.¹⁰:⁷⁷

They said: Hadst thou drawn near to us to turn us from what we found our fathers on so that the domination on the earth might be for you two? We are not ones who believe in both of you.¹⁰:⁷⁸

And Pharaoh said: Bring to me everyone who is a knowing sorcerer.¹⁰:⁷⁹

And when the ones who are sorcerers drew near, Moses said to them: Cast down with ones who cast.¹⁰:⁸⁰

Then, when they cast Moses said: What you brought about is sorcery. Truly, God will render it untrue. Truly, God makes not right the actions of the ones who make corruption.¹⁰:⁸¹

And God will verify The Truth by His Words, although the ones who sin disliked it much!¹⁰:⁸²

But none believed Moses but the offspring of his folk because of the fear of Pharaoh and his Council that he persecute them. And, truly, Pharaoh was one who exalted himself on the earth. And he was, truly, of the ones who are excessive.¹⁰:⁸³

And Moses said: O my folk! If you had been believing in God, then, put your trust in Him, if you had been ones who submit to God.¹⁰:⁸⁴

Then, they said: We put our trust in God. Our Lord! Make us not a temptation for the folk, the ones who are unjust.¹⁰:⁸⁵

And deliver us by Thy Mercy from the folk, the ones who are ungrateful.¹⁰:⁸⁶

And We revealed to Moses and his brother: Take as your dwellings, houses for your folk in Egypt. Make your houses a direction of formal prayer. And perform the formal prayer. And give good tidings to the ones who believe.¹⁰:⁸⁷

And Moses said: Our Lord! Thou hadst given to Pharaoh and his Council adornment and wealth in this present life. Our Lord! Cause them to go astray from Thy way. Our Lord! Obliterate their wealth and harden their hearts so that they believe not until they consider the painful punishment.¹⁰:⁸⁸

He said: Surely, you both were answered, so go straight both of you and follow not the way of those who know not.[10:89]

And We brought the Children of Israel over the sea. And Pharaoh and his army pursued them in insolence and acting impulsively until when, overtaken by drowning, he said: I believed that there is no god but He in Whom the Children of Israel believed and I am among ones who submit to God.[10:90]

It was said: Now, surely, thou hadst rebelled before and had been among the ones who make corruption.[10:91]

On this day We will deliver thee with thy physical form that thou be a sign to whoever is after thee. And, truly, many among humanity are ones who are heedless of Our signs.[10:92]

And, certainly, We placed the Children of Israel in a sound place of settlement and provided them with what is good. And they are not at variance until the knowledge drew near them. Truly, thy Lord will decree between them on the Day of Resurrection about what they had been at variance in it.[10:93]

So if thou hadst been in uncertainty about what We caused to descend to thee, then, ask those who recited the Book before thee. Certainly, The Truth drew near thee from thy Lord so thou hast not been among the ones who contest.[10:94]

Thou hast not been among those who denied the signs of God, for, then, thou wouldst be among the ones who are losers.[10:95]

Truly, those against whom is realized through the Word of thy Lord, will not believe[10:96]—even if every sign drew near them—until they consider the painful punishment.[10:97]

And had there been a town that believed and profited from its belief other than the folk of Jonah?

When they believed, We removed from them the punishment of degradation in this present life and gave them enjoyment for awhile.[10:98]

And if thy Lord willed, all would have believed who are on the earth altogether. So wouldst thou compel humanity against their will until they become ones who believe?[10:99]

And it would not have been for any person to believe but by the permission of God. And He lays disgrace on those who are not reasonable.[10:100]

Say: Look on what is in the heavens and the earth.

And neither the signs nor the warning avail a folk who believe not.[10:101]

So wait they awhile but like in the days of those who passed away before them? Say: So wait awhile. I am with you among the ones waiting awhile![10:102]

Again, We rescue Our Messengers and those who believed. Thus, it is an obligation upon Us to deliver the ones who believe.[10:103]

Say: O humanity! If you were in uncertainty as to my way of life, then, I will not worship those whom you worship other than God. Rather, I worship only God Who will call you to Himself. And I was commanded that I be among the ones who believe[10:104] and that: Settest thou thy face to the way of life of a monotheist. And be thou not among the ones who are polytheists.[10:105]

And call not to other than God what neither profits nor hurts thee. And if thou wert to accomplish that, truly, thou wouldst be among the ones who are unjust.[10:106]

And if God afflicts thee with harm, there is no one who removes it but He. And if He wants good for thee, there is no one who repels His grace. It lights on whomever He wills of His servants. And He is The Forgiving, The Compassionate.[10:107]

Say: O humanity! Surely, The Truth drew near you from your Lord so whoever was truly guided, then, he is only truly guided for his own self. And whoever went astray, then, he only goes astray to his own loss. And I am not a trustee over you.[10:108]

And follow thou what is revealed to thee. And have thou patience until God gives judgment. And He is Best of the ones who judge.[10:109]

CHAPTER 11 HUD

In the Name of God The Merciful, The Compassionate Alif Lām Rā.

A Book, the signs in it were set clear. Again, they were explained distinctly from that which proceeds from the Presence of the Wise, Aware, [11:1] that you not worship any but God.

Truly, I am a warner to you from Him and a bearer of good tidings[11:2] and that: Ask for forgiveness from your Lord. Again, repent to Him that He give you fairer enjoyment for a term that which is determined. He gives His grace to every possessor of grace. And if they turn away, I fear for you the punishment of a Great Day.[11:3]

To God is your return. And He is Powerful over everything.[11:4]

But they fold up their breasts that they conceal themselves from Him. No doubt at the time when they cover themselves with their garments, He knows what they keep secret and what they speak openly. Truly, He is Knowing of what is in their breasts.[11:5]

And there is no moving creature on earth but its provision is from God. And He knows its appointed time and its repository. All is in a clear Book.[11:6]

And it is He Who created the heavens and the earth in six days. And His Throne had been upon the waters that He try you—which of you is fairer in actions. And if thou wert to say to them: Truly, you are ones who will be raised up after death. Those who were ungrateful would be sure to say: This is nothing but clear sorcery.[11:7]

If We postponed the punishment for them for a period of time, that which is numbered, they will, surely, say: What detains it?

Certainly, the day it approaches them, there is not of that which will be turned away from them and surrounded them was what they had been ridiculing of it.[11:8]

And if We caused the human being to experience mercy from Us, then, again, We tear it out from him, truly, he is hopeless, ungrateful.[11:9]

And if We caused him to experience favor after tribulation afflicted him, he is certain to say: Evil deeds went from me! Truly, he becomes glad, boastful.[11:10]

But those who endured patiently and did as the ones in accord with morality, those, for them is forgiveness and a great compensation.[11:11]

So wouldst thou perhaps be one who leaves some of what is revealed to thee?

Or is thy breast that which is narrowed by it because they say: Why was a treasure not caused to descend to him or an angel drew near him?

Truly, thou art only a warner. And God is a Trustee over everything. Or they say: He devised it.[11:12]

Say: Approach you, then, with ten chapters of the Quran like it, that which is forged, and call to whomever you were able other than God if you had been ones who are sincere.[11:13]

If they respond not to you, then, know that it was only caused to descend by the knowledge of God and that there is no god but He. Are you, you, then, ones who submit to God?[11:14]

Whoever had been wanting this present life and its adornment, We pay their account in full to them for their actions in it. And they will not be diminished in it.[11:15]

Those are those for whom there is nothing in the world to come but fire. And what they crafted here was fruitless. And what they had been doing is in vain.[11:16]

Is he, then, who had been on a clear portent from his Lord, and recounts it from Him as one who bears witness—and before it was the Book of Moses, a leader and a mercy—like them? Those believe in it. Whoever is ungrateful for it among the confederates, he is promised the fire! So be thou not hesitant about it. Truly, it is The Truth from thy Lord, except most of humanity believes not.[11:17]

Who does greater wrong than he who devised a lie against God? Those will be presented before their Lord.

And the ones who bear witness will say: These are those who lied against their Lord. But the curse of God is upon the ones who are unjust—[11:18] they who bar from the way of God and desire in it crookedness. And they, in the world to come, they are ones who disbelieve.[11:19]

Those will not be ones who frustrate Him on the earth, nor had there been for them—other than God—any protectors. The punishment is multiplied for them. Not had they been able to have the ability to hear, nor had they been perceiving.[11:20]

Those are those who lost their souls. What they had been devising had gone astray.[11:21]

Without a doubt they in the world to come, they are the ones who are losers.[11:22]

Truly, those who believed and did as the ones in accord with morality and humbled themselves before their Lord, those will be the Companions of the Garden. They, ones who will dwell in it forever.[11:23]

The parable of the two groups of people is as the one unwilling to see, unwilling to hear and the other, seeing and hearing. They are not on the same level in likeness. Will you not, then, recollect?[11:24]

And, certainly, We sent Noah to his folk: Truly, I am a clear warner to you[11:25] that you worship none but God. Truly, I fear for you the punishment of a painful Day.[11:26]

Then, the Council of those who were ungrateful said from among his folk: We see thee only as a mortal like us. We see none followed thee but those, they who are visibly our most wretched, simple minded. Nor we see you as having any merit above us. Nay! We think that you are ones who lie.[11:27]

He said: O my folk! Considered you that I had been with a clear portent from my Lord and that He gave me mercy from Himself but it was invisible to you? Then, will we fasten you to it when you are ones who dislike it?[11:28]

And O my folk! I ask not of you wealth for it. My compensation is but with God. And I will not be one who drives away those who believed. Truly, they are ones who will encounter their Lord while I see you a folk who are ignorant.[11:29]

And O my folk! Who would help me against God if I drove them away?

Will you not, then, recollect?[11:30]

And I say not to you: The treasures of God are with me nor that I know the unseen nor I say: Truly, I am an angel nor I say of those whom your eyes look down upon: God will never give them good. God is greater in knowledge of what is within their souls for, then, I would be of the ones who are unjust.[11:31]

They said: O Noah! Surely, thou hadst disputed with us, then, made much of the dispute with us. Now approach us with what thou hadst promised us if thou hadst been among the ones who are sincere.[11:32]

He said: Only God will bring it on you if He willed. And you will not be ones who frustrate Him.[11:33] And my advice will not profit you—even if I wanted to advise you—if God hadst been wanting to lead you into error. He is your Lord and to Him you will return.[11:34]

Or they say: He devised it.

Say: If I devised it, my sin is upon me and I am free of your sins.[11:35]

And it was revealed to Noah: Truly, none of thy folk will believe but who had already believed. So be thou not despondent at what they have been accomplishing.[11:36]

And craft thou the boat under Our Eyes and by Our Revelation and address Me not for those who did wrong. They are, truly, ones who are drowned.[11:37]

And he crafts the boat. Whenever the Council passed by him of his folk, they derided him.

He said: If you deride us, then, we will deride you just as you deride us.[11:38] And you will know to whom will approach a punishment covering with shame and on whom an abiding punishment will alight![11:39]

Until when Our command drew near and the oven boiled, We said: Carry in it of every living thing, two, a pair and thy people, but him against whom the saying has preceded and who believed. And none but a few believed with him.[11:40]

And he said: Embark in it. In the Name of God will be the course of the ship and its berthing. Truly, my Lord is Forgiving, Compassionate.[11:41]

So it runs with them amidst waves like mountains. And Noah cried out to his son and he had been standing apart: O my son! Embark with us and be thou not with the ones who are ungrateful![11:42]

He said: I will take shelter for myself on a mountain. It will be what saves me from the harm of the water.

Noah said: No one saves from the harm this day from the command of God but him on whom He had mercy. And a wave came between them so he had been of the ones who are drowned.[11:43]

And it was said: O earth! Take in thy water! And O heaven: Desist!

And the water was shrunken and the command of God was satisfied and it was on the same level as Al-Judi. And it was said: Away with the folk, the ones who are unjust![11:44]

And Noah cried out to his Lord and said: My Lord! Truly, my son is of my people. And, truly, Thy promise is The Truth. And Thou art the Most Just of the ones who judge.[11:45]

He said: O Noah! Truly, he is not of thy people. Truly, he, his actions are not in accord with morality. So ask not of Me what thou hast no knowledge. Truly, I admonish thee so that thou not be of the ones who are ignorant.[11:46]

He said: My Lord! Truly, I take refuge with Thee so that I not ask Thee of what I am without knowledge. Unless Thou art to forgive me and have mercy on me, I would be of the ones who are losers.[11:47]

It was said: O Noah! Get thee down with peace from Us and blessings on thee and on communities from whoever are with thee, and communities to whom We will give enjoyment. And, again, they will be afflicted by Us with a painful punishment.[11:48]

That is of the tidings of the unseen that We reveal to thee. Thou hast not been knowing of them nor thy folk before this. So have thou patience. Truly, the Ultimate End is for the ones who are Godfearing.[11:49]

And to Ad, their brother Hud. He said: O my folk! Worship God! You have no god other than He. You are nothing but ones who devise.[11:50]

O my folk! I ask not of you any compensation. My compensation is but with Who originated me. Will you not, then, be reasonable?[11:51]

And O my folk! Ask your Lord for forgiveness. Again, repent to Him. He will send abundant rain to you from heaven and increase you, adding strength to your strength. So turn not away as ones who sin.[11:52]

They said: O Hud! Hadst thou brought about any clear portent for us? We will not be ones who leave our gods for thy saying? And we are not ones who believe in thee.[11:53]

Truly, we say nothing but that some of our gods inflicted thee with evil.

He said: Truly, I call God to witness and bear you witness that I am free from partners you ascribe[11:54] other than Him. So try to outwit me altogether. Again, give me no respite.[11:55]

Truly, I put my trust in God, my Lord and your Lord. There is not a moving creature but He is One Who Takes of its forelock. Truly, my Lord is on a straight path.[11:56] But if you turn away, that is your decision. Then, surely, I expressed to you what I was sent with to you. And my Lord will make successors a folk other than you and you will not injure Him at all. Truly, My Lord is Guardian over everything.[11:57]

And Our command drew near. We delivered Hud and those who believed with him by a mercy from Us. And We delivered them from a harsh punishment.[11:58]

And that was Ad. They negated the signs of their Lord and rebelled against His Messengers. And they followed the command of every haughty and stubborn one.[11:59] And they were pursued in the present life by a curse. And on the Day of Resurrection, no doubt, truly, Ad were ungrateful to their Lord. Away with Ad, a folk of Hud![11:60]

And We sent to Thamud their brother Salih. He said: O my folk! Worship God. You have no god other than He. He caused you to grow from the earth and settled you on it. So ask for His forgiveness. Again, repent to Him. Truly, my Lord is Near, One Who Answers.[11:61]

They said: O Salih! Surely, thou hadst been one who is a source of hope to us before this. Hast thou prohibited us that we worship what our fathers worship? And, truly, we are in uncertainty about what thou hast called us to, in grave doubt.[11:62]

He said: O my folk! Considered you that I had been with a clear portent from my Lord and that He gave me a mercy from Himself so who, then, would help me against God if I rebelled against Him? Then, you would increase me not but in decline.[11:63]

And: O my folk! This is the she-camel of God, a sign for you. So let her eat on God's earth and afflict her not with evil so that a near punishment take you.[11:64]

But they crippled her. So he said: Take joy in your abode for three days. That is a promise, one that will not be belied.[11:65]

Then, Our command drew near. We delivered Salih and those who believed with him by a mercy from Us and from the degradation of that Day. Truly, thy Lord, He is Strong, Almighty.[11:66]

The Cry took those who did wrong. It came to be in the morning in their abodes, ones who are fallen prostrate,[11:67] as if they dwelt not in them. No doubt, truly, Thamud were ungrateful to their Lord. Away with Thamud.[11:68]

And, certainly, Our messengers drew near Abraham with good tidings. They said: Peace.

He said: Peace.

And he presently brought about a roasted calf.[11:69]

Then, when he saw their hands reach not out towards it, he became suspicious and sensed awe of them.

They said: Fear not. We were sent to the folk of Lot.[11:70]

Abraham's woman, one who is standing up, laughed when We gave her good tidings of Isaac and besides Isaac, Jacob.[11:71]

She said: Woe to me! Will I give birth when I am an old woman and this, my husband, is an old man? Truly, this is a strange thing![11:72]

They said: Marvel thou at the command of God? The mercy of God and His blessings be upon you, O People of the House: Truly, He is Worthy of Praise, Glorious.[11:73]

And when the panic went from Abraham and the good tidings drew near to him, he disputes with Us for the folk of Lot.[11:74] Truly, Abraham was forbearing, sympathetic, one who turns in repentance.[11:75]

O Abraham! Turn aside from this. Truly, the command of thy Lord drew near. And, truly, that which arrives for them is a punishment, one that is not to be repelled.[11:76]

And when Our messengers drew near Lot, he was troubled for them and was concerned for them, being distressed. And he said: This is a distressful day![11:77]

Then, drew near his folk, running toward him because they had been doing evil deeds before. He said: O my folk! These are my daughters! They are purer for you. So be Godfearing of God. And cover me not with shame as regards my guests. Is there not among you a well-intentioned man?[11:78]

They said: Certainly, thou hadst known we have no right to thy daughters. And, truly, thou hast known well what we want.[11:79]

He said: Would that I had strength against you or take shelter with stauncher support![11:80]

They said: O Lot! Truly, we are Messengers of thy Lord. They will not reach out to thee so set thou forth with thy people in a part of the night and let not any of you look back, but thy woman. Truly, that which lights on them will light on her. Truly, what is promised to them is in the morning. Is the morning not near?[11:81]

So when Our command drew near, We made its high part low and We rained down on it rocks of baked clay, one upon another,[11:82] ones that are distinguished, and not far from the ones who are unjust.[11:83]

And We sent to Midian their brother Shuayb. He said: O my folk! Worship God. You have no god other than He. And reduce not the measuring vessel and balance. Truly, I consider you as good. And, truly, I fear for you the punishment of an Enclosing Day.[11:84]

And O my folk! Live up to the measuring vessel and balance in equity. And diminish not of humanity their things. And do no mischief in and on the earth as ones who make corruption.[11:85] God's abiding wisdom is best for you if you had been ones who believe. And I am not a Guardian over you.[11:86]

They said: O Shuayb! Is it that thy formal prayer commands thee that we leave what our fathers worship or that we accomplish not with our possibilities whatever we will? Truly, thou art the forbearing, the well-intentioned.[11:87]

He said: O my folk! Considered you that I had been with a clear portent from my Lord. He provided me fairer provision from Himself. And I want not to go against you in what I prohibit you. I want only making things right so far as I was able. And my success is not but from God. In Him I put my trust and to Him I am penitent.[11:88]

And O my folk! Let not your breach with me drive you into being lighted on by the like of what lit on a folk of Noah or a folk of Hud or a folk of Salih. And a folk of Lot are not far from you.[11:89] And ask for forgiveness from your Lord. Again, repent to Him. Truly, my Lord is Compassionate, Loving.[11:90]

They said: O Shuayb! We understand not much of what thou sayest. And, truly, we see thee weak among us. If it had not been for thy extended family, we would have stoned thee. And thou art not mighty against us.[11:91]

He said: O my folk! Is my extended family mightier to you than God whom you took to yourselves to disregard? Truly, my Lord is One Who Encloses whatever you do.[11:92]

O my folk! Act according to your ability and, truly, I am one who acts. You will know to whom approaches a punishment covering him with shame and who, he is one who lies. And be on the watch! Truly, I am watching with you.[11:93]

And Our command drew near. We delivered Shuayb and those who believed with him by a mercy from Us. And the Cry took those who did wrong. It came to be in the morning in their abodes ones who are fallen prostrate,¹¹:⁹⁴ as if they had not been dwelling in them.

Away with Midian just as Thamud was done away.¹¹:⁹⁵

And, certainly, We sent Moses with Our signs and a clear authority¹¹:⁹⁶ to Pharaoh and his Council but they followed the command of Pharaoh. And the command of Pharaoh was not well-intended.¹¹:⁹⁷ He will go before his folk on the Day of Resurrection and they will be led down into the fire. Miserable will be the watering place, that to which they are led down!¹¹:⁹⁸ And they were pursued by a curse in this life and on the Day of Resurrection! Miserable will be, the oblation, that which is offered!¹¹:⁹⁹

That is from the tidings of the towns that We relate to thee. Of them, some are ones that are standing up and some are stubble.¹¹:¹⁰⁰ And it was not that We did wrong to them. Rather, they did wrong themselves. And their gods availed them not whom they call to besides God at all. When the command of thy Lord drew near they increased them not other than in ruination.¹¹:¹⁰¹

And, thus, is the taking of thy Lord when He took the towns while they are ones who are unjust. Truly, His taking is painful, severe.¹¹:¹⁰²

In that, truly, there is a sign for whoever feared the punishment of the world to come. That Day humanity will be one that is gathered together for it and that will be a witnessed Day.¹¹:¹⁰³

And We postpone it not but for the numbered term.¹¹:¹⁰⁴

On the Day it approaches no person will assert anything but with His permission. Then, among them will be the disappointed and the happy.¹¹:¹⁰⁵

As for those who were in despair, they will be in the fire. For them in it is sobbing and sighing,¹¹:¹⁰⁶ ones who will dwell in it for as long as the heavens and the earth continued, but what thy Lord willed. Truly, thy Lord is Achiever of what He wants.¹¹:¹⁰⁷

And as for those who were happy, they will be in the Garden, ones who will dwell in it for as long as the heavens and the earth continued, but what thy Lord willed, a gift that will not be that which is broken.¹¹:¹⁰⁸

So be thou not hesitant as to what these worship. They worship nothing but what their fathers worship before. And We are the ones who pay their share in full without being that which is reduced.¹¹:¹⁰⁹

And, certainly, We gave Moses the Book, but they were at variance about it. And if it were not for a Word that preceded from thy Lord, it would be decided between them. And, truly, they were uncertain about it, ones in grave doubt.¹¹:¹¹⁰

And, truly, to each his account will be paid in full by thy Lord for their actions. Truly, He is Aware of what they do.¹¹:¹¹¹

So go thou straight as thou wert commanded and those who repented with thee and be not defiant. Truly, He is Seeing of what you do.¹¹:¹¹²

Then, incline not to those who did wrong so the fire afflict you and there will not be for you any protectors other than God. Again, you will not be helped.¹¹:¹¹³

And perform the formal prayer at the two ends of the daytime and at nearness of the nighttime. Truly, benevolence causes evil deeds to be put away. That is a reminder for the ones who remember.¹¹:¹¹⁴

And have thou patience, for, truly, God wastes not the compensation of the ones who are doers of good.¹¹:¹¹⁵

Why had there not been among the generations before you imbued with abiding wisdom, prohibiting corruption in and on the earth, but a few of those whom We rescue from among them? And those who did wrong followed what they were given ease in it. And they had been ones who sin.¹¹:¹¹⁶ Thy Lord had not been causing the towns to perish unjustly while their people are ones who make things right.¹¹:¹¹⁷

And if thy Lord willed, He would have made humanity one community. But they cease not to be ones who are at variance,¹¹:¹¹⁸ but on whom thy Lord had mercy. And for that, He created them, and completed was the Word of thy Lord. Certainly, I will fill hell with genie and humanity one and all.¹¹:¹¹⁹

And all that We relate to thee of the tidings of the Messengers is so that We make thy mind firm by it. And The Truth drew near thee in this, and an admonishment and a reminder for the ones who believe.¹¹:¹²⁰

And say to those who believe not: Act according to your ability. Truly, We are ones who act.¹¹:¹²¹ And wait awhile. We, too, are ones who are waiting awhile.¹¹:¹²²

And to God belongs the unseen of the heavens and the earth. And to Him is the return of every command, so worship Him and put thy trust in Him. And thy Lord is not One Who is Heedless of what you do.¹¹:¹²³

CHAPTER 12 JOSEPH

In the Name of God, The Merciful, The Compassionate
Alif Lām Rā.

That are the signs of the clear Book.¹²:¹

Truly, We caused to descend a Recitation in Arabic so that perhaps you will be reasonable.¹²:²

We relate to thee the fairer of narratives through what We revealed to thee of this, the Quran, although thou hadst been before this among the ones who are heedless.¹²:³

Mention when Joseph said to his father: O my father! Truly, I saw eleven stars and the sun and the moon. I saw them as ones prostrating themselves to me.¹²:⁴

He said: O my son! Relate not thy dream to thy brothers so that they contrive cunning against thee. Truly, Satan is a clear enemy to the human being.¹²:⁵

And, thus, thy Lord will elect thee and teach thee of the interpretation of events. And He will fulfill His divine blessing on thee and on the people of Jacob just as He fulfilled it on thy two fathers before, Abraham and Isaac. Truly, thy Lord is Knowing, Wise.¹²:⁶

Certainly, there had been in Joseph and his brothers signs for the ones who ask.¹²:⁷ When they said: Certainly, Joseph and his brother are more beloved to our father than we, although we are many. Truly, our father is clearly wandering astray.¹²:⁸ Kill Joseph or fling him to some other region to free the face of your father for you. You be a folk after that ones in accord with morality!¹²:⁹

Said one who says: Kill not Joseph, but cast him into the bottom of a well. Some company of travelers will pick him out, if you had been ones who do this.¹²:¹⁰

They said: O our father! Why wilt thou not entrust us with Joseph when we are, truly, ones who will, certainly, look after him?¹²:¹¹ Send him with us tomorrow to frolic and play. And, truly, we are ones who guard him.¹²:¹²

He said: Truly, it disheartens me that you go with him. And I fear that a wolf eat him while you are ones who are heedless of him.¹²:¹³

They said: If a wolf ate him while we are many, truly, then, we are ones who are losers.¹²:¹⁴

So they went with him, and they agreed to lay him in the bottom of the well.

And We revealed to him: Certainly, thou wilt tell them of this, their affair, when they are not aware.¹²:¹⁵

And they drew near their father in the time of night, weeping.¹²:¹⁶

They said: O our father! Truly, we went racing and we left Joseph with our sustenance and a wolf ate him and thou wilt not be one who believes us, even if we had been ones who are sincere.¹²:¹⁷ And they brought about his long shirt with false blood.

He said: Nay! Your souls enticed you with a command. Having patience is graceful. And it is God, One Whose Help is being sought against what you allege.¹²:¹⁸

And there drew near a company of travelers so they sent their water-drawer to let down his bucket. He said: What good tidings! This is a boy!

So they kept him secret as merchandise. And God is Knowing of what they do.¹²:¹⁹ And they sold him for a meager price of coins, ones that are numbered. And they had been of him among the ones who hold him in low esteem.¹²:²⁰

One from Egypt who bought him said to his woman: Honor him as a guest with a place of lodging. Perhaps he will profit us or we will take him to ourselves as a son.

And, thus, We established Joseph firmly in the earth that We teach him the interpretation of events. God is One Who is Victor over His command, except most of humanity knows not.¹²:²¹

And when he had fully grown and come of age, We gave him critical judgment and knowledge. And, thus, We give recompense to the ones who are doers of good.¹²:²²

And she in whose house he was solicited him, enticing him to evil. And she shut the doors and said: Come thou!

He said: God be my safe place. Truly, he, thy husband, is my master and He gave me a goodly place of lodging. Truly, the ones who are unjust will not prosper.¹²:²³

She, certainly, was about to act on her desire for him and he was about to act on his desire for her, if it were not that he saw proof of his Lord. Thus, it was that We turn away from him evil and depravity. And, truly, he was among Our servants, ones who are devoted.¹²:²⁴ So they raced to the door and she tore his long shirt from behind. And they both discovered her chief at the door.

She said: What is the recompense of him who wanted evil for thy household, but that he be imprisoned or a painful punishment?¹²:²⁵

He said: She solicited me, enticing me to evil. And one who bears witness bore witness from her household and said: If his long shirt had been torn from the front, then, she was sincere, and he was among the ones who lie.¹²:²⁶

But if his long shirt had been torn from behind, she lied against herself; he was among ones who are sincere.¹²:²⁷

When her husband saw his long shirt was torn from behind, he said: It is of your (f) cunning; truly, your (f) cunning is serious.¹²:²⁸ Joseph! Turn aside from this!

To his wife he said: Ask thou for forgiveness for thy (f) impiety; truly, thou (f) hadst been of the ones who are inequitable.¹²:²⁹

And the ladies in the city said: The woman of the great one solicits her spiritual warrior, enticing him to evil. Surely, he captivated her longing. Truly, we consider her to be clearly wandering astray.¹²:³⁰

So when she heard of their planning, she sent for them (f), and made ready for them a banquet. And she gave each one of them (f) a knife, and said to Joseph: Go forth before them (f). Then, when they saw him, they admired him and cut their hands. And they (f) said: God save us! This is not a mortal. This is nothing but a generous angel!¹²:³¹

She said: This is he about whom you (f) blamed me. And, certainly, I solicited him, enticing him to evil, but he preserved himself from sin. And now if he accomplishes not what I command, he will, certainly, be imprisoned and will be among the ones who are disgraced.¹²:³²

He said: O my Lord! Prison is more beloved to me than what they call me to. Unless Thou hast turned away their

(f) cunning from me, I will yearn towards them (f) and I will be among the ones who are ignorant.¹²:³³

So his Lord responded to him and turned away their (f) cunning from him. Truly, He, He is The Hearing, The Knowing.¹²:³⁴

Again, it showed itself to them. And after they saw the signs, it seemed that they should imprison him for awhile.¹²:³⁵

And there entered with him in the prison two male spiritual warriors. One of them said: Truly, I see myself pressing grapes in season. And the other said: Truly, I see myself carrying bread over my head from which birds are eating. They said: Tell us the interpretation of this. Truly, we consider thee among the ones who are doers of good.¹²:³⁶

He said: The food you both are provided approaches you not, but I will tell you of its interpretation before it approaches. That is of what my Lord taught me. Truly, I left the creed of a folk who believe not in God and they, in the world to come, they are ones who disbelieve.¹²:³⁷

And I followed the creed of my fathers, Abraham and Isaac and Jacob. It had not been for us that we ascribe anything as partners with God. That is from the grace of God to us and to humanity, except most of humanity gives not thanks.¹²:³⁸

O my two prison companions! Are ones that are different masters better or God, The One, The Omniscient?¹²:³⁹

Whomever you worship other than He are nothing but names that you named—you and your fathers for which God caused not to descend any authority. The determination is from God alone. He commanded that you worship none but Him. That is the truth-loving way of life, except most of humanity knows not.¹²:⁴⁰

O my two prison companions! As for one of you, he will give intoxicants to drink to his master. And as for the other, he will be crucified. And birds will eat from his head. The matter was decided about which you ask for advice.¹²:⁴¹

And he said to the one of them whom he thought should be the one who is saved of the two: Remember me to thy master. Then, Satan caused him to forget the remembrance of him to his master so Joseph lingered in expectation in prison for a certain number of years.¹²:⁴²

And the king said: Truly, I, I see seven fattened cows eating seven lean ones and seven ears of green wheat and others dry. O Council: Render an opinion to me about my dream if you had been able to expound dreams.¹²:⁴³

They said: Jumbled nightmares. And we are not of the interpretation of nightmares ones who know.¹²:⁴⁴

And said the man of the two of them who was delivered and recalled after a period of time: I will tell you its interpretation so send me.¹²:⁴⁵

Joseph, O thou just person! Render an opinion to us about seven fattened cows eaten by seven lean ones and seven ears of green wheat and others dry so that perhaps I will return to the personages so that perhaps they will know about thee.¹²:⁴⁶

He said: You will sow for seven years in like previous manner and of what you reaped, then, forsake ears of wheat, but a little of it that you may eat.¹²:⁴⁷ Again, seven severe years will approach after that. You will eat what you put forward, but a little of what you keep in store.¹²:⁴⁸ Again, after that, will approach a year in which humanity will be helped with rain and they will press in season.¹²:⁴⁹

And the king said: Bring him to me. Then, when the Messenger brought about, he said: Return to thy master and ask him: What of the ladies, those who cut their hands? Truly, my Lord is Knowing of their (f) cunning.¹²:⁵⁰

He said: What was your (f) business when you solicited Joseph, enticing him to evil?

They (f) said: God save us! We knew not any evil against him.

The woman of the great one said: Now The Truth was discovered! I sought to solicit him, enticing him to evil. And, truly, he is among the ones who are sincere.[12:51]

Joseph said: That is so that the great one know that I betray him not in his absence. And that God guides not the cunning of the ones who are traitors.[12:52]

And I declare my soul not innocent. Truly, the soul is that which incites to evil, but when my Lord had mercy. Truly, my Lord is Forgiving, Compassionate.[12:53]

And the king said: Bring him to me so that I attach him to myself.

Then, when he spoke to him he said: Truly, this day thou art with us secure, trustworthy.[12:54]

Joseph said: Assign me over the storehouses of the region. Truly, I will be a knowing guardian.[12:55]

And, thus, We established Joseph firmly in the region to take his dwelling in it when or where he wills. We light Our mercy on whom We will and We waste not the compensation of ones who are doers of good.[12:56]

Truly, the compensation of the world to come is better for those who believed and had been Godfearing.[12:57]

And Joseph's brothers drew near and they entered before him. He recognized them, but they are ones who know him not.[12:58]

And when he equipped them with their food supplies, he said: Bring me a brother of yours from your father. See you not that I live up to full measure and that I am best of the ones who host?[12:59] Then, if you bring him not to me, there will be no full measure for you with me, nor will you come near me.[12:60]

They said: We will solicit his father for him and, truly, we are ones who do it.[12:61]

And Joseph said to his spiritual warriors: Lay their merchandise into their saddlebags so that perhaps they will recognize it when they turned about to their household so that perhaps they will return.[12:62]

So when they returned to their father, they said: O our father! The full measure was refused to us so send our brother with us that we will obtain our measure. And, truly, we will be ones who guard him.[12:63]

Jacob said: How will I entrust him to you as I entrusted you with his brother before? But, then, God is Best of One Who Guards. And He is One Who is the Most Merciful of the ones who are the most merciful.[12:64]

And when they opened their sustenance, they found their merchandise was returned to them. They said: O our father, this is what we desire. Our merchandise was returned to us and we will get provision for our household and we will keep our brother safe and add a camel's load of full measure. That is an easy full measure.[12:65]

He said: I will not send him with you until you give me a pledge by God that you will bring him back to me, unless you are enclosed yourselves. And when they gave him their pledge, he said: God is Trustee over what we say.[12:66]

And he said: O my sons! Enter not by one door, but enter by different doors. I will not avail you against God in anything. Truly, the determination is but with God. In Him I put my trust. And in Him put their trust the ones who put their trust.[12:67]

And when they entered from where their father commanded, it had not been availing them against God in anything, but it was a need of Jacob's inner self which he satisfied. And, truly, he was a possessor of knowledge because We taught him, except most of humanity knows not.[12:68]

And when they entered before Joseph, he himself gave refuge to his brother. He said: Truly, I am thy brother, so be not despondent for what they had been doing.[12:69]

So when he equipped them with their food supplies, he laid the drinking cup into their brother's saddlebag. Again, one who announces announced: O you in the caravan! Truly, you are ones who are thieves.[12:70]

They said coming forward: What is it that you are missing?[12:71]

They said: We are missing the king's drinking cup and for him who brought it about is a camel's load and I am the guarantor for it.[12:72]

They said: By God, certainly, you knew we drew not near making corruption in the region. And we had not been ones who are thieves.[12:73]

They said: What, then, will be the recompense for him if you had been ones who lie?[12:74]

They said: The recompense for it will be that he in whose saddlebag it was located will be the recompense. Thus, we give recompense to the ones who are unjust.[12:75]

So he began with their sacks before the sack of his brother. Again, he pulled it out of his brother's sack. Thus, We contrived for Joseph. He would not have taken his brother into the judgment of the king unless God wills it. We exalt in degree whomever We will, and above all those possessors of knowledge is One Who is Knowing.[12:76]

They said: If he steals, surely, a brother of his stole before. But Joseph kept it secret within himself, not showing it to them. He said: You are in a worse place. And God is greater in knowledge of what you allege.[12:77]

They said: O the great one! Truly, for him is an old man as his father so take one of us in his place. Truly, we consider thee among the ones who are doers of good.[12:78]

He said: God be my safe place that we take but him with Whom we found our sustenance. Truly, we, then, would be of the ones who are unjust.[12:79]

So when in regard to him they became hopeless, they conferred privately. The eldest of them said: Know you not that your father, surely, took a pledge from you by God and before that you neglected your duty with Joseph. So I never quit this region until my father gives me permission or God gives judgment in my case. And He is Best of the ones who judge.[12:80]

Return to your father and say: O our father! Truly, thy son stole and we bore witness only to what we knew. And we had not been ones who guard the unseen.[12:81] And ask the people of the town where we had been and the people of the caravan in which we came forward. And, truly, we are ones who are sincere.[12:82]

He said: You were enticed by your souls into an affair. So patience is graceful. Perhaps God will bring me them altogether. Truly, He, He is The Knowing, The Wise.[12:83]

And he turned away from them and said: O my bitterness for Joseph! And his eyes brightened because of the sorrow that was choking him.[12:85]

They said: By God! Thou wilt never discontinue remembering Joseph until thou hast ruined thy health. Thou wouldst be among the ones who are perishing.[12:85]

He said: I make not complaint of my anguish and sorrow but to God. And I know from God what you know not.[12:86] O my sons! Go and search for Joseph and his brother. And give not up hope of the solace of God. Truly, no one gives up hope of the solace of God but the folk, ones who are ungrateful.[12:87]

Then, when they entered to him, they said: O the great one! Harm afflicted us and our household. We drew near merchandise of scant worth so live up to the full measure and be charitable to us. Truly, God gives recompense to the ones who give in charity.[12:88]

He said: Knew you what you accomplished with Joseph and his brother when you are ones who are ignorant?[12:89]

They said: Art thou, truly, Joseph?

He said: I am Joseph and this is my brother. Surely, God showed us grace. Truly, He Who is Godfearing and endures patiently, then, surely, God will not waste the compensation of the ones who are doers of good.¹²:⁹⁰

They said: By God! Certainly, God held thee in greater favor above us. And, truly, we had been ones who are inequitable.¹²:⁹¹

He said: No censure on you this day. God forgive you. And He is One Who is Most Merciful of the ones who are most merciful.¹²:⁹² Go with this, my long shirt and cast it over the face of my father. He will become seeing. And bring me your household one and all.¹²:⁹³

And when they set forward with the caravan their father said: Truly, I find the scent of Joseph if you think me not weak of mind.¹²:⁹⁴

They said: By God! Truly, thou art long possessed by thy wandering astray.¹²:⁹⁵

Then, when the bearer of good tidings drew near, he cast it over his face and he went back, seeing.

He said: Did I not say to you, truly, I know from God what you know not?¹²:⁹⁶

They said: O our father! Ask forgiveness for us for our impieties. Truly, we had been ones who are inequitable.¹²:⁹⁷

He said: I will ask forgiveness for you with my Lord. Truly, He, He is The Forgiving, The Compassionate.¹²:⁹⁸

Then, when they entered to Joseph, he gave refuge to his parents and said: Enter Egypt, if God willed, as ones who are safe!¹²:⁹⁹

And he exalted his parents to the throne. And they fell down before him as ones who prostrate themselves.

And he said: O my father! This is the interpretation of my dream from before. My Lord has made it a reality. And, surely, He did good to me when He brought me out of the prison and drew you near out of the desert after Satan had sown enmity between me and between my brothers. Truly, my Lord is Subtle in what He wills. Truly, He is The Knowing, The Wise.¹²:¹⁰⁰

My Lord! Surely, Thou hadst given me of the dominion. Thou hadst taught of the interpretation of events. One Who is Originator of the heavens and the earth, Thou art my protector in the present and in the world to come. Call me to Thyself as one who submits to Thee and cause me to join with the ones in accord with morality.¹²:¹⁰¹

That is of the tidings of the unseen that We reveal to thee. And thou hadst not been in their presence when they agreed to their affair. And they plan.¹²:¹⁰² And most of humanity is not ones who believe, even if thou wert eager.¹²:¹⁰³ Thou hast asked them not for any compensation. It is but a Remembrance to the worlds.¹²:¹⁰⁴

And how many signs of the heavens and the earth they pass by while they are ones who turn aside from them!¹²:¹⁰⁵

And most of them believe not in God, but they be ones who are polytheists.¹²:¹⁰⁶

Were they safe from the approach to them of the overwhelming event of the punishment from God or the approach on them of the Hour suddenly while they are not aware?¹²:¹⁰⁷

Say: This is my way. I call to God. I and whoever followed me are on clear evidence. And glory be to God! And I am not among the ones who are polytheists.¹²:¹⁰⁸

And We sent not before thee as Messengers, but men to whom We reveal from among the people of the towns. So journey they not through the earth and look on how had been the Ultimate End of those who were before them? And, truly, the abode of the world to come is better for those who were Godfearing. Will you not, then, be reasonable?¹²:¹⁰⁹

When the Messengers became hopeless and thought that they were lied against, then, Our help drew near. So We were to deliver whomever We will. And Our Might will not be repelled from the folk, the ones who sin.¹²:¹¹⁰

Certainly, there had been in their narratives a lesson for those imbued with intuition. It had not been a discourse that is devised except it established as true what was before and decisively explained everything and is a guidance and a mercy for a folk who believe.¹²:¹¹¹

CHAPTER 13 THUNDER

In the Name of God, The Merciful, The Compassionate
Alif Lām Mīm Rā.

That are the signs of the Book, and what were caused to descend to thee from thy Lord is The Truth, except most of humanity believes not.¹³:¹

It is He Who exalted the heavens without any pillars so that you see them. Again, He turned his attention to above the Throne. And He caused to become subservient the sun and the moon, each run for a term, that which is determined. He manages the command. He explains distinctly the signs so that perhaps of the meeting with your Lord you would be certain.¹³:²

And it is He Who stretched out the earth and made on it firm mountains and rivers. And with all kinds of fruits, he made in it two, a pair. He covers the nighttime with the daytime. Truly, in that are signs for a folk who reflect.¹³:³

And in the earth there are strips, that which neighbor one another and gardens of grapevines and plowed lands and date palm trees coming from the same root and not coming from the same root that are given to drink from one water. And We give advantage to some of them over some others in produce. Truly, in these things there are signs for a folk who are reasonable.¹³:⁴

And if thou hast marveled, then, wonder at their saying: When we had been earth dust, will we, truly, be in a new creation?

And those are those who were ungrateful to their Lord. Those will have yokes around their necks. And those will be the Companions of the Fire. They, ones who will dwell in it forever.¹³:⁵

And they seek thee to hasten on evil deeds before the benevolence. And, surely, passed away before them exemplary punishments. But, truly, thy Lord is certainly, The Possessor of Forgiveness for humanity in spite of their injustice. And, truly, thy Lord is Severe in repayment.¹³:⁶

And those who were ungrateful say: Why was a sign not caused to descend to him from his Lord? Thou art only one who warns, and one who guides every folk.¹³:⁷

God knows what every female carries and how much her womb absorbs and what they add. And everything with Him is in proportion.¹³:⁸

He is One Who Knows the unseen and the visible, The Great, The One Who is Raised High.¹³:⁹

It is equal to Him whether you kept secret his saying or you published it. Or whoever he be, one who conceals himself by nighttime or one who goes about carelessly in the daytime.¹³:¹⁰

For him there are Ones Who Postpone from before him and from behind him to keep him safe by the command of God. Truly, God alters not a folk until they alter what is within themselves.

And when God wanted evil for a folk, then, there is no turning it back. And there is not for them other than He anyone who is a safeguarder.¹³:¹¹

It is He Who causes you to see the lightning in fear and in hope. And it is He Who causes the clouds to grow heavy,¹³:¹² and thunder glorifies His praise and the angels, because of their awe of Him. And He sends thunderbolts and He lights on whom He wills. And they dispute about God, and He is a Severe Force.^{13:13}

For Him is the call of The Truth. And those whom they call to other than Him, they respond not to them at all, but like one who stretches out the palms of his hands for water so that it should reach his mouth, but it is not that which reaches it. And supplication of the ones who are ungrateful is only wandering astray.^{13:14}

And to God prostrates whatever is in the heavens and the earth, willingly or unwillingly as does their shade at the first part of the day and the eventide.^{13:15}

Say: Who is the Lord of the heavens and the earth?

Say: God!

Say: Took you to yourselves other than Him protectors? They control not themselves, neither profiting nor hurting.

Say: Are the unwilling to see on the same level as the seeing?

Are the shadows on the same level as the light?

Made they ascribed associates with God who created as His creation so that creation resembled one another to them?

Say: God is One Who is Creator of everything. And He is The One, The Omniscient.^{13:16}

He caused water to descend from heaven and it flowed into valleys according to their measure. Then, the flood bears away the froth. And from what they kindle in a fire, looking for glitter or sustenance, there is a froth the like of it. Thus, God compares The Truth and falsehood. Then, as for the froth, it goes as swelling scum while what profits humanity abides on the earth. Thus, God propounds parables.^{13:17}

For those who responded to their Lord there is the fairer. And for those who respond not to Him, if they had all that is in and on the earth and its like with it, they would offer it as ransom. Those, for them will be a dire reckoning and their place of shelter will be hell. Miserable will be the cradling!^{13:18}

Then, is he who knows what was caused to descend to thee from thy Lord to be The Truth like he who is unwilling to see?

It is only those imbued with intuition who recollect.^{13:19}

Those who live up to their compact with God and break not their solemn promise^{13:20} and those who reach out to what God commanded be joined and dread their Lord and they fear the dire reckoning^{13:21} and those who endured patiently, looking for the Countenance of their Lord and who performed the formal prayer and spent out of what We have provided them in secret and in public, and they drive off the evil deed with benevolence—those, for them is the Ultimate Abode:^{13:22} Gardens of Eden which they will enter along with whoever was in accord with morality from among their fathers and their spouses and their offspring.

And angels will enter to them from every door saying:^{13:23} Peace be to you for what you endured patiently. How excellent is the Ultimate Abode!^{13:24}

But those who break the compact of God after its solemn promise and sever what God commanded to be joined and make corruption in and on the earth, those, for them is the curse and for them is the Dire Abode.^{13:25}

God extends the provision for whom He wills and measures it. They were glad in this present life. And there is nothing in this present life like the world to come but a brief enjoyment.^{13:26}

And those who were ungrateful say: Why was a sign not caused to descend to him from his Lord?

Say: Truly, God causes to go astray whom He wills and guides to Himself whomever was penitent,^{13:27} those who believed and their hearts are at rest in the remembrance of God, no doubt in the remembrance of God hearts are at rest.^{13:28}

Those who believed and did as the ones in accord with morality, there is joy for them and a goodness of destination.^{13:29}

Thus, We sent thee to a community. Surely, passed away other communities before it so that thou wouldst recount to them what We revealed to thee and they are ungrateful to The Merciful.

Say: He is my Lord. There is no god but He. In Him I put my trust and to Him I am turning in repentance.^{13:30}

If there were a Recitation that would have set mountains in motion with it, or the earth would be cut off with it or the dead would be spoken to with it, nay! The command is altogether with God. Do those who believed not have knowledge that if God wills He would have guided humanity altogether. Will cease not to light on those who were ungrateful disaster because of what they crafted?

Or will it alight close to their abode until the promise of God approaches? Truly, God breaks not His solemn declaration.^{13:31}

And, certainly, Messengers were ridiculed before thee, but I granted indulgence to those who were ungrateful. Again, I took them. How had been My repayment!^{13:32}

Is He, then, One Who Sustains Every Soul for what it earned?

And yet they ascribe associates with God!

Say: Name them! Or will you tell Him of what He knows not in the earth?

Or name you only them in the manifest sayings?

Nay! Made to appear pleasing to those who were ungrateful was their planning and they were barred from the way. And whomever God causes to go astray, for him there is no one who guides.^{13:33}

For them is a punishment in this present life and, certainly, punishment in the world to come will be one that presses hard. And for them is no one who is a defender against God.^{13:34}

A parable of the Garden which was promised to the ones who are Godfearing; beneath it rivers run. Its produce is one that continues as is its shade. That is the Ultimate End of those who were Godfearing; and the Ultimate End of the ones who are ungrateful is the fire.^{13:35}

And those to whom We gave the Book are glad at what was caused to descend to thee. And there are among the confederates some who reject some of it.

Say: I was commanded to worship only God and not to ascribe partners with Him. I call to Him and to Him is my destination.^{13:36}

And, thus, We caused to descend an Arabic determination. If thou hadst followed their desires after what drew near thee of the knowledge, thou wouldst not have against God either a protector or one who is a defender.^{13:37}

And, certainly, We sent Messengers before thee and We assigned for them spouses and offspring. And it had not been for a Messenger to bring a sign but with the permission of God. For every term there is a Book.^{13:38}

God blots out what He wills and brings to a standstill what He wills; and with Him is the essence of the Book.^{13:39}

And whether We cause thee to see some of what We have promised them or call thee to Ourselves, on thee is delivering the message and on Us is the reckoning.^{13:40}

Consider they not that We approach the earth, reducing it from its outlying parts?

And God gives judgment. There is no one who postpones His determination. And He is Swift in reckoning.^{13:41}

And, surely, those who were before them planned, but to God is the plan altogether. He knows what every person earns. And the ones who are ungrateful will know for whom will be the Ultimate Abode.^{13:42}

And those who were ungrateful say: Thou art not one who is sent.

Say: God sufficed as a witness between me and between you and whoever has knowledge of the Book.^{13:43}

CHAPTER 14 ABRAHAM

In the Name of God, The Merciful, The Compassionate
Alif Lām Rā.

This is a Book We caused to descend to thee so that thou hast brought humanity out from the shadows into the light with the permission of their Lord to the path of The Almighty, The Worthy of Praise.¹⁴:¹

God! To Him belongs whatever is in the heavens and whatever is in and on the earth, and woe to the ones who are ungrateful. For them is the severe punishment,¹⁴:² those who embrace this present life instead of the world to come and bar from the way of God, and desire in it crookedness. Those are wandering far astray.¹⁴:³

We sent not any Messenger but with the tongue of his folk in order that he make it manifest for them. Then, God causes to go astray whom He wills and guides whom He wills. And He is The Almighty, The Wise.¹⁴:⁴

And, certainly, We sent Moses with Our signs saying: Bring out thy folk from the shadows into the light and remind them of the Days of God. Truly, in that are signs for every enduring, grateful one.¹⁴:⁵

And mention when Moses said to his folk: Remember the divine blessing of God to you when He rescued you from the people of Pharaoh who cause an affliction to befall you—a dire punishment—and slaughter your children and save alive your women. And in it was a serious trial from your Lord.¹⁴:⁶

And mention when your Lord caused to be proclaimed: If you gave thanks, I will increase your blessings. And if you were ungrateful, truly, My punishment will be severe.¹⁴:⁷

And Moses said: Even if you are ungrateful, you and what is in and on the earth altogether, then, truly, God is Sufficient, Worthy of Praise.¹⁴:⁸

Approach not to you the tidings of those before you: The folk of Noah and Ad and Thamud and of those after them. None knows them but God. Their Messengers drew near them with the clear portents, but they shoved their hands into their mouths in denial.

Then, they said: Truly, we disbelieved in what you were sent and we are in uncertainty about that to which you call us. We are in grave doubt.¹⁴:⁹

Their Messengers said: Is there any uncertainty about God, One Who is Originator of the heavens and the earth? He calls you so that He would forgive you your impieties and postpone for you a term, that which is determined. They said: You are only mortal like us. You want to bar us from what our fathers had been worshipping. Then, bring us a clear authority.¹⁴:¹⁰

Their Messengers said to them: We are only mortals like you except God shows His grace on whom He wills of His servants. And it had not been for us that we bring you an authority, but by the permission of God. And in God let the ones who believe put their trust.¹⁴:¹¹

And why should we not put our trust in God while, surely, He guided us to our ways? And we will endure patiently however you maligned us. And in God let the ones who trust, put their trust.¹⁴:¹²

And those who were ungrateful said to their Messengers: Certainly, we will drive you out of our region unless you revert to our creed. So their Lord revealed to them: Truly, We will cause to perish the ones who are unjust.¹⁴:¹³

Certainly, We will cause you to dwell in the region after them. This is for whoever feared My station and feared My threat.¹⁴:¹⁴

And the Messengers sought judgment and frustrated was every haughty, stubborn one.¹⁴:¹⁵ And hell is ahead of him. He will be given to drink of watery pus.¹⁴:¹⁶ He will gulp it and he will be about to swallow it easily when death will approach him from every place, yet he will not be dead. And ahead of him will be a harsh punishment.¹⁴:¹⁷

A parable of those who were ungrateful to their Lord, their actions are as ashes over which the wind blew strongly on a tempestuous day. They will have no power over anything they earned. That is the wandering far away, astray.¹⁴:¹⁸

Hast thou not considered that God created the heavens and the earth in Truth? If He wills, He will cause you to be put away and bring a new creation.¹⁴:¹⁹

And that is not a great matter for God.¹⁴:²⁰

And they will depart to God altogether. Then, the weak would say to those who grew arrogant: Truly, we had been followers of yours. Have you ones who avail us at all against the punishment of God?

They would say: If God would have guided us, we would have guided you. It is equal to us whether we were patientless or endured patiently. There is no asylum for us.¹⁴:²¹

Satan would say when the command would be decided: Truly, God promised you a promise of the Truth. And I promised you, but I broke it. And I had been no authority over you, but that I called to you and you responded to me. So blame me not, but blame yourselves. I am not one who assists you nor are you one who assists me. Truly, I was ungrateful for your ascribing me as partner with God before. Truly, the ones who are unjust, for them is a painful punishment.¹⁴:²²

And will be caused to enter those who believed and did as the ones in accord with morality into Gardens beneath which rivers run. They, ones who will dwell in them forever with the permission of their Lord. And their greeting in it will be: Peace!¹⁴:²³

Hast thou not considered how God propounded a parable? What is like a good word is what is like a good tree. Its root is one that is firm and its branches are in heaven.¹⁴:²⁴

It gives all its produce for awhile with the permission of its Lord.

And God propounds parables for humanity so that perhaps they will recollect.¹⁴:²⁵

And the parable of a bad word is that of a bad tree, that was uprooted from above the earth, so it has no stability.¹⁴:²⁶

God makes firm those who believed with the saying, one that is firm in this present life and in the world to come. And God will cause to go astray the ones who are unjust. And God accomplishes what He wills.¹⁴:²⁷

Hast thou not considered those who substituted ingratitude for the divine blessing of God and caused their folk to live in abodes of nothingness?¹⁴:²⁸

They will roast in hell. Miserable will be the stopping place!¹⁴:²⁹

And they made rivals with God, causing others to go astray from His way.

Say: Take joy, but, truly, your homecoming is the fire!¹⁴:³⁰

Say to My servants who believed that they should perform the formal prayer and spend from what We provided them secretly and in public before a Day approaches in which there is neither trading nor befriending.¹⁴:³¹

God is He Who created the heavens and the earth and caused water to descend from heaven and brought out thereby fruits as provision for you. And He caused boats to be subservient to you that they run through the sea by His command. And He caused rivers to be subservient to you.¹⁴:³²

And He caused the sun to be subservient to you and the moon, both, ones that are constant in their work. And He caused the nighttime to be subservient to you and the daytime.¹⁴:³³

And He gave you all that you asked of Him. And if you were to number the divine blessing of God, you would not count them, truly, the human being is wrongdoing and an ingrate.¹⁴:³⁴

And when Abraham said: My Lord! Make this land that which is safe and cause me and my children to turn away from worshipping idols.¹⁴:³⁵

My Lord! Truly, they caused to go astray many among humanity; so whoever heeded me, truly, he is of me. And whoever rebelled against me, then Thou art, truly, Forgiving, Compassionate.¹⁴:³⁶

Our Lord! Truly, I caused to dwell some of my offspring in an unsown valley by Thy Holy House, O our Lord, they, certainly, perform the formal prayer. So make the minds among humanity yearn for them and provide them with fruits so that perhaps they will give thanks.¹⁴:³⁷

Our Lord! Truly, Thou hast known what we conceal and what we speak openly. And nothing is hidden from God in or on the earth or in heaven.¹⁴:³⁸

The Praise belongs to God Who bestowed on me in my old age Ishmael and Isaac. And, truly, my Lord is Hearing the supplication.¹⁴:³⁹

My Lord! Make me one who performs the formal prayer and from my offspring also. Our Lord! Receive my supplication.¹⁴:⁴⁰

Our Lord! Forgive Thou me and the ones who are my parents and the ones who believe on the Day the reckoning arises.¹⁴:⁴¹

And assume not that God is One Who is Heedless of what the ones who are unjust do. He only postpones their reckoning to a Day when their sight will be fixed in horror,¹⁴:⁴² ones who run forward with eyes fixed in horror, ones who lift up their heads. Their glance goes not back to them. And their minds are void.¹⁴:⁴³

And warn humanity of a Day the punishment will approach them. So those who did wrong will say: Our Lord! Postpone for us a near term so that we answer Thy call and follow the Messengers.

Yet swore you not an oath before that there would be no ceasing for you?¹⁴:⁴⁴

And you inhabited the dwellings of those who did wrong to themselves. And it became clear to you how We accomplished against them and We propounded for you parables.¹⁴:⁴⁵

And, surely, they planned their plan and their plan was with God, even if their plan had been to displace mountains.¹⁴:⁴⁶

So assume not that God will be one who breaks His promise to His Messengers. Truly, God is Almighty, Possessor of Requital.¹⁴:⁴⁷

On a Day when the earth will be substituted for other than this earth and the heavens, they will depart to God, The One, The Omniscient God,¹⁴:⁴⁸ and thou wilt consider the ones who sin that Day, ones who are chained in bonds,¹⁴:⁴⁹ their tunics are made of pitch and the fire will overcome their faces¹⁴:⁵⁰ so that God would give recompense to every soul for what it earned. Truly, God is Swift in reckoning.¹⁴:⁵¹

This is the delivering of the message to humanity so that they be warned by it and that they know that He is One God so that those imbued with intuition recollect.¹⁴:⁵²

CHAPTER 15
THE ROCKY TRACT

In the Name of God, The Merciful, The Compassionate
Alif Lām Rā.

That are the signs of the Book and of a clear Recitation.¹⁵:¹

It may be those who were ungrateful would wish that they had been ones who submit to God.¹⁵:² Forsake them to

eat and let them take joy and be diverted with hopefulness. Then, they will know.¹⁵:³

And We caused not a town to perish but there was for it a known prescription.¹⁵:⁴ No community precedes its term nor delays it.¹⁵:⁵

And they say: O thou to whom was sent down the Remembrance, truly, thou art one who is possessed.¹⁵:⁶

Why hast thou not brought angels to us if thou hadst been the ones who are sincere?¹⁵:⁷

We send angels down not but with The Truth. If they come to the ungrateful, they would not have been ones who are given respite.¹⁵:⁸

Truly, We, We sent down the Remembrance and, truly, We are ones who guard it.¹⁵:⁹

And, certainly, We sent Messengers before thee to partisans of the ancient ones.¹⁵:¹⁰

And approach them not any Messenger but they had been ridiculing him.¹⁵:¹¹

Thus, We thrust it into the hearts of the ones who sin.¹⁵:¹²

They believe not in it. Surely, passed away before them a custom of the ancient ones.¹⁵:¹³

And even if We opened for them a door from heaven and they continued going up to it,¹⁵:¹⁴ they would say: Truly, our sight was dazzled. Nay! We were a bewitched folk.¹⁵:¹⁵

And, certainly, We made constellations in the heavens and We made them appear pleasing to the ones who look.¹⁵:¹⁶ And We kept them safe from every accursed satan,¹⁵:¹⁷ but he who had the ability to hear by eavesdropping. Then, a clear flame pursued him.¹⁵:¹⁸

And We stretched out the earth and We cast on it firm mountains and We caused to develop on it that which was well-balanced of everything.¹⁵:¹⁹

And We made on it for you a livelihood and for whomever you are not ones who provide.¹⁵:²⁰

And there is not a thing, but its treasures are with Us and We send it down not but in a known measure.¹⁵:²¹

And We sent fertilizing winds. Then, We caused water to descend from heaven, then, We satiated you, and you are not ones who are its keepers.¹⁵:²²

And, truly, it is We Who give life and cause to die and We are the ones who inherit.¹⁵:²³ And, certainly, We knew the ones who precede among you and, certainly, We knew the ones who come later.¹⁵:²⁴ And, truly, thy Lord is He Who assembles. Truly, He is Wise, Knowing.¹⁵:²⁵

And, certainly, We created the human being out of earth-mud of soft wet earth.¹⁵:²⁶

And We created the ones who are spirits before from the fire of a burning wind.¹⁵:²⁷

And mention when thy Lord said to the angels: Truly, I am One Who is Creator of mortals out of earth-mud of soft wet earth.¹⁵:²⁸ That is when I shaped him and breathed into him of My Spirit. So fall down before him as ones who prostrate themselves.¹⁵:²⁹

The angels prostrated themselves, one and all,¹⁵:³⁰ but Iblis. He refused to be with the ones who prostrate themselves.¹⁵:³¹

He said: O Iblis! What is with thee that thou be not with the ones who prostrate themselves?¹⁵:³²

Iblis said: I will not be prostrating myself before a mortal whom Thou hadst created out of earth-mud of soft wet earth.¹⁵:³³

It was said: Go thou forth from here, for, truly, thou art accursed!¹⁵:³⁴

And, truly, a curse will be upon thee until the Day of Judgment.¹⁵:³⁵

Iblis said: O my Lord! Give me respite until the Day they are raised up.¹⁵:³⁶

He said: Then, truly, thou art among the ones who are given respite¹⁵:³⁷ until the Day of the known time.¹⁵:³⁸

Iblis said: My Lord! Because Thou hadst led me into error I will, certainly, make the earth appear pleasing to them and I will lead them one and all into error,[15:39] but Thy servants among them, the ones who are devoted.[15:40]

He said: This is the straight path to Me.[15:41]

Truly, as for My servants there is no authority for thee over them, but ones who are in error followed thee.[15:42]

And, truly, hell is promised to them one and all.[15:43] It has seven doors. Then, for everyone, a door set apart, is for them.[15:44]

Truly, the ones who are Godfearing will be amidst gardens and springs.[15:45] Enter them in peace as ones who are safe![15:46] And We will tear out any grudges from their breasts. They will be as brothers/sisters on couches, one facing the other.[15:47] In it neither fatigue will afflict them nor will they be ones who are driven out.[15:48]

Tell My servants that I am The Forgiving, The Compassionate[15:49] and that My punishment, it is a painful punishment.[15:50]

And tell them about the guests of Abraham[15:51] when they entered upon him and said: Peace! He said: Truly, we are afraid of you.[15:52]

They said: Take no notice. Truly, we give thee good tidings of a knowing boy.[15:53]

He said: Gave you good tidings to me even though old age afflicted me? So of what give you good tidings?[15:54]

They said: We gave thee good tidings of The Truth, so thou art not of the ones who despair.[15:55]

He said: Who despairs of the mercy of his Lord, but the ones who go astray?[15:56]

He said: Then, what is your business, O the ones who are sent?[15:57]

They said: We were sent to a folk, ones who sin,[15:58] but the family of Lot. Truly, we are ones who will deliver them one and all,[15:59] but his woman. We ordained that she be of the ones who stay behind.[15:60]

Then, when the ones who are sent drew near the people of Lot,[15:61] he said: Truly, you are folk, ones unlawful to me.[15:62]

They said: Nay! We drew near thee with what they had been contesting in it.[15:63] We approached thee with The Truth and, truly, we are ones who are sincere.[15:64] Then, set forth with thy family in a part of the night and follow thou their backs and look not back any of you, but pass on to where you are commanded.[15:65]

And We decreed the command to him that the last remnant of these would be that which is severed, in that which is morning.[15:66] The people of the city drew near rejoicing at the good tidings.[15:67]

Lot said: Truly, these are my guests, so put me not to shame.[15:68] Be Godfearing of God and cover me not with shame.[15:69]

They said: Prohibit we thee not from some beings?[15:70]

Lot said: These are my daughters if you hadst been ones who do something.[15:71]

By thy life, truly, they were in a daze, wandering unwilling to see.[15:72] So the Cry took them at sunrise.[15:73] And We made its high part low and We rained down on them rocks of baked clay.[15:74] Truly, in this are signs for the ones who read marks.[15:75] And, truly, they are ones who are on an abiding way.[15:76] Truly, in it is a sign for the ones who believe.[15:77]

And, truly, the Companions of the Thicket had been ones who are unjust[15:78] so We requited them and they were both on a clear high road.[15:79]

Certainly, the Companions of the Rocky Tract denied the ones who are sent.[15:80] And We gave them Our signs. Then, they had been ones who turn aside from them.[15:81] And they had been carving out safe houses from mountains,[15:82] but the Cry took them in that which is morning.[15:83] And availed them not what they had been earning.[15:84]

And We created not the heavens and the earth and whatever is in between them but with The Truth. And, truly, the Hour is one that arrives. So overlook with a graceful overlooking.[15:85] Truly, thy Lord is The Knowing Creator.[15:86]

And, certainly, We gave thee seven often repeated parts of the sublime Quran.[15:87]

And stretch not out thy eyes for what We gave of enjoyment in this life to spouses among them, nor feel remorse for them, but make low thy wing in kindness to the ones who believe.[15:88]

And say: Truly, I am a clear warner,[15:89] even as We caused to descend on the ones who are partitioners,[15:90] those who made the Quran into fragments.[15:91]

So by thy Lord, We will, certainly, ask them one and all[15:92] about what they had been doing.[15:93]

So call aloud what thou art commanded: Turn aside from the ones who are polytheists![15:94] Truly, We sufficed thee against the ones who ridicule,[15:95] those who make with God another god. But they will know.[15:96]

And, certainly, We know that thy breast became narrowed, injured in spirit, because of what they say.[15:97] So glorify the praises of thy Lord and be among the ones who prostrate themselves[15:98] and worship thy Lord until the certainty approaches thee.[15:99]

CHAPTER 16 THE BEE

In the Name of God, the Merciful, the Compassionate

Approached the command of God? Seek not to hasten it. Glory be to Him and exalted is He above partners they ascribe with God.[16:1]

He sends down the angels with the Spirit of His command on whom He wills of His servants to warn that there is no god but I, so be Godfearing of Me.[16:2]

He created the heavens and the earth with The Truth. Exalted is He above partners they ascribe.[16:3]

He created the human being from seminal fluid. That is when he is a clear adversary.[16:4]

And He created the flocks, for you in which there is warmth and profits and of them you eat[16:5] and in them is a beauty for you when you give them rest and when you drive forth flocks to pasture.[16:6] And they carry your lading to a land, being that which reaches you not but under adverse circumstances to yourselves. Truly, your Lord is Gentle, Compassionate.[16:7]

And He creates horses, mules and donkeys for you to ride and as an adornment. And He creates what you know not.[16:8]

And with God is showing of the way yet some of them are ones who swerve. If He willed, He would have guided you one and all.[16:9]

It is He Who caused water to descend from heaven for you to drink from it and from it, trees wherein you pasture your herds.[16:10]

He caused crops to develop for you with it, and the olives and the date palms and the grapevines, and all kinds of fruits. Truly, in that is a sign for a folk who reflect.[16:11]

And He caused to be subservient to you the nighttime and the daytime and the sun and the moon, and the stars, ones caused to be subservient by His command. Truly, in that are signs for a folk who are reasonable.[16:12]

And whatever He made numerous for you in and on the earth of hues, ones that are at variance, truly, in that is a sign for a folk who recollect.[16:13]

And He it is Who caused the sea to be subservient to you so that you eat from it succulent flesh and pull out of it glitter to wear and thou seest the boats, ones that plow through the waves, that you be looking for His grace and so that perhaps you will give thanks.¹⁶:¹⁴

And He cast on to the earth firm mountains so that it not vibrate with you and rivers and roads so that perhaps you will be truly guided¹⁶:¹⁵ and landmarks.

And they are truly guided by the stars.¹⁶:¹⁶

Is, then, He Who creates as he who creates not?

Will you not, then, recollect?¹⁶:¹⁷

And if you try to number the divine blessing of God, you will not be able to count it. Truly, God is Forgiving, Compassionate.¹⁶:¹⁸

And God knows what you keep secret and what you speak openly.¹⁶:¹⁹

And those whom you call to other than God, they created not anything but they are themselves created.¹⁶:²⁰ They are lifeless, not living. And they are not aware when they will be raised up.¹⁶:²¹

Your God is One God. But for those who believe not in the world to come, their hearts are ones that know not and they are ones who grow arrogant.¹⁶:²²

Without a doubt God knows what they keep secret and what they speak openly. Truly, He loves not the ones who grow arrogant.¹⁶:²³

And when it is said to them: What is that your Lord caused to descend, they would say: Fables of the ancient ones!¹⁶:²⁴

They will carry their own heavy loads, that which is complete, on the Day of Resurrection, and of the heavy loads of whomever they cause to go astray without knowledge. How evil is what they will bear!¹⁶:²⁵

Surely, those who were before them planned, then, God approached their structures from the foundations and the roof fell down upon them from above and the punishment approached them from where they are not aware.¹⁶:²⁶

Again, on the Day of Resurrection He will cover them with shame and will say: Where are My ascribed associates with whom you had been making a breach with them?

Those who were given the knowledge will say: Truly, degradation this Day and evil upon the ones who are ungrateful.¹⁶:²⁷

Those whom the angels call to themselves while they are ones who are unjust to themselves. Then, they will give a proposal of surrender: We had not been doing any evil. Yea! Truly, God is Knowing of what you had been doing.¹⁶:²⁸ So enter the doors of hell—ones who will dwell in it forever; and, certainly, it will be a miserable place of lodging. It is for the ones who increase in pride!¹⁶:²⁹

And when it was said to those who were Godfearing: What is it that your Lord caused to descend? They will say: Good or for those who did good in the present, there is benevolence. And the abode of the world to come is better. And how excellent will be the abode of the ones who are Godfearing!¹⁶:³⁰ Gardens of Eden which they will enter beneath which rivers run. They have in them all that they will. Thus, God gives recompense to the ones who are Godfearing.¹⁶:³¹

Those whom the angels call to themselves while they are ones who are good. They say to them: Peace be unto you! Enter the Garden because of what you had been doing.¹⁶:³²

Look they not on but that the angels approach them or the command of thy Lord approach? Thus, accomplished those before them. And God did not wrong them. Rather, they had been doing wrong to themselves.¹⁶:³³

Then, their evil deeds lit on them for what their hands did. And surrounded them is what they had been ridiculing.¹⁶:³⁴

And those who ascribed partners with God said: If God willed neither would we have worshiped other than Him anything, we nor our fathers, nor would we have held sacred anything other than what He forbade. Thus, accomplished those who were before them. Then, what is upon the Messengers, but the delivering of the clear message?¹⁶:³⁵

And, certainly, We raised up in every community a Messenger saying that: Worship God and avoid false deities.

Then, of them were some whom God guided and of them were some upon whom their fallacy was realized.

So journey through the earth; then, look on how had been the Ultimate End of the ones who deny.¹⁶:³⁶

If thou be eager for their guidance, then, truly, God will not guide whom He causes to go astray. And they will have no ones who help.¹⁶:³⁷

And they swore by God their most earnest oaths: God will not raise up him who dies. Yea! It is a promised obligation upon Him—except most of humanity knows not—¹⁶:³⁸ in order to make manifest for them about what they are at variance in it and so that those who were ungrateful know that they had been ones who lie.¹⁶:³⁹

Our saying to a thing when We wanted it is that We say to it: Be! Then, it is!¹⁶:⁴⁰

As for those who emigrated for God after they were wronged, We will, certainly, have a place of settlement for them with benevolence in the present. And the compensation of the world to come will be greater, if they had been knowing.¹⁶:⁴¹

Those who endured patiently, they put their trust in their Lord.¹⁶:⁴²

And We sent not before thee but men to whom We reveal revelation. So ask the People of Remembrance if you had not been knowing.¹⁶:⁴³

With the clear portents and the ancient scrolls, We caused to descend the Remembrance to thee that thou wilt make manifest to humanity what was sent down to them and so that perhaps they will reflect.¹⁶:⁴⁴

Were those who planned evil deeds safe that God will not cause the earth to swallow them or that the punishment will not approach them from where they are not aware?¹⁶:⁴⁵

Or that He take them in their going to and fro where they will not be ones who frustrate Him?¹⁶:⁴⁶

Or that He take them, destroying them little by little? Truly, thy Lord is Gentle, Compassionate.¹⁶:⁴⁷

Consider they not that whatever things God created casts its shadow to the right and to the left, ones who prostrate themselves to God. And they are ones in a state of lowliness?¹⁶:⁴⁸

And to God prostrates whatever is in the heavens and all that is in and on the earth of moving creatures and the angels and they grow not arrogant.¹⁶:⁴⁹ They fear their Lord above them and accomplish what they are commanded.¹⁶:⁵⁰

And God said: Take not two gods to yourselves. Truly, He is One God. Then, have reverence for Me.¹⁶:⁵¹

And to Him belongs whatever is in the heavens and the earth and His is the way of life, that which is forever. Are you Godfearing of other than God?¹⁶:⁵²

And whatever you have of divine blessing is from God. After that when harm afflicted you, you make entreaties to Him.¹⁶:⁵³

Again, when He removed the harm from you, that is when a group of people among you ascribe partners with their Lord.¹⁶:⁵⁴ They are ungrateful for what We gave them. So let them take joy. They will know.¹⁶:⁵⁵

And they assign to what they know not a share from what We provided them. By God! You will, certainly, be asked about what you had been devising.¹⁶:⁵⁶

And they assign daughters to God! Glory be to Him! And for themselves, that for which they lust.¹⁶:⁵⁷ And when any of them was given good tidings of a female, his face stayed one that is clouded over and he chokes.¹⁶:⁵⁸ He is secluded from the folk because of the dire tidings he was given. Will he hold it back with humiliation or will he trample it in the earth dust?

Truly, how evil is the judgment they give! [16:59]

For those who believe not in the world to come there is the reprehensible evil description while the loftiest description belongs to God. And He is The Almighty, The Wise. [16:60]

And if God were to take humanity to task for their injustice, He would not leave on it a moving creature. Rather, He postpones them for a term, that is determined. And when their term drew near, neither will they delay it an hour, nor press it forward. [16:61]

And they assign to God what they dislike. Their tongues allege the lie that the fairer things will be theirs. Without a doubt, for them is the fire, and they will be ones made to hasten to it. [16:62]

By God! We, certainly, sent Messengers to communities before thee.

Satan made their actions appear pleasing to them. So he is their protector on this Day and theirs will be a painful punishment. [16:63]

And We caused the Book to descend to thee, but that thou wilt make manifest to them those things in which they were at variance in it and as a guidance and a mercy for a folk who believe. [16:64] And God caused water to descend from heaven and from it gave life to the earth after its death. Truly, in this is a sign for a folk who hear. [16:65]

And, truly, for you in the flocks is a lesson. We satiate you from what is in their bellies—between waste and blood—exclusively milk, that which is delicious to the ones who drink. [16:66] From fruits of the date palm trees and grapevines you take to yourselves of it what obscures the mind and fairer provisions. Truly, in it is a sign for a folk who be reasonable. [16:67]

And thy Lord revealed to thee the bee: Take to thyself houses from the mountains and in the trees and in what they construct. [16:68]

Again, eat of all the fruits and insert thyself submissively into the ways of thy Lord. Drink goes forth from their bellies in hues, ones that are at variance, wherein is healing for humanity. Truly, in this is, certainly, a sign for a folk who reflect. [16:69]

And God created you. Again, He calls you to Himself. And of you there are some who are returned to the most wretched of lifetimes so that he knows nothing after having knowledge of something. Truly, God is Knowing, Powerful. [16:70]

God gave advantage to some of you over some others in provision. But those who were given advantage are not ones who give over their provision to what their right hands possessed so that they are equal in it. Why negate they the divine blessing of God? [16:71]

And God assigned to you spouses (f) of your own kind and has assigned you from your spouses (f), children and grandchildren and provided you with what is good. Believe they, then, in falsehood and are ungrateful for the divine blessing of God? [16:72]

They worship other than God what has no sway, no power to provide for them anything from the heavens and the earth, nor are they able to do so. [16:73]

So propound not parables for God. Truly, God Knows and you know not. [16:74]

God propounded a parable of a chattel servant who has no power over anything and one to whom We provided from Us a fairer provision. And he spends from it secretly and openly publishing it. Are they on the same level? The Praise belongs to God. Nay! Most of them know not! [16:75]

And God propounded a parable of two men, one of them unwilling to speak. He has no power over anything and he is a heavy burden to his defender. Whichever way he turns his face, he brings no good. Is he on the same level as the one who commands justice and he who is on a straight path? [16:76]

And to God belongs the unseen of the heavens and the earth. And the command of the Hour is not but the twinkling of an eye to one's sight or it is nearer. Truly, God is Powerful over everything. [16:77]

And God brought you out from the wombs of your mothers and you know nothing. And He assigned to you the ability to hear and sight and mind so that perhaps you will give thanks. [16:78]

Consider you not the birds, the ones caused to be subservient in the firmament of the heavens? None holds them back but God. Truly, in this are the signs for a folk who believe. [16:79]

And God assigned for you your houses as places of comfort and rest and assigned for you the hides of flocks for your houses which you find light on the day of your departure and the day of your halting and of their wool and furs and hair—furnishing and enjoyment for awhile. [16:80]

And God made for you shade out of what He created and made for you the mountains as a refuges in the time of need and has made for you tunics to protect you from the heat and tunics to protect you from your violence. Thus, He fulfills His divine blessing to you so that perhaps you will submit to God. [16:81]

Then, if they turned away, for thee is only the delivering of the clear message. [16:82]

They recognize the divine blessing of God. Again, they reject it and most of them are the ones who are ungrateful. [16:83]

On the Day We will raise up from every community a witness again, no permission will be given to those who are ungrateful nor will they ask to be favored. [16:84]

And when those who did wrong consider the punishment, then, it will not be lightened for them nor will they be given respite. [16:85]

And when those who ascribed partners saw their ascribed associates with God, they will say: Our Lord, these are our ascribed associates whom we had been calling to other than Thee. Then, they will cast their saying back to them: Truly, you are ones who lie! [16:86]

They will give a proposal to God on that day of surrender. Gone astray from them will be what they had been devising. [16:87]

Those who were ungrateful and barred from the way of God, We increased them in punishment above their punishment because they had been making corruption. [16:88]

On the Day We raise up in every community a witness against them from among themselves and We will bring thee about as a witness against these. And We sent down to thee the Book as an exposition that makes everything clear and as a guidance and as a mercy and as good tidings for the ones who submit to God. [16:89]

Truly, God commands justice and kindness and giving to one who is a possessor of kinship and He prohibits depravity and ones who are unlawful and insolent. He admonishes you so that perhaps you will recollect. [16:90]

And live up to the compact of God when you have made a contract. And break not the oaths after ratification. And, surely, you made God surety over you. Truly, God knows what you accomplish. [16:91]

And be not like she who would break what she spun after firming its fibers by taking to yourselves your oaths in mutual deceit among yourselves so that one community be one that is swelling more than another community. God tries you but by this. And He will make manifest to you on the Day of Resurrection about what you had been at variance in it. [16:92]

If God willed, He would have made you one community, but He causes to go astray whom He wills and guides whom

He wills. And, certainly, you will be asked about what you had been doing.¹⁶·⁹³

Take not your oaths to yourselves in mutual deceit among yourselves, that your footing should not backslide after standing firm and you experience the evil of having barred from the way of God. And for you will be a serious punishment.¹⁶·⁹⁴

And exchange not the compact for a little price. Truly, what is with God is better for you if you had been knowing.¹⁶·⁹⁵

Whatever is with you will come to an end. And whatever is with God is that which endures. And We will, certainly, give recompense to those who endured patiently their fairer compensation for what they had been doing.¹⁶·⁹⁶

Whoever does as one in accord with morality, whether male or female, while being one who believes, We will give life—this good life. And We will give recompense to them—their compensation—for the fairer for what they had been doing.¹⁶·⁹⁷

So when thou hadst recited the Quran, seek refuge with God from the accursed Satan.¹⁶·⁹⁸ Truly, he is not an authority over those who believed and in their Lord they put their trust.¹⁶·⁹⁹ His authority is only over those who turn away to him and they, those are ones who are polytheists.¹⁶·¹⁰⁰

And when We substituted a sign in place of another sign—and God is greater in knowledge of what He sends down—they said: Thou art only one who devises! But most of them know not.¹⁶·¹⁰¹

Say: The hallowed Spirit sent it down from thy Lord with The Truth to make firm those who believed and as a guidance and good tidings to the ones who submit to God.¹⁶·¹⁰²

And, certainly, We know that they say: It is only a mortal who teaches him.

The tongue of him whom they hint at is non-Arab, while this is in a clear Arabic tongue.¹⁶·¹⁰³

Truly, those who believe not in the signs of God, God will not guide them and for them is a painful punishment.¹⁶·¹⁰⁴

Devising falsity is only by those who believe not in the signs of God. And those, they are the ones who lie.¹⁶·¹⁰⁵ Whoever disbelieved in God after his belief—other than whoever was compelled to do it against his will while his heart is one that is at peace in belief—but whoever's breast is expanded to disbelief, on them is the anger of God and for them is a serious punishment.¹⁶·¹⁰⁶ That is because they embraced this present life instead of the world to come.

And God guides not the folk, the ones who disbelieve,¹⁶·¹⁰⁷ those are those who God set a seal upon their hearts and upon their ability to hear and their sight. And those, they are the ones who are heedless.¹⁶·¹⁰⁸ Without a doubt they will be in the world to come, the ones who are losers.¹⁶·¹⁰⁹

Again, truly, thy Lord, for those who emigrated after they were persecuted and, again, struggled and endured patiently. Truly, after that, thy Lord is Forgiving, Compassionate.¹⁶·¹¹⁰

On a Day every soul will approach, disputing for itself and for every soul, its account will be paid in full for what it did they will not be wronged.¹⁶·¹¹¹ And God propounded a parable of a town—that which had been safe, one that is at peace, its provision approaches it freely from every place. Then, it was ungrateful for the divine blessings of God and so God caused it to experience extreme hunger and fear because of what they had been crafting.¹⁶·¹¹²

And, certainly, drew near them a Messenger from among them, but they denied him, so the punishment took them while they are ones who are unjust.¹⁶·¹¹³

So eat of what God provided you as lawful, what is good and give thanks for the divine blessing of God if it had been Him that you worship.¹⁶·¹¹⁴

He only forbade to you carrion and blood and flesh of swine and what was hallowed to other than God. But if one was compelled, without being one who is willfully disobedient, nor one who turns away, then, truly, God is Forgiving, Compassionate.¹⁶·¹¹⁵

And say not to what your lying tongues allege: This is lawful and this is unlawful so as to devise lies against God. Truly, those who devise against God lies will not prosper,¹⁶·¹¹⁶ but a little enjoyment and for them is a painful punishment.¹⁶·¹¹⁷

We forbade those who became Jews what We related to thee before and We did not wrong them, except they had been doing wrong to themselves.¹⁶·¹¹⁸

Again, truly, thy Lord—to those who did evil in ignorance, again, repented after that and made things right—truly, thy Lord after that is Forgiving, Compassionate.¹⁶·¹¹⁹

Abraham had been a community obedient to God—a monotheist—he is not among the ones who are polytheists.¹⁶·¹²⁰

He was one who is thankful for His divine blessings. He elected him and guided him to a straight path.¹⁶·¹²¹ And We gave him in the present benevolence. And, truly, in the world to come he will be among the ones in accord with morality.¹⁶·¹²²

Again, we revealed to thee that thou follow the creed of Abraham—a monotheist. And he had not been among the ones who are polytheists.¹⁶·¹²³

Truly, the Sabbath was made for those who are at variance about it. Truly, thy Lord will give judgment between them on the Day of Resurrection about what they had been at variance in it.¹⁶·¹²⁴

Call thou to the way of thy Lord with wisdom and fairer admonishment. And dispute with them in a way that is fairer. Truly, thy Lord is He Who is greater in knowledge of whoever went astray from His way. And He is greater in knowledge of the ones who are truly guided.¹⁶·¹²⁵

And if you chastised, then, chastise with the like of that with which you were chastised. But if you endured patiently, certainly, it is better for the ones who remain steadfast.¹⁶·¹²⁶

And have thou patience and thy patience is only from God. And feel not remorse over them, nor be thee troubled about what they plan.¹⁶·¹²⁷ Truly, God is with those who were Godfearing and those, they are ones who are doers of good.¹⁶·¹²⁸

CHAPTER 17 THE JOURNEY BY NIGHT

In the Name of God, The Merciful, The Compassionate

Glory be to Him Who caused His servant to set forth night from the Masjid al-Haram to the Masjid al-Aqsa around which We blessed so that We cause him to see Our signs. Truly, He, He is The Hearing, The Seeing.¹⁷·¹

And We gave Moses the Book and made it a guidance for the Children of Israel: Take not to yourselves a Trustee other than Me.¹⁷·²

O offspring of whomever We carried with Noah: Truly, he had been a grateful servant.¹⁷·³

And We decreed for the Children of Israel in the Book: Certainly, you will make corruption in and on the earth two times. And, certainly, you will exalt yourselves in a great self-exaltation.¹⁷·⁴

So when the promise drew near for the first of the two, We raised up against you servants of Ours imbued with severe might. They ransacked in the midst of your abodes. And the promise had been one that is accomplished.¹⁷·⁵

Again, We returned to you a turn of luck over them and We furnished you relief with children and wealth and made you more in soldiery:¹⁷·⁶ If you did good, you would be doing good for yourselves. And if you did evil, then, it is against yourselves.

Then, when the last promise drew near, We sent your enemies; they raise anger on your faces and they enter the place of prostration just as they entered it the first time, to shatter all that they ascended to with a shattering.17:7

Perhaps your Lord will have mercy on you. But if you reverted, We will revert. And We made hell a jail for the ones who are ungrateful.17:8

Truly, this, the Quran, guides to what is upright and gives good tidings to the ones who believe, those who are as the ones in accord with morality, that they will have a great compensation.17:9 And as for those who believe not in the world to come, We made ready for them a painful punishment.17:10

And the human being calls to worse as much as he supplicates for good. And the human being had been hasty.17:11

We made the nighttime and the daytime as two signs. Then, We blotted out the sign of nighttime and We made the sign of daytime for one who perceives that you be looking for grace from your Lord and that you know the number of years and the reckoning. And We explained everything distinctly, with a decisive explanation.17:12

For every human being We fastened his omen to his neck and We will bring out for him on the Day of Resurrection a book in which he will meet that which unfolded.17:13

Recite thy book! This day thy soul sufficed thee as thy reckoner against thee.17:14

Whoever was truly guided is truly guided only for his own soul. And whoever went astray, then, only goes astray against it. And no burdened soul bears the heavy load of another, nor would We have been ones who punish until We raised up a Messenger.17:15

And when We wanted to cause a town to perish, We commanded ones who are given ease, but they disobeyed therein. So the saying was realized against it. Then, We destroyed it with utter destruction.17:16

How many generations have We caused to perish after Noah? And thy Lord sufficed as Aware, Seeing the impieties of His servants.17:17

Whoever had been wanting that which hastens away, We quicken it for him, whatever We will to whomever We want. Again, We assigned hell for him. He will roast in it, one who is condemned, one who is rejected.17:18

And whoever wanted the world to come and endeavored for it, endeavoring, while he is one who believes, then, those, their endeavoring had been appreciated.17:19

To each We furnish relief, these and these, with the gift of thy Lord. And this gift of thy Lord has not been that which is confined.17:20

Look on how We gave advantage to some of them over some others. And, certainly, the world to come will be greater in degrees and greater in excellence.17:21

Assign not another god with God for, then, thou wilt be put as one who is condemned, one who is damned.17:22

And thy Lord decreed that you worship none but Him! And kindness to the ones who are one's parents. If they reach old age with thee—one of them or both of them—then, thou wilt not say to them a word of disrespect nor scold them, but say a generous saying to them.17:23 And make thyself low to them, the wing of the sense of humility through mercy. And say: O my Lord! Have mercy on them even as they raised me when I was small.17:24

Your Lord is greater in knowledge of what is within yourselves. If you be ones in accord with morality, truly, He is Forgiving to those who had been penitent.17:25

And give to the possessor of kinship his right and to the needy and to the traveler of the way. And spend not extravagantly an extravagant spending.17:26

Truly, the ones who spend extravagantly had been brothers/sisters of the satans and Satan had been ungrateful to his Lord.17:27

And if thou hast turned aside from them, looking for mercy from thy Lord for which thou hast hoped, then, say to them a saying softly.17:28

And make not thy hand be one that is restricted to thy neck as a miser nor extend it to its utmost expansion as a prodigal so that thou wilt sit as one who is reproached, one who is denuded.17:29 Truly, thy Lord extends the provision for whom He wills and He tightens for whom He wills. Truly, He, He had been Aware, Seeing of His servants.17:30

And kill not your children dreading want. We will provide for them and for you. Truly, the killing of them had been a grave inequity.17:31

And come not near committing adultery. Truly, it had been a great indecency! How evil a way!17:32

And kill not a soul that God forbade, but rightfully. And whoever was slain as one who is treated unjustly, surely, We assigned for his protector, authority, but he should not exceed all bounds in killing. Truly, he would be one who is helped by the Law.17:33

And come not near the property of the orphan, but with what is fairer until he reaches the coming of age. And live up to the compact. Truly, the compact had been that which will be asked about.17:34

And live up to the full measure when you wanted to measure. And weigh with a scale, one that is straight. That is best and fairer in interpretation.17:35

And follow up not of what there is not for thee knowledge of it. Truly, having the ability to hear and sight and mind, each of those will have been that which is asked.17:36

And walk not on the earth exultantly. Truly, thou wilt never make a hole in the earth and wilt never reach the mountains in height.17:37

All of that had been bad deeds, ones that are disliked by thy Lord.17:38

That is of what thy Lord revealed to thee of wisdom. So make not up with God another god that thou wouldst be cast down into hell as one who is reproached, as one who is rejected.17:39

Selected your Lord for you sons and taken for Himself females from among the angels? Truly, you, you say a serious saying!17:40

And, certainly, We diversified in this, the Quran, that they recollect. And it increases them only in aversion.17:41

Say: If there had been gods along with Him as they say, then, they would, certainly, be looking for a way to the Possessor of the Throne.17:42 Glory be to Him! And exalted is He above what they say, greatly exalted.17:43

The seven heavens glorify Him and the earth and whatever is in and on them. There is not a thing but it glorifies His praise, except you understand not their glorification. Truly, He had been Forbearing, Forgiving.17:44

And when thou hadst recited the Quran, We made between thee and between those who believe not in the world to come a partition obstructing their vision.17:45 And We laid sheaths on their hearts so that they not understand it and heaviness in their ears. And when thou hadst remembered thy Lord in the Quran that He is One, they turned their backs in aversion.17:46

We are greater in knowledge of what they listen for when they listen to thee.

And when they conspire secretly, when the ones who are unjust say: You follow but a bewitched man.17:47

Look on how they propounded parables for thee. So they went astray and they are not able to be on a way.17:48

And they say: When we had been bones and broken bits will we be ones who are raised up in a new creation?.17:49

Say: Should you be rocks or iron,17:50 or any creation that is more troublesome in your breasts to raise up?

Then, they will say: Who will cause us to return?

Say: He Who originated you the first time.

Then, they will nod their heads at thee and say: When will it be?

Say: Perhaps it is near.17:51

It will be a Day when He will call to you and you will respond to Him with His praise and you will think that you lingered in expectation but a little.17:52

And say to My servants they should say what is fairer. Truly, Satan sows enmity among them. Truly, Satan had been to the human being, a clear enemy.17:53

Your Lord is greater in knowledge of you. If He wills, He will have mercy on you. And if He wills, He will punish you. And We sent thee not as a trustee over them.17:54

And thy Lord is greater in knowledge of whoever are in the heavens and in and on the earth. And, certainly, We gave advantage to some of the Prophets over others. And to David We gave Psalms.17:55

Say: Call to those whom you claimed other than Him. Then, they are neither in control to remove harm from you nor revise it.17:56

Those are those to whom they call to, they are looking for an approach to their Lord—whoever is nearer—and they hope for His mercy and they fear His punishment. Truly, the punishment of thy Lord had been one to beware.17:57

And there is not a town but We will be ones who cause it to perish before the Day of Resurrection, or We will be ones who punish it with a severe punishment—that which had been inscribed in the Book.17:58

And nothing prevented Us from sending the signs, but that the ancient ones denied them. And We gave to Thamud the she-camel—the one who perceives—but they did wrong to her. And We send not the signs, but as a deterrence.17:59

And mention when We said to thee: Truly, thy Lord enclosed humanity. And We made not the dream that We caused thee to see, but as a test for humanity—and the tree—one that was cursed in the Quran. And We frighten them, but it only increases them in great defiance.17:60

And mention when We said to the angels: Prostrate yourselves to Adam! so they prostrated themselves, but Iblis. He said: Will I prostrate myself to one whom Thou hadst created from clay?17:61

He said: Hadst Thou considered this whom Thou hadst held in esteem above me? If Thou hadst postponed for me to the Day of Resurrection, I will, certainly, bring under full control his offspring, but a few.17:62

He said: Go thou! And whoever of them heeded thee, then, truly, hell will be your recompense, an ample recompense.17:63 And hound whom thou wert able to of them with thy voice and rally against them with thy horses and thy foot soldiers and share with them in their wealth and children and promise them. And Satan promises them nothing but delusion.17:64

Truly, My servants, over them there is no authority for thee. And thy Lord sufficed as a Trustee.17:65

Your Lord is He Who propels for you the boats on the sea so that you be looking for His grace. Truly, He had been Compassionate towards you.17:66

And when harm afflicted you upon the sea, whomever you call to besides Him went astray. But when He delivered you to dry land, you turned aside. And the human being had been ungrateful.17:67

Were you safe that He causes not the shore of dry land to swallow you up or send a sand storm against you?

Again, you will find no trustee for you.17:68

Or were you safe that He will not cause you to return to it another time and send against you a hurricane of wind and drown you because you were ungrateful?

Again, you will not find for yourselves an advocate against Us in it.17:69

And, certainly, We held the Children of Adam in esteem. And We carried them on dry land and on the sea and provided them with what is good. And We gave them advantage over many of whomever We created with excellence.17:70

On a Day when We will call to every clan with their leader, then, whoever was given his book in his right hand, those will recite their book and they will not be wronged in the least.17:71

And whoever had been unwilling to see here, will be unseeing in the world to come and one who goes astray from the way.17:72

And, truly, they were about to persecute thee for what We revealed to thee so that thou wouldst devise against Us other than it. And, then, they would take thee to themselves as a friend.17:73

And if We made thee not firm, certainly, thou wast about to incline to them a little.17:74 And, then, We would have caused thee to experience a double of this life and a double after dying. Again, thou wouldst find for thyself no helper against Us.17:75

They were about to hound thee from the region that they drive thee out of it. Then, they would not linger in expectation behind thee but for a little while.17:76 This is, surely, a custom with whomever We sent before thee of Our Messengers. And thou wilt not find in Our custom any revision.17:77

Perform the formal prayer from the sinking sun until the darkening of the night and the recital at dawn. Truly, the dawn recital had been one that is witnessed.17:78

And keep vigil with it in the night as a work of supererogation for thee. Perhaps thy Lord will raise thee up to a station of one who is praised.17:79

And say: My Lord! Cause me to enter a gate in sincerity. And bring me out as one who is brought out in sincerity. And assign me from that which proceeds from Thy Presence a helping authority.17:80

And say: The Truth drew near and falsehood is vanishing! Truly, falsehood had been made to vanish away.17:81

We send down in the Quran what is a healing and a mercy for the ones who believe. And it increases not the ones who are unjust, but in a loss.17:82

And when We were gracious to the human being, he turned aside and withdrew aside. And when worse afflicted him, he had been hopeless.17:83

Say: Each does according to his same manner. And thy Lord is greater in knowledge of him who is better guided on the way.17:84

And they will ask thee about the spirit.

Say: The spirit is of the command of my Lord. And you were not given the knowledge but a little.17:85

And if We willed, We would, certainly, take away what We revealed to thee. Again, thou wouldst not find for thee in that any trustee against Us,17:86 but a mercy from thy Lord. Truly, His grace had been great upon thee.17:87

Say: If humankind were gathered together and jinn to bring the like of this Quran, they would not approach the like of it even if some of them had been sustainers of some others.17:88

And, certainly, We diversified for humanity in this, the Quran, every kind of parable, but most of humanity refused all but disbelief.17:89

And they would say: We will never believe in thee until thou hast a fountain gush out of the earth for us.17:90

Or will there be a garden for thee of date palms and grapevines and Thou hast caused rivers to gush forth in its midst with a gushing forth?·17:91

Or hast thou caused heaven to drop on us in pieces as thou hadst claimed?

Or hast thou brought God and the angels as a warranty?·17:92

Or is there a house of ornament for thee?

Or hast thou ascended up into heaven?

And we will not believe in thy ascension until thou hast sent down for us a Book that we recite.

Say: Glory be to my Lord! Had I been but a mortal Messenger?·17:93

And nothing prevented humanity from believing when the guidance drew near them, but that they said: Raised God up a mortal as a Messenger?·17:94

Say: If there had been angels on earth walking around, ones who are at peace, then, We would certainly have sent down for them from heaven an angel as a Messenger.·17:95

Say: God sufficed as a Witness between me and between you. Truly, He had been of His servants Aware, Seeing.·17:96

And he whom God guides is one who is truly guided. And whomever He causes to go astray, thou wilt never find for them protectors other than Him.

And We will assemble them on the Day of Resurrection on their faces, unseeing and unspeaking and unhearing. Their place of shelter will be hell. Whenever it declined, We will increase the blaze for them.·17:97

That is their recompense because they were ungrateful for Our signs.

And they said: When we had been bones and broken bits, will we be ones who are raised up as a new creation?·17:98

Consider they not God Who created the heavens and the earth is One Who Has Power to create the like of them? And He assigned a term for them whereof there is no doubt in it, but the ones who are unjust refused all but disbelief.·17:99

Say: If you possessed the treasures of the mercy of my Lord, then, you would hold back for dread of spending. And the human being had been ever stingy.·17:100

And, certainly, We gave Moses nine signs, clear portents. Then, ask the Children of Israel when he drew near them. Then Pharaoh said to him: Truly, O Moses, I think that thou art one who is bewitched.·17:101

He said: Certainly, thou knewest no one caused these to descend but the Lord of the heavens and the earth as clear evidence. And, truly, O Pharaoh, I think that thou be one who is accursed.·17:102

So he wanted to hound them in the region, but We drowned him and those who were with him altogether.·17:103

And We said to the Children of Israel after him: Inhabit the region. So when drew near the promise of the world to come, We will bring you about a mixed group.·17:104

And We caused it to descend with The Truth. And it came down with the Truth. And We sent it not to thee, but as one who gives good tidings and as a warner.·17:105

And it is a Recitation. We separated it in order that thou recitest it to humanity at intervals. And We sent it down a sending successively down.·17:106

Say: Believe in it, or believe not.

Truly, those who were given the knowledge before it, when it is recounted to them, they fall down on their visages, ones who prostrate.·17:107

And they say: Glory be to our Lord! Truly, the promise of our Lord had been one that is accomplished.·17:108

And they fall down on their visage weeping. And it increases them in humility.·17:109

Say: Call to God or call to the Merciful. By whatever you call Him, to Him are the Fairer Names. And be thou not loud in thy formal prayer nor speak in a low tone and look for a way between.·17:110

And say: The Praise belongs to God Who takes not a son to Himself and there be no associates ascribed with Him in the dominion nor there be for Him need for a protector from humility. And magnify Him a magnification!·17:111

CHAPTER 18 THE CAVE

In the Name of God, the Merciful, the Compassionate

The Praise belongs to God Who caused the Book to descend to His servant and makes not for it any crookedness,·18:1 truth-loving, to warn of severe violence from that which proceeds from His Presence and to give good tidings to the ones who believe, those who do as the ones in accord with morality, that they will have a fairer compensation,·18:2 ones who will abide in it eternally·18:3 and to warn those who said: God took to Himself a son.·18:4

They have no knowledge about it, nor had their fathers. Troublesome is a word that goes forth from their mouths. And they say nothing but a lie·18:5 so that perhaps thou wilt be one who consumes thyself with grief for their sake if they believe not in this discourse out of bitterness.·18:6

Truly, We assigned whatever is in and on the earth as adornment for it so that We try them with it as to which of them are fairer in actions.·18:7

And, truly, We are ones who make whatever is on it, barren dust, dry earth.·18:8

Hast thou assumed that the Companions of the Cave and the Bearers of Inscription had been a wonder among Our signs?·18:9

And when the spiritual warriors took shelter in the Cave, then, they said: Our Lord! Give us mercy from Thy Presence and furnish us with right mindedness in our affair.·18:10

So We sealed their ears in the Cave for a number of years.·18:11

Again, We raised them up so that We might know which of the two confederates was better in calculating the space of time they lingered in expectation.·18:12

We relate this tiding to thee with The Truth. Truly, they were male spiritual warriors who believed in their Lord and We increased them in guidance.·18:13 And We invigorated their hearts when they stood up and said: Our Lord is Lord of the heavens and the earth. We will never call to any god other than He. Certainly, we would have said an outrageous thing.·18:14 These, our folk, took to themselves gods other than Him. Why bring they not a clear portent of authority with them? And who does greater wrong than he who devised a lie against God?·18:15

And when you withdrew from them and from what they worship but God, then, take shelter in the cave. Your Lord will unfold for you from His mercy and will furnish you with a gentle issue in your affair.·18:16

Thou wouldst have seen the sun when it came up. It inclines from their cave towards the right and when it began to set, it passed them towards the left while they were in a fissure. That is of the signs of God. He whom God guides, he is one who is truly guided. And he whom He causes to go astray, thou wilt never find for him a protector or one who will show him the way.·18:17

Thou wouldst assume them to be awake while they are ones who are sleeping. We turn them around and around towards the right and towards the left and their dog, one who stretches out its paws at the threshold. And if thou wert to peruse them, thou wouldst have turned from them, running away, and wouldst, certainly, be filled with alarm of them.·18:18

And, thus, it was that We raised them up that they might demand of one another. Said one who speaks among them: How long lingered you in expectation?

They said: We lingered in expectation a day or a part of a day. They said: Your Lord is greater in knowledge of how long you lingered in expectation. So raise up one of you and with this, your money, send him to the city and let him look on which is the purest food. Then, let him bring you provision from there. And let him be courteous and cause not anyone to realize.¹⁸:¹⁹

Truly, if you become manifest to them, they will stone you, or they will cause you to return to their creed and you would not ever prosper.¹⁸:²⁰

And, thus, We made their case known that they know that the promise of God is true and that, as for the Hour, there is no doubt about it. Mention when they contend with one another about their affair.

They said: Build over them a structure.

Their Lord is greater in knowledge about them. Those who prevailed over their affair said: We, certainly, will take to ourselves over them a place of prostration.¹⁸:²¹

They will say: They were three, the fourth of them being their dog. And they will say: They were five, the sixth of them being their dog, guessing at the unseen. And they will say: They were seven, the eighth of them being their dog. Say: My Lord is greater in knowledge of their amount. No one knows them but a few, so altercate not about them but with a manifest argumentation and ask not for advice about them of anyone of them.¹⁸:²²

And, surely, he will not say about something: Truly, I will be one who does that tomorrow,¹⁸:²³ but that you add: If God wills.

And remember thy Lord when thou hadst forgotten. And say: Perhaps my Lord will guide me nearer to right mindedness than this.¹⁸:²⁴

And they lingered in expectation in their cave three hundred years, and they added nine.¹⁸:²⁵

Say: God is greater in knowledge of how long they lingered in expectation. And to Him belongs the unseen of the heavens and the earth. How well He perceives and how well He hears! Other than him, they have no protector and He ascribes no one partners in His determination.¹⁸:²⁶

And recount what was revealed to thee from the Book of Thy Lord. There is no one who changes His Words. And thou wilt never find other than Him, that which is a haven.¹⁸:²⁷

And have thou patience thyself with those who call to their Lord in the morning and the evening, wanting His Countenance. And let not thy eyes pass over them wanting the adornment of this present life. And obey not him whose heart We made neglectful of Our Remembrance and who followed his own desires and whose affair had been excess.¹⁸:²⁸

And say: The Truth is from your Lord. Then, let whoever willed, believe, and let whoever willed, disbelieve. Truly, We made ready a fire for the ones who are unjust. They will be enclosed by its large tent. And if they cry for help, they will be helped with rain, water like molten copper that will scald their faces. Miserable was the drink and how evil a place of rest!¹⁸:²⁹

Truly, those who believed and did as the ones in accord with morality, truly, We will not waste the compensation of him who did good actions.¹⁸:³⁰

Those, for them are Gardens of Eden beneath which rivers run. They will be adorned in them with bracelets of gold and they will wear green garments of fine silk and brocade. They will be ones who are reclining in it on raised benches. Excellent is the reward for good deeds and how excellent a place of rest!¹⁸:³¹

And propound to them the parable of two men: We assigned to one of them two gardens of grapevines and We encircled them with date palm trees and We made crops between them.¹⁸:³²

Both the gardens gave their produce and fail nothing at all. We caused a river to gush forth in the midst of them.¹⁸:³³ And there had been fruit for him.

Then, he said to his companion while he converses with him: I have more wealth than thee and am mightier than a group of men or jinn.¹⁸:³⁴

And he entered his garden while he is one who is unjust to himself. He said: I think that this will not be destroyed ever.¹⁸:³⁵ And I think that the Hour will not be one that arises. And if I would be returned to my Lord, I would, surely, find better than this as an overturning.¹⁸:³⁶

And his companion said to him while he converses with him: Wert thou ungrateful to Him Who created thee out of earth dust, again, out of seminal fluid and, again, shaped thee into a man?¹⁸:³⁷ Certainly, He is God, my Lord, and I will not ascribe partners with my Lord anyone.¹⁸:³⁸ Would that when thou hadst entered thy garden thou hadst said: What God willed! There is no strength but with God! If thou hast seen I am less than you in wealth and children.¹⁸:³⁹ Then, perhaps my Lord will give me better than thy garden and will send on it a thunderclap from heaven. And it will come to be in the morning a place of slippery earth.¹⁸:⁴⁰

Or it will come to be in the morning that its water will be sinking into the ground so that thou wilt never be able to seek it out.¹⁸:⁴¹

And its fruit was enclosed. It came to be in the morning he turns around and around the palms of his hands in wretchedness for what he spent on it while it was one that has fallen down in ruins. And he says: Would that I not ascribe partners with my Lord anyone!¹⁸:⁴² And there is no faction to help him other than God. And he had been one who is helpless.¹⁸:⁴³

All protection there belongs to God, The Truth. He is Best in rewarding for good deeds and Best in consequence.¹⁸:⁴⁴

And propound for them the parable of this present life: It is like water that We caused to descend from heaven. Then, plants of the earth mingled with it and it becomes straw in the morning that winnows in the winds. And God had been over everything One Who is Omnipotent.¹⁸:⁴⁵

Wealth and children are the adornment of this present life. But that which endures are ones in accord with morality. These are better with thy Lord in reward for good deeds and better for hopefulness.¹⁸:⁴⁶ And on a Day We will set in motion the mountains and thou wilt see the earth as that which will depart. And We will assemble them and not leave out anyone of them.¹⁸:⁴⁷

And they were presented before thy Lord ranged in rows. Certainly, you drew near Us as We created you the first time. Nay! You claimed that We never assign for you something that is promised.¹⁸:⁴⁸

And the Book was set in place and thou wilt see the ones who sin being ones who are apprehensive as to what is in it. And they will say: Woe to us! What is this Book? It neither leaves out anything small or great, but counted everything. They will find present what their hands had done. And thy Lord does not wrong anyone.¹⁸:⁴⁹

And mention when We said to the angels: Prostrate yourselves to Adam! So they prostrated themselves but Iblis. He had been among the jinn and he disobeyed the command of His Lord. Will you, then, take him to yourselves and his offspring to be protectors other than Me while they are an enemy to you?

Miserable was it to give in place ones who are unjust!¹⁸:⁵⁰

I called them not to witness the creation of the heavens and the earth nor to their own creation of themselves nor took I to myself the ones who are led astray as assistants.[18:51]

And on a Day when He will say: Cry out to My associates, those who you claimed. Then, they will call out to them, but they will not respond to them and We will make a gulf of doom between them.[18:52]

And the unjust will see the ones who sin in the fire. They thought that they are ones who are about to fall in it and they will not find a place to turn from it.[18:53]

And, certainly, We diversified in this, the Quran, every kind of example for humanity. And the human being had been more than anything argumentative.[18:54]

Nothing prevented humanity from believing when the guidance drew near to them or from asking forgiveness of their Lord, but that approaches them a custom of the ancient ones or approaches them the punishment face to face.[18:55]

We send not the ones who are sent, but as ones who give good tidings and as ones who warn.

And those who were ungrateful dispute with falsehood in order to refute The Truth by it. And they took My signs to themselves—and what they were warned of—in mockery.[18:56]

And who does greater wrong than he who was reminded of the signs of his Lord, then, turned aside from them and forgot what his hands put forward?

Truly, We laid sheathes on their hearts so that they should not understand it and heaviness in their ears. And if thou hast called them to the guidance, yet they will not be truly guided ever.[18:57]

And thy Lord is Forgiving, Possessor of Mercy. If He were to take them to task for what they earned, He will quicken the punishment for them. But for them is what they are promised, from which they will never find a way to elude it.[18:59]

And these towns, We caused them to perish when they did wrong and We assigned for their destruction what is promised.[18:59]

Mention when Moses said to his spiritual warrior: I will not quit until I reach the place of meeting of the two seas even if I will go on for many years.[18:60]

But when they reached the place of the meeting between them, then, they both forgot their great fish and it took to itself a way through the sea, burrowing.[18:61]

Then, when they crossed, he said to his spiritual warrior: Give us our breakfast. Certainly, we met fatigue from our journey.[18:62]

He said: Hadst thou considered? When we took shelter at the rock, truly, I forgot the great fish. And none but Satan caused me to forget to remember it. And it took to itself to a way into the sea in a wondrous way.[18:63]

He said: That is what we had been looking for! So they went back following their footsteps.[18:64]

Then, they found a servant among Our servants to whom We gave mercy from Us and We taught him knowledge which proceeds from Our Presence.[18:65]

Moses said to him: May I follow thee so that thou wilt teach me something of what thou wert taught of right judgment?[18:66]

He said: Truly, thou wilt never be able to have patience with me.[18:67] And how wilt thou endure a thing patiently when thou hast not comprehended any awareness of it?[18:68]

Moses said: Thou wilt find me, if God willed, one who remains steadfast and I will not rebel against thy command.[18:69]

He said: Then, if thou hadst followed me, ask me not about anything until I cause to be evoked in thee a remembrance of it.[18:70]

So they both set out until when they embarked in a vessel. He made a hole in it.

Moses said: Hadst thou made a hole in it in order to drown the people? Certainly, thou hadst brought about a dreadful thing![18:71]

He said: Said I not that thou wilt never be able to have patience with me?[18:72]

Moses said: Take me not to task for what I forgot and constrain me not with hardship for my affair.[18:73]

Then, they both set out until when they met a boy; then, he killed him.

Moses said: Hadst thou killed a pure soul without his having slain a soul? Certainly, thou hadst brought about a horrible thing![18:74]

He said: Said I not that thou wilt never be able to have patience with me?[18:75]

Moses said: If I asked thee about anything after this, then, keep not company with me, surely, thou hadst reached enough of excusing from my presence![18:76]

Then, they both set out until when they approached a people of a town. They asked its people for food. But they refused to receive them as guests. Then, they found in it a wall that wants to tumble down, so he repaired it.

Moses said: If thou hadst willed, certainly, thou wouldst have taken compensation to thyself for it.[18:77]

He said: This is the parting between me and between thee! I will tell thee the interpretation of what thou wert not able to have patience for it.[18:78] As for the vessel, it had been of some needy people who toil in the sea, so I wanted to mar it as there had been a king behind them taking every vessel forcefully.[18:79] And as for the boy, both his parents had been ones who believe, and we dreaded that he should constrain them with defiance and ingratitude,[18:80] so we wanted their Lord to cause for them in exchange one better than he in purity and nearer in sympathy.[18:81] As for the wall, it had been that of two orphan boys in the city and beneath it had been a treasure for them. The father of both of them had been one in accord with morality so thy Lord wanted they be fully grown, having come of age, and pull out their treasure as a mercy from thy Lord. And I accomplished that not of my own command. This is the interpretation of what thou wert not able to have patience for it.[18:82]

And they will ask thee about Dhu-l Qarnayn.

Say: I will recount to you a remembrance of him.[18:83]

Truly, We established him firmly on the earth and gave him a route to everything.[18:84] So he pursued a route [18:85] until when he reached the setting of the sun. He found it beginning to set in a spring of muddy water. And he found near it a folk.

We said: O Dhu-l Qarnayn! Either thou wilt punish them or thou wilt take them to thyself with goodness.[18:86]

He said: As for him who did wrong, we will punish him. Again, he will be returned to his Lord Who will punish him with a horrible punishment.[18:87]

But as for him who believed and did as one in accord with morality, he will have the fairer recompense. And we will say to him of our command with ease.[18:88]

Again, he pursued a route [18:89] until when he reached the rising place of the sun. He found it coming up on a folk for whom We make not any obstruction against it.[18:90] Thus, We, surely, enclosed whatever was near him through awareness.[18:91]

Again, he pursued a route[18:92] until when he reached between two embankments. He found behind them a folk who would almost not understand any saying.[18:93]

They said: O Dhu-l Qarnayn! Truly, Gog and Magog are ones who make corruption in and on the earth. Will we assign to thee payment if thou hast made an embankment between us and between them?[18:94]

He said: What my Lord established firmly for me is better, so assist me with strength. I will make a fortification between you and between them.¹⁸ː⁹⁵ Give me ingots of iron, until when he made level between the two cliffs.

He said: Blow, until when he made it a fire.

He said: Give me molten brass to pour out over it.¹⁸ː⁹⁶

So they were not able to scale it nor were they able to dig through it.¹⁸ː⁹⁷

He said: This is a mercy from my Lord. So when the promise of my Lord drew near, He made it powder. And the promise of my Lord had been true.¹⁸ː⁹⁸

And that Day We will leave some of them to surge like waves on some others. And the trumpet will be blown, then, We will gather them altogether.¹⁸ː⁹⁹

We will present the depths of hell on that Day in plain view to ones who are ungrateful,¹⁸ː¹⁰⁰ to those whose eyes had been screened from My Remembrance and who had not been able to hear.¹⁸ː¹⁰¹

Assumed ones who were ungrateful that they take My servants to themselves as protectors instead of Me? Truly, We made hell ready with hospitality for ones who are ungrateful.¹⁸ː¹⁰²

Say: Shall We tell you who will be ones who are losers by their actions?¹⁸ː¹⁰³

It is those whose endeavoring went astray in this present life while they assume that they are doing good by their handiwork.¹⁸ː¹⁰⁴

Those were those who were ungrateful for the signs of their Lord and the meeting with Him so their actions were fruitless. And so We will not perform for them on the Day of Resurrection, any weighing.¹⁸ː¹⁰⁵

That will be their recompense—hell—because they were ungrateful and took to themselves My signs and My Messengers in mockery.¹⁸ː¹⁰⁶

Truly, those who believed and did as ones in accord with morality, their hospitality had been in the Gardens of Paradise,¹⁸ː¹⁰⁷ ones who will dwell in them forever. They will have no desire for relocation from there.¹⁸ː¹⁰⁸

Say: If the sea had been ink for the Words of my Lord, the sea would come to an end before the Words of my Lord came to an end even if We brought about replenishment the like of it.¹⁸ː¹⁰⁹

Say: I am only a mortal like you. It is revealed to me that your God is One, so whoever had been hoping for the meeting with his Lord, let him do with his actions as one in accord with morality and ascribe no partners—in the worship of his Lord, ever.¹⁸ː¹¹⁰

CHAPTER 19 MARY

In the Name of God, the Merciful, the Compassionate
*Kāf Hā Yā Aīn Sād.*¹⁹ː¹

A remembrance of the mercy of thy Lord to His servant Zechariah¹⁹ː² when he cried out to his Lord, secretively crying out.¹⁹ː³

He said: My Lord! Truly, I—my bones became feeble and my head became studded with grayness of hair and I be not disappointed in my supplication to Thee, O my Lord.¹⁹ː⁴

And, truly, I feared for my defenders after me. And my woman had been a barren woman. So bestow on me from that which proceeds from Thy Presence a protector.¹⁹ː⁵

He will inherit from me and inherit from the family of Jacob. And make him, my Lord, pleasing.¹⁹ː⁶

O Zechariah! Truly, We give thee the good tidings of a boy. His name will be Yahya and We assigned it not as a namesake for anyone before.¹⁹ː⁷

He said: My Lord! How will I have a boy while my woman had been a barren woman and, surely, I reached an advanced old age?¹⁹ː⁸

He said: It is about to be! Thy Lord said: It is insignificant for Me and, surely, I created thee before when thou wast nothing.¹⁹ː⁹

Zechariah said: My Lord! Assign for me a sign.

He said: Thy sign is that thou wilt not speak to humanity for three nights, although being without fault.¹⁹ː¹⁰

So he went forth to his folk from the sanctuary. Then, he revealed to them: Glorify in the early morning dawn and evening.¹⁹ː¹¹

O Yahya! Take the Book with strength. And We gave him critical judgment while a lad,¹⁹ː¹² and Our continuous mercy from that which proceeds from Our Presence and purity and he had been devout¹⁹ː¹³ and pious to ones who are his parents and be not haughty nor rebellious.¹⁹ː¹⁴

And peace be on him the day on which he was given birth and the day he dies and the day he is raised up, living.¹⁹ː¹⁵

And remember Mary in the Book when she went apart from her people to an eastern place.¹⁹ː¹⁶

Then, she took to herself a partition away from them, so We sent Our Spirit to her and he presented himself before her as a mortal without fault.¹⁹ː¹⁷

She said: Truly, I take refuge in The Merciful from thee; come not near me if thou hadst been devout.¹⁹ː¹⁸

He said: I am only a messenger from thy Lord that I bestow on thee (f) a pure boy.¹⁹ː¹⁹

She said: How will I have a boy when no mortal touches me, nor am I an unchaste woman?¹⁹ː²⁰

He said: Thus, it will be.

Thy Lord said: It is for Me insignificant. And: We will assign him as a sign for humanity and as a mercy from Us. And it had been that which is a decreed command.¹⁹ː²¹

So she conceived him and she went apart with him to a farther place.¹⁹ː²² And the birth pangs surprised her at the trunk of a date palm tree.

She said: O would that I had died before this and I had been one who is forgotten, a forgotten thing!¹⁹ː²³

So he cried out to her from beneath her: Feel not remorse! Surely, thy Lord made under thee (f) a brook.¹⁹ː²⁴ And shake towards thee (f) the trunk of the date palm tree. It will cause ripe, fresh dates to fall on thee.¹⁹ː²⁵ So eat and drink and thy eyes be refreshed.

If thou hast seen any mortal, say: I vowed formal fasting to The Merciful so I will never speak to any human being this day.¹⁹ː²⁶

Then, she approached her folk with him, carrying him.

They said: O Mary! Surely, thou hadst drawn near a monstrous thing!¹⁹ː²⁷ O sister of Aaron! Thy father had not been a reprehensible man nor was thy mother an unchaste woman.¹⁹ː²⁸

Then, she pointed to him.

They said: How speak we to one who had been in the cradle, a lad?¹⁹ː²⁹

Jesus said: Truly, I am a servant of God. He gave me the Book and He made me a Prophet.¹⁹ː³⁰ And He made me one who is blessed wherever I had been and He bequeathed to me the formal prayer and the purifying alms as long as I continue living,¹⁹ː³¹ and He makes me pious toward one who is my mother and He makes me not haughty nor disappointed.¹⁹ː³² And peace be on me the day I was given birth and the day I die and the day I am raised up, living.¹⁹ː³³

That is Jesus son of Mary, a saying of The Truth. They contest what is in it.¹⁹ː³⁴

It had not been for God that He takes to Himself a son. Glory be to Him! When He decreed a command, He not but says to it: Be! Then, it is!¹⁹ː³⁵

And, truly, God is my Lord and your Lord, so worship Him. This is a straight path.¹⁹ː³⁶

There was variance among the confederates, so woe to those who were ungrateful from the scene of a tremendous Day!¹⁹ː³⁷

Hear well and perceive well. On that Day they will approach Us, but today the ones who are unjust are in a clear wandering astray!¹⁹:³⁸

And warn thou them of the Day of Regret when the command would be decided. Yet they are heedless and they believe not.¹⁹:³⁹

Truly, We will inherit the earth and whatever is in and on it and to Us they will be returned.¹⁹:⁴⁰

And remember Abraham in the Book. Truly, he had been a just person, a Prophet.¹⁹:⁴¹

That is when he said to his father: O my father! Why wilt thou worship what hears not, and perceives not, and avails thee not anything?¹⁹:⁴² O my father! Truly, I, there drew near me of the knowledge of what approaches thee not. So follow me and I will guide thee to a path without fault.¹⁹:⁴³ O my father! Worship not Satan. Truly, Satan had been rebellious towards The Merciful!¹⁹:⁴⁴ O my father! Truly, I fear that a punishment should afflict thee from The Merciful so that thou become a protector of Satan.¹⁹:⁴⁵

He said: Art thou one who shrinks from my gods, O Abraham? If thou wilt not refrain thyself, certainly, I will stone thee, so abandon me for some while.¹⁹:⁴⁶

He said: Peace be to thee. I will ask for forgiveness from my Lord for thee. Truly, He had been One Who is Gracious to me.¹⁹:⁴⁷ And I will withdraw from you and what you call to other than God and I will call to my Lord. Perhaps I will not be disappointed in my supplication to my Lord.¹⁹:⁴⁸

So he withdrew from them and what they worship other than God. And We bestowed on him Isaac and Jacob. And each of them We made a Prophet.¹⁹:⁴⁹

And We bestowed on them from Our mercy and We assigned them the tongue of lofty sincerity.¹⁹:⁵⁰

And remember Moses in the Book. Truly, he had been one who was devoted and he had been a Messenger, a Prophet.¹⁹:⁵¹

And We proclaimed to him from the right edge of the mount and We brought him near privately.¹⁹:⁵²

And We bestowed on him out of Our mercy his brother Aaron, a Prophet.¹⁹:⁵³

And remember Ishmael in the Book. Truly, he had been one who is sincere in his promise, and he had been a Messenger, a Prophet.¹⁹:⁵⁴

He had been commanding his people to formal prayer and the purifying alms and he had been with His Lord one who is well-pleasing.¹⁹:⁵⁵

And remember Enoch in the Book. Truly, he had been a just person, a Prophet.¹⁹:⁵⁶ And We exalted him to a lofty place.¹⁹:⁵⁷

Those are those to whom God was gracious from among the Prophets of the offspring of Adam and whomever We carried with Noah and of the offspring of Abraham and Israel, Jacob, from among whomever We guided and elected. When are recounted to them the signs of the Merciful they fell down, crying, ones who prostrate themselves.¹⁹:⁵⁸

Then, after them succeeded a succession who wasted the formal prayer and followed their lusts. So they will meet error,¹⁹:⁵⁹ but the ones who repented and believed and did as ones in accord with morality.

For those will enter the Garden and they will not be wronged at all,¹⁹:⁶⁰ Gardens of Eden which The Merciful promised His servants in the unseen. Truly, He, His promise had been that which is kept.¹⁹:⁶¹

They will not hear in them idle talk, nothing but: Peace. And they will have their provision in them in the early morning dawn and evening.¹⁹:⁶² This is the Garden which We will give as inheritance to whomever of Our servants who had been devout.¹⁹:⁶³

And we come forth not but by the command of thy Lord. To Him belongs whatever is in advance of us and whatever is behind us and whatever is in between that.

And thy Lord had not been forgetful,¹⁹:⁶⁴ the Lord of the heavens and the earth, and what is between them! So worship Him and maintain thou patience in His worship. Hast thou known any namesake for Him?¹⁹:⁶⁵

And the human being says: When I am dead, will I be brought out living?¹⁹:⁶⁶

Will the human being not remember that We created him before when he be of nothing?¹⁹:⁶⁷

So by thy Lord, certainly, We will assemble them and the satans. Again, We will parade them around hell, ones who crawl on their knees.¹⁹:⁶⁸ Again, We will tear out every partisan, whoever of them was more severe in stubborn rebellion against The Merciful.¹⁹:⁶⁹ After that We are greater in knowledge of those, they who are most deserving of roasting in it.¹⁹:⁷⁰

There is none of you, but ones who go down to it. This had been a thing decreed, that decreed by thy Lord.¹⁹:⁷¹

Again, We will deliver those who were Godfearing and We will forsake the ones who are unjust, in it, ones who crawl on their knees.¹⁹:⁷²

And when are recounted to them Our signs, clear portents, those who were ungrateful would say to those who believed: Which of the two groups of people is best in station and fairer in alliance?¹⁹:⁷³

How many before them We caused to perish whose generation was fairer in furnishing and outward show?¹⁹:⁷⁴

Say: Whoever had been in fallacy, The Merciful will prolong his prolonging for him. Until when they would see what they are promised, either the punishment or the Hour, then, they will know whose place is worse and whose army is weak.¹⁹:⁷⁵

And God increases in guidance those who were truly guided and endure in accord with morality. They are better with thy Lord in reward for good deeds and better for turning back.¹⁹:⁷⁶

Hadst thou seen him who was ungrateful for Our signs, who said: Will I be given wealth and children?¹⁹:⁷⁷

Perused he the unseen or took he to himself a compact from The Merciful?¹⁹:⁷⁸ No indeed! We will write down what he says. We will cause the punishment to increase for him, prolonging it.¹⁹:⁷⁹

And We will inherit from him all that he says and he will approach Us individually.¹⁹:⁸⁰ And they took to themselves gods other than God that there be a triumph for them.¹⁹:⁸¹ No indeed! They will disbelieve in what they worship and they will be taking a stand against them.¹⁹:⁸²

Hast thou not considered that We sent the satans against the ones who were ungrateful to confound them with confusion?¹⁹:⁸³ So hasten thou not against them. We only number for them a sum.¹⁹:⁸⁴

On the Day We will assemble the ones who are Godfearing to The Merciful like an entourage.¹⁹:⁸⁵ And We will drive the ones who sin to hell, herding them.¹⁹:⁸⁶

None of them will possess the power of intercession but such a one who took to himself a compact with The Merciful.¹⁹:⁸⁷

And they said: The Merciful took to Himself a son!¹⁹:⁸⁸

Certainly, you brought about a disastrous thing¹⁹:⁸⁹ whereby the heavens are almost split asunder and the earth is split and the mountains fall crashing down ¹⁹:⁹⁰ that they attributed a son to The Merciful.¹⁹:⁹¹

It is not fit and proper for The Merciful that He should take a son to Himself!¹⁹:⁹²

There is none at all in the heavens and the earth but he be one who arrives to The Merciful as a servant.¹⁹:⁹³

Certainly, He counted for them and numbered up a sum!¹⁹:⁹⁴

And everyone of them will be ones who arrive to Him individually on the Day of Resurrection.¹⁹:⁹⁵

Truly, those who believed and did as the ones in accord with morality, The Merciful will assign ardor for them.¹⁹:⁹⁶

So, truly, We made this easy on thy tongue. Certainly, thou wilt give good tidings with it to the ones who are Godfearing and thou wilt warn a most stubborn folk with it.¹⁹:⁹⁷

How many a generation caused We to perish before them? Art thou conscious of anyone of them or hear you so much as a whisper from them?

CHAPTER 20 TA HA

In the Name of God, The Merciful, The Compassionate
*Tā Hā.*²⁰:¹

We caused not the Quran to descend to thee that thee be in despair,²⁰:² but as an admonition to him who dreads²⁰:³ a sending down successively from Him Who created the earth and the lofty heavens.²⁰:⁴

The Merciful turned His attention to the Throne.²⁰:⁵

To Him belongs whatever is in the heavens and whatever is on the earth and whatever is between them and whatever is beneath the soil.²⁰:⁶

And if thou art to publish a saying, yet, truly, He knows the secret and what is more secret.²⁰:⁷

God, there is no god but He. To Him belongs the Fairer Names.²⁰:⁸

Has the conversation of Moses approached thee?²⁰:⁹

When he saw a fire, he said to his people: Abide! Truly, I observed a fire so that perhaps I will bring you some firebrand from it or I find guidance at the fire.²⁰:¹⁰

When he approached it, it was proclaimed: O Moses!²⁰:¹¹ Truly, I—I am thy Lord! So take off thy shoes; truly, thou art one who is in the sanctified valley of Tuwa.²⁰:¹² And I chose thee so listen to what is revealed:²⁰:¹³

Truly, I—I am God. There is no god but Me. So worship Me and perform the formal prayer of My Remembrance.²⁰:¹⁴ Truly, the Hour is that which arrives. I am about to conceal it so that every soul is given recompense for what it endeavors.²⁰:¹⁵ So let none bar thee from it—whoever believes not in it and followed his own desires—so that thee not survive.²⁰:¹⁶

And what is that in thy right hand O Moses?²⁰:¹⁷

Moses said: This is my staff. I lean on it, and beat down leaves from a tree with it for my herd of sheep and for me in it are other uses.²⁰:¹⁸

He said: Cast it, O Moses!²⁰:¹⁹

So he cast it. That is when it was a viper sliding.²⁰:²⁰

He said: Take it and fear not. We will cause it to return to its first state.²⁰:²¹ And clasp thy hand to thy armpit. It will go forth shimmering white without any evil as another sign²⁰:²² that We cause thee to see of Our greater signs.²⁰:²³ Go thou to Pharaoh! Truly, he was defiant.²⁰:²⁴

Moses said: My Lord!²⁰:²⁵ Expand my breast for me and make Thou my affair easy for me²⁰:²⁶ and untie the knot from my tongue²⁰:²⁷ so they understand my saying²⁰:²⁸ and assign to me a minister from my people—²⁰:²⁹ Aaron, my brother.²⁰:³⁰ Strengthen my vigor with him²⁰:³¹ and ascribe him as a partner in my affair²⁰:³² that we glorify Thee much²⁰:³³ and we remember Thee frequently.²⁰:³⁴ Truly, Thou, Thou alone hadst been seeing of us.²⁰:³⁵

He said: Surely, thou wert given thy petition, O Moses!²⁰:³⁶ Certainly, We showed grace on thee another time²⁰:³⁷ when We revealed to thy mother what is revealed:²⁰:³⁸ Cast him adrift in the ark. Then, cast it adrift into the water of the sea.

Then, the water of the sea will cast him up on the bank and he will be taken by an enemy of Mine and an enemy of his. And I cast on thee fondness from Me that thou be trained under My Eye.²⁰:³⁹

Mention when thy sister walks saying: Shall I point you to one who will take control of him?

So We returned thee to thy mother that her eyes settle down and she not feel remorse. And thou hast killed a soul, but We delivered thee from lament and We tried thee with an ordeal. Then, thou hadst lingered in expectation years among the people of Midian. Again, thou hadst drawn near according to a measure, O Moses!²⁰:⁴⁰ And I chose thee for service for Myself.²⁰:⁴¹

Go thou and thy brother with My signs and you both not be inattentive in My Remembrance.²⁰:⁴² So go both of you to Pharaoh. Truly, he had become defiant.²⁰:⁴³ And both say to him a saying gently, so that perhaps he will recollect or dread.²⁰:⁴⁴

They both said: Our Lord! Truly, we fear that he should exceed against us or that he be defiant.²⁰:⁴⁵

He said: Fear not. Truly, I am with both of you. I hear and I see.²⁰:⁴⁶

So approach you both to him and say: Truly, we are Messengers of thy Lord. So send the Children of Israel with us and punish them not. Surely, we drew near thee with a sign from thy Lord. And peace be to him who followed the guidance.²⁰:⁴⁷

Surely, it was revealed to us that the punishment is on him who denied and turned away.²⁰:⁴⁸

He said: Then, who is the Lord of you two, O Moses?²⁰:⁴⁹

He said: Our Lord is He Who gave everything its creation; again, He guided it.²⁰:⁵⁰

Pharaoh said: Then, what of the first generations?²⁰:⁵¹

Moses said: The knowledge of them is with my Lord in a Book. My Lord neither goes astray nor forgets.²⁰:⁵² He it is Who assigned for you the earth as a cradle and threaded ways for you in it and caused water to descend from heaven. And We brought out from it diverse pairs of plants:²⁰:⁵³ Eat and give attention to your flocks. Truly, in this are signs for the people imbued with sense.²⁰:⁵⁴

We created you from it and into it We will cause you to return and from it We will bring you out another time.²⁰:⁵⁵

And, certainly, We caused Pharaoh to see Our signs—all of them—but he denied and refused.²⁰:⁵⁶

He said: Hast thou drawn near us to drive us out of our region with thy sorcery, O Moses?²⁰:⁵⁷ Then, truly, we will bring for thee sorcery like it. So make something that is promised between us and thee—neither we nor thou will break it—at a mutually agreeable place.²⁰:⁵⁸

He said: That promised will be for the Day of Adornment and let humanity be assembled in the forenoon.²⁰:⁵⁹

So Pharaoh turned away. Then, he gathered his cunning. After that he approached.²⁰:⁶⁰

Moses said to them: Woe to you! Devise you not a lie against God so that He put an end to you with a punishment. And, surely, he who devised will be frustrated.²⁰:⁶¹

So they contended between each other about their affair and they kept secret, conspiring secretly.²⁰:⁶²

They said: Truly, these two are the ones who are sorcerers who want to drive you out from your region with their sorcery and take away your most ideal behavior.²⁰:⁶³ So summon up your cunning. Again, approach ranged in rows. And, truly, he who gained the upper hand will prosper this day.²⁰:⁶⁴

They said: O Moses! Either thou wilt cast or let us be the first to cast.²⁰:⁶⁵

He said: Nay! You cast.

That is when their ropes and their staffs seem to him to be, by their sorcery, as though they are sliding.²⁰:⁶⁶

So Moses sensed awe in himself.20:67

We said: Fear not! Truly, thou, thou art lofty!20:68 And cast what is in thy right hand. It will swallow what they crafted. What they crafted is not but the cunning of one who is a sorcerer. And the one who is a sorcerer will not prosper in whatever he approached.20:69

Then, the ones who are sorcerers were cast down, ones who prostrate themselves.

They said: We believed in the Lord of Aaron and Moses.20:70

Pharaoh said: Believed you in Him before I give you permission? Truly, he is your teacher who taught you the sorcery. So, certainly, I will cut off your hands and your feet on opposite sides and, certainly, I will cause you to be crucified on the trunks of date palm trees, and, certainly, you will know which of us is more severe in punishment and one who endures.20:71

They said: We will never hold thee in greater favor over the clear portents that drew near us nor over Who originated us. So decide whatever thou wilt as one who decides. Thou wilt decide not but about this present life.20:72 For us, truly, we believed in our Lord that He forgive us our transgressions and what thou hadst compelled us to do because of the sorcery. And God is Best of one who endures.20:73

Truly, whoever approaches his Lord as one who sins, then, truly, for him is hell. Neither will he die in it nor will he live.20:74

And whoever approaches Him as one who believes, who, surely, did as the one in accord with morality, then, for those, they are of lofty degrees,20:75 Gardens of Eden, beneath which rivers run, ones who will dwell in them forever. And that is the recompense of whoever purified himself.20:76

And, certainly, We revealed to Moses that set thou forth with My servants. Then, strike for them a dry road in the sea, neither fearing to be overtaken, nor dreading that.20:77

Then, Pharaoh and his army pursued them. Then, overcame them the water of the sea by what overcame.20:78

And Pharaoh caused his folk to go astray and he guided them not.20:79

O Children of Israel! Surely, We rescued you from your enemy and We appointed someone with you on the right edge of the mount and We sent down to you the manna and the quails.20:80 Eat from what is good that We provided you, and be not defiant in it so that My anger not alight on you. And he on whom My anger alights surely, will be hurled to ruin.20:81 And, truly, I am a Forgiver of whoever repented and believed and did as one in accord with morality. Again, he was truly guided.20:82

And what caused thee to hasten from thy folk, O Moses?20:83

Moses said: They are those who are close on my footsteps and I hastened to Thee, my Lord that I please thee.20:84

He said: Then, truly, We tried thy folk after thee and the Samaritan caused them to go astray.20:85

Then, Moses returned to his folk enraged, grieved. He said: O my folk! Promise you not with your Lord a fairer promise? Was the compact too long for you to wait? Or wanted you that the anger of your Lord alight on you, so you broke what you were to have promised me?20:86

They said: We broke not what was promised to thee from what is within our power, but we were charged with a heavy load of the adornments of the folk. Surely, we hurled them because the Samaritan cast.20:87

Then, he brought out for them a calf, a lifeless body that had the lowing sound of flocks.

Then, they said: This is your god and the God of Moses whom he forgot.20:88

Then, see they not that it returns not to them a saying and it possesses for them neither hurt nor profit?20:89

And, certainly, Aaron said to them before: O my folk! You were only tempted by it. And, truly, your Lord is The Merciful. So follow me and obey my command.20:90

They said: We will never quit it as ones who give ourselves up until Moses returns to us.20:91

He said: O Aaron! What prevented thee when thou hadst seen them going astray20:92 that thou hast followed me not? Hast thou, then, rebelled against my command?20:93

Aaron said: O son of my mother! Take me not by my beard nor by my head. Truly, I dreaded that thou hast said: Thou hadst separated and divided between the Children of Israel and thou hast not regarded my saying.20:94

Moses said: Then, what is thy business O Samaritan?20:95

He said: I kept watch over what they keep not watch, so I seized a handful of dust from the foot prints of the Messenger and cast it forth. And thus my soul enticed me.20:96

Moses said: Then go off! Truly for thee in this life is that thou mayest say: Untouchable; there is for thee something promised that thou shalt never break; and look on thy god that thou hast stayed with and given thyself up to; certainly we will burn it. After that we will certainly scatter it in the water of the sea in a scattering.20:97 Your God is only God Whom there is no god but He. He encompassed everything in His knowledge.20:98

Thus We relate to thee some tiding of what preceded.

And surely We gave thee from that which proceeds from Our Presence a Remembrance.20:99 Whoever turned aside from it, then truly he will carry a heavy load on the Day of Resurrection, ones who will dwell in it forever.

How evil for them on the Day of Resurrection20:100 ones who will dwell in it forever; how evil for them on the Day of Resurrection will be the load20:101 on the Day the trumpet will be blown. We will assemble the ones who sin, white eyed on that Day.20:102 They will whisper among themselves: You lingered in expectation but ten days.20:103 We are greater in knowledge of what they will say when the most ideal of them in tradition says: You lingered in expectation not but a day!20:104

And they will ask thee about the mountains. Then, say: My Lord will scatter them a scattering.20:105 Then, He will forsake it as a leveled spacious plain.20:106 Then, thou wilt see not in it any crookedness nor unevenness.20:107 On that Day they will follow one who calls. There will be no crookedness in him. And voices will be hushed for The Merciful so thou wilt hear nothing but a murmuring.20:108

On a Day intercession will not profit anyone but him to whom gave permission The Merciful and with whose saying He was well-pleased.20:109 He knows what is in advance of them and what is behind them and they will not comprehend Him in knowledge.20:110 And faces will be humbled before The Living, The Eternal while, surely, will be frustrated whoever was burdened by doing injustice.20:111

Whoever does as the one in accord with morality and he is one who believes, then, he will neither fear injustice nor unfairness.20:112

And, thus, We caused it to descend as an Arabic Recitation. And We diversified the threats in it so that perhaps they will be Godfearing or cause the Remembrance to be evoked by them.20:113

Then, exalted be God, The True King, and hasten not the Recitation before its revelation is decreed to thee. And say: My Lord! Increase me in knowledge!20:114

And, certainly, We made a compact with Adam before. Then, he forgot and We find no constancy in him.20:115

And when We said to the angels: Prostrate yourselves to Adam! They prostrated themselves, but Iblis who refused.20:116

Then, We said: O Adam! Truly, this is an enemy to thee and to thy spouse, so let him not drive you both out from the Garden so that thou wouldst be in despair.²⁰:¹¹⁷ Truly, it is not for thee that thou hunger in it nor to be naked.²⁰:¹¹⁸ And, truly, thou wilt not thirst in it nor suffer the heat of the sun.²⁰:¹¹⁹

Then, Satan whispered evil to him. He said: O Adam! Will I point thee to the Tree of Infinity and a dominion that will not decay?²⁰:¹²⁰

Then, they both ate from that so the intimate parts of both showed to both themselves. Both of them took to doing stitching together over both from the leaves of the Garden. And Adam rebelled against his Lord and he erred.²⁰:¹²¹ Again, his Lord elected him. Then, He turned in forgiveness to him and guided him.²⁰:¹²² He said: Get you both down from here altogether, some of you an enemy to some others. Then, if guidance approaches you from Me, then, whoever followed My Guidance, neither will he go astray, nor will he be in despair.²⁰:¹²³

And whoever turned aside from My Remembrance, then, truly, for him is a livelihood of narrowness. And We will assemble him on the Day of Resurrection unseeing.²⁰:¹²⁴

He would say: My Lord! Why hadst Thou assembled me with the unseeing when, surely, I had been seeing?²⁰:¹²⁵

He would say: It is thus: Our signs approached thee, but thou hadst forgotten them and, thus, this Day thou wilt be forgotten.²⁰:¹²⁶

And, thus, We give recompense to him who exceeded all bounds and believes not in signs of his Lord. And, surely, punishment in the world to come is more severe and one that endures.²⁰:¹²⁷

Guide He not them? How many generations We caused to perish before them amidst whose dwellings they walk. Truly, in this are signs for the people imbued with sense.²⁰:¹²⁸

And if a Word preceded not from thy Lord for a term that was determined, it would be close at hand.²⁰:¹²⁹ So have thou patience with what they say and glorify the praises of thy Lord before the coming up of the sun and before sunset and during the nighttime night watch and glorify at the end of the daytime, so that perhaps thou wilt be well-pleased.²⁰:¹³⁰

And stretch not out thy eyes for what We gave of enjoyment in this life to spouses among them as the luster of this present life so that We try them by it. And provision of thy Lord is Best and that which endures.²⁰:¹³¹

And command thy people to the formal prayer, and to maintain patience in it. We ask not of thee for any provision. We provide for thee and the Ultimate End will be for the God-conscious.²⁰:¹³²

And they said: Why brings he not to us a sign from his Lord? Approaches them not clear portents that were in the first scrolls?²⁰:¹³³ And if We caused them to perish with a punishment before this, certainly, they would have said: Our Lord! Why hadst Thou not sent to us a Messenger so that we follow Thy signs before we are degraded and humiliated!²⁰:¹³⁴

Say: Each is one who is waiting so watch. Then, you will know who are the Companions of the Path without fault and who were truly guided.²⁰:¹³⁵

CHAPTER 21
THE PROPHETS

In the Name of God, the Merciful, the Compassionate

The reckoning for humanity was near while they are ones who turn aside in heedlessness.²¹:¹

Approaches them not a remembrance from their Lord, that which is renewed, but they listened to it while they play²¹:²

being ones whose hearts are ones that are diverted, and they kept secret, conspiring secretly those who did wrong? Is this other than a mortal like you?

Then, will you approach sorcery while you perceive?²¹:³

He said: My Lord knows The Word of the heavens and the earth. And He is The Hearing, The Knowing.²¹:⁴

Nay! They said: Jumbled nightmares! Nay! He but devised it! Nay! He is but a poet! Let him bring us a sign as the ancient ones were sent!²¹:⁵

No town believed before them of whom We caused to perish. Will they, then, believe?²¹:⁶

And We sent not before thee but men to whom We reveal. So ask the People of the Remembrance if you had not been knowing.²¹:⁷

And We made them not lifeless bodies that eat not food nor had they been ones who will dwell forever.²¹:⁸

Again, We were sincere in the promise. So We rescued them and whom We will. We caused the ones who are excessive to perish.²¹:⁹

Surely, We caused a Book to descend to you in which is your Remembrance. Will you not, then, be reasonable?²¹:¹⁰

How many a town We damaged that had been one that is unjust and caused to grow after them another folk?²¹:¹¹ Then, when they were conscious of Our might, that is when they make haste from it!²¹:¹² Make not haste, but return to what you were given of ease in it and to your dwellings, so that perhaps you will be asked.²¹:¹³

They said: O woe to us! Truly, we had been ones who are unjust!²¹:¹⁴

Then, truly, they ceased not calling that out until We made them as stubble, ones silent and stilled.²¹:¹⁵

And We created not the heavens and the earth and what is between them as ones in play.²¹:¹⁶ If We wanted We would have taken some diversion. We would take it to Ourselves from that which proceeds from Our Presence if We had been ones who do so.²¹:¹⁷

Nay! We hurl The Truth against falsehood so it prevails over it. That is when falsehood is that which vanishes away. And woe to you for what you allege.²¹:¹⁸

And to Him belongs whoever is in the heavens and the earth. And whoever is near Him, they grow not arrogant to worship Him, nor they be weary.²¹:¹⁹ They glorify Him nighttime and daytime. They never decrease.²¹:²⁰

Or took they gods to themselves from the earth, they, ones who revive the dead?²¹:²¹

If there had been gods in it—other than God—certainly, both would have gone to ruin. Then, glory be to God! Lord of the Throne! High above what they allege.²¹:²²

He will not be asked as to what He accomplishes, but they will be asked.²¹:²³

Or took they gods to themselves other than He?

Say: Prepare your proof. This is a Remembrance for him who is with me and a Remembrance of him before me. Nay! Most of them know not The Truth, so they are ones who turn aside.²¹:²⁴

And We sent not before thee any Messenger, but We reveal to him that there is no god but I, so worship Me.²¹:²⁵

And they said: The Merciful took to Himself a son. Glory be to Him! Nay! Honored servants!²¹:²⁶ They precede Him not in saying and they act by His command.²¹:²⁷ He knows what is in advance of them and what is behind them and they intercede not but for him with whom He was content. And they are dreading Him, ones who are apprehensive.²¹:²⁸

And whoever says of them: Truly, I am a god other than He, then, We will give recompense to him with hell. Thus, We give recompense to the ones who are unjust.²¹:²⁹

Consider not those who were ungrateful that the heavens and the earth had been interwoven and We unstitched them? And We made every living thing of water. Will they, then, not believe?²¹·³⁰

And We made firm mountains on the earth so that it should not vibrate with them. And We made in it ravines as ways, so that perhaps they will be truly guided.²¹·³¹

And We made heaven as a guarded roof. Yet they are ones who turn aside from its signs.²¹·³²

And it is He Who created the nighttime and the daytime, the sun and the moon, each swimming in orbit.²¹·³³

And We assigned not to any mortal before thee immortality. If thou wert to die will they be ones who dwell forever?²¹·³⁴ Every soul is one that experiences death. And We will try you with the worst and good as a test. And to Us you will be returned.²¹·³⁵

And when those who were ungrateful saw thee, they take thee to themselves not but in mockery:

Ha! Is this he who mentions your gods?

And they, for Remembrance of The Merciful, they are ones who are ungrateful.²¹·³⁶

The human being was created of haste. I will cause you to see My signs, so seek not to hasten!²¹·³⁷

And they say: When will this promise be if you had been ones who are sincere?²¹·³⁸

If those who were ungrateful but know at the time when they will not limit the fire from their faces, nor from their backs and they will not be helped!²¹·³⁹ Nay! It will approach them suddenly. Then, it will dumfound them so they will not be able to come back nor will they be given respite.²¹·⁴⁰

And, certainly, Messengers were ridiculed before thee. Then, those who derided them were surrounded by what they had been ridiculing.²¹·⁴¹

Say: Who will guard you in the nighttime and the daytime from The Merciful? Nay! They, from the Remembrance of their Lord, are ones who turn aside.²¹·⁴²

Or secure them their gods from Us? They are not able to help themselves, nor will they be rendered safe from Us.²¹·⁴³

Nay! We gave enjoyment to these, their fathers until their lifetime was long for them.

Consider they not that We approach the earth? We reduce it of its outlying parts. Or will they be the ones who are the victors?²¹·⁴⁴

Say: I warn you only by the revelation. But hear not the unwilling to hear, the calling to them when they are warned.²¹·⁴⁵

And if a breath afflicted them of punishment of thy Lord, they would, surely, say: O woe to us! Truly, we had been ones who are unjust.²¹·⁴⁶

And We will lay down the balances of equity on the Day of Resurrection. Then, no soul will be wronged at all. And even if it had been the weight of a grain of a mustard seed We will bring it. And We sufficed as Ones Who Reckon.²¹·⁴⁷

And, certainly, We gave Moses and Aaron the Criterion between right and wrong and an illumination and a Remembrance for the ones who are Godfearing,²¹·⁴⁸ those who dread their Lord in the unseen while they are ones who are apprehensive of the Hour. ²¹·⁴⁹ This is a blessed Remembrance We caused to descend. Are you, then, ones who know not of it?²¹·⁵⁰

Certainly, We gave Abraham his right judgment before. And We had been ones who know of him²¹·⁵¹ when he said to his father and his folk: What are these images to which you be ones who give yourselves up to?²¹·⁵²

They said: We found our fathers as ones who are worshippers of them.²¹·⁵³

He said: Certainly, you and your fathers had been in a clear wandering astray.²¹·⁵⁴

They said: Hadst thou drawn near The Truth or art thou of the ones who play?²¹·⁵⁵

He said: Nay! Your Lord is the Lord of the heavens and the earth, Who originated them. And I am of the ones who bear witness to this:²¹·⁵⁶ And by God, I will contrive against your idols after you turn as ones who draw back.²¹·⁵⁷

So he made them broken pieces—but the greatest of them—so that perhaps they will return to it.²¹·⁵⁸

They said: Who accomplished this with our gods? Truly, he is of the ones who are unjust!²¹·⁵⁹

They said: We heard a spiritual warrior (m) mention them. It is said he is Abraham.²¹·⁶⁰

They said: Then, approach with him before the eyes of personages so that perhaps they will bear witness.²¹·⁶¹

They said: Hast thou accomplished this with our gods O Abraham?²¹·⁶²

He said: Nay! It was accomplished by the greatest of them—this. So ask them if they had been able to speak for themselves.²¹·⁶³

Then, they returned to one another.

Then, they said: Truly, you, you are the ones who are unjust.²¹·⁶⁴

Again, they were put into confusion: Certainly, thou hadst known that these speak not for themselves!²¹·⁶⁵

He said: Worship you, then, other than God what neither profits you nor hurts you at all?²¹·⁶⁶ Fie on you on what you worship other than God. Will you not, then, be reasonable?²¹·⁶⁷

They said: Burn him and help your gods if you had been ones who do so!²¹·⁶⁸

We said: O fire! Be coolness and peace for Abraham!²¹·⁶⁹

And they wanted to use cunning against him, but We made them the ones who are losers.²¹·⁷⁰

And We delivered him and Lot to the region which We blessed for the worlds.²¹·⁷¹

And We bestowed Isaac on him and Jacob as an unexpected gift. And We made both of them ones in accord with morality.²¹·⁷² And We made them leaders, guiding by Our command. And We revealed to them the accomplishing of good deeds and the performing of the formal prayer and the giving of the purifying alms. And they had been ones who worship Us.²¹·⁷³

And to Lot We gave him critical judgment and knowledge and We delivered him from the town which had been doing deeds of corruption. Truly, they had been a reprehensible folk, ones who disobey.²¹·⁷⁴ And We caused him to enter into Our Mercy. Truly, he was among the ones in accord with morality.²¹·⁷⁵

And mention Noah, when he cried out before and We responded to him. And We delivered him and his people from the tremendous distress.²¹·⁷⁶ And We helped him against the folk who denied Our signs. Truly, they had been a reprehensible folk. So We drowned them one and all.²¹·⁷⁷

And mention David and Solomon, when they give judgment about cultivation when a herd of the sheep of his folk strayed. And to their critical judgment We had been ones who bear witness.²¹·⁷⁸

So We caused Solomon to understand it.

And We gave each of them critical judgment and knowledge. And We caused to become subservient to David, the mountains and the birds to glorify God. And We had been ones who do such things.²¹·⁷⁹ We taught him the art of making garments of chain mail for you to fortify you from your violence. Will you, then, be ones who are thankful?²¹·⁸⁰

And to Solomon, the wind tempest runs by His command toward the earth which We blessed. We had been ones who know everything.²¹·⁸¹

Among the satans are some who dive for him and do actions other than that. And We had been ones who guard over them.²¹:⁸²

And Job, when he cried out to his Lord: Truly, harm afflicted me and Thou art One Who is Most Merciful of the ones who are merciful.²¹:⁸³

So We responded to him. Then, We removed his harm. And We gave him back his people and the like of others with them as a mercy from Us and as a reminder of ones who worship.²¹:⁸⁴

And Ishmael and Enoch and Dhul-Kifl, all were of the ones who remain steadfast.²¹:⁸⁵ And We caused them to enter into Our mercy. They are the ones in accord with morality.²¹:⁸⁶

And Jonah, when he went as one who is enraged, and thought that We would never have power over him. And, then, he cried out through the shadows that: There is no god, but Thou! Glory be to Thee! Truly, I had been of the ones who are unjust.²¹:⁸⁷

So We responded to him. And We delivered him from the lament. And, thus, We rescue the ones who believe.²¹:⁸⁸

And mention Zechariah when he cried out to his Lord: My Lord! Forsake me not unassisted and Thou art Best of the ones who inherit.²¹:⁸⁹

So We responded to him and We bestowed Yahya on him. And We made things right for his spouse and for him. Truly, they had been competing with one another in good deeds and they would call to Us with yearning and reverence. And they had been ones who are humbled before Us.²¹:⁹⁰

And she who guarded her private parts, then, We breathed into her Our Spirit and We made her and her son a sign for the worlds.²¹:⁹¹

Truly, this, your community, is one community and I am your Lord so worship Me.²¹:⁹²

But they cut asunder their affair between them. Yet all of them are ones who return to Us.²¹:⁹³

So whoever does as the ones in accord with morality and he is one who believes, then, his endeavoring will not be rejected. And, truly, We will be One Who Inscribes it for him.²¹:⁹⁴

And there is a ban on the town that We caused to perish. They will not return²¹:⁹⁵ until Gog and Magog are let loose and they slide down from every slope.²¹:⁹⁶ And the true promise **will be** near.

That is when the sight will be that which fixed in horror of those who were ungrateful! O woe to us. Surely, we had been in heedlessness of this. Nay! We had been ones who were unjust.²¹:⁹⁷

Truly, you and what you worship other than God are fuel material for hell. You are the ones who go down to it.²¹:⁹⁸

If these had been gods, they would never have gone down to it.

All are ones who will dwell in it forever.²¹:⁹⁹

There will be sobbing in it for them and they, their gods, will not hear in it.²¹:¹⁰⁰

Truly, those to whom there has preceded the fairer from Us, those are ones who are far removed from it.²¹:¹⁰¹ They will not hear even the low sound of it. And they, in that for which their souls lusted, will be ones who will dwell in it forever.²¹:¹⁰² The greater terror will not dishearten them and the angels will admit them: This is your day that you had been promised!²¹:¹⁰³

On a Day when We roll up the heavens like the rolling up of the written scroll of manuscripts, as We began the first creation, We will cause it to return. It is a promise from Us. Truly, We had been ones who do.²¹:¹⁰⁴

And, certainly, We wrote down in the Psalms after the Remembrance that the earth will be inherited by My servants—the ones who are in accord with morality.²¹:¹⁰⁵

Truly, in this is the delivering of this message for the folk, ones who worship.²¹:¹⁰⁶

And We sent thee not but as a mercy for the worlds.²¹:¹⁰⁷

Say: It is only revealed to me that your god is One God. Will you, then, be ones who submit to God?²¹:¹⁰⁸

But if they turned away, then, say: I proclaimed to you all equally. And I am not informed whether what you are promised is near or far.²¹:¹⁰⁹ Truly, He knows the openly published saying and He knows what you keep back.²¹:¹¹⁰ And I am not informed so that perhaps it will be a test for you and an enjoyment for awhile.²¹:¹¹¹

He said: My Lord! Give Thou judgment between us with The Truth. And our Lord is The Merciful, He Whose help is being sought against what you allege.²¹:¹¹²

CHAPTER 22 THE PILGRIMAGE

In the Name of God, the Merciful the Compassionate

O humanity! Be Godfearing of your Lord. Truly, the earthquake of the Hour is a tremendous thing. On a Day you will see it,²²:¹ everyone who is breast feeding will be negligent of whoever she breast fed. And every pregnant woman will bring forth a foetus and thou wilt see humanity intoxicated yet they will not be intoxicated. But the punishment of God will be severe.²²:²

And among humanity is he who disputes about God without knowledge and follows every rebel satan.²²:³

It was written down about him that whoever turned away to him as a friend, truly, he will cause him to go astray and will guide him to the punishment of the blaze.²²:⁴

O humanity! If you had been in doubt about the Uprising, truly, We created you from earth dust and, again, from seminal fluid and, again, from a clot and, again, from tissue that was formed and that was not formed so that We make it manifest to you. We establish in the wombs whom We will for a term, that which is determined. And, again, We bring you out as infant children and, again, you may reach the coming of age. And among you there is he whom death will call to itself. And among you there is he who is returned to the most wretched lifetime so that he knows not anything after some knowledge.

And thou hast seen the earth as that which is lifeless. Yet when We caused water to descend on it, it quivered and it swelled and put forth every lovely pair.²²:⁵ That is because God, He is The Truth, and it is He Who gives life to the dead and He is Powerful over everything.²²:⁶

And, truly, the Hour is that which arrives. There is no doubt about it and that God will raise up whoever is in the graves.²²:⁷

And among humanity is such a one who disputes about God without knowledge nor guidance nor an illuminating Book,²²:⁸ turning to his side as one who turns away to cause to go astray from the way of God. For him in the present is degradation. And We will cause him to experience—on the Day of Resurrection—the punishment of the burning.²²:⁹ That is because of what thy two hands put forward! And, truly, God is not unjust to His servants.²²:¹⁰

And among humanity is he who worships God on the fringes. If good lit on him, he is at rest with it. And if a test lit on him, he turned completely about. He lost the present and the world to come. That, it is the clear loss.²²:¹¹

He calls to other than God what neither hurts him nor profits him. That it is a far wandering astray.²²:¹² He calls to him whose hurting is nearer than his profiting. Miserable was the defender and miserable was the acquaintance.²²:¹³

Truly, God will cause to enter those who have believed and did as the ones accord with morality, Gardens beneath which rivers run. Truly, God accomplishes what He wants.²²:¹⁴

Whoever had been thinking that God will never help him, in the present and in the world to come, let him stretch out a cord to heaven. Again, let him sever it. Then, let him look on whether his cunning causes to put away what enrages him.²²:¹⁵

And, thus, We caused signs to descend, clear portents. And that God guides whom He wants.²²:¹⁶

Truly, those who believed and those who became Jews and the Sabeans and the Christians and the Zoroastrians and those who ascribed partners—truly, God will distinguish between them on the Day of Resurrection. Truly, God over everything is a Witness.²²:¹⁷

Hast thou not considered that to God prostrates to Him whoever is in the heavens and whoever is in and on the earth and the sun and the moon and the stars, the mountains, the trees and the moving creatures, and many of humanity while there are many on whom the punishment will be realized. And He whom God despises, then, there is no one who honors him. Truly, God accomplishes whatever He wills.²²:¹⁸

These two disputants strove against one another about their Lord. Then, for those who were ungrateful garments of fire will be cut out for them. Over their heads, scalding water will be unloosed²²:¹⁹ whereby what is in their bellies will be dissolved and their skins.²²:²⁰

And for them are maces of iron.²²:²¹ Whenever they wanted to go forth from there because of lament, they will be caused to return to it and experience the punishment of the burning.²²:²²

Truly, God will cause to enter those who believed and did as ones in accord with morality, Gardens beneath which rivers run. They are adorned in them with bracelets of gold and pearls. And their garments in it will be of silk.²²:²³

And they were guided to what is good of the saying and they were guided to the Path of Him Who is Worthy of Praise.²²:²⁴

Truly, those who were ungrateful and bar from the way of God and from the Masjid al-Haram that We made for humanity—equal for the ones who give themselves up and the ones who are desert dwellers—and whoever wants to violate it with injustice, We will cause him to experience a painful punishment.²²:²⁵

And mention when We placed Abraham in the place of the House that: Thou wilt ascribe nothing as partners with Me. And Thou purify My House for the ones who circumambulate it and the ones who are standing up, and the ones who bow down and the ones who prostrate themselves.²²:²⁶

Announce to humanity the pilgrimage to Makkah. They will approach thee on foot and on every thin camel. They will approach from every deep ravine²²:²⁷ that they bear witness to what profits them and remember the Name of God on known days over whatever He provided them from flocks of animals. Then, eat of it and feed the ones who are in misery and the poor.²²:²⁸

Again, let them finish their ritual cleanliness and live up to their vows and circumambulate the Ancient House.²²:²⁹

That was commanded! Whoever holds the sacred things of God in honor, then, that is better for him with his Lord.

And permitted to you were the flocks, but what will be recounted to you. So avoid the disgrace of graven images and avoid saying the untruth.²²:³⁰

Turn to God as monotheists not with Him as ones who are polytheists. And whoever ascribes partners with God, it is as if he fell down from heaven and the birds snatch him or the wind hurled him to ruin in a place far away.²²:³¹

That was commanded! Whoever holds the waymarks of God in honor, then, it is, truly, from hearts filled with God-consciousness.²²:³²

For you in that is what profits for a term, that which is determined. Again, their place of sacrifice is at the Ancient House.²²:³³

And for every community We assigned devotional acts that they may remember the Name of God over what We provided them of flocks of animals. And your God is One God. Submit to Him, and give thou good tidings to the ones who humble themselves,²²:³⁴ those who, when God was remembered, their hearts took notice and the ones who remain steadfast against whatever lit on them and the ones who perform the formal prayer and who spends out of what We provided them.²²:³⁵

We made for you the beasts of sacrifice among the way-marks of God. You have in them much good so remember the Name of God over them, ones who are standing in ranks. Then, when they collapsed on their sides, eat from them and feed the ones who are paupers and the ones who are poor persons who beg not. Thus, We caused them to be subservient to you so that perhaps you will give thanks.²²:³⁶

Neither their flesh nor their blood attains to God, rather, God-consciousness from you attains Him. Thus, He caused them to be subservient to you that you magnify God in that He guided you. And give thou good tidings to the ones who are doers of good.²²:³⁷ Truly, God defends those who believed. Truly, God loves not any who is an ungrateful betrayer.²²:³⁸

Permission was given to those who are fought against because they, they were wronged. And, truly, Powerful is God to help them,²²:³⁹ those who were driven out from their abodes without right because they say: Our Lord is God! If not for God driving back humanity, some by some other, cloisters would be demolished and churches and synagogues and mosques in which is remembered in it the Name of God frequently.

Truly, God will help whoever helps Him. Truly, God is Strong, Almighty.²²:⁴⁰

Those who, if We established them firmly on the earth, they performed the formal prayer and they gave the purifying alms and they commanded to that which is honorable and they prohibited that which is unlawful. And with God is the Ultimate End of the command.²²:⁴¹

And if they deny thee, surely, the folk of Noah denied before thee and Ad and Thamud²²:⁴² and the folk of Abraham and the folk of Lot²²:⁴³ and the companions of Midian. And Moses was denied, but I granted indulgence to the ones who are ungrateful. Again, I took them and how had been My disapproval!²²:⁴⁴

And how many a town We caused to perish while they are ones who are unjust so that it be one that had fallen down in ruins and how much well water ignored and a tall palace!²²:⁴⁵

Journey they not through the earth? Have they not hearts with which to be reasonable or ears with which to hear? Truly, it is not their sight that is in darkness, but their hearts that are within their breasts that are in darkness!²²:⁴⁶

And seek they that then hasten the punishment? And God never breaks His Promise. And, truly, a day with thy Lord is as a thousand years of what you number.²²:⁴⁷

How many a town I granted indulgence while it is one that is unjust. Again, I took it and to Me was the Homecoming.²²:⁴⁸

Say: O humanity! Truly, I am only a clear warner to you.²²:⁴⁹ So those who believed and did as ones in accord with morality, for them is forgiveness and a generous provision.²²:⁵⁰

And those who endeavored against Our signs, ones who strive to thwart, those are the Companions of Hellfire.²²:⁵¹

And We sent not before thee any Messenger nor Prophet, but when he fantasized, Satan cast fantasies into him. But

God nullifies what Satan casts. Again, God set clear His signs. And God is Knowing, Wise,²²:⁵² for He makes what Satan casts a test for those who in their hearts is a sickness and their hearts, ones that harden. And, truly, the ones who are unjust are in a wide breach.²²:⁵³

And those who were given the knowledge know that it is The Truth from thy Lord, so that they believe in it and humble their hearts to Him. And, truly, God is One Who Guides those who believed to a straight path.²²:⁵⁴

And those who were ungrateful cease not to be hesitant about it until the Hour approaches them suddenly or the punishment approaches them on a withering Day.²²:⁵⁵ On that Day the dominion will belong to God. He will give judgment between them. So those who believed and did as the ones accord with morality will be in Gardens of Bliss.²²:⁵⁶ And those who were ungrateful and denied Our signs, for them will be a despised punishment.²²:⁵⁷

And those who emigrated in the way of God, then, they were slain or died, certainly, God will provide them a fairer provision. And, truly, God, certainly, He is Best of the ones who provide.²²:⁵⁸ Certainly, He will cause them to enter a gate with which they will be well-pleased. And, truly, God is, certainly, Knowing, Forbearing.²²:⁵⁹

That is so! And whoever chastises for injustice with the like of what he was chastised, and, again, suffered an injustice, God will, certainly, help him. Truly, God is Pardoning, Forgiving.²²:⁶⁰

That is because God causes the nighttime to be interposed into the daytime and He causes the daytime to be interposed into the nighttime. And, truly, God is Hearing, Seeing.²²:⁶¹ That is because God, He is The Truth. And what they call to other than Him, it is falsehood. And that God, He is The Lofty, The Great.²²:⁶²

Hast thou not considered that God caused water to descend from heaven? Then, in the morning, the earth becomes green. Truly, God is Subtle, Aware.²²:⁶³

To Him belongs whatever is in the heavens and whatever is in and on the earth. And, truly, God, He is The Sufficient, The Worthy of Praise.²²:⁶⁴

Hast thou not considered that God caused to be subservient to you what is in and on the earth?

And the boats run through the sea by His command. And He holds back the heaven so that it not fall on the earth, but by His permission. Truly, to humanity God is Gentle, Compassionate.²²:⁶⁵

And it is He Who gave you life and, again, He will cause you to die and, again, He will give you life. Truly, the human being is ungrateful.²²:⁶⁶

For every community We assigned devotional acts so that they be ones who perform rites. So let them not bicker with thee in the command. And call thou to thy Lord. Truly, Thou art on a guidance, that which is straight.²²:⁶⁷

And if they disputed with thee, then, thou say: God is greater in knowledge about what you do.²²:⁶⁸ God will give judgment among you on the Day of Resurrection about what you had been at variance in it.²²:⁶⁹

Hast thou not known that God knows what is in the heaven and the earth? Truly, that is in a Book. Truly, that is easy for God.²²:⁷⁰ And they worship other than God, that for which He sent not down any authority and of what they have no knowledge. And there is no helper for the ones who are unjust.²²:⁷¹ And when Our signs are recounted to them, clear portents, thou wilt recognize on the faces of those who were ungrateful, that they are the ones who are rejected. They are about to rush upon those who recount Our signs to them. Say: Shall I tell you of worse than that? God promised the fire to those who were ungrateful. And miserable will be the Homecoming!²²:⁷²

O humanity! A parable was propounded, so listen to it. Truly, those whom you call to other than God will never create a fly, even if they were gathered together for it. And when the fly is to rob them of something, they would never seek to deliver it from the fly. Weak were the ones who are seekers and the ones who are sought.²²:⁷³ They duly measured not the measure of God. Truly, God is Strong, Almighty.²²:⁷⁴

God favors from the angels messengers and from humanity. Truly, God is Hearing, Seeing.²²:⁷⁵

He knows what is in advance of them, and what is behind them, and to God all matters are returned.²²:⁷⁶

O those who believed! Bow down and prostrate yourselves, and worship your Lord, and accomplish good so that perhaps you will prosper.²²:⁷⁷

And struggle for God in a true struggling. He elected you and made not for you in your way of life any impediment. It is the creed of your father Abraham. He named you the ones who submit to God before and in this Recitation that the Messenger be a witness over you and you you are witnesses over humanity. So perform the formal prayer and give the purifying alms and cleave firmly to God. He is your Defender. How excellent a Defender and how excellent a Helper!²²:⁷⁸

CHAPTER 23 THE BELIEVERS

In the Name of God, The Merciful, The Compassionate

Surely, the ones who believe prospered,²³:¹ those, they, who in their formal prayers are ones who are humble²³:² and they, those who from idle talk, are ones who turn aside²³:³ and they, those who the purifying alms are ones who do give²³:⁴ and they, those who of their private parts, are ones who guard,²³:⁵ but from their spouses or from what their right hands possessed. Truly, they are ones who are irreproachable.²³:⁶

Whoever was looking for something beyond that, then, those, they are the ones who turn away.²³:⁷ And those, they who their trusts and their compacts are ones who shepherd²³:⁸ and those, they who over their formal prayers are watchful,²³:⁹ those, they are ones who will inherit,²³:¹⁰ those who will inherit Paradise, they are ones who will dwell in it forever.²³:¹¹

And, certainly, We created the human being from an extraction of clay.²³:¹² Again, We made him into seminal fluid in a stopping place, secure.²³:¹³ Again, We created a clot from seminal fluids. Then, We created tissue from the clot. Then, We created bones from tissue. Then, We clothed the bones with flesh. Again, We caused another creation to grow. So blessed be God, the Fairer of the ones who are creators!²³:¹⁴

Again, truly, after that, you will die.²³:¹⁵ Again, truly, you will be raised up on the Day of Resurrection.²³:¹⁶

Certainly, We created above you seven tiers. We had not been ones who are heedless of the creation.²³:¹⁷

We caused water to descend from heaven in measure and We ceased it to dwell in the earth. And We certainly are ones who have power to take away.²³:¹⁸

And We caused to grow for you gardens of date palm trees and grapevines where there is much sweet fruit for you and you eat of it²³:¹⁹ and a tree that goes forth from Mount Sinai that bears oil and a seasoning for the ones who eat it.²³:²⁰

And, truly, for you in the flocks there is a lesson. We satiate you with what is in their bellies. In them are many profits and of them you eat²³:²¹ and on them and on boats you are carried.²³:²²

And, certainly, We sent Noah to his folk. And he said: O my folk! Worship God! You have no other god but Him. Will you not, then, be Godfearing?²³:²³

But said the Council who were ungrateful among his folk: This is nothing but a mortal like you. He wants to gain superiority over you.²³:²⁴ If God willed He would have caused angels to descend. We heard not such a thing from our fathers, the ancient ones.²³·²⁵ He is nothing but a man in whom there is madness. So watch him for awhile.²³·²⁶

He said: My Lord! Help me because they denied me.²³·²⁶

So We revealed to him: Craft thou the boat under Our eyes and by Our revelation. Then, when Our command drew near and the oven boiled, then, insert two pairs of each kind and thy people, but whomever against whom the saying has preceded. And address Me not for those who did wrong. Truly, they are ones who are drowned.²³·²⁷

When thou and whoever is with thee art seated in the boat, then, say: All Praise belongs to God Who delivered us from the folk, the ones who are unjust.²³·²⁸

And say: My Lord! Land Thou me with a blessed landing for Thou art Best of the landing-places.²³·²⁹ Truly, in this there are signs and, truly, We had been ones who test.²³·³⁰

Again, We caused to grow another generation after them.²³·³¹ We sent a Messenger to them from among them saying that: Worship God! You have no god other than Him. Will you, then, not be Godfearing?²³·³²

And said the Council of his folk to those who were ungrateful and denied the meeting in the world to come, and to whom We gave ease in this present life: This is nothing but a mortal like you. He eats of what you eat and he drinks of what you drink.²³·³³ And if you obeyed a mortal like yourselves, truly, then, you are ones who are losers.²³·³⁴ Promises He that when you died and had been earth dust and bones, that you will be ones who are brought out?²³·³⁵ Begone! Begone with what you are promised!²³·³⁶ There is nothing but this present life. We die and we live and we shall not be ones who are raised up.²³·³⁷ He is nothing but a man. He devised a lie against God and we are not ones who will believe in him.²³·³⁸

He said: My Lord! Help me because they denied me.²³·³⁹

He said: In a little while they will become ones who are remorseful.²³·⁴⁰

Then, a Cry duly took them so We made them into refuse. So away with the folk, the ones who are unjust!²³·⁴¹

Again, We caused to grow after them other generations.²³·⁴² No community precedes its term, nor delays it.²³·⁴³ Again, We sent Our Messengers one after another.

Whenever drew near a community a Messenger to them, they denied him. So We caused some of them to pursue others and We made them tales. So away with the folk who believe not!²³·⁴⁴

Again, We sent Moses and his brother Aaron with Our signs and clear authority²³·⁴⁵ to Pharaoh and his Council. Then, they grew arrogant and they had been a folk, ones who exalt themselves.²³·⁴⁶

Then, they said: Will we believe in two mortals like ourselves while their folk are ones who worship us?²³·⁴⁷

So they denied both of them. They had been among the ones who are caused to perish.²³·⁴⁸

And, certainly, We gave Moses the Book so that perhaps they will be truly guided.²³·⁴⁹

And We made the son of Mary and his mother a sign, and We gave them refuge on a hillside, a stopping place, and a spring of water.²³·⁵⁰

O you Messengers! Eat of what is good and do as one in accord with morality. Truly, I am Knowing of what you do.²³·⁵¹

And, truly, this, your community is one community and I am your Lord so be Godfearing.²³·⁵²

Then, they cut their affair of unity asunder into sects among them, each party glad with what was with them.²³·⁵³ So forsake thou them for awhile in their obstinacy.²³·⁵⁴

Assume they that with the relief We furnish them of wealth and children²³·⁵⁵ We compete for good deeds for them? Nay! They are not aware.²³·⁵⁶

Truly, those, they are dreading their Lord, ones who are apprehensive.²³·⁵⁷ And those, they who believe in the signs of their Lord²³·⁵⁸ and those, they who ascribe nothing as partners with their Lord,²³·⁵⁹ and those who give what they gave with their hearts afraid because they are ones who will return to their Lord,²³·⁶⁰ are those who compete with one another in good deeds and they, in them, are ones who take the lead.²³·⁶¹

And We place not a burden on any soul but to its capacity. And from Us is a Book that speaks The Truth for itself. And they will not be wronged.²³·⁶²

Nay! Their hearts are in obstinacy towards this Quran and they have other actions besides as they are ones who act²³·⁶³ until, when We took ones who are given ease with the punishment. That is when they make entreaties.²³·⁶⁴

Make not entreaties this Day. Truly, you will not be helped from Us.²³·⁶⁵

Surely, My signs had been recounted to you, but you had been receding on your heels²³·⁶⁶ as ones who grow arrogant regarding it and ones who nightly talk nonsense, talking foolishly.²³·⁶⁷

Meditate they not on the saying or drew not near them anything that approaches not their fathers, the ancient ones?²³·⁶⁸

Or is it they recognize not their Messenger so that they are ones who reject him?²³·⁶⁹

Or say they: There is madness in him?

Nay! He drew near them with The Truth, but most of them are ones who dislike The Truth.²³·⁷⁰ And if The Truth followed their desires, the heavens and the earth would have gone to ruin and whoever is in it.

Nay! We brought them their Remembrance, but they, from their Remembrance, are ones who turn aside.²³·⁷¹

Or is it that thou hast asked them for payment?

Yet the revenue from thy Lord is better. And He is Best of the ones who provide.²³·⁷²

And, truly, thou hast called them to a straight path.²³·⁷³

And, truly, those who believe not in the world to come are ones who move away from the path.²³·⁷⁴ And even if We had mercy on them and removed the harm which is on them, they would still be resolute in their defiance, wandering unwilling to see.²³·⁷⁵ And, certainly, We took them with the punishment. Then, they gave not into their Lord nor lower themselves²³·⁷⁶ until, when we opened a door for them of a severe punishment. That is when they were ones who are seized with despair!²³·⁷⁷

And He it is Who caused you to grow, have the ability to hear and sight and mind. But you give little thanks!²³·⁷⁸

It is He Who made you numerous on the earth and to Him you will be assembled.²³·⁷⁹ And it is He Who gives life and causes to die and His is the alteration of nighttime and daytime. Will you not, then, be reasonable?²³·⁸⁰

Nay! They said the like of what the ancient ones said.²³·⁸¹

They said: When we are dead and had been earth dust and bones, will we be ones who are raised up?²³·⁸² Certainly, we were promised this—we and our fathers—before this. This is nothing but the fables of the ancient ones.²³·⁸³

Say: To whom belongs the earth and whoever is in it if you had been knowing?²³·⁸⁴

They will say: To God!

Say: Then, will you not recollect?²³·⁸⁵

Say: Who is the Lord of the seven heavens and Lord of the Sublime Throne?²³·⁸⁶

They will say: It belongs to God!

Say: Then, will you not be Godfearing?²³·⁸⁷

Say: In whose hand is the kingdom of everything and He grants protection? No one is granted protection against Him if you had been knowing.²³·⁸⁸

They will say: It belongs to God! Say: How, then, are you under a spell!²³:⁸⁹

Nay! We brought them The Truth and, truly, they are ones who lie.²³:⁹⁰

God took not to Himself any son, nor had there been any god with Him. For, then, each god would have taken away what he created. And some of them would have ascended over some others. Glory be to God above all that they allege!²³:⁹¹

He is the One Who Knows the unseen and the visible. Exalted be He above partners they ascribe.²³:⁹²

Say: My Lord! If Thou wilt cause me to see what they are promised,²³:⁹³ then, assign me not, my Lord, to the folk, the ones who are unjust.²³:⁹⁴

And, truly, We cause thee to see what We promise them as certainly ones who have power.²³:⁹⁵ Drive thou back evil deeds with what is fairer. We are greater in knowledge of what they allege.²³:⁹⁶

And say: My Lord! I take refuge with Thee from the evil suggestions of the satans.²³:⁹⁷ And my Lord, I take refuge with Thee so that they not attend me.²³:⁹⁸

Until when death drew near one of them, he said: My Lord! Return me²³:⁹⁹ so that perhaps I will do as one in accord with morality in what I left behind.

No indeed! Truly, it is only a word that one who converses says.

And ahead of them is a barrier until the Day they are raised up.²³:¹⁰⁰

When the trumpet will be blown, there will be no talk of kindred among them that Day nor will they demand anything of one another.²³:¹⁰¹

Then, whose balance was heavy with good deeds, those, they are the ones who prosper.²³:¹⁰²

And among ones whose balance was made light, then, those are those who lost themselves. They will be ones who will dwell in hell forever.²³:¹⁰³ Their faces will fry in the fire. And they will be ones who are morose in it.²³:¹⁰⁴

Be not My signs recounted to you, yet you had been denying them?²³:¹⁰⁵

They will say: Our Lord! Our misgiving prevailed over us. We had been a folk, ones who go astray.²³:¹⁰⁶ Our Lord! Bring us out of this. Then, if ever we reverted, truly, we will be ones who are unjust.²³:¹⁰⁷

He would say: Be driven away in it and speak not to Me.²³:¹⁰⁸

Truly, there had been a group of people of My servants who say: Our Lord! We believed, so forgive us and have mercy on us for Thou art Best of the ones who are most merciful.²³:¹⁰⁹

But you took them to yourselves as a laughing-stock until they caused you to forget My Remembrance and you had been laughing at them.²³:¹¹⁰

Truly, I gave recompense this Day for what they endured patiently. Truly, they, they are the ones who are victorious!²³:¹¹¹

He said: Lingered you in expectation on the earth for what number of years?²³:¹¹²

They said: We lingered in expectation a day or some of a day. So ask the ones who count.²³:¹¹³

He said: You lingered in expectation not but a little. If you had but been knowing.²³:¹¹⁴

Assumed you that We created you in amusement and that to Us you would not be returned?²³:¹¹⁵

So exalted be God! The King, The Truth. There is no god but He, the Lord of the Generous Throne!²³:¹¹⁶

And whoever calls to another god with God of which he has no proof, then, truly, his reckoning is with his Lord. Truly, the ones who are ungrateful will not prosper.²³:¹¹⁷

And say: My Lord! Forgive and have mercy and Thou art Best of the ones who are most merciful.²³:¹¹⁸

CHAPTER 24 THE LIGHT

In the Name of God, The Merciful, The Compassionate

This is a chapter of the Quran that We caused to descend and We imposed laws in it. We caused to descend signs, clear portents, so that perhaps you will recollect.²⁴:¹

The one who is an adulteress and the one who is an adulterer, scourge each one of them one hundred strokes. And let not tenderness for them take you from the judgment of God, if you had been believing in God and the Last Day. And let them bear witness to their punishment by a section of the ones who believe.²⁴:²

The one who is an adulterer will not marry but one who is an adulteress, or one who is a female polytheist. And the one who is an adulteress will not marry but one who is an adulterer, or one who is a male polytheist. All that was forbidden to the ones who believe.²⁴:³

And those who accuse the ones who are free, chaste (f) and, again, bring not four witnesses, then, scourge them eighty strokes and never accept their testimony. And those, they are the ones who disobey.²⁴:⁴

But those who repented after that and made things right, so, truly, God is Forgiving, Compassionate.²⁴:⁵

And those who accuse their spouses—and there be no witnesses but themselves—let the testimony of one of them be four testimonies sworn to God that he is among the ones who are sincere²⁴:⁶ and a fifth that the curse of God be on him, if he had been among the ones who lie.²⁴:⁷

And it will drive off the punishment from her if she bears witness with four testimonies sworn to God that he is among the ones who lie ²⁴:⁸ and the fifth, that the anger of God be on her if he had been among the ones who are sincere.²⁴:⁹

And if it were not for the grace of God on you and His mercy and that God is Accepter of Repentance, Wise—²⁴:¹⁰

truly, those who drew near with the calumny are many among you. Assume it not worse for you. Nay! It is good for you. To every man of them is what he deserved of sin. And as for those who turned away towards the greater part from among them, there will be a tremendous punishment for him.²⁴:¹¹

Why not when you heard about it, thought not the ones who are male believers and the ones who are female believers the better of themselves and have said: This is a clear calumny?²⁴:¹²

Why brought they not about four witnesses for it? As they bring not about witnesses, then, with God, those, they are the ones who lie.²⁴:¹³

If it not were for the grace of God on you and His mercy in the present and in the world to come, certainly, would have afflicted you a tremendous punishment for what you muttered.²⁴:¹⁴

When you received it on your tongues and said with your mouths of what there is no knowledge, you assume it insignificant while it is serious with God.²⁴:¹⁵

And why, when you heard it, said you not: It will not be for us to assert this. Glory be to Thee! This is a serious false charge to harm the reputation of another.²⁴:¹⁶

God admonishes you that you shall never revert to the like of it, if you had been ones who believe.²⁴:¹⁷

And He makes manifest for you the signs. And God is Knowing, Wise.²⁴:¹⁸

Truly, those who love that indecency be spread about those who believed, they will have a painful punishment in the present and in the world to come. And God knows and you know not.²⁴:¹⁹

And if it were not for the grace of God on you and His mercy, you would be ruined, and that God is Gentle, Compassionate.²⁴:²⁰

O those who believed! Follow not in the steps of Satan. And whoever follows in the steps of Satan, then, truly, he commands depravity, and that which is unlawful. And if it were not for the grace of God on you and His mercy, none of you would ever be pure in heart, but God makes pure whom He wills. And God is Hearing, Knowing.24:21

Let those imbued with grace not forswear—and those with plenty among you—to give to those imbued with kinship and to the needy and the ones who emigrate in the way of God. And let them pardon and let them overlook. Love you not that God should forgive you? And God is Forgiving, Compassionate.24:22

Truly, those who accuse the ones who are free, unwary, chaste female believers were cursed in the present and the world to come and for them will be a serious punishment24:23 on a Day when their tongues bear witness against them and their hands and their feet as to what they had been doing.24:24

On that Day God will pay them their account in full, what is their just due. And they will know that God, He is The Clear Truth.24:25

The bad females are for the bad males and the bad males are for the bad females. And who are good females are for who are good males and who are good males are for who are good females. Those are ones declared innocent of what others say. For them is forgiveness and generous provision.24:26

O those who believed! Enter not houses other than your houses until you announced your presence and greeted the people within. That is better for you so that perhaps you will recollect.24:27

And if you find not in it anyone, then, enter them not until permission be given to you. And if it was said to you: Return, then, return. It is purer for you. And God is Knowing of what you do.24:28

There is no blame on you in entering houses without ones who are inhabitants wherein you have enjoyment. And God knows what you show and what you keep back.24:29

Say to the males, ones who believe, to lower their sight and keep their private parts safe. That is purer for them. Truly God is Aware of what they craft.24:30

And say to the females, ones who believe to lower their (f) sight and keep their (f) private parts safe and show not their (f) adornment but what is manifest of it. And let them (f) draw their head coverings over their (f) bosoms; and not show their (f) adornment but to their (f) husbands or their (f) fathers or the fathers of their (f) husbands or their sons or the sons of their (f) husbands or their (f) brothers or the sons of their (f) brothers or the sons of their (f) sisters or their (f) women, or what their (f) right hands possessed, or the ones who heed, imbued with no sexual desire among the men or small male children to whom was not manifest nakedness of women. And let them (f) not stomp their feet so as to be known what they (f) conceal of their adornment. And turn to God altogether for forgiveness. O the ones who believe, so that perhaps you will prosper.24:31

And wed the single among you to the ones in accord with morality of your male bond servants and your female bond servants. If they be poor, God will enrich them of His grace. And God is One Who is Extensive, Knowing.24:32

Let those who find not the means for marriage have restraint until God enriches them of His grace.

And for those who are looking for emancipation from among what your right hands possessed, contract with them if you knew good in them. And give them of the wealth of God which He gave you.

Compel not your spiritual warriors (f) against their will to prostitution when they (f) wanted chastity, that you be looking for the advantage of this present life. And whoever

compels them (f) to it against their (f) will, yet after their (f) compulsion, God will be of them (f), the female, Forgiving, Compassionate.24:33

And, certainly, We caused to descend to you manifest signs and a parable of those who passed away before you and an admonishment for ones who are Godfearing.24:34

God is the Light of the heavens and the earth. The parable of His Light is as a niche in which there is a lamp. The lamp is in a glass. The glass is as if it had been a glittering star, kindled from a blessed olive tree, neither eastern nor western, whose oil of the olive is about to illuminate although no fire touches it. Light on light, God guides to His Light whom He wills! And God propounds parables for humanity, and God is Knowing of everything.24:35 The Light is lit in houses God gave permission to be lifted up and that His Name be remembered in it.

Glorifying Him at the first part of the day and the eventide24:36 are men whom neither trade nor trading diverts from the remembrance of God and the performing the formal prayer and the giving of purifying alms for they fear a Day when the hearts will go to and fro and their sight,24:37 that God gives recompense to them according to the fairer of what they did and increases even more for them from His grace. And God provides to whom He wills without reckoning.24:38

As for those who were ungrateful, their actions are like a mirage in a spacious plain. The thirsty one assumes it to be water until he drew near it. He finds it to be nothing. Instead, he found God with him Who paid his account in full, reckoning and God is Swift at reckoning.24:39

Or they are like the shadows in an obscure sea, overcome by a wave, above which is a wave, above which are clouds, shadows, some above some others. When he brought out his hand he almost sees it not. And whomever God assigns no light for him, there is no light for him.24:40

Hast thou not considered that glorifies God whatever is in the heavens and the earth and the birds, ones standing in ranks? Each knew its formal prayer and its glorification. And God is Knowing of what they accomplish.24:41

And to God belongs the dominion of the heavens and the earth. And to God is the Homecoming.24:42

Hast thou not considered how God propels clouds and, again, brings what is between them together?

Again, He lays them into a heap. Thou hast seen the rain drops go forth in the midst. And He sends down from the heaven mountains of rain in which there is hail.

And He lights it on whom He wills and turns away from it whom He wills. The gleams of His lightning almost take away the sight.24:43

God turns around and around the nighttime and the daytime. Truly, in this is a lesson for those imbued with insight.24:44

God created every moving creature from water. Among them there is what walks on its belly and of them there is what walks on two feet and of them there is what walks on four. God creates what He wills. Truly, God is Powerful over everything.24:45

Certainly, We caused manifest signs to descend. And God guides whom He wills to a straight path.24:46

And they say: We believed in God and the Messenger, and we obeyed. Again, a group of people among them turn away after this. And those are not of the ones who believe.24:47

And when they were called to God and His Messenger to give judgment among them, then, a group of people among them are ones who turn aside.24:48 But if they would be in the right, they would approach him as ones who are yielding.24:49

Is there a sickness in their hearts? Or were they in doubt? Or be they fearful that God and His Messenger will be unjust to them? Nay! Those, they are the ones who are unjust.24:50

The only saying of the ones who believe had been—when they were called to God and His Messenger that He give judgment between them—to say: We heard and obeyed. And those, they are the ones who prosper.²⁴:⁵¹

And whoever obeys God and His Messenger and dreads God and is Godfearing, those, they are the ones who are victorious.²⁴:⁵²

And they swore by God their most earnest oaths that if thou wouldst command them, they would go forth.

Say: Swear not; honorable obedience is better. Truly God is Aware of what you do.²⁴:⁵³

Say: Obey God and obey the Messenger. But if you turn away, then, on him was only what was loaded on him, and on you was only what was loaded on you. And if you obey him, you will be truly guided. And there is not a duty on the Messenger but the delivering of the clear message.²⁴:⁵⁴

God promised those who have believed among you and did as the ones in accord with morality, that He will make them successors in the earth, even as He made of those before them successors and He will establish for them their way of life firmly by which He was content with them and He will substitute a place of sanctuary in place of their fear: They shall worship Me—ascribe nothing as partners with Me.

And whoever was ungrateful after that, then, those, they are the ones who disobey.²⁴:⁵⁵

And perform the formal prayer and give the purifying alms and obey the Messenger so that perhaps you will find mercy.²⁴:⁵⁶

Assume not those who were ungrateful that they are ones who will frustrate Him in the region. Their place of shelter will be the fire and how miserable the Homecoming!²⁴:⁵⁷

O those who believed! Let them ask permission—those whom your right hands possessed (f) and those who reach not puberty—three times: Before the dawn formal prayer, when you lay down your garments at the time of noon and after the time of night formal prayer. These are the three times of privacy for you. There is not on you nor on them blame after these. Other than these, go about some of you with some others. Thus, God makes manifest to you the signs. And God is Knowing, Wise.²⁴:⁵⁸

When infant children were fully grown among you, then, let them ask permission as asked permission those who were before them. Thus, God makes manifest for you His signs. And God is Knowing, Wise.²⁴:⁵⁹

And women who are past child-bearing, those who hope not for marriage, there is no blame on them (f) if they lay down their (f) garments, not as ones who flaunt themselves and their (f) adornment. And that they have restraint is better for them (f), and God is Hearing, Knowing.²⁴:⁶⁰

There is no fault on the blind nor fault on the lame nor fault on the sick nor on yourselves that you eat from your houses or the houses of your fathers or the houses of your mothers or the houses of your brothers or the houses of your sisters or the houses of your paternal uncles or the houses of your paternal aunts or the houses of your maternal uncles or the houses of your maternal aunts or of that for which you possess its keys or your ardent friend.

There is no blame on you that you eat altogether or separately. But when you entered houses, then, greet one another with a greeting from God, one that is blessed and what is good. Thus, God makes manifest for you the signs so that perhaps you will be reasonable.²⁴:⁶¹

The ones who believe are only those who believe in God and His Messenger. And when they had been with him on a collective matter, they go not until they asked his permission. Truly, those who ask thy permission, those are those who believed in God and His Messenger. So when they ask thy permission for some of their affairs, give permission to whom thou hadst willed of them, and ask God for forgiveness for them. Truly, God is Forgiving, Compassionate.²⁴:⁶²

The supplication of the Messenger among you is not as the supplication of some of you on some other. Surely, God knows those who slip away under cover.

And let those who go against his command beware so that a test should not light on them or a painful punishment not light on them.²⁴:⁶³

Surely, to God belongs whatever is in the heavens and the earth. Surely, He knows what you did. And on the Day when they are returned to Him, then, He will tell them what their hands did, and God is Knowing of everything.²⁴:⁶⁴

CHAPTER 25 THE CRITERION

In the Name of God, The Merciful, The Compassionate

Blessed be He Who sent down the Criterion between right and wrong to His servant so that he be a warner to the worlds,²⁵:¹ He to Whom belongs the dominion of the heavens and the earth, and Who takes not to Himself a son.

There be no ascribed associate with Him in the dominion. And He created everything and ordained it a foreordaining.²⁵:²

Yet they took gods to themselves other than Him who create nothing and are themselves created. And they neither possess for themselves hurt nor profit nor have they dominion over death, nor this life, nor rising up.²⁵:³

And those who were ungrateful said: This is nothing but a calumny he devised and other folk assisted him. So, surely, they brought about injustice and untruth.²⁵:⁴

And they said: Fables of the ancient ones that he caused to be written down! And they are to be related from memory to him at early morning dawn and eventide.²⁵:⁵

Say: It was caused to descend by He who knows the secret in the heavens and the earth. Truly, He had been Forgiving, Compassionate.²⁵:⁶

And they said: What Messenger is this that he eats food and walks in the markets? Why was an angel not caused to descend to him to be a warner with him?²⁵:⁷

Or why is not a treasure cast down to him or why is there not a garden for him so that he may eat from it?

And the ones who are unjust said: You follow nothing but a bewitched man.²⁵:⁸

Look on how they propounded for thee parables for they went astray and are not able to find a way.²⁵:⁹

Blessed be He Who, had He willed, assigned for thee better than that, Gardens beneath which rivers run and He will assign for thee palaces.²⁵:¹⁰

Nay! They denied the Hour. And We made ready a blaze for whoever denied the Hour.²⁵:¹¹ When it saw them from a far place, they heard it raging furiously and roaring.²⁵:¹² And when they were cast down into it, a troubling place, ones who are chained, they called for damnation.²⁵:¹³

It will be said to them: Call not today for a single damnation, but call for many damnations!²⁵:¹⁴

Say: Is that better or the Garden of Infinity that was promised the ones who are Godfearing?

It had been a recompense for them and a Homecoming.²⁵:¹⁵

For them in it will be whatever they will, ones who will dwell in it forever. That had been from thy Lord a promise, one that is besought.²⁵:¹⁶

And on the Day He will assemble them and what they worship other than God.

To them He will say: Was it you who caused these My servants to go astray?

Or went they astray from the way?²⁵:¹⁷

They would say: Glory be to Thee! It had not been fit and proper for us to take to ourselves any protectors other than Thee. But Thou hadst given them enjoyment and their fathers until they forgot the Remembrance and had been a lost folk.²⁵:¹⁸

So, surely, they denied you in what you say. Then, you will neither be able to turn away from it, nor help. And whoever does wrong among you, We will cause him to experience the great punishment.²⁵:¹⁹

And We sent not before thee any ones who are sent but that, truly, they eat food and walk in the markets. And We made some of you as a test for some others. Will you endure patiently, and thy Lord had been Seeing.²⁵:²⁰

Those who hope not for a meeting with Us said: Why were angels not caused to descend to us and why see we not our Lord? Surely, they grew arrogant among themselves, defiant, turning in great disdain.²⁵:²¹

On a Day they will see the angels there will be no good tidings for the ones who sin. And they will say: Unapproachable! Banned!²⁵:²²

We will advance on whatever actions they did. We will make them as scattered dust.²⁵:²³

The Companions of the Garden on that Day will have the best resting place and the fairer place of noonday rest.²⁵:²⁴

On a Day when heaven will be split open with the cloud shadows and the angels were sent down, a sending down successively,²⁵:²⁵ on that Day the true dominion will belong to The Merciful.

And it will be a Day difficult for the ones who are ungrateful.²⁵:²⁶

And on a Day when one who is unjust will bite his hands, he will say: Would that I took myself to a way with the Messenger!²⁵:²⁷ Ah! Woe is me! Would that I take not to myself so-and-so as a friend!²⁵:²⁸ Certainly, he caused me to go astray from the Remembrance after it drew near me.

And Satan had been a betrayer of the human being.²⁵:²⁹

And the Messenger said: O my Lord! Truly, my folk took this, the Quran to themselves, as that which is to be abandoned!²⁵:³⁰

And, thus, We assigned for every Prophet an enemy of the ones who sin. And thy Lord sufficed as one who guides and as a helper.²⁵:³¹

And those who were ungrateful said: Why was the Quran not sent down to him all at once?

Thus, We will make firm thy mind by it. And We chanted a chanting.²⁵:³²

And they bring thee no parable. We brought about The Truth to thee and fairer exposition.²⁵:³³

Those who will be assembled on their faces in hell, those are worse placed, ones who go astray from the way.²⁵:³⁴

And, certainly, We gave Moses the Book and assigned his brother Aaron to him as a minister.²⁵:³⁵

And We said: You both go to the folk who denied Our signs. Then, We destroyed them, an utter destruction.²⁵:³⁶

And the folk of Noah when they denied the Messengers, We drowned them. And We made them as a sign for humanity. And We made ready for the ones who are unjust a painful punishment,²⁵:³⁷ and Ad and Thamud and the Companions of Rass and many generations in between that.²⁵:³⁸

And We propounded parables for each of them. And We shattered each a shattering.²⁵:³⁹

And, certainly, they approached the town where the reprehensible rain was rained down on them. Is it that they see it not?

Nay! They had been not hoping for any rising up. And when they saw thee,²⁵:⁴⁰ they take thee to themselves but in mockery: Is this the one whom God raised up as a Messenger?²⁵:⁴¹

He was about to cause us to go astray from our gods, if it were not that we endured patiently in them! And they will know at the time when they see the punishment, who is one who goes astray from the way.²⁵:⁴²

Hadst thou considered him who took to himself his own desires as his god?

Wouldst thou, then, be over him a trustee?²⁵:⁴³

Or assume thou that most of them hear or are reasonable?

They are not but as flocks. Nay! They are ones who go astray from a way.²⁵:⁴⁴

Hast thou not considered how thy Lord stretched out the shade?

If He willed, He would make it a place of rest.

Again, We made the sun an indicator over it.²⁵:⁴⁵

Again, We seized it to Us an easy seizing.²⁵:⁴⁶

And it is He Who made the nighttime a garment for you and sleep a rest and made the daytime for rising.²⁵:⁴⁷

And it is He Who sent the winds, bearers of good tidings in advance of His Mercy.

And We caused to descend undefiled water from heaven²⁵:⁴⁸ that We give life by it to a lifeless land and with it We satiate. We created flocks on it and many humans.²⁵:⁴⁹

And, certainly, We diversified among them so that they recollect. Then, most of humanity refused everything, but disbelief.²⁵:⁵⁰

And if We willed, We would have raised up a warner in every town.²⁵:⁵¹

So obey not the ones who are ungrateful and struggle against them thereby with a great struggle.²⁵:⁵²

And it is He Who let forth the two seas—this, agreeable and water of the sweetest kind and this, salty, bitter. He made between the two that which was unapproachable, a banned barrier.²⁵:⁵³

And it is He Who created a mortal from water and made for him kindred by blood and kin by marriage. And thy Lord had been ever Powerful.²⁵:⁵⁴

And they worship other than God what neither profits them nor hurts them.

And the one who is ungrateful had been ever a sustainer against his Lord.²⁵:⁵⁵

And We sent thee not, but as one who gives good tidings and as a warner.²⁵:⁵⁶

Say: I ask of you no compensation for this but that whoever willed should take himself on a way to his Lord.²⁵:⁵⁷

And put thy trust in the Living Who is Undying and glorify His praise. And He sufficed to be aware of the impieties of His servants,²⁵:⁵⁸

He Who created the heavens and the earth and whatever is between the two in six days, again, He turned His attention to the Throne. The Merciful! Ask the aware, then, about Him.²⁵:⁵⁹

And when it was said to them: Prostrate yourselves to The Merciful, they said: And what is The Merciful? Will we prostrate ourselves to what thou hast commanded us? And it increased aversion in them.²⁵:⁶⁰

Blessed be He Who made constellations in the heaven and made in it a light-giving lamp and an illuminating moon.²⁵:⁶¹

And He it is Who made the nighttime and the daytime to follow in succession for who wanted to recollect, or who wanted thankfulness.²⁵:⁶²

And the servants of The Merciful are those who walk on the earth in meekness.

And when the ones who are ignorant addressed them, they said: Peace!²⁵:⁶³

And those who spend the night with their Lord as ones who prostrate themselves and are upright,²⁵:⁶⁴ and those who say: Our Lord! Turn Thou away the punishment of hell from us. Truly, its punishment will be continuous torment.²⁵:⁶⁵ How evil a habitation and resting place.²⁵:⁶⁶

And those who, when they spent, neither exceed all bounds, nor are they tightfisted, but had been between that, a just stand:²⁵:⁶⁷ Those who call not to another god with God nor kill the soul which God forbade but rightfully, nor commit adultery. And whoever disregards and commits this will meet sinfulness.²⁵:⁶⁸

The punishment will be multiplied for him on the Day of Resurrection. And he will dwell in it forever, as one who is despised.²⁵:⁶⁹

Whoever has repented and believed and whose actions were done as one in accord with morality, for those God will substitute for their evil deeds benevolence. And God had been Forgiving, Compassionate.²⁵:⁷⁰

And whoever repented and did as one in accord with morality, he, truly, repents to God, turning in repentance.²⁵:⁷¹

And those who bear not witness to untruth and if they passed by idle talk, they passed by nobly,²⁵:⁷² and those who, when they were reminded of the signs of their Lord, fall not down unwilling to hear and unwilling to see²⁵:⁷³ and those who say: Our Lord! Bestow on us from our spouses and our offspring the comfort of our eyes and make us leaders of the ones who are Godfearing,²⁵:⁷⁴ those will be given recompense in the highest chambers because they endured patiently. They will be in receipt of greetings and peace,²⁵:⁷⁵ ones who will dwell in it forever. Excellent it is for habitation and as a resting place!²⁵:⁷⁶

Say: My Lord would not concern Himself with you if it had not been for your supplication, for, surely, you denied so it will be close at hand.²⁵:⁷⁷

CHAPTER 26 THE POETS

In the Name of God, the Merciful, the Compassionate
*Tā Sīn Mīm.*²⁶:¹

That are the signs of the clear Book.²⁶:²

Perhaps thou wouldst be one who consumes thyself in grief because they become not ones who believe.²⁶:³

If We will, We send down to them from heaven a sign so that perhaps their necks would stay to it, ones that are bent in humility.²⁶:⁴

And there approaches them not any renewed Remembrance from The Merciful but that they had been ones who turn aside from it.²⁶:⁵ Surely, they denied it. So soon the tiding will approach them about what they had been ridiculing.²⁶:⁶

Consider they the earth, how much We caused to develop in and on it of every generous pair?²⁶:⁷ Truly, in that is a sign. Yet most of them had not been ones who believe.²⁶:⁸ Truly, thy Lord, He is, certainly, The Almighty, The Compassionate.²⁶:⁹

And when thy Lord proclaimed to Moses saying that: Approach the unjust folk,²⁶:¹⁰ a folk of Pharaoh saying: Will they not be Godfearing?²⁶:¹¹

He said: My Lord! Truly, I fear that they will deny me²⁶:¹² and my breast be narrowed and my tongue will not be loosened. So send for Aaron.²⁶:¹³ And they charge an impiety against me. I fear that they will kill me.²⁶:¹⁴

He said: No indeed! Both of you go with Our signs. Truly, We will be with you, ones who are listening.²⁶:¹⁵ And both of you approach Pharaoh and say: We are the Messengers of the Lord of the worlds,²⁶:¹⁶ so send the Children of Israel with us.²⁶:¹⁷

Pharaoh said: Raise not we thee up among us as a child? Hadst thou not lingered in expectation with us for many years of thy lifetime?²⁶:¹⁸ And thou hadst accomplished thy accomplishment that thou hadst accomplished and thou art among the ones who are ungrateful.²⁶:¹⁹

Moses said: I accomplished it when I was of the ones who go astray.²⁶:²⁰ So I ran away from you when I feared you. Then, my Lord bestowed on me critical judgment and made me among the ones who are sent.²⁶:²¹ Beyond this past favor with which thou hast reproached me, thou hadst enslaved the Children of Israel.²⁶:²²

Pharaoh said: And what is the Lord of the worlds?²⁶:²³

Moses said: The Lord of the heavens and the earth and whatever is between the two of them if you had been ones who are certain.²⁶:²⁴

Pharaoh said to whoever was around him: Listen you not?²⁶:²⁵

Moses said: Your Lord and the Lord of your fathers, the ancient ones.²⁶:²⁶

Pharaoh said: Truly, your Messenger who was sent to you is one who is possessed!²⁶:²⁷

Moses said: The Lord of the East and the West and whatever is between the two of them if you had been reasonable!²⁶:²⁸

Pharaoh said: If thou hadst taken to thyself a god other than me. I will, certainly, assign thee to be imprisoned!²⁶:²⁹

Moses said: What if I drew near thee with something that makes it clear?²⁶:³⁰

Pharaoh said: Bring it, if thou hast been among the ones who are sincere.²⁶:³¹

So he cast his staff; that is when it was a clear serpent.²⁶:³² And he drew out his hand and that is when it was shimmering white to the ones who look.²⁶:³³

He said to the Council around him: Truly, this is one who is a knowing sorcerer!²⁶:³⁴ He wants to drive you out from your region by his sorcery. What is it, then, that you suggest?²⁶:³⁵

They said: Put him and his brother off and raise up ones who summon in the cities.²⁶:³⁶ They will bring every knowing witch to thee.²⁶:³⁷

So the ones who were sorcerers were gathered at a time appointed on a known day²⁶:³⁸ and it was said to humanity: Will you, you be ones who gather together²⁶:³⁹ so that perhaps we follow the ones who are sorcerers if they had been the ones who are victors?²⁶:⁴⁰

So when the ones who are sorcerers drew near, they said to Pharaoh: Is there a compensation for us if we had been the ones who are victors?²⁶:⁴¹

Pharaoh said: Yes! Truly, you will be the ones who are brought near to me.²⁶:⁴²

Moses said to them: Cast what you will as ones who cast.²⁶:⁴³

So they cast their ropes and their staffs and said: By the vainglory of Pharaoh, we, we will, surely, be the ones who are victors!²⁶:⁴⁴

Then, Moses cast down his staff. That is when it swallows what they faked.²⁶:⁴⁵

The ones who are sorcerers were cast down, ones who prostrate themselves.²⁶:⁴⁶

They said: We believed in the Lord of the worlds,²⁶:⁴⁷ the Lord of Moses and Aaron.²⁶:⁴⁸

Pharaoh said: You believed in him before I give permission to you? He is, truly, your foremost master who taught you sorcery. Then, you will know. I will, certainly, cut off your hands and your feet on opposite sides, and I will cause you to be crucified one and all.²⁶:⁴⁹

They said: No grievance. Truly, to our Lord we are ones who are turning.²⁶:⁵⁰ Truly, we are desirous that Our Lord forgive us our transgressions that we had been the first of the ones who believe.²⁶:⁵¹

And We revealed to Moses saying that: Set thou forth by night with My servants. Truly, you are ones who will be followed.²⁶:⁵² Then, Pharaoh sent to the cities, ones who summon.²⁶:⁵³

They said: These are, truly, a small crowd[26:54] and, truly, they are ones who enrage us.[26:55] We are altogether, truly, ones who are cautious.[26:56] So We drove them out from the gardens and springs[26:57] and treasures and a generous station.[26:58] And We, thus, gave them as inheritance to the Children of Israel.[26:59]

So they pursued them at sunrise.[26:60] Then, when the two multitudes sighted each other, the Companions of Moses said: Truly, we are ones who are to be overtaken.[26:61]

Moses said: No indeed. Truly, my Lord is with me and He will guide me.[26:62]

Then, We revealed to Moses saying that: Strike the sea with thy staff and it divided and each had been a separate part like a high, tremendous mountain.[26:63]

And, again, We brought the others close[26:64] and We rescued Moses and whoever was with him, one and all.[26:65]

Again, We drowned the others.[26:66]

Truly, in this is a sign and yet most of them had not been ones who believe.[26:67]

And, truly, thy Lord, He is The Almighty, The Compassionate.[26:68]

And recount to them the tidings of Abraham[26:69] when he said to his father and his folk: What is it you worship?[26:70]

They said: We worship idols. We will stay ones who give ourselves up to them.[26:71]

He said: Hear they when you call them?[26:72]

Or are they profiting you or hurting you?[26:73]

They said: Nay! But we found our fathers acting likewise.[26:74]

He said: Then, considered what you had been worshipping,[26:75] you and your fathers, the elders?[26:76] Truly, they are an enemy to me, but not so the Lord of the worlds[26:77] Who created me. And it is He Who guides me.[26:78] And that He Who feeds me and gives me drink.[26:79] And when I was sick, it is He Who heals me[26:80] and Who causes me to die, again, will give me life,[26:81] and from Whom I am desirous that He will forgive me my transgressions on the Day of Judgment.[26:82]

My Lord! Bestow on me critical judgment and cause me to join with the ones in accord with morality.[26:83] And assign me a good name of good repute with the later ones[26:84] and make me one who inherits the Garden of Bliss.[26:85] And forgive my father. Truly, he had been among the ones who go astray.[26:86] And cover me not with shame on a Day they will be raised up,[26:87] on a Day neither wealth will profit nor children[26:88] but he who approached God with a pure-hearted heart.[26:89]

And the Garden will be brought close for the ones who are Godfearing[26:90] and hellfire will be advanced for the ones who are in error.[26:91]

And it will be said to them: Where is what you had been worshipping[26:92] instead of God?

Are you helped by them?

Or help they themselves?[26:93]

Then, they were thrown down into it, they and the ones who are in error,[26:94] and the army of Iblis, one and all.[26:95]

And they said while they are in it striving against one another:[26:96] By God! Truly, we had been clearly wandering astray[26:97] when we made you equal with the Lord of the worlds.[26:98] And no one caused us to go astray but the ones who sin.[26:99]

Now we have not ones who are intercessors[26:100] nor an ardent friend, a loyal friend.[26:101] Would that there were for us a return again. Then, we would be among the ones who believe![26:102]

Truly, in this is a sign; yet most of them had not been ones who believe.[26:103]

And, truly, thy Lord, He is The Almighty, The Compassionate.[26:104]

The folk of Noah denied the ones who are sent[26:105] when their brother, Noah, said to them: Will you not be Godfearing?[26:106]

Truly, I am a trustworthy Messenger to you[26:107] so be Godfearing of God and obey me.[26:108]

And I ask you not for any compensation for it. My compensation is only from the Lord of the worlds.[26:109] So be Godfearing of God and obey you me.[26:110]

They said: Will we believe in thee when it is the most wretched that followed thee?[26:111]

He said: And what knowledge have I of what they had been doing?[26:112] Truly, their reckoning is but with my Lord if you be aware.[26:113] I am not one who drives away the ones who believe.[26:114] I am not but a clear warner.[26:115]

They said: If thou hast not refrained thyself, O Noah, thou wilt, certainly, be among the ones who are stoned![26:116]

He said: My Lord! My folk denied me,[26:117] so give Thou deliverance between me and them and victory and deliver me and whoever is with me among the ones who believe.[26:118]

And We rescued him and whoever was with him in the laden boat.[26:119]

Again, We drowned after that the ones who remained.[26:120]

In this is, truly, a sign, yet most of them had not been ones who believe.[26:121]

Thy Lord, He, truly, is The Almighty, The Compassionate.[26:122]

Ad denied the ones who are sent[26:123] when their brother Hud said to them: Will you not be Godfearing?[26:124] Truly, I am a trustworthy Messenger to you,[26:125] so be Godfearing of God and obey me.[26:126] And I ask you not for any compensation for it. My compensation is only from the Lord of the worlds.[26:127] Build you a sign on every high hill to amuse?[26:128] And take you for yourselves castles so that perhaps you will dwell in them forever?[26:129] And when you seized by force, seized you by force haughtily?[26:130] So be Godfearing of God and obey me.[26:131] Be Godfearing of Him Who furnished relief to you with all that you know.[26:132] He furnished relief to you with flocks and children[26:133] and gardens and springs.[26:134] Truly, I fear for you the punishment of a tremendous Day.[26:135]

They said: It is equal to us whether thou wert to admonish or thou hast not been among the ones who admonish.[26:136] Truly, this is nothing but morals of the ancient ones[26:137] and we are not ones who are punished.[26:138]

So they denied him and We caused them to perish. Truly, in this is a sign yet most of them had not been ones who believe.[26:139] And, truly, thy Lord, He is, certainly, The Almighty, The Compassionate.[26:140]

And Thamud denied the ones who are sent[26:141] when their brother Salih said to them: Will you not be Godfearing?[26:142] Truly, I am a trustworthy Messenger to you,[26:143] so be Godfearing of God and obey me.[26:144]

And I ask you not for any compensation for it. My compensation is only from the Lord of the worlds.[26:145] Will you be left ones who are safe in what you have here[26:146] in gardens and springs[26:147] and crops of slender spathes of date palm trees?[26:148] Will you carve houses out of the mountains as ones who are skillful?[26:149] So be Godfearing of God and obey me.[26:150] Obey not the command of the ones who are excessive,[26:151] who make corruption in and on the earth and make not things right.[26:152]

They said: Truly, thou art only of the ones against whom a spell is cast.[26:153] Thou art not but a mortal like us. So bring us a sign if thou hadst been of the ones who are sincere.[26:154]

He said: This is a she camel. She has a right to drink and you have a right to drink on a known day.[26:155] And afflict her not with evil so that you should take the punishment of a tremendous Day.[26:156]

But they crippled her and, then, it came to be in the morning that they are ones who are remorseful.[26:157] So the punishment took them. Truly, in this is a sign yet most of them had not been ones who believe.[26:158] And, truly, thy Lord! He is, certainly, The Almighty, The Compassionate.[26:159]

The folk of Lot denied the ones who are sent[26:160] when their brother, Lot, said to them: Will you not be Godfearing?[26:161] Truly, I am a trustworthy Messenger to you[26:162] so be Godfearing of God and obey me. [26:163] And I ask you not for any compensation for it. My compensation is only from the Lord of the worlds. [26:164] You approach males among worldly beings[26:165] forsaking spouses whom your Lord created for you? Nay! You are a folk ones who turn away. [26:166]

They said: If thou hast not refrained thyself, O Lot, thou wilt, certainly, be among ones who are driven out. [26:167]

He said: I am of the ones with hatred for your actions. [26:168] My Lord! Deliver me and my people from what they do! [26:169] So We delivered him and his people one and all [26:170] but an old woman of the ones who stay behind. [26:171] Again, We destroyed the others[26:172] and We rained down on them a rain. And how evil was the rain for the ones who are warned! [26:173] Truly, in this is a sign. Yet most of them had not been ones who believe. [26:174] And, truly, thy Lord, He is, certainly, The Almighty, The Compassionate. [26:175]

The Companions of the Thicket denied the ones who are sent. [26:176]

When Shuayb said to them: Will you not be Godfearing? [26:177] Truly, I am a trustworthy Messenger to you[26:178] so be Godfearing of God and obey me. [26:179] And I ask you not for any compensation for it. My compensation is only from the Lord of the worlds. [26:180] Live up to the full measure and be not of the ones who cause loss to others by fraud. [26:181] And weigh with a straight scale[26:182] and diminish not to humanity their things nor do mischief in or on the earth as ones who make corruption. [26:183] And be Godfearing of Him Who created you and the array of the ancient ones. [26:184]

They said: Thou art only ones against whom a spell is cast. [26:185] And thou art nothing but a mortal like us. And, truly, we think thee to be among the ones who lie. [26:186] So cause pieces of heaven to drop on us, if you had been among the ones who are sincere. [26:187]

He said: My Lord is greater in knowledge of what you do. [26:188] But they denied him. So took them the punishment on the overshadowing day. Truly, that had been the punishment of a tremendous Day! [26:189] Truly, in this is a sign. Yet most of them had not been ones who believe. [26:190] And, truly, thy Lord, He is, certainly, The Almighty, The Compassionate. [26:191]

And this, truly, is the sending down successively of the Lord of the worlds[26:192] that the Trustworthy Spirit brought down[26:193] on thy heart that thou be among the one who warn[26:194] in a clear Arabic tongue. [26:195] And, truly, it is in the ancient scrolls of the ancient ones. [26:196]

Would it not be a sign for them that is known to the knowing among the Children of Israel? [26:197]

And if We sent it down to some of the non-Arabs, [26:198] and he recited it to them, they had not been ones who believe in it. [26:199]

Thus, We thrust it into the hearts of the ones who sin. [26:200] They will not believe in it until they see the painful punishment. [26:201] Then, it will approach them suddenly while they are not aware. [26:202]

Then, they will say: Are we ones who are given respite? [26:203] Seek they to hasten Our punishment? [26:204]

Hadst thou considered that if We gave them enjoyment for years[26:205] and, again, there drew near them what they had been promised, [26:206] they would not be availed by what they had been given of enjoyment? [26:207]

We caused no town to perish but that it had ones who warn[26:208] as a reminder. And We had not been ones who are unjust. [26:209] It came not forth by the satans[26:210] and neither is it fit and proper for them nor are they able. [26:211] Truly, they, from having the ability to hear, are the ones who are set aside. [26:212]

So call thou not to any god with God so that thou be among the ones who are punished. [26:213]

And warn thy nearest kin, the kinspeople. [26:214] And make low thy wing to whoever followed thee among the ones who believe. [26:215]

Then, if they rebelled against thee, then, say: Truly, I am free of what you do. [26:216]

And put thy trust in The Almighty, The Compassionate, [26:217] Who sees thee at the time thou hast stood up[26:218] and thy going to and fro of the ones who prostrate themselves? [26:219] Truly, He is The Hearing, The Knowing. [26:220]

Will I tell you in whom the satans come forth? [26:221] They come forth in every sinful false one who gives listen, [26:222] but most of them are ones who lie. [26:223]

As for the poets, the ones who are in error follow them. [26:224] Hast thou not considered that they wander in every valley[26:225] and that they say what they accomplish not? [26:226]

But those who believed and did as the ones in accord with morality remembered God frequently and helped themselves after they were wronged. And those who did wrong will know by which overturning they will be turned about! [26:227]

CHAPTER 27 THE ANT

In the Name of God, the Merciful, the Compassionate
Tā Sīn.

That are the signs of the Quran and a clear Book, [27:1] a guidance and good tidings for the ones who believe, [27:2] those who perform the formal prayer and give the purifying alms so that they of the world to come, they are certain. [27:3]

Truly, as for those who believe not in the world to come, We made their actions appear pleasing to them so that they wander unwilling to see. [27:4] Those are those for whom is the dire punishment and they, in the world to come, they are the ones who are the losers. [27:5]

And, truly, thee, thou art in receipt of the Quran, that which proceeds from the Presence of One who is Wise, Knowing. [27:6]

Mention when Moses said to his people: Truly, I, I observed a fire! I will bring you news from it or I will approach you with a flaming firebrand so that perhaps you would warm yourselves. [27:7]

But when he drew near it, it was proclaimed that: Blessed be He Who is in the fire and Who is around it, and glory be to God, the Lord of the worlds. [27:8] O Moses! Truly, I alone am God, The Almighty, The Wise. [27:9] Cast down thy staff.

But when he saw it quiver as if it were a snake, he turned as one who draws back to retrace his steps.

O Moses! Fear not! The ones who are sent fear not My nearness[27:10] but whoever did wrong does. Again, he substituted goodness after evil and, truly, I am Forgiving, Compassionate. [27:11] Cause thy hand to enter into thy bosom. It will go forth shimmering white without evil. These are among nine signs to Pharaoh and his folk. Truly, they had been a folk, ones who disobey. [27:12]

But when Our signs drew near them, ones who perceive, they said: This is clear sorcery. [27:13] And they negated them—although their souls confessed to them—out of injustice and self-exaltation. So look on how had been the Ultimate End of the ones who make corruption. [27:14]

Certainly, We gave David and Solomon knowledge; and they said: All Praise belongs to God Who gave us advantage over many of His servants, ones who believe. [27:15]

And Solomon inherited from David and he said: O humanity! We were taught the utterance of the birds and everything was given to us. Truly, this is clearly grace. [27:16]

And there was assembled before Solomon his armies of jinn and humankind and birds and they are marching in rank²⁷:¹⁷ until when they approached the Valley of the Ants.

One ant said: O ants! Enter your dwellings so that Solomon and his armies not crush you while they are not aware.²⁷:¹⁸

So Solomon smiled as one who laughs at its saying and he said: My Lord! Arouse me that I give thanks for Thy divine blessing with which Thou wert gracious to me and ones who are my parents and that I do as one in accord with morality. May Thou be well-pleased and cause me to enter by Thy Mercy among Thy servants, ones in accord with morality.²⁷:¹⁹

And he reviewed the birds and said: Why see I not the hoopoe bird? Had it been among the ones who are absent?²⁷:²⁰ I will, certainly, punish him with a severe punishment or deal a death blow to it unless it brings me a clear authority!²⁷:²¹

But it was not long in coming. Then, it said: I comprehended what thou hast not comprehended of it. And I drew near thee from Sheba with certain tidings.²⁷:²² Truly, I found a woman controlling them. And she was given everything and for her is a sublime throne.²⁷:²³ I found her and her folk prostrating herself to the sun—instead of God—and Satan made to appear pleasing to them their actions and barred them from the way so they are not truly guided.²⁷:²⁴ So they prostrate themselves not to God Who brings out that which is hidden in the heavens and the earth and knows what you conceal and what you speak openly.²⁷:²⁵ God, there is no god but He, the Lord of the Sublime Throne.²⁷:²⁶

Solomon said: We will look on if thou hadst been sincere or thou art of the ones who lie.²⁷:²⁷ Go thou with this letter of mine and cast it to them. Again, turn away from them and look on what they return.²⁷:²⁸

She said: O Council! Truly, a generous letter was cast down to me.²⁷:²⁹ Truly, it is from Solomon and, truly, it is in the Name of God, The Merciful, The Compassionate.²⁷:³⁰ Rise not up against me, but approach me as ones who submit to God.²⁷:³¹

She said: O Council! Render me an opinion in my affair. I had not been one who resolves unless you bear witness.²⁷:³²

They said: We are imbued with strength and vigorous might, but the command is for thee. So look on what thou wilt command.²⁷:³³

She said: Truly, when kings entered a town, they made corruption in it and made the most mighty of its people humiliated in spirit. Thus, this is what they accomplish.²⁷:³⁴ But, truly, I am one who will send to them a present and will be one who looks with what returns the ones who are sent.²⁷:³⁵

So when they drew near Solomon, he said: Are you furnishing me relief with wealth? What God gave me is better than what He gave you. Nay! It is you who should be glad with your present!²⁷:³⁶ Return thou to them and We, truly, will approach them with armies against which they will not be capable and we will drive them out from there as ones who are disgraced and they, humble-spirited.²⁷:³⁷

He said: O Council! Which of you will bring me her throne before they approach me as ones who submit to God?²⁷:³⁸

A demon from among the jinn said: I will bring it to thee before thou wilt stand up from thy station. And, truly, I am strong, trustworthy.²⁷:³⁹

Said he who has knowledge of the Book: I will bring it to thee before thy glance goes back to thee.

And, then, when he saw that which is settled before him, he said: This is from the grace of my Lord to try me whether I give thanks or am ungrateful. And whoever gave thanks, truly, he gives thanks for himself. And whoever was ungrateful, then, truly, my Lord is Rich, Generous.²⁷:⁴⁰

He said: Disguise her throne for her that we look on whether she will be truly guided or she will be of those who are not truly guided.²⁷:⁴¹

So when she drew near, it was said: Is thy throne like this? She said: It is as though it had been it.

Solomon said: The knowledge was given us before her and we had been ones who submit to the One God.²⁷:⁴²

She was barred from worshipping God by what she had been worshipping other than God for, truly, she had been of a folk, ones who are ungrateful.²⁷:⁴³

It was said to her: Enter the pavilion.

And when she saw it, she assumed it to be a pool and she bared her legs.

He said: Truly, it is a smooth, crystal pavilion.

She said: My Lord! Truly, I did wrong to myself and I submitted with Solomon to God, the Lord of the worlds.²⁷:⁴⁴

And, certainly, We sent to Thamud their brother, Salih that they worship God!

Then, when they became two groups of people striving against one another,²⁷:⁴⁵ he said: O my folk! Why seek you to hasten the evil deed before benevolence?

Why ask you not for forgiveness of God so that perhaps you will find mercy?²⁷:⁴⁶

They said: We auger ill of thee and whoever is with thee.

He said: That which is your omen is with God. Nay! You are a folk who are being tried.²⁷:⁴⁷

And there had been nine groups of persons in the city who make corruption in the earth and make not things right.²⁷:⁴⁸

They said: Swear to one another by God: We will, certainly, attack him by night and his people.

Again, we will, certainly, say to his protector: We bore not witness to the destruction of his people and, truly, we are ones who are sincere.²⁷:⁴⁹

So they planned a plan and We planned a plan while they were not aware.²⁷:⁵⁰

So look on how had been the Ultimate End of their planning! Truly, We destroyed them and their folk one and all.²⁷:⁵¹

And that are their houses, ones that have fallen down for what they did wrong. Truly, in this is a sign for a folk who know.²⁷:⁵²

And We rescued those who believed and had been God-fearing.²⁷:⁵³

And Lot, when he said to his folk: You approach indecency and you perceive what you do.²⁷:⁵⁴ Why approach you men with lust instead of women? Nay! You are a folk who are ignorant.²⁷:⁵⁵

Then, there had been no answer by his folk, but that they said: Drive the people of Lot out from your town. Truly, they are a clan to cleanse themselves.²⁷:⁵⁶

So We rescued him and his people, but his woman. We ordained her to be among the ones who stay behind.²⁷:⁵⁷ And We rained down on them a rain. How evil was the rain to the ones who are warned!²⁷:⁵⁸

Say: The Praise belongs to God and peace be on His servants, those whom He favored. Is God better or what they ascribe as partner with God?²⁷:⁵⁹

Who created the heavens and the earth and caused to descend for you from the heavens, water? With it We caused joyous, fertile gardens to develop. It had not been for you to cause their trees to develop. Is there any god besides God? Nay! They are a folk who equate others with God.²⁷:⁶⁰

Who made the earth a stopping place and made rivers in the midst and made firm mountains for it and made between the two sees that which hinders? Is there a god besides God? Nay! But most of them know not!²⁷:⁶¹

Who answers one who is constrained when he called to Him and He removes the evil and assigns you as vice-regents on the earth? Is there a god besides God? Little is what you recollect!27:62

Who guides you in the shadows of the dry land the sea and Who sends the winds, bearer of good news in advance of His mercy? Is there a god besides God? Exalted is God above partners they ascribe with God.

Say: The Praise belongs to God and peace be on His servants, those whom He favored. Is God better, or what they ascribe as partner with God? Is there a god besides God? Exalted is God above partners they ascribe with God!27:63

Who begins creation, again, will cause it to return and Who provides you from the heaven and the earth. Is there a god besides God?

Say: Prepare your proof if you had been ones who are sincere!27:64

Say: None knows who is in the heaven and the earth, nor the unseen but God. Nor are they aware when they will be raised up.27:65

Nay! Their knowledge of the world to come failed.

Nay! They are in uncertainty about it. Nay! They are in the dark about it.27:66

And those who were ungrateful said: When we had been earth dust like our fathers will we, truly, be ones who are brought out?27:67 Certainly, we were promised this, we and our fathers before. Truly, this is nothing but fables of the ancient ones.27:68

Say: Journey through the earth; then, look on how had been the Ultimate End of the ones who sin.27:69 And feel thou not remorse for them, nor be troubled by what they plan.27:70

And they say: When is the promise if you had been ones who are sincere?27:71

Say: Perhaps coming close behind you be some of that which you seek to hasten.27:72 And, truly, thy Lord is Possessor of Grace for humanity, but most of them give not thanks.27:73 And, truly, thy Lord knows what their breasts hide and what they speak openly.27:74

Not is that which is absent in the heaven and the earth, but that it is in the clear Book.27:75 Truly, this, the Quran, relates about the Children of Israel and most of what they are at variance in it.27:76 And, truly, it is a guidance and a mercy for the ones who believe.27:77 Truly, thy Lord will decree between them with His determination. And He is The Almighty, The Knowing.27:78

So put thy trust in God. Truly, thou art on The Clear Truth.27:79

Truly, thou wilt not cause the dead to hear nor wilt thou cause to hear the unwilling to hear the calling to them when they turned as ones who draw back.27:80

Nor wilt thou be one who guides the unwilling to see out of their fallacy. Thou wilt not cause to hear, but whoever believes in Our signs and so they are ones who submit to God.27:81

And when the saying fell on them, We will bring out a moving creature for them from the earth that will speak to them, that: Humanity had not been certain of Our signs.27:82

And on a Day We will assemble a unit out of every community of whoever denies Our signs and they will be marching in rank.27:83 Until when they drew near, He will say: Denied you My signs without comprehending them in knowledge, or what is it that you had been doing?27:84

And the saying will fall on them because they did wrong. And they will speak nothing for themselves.27:85

Considered they not? We made the nighttime for them to rest in it and the daytime for ones who perceive. Truly, in that are signs for a folk who believe.27:86

On a Day on which the trumpet will be blown, whoever is in the heavens will be terrified and whoever is on the earth, but him whom God willed. And all will approach Him as ones who are in a state of lowliness.27:87

And thou wilt see the mountains thou hast assumed to be that which are fixed. But they will pass by as the passing of the clouds. This is the handiwork of God Who created everything very well. Truly, He is Aware of what you accomplish.27:88

Whoever drew near with benevolence, for him will be better than it and they would be from the terror ones who are safe on that Day.27:89

And whoever drew near with evil deeds, they would be slung on their faces in the fire: Are you given recompense but for what you had been doing?27:90

Truly, I was commanded to worship the Lord of this land which He made sacred and to Whom everything belongs. And I was commanded that I be among the ones who submit to God27:91 and to recount the Recitation. So whoever was truly guided, then, he is truly guided only for himself.

And to whoever went astray say: Truly, I am among the ones who warn.27:92

And say: The Praise belongs to God. He will cause you to see His signs and you will recognize them. Thy Lord is not One Who is Heedless of what you do.27:93

CHAPTER 28 THE STORY

In the Name of God, The Merciful, The Compassionate
*Tā Sīn Mīm.*28:1

That are the signs of the clear Book.28:2 We recount to thee the tiding of Moses and Pharaoh with The Truth for a folk who believe.28:3 Truly, Pharaoh exalted himself on the earth and made his people partisans, taking advantage of due to their weakness, a section among them. He slaughters their children and saves alive their women. Truly, he had been of the ones who make corruption.28:4

And We want to show grace to those who were taken advantage of due to their weakness on the earth and to make them leaders and to make them the ones who inherit28:5 and to establish them firmly on the earth.

And We cause Pharaoh and Haman to see—and their armies from them—that of which they had been fearful.28:6

And We revealed to the mother of Moses: Breast feed him. But if thou hadst feared for him, then, cast him into the water of the sea and neither fear nor feel remorse. Truly, We will be ones who restore him to thee, ones who make him among the ones who are sent.28:7 Then, the people of Pharaoh picked him out to be an enemy to them and a cause of grief. Truly, Pharaoh and Haman and their armies had been ones who are inequitable.28:8

And the woman of Pharaoh said: He will be a comfort to our eyes for me and for thee. Kill him not. Perhaps he may profit us or we may take him to ourselves as a son. But they are not aware.28:9

And it came to be in the morning that the mind of the mother of Moses was that which is empty. Truly, she was about to show him, if We had not invigorated her heart so that she became among the ones who believe.28:10

And she said to his sister: Track him.

So she kept watching him from afar while they are not aware.28:11

And We forbade any breast feeding female for him before. Then, she said: Shall I point you to the people of a house who will take control of him for you and they will be ones who will look after him?28:12

So We returned him to his mother that her eyes settle down and she not feel remorse and that she knows that the Promise of God is true. But most of them know not.28:13

And when he was fully grown, come of age and he straightened himself up, We gave him critical judgment and knowledge. And, thus, We give recompense to the ones who are doers of good.[28:14]

And he entered the city at a time of heedlessness of its people. He found in it two men fighting one against the other. This who was from among his partisans and this who was from among his enemies. The one who was among his partisans cried for help against him who was among his enemies. So Moses struck him with his fist and Moses made an end of him.

He said: This is the action of Satan. Truly, he is a clear enemy, one who leads astray.[28:15]

He said: My Lord! Truly, I did wrong to myself so forgive me and He forgave him. Truly, He is The Forgiving, The Compassionate.[28:16]

He said: My Lord! For that with which Thou wert gracious to me I will never be a sustainer of the ones who sin.[28:17]

So he came to be in the morning in the city one who is fearful and is vigilant. That is when the one who had asked for help yesterday cries out aloud to him.

Moses said to him: Truly, thou art clearly a hothead.[28:18]

Then, when he wanted to seize by force the one who he was an enemy of both of them—he said: O Moses! Wouldst thou want to kill me as thou hadst killed a soul yesterday? Thou wouldst want nothing, but to be haughty on the earth? And thou wouldst want not to be among the ones who make things right?[28:19]

A man drew near from the farther part of the city, coming eagerly, he said: O Moses! Truly, the Council is conspiring against thee to kill thee, so go forth. Truly, I am the one who gives advice to thee.[28:20]

So Moses went forth from there as one who is fearful, is vigilant.

He said: My Lord! Deliver me from the folk, ones who are unjust.[28:21]

When of his own accord he turned his face toward Midian he said: Perhaps my Lord guides me to the right way.[28:22]

And when he went down to the well of Midian, he found a community there of personages drawing water and he found other than them two women who keep away.

He said: What is your business?

They both said: We draw not water until the ones who are shepherds move on. And our father is an aged, old man.[28:23]

So he drew water for them.

Again, he turned away to the shade and said: My Lord! Truly, I am, certainly, of whatever Thou caused to descend of good to me, in need.[28:24]

Then, drew near him one of the two women, walking bashfully.

She said: Truly, my father calls to thee that he may give thee recompense of compensation because thou hadst drawn water for us.

So when he drew near him and related to him the narrative, he said: Fear not. Thou wert delivered from the folk, ones who are unjust.[28:25]

One of the two women said: O my father! Employ him. Truly, best is that thou wouldst employ the strong, the trustworthy.[28:26]

He said: Truly, I want to wed thee to one of my two daughters if that thou wilt hire thyself to me for eight years. But if thou wert to fulfill ten years, then, it will be from thee, for I want not to press thee hard. Thou wilt find me, if God willed, among the ones in accord with morality.[28:27]

He said: That is between thee and between me whichever of the two terms I satisfied. There will be no deep seated dislike from me. And God is Trustee over what we say.[28:28]

Then, when Moses satisfied the term and journeyed with his people, he observed at the edge of the mount a fire.

He said to his people: Abide! Truly, I, I observed a fire so that perhaps I will bring you some news from there or burning wood of fire so that perhaps you will warm yourselves.[28:29]

So when he approached it, it was proclaimed from the right side of the ridge of the valley, in a corner of the blessed ground from the tree: O Moses! Truly, I am God, the Lord of the worlds.[28:30]

Cast thy staff. But when he saw it quiver as if it were a snake, he turned as one who draws back, and he retraces his steps.

O Moses! Come forward and fear not. Truly, thou art among the ones who are safe.[28:31] Insert thy hand into thy bosom. It will go forth shimmering white without evil and clasp thy arm pits against fright. These are two proofs from thy Lord to Pharaoh and his Council. Truly, they had been a folk, ones who disobey.[28:32]

He said: My Lord! Truly, I killed a soul among them and I fear that they will kill me.[28:33] And my brother Aaron, he is more oratorical in language than I, so send him with me as a helpmate to establish me as true. Truly, I fear that they will deny me.[28:34]

He said: We will strengthen thy arm through thy brother and assign to you both authority so that they reach not out to you both. With Our signs, you two and whoever followed you two will be the ones who are victors.[28:35]

Then, when Moses drew near them with Our signs, clear portents, they said: This is nothing but forged sorcery. We heard not of this from our fathers, the ancient ones.[28:36]

Moses said: My Lord is greater in knowledge of who drew near with guidance from Him and what will be the Ultimate End in the Abode. Truly, the ones who are unjust will not prosper.[28:37]

And Pharaoh said: O Council! I knew not of any god for you other than me so kindle for me, O Haman, a fire on the clay and make a pavilion for me so that perhaps I will puruse the God of Moses. And, truly, I think that he is among the ones who lie.[28:38]

And he grew arrogant, he and his armies, on the earth without right and they thought that they would not be returned to Us.[28:39]

So We took him and his armies and We cast them forth in the water of the sea. So look on how had been the Ultimate End of the ones who are unjust.[28:40]

We made them leaders. They call to the fire. And on the Day of Resurrection, they will not be helped.[28:41]

And a curse pursued them in the present. And on the Day of Resurrection they will be of the ones who are spurned.[28:42]

And, certainly, We gave Moses the Book, after We caused previous generations to perish as clear evidence for humanity and a guidance and a mercy so that they recollect.[28:43]

And thou hadst not been on the western edge when We decreed the command to Moses and thou hadst not been among the ones who bear witness.[28:44]

But We caused generations to grow and their lifetimes continued to be long. And thou hadst not been one who is a dweller with the people of Midian who recount Our signs to them, but it is We Who had been ones who send.[28:45]

And thou hadst not been at the edge of the mount when We proclaimed, but as a mercy from thy Lord, that thou wast to warn a folk to whom no warner approached them before thee so that perhaps they will recollect.[28:46]

So that if affliction lights on them for what their hands put forward, they say: Our Lord! Why hadst Thou not sent a Messenger to us that we would have followed Thy signs and we would be among the ones who believe?[28:47]

But when The Truth drew near them from Us they said: Why was he not given the like of what was given to Moses before?

They are ones who are ungrateful for what was given to Moses before.

They said: Two kinds of sorcery, each helped one against the other.

And they said: Truly, we disbelieve in all of it.²⁸:⁴⁸

Say: Then, bring a Book from God that is better guided than these two that I follow it, if you had been ones who are sincere.²⁸:⁴⁹

But if they respond not to thee, then, know that they only follow their own desires. And who is one who goes astray than whoever followed his own desires without guidance from God?

Truly, God guides not the folk, the ones who are unjust.²⁸:⁵⁰

And, certainly, We caused the saying to reach them so that perhaps they will recollect.²⁸:⁵¹

Those to whom We gave the Book before it, they believe in it.²⁸:⁵² And when it is recounted to them, they say: We believed in it. Truly, it is The Truth from our Lord. Truly, even before it we had been ones who submit to God.²⁸:⁵³

Those will be given their compensation two times because they patiently endured and drive off evil deeds with benevolence and they spend out of what We provided them.²⁸:⁵⁴

And when they heard idle talk, they turned aside from it and said: To us are our actions and to you are your actions. Peace be to you! We are not looking for the ones who are ignorant.²⁸:⁵⁵

Truly, thou hast not guided whom thou hast loved but God guides whomever He wills. And He is greater in knowledge of the ones who are truly guided.²⁸:⁵⁶

They said: If we follow the guidance with thee, we would be snatched away from our region.

Establish We not firmly for them a holy, safe place where all kinds of fruits are collected as provision from that which proceeds from Our Presence? But most of them know not.²⁸:⁵⁷

And how many a town that We caused to perish boasted about its livelihood. And these are their dwellings, not to be inhabited after them but a little. And, truly, We, We had been the ones who inherit.²⁸:⁵⁸

Thy Lord had not been One Who Causes towns to perish until He raises up to their mother-town a Messenger who recounts Our signs to them. We never had been Ones Who Cause towns to perish unless their people are ones who are unjust.²⁸:⁵⁹

And whatever things you were given are enjoyment for this present life and its adornment. And what is with God is better for one who endures. Will you not, then, be reasonable?²⁸:⁶⁰

Is he to whom We promised a fairer promise—and it is one that reaches fulfillment—like him to whom We gave the enjoyment of enjoyment for this present life?

Again, on the Day of Resurrection he will be among the ones who are charged?²⁸:⁶¹

And on that Day He will proclaim to them and will say: Where are My ascribed associates whom you had been claiming?²⁸:⁶²

They would say about whom will be realized the saying: Our Lord! These are they whom we led into error. We led them into error even as we erred. We clear ourselves with Thee. They had never been worshipping us.²⁸:⁶³

And it would be said: Call to your ascribed associates.

Then, they will call to them, but they will not respond to them and they will see the punishment. If only they had been truly guided!²⁸:⁶⁴

And on a Day when He would proclaim to them and He would say: What have you answered to the ones who are sent?²⁸:⁶⁵

Then, the tidings of that day will be in darkness and they will not demand anything of one another.²⁸:⁶⁶ As for him who

repented and believed and did as one in accord with morality, then, perhaps he will be among the ones who prosper.²⁸:⁶⁷

And thy Lord creates whatever He wills and chooses. Not for them had there been a choice. Glory be to God and exalted is He above partners they ascribe!²⁸:⁶⁸

And thy Lord knows what their breasts hide and what they speak openly.²⁸:⁶⁹

And He, God, there is no god but He. His is all Praise in the First and in the Last. And His is the determination. And to Him you will be returned.²⁸:⁷⁰

Say: Considered you what if God made the nighttime endless for you until the Day of Resurrection? What god other than God brings you illumination? Will you not, then, hear?²⁸:⁷¹

Say: Considered you what if God made the daytime endless for you until the Day of Resurrection? What god other than God brings you nighttime wherein you rest? Will you not, then, perceive?²⁸:⁷²

And it is out of His mercy that He assigned for you the nighttime and the daytime that you rest in it and that you be looking for His grace and so that perhaps you will give thanks.²⁸:⁷³

And on a Day He will proclaim to them and say: Where are My ascribed associates whom you had been claiming?²⁸:⁷⁴ And We will tear out a witness from every community and We will say: Prepare your proof. Then, they will know that The Truth is with God and will go astray from them what they had been devising.²⁸:⁷⁵

Truly, Korah had been of the folk of Moses, but he was insolent towards them. And We gave him of the treasures which truly, the keys of it were a heavy ordeal to many imbued with strength.

Mention when His folk said to him: Exult not. Truly, God loves not the exultant.²⁸:⁷⁶

Look for what God gave thee for the Last Abode. And forget not thy share of the present and do good even as God did good to thee. And be not insolent, corrupting in and on the earth. Truly, God loves not the ones who make corruption.²⁸:⁷⁷

Korah said: I was only given it because of the knowledge with me. Knows he not that God caused to perish before him some of the generations who were more vigorous in strength than he and more numerous in multitude yet the ones who sin will not be asked about their impieties?²⁸:⁷⁸

So he went forth to his folk in his adornment. And said those who want this present life: O would that we had the like of what was given to Korah! Truly, he is the possessor of a sublime allotment.²⁸:⁷⁹

And those who were given the knowledge said: Woe to you! The reward for good deeds from God is better for whoever believed and did as ones in accord with morality. And none will be in receipt of it, but the ones who remain steadfast.²⁸:⁸⁰

So We caused to swallow him the earth and his abode! Then, there had been not any faction to help him against God. And he had been of the ones who are helpless.²⁸:⁸¹

And it came to be in the morning those who had coveted his place but yesterday, say: God extends the provision to whomever He wills of His servants and confines it to whomever He wills. Were it not that God showed grace to us, He would have caused the earth to swallow us; O how the ones who are ungrateful will not prosper!²⁸:⁸²

This is the Last Abode that We will assign to those who want not self-exaltation in the earth, nor corruption. And the Ultimate End is for the ones who are Godfearing.²⁸:⁸³

Whoever brought about benevolence, for him there will be better than it. And whoever brought about an evil deed, then, not will be given recompense to those who did evil deeds other than for what they had been doing.²⁸:⁸⁴

Truly, He Who imposed the Quran for thee will be one who restores thee to the place of return. Say: My Lord is greater in knowledge of whoever drew near guidance and whoever is clearly wandering astray.²⁸:⁸⁵

And thou hadst been without hope that the Book would be cast down to thee, but as a mercy from thy Lord. Be thou not a sustainer of the ones who are ungrateful.²⁸:⁸⁶

And let them not bar thee from the signs of God after they were caused to descend to thee. And call to thy Lord. And be thou not among the ones who are polytheists.²⁸:⁸⁷

And call not to any god other than God. There is no god but He! Everything is that which perishes, but His Countenance. To Him is the determination and to Him you will be returned.²⁸:⁸⁸

CHAPTER 29 THE SPIDER

In the Name of God, The Merciful, The Compassionate
*Alif Lām Mīm.*²⁹:¹

Assumed humanity that they will be left because they say: We believed and they will not be tried?²⁹:²

And, certainly, We tried those who were before them. Then, certainly, God knows those who were sincere and knows the ones who lie.²⁹:³

Or assumed those who do evil deeds that they will out do Us?

How evil is that about which they give judgment!²⁹:⁴

Whoever had been hoping for the meeting with God, then, truly, the term of God is that which arrives. And He is The Hearing, The Knowing.²⁹:⁵

Whoever struggled, he struggles only for himself. Then, truly, God is Sufficient for the worlds.²⁹:⁶

And those who believed and do as ones in accord with morality, certainly, We will absolve them of their evil deeds and We will give recompense for the fairer of what they had been doing.²⁹:⁷

And We charged the human being with goodness to ones who are his parents and if they struggled with thee that thou ascribest partners with Me, that of which for thee there is no knowledge, then, obey them not. To Me is your return and I will tell you of what you had been doing.²⁹:⁸

And those who believed and did as the ones in accord with morality, We will, certainly, cause them to enter among the ones in accord with morality.²⁹:⁹

And of humanity is he who says: We believed in God. But, when he was maligned for the sake of God, he mistook the persecution by humanity for a punishment by God.

And if help drew near from thy Lord, they would, surely, say: We had been with you. Is not God greater in knowledge of what is in the breasts of beings?²⁹:¹⁰

And, certainly, God knows those who believed and, certainly, He knows the ones who are hypocrites.²⁹:¹¹

And those who were ungrateful said to those who believed: Follow our way and we will, certainly, carry your transgressions while they are not ones who carry any of their own transgressions. Truly, they are the ones who lie.²⁹:¹²

And, certainly, they will carry their own lading and other ladings with their own ladings. And, certainly, they will be asked on the Day of Resurrection about what they had been devising.²⁹:¹³

And, certainly, We sent Noah to his folk and he lingered in expectation among them a thousand years less fifty years. And the Deluge took them while they were the ones who are unjust. ²⁹:¹⁴ Then, We rescued him and the Companions of the Vessel and made it a sign for the worlds.²⁹:¹⁵

And when Abraham said to his folk: Worship God and be Godfearing of Him. That would be better for you if you had been knowing.²⁹:¹⁶ You only worship graven images and not God? And you create calumny? Truly, those whom you worship other than God possess not for you any power to provide for you.

So look for the provision from God and worship Him and give thanks to Him. To Him you will be returned.²⁹:¹⁷

And if you deny, then, surely, communities denied before you. And for the Messenger is not but the delivering of the clear message.²⁹:¹⁸

Consider they not how God causes the creation to begin and, again, He causes it to return? Truly, that for God is easy.²⁹:¹⁹

Say: Journey through the earth; then, look on how He began the creation. Again, God will cause the last growth to grow. Truly, God is Powerful over everything.²⁹:²⁰

He punishes whom He wills and has mercy on whom He wills. And to Him you will come back.²⁹:²¹

You will not be ones who frustrate Him on the earth nor in the heaven and there is not for you, other than God, either a protector or a helper.²⁹:²²

And those who disbelieved in the signs of God and the meeting with Him, those gave up hope of My mercy and those, for them there will be a painful punishment.²⁹:²³

So the answer of his folk had been not but that they said: Kill him or burn him! Then, God rescued him from the fire. Truly, in this are, certainly, signs for a folk who believe.²⁹:²⁴

And he said: You take only to yourselves graven images instead of God because of affection among yourselves for this present life. Again, on the Day of Resurrection some of you will disavow some others and some of you will curse some others and your place of shelter will be the fire. And for you there will be no ones who help.²⁹:²⁵

So Lot believed in him.

And Abraham said: Truly, I am one who emigrates for my Lord. Truly, He, He is The Almighty, The Wise.²⁹:²⁶

And We bestowed Isaac and Jacob on him and We assigned to his offspring prophethood and the Book. We gave him his compensation in the present. And, truly, in the world to come he will be, certainly, among the ones in accord with morality.²⁹:²⁷

And Lot, when he said to his folk: Truly, you approach indecency which none who preceded you committed in the worlds.²⁹:²⁸ You approach men with lust and sever the way and approach that which is unlawful in your conclave.

Then, the answer of his folk had not been but that they said: Bring on us the punishment of God if thou hadst been among the ones who are sincere.²⁹:²⁹

He said: My Lord! Help me against the folk, ones who make corruption.²⁹:³⁰

And when Our messengers drew near Abraham with the good tidings, they said: Truly, We are ones who will cause to perish the people of this town. Truly, its people had been ones who are unjust.²⁹:³¹

He said: Truly, in it is Lot.

They said: We are greater in knowledge of who is in it. We will, truly, deliver him and his family, but his woman. She had been among the ones who stay behind.²⁹:³²

And when Our messengers drew near Lot, he was troubled because of them and he was concerned for them, distressed, and they said: Neither fear nor feel remorse. Truly, we are ones who will deliver thee and thy family but thy woman. She had been among the ones who stay behind.²⁹:³³

Truly, we are ones who will cause to descend on the people of this town wrath from heaven because they had been disobeying.²⁹:³⁴

And, certainly, We left in it a sign, clear portents for a folk who be reasonable.²⁹:³⁵

And to Midian, their brother Shuayb.

He said: O my folk! Worship God and hope for the Last Day and do not mischief in and on the earth as ones who make corruption.²⁹:³⁶

And they denied him. So the quaking of the earth took them and it came to be in the morning in their abodes, ones who are fallen prostrate.²⁹:³⁷

And Ad and Thamud, surely, it became clear to you from their dwellings. Satan made their actions appear pleasing to them and barred them from the way and they had been ones who see clearly.²⁹:³⁸

And Korah and Pharaoh and Haman and, certainly, Moses drew near to them with the clear portents, but they grew arrogant on the earth and they had not been ones who take the lead from Us.²⁹:³⁹

So We took each of them in his impiety. And of them was he on whom We sent a sand storm and of them was he whom the Cry took and of them was he whom We caused the earth to swallow and of them were some whom We drowned. And God had not been doing wrong to them, but they had been doing wrong themselves.²⁹:⁴⁰

The parable of those who took other than God to themselves as protectors is that of the spider who took a house to itself. But, truly, the frailest of houses is the house of the spider if they had but been knowing.²⁹:⁴¹

Truly, God knows what thing they call to other than Him. And He is The Almighty, The Wise.²⁹:⁴²

And We propound these parables for humanity. And no one is reasonable among them but the ones who know.²⁹:⁴³

God created the heavens and the earth with The Truth. Truly, in that is a sign for the ones who believe.²⁹:⁴⁴

Recount what was revealed to thee of the Book and perform the formal prayer. Truly, the formal prayer prohibits depravity and that which is unlawful, and, truly, the remembrance of God is greater. And God knows what you craft.²⁹:⁴⁵

And dispute not with the People of the Book unless in a way that is fairer, but with those who did wrong among them. And say: We have believed in what was caused to descend to us and was caused to descend to you and our God and your God is One and we are ones who submit to Him.²⁹:⁴⁶

And, thus, We caused the Book to descend to thee. And those to whom We gave the Book before will believe in it. And of these, the people of Makkah, there are some who believe in it. And none negates Our signs but the ones who are ungrateful.²⁹:⁴⁷

And neither hadst thou been recounting from any Book before it nor writest thou it with thy right hand for then, certainly, they would have been in doubt, the ones who deal in falsehood.²⁹:⁴⁸

Nay! It is clear portents, signs in the breasts of those who were given the knowledge. And none negate Our signs but ones who are unjust.²⁹:⁴⁹

And they said: Why were signs not caused to descend to him from his Lord?

Say: The signs are only with God. I am only a warner, one who makes clear.²⁹:⁵⁰

Suffices for them not that We caused the Book to descend to thee which is recounted to them? Truly, in that is a mercy and a reminder for a folk who believe.²⁹:⁵¹

Say: God sufficed as a witness between me and between you. He knows whatever is in the heavens and the earth. And those who believed in falsehood and were ungrateful to God, those, they are the ones who are losers.²⁹:⁵²

And they seek thee to hasten the punishment! And were it not for a term, that which is determined, the punishment would have drawn near them. And, certainly, it will approach them suddenly while they are not aware.²⁹:⁵³

They seek to hasten the punishment and, truly, hell will be that which encloses the ones who are ungrateful.²⁹:⁵⁴

On a Day when the punishment overcomes them from above them and from beneath their feet, He will say: Experience what you had been doing!²⁹:⁵⁵ O my servants who have believed, My earth, truly, is that which is extensive, so worship Me!²⁹:⁵⁶

Every soul is one that experiences death. Again, to Us you will return.²⁹:⁵⁷

And those who believed and did as the ones in accord with morality, We will certainly place them in a settlement in the highest chambers in the Garden, beneath which rivers run, ones who will dwell in it forever. How excellent is the compensation for the ones who work,²⁹:⁵⁸ those who endured patiently and they put their trust in their Lord.²⁹:⁵⁹

And how many a moving creature carries not its own provision, but God provides for it and for you. And He is The Hearing, The Knowing.²⁹:⁶⁰ And if thou hadst asked them: Who created the heavens and the earth and caused the sun and the moon to be subservient? They will, certainly, say: God. Then, how they are misled!²⁹:⁶¹

God extends the provision for whom He wills of His servants and confines it for whom He wills. Truly, God is Knowing of everything.²⁹:⁶²

And if thou hadst asked them: Who sent down water from heaven and gave life by it to the earth after its death, certainly, they would say: God!

Say: The Praise belongs to God! Nay! Most of them are not reasonable.²⁹:⁶³

And this present life is not, but a diversion and a pastime. And, truly, the Last Abode is the eternal life if they had been knowing!²⁹:⁶⁴

And when they embarked on the boats, they called to God, ones who are sincere and devoted in the way of life to Him. Then, when He delivered them to dry land, that is when they ascribed partners with God,²⁹:⁶⁵ being ungrateful for what We gave them. So let them take joy for soon they will know!²⁹:⁶⁶

Consider they not that We made a safe, holy place while humanity is being snatched away all around them? Believe they, then, in falsehood and are they ungrateful for the divine blessing?²⁹:⁶⁷

And who does greater wrong than he who devised a lie against God?

Or denied The Truth when it drew near him?

Is there not in hell a place of lodging for the ones who are ungrateful?²⁹:⁶⁸

And as for those who struggled for Us, We will truly guide them to Our ways. And, truly, God is with ones who are doers of good.²⁹:⁶⁹

CHAPTER 30 THE ROMANS

In the Name of God, The Merciful, The Compassionate
*Alif Lām Mīm.*³⁰:¹

The Romans were vanquished³⁰:² in the closer region, and they, after being vanquished, will prevail³⁰:³ within a certain number of years.

To God belongs the command before and after. And that Day ones who believe will be glad³⁰:⁴ with the help of God. He helps whom He wills. And He is The Almighty, The Compassionate.³⁰:⁵

It is the promise of God. God breaks not His Promise, but most of humanity knows not.³⁰:⁶ They know only that which is manifest in this present life. And of the world to come, they are ones who are heedless.³⁰:⁷

Or if they reflect not in themselves, God created not the heavens and the earth and whatever is between the two but with The Truth and for a term that is determined. And, truly, most of humanity, in the meeting with their Lord, are, certainly, ones who disbelieve.³⁰:⁸

Or journey they not through the earth and look on how had been the Ultimate End of those who were before them? They had been superior to them in strength. And they plowed the earth and frequented it more than they frequented it. And drew near them their Messengers with the clear portents. Then, it had not been God doing wrong to them, but they had been doing wrong to themselves.³⁰:⁹

Again, the Ultimate End had been misdeeds for those who did evil, because they denied the signs of God and had been ridiculing them.³⁰:¹⁰

God begins the creation. Again, He causes it to return. Again, you will be returned to Him.³⁰:¹¹

And on a Day when the Hour will be secure, the ones who sin will be seized with despair.³⁰:¹²

And for them among their ascribed associates will not be intercessors and their ascribed associates with God will be ones who disavow them.³⁰:¹³

And on a Day when the Hour will be secure, that Day they will be split up.³⁰:¹⁴ Then, as for those who believed and did as the ones in accord with morality, they will be walking with joy in a well-watered meadow.³⁰:¹⁵

And as for those who are ungrateful and denied Our signs and the meeting of the world to come, those are ones who are charged with the punishment.³⁰:¹⁶ So glory be to God at the time of the evening hour and at the time when it comes to be the morning!³⁰:¹⁷

To Him be The Praise in the heavens and the earth and in the evening and at the time of noon.³⁰:¹⁸ He brings out the living from the dead. And He brings out the dead from the living. And He gives life to the earth after its death. And, thus, you will be brought out.³⁰:¹⁹

And among His signs are that He created you from earth dust, when, again, you were mortals dispersed.³⁰:²⁰

And among His signs are that He created for you spouses from among yourselves, that you rest in them. And He made affection and mercy among you. Truly, in that are certainly signs for a folk who reflect.³⁰:²¹

And among His signs are the creation of the heavens and the earth and the alteration of your languages and hues. Truly, in that are certainly signs for ones who know.³⁰:²²

And among His signs are your slumbering by nighttime and by daytime and your looking for His grace. Truly, in that are, certainly, signs for a folk who hear.³⁰:²³

And among His signs are that He causes you to see the lightning in fear and in hope. And He sends water down from heaven and gives life by it to the earth after its death. Truly, in that are, certainly, signs for a folk who are reasonable.³⁰:²⁴

And among His signs are that the heaven and the earth are secured for you by His command. When He will call you by a call again from the earth, that is when you will go forth!³⁰:²⁵

And to Him belongs whoever is in the heavens and the earth. All are ones who are morally obligated to Him.³⁰:²⁶

And He it is Who begins the creation. Again, He causes it to return and this is insignificant for Him. And His is the Lofty Parable in the heavens and the earth. And He is The Almighty, The Wise.³⁰:²⁷

He propounds a parable for you from yourselves. Have you—among those whom your right hands possessed—ascribed associates in what We provided you so that you share as equals and you fear them like your awe for each other? Thus, We explain distinctly the signs to a folk who are reasonable.³⁰:²⁸

Nay! Those who did wrong followed their own desires without knowledge. Then, who will guide whom God caused to go astray? And they will not have ones who help.³⁰:²⁹

So set thy face towards a way of life as a monotheist. It is the nature originated by God in which He originated humanity. There is no substitution for the creation of God. That is the truth-loving way of life, but most of humanity knows not.³⁰:³⁰

Be ones who turn in repentance to Him and be Godfearing and perform the formal prayer and be not among the ones who are polytheists³⁰:³¹ or of those who separated and divided their way of life and had been partisans, each party is glad with what they have.³⁰:³²

And when harm afflicted humanity, they call to their Lord as ones who turn in repentance to Him. When He caused them, again, to experience His mercy, that is when a group of people among them ascribe partners with their Lord,³⁰:³³ for they are ungrateful for what We gave them. Then, take joy; you will know.³⁰:³⁴

Or caused We to descend to them an authority that it assert what they had been ascribing as partners with Him?³⁰:³⁵

And when We caused humanity to experience mercy, they were glad of it. But when an evil deed lights on them because of what their hands put forward, that is when they are in despair.³⁰:³⁶

Consider they that God extends the provision for whom He wills and confines it for whom He wills?

Truly, in that are signs for a folk who believe.³⁰:³⁷

So give to possessors of kinship rightfully and to the needy and to the traveler of the way. That is better for those who want the Countenance of God. And those, they are the ones who prosper.³⁰:³⁸

And what you gave in usury in order that it swell the wealth of humanity swells not with God. And what you gave in purifying alms, wanting the Countenance of God, then, those, they are the ones who will receive manifold.³⁰:³⁹

God is He Who created you. Again, He provided for you and, again, He will cause you to die. Again, He will give you life. Is there among your ascribed associates with Him who accomplish anything of that? Glory be to Him! Exalted is He above partners they ascribe!³⁰:⁴⁰

Corruption was manifested on the dry land and the sea because of what the hands of humanity earned. He causes them to experience some of what they did, so that perhaps they will return repentant.³⁰:⁴¹

Say: Journey through the earth; then, look on how had been the Ultimate End of those who were before. Most of them had been ones who are polytheists.³⁰:⁴²

So set thy face to the truth-loving way of life before that Day approaches from God and there is no turning back. They will be split up on that Day.³⁰:⁴³

Whoever was ungrateful, his ingratitude is on him. Whoever did as one in accord with morality will be arranging provision for themselves.³⁰:⁴⁴

And He gives recompense to those who believed and did as the ones in accord with morality from His grace. Truly, He loves not the ones who are ungrateful.³⁰:⁴⁵

Among His signs are that He sends the winds as ones that give good tidings and causes you to experience His mercy and so that the boats run at His command and that you be looking for His grace so that perhaps you will give thanks.³⁰:⁴⁶

And, certainly, We sent Messengers before thee to their own folk. They drew near them with the clear portents. Then, We requited those who sinned. And it had been an obligation on Us to help ones who believe.³⁰:⁴⁷

God is He Who sends the winds so they raise clouds. He extends them in the heaven how He wills and He makes them into pieces until thou hast seen rain drops go forth from their midst. That is when He lit it on whomever He wills of His servants. That is when they rejoice at the good tidings.³⁰:⁴⁸

And, truly, they had been—even before it is sent down on them—before that, ones who are seized with despair.³⁰:⁴⁹

Look on the effects of the mercy of God, how He gives life to the earth after its death! Truly, that! He is One Who Gives Life to the dead and He is Powerful over everything.³⁰:⁵⁰

And if We sent a wind and they saw fields, ones that are yellowing, they would stay ungrateful after that.³⁰:⁵¹

Then, truly, thou wilt not cause the dead to hear nor wilt thou cause the unwilling to hear, to hear the calling to them when they turned as ones who draw back.³⁰:⁵²

And thou art not one who guides the unwilling to see from their fallacy. Thou hast caused none to hear but those who believe in Our signs. And they are ones who submit to God.³⁰:⁵³

God is He Who created you in your weakness. Again, after that weakness, He assigned strength; again, after that strength, He assigned weakness and grayness of hair. And He creates what He wills. And He is The Knowing, The Powerful.³⁰:⁵⁴

And on a Day when the Hour is secured for you, the ones who sin will swear that they lingered in expectation not but an hour. Thus, they had been misled.³⁰:⁵⁵

And said those who were given the knowledge and the belief: Certainly, you lingered in expectation by what is prescribed by God until the Day of the Uprising. This is the Day of Uprising, but you had not been knowing.³⁰:⁵⁶

So on that Day will not profit them, those who did wrong, their excuses nor will they ask to be favored.³⁰:⁵⁷

And, certainly, We propounded for humanity in this, the Quran, every kind of parable. But if thou wert to bring about any sign to them, certainly, they who were ungrateful would say: Truly, you are nothing but ones who deal in falsehood.³⁰:⁵⁸

Thus, God sets a seal on the hearts of those who know not.³⁰:⁵⁹ So have thou patience. Truly, the promise of God is True. And let them not irritate thee, those who are not certain in belief.³⁰:⁶⁰

CHAPTER 31 LUQMAN

In the Name of God, The Merciful, The Compassionate
*Alif Lām Mīm.*³¹:¹

There are the signs of the wise Book,³¹:² a guidance and a mercy to the ones who are doers of good,³¹:³ those who perform the formal prayer and give the purifying alms and they are certain of the world to come.³¹:⁴ Those are on a guidance from their Lord. And those, they are the ones who prosper.³¹:⁵

And of humanity is he who exchanges diversionary conversation to cause others to go astray from the way of God without any knowledge. And he takes it to himself in mockery. Those, for them will be a despised punishment.³¹:⁶

When Our signs are recounted to him, he turned as one who grows arrogant, as if he had not been hearing them, as if there had been heaviness in his ears. So give him the good tidings of a painful punishment.³¹:⁷

Truly, those who believed and did as the ones in accord with morality, for them are Gardens of Bliss,³¹:⁸ ones who will dwell in them forever. The promise of God is true. And He is The Almighty, The Wise.³¹:⁹

He created the heavens without any pillars so that you see the heavens. And He cast firm mountains on the earth so that the earth should not vibrate with you. And He disseminated in and on it of all moving creatures. And We caused water to descend from heaven. We caused all generous, diverse pairs to develop in it.³¹:¹⁰

This is the creation of God. Then, cause me to see what other than He created? Nay! The ones who are unjust are clearly wandering astray.³¹:¹¹

And, certainly, We gave Luqman wisdom that: Give thanks to God. And whoever gives thanks, gives thanks only for himself. And whoever was ungrateful—then, truly, God is Sufficient, Worthy of Praise.³¹:¹²

And when Luqman said to his son as he admonishes him: O my son! Ascribe not partners with God. Truly, association with God is, certainly, a tremendous injustice.³¹:¹³

And We charged the human being about ones who are his parents. His mother carried him in feebleness on feebleness and his weaning is in two years. Give thanks to Me and to ones who are thy parents. And to Me is the Homecoming.³¹:¹⁴

But if they both struggled with thee that thou hast ascribed partners with Me of what for thee is no knowledge, then, obey them not. And keep their company in the present as one who is honorable but follow the way of him who was penitent to Me. Again, to Me will be your return and I will tell you of what you had been doing.³¹:¹⁵

O my son! Truly, even if it be the weight of a grain of a mustard seed and though it be in a rock or in the heavens or in or on the earth God will bring it. Truly, God is Subtle, Aware.³¹:¹⁶

O my son! Perform the formal prayer. And command that which is honorable. And prohibit that which is unlawful. And have thou patience with whatever lit on thee. Truly, that is the constancy of affairs.³¹:¹⁷ And turn not thy cheek away from humanity nor walk through the earth exultantly. Truly, God loves not any proud boaster.³¹:¹⁸

And be moderate in thy walking and lower thy voice. Truly, the most horrible of voices is, certainly, the voice of the donkey.³¹:¹⁹

Consider you not that God caused to become subservient to you whatever is in the heavens and whatever is in and on the earth and lavished on you His divine blessing, that which is manifest and that which is inward and yet most of humanity is he who disputes about God without knowledge and with no guidance and without an illuminating Book.³¹:²⁰

And when it was said to them: Follow what God caused to descend. They said: Nay! We will follow what we found our fathers on.

Even if it Satan had been calling them to the punishment of the blaze?³¹:²¹

And whoever submits his face to God while he is one who is a doer of good, then, surely, he held fast to the most firm handhold. And to God is the Ultimate End of affairs.³¹:²²

And whoever was ungrateful, let not his ingratitude dishearten thee. To Us is their return and We will tell them what they did. Truly, God is Knowing of what is in the breasts.³¹:²³ We give them enjoyment for a little while. Again, We will compel them to a harsh punishment.³¹:²⁴

And if thou hadst asked them who created the heavens and the earth, they will certainly say: God! Say: The Praise belongs to God! But most of them know not.³¹:²⁵

To God belongs whatever is in the heavens and the earth. Truly, God, He is The Sufficient, The Worthy of Praise.³¹:²⁶

And if trees on the earth were only pens and the sea causes to increase after that with seven more seas that were ink, yet the Words of God would not come to an end. Truly, God is Almighty, Wise.³¹:²⁷

Your creation and your Uprising are not but like that of a single soul. Truly, God is Hearing, Seeing.³¹:²⁸

Hast thou not considered that God causes the nighttime to be interposed into the daytime and causes the daytime to be interposed into the nighttime and caused the sun to become subservient and the moon, each run for a term, that which is determined and that God is Aware of what you do?31:29

That is because God, He is The Truth and what they call to other than Him is falsehood. And that God, He is The Lofty, The Great!31:30

Hast thou not considered that the boats run through the sea by the divine blessing of God that He causes you to see His signs? Truly in that are signs for every enduring, grateful one.31:31

And when a wave overcame them like an overshadowing, they called to God as ones who are sincere and devoted in the way of life to Him. Then, when He delivered them to dry land among them are ones who halt between two opinions. And none negates Our signs but every ungrateful turncoat.31:32

O humanity! Be Godfearing of your Lord, and dread a Day when recompense will not be given by a child to one to whom the child is born, nor will one to whom a child is born be one who gives recompense for the one who is born at all. Truly, the promise of God is True so let not this present life delude you nor let the deluder delude you about God.31:33

Truly, the knowledge of the Hour is with God. And He sends plenteous rain water down. And He knows what is in the wombs. And no soul is informed of what it will earn tomorrow. And no soul is informed in what region it will die. Truly, God is Knowing, Aware.31:34

CHAPTER 32
THE PROSTRATION

In the Name of God, The Merciful, The Compassionate
*Alif Lām Mīm.*32:1

The sending down successively of the Book, there is no doubt in it. It is from the Lord of the worlds.32:2

Or they say: He devised it.

Nay! It is The Truth from thy Lord that thou warnest a folk to whom no warner approached them before thee, so that perhaps they will be truly guided.32:3

God! It is He Who created the heavens and the earth and whatever is between them in six days.

Again, He turned His attention to the Throne.

You will have none other than Him as protector and no intercessor. Will you not, then, recollect?32:4

He manages every command from the heaven to the earth. Again, it will go up to Him in a day, the span of which had been a thousand years of what you number.32:5

That is the One Who Knows of the unseen and the visible, The Almighty, The Compassionate32:6 Who did everything that He created well.

And He began the creation of the human being from clay.32:7

Again, He made human progeny from the extraction of despicable water.32:8

Again, He shaped him and breathed into him His Spirit. And He made for you the ability to hear and sight and minds. But you give little thanks!32:9

They said: When we went astray on the earth will we be in a new creation?

Nay! In the meeting with their Lord they are ones who disbelieve.32:10

Say: The angel of death who was charged with you, will call you to itself. Again, you will be returned to your Lord.32:11

And if thou but see when the ones who sin become ones who bend down their heads before their Lord: Our Lord! We perceived and heard. So return us. We will do as ones in accord with morality. Truly, we are now ones who are certain.32:12

And if We willed it, We would have, surely, given every soul its guidance, but My saying will be realized. I will fill hell with genies and humanity one and all.32:13 Then, experience it.

As you forgot the meeting of this Day of yours, truly, We forgot you. And experience the infinite punishment for what you had been doing.32:14

Only those believe in Our signs who, when they were reminded of them, fell down, ones who prostrate themselves and glorified the praise of their Lord and they grow not arrogant,32:15 whose sides deliberately avoided their sleeping places to call to their Lord in fear and hope. And they spend of what We provided them.32:16

No soul knows what was concealed for them of comfort for their eyes as a recompense for what they had been doing.32:17

Is he who had been one who believes like he who had been one who disobeys? They are not on the same level.32:18

As for those who believed and did as the ones in accord with morality, for them are Gardens as places of shelter, hospitality for them for what they had been doing.32:19

And as for those who disobeyed, their place of shelter will be the fire. Every time they would want to go forth from there, they would be caused to return to it.

And it will be said to them: Experience the punishment of the fire which you had been denying!32:20

And, certainly, We will cause them to experience the closer punishment other than the greater punishment so that perhaps they will return.32:21

And who does greater wrong than he who was reminded of the signs of His Lord, then, he turned aside from them? Truly, on the ones who sin, We are ones who requite.32:22

And, certainly, We gave Moses the Book. So be you not hesitant about meeting Him. And We assigned it as a guidance for the Children of Israel.32:23

And We assigned leaders from among them to guide under Our command when they endured patiently. And they had been certain of Our signs.32:24 Truly, thy Lord is He Who will distinguish among them on the Day of Resurrection about what they had been at variance in it.32:25

Guides them not how many We caused to perish of generations before them amidst whose dwellings they walk?

Truly, in that are the signs. Will they not then hear?32:26

Consider they not that We drive water to the barren dust of earth?

We drive out crops with it from which their flocks eat and they themselves. Will they not, then, perceive?32:27

And they say: When is this victory if you had been ones who are sincere?32:28

Say: On the Day of Victory there will be no profit for those who disbelieved if they, then, have belief nor will they be given respite.32:29 So turn thou aside from them and wait awhile. Truly they are ones who are waiting awhile.32:30

CHAPTER 33
THE CONFEDERATES

In the Name of God, The Merciful, The Compassionate

O Prophet! Be Godfearing of God and obey not the ones who are ungrateful and the ones who are hypocrites. Truly, God had been Knowing, Wise.33:1

And follow what is revealed to thee from thy Lord. Truly, God is Aware of what you had been doing.33:2

And put thy trust in God. And God sufficed as a Trustee.33:3

And God made not two hearts for any man in his interior. Nor made He your spouses those whom you divorced saying:

Be as the back of my mother! Nor made He your adopted sons, your sons. That is but a saying of your mouths. And God says The Truth and He guides to the way.^{33:4}

Call to them by the names of their fathers. That is more equitable with God. But if you know not their fathers, they are your brothers in the way of life and your defenders. And there is no blame on you in what mistake you made in it, but what your hearts premeditated. And God had been Forgiving, Compassionate.^{33:5}

The Prophet is closer to the ones who believe than their own souls. And his spouses are their mothers and those imbued through the wombs, blood relations, some of them are closer to some other in what is prescribed by God than the other ones who believe and ones who emigrate, but accomplish what you may for your protectors as ones who are honorable—that which had been inscribed in the Book.^{33:6}

Mention when We took a solemn promise from the Prophets and from thee and from Noah and Abraham and Moses and Jesus son of Mary. We took an earnest solemn promise from them^{33:7} so that He ask the ones who are sincere about their sincerity.

He prepared for the ones who are ungrateful a painful punishment.^{33:8}

O those who believed! Remember the divine blessing of God to you when armies drew near you and We sent the winds against them and armies you see not. And God had been Seeing of what you do.^{33:9}

When they drew near you from above you and from below you and when the sight swerved and the hearts reached the throats and you think thoughts about God,^{33:10} there the ones who believe were tested and were convulsed with a severe convulsing.^{33:11}

And when the ones who are hypocrites say, as well as those who in their hearts is a sickness: What God and His Messenger promised is nothing but delusion.^{33:12}

And when a section of them said: O people of Yathrib! There is no habitation for you, so return.

A group of people ask permission of the Prophet among them saying: Truly, Our houses are exposed.

But they were not exposed. They want only to run away.^{33:13}

And if entry was forced against them from all areas and, again, they were asked to dissent, they would have given into it and they would not have but briefly hesitated^{33:14} although, certainly, they made a contract with God before that they would not turn their backs to the enemy. And about their compact with God that had been, they are ones who will be asked.^{33:15}

Say: Running away will never profit you that you ran away from death or killing, then, you will be given enjoyment but for a little.^{33:16}

Say: Who will save you from harm from God if He wanted evil for you or wanted mercy for you?

And they will not find for themselves other than God a protector or a helper.^{33:17}

Surely, God knows the ones of you who hold off and the ones who converse with their brothers saying to us: Come on! And they approach not the battle themselves but a little,^{33:18} being covetous of you. Then, when fear drew near, thou wilt see them looking on thee, their eyes rolling like he who is overcome by death. But when their fear went, they abused you with sharp tongues in their covetousness for good things. Those believe not and God caused their actions to fail. And that had been easy for God.^{33:19}

They assume the confederates go not, withdrawing. And if the confederates approach you, returning, they would wish they were nomads among the ones who are desert dwellers, asking tidings about you. And if they had been among you, they would fight but a little.^{33:20}

Surely, in the Messenger of God there is for you a fairer, good example for those whose hope had been in God and the Last Day and remembered God frequently.^{33:21}

When the ones who believe saw the confederates, they said: This is what God and His Messenger promised us and God and His Messenger were sincere. And it increased them not but in belief and to resign themselves to submission to God.^{33:22}

Among the ones who believe are men who were sincere in the contracts they made with God. Of them are some who satisfied by fulfilling their vow with death and of them are some who wait awhile. And they substituted not any substitution^{33:23} so that God gives recompense to the ones who are sincere for their sincerity and punish the ones who are hypocrites had He willed or He turns to them in forgiveness. Truly, God had been Forgiving, Compassionate.^{33:24}

God repelled those who were ungrateful in their rage without their attaining any good. And God spared the ones who believe in fighting. And God had been Strong, Almighty.^{33:25}

And He caused to descend those who were behind among the People of the Book from their strongholds and He hurled alarm into their hearts so that you kill a group of people and make captives of another group of people.^{33:26}

And He gave you their region as an inheritance and their abodes and their wealth and a region you tread not. And God had been Powerful over everything!^{33:27}

O Prophet! Say to thy spouses: If you had been wanting this present life and its adornment, then, approach now. I will give you enjoyment and set you (f) free, releasing gracefully.^{33:28}

And if you had been wanting God and His Messenger, and the Last Abode, then truly God prepared for the ones who are doers of good among you a sublime compensation.^{33:29}

O wives of the Prophet! Whoever of you (f) approaches a manifest indecency her punishment will be multiplied for her twofold. And that would have been easy for God.^{33:30}

And whoever of you (f) is morally obligated to God and His Messenger and do as ones (f) in accord with morality, We will give her her compensation two times over. We made ready a generous provision for her.^{33:31}

O wives of the Prophet! There is not among the wives any like you. If you (f) were Godfearing, then, be not soft in your saying so that he become desirous he in whose heart is a sickness, but say (f) a saying of one who is honorable.^{33:32}

And settle down (f) in your (f) houses and flaunt (f) not your (f) finery as those who flaunted their finery in the previous Age of Ignorance. And perform (f) the formal prayer and give (f) the purifying alms and obey (f) God and His Messenger. God only wants to cause disgrace to be put away from you—People of the House—and purify you with a purification.^{33:33}

And remember (f) what is recounted in your (f) houses of the signs of God and wisdom. Truly, God had been Subtle, Aware.^{33:34} Truly, the males, ones who submit to God and the females, ones who submit to God and the males, ones who believe and the females, ones who believe and the males, ones who are morally obligated and the females, ones who are morally obligated and the males, ones who are sincere and the females, ones who are sincere and the males, ones who remain steadfast and the females, ones who remain steadfast and the males, ones who are humble and the females, ones who are humble and the males, ones who are charitable and the females, ones who are charitable and the males, ones who fast and the females, ones who fast and the males, ones who guard their private parts and the females, ones who guard and the males, ones who remember God frequently and the females, ones who remember, God prepared for them forgiveness and a sublime compensation.³³:³⁵

It had not been for a male, one who believes and a female, one who believes, when God and His Messenger decreed an affair that there be any choice for them in their affair. And whoever rebels against God and His Messenger, certainly, he went astray, clearly wandering astray.³³:³⁶

And mention when thou hast said to him to whom God was gracious and to whom thou wert gracious: Hold back thy spouse to thyself and be Godfearing of God. But thou hast concealed in thyself what God is One Who Shows and thou hast dreaded humanity whereas God has a better right that thou hast dreaded Him.

So when Zayd satisfied the necessary formality, We gave her to thee in marriage so that there be no fault for ones who believe in respect of the spouses of their adopted sons when they (m) satisfied the necessary formality. And the command of God had been one that is accomplished.³³:³⁷

There had been no fault with the Prophet in what is undertaken by him as a duty from God. This is a custom of God with those who passed away before. And the command of God had been a measured measure³³:³⁸ for those who state the messages of God and dread Him and dread none but God, and God sufficed as a Reckoner.³³:³⁹

Muhammad had not been the father of any men from among you, but he is the Messenger of God and the Seal of the Prophets. And God had been Knowing of everything.³³:⁴⁰

O those who believed! Remember God with a frequent remembrance³³:⁴¹ and glorify Him at early morning dawn and eventide.³³:⁴² He it is Who gives blessings to you and His angels that He bring you out of the shadows into the light. And He had been Compassionate to ones who believe.³³:⁴³ Their greetings on the Day they will meet Him will be: Peace! And He prepared for them a generous compensation.³³:⁴⁴

O Prophet! Truly, We sent thee as one who bears witness and as one who gives good tidings and as a warner³³:⁴⁵ and as one who calls to God with His permission and as a light-giving illuminating lamp.³³:⁴⁶

And give good tidings to the ones who believe that for them is a great grace from God.³³:⁴⁷

And obey not the ones who are ungrateful and the ones who are hypocrites and heed not their annoyance and put thy trust in God. And God sufficed as a Trustee.³³:⁴⁸

O those who believed! If you married the females, ones who believe, and, again, divorced them before you touch them (f), then, there is no waiting period to reckon against; so make provision for them (f), and set them (f) free, releasing gracefully.³³:⁴⁹

O Prophet! Truly, We have permitted to thee thy spouses (f), those whom thou hadst given their (f) compensation and whom thy right hand possessed from that God gave thee as spoils of war and the daughters of thy paternal uncles and the daughters of thy paternal aunts and the daughters of thy maternal uncles and the daughters of thy maternal aunts those who emigrated with thee and a woman, one who believes, if she bestowed herself on the Prophet.

And if the Prophet wanted to take her in marriage—that is exclusively for thee—not for the other ones who believe. Surely, We know what We imposed on them about their spouses and whom their right hands possessed (f) that there be no fault on thee. And God had been Forgiving, Compassionate.³³:⁵⁰

Thou wilt put off whom thou wilt of them (f) and thou will give refuge to whom thou wilt. And whomever thou wilt be looking for of whom thou hadst set aside, there is no blame on thee to receive her again. That is likelier that will be refreshed their (f) eyes and they (f) not feel remorse and may

they (f) be well-pleased with what thou hadst given them (f), all of them (f). And God knows what is in your hearts. And God had been Knowing, Forbearing.³³:⁵¹

Women are not lawful for thee in marriage after this, nor that thou wert taking them (f) in exchange for other spouses, even though their (f) goodness impressed thee, but whom thy right hand possessed (f). And God had been watching over everything.³³:⁵²

O those who believed! Enter not the houses of the Prophet for food unless permission be given to you without being ones who look for the proper time. And when you were called to enter, when you have eaten your meal, then, disperse, and be not one who lingers for conversation. Truly, such had been to harass the Prophet and he is ashamed to ask you to leave. But God is not ashamed before The Truth.

And when you asked his wives for sustenance, then, ask them (f) from behind a partition. That is purer for your hearts and their (f) hearts.

And it had not been for you to harass the Messenger of God nor marry you his spouses after him ever. Truly, that would have been serious with God.³³:⁵³

Whether you show anything or conceal it, truly, God had been Knowing of everything.³³:⁵⁴

There is no blame on them (f) to converse freely with their (f) fathers nor their (f) sons nor their (f) brothers, nor the sons of their (f) brothers nor the sons of their (f) sisters, nor their (f) women, nor what their (f) right hands possessed. And be Godfearing of God. Truly, God had been Witness over everything.³³:⁵⁵

Truly, God and His angels give blessings to the Prophet. O those who believed! Give your blessings to him and blessings of peace and invoke peace for him.³³:⁵⁶

Truly, those who malign God and His Messenger, God cursed them in the present and in the world to come and prepared for them a despised punishment.³³:⁵⁷

And those who malign the males, ones who believe and the females, ones who believe without their deserving it, surely, they lay a burden on themselves of false charges to harm another's reputation and a clear sin.³³:⁵⁸

O Prophet! Say to thy spouses (f) and thy daughters and the females, ones who believe to draw closer their (f) outer garments over themselves (f). That is more fitting so that they (f) be recognized and not be maligned. And God had been Forgiving, Compassionate.³³:⁵⁹

If the ones who are hypocrites refrain not themselves and those who in their hearts is a sickness and the ones who make a commotion in the city, We will stir thee up against them. Again, they will not be thy neighbors in it, but a little while.³³:⁶⁰

They are ones who are cursed. Whenever they were come upon, they were taken and were killed with a terrible slaying.³³:⁶¹

This is a custom of God with those who passed away before. And thou wilt never find in a custom of God any substitution.³³:⁶²

Humanity asks thee about the Hour.

Say: The knowledge of it is only with God.

And what will cause thee to recognize that perhaps the Hour be near?³³:⁶³

Truly, God cursed the ones who are ungrateful and prepared a blaze for them, ³³:⁶⁴ ones who will dwell in it forever, eternally. They shall not find a protector nor a helper.³³:⁶⁵

On a Day when will be turned upside down, their faces in the fire, they will say: O would that we obeyed God and obeyed the Messenger!³³:⁶⁶

And they will say: Our Lord! Truly, we obeyed our chiefs and our great ones. They caused us to go astray from the way.³³:⁶⁷

Our Lord! Give them double the punishment and curse them with a great cursing!³³:⁶⁸

O those who believed! Be not like those who maligned Moses. God declared him innocent of what they said. And he had been well-esteemed with God.³³:⁶⁹

O those who believed! Be Godfearing of God and say an appropriate saying.³³:⁷⁰

He will make your actions right for you and forgive you your impieties. And whoever obeys God and His Messenger surely, won a triumph, a sublime triumph!³³:⁷¹

Truly, We presented the trust to the heavens and the earth and the mountains, but they refused to carry it and were apprehensive of it. But the human being carried it. Truly, he had been wrongdoing, very ignorant.³³:⁷²

God punishes the males, ones who are hypocrites and the females, ones who are hypocrites and the males, ones who are polytheists and the females, ones who are polytheists and God will turn to forgiveness toward the males, ones who believe and the females, ones who believe. And God had been Forgiving, Compassionate.³³:⁷³

CHAPTER 34 SHEBA

In the Name of God, The Merciful, The Compassionate

The Praise belongs to God. To Him belongs whatever is in the heavens and whatever is in and on the earth. And His is The Praise in the world to come. And He is The Wise, The Aware.³⁴:¹

He knows whatever penetrates into the earth and what goes forth out of it and what comes down from the heaven and what goes up to it. And He is The Compassionate, The Forgiving.³⁴:²

And those who were ungrateful said: The Hour will not approach us.

Say: Yea! By my Lord, it will, certainly, approach you. He is One Who Knows of the unseen. Not an atom's weight escapes from Him in the heavens or in and on the earth, be it smaller than that or greater, but that it had been in a clear Book ³⁴:³ that He may give recompense to those who believed and did as the ones in accord with morality.

Those, for them there is forgiveness and a generous provision.³⁴:⁴

But those who endeavored against Our signs as ones who strive to thwart, those, for them there is a punishment of painful wrath.³⁴:⁵

And consider those who were given the knowledge that what was caused to descend to thee from thy Lord. It is The Truth and it guides to a path of The Almighty, The Worthy of Praise.³⁴:⁶

Those who were ungrateful said: Shall we point you to a man who will tell you when you were torn to pieces, ones who are totally torn to pieces? Then, you will be, truly, in a new creation.³⁴:⁷

Devised he a lie against God or is there a madness in him? Nay! Those who believe not in the world to come there is a punishment and a going far astray.³⁴:⁸

Consider they not what is in advance of them and what is behind them of the heaven and the earth? If We will, We could cause the earth to swallow them, or cause to drop on them pieces of heaven. Truly, in this is a sign for every servant, one who turns in repentance.³⁴:⁹

And, certainly, We gave David grace from Us. O mountains! Echo psalms of praise with him and the birds. And We softened iron for him,³⁴:¹⁰ saying that: Work on full coats of mail and calculate the links. And do as one in accord with morality. Truly, I am Seeing of what you do.³⁴:¹¹

And to Solomon We subjected the wind. The first part of the day was a month's journey and the evening course was a month's journey. We caused a spring of molten brass to flow for him. And We gave him of the jinn who work in advance of him with the permission of his Lord. Whoever of them swerved from Our command We caused him to experience the punishment of the blaze.³⁴:¹²

They worked for him whatever of sanctuaries he wills—images and basin-like cisterns like water-troughs and cooking pots—ones firmly fixed.

People of David! Act with thankfulness. But few of My servants are grateful.³⁴:¹³

Then, when We decreed death for Solomon, nothing pointed out his death to the jinn, but a moving creature of the earth that consumes his scepter. So when he fell down, it became clear to the jinn that if they had been knowing the unseen, they would not have lingered in expectation in the despised punishment.³⁴:¹⁴

There had, certainly, been for Sheba a sign in their dwelling place. Two gardens on the right and on the left. Eat of the provision of your Lord and give thanks to Him: A good land and a forgiving Lord.³⁴:¹⁵

But they turned aside, so We sent against them the overwhelming flood, and We substituted for their two gardens, two gardens yielding a sour harvest, and tamarisks, and something of lote-trees here and there.³⁴:¹⁶

That is how We gave recompense to them because they were ungrateful. And we recompense, but the ungrateful.³⁴:¹⁷

And We made between them and between the towns which We blessed, that which are manifest towns and We ordained journeying in them.

Journey through them as ones who are safe night and day.³⁴:¹⁸

But they said: Our Lord! Cause a distance between our journeys and they did wrong to themselves.

So We made them as tales and We tore them to pieces, a total tearing to pieces. Truly, in that are signs for every enduring grateful one.³⁴:¹⁹

And, certainly, established as true about them was the opinion of Iblis and they followed him, but a group of people among the ones who believe.³⁴:²⁰

There had not been for him any authority over them, but that We know who believe in the world to come from who is in uncertainty of it. And thy Lord is Guardian over everything.³⁴:²¹

Say: Call on those whom you claimed other than God. They possess not the weight of an atom in the heavens nor on the earth, nor have they in either any association, nor among them is there any sustainer of Him.³⁴:²²

No intercession profits with Him, but for him to whom He gave permission. Until when their hearts were freed from terror, they said: What is it that your Lord said. They said: The Truth. And He is the Lofty, the Great.³⁴:²³

Say: Who provides for you from the heavens and the earth? Say: God. And, truly, we or you are either on guidance or clearly going astray.³⁴:²⁴

Say: You will not be asked of what we sinned, nor will we be asked about what you do.³⁴:²⁵

Say: Our Lord will gather us. Again, He will explain The Truth among us and He is The Opener, The Knowing.³⁴:²⁶

Say: Cause me to see those whom you caused to join with Him as ascribed associates. No indeed! Nay! He is God, The Almighty, The Wise.³⁴:²⁷

And We sent thee not, but collectively for humanity as a bearer of good tidings and a warner, but most of humanity knows not.³⁴:²⁸

And they say: When is this promise if you had been ones who are sincere?³⁴:²⁹

Say: Yours is the solemn declaration of a Day which you delay not for an hour nor press forward.³⁴:³⁰

And those who were ungrateful said: We will never believe in this, the Quran, nor in what was in advance of it, but if thou hast considered when the ones who are unjust who are stationed before their Lord, returning the saying, some of them to some others.

Say to those who were taken advantage of due to their weakness to those who grew arrogant: If it were not for you, we would have been ones who believe.³⁴:³¹

Those who grew arrogant would say to those who were taken advantage due to their weakness: Barred we you from guidance after it drew near you?

Nay! You had been ones who sin.³⁴:³²

And would say those who were taken advantage due to their weakness to those who grew arrogant: Nay! It was your planning by nighttime and daytime when you commanded us to be ungrateful to God and to assign rivals to Him.

And they will keep their self-reproach secret when they will see the punishment and We assigned yokes around the necks of those who were ungrateful. Are they given recompense but for what they had been doing?³⁴:³³

We sent not any warner to a town, but that the ones who are given ease said: Truly, in what you were sent, we are ones who disbelieve it.³⁴:³⁴

And they said: We are more than you in wealth and in children and we are not ones who are punished!³⁴:³⁵

Say: Truly, my Lord extends the provision for whomever He wills and confines it for whom He wills, but most of humanity knows not.³⁴:³⁶

And it is not your wealth nor your children that will bring you near to Us, but whoever believed and did as one in accord with morality. As for those, for them, the recompense is doubled for what they did and they will live in the highest chambers as one who is safe.³⁴:³⁷

And those who endeavor against Our signs, as ones who strive to thwart them, those are ones who are charged with the punishment.³⁴:³⁸

Say: Truly, my Lord extends the provision for whomever He wills of His servants and confines for him what He wills. And whatever you spent of anything, He will replace it. And He is Best of the ones who provide.³⁴:³⁹

And on a Day He will assemble them altogether. Again, He will say to the angels: Was it these who had been worshipping you?³⁴:⁴⁰

They would say: Glory be to Thee! Thou art our Protector and not they. Nay! They had been worshipping the jinn. Most of them were ones who believe in them.³⁴:⁴¹

Then, today none of you will possess the power over some others to profit nor hurt and We will say to those who did wrong: Experience the punishment of the fire which you had been denying.³⁴:⁴²

When are recounted to them Our signs, clear portents, they said: This is not but a man who wants to bar you from what your fathers had been worshipping.

And they said: This is not but a forged calumny.

And those who were ungrateful for The Truth said when it drew near them: Truly, this is but clear sorcery.³⁴:⁴³

And We gave them not any Books that they study them nor sent We to them any warner before thee.³⁴:⁴⁴

Those that were before them denied and they reached not one-tenth of what We gave them. Yet they denied My Messengers. So how had My disapproval of them been!³⁴:⁴⁵

Say: I admonish you in but one thing: That you stand up for God by twos and one by one. Again, reflect. There is not in your companion any madness. He is only a warner to you of a severe punishment in advance of you.³⁴:⁴⁶

Say: Whatever compensation I asked of you, that is for you. My compensation is only from God. And He is a Witness over everything.³⁴:⁴⁷

Say: Truly, my Lord hurls The Truth. He is The Knower of the unseen.³⁴:⁴⁸

Say: The Truth drew near and falsehood neither causes to begin nor causes to return.³⁴:⁴⁹

Say: If I went astray, truly, I will only go astray with loss for myself. And if I was truly guided, it is because of what my Lord reveals to me. Truly, He is Hearing, Ever Near.³⁴:⁵⁰

And if thou wouldst see when they would be terrified, when there is no escape and they would be taken from a near place,³⁴:⁵¹ they would say: We believed in it! But how could they reach it from a place so far away?³⁴:⁵²

And, surely, they were ungrateful for it before. And they hurl at the unseen from a far place.³⁴:⁵³

And a barrier was set up between them and between that for which they lust just as was accomplished with partisans before. Truly, they had been uncertain, in grave doubt.³⁴:⁵⁴

CHAPTER 35 THE ORIGINATOR

In the Name of God, The Merciful, The Compassionate

The Praise belongs to God, One Who is the Originator of the heavens and the earth, the One Who Makes the angels messengers imbued with wings by twos and in threes and fours. He increases in creation what He wills. Truly, God is Powerful over everything.³⁵:¹

Whatever God may open of mercy to humanity, there is not one who holds it back. And what He holds back, there is not one who sends it after that. And He is The Almighty, The Wise.³⁵:²

O humanity! Remember the divine blessing of God on you! Is there anyone who is a creator other than God Who provides for you from the heaven and the earth? There is no god but He. Then, how you are misled!³⁵:³

And if they deny thee, surely, Messengers before thee were denied. And to God all affairs are returned.³⁵:⁴

O humanity! Truly, the promise of God is true. So let not this present life delude you. And let not the deluder delude you about God.³⁵:⁵

Truly, Satan is an enemy to you so take him to yourselves as an enemy. He calls only his party that they be among the Companions of the Blaze.³⁵:⁶

Those who were ungrateful, for them will be a severe punishment. And those who believed and did as the ones in accord with morality, for them there is forgiveness and a great compensation.³⁵:⁷

Then, who is there that was made to appear pleasing to him the direness of his actions so that, then, he saw it as fairer. Truly, God causes to go astray whomever He wills and guides whomever He wills. So let not thy soul be wasted in regret for them. Truly, God is Knowing of what they craft!³⁵:⁸

And it is God Who sent the winds so that they raise clouds and We drove them to a dead land and We gave life by them to the earth after its death. Thus, will be the rising!³⁵:⁹

Whoever had been wanting great glory, great glory belongs to God altogether. To Him Words of what is good rise. He exalts the actions of one in accord with morality. But those who plan evil deeds, for them will be a severe punishment. And the planning of those, it will come to nothing.³⁵:¹⁰

And God created you from earth dust: Again, from seminal fluid.

Again, He made you pairs.

And no female carries nor brings forth her burden but with His Knowledge. No one who is given a long life is given a long life, nor is anything reduced from his lifetime but it is in a Book. Truly, that is easy for God.³⁵:¹¹

The two bodies of water are not on the same level. This is agreeable, water of the sweetest kind, that which is delicious to drink, and the other is salty, bitter. But from each you eat succulent flesh and pull out glitter that you wear. And thou wilt see the boats, that which plows through the waves on it, that you be looking for His grace and so that perhaps you will give thanks.³⁵:¹²

He causes the nighttime to be interposed in the daytime and He causes the daytime to be interposed into the night-time and He caused the sun to be subservient and the moon. Each runs its course for a term, that is determined. That is God, your Lord. For Him is the dominion! And those whom you call to other than Him possess not even the white spot of a date stone.³⁵:¹³

If you call to them, they would not hear your supplication. Even if they heard, they would not respond to you. And on the Day of Resurrection they will disbelieve in your association with them. And none tells thee like One Who is Aware.³⁵:¹⁴

O humanity! It is you who are poor in relation to God. And God—He is Sufficient, Worthy of Praise.³⁵:¹⁵

If He wills, He would cause you to be put away and bring a new creation.³⁵:¹⁶

And that for God is not a great matter.³⁵:¹⁷ And no burdened soul will bear another's load. If one who is weighed down calls for help for his heavy load, nothing of it is carried for him, even if he had been possessor of kinship. Hast thou warned only those who dread their Lord in the unseen and performed the formal prayer. And he who purified himself, then, only purifies for himself. And to God is the Homecoming.³⁵:¹⁸

Not on the same level are the unwilling to see and the seeing³⁵:¹⁹ nor are shadows and light³⁵:²⁰ nor are the shade and the torrid heat.³⁵:²¹

Nor are the living and the lifeless on the same level. Truly, God causes to hear whom He wills. And thou art not one who causes to hear whoever is in graves.³⁵:²²

Thou art but a warner.³⁵:²³

Truly, We sent thee with The Truth, a bearer of good tidings and a warner.

And there is not any community, but a warner passed away among them.³⁵:²⁴

And if they deny thee, so, surely, those who were before them denied. Their Messengers drew near them with the clear portents and with the Psalms and the illuminating Book.³⁵:²⁵ Again, I took those who were ungrateful. And how had My disapproval of them been!³⁵:²⁶

Hast thou not considered that God caused water to descend from the heavens? And, then, We brought out fruits, the ones of varying hues. Among the mountains are white and red streaks—the ones of varying hues—and others raven black,³⁵:²⁷ and of humanity and moving creatures and flocks, thus, they are likewise of hues, ones at variance. Only His servants who dread God are knowing. Truly, God is Almighty, Forgiving.³⁵:²⁸

Truly, those who recount the Book of God and performed the formal prayer and spent out of what We provided for them secretly and in public, they hope for a trade that will never come to nothing.³⁵:²⁹ He will, certainly, pay them their account in full as their compensation and increase them more out of His grace. Truly, He is Forgiving, Ready to Appreciate.³⁵:³⁰

And what We revealed to thee of the Book is The Truth, that establishes as true what was in advance of it. Truly, God is Aware, Seeing of His servants.³⁵:³¹

Again, We gave the Book as an inheritance to those whom We favored of Our servants. Then, of them are ones who are unjust to themselves and of them are ones who halt between two opinions and some of them are ones who take the lead with good deeds by permission of God. That is the greater grace.³⁵:³²

Gardens of Eden—they will enter them. They will be adorned in them with bracelets of gold and pearls. And their garments in them will be silk.³⁵:³³

And they would say: The Praise belongs to God Who caused grief to be put away from us. Truly, our Lord is Forgiving, Ready to Appreciate.³⁵:³⁴

He Who caused us to live in the inhabited Abode out of His grace, fatigue will not afflict us in it, nor will we be afflicted with exhaustion in it.³⁵:³⁵

And those who were ungrateful, for them will be the fire of hell: Neither will it be decided a term for them so that they die nor will its punishment be lightened for them. Thus, We give recompense to every ungrateful one.³⁵:³⁶

And they will shout aloud in it: Our Lord! Bring us out and we shall do as ones in accord with morality, not what we had been doing! Give We not you a long enough life so that whoever recollects would recollect there? And the warner drew near you, so experience it because there is no helper for ones who are unjust.³⁵:³⁷

Truly, God is One Who Knows the unseen of the heavens and the earth. Truly, He is Knowing of what is in the breasts.³⁵:³⁸ He it is Who made you viceregents on the earth. So whoever was ungrateful, then, his ingratitude will be against him. And the ones who are ungrateful increase not their ingratitude to their Lord, but in repugnance. And the ones who are ungrateful increase not their ingratitude to their Lord, but in loss.³⁵:³⁹

Say: Considered you your ascribed associates to whom you call to other than God?

Cause me to see what they created in the earth or have they any association in creation of the heavens?

Or gave We them a Book so that they have a clear portent from there?

Nay! The ones who are unjust promise nothing—some of them to some others—but delusion.³⁵:⁴⁰

Truly, God holds back the heavens and the earth so that they are not displaced. And if they were displaced, there is none who held them back after Him. Truly, He had been Forbearing, Forgiving.³⁵:⁴¹

And they swore by God the most earnest oaths, that if a warner drew near them, they would be better guided than any of the other communities. Yet when a warner drew near to them, it increased nothing in them but aversion,³⁵:⁴² growing arrogant on the earth and planning evil deeds. The plan of bad deeds surround none but people themselves.

Then, look they on but a custom of the ancient ones?

Thou wilt never find in a custom of God any substitution. And thou wilt never find in a custom of God any revision.³⁵:⁴³

Journey they not through the earth and look on how had been the Ultimate End of those before them? They had been stronger than they are in strength. And God had not been weakened by anything in the heavens nor in or on the earth. Truly, He had been Knowing, Powerful.³⁵:⁴⁴

And if God takes humanity to task for what they earned, He would not leave on the back of the earth any moving creature, but He postpones to a term, that is determined.

And when their term drew near, then, truly, God had been Seeing of His servants.³⁵:⁴⁵

CHAPTER 36 YA SIN

In the Name of God, The Merciful, The Compassionate
*Yā Sīn.*³⁶:¹

By the Wise Quran,³⁶:² truly, thou art among the ones who are sent³⁶:³ on a straight path,³⁶:⁴ sent down successively by The Almighty, The Compassionate that³⁶:⁵ thou warnest a folk whose fathers were not warned, so they were ones who were heedless.³⁶:⁶

Certainly, the saying was realized against most of them for they believe not.³⁶:⁷ We laid yokes on their necks up to the chins, so that they are ones who are stiff-necked.³⁶:⁸ And We laid in advance of them an embankment and behind them an embankment. Then, We covered them so they perceive not.³⁶:⁹ And equal it is to them whether thou warn them, or thou warn them not. They will not believe.³⁶:¹⁰

Thou hast only warned whoever followed the Remembrance and dreaded The Merciful in the unseen, so give him good tidings of forgiveness and a generous compensation.³⁶:¹¹

Truly, We give life to the dead and We write down what they put forward and their effects. We counted everything in a clear record.³⁶:¹²

And propound a parable for them: The Companions of the Town when ones who were sent drew near them.³⁶:¹³ When We sent to them two, they denied them both, so We replenished them with the third. And they said: Truly, We are ones who are sent to you.³⁶:¹⁴

They said: You are nothing but mortals like ourselves and The Merciful caused not to descend anything. You are but lying!³⁶:¹⁵

They said: Our Lord knows that we are ones who are sent to you.³⁶:¹⁶ On us is only the delivering of the clear message.³⁶:¹⁷

They said: Truly, we augered ill of you. If you refrain not yourselves, we will, certainly, stone you. Certainly, a painful punishment will afflict you from us.³⁶:¹⁸

They said: Ones who auger ill will be with you!

Is it because you were reminded?

Nay! You are a folk, ones who are excessive.³⁶:¹⁹

A man drew near from the farther part of the city, coming eagerly. He said: O my folk! Follow the ones who are sent!³⁶:²⁰ Follow whoever asks not of you any compensation and they are ones who are truly guided.³⁶:²¹

What is it for me that I worship not Him Who originated me and to Whom you will be returned?³⁶:²² Will I take gods to myself other than He when, if The Merciful wants any harm for me, their intercession will not avail me at all nor will they save me.³⁶:²³ Truly, I would, then, be clearly going astray.³⁶:²⁴ Truly, I believed in your Lord so hear me!³⁶:²⁵

It was said: Enter the Garden.

He said: O would that my folk know³⁶:²⁶ that my Lord forgave me and made me one who is honored!³⁶:²⁷

After him We caused not to descend on his folk an army from heaven, nor had We been ones who need to cause to descend again.³⁶:²⁸ It would be but one Cry and that is when they were ones who are silent and still.³⁶:²⁹

O how regrettable of the servants! A Messenger approaches them not, but they had been ridiculing him.³⁶:³⁰

Consider they not how many generations We caused to perish before them who, truly, return not to them.³⁶:³¹ And, truly, all of them will be altogether, ones who are charged in Our Presence.³⁶:³²

And a sign for them is the dead body of the earth. We gave life to it and We brought out grain from it so that they eat from it.³⁶:³³ We made in them gardens of date palm trees and grapevines and We caused a spring to gush forth in it³⁶:³⁴ so that they may eat of the fruit from there that are not what their hands did. Will they, then, not give thanks?³⁶:³⁵

Glory be to Him Who created pairs, all of them, of what the earth causes to develop as well as of themselves and of what they know not!³⁶:³⁶

And a sign for them is the nighttime. We pluck the daytime from it and that is when they are ones in darkness!³⁶:³⁷ And the sun runs to a resting place for it. That is foreordained by The Almighty, The Knowing.³⁶:³⁸

And for the moon We ordained mansions until it reverted like an ripe aged, dry, date stalk.³⁶:³⁹

It is not fit and proper for the sun to overtake the moon nor the nighttime one to take the lead over the daytime. They each swim in an orbit.³⁶:⁴⁰

A sign for them is that We carried their offspring in a laden boat.³⁶:⁴¹ And We created for them of its like that they ride.³⁶:⁴² And if We will, We drown them with none for them to whom they cry aloud for help nor will they be saved³⁶:⁴³ unless it be a mercy from Us and as an enjoyment for awhile.³⁶:⁴⁴

And when it was said to them: Be Godfearing of what is in advance of you and what is behind you, so that perhaps you will find mercy,³⁶:⁴⁵ there never approaches them any sign from the signs of their Lord, but they had been ones who turn aside from it.³⁶:⁴⁶

And when it was said to them: Spend of whatever God provided you, those who were ungrateful said to those who believed: Will we feed him whom He would have fed, if He wills? You are nothing, but in a clear going astray.³⁶:⁴⁷

And they say: When is this promise if you had been ones who are sincere?³⁶:⁴⁸

They expect but one Cry which will take them while they strive against one another.³⁶:⁴⁹ Then, they will not be able to leave a legacy nor will they return to their people.³⁶:⁵⁰

And the trumpet would be blown! That is when they will be sliding down to their Lord from their tombs.³⁶:⁵¹

They would say: Woe on us! Who raised us up from our place of sleep? This is what The Merciful promised and the ones who are sent were sincere.³⁶:⁵²

It would be but one Cry. That is when they will be in Our Presence altogether, ones who are charged.³⁶:⁵³

This Day no soul will be wronged at all nor will you be given recompense but for what you had been doing.³⁶:⁵⁴

Truly, the Companions of the Garden that Day are ones who are joyful in their engagements.³⁶:⁵⁵ They and their spouses, in shade on raised benches, ones who are reclining.³⁶:⁵⁶ They will have in it sweet fruits and they will have whatever they call for:³⁶:⁵⁷ Peace! A saying from the Compassionate Lord.³⁶:⁵⁸ And be separated on this Day, O ones who sin!³⁶:⁵⁹

Make I not a compact with you, O Children of Adam, that you not worship Satan? Truly, he is a clear enemy³⁶:⁶⁰ and that you should worship Me. This is a straight path.³⁶:⁶¹ And, certainly, He caused to go astray many an array of you. Be you not, then, reasonable?³⁶:⁶²

This is hell which you had been promised.³⁶:⁶³ Roast in it this Day because you had been ungrateful.³⁶:⁶⁴ On this Day We will seal over their mouths and their hands will speak to Us and their feet will bear witness to what they had been earning.³⁶:⁶⁵ And if We will, We would, certainly, have obliterated their eyes. Then, they would race towards the path. How would they have perceived?³⁶:⁶⁶

And if We will, We would, certainly, have transformed their ability. Then, they would not have been able to pass on, nor would they return.³⁶:⁶⁷

And he to whom We give a long life, We bend him over in his constitution. Will they not, then, be reasonable?³⁶:⁶⁸

We taught him not poetry, nor is it fit and proper for him. It is but a Remembrance and a clear Recitation.36:69 to warn whoever had been living and that the saying be realized against the ones who are ungrateful.36:70

Consider they not how We created for them—out of what Our hands did—flocks, so they were of them ones who are owners?36:71 And We subdued them for them so that of them, some are riding animals and some of them, they eat.36:72

And they have profits from them and providing a place from which to drink. Will they not, then, give thanks?36:73 And they took to themselves gods other than God so that perhaps they will be helped.36:74 They are not able to help them while they are to them as a charged army.36:75 So let not their saying dishearten thee.

Truly, We know what they keep secret and what they speak openly.36:76

Consider not the human being that We created him from seminal fluid?

That is when he is a clear adversary.36:77 He propounded parables for Us and forgot his own creation.

He said: Who will give life to these bones when they decayed?36:78

Say: He will give life to them Who caused them to grow the first time and He is The Knowing of every creation.36:79

It is He Who made for you fire out of a green tree. That is when you kindle from it.36:80

Is not He Who created the heavens and the earth One Who Has Power to create the like of them?

Yea! And He is The Knowing Creator.36:81

Truly, His command when He wanted a thing is but to say to it: Be! Then, it is!36:82 Then, Glory be to Him in whose hand is the Kingdom of everything! And to Him you will be returned.36:83

CHAPTER 37 THE ONES STANDING IN RANKS

In the Name of God, The Merciful, The Compassionate

By the ones standing in ranks, ranged in rows37:1 then, ones who scare in a scaring37:2 then, ones who recount the Remembrance,37:3 truly, your God is One,37:4 the Lord of the heavens and the earth and whatever is between them and the Lord of the sunrise.37:5

Truly, We made to appear pleasing the present heaven with the adornment of the stars37:6 and keeping it safe from every emboldened Satan.37:7

They pay no attention to the lofty Council for they are hurled at from every edge,37:8 rejected. And for them is a punishment, that which lasts forever,37:9 but for him who snatched a fragment, then, a piercing flame pursued him.37:10

So ask them for advice: Are they stronger in constitution or those others whom We created?

Truly, We created them of clinging clay.37:11

Nay! Thou hadst marveled while they deride.37:12 And when they were reminded, they remember not.37:13

And when they saw a sign, they scoff at it.37:14

And they said: This is not but clear sorcery.37:15

Is it when we were dead and had been earth dust and bones that we will, truly, be ones who are raised up37:16 and our fathers, the ancient ones?37:17

Say: Yes, you will be ones in a state of lowliness.37:18 There will be only one Scare.

So when they will be looking on it,37:19 they will say: Woe to us! This is the Day of Judgment!37:20

This is the Day of Decision which you had been denying.37:21

Assemble those who did wrong and their spouses, and what they had been worshipping37:22—other than God—and guide them to the path to hellfire.37:23 And stop them for they are ones who will be asked:37:24

What is the matter with you that you help not one another?37:25

Nay! They are on that Day ones who will resign themselves to submission to God.37:26

And some of them came forward to some others, demanding of one another.37:27 They would say: Truly, you, you had been approaching us from the right.37:28

They would say: Nay! You are not ones who believe37:29 and we had not been any authority over you.

Nay! You had been a folk, ones who are defiant.37:30

So the saying was realized against us of our Lord. That, truly, we are ones who experience the punishment.37:31 So we led you into error. Truly, we had been ones who are in error.37:32 Then, truly, they will be on that Day ones who are partners in the punishment.37:33 We accomplish, thus, with the ones who sin.37:34

Truly, when it had been said to them: There is no god but God, they grow arrogant.37:35

And they said: Are we ones who leave our gods for a possessed poet?37:36

Nay! He drew near with The Truth and he established as true the ones who are sent.37:37 Truly, you are ones who will experience the painful punishment37:38 and you will be given recompense but for what you had been doing.37:39

But the devoted servants of God,37:40 those, for them was a known provision37:41—sweet fruits—and they will be ones who are honored37:42 in the Gardens of Bliss,37:43 on couches—ones who face one another.37:44

A cup from a spring of water will be passed around,37:45 white, a delight to ones who drink it.37:46 In that is neither headache, nor are they intoxicated by it.37:47 And with them are ones who are restraining their (f) glance, lovely eyed37:48 as if they are well-guarded pearls.37:49

So some of them will come forward to some others, demanding of one another.37:50

One of them who converses would say: Truly, I had a comrade37:51 who would say: Art thou of the ones who establish the Resurrection as true?37:52 When we are dead and had been earth dust and bones, will we be ones who are judged?37:53

He said: Will you be ones who puruse?37:54 So he perused and saw him amidst hellfire.37:55

He said: By God, thou wert about to deal me destruction!37:56 Had it not been for the divine blessing of my Lord I would have been of the ones who are charged.37:57

Are we not, then, to be dead again37:58 but for our first death and will we not be ones who are punished?37:59

Truly, this, it is the winning the sublime triumph.37:60 For the like of this, let the ones who work, work.37:61

Is this better as hospitality or the tree of Zaqqum?37:62 Truly, We made it a test for the ones who are unjust.37:63 Truly, it is a tree that goes forth, its root in hellfire,37:64 its spathes have been like the heads of satans.37:65 So, truly, they, they are ones who eat from it, ones who fill their bellies with it.37:66 Again, truly, on top of that for them is a brew of scalding water.37:67 Again, truly, their return is to hellfire.37:68

They discovered their fathers ones who go astray,37:69 yet they are running in their footsteps.37:70 And, certainly, went astray most of the ancient ones before them.37:71 And, certainly, We sent among them ones who warn.37:72 Then, look on how had been the Ultimate End of the ones who are warned,37:73 but the devoted servants of God.37:74

And, certainly, Noah cried out to Us. And how excellent were the ones who answer!^{37:75} And We delivered him and his people from tremendous distress.^{37:76} And We made his offspring—they, the ones who remain.^{37:77} And We left for him to say with the later ones:^{37:78}

Peace be on Noah among the worlds.^{37:79}

Thus, We give recompense to the ones who are doers of good.^{37:80}

Truly, he is one of Our believing servants.^{37:81}

Again, We drowned the others.^{37:82}

And, truly, among his partisans was Abraham.^{37:83} When he drew near his Lord with a pure-hearted heart,^{37:84} when he said to his father and to his folk: What is it that you worship?^{37:85}

Is it a calumny that you want gods other than God!^{37:86}

Then, what is your opinion about the Lord of the worlds?^{37:87}

And he looked on them with a glimpse at the stars^{37:88} and he said: Truly, I am ill!^{37:89}

But they turned away from him as ones who draw back^{37:90} and he turned upon their gods then, said: Will you not eat?^{37:91}

Why speak you not for yourselves?^{37:92}

Then, he turned upon them, striking them with his right hand.^{37:93}

Then, the people came forward towards him rushing.^{37:94}

He said: Worship you what you yourselves carve out^{37:95} while God created you and what you do?^{37:96}

They said: Build for him a structure. Then, cast him into hellfire.^{37:97}

So they wanted to use cunning against him, but We made them the lowest.^{37:98}

He said: Truly, I am one who goes to my Lord. He will guide me.^{37:99}

My Lord! Bestow on me among the ones in accord with morality.^{37:100} So We gave him the good tidings of a forbearing boy.^{37:101} And when he reached maturity endeavoring with him, he said: O my son! Truly, I see while slumbering that I am sacrificing thee. So look on what thou hast considered? He said: O my father! Accomplish whatever thou art commanded. Thou wilt find me, if God willed, of the ones who remain steadfast.^{37:102}

Then, when they both submitted themselves to God and he flung him on his brow^{37:103}

We cried out to him: O Abraham!^{37:104} Surely, thou hadst established the dream as true. Thus, We give recompense to the ones who are doers of good.^{37:105} Truly, that was, certainly, the clear trial.^{37:106}

And, then, We took ransom for him with a sublime slaughter^{37:107} and We left for him a good name with the later ones:^{37:108} Peace be on Abraham!^{37:109}

Thus, We give recompense to the ones who are doers of good.^{37:110} Truly, he is one of Our believing servants.^{37:111} And We gave him the good tidings of Isaac, a Prophet, among the ones in accord with morality.^{37:112}

And We blessed him and Isaac. And of their offspring are ones who are doers of good and ones who are clearly unjust to themselves.^{37:113}

And, certainly We showed Our grace to Moses and Aaron.^{37:114} And We delivered them and their folk from the tremendous distress^{37:115} and helped them so that they, they had been the ones who are victors.^{37:116} And We gave them the manifest Book^{37:117} and guided them to the straight path.^{37:118} We left for them a good name with the later ones:^{37:119} Peace be on Moses and Aaron!^{37:120}

Truly, thus, We give recompense to the ones who are doers of good.^{37:121} Truly, they were of Our servants, ones who believe.^{37:122}

And, truly, Elijah was of the ones who are sent^{37:123} when he said to his folk: Will you not be Godfearing?^{37:124}

Will you call to Baal and forsake the fairer of ones who are the creators,^{37:125} God, your Lord and the Lord of your ancient fathers?^{37:126}

But they denied him, so they, truly, were ones who are charged.^{37:127} As for the devoted servants of God among them,^{37:128} We left for him a good name with the later ones:^{37:129} Peace be on Elijah!^{37:130}

Thus, We give recompense to the ones who are doers of good.^{37:131} Truly, he was of Our servants, ones who believe.^{37:132}

And, truly, Lot was of the ones who are sent.^{37:133} We delivered him and his people, one and all,^{37:134} but an old woman of the ones who stay behind.^{37:135} Again, We destroyed the others.^{37:136}

And, truly, you pass by them in that which is morning^{37:137} and at night. Will you not, then, be reasonable?^{37:138}

And, truly, Jonah was of the ones who are sent^{37:139} when he fled, without his Lord's permission, to the laden boat.^{37:140} He cast lots with them and he had been of the ones who are refuted.^{37:141} Then, the great fish engulfed him while he was one who is answerable.^{37:142} If he had not been of the ones who glorify,^{37:143} he would have lingered in expectation in its belly until the Day they are raised up.^{37:144} Then, We cast him forth on the naked shore while he was ill.^{37:145} We caused a vine of gourd to develop over him.^{37:146} We sent him to a community of a hundred thousand, or they even exceed that.^{37:147} And they believed, so We gave them enjoyment for awhile.^{37:148}

Then, ask them for advice: Are daughters for thy Lord and for them, sons?^{37:149}

Or created We female angels while they were ones who bear witness?^{37:150}

Truly, it is out of their calumny that they say:^{37:151} God procreated! And, truly, they are ones who lie.^{37:152}

Favored He daughters over sons?^{37:153}

What is the matter with you?

How you give judgment!^{37:154}

Will you not, then, recollect?^{37:155}

Or is there for you a clear authority?^{37:156} Then, bring your Book if you would be ones who are sincere.^{37:157}

And they made kindred between him and between the genies. But, surely, the genies knew well that they were ones who will be charged.^{37:158}

Glory be to God from what they allege,^{37:159} but not the devoted servants of God.^{37:160}

So, truly, you and those whom you worship^{37:161} will not be ones who are tempters against Him,^{37:162} but he who would be one who roasts in hellfire.^{37:163}

There is not any of us but he has a known station.^{37:164} And we are ones who are standing in ranks.^{37:165} And we are the ones who glorify.^{37:166} And, truly, they had been saying:^{37:167} Had been with us a Remembrance from the ancient ones,^{37:168} we would have been servants of God, ones who are devoted,^{37:169} but they were ungrateful for it. and soon they will know.^{37:170}

And, certainly, Our Word preceded for Our servants, the ones who are sent.^{37:171} They, truly, they are ones who shall be helped.^{37:172}

And, truly, Our armies are the ones who are victors.^{37:173} So turn thou away from them for awhile^{37:174} and perceive them and soon they will perceive.^{37:175}

Are they impatient for Our punishment?^{37:176} Then, when it would come down into their courtyard, how evil will be the morning daybreak of the ones who are warned!^{37:177} So turn thou away from them for awhile,^{37:178} and perceive and they will perceive.^{37:179}

Glory be to thy Lord, the Lord of Great Glory, from what they allege about Him.^{37:180} And peace be to the ones who are sent.^{37:181} And The Praise belongs to God, the Lord of the worlds!^{37:182}

CHAPTER 38 SAD

In the Name of God, The Merciful, The Compassionate
Sad.

By the Quran, Possessor of the Remembrance.38:1

Nay! Those who were ungrateful are in vainglory and breach.38:2

How many before them have We caused to perish of generations! And they cried out but there was no time for escape for awhile.38:3

And they marveled that drew near them one who warns from among themselves. And the ones who are ungrateful said: This is one who is a sorcerer, a liar.38:4 Made He all gods One God? Truly, this is an astounding thing!38:5

And the Council set out from them, saying: Be gone! And have patience with your gods. Truly, this is a thing to be wanted!38:6

We heard not the like of this in the later creed. This is only made up tales!38:7

Was the Remembrance only caused to descend to him from among us?

Nay! They are in uncertainty about My Remembrance. Nay! They experience not My punishment!38:8

Or are they owners of the treasures of mercy of thy Lord, The Almighty, The Giver?38:9

Or is theirs the dominion of the heavens and the earth and what is between them? Let them climb up with cords!38:10 Their army is one that is put to flight among the confederates.38:11

The folk of Noah before them denied and Ad and Pharaoh, the possessor of the stakes,38:12 and Thamud and a folk of Lot and the Companions of the Thicket. Those were the confederates.38:13

All of them denied the Messengers so My repayment was realized.38:14

These expect not but one Cry. There was no holding it back.38:15

And they said: Our Lord! Quicken the sentence of the judge on us before the Day of Reckoning.38:16

Have patience with what they say, and remember Our servant David, the possessor of potency. Truly, he was penitent.38:17 Truly, We caused the mountains to be subservient to glorify with him in the evening and the rising of the sun.38:18 And the birds were ones who are assembled, all penitent to Him.38:19 And We strengthened his dominion and gave him wisdom and decisiveness in argument.38:20

Approached thee the tiding of the disputants when they climbed over the wall of a sanctuary?38:21 When they entered in on David, he was terrified of them. They said: Fear not. Two disputants were insolent, one of us against the other. So give judgment duly between us and transgress not and guide us to the right path.38:22 Truly, this is my brother. He has ninety-nine ewe, while I have one ewe. And he said: Place it in my charge and he triumphed over me in argument.38:23

David said: Certainly, he did wrong to thee in asking for thy ewe in addition to his ewes. And, truly, many partners in business are insolent, one to another, but those who believed and did as the ones in accord with morality, and they are few.

And David thought that We tried him and he asked for forgiveness of his Lord and fell down as one who bows down penitent.38:24 So We forgave him that. And, truly, for him is nearness with Us and goodness of destination.38:25

O David! Truly, We made thee a viceregent on the earth so give judgment duly among humanity and follow not your desire for it will cause thee to go astray from the way of God. Truly, those who go astray from the way of God, for them there is a severe punishment because they forgot the Day of Reckoning.38:26

And We created not the heaven and the earth and whatever is between the two in falsehood. That is the opinion of those who were ungrateful. Then, woe to those who disbelieved in the fire!38:27

Or will We make those who believed and did as the ones in accord with morality like the ones who make corruption in and on the earth or will We make the ones who are God-fearing as the ones who acted immorally?38:28

It is a blessed Book that We caused to descend to thee, so that they meditate on its signs and those imbued with intuition recollect.38:29

And We bestowed Solomon on David. How excellent a servant. Truly, he was penitent.38:30 When they were presented before him in the evening—steeds standing with one foot slightly raised—38:31 he said: Truly, I cherished and loved the good instead of remembering my Lord when the sun secluded itself behind the partition of the night.38:32 Return them to me. Then, he took wiping over their legs and their necks.38:33

And, certainly, We tried Solomon. We cast a lifeless body on his seat. Again, he was penitent.38:34

He said: My Lord! Forgive me and bestow on me a dominion such will not be fit and proper for another after me. Truly, Thou art The Giver.38:35

So We caused the wind to be subservient to him. It runs at his command, a gentle wind, wherever it lit.38:36 And We made subservient the satans and every builder and diver38:37 and others, ones who are chained in bonds.38:38

This is Our gift. Then, hast thou shown grace or hast thou held back without reckoning?38:39 Truly, for him is nearness with Us, and goodness of destination.38:40

And remember Our servant Job when he cried out to his Lord: Truly, Satan afflicted me with fatigue and punishment!38:41 It is said: Stomp with thy foot. This is a place of washing that is cool and from which to drink.38:42 And We bestowed on him, his people, and the like of them along with them as a mercy from Us, a reminder for those imbued with intuition.38:43 And take in thy hand a bundle of rushes and strike with it and fail not thy oath. Truly, We found him one who remains steadfast. How excellent a servant. Truly, he was penitent.38:44

And remember Our servants Abraham, and Isaac and Jacob, all imbued with dynamic energy and insight.38:45 And, truly, We made them sincere with that which is pure, a reminder of the Abode.38:46 And, truly, they are to Us among ones who are favored and good.38:47

And remember Ishmael, Elisha, and Dhu-l Kifl. And all are among the good.38:48

This is a Remembrance. And, truly, for ones who are Godfearing this is, certainly, a goodly destination,38:49 the Gardens of Eden, the doors, ones that are opened up for them.38:50 Ones who are reclining in them. They will call for many sweet fruits and drink in it.38:51 And with them will be ones who are restraining their (f) glance, persons of the same age.38:52 This is what you are promised for the Day of Reckoning.38:53 Truly, this is Our provision. For it, there is no coming to an end. 38:54 This is so.

And, truly, for ones who are defiant, there will be a worse destination,38:55 hell, where they will roast. And miserable will be the cradling!38:56 This is so! Then, let them experience this—scalding water and filth38:57 and other torment of a like kind in pairs.38:58 This is an army unit, one that rushes in with you. There is no welcome for them! Truly, they are ones who roast in the fire.38:59

They said: Nay! You! There is no welcome for you. It is you who put this forward on us. Miserable will be the stopping place!38:60

They said: Our Lord! Whoever put this forward for us, increase him with a double punishment in the fire.³⁸ᐟ⁶⁰

And they said: What is the matter with us that we see not men whom we had been numbering among the worst?³⁸ᐟ⁶² Took We them to ourselves as a laughing-stock or swerved our sight from them?³⁸ᐟ⁶³

Truly, this is true of the disagreement of the people of the fire.³⁸ᐟ⁶⁴

Say: I am only one who warns. And there is no god but God, The One, The Omniscient,³⁸ᐟ⁶⁵ the Lord of the heavens and the earth and whatever is between them, The Almighty, The Forgiver.³⁸ᐟ⁶⁶

Say: It is a serious tiding³⁸ᐟ⁶⁷ from which you are ones who turn aside.³⁸ᐟ⁶⁸ I had been without knowledge of the lofty Council when they are striving against one another.³⁸ᐟ⁶⁹ It is revealed to me only that I am a warner, one who makes clear.³⁸ᐟ⁷⁰

Thy Lord said to the angels: Truly, I am one who is Creator of a mortal from clay.³⁸ᐟ⁷¹ So when I shaped him and breathed into him My Spirit, then, fall to him, ones who prostrate themselves.³⁸ᐟ⁷²

So the angels prostrated themselves, one and all, altogether³⁸ᐟ⁷³ but Iblis. He grew arrogant and had been among the ones who are ungrateful.³⁸ᐟ⁷⁴

He said: O Iblis! What prevented thee from prostrating thyself to what I created with My two hands?

Hadst thou grown arrogant?

Or hadst thou been among the ones who exalt themselves?³⁸ᐟ⁷⁵

Iblis said: I am better than he. Thou hadst created me from fire while Thou hadst created him from clay.³⁸ᐟ⁷⁶

He said: Then, go thou forth from here; for, truly, thou art accursed.³⁸ᐟ⁷⁷ And, truly, on thee is My curse until the Day of Judgment.³⁸ᐟ⁷⁸

Iblis said: My Lord! Then, give me respite until the Day to be raised up.³⁸ᐟ⁷⁹

He said: Truly, thou art among the ones who are given respite ³⁸ᐟ⁸⁰ until the Day of the known time.³⁸ᐟ⁸¹

Iblis said: By Thy Great Glory, then, I will certainly lead them one and all into error,³⁸ᐟ⁸² but Thy devoted servants among them.³⁸ᐟ⁸³

He said: This is The Truth and The Truth I say³⁸ᐟ⁸⁴ that I will fill hell with thee and with one and all of whoever heeded thee.³⁸ᐟ⁸⁵

Say: I ask of you not for any compensation for this nor am I among the ones who take things upon themselves.³⁸ᐟ⁸⁶ It is nothing other than a Remembrance for the worlds³⁸ᐟ⁸⁷ and you will, certainly, know its tidings after awhile.³⁸ᐟ⁸⁸

CHAPTER 39 THE TROOPS

In the Name of God, The Merciful, The Compassionate

The sending down successively of this Book is from God, The Almighty, The Wise.³⁹ᐟ¹

Truly, We caused to descend to thee the Book with The Truth so worship God as one who is sincere and devoted in the way of life to Him.³⁹ᐟ²

The way of life is exclusively for God. And those who took to themselves protectors other than Him say: We worship them not, but that they bring us nearness to God. Truly, God gives judgment between them about what they are at variance in it. Truly, God guides not him, one who lies and is an ingrate.³⁹ᐟ³

If God wanted to take to Himself a son, He would have favored from what He creates of what He wills. Glory be to Him. He is God, The One, The Omniscient.³⁹ᐟ⁴

He created the heavens and the earth with The Truth. He wraps the nighttime around the daytime and wraps the daytime around the nighttime. And He caused to be subservient the sun and the moon, each run for a term, that which is determined. Is He not The Almighty, The Forgiver?³⁹ᐟ⁵

He creates you from one soul.

Again, He made its mate from it and He caused to descend for you eight pairs of flocks.

He creates you in the wombs of your mothers, creation after creation, in threefold shadows.

Such is God your Lord. His is the dominion. There is no god but He. Why, then, turn you away?³⁹ᐟ⁶

If you are ungrateful, truly, God is Independent of you. And He is not well-pleased with ingratitude from His servants. And if you give thanks, He will be well-pleased with you.

No burdened soul will bear the heavy load of another. Again, to your Lord is the return, so He will tell you what you had been doing. Truly, He is Knowing of what is in the breasts.³⁹ᐟ⁷

And when some distress afflicted the human being, he calls to his Lord as one who turns in repentance to Him. Again, when He granted him divine blessing from Himself, he forgets that for which he had been calling to Him before and he laid on rivals to God to cause others to go astray from His way.

Say: Take joy in thy ingratitude for awhile. Truly, thou art of the Companions of the Fire.³⁹ᐟ⁸

Is he one who is morally obligated during the night watch, one who prostrates himself or one who is standing up in prayer being fearful of the world to come and hoping for the mercy of his Lord?

Say: Are those who know on the same level as those who know not? Only those imbued with intuition recollect.³⁹ᐟ⁹

Say: O My servants who believed! Be Godfearing of your Lord. For those who did good in the present, there is benevolence, and the earth of God is One Who is Extensive. Only ones who remain steadfast will have their compensation without reckoning.³⁹ᐟ¹⁰

Say: Truly, I was commanded to worship God, one who is sincere and devoted in the way of life to Him.³⁹ᐟ¹¹ And I was commanded that I be the first of the ones who submit to God.³⁹ᐟ¹²

Say: Truly, I fear if I rebelled against my Lord the punishment of a tremendous Day.³⁹ᐟ¹³

Say: God alone I worship as one sincere and devoted in the way of life to Him.³⁹ᐟ¹⁴ So worship what you would other than Him.

Say: Truly, the ones who are losers are those who lost themselves and their people on the Day of Resurrection. Truly, that is a clear loss.³⁹ᐟ¹⁵ They will have overshadowings above from the fire and beneath them, overshadowings. With that, God frightens His servants. O my servants! Be Godfearing of Me!³⁹ᐟ¹⁶

And those who avoided false deities so that they worship them not and were penitent to God, for them are good tidings. So give good tidings to My servants,³⁹ᐟ¹⁷ those who listen to the saying of the Quran and follow the fairer of it. Those are those whom God guided. And those, they are imbued with intuition.³⁹ᐟ¹⁸

Against whom was realized the word of punishment? Wilt thou be saving him from the fire?³⁹ᐟ¹⁹

But those who were Godfearing of their Lord, for them are the highest chambers with the highest chambers built above them, beneath which rivers run. This is the solemn declaration of God. God never breaks His promise.³⁹ᐟ²⁰

Hast thou not considered that God caused to descend water from heaven and threaded fountains in the earth, again, brings out crops by it of hues, ones that are at variance? Again, they wither so thou seest them as ones that are growing yellow.

Again, He makes them chaff. Truly, in this is a reminder for those imbued with intuition.³⁹:²¹

So is whose breast God has expanded for submission to God, in a light from His Lord?

So woe to their hearts, ones that harden against the Remembrance of God. Those are clearly going astray.³⁹:²²

God sent down the fairer discourse, a Book, one that is consistent in its often repeated parts of the Quran by which shiver the skins of those who dread their Lord.

Again, their skins and their hearts become gentle with the Remembrance of God. That is the guidance of God. With it He guides whom He wills. And whomever God causes to go astray, there is not for him anyone who guides.³⁹:²³

Is he, then, one who fends off a dire punishment with his face on the Day of Resurrection?

And it will be said to the ones who are unjust: Experience what you had been earning!³⁹:²⁴ Those before them denied and so the punishment approached them from where they are not aware.³⁹:²⁵ So God caused them to experience degradation in this present life. But the punishment of the world to come is greater if they had been knowing!³⁹:²⁶

And, certainly, We propounded for humanity in this, the Quran, every kind of parable so that perhaps they will recollect,³⁹:²⁷ an Arabic Recitation without any crookedness so that perhaps they would be Godfearing.³⁹:²⁸

God propounded a parable of a man owned by quarreling ascribed associates and a man belonging to another man. Are they both equal in likeness? The Praise belongs to God. But most of them know not.³⁹:²⁹

Truly, thou art mortal and, truly, they are mortal.³⁹:³⁰

Again, truly, on the Day of Resurrection before your Lord you will strive against one another.³⁹:³¹

Then, who does greater wrong than one who lied against God and denied sincerity when it drew near him? Is there not in hell a place of lodging for the ones who are ungrateful?³⁹:³²

And he who brought about sincerity and he who established it as true, those, they are the ones who are Godfearing.³⁹:³³ For them is all that they will with their Lord. That is the recompense of the ones who are doers of good.³⁹:³⁴ Certainly, God absolves them of bad deeds of what they do and gives them recompense in compensation for the fairer of what they had been doing.³⁹:³⁵

Is not God One Who Suffices for His servants?

They frighten thee with those other than Him.

And whom God causes to go astray, there is not for him anyone who guides.³⁹:³⁶

And whomever God guides, there is not for him anyone who leads astray. Is not God Almighty, The Possessor of Requital?³⁹:³⁷

And, truly, if thou hadst asked them: Who created the heavens and the earth? They would, certainly, say: God.

Say: Considered you what you call to other than God?

If God wanted some harm for me, would they be ones who remove His harm from me?

Or if He wanted mercy for me would they (f) be ones who hold back His mercy?

Say: God is enough for me. In Him put their trust the ones who put their trust.³⁹:³⁸

Say: O my folk! Truly, act according to your ability. I am one who acts.

You will know³⁹:³⁹ to whom punishment approaches covering him with shame and on whom alights an abiding punishment.³⁹:⁴⁰

Truly, We caused the Book to descend to thee for humanity with The Truth. So whoever was truly guided, it is only for himself. And whoever went astray, goes astray but for himself. Thou art not over them a trustee.³⁹:⁴¹

God calls the souls to Himself at the time of their death and those that die not during their slumbering. He holds back those for whom He decreed death and sends the others back for a term, that which is determined. Truly, in that are signs for a folk who reflect.³⁹:⁴²

Or took they to themselves other than God intercessors?

Say: Even though they had not been possessing anything and they are not reasonable?³⁹:⁴³

Say: To God belongs all intercession. His is the dominion of the heavens and the earth. Again, to Him you will be returned.³⁹:⁴⁴

And when God alone was remembered, the hearts shuddered of those who believe not in the world to come. But when those who, other than Him, were remembered, that is when they rejoice at the good tidings!³⁹:⁴⁵

Say: O God! One Who is Originator of the heavens and the earth! One Who Knows of the unseen and the visible! Thou wilt give judgment among Thy servants about what they had been at variance in it.³⁹:⁴⁶

And if those who did wrong had whatever is in and on the earth altogether and the like with it, they would, truly, have offered it as ransom for the evil punishment on the Day of Resurrection. And it will show itself to them from God what they not be anticipating.³⁹:⁴⁷ And it will show itself to them, the evil deeds that they earned and they will be surrounded by what they had been ridiculing.³⁹:⁴⁸

Then, when harm afflicted the human being, he called to Us. Again, We granted him divine blessing from Us.

He would say: I was only given this because of my knowledge.

Nay! It is only a test, but most of them know not.³⁹:⁴⁹

Truly, those who were before them said it so what they had been earning availed them not.³⁹:⁵⁰ The evil deeds they earned lit on them. And as for those who did wrong among these, evil deeds of what they earned will light on them. They will not be ones who frustrate Him.³⁹:⁵¹

Know they not that God extends the provision for whomever He wills and tightens it for whom He wills. Truly, in this are, certainly, signs for a folk who believe.³⁹:⁵²

Say: O My servants who exceeded all bounds against themselves, despair not of the mercy of God. Truly, God forgives all impieties. Truly, He is The Forgiving, The Compassionate.³⁹:⁵³

Be penitent to your Lord and submit to Him before the punishment approaches you. Again, you will not be helped.³⁹:⁵⁴

And follow the fairer of what was caused to descend to you from your Lord before the punishment approaches you suddenly while you are not aware³⁹:⁵⁵ so that a soul not say: O me that I am regretful for what I neglected in my responsibility to God and that I had, truly, been among the ones who deride.³⁹:⁵⁶

Or he may say: If God guided me, I would, certainly, have been among the ones who are Godfearing.³⁹:⁵⁷

Or he say at the time he sees the punishment: If only I might return again, then, be among the ones who are doers of good.³⁹:⁵⁸

Yea! My signs drew near thee and thou hadst denied them and hadst grown arrogant. Thou hadst been among the ones who are ungrateful.³⁹:⁵⁹

And on the Day of Resurrection thou wilt see those who lied against God, their faces, ones that are clouded over. Is there not in hell a place of lodging for ones who increase in pride?³⁹:⁶⁰

And God delivers those who were Godfearing, keeping them safe. No evil will afflict them, nor will they feel remorse.³⁹:⁶¹

God is One Who is Creator of everything. And He is Trustee over everything.³⁹:⁶² To Him belongs the pass keys of the heavens and the earth.

And those who were ungrateful for the signs of God, those, they are the ones who are the losers.39:63

Say: Commanded you me to worship other than God, O ones who are ignorant?39:64

And, certainly, it was revealed to thee and to those who were before thee that if thou hast ascribed partners with God, certainly, thy actions will be fruitless and thou wilt, certainly, be among the ones who are losers.39:65

Nay! Worship thou God and be thou among the ones who are thankful!39:66

And they measured not God with His true measure.

And the earth altogether will be His handful on the Day of Resurrection when the heavens will be rolled up in His right hand. Glory be to Him! And exalted is He above partners they ascribe!39:67

And the trumpet will be blown. Then, whoever is in the heavens will swoon and whoever is in and on the earth, but he whom God willed. Again, it will be blown another time. Then, they will be upright looking on.39:68

And the earth will shine with the Light of its Lord and the Book will be laid down and the prophets and the witnesses will be brought about. And it will be decided among them with The Truth. And they, they will not be wronged.39:69

The account of each soul will be paid in full for what it did. He is greater in knowledge of what they accomplish.39:70

Those who were ungrateful will be ones driven to hell in troops until when they drew near it, then, the doors of it will be flung open. Ones who are its keepers will say to them: Approach not Messengers from among you who recount to you the signs of your Lord to warn you of the meeting of this your Day?

They would say: Yea.

But the word of punishment was realized against the ones who are ungrateful.39:71

It will be said: Enter the doors of hell as ones who will dwell in it forever. Miserable it will be as a place of lodging for the ones who increase in pride.39:72

Those who were Godfearing will be ones driven to their Lord in the Garden in troops until when they drew near it and its doors were let loose, ones who are its keepers will say to them: Peace be on you! You fared well! So enter it, ones who dwell in it forever.39:73

They would say: The Praise belongs to God Who was sincere in His promise to us and gave us the earth as inheritance that we take our dwelling in the Garden wherever we will. How excellent a compensation for the ones who work!39:74

And thou wilt see the angels as ones who encircle around the Throne glorifying their Lord with praise. And it would be decided in Truth among them.

And it would be said: The Praise belongs to God, the Lord of the worlds.39:75

CHAPTER 40 THE ONE WHO FORGIVES

In the Name of God, The Merciful, The Compassionate
*Hā Mīm*40:1

The sending down successively of this Book is from God, The Almighty, The Knowing,40:2 The One Who Forgives impieties, The One Who Accepts remorse, The Severe in Repayment, The Possessor of Bounty. There is no god but He. To Him is the Homecoming.40:3

No one disputes the signs of God, but those who were ungrateful. So be thou not disappointed with their going to and fro in the land.40:4

The folk of Noah denied before them and the confederates after them.

And every community is about to take its Messenger and they dispute with falsehood to refute The Truth. So I took them. And how had been My repayment!40:5

And, thus, was the Word of thy Lord realized against those who were ungrateful that they will be the Companions of the Fire.40:6

Those who carry the Throne and whoever is around it glorify the praises of their Lord and believe in Him and ask for forgiveness for those who believed: Our Lord! Thou hadst encompassed everything in mercy and in knowledge. So forgive those who repented and followed Thy way and guard them from the punishment of hellfire.40:7

Our Lord! And cause them to enter the Gardens of Eden which Thou hadst promised them and whomever was in accord with morality among their fathers and their spouses and their offspring. Truly, Thou, Thou alone art The Almighty, The Wise.40:8

And guard them from the evil deeds. And whomever Thou hast guarded from the evil deeds on that Day. Surely, Thou hadst had mercy on him. And that, it is the winning the sublime triumph!40:9

It will be proclaimed to those who were ungrateful: Certainly, the repugnance of God is greater than your repugnance of yourselves when you are called to belief, but you are ungrateful.40:10

They said: Our Lord! Thou hadst caused us to die two times and Thou hadst given us life two times. We acknowledged our impieties. Then, is there any way of going forth?40:11

It will be said: That is because when God alone was called to, you disbelieved. But when partners are ascribed with Him, you believe. And the determination is with God alone, The Lofty, The Great.40:12

It is He Who causes you to see His signs and sends down provision for you from heaven. And none recollect but whoever is penitent.40:13 So call you on God ones who are sincere and devoted in the way of life to Him although the ones who are ungrateful disliked it.40:14

Exalter of Degrees, Possessor of the Throne, He casts the Spirit by His command on whom He wills of His servants to warn of the Day of the Encounter,40:15 a Day when they are ones who depart.

Nothing about them will be hidden from God. Whose is the dominion this Day. It is to God, The One, The Omniscient.40:16

On this Day every soul will be given recompense for what it earned. There will be no injustice today. God is Swift in reckoning.40:17

And warn them of The Impending Day when the hearts will be near the throats, ones who choke. There will not be a loyal friend for ones who are unjust, nor an intercessor be obeyed.40:18

He knows that which is the treachery of the eyes and whatever the breasts conceal.40:19

And God decrees by The Truth. And those whom they call to other than Him decide not anything. Truly, God, He is The Hearing, The Seeing.40:20

Journey they not through the earth and look on how had been the Ultimate End of those who had been before them?

They, they had been superior to them in strength and in traces they left on the earth, but God took them for their impieties and there had not been for them one who is a defender from God.40:21

That had been because their Messengers approached them with the clear portents, but they were ungrateful so God took them. Truly, He is Strong, Severe in Repayment.40:22

And, certainly, We sent Moses with Our signs and a clear authority^{40:23} to Pharaoh and Haman and Korah.

But they said: He is one who is a lying sorcerer.^{40:24}

Then, when he drew near with The Truth from Us, they said: Kill the children of those who believed with him and save alive their women.

And the cunning of the ones who are ungrateful is but going astray.^{40:25}

And Pharaoh said: Let me kill Moses and let him call to his Lord. Truly, I fear that he substitute for your way of life or that he cause to appear in and on the earth corruption.^{40:26}

And Moses said: Truly, I took refuge in my Lord and your Lord from everyone who increases in pride and who believes not in the Day of Reckoning.^{40:27}

Said a believing man of the family of Pharaoh, who keeps back his belief: Would you kill a man because he says: My Lord is God, and he drew near you with the clear portents from your Lord? And if he be one who lies, then, on him will be his lying. And if he be one who is sincere, then, will light on you some of what he promises. Truly, God guides not him who is one who is excessive, a liar.^{40:28}

O my folk! Yours is the dominion this day, ones who are prominent on the earth. But who will help us from the might of God if it drew near us?

Pharaoh said: I cause you to see not but what I see and what I guide you to is not but the way of rectitude.^{40:29}

And he who believed said: O my folk! Truly, I fear for you like a Day of the confederates,^{40:30} in like manner of a folk of Noah and Ad and Thamud and those after them. And God wants not injustice for His servants.^{40:31}

And O my folk! Truly, I fear for you a Day when they would call to one another^{40:32} a Day when you will turn as ones who draw back. No one saves you from harm from God. And for whomever God causes to go astray, there is not anyone who guides.^{40:33}

And, certainly, Joseph drew near you before with the clear portents, but you ceased not in uncertainty as to what he brought about to you. Until when he perished you said: God will never raise up a Messenger after him. Thus, God causes him to go astray, one who is excessive, one who is a doubter,^{40:34} those who dispute the signs of God without any authority having approached them. It is troublesome, repugnant with God and with those who believed. Thus, God sets a seal on every heart of one who increases in pride, haughtiness.^{40:35}

And Pharaoh said: O Haman! Build for me a pavilion so that perhaps I will reach the routes,^{40:36} the routes to the heavens, and that I may peruse The God of Moses but, truly, I think that he is one who lies.

Thus, it was made to appear pleasing to Pharaoh, the evil of his actions. And he was barred from the way. And the cunning of Pharaoh was not but in defeat.^{40:37}

And he who believed said: O my folk! Follow me; I will guide you to the way of rectitude.^{40:38}

O my folk! Truly, this present life is nothing but transitory enjoyment and that the world to come is the stopping place, the Abode.^{40:39} Whoever did an evil deed will not be given recompense but the like of it. But whoever did as one in accord with morality, whether male or female, and such is one who believes, then, those will enter the Garden where they will be provided in it without reckoning.^{40:40}

And O my folk! What is it to me that I call to you for deliverance and you call to me for the fire?^{40:41}

You call to me to be ungrateful to God and to ascribe partners with Him of what there is no knowledge, while I call you to The Almighty, The Forgiver.^{40:42} Without a doubt what you call me to has no merit. It is not a call to the present or to the world to come. And our turning back is to God. And, truly, the ones who are excessive, they will be Companions of the Fire.^{40:43} And you will remember what I say to you. I commit my affair to God. Truly, God is Seeing of the servants.^{40:44}

So God guarded him from the evil deeds that they planned while surrounded the people of Pharaoh an evil punishment:^{40:45} The fire to which they are presented the first part of the day and evening.

And on a Day when the Hour is secure it is said: Cause the people of Pharaoh to enter the severest punishment.^{40:46}

And when they dispute with one another in the fire, the weak will say to those who grew arrogant: Truly, we had been followers of you so will you be ones who avail us from a share of the fire?^{40:47}

Those who grew arrogant would say: Truly, we are all in it. Truly, God, surely, gave judgment among His servants.^{40:48}

And those in the fire would say to ones who are keepers of hell: Call to your Lord to lighten the punishment for us for a day.^{40:49}

They would say: Be bringing not your Messengers the clear portents.

They would say: Yea!

They would say: Then, you call.

And the supplication of the ones who are ungrateful only goes astray.^{40:50}

Truly, We will, certainly, help Our Messengers and those who believed in this present life and on a Day when the ones who bear witness will stand up,^{40:51} a Day when their excuses will not profit the ones who are unjust. And for them will be the curse and for them will be an evil abode.^{40:52}

And, certainly, We gave Moses the guidance and We gave as inheritance to the Children of Israel the Book^{40:53} as a guidance and a reminder for those imbued with intuition.^{40:54}

So have thou patience. Truly, the promise of God is true. And ask for forgiveness for thy impiety. And glorify thy Lord with praise in the evening and the early morning.^{40:55}

Truly, those who dispute about the signs of God without any authority having approached them, there is nothing but having pride in their breasts. They will never be ones who reach its satisfaction. So seek refuge in God. Truly, He, He is The Hearing, The Seeing.^{40:56}

Certainly, the creation of the heavens and the earth is greater than the creation of humanity, yet most of humanity knows not.^{40:57}

Not on the same level are the unwilling to see and the seeing nor those who believed and did as the ones in accord with morality and the ones who are evil doers. Little do they recollect.^{40:58}

Truly, the Hour is that which arrives. There is no doubt about it, yet most of humanity believes not.^{40:59}

And your Lord said: Call to Me; I will respond to you. Truly, those who grow arrogant toward My worship, they will enter hell as ones who are in a state of lowliness.^{40:60}

God is He Who made for you the nighttime so that you may rest in it and the daytime for one who perceives. Truly, God is Possessor of Grace to humanity, but most of humanity gives not thanks.^{40:61}

That is God, your Lord, the One Who is Creator of everything. There is no god but He. Then, how you are misled!^{40:62}

Thus, are misled those who had been negating the signs of God.^{40:63}

God is He Who made the earth for you as a stopping place and the heaven as a canopy. And He formed you and formed you well and He provided you of what is good. That is God, your Lord. Then, blessed be God, the Lord of the worlds!⁴⁰:⁶⁴ He is The Living! There is no god but He! So call to Him, ones sincere and devoted in the way of life to Him. The Praise belongs to God, the Lord of the worlds!⁴⁰:⁶⁵

Say: Truly, I was prohibited from worshipping those whom you call to other than God, because the clear portents drew near me from my Lord. And I was commanded to submit to the Lord of the worlds.⁴⁰:⁶⁶

He it is Who created you from earth dust, again, from seminal fluid, again, from a clot.

Again, He brings you out as infant children.

Again, you come of age and are fully grown.

Again, you be an old man.

And of you is he whom death calls to itself before, and that you reach a term, that which is determined so that perhaps you will be reasonable.⁴⁰:⁶⁷

He it is Who gives life and causes to die.

And when He decreed an affair, He only says to it: Be! Then, it is!⁴⁰:⁶⁸

Hast thou not considered those who dispute about the signs of God, where they are turned away:⁴⁰:⁶⁹ Those who denied the Book and that with which We sent Our Messengers?

Then, they will know.⁴⁰:⁷⁰

When yokes are on their necks and the chains, they will be dragged⁴⁰:⁷¹ into scalding water. Again, they will be poured forth into the fire as fuel.⁴⁰:⁷² Again, it will be said to them: Where are what you had been ascribing as partners⁴⁰:⁷³ other than God?

They would say: They went astray from us. Nay! We be not calling to anything before.

Thus, God causes to go astray ones who are ungrateful.⁴⁰:⁷⁴

That was because you had been exultant on the earth without right and that you had been glad. ⁴⁰:⁷⁵ Enter the doors of hell as ones who will dwell in it forever. Then, miserable it will be as a place of lodging for the ones who increase in pride!⁴⁰:⁷⁶

So have thou patience. Truly, the promise of God is true. And whether We cause thee to see some part of what We promise them or We call thee to Us, then, it is to Us they will be returned.⁴⁰:⁷⁷

And, certainly, We sent Messengers before thee among whom We related to thee and of whom We relate not to thee. And it had not been for any Messenger that he bring a sign, except with the permission of God. So when the command of God drew near, the matter would be decided rightfully. And lost here are these, the ones who deal in falsehood.⁴⁰:⁷⁸

God is He Who has made for you flocks among which you may ride on them and among which you eat of them.⁴⁰:⁷⁹ And you have what profits from them and that with them you reach the satisfaction of a need that is in your breasts and you are carried on them and on boats.⁴⁰:⁸⁰

And He causes you to see His signs. So which of the signs of God do you reject?⁴⁰:⁸¹

Journey they not through the earth and look on how had been the Ultimate End of those before them? They had been more than them and were more vigorous in strength and in regard to the traces they left on the earth. Then, availed them not what they had been earning.⁴⁰:⁸²

Then, when their Messengers drew near them with the clear portents, they were glad in the knowledge that they had and surrounded them was what they had been ridiculing.⁴⁰:⁸³ So when they saw Our might, they said: We believed in God alone and we were ungrateful in that we had been ones who are polytheists.⁴⁰:⁸⁴

But their belief be not what profits them once they saw Our might. This is a custom of God which was, surely, in force among His servants. And lost here are the ones who are ungrateful.⁴⁰:⁸⁵

CHAPTER 41 THEY WERE EXPLAINED DISTINCTLY

In the Name of God, The Merciful, The Compassionate Hā Mīm.⁴¹:¹

A sending down successively from The Merciful, The Compassionate,⁴¹:² a Book in which its signs were explained distinctly, an Arabic Recitation for a folk who know, ⁴¹:³ a bearer of glad tidings and a warner, but most of them turned aside so they hear not.⁴¹:⁴

And they said: Our hearts are sheathed from that to which thou hast called us and in our ears is a heaviness and between us and between thee is a partition. So work. Truly, we, too, are ones who work.⁴¹:⁵

Say: I am only a mortal like you. It is revealed to me that your God is God, One; so go straight to Him and ask for forgiveness from Him, and woe to the ones who are polytheists—those who give not the purifying alms⁴¹:⁶ and who in the world to come are ones who disbelieve.⁴¹:⁷

Truly, those who believed and did as the ones in accord with morality, for them will be compensation, that which is unfailing.⁴¹:⁸

Say: Truly, are you ungrateful to Him Who created the earth in two days?

And assign you to Him rivals?

That is the Lord of the worlds!⁴¹:⁹

And He made on it firm mountains from above it and He blessed it and ordained its subsistence within it in four days equally for the ones who ask.⁴¹:¹⁰

Again, He turned His attention to the heaven while it was smoke and He said to it and to the earth: Approach both of you willing or unwilling.

They both said: We approached as ones who are obedient.⁴¹:¹¹

Then, foreordaining seven heavens in two days, He revealed in each heaven its command. We made the present heaven appear pleasing with lamps and keeping them safe. Thus, decreed the Almighty, The Knowing.⁴¹:¹²

But if they turned aside, then, say: I warned you of a thunderbolt like the thunderbolt of Ad and Thamud.⁴¹:¹³

And when the Messengers drew near before them and from behind them saying: Worship none but God, they said: If our Lord willed, He would have caused angels to descend. Then, truly, in what you were sent, we are ones who disbelieve.⁴¹:¹⁴

As for Ad, they grew arrogant on the earth without right and they said: Who is more vigorous than us in strength?

Consider they not that God Who created them, He was more vigorous than they in strength?

And they had been negating Our signs.⁴¹:¹⁵

So We sent on them a raging wind in days of misfortune that We might cause them to experience the punishment of degradation in this present life. And the punishment in the world to come will be more degrading; and they will not be helped.⁴¹:¹⁶

And as for Thamud, We guided them, but they embraced blindness of heart instead of guidance. Then, a thunderbolt took them with a humiliating punishment because of what they had been earning.⁴¹:¹⁷

We delivered those who believed and had been Godfearing.⁴¹:¹⁸

On a Day when will be assembled the enemies of God to the fire, then, they will be marching in rank⁴¹:¹⁹ until when they drew near it. Witness will be borne against them by their having the ability to hear, and by their sight and by their skins as to what they had been doing.⁴¹:²⁰

And they will say to their skins: Why bore you witness against us?

They will say: We were given speech by God Who gave speech to all things.

And He created you the first time and to Him you will be returned.⁴¹:²¹

And you had not been covering yourselves so that witness be borne against you by your having the ability to hear or by your sight or by your skins but that you thought that God knows not much of what you do.⁴¹:²²

And that your thought, which you thought about your Lord has dealt destruction to you. Then, you became among the ones who are losers.⁴¹:²³

Then, even if they endure patiently, yet the fire will be the place of lodging for them. And if they ask for favor, yet they will not be of the ones to whom favor is shown.⁴¹:²⁴

And We allotted for them comrades who were made to appear pleasing to them whatever was before them and whatever was behind them. And the saying was realized against them in communities that passed away before them of jinn and humankind. Truly, they, they had been ones who are losers.⁴¹:²⁵

And those who are ungrateful said: Hear not this, the Quran, but talk idly about it while it is being recited so that perhaps you will prevail.⁴¹:²⁶

We will cause those who were ungrateful to experience a severe punishment. And We will give recompense to them for the bad deeds of what they had been doing.⁴¹:²⁷ That is the recompense of the enemies of God: The fire. For them is the infinite abode in it, recompense because they had been negating Our signs.⁴¹:²⁸

And those who were ungrateful would say: Our Lord! Cause us to see those who caused us to go astray among jinn and humankind. We will lay them both beneath our feet so that they become of the lowest.⁴¹:²⁹

Truly, those who said: Our Lord is God, again, they went straight, the angels come forth to them: Neither fear nor feel remorse, but rejoice in the Gardens which you had been promised.⁴¹:³⁰

We were protectors in this present life and in the world to come. And you will have in it that for which your souls lust and in it is what you call for,⁴¹:³¹ a hospitality from the Forgiving, Compassionate.⁴¹:³²

And who has a fairer saying than he who called to God and did as one in accord with morality, and said: I am one of the ones who submit to God.⁴¹:³³ Not on the same level are benevolence or the evil deed. Drive back with what is fairer. Then, behold he who between thee and between him was enmity as if he had been a protector, a loyal friend.⁴¹:³⁴

And none will be in receipt of it but those who endured patiently. And none will be in receipt of it but the possessor of a sublime allotment.⁴¹:³⁵

But if Satan sows enmity, sowing enmity in thee, then, seek refuge in God. Truly, He is The Hearing, The Knowing.⁴¹:³⁶

And of His signs are the nighttime and the daytime and the sun and the moon. Prostrate not yourselves to the sun nor to the moon, but prostrate yourselves to God Who created both of them if it is He you had been worshipping.⁴¹:³⁷

But if they grew arrogant, then, those who are with thy Lord glorify Him during the nighttime and the daytime and they never grow weary.⁴¹:³⁸

And among His signs are that thou hast seen the earth as that which is humble. But when We caused water to descend to it, it quivered and swelled. Truly, He Who gives life to it is the One Who Gives Life to the dead. Truly, He is Powerful over everything.⁴¹:³⁹

Truly, those who blaspheme Our signs are not hidden from Us. Is he who is cast down into the fire better off, or he who approaches as one who is safe on the Day of Resurrection?

Do as you willed. Truly, He is Seeing of what you do.⁴¹:⁴⁰

Truly, those who were ungrateful for the Remembrance when it drew near them are not hidden from Us. And, truly, it is a mighty Book!⁴¹:⁴¹

Falsehood approaches it not from before it, nor from behind it. It is a sending down successively from The Wise, The Worthy of Praise.⁴¹:⁴²

Nothing is said to thee but what, truly, was said to the Messengers before thee. Truly, thy Lord is, certainly, the Possessor of Forgiveness, and the Possessor of Painful Repayment.⁴¹:⁴³

And if We made this a non-Arabic Recitation, they would have said: Why were His signs not explained distinctly: A non-Arab tongue and an Arab!

Say: It is a guidance for those who believe and a healing. And as for those who believed not, there is a heaviness in their ears and blindness in their hearts. Those are given notice from a far place.⁴¹:⁴⁴

And, certainly, We gave Moses the Book. Then, they were at variance about it. And if it were not for a Word that had preceded from thy Lord, it would have been decided between them. But, truly, they are in uncertainty, ones in grave doubt about it.⁴¹:⁴⁵ Whoever did as one in accord with morality, it is for himself. And whoever did evil, it is against himself, and thy Lord is not unjust to His servants.⁴¹:⁴⁶

To Him is returned the knowledge of the Hour. No fruits go forth from its sheath and no female conceives or brings forth offspring but with His knowledge.

And on a Day He will cry out to them: Where are My ascribed associates? They would say: We proclaimed to Thee that none of us was a witness to that.⁴¹:⁴⁷

Gone astray from them is what they had been calling to before. They would think that there is for them no asylum.⁴¹:⁴⁸

The human being grows not weary of supplicating for good, but if the worst afflicted him, then, he is hopeless, desperate.⁴¹:⁴⁹

And, truly, if We caused him to experience mercy from Us, after some tribulation afflicted him, he will, certainly, say: This is due to me. And I think not that the Hour will be one that arises, but if I were returned to my Lord, truly, with Him will be the fairer for me.

Then, certainly, We will tell those who were ungrateful of what they did. And We will cause them to experience a harsh punishment.⁴¹:⁵⁰

And when We were gracious to the human being, he turned aside, withdrew aside. But when the worst afflicted him, then, he is full of supplication.⁴¹:⁵¹

Say: Considered you that even though it had been from God, again, you were ungrateful for it. Who is one who goes more astray than he who is in wide breach?⁴¹:⁵²

We will cause them to see Our signs on the horizons and within themselves until it becomes clear to them that it is The Truth. Suffices not thy Lord that, truly, He is Witness over all things?⁴¹:⁵³

They are hesitant about the meeting with their Lord. Truly, He is who One Who Encloses everything.⁴¹:⁵⁴

CHAPTER 42
THE CONSULTATION

In the Name of God, The Merciful, The Compassionate
*Hā Mīm.*⁴²:¹ *Ayn Sīn Qāf:*⁴²:²

Thus, He reveals to thee and to those who were before thee, God is The Almighty, The Wise.⁴²:³

To Him belongs whatever is in and on the heavens and whatever is in and on the earth. And He is The Lofty, The Sublime.⁴²:⁴

The heavens are about to split asunder from above them while the angels glorify the praise of their Lord and ask forgiveness for whoever is on the earth. Truly, God, He is The Forgiving, The Compassionate.⁴²:⁵

As for those who took to themselves other than Him as protectors, God is Guardian over them and thou art not a Trustee over them.⁴²:⁶

And, thus, We revealed to thee an Arabic Recitation that thou wilt warn the Mother of the Towns and whoever is around it. And warn of the Day of Amassing. There is no doubt about it. A group of people will be in the Garden and a group of people will be in the blaze.⁴²:⁷

And if God willed, He would have made them one community but He causes to enter whom He wills into His mercy. And the ones who are unjust, there is not for them either a protector or a helper.⁴²:⁸

Or they took other than Him to themselves as protectors. But God, He alone is The Protector. And He gives life to the dead. And He is Powerful over everything.⁴²:⁹

Whatever thing about which you were at variance in it, then, its determination is with God. That is God, my Lord in Whom I put my trust and to Him I am penitent,⁴²:¹⁰

One Who is Originator of the heavens and the earth. He made for you spouses of yourselves and of the flocks, pairs by which means He makes you numerous in it.

There is not like Him anything. And He is The Hearing, The Seeing.⁴²:¹¹

To Him belongs the pass keys of the heavens and the earth. He extends provision for whomever He wills and measures it. Truly, He is The Knowing of everything.⁴²:¹²

He laid down the law of the way of life for you, that with which He charged Noah and what We revealed to thee and that with which We charged Abraham and Moses and Jesus.

Perform the prescribed way of life and be not split up in it.

Troublesome for the ones who are polytheists is that to which thou hast called them.

God elects for Himself whomever He wills and guides the penitent to Himself.⁴²:¹³

And they split not up until after the knowledge drew near them through insolence between themselves.

And if it were not for a Word that preceded from thy Lord—until a term, that which is determined—it would be decided between them. And, truly, those who were given as inheritance the Book after them are in uncertainty, in grave doubt about it.⁴²:¹⁴

Then, for that, call to this. And go thou straight as thou wert commanded. And follow not their desires.

And say: I believed in what God caused to descend from a Book. And I was commanded to be just among you. God is our Lord and your Lord. For us are our actions and for you, your actions. There is no disputation between us and between you. God will gather us together. And to Him is the Homecoming.⁴²:¹⁵

And those who argue with one another about God, after He was assented to, their disputations are null and void with their Lord, and on them is His anger. And for them will be a severe punishment.⁴²:¹⁶

It is God Who caused the Book to descend with The Truth and the Balance.

And what causes thee to recognize it so that perhaps the Hour is near?⁴²:¹⁷ Seeking to hasten are those who believe not in it. Those who believed are ones who are apprehensive of it. And they know that it is The Truth, those who altercate, truly, about the Hour are, certainly, going far astray.⁴²:¹⁸

God is Subtle with His servants. He provides to whom He wills. And He is The Strong, The Almighty.⁴²:¹⁹

Whoever had been wanting cultivation of the world to come, We increase his cultivation for him. Whoever had been wanting cultivation of the present, We give him of it. And he has not a share in the world to come.⁴²:²⁰

Or ascribe they associates who laid down the law of the way of life for them for which God gives not permission?

Were it not for a decisive word, it would be decided among them.

And, truly, the ones who are unjust, for them is a painful punishment.⁴²:²¹

Thou wilt see the ones who are unjust as ones who are apprehensive of what they earned and it is that which falls on them.

And those who believed and did as the ones in accord with morality, are in the well-watered meadows of the Gardens. For them will be whatever they will from their Lord. That it is the great grace.⁴²:²²

That is what God gives as good tidings to His servants who believed and did as the ones in accord with morality.

Say: I ask you not for compensation, but for the affection for any kin.

And whoever gains benevolence, We will increase for him goodness in it. Truly, God is Forgiving, Most Ready to Appreciate.⁴²:²³

Or they say: He devised against God a lie. But if God wills He would have sealed over thy heart.

And God blots out falsehood and verifies The Truth by His Words. Truly, He is Knowing of what is in the breasts.⁴²:²⁴

And He accepts the remorse of His servants and pardons their evil deeds. And He knows what you accomplish.⁴²:²⁵

And He responds to those who believed and did as the ones in accord with morality, and increases them of His grace.

And as for the ones who are ungrateful, theirs will be a severe punishment.⁴²:²⁶

And if God extended the provision for His servants, they would be insolent in the earth, but He sends down by measure whatever He wills. Truly, He is The Aware, The Seeing of His servants.⁴²:²⁷

And He it is Who sends down plenteous rain water after they despaired and He unfolds His mercy. And He is The Protector, The Worthy of Praise.⁴²:²⁸

And among His signs are the creation of the heavens and the earth and whatever of moving creatures He disseminated in them. And He has the power of amassing them when He wills.⁴²:²⁹

And whatever affliction lit on you is because of what your hands earned. And He pardons much.⁴²:³⁰

And you are not ones who frustrate Him on the earth. And there is not for you other than God either a protector or a helper.⁴²:³¹

And among His signs are the ones that run on the sea like landmarks.⁴²:³² If He wills, He stills the wind. Then, they would stay, that which is motionless on the surface. Truly, in that are signs for every enduring and grateful one.⁴²:³³

Or He wreck them because of what they earned. And He pardons them from much.⁴²:³⁴

And those who dispute Our signs know that there is no asylum for them.⁴²:³⁵

So whatever thing you were given is the enjoyment of this present life. And what is with God is better and is that which endures for those who believed and put their trust in their Lord⁴²:³⁶ and those who avoid the major sins and the indecencies and they forgive when they were angry⁴²:³⁷ and those who responded to their Lord and performed their formal prayer and their affairs are by counsel among themselves, and who spend of what We provided them,⁴²·³⁸ and those who, when insolence lit on them, they help each other.⁴²·³⁹

And the recompense for an evil deed is the like of an evil deed. Then, whoever pardoned and made things right, his compensation is due from God. Truly, He loves not the ones who are unjust.⁴²·⁴⁰

As whoever helped himself after an injustice, so those, there is not any way against them.⁴²·⁴¹ The way is only against those who do wrong to humanity and are insolent in and on the earth unrightfully. Those, for them is a painful punishment.⁴²·⁴²

And whoever endured patiently and forgave, truly, that is, certainly, a sign of constancy of affairs.⁴²·⁴³

And whomever God causes to go astray has no protector apart from Him. And thou wilt see the ones who are unjust when they would see the punishment. They will say: Is there any way of turning it back?⁴²·⁴⁴

And thou wilt see them being presented to it as ones who are humbled by a sense of humility looking on with secretive glances.

And those who believed will say: Truly, the ones who are losers are those who lost themselves and their people on the Day of Resurrection. Truly, the ones who are unjust will be in an abiding punishment⁴²·⁴⁵ that there had not been for them any protector to help them other than God. And he whom God causes to go astray, there is not for him any way.⁴²·⁴⁶

Respond to the call of your Lord before a Day approaches for which there is no turning back from God. There will be no shelter for you on that Day, nor is there for you any refusal.⁴²·⁴⁷

But if they turned aside, We put thee not forward as a guardian over them. It is for thee not but the delivering of the message.

And, truly, when We caused the human being to experience mercy from Us, he was glad in it. But when evil deeds light on him—because of what his hands sent—then, truly, the human being is ungrateful.⁴²·⁴⁸

To God belongs the dominion of the heavens and the earth. He creates what He wills. He bestows females on whom He wills. And He bestows males on whom He wills.⁴²·⁴⁹ And He couples them, males and females. And He makes barren whom He wills. Truly, He is Knowing, Powerful.⁴²·⁵⁰

And it had not been for a mortal that God speak to him, but by revelation or from behind a partition or that He send a Messenger to reveal by His permission what He wills. Truly, He is Lofty, Wise.⁴²·⁵¹

And, thus, We revealed to thee the Spirit of Our command. Thou hadst not been informed what the Book is nor what is belief, but We made it a light by which We guide whomever We will of Our servants. And, truly, thou, thou hast guided to a straight path—⁴²·⁵² the path of God, to whom belongs whatever is in the heavens and whatever is in and on the earth. Truly, will not all affairs come home to God?⁴²·⁵³

CHAPTER 43 THE ORNAMENTS

In the Name of God, The Merciful, The Compassionate
*Hā Mīm.*⁴³·¹

By the clear Book,⁴³·² We, truly, made it an Arabic Recitation so that perhaps you will be reasonable.⁴³·³

Truly, it is in the essence of the Book from Our Presence, Lofty, Wise.⁴³·⁴

Will We turn away the Remembrance from you, overlooking as you had been a folk, ones who are excessive?⁴³·⁵

And how many a Prophet sent We among the ancient ones!⁴³·⁶

And approaches them not a Prophet, but that they had been ridiculing him.⁴³·⁷

Then, We caused to perish the more vigorous in courage than them and the example of the ancient ones passed.⁴³·⁸

And, certainly, if thou hadst asked them: Who created the heavens and the earth?

They will, certainly, say: The Almighty, The Knowing created them,⁴³·⁹ Who made the earth a cradle for you and made in it ways for you so that perhaps you would be truly guided⁴³·¹⁰ and Who sent down water from heaven in measure. Then, We revived with it a lifeless land. Thus, you are brought out.⁴³·¹¹

And it is He Who created all the pairs and assigned for you the boats and the flocks on which you ride⁴³·¹² so that you sit upon their backs.

And, again, remember the divine blessing of your Lord when you are seated on them and you say: Glory be to Him Who caused this to be subservient to us and we had not been ones who are equal to it!⁴³·¹³ And, truly, we, certainly, are to our Lord ones who are turning.⁴³·¹⁴

Yet they assigned with Him a part of some of His servants. Truly, the human being is clearly ungrateful.⁴³·¹⁵

Or took He to Himself daughters from what He creates and selected He sons for you?⁴³·¹⁶

And if good tidings were given to one of them of what he cited as an example from The Merciful, his face stayed one that is clouded over and he chokes.⁴³·¹⁷

Is whoever is brought up amid glitter one who is without clarity when he is in an altercation?⁴³·¹⁸

And made they the angels—who themselves are servants of The Merciful—females?

Bore they witness to their creation? Their giving testimony will be written down. And they will be asked about it.⁴³·¹⁹

And they would say: If willed The Merciful, we would not have worshiped them.

And they have no knowledge of that. They do nothing but guess.⁴³·²⁰

Or gave We them any Book before this so they are ones who hold fast to it?⁴³·²¹

Nay! They said: We found our fathers in a community holding to a way of life and we are, truly, in their footsteps ones who are truly guided.⁴³·²²

And, thus, We sent not a warner to any town before thee without ones who are given ease saying: We found our fathers in a community. We are, certainly, ones who imitate their footsteps.⁴³·²³

He said: Even if I brought about better guidance for you than what you found your fathers on.

They would say: Truly, we, in that with which you were sent are ones who disbelieve.⁴³·²⁴

So We requited them. Then, look on how had been the Ultimate End of the ones who deny.⁴³·²⁵

Mention when Abraham said to his father and his folk: Truly, I am released from obligation to what you worship⁴³·²⁶ other than He Who originated me and, truly, He will guide me.⁴³·²⁷

And He made it an enduring Word among his posterity, so that perhaps they will return.⁴³·²⁸

Nay! I gave enjoyment to these and to their fathers until The Truth drew near them and a clear Messenger.⁴³·²⁹

And when The Truth drew near them, they said: This is sorcery and we are ones who disbelieve in it.⁴³·³⁰

They said: Why was this, the Quran, not sent down to some eminent man of the two towns?⁴³·³¹

Would they divide the mercy of thy Lord? It is We Who divided out among them their livelihood in this present life. Exalted are some of them above some others in degree so that some take to themselves others in their bondage. And the mercy of thy Lord is better than what they gather.⁴³·³²

And were it not that humanity be one community, would We have made for whoever is ungrateful for The Merciful, roofs of silver for their houses, and stairways which they would scale up[43:33] and for their houses, doors, and couches on which they would recline[43:34] and ornaments? Yet all this would have been nothing, but enjoyment of this present life.

And the world to come with your Lord is for the ones who are Godfearing.[43:35]

And whoever withdraws from the Remembrance of The Merciful, We allotted for him a satan, so he is a comrade for him.[43:36] And, truly, they bar them from the way, but they assume that they are ones who are truly guided.[43:37]

Then, when he drew near us he would say: Would that there were a distance between me and between thee of two sunrises! Miserable was the comrade.[43:38]

And it will never profit you this Day as you did wrong. You will be ones who are partners in the punishment.[43:39]

So hast thou caused someone unwilling to hear, to hear or wilt thou guide the unwilling to see, or someone who had been clearly going astray?[43:40]

And even if We take thee away, We will, truly, be ones who requite them[43:41] or We will cause thee to see what We promised them. Then, We are ones who are omnipotent over them.[43:42] So hold thee fast to what was revealed to thee. Truly, thou art on a straight path.[43:43] And, truly, this is a remembrance for thee and thy folk. And you will be asked.[43:44]

And ask ones whom We sent before thee of Our Messengers: Made We gods other than the Merciful to be worshiped?[43:45]

And, certainly, We sent Moses with Our signs to Pharaoh and his Council. So he said: Truly, I am a Messenger of the Lord of the worlds.[43:46]

But when he drew near them with Our signs, that is when they laugh at them.[43:47]

And We cause them not to see any sign, but it was greater than its sister's sign. And We took them with the punishment so that perhaps they would return.[43:48]

And they said: O one who is a sorcerer! Call for us to thy Lord by the compact He made with thee. Truly, We will be ones who are truly guided.[43:49]

But when We removed the punishment from them, that is when they break their oath![43:50]

And Pharaoh proclaimed to his folk. He said: O my folk! Is not the dominion of Egypt for me and these rivers run beneath me? Will you not, then, perceive?[43:51]

Or am I better than this one who is despicable, who scarcely makes things clear?[43:52]

Why were bracelets of gold not cast down on him or the angels drawn near to him as ones who are connected with one another?[43:53]

Thus, he irritated his folk. Then, they obeyed him. Truly, they had been a folk, ones who disobey.[43:54]

So when they provoked against Us, We requited them and drowned them one and all[43:55] and We made them a thing of the past and a parable for later ages.[43:56]

And when the son of Mary was cited as an example, that is when thy folk cry aloud[43:57] and said: Are our gods better or is he?

They cited him to thee not but to be argumentative. Nay! They are a contentious folk.[43:58]

He was but a servant to whom We were gracious, and We made him an example to the Children of Israel.[43:59] And if We will, We would have assigned angels to succeed among you on the earth.[43:60] And, truly, he is with the knowledge of the Hour, so contest not about it and follow Me. This is a straight path.[43:61]

And let not Satan bar you. Truly, he is a clear enemy to you.[43:62]

And when Jesus drew near with the clear portents, he said: Truly, I drew near you with wisdom and in order to make manifest to you some of that about which you are at variance in it. So be Godfearing of God and obey me.[43:63] Truly, God He is my Lord and your Lord so worship Him. This is a straight path.[43:64]

The confederates were at variance among themselves. So woe to those who did wrong from the punishment of a painful Day.[43:65]

Looked they on but for the Hour that will approach them suddenly while they are not aware?[43:66]

Friends on that Day will be enemies some to some others, but ones who are Godfearing.[43:67]

O My servants! This Day there shall be no fear in you nor will you feel remorse.[43:68]

It will be said to those who believed in Our signs and had been ones who submit to God:[43:69] Enter the Garden, you and your spouses, to be walking with joy![43:70]

There will be passed around among them platters of gold and goblets. And in it will be whatever souls lust for and all that in which the eyes delight. And you will be ones who dwell in it forever.[43:71] This is the Garden that you were given as inheritance because of what you had been doing.[43:72] For you there will be much sweet fruit from which you will eat.[43:73]

Truly, ones who sin will be in the punishment of hell, ones who will dwell in it forever.[43:74] It will not be decreased for them and they will be ones who are seized with despair in it.[43:75] And We did not wrong them, but they had been ones who are unjust.[43:76]

And they would cry out: O Malik! Let thy Lord finish us.

He would say: Truly, you will be ones who abide.[43:77]

Certainly, We brought about The Truth to you, but most of you are ones who dislike The Truth.[43:78]

Or fixed they on some affair?

Then, We, too, are ones who fix some affair.[43:79]

Assume they that We hear not their secret thoughts and their conspiring secretly?

Yea! Our messengers are near them writing down.[43:80]

Say: If The Merciful had had a son, then, I would be first of the ones who worship.[43:81]

Glory be to the Lord of the heavens and the earth, the Lord of the Throne, from all that they allege![43:82]

So let them engage in idle talk and play until they encounter their Day which they are promised.[43:83]

And it is He Who is in the heaven, God, and on the earth, God. And He is The Wise, The Knowing.[43:84]

Blessed be He to whom belongs the dominion of the heavens and the earth and whatever is between them and with Whom is the knowledge of the Hour and to Whom you will be returned.[43:85]

And those whom they call to possess no power other than Him for intercession, only whoever bore witness to The Truth, and they know.[43:86]

And if thou hadst asked them: Who created them?

They would, certainly, say: God. Then, how are they misled?[43:87]

And his saying: O my Lord! Truly, these are a folk who believe not,[43:88] so overlook them and say: Peace. And they will know.[43:89]

CHAPTER 44 THE SMOKE

In the Name of God, The Merciful, The Compassionate
Hā Mīm.[44:1]

By the clear Book[44:2] truly, We caused it to descend on a blessed night. Truly, We had been ones who warn.[44:3]

Every wise command is made clear in it,⁴⁴:⁴ a command from Us. Truly, We had been ones who send it⁴⁴:⁵ as a mercy from thy Lord. Truly, He is The Hearing, The Knowing,⁴⁴:⁶ Lord of the heavens and the earth and whatever is between them. If you had been ones who are certain.⁴⁴:⁷

There is no god but He. It is He Who gives life and causes to die. He is your Lord and the Lord of your ancient fathers.⁴⁴:⁸

Nay! They play in uncertainty.⁴⁴:⁹

Then, thou be on the watch for a Day when the heavens will bring a clear smoke⁴⁴:¹⁰ overcoming humanity. This is a painful punishment.⁴⁴:¹¹

Our Lord! Remove thou the punishment from us! Truly, we are ones who believe.⁴⁴:¹²

What will there be as a reminder for them? A clear Messenger drew near them.⁴⁴:¹³

Again, they turned away from him and they said: He is one who is taught by others, one who is possessed.⁴⁴:¹⁴

Truly, We are ones who remove the punishment for a little. Truly, you are ones who revert to ingratitude.⁴⁴:¹⁵

On the Day when We will seize by force with the greatest attack, truly, We will be ones who requite.⁴⁴:¹⁶

And, certainly, We tried a folk of Pharaoh before them when there drew near them a generous Messenger:⁴⁴:¹⁷ Give back to me the servants of God, the Children of Israel. Truly, I am a trustworthy Messenger to you.⁴⁴:¹⁸ And rise not up against God. Truly, I am one who arrives with a clear authority.⁴⁴:¹⁹ Truly, I took refuge in my Lord and your Lord so that you not stone me.⁴⁴:²⁰ But if you believe not in me, then, withdraw.⁴⁴:²¹

So he called on his Lord: Truly, these are a folk, ones who sin.⁴⁴:²²

He said: Set thou forth with my servants by night. Truly, you will be ones who are followed.⁴⁴:²³ And leave the sea calmly as it is. Truly, they will be an army, one that is drowned.⁴⁴:²⁴

How many they left behind of gardens and springs⁴⁴:²⁵ and crops and generous stations⁴⁴:²⁶ and prosperity in which they had been, ones who are joyful!⁴⁴:²⁷ And, thus, We gave it as inheritance to another folk.⁴⁴:²⁸ And neither the heavens wept for them nor the earth nor had they been ones who are given respite.⁴⁴:²⁹

And, certainly, We delivered the Children of Israel from the despised punishment⁴⁴:³⁰ of Pharaoh. Truly, He had been one who exalts himself and was of the ones who are excessive.⁴⁴:³¹

And, certainly, We chose them with knowledge above the worlds⁴⁴:³² and gave them the signs in which there was a clear trial.⁴⁴:³³

Truly, these say:⁴⁴:³⁴ There is nothing but our first singled out death and we will not be ones who are revived.⁴⁴:³⁵ Then, bring our fathers back if you had been ones who are sincere.⁴⁴:³⁶

Are they better or a folk of Tubba and those who were before them? We caused them to perish. They, truly, had been ones who sin.⁴⁴:³⁷

And We created not the heavens and the earth and whatever is between them as ones who play!⁴⁴:³⁸

We created them not but with The Truth but most of them know not.⁴⁴:³⁹

Truly, the Day of Decision is the time appointed for them one and all,⁴⁴:⁴⁰ a Day when a defender will not avail another defender at all nor will they be helped⁴⁴:⁴¹ but him on whom God had mercy. Truly, He is The Almighty, The Compassionate.⁴⁴:⁴²

Truly, the tree of Zaqqum⁴⁴:⁴³ will be the food of the sinful.⁴⁴:⁴⁴ Like molten copper it will bubble in the bellies,⁴⁴:⁴⁵ like boiling, scalding water.⁴⁴:⁴⁶

It will be said: Take him and drag him violently into the depths of hellfire.⁴⁴:⁴⁷ Again, then, unloose over his head the punishment of scalding water!⁴⁴:⁴⁸ Experience this! Truly,

thou, thou art seemingly the mighty, the generous.⁴⁴:⁴⁹ Truly, this is what you had been contesting.⁴⁴:⁵⁰

Truly, the ones who are Godfearing will be in the station of trustworthiness⁴⁴:⁵¹ among Gardens and springs⁴⁴:⁵² wearing fine silk and brocade, ones who face one another.⁴⁴:⁵³ Thus, it is so. We will give in marriage lovely, most beautiful eyed ones.⁴⁴:⁵⁴ They will call therein for every kind of sweet fruit, ones that are safe.⁴⁴:⁵⁵ They will not experience death with them but the first singled out death. And He will protect them from the punishment of hellfire,⁴⁴:⁵⁶ a grace from thy Lord. That, it is the winning the sublime triumph!⁴⁴:⁵⁷

Truly, We made this easy in thy language so that perhaps they will recollect.⁴⁴:⁵⁸ So be on the watch! Truly, they are ones who watch.⁴⁴:⁵⁹

CHAPTER 45
THE ONES WHO KNEEL

In the Name of God, The Merciful, The Compassionate
*Hā Mīm.*⁴⁵:¹

The sending down the Book successively is from God, The Almighty, The Wise.⁴⁵:² Truly, in the heavens and the earth are signs for the ones who believe.⁴⁵:³ And in your creation and what He disseminates of moving creatures are signs for a folk who are certain,⁴⁵:⁴ the alternation of the nighttime and the daytime and what God caused to descend from the heaven of provision. He gave life with it to the earth after its death and the diversifying of the winds—signs for a folk who are reasonable.⁴⁵:⁵

These are the signs of God We recount to thee with The Truth. Then, in which discourse, after God and His signs, will they believe?⁴⁵:⁶

Woe to every false, sinful one!⁴⁵:⁷ He hears the signs of God being recounted to him. Again, he persists as one who grows arrogant as if he hears them not. So give him good tidings of a painful punishment!⁴⁵:⁸ And if he knew anything about Our signs, he took them to himself in mockery. Those, for them is a despised punishment.⁴⁵:⁹ Behind them there is hell. What they earned will avail them not at all nor whatever they took to themselves other than God as protectors. And for them will be a tremendous punishment.⁴⁵:¹⁰

This is a guidance. Those who were ungrateful for the signs of their Lord, for them there is a punishment of painful wrath.⁴⁵:¹¹

God! It is He Who caused the sea to be subservient to you that the boats may run through it by His command and so that you be looking for His grace and so that perhaps you will give thanks.⁴⁵:¹²

And He caused to be subservient to you whatever is in the heavens and whatever is in and on the earth. All is from Him.

Truly, in that are signs for a folk who reflect.⁴⁵:¹³

Say to those who believed: Forgive those who hope not for the Days of God that He give recompense to a folk according to what they had been earning.⁴⁵:¹⁴

Whoever did as one in accord with morality, it is for himself and whoever did evil, it is against himself. Again, to your Lord you will be returned.⁴⁵:¹⁵

And, certainly, We gave the Children of Israel the Book, the critical judgment and the prophethood and We provided them from what is good and We gave them advantage over the worlds⁴⁵:¹⁶ and We gave them clear portents of the command. And they are not at variance until after the knowledge drew near them through insolence among themselves. Truly, thy Lord will decree between them on the Day of Resurrection about what they had been at variance in it.⁴⁵:¹⁷

Again, We assigned thee an open way of the command so follow it and follow not the desires of those who know not.⁴⁵:¹⁸ Truly, they will never avail thee against God at all.

And, truly, the ones who are unjust, some of them are protectors of some others.

But God is Protector of the ones who are Godfearing.⁴⁵:¹⁹

This is a clear evidence for humanity and a guidance and a mercy for a folk who are certain.⁴⁵:²⁰

Assumed those who sought to do evil deeds that We will make them equal with those who believed and did as the ones in accord with morality?

Are their living and dying equal?

How evil is the judgment they give!⁴⁵:²¹

And God created the heavens and the earth with The Truth so that every soul would be given recompense for what it earned and they, they will not be wronged.⁴⁵:²²

Hadst thou considered he who took to himself his own desire as his god and whom God caused to go astray out of a knowledge, sealed over his having the ability to hear and his heart and laid a blindfold on his sight?

Who, then, will guide him after God?

Will you not, then, recollect?⁴⁵:²³

And they said: There is nothing, but this present life of ours. We die and we live and nothing causes us to perish but a long course of time.

And there is for them not any knowledge. Truly, they are but surmising.⁴⁵:²⁴ And when are recounted to them Our signs, clear portents, then, disputation had not been but that they said: Bring our fathers if you had been ones who are sincere.⁴⁵:²⁵

Say: God gives you life. Again, He causes you to die. Again, He will gather you on the Day of Resurrection in which there is no doubt but most of humanity knows not.⁴⁵:²⁶

And to God belongs the dominion of the heavens and the earth. And on a Day that the Hour will be secure, on that Day the ones who deal in falsehood will lose.⁴⁵:²⁷ Thou wilt see each community one who crawls on its knees. Each community will be called to its book: This Day you will be given recompense for what you had been doing.⁴⁵:²⁸ This is Our Book that speaks for itself against you with The Truth. Truly, We registered what you had been doing.⁴⁵:²⁹

Then, as for those who believed and did as the ones in accord with morality, their Lord will cause them to enter in His mercy. That will be the winning the clear triumph.⁴⁵:³⁰

But as for those who were ungrateful: Be not My signs recounted to you?

Then, you grew arrogant and you had been a folk, ones who sin!⁴⁵:³¹

And when it was said: Truly, the promise of God is true and the Hour, there is no doubt about it. You said: We are not informed about the Hour. Truly, We think it but an opinion and we are not ones who ascertain it.⁴⁵:³²

And shown to themselves will be the evil deeds they did. They will be surrounded by what they had been ridiculing.⁴⁵:³³

It would be said: This Day We will forget you as you forgot the meeting of this your Day. Your place of shelter will be the fire and there is not for you anyone who helps.⁴⁵:³⁴ This is because you took to yourselves the signs of God in mockery and this present life deluded you. So this Day they will not be brought out from there nor will they ask to be favored.⁴⁵:³⁵

So The Praise belongs to God, the Lord of the heavens and the Lord of the earth, and the Lord of the worlds.⁴⁵:³⁶ And His is the domination of the heavens and the earth. And He is The Almighty, The Wise.⁴⁵:³⁷

CHAPTER 46
THE CURVING SANDHILLS

In the Name of God, The Merciful, The Compassionate
*Hā Mīm.*⁴⁶:¹

The sending down successively of the Book is from God The Almighty, The Wise.⁴⁶:²

We created not the heavens and the earth and whatever is between the two, but with The Truth and for a term, that which is determined.

And those who disbelieved in what they were warned about are ones who turn aside.⁴⁶:³

Say: Considered you what you call to other than God?

Cause me to see what of the earth they created.

Have they an association in the heavens?

Bring me a Book from before this, or a vestige of knowledge if you had been ones who are sincere.⁴⁶:⁴

And who is one who has gone more astray than one who calls to other than God, one who responds not to him until the Day of Resurrection?

And they are of their supplication to them, ones who are heedless.⁴⁶:⁵

And when humanity will be assembled, they will become their enemies and will be ones who disavow their worship.⁴⁶:⁶

And when Our signs are recounted, clear portents, those who were ungrateful for The Truth said when it drew near them: This is clear sorcery!⁴⁶:⁷

Or they say: He devised it.

Say: If I devised it, you still possess nothing for me against God. He is greater in knowledge of what you press on about. He sufficed as a Witness between me and between you. And He is The Forgiving, The Compassionate.⁴⁶:⁸

Say: I had not been an innovation among the Messengers, nor am I informed of what will be wreaked on me, nor with you. I follow only what is revealed to me and I am only a clear warner.⁴⁶:⁹

Say: Considered you if this had been from God and you were ungrateful for it and bore witness as one who bears witness from among the Children of Israel to its like and believed in it, yet you grew arrogant, how unjust you are; truly, God guides not the folk, the ones who are unjust.⁴⁶:¹⁰

Those who were ungrateful said of those who believed: If it had been good, they would not have preceded us towards it. And when they are not truly guided by it, they say: This is a ripe, aged calumny.⁴⁶:¹¹

Yet before it was the Book of Moses for a leader and as a mercy. And this is a Book, that which establishes as true in the Arabic language to warn those who did wrong and as good tidings to the ones who are doers of good.⁴⁶:¹²

Truly, those who say: Our Lord is God again, go straight, neither will there be fear in them, nor will they feel remorse.⁴⁶:¹³ Those are the Companions of the Garden, ones who will dwell in it forever as a recompense for what they had been doing.⁴⁶:¹⁴

And We charged the human being with kindness to ones who are his parents. His mother carried him painfully and she painfully brought him forth. And the bearing of him and the weaning of him are thirty months.

When he was fully grown, having come of age and reached forty years he said: My Lord! Arouse me that I may give thanks for Thy divine blessing, that with which Thou wert gracious to me and to ones who are my parents and that I do as one in accord with morality so that Thou be well-pleased and make things right for me and my offspring. Truly, I repented to Thee and, truly, I am of the ones who submit to God.⁴⁶:¹⁵

Those are those from whom We will receive the fairer of what they did and we will pass on by their evil deeds. They are among the Companions of the Garden. This is the promise of sincerity that they had been promised.⁴⁶:¹⁶

But he who would say to ones who are his parents a word of disrespect to both of them: Promise you me that I will be brought out when generations before me passed away?

And they will both cry to God for help: Woe unto thee! Believe! Truly, the promise of God is true.

But he said: This is only the fables of the ancient ones.⁴⁶:¹⁷

Those are those against whom the saying was realized about the communities that passed away before of the jinn and humankind. Truly, they had been ones who are losers.⁴⁶:¹⁸

And for each there will be degrees according to what he did and He will pay them their account in full for their actions and they, they will not be wronged.⁴⁶:¹⁹

On a Day when they will be presented—those who were ungrateful—to the fire, it will be said: You caused what is good to be put away in your present life while you enjoyed it. Then, you will be given recompense with a punishment of humiliation because you had been growing arrogant on the earth without right and because you had been disobeying.⁴⁶:²⁰

And remember the brother of Ad when he warned his folk in the curving sandhills. Warnings passed away before and after him from: Worship nothing but God. Truly, I fear for you the punishment of a tremendous Day.⁴⁶:²¹

They said: Hadst thou drawn near to us to mislead us from our gods? Then, bring us that which thou hast promised us if thou hadst been among the ones who are sincere.⁴⁶:²²

He said: The knowledge is only with God and I state to you what I was sent with, but I see that you are a folk who are ignorant.⁴⁶:²³

Then, when they saw it as a dense cloud proceeding towards their valleys, they said: This is a dense cloud, that which gives rain to us.

Nay! It is what you seek to hasten, a wind in which there is a painful punishment.⁴⁶:²⁴ It will destroy everything at the command of its Lord. So it came to be in the morning nothing was seen but their dwellings. Thus, We give recompense to the folk, ones who sin.⁴⁶:²⁵

And, certainly, We established them firmly in what We established you firmly not and We made for them the ability to hear and sight and minds. Yet having the ability to hear availed them not, nor their sight, nor their minds at all since they had been negating the signs of God. And surrounded were they by what they had been ridiculing.⁴⁶:²⁶

And, certainly, We caused to perish towns around you and We diversified the signs so that perhaps they will return.⁴⁶:²⁷ Then, why helped them not those whom they took to themselves other than God as gods as a mediator.

Nay! They went astray from them. And that was their calumny and what they had been devising.⁴⁶:²⁸

And when We turned away from thee groups of men or jinn who listen to the Quran, when they found themselves in its presence, they said: Pay heed.

And when it was finished, they turned to their folk, ones who warn.⁴⁶:²⁹

They said: O our folk! Truly, We heard a Book was caused to descend after Moses, that which establishes as true what was in advance of it. It guides to The Truth and to a straight road.⁴⁶:³⁰

O our folk! Answer one who calls to God and believe in Him. He will forgive you your impieties and will grant protection to you from a painful punishment.⁴⁶:³¹

And who answers not to one who calls to God? He is not one who frustrates Him in and on the earth. And there will not be for him other than God any protectors. Those are clearly gone astray.⁴⁶:³²

Considered they not that God Who created the heavens and the earth and is not wearied by their creation—is One Who Has Power to give life to the dead? Yea! He, truly, is Powerful over everything.⁴⁶:³³

And on a Day when will be presented those who were ungrateful to the fire saying: Is not this The Truth?

They would say: Yea! By our Lord!

He will say: Then, experience the punishment because you had been ungrateful!⁴⁶:³⁴

So have thou patience as endured patiently those imbued with constancy of the Messengers and let them not seek to hasten the Judgment. As, truly, on a Day they will see what they are promised as if they lingered not in expectation but for an hour of daytime. This is delivering the message! Will any be caused to perish but the folk, the ones who disobey?⁴⁶:³⁵

CHAPTER 47 MUHAMMAD

In the Name of God, The Merciful, The Compassionate

Those who were ungrateful and who barred from the way of God—He caused their actions to go astray.⁴⁷:¹

And those who believed and did as the ones in accord with morality and believed in what was sent down to Muhammad—for it is The Truth from their Lord—He will absolve them of their evil deeds and will make right their state of mind.⁴⁷:²

That is because those who were ungrateful followed falsehood, while those who believed followed The Truth from their Lord. Thus, God propounds for humanity their parables.⁴⁷:³

So when you met those who were ungrateful, then, strike their thick necks until you gave them a sound thrashing. Then, tie them fast with restraints. And afterwards either have good will towards them or take ransom for them until the war ends, laying down its heavy load. Thus, it is so! But if God willed, He Himself would have, certainly, avenged you. But it is to try some of you with some others. As for those who were slain in the way of God, He will never cause their actions to go astray.⁴⁷:⁴ He will guide them and He will make right their state of mind.⁴⁷:⁵ And He will cause them to enter the Garden with which He acquainted them.⁴⁷:⁶

O those who believed! If you help God, He will help you and make firm your feet.⁴⁷:⁷ As for those who are ungrateful, for them is falling into ruin! And He caused their actions to go astray.⁴⁷:⁸ That is because they disliked what God caused to descend so He caused their actions to fail.⁴⁷:⁹

Journey they not through the earth and look on how had been the Ultimate End of those who were before them? God destroyed them. And for ones who are ungrateful is its likeness.⁴⁷:¹⁰

That is because God is the Defender of those who believed. And for the ones who are ungrateful, there is no defender of them.⁴⁷:¹¹

Truly, God will cause to enter those who believed and did as the ones in accord with morality, gardens beneath which rivers run.

While those who were ungrateful, take joy in eating as the flocks eat, the fire will be the place of lodging for them.⁴⁷:¹²

And how many a town had there been which was stronger in strength than thy town which drove thee out, that We have caused to perish? And there was no one who helps them!⁴⁷:¹³

Is he who had been on a clear portent from his Lord like him for whom was made to appear pleasing his dire actions and they followed their own desires?47:14

This is the parable of the Garden which was promised the ones who are Godfearing: In it are rivers of unpolluted water and rivers of milk, the taste of which is not modified and rivers of intoxicants delightful to ones who drink and rivers of clarified honey, and in it for them all kinds of fruits and forgiveness from their Lord.

Is this like ones who will dwell forever in the fire and they were given scalding water to drink so that it cuts off their bowels?47:15

And among them are some who listen to thee until when they went forth from thee. They said to those who were given the knowledge: What was that he said just now?

Those are those upon whose hearts God set a seal. And they followed their own desires.47:16

And those who were truly guided, He increased them in guidance and He gave to them their God-consciousness.47:17

Look, then, on not but the Hour, that it approach them suddenly?

Certainly, its tokens drew near. Then, what will it be like for them when their reminder drew near to them?47:18

So know thou that there is no god but God and ask forgiveness for thy impieties and also for the males, ones who believe and the females, ones who believe, and God knows your place of turmoil and your place of lodging.47:19

And those who believed say: Why was a chapter of the Quran not caused to descend?

But when was caused to descend a definitive chapter of the Quran and fighting was remembered in it, thou hadst seen those who in their hearts is a sickness looking on thee with the look of one who is fainting at death.47:20 But better for them would be obedience and an honorable saying! And when the affair was resolved, then, if they were sincere to God, it would have been better for them.47:21

Will it be that if you turned away, you would make corruption in the earth and cut off your ties with blood relations?47:22 Those are those whom God cursed, so He made them unwilling to hear and their sight, unwilling to see.47:23

Meditate they not, then, on the Quran or are there locks on their hearts?47:24 Truly, those who went back—turn their back—after the guidance became clear to them, it was Satan who enticed them and He granted them indulgence.47:25

That is because they said to those who disliked what God sent down: We will obey you in some of the affair.

And God knows what they keep secret.47:26

Then, how will it be for them when the angels will call them to themselves, striking their faces and their backs?47:27

That is because they followed what displeased God and they disliked His contentment so He caused their actions to fail.47:28

Or assumed those who in their hearts is a sickness that God will never bring out their rancor?47:29

If We will, We would have caused thee to see them. Thou wouldst have recognized them by their mark. But, certainly, thou wilt recognize them by the twisting of sayings. And God knows all your actions.47:30

And, certainly, We will try you until We know the ones who struggle among you and the ones who remain steadfast and We will try your reports.47:31 Truly, those who were ungrateful and barred from the way of God and made a breach with the Messenger after guidance became clear to them, they never hurt or profit God at all, but He will cause their actions to fail.47:32

O those who believed! Obey God and obey the Messenger and render not your actions untrue.47:33

Truly, those who were ungrateful and barred from the way of God, again, they died while they were ones who are ungrateful, then, God will never forgive them.47:34

So be not faint and call for peace while you have the upper hand. God is with you and He will never cheat you out of your actions.47:35

This present life is only a pastime and a diversion. But if you believe and are Godfearing, He will give you your compensation and will not ask of you for your property.47:36

When He asks it of you and, then, urges persistently, you would be a miser and He will bring out your rancor.47:37

Lo and behold! These are being called to spend in the way of God, yet among you are some who are misers. And whoever is miser, then, he is a miser only to himself. God is Sufficient and you are poor. And if you turn away, He will have a folk other than you in exchange. Again, they will not be the like of you.47:38

CHAPTER 48 THE VICTORY

In the Name of God, The Merciful, The Compassionate

Truly, We gave victory to thee, a clear victory,48:1 that God forgive thee what was former of thy impiety and what remained behind that He fulfill His divine blessing on thee and guide thee on a straight path48:2 and that God help thee with a mighty help.48:3

He it is Who caused the tranquility to descend into the hearts of the ones who believe that they add belief to their belief.

And to God belongs the armies of the heavens and the earth.

And God had been Knowing, Wise48:4 that He causes to enter the males, ones who believe and the females, ones who believe Gardens beneath which rivers run, ones who will dwell in them forever, and that He absolve them of their evil deeds. And that had been with God a winning a sublime triumph.48:5

And that He punish the males, ones who are hypocrites and the females, ones who are hypocrites and the males, ones who are polytheists and the females, ones who are polytheists, the ones who think an evil thought about God, a reprehensible thought, for them is the reprehensible turn of fortune. And God was angry with them. And He cursed them and prepared hell for them. And how evil a Homecoming!48:6

And to God belongs the armies of the heavens and the earth. And God had been Almighty, Wise.48:7

Truly, We sent thee as one who bears witness and one who gives good tidings and as a warner,48:8 so that you believe in God and His Messenger and that you support him and revere Him and glorify Him at early morning dawn and eventide.48:9

Truly, those who take the pledge of allegiance to thee, take the pledge of alliance only to God. The hand of God is over their hands. Then, whoever broke his oath, breaks his oath only to the harm of himself. And whoever lived up to what he made as a contract with God, He will give him a sublime compensation.48:10

The ones who are left behind will say to thee among the nomads: Our property and our people occupied us, so ask forgiveness for us.

They say with their tongues what is not in their hearts.

Say: Who, then, has sway over you against God at all if He wanted to harm you or wanted to bring you profit? Nay! God had been aware of what you do.48:11 Nay! You thought that the Messenger would never turn about and the ones who believe to their people ever, and that was made to appear pleasing in your hearts. But you thought a reprehensible thought, and you had been a lost folk.48:12

And whoever believes not in God and His Messenger, truly, We made ready a blaze for the ones who are ungrateful.48:13

And to God belongs the dominion of the heavens and the earth. He forgives whom He wills and punishes whom He wills. And God had been Forgiving, Compassionate.⁴⁸ʲ¹⁴

The ones who are left behind will say when you set out to take the gains: Let us follow you. They want to substitute for the assertion of God. Say: You will not follow us. Thus, God said before; then, they will say: Nay! You are jealous of us. Nay! They had not been understanding, but a little.⁴⁸ʲ¹⁵

Say to the ones who are left behind among the nomads: You will be called against a folk imbued with severe might. You will fight them or they will submit to God. Then, if you obey, God will give you a fairer compensation. But if you turn away as you turned away before, He will punish you with a painful punishment.⁴⁸ʲ¹⁶

There is neither a fault on the blind, nor a fault on the lame, nor a fault on the sick, and whoever obeys God and His Messenger, He will cause him to enter Gardens beneath which rivers run. And whoever turns away, He will punish him with a painful punishment.⁴⁸ʲ¹⁷

God was well-pleased with the ones who believe (f) when they take the pledge of allegiance to thee beneath the tree for He knew what was in their hearts and He caused the tranquility to descend on them and He repaid them with a victory near at hand.⁴⁸ʲ¹⁸ And they will take much gain. And God had been Almighty, Wise.⁴⁸ʲ¹⁹

God promised you much gain that you will take and He quickened this for you. He limited the hands of humanity from you so that perhaps it will be a sign to the ones who believe and that He guide you to a straight path⁴⁸ʲ²⁰ and other gains which are not yet within your power. Surely, God enclosed them. And God had been over everything Powerful.⁴⁸ʲ²¹

And if those who were ungrateful fought you, they would have turned their backs. Again, they would not have found a protector or a helper.⁴⁸ʲ²² This is a custom of God which was, surely, in force before. Thou wilt never find in a custom of God any substitution.⁴⁸ʲ²³

And He it is who limited their hands from you and your hands from them in the hollow of Makkah after He made you victors over them. And God had been Seeing of what you do.⁴⁸ʲ²⁴

They were ungrateful, and they barred you from the Masjid al-Haram, and were ones who detained the sacrificial gift from reaching its place of sacrifice. If it had not been for men, ones who believe, and for women, ones who believe, whom you know not that you tread on them and guilt should light on you without your knowledge. This was so that God may cause to enter into His mercy whomever He wills. If they were clearly apart, separated, We would have punished those who were ungrateful among them with a painful punishment.⁴⁸ʲ²⁵

Mention when those who were ungrateful laid zealotry in their hearts, like the zealotry of the Age of Ignorance. Then, God caused to descend His tranquility on His Messenger and on the ones who believe and fastened on them the Word of God-consciousness. They had been with right to it and were more worthy of it. And God had been Knowing.⁴⁸ʲ²⁶

Certainly, God was sincere to the dream of His Messenger with The Truth: You will enter the Masjid al-Haram, if God willed, as ones who are safe, as ones who shaved your heads or as ones whose hair is cut short. You will fear not. He knew what you know not and He assigned other than that a victory near at hand.⁴⁸ʲ²⁷

He it is Who sent His Messenger with guidance and the way of life of The Truth that He uplift it over all of the ways of life. And God sufficed as a witness.⁴⁸ʲ²⁸

Muhammad is the Messenger of God. And those who are with him are severe against the one who is ungrateful, but compassionate among themselves. Thou hast seen them as ones who bow down as ones who prostrate themselves. They are looking for grace from God and contentment. Their mark is on their faces from the effects of prostration.

This is their parable in the Torah. And their parable in the Gospel is like sown seed that brought out its shoot, energized. It, then, became stout and rose straight on its plant stalk impressing the ones who sow so that He enrage by them the ones who are ungrateful, God promised those who believed and did as the ones in accord with morality, for them forgiveness and a sublime compensation.⁴⁸ʲ²⁹

CHAPTER 49 THE INNER APARTMENTS

In the Name of God, The Merciful, The Compassionate

O those who believed! Put not yourselves forward in advance of God and His Messenger. And be Godfearing of God. Truly, God is Hearing, Knowing.⁴⁹ʲ¹

O those who believed! Exalt not your voices above the voice of the Prophet nor publish a saying to him as you would openly publish something to some others so that your actions not be fruitless while you are not aware.⁴⁹ʲ² Truly, those who lower their voices near the Messenger of God, those are those who are ones God put to test their hearts for God-consciousness. For them is forgiveness and a sublime compensation.⁴⁹ʲ³

Truly, those who cry out to thee from behind the inner apartments, most of them are not reasonable.⁴⁹ʲ⁴ And if they endured patiently until thou wouldst go forth to them, it would have been better for them. And God is Forgiving, Compassionate.⁴⁹ʲ⁵

O those who believed! If one who disobeys drew near to you with a tiding, then, be clear so that you not light on a folk out of ignorance. Then, you would become ones who are remorseful for what you accomplished.⁴⁹ʲ⁶

Know you that the Messenger of God is of you. If he obeys you in much of the affairs, you would, certainly, fall into misfortune. But God endeared belief to you and made it appear pleasing to your hearts. And He caused to be detestable to you ingratitude and disobedience and rebellion. Those, they are the ones who are on the right way.⁴⁹ʲ⁷ This is a grace from God and His divine blessing. And God is Knowing, Wise.⁴⁹ʲ⁸

And if two sections among the ones who believe fought one against the other, then, make things right between them both. Then, if one of them was insolent against the other, then, fight the one who is insolent until it changed its mind about the command of God. Then, if it changes its mind, make things right between them justly. And act justly. Truly, God loves the ones who act justly.⁴⁹ʲ⁹

Only the ones who believe are brothers/sisters, so make things right between your two brothers/sisters. And be Godfearing of God so that perhaps you will find mercy.⁴⁹ʲ¹⁰

O those who believed! Let not a folk deride another folk. Perhaps they be better than they, nor women deride other women. Perhaps they be better than they. Nor find fault with one another nor insult one another with nicknames. Miserable was the name of disobedience after belief! And whoever repents not, then, those, they are the ones who are unjust.⁴⁹ʲ¹¹

O those who believed! Avoid suspicion much. Truly, some suspicion is a sin. And spy not nor backbite some by some other. Would one of you love to eat the flesh of his lifeless brother? You would have disliked it. And be Godfearing of God. Truly, God is Accepter of Repentance, Compassionate.⁴⁹ʲ¹²

O humanity! Truly, We created you from a male and a female and made you into peoples and types that you recognize one another. Truly, the most generous of you with God is the most devout. Truly, God is Knowing, Aware.49:13

The nomads said: We believed.

Say to them: You believe not.

But say: We submitted to God, for belief enters not yet into your hearts. But if you obey God and His Messenger, He will not withhold your actions at all. Truly, God is Forgiving, Compassionate.49:14

The ones who believe are not but those who believed in God and His Messenger. Again, they were not in doubt and they struggled with their wealth and themselves in the way of God. Those, they are the ones who are sincere.49:15

Say: Would you teach God about your way of life while God knows whatever is in the heavens and whatever is in and on the earth?

And God is Knowing of everything.49:16

They show grace to thee that they submitted to God.

Say: Show you submission to God as grace to me? Nay! God shows grace to you in that He guided you to belief if you, truly, had been ones who are sincere.49:17

Truly, God knows the unseen of the heavens and the earth. And God is Seeing of what you do.49:18

CHAPTER 50 QAF

In the Name of God, The Merciful, The Compassionate
Qaf.

By the glorious Quran!50:1

Nay! They marveled that there drew near them one who warns from among themselves. So the ones who are ungrateful said: This is a strange thing.50:2 When we died and had been earth dust, that is a far-fetched returning!50:3

Surely, We knew what the earth reduces from them. And with Us is a guardian Book.50:4

Nay! They denied The Truth when it drew near them, so they are in a confused state of affairs.50:5

Look they not on the heaven above them, how We built it and made it appear pleasing?

And there are not any gaps in it.50:6

And the earth, We stretched it out and cast on it firm mountains and caused in it to develop every lovely, diverse pair50:7 for contemplation and as a reminder to every servant, one who turns in repentance.50:8

And We sent down blessed water from heaven. Then, We caused gardens to develop from it and reaped grains of wheat50:9 and high-reaching date palm trees with ranged spathes50:10 as provision for My servants. And We gave life by them to a lifeless land. Thus, will be the going forth.50:11

The folk of Noah denied what came before them, and the Companions of the Rass and Thamud,50:12 and Ad and Pharaoh and the brothers of Lot,50:13 and the Companions of the Thicket and the folk of Tubba.

Everyone denied the Messengers, so My threat was realized.50:14

Were We wearied by the first creation?

Nay! They are perplexed about a new creation.50:15

And, certainly, We created the human being. We know what evil his soul whispers to him. We are nearer to him than the jugular vein.50:16

When the two receivers are ones who receive, seated on the right and on the left,50:17 he utters not a saying but that there is one ready, watching over near him50:18 when the agony of death drew near with The Truth. That is what thou hadst been shunning.50:19

And the trumpet will be blown. That is the Day of The Threat.50:20 And every person will draw near with an angel,

one who drives, and an angel witness.50:21 Certainly, thou hadst been heedless of this so We removed thy screen from thee so that thy sight this Day will be sharp.50:22 And his comrade angel would say: This is what is ready near me of his record:50:23 Cast into hell every stubborn ingrate50:24 who delays the good, one who exceeds the limits, one who is in grave doubt,50:25 he who made another god with God! Then, cast him into the severe punishment!50:26

His comrade Satan would say: Our Lord! I made him not overbold, but he had been going far astray.50:27

He would say: Strive not against one another in My presence, for, surely, I will put forward The Threat to you.50:28

The statement is not substituted in My presence and I am not unjust to the servants.50:29

On a Day when We will say to hell: Art thou full?

And it will say: Are there any additions?50:30

And the Garden was brought close to the ones who are Godfearing, not far off.50:31 This is what is promised you, for every penitent and guardian50:32 who dreaded The Merciful in the unseen and drew near with a heart of one who turns in repentance:50:33 Enter you there in peace. That is the Day of Eternity!50:34 They will have what they will in it and with Us there is yet an addition.50:35

And how many We caused to perish before them of generations who were stronger than they in courage so that they searched about on the land. Was there any asylum?50:36

Truly, in that is a reminder for him, for whoever had a heart or, having the ability to hear, gave listen. He is a witness.50:37

And, certainly, We created the heavens and the earth and whatever is between in six days, and no exhaustion afflicted Us.50:38 So have thou patience with whatever they say and glorify with the praise of thy Lord before the coming up of the sun and before sunset.50:39

And in the night glorify Him and at the end part of the prostrations.50:40

And listen thou on a Day when one who calls out will cry out from a near place.50:41

On a Day when they will hear the Cry with The Truth. That will be the Day of going forth.50:42 Truly, it is We who give life and cause to die and to Us is the Homecoming50:43 on a Day when the earth will be split open swiftly. That will be an easy assembling for Us.50:44

We are greater in knowledge as to what they say. And thou art not haughty over them so remind by the Quran whoever fears My threat.50:45

CHAPTER 51
THE WINNOWING WINDS

In the Name of God, The Merciful, The Compassionate

By the winnowing winds of ones that winnow51:1 by the burden-bearers, the ones who carry a heavy burden51:2 and the ones that run with ease51:3 and the ones who distribute the command,51:4 truly, what you are promised is that which is sincere.51:5 And, truly, the judgment is that which falls.51:6

By the heaven that is full of tracks,51:7 you are ones who are at variance in your sayings.51:8 He is misled there by he who was misled.51:9 Perdition to those who guess,51:10 ones who are inattentive because of obstinacy.51:11 They ask: When will the Day of Judgment be?51:12

A Day when they are tried over the fire:51:13 Experience your test. This is that for which you had been seeking to hasten.51:14

Truly, the ones who are Godfearing will be in the Garden and springs,51:15 ones who take what their Lord gave them. Truly, they had been before this—ones who are doers of good.⁵¹:¹⁶ They had been slumbering little during the night.⁵¹:¹⁷ And at the breaking of the day, they ask for forgiveness.⁵¹:¹⁸

And there is an obligation from their wealth for the one who begs and the one who is deprived.⁵¹:¹⁹ On the earth are signs, for the ones that are certain⁵¹:²⁰ and in yourselves. Will you not, then, perceive?⁵¹:²¹

And in the heaven is your provision as you are promised⁵¹:²² by the Lord of the heaven and the earth. It is, truly, The Truth just as you yourselves speak.⁵¹:²³

Truly, approached thee the discourse of guests of Abraham, the ones who are honored?⁵¹:²⁴ When they entered to him they said: Peace.

He said: Peace, to a folk, ones who are unknown.⁵¹:²⁵

Then, he turned upon his people and brought about a fattened calf⁵¹:²⁶ so he brought it near to them. He said: Will you not eat?⁵¹:²⁷

Then, he sensed a fear of them; they said: Be not in awe. They gave him good tidings of a knowing boy.⁵¹:²⁸

Then, his woman came forward with a loud cry. She slapped her face and said: I am an old barren woman!⁵¹:²⁹

They said: Thus, spoke thy Lord. Truly, He is The Wise, The Knowing.⁵¹:³⁰

Abraham said: O ones who are sent, what is your business?⁵¹:³¹

They said: That we were sent to a folk, ones who sin,⁵¹:³² to send on them rocks of clay,⁵¹:³³ ones distinguished by thy Lord for ones who are excessive.⁵¹:³⁴

So We brought out whoever had been in it of the ones who believe.⁵¹:³⁵ But We found in it nothing but a house of ones who submit to God.⁵¹:³⁶ And We left a sign in it for those who fear the painful punishment.⁵¹:³⁷

And in Moses, then, We sent him to Pharaoh with a clear authority.⁵¹:³⁸

Then, Pharaoh turned away to his court. He said: One who is a sorcerer, one who is possessed!⁵¹:³⁹

So We took him and his armies and cast them forth into the water of the sea and he is one who is answerable.⁵¹:⁴⁰

And in Ad, when We sent against them the withering wind.⁵¹:⁴¹ It forsakes not anything it approached, but made it like it was decayed.⁵¹:⁴²

And in Thamud, when it was said to them: Take joy for awhile.⁵¹:⁴³ Yet they defied the command of their Lord so the thunderbolt took them while they look on.⁵¹:⁴⁴ They were neither able to stand up nor had they been ones who are aided.⁵¹:⁴⁵

And the folk of Noah from before. Truly, they had been a folk, ones who disobey.⁵¹:⁴⁶

And We built the heaven with potency. And, truly, We are ones who extend wide.⁵¹:⁴⁷ And the earth, We spread it forth. How excellent are the ones who spread!⁵¹:⁴⁸ And of everything We created pairs so that perhaps you will recollect.⁵¹:⁴⁹

So run away towards God. Truly, I am to you a clear warner from Him.⁵¹:⁵⁰ And make not with God any other god. Truly, I am to you a clear warner from Him.⁵¹:⁵¹ There approached not those who were before them any Messenger but that they said: One who is a sorcerer or one who is possessed!⁵¹:⁵²

Counseled they this to one another?

Nay! They are a folk, ones who are defiant!⁵¹:⁵³ So turn thou away from them that thou be not one who is reproached.⁵¹:⁵⁴ And remind, for, truly, the reminder profits the ones who believe.⁵¹:⁵⁵

And I created not jinn and humankind but that they worship Me.⁵¹:⁵⁶ I want no provision from them nor want I that they feed Me.⁵¹:⁵⁷ Truly, God, He is The Provider, The Possessor of Strength, The Sure.⁵¹:⁵⁸

And, truly, the impiety of those who did wrong is like the impiety of their companions. So let them not seek to hasten the Judgment.⁵¹:⁵⁹ Then, woe to those who disbelieved in that Day of theirs that they are promised.⁵¹:⁶⁰

CHAPTER 52 THE MOUNT

In the Name of God, The Merciful, The Compassionate

By the mount⁵²:¹ and by a Book inscribed⁵²:² on an unrolled scroll of parchment⁵²:³ and by the frequented House⁵²:⁴ and by the exalted roof⁵²:⁵ and that which is poured forth over the seas,⁵²:⁶ truly, the punishment of Thy Lord is that which falls.⁵²:⁷ There is no one who averts it.⁵²:⁸

On a Day when the heaven will spin a spinning⁵²:⁹ and the mountains will journey a journey.⁵²:¹⁰

Then, woe on a Day to the ones who deny,⁵²:¹¹ they, those are engaging in idle talk, play,⁵²:¹² on a Day they will be driven away with force to the fire of hell with a driving away:⁵²:¹³ This is the fire which you had been denying!⁵²:¹⁴

Is this, then, sorcery or is it that you perceive not?⁵²:¹⁵

Roast you in it! Then, have patience, or you endure patiently not, it is all the same to you. You will be only given recompense for what you had been doing.⁵²:¹⁶

Truly, the ones who are Godfearing will be in Gardens and bliss,⁵²:¹⁷ ones who are joyful for what their Lord gave them. And their Lord protected them from the punishment of hellfire.⁵²:¹⁸ Eat and drink wholesomely because of what you had been doing.⁵²:¹⁹ They will be ones who are reclining on couches arrayed. And We will give in marriage to them lovely, most beautiful eyed ones.⁵²:²⁰

And those who believed and their offspring who followed them in belief, We caused them to join their offspring. And We deprived them not of anything of their actions. Every man will be pledged for what he earned.⁵²:²¹ And We furnished relief to them with sweet fruit and meat such as that for which they lust.⁵²:²² They will contend with one another for a cup around which there is no idle talk nor accusation of sinfulness.⁵²:²³ And boys of theirs will go around them as if they had been well-guarded pearls.⁵²:²⁴ And some of them will come forward to some others demanding of one another.⁵²:²⁵

They would say: Truly, we had been before ones who are apprehensive among our people,⁵²:²⁶ but God showed grace to us and protected us from the punishment of the burning wind.⁵²:²⁷

Truly, we had been calling to Him before. Truly, He, He is The Source of Goodness, The Compassionate.⁵²:²⁸

So remind! Thou art not, by the divine blessing of thy Lord, a soothsayer nor one who is possessed.⁵²:²⁹

Or they say: A poet! We await for the setback of fate for him.⁵²:³⁰

Say: Await for I am with the ones who are waiting.⁵²:³¹

Or command their faculties of understanding to this? Or are they a folk, ones who are defiant?⁵²:³²

Or say they: He fabricated it? Nay! They believe not.⁵²:³³

Then, let them bring a discourse like it, if they had been ones who are sincere.⁵²:³⁴

Or were they created out of nothing? Or are they ones who are creators of themselves?⁵²:³⁵

Or created they the heavens and the earth? Nay! They are not certain.⁵²:³⁶

Or are the treasures of thy Lord with them? Or are they ones who are registrars?⁵²:³⁷

Or have they a ladder by means of which they listen? Then, let ones who are listening bring a clear authority.⁵²:³⁸

Or has He daughters and they have sons?⁵²:³⁹

Or hast thou asked them for a compensation so that they are from something owed ones who will be weighed down?⁵²:⁴⁰

Or is the unseen with them and they write it down?⁵²:⁴¹

Or want they cunning?

But it is those who were ungrateful, they are the ones who are outwitted.⁵²:⁴²

Or have they a god other than God?

Glory be to God above partners they ascribe!⁵²:⁴³

And if they consider pieces of the heaven descending, they would say: Heaped up clouds!⁵²:⁴⁴ So forsake them until they encounter their day in which they will be swooning.⁵²:⁴⁵ A Day when their cunning will avail them not at all nor will they be helped.⁵²:⁴⁶ And, truly, for those who did wrong there is a punishment besides that, but most of them know not.⁵²:⁴⁷

So have thou patience for the determination of thy Lord, for, truly, thou art under Our eyes; and glorify the praises of thy Lord when thou hast stood up at the time of dawn,⁵²:⁴⁸ and glorify at night and the drawing back of the stars.⁵²:⁴⁹

CHAPTER 53 THE STAR

In the Name of God, The Merciful, The Compassionate

By the star when it hurled to ruin,⁵³:¹ neither your companion went astray, nor he erred⁵³:² nor speaks he for himself out of desire.⁵³:³ It is but a revelation that is revealed,⁵³:⁴ taught to him by The One Stronger in Strength,⁵³:⁵ Possessor of Forcefulness.

Then, he stood poised⁵³:⁶ while he was on the loftiest horizon.⁵³:⁷ Again, he came to pass near and hung suspended⁵³:⁸ until he had been at a distance of two bow lengths or closer.⁵³:⁹ Then, He revealed to His servant what He revealed.⁵³:¹⁰ The mind lied not against what it saw.⁵³:¹¹

Will you altercate with him about what he sees?⁵³:¹²

And, certainly, he saw it another time⁵³:¹³ near the Lote Tree of the Utmost Boundary⁵³:¹⁴ near which is the Garden of the Place of Shelter,⁵³:¹⁵ when overcomes the Lote Tree what overcomes it.⁵³:¹⁶

The sight swerved not, nor was it defiant.⁵³:¹⁷

Certainly, he saw some of the greatest signs of his Lord.⁵³:¹⁸

Saw you, then, al-Lat and al-Uzza⁵³:¹⁹ and Manat, the third, the other?⁵³:²⁰ Have you males and has He, females?⁵³:²¹ That, then, is an unfair division.⁵³:²² They are but names that you named, you and your fathers, for which God caused not to descend any authority. They follow nothing but opinion and that for which their souls yearn. And, certainly, drew near them the guidance from their Lord.⁵³:²³

Or will the human being have what he coveted?⁵³:²⁴

Then, to God belongs the Last and the First.⁵³:²⁵

And how many an angel in the heavens is there whose intercession will avail nothing at all, but after God gives permission to whom He wills and He is well-pleased.⁵³:²⁶ Truly, those who believe not in the world to come naming the angels with female names,⁵³:²⁷ while they have no knowledge of it, they follow nothing but opinion. And, truly, opinion avails them not at all against The Truth.⁵³:²⁸

So turn thou aside from him who turns away from Our Remembrance and he wants nothing but this present life.⁵³:²⁹ That is their attainment of the knowledge. Truly, thy Lord, He is the One Who is greater in knowledge of whoever went astray from His way. And He is greater in knowledge of whoever were truly guided.⁵³:³⁰

And to God belongs whatever is in the heavens and whatever is in and on the earth that He may give recompense to those who did evil for what they did and give recompense fairer to those who did good,⁵³:³¹ those who avoid the major sins and the indecencies but the lesser offenses. Truly, thy Lord is One Who is Extensive in forgiveness. He is greater in knowledge of you when He caused you to grow from the earth and when you were an unborn child in the wombs of your mothers. So you make not pure yourselves. He is greater in knowledge of him who was Godfearing.⁵³:³²

Hadst thou considered him who turned away⁵³:³³ and gave a little, giving grudgingly?⁵³:³⁴

Is the knowledge of the unseen with him so that he sees it?⁵³:³⁵ Or is he told what is in the scrolls of Moses⁵³:³⁶ and of Abraham who paid his account in full?⁵³:³⁷

The burdened soul will not bear the heavy load of another.⁵³:³⁸

The human being is not but what he endeavored for⁵³:³⁹ and that his endeavoring will be seen.⁵³:⁴⁰ Again, he will be given recompense for it with a more true recompense,⁵³:⁴¹ and that towards thy Lord is the Utmost Boundary,⁵³:⁴² and that He caused laughter and caused weeping,⁵³:⁴³ and that He caused to die and gave life⁵³:⁴⁴ and it is He, He created the pairs, the male and the female⁵³:⁴⁵ from seminal fluid when it is emitted,⁵³:⁴⁶ and that with Him is another growth⁵³:⁴⁷ and it is He, He Who Enriched and made rich⁵³:⁴⁸ and that He, He is the Lord of Sirius⁵³:⁴⁹ and that He caused to perish the previous Ad⁵³:⁵⁰ and Thamud. He caused none to remain⁵³:⁵¹—and the folk of Noah before.

Truly, they had been they who do greater wrong and ones who are defiant.⁵³:⁵² He caused to tumble that which are cities overthrown,⁵³:⁵³ then, enwrapped them with what enwrapped.⁵³:⁵⁴

Then, which of the benefits of thy Lord wilt thou quarrel with?⁵³:⁵⁵

This is a warner among the previous warnings.⁵³:⁵⁶ The Impending Day is impending.⁵³:⁵⁷ There is not other than God, One Who Uncovers it.⁵³:⁵⁸ Then, at this discourse you marvel?⁵³:⁵⁹

And will you laugh and not weep⁵³:⁶⁰ while you are ones who pass life in enjoyment?⁵³:⁶¹

So prostrate yourselves to God and worship Him.⁵³:⁶²

CHAPTER 54 THE MOON

In the Name of God, The Merciful, The Compassionate

The Hour neared and the moon was split.⁵⁴:¹

And if they see a sign, they turn aside and say: Incessant sorcery!⁵⁴:² And they denied and followed their own desires. And every affair is that which is settled.⁵⁴:³ And, certainly, the tidings drew near them wherein was that which is to deter⁵⁴:⁴—namely, that which is far reaching wisdom—yet warnings avail not.⁵⁴:⁵ So turn thou away from them on a Day when One Who Calls will call to a horrible thing.⁵⁴:⁶ Their sight will be that which is humbled and they will go forth from the tombs as if they had been dispersed locusts,⁵⁴:⁷ ones who run forward with their eyes fixed in horror towards The One Who Calls. The ones who are ungrateful will say: This is a difficult Day!⁵⁴:⁸

The folk of Noah denied before them. They denied Our servant and said: One who is possessed! And he was deterred.⁵⁴:⁹

So he called to his Lord saying: I am one who is vanquished, so Thou help me.⁵⁴:¹⁰ So We opened the doors of heaven with torrential water.⁵⁴:¹¹ And We caused the earth to gush forth with springs so the waters were to meet one another from a command that was measured.⁵⁴:¹² And We carried him on a vessel of planks and caulked,⁵⁴:¹³ running under Our eyes, a recompense for Noah who had been disbelieved.⁵⁴:¹⁴ And, certainly, We left this as a sign. Then, is there one who recalls?⁵⁴:¹⁵

So how had been My punishment and My warning?⁵⁴:¹⁶

And, certainly, We made the Quran easy as a Remembrance. Then, is there one who recalls?⁵⁴:¹⁷

Ad denied. So how had been My punishment and My warning?⁵⁴:¹⁸

Truly, We sent a raging wind against them on a day of continuous misfortune,⁵⁴:¹⁹ tearing out humanity as if they had been uprooted palm trees, uprooted.⁵⁴:²⁰

So how had been My punishment and My warning?⁵⁴:²¹

And, certainly, We made the Quran easy as a Remembrance. Then, is there one who recalls?⁵⁴:²²

Thamud denied the warning⁵⁴:²³ for they said: Follow we a lone mortal from among us?

Truly, we would be going astray and insane.⁵⁴:²⁴

Is it that the Remembrance was cast down to Salih from among us?

Nay! He is a rash liar!⁵⁴:²⁵

They will know tomorrow who the rash liar is!⁵⁴:²⁶

Truly, We are ones who sent the she-camel as a test for them. So thou be on the watch for them and maintain patience.⁵⁴:²⁷ And tell them that the division of the water is between them. Every drink was that which is divided in turn.⁵⁴:²⁸ But they cried out to their companion, and he took her in hand and crippled her.⁵⁴:²⁹

So how had been My punishment and My warning?⁵⁴:³⁰

Truly, We sent against them one Cry and they had been like straw for the one who is a builder of animal enclosures.⁵⁴:³¹ And, certainly, We made the Quran easy as a Remembrance. Then, is there one who recalls?⁵⁴:³²

The folk of Lot denied the warning.⁵⁴:³³ Truly, We sent against them a sand storm, but the family of Lot. We delivered them at the breaking of day⁵⁴:³⁴ as a divine blessing from Us. Thus, We gave recompense to him who gave thanks.⁵⁴:³⁵ And, certainly, he warned them of Our attack but they quarreled over the warning.⁵⁴:³⁶ And, certainly, they solicited his guests, so We obliterated their eyes. Then, experience My punishment and My warning.⁵⁴:³⁷ And, certainly, it came in the morning, early morning at dawn, a settled punishment.⁵⁴:³⁸ Then, experience My punishment and My warning.⁵⁴:³⁹

And, certainly, We made the Quran easy as a Remembrance. Then, is there one who recalls?⁵⁴:⁴⁰

And, certainly, drew near the warning to the people of Pharaoh.⁵⁴:⁴¹ They denied Our signs, all of them. So We took them with a taking, One Who is Almighty, Omnipotent.⁵⁴:⁴²

Are ones who are ungrateful better than those?

Or have you an immunity in the ancient scrolls?⁵⁴:⁴³

Or say they: We are aided altogether.⁵⁴:⁴⁴

Their multitude will be put to flight and they will turn their backs.⁵⁴:⁴⁵

Nay! The Hour is what is promised them and the Hour will be more calamitous and more distasteful.⁵⁴:⁴⁶

Truly, ones who sin are going astray and insane.⁵⁴:⁴⁷

On a Day they will be dragged into the fire on their faces: Experience the touch of Saqar!⁵⁴:⁴⁸

Truly, We created all things in measure⁵⁴:⁴⁹ and Our command is not but one as the twinkling of the eye.⁵⁴:⁵⁰

And, certainly, We caused to perish their partisans. Is there, then, one who recalls?⁵⁴:⁵¹

And everything they accomplished is in the ancient scrolls.⁵⁴:⁵² And every small and great thing is that which is written.⁵⁴:⁵³

Truly, the ones who are Godfearing will be in Gardens and rivers,⁵⁴:⁵⁴ in positions of sincerity near an Omnipotent King.⁵⁴:⁵⁵

CHAPTER 55 THE MERCIFUL

In the Name of God, The Merciful, The Compassionate

The Merciful.⁵⁵:¹

He taught the Quran.⁵⁵:²

He created the human being.⁵⁵:³

He taught him the clear explanation.⁵⁵:⁴

The sun and the moon are to keep count.⁵⁵:⁵

And the stars and the trees both prostrate.⁵⁵:⁶

And the heaven He exalted. And He set in place the Balance⁵⁵:⁷ that you be not defiant in the Balance.⁵⁵:⁸

Set up the weighing with justice and skimp not in the Balance.⁵⁵:⁹

And He set the earth in place for the human race.⁵⁵:¹⁰ On and in it are many kinds of sweet fruit and date palm trees with sheathed fruit trees⁵⁵:¹¹ and grain possessor of husks and fragrant herbs.⁵⁵:¹² So which of the benefits of the Lord of you both will you both deny?⁵⁵:¹³

He created the human being from earth mud like potter's clay.⁵⁵:¹⁴ He created the ones who are spirits from a smokeless flame of fire.⁵⁵:¹⁵

So which of the benefits of the Lord of you both will you both deny?⁵⁵:¹⁶

The Lord of the Two Easts, and the Lord of the Two Wests!⁵⁵:¹⁷

So which of the benefits of the Lord of you both will you both deny?⁵⁵:¹⁸

He let forth the two seas to meet one another.⁵⁵:¹⁹ Between them is a barrier which they wrong not.⁵⁵:²⁰

So which of the benefits of the Lord of you both will you both deny?⁵⁵:²¹

From both of them go forth pearls and coral.⁵⁵:²²

So which of the benefits of the Lord of you both will you both deny?⁵⁵:²³

His are ones that run with that which is displayed in the sea like landmarks.⁵⁵:²⁴

So which of the benefits of the Lord of you both will you both deny?⁵⁵:²⁵

All who are in or on it are ones who are being annihilated,⁵⁵:²⁶ yet the Countenance of thy Lord will remain forever, Possessor of The Majesty and The Splendor.⁵⁵:²⁷

So which of the benefits of the Lord of you both will you both deny?⁵⁵:²⁸

Of Him asks whoever is in the heavens and in and on the earth. Every day He is on some matter.⁵⁵:²⁹

So which of the benefits of the Lord of you both will you both deny?⁵⁵:³⁰ We will attend to you at leisure, O you two dependents.⁵⁵:³¹

So which of the benefits of the Lord of you both will you both deny?⁵⁵:³²

O you both, assembly of jinn and humankind! If you were able to pass through the areas of the heavens and the earth, then, pass through them! But you will not pass through, but with an authority.⁵⁵:³³

So which of the benefits of the Lord of you both will you both deny?⁵⁵:³⁴

There will be sent against you both a flame of fire and heated brass. Will you not, then, help yourselves?⁵⁵:³⁵

So which of the benefits of the Lord of you both will you both deny?⁵⁵:³⁶

Then, when the heaven was split then, it had been crimson like red leather,⁵⁵:³⁷ so which of the benefits of the Lord of you both will you both deny?⁵⁵:³⁸

On that Day no one will be asked about his impiety neither humankind nor ones who are spirits.⁵⁵:³⁹

So which of the benefits of the Lord of you both will you both deny?⁵⁵:⁴⁰

Ones who sin will be recognized by their mark and they will be taken by their forelocks and their feet.⁵⁵:⁴¹

So which of the benefits of the Lord of you both will you both deny?⁵⁵:⁴² This is hell which the ones who sin deny!⁵⁵:⁴³ They will go around between it and between scalding boiling water!⁵⁵:⁴⁴

So which of the benefits of the Lord of you both will you both deny?⁵⁵:⁴⁵

For him who feared the station before his Lord are two Gardens.⁵⁵:⁴⁶

So which of the benefits of the Lord of you both will you both deny?⁵⁵:⁴⁷

Possessor of wide shade.⁵⁵:⁴⁸

So which of the benefits of the Lord of you both will you both deny?⁵⁵:⁴⁹

Two springs will be running.⁵⁵:⁵⁰

So which of the benefits of the Lord of you both will you both deny?⁵⁵:⁵¹

In them both every kind of sweet fruit of diverse pairs.⁵⁵:⁵²

So which of the benefits of the Lord of you both will you both deny?⁵⁵:⁵³

Ones who are reclining on places of restfulness the inner linings of which are of brocade. And the fruit plucked from trees while fresh, that which draws near from the two Gardens.⁵⁵:⁵⁴

So which of the benefits of the Lord of you both will you both deny?⁵⁵:⁵⁵

In them both are ones who are restraining their (f) glance. No humankind touched them (f) sexually before nor ones who are spirits.⁵⁵:⁵⁶

So which of the benefits of the Lord of you both will you both deny?⁵⁵:⁵⁷ They are as if they were like rubies and coral.⁵⁵:⁵⁸

So which of the benefits of the Lord of you both will you both deny?⁵⁵:⁵⁹

Is the recompense for kindness other than kindness?⁵⁵:⁶⁰

So which of the benefits of the Lord of you both will you both deny?⁵⁵:⁶¹

Besides these are two other Gardens.⁵⁵:⁶²

So which of the benefits of the Lord of you both will you both deny?⁵⁵:⁶³

Dark green.⁵⁵:⁶⁴

So which of the benefits of the Lord of you both will you both deny?⁵⁵:⁶⁵

In them both are two springs gushing.⁵⁵:⁶⁶

So which of the benefits of the Lord of you both will you both deny?⁵⁵:⁶⁷

In them both are sweet fruits and date palm trees and pomegranates.⁵⁵:⁶⁸

So which of the benefits of the Lord of you both will you both deny?⁵⁵:⁶⁹

In them both are the good deeds, fairer.⁵⁵:⁷⁰

So which of the benefits of the Lord of you both will you both deny?⁵⁵:⁷¹

Most beautiful eyed ones who will be restrained in edifices.⁵⁵:⁷²

So which of the benefits of the Lord of you both will you both deny?⁵⁵:⁷³

No humankind touched them (f) sexually before nor ones who are spirits.⁵⁵:⁷⁴

So which of the benefits of the Lord of you both will you both deny?⁵⁵:⁷⁵

Ones who are reclining on green pillows and fairer carpets.⁵⁵:⁷⁶

So which of the benefits of the Lord of you both will you both deny?⁵⁵:⁷⁷

Blessed be the Name of thy Lord, Possessor of The Majesty and The Splendor.⁵⁵:⁷⁸

CHAPTER 56 THE INEVITABLE

In the Name of God, The Merciful, The Compassionate

When The Inevitable came to pass,⁵⁶:¹ its descent is not like that which lies.⁵⁶:² It will be one that abases, one that exalts.⁵⁶:³

When the earth will rock with a rocking⁵⁶:⁴ and the mountains be crumbled to dust, crumbling,⁵⁶:⁵ then, they had been dust scattered about.⁵⁶:⁶

And you had been of three diverse pairs.⁵⁶:⁷

Then, the Companions of the Right—who are the Companions of the Right?⁵⁶:⁸

And the Companions of the Left—who are Companions of the Left?⁵⁶:⁹

Ones who take the lead are the ones who take the lead.⁵⁶:¹⁰ Those are the ones who are brought near⁵⁶:¹¹ in the Gardens of Bliss.⁵⁶:¹² A throng of the ancient ones⁵⁶:¹³ and a few of the later ones⁵⁶:¹⁴ are on lined couches,⁵⁶:¹⁵ ones who are reclining on them, ones who are facing one another.⁵⁶:¹⁶ Immortal children go around them⁵⁶:¹⁷ with cups and ewers and goblets from a spring of water.⁵⁶:¹⁸ Neither will they suffer headaches nor will they be intoxicated,⁵⁶:¹⁹ and sweet fruit of what they specify⁵⁶:²⁰ and the flesh of birds for which they lust⁵⁶:²¹ and most beautiful eyed ones,⁵⁶:²² like the parable of the well-guarded pearls,⁵⁶:²³ a recompense for what they had been doing.⁵⁶:²⁴ They will not hear any idle talk in it nor accusation of sinfulness,⁵⁶:²⁵ but the saying of: Peace! Peace!⁵⁶:²⁶

And the Companions of the Right—who are the Companions of the Right?⁵⁶:²⁷ They will be among thornless lote-trees⁵⁶:²⁸ and acacias, one on another,⁵⁶:²⁹ and spread out shade⁵⁶:³⁰ and outpoured water⁵⁶:³¹ and many sweet fruit.⁵⁶:³² There will be neither that which is severed nor that which is inaccessible.⁵⁶:³³ And it is an exalted place of restfulness.⁵⁶:³⁴ Truly, We caused them (f) to grow, a good forming,⁵⁶:³⁵ and made them (f) virgins,⁵⁶:³⁶ full of love, of the same age,⁵⁶:³⁷ for the Companions of the Right.⁵⁶:³⁸

A throng of the ancient ones⁵⁶:³⁹ and a throng from the later ones,⁵⁶:⁴⁰ and the Companions of the Left—who are the Companions of the Left?⁵⁶:⁴¹ Those who are in burning wind and scalding water⁵⁶:⁴² and shade of black smoke⁵⁶:⁴³ neither that which is cool nor generous.⁵⁶:⁴⁴ Truly, they had been before that ones who are given ease⁵⁶:⁴⁵ and they had been persisting in tremendous wickedness.⁵⁶:⁴⁶

And they had been saying: When we died and had been earth dust and bones, will we, then, be ones who are raised up?⁵⁶:⁴⁷

And our ancient fathers?⁵⁶:⁴⁸

Say: Truly, the ancient ones and the later ones⁵⁶:⁴⁹ will be ones who will be gathered to a time appointed on a known Day.⁵⁶:⁵⁰ Again, you, O ones who go astray, are the ones who deny.⁵⁶:⁵¹ Certainly, you will be ones who eat from the Zaqqum tree.⁵⁶:⁵² Then, you will be ones who fill your bellies from it,⁵⁶:⁵³ then, ones who drink scalding water after it.⁵⁶:⁵⁴ So you will be ones who drink like the drinking of thirsty camels.⁵⁶:⁵⁵ This will be their hospitality on the Day of Judgment!⁵⁶:⁵⁶ We, We created you. Why establish it not as true?⁵⁶:⁵⁷

Considered you what you spill of human seed?⁵⁶:⁵⁸

Is it you who create it?

Or are We the ones who are the creators?⁵⁶:⁵⁹

We ordained death among you and We will not be ones who will be outrun⁵⁶:⁶⁰ in that We will substitute your likeness and We caused you to grow in a way you know not.⁵⁶:⁶¹ And, certainly, you knew the first growth.

Will you not, then, recollect?⁵⁶:⁶²

Considered you the soil that you till?⁵⁶:⁶³

Is it you who sows it?

Or are We the ones who sow?⁵⁶:⁶⁴

If We will, We would make it into chaff and you would continue to joke saying:⁵⁶:⁶⁵

We are ones who are debt-loaded!⁵⁶:⁶⁶

Nay! We are ones who are deprived.⁵⁶:⁶⁷ Considered you the water that you drink?⁵⁶:⁶⁸

Is it you who caused it to descend from the cloud vapors?

Or are We the ones who caused it to descend?⁵⁶:⁶⁹

If We will, We would make it bitter.

Why, then, give you not thanks?⁵⁶:⁷⁰

Considered you the fire which you strike?⁵⁶:⁷¹

Is it you who caused the tree to grow?

Or are We the ones who cause it to grow?⁵⁶:⁷²

We made it an admonition and sustenance for ones who are desert people.⁵⁶:⁷³

Then, glorify with the name of thy Lord, The Sublime.⁵⁶:⁷⁴

But no! I swear by the orbit of the stars⁵⁶:⁷⁵ and, truly, that is an oath to be sworn if you know, sublime.⁵⁶:⁷⁶ Truly, it is a generous Recitation⁵⁶:⁷⁷ in a well-guarded Book.⁵⁶:⁷⁸ None touches it but the ones who are purified,⁵⁶:⁷⁹ a sending down successively from the Lord of the worlds.⁵⁶:⁸⁰

Then, is it this discourse that you are ones who scorn?⁵⁶:⁸¹

And you make it your provision that you, you deny the Recitation.⁵⁶:⁸²

Then, why not intervene when it reached the wind-pipe⁵⁶:⁸³ and you are looking on at the time?⁵⁶:⁸⁴

And We are nearer to him than you, yet you perceive not.⁵⁶:⁸⁵

Then, why had you not been—if you are not ones to be judged—⁵⁶:⁸⁶ returning the soul to the body, if you had been ones who are sincere?⁵⁶:⁸⁷

If he had been among the ones who are brought near,⁵⁶:⁸⁸ there is solace and fragrant herbs and a Garden of Bliss.⁵⁶:⁸⁹ And if he had been of the Companions of the Right,⁵⁶:⁹⁰ then: Peace for thee from the Companions of the Right.⁵⁶:⁹¹

And yet if he had been of the ones who go astray, ones who deny,⁵⁶:⁹² then, a hospitality of scalding water⁵⁶:⁹³ and broiling in hellfire.⁵⁶:⁹⁴

Truly, this is The Truth of certainty.⁵⁶:⁹⁵ So glorify the Name of thy Lord, The Almighty.⁵⁶:⁹⁶

CHAPTER 57 IRON

In the Name of God, The Merciful, The Compassionate

Whatever is in the heavens glorified God and whatever is in and on the earth. And He is The Almighty, The Wise.⁵⁷:¹

To Him belongs the dominion of the heavens and the earth. He gives life and causes to die. And He is Powerful over everything.⁵⁷:²

He is The First and The Last, The One Who is Outward and The One Who is Inward. And He is Knowing of everything.⁵⁷:³

It is He Who created the heavens and the earth in six days. Again, He turned His attention to the Throne. He knows what penetrates into the earth and what goes forth from it, and what comes down from the heaven and what goes up to it. And He is with you wherever you had been. And God is Seeing of what you do.⁵⁷:⁴

To Him belongs the dominion of the heavens and the earth. All commands are returned to God.⁵⁷:⁵

He causes the nighttime to be interposed into the daytime and causes the daytime to be interposed into the nighttime. And He is Knowing of whatever is in the breasts.⁵⁷:⁶

Believe in God and His Messenger and spend out of what He made you ones who are successors in it. Those among you who believed and spent, for them is a great compensation.⁵⁷:⁷

And what is the matter with you that you believe not in God while the Messenger calls to you to believe in your Lord? And He took your solemn promise, if you had been ones who believe.⁵⁷:⁸

It is He Who sends down to His servant clear portents, signs, that He brings you out from the shadows into the light. And, truly, God is to you Gentle, Compassionate.⁵⁷:⁹

And what is the matter with you that you spend not in the way of God?

And to God belongs the heritage of the heavens and the earth?

Not on the same level among you are whoever spent before the victory and fought. Those are more sublime in degree than those who spent afterwards and fought. And God promised the fairer to all. And God is Aware of what you do.⁵⁷:¹⁰

Who is he who will lend to God a fairer loan that He multiply it for him and he will have a generous compensation?⁵⁷:¹¹

On a Day thou wilt see the males, ones who believe and the females, ones who believe, their light coming eagerly in advance of them and on their right: Good tidings for you this Day, Gardens beneath which rivers run, ones who will dwell in them forever. That, it is the winning the sublime triumph!⁵⁷:¹²

On a Day will say the males, ones who are hypocrites and females, the ones who are hypocrites to those who believed: Wait for us that we will borrow from your light.

It will be said: Return behind and search out for a light.

There would be a fence between them for which there is a door. That which is inward is mercy and that which is outward is towards the punishment.⁵⁷:¹³

The hypocrites will cry out to the believers: Have we not been with you?

They will say: Yea! And you let yourselves be tempted and you awaited and you were in doubt and you were deluded by following your fantasies until the command of God drew near and the deluder deluded you in regard to God.⁵⁷:¹⁴ So this Day ransom will not be taken from you nor from those who were ungrateful. Your place of shelter will be the fire. It is your defender. And miserable will be the Homecoming!⁵⁷:¹⁵

Is it not time for those who believed that their hearts be humbled by the Remembrance of God and to The Truth that came down to them and that they not be like those who were given the Book before?

Then, the space of time was long for them so their hearts became hard. And many of them were ones who disobey.⁵⁷:¹⁶

Know you that God gives life to the earth after its death. Surely, We made manifest the signs to you so that perhaps you will be reasonable.⁵⁷:¹⁷ Truly, the males, ones who are charitable and the females, ones who are charitable and who lent a fairer loan to God, it will be multiplied for them and for them there is a generous compensation.⁵⁷:¹⁸

And those who believed in God and His Messengers, those, they are the just persons. And the witnesses to their Lord. For them is their compensation and their light. And those who were ungrateful and denied Our signs, those are the Companions of Hellfire.⁵⁷:¹⁹

Know that this present life is only a pastime, a diversion and an adornment and a mutual boasting among you and a rivalry in respect to wealth and children as the likeness of plenteous rain water. The plants impressed ones who are ungrateful. Again, it withers; then, thou hast seen it yellowing. Again, it becomes chaff while in the world to come there is severe punishment and forgiveness from God and contentment. And this present life is nothing but a delusion of enjoyment.⁵⁷:²⁰

Move quickly towards forgiveness from your Lord and the Garden whose depth is as the breadth of the heavens and earth. It was prepared for those who believed in God and His Messengers. That is the grace of God. He gives it to whom He wills. And God is The Possessor of the Sublime Grace.⁵⁷:²¹

And no affliction lit on the earth nor on yourselves but it is in a Book that We fashion before. Truly, that is easy for God,⁵⁷:²² so that you not grieve over what slipped away from you nor be glad because of what was given to you. And God loves not any proud, boaster,⁵⁷:²³ those who are misers and who command humanity to miserliness, and whoever turns away then, God, He is The Sufficient, The Worthy of Praise.⁵⁷:²⁴

Certainly, We sent Our Messengers with the clear portents and We caused the Book to descend with them and the Balance so that humanity may uphold equity. And We caused iron to descend in which is vigorous might and profits for humanity that perhaps God would know whoever helps Him and His Messengers in the unseen. Truly, God is Strong, Almighty.⁵⁷:²⁵

And, certainly, We sent Noah and Abraham and We assigned to their offspring prophethood and the Book. And of them are ones who are truly guided while many of them are ones who disobey.⁵⁷:²⁶

Again, We sent Our Messengers following their footsteps. And We sent following them Jesus son of Mary. And We gave him the Gospel. And We assigned in the hearts of those who followed him, tenderness and mercy. But as for monasticism, they made it up themselves. We prescribed it not for them but that they were seeking for the contentment of God. Then, they gave it not the attention giving its right attention so We gave those who believed among them their compensation. And many of them are ones who disobey.⁵⁷:²⁷

O those who believed! Be Godfearing of God and believe in His Messenger. He will give you a double like part of His mercy. And He assigns you a light to walk by. And He will forgive you. And God is Forgiving, Compassionate.⁵⁷:²⁸

Certainly, the People of the Book know that they have no power over anything of the grace of God and that the grace of God is in the hand of God. He gives it to whomever He wills. And God is Possessor of the Sublime Grace.⁵⁷:²⁹

CHAPTER 58
SHE WHO DISPUTES

In the Name of God, The Merciful, The Compassionate

Surely, God heard the saying of she who disputes with thee about her spouse and she complains to God and God hears conversing between you both. Truly, God is Hearing, Seeing.⁵⁸:¹

Those who say to their wives: Be as my mother's back, they (f) are not their mothers. Their mothers are only those (f) who gave them birth. And, truly, they say that which is unlawful among their sayings and an untruth. And, truly, God is Pardoning, Forgiving.⁵⁸:²

And those who say: Be as my mother's back, to their wives and again, retract what they said, then, the letting go of a bondsperson before they both touch one another. That is of what you are admonished. And God is Aware of what you do.⁵⁸:³

He who finds not such means then, formal fasting for two successive months before they both touch one another. And for him who is unable to fast, the feeding of sixty needy persons. That is so that you believe in God and His Messenger. And those are the ordinances of God. And for the ones who are ungrateful, a painful punishment.⁵⁸:⁴

Truly, those who oppose God and His Messenger, they were suppressed as those who before them were suppressed. And, surely, We caused clear portents, signs to descend. For the ones who are ungrateful is a despised punishment⁵⁸:⁵ on a Day when God will raise them up altogether and tell them of what they did. God counted it while they forgot it. And God is a Witness over everything.⁵⁸:⁶

Hast thou not considered that God knows whatever is in the heavens and whatever is in and on the earth. There will be no conspiring secretly of three, but He is their fourth nor of five, but He is the sixth, nor of fewer than that nor of more, but He is with them wherever they had been. Again, He will tell them of what they did on the Day of Resurrection. Truly, God is Knowing of everything.⁵⁸:⁷

Hast thou not considered those who were prohibited from conspiring secretly?

Again, they revert to what they were prohibited from and hold secret counsel in sin and deep-seated dislike and in opposition to the Messenger?

And when they drew near thee they gave thee greetings with that with which God gives not as a greeting to thee and they say to themselves: Why punishes us not God for what we say?

Hell will be enough for them. They will roast in it. Then, miserable will be the Homecoming!⁵⁸:⁸

O those who believed! When you hold secret counsel, hold not secret counsel in sin and deep-seated dislike and in opposition to the Messenger. But hold secret counsel for virtuous conduct and God-consciousness and be Godfearing of God before Whom you will be assembled.⁵⁸:⁹

Conspiring secretly is only from Satan that he dishearten those who believed. But he is not one who injures them at all, but with the permission of God.

In God let the ones who believe put their trust.⁵⁸:¹⁰

O those who believed! When it was said to you: Make ample space in the assemblies, then, make room. God will make room for you.

And when it was said: Move up, then, move up.

God will exalt those among you who believed and those who were given the knowledge in degrees. And God is Aware of what you do.⁵⁸:¹¹

O those who believed! When you consulted with the Messenger, put charity forward in advance of your conversing privately. That is better for you and purer. But if you find not the means, then, truly, God is Forgiving, Compassionate.⁵⁸:¹²

Are you apprehensive to put forward charity in advance of your conversing privately?

If, then, you accomplish it not, God turned in forgiveness to you.

Perform the formal prayer and give the purifying alms and obey God and His Messenger. And God is Aware of what you do.⁵⁸:¹³

Hast thou considered those who turned in friendship to a folk against whom God was angry?

They are not of you, nor are you of them and they swear to a lie while they know.⁵⁸:¹⁴ God prepared a severe punishment for them. Truly, they, how evil is what they had been doing!⁵⁸:¹⁵ They took their oaths to themselves as a pretext and they barred from the way of God. So for them is a despised punishment.⁵⁸:¹⁶ Avails them not their wealth and their children against God at all. Those will be the Companions of the Fire. They are ones who will dwell in it forever.⁵⁸:¹⁷

On a Day when God will raise them up altogether, then, they will swear to Him as they swear to you, assuming that they are something. They, they are ones who lie.⁵⁸:¹⁸

Satan gained mastery over them, so he caused them to forget the Remembrance of God. Those are of the Party of Satan. Regard the Party of Satan, they will be the ones who are losers.⁵⁸:¹⁹

Truly, those who oppose God and His Messenger, those are among the humiliated in spirit.⁵⁸:²⁰

God prescribed: I will prevail, truly, I and My Messengers. Truly, God is Strong, Almighty.⁵⁸:²¹

Thou wilt not find any folk who believe in God and the Last Day who make friends with whoever opposed God and His Messenger even if they had been their fathers or their sons or their brothers or their kinspeople.

Those, He prescribed belief in their hearts, and confirmed them with a Spirit from Himself. And He will cause them to enter Gardens beneath which rivers run as ones who will dwell in them forever. God was well-pleased with them and they were well-pleased with Him. Those are the Party of God. Lo! the Party of God. They are the ones who prosper.⁵⁸:²²

CHAPTER 59
THE BANISHMENT

In the Name of God, The Merciful, The Compassionate

Whatever is in the heavens glorified God and whatever is in and on the earth. And He is The Almighty, The Wise.⁵⁹:¹

It is He Who drove out those who were ungrateful—among the People of the Book—from their abodes at the first assembling. You thought that they would not go forth. And they thought that they are ones who are secure in their fortresses from God. But God approached them from where they anticipate not. And He hurled alarm into their hearts. They devastate their own houses with their own hands and the hands of the ones who believe. Then, take warning, O those imbued with insight!⁵⁹:²

If God prescribed not banishment for them, He would have punished them in the present. And for them in the world to come would be the punishment of the fire.⁵⁹:³ That is because they make a breach with God and His Messenger. And whoever made a breach with God, then, truly, God is Severe in repayment.⁵⁹:⁴

Whatever palm trees you severed or left them as ones that arise from their roots, it was with the permission of God and so that He might cover with shame the ones who disobey.⁵⁹:⁵

And what God gave as spoils of war to His Messenger from them, you spurred not an animal for an expedition, neither any horse nor riding camel, but God gives authority to His Messengers over whomever He wills. And God is Powerful over everything.⁵⁹:⁶

What God gave to His Messenger as spoils of war from the people of the towns is for God and His Messenger and the possessors of kinship and the orphans and the needy and the traveler of the way so that it be changing not hands between the rich among you.

And whatever the Messenger gave you, take it. And refrain yourselves from what he prohibited you. And be Godfearing of God. Truly, God is Severe in repayment.⁵⁹:⁷

For the poor who were of the ones who emigrate, those who were driven out from their abodes and their property, looking for grace from God and His contentment and they help God and His Messenger, there is also a share. Those, they are the ones who are sincere.⁵⁹:⁸

And those who took their abodes as dwellings and had belief before them, love them who emigrated to them and they find not in their breasts any need for what the emigrants were given and hold them in greater favor over themselves even though they themselves had been in destitution. And whoever is protected from his own stinginess, then, those, they are the ones who prosper.⁵⁹:⁹

And those who drew near after them, they say: Our Lord! Forgive us and our brothers/sisters who preceded us in belief and make not in our hearts any grudge against those who believed. Our Lord! Truly, Thou art Gentle, Compassionate.⁵⁹:¹⁰

Hast thou not considered those who are ones who are hypocrites?

They say to their brothers—those who were ungrateful—among the People of the Book: If you were driven out, we, certainly, will go forth with you and we will never obey anyone against you ever. And if you were fought against, we will, certainly, help you.

And God bears witness that they, truly, are ones who lie.⁵⁹:¹¹

Certainly, if they were driven out, they would not go forth with them. And if they were fought against they would not help them. And if they had helped them, they would turn their backs. Again, they would not be helped by them.⁵⁹:¹²

Truly, you are a more severe fright in their breasts than God. That is because they are a folk who understand not.⁵⁹:¹³ They

fight not against you altogether, but in fortified towns or from behind walls. Their might among themselves is very severe. You would assume them united, but their hearts are diverse. That is because they are a folk who are not reasonable.⁵⁹:¹⁴

As the likeness of those who were before them, they experienced the immediate mischief of their affair and for them is a painful punishment.⁵⁹:¹⁵

As the likeness of Satan when he said to the human being: Be Ungrateful! Then, when he was ungrateful, Satan said: I am free of thee. I fear God, the Lord of the worlds.⁵⁹:¹⁶

The Ultimate End of both of them will be that they be in the fire, ones who will dwell in it forever. And that is the recompense of the ones who are unjust.⁵⁹:¹⁷

O those who believed! Be Godfearing of God and let every soul look on what is put forward for tomorrow. And be Godfearing of God. Truly, God is Aware of what you do.⁵⁹:¹⁸

And be not like those who forgot God and He caused them to forget themselves. Those, they are the ones who disobey.⁵⁹:¹⁹

The Companions of the Fire are not equal to the Companions of the Garden.

The Companions of the Garden, they are the ones who are victorious.⁵⁹:²⁰

If We had caused this, the Quran, to descend on a mountain, thou wouldst have seen it as that which is humbled, one that is split open from dreading God.

And there are the parables that We propound for humanity so that perhaps they will reflect.⁵⁹:²¹

He is God; there is no god but He, One Who Knows of the unseen and the visible. He is The Merciful, The Compassionate.⁵⁹:²²

He is God besides whom there is no god but He, The King, The Holy, The Peaceable, One Who is The Bestower, Preserver, The Almighty, The Compeller, The One Who is The Supreme. Glory be to God above partners they ascribe.⁵⁹:²³

He is God, the One Who is Creator, The One Who Fashions, The One Who is The Giver of Form. To Him belongs the Fairer Names. Whatever is in the heavens glorifies Him and whatever is in and on the earth and He is The Almighty, The Wise.⁵⁹:²⁴

CHAPTER 60 SHE WHO
IS PUT TO A TEST

In the Name of God, The Merciful, The Compassionate

O those who believed! Take not My enemies to yourselves and your enemies as protectors, giving a proposal of affection towards them while they were ungrateful for what drew near you of The Truth. They drive out the Messenger and you because you believe in God, your Lord. If you had been going forth struggling in My way and looking for My goodwill, you keep secret affection for them. Yet I am greater in knowledge of what you concealed and what you spoke openly. And whoever accomplishes that among you, surely, he went astray from the right path.⁶⁰:¹

If they come upon you, they will be enemies against you. They extend their hands against you and their tongues with evil. And they wished that you be ungrateful.⁶⁰:² Your blood relations will never profit you nor your children. On the Day of Resurrection, He will distinguish among you. And God is Seeing of what you do.⁶⁰:³

Surely, there had been a fairer, good example for you in Abraham and those with him when they said to their folk: Truly, we are released from obligation to you and whatever you worship other than God. We disbelieved in you. Shown itself between us and between you was enmity and hatred eternally until you believe in One God, but for Abraham saying to his father: Truly, I will ask for forgiveness for thee and I possess not anything for thee before God.

Our Lord! In Thee we put our trust and to Thee we were penitent and to Thee is the Homecoming!⁶⁰:⁴

Our Lord! Make us not be a cause of their pleasure for those who were ungrateful and forgive us. Our Lord; truly, Thou, Thou alone art The Almighty, The Wise.⁶⁰:⁵

Certainly, there had been a fairer, good example in them for you for whoever had been hoping for God and the Last Day. And whoever turns away, then, truly, God, He is Sufficient, Worthy of Praise.⁶⁰:⁶

Perhaps God will assign between you and between those to whom you were at enmity with them, affection. And God is Powerful. And God is Forgiving, Compassionate.⁶⁰:⁷

God prohibits you not from those who fight not against you because of your way of life nor drive you out of your abodes so be good and act justly towards them. Truly, God loves the ones who act justly.⁶⁰:⁸

God prohibits you only from those who fought against you in your way of life and drove you out of your abodes and were behind expelling you, that you turn to them in friendship. And whoever turns to them in friendship, then, those, they are the ones who are unjust.⁶⁰:⁹

O those who believed! When the females, ones who believe, drew near to you, ones who emigrate (f), put them (f) to a test. God is greater in knowledge as to their (f) belief. Then, if you knew them (f) as ones who believe (f), return them (f) not to the ones who are ungrateful. They (f) are not allowed to them (m) nor are they (m) lawful for them (f). And give them (m) what they (m) have spent. There is no blame on you that you (m) marry them (f) when you have given them (f) their compensation. And hold back conjugal ties with the ones who are ungrateful and ask for what you (m) spent and let them ask for what they (m) spent. That is the determination of God. He gives judgment among you. And God is Knowing, Wise.⁶⁰:¹⁰

And if any slipped away from you of your spouses to the ones who are ungrateful, then, you retaliated and give the like to whose spouses went of what they (m) spent. And be Godfearing of God in Whom you are ones who believe.⁶⁰:¹¹

O Prophet! When drew near thee the females, ones who are believers, to take the pledge of allegiance to thee that they will ascribe nothing as partners with God nor will they steal nor will they commit adultery nor will they kill their children, nor will they approach making false charges to harm another's reputation that they devise between their (f) hands and their (f) feet, and that they rebel not against thee in anything that is honorable. Then, take their (f) pledge of allegiance and ask forgiveness from God for them (f). Truly, God is Forgiving, Compassionate.⁶⁰:¹² O those who believed! Turn not in friendship to a folk against whom God was angry. Surely, they gave up hope for the world to come, just as gave up hope the ones who are ungrateful of the occupants of the graves.⁶⁰:¹³

CHAPTER 61 THE RANKS

In the Name of God, The Merciful, The Compassionate
Whatever is in the heavens glorified God and whatever is in and on the earth. And He is The Almighty, The Wise.⁶¹:¹

O those who believed! Why say you what you accomplish not?⁶¹:² It was most troublesome, repugnant to God that you say what you accomplish not.⁶¹:³

Truly, God loves those who fight in His way, ranged in rows as if they were a well-compacted structure.⁶¹:⁴

And when Moses said to his folk: O my folk! Why malign me while, surely, you know that I am the Messenger of God to you? So when they swerved, God caused their hearts to swerve. And God guides not the folk, the ones who disobey.⁶¹:⁵

And when Jesus son of Mary said: O Children of Israel! I am the Messenger of God to you, one who establishes as true what was in advance of me in the Torah and one who gives good tidings of a Messenger to approach after me. His name will be Ahmad. But when he brought about the clear portents to them, they said: This is clear sorcery!⁶¹:⁶

And who does greater wrong than he who devised the lie against God while he is being called to submission to God? And God guides not the folk, ones who are unjust.⁶¹:⁷ They want to extinguish the light of God with their mouths but God is One Who Fulfills His light even though the ones who are ungrateful disliked it.⁶¹:⁸ He it is Who sent His Messenger with guidance and the way of life of The Truth to uplift it over all other ways of life even though the ones who are polytheists disliked it.⁶¹:⁹

O those who believed! Shall I point you to a transaction that will rescue you from a painful punishment?⁶¹:¹⁰ You believe in God and His Messenger and struggle in the way of God with your wealth and your lives. That is better for you if you had been knowing.⁶¹:¹¹ He will forgive you your impieties and cause you to enter into Gardens beneath which rivers run, and into good dwellings in the Gardens of Eden, the winning the sublime triumph.⁶¹:¹² And He gives another thing you love, help is from God and victory in the near future, so give good tidings to the ones who believe.⁶¹:¹³

O those who believed! Be helpers of God as Jesus son of Mary said to the disciples: Who are my helpers for God?

The disciples said: We are the helpers for God.

Then, a section believed of the Children of Israel and a section were ungrateful. So We confirmed those who believed against their enemies. And they became ones who are prominent.⁶¹:¹⁴

CHAPTER 62
THE CONGREGATION

In the Name of God, The Merciful, The Compassionate
Whatever is in the heavens glorifies God and whatever is in and on the earth, The King, The Holy, The Almighty, The Wise.⁶²:¹

He it is Who raised up among the unlettered a Messenger from among them who recounts His signs to them and makes them pure and teaches them the Book and wisdom even though they had been before certainly, clearly going astray⁶²:² and to others among them who join them not. And He is The Almighty, The Wise.⁶²:³

That is the grace of God. He gives it to whom He wills. And God is Possessor of the Sublime Grace.⁶²:⁴

The parable of those who were entrusted with the Torah, and, again, carries it not is as the parable of a donkey who carries writings. Miserable was the parable of a folk who denied the signs of God! And God guides not the folk, the ones who are unjust.⁶²:⁵

Say: O those who became Jews! If you claimed that you are the protectors of God to the exclusion of humanity, then, covet death if you had been ones who are sincere.⁶²:⁶

But they will not covet it ever because of what their hands put forward. And God is Knowing of the ones who are unjust.⁶²:⁷

Say: Truly, the death that you run away from, then, it will be, truly, that which you encounter. Again, you will be returned to the One Who Knows of the unseen and the visible and He will tell you what you had been doing.^{62:8}

O those who believed! When the formal prayer was proclaimed on the day of congregation, then, hasten about to the Remembrance of God and forsake trading. That is better for you if you had been knowing.^{62:9} Then, when the formal prayer had ended, disperse through the earth looking for the grace of God.

And remember God frequently so that perhaps you will prosper.^{62:10}

And when they considered a transaction or a diversion, they broke away toward it, and left thee as one who is standing up.

Say: What is with God is better than any diversion or than any transaction. And God is Best of the ones who provide.^{62:11}

CHAPTER 63
THE HYPOCRITES

In the Name of God, The Merciful, The Compassionate

When the ones who are hypocrites drew near thee.

They said: We bear witness that thou art, truly, the Messenger of God.

And God knows that thou art, truly, His Messenger and God bears witness that the ones who are hypocrites are ones who lie.^{63:1}

They took their oaths to themselves as a pretext. Then, they barred from the way of God. Truly, they, how evil is what they had been doing!^{63:2} That is because they believed and, again, disbelieved, so a seal was set on their hearts so they understand not.^{63:3}

When thou hast seen them, their physiques impress thee. And when they speak, thou hast heard their saying. It is as if they had been propped up timber. They assume that every Cry is against them. They are the enemy so beware of them. God took the offensive. How they are misled!^{63:4}

And when it was said to them: Approach now. The Messenger of God asks forgiveness for you.

They twist their heads and thou hadst seen them dissuading while they are ones who grow arrogant.^{63:5}

It is the same to them whether thou hadst asked for forgiveness for them or thou hadst not asked for forgiveness for them. God will never forgive them. Truly, God guides not the folk, the ones who disobey.^{63:6}

They, those who say: Spend not on such ones who are with the Messenger of God until they break away.

And to God belongs the treasures of the heavens and the earth but the ones who are hypocrites understand not.^{63:7}

They say: If we returned to the city, certainly, would drive out the more mighty, the ones humble spirited from it.

Yet to God belongs the great glory and to His Messenger and to the ones who believe. But the ones who are hypocrites know not.^{63:8}

O those who believed! Let not your wealth divert you nor your children from the Remembrance of God. And whoever accomplishes that, then, those, they are the ones who are losers.^{63:9}

And spend of what We provided you before approaches death to any of you. Then, he will say: My Lord! If only Thou wouldst postpone it for a little term then, I would be charitable and be among the ones in accord with morality.^{63:10}

But God never postpones it for a soul when its term drew near. And God is Aware of what you do.^{63:11}

CHAPTER 64 THE MUTUAL LOSS AND GAIN

In the Name of God, The Merciful, The Compassionate

Whatever is in the heavens glorifies God and whatever is in and on the earth. His is the dominion and to Him belongs all the praise. And He is Powerful over everything.^{64:1}

He it is Who created you: So some of you are ones who disbelieve and some of you are ones who believe. And God is Seeing of what you do.^{64:2}

He created the heavens and the earth with The Truth and He formed you and formed your forms well. And to Him is the Homecoming!^{64:3}

He knows what is in the heavens and the earth and He knows what you keep secret and what you speak openly. And God is Knowing of what is in the breasts.^{64:4}

Approaches you not the tiding of those who were ungrateful before? They experienced the mischief of their affair and there is a painful punishment for them.^{64:5}

That had been because their Messengers approach them with the clear portents, but they said: Will mortals guide us? So they were ungrateful and turned away. And God is Self-Sufficient. And God is Rich, Worthy of Praise.^{64:6}

Those who were ungrateful claimed that they will never be raised up.

Say: Yea! By my Lord, you will, certainly, be raised up. Again, you will be told of what you did. And that is easy for God.^{64:7}

So believe in God and His Messenger, and in the Light which We caused to descend. And God is Aware of what you do.^{64:8}

On a Day when He will amass you for the Day of Gathering, that will be the day of the mutual loss and gain, and whoever believes in God and does as one in accord with morality, He will absolve him of his evil deeds and He will cause him to enter Gardens beneath which rivers run as ones who will dwell in them forever, eternally. That will be winning the sublime triumph.^{64:9}

But for those who were ungrateful and denied Our signs, those are the Companions of the Fire, ones who will dwell in it forever. And miserable will be the Homecoming!^{64:10}

No affliction lit but with the permission of God. Whoever believes in God, He guides his heart. And God is Knowing of everything.^{64:11}

And obey God and obey the Messenger. Then, if you turned away, then, it is only for Our Messenger the delivering the clear message.^{64:12}

God, there is no god but He. And in God let the ones who believe put their trust.^{64:13}

O those who believed! Truly, there are among your spouses and your children enemies for you, so beware of them. And if you would pardon, overlook and forgive, then, truly, God is Forgiving, Compassionate.^{64:14}

Your wealth and your children are only a test. And God, with Him is a sublime compensation.^{64:15}

So be Godfearing of God as much as you were able and hear and obey and spend. That is good for yourselves, and whoever is protected from his own stinginess, then, those, they are the ones who prosper.^{64:16}

If you lend to God a fairer loan, He will multiply it for you and will forgive you. And God is Ready to Appreciate, Forbearing,^{64:17} One Who Knows the unseen and the visible, The Almighty, The Wise.^{64:18}

CHAPTER 65 DIVORCE

In the Name of God, The Merciful, The Compassionate

O Prophet! When you divorced your wives, then, divorce them (f) after their (f) waiting periods and count their (f) waiting periods. And be Godfearing of God, your Lord. And drive them (f) not out from their (f) houses nor let them (f) go forth unless they approach a manifest indecency. These are the ordinances of God. And whoever violates the ordinances of God, then, truly, he did wrong to himself. Thou art not informed so that perhaps God will cause to evoke something after that affair.⁶⁵:¹

Then, when they (f) reached their (f) term, either hold them (f) back as one who is honorable or part from them (f) as one who is honorable and call to witnesses from two possessors of justice from among you and perform testimony for God. That is admonished for whomever had been believing in God and the Last Day. And he who is Godfearing of God, He will make a way out for him.⁶⁵:²

And He will provide him with where he not anticipate. And whoever puts his trust in God, then, He will be enough for him. God is One Who Reaches Through His command. Surely, God assigned a measure to everything.⁶⁵:³

And as for those who gave up hope of menstruation among your women, if you were in doubt, their (f) waiting period is three months and for those who have not yet menstruated. As for those (f) who are imbued with pregnancy, their (f) term is that they (f) bring forth their (f) burden. And whoever is Godfearing of God, He will make his affair with ease for him.⁶⁵:⁴

That is the command of God which He caused to descend to you. And whoever is Godfearing of God, He will absolve him of his evil deeds and will enhance for him a compensation.⁶⁵:⁵

Cause them (f) to dwell where you inhabited according to what you are able to afford and be not pressing them (f), putting them (f) in straits. And if they (f) had been imbued with pregnancy, then, spend on them (f) until they bring forth their (f) burden. Then, if they (f) breast feed for you, give them (f) their compensation. And each of you take counsel between you as one who is honorable.

But if you make difficulties for one another, then, another would breast feed on behalf of the father.⁶⁵:⁶ The possessor of plenty spends from his plenty.

And he whose provisions were measured, he will spend out of what God gave him. And God places not a burden on any person beyond what He gave him. God will make ease after hardship.⁶⁵:⁷

How many a town defied the command of its Lord and His Messengers, so we made a reckoning, a severe reckoning and We punished it with a horrible punishment.⁶⁵:⁸ So it experienced the mischief of its affair and the Ultimate End of its affair had been loss.⁶⁵:⁹

God prepared for them a severe punishment. So be Godfearing of God, O those imbued with intuition, those who believed! Surely, God caused to descend to you a Remembrance,⁶⁵:¹⁰ a Messenger who recounts to you the signs of God, ones that are made manifest, that he brings out those who believed and did as the ones in accord with morality from the shadows to the light.

And whoever believes in God and does as one in accord with morality, He will cause him to enter into Gardens beneath which rivers run, ones who will dwell in them forever, eternally. Surely, God did good with provision for him.⁶⁵:¹¹

It is God Who created the seven heavens and of the earth, a similar number like them. The command comes forth between them so that perhaps you would know that God is Powerful over everything and that God, truly, enclosed everything in His Knowledge.⁶⁵:¹²

CHAPTER 66 THE FORBIDDING

In the Name of God, The Merciful, The Compassionate

O Prophet! Why hast thou forbidden what God permitted to thee. Looking for the goodwill of thy spouses? And God is Forgiving, Compassionate.⁶⁶:¹

God imposed on you the dissolution of such of your oaths. And God is your Defender. And He is The Knowing, The Wise.⁶⁶:²

And mention when the Prophet confided to one of his spouses a discourse, she, then, told it to another. God disclosed to him of it. He acquainted her with some of it and turned aside some of it. When he told her about it, she said: Who communicated this to thee?

He said: The Knowing, The Aware told me.⁶⁶:³

If you two repent to God, the hearts of you both will be bent towards it. And if you helped one another against him, then, truly, God, He is his Defender and Gabriel and ones in accord with morality. And the angels after that are his sustainers.⁶⁶:⁴

Perhaps if he divorced you (f), his Lord will cause in exchange for him spouses better than you (f), ones who submit (f) to One God, ones who believe (f), ones who are morally obligated (f), ones who repent, ones who worship (f), ones who are inclined to fasting (f), women previously married and virgins.⁶⁶:⁵

O those who believed! Protect yourselves and your people from a fire whose fuel is humanity and rocks over which are angels, harsh, severe who rebel not against whatever God commanded them and they accomplish what they are commanded.⁶⁶:⁶

O those who were ungrateful! Make not excuses this Day. You are only given recompense for what you had been doing.⁶⁶:⁷

O those who believed! Turn to God for forgiveness remorsefully, faithfully. Perhaps your Lord will absolve you of your evil deeds and cause you to enter into Gardens beneath which rivers run. On the Day God will not cover the Prophet with shame and those who believed with him. Their light will hasten about between them and on their right.

They will say: Our Lord! Fulfill for us our light and forgive us. Truly, Thou art Powerful over everything.⁶⁶:⁸

O Prophet! Struggle against the ones who are ungrateful and the ones who are hypocrites and be thou harsh against them. And their place of shelter will be hell. And miserable will be the Homecoming!⁶⁶:⁹

God propounded an example for those, ones who are ungrateful like the woman of Noah and the woman of Lot. They both had been beneath two servants of Our servants, ones who are in accord with morality. But they both (f) betrayed them so they avail them not against God at all. And it was said: Enter the fire along with ones who enter.⁶⁶:¹⁰

And God propounded an example for those who believed: Behold the woman of Pharaoh; she said: My Lord, build for me near Thee a house in the Garden and deliver Thou me from Pharaoh and his actions and deliver me from the folk, the ones who are unjust.⁶⁶:¹¹

And Mary, the daughter of Imran, who guarded her private parts, so We breathed into it of Our Spirit and she established as true the Words of her Lord and His Books and she had been among the ones who are morally obligated.⁶⁶:¹²

CHAPTER 67 THE DOMINION

In the Name of God, The Merciful, The Compassionate

Blessed be He in whose hands is the dominion and He is Powerful over everything!⁶⁷:¹

He Who created death and this life that He try you as to which of you is fairer in action. And He is The Almighty, The Forgiving,⁶⁷:²

Who created the seven heavens one on another?

Thou hast not seen any imperfection in the creation of The Merciful. Then, return thy sight! Hast thou seen any flaw?⁶⁷:³

Again, return thy sight twice again and thy sight will turn about to thee, one that is dazzled while it is weary.⁶⁷:⁴

And, certainly, We made to appear pleasing the lower heaven with lamps and We assigned them things to stone satans. We made ready for them the punishment of the blaze.⁶⁷:⁵

And for those who were ungrateful to their Lord is the punishment of hell. Miserable will be the Homecoming!⁶⁷:⁶ When they were cast down into it, they would hear it sighing while it is boiling⁶⁷:⁷ and about to burst with rage.

As often as a unit of them were cast down into it, the ones who are keepers there asked them: Approaches not a warner to you?⁶⁷:⁸

They will say: Yea! A warner drew near us, but we denied him. And we said: God sent not down anything. You are not but in a great going astray.⁶⁷:⁹

And they would say: If we had been hearing or are reasonable, we would not have been Companions of the Blaze.⁶⁷:¹⁰

And they would acknowledge their impiety. Then, hell for the Companions of the Blaze!⁶⁷:¹¹ Truly, those who dread their Lord in the unseen, for them is forgiveness and a great compensation.⁶⁷:¹²

Keep your saying secret or publish it, truly, He is Knowing of what is in your breasts.⁶⁷:¹³

Would He who created not know?

And He is The Subtle, The Aware.⁶⁷:¹⁴

It is He who made the earth submissive to you, so walk in its tracts and eat of His provision. To Him is the rising.⁶⁷:¹⁵ Were you safe from He Who is in the heaven that He will not cause the earth to swallow you up when it spins?⁶⁷:¹⁶

Were you safe from He Who is in the heavens that He will not send against you a sand storm? You will know how My warner has been right!⁶⁷:¹⁷

And, certainly, those who were before them denied. Then, how horrible had been My reproach!⁶⁷:¹⁸

Consider they not the birds above them ones standing in ranks and closing their wings? Nothing holds them back but The Merciful. Truly, He is Seeing of everything.⁶⁷:¹⁹

Who is this who would be an army for you to help you other than The Merciful? Truly, ones who are ungrateful are not but in delusion.⁶⁷:²⁰

Or who is this who will provide for you if He held back His provision? Nay! They were resolute, turning in disdain and aversion.⁶⁷:²¹

Then is whoever walks as one who is prone on his face better guided, or he who walks without fault on a straight path?⁶⁷:²²

Say: It is He who caused you to grow and assigned you the ability to hear, sight, and minds. But you give little thanks!⁶⁷:²³

Say: It is He who made you numerous on the earth and to Him you will be assembled.⁶⁷:²⁴

And they say: When is this promise if you had been ones who are sincere?⁶⁷:²⁵

Say: The knowledge of this is only with God and I am only a clear warner.⁶⁷:²⁶

But when they saw the punishment nigh, the faces were troubled of those who were ungrateful.

And it will be said to them: This is what you had been calling for.⁶⁷:²⁷

Say: Considered you if God would cause me to perish and whoever is with me or had mercy on us, who will grant protection to the ones who are ungrateful from a painful punishment?⁶⁷:²⁸

Say: He is The Merciful. We believed in Him and in Him we put our trust. Then, you will know who he is, one who is clearly gone astray.⁶⁷:²⁹

Say: Considered you? If it came to be in the morning that your water be sinking into the ground, who approaches you with assistance from water springs ?⁶⁷:³⁰

CHAPTER 68 THE PEN

In the Name of God, The Merciful, The Compassionate

Nun! By the pen and what they inscribe:⁶⁸:¹ Thou art not, by the divine blessing of thy Lord, one who is possessed.⁶⁸:² And, truly, there is for thee certainly, compensation, that which is unfailing.⁶⁸:³ And, truly, thou art of sublime morals.⁶⁸:⁴ Thou wilt perceive and they will perceive⁶⁸:⁵ which of you is the one who is demented.⁶⁸:⁶ Truly, thy Lord, He is greater in knowledge of whoever went astray from His Way and He is greater in knowledge of ones who are truly guided.⁶⁸:⁷ Then, obey not ones who deny.⁶⁸:⁸

They wished that thou wouldst compromise with them and they would compromise with thee.⁶⁸:⁹ But obey thou not every worthless swearer, defamer,⁶⁸:¹⁰ one who goes about with slander, slandering,⁶⁸:¹¹ who delays good, a sinful, exceeder of limits,⁶⁸:¹² cruel and after that, ignoble,⁶⁸:¹³ because he had been possessor of wealth and children.⁶⁸:¹⁴

When Our signs are recounted to him, he said: Fables of the ancient ones!⁶⁸:¹⁵

We will mark him on the snout!⁶⁸:¹⁶

Truly, We tried them as We tried the Companions of the Garden when they swore an oath that they would pluck fruit, in that which is happening in the morning.⁶⁸:¹⁷

They make no exception by saying if God wills.⁶⁸:¹⁸

Then, a visitation from thy Lord visited it while they were ones who sleep,⁶⁸:¹⁹ in that which is happening in the morning, it was like a plucked garden!⁶⁸:²⁰

And they called to one another in that which is morning:⁶⁸:²¹ Set forth in the early morning dawn to your cultivation if you had been ones who pluck fruit.⁶⁸:²²

So they set out and they whisper, saying:⁶⁸:²³ There will, truly, not enter it today on you any needy person.⁶⁸:²⁴

And they set forth in the early morning, designing, assuming they were ones who have the power.⁶⁸:²⁵

But when they saw it, they said: We are, certainly, ones who go astray!⁶⁸:²⁶ Nay! We are ones who are deprived.⁶⁸:²⁷

The most moderate of them said: Say I not to you: Why glorify you not God?⁶⁸:²⁸

They said: Glory be to God, our Lord! Truly, we had been ones who are unjust.⁶⁸:²⁹

Then, they came forward, some with some others blaming one another.⁶⁸:³⁰

They said: O woe be to us! Truly, we had been ones who are defiant.⁶⁸:³¹ Perhaps our Lord will cause to exchange for us better than it. Truly, we are ones who quest our Lord.⁶⁸:³²

Thus, this is the punishment of this present life, but the punishment of the world to come is greater, if they had been knowing!⁶⁸:³³

Truly, for ones who are Godfearing are Gardens of Bliss with their Lord.⁶⁸:³⁴ Will We make ones who submit to God as ones who sin?⁶⁸:³⁵

What is the matter with you?

How you give judgment!⁶⁸:³⁶ Or have you a Book by which you study⁶⁸:³⁷ that you will have in it whatever you specify?⁶⁸:³⁸

Or are there oaths from Us, ones that reach through to the Day of Resurrection providing that you will have what you yourselves give as judgment?⁶⁸:³⁹

Ask them, then, which of them will be a guarantor for that.⁶⁸:⁴⁰

Or have they ones they ascribe as associate with God?

Then, let them approach with their ascribed associates if they had been ones who are sincere.⁶⁸:⁴¹

On a Day the great calamity will be uncovered and they will be called to prostration, then, they will not be able to do so.⁶⁸:⁴² Their sight will be that which is humbled. Abasement will come over them and they had before this been called to prostration while they were ones who are healthy.⁶⁸:⁴³ So forsake Me and whoever denies this discourse. We will draw them on gradually from where they know not⁶⁸:⁴⁴ and I will grant indulgence to them. Truly, My cunning is sure.⁶⁸:⁴⁵

Or hast thou asked them for a compensation, so that they would be weighed down from something owed?⁶⁸:⁴⁶

Or have they knowledge of the unseen with them so that they write it down?⁶⁸:⁴⁷

So be thou patient until the determination of thy Lord and be not like the Companion of the Great Fish when he cried out, one who is suppressed by grief.⁶⁸:⁴⁸

If a divine blessing not followed him one after another, from His Lord he would be cast forth on the naked shore while he was one who is condemned.⁶⁸:⁴⁹ But his Lord elected him and made him among the ones in accord with morality.⁶⁸:⁵⁰

It was almost as if those who were ungrateful looked at thee sternly with their sight when they heard the Remembrance, and they say: He is one who is possessed!⁶⁸:⁵¹

And it is, certainly, not but a Remembrance to the worlds.⁶⁸:⁵²

CHAPTER 69 THE REALITY

In the Name of God, The Merciful, The Compassionate

The Reality!⁶⁹:¹

What is The Reality?⁶⁹:²

And what would cause thee to recognize what The Reality is?⁶⁹:³ Thamud and Ad denied the Day of Disaster.⁶⁹:⁴

Then, as for Thamud, they were caused to perish by a storm of thunder and lightning.⁶⁹:⁵

As for Ad, they were caused to perish by a fierce and roaring, raging wind.⁶⁹:⁶

It compelled against them for seven uninterrupted nights and eight days so wilt thou see the folk in it laid prostrate as if they had been uprooted fallen down date palm trees?⁶⁹:⁷

Then, wilt thou see of them any ones who endure?⁶⁹:⁸

Pharaoh and whoever draw near before him and the ones that are cities overthrown were ones of inequity⁶⁹:⁹ and they rebelled against the Messenger of their Lord, so He took them with a swelling, taking.⁶⁹:¹⁰

When the waters became turbulent, we carried you in that which runs on water,⁶⁹:¹¹ that We make it an admonition for you, and attentive ears would hold onto it.⁶⁹:¹²

And when the trumpet will be blown with one gust,⁶⁹:¹³ and the earth and the mountains will be mounted, then, will be ground to powder in one grinding,⁶⁹:¹⁴ so on that Day will have come to pass The Reality⁶⁹:¹⁵ and the heaven will be split.

For on that day they will be as ones who are frail,⁶⁹:¹⁶ and the angels will be at its borders.

The Throne of thy Lord above them will be carried by eight on that Day.⁶⁹:¹⁷ That Day you will be presented. Your private matters will not be hidden.⁶⁹:¹⁸

And for him who will be given his book in his right hand he will say: Lo and behold! Recite my book!⁶⁹:¹⁹ Truly, I thought that I would be one who encounters my reckoning.⁶⁹:²⁰

And he will have a well-pleasing, pleasant life⁶⁹:²¹ in a magnificent Garden.⁶⁹:²² Its clusters, that which draws near.⁶⁹:²³ Eat and drink wholesomely for what you did in the past, in the days, that which have gone by.⁶⁹:²⁴

But as for him who is given his book to his left he will say: O would that I was not given my book,⁶⁹:²⁵ and that I was not informed of my reckoning!⁶⁹:²⁶ O would that my death had been my expiry!⁶⁹:²⁷ My wealth availed me not.⁶⁹:²⁸ Perished from me is my authority.⁶⁹:²⁹

It will be said: Take him and restrict him.⁶⁹:³⁰ Again, broil him in hellfire⁶⁹:³¹ and after that in a chain of the length of seventy cubits. So insert him in it.⁶⁹:³² Truly, he had not been believing in God, The Sublime,⁶⁹:³³ nor did he urge food for the needy.⁶⁹:³⁴ This day he is not to have any loyal friend here⁶⁹:³⁵ and no food, but foul pus⁶⁹:³⁶ which none eat but ones of inequity.⁶⁹:³⁷

So I swear an oath by what you perceive⁶⁹:³⁸ and what you perceive not.⁶⁹:³⁹

Truly, it is the saying of a generous Messenger,⁶⁹:⁴⁰ and not the saying of a poet.

Little do you believe!⁶⁹:⁴¹ Nor is it the saying of a soothsayer. Little do you recollect!⁶⁹:⁴²

It is a sending down from the Lord of the worlds.⁶⁹:⁴³ And if he fabricated against Us some sayings,⁶⁹:⁴⁴ truly, We would have taken him by the right hand⁶⁹:⁴⁵ and, again, We would have severed his life-vein.⁶⁹:⁴⁶ And there is none of you who would be ones who hinder Us from him.⁶⁹:⁴⁷ And, truly, it is an admonition to ones who are Godfearing.⁶⁹:⁴⁸

And We well know that there are among you, ones who deny.⁶⁹:⁴⁹ And, truly, it will be a regret for ones who are ungrateful.⁶⁹:⁵⁰

And, truly, it is The Truth of certainty.⁶⁹:⁵¹ So glorify the Name of thy Lord, The Sublime.⁶⁹:⁵²

CHAPTER 70
THE STAIRWAYS OF ASCENT

In the Name of God, The Merciful, The Compassionate

One who supplicates asked for a punishment that will fall⁷⁰:¹ on the ones who are ungrateful for which there will be no one to avert⁷⁰:² from God, the Possessor of the Stairways of Ascent.⁷⁰:³

The angels and the Spirit go up to Him on a Day whose measure had been fifty thousand years.⁷⁰:⁴ So have thou patience with a graceful patience.⁷⁰:⁵ Truly, they see it as distant,⁷⁰:⁶ but We see it as near at hand.⁷⁰:⁷

On a Day the heaven will become as molten copper⁷⁰:⁸ and the mountains be as wool clusters⁷⁰:⁹ and no loyal friend will ask a loyal friend,⁷⁰:¹⁰ although they are given sight of them. One who sins would wish that he offer for ransom—from the punishment of that day—his children⁷⁰:¹¹ or his companion wife, or his brother⁷⁰:¹² or his relatives who gave him refuge,⁷⁰:¹³ or whoever is on the earth altogether, again, if that would rescue him.⁷⁰:¹⁴

No indeed. Truly, it is the furnace of hell⁷⁰:¹⁵ removing their scalps,⁷⁰:¹⁶ calling whoever drew back and turned away⁷⁰:¹⁷ and gathered wealth and amassed.⁷⁰:¹⁸ Truly, the human being was created fretful.⁷⁰:¹⁹

When the worst afflicted him, he is impatient.⁷⁰:²⁰ And when the good afflicted him, begrudging.⁷⁰:²¹

But the ones who formally pray,⁷⁰:²² those, they are ones who continue with their formal prayers⁷⁰:²³ and those who in their wealth there is a known obligation towards⁷⁰:²⁴ the one who begs and the one who is deprived⁷⁰:²⁵ and those who sincerely validate the Day of Judgment.⁷⁰:²⁶

And those, they are ones who are apprehensive of the punishment of their Lord.⁷⁰:²⁷ Truly, as to the punishment of their Lord, there is no one who is safe from it.⁷⁰:²⁸

Those, they are ones who guard their private parts,⁷⁰:²⁹ but not from their spouses or what their right hands possessed. Truly, they are not ones who will be reproached.⁷⁰:³⁰

But whoever was looking beyond that, those, they are ones who turn away.⁷⁰:³¹

And those, they, who in their trusts and to their compacts are ones who shepherd.⁷⁰:³² And they, those are who, giving their testimony, are ones who uphold.⁷⁰:³³ And those, they who over their formal prayers are watchful.⁷⁰:³⁴ Those will be in Gardens, ones who are honored.⁷⁰:³⁵

What is with those who were ungrateful—ones who run forward towards thee, eyes fixed in horror,⁷⁰:³⁶ to the right and the left, tied in knots.⁷⁰:³⁷

Is not every man of them desirous of being caused to enter into a Garden of Bliss?⁷⁰:³⁸

No indeed. Truly, We created them out of what they know.⁷⁰:³⁹

So I swear an oath by the Lord of the rising places and the setting places, that We certainly are ones who have power⁷⁰:⁴⁰ to substitute better for them. And We are not ones who are outrun.⁷⁰:⁴¹

So let them engage in idle talk and play until they encounter the Day of theirs that they are promised,⁷⁰:⁴² the Day when they will go forth swiftly from their tombs as though they had been hurrying to a goal⁷⁰:⁴³ with their sight, that which is humbled. Abasement will come over them. That is the Day which they had been promised.⁷⁰:⁴⁴

CHAPTER 71 NOAH

In the Name of God, The Merciful, The Compassionate

Truly, We sent Noah to his folk saying: Warn thy folk before a painful punishment approaches them.⁷¹:¹

He said: O my folk! Truly, I am a clear warner to you:⁷¹:² Worship God and be Godfearing of Him and obey me.⁷¹:³ He forgives you some of your impieties and postpones for you a term, that which is determined. Truly, when the term of God drew near, it will not be postponed if you had been but knowing.⁷¹:⁴

He said: My Lord! Truly, I called to my folk nighttime and daytime,⁷¹:⁵ but my supplication increases not but their running away.⁷¹:⁶ And, truly, as often as I called to them that Thou wouldst forgive them, they laid their finger tips over their ears and covered themselves with their garments. And they maintained growing arrogant as they grew arrogant.⁷¹:⁷ Again, truly, I called to them with openness.⁷¹:⁸

Again, I spoke openly to them and confided in them, keeping secret our converse.⁷¹:⁹ And I said: Ask for forgiveness of your Lord. Truly, He had been a Forgiver.⁷¹:¹⁰ He sends from heaven abundant rain for you.⁷¹:¹¹ He will furnish you relief with wealth and children. And He will assign for you Gardens and will assign for you rivers.⁷¹:¹² What is it with you that you hope not for dignity from God?⁷¹:¹³

And, surely, He created you in stages?⁷¹:¹⁴

Consider you not how God created the seven heavens, one on another?⁷¹:¹⁵

And how He made the moon in them as a light and how He made the sun as a light-giving lamp?⁷¹:¹⁶

And how God caused you to develop, bringing you forth from the earth.⁷¹:¹⁷ Again, He will cause you to return into it and bring you out in an expelling.⁷¹:¹⁸

And how God made for you the earth as a carpet⁷¹:¹⁹ that you may tread in it ways through ravines.⁷¹:²⁰

Noah said: My Lord! Truly, they rebelled against me. They followed such a one whose wealth and children increase him not, but in loss.⁷¹:²¹ And they planned a magnificent plan⁷¹:²²

And they said: You will by no means forsake your gods, nor will you forsake Wadd nor Suwa nor Yaghuth nor Yauq nor Nasr.⁷¹:²³

And, truly, they are going much astray. And increase Thou not ones who are unjust but in causing them to go astray.⁷¹:²⁴ Because of their transgressions, they were drowned and were caused to enter into a fire. And they find not for themselves any helpers other than God.⁷¹:²⁵

And Noah said: My Lord! Allow not even one on the earth from among the ones who are ungrateful!⁷¹:²⁶ Truly, Thou, if Thou wert to allow them, they would cause Thy servants to go astray and they will but procreate immoral ingrates.⁷¹:²⁷

My Lord! Forgive me and ones who are my parents and whoever entered my house as one who believes—the males, ones who believe and the females, ones who believe and increase not the ones who are unjust, but in ruin.⁷¹:²⁸

CHAPTER 72 THE JINN

In the Name of God, The Merciful, The Compassionate

Say: It was revealed to me that a group of jinn listened to me. They said: Truly, we heard a wondrous Recitation.⁷²:¹ It guides to the right judgment, so we believed in it.

And we will never ascribe partners with our Lord anyone.⁷²:² Truly, He, exalted be the grandeur of our Lord. He took no companion (f) to Himself, nor a son,⁷²:³ and yet a foolish one among us had been saying an outrageous lie about God!⁷²:⁴

But we, truly, thought that the humankind, nor the jinn would ever say a lie about God⁷²:⁵ and that there had been men of humankind who would take refuge with the masculine of the jinn, but they increased them in vileness.⁷²:⁶

And they thought as you thought, that God will never raise up anyone.⁷²:⁷

And we stretched towards the heaven. Then, we found it was filled with stern guards and burning flames.⁷²:⁸

And we had been sitting in positions having the ability to hear. But whoever listens now will find a burning flame and watchers for him.⁷²:⁹

And we were not informed whether the worst was intended for those who are on earth or whether their Lord intended for them right mindedness.⁷²:¹⁰ There are among us, the ones in accord with morality. And there are among us other than that. We had been of ways differing from one another.⁷²:¹¹

And we, truly, thought that we will never be able to weaken God on the earth and we will never weaken Him by flight.⁷²:¹² So, truly, when we heard the guidance, we believed in it. And whoever believes in his Lord, he will fear neither meagerness nor vileness.⁷²:¹³

And, truly, we are the ones who submit to God. Among us there are the ones who swerve from justice. And whoever submitted to God, then, those sought right mindedness.⁷²:¹⁴

As for the ones who swerve from justice, they had been as firewood for hell.⁷²:¹⁵ If they went straight on the way, We would have satiated them with copious water⁷²:¹⁶ so that We try them in it.

But whoever turns aside from the Remembrance of his Lord, He will dispatch him to a rigorous punishment.⁷²:¹⁷

Truly, the places of prostration belong to God so call not to anyone with God.⁷²:¹⁸ And, truly, when the servant of God stood up, calling to Him, they be about to swarm upon him.⁷²:¹⁹

Say: Truly, I call only to my Lord, and I ascribe not as partners with Him anyone.[72:20]

Say: Truly, I possess not the power to hurt nor to bring right mindedness for you.[72:21]

Say: Truly, none would grant me protection from God—not anyone! And I will never find other than Him that which is a haven[72:22] unless I be delivering messages from God, His messages.

And whoever disobeys God and His Messenger, then, for him is the fire of hell, ones who will dwell in it forever, eternally.[72:23]

Until when they saw what they are promised, then, they will know who is weaker of ones who help and fewer in number.[72:24]

Say: I am not informed if what you are promised is near, or if my Lord will assign for it a space of time.[72:25] He is The One Who Knows of the unseen! And He discloses not the unseen to anyone,[72:26] but a Messenger with whom He was content. Then, truly, He dispatches in advance of him and from behind him, watchers[72:27] that He know that they expressed the messages of their Lord. He enclosed whatever is with them and He counted everything with numbers.[72:28]

CHAPTER 73 THE ONE WHO IS WRAPPED

In the Name of God, The Merciful, The Compassionate

O thou, the one who is wrapped,[73:1] stand up during the night, but for a little part,[73:2] for half of it or reduce it a little.[73:3] Or increase it and chant the Quran, a good chanting,[73:4] for We will cast on thee a weighty saying.[73:5]

Truly, one who begins in the night, is when impression is strongest and speech more upright.[73:6] Truly, for thee in the daytime is a lengthy occupation.[73:7]

And remember thou the Name of thy Lord. And devote thyself to Him with total devotion.[73:8]

The Lord of the East and of the West, there is no god but He. So take Him to thyself as thy Trustee.[73:9] And have thou patience with regard to what they say and abandon them with a graceful abandoning.[73:10] Forsake to Me the ones who deny, those imbued with prosperity and respite them for a little.[73:11]

Truly, with Us are shackles and hellfire[73:12] and food which sticks in the throat and chokes and a painful punishment.[73:13]

On a Day when the earth will quake and the mountains, and the mountains will become a poured forth heap of sand.[73:14]

Truly, We sent you a Messenger, one who bears witness to you, as We sent to Pharaoh a Messenger.[73:15] But Pharaoh rebelled against the Messenger so We took him a taking remorselessly.[73:16]

How will you fend off a day if you were ungrateful, that will make the children gray haired?[73:17]

The heaven will be that which is split apart from it. His promise had been one that is accomplished.[73:18] Truly, this is an admonition; so let whoever willed take himself a way to his Lord.[73:19]

Truly, thy Lord knows that thou be standing up for nearly two thirds of the nighttime, or a half of it or a third of it along with a section of those who are with thee. And God ordains the nighttime and the daytime. He knew that you would not be able to keep count of it, so He turned towards you in forgiveness, then recite of the Quran as much as was easy.

He knew that some of you are sick and others travel on the earth looking for the grace of God and others fight in the way of God. So recite of it as much as was easy.

And perform the formal prayer and give the purifying alms and lend to God a fairer loan. For whatever of good you put forward for your souls, you will find the same with God. It is good and a sublime compensation. And ask God for forgiveness. Truly, God is Forgiving, Compassionate.[73:20]

CHAPTER 74 THE ONE WHO WRAPPED HIMSELF IN A CLOAK

In the Name of God, The Merciful, The Compassionate

O thou, the one who wrapped himself in a cloak![74:1] Stand up and warn![74:2] And magnify thy Lord[74:3] and purify thy garments[74:4] and abandon contamination![74:5] And reproach not others to acquire more for yourself.[74:6] And for thy Lord, then, have thou patience.[74:7]

Then, when the horn is sounded,[74:8] truly, that Day will be a difficult day,[74:9] and not easy for the ones who are ungrateful.[74:10]

Forsake to Me whom I alone created.[74:11] I assigned to him the spreading out of wealth[74:12] and children as ones who bear witness.[74:13] And I made smooth for him, a making smooth.[74:14] Again, he is desirous that I increase it.[74:15] No indeed; he had been stubborn about Our signs.[74:16] I will constrain him with a hard ascent.[74:17] Truly, he deliberated and calculated.[74:18] Then, perdition to him! How he calculated![74:19] Again, perdition to him! How he calculated![74:20] Again, he looked on[74:21] and, again, he frowned and scowled.[74:22] Again, he drew back and grew arrogant.[74:23]

And he said: This is nothing but fabricated old sorcery.[74:24] This is nothing but the saying of a mortal.[74:25]

I will scorch him in Saqar.[74:26]

And how will thee recognize what Saqar is?[74:27]

It forsakes not nor causes anything to remain,[74:28] scorching the mortal.[74:29] Over it there are nineteen.[74:30]

We assigned none but angels to be wardens of the Fire and We made the amount of them not but as a test for those who were ungrateful.

So those who were given the Book are reassured and those who believed, add to their belief. And will not doubt those who were given the Book and the ones who believe. And say to those who in their hearts is a sickness and the ones who are ungrateful: What had God wanted by this example?

Thus, God causes to go astray whom He wills, and He guides whom He wills. And none knows the armies of thy Lord but He. And it is not other than a reminder for the mortals.[74:31]

No indeed! By the moon[74:32] and the night when it drew back[74:33] and polished is the morning.[74:34] Truly, it is one of the greatest of all things[74:35] as a warner to the mortals,[74:36] to whomever willed among you that he go forward or remain behind.[74:37]

Every soul is a pledge for what it earned[74:38] but the Companions of the Right[74:39] will be in Gardens and will demand of one another[74:40] about the ones who sin:[74:41]

What thrust you into Saqar?[74:42]

They would say: We be not among the ones who formally pray[74:43] and we were not those who feed the poor.[74:44] And we had been ones who engage in idle talk along with the ones who engage in idle talk.[74:45] And we had been denying the Day of Judgment[74:46] until the certainty of the Hour approached us.[74:47]

Then, intercession will not profit them from the ones who are intercessors.[74:48] Then, what is the matter with them that they are ones who turn aside from the admonition,[74:49] as though they had been frightened donkeys[74:50] that ran away from a lion?[74:51]

Nay! Every man among them wants to be given unrolled scrolls.[74:52]

No indeed! Nay! They fear not the world to come.⁷⁴:⁵³

No indeed! Truly, it is an admonition.⁷⁴:⁵⁴

So let whoever willed, remember it.⁷⁴:⁵⁵ But they will not remember unless God wills. He is Worthy of God-consciousness and He is Worthy of granting The Forgiveness.⁷⁴:⁵⁶

CHAPTER 75
THE RESURRECTION

In the Name of God, The Merciful, The Compassionate

I swear an oath by the Day of Resurrection.⁷⁵:¹ And I swear an oath by the reproachful soul.⁷⁵:²

Assumes the human being that We will never gather his bones?⁷⁵:³

Yea! We are ones who have power to shape his fingers again.⁷⁵:⁴

Nay! The human being wants to act immorally in front of him.⁷⁵:⁵

He asks: When is this Day of Resurrection?⁷⁵:⁶

But when their sight will be astonished⁷⁵:⁷ and the moon will cause the earth to be swallowed⁷⁵:⁸ and the sun and the moon will be gathered,⁷⁵:⁹ the human being will say on that Day: Where is a place to run away to?⁷⁵:¹⁰

No indeed! There is no refuge.⁷⁵:¹¹ With thy Lord on this Day will be thy recourse.⁷⁵:¹² The human being will be told on that Day what he put forward and what he postponed.⁷⁵:¹³ Nay! The human being is clear evidence against himself.⁷⁵:¹⁴ And although he would cast his excuses,⁷⁵:¹⁵ impel not thy tongue to hasten it.⁷⁵:¹⁶

Truly, on Us is his amassing and its Recitation.⁷⁵:¹⁷

But when We recited it, follow thou its Recitation.⁷⁵:¹⁸ From Us after that is its clear explanation.⁷⁵:¹⁹

No indeed! Nay! You love that which hastens away⁷⁵:²⁰ and forsake the world to come.⁷⁵:²¹

Faces on that Day will be ones that beam,⁷⁵:²² ones that look towards their Lord.⁷⁵:²³

And faces on that day will be ones that scowl.⁷⁵:²⁴

Thou will think that against them is wreaked a crushing calamity.⁷⁵:²⁵ No indeed! When it reached the collar bones at death⁷⁵:²⁶ and it was said: Where is one who is a wizard to save me?⁷⁵:²⁷

And he thought it to be his parting⁷⁵:²⁸ and one leg was intertwined with the other leg,⁷⁵:²⁹ that Day he will be driving toward thy Lord⁷⁵:³⁰ for he established not the true nor invoked blessings⁷⁵:³¹ and he denied and turned away.⁷⁵:³² He went to his people again, going arrogantly.⁷⁵:³³ Closer to thee! And closer to thee!⁷⁵:³⁴ Again closer to thee! And closer to thee!⁷⁵:³⁵

Assumes the human being that he will be left aimless?⁷⁵:³⁶

Was he not a sperm-drop to be emitted in seminal fluid?⁷⁵:³⁷ Again, he had been a clot and He created him and shaped him.⁷⁵:³⁸ Then, He made of him two pairs, the male and the female.⁷⁵:³⁹

Is not that One Who Has Power over that able to give life to the dead?⁷⁵:⁴⁰

CHAPTER 76
THE HUMAN BEING

In the Name of God, The Merciful, The Compassionate

Approached the human being a long course of time when he will be nothing remembered?⁷⁶:¹

Truly, We made the human being of a mingling of seminal fluid that We may test him. So We made him hearing, seeing.⁷⁶:²

Truly, We guided him on the way, whether he be one who is thankful or ungrateful.⁷⁶:³

Truly, We made ready for ones who are ungrateful chains and yokes and a blaze.⁷⁶:⁴

Truly, the pious will drink from a cup that had been a mixture of camphor,⁷⁶:⁵ a spring where the servants of God will drink, causing it to gush forth, a great gushing.⁷⁶:⁶ They live up to their vows and they fear a Day when the worst will be that which flies far and wide.⁷⁶:⁷

In spite of their love for it, they feed with food one who is needy and the orphan and the prisoner of war saying:⁷⁶:⁸ We feed you only for the Countenance of God. We want no recompense from you nor any thankfulness.⁷⁶:⁹ Truly, we fear our Lord on a frowning, inauspicious Day.⁷⁶:¹⁰

So God would protect them from worse on that day, and would make them find radiancy and joyfulness.⁷⁶:¹¹ And He will give them recompense for their enduring patiently with a Garden and silk,⁷⁶:¹² and ones who are reclining in it on raised benches. In it they will see neither sun nor excessive cold of the moon.⁷⁶:¹³ And that which draws near them is its shade and clusters of grapes will be subdued, a subduing.⁷⁶:¹⁴ And are passed around among them receptacles of silver and goblets that had been of crystal,⁷⁶:¹⁵ crystal like silver, and that they calculated a calculating.⁷⁶:¹⁶ And they are given to drink in it a cup that had been with a mixture of ginger.⁷⁶:¹⁷

There is a spring in it named Salsabil.⁷⁶:¹⁸ And ones who are immortal youths will go around them whom, when thou hadst seen them, thou wouldst assume them to be scattered pearls.⁷⁶:¹⁹ And when thou hadst seen them, again, thou wilt have seen bliss and a great dominion.⁷⁶:²⁰ Upon them are garments of fine green silk and brocade. And they will be adorned with bracelets of silver. Their Lord will give to drink undefiled drink.⁷⁶:²¹ Truly, this had been your recompense. What had been that which is your endeavoring.⁷⁶:²²

Truly, We sent down to thee the Quran, a sending down successively.⁷⁶:²³ So have thou patience for the determination of thy Lord and obey not anyone of them, not the ones who are perverted nor the ungrateful.⁷⁶:²⁴

And remember thou the Name of thy Lord at early morning dawn and eventide.⁷⁶:²⁵

And during the night, prostrate thyself to Him and glorify Him a lengthy part of the night.⁷⁶:²⁶

Truly, these are they who love that which hastens away and they forsake a weighty day behind them.⁷⁶:²⁷

We created them and We strengthened their frame. And when We willed, We will substitute their likes with a substitution.⁷⁶:²⁸ Truly, this is an admonition.

And whoever willed, he took himself on a way to his Lord.⁷⁶:²⁹ But you will it not unless God wills it. For God had been Knowing, Wise.⁷⁶:³⁰ He causes to enter whom He wills into His mercy.

And the ones who are unjust, He prepared for them a painful punishment.⁷⁶:³¹

CHAPTER 77
THE ONES WHO ARE SENT

In the Name of God, The Merciful, The Compassionate

By ones who are sent successively,⁷⁷:¹ by the storm and raging tempest,⁷⁷:² by that which causes vegetation to revive, unfolding⁷⁷:³ by the ones who separate a separating⁷⁷:⁴ by ones who cast a remembrance⁷⁷:⁵ as excusing or warning,⁷⁷:⁶ truly, what you are promised will be that which falls.⁷⁷:⁷

Then, when the stars will be obliterated⁷⁷:⁸ and when the heaven will be cleaved asunder⁷⁷:⁹ and when the mountains will be scattered[77:10] and when the time will be set for the Messengers,[77:11] for which Day were these appointed?[77:12]

For the Day of Decision.[77:13]

And what would cause thee to recognize what the Day of Decision is?[77:14]

Woe on that Day to the ones who deny![77:15]

Caused We not the ancient ones to perish?[77:16]

Again, We will pursue the later ones.[77:17] Thus, We accomplish this with the ones who sin.[77:18]

Woe on that Day to the ones who deny![77:19]

Create We you not of despicable water?[77:20] Then, We made it in a secure stopping place[77:21] for a known measuring?[77:22] And We measured. How bountiful are the ones who measure![77:23]

Woe on that Day to the ones who deny![77:24]

Make We not the earth a place of drawing together[77:25] the living and the lifeless?[77:26]

We made on it soaring, firm mountains. We satiated you with water of the sweetest kind.[77:27]

Woe on that Day to the ones who deny![77:28]

Set out toward what you had been in it denying.[77:29]

Set out to the shade. It is possessor of three columns,[77:30] having no shade nor availing you against the flaming![77:31]

Truly, it will throw up sparks of fire like the palace,[77:32] as though it was a string of saffron-colored male camels.[77:33]

Woe on that Day to the ones who deny![77:34]

This Day they will not speak for themselves[77:35] nor will they be given permission so that they make excuses.[77:36]

Woe on that Day to the ones who deny![77:37]

This is the Day of Decision; We gathered you and the ancient ones.[77:38] So if you had been cunning, then, try to outwit Me.[77:39]

Woe on that Day to the ones who deny![77:40]

Truly, the ones who are Godfearing will be amidst shade and springs[77:41] and sweet fruit for which they lust:[77:42]

Eat and drink wholesomely for what you had been doing.[77:43]

Truly, We, thus, give recompense to the ones who are doers of good.[77:44]

Woe on that Day to the ones who deny![77:45]

Eat, take joy for a little. You are ones who sin.[77:46]

Woe on that Day to the ones who deny![77:47] When it will be said: Bow down, they bow not down.[77:48]

Woe on that Day to the ones who deny![77:49]

Then, in which discourse after this will they believe?[77:50]

CHAPTER 78 THE TIDING

In the Name of God, The Merciful, The Compassionate

About what demand you of one another?[78:1] Of the sublime tiding[78:2] about which they are ones who are at variance in it?[78:3]

No indeed! Soon they will know.[78:4]

Again, no indeed! Soon they will know.[78:5]

Make We not the earth for a cradling[78:6] and the mountains as stakes?[78:7]

And We created not you in pairs[78:8] and We made your sleep as a rest.[78:9]

And We made the nighttime as a garment.[78:10]

And We made the daytime for you to earn a living.[78:11]

And We built over you seven superior ones.[78:12]

And We made a bright, light-giving lamp.[78:13]

And We caused to descend that which are clouds bringing rain, water cascading,[78:14] with which We bring about grain and plants[78:15] and luxuriant Gardens.[78:16]

Truly, the Day of Decision[78:17] would be a time appointed,[78:17] a Day the trumpet is blown. Then, you approach in units[78:18] and the heaven will be let loose and will be all doors.[78:19] And the mountains will be set in motion and will be as vapor.[78:20]

Truly, hell will be on the watch,[78:21] a destination for the ones who are defiant,[78:22] one who lingers in expectation in it for many years.[78:23] They experience in it not any coolness nor any drink,[78:24] but scalding water and filth,[78:25] a suitable recompense![78:26] Truly, they had been not hoping not for a reckoning[78:27] and they denied Our signs with a denial.[78:28]

But We counted everything in a Book.[78:29] Experience it! We will never increase you but in punishment.[78:30]

Truly, for the ones who are Godfearing, there is a place of security;[78:31] fertile gardens and grapevines,[78:32] and full breasted maidens of the same age[78:33] and a cup overflowing.[78:34]

No idle talk will they hear in it nor any denial,[78:35] a recompense from thy Lord, a gift, a reckoning[78:36] from the Lord of the heavens and the earth and of whatever is between them, The Merciful against Whom they possess no argument.[78:37]

On a Day when the Spirit and the angels will stand up ranged in rows. They will not assert themselves but he to whom the Merciful gave permission and who said what is correct.[78:38]

That is the Day of The Truth; so whoever willed took his Lord to himself as the destination.[78:39] We warned you of a near punishment on a Day when a man will look on what his hands put forward and the ones who are ungrateful will say: O would that I had been earth dust![78:40]

CHAPTER 79
THE ONES WHO TEAR OUT

In the Name of God, The Merciful, The Compassionate

By the ones who tear out vehemently,[79:1] by the ones who draw out a drawing out,[79:2] by the ones who are swimmers, swimming,[79:3] the ones who take the lead, taking the lead,[79:4] by the ones who manage a command,[79:5] on a Day when the quake quakes,[79:6] succeeds the one that comes close behind it,[79:7] hearts beating painfully on that Day,[79:8] their sight, that which is humble.[79:9]

They say: Will we be restored to our original state[79:10] when we had been crumbled bones?[79:11]

They said: That is a return again of one who is a loser.[79:12] Truly, there will be but one scare.[79:13] That is when they would be the ones awakening.[79:14]

Approached thee the discourse of Moses[79:15] when his Lord cried out to him in the sanctified valley of Tuwa:[79:16] Be thou gone to Pharaoh. Truly, he was defiant.[79:17]

And say: Wouldst thou purify thyself?[79:18] And I will guide thee to thy Lord, then, thou wilt dread Him.[79:19]

And he caused him to see the greater sign.[79:20]

But Pharaoh denied and rebelled.[79:21]

Again, Pharaoh drew back, hastening about.[79:22]

Then, Pharaoh assembled them; then, proclaimed.[79:23] Then, Pharaoh said: I am your lofty lord.[79:24] So God took him with an exemplary punishment for the last and for the first.[79:25] Truly, in that is a lesson for whoever dreads God.[79:26]

Is your constitution harder to create or the heaven which He built?[79:27] He exalted its vault and shaped it[79:28] and He made its night dark and brought out its forenoon.[79:29] And, after that, He spread out the earth.[79:30] He brought out from it its water and its pasture.[79:31] And the mountains He set firm,[79:32] an enjoyment for you and for your flocks.[79:33]

When the Greater Catastrophe would draw near,[79:34] on that Day the human being will recollect for what he endeavored.[79:35] Hellfire will be advanced for whoever sees.[79:36] As for whoever was defiant[79:37] and held this present life in greater favor,[79:38] then, truly, hellfire will be the place of shelter![79:39]

And as for him who feared the Station of his Lord and prohibited desire from his soul,[79:40] truly, the Garden will be the place of shelter![79:41]

They ask thee about the Hour. When will it berth?⁷⁹:⁴² Then, what art thou about that thou remind of it?⁷⁹:⁴³

To thy Lord is the Utmost Boundary of it.⁷⁹:⁴⁴ And thou art only one who warns to such a one whoever dreads it.⁷⁹:⁴⁵ It will be as though a Day they see it, they linger not in expectation but an evening or a forenoon.⁷⁹:⁴⁶

CHAPTER 80 HE FROWNED

In the Name of God, The Merciful, The Compassionate
He frowned and turned away ⁸⁰:¹ that the blind man drew near him.⁸⁰:²

And what will cause thee to recognize so that perhaps he will purify himself⁸⁰:³ or yet recollect and a reminder profit him?⁸⁰:⁴

But as for he who was self-complacent,⁸⁰:⁵ then, thou hast attended to him⁸⁰:⁶ and not upon thee is any blame if he purifies not himself.⁸⁰:⁷

Yet as for him who drew near to thee, coming eagerly for knowledge⁸⁰:⁸ and he dreads God,⁸⁰:⁹ then, thou hast paid no heed to him?⁸⁰:¹⁰

No indeed! Truly, this is an admonition.⁸⁰:¹¹

So let whoever willed, remember it⁸⁰:¹² in scrolls to be held in esteem,⁸⁰:¹³ ones that are exalted and ones that are purified⁸⁰:¹⁴ by the hands of generous writers⁸⁰:¹⁵ and ones who are kindly, generous.⁸⁰:¹⁶

Perdition to the human being! How ungrateful he is!⁸⁰:¹⁷

From which thing did He create him?⁸⁰:¹⁸ He created him from seminal fluid then, ordained that he be.⁸⁰:¹⁹ He made the way easy for him again.⁸⁰:²⁰ Again, He caused him to die and be buried.⁸⁰:²¹ Again, when He willed, He will revive him.⁸⁰:²² No indeed! The human being finishes not what He commanded him.⁸⁰:²³

Then, let the human being look on his food—⁸⁰:²⁴ how We, truly, unloosed rain water with a pouring out.⁸⁰:²⁵ Again, We split the earth, a splitting.⁸⁰:²⁶ And We put forth in it grain⁸⁰:²⁷ and grapevines and reeds⁸⁰:²⁸ and olives and date palm trees⁸⁰:²⁹ and dense fertile gardens⁸⁰:³⁰ and sweet fruits and whatever grows on the earth,⁸⁰:³¹ an enjoyment for you and your flocks.⁸⁰:³²

Then, when the blare drew near,⁸⁰:³³ that Day a man will run away from his brother⁸⁰:³⁴ and his mother and his father⁸⁰:³⁵ and his companion wife and his children.⁸⁰:³⁶ For every man of them on that Day will be a matter that will preoccupy him.⁸⁰:³⁷ Faces that Day will be ones that are polished,⁸⁰:³⁸ ones who are laugh and ones who rejoice at good tidings.⁸⁰:³⁹

And faces on that Day will be dust-stained.⁸⁰:⁴⁰ Gloom will come over them.⁸⁰:⁴¹ Those, they are the ones who are ungrateful, ones who act immorally.⁸⁰:⁴²

CHAPTER 81 THE DARKENING

In the Name of God, The Merciful, The Compassionate
When the sun will be darkened⁸¹:¹ and when the stars plunge down⁸¹:² and when the mountains will be set in motion⁸¹:³ and when the pregnant camels are ignored⁸¹:⁴ and when the savage beasts will be assembled together⁸¹:⁵ and when the seas are caused to overflow⁸¹:⁶ and when the souls will be mated⁸¹:⁷ and when the buried infant girl will be asked⁸¹:⁸ for which impiety she was slain⁸¹:⁹ and when the scrolls will be unfolded⁸¹:¹⁰ and when the heaven is stripped off⁸¹:¹¹ and when hellfire will be caused to burn fiercely⁸¹:¹² and when the Garden will be brought close,⁸¹:¹³ every soul will know to what it was prone.⁸¹:¹⁴

So no! I swear an oath by the stars that recede,⁸¹:¹⁵ by the ones that run, the setting stars⁸¹:¹⁶ and by the night when it swarmed⁸¹:¹⁷ and by the morning, when it sighed,⁸¹:¹⁸ truly, the Quran is a saying from a generous Messenger,⁸¹:¹⁹ possessed of strength, with the Possessor of the Throne, secure,⁸¹:²⁰ one who is obeyed and, again, trustworthy.⁸¹:²¹

And your companion is not one who is possessed.⁸¹:²²

And, certainly, he saw him on the clear horizon.⁸¹:²³ And he is not avaricious for the unseen,⁸¹:²⁴ nor is it the saying of the accursed Satan.⁸¹:²⁵ So where are you going?⁸¹:²⁶

Truly, it is not but a Remembrance to the worlds⁸¹:²⁷ to whoever among you willed to go straight.⁸¹:²⁸ But you will not, unless God wills, the Lord of the worlds.⁸¹:²⁹

CHAPTER 82
THE SPLITTING APART

In the Name of God, The Merciful, The Compassionate
When the heaven will be split apart⁸²:¹ and when the stars will be scattered⁸²:² and when the seas will be caused to gush forth⁸²:³ and when the graves will be scattered about⁸²:⁴ every soul would know what it put forward and what it postponed.⁸²:⁵

O human being! What deluded thee as to thy generous Lord,⁸²:⁶ He Who created thee, then, shaped thee in proportion.⁸²:⁷

He composed thee in whichever form He willed.⁸²:⁸

No indeed! Nay! You deny this way of life!⁸²:⁹

And, truly, there are ones who guard over you,⁸²:¹⁰ ones who are generous scribes.⁸²:¹¹ They know whatever you accomplish.⁸²:¹²

Truly, the pious will be in bliss.⁸²:¹³

And, truly, the ones who act immorally will be in hellfire.⁸²:¹⁴ They will roast on the Day of Judgment.⁸²:¹⁵ And they will not be of ones who are absent.⁸²:¹⁶

And what will cause thee to recognize what the Day of Judgment is?⁸²:¹⁷ Again, what will cause thee to recognize what the Day of Judgment is?⁸²:¹⁸

It is a Day whereon a soul will not possess anything to avail another soul and the command on that Day will belong to God.⁸²:¹⁹

CHAPTER 83 THE ONES WHO
GIVE SHORT MEASURE

In the Name of God, The Merciful, The Compassionate
Woe be to the ones who give short measure,⁸³:¹ those who when they measure against humanity obtained full measure.⁸³:² Yet when they wanted to measure for them, or weigh for them, they skimp.⁸³:³ Think those not that they will be ones who are raised up⁸³:⁴ on the sublime Day,⁸³:⁵ a Day when humanity will stand up for the Lord of the worlds?⁸³:⁶

No indeed! Truly, the Book of the ones who act immorally is in Sijjin.⁸³:⁷

And what will cause thee to recognize what Sijjin is?⁸³:⁸

It is a written book.⁸³:⁹

Woe on that Day to the ones who deny—⁸³:¹⁰ those who deny the Day of Judgment!⁸³:¹¹

And none denies it but every sinful, exceeder of limits,⁸³:¹² who, when Our signs are recounted to him, he said: Fables of the ancient ones!⁸³:¹³

No indeed! Nay! Their hearts will be overcome with rust from what they had been earning.⁸³:¹⁴

No indeed! They will be from their Lord on that Day ones who are alienated.⁸³:¹⁵ Truly, again, they will be ones who roast in hellfire.[83:16] Again, it will be said to them after that: This is what you had been denying.[83:17]

No indeed! Truly, the book of the pious is in Illiyyun.[83:18]

And what will cause thee to recognize what Illiyyun is?[83:19]

It is a written book.[83:20] Bearing witness to it are the ones who are brought near to God.[83:21] Truly, the pious will be in bliss,[83:22] on raised benches, looking on.[83:23] Thou wilt recognize on their faces the radiancy of bliss.[83:24] They will be given to drink sealed over exquisite wine.[83:25] Its seal will have the lingering smell of musk. So for that, then, the ones who strive, strive.[83:26] And the mixture will be of Tasnim,[83:27] a spring from which will drink the ones who are brought near to it.[83:28]

Truly, those who sinned—at those who believed—had been laughing.[83:29] And when they passed by them, they would wink at one another,[83:30] and when they would turn about to their people, they would turn about acting as ones who are unconcerned.[83:31]

And when they saw them, they would say: Truly, these are ones who go astray.[83:32] They were sent as ones who guard over them.[83:33]

Then, on this Day, those who believed laugh at the ones who are ungrateful,[83:34] seated on raised benches, they look on.[83:35] Were the ones who are ungrateful not rewarded for what they had been accomplishing?[83:36]

CHAPTER 84
THE SPLITTING OPEN

In the Name of God, The Merciful, The Compassionate

When the heaven was split open[84:1] and gave ear to its Lord as it will be justly disposed to do[84:2] and when the earth stretches out[84:3] and cast what is in it and voided itself[84:4] and gave ear to its Lord as it will be justly disposed to do,[84:5] O human being! Truly, thou art one who is laboring towards thy Lord laboriously and thou wilt be one who encounters Him.[84:6]

And as for him who will be given his book in his right hand,[84:7] then, he will be made a reckoning, an easy reckoning,[84:8] and will turn about to his people as one who is joyous.[84:9]

But for whoever will be given his book behind his back,[84:10] he will call for damnation[84:11] and roast in a blaze.[84:12] He had been one who is joyous with his people.[84:13] Truly, he thought he would never retreat.[84:14] Yea! Truly, his Lord had been seeing him.[84:15]

So no! I swear an oath by the twilight[84:16] and by the night and whatever it enveloped[84:17] and by the moon when it was full[84:18] that you will, truly, ride plane after plane.[84:19]

Then, what is for them who believe not[84:20] when the Quran was recited to them, they prostrate not themselves?[84:21]

Nay! Those who were ungrateful deny,[84:22] but God is greater in knowledge of what they amass.[84:23] So give them good tidings of a painful punishment.[84:24]

But those who believed and did as the ones in accord with morality, for them is compensation, that which is unfailing.[84:25]

CHAPTER 85
THE CONSTELLATIONS

In the Name of God, The Merciful, The Compassionate

By the heaven possessing the constellations,[85:1] by the promised Day,[85:2] by ones who bear witness and ones who are witnessed,[85:3] the Companions of the Ditch were slain,[85:4] possessors of the fuel of the fire[85:5] above which they were

ones who sit,[85:6] as they were, in what they accomplish against the ones who believe, ones who bore witness.[85:7]

And they sought revenge on them only because they believe in God, The Almighty, The Worthy of Praise,[85:8] Him to whom belongs the dominion of the heavens and the earth. And God is Witness over everything.[85:9]

Truly, those who persecuted the males, ones who believe and the females, ones who believe and again repent not after that, for them is the punishment of hell and for them is the punishment of the burning.[85:10]

Truly, those who believed and did as the ones in accord with morality, for them will be Gardens beneath which rivers run. That will be the Great Triumph.[85:11]

Truly, the seizing by force by thy Lord is severe.[85:12] Truly, He causes to begin and He causes to return.[85:13] And He is The Forgiving, The Loving,[85:14] the Possessor of the Glorious Throne[85:15] Achiever of what He wants.[85:16]

Approached thee the discourse of the armies[85:17] of Pharaoh and of Thamud?[85:18]

Nay! Those who were ungrateful are belying[85:19] and God is One Who Encloses them from behind.[85:20]

Nay! It is a glorious Recitation[85:21] inscribed on the Guarded Tablet.[85:22]

CHAPTER 86
THE NIGHT VISITOR

In the Name of God, The Merciful, The Compassionate

By the heaven and the night visitor,[86:1] what will cause thee to recognize what the night visitor is?[86:2]

It is the piercing star.[86:3] Truly, every soul has one who guards it.[86:4]

So let the human being look on of what he was created.[86:5] He was created of water, that which gushes forth,[86:6] going forth from between the loins and the breast bone.[86:7]

Truly, He, in returning him, certainly is One Who Has Power.[86:8]

On a Day all secret thoughts will be tried,[86:9] then, there will not be for him any strength nor one who helps.[86:10]

By the heaven possessing the returning[86:11] and by the earth splitting with verdure,[86:12] truly, the Quran is a decisive saying[86:13] and it is not for mirth.[86:14]

Truly, they are strategizing a strategy.[86:15] And I am strategizing a strategy.[86:16]

So respite the ones who are ungrateful! Grant thou them a delay for awhile.[86:17]

CHAPTER 87 THE LOFTY

In the Name of God, The Merciful, The Compassionate

Glorify the Name of thy Lord, The Lofty[87:1] Who created and shaped[87:2] and who ordained and, then, guided[87:3] and who brought out the pasture[87:4] then, made it dark colored refuse.[87:5]

We will make thee recite and thou wilt not forget[87:6] but what God willed. Truly, He knows the openly published and whatever is hidden.[87:7]

And We will make easy for thee an easing.[87:8]

So remind if a reminder profited them.[87:9] Whoever dreads God will recollect,[87:10] but the disappointed will scorn it—[87:11] even he who will roast in the great fire,[87:12] again, neither dying in it nor living.[87:13]

He, surely, prospered, he who purified himself,[87:14] and remembered the Name of his Lord and invoked blessings.[87:15]

Nay! You hold this present life in greater favor,[87:16] yet the world to come is better, and one that endures.[87:17] Truly, this is in the previous scrolls,[87:18] the scrolls of Abraham and Moses.[87:19]

CHAPTER 88 THE OVERWHELMING EVENT

In the Name of God, The Merciful, The Compassionate

Approached thee the discourse of the Overwhelming Event?[88:1] Faces on that Day will be ones that are humbled,[88:2] ones that work and ones that are fatigued,[88:3] roasting in a hot fire.[88:4] They will be given to drink from boiling receptacles.[88:5] Is it not that there is no food for them but a thorny fruit.[88:6] It will not fatten nor will it avail hunger.[88:7]

Faces on that Day will be ones that are pleasant,[88:8] ones who are well-pleased by their endeavoring[88:9] in a magnificent Garden.[88:10] They will hear no babble in it.[88:11] In it is a running spring.[88:12] In it are exalted couches[88:13] and goblets that are set down[88:14] and cushions arrayed[88:15] and rugs, ones that are dispersed.[88:16]

Will they not, then, look on the camel, how it was created?[88:17]

And of the heaven, how it was lifted up?[88:18]

And the mountains, how they were hoisted up?[88:19]

And the earth, how it was stretched out?[88:20]

Then, remind for thou art only one who reminds.[88:21] Thou art not over them one who is a register of their deeds.[88:22] But whoever turned away and is one who is ungrateful,[88:23] God will punish him with the greater punishment.[88:24] Truly, to Us is their reversion.[88:25] Again, truly, on Us is their reckoning.[88:26]

CHAPTER 89 THE DAWN

In the Name of God, The Merciful, The Compassionate

By the dawn [89:1] and the ten nights,[89:2] by the even number and the odd number [89:3] and at night when it sets out.[89:4]

Is there not in that an oath to be sworn for a possessor of intelligence?[89:5]

Hast thou not considered how thy Lord accomplished with Ad,[89:6] with Iram of the pillars[89:7] of which are not created the likes in the land?[89:8]

And with Thamud, those who hollowed out the rocks in the valley?[89:9]

And with Pharaoh, the possessor of the stakes,[89:10] those who were defiant in the land[89:11] and made much corruption in it?[89:12]

So thy Lord unloosed on them a scourge of punishment.[89:13] Truly, thy Lord is, surely, on the watch.[89:14]

Then, as for the human being, when his Lord tested him and honored him and lauded him, he says: My Lord honored me.[89:15]

But whenever He tested him and constricted his provision for him, he says: My Lord despised me.[89:16]

No indeed! Nay! You honor not the orphan[89:17] and you encouraged not one another about food for the needy[89:18] and you consume the inheritance, a greedy consuming,[89:19] and you love wealth with an ardent cherishing.[89:20]

No indeed! When the earth will be ground to powder, ground to powder, ground to powder,[89:21] and thy Lord will draw near, and the angels, ranged in rows,[89:22] on the Day hell is brought about. On that Day the human being will recollect.

And how will the reminder be for him?[89:23] He will say: O would that I had put forward from this life for the world to come![89:24]

Then, on that Day, He will punish no one the like of His punishment.[89:25] And no one will bind as His restraints.[89:26] O soul, one that is at peace![89:27]

Return to thy Lord, one that is well-pleasing, well-pleased:[89:28] Enter thou among My servants[89:29] and thou enter My Garden![89:30]

CHAPTER 90 THE LAND

In the Name of God, The Merciful, The Compassionate

I swear an oath by this land[90:1] thou art allowed in this land[90:2] and by ones who are your parents and what is procreated,[90:3] truly, We created the human being in trouble.[90:4]

Assumes he that none has power over him?[90:5]

He says: I have caused abundant wealth to perish.[90:6]

Assumes he that none sees him?[90:7]

Make we not two eyes for him[90:8] and a tongue and two lips[90:9] and guided him to the two open highways?[90:10]

Yet he rushed not onto the steep ascent.[90:11]

What will cause thee to recognize what the steep ascent is?[90:12]

It is the liberating of a bondsperson[90:13] or feeding on a day possessing famine[90:14] an orphan, possessor of kinship,[90:15] or a needy, possessor of misery.[90:16]

Again, it had been among those who believed and counseled one another to having patience and counseled one another to clemency.[90:17]

Those will be the Companions of the Right.[90:18]

But they who were ungrateful for Our signs they will be the Companions of the Left[90:19] and over them will be fire, that which is closing in.[90:20]

CHAPTER 91 THE SUN

In the Name of God, The Merciful, The Compassionate

By the sun and its forenoon[91:1] and by the moon when it related to it[91:2] and by the daytime when it displayed it[91:3] and by the nighttime when it overcomes it[91:4] and by the heaven and what built it[91:5] and by the earth and what widened it[91:6] and by the soul and what shaped it[91:7] and, then, inspired it to its acting immorally and God-consciousness,[91:8] he who made it pure prospered.[91:9]

Surely, is frustrated whoever seduced it.[91:10]

Thamud denied because of their overboldness.[91:11] When the disappointed among them were aroused,[91:12] and the Messenger of God said to them: Allow watering to the she-camel of God.[91:13] Then, they denied him; then, they crippled her. So their Lord doomed them for their impiety.[91:14] Then, He leveled them. And He fears not its Ultimate End.[91:15]

CHAPTER 92 THE NIGHT

In the Name of God, The Merciful, The Compassionate

By the nighttime when it overcomes,[92:1] by the daytime when it self-disclosed,[92:2] by Him Who created the male and the female,[92:3] truly, your endeavoring is diverse.[92:4]

As for him who gave and was Godfearing[92:5] and established the fairer as true,[92:6] We will make easy for him the easing.[92:7]

And as for him who was a miser and was self-sufficient[92:8] and denied the fairer,[92:9] We will make falling into difficulty easy for him.[92:10]

And his wealth will not avail him when he succumbed.[92:11] Truly, guidance is from Us[92:12] and, truly, to Us belongs the last and the first.[92:13]

I warned you of a fire that blazes fiercely.⁹²:¹⁴ It roasts none but the vile⁹²:¹⁵ who denied and turned away.⁹²:¹⁶ But the devout will be caused to turn aside from it.⁹²:¹⁷

He who gives of his wealth to purify himself,⁹²:¹⁸ and with him there is none for which recompense is expected to be given for divine blessing,⁹²:¹⁹ but looking for the Countenance of his Lord, The Lofty,⁹²:²⁰ he will be well-pleased.⁹²:²¹

CHAPTER 93 THE FORENOON

In the Name of God, The Merciful, The Compassionate

By the forenoon⁹³:¹ and by the night when it brooded,⁹³:² thy Lord deserted thee not, nor is He in hatred of thee.⁹³:³

Truly, the last will be better for thee than the first.⁹³:⁴

And thy Lord will give to thee. Then, thou wilt be well-pleased.⁹³:⁵

Found He thee not an orphan and He gave thee refuge?⁹³:⁶ And found He thee one who goes astray, then, He guided thee?⁹³:⁷

And found He thee one who wants, then, He enriched thee?⁹³:⁸

So as for the orphan, oppress him not.⁹³:⁹

And as for one who begs, scold him not.⁹³:¹⁰

And as for the divine blessing of thy Lord, divulge it!⁹³:¹¹

CHAPTER 94 THE EXPANSION

In the Name of God, The Merciful, The Compassionate

Expand We not thy breast⁹⁴:¹ and lifted from thee the heavy loaded burden,⁹⁴:² that weighed heavily on thy back?⁹⁴:³

Exalted We not thy remembrance?⁹⁴:⁴ So, truly, with hardship, ease.⁹⁴:⁵ Truly, with hardship, ease.⁹⁴:⁶

When thou hadst finished thy duties, then, work on supplication,⁹⁴:⁷ and quest thy Lord.⁹⁴:⁸

CHAPTER 95 THE FIG

In the Name of God, The Merciful, The Compassionate

By the fig and the olive⁹⁵:¹ and by Mount Sinai⁹⁵:² and by this trustworthy land,⁹⁵:³ truly, We have created the human being of the fairer symmetry.⁹⁵:⁴

Again, We returned him to the lowest of the low.⁹⁵:⁵

But those who believed and did as the ones in accord with morality, for them is compensation, that which is unfailing.⁹⁵:⁶

What will cause thee to deny the Judgment after that?⁹⁵:⁷

Is not God The Most Just of ones who judge?⁹⁵:⁸

CHAPTER 96 THE BLOOD CLOT

In the Name of God, The Merciful, The Compassionate

Recite in the Name of thy Lord Who created.⁹⁶:¹ He created the human being from a clot.⁹⁶:²

Recite: Thy Lord is the Most Generous,⁹⁶:³ He Who taught by the pen.⁹⁶:⁴ He taught the human being what he knows not.⁹⁶:⁵

No indeed! The human being is, truly, defiant.⁹⁶:⁶ He considered himself self-sufficient.⁹⁶:⁷

Truly, to thy Lord is the returning.⁹⁶:⁸

Hast thou thyself considered he who prohibits⁹⁶:⁹ a servant when he invoked blessings?⁹⁶:¹⁰

Hast thou considered if he had been on guidance⁹⁶:¹¹ or commanded God-consciousness?⁹⁶:¹²

Hast thou considered if he denied and turned away?⁹⁶:¹³ Knows he not that God sees?⁹⁶:¹⁴

No indeed! Truly, if he refrains himself not, We will, surely, lay hold of him by the forelock,⁹⁶:¹⁵ a lying, inequitable forelock. ⁹⁶:¹⁶

And let him call to his conclave.⁹⁶:¹⁷ We will call to the guards of hell.⁹⁶:¹⁸

No indeed! Truly, obey thou him not but prostrate thyself to God and be near to Him.⁹⁶:¹⁹

CHAPTER 97 THE NIGHT OF POWER

In the Name of God, The Merciful, The Compassionate

Truly, We caused it to descend on the night of power.⁹⁷:¹

And what will cause thee to recognize what is the night of power?⁹⁷:²

The night of power is better than a thousand months.⁹⁷:³ The angels come forth and the Spirit during it with their Lord's permission, with every command.⁹⁷:⁴ Peace it is until the time of the rising dawn.⁹⁷:⁵

CHAPTER 98 THE CLEAR PORTENT

In the Name of God, The Merciful, The Compassionate

Not would those who were ungrateful from among the People of the Book, nor the ones who are polytheists to be ones who set aside their beliefs until the clear portent approaches them⁹⁸:¹ A Messenger from God, who recounts to them purified scrolls⁹⁸:² wherein are truth-loving Books.⁹⁸:³ Split up not among themselves those to whom the Book was given until after the clear portent drew near them.⁹⁸:⁴ They were commanded but to worship God as ones who are sincere and devoted in the way of life to Him, as monotheists and they perform the formal prayer and they give the purifying alms. That is the truth-loving way of life.⁹⁸:⁵

Truly, those who were ungrateful among the People of the Book and the ones who are polytheists will be in the fire of hell, ones who will dwell in it forever. Those are the worst of creatures.⁹⁸:⁶

But those who believed and did as the ones in accord with morality, those are the best of creatures.⁹⁸:⁷ Their recompense is with their Lord—Gardens of Eden, beneath which rivers run, ones who will dwell in them forever, eternally. God was well-pleased with them and they were well-pleased with Him. That is for him who dreaded his Lord.⁹⁸:⁸

CHAPTER 99 THE CONVULSION

In the Name of God, The Merciful, The Compassionate

When the earth will be convulsed with a convulsion,⁹⁹:¹ and the earth brought out its ladings⁹⁹:² and the human being said: What is with it?⁹⁹:³

On that Day it will divulge its news⁹⁹:⁴ for your Lord revealed it.⁹⁹:⁵

On that Day humanity will issue, separately, that they may be caused to see their actions.⁹⁹:⁶ And whoever does the weight of an atom of good will see it.⁹⁹:⁷ And whoever does the weight of an atom of the worst will see it.⁹⁹:⁸

CHAPTER 100 THE CHARGERS

In the Name of God, The Merciful, The Compassionate

By the chargers, panting,[100:1] by ones who strike a fire, striking fire,[100:2] by the ones who are raiders in the morning,[100:3] then, they plowed it to a trail of dust,[100:4] and they penetrated the center with it, a multitude.[100:5]

Truly, the human being is unthankful to his Lord.[100:6] And, truly, he is a witness to that.[100:7] And he is more severe in the cherishing of good.[100:8] Knows he not that when all that is in the graves will be scattered about[100:9] and will be shown forth what is in the breasts?[100:10] Truly, their Lord on that Day is Aware of them.[100:11]

CHAPTER 101 THE DISASTER

In the Name of God, The Merciful, The Compassionate

The Disaster![101:1] What is the Disaster?[101:2] And what will cause thee to recognize what the Disaster is?[101:3]

On a Day humanity will be like dispersed moths[101:4] and the mountains will be like plucked wool clusters.[101:5]

Then, for him whose balance was heavy will be[101:6] one whose life is pleasant, well-pleasing.[101:7]

But he whose balance was made light,[101:8] his abode of rest will be the pit.[101:9]

What will cause thee to recognize what it is?[101:10] It is a hot fire.[101:11]

CHAPTER 102 THE RIVALRY

In the Name of God, The Merciful, The Compassionate

Rivalry diverted you[102:1] until you stopped by the cemetery.[102:2] No indeed! You will know![102:3] Again, no indeed! You will know![102:4]

No indeed! If you will know with the knowledge of certainty,[102:5] you will, certainly, see hellfire.[102:6]

Again, you will see it with the eye of certainty.[102:7]

Again, you will, certainly, be asked on that day about the bliss.[102:8]

CHAPTER 103 BY TIME

In the Name of God, The Merciful, The Compassionate

By time through the ages,[103:1] truly, the human being is, surely, in a loss[103:2] but those who believed and did as the ones in accord with morality, and counseled one another to The Truth, and counseled one another to having patience.[103:3]

CHAPTER 104 THE SLANDERER

In the Name of God, The Merciful, The Compassionate

Woe to every slandering backbiter[104:1] who gathered wealth and counted it over and over![104:2] He assumes that his wealth made him immortal.[104:3]

No indeed! He will be cast forth into the Crusher.[104:4] And what will cause thee to recognize what the Crusher is?[104:5] It is the fire of God, that which is kindled eternally,[104:6] that puruses the minds,[104:7] that which will be closing in on them[104:8] with its pillars, ones that are outstretched.[104:9]

CHAPTER 105 THE ELEPHANT

In the Name of God, The Merciful, The Compassionate

Hast thou not considered what thy Lord accomplished with the Companions of the Elephant?[105:1]

Makes He not their cunning leading to nothing?[105:2]

And He sent upon them flocks of birds,[105:3] throwing at them rocks of baked clay.[105:4] Then, made He them like ones who are consumed by stalks of husked grain.[105:5]

CHAPTER 106 THE QURAYSH

In the Name of God, The Merciful, The Compassionate

For the solidarity of the Quraysh,[106:1] their solidarity is the winter and the summer travel.[106:2]

Let them worship the Lord of this House[106:3] Who fed them against hunger and secured them against fear.[106:4]

CHAPTER 107 ASSISTANCE

In the Name of God, The Merciful, The Compassionate

Hadst thou considered one who denies this way of life?[107:1] And that is he who drives away with force the orphan[107:2] and urges not to give food to the needy.[107:3]

So woe to ones who formally pray,[107:4] ones who are inattentive to their formal prayers,[107:5] those who make display,[107:6] yet they repulse giving the assistance.[107:7]

CHAPTER 108 THE ABUNDANCE

In the Name of God, The Merciful, The Compassionate

Truly, We gave thee the abundance.[108:1] So invoke blessings for thy Lord and make sacrifice.[108:2] Truly, the one who detests thee, he is the one who is cut off.[108:3]

CHAPTER 109 THE UNGRATEFUL

In the Name of God, The Merciful, The Compassionate

Say: O ones who are ungrateful![109:1] I worship not what you worship;[109:2] and you are not ones who worship what I worship.[109:3] And I am not one who worships what you worshipped.[109:4] And you are not ones who worship what I worship.[109:5] For you is your way of life, and for me is my way of life.[109:6]

CHAPTER 110 THE HELP

In the Name of God, The Merciful, The Compassionate

When the help of God drew near and the victory[110:1] and thou hadst seen humanity entering into the way of life of God in units,[110:2] then, glorify the praise of thy Lord and ask for His forgiveness. Truly, He had been ever The Accepter of Repentance.[110:3]

CHAPTER 111
ROPE OF PALM FIBERS

In the Name of God, The Merciful, The Compassionate
Ruined were the hands of Abu Lahab and he was ruined.[111:1] His wealth availed him not nor whatever he earned.[111:2] He will roast in a fire, possessing flames[111:3] and his woman, the carrier of firewood,[111:4] around her long neck is a rope of palm fibers.[111:5]

CHAPTER 112
THE SINCERE EXPRESSION

In the Name of God, The Merciful, The Compassionate
Say: He is God, One,[112:1] God, the Everlasting Refuge.[112:2] He procreated not nor was He procreated[112:3] and there be not anything comparable with Him.[112:4]

CHAPTER 113 THE DAYBREAK

In the Name of God, The Merciful, The Compassionate
Say: I take refuge with the Lord of Daybreak[113:1]
from the worst of things that He created[113:2]
and from the worst of the darkness of the night when the dark intensified,[113:3]
and from the worst of the women who practice magic, blowing on the knots[113:4]
and from the worst of one who is jealous when jealous.[113:5]

CHAPTER 114 HUMANITY

In the Name of God, The Merciful, The Compassionate
Say: I take refuge with the Lord of humanity,[114:1]
King of humanity,[114:2]
God of humanity,[114:3]
from the worst of the sneaking whisperer of evil[114:4]
who whispers evil in the breasts of humanity,[114:5]
from among the genie and humanity.

epilogue

The Book of the People

T HE SCRIPTURES OF ABRAHAM'S FAMILY ARE PUBLISHED TOGETHER HERE FOR THE FIRST TIME. In this context they provide something of a paradigm shift, as understandings of Jewish monotheism, the Christian Savior and Islam's People of the Book are each presented in new light for our mutual consideration. Among Jews, Christians and Muslims, attempts at mutual understanding based on history have largely failed, since each group has its own ingrained historical perspective on events like the Crusades, much less more recent history. Attempts based on culture have likewise proven futile when practices seen as unacceptable in others are set in the context of questionable practices of one's own (female genital circumcision being no more specifically Muslim than breast augmentation is specifically Christian or Jewish, but the reasons for such practices in each culture are abhorrent to others, while their own practices are regarded as benign or desirable). Even attempts at reciprocal understanding based on the study of each other's religions, as evolved historically and culturally, have been undertaken in the face of defensive posturing and bigotry—no examples being necessary since everyone has some such story. The attempts at reciprocity based on an appreciation of each other's Scripture are more basic, and they are possibly laden with greater potential. As the first instance in which the Torah, Gospel and Quran have been published together in a mutually appreciative context, the general response of contributors, collaborators and first reviewers has been acknowledgment that this exercise succeeds in expanding the appreciation of each reader's own tradition, as well as promoting a positive reception of the related traditions.

We would dare hope that in a modest manner, *Three Testaments* may be regarded as "the book of the people" for "the people of the book," at least as it witnesses to that ineffable Word of God that is embodied in the people for Jews as reported in the Torah, embodied in Jesus Christ for Christians as reported in the Gospel and embodied in the very breath of the recitation for Muslims as reported in the Quran. At the same time, this book may be of interest in linking East and West as Jews, Christians and Muslims reconnect with Zoroastrians, traditionally identified as also being people of the book, as reported in the Avesta, extending through Zoroaster to all people of the world.

The discovery of the Cyrus Cylinder in 1879 transformed the tradition of that monarch's emphasis on human rights from its image as an idealistic myth to a fact of history. At about the same time, Heinrich Schliemann discovered the city of Troy, excavating the site between 1871 and 1873, proving to the world that Homer's "mythical" *Iliad* was based on events that actually happened in history. In research from 2008 to 2011, University of Hartford professor Richard Freund claimed to have matched the city map of Atlantis described in Plato's *Timaeus* to satellite photos of circles in a swampy field north of Cadiz in Spain, discovering what is increasingly regarded as the ruins of the "mythical" Atlantis, obliterated by a tsunami. In a manner similar to these discoveries, this book puts skin and bone to the almost mythical figure of Zoroaster and demonstrates the impact of Zoroastrianism on the Torah, the Gospel and the Quran at various levels of our excavation.

We know that Schliemann destroyed some of the evidence in his clumsy but successful dig, and we realize that years of painstaking research must now go into the excavation of the putative site of Atlantis. So we humbly acknowledge that careful work also lies ahead for scholars (1) to verify that Zoroaster got his monotheism from Israeli exiles in the time of the prophet, Jeremiah; (2) to recognize that the travels of Jesus in Zoroastrian territory impacted his messianic mission, whether or not he ever reached India; and (3) to verify that the Sabaeans in the Quran are Zoroastrians whose beliefs are critiqued both positively and negatively in the Quran, which itself confirms both the monotheism of the Jews and the messianic title of Jesus as the precursor of judgment for the whole world, rather than as merely the restorer of the throne of David. In this particular "dig," we recall our allusion to the astronauts in space who can see the outlines of Roman villages in Britain, and we recognize that the harvest in this Scriptural quest will be eventually reaped by "scholar-farmers" who know every stick and stone on this landscape but have not yet seen the outlines of what we have observed from a great distance.

We avoided any seeming syncretism of Judaism, Christianity and Islam in this book by using the format of Books One, Two and Three to appreciate both the links and the differences between these three related religions. But we might finally welcome some greater understanding of what they share with each other.

For example, in the first place the three are united in monotheism and in opposition to polytheism in general, and to dualism in particular. The central Zoroastrian concept that human beings are continually faced with a choice between the paths of "good" and "evil," represented by the contrasting figures of Ahura Mazda and Ahriman (or Satan) has inspired thinkers as diverse as François-Marie Arouet Voltaire, Wolfgang Amadeus Mozart and Friedrich Nietzsche in recent centuries. Some may contend that Zoroastrianism does not degenerate into dualism but rather develops into balance, suggesting that there is no difference between right and wrong, only "what is" or "reality." Others of Oriental Vedic heritage contend that both good and evil are illusions. Neither of these represents what Jews, Christians and Muslims believe, nor what Zoroaster himself believed. Jews, Christians and Muslims do believe in right and wrong, rather than either relativism or illusion, and they also believe that right and wrong are not defined in terms of utilitarianism, government policy, majority consensus or self-serving pleasure. Jews, Christians and Muslims believe that right and wrong are defined by a justice that is pleasing to God, to whose will believers must sincerely subscribe, beginning with the study of Scriptures revealed by God.

Second, Jews, Christians and Muslims all believe that their one God is both Creator and Redeemer, ultimately blessing all who put their trust in God's mercy and grace. Since Second Isaiah, Jews have seen God specifically as Redeemer. Christians see the redemptive action of God in Jesus Christ. In the Quran the redemption motif appears consistently in the "*Basmala* phrase," which recurs in 113 of 114 chapters as "In the name of God, Most Gracious, Most Merciful" (*b-ismi-llāhi r-raḥmāni r-raḥ īmi*), recited also in the daily prayers of Muslims.

Third, Judaism, Christianity and Islam are united in acceptance and promotion of the original and seminal Zoroastrian belief that time is linear, rather than cyclical or meandering, and that it progresses toward a purpose or goal in the community of God (Holy Nation, Kingdom of God, City of God or Ummah) in paradise, the objective toward which believers are called to work on earth. For better or worse, this is the origin of the Western view of progress that eluded the Orient until Islamic and European empires and communism (with its Judeo-Christian perspective of history) grafted it onto Indian, Chinese and other political and economic systems.

The contextual commentaries of this book have premised that in addition to being a key link between Judaism, Christianity and Islam, Zoroastrianism also links Western monotheism with the main religions of the Orient: Buddhism, Hinduism and others. We may not yet be as ready or as able to articulate these connections as we have been able to do with Judaism, Christianity and Islam, but we do know now that Rudyard Kipling was wrong when he said, "East is east and west is west and never the twain shall meet." They met eons ago in Persia, they separated for millennia and they are destined to get reacquainted in the twenty-first century.

Simply put in summary, out of his revelatory experience Zoroaster took the Aryan "aboriginal" understanding of the Divine, as Brahmanic tradition had already begun to refine it, and made it personal in ways that could later be applied to the spectrum of religious communities, both within and beyond the fringes of the Persian Empire, over the next hundred years. Creaturely dependence was replaced by partnership with the Divine in a phenomenon that spread like wildfire in what has come to be known as the Axial Age. Zoroaster was the axis of the Axial Age. Now that his dates are increasingly accepted as 628–551 BCE, we realize that in all probability Zoroaster also had personal experience, direct or indirect, with monotheistic Israel, making monotheism the starting point of his reforms.

As the connection between pre-Zoroastrian Indo-Oriental religions and post-Zoroastrian Occidental religions becomes more apparent in reference to their common Vedic ancestor, we may be able to speak at last of "world religion" rather than "world religions." Properly understood, religion may now be seen as one vast system of oceans around the world, each with different temperatures and powerful currents of their own. The Arctic Ocean is not the South Pacific, and we cannot imagine them becoming the same. Indeed, each ocean has an essential and unique role to play in the ecosystem, but all are connected. Likewise, religious currents contribute to each other in important ways in the twenty-first century, not as inland lakes completely separated from each other, but as interrelated bodies of vast spiritual oceans.

This separate ocean metaphor means respect for Jews who do not seek to convert others, and who do not wish to be assimilated into other religious cultures, but it also means that the world might more gratefully recognize the source of monotheism as treasured by most of humanity. It means that Christians might be share the warm currents from Israel's most famous son without hoping that Jews will become swallowed in the Christian ocean, or that Muslims will "join the church" as the outcome of evangelism, but rather "follow" the Jesus whom they already know and love in ways appropriate for them. Muslims have the great challenge of living up to the Quran in this new era of mutual respect and understanding by acknowledging that Islam is by no means the only valid religion and that others must be given generous respect in political and social life in both Muslim-majority cultures and mixed societies where Muslims are in the minority.

People ask about the future of religion in a skeptical age in which books on atheism abound. In fact, as Salman Rushdie once put it, "atheists are obsessed with God,"[1] and while some believers are prepared to dialogue constructively with intellectual atheism, its current proponents appear to offer little advance beyond the classic views of Sigmund Freud, Karl Marx, Friedrich Nietzsche and Bertrand Russell. Conversations about the question of the existence of transcendence could be helpful. For example, is Transcendence the Divinity, as opposed to the tyrant in the sky so rightly rejected by modern atheists? Does this Transcendence exert magnetism toward some purpose or order that may include a human destiny? Does this Transcendence somehow invite human partnership? Can Transcendence even act redemptively in relation to mortals? Instead of such a discussion, a seeming deterioration in godless philosophy appears in the form of an increased vitriol against organized religion. This may be attributed to abhorrence of the way many Jews, Christians and Muslims live their religion, but it does little to advance the discussion, and believers themselves frequently exhibit a similar unworthy testiness toward atheists.[2]

If we could differentiate between those "practicing no religion" and "atheists," the latter appear limited to elderly white males in eastern North America and Northern Europe, as represented by authors and media spokespersons of such a movement. Few women are atheists, and the African American comedic commentator, D. L. Hughley, has remarked more than once that he has "never met a black atheist,"[3] an observation that, while not literally true, might be as valid in Africa as it is in America. Practically no atheists can be found in India, and formerly atheistic China appears to be moving headlong into belief, even as Russia recovers its faith perspective. In the meanwhile, the world has changed in the twenty-first century, and the religious constituency is in the process of learning how to accommodate the changes and to accommodate each other. The understanding of each other's Scriptures may be one way to learn to cherish each other.

Indeed, the growth of religion may be one of the most important sociopolitical facts of the twenty-first century. Tony Blair, the former prime minister of Great Britain, described this phenomenon on a world tour introducing and establishing his Faith Foundation:

> For years, it was assumed, certainly in the West, that, as society developed, religion would wither away. But it hasn't and, at the start of a new decade, it is time for policy-makers to take religion seriously. The number of people proclaiming their faith worldwide is growing.

Blair could have used the examples of Judaism, Hinduism or Buddhism, but because they are more in the news of late, he continued by referencing Islam and Christianity:

> This is clearly so in the Islamic world. Whereas Europe's birth rate is stagnant, the Arab population is set to double in the coming decades, and the population will also rise in many of the Asian Muslim-majority countries. Christianity is also growing rapidly—in odd ways and in surprising places. Religion's largest growth is in China. There are more Muslims in China than in Europe. There are more Protestants in China than in England. There are more Catholics in China than in Italy.[4]

Blair goes on to talk of the booming religions of Africa and South America before turning to the burgeoning spirituality of North America and Europe in the face of a seeming decline in "organized religion." Since spirituality usually gets organized, the decline may be a temporary phenomenon, just like the collapse of organized religion in Russia nearly one hundred years ago and the dissolution of "missions" in China just over fifty years ago. Both of these might now be seen as passing phenomena related to political and social upheavals rather than changes in human nature.

Yet religion remains problematic in our time. At the beginning of the twenty-first century, the family of Abraham, Sarah and Hagar is associated with many of the world's most serious problems and conflicts, and "there is no feud like a family feud." The Jews are paranoid about their security, and they have every reason to be so, given their experiences in history, but their best friends are joining their own wisest commentators to urge a peaceful accommodation in a situation that must be resolved in the Middle East. Christians claim to follow Jesus as the "Prince of Peace," but they own more guns and "weapons of mass destruction" than anyone else, and it seems to many that they are too ready, too willing and too able to use them in "defense" of their geopolitical and economic interests. Muslims use the peaceful greeting of "Salam" even more often than Christians speak of peace or Jews of *Shalom*, but the brutality between Muslims is as regrettable as the current association of the word *Islamic* with "extremism" or *Muslim* with "terrorism."

Part of the purpose of this book is to address these matters frankly and to seek remedial amelioration through understanding of the spiritual dynamics we derive from our Scriptures. Monotheism should now be seen as the particular and original hallmark of Judaism, supplanting the image of Jews as "God-killers" so abhorrently promoted by injudicious Christians. Christians themselves might assume a disposition of less talk and more action in a world that is now less disposed to find "the Savior of the World" in the words of preaching and argument than in the deeds of those who might simply model Jesus. It is now incumbent upon Muslims to appreciate the cultural mores of others who have submitted to God in other religious traditions, so that the Quran might be increasingly appreciated as confirming, critiquing and amplifying the previously revealed Scriptures in a context of mutual respect.

Finally, regarding the miniscule and still contracting Zoroastrian community in Iran, India and elsewhere in the world, we offer recognition from the extended family of Abraham, Sarah and Hagar to this continuing bridge between East and West. Zoroastrianism has more to present to the participants in this spiritual "trialogue" than has been acknowledged in this book. Judaism and Christianity have both benefited from continu-

An Ancient Image, Taken to Be That of Zoroaster

ing scholarly investigations of the historicity of their principal figures, Moses and Jesus, and there have been more works written on the life of Muhammad in the first decade of the twenty-first century than in the whole previous century. We now call for a quest for the historical Zoroaster as a feature of the next era. This would happen in conjunction with a quest to find complete copies of the Avesta material prior to the time of Alexander the Great and copies of the Avesta material existing in the time of Christ and in the time of Muhammad. This is entirely possible, and even likely, though we may not get the full picture, even when the Avesta is found, any more than we did during those other historical quests. But we may gain spiritual insight in the process and contribute to the reconnecting of the dysfunctional family of Abraham, Sarah and Hagar with each other, and with their first and second cousins further east in India, China and elsewhere. "The people of the book" may someday appreciate "the book of the people" in its manifestations in every age and in all parts of the world.

notes

foreword

1. Quran 3:7.
2. Ibid., 3:7. See also the Pickthall scholarly interpretation where this term is rendered "allegorical."
3. John Porter, *The Vertical Mosaic*, 519.
4. Jews, Muslims and others wary of conversations with Christians might Google "A Song of Faith" or visit www.united -church.ca/beliefs/statements/songfaith to find an acceptable starting point for such interfaith discussions, based on an engaging poetic exposition of this creed.
5. Deuteronomy 6:4.
6. The first pillar of Islam.
7. Mark 12:29.

prologue

1. The standard Yusuf Ali English edition, for example, contains 6265 footnotes.
2. The method developed for *Good News for Modern Man* (*The Good News Bible*) of 1966 by the late Eugene Nida, who led the translation program of the American Bible Society for nearly fifty years.
3. While its parts were often identified as the JPS Version, the revised compendium of 1987 became known as the NJPS, for *New Jewish Publication Society* translation, or sometimes the NJV, for *New Jewish Version*.
4. A legal requirement in this case is fulfilled by the acknowledgment of these quotations by the endnote designation NRSV on the pages in which they occur.
5. Mathew 16, Mark 7 and elsewhere.
6. Ezekiel 37:1–6.
7. Jenny Rose, *Zoroastrianism* (London: I.B. Taurus, 2011), 58.

book one: torah

PREFACE TO THE TORAH

1. Midrash Tehillim 90:12.
2. Midrash Genesis Rabbah 1:1.
3. See *Forensic Scriptures* by Brian Arthur Brown, page 53, for the Hymn to Inanna as the earliest sacred feminist literature.
4. B. Eruvin 13b.

CHAPTER 1

1. Jeremiah 1:4–8, a prophetic utterance no doubt repeated many times, in the usual style of preachers, but actually fitting best here, when first uttered by the prophet as a young man.
2. Jeremiah 12:7–8.
3. Deuteronomy 6:4–7.
4. Jeremiah 18:13–14.
5. Arnold J. Toynbee, *A Study of History*, 387.
6. Jeremiah 17:15.
7. See Jeremiah 31:1–2.
8. Zadspram 20–21.
9. Yasna 31:8, 33:6–7, 43:5.
10. Denkard 7:3.2 and 7:3.8.
11. Yasna 33:6 and 13:94.
12. Genesis 5:27.
13. Genesis 9:29.
14. This delightful illustration was introduced by Jenny Brown to students in one of my seminary classes who were having difficulty recognizing the potential for confusion in the ancient world's change from lunar to solar dating.
15. See bibliographical references to Ernst E. Herzfeld, W. B. Henning, Gore Vidal, *The Journal of the American oriental Society* of 1994 and *The Bulletin of the School of Oriental and African Studies* of 1997.
16. Aryan dynamic creativity contributed to one of the most egregious errors in world history, the canard of the Aryan super "race." Aryan dynamism came from many factors, one being the aggressive absorption of widespread clans and tribes into an avaricious new hybrid gene pool. The Aryan "race" was anything but "pure," and its diversity was perhaps a source of strength. Hitler's Aryan "super race" mistake would have been comical, were it not tragic, like a child who hears his father say that their new dog is a mongrel and goes forth to boast to friends that his beloved pet is indeed a "pure mongrel." (Modern nations struggling with diversity might take note.) Aryans were connected more by language and inclusive religious developments than by race. The linguistic foundations of this connection have been documented as the precursor of Greek and Latin, with German, English and other offshoots, as well as Sanskrit, with Hindi, Persian and other off-shoots. This study may help establish the religious connection.
17. Ernest Brandewie, *Wilhelm Schmidt and the Origin of the Idea of God*.
18. Karen Armstrong, *The Great Transformation*, 8.
19. Daniel 8:16.
20. Luke 1:19.
21. Luke 1:26.
22. Quran 96:1–3.
23. Genesis 12:1.
24. Genesis 28:12.
25. Genesis 32:24–28.
26. Exodus 3:2.
27. Exodus 19.
28. Acts 9.
29. *Achsenseit* or "axistime" in Karl Jaspers, *Vom Ursprung und Ziel der Geschichte* (*Origin and Goal of History*), translated by Michael Bullock.
30. Jaspers's use of the German word *Achse* is translated equally well as "axis" or "pivot."

CHAPTER 2

1. Daniel 5.
2. William Barclay, *The Revelation of John*, vol. 1, 122.
3. II Chronicles 36:22–23.
4. Ezra 5:17.
5. Ezra 6:2b–5.
6. Ezra 7:11–20.
7. Flavius Josephus, *Antiquities of the Jews*, 382–87.
8. Yasna 27:13.
9. Isaiah 45:1–7.

10. Ezra 1:1–4.
11. Genesis 1.
12. The Creation as summarized in Yajurveda Taittiriya Upanishad 1–2–1.
13. Richard Elliott Friedman, *The Bible with Sources Revealed*.
14. Herodotus, *The Histories*, chapters 1 and 7.
15. Ronald G. Kent, *Old Persian Grammar, Texts, Lexicon*, 2nd rev. ed.
16. Herodotus, *The Histories*, chapter 7.
17. Nehemiah 5:14 and 10:1.
18. Ezra 7:11–26.
19. Nehemiah 8:1.
20. See also *Who Wrote the Bible?* by Richard Elliott Friedman.

CHAPTER 3

1. Conversations with Mary Boyce in October 2005.
2. Exodus 3:14, 15, King James Version, most other versions and translated as such in footnotes to these verses in the Tanakh, which transliterates the original Ehweh-Asher-Ehyeh (I Am That I Am) and Ehweh (I Am) in the text itself.
3. An insight that is featured in several books by Richard Elliott Friedman, listed in the bibliography.
4. H. P. Blavatsky, *Theosophical Glossary*, 168.
5. Ibid., 167.
6. Steve Mason, "Did the Essenes Write the Dead Sea Scrolls? Don't Rely on Josephus," *Biblical Archaeology Review* 34, no. 6 (November/December 2008).
7. V:1–VI:23.
8. Jacob Neusner, *A History of the Jews in Babylonia* (Leiden: E. J. Brill, 1969), especially volume 4.
9. Brochure of Center for Jewish Studies, UCLA, May 6–7, 2007.
10. Douglas Roper Krotz, *The Man Who Sent the Magi*.
11. Carol Meyers and Eric Meyers, *Haggai, Zechariah 1–8* and *Zechariah 9–14*.
12. Carol Meyers and Eric Meyers, *Haggai, Zechariah 1–8*, 9.
13. Ibid., 10.
14. Ibid., 9.
15. Ibid., 9, where Meyers contends that *Zeru* is merely the Jewish East Semetic equivalent of the Babylonian-area West Semetic *Zera*.
16. "The Life of Thomas Edison," MemoryLoc.gov, accessed at http://memory.loc.gov/ammem/edhtml/edbio.html.
17. "History of Mazda," ILoveIndia.com, accessed at http://lifestyle.iloveindia.com/lounge/history-of-mazda-8927.html.

CHAPTER 4

1. This argument was developed in Brown, *Forensic Scriptures*, 57, 60–63.
2. Daniel 12:2.
3. Matthew 22:23.
4. Haggai 2:11–13.
5. Haggai 2:21.
6. Hebrews 12:26.
7. Ezra 6:14–15.
8. Nehemiah 12:4.
9. Zechariah 6:1–14.
10. Conversations, January 2006.
11. Malachi 1:11.
12. Isaiah 1–39.
13. Flavius Josephus, *Antiquities of the Jews* 11:5–7.
14. Isaiah 40–55.
15. Isaiah 40:1 (King James Version).
16. Isaiah 41:2.
17. Isaiah 52:9–10.

18. Isaiah 52:11; see also Ezra 1:7–8 and 5:14–15.

19. Isaiah 56–66.

20. Yasna 44.3:4–5.

21. Isaiah 40:26.

22. Yasna 44.4:1–3.

23. Isaiah 40:12.

24. Yasna 44.5:1–3.

25. Isaiah 45:7.

26. Nehemiah 2:1–8.

27. Joseph H. Peterson, ed., *Avestan Dictionary* (1995): m. benefactor, strengthener, saviour, redeemer [lit. "who sets about benefitting, etc."] (Hum 11); beneficent (lit.); a prophet, religious leader; future savior or messiah (k517).

28. For example, see John Barton in an entry on "Source Criticism," in David Noel Friedman et al., *The Anchor Bible Dictionary*, vol. 6.

29. Conversations with Mary Boyce, January 2006, in support of her observations in her 1982 *History of Zoroastrianism*, then in revision despite her ill health.

30. Job 1:6 and 2:1.

31. Job 19:25 King James Version, familiar phraseology from Handel's *Messiah*.

32. Job 19:26.

33. Isaiah 45:1.

INTRODUCTION TO THE TORAH

1. Genesis 11:27.

2. "The Ten Sayings" are often misnamed "The Ten Commandments"; "I the LORD am your God" is the first saying of the Decalogue according to Talmudic and later Jewish tradition, but these words are not phrased as a commandment. Thus, the name *The Ten Commandments* assumes a non-Jewish stance.

3. Genesis 2:2–3.

4. Exodus 25–40.

5. Proverbs 1:8.

6. Exodus 24:18; 34:28; Deuteronomy 9:9; 10:10.

7. See, for example, Otto Eissfeldt, *The Old Testament: An Introduction* (New York: Harper & Row, 1965), 159.

8. See Thomas Hobbes, *Leviathan* (New York: Barnes and Noble, 2004), 248–56 (ch. 33), and Baruch Spinoza, *Tractatus Theologico-Politicus* (Leiden: Brill, 1991), 14–172 (chs. 7–8).

9. Julius Wellhausen, *Prolegomena to the History of Ancient Israel* (Gloucester, MA: Peter Smith, 1973).

10. Traditional Jews, already from the early postbiblical period, do not pronounce the name *Yahweh*, viewing it as too holy, and they replace it with *Adonai*, which means "my Lord."

11. Most biblical verses are divided into two parts, with "a" representing the first, and "b" the second.

12. Genesis 9:11.

13. Exodus 21:6.

14. Deuteronomy 15:17.

15. Leviticus 25.

16. Leviticus 25:40.

17. Genesis 3:8.

18. Genesis 3:21.

19. See Genesis 1.

20. Deuteronomy 4:12.

21. Deuteronomy 12:11.

22. See especially Deuteronomy 12.

23. Even the Babylonian Laws of Hammurabi, which predate the Bible, are now recognized as a collection rather than a code; see the title of Martha T. Roth, *Law Collections from Mesopotamia and Asia Minor* (Atlanta: Scholars Press, 1995).

24. Leviticus 19:2.

25. See Exodus 15:20–21.

26. See the survey of Jean-Loius Ska, *Introduction to Reading the Pentateuch* (Winona Lake: Eisenbrauns, 2006), and Reinhard G. Kratz, *The Composition of the Narrative Books of the Old Testament* (London: T & T Clark, 2000), who speaks only of Priestly and non-Priestly material.

27. See Numbers 21:14, 27.
28. As elaborated by Brian Arthur Brown in chapters 3 and 4.
29. Genesis 2–3.
30. Genesis 6–9.
31. Genesis 11:1–9.
32. Numbers 36:13.
33. Genesis 12:2–3.
34. Leviticus 19:18b.
35. Leviticus 26.
36. Deuteronomy 34:10–11.
37. These states are known to us today as Lebanon, Syria and Jordan, and they appear by different names again in Book Two, possibly exerting a similar influence on the ideas formulating in the Christian Scriptures.
38. An instructive, if perhaps extraneous, example of the kind of "linguistic markers" used by Brian Arthur Brown to identify Zoroastrian key words used in the Hebrew, Christian and Muslim Scriptures.
39. The *Shema* contains three paragraphs of the Torah, beginning with Deuteronomy 6:4–9; it became a standard statutory prayer late in the Second Temple period.
40. A dialogue fully developed by Brown in chapter 4.
41. Exodus 20:3; Deuteronomy 5:7.
42. Deuteronomy 4:35, perhaps reflecting final Torah emendations following the experience in Exile in which the Jewish community had been influenced to return to a stricter articulation of the burning bush revelation.
43. Genesis 39:9.
44. The Second Temple, built from 520–516 BCE, was destroyed by the Romans in 70 CE.
45. Psalm 1:2.

book two: gospel

PREFACE TO THE GOSPEL

1. Luke 10:25–37.
2. Luke 15:11–32.
3. For example, Isaiah 51.
4. *Euangelion*: gospel.
5. Genesis 1:1–2:4a and Genesis 2:4b–2:25.

CHAPTER 5

1. Matthew 2:1–12.
2. As in Matthew 4:15–16, John 19:37 and I Corinthians 15:54.
3. Flavius, *Antiquities of the Jews*, XVIII, 3.3.
4. Finalized as used today in 363 CE by the Council of Laodocia.
5. Matthew 22:36–40.
6. Deuteronomy 6:5.
7. Leviticus 19:18.
8. Deuteronomy 8:3 as quoted by Northrop Frye, *Double Vision: Language and Meaning in Religion* (Toronto: University of Toronto Press, 1991), 7.
9. Genesis 2:8–9.
10. Revelation 21:2 and 22:1–2.
11. Luke 1:17.
12. Quran 3, commented upon by Frye in *The Great Code: The Bible and Literature* (Orlando, FL: First Harvest Edition, 1982), 172.
13. Luke 1:46–56.
14. I Samuel 2:1–12.
15. By a female writer, according to Marc Brettler, in "A Woman's Voice in the Psalter: A New Understanding of Psalm 113," *Biblical Archaeological Review* (May/June 2008): 28.
16. Genesis 11:1–9.
17. Acts of the Apostles 2:1–12.

CHAPTER 6

1. John 21:25 New Revised Standard Version.

2. Jawaharlal Nehru, *Glimpses of World History*, 84.

3. Luke 2:12.

4. Luke 2:52 King James Version.

5. Luke 2:52 New Revised Standard Version.

6. Ibid., as in "Jesus increased in wisdom and in years, and in divine and human favour."

7. Bhavishyat Maha Purana 9:17–32.

8. In the Hindu Kush.

9. Son of God.

10. A name for *God* in Sanskrit.

11. Abubakr Salahuddin, *Saving the Savior: Did Christ Survive the Crucifixion?* (Kashmir, India: Jammu Press, 2000).

12. Edgar Goodspeed, *Modern Apocrypha: Famous Biblical Hoaxes* (Grand Rapids, MI: Baker Book House, 1956).

13. Swami Abhedananda, *Journey into Kashmir and Tibet (the English translation of Kashmiri o Tibbate)* (Calcutta: Ramakrishna Vivekananda Math, 1987).

14. Swami Satyasanganananda Saraswati, *Light on the Guru and Disciple Relationship* (Bihar, India: Bihar School of Yoga, 1984).

15. Elizabeth Clare Prophet, *The Lost Years of Jesus: Documentary Evidence of Jesus' 17-Year Journey to the East* (Gardiner, MT: Summit University Press, 1988), 468.

16. "Jesus, son of Joseph" in Aramaic.

17. "Son of Joseph" in Hindi.

18. Luke 2:47 New Revised Standard Version.

19. Luke 2:48 New Revised Standard Version.

20. Luke 2:49 New Revised Standard Version.

21. Luke 4:22 New Revised Standard Version.

22. Mark 6:2 New Revised Standard Version (our italics).

23. Matthew 13:55–56 New Revised Standard Version.

24. Luke 2:51 New Revised Standard Version.

25. John 4:6–26.

26. As will be shown later, the Muslim Hadith records the tradition of memories of Jesus in the Damascus region, and we will shortly submit the Christian Scriptural references to that effect.

27. Mark 7:24–30.

28. Mark 7:24 New Revised Standard Version.

29. Loose translation of Mark 7 and more explicit in the Matthew 15 parallel.

30. Matthew 16:13–23 New Revised Standard Version, Mark 8:27–33 New Revised Standard Version and Luke 9:18–22 New Revised Standard Version ("who do the crowds say that I am?").

31. Luke 8:26 New Revised Standard Version.

32. Luke 8:40 New Revised Standard Version.

33. Matthew 17:1–13, Mark 9:2–9 and Luke 9:28–36 New Revised Standard Version.

34. Deepak Chopra, *Jesus*.

35. As also at Matthew 11:21.

36. Luke 4:24–26 New Revised Standard Version.

37. Luke 4:27 New Revised Standard Version.

38. Luke 10:13 New Revised Standard Version.

39. John 6:35, 41, 48–51 New Revised Standard Version.

40. John 8:12 and 9:5 New Revised Standard Version.

41. John 10:7–9.

42. John 10:11–14 New Revised Standard Version.

43. John 11:25 New Revised Standard Version.

44. John 14:6 New Revised Standard Version.

45. John 15:1–5 New Revised Standard Version.

46. John 8:51 New Revised Standard Version.

47. John 8:52–53 New Revised Standard Version.

48. John 8:54–56 New Revised Standard Version.

49. John 8:57 New Revised Standard Version.

50. John 8:58 New Revised Standard Version.

51. John 14:6 New Revised Standard Version.
52. Brent Landau, *Revelation of the Magi.*
53. Matthew 3:16; Mark 1:10; Luke 3:21 and John 1:32.
54. Job 33:24 New Revised Standard Version and Tanakh.
55. Matthew 20:28 and Mark 10:45 New Revised Standard Version.
56. Timothy 2:5–6 New Revised Standard Version.
57. Job 19:25, again in the familiar King James Version.
58. Mark 14:62 New Revised Standard Version.
59. Daniel 7:13 Tanakh.
60. John 8:12 and 9:5 New Revised Standard Version.
61. Luke 23:43 New Revised Standard Version.

CHAPTER 7

1. Exodus 12:5 Tanakh, a reference to Passover.
2. John 1:29 New Revised Standard Version, a reference to Jesus.
3. I Peter 1:18–19 New Revised Standard Version.
4. Sathpathbrahmana III.
5. Rig Veda 9:113.7–11.
6. Rig Veda 4:5.5 and 7:104.3.
7. Rig Veda 9:44.
8. Contra Celsus.
9. In a lengthy inscription on the cliff face at Bisutun, just east of Kermanshah on the principal route through the mountains from Baghdad to Tehran, Darius reminds passersby of how Ahura Mazda helped him consolidate power by defeating Gaumata and banishing a form of the emerging religion that looks suspiciously like Buddhism.
10. Luke 2:46 New Revised Standard Version.
11. Philo, *On the Contemplative Life*, 1, published in 10 CE, found in all standard collections of Philo's works.
12. Will Durant and Ariel Durant, *The Story of Civilization: Our Oriental Heritage*, vol. 1 (New York: Simon and Schuster, 1935), 449.
13. Muller quoted in John R. Remsburg, *The Christ: A Critical Review and Analysis of the Evidences of His Existence* (New York: Truth Seeker Company, 1909), 510.
14. Quoted by Marcus Borg, *Jesus and Buddha,* 13.
15. Wilhelm Bousset, *Kyrios Christos* (english translation) (Nashville, TN: Abingdon Press, 1970), 245.
16. Richard Reitzenstein, *Poimandres* (Darmstadt: Wissenschaftliche Buchgesellschaft, 1966).
17. The famous *Religionsgeschichtliche Schule.*
18. Luke 2:22–33.
19. Sutta-Nipata 689–91.
20. Richard Garbe, *Indien und Das Christentum: Eine Untersuchung der Religions-Geschichtlichen Zusammenhänge* (Charleston, SC: Nabu Press, 2010), 49f.
21. Suttanipata Nalakasutta.
22. Numbers 3:13.
23. Dhammapada 10.1.
24. Luke 6:31 New Revised Standard Version.
25. Majjhima Nikaya 21.6.
26. Luke 6:29 New Revised Standard Version.
27. Udanavarga 27.1.
28. Luke 6:41 New Revised Standard Version.
29. Lalitavistara Sutra 18.
30. Luke 4:13 New Revised Standard Version.
31. Majjhima Nikaya 22.47.
32. Mark 13:31 New Revised Standard Version.
33. Anguttara Nikaya 6.24.
34. Mark 13:31 New Revised Standard Version.
35. Anguttara Nikaya 6.24.
36. Matthew 17:20 New Revised Standard Version.
37. Dhammapada 13.11.
38. Matthew 19:21 New Revised Standard Version.

39. Dhammapada 15.4.
40. Luke 6:20 New Revised Standard Version.
41. Sutta Nipata 149–50.
42. John 15:12–13 New Revised Standard Version.
43. Dhammapada 7.3–4.
44. Matthew 6:25–26 New Revised Standard Version.
45. Dhammapada 7.3–4.
46. Matthew 5:45 New Revised Standard Version.
47. Khuddakapatha 8.9.
48. Matthew 6:19–20 New Revised Standard Version.
49. Digha Nikaya 13.15.
50. Luke 6:39–40 New Revised Standard Version.
51. Borg, *Jesus and Buddha*, xvi.
52. Digha Nikaya 19.43.
53. Matthew 5:8 New Revised Standard Version.
54. Revelation 5:1–12.
55. Tin Htut, "Is Jesus a Buddhist?," in *The Perfection of Wisdom*, translated by R. C. Jamieson (London: The Book Studio, 2000).

CHAPTER 8

1. Introduction to *Deus Caritas Est.*
2. Quran 6:101.
3. Quran 19:89–92.
4. Matthew 8:20; 9:6; 10:23; 12:8, 32, 40; 13:37, 41; 16:27, 28; 17:9, 12, 22; 18:11; 19:28; 20:18, 28; 24:27, 30, 37, 39, 44; 25:31; 26:2, 24, 45; Matthew parallels in Mark and Luke, plus John 1:51; 5:27; 6:27, 62; 8:28; 9:35; 12:23; and 13:31 New Revised Standard Version.
5. Matthew 1:20 New Revised Standard Version.
6. John 1:12 King James Version.
7. Luke 3:38.
8. Exodus 4:22.
9. Psalms 2:7.
10. Matthew 28:19 New Revised Standard Version.
11. II Corinthians 13:13 New Revised Standard Version.
12. Quran 4:171.
13. Quran 5:76.
14. Quran 5:119.
15. Edward Hulmes, "Qur'an and the Bible, The," entry in the *Oxford Companion to the Bible.*
16. David Thomas, "Trinity," in the *Encyclopaedia of the Qur'ān.*
17. Some, including Todd Lawson and Nevin Reda at the University of Toronto, prefer the word *duality.* See Todd Lawson, "Duality, Opposition and Typology in the Qur'an: The Apocalyptic Substrate," 23–49.
18. Christian theologians and other critics may mistake this for "modalism," an ancient heresy limiting God to one persona at a time, whereas the Gospel shows Jesus praying to the Father in a divine dynamism unique to God.
19. Mark 14:50 New Revised Standard Version.
20. Quran 4:157–58.
21. Quran 19:33.
22. John 10:17b–18 New Revised Standard Version.
23. An expression used frequently in *Noah's Other Son* and *Forensic Scriptures* by Brian Arthur Brown and subsequently quoted elsewhere.
24. Against Heresies 4.32.
25. Acts 15:36.
26. Abbas Mahmoud El Akkad, *Haejat al-Masih*, 45.
27. John 14:12.
28. Jeremiah 8:22 Tanakh et al.
29. Matthew 13:46 New Revised Standard Version.
30. Matthew 10:27 New Revised Standard Version.
31. Author unknown.

INTRODUCTION TO THE GOSPEL

1. Corinthians 7:1–20.
2. Mark 1:1 New Revised Standard Version.
3. Martin Hengel, *The Four Gospels and the One Gospel of Jesus Christ* (Harrisburg, PA: Trinity International Press, 2000).
4. Mark 14:24 New Revised Standard Version.
5. Many Jewish scholars such as Amy-Jill Levine express satisfaction with the term *Old Testament*, so long as there is no intended denigration of their integrity. In this usage, the Hebrew Scriptures serve as an "old" or "earlier" covenant giving birth for Jews to the Talmud and for Christians to their "New Testament."
6. John Webster, "Resurrection and Scripture," in Andrew T. Lincoln, and Angus Paddison, *Christology and Scripture: Interdisiciplinary Perspectives* (London: T&T Clark, 2007).
7. See R. A. Burridge, *What Are the Gospels? A Comparison with Graeco-Roman Biography* (New York: Cambridge University Press, 1992); Jan Vansina, *Oral Tradition as History* (Madison, WI: University of Wisconsin Press, 1985).
8. See Francis Schüssler-Fiorenza, *Foundational Theology and the Church* (New York: Crossroad, 1984); Richard Bauckham, *Jesus and the Eyewitnesses: The Gospels as Eyewitness Testimony* (Grand Rapids, MI: William B. Eerdmans Publishing, 2006).
9. See Birger Gerhardsson, *Memory and Manuscript* (Copenhagen: Ejnar Munksgaard, 1961); Samuel Byrskog, *Story as History—History as Story: The Gospel Tradition in the Context of Ancient Oral History* (Boston: Brill Academic Publishers, Inc., 2002).
10. Revelation 22:16 New Revised Standard Version.
11. Brown, *Forensic Scriptures*, 114–18.
12. Ibid., 105–13.
13. Acts 1:1 New Revised Standard Version.
14. See Ernest Renan, *The Life of Jesus* (New York: Modern Library, 1927).
15. John 21:24 New Revised Standard Version.
16. Revelation 1:2 New Revised Standard Version.
17. The standard treatment of this can be found in Burton Throckmorton, *Gospel Parallels, NRSV Edition* (New York: Thomas Nelson, 1993).
18. See John S. Kloppenborg Verbim, *Excavating Q: The History and Setting of the Sayings Gospel* (Minneapolis, MN: Fortress Press, 2000).
19. Mark 12:28–34; Matthew 22:34–40; Luke 10:25–28 New Revised Standard Version.
20. David Bruce, *Jesus 24/7: Guide to the Bible*, 78.
21. Matthew 28:18 New Revised Standard Version.
22. While all the other items in this format are direct quotes from *Jesus 24/7: Guide to the Bible* by David Bruce, this brief exposition of Mark's Gospel is original to this book, printed in the format of adjoining material for conformity.
23. Mark 1:1 New Revised Standard Version.
24. Mark 9:7 New Revised Standard Version.
25. Bruce, *Jesus 24/7: Guide to the Bible*, 90.
26. Luke 4:18–19 New Revised Standard Version.
27. Luke 15 New Revised Standard Version.
28. Bruce, *Jesus 24/7: Guide to the Bible*, 90.
29. John 1:14 New Revised Standard Version.
30. John 19:11 New Revised Standard Version.
31. John 20:30–31 New Revised Standard Version.
32. See N. T. Wright, *The Resurrection of the Son of God* (Minneapolis, MN: Fortress Press, 2003).
33. Elisabeth Schüsller Fiorenza, *Jesus, Miriam's Child, Sophia's Prophet: Critical Issues in Feminist Christology* (New York: Continuum, 1995).
34. Bruce, *Jesus 24/7: Guide to the Bible*, 102.
35. Acts 2:4 New Revised Standard Version.
36. Acts 9:27 New Revised Standard Version.
37. Acts 15.
38. The Council at Jerusalem was presided over by "James," whom most scholars agree was not the apostle by that name, but James the Just.
39. Bruce, *Jesus 24/7: Guide to the Bible*, 114.
40. Bruce, *Jesus 24/7: Guide to the Bible*, 126.

41. Bruce, *Jesus 24/7: Guide to the Bible*, 138.

42. The placement of Matthew as first in the canonical order of the Christian Scriptures has long been construed as a deliberate attempt to form linkages with the Hebrew Scriptures, especially given Matthew's predilection for regarding as events in and around Jesus' life as "fulfilling" of promises and shadows. It may be the case, as Brown suggests, that the placement of the Book of Revelation at the end of the collection of Christian Scriptures gave it the position of a climax, engendering the inference that any further revelation from God would be apocalyptic in tone, a suggestion that may have influenced the reception of the Quran, either by Muhammad or at least by those to whom he related the revelations he received.

book three: the quran

PREFACE TO THE SUBLIME QURAN

1. Quran 7:172.

2. In the Arab-speaking world, in Iran and in Turkey, a woman is not permitted to recite the Arabic Quran in public. This prevents women from learning the traditional method of reciting the Quran. Only a few are able to learn from their father or another close relative, and then they are not allowed to recite in public. This also denies women the right to listen to a woman reciting the Quran. This is not the case in other Muslim countries such as Malaysia and Indonesia.

3. When it comes to a woman reciting the Quran in translation, there does not appear to be any restrictions as to who can listen to it. As a result, I have recorded the entire *Sublime Quran* on DVD. My hope is that women who translate the Quran into other languages will then recite it themselves or find a woman to recite it so that women throughout the Muslim world have a chance to hear a woman recite the meaning of the Quran in their language.

4. Quran 41:53.

5. Quran 17:82.

6. Quran 26:80.

7. Quran 7:156.

8. Quran 21:107.

9. Quran 3:132.

10. Quran 4:34.

CHAPTER 9

1. Yasna 28:1–7.

2. Yasna 33:1–7 and 10–14.

3. Yasna 43:5–8.

4. Yasna 44:1–5 and 8–12.

5. Yasna 46:1–3.

6. Yasna 48:1–12.

7. Quran 2:62.

8. Quran 22:17. *The Sublime Quran*, a twenty-first-century translation, at least identifies the Magi as Zoroastrians and points the direction to which we subscribe in references to Sabaeans as another branch of the same.

9. Those who "ascribe partners" to God are rendered "polytheists" in some interpretations, a reference to Babylonians.

10. Mahmoud Ayoub, "Religious Pluralism and Islam," a paper for the International Institute of Islamic Thought, 2007, 3.

CHAPTER 10

1. Genesis 15:2. Abraham's "chief of staff" was almost like a relative to him. Identified as the first person in the Bible to ever pray for personal divine guidance (Genesis 24:12), it was he who arranged marriage for Isaac and Rebecca.

2. Genesis 15:5.

3. An Egyptian system of time measurement by crop cycles (two per solar year) makes perfect sense of the ages ascribed to Sarah and Abraham, as described by Brian Arthur Brown in *Noah's Other Son*, 70.

4. Genesis 16:3 ("concubine" in Tanakh version; "wife" in this context in New Revised Standard Version, King James Version and most others).

5. Genesis 16:4–15.

6. Genesis 17:18.

7. Genesis 17:20.

8. Genesis 17:23–27.

9. Jewish boys, including Jesus (Luke 2:21), have been circumcised on the eighth day ever since, whereas Muslim boys are circumcised at any age, usually at puberty, close to thirteen. The practice is not mentioned in the Quran, but because of Muhammad's teaching about it, it has the status of *Sunnah*, a tradition of the Prophet, and it is practiced universally.

10. Genesis 21:11–13.

11. Genesis 21:15.

12. Several Hadith develop the theme of Hagar's repeated attempts to find water for her son by running between the hills known as Safa and Marwah. During the two Muslim pilgrimages, the Hajj and Umra, pilgrims walk between the hills seven times in memory of Hagar's quest, a rite celebrating both motherhood and the leadership of women.

13. Genesis 21:14–16.

14. Genesis 21:17–21.

15. Quran 2:127.

16. Quran 21:57–71.

17. Genesis 22:1–19 and Quran 37:99–113.

18. Psalm 84:6–7.

19. Bukhari Book I, Hadith 002.

20. Deuteronomy 18:18.

21. Quran 7:157.

22. Martin Lings, *Muhammad: His Life Based on the Earliest Sources*.

23. Ibid., 29–30.

24. Ibid., 33–37.

25. English and Arabic spellings here reflect current usages in the very mixed Muslim community in North America, as heard in the schoolyards of any community.

26. Quran 12:4–102.

27. Genesis 37–50.

28. Quran 20:80.

29. Quran 32:23.

30. Quran 45:16.

31. Quran 3:113–15.

32. Luke 2:12.

33. I Corinthians 13:1.

34. Deuteronomy 6:4.

35. Genesis 2:1–3.

36. Waraqah bin Nawfal in Lings, *Muhammad*, 16, 29, and 45.

37. WikiAnswers.com (What are the reasons to doubt the Quran?), January 24, 2011.

38. Please note references to "different" modes of expression for later consideration of Furqan, "The Criterion."

39. Bukhari: V6B61N561.

40. New support for Harold Bloom's thesis that David's daughter wrote the Book of J, and the *Forensic Scriptures* thesis by Brown that Q was written by the wife of Saint James.

CHAPTER 11

1. Asserted by Abubakr ben Ishmael Salahuddin in *Saving the Savior: Did Christ Survive the Crucifixion?*.

2. Miracles of the animation of birds reported in the Gospel of Thomas, the Infancy Gospel of Thomas and Thomas the Israelite, are echoed also in Quran 3:49 and Quran 5:113, reflecting a high Christology in which the youthful messiah creates life from clay.

3. Quran 3:49–51.

4. *The Book of Asceticism and Tender Mercies* (Kitab al-Zuhd wa'l Raqa'iq) by Ibn al-Mubarak, who died in 797 CE, and *The Book of Asceticism* (Kitab al-Zuhd) by Ibn Hanbal, who lived until 855 CE.

5. Published in 1896 by the English orientalist, David Margoliouth.

6. *Logia et agrapha Domini Jesu* by Miguel Asin y Palacios in 1919, *Aqwal al-Sayyid al-Masih* by Hanna Mansur in 1978 and *Christ in Islam* by James Robson in 1929.

7. No real parallel exists, but this opener comes from possibly the earliest Hadith collection and illustrates the early interest in Jesus as one who cautioned against judging one another.

8. Matthew 6:17, Matthew 6:3, Matthew 6:6.

9. Matthew 5:44 and somewhat differently at Luke 6:28.

10. Matthew 10:25 and Luke 18:25.

11. Matthew 5:16 and 42.

12. Matthew 26:39.

13. Matthew 5:22 and refers to Peter as "the pure," *al-safi* in Arabic, almost certainly a gloss on *al-safa*, "the rock."

14. No parallel, but so like Jesus in content and style and so popular among Muslims that it may be a candidate for consideration as an authentic saying of Jesus not recorded elsewhere. Al-Ghazali, a giant of Islamic literature, had a special love for Jesus, whom he referred to as "The Prophet of the Heart."

15. Matthew 5:26–29, with an imagery also reflected in Quran 24:30–31.

16. Somewhat similar to biblical comments by Jesus about dogs, but a favorable comment by him about a dog in a Muslim collection would be quite offensive, and its retention might therefore cause it to be seen as authentic.

17. Likewise plausible and possibly authentic for the same reason.

18. Matthew 11:17 and Luke 7:32.

19. Matthew 5:39.

20. Matthew 5:7.

21. Mark 12:18–26 is a possible connection to a subject of some interest in the traditional Muslim community.

22. Matthew 5:27–28 and Matthew 5:34–37, verses only connected tenuously here as they are also in the Gospel.

23. Matthew 5:26–28.

24. Luke 6:28.

25. Matthew 13:4–9.

26. Matthew 7:15, except that the "false prophets" in the Gospel have become monks, reflecting possible Arab experience.

27. Matthew 26:39 and Luke 22:44.

28. An Arab recollection of Jesus traveling at least as far as the Gutta Valley, within sight of Damascus.

29. A parallel only to the extent that Jesus so frequently condemns hypocrisy in the Gospel.

30. Matthew 5:45.

31. John 13:1–16.

32. Matthew 16:25–29.

33. *masih* (Messiah) 3:45; 4:157, 171, 172; 5:17, 72, 75; 9:30, 31.

34. *nabi* (Prophet) 2:136, 3:84, 33:7.

35. *rasul ullah* 4:157, 171; 5:75, 111; 61:6.

36. *ruh minhu* (spirit of God) 4:171.

37. *min al-salihin* (the Righteous) 3:46; 6:85.

38. Quran 4:171.

39. Quran 19:1–15 and Quran 19:16–40.

40. Quran 3:35–37.

41. Pope John Paul II, General Audience, June 30, 1993.

42. Ibn Ishaq, *The Life of Mohammed*, translated by A. Guillaume (Pakistan: Oxford University Press, 1967), 552.

43. Quran 3:38–41 and 19:2–15.

44. Luke 1:5–80 and 3:1–22.

45. See Abdullah Yusuf Ali, *The Meaning of the Holy Qur'ān*, footnote 3957.

46. Quran 36:14.

47. Quran 61:6.

48. John 14:16, 14:26, 15:26, and 16:7.

49. Matthew 16:18.

50. Brought out in book form in 1993 by Orbis Books as *Christianity and World Religions: Paths of Dialogue with Islam, Hinduism and Buddism*.

51. Rt. Rev. George Carey, former archbishop of Canterbury, 1991–2002, in a 1993 book review of *Islam: Past, Present and Future* (final volume in Küng's trilogy on *Judaism, Christianity and Islam*), published on Amazon .com and elsewhere.

52. Hans Küng, *Islam: Past, Present and Future*.

53. Karen Armstrong, *Muhammad, A Prophet for Our Time* (New York: HarperOne, 2007).

54. Quran 33:40.

55. Revelation 10:1–2.

56. Revelation 10:3.

57. Revelation 10:4.

CHAPTER 12

1. Although the word *Babilla* in chapter 2:102 is understood as Babylon, this is in the discussion of the angels Harut and Marut, who taught sorcery as part of the Tower of Babylon story amplified in the Quran.

2. www.BrianArthurBrown.com.

3. Quran 1:1–7.

4. Quran 13:12–13.

5. Quran 25:59–65.

6. Quran 36:51–58.

7. Quran 44:51–57.

8. Quran 57:1–7, and verse 1 of both 59 and 61.

9. Quran 82:1–19.

10. Quran 91:1–10.

11. Ibn Masood and The Two Last Surahs of the Quran, Gift2shias.com. Accessed at http://gift2shias.com/2009/11/01/ibn-masood-and-two-last-surahs-of-quran.

12. Quran 113 and 114.

INTRODUCTION TO THE QURAN

1. Arabic is a language of roots and patterns, both of which shape the meaning of each individual word. Most classical dictionaries organize words according to their roots, thereby showing the various shades of meaning encompassed by each root. Patterns have historically not received as much scholarly attention and remain in need of further research. Qur'an follows the pattern *fu'lan*, and it seems to denote the object, which has the function or condition described by the ongoing action of the root verb. Thus, the Quran is not "that which has been read out loud, recited" or *maqru'*, but rather "that of which the function/condition is to be read out loud, recited." The same pattern occurs elsewhere in the Quran; for example, in the word *furqan*, usually rendered "criterion" or "piecemeal revelation"—that is, "that of which the function/condition is to differentiate [between right and wrong]" or "that of which the condition was [to be revealed] in a piecemeal fashion," a key element of this study, as has been noted.

2. All Quran translations are by Laleh Bakhtiar unless otherwise stated. Here, I have added the word *read*.

3. Quran 96:1.

4. See, for example, Isaiah 29:12.

5. This ritual entails going around and around the ancient house in a circular fashion. It is called *tawaf*.

6. See Ibn Hisham, *al-Sira al-Nabawiyya*, 3rd ed., edited by Sa'id Muhammad al-Lahham (Bayrut: Dar al-Fikr, 1998), 178–86.

7. For more about Hanifs, see Uri Rubin, "Hanif," in *Encyclopaedia of the Qur'ān* (EQ), vol. 2, edited by Jane McAuliffe (Leiden: Brill, 2001–2006), 402–4. .

8. Quran 1:1–7.

9. Quran 2:1–2.

10. Perhaps particularly those of the Zoroastrian-Jewish-Christian genres within the framework of ancient Arabia.

11. For more on the structure and composition of suras, see the work of Angelika Neuwirth, "Sura(s)," in *Encyclopaedia of the Qur'ān*, vol. 5, 166–77.

12. The sole exception to this rule is chapter 9 (al-Tawba). Early Muslims weren't clear as to whether it was an independent chapter or part of the preceding one. They decided to count it as an independent chapter without the initial basmallah.

13. *Iyjaz wa tafsil*. See, for example, Abd al-Razzaq Ghalib al-Mahdi, ed., *Biqa'i Nazm al-durar fi tanasub al-Ayat wa'l-suwar*, 3rd ed. (Bayrut: Dar al-Kutub al 'Ilmiyya, 2006), 40; 'Abd Allah Muhammad al-Darwish, ed., *Suyuti, Tanasuq al-durar fi tanasub al-suwar*, 2nd ed. (Bayrut: 'Alam al-Kutub, 1987), 41–45.

14. Lawson, "Duality, Opposition and Typology in the Qur'an," 23–49. Lawson points to one of the distinctive features of this genre, duality and opposition, such as the duality of styles, "narrative" and "antinarrative,"

and the pairs that are often mentioned in the Quran—day and night, heaven and hell, man and woman, and more. There is even a duality of dualities, contrasting these pairs with the One who is one. He also discusses another feature, typological figuration, in the way the text illustrates prophethood and Muhammad's belonging to that type of figure.

15. Brian Brown adds *furqan* (3:4) to this list, noting linguistic similarities between this term and the Zoroastrian Scripture, *Fargan*, both meaning "criterion."

16. The position of Mary as a prophet has been debated in the classical literature and is not universally accepted. Abraham's wife, Sarah, and Moses's mother are also portrayed as receiving divine revelation.

17. Quran 111:1.

18. Quran 30:1–6.

19. There are no verses in the Quran that prescribe stoning as a punishment for adultery; the punishment for adultery is clearly delineated as whipping a certain number of lashes (24:2; 4:25). Stoning has been criticized in both the classical and modern Islamic scholarship; however, the surviving schools of jurisprudence still adhere to this law. It derives from outside the Quran. For more, see the work of John Burton, for example, "Law and Exegesis: The Penalty for Adultery in Islam."

20. See, for example, Quran 41:33–35; 2:109; 3:186.

21. While this idea occurs in Quran 2:190–95, it is more clearly elaborated in 60:8–9.

22. Quran 36:69; 21:5; 69:41.

23. For more on rhymed prose, see Devin J. Stewart, "Saj'," in "The Qur'an: Prosody and Structure," *Journal of Arabic Literature* 21 (1990): 101–39.

24. Quran, 52:29–34; 69:40–43.

25. See, in particular, Michael Zwettler, "A Mantic Manifesto: The Sura of 'The Poets' and the Qur'anic Foundations of Prophetic Authority."

26. See Mustafā al-A'zami, *The History of the Qur'anic Text*, 70–76.

27. (96:1, 3–5); I have added "read" to Laleh Bakhtiar's translation in order to bring out the nuance that connects this word with "the pen."

28. Ahmad 'Abd al-Rahman al-Banna, *Al-Fath al-rabbani li-tartib musnad al-imam Ahmad ibn Hanbal al-Shaybani ma' sharhih bulugh al-amani*, vol. 5 (3) (Bayrut: Dar Ihya' al-Turath al-'Arabi, n.d.), 1375; ibn Sa'd, *Kitab al-tabaqat al-kabir*, vol. 8 (Bayrut: Dar Sadir, 1958), 457. See also Jalal al-Din al-Suyuti, *al-Itqan fi 'ulum al-Qur'an*, vol. 1, 203–4.

29. There is some confusion in the sources as to this master document. It could have been her own copy, which she wrote herself on loose sheets of parchment or similar material (*suhuf*). It could also be a second copy, collected under the supervision of Zayd ibn Thabit and possibly transcribed by him on loose sheets. The sources are also not entirely clear as to what role her copy played in the 'Uthmanic codex. One popular source records that the 'Uthmanic "books" were copied directly from that one document. A more widely accepted version places the collection of the master document from various fragments in the reign of 'Uthman, while Hafsah's copy was used to verify the final text produced in book form (*mushaf*). In all these versions, she is accredited with keeping the official state document for some time. For more, see Suyuti, *Itqan*, vol. 1, 164–72.

30. These literate women in the Prophet's own household (educated at his behest) are held up by Brian Brown as examples of literate women in leadership households in the ancient world. In some of the earlier religious traditions, such women were also typically anonymous, as were most male writers, but, unlike their male counterparts, they did not receive their fair share in acknowledgment and have remained unreported and unidentified in subsequent history. See chapter 9 of this volume and *Forensic Scriptures*. It is noteworthy that Umm Waraqa also seems to have been forgotten until she was rediscovered by Suyuti (d. 1515 CE). See Suyuti, *Itqan*, vol. 1, 203–4.

31. For more on the collection of the Quran, see Ibn Hajar al'Asqalani, *Fath al-bari bi-sharh sahih al-Bukhari*, 627–63; Suyuti, *Itqan*, vol. 1, 164–68; and Al-A'zami, *History*.

32. For a brief summary of Western approaches to the Quran's formation, see Harald Motzki, "Alternative Accounts of the Qur'an's Formation." For a description of the tradition-critical and other approaches, see Fred Donner, *Narratives of Islamic Origins*.

33. John Wansbrough, *Qur'anic Studies: Sources and Methods of Scriptural Interpretation* (Oxford: Oxford University Press, 1977).

34. Andrew Rippin, "Literary Analysis of the Qur'ān, Tafsīr and Sīra," 151–63, 227–32. For "conjecture and verification," see 157–58.

35. This codex was found in the cache under the grand mosque in the city of Sanaa in Yemen, containing some of the oldest manuscripts in the world. Carbon dating has placed it between 657 and 690 CE, while Hans-Caspar Graf von Bothmer has dated it to 710–715 CE, arguing that some of the illustrations and orthography are likely a little later and pointing out that Quran manuscripts sometimes took years to complete. Both of

these dates place this manuscript within the first century of Islam. Hans-Caspar Graf von Bothmer, "Neue Wege der Koranforschung," *Universität des Saarlandes Magazinforschung* 1 (1999): 33–46.

36. Al-A'zami, *History*, 315–18.

37. When showing that the early dating of some of these manuscripts has not been generally acknowledged, scholars writing in Wansbrough's day (1977) and Motzki's day (2001) cite a 1958 article: Adolf Grohmann, "The Problem of Dating Early Qur'ans," *Der Islam*: 213–31. See Harald Motzki, "The Collection of the Qur'an: Reconsideration of Western Views in Light of Recent Methodological Developments," *Der Islam* 78, no. 1 (2001): 1–34, see 2. The dating of these manuscripts needs careful reevaluation.

38. Dialectal differences have contributed to the variation in pronouncing this weak consonant: Western Arabians tended to assimilate it, while Eastern Arabians were known to emphasize it. In addition, the orthography of this letter developed relatively late, thereby leaving room for differences to develop in the interim. For more on the pronunciation of the guttural stop, see Sibawayhi, *al-Kitab*, vol. 3 (al-Qahirah: Maktabat al-Khanji, 1992), 541–57.

39. For more, see Suyuti, *Itqan*, vol. 1, 204–6.

40. The strong stop indicates a grammatical Form IV (*adraba, yudribu, idraban*, of which the imperative is *adrib*), while the weak stop indicates a grammatical Form I (*daraba, yadribu, darban*, of which the imperative is *idrib* (classical) or *idrab* (colloquial). When adding the conjunction *w* with the short *a* vowel (*fathah*), Form I's weak hamzah will become assimilated into the short *a* vowel, while in theory, the Form IV's strong stop will be articulated, preceded and followed by a short *a* vowel. However, in practice, both will sound the same, particularly in the pronunciation of the Prophet's tribe and Eastern Arabia, which tended to assimilate such consonants. They do not even seem to have emphasized the guttural stop in words like *sa'ala*, "he asked," where the guttural stop is a root consonant. See Sibawayhi, *al-Kitab*, 541–42.

41. It is unclear what methods they used in their interpretations, but "beat/strike" is a popular traditional interpretation in the classical literature. The Quran supports a meaning of "go away from," since there is a supporting verse: the iyla' verse in 2:226. There is no supporting verse for the meaning "beat [your wives]" anywhere in the Quran. Hence, if one were to follow the method of using the Quran to interpret the Quran, "go away from" would be the more likely interpretation.

42. See Bakhtiar's translation of verse 4:34 in Bakhtiar, *The Sublime Quran*, the translation featured in this text.

43. There are some allegations of falsification within early and Safavid Shia sources; however, they diminish in the Buyid period and in modern times. For the early period, see Meir Bar-Asher, *Scripture and Exegesis in Early Imami Shiism* (Leiden: Brill, 1999). For the Safavid period, see Todd Lawson, "Akhbari Shi'i Approaches to Tafsir," 173–210.

44. The witnessing system is known as *shahadah*, while the tradent system with its chains of transmission is known as *riwayah*. According to Islamic law, while shahadah is admissible in court—for example, in testimonies against persons committing crimes—riwayah is not admissible in court, similar to the way we would consider hearsay evidence today.

45. For the format of these reports, see, for example, 'Asqalani, *Fath*.

46. For more on the use of writing in the process of transmission, see Gregor Schoeler, "Schreiben und Veröffentlichen: Zur Verwendung und Funktion der Schrift in den ersten islamischen Jahrhunderten," *Der Islam* 69 (1992): 1–43.

47. This popular kind of commentary is called *tafsir musalsal*. Jarir al-Tabari's work is one of the earliest and most famous works in this genre. See Tabari's monumental *Jami' al-bayan 'an ta'wil ay al-Qur'an*, edited by Mahmud Muhammad Shakir (al-Qahirah: Dar al-Ma'arif, 1958–).

48. These narratives are known as *isra'iliyyat*, "Israelite material."

49. See Walid Saleh, *The Formation of the Classical Tafsir Tradition: The Qur'an Commentary of al-Tha'labi* (d. 427/1035) (Leiden: Brill, 2004), 14–23.

50. For a traditionalist Sunni focus, see the commentary of Tabari (d. 923 CE); for mystical content, Sulami (d. 1021 CE); for legal expertise, Jassas (d. 982 CE), Abu Bakr Ibn al-'Arabi (d. 1148 CE) and Qurtubi (d. 1272 CE); for linguistic knowledge, Abu Hayyan al-Andalusi (d. 1353 CE) and Zamakhshari (d. 1144 CE); for Shiate content, Tusi (d. 1067 CE) and Tabarsi (or Tabrisi) (d. 1154 CE); for a focus on the Quran's internal connections, Biqa'i (d. 1480 CE).

51. See Saleh, *Formation*, 16.

52. For more on this topic, see the work of John Burton, "Abrogation," in *Encyclopaedia of the Qur'ān*, vol. 1, 11–19.

53. Translation of the dialogue, including Asma' and Umm Salamah's words, is mine, except for the Quranic verse, which is by Laleh Bakhtiar. For more, see Wahidi (d. 1076 CE), *Asbab al-nuzul* (Bayrut: Dar al-Kutub al-'Ilmiyyah, 1999), 202. See also Tantawi, *al-Tafsir al-wasit li'l-Qur'an al-karim*, vol. 11 (Madinat al-Sadis min Uktubar: Nahdat Misr, 1997), 209–10.

54. Quran 33:35.

55. See Suyuti, *Itqan*. There is another well-known book of this genre: Zarkashi (d. 794/1391), *al-Burhan fi 'ulum al-Qur'an*, edited by Muhammad Abu al-Fadl Ibrahim (al-Qahirah: Dar al-Turath, n.d.). However, it is earlier and not as widely in use. For example, Ahmad von Denffer's book relies exclusively on Suyuti. See Ahmad von Denffer, *'Ulūm al-Qur'ān: An Introduction to the Sciences of the Qur'ān*.

56. Ibn Taymiyyah, *Muqaddimah fi usul al-tafsir* (al-Qahirah: Maktabat al-Turath al-Islami, 1988), 93–105; Zarkashi, *Burhan*, vol. 2, 175–76; Suyuti, *Itqan*, vol. 4, 174.

57. Some of the names that stand out in the literary approach include Amin al-Khuli (d. 1967) and 'A'ishah 'Abd al-Rahman (d. 1998) (also known by a pen name, Bint al-Shati', "Daughter of the Riverbank"), who wrote the first consciously literary exegetical work.

58. See, for example, Hassan Hanafi, "Method of Thematic Interpretation of the Qur'an."

59. For more, see Nevin Reda, "Holistic Approaches to the Quran: A Historical Background," 495–506.

60. Names that stand out in this trend include Tantawi Jawhari (d. 1940) and Mustafa Mahmud (d. 2009).

61. Quran 24:40.

62. Amina Wadud, *Qur'an and Woman: Rereading the Sacred Text from a Woman's Perspective*, 2nd ed.

63. Asma Barlas, "Believing Women."

64. Nimat Hafez Barazangi, *Woman's Identity and the Qur'an: A New Reading*.

65. Ibn Kathir, *Tafsir al-Qur'an al-'azim* ([al-Qahirah]: 'Isa al-Babi al-Halabi, n.d.).

66. See Muhammad Kurayyim Rajih, ed., *Mukhtasar tafsir ibn Kathir* (Bayrut: Dar al-Ma'rifah, 1983); Muhammad 'Ali al-Sabuni, ed., *Mukhtasar tafsir ibn Kathir* (Bayrut: Dar al-Qur'an al-Karim, 1393 [1973 or 1974]); and Safi al-Rahman Mubarakfuri, *al-Misbah al-munir fi tahdhib tafsir ibn Kathir* (al-Riyad: Darussalam, 2000). An English translation of the latter is also available; see below.

67. Safi al-Rahman Mubarakfuri, *Tafsir ibn Kathir: Abridged by a Group of Scholars under the Supervision of Safi-ur-Rahman al-Mubarakpuri* (Riyadh: Darussalam, 2000).

epilogue

1. *Faith and Reason*, with Bill Moyers on PBS, June 23, 2006.

2. A notable exception is found in the leadership of Frank Fredericks of New York, founder of World Faith.

3. *D. L. Hughley Breaks the News*, on CNN November 18, 2008, and March 7, 2009.

4. Tony Blair, *Toronto Star*, December 23, 2010.

selected bibliography

Abdul Rauf, Imam Feisal. *What's Right with Islam: A New Vision for Muslims and the West*. New York: Harper-Collins, 2004.

al'Asqalani, Ibn Hajar. *Fath al-bari bi-sharh sahih al-Bukhari*. Vol. 8. Edited by Muhibb al-Din al-Khatib. al-Qahira: Dar al-Rayyan li'l-Turath, 1988.

Al-A'zami, Muhammad Mustafā. *The History of the Qur'ānic Text: From Revelation to Compilation; A Comparative Study with the Old and New Testaments*. Leicester: UK Islamic Academy, 2003.

Al-Biruni. *The Chronology of Ancient Nations*. Athens: Aristide D. Caratzas, 1984.

Ali, Abdullah Yusuf. *The Meaning of the Holy Qur'ān*. Brentwood, MD: Amana, 1991.

al-Suyuti, Jalal al-Din. *al-Itqan fi 'ulum al-Qur'an*. Vol. 1. Edited by Muhsin Abu al-Fadl Ibrahim. al-Qahira: Maktaba al-Turath, n.d.

Al-Wahidi, Abul Hasan Ali ibn Ahmad ibn Muhammad ibn Ali. *Asbab al-Nuzul: Great Commentaries of the Holy Qur'an*. Bayrut: Dar al-Kutub al-'Ilmiyyah, 1999.

Armstrong, Karen. *The Great Transformation: The Beginning of Our Religious Traditions*. New York: Anchor, 2007.

Ayoub, Mahmoud. *A Muslim View of Christianity: Essays on Dialogue*. Edited by Irfan A. Omar. New York: Orbis, 2007.

Bakhtiar, Laleh, trans. *The Sublime Quran*. Rev. ed. Chicago: Kazi, 2011.

Bakhtiar, Laleh, and Shaykh Muhammad Hisham Kabbani, eds. *Encyclopedia of Muhammad's Women Companions: And the Traditions They Related*. Chicago: ABC International Group, Inc., 1998.

Barazangi, Nimat Hafez. *Woman's Identity and the Qur'an: A New Reading*. Gainsville: University Press of Florida, 2004.

Barclay, William. *The Revelation of John*. Vol. I. Philadelphia: Westminster Press, 1976.

Barlas, Asma. "Believing Women." In *Islam: Unreading Patriarchal Interpretations of the Qur'an*. Austin: University of Texas Press, 2002.

Benveniste, Émile. *The Persian Religion according to the Chief Greek Texts*. Paris: Paul Geuthner, 1929.

Berlin, Adele, and Marc Brettler, eds. *The Jewish Study Bible*. London: Oxford, 2004.

Blavatsky, H. P. *Theosophical Glossary*. Kilka, MT: Kessinger, 2010,

Bleeck, Arthur H. *Avesta: The Religious Books of the Parsees*. 3 vols. Lexington: Elibron Classics, 2005.

Borg, Marcus. *Jesus and Buddha: The Parallel Sayings*. Berkeley: Ulysses, 1997.

Boyce, Mary. *A Persian Stonghold of Zoroastrianism*. Oxford: Clarendon Press. 1977.

———. *Textual Sources for the Study of Zoroastrianism*. Chicago: University of Chicago Press, 1990.

———. *Zoroastrians: Their Religious Beliefs and Practices*. London: Routledge, 1979.

Brandewie, Ernest. *Wilhelm Schmidt and the Origin of the Idea of God*. Lanham, MD: Rowman & Littlefield, 1983.

Brettler, Marc, ed. *The Jewish Study Bible*. London: Oxford, 2004.

———. "A Woman's Voice in the Psalter: A New Understanding of Psalm 113." *Biblical Archaeological Review* (May/June 2008): 28.

Brown, Brian Arthur. *Forensic Scriptures: Critical Analysis of Scripture and What the Qur'an Reveals about the Bible*. Eugene, OR: Cascade, 2009.

———. *Noah's Other Son: Bridging the Gap between the Bible and the Qur'an*. New York: Continuum, 2007.

Bruce, David. *Jesus 24/7: Guide to the Bible*. Toronto: United Church Publishing House, 2010.

Burton, John. "Abrogation." In *Encyclopaedia of the Qur'ān*, edited by Jane Dammen McAuliffe. Leiden: Brill, 2001–2006.

———. "Law and Exegesis: The Penalty for Adultery in Islam." In *Approaches to the Qur'an*, edited by Gerald Hawting and Abdul-Kader A. Shareef. London: Routledge, 1993.

Carter, George William. *Zoroastrianism and Judaism*. Boston: Gorham Press, 1918.

Chittister, Joan. *Becoming Fully Human: The Greatest Glory of God*. Lanham, MD: Sheed & Ward, 2005.

Chopra, Deepak. *Jesus: A Story of Enlightenment*. New York: HarperOne, 2008.

Dallah, Maneckji N. *History of Zoroastrianism*. Brooklyn, NY: Ams Press, 1938.

Denffer, Ahmad von. *'Ulum al-Qur'ān: An Introduction to the Sciences of the Qur'ān*. United Kingdom: The Islamic Foundation, 2000.

Doi, Abdur Rahman. *Hadith: An Introduction*. Chicago: Kazi, 1980.

Donner, Fred M. *Narratives of Islamic Origins: The Beginnings of Islamic Historical Writing*. Princeton, NJ: Darwin Press, 1998.

El Akkad, Abbas Mahmoud. *Haejat al-Masih*. Cairo: Community Books, 1958.

Freedman, David Noel, et al., eds. *Anchor Bible Dictionary*. New York: Doubleday, 1992.

Friedman, Richard Elliott. *The Bible with Sources Revealed: A New View into the Five Books of Moses*. New York: HarperOne, 2005.

———. *Who Wrote the Bible?* New York: HarperCollins, 1997.

Frost, Stanley B. *The Beginning of the Promise*. London: SPCK, 1960.

Gilliot, Claude. "Creation of a Fixed Text." In *The Cambridge Companion to the Qur'ān*, edited by Jane Dammen McAuliffe. Cambridge: Cambridge University Press, 2006.

Gruber, Elmar R., and Holger Kersten. *The Original Jesus: The Buddhist Sources of Christianity*. Shaftsbury: Element Books, 1996.

Hanafi, Hassan. "Method of Thematic Interpretation of the Qur'an." In *The Qur'an as Text*, edited by Stefan Wild. Leiden: Brill, 1996.

Hassnain, Fida, and Dahan Levi. *The Fifth Gospel: New Evidence from the Tibetan, Sanskit, Arabic, Persian and Urdu Sources about the Historical Life of Jesus Christ after the Crucifixion*. Nevada City, CA: Blue Dolphin, 2006.

Hassnain, Fida, and Suzanne Olsson. *Roza Bal: The Tomb of Jesus*. Lexington: Booksurge, 2010.

Henning, W. B. *Zoroaster: Politician or Witch-Doctor?* Oxford: Oxford University Press, 1951.

Herzfeld, Ernst E. *Zoroaster and His World*. Princeton, NJ: Princeton University Press, 1947.

Holy Bible: New Revised Standard Version. Iowa Falls: World Bible Publishers, Inc., 1989.

Hussain, Amir. *Oil & Water; Two Faiths: One God*. Kelowna: CopperHouse, 2006.

Hussain, Amir, and Willard G. Oxtoby, eds. *World Religions: Western Traditions*. 3rd ed. New York: Oxford University Press, 2010.

Jacobs, Alan. *When Jesus Lived in India; The Quest for the Aquarian Gospel: The Mystery of the Missing Years*. London: Watkins Publishing, 2009.

Jamieson, R. C., trans. *The Perfection of Wisdom*. London: The Book Studio, 2000.

Jaspers, Karl. *Vom Ursprung und Ziel der Geschichte (The Origin and Goal of History)*. Translated by Michael Bullock. New Haven, CT: Yale University Press, 1955.

Jones, Serene. *Trauma and Grace: Theology in a Ruptured World*. Louisville, KY: Westminster John Knox Press, 2000.

Josephus, Flavius. *Antiquities of the Jews*. Grand Rapids, MI: Kregel, 1960.

Kaiser, Ward. *How Maps Change Things*. Amherst, MA: ODT Inc., 2012 (a Kindle book).

Kent, Ronald G. *Old Persian Grammar, Texts, Lexicon*. 2nd rev. ed. New Haven, CT: American Oriental Society, 1953.

Kersten, Holger. *Jesus Lived in India: His Unknown Life before and after the Crucifixion*. New Delhi: Penguin, 2001.

Khalidi, Tarif, ed. and trans. *The Muslim Jesus: Sayings and Stories in Islamic Literature*. Cambridge, MA: Harvard University Press, 2001.

Knitter, Paul F. *Without Buddha I Could Not Be a Christian*. Oxford: Oneworld, 2009.

Krotz, Douglas Roper. *The Man Who Sent the Magi: A Religious Rosetta Stone*. Peoria, AZ: Intermedia, 2011.

Küng, Hans. *Islam: Past, Present and Future*. Oxford: Oneworld, 2007.

Landau, Brent. *Revelation of the Magi: The Lost Tale of the Wise Men's Journey to Bethlehem*. New York: HarperOne, 2010.

Lawson, Todd. "Akhbari Shi'i Approaches to Tafsir." In *Approaches to the Qur'an*, edited by G. R. Hawting and Abdul-Kader A. Shareef. London: Routledge, 1993.

———. "Duality, Opposition and Typology in the Qur'an: The Apocalyptic Substrate." *Journal of Qur'anic Studies* 10, no. 2 (2008).

Lings, Martin. *Muhammad: His Life Based on the Earliest Sources*. 2nd U.S. ed. Rochester, VT: Inner Traditions, 2006.

Madigan, Daniel. "Themes and Topics." In *The Cambridge Companion to the Qur'ān*, edited by Jane Dammen McAuliffe. Cambridge: Cambridge University Press, 2006.

Malandra, William W. *An Introduction to Ancient Iranian Religion: Readings from the Avesta and the Achaemenid Inscriptions*. Minneapolis: University of Minnesota Press, 1983.

Martin, Edward T. *King of Travelers: Jesus' Lost Years in India* (and the motion picture of the same name). Los Angeles: Yellow Hat Productions, 2008.

McAuliffe, Jane Dammen, et al. *Encyclopaedia of the Qur'ān*. 1st ed., 5 vols. plus index. Leiden: Brill, 2001–2006.

Meyers, Carol, and Eric Meyers. *Haggai, Zechariah 1–8*. Anchor Bible Series. New York: Doubleday, 1987.

———. *Zechariah 9–14*. Anchor Bible Series. New York: Doubleday, 1993.

Motzki, Harald. "Alternative Accounts of the Qur'an's Formation." In *The Cambridge Companion to the Qur'ān*, edited by Jane Dammen McAuliffe. Cambridge: Cambridge University Press, 2006.

Nanavutty, Piloo. *The Gathas of Zarathushtra: Hymns in Praise of Wisdom*. Ahmedabad: Mapin Publishing, 1999.

Nehru, Jawaharlal. *Glimpses of World History*. New York: John Day Company, 1942.

Nigosian, S. A. *The Zoroastrian Faith: Tradition and Modern Research*. Montreal: McGill-Queens, 2007.

Notovitch, Nicolas. *The Unknown Life of Jesus Christ*. Radford, VA: Wilder, 2008.

Pagels, Elaine. *The Gnostic Gospels*. New York: Random House, Inc., 1979.

Pickthall, Muhammad M. *The Glorious Quran*. Elmhurst, NY: Tahrike Tarsile Qur'an Inc., 2001.

Porter, John. *The Vertical Mosaic: An Analysis of Social Class and Power in Canada*. Toronto: University of Toronto Press, 1965.

Ragg, Lonsdale, and Laura Ragg, eds. and trans. *The Gospel of Barnabas*. Oxford: Clarendon Press, 1907.

Reda, Nevin. "Holistic Approaches to the Quran: A Historical Background." *Religion Compass* 4, no. 8 (2010).

Rippin, Andrew. "Literary Analysis of the Qur'ān, Tafsīr and Sīra: The Methodologies of John Wansbrough." In *Approaches to Islam in Religious Studies*, edited by Richard C. Martin. London: Oneworld, 2001.

Rose, Jenny. *Zoroastrianism: An Introduction*. London: I. B. Tauris, 2011.

Sells, Michael. "A Literary Approach to the Hymnic Sūras of the Qur'ān: Spirit, Gender and Aural Intertextuality." In *Literary Structures of Religious Meaning in the Qur'ān*, edited by Issa J. Boullata. Richmond: Curzon, 2000.

Stein, David E. S., et al., eds. *The Contemporary Torah: A Gender-Sensitive Adaptation of the JPS Translation*. Philadelphia: Jewish Publication Society, 2006.

Takyi, H. K., and K. J. Khubchandani. *Words of Jesus and Sathya Sai Baba*. Madras: Sai Shriram, 1995.

Tanakh, The Holy Scriptures. Philadelphia: The Jewish Publication Society, 1985.

Toynbee, Arnold J. *A Study of History*. Abridgement of volumes I–VI by D. C. Somervell. Oxford: New York, 1974.

Vaux, Kenneth L. *Journey into an Interfaith World: Jews, Christians, and Muslims in a World Come of Age*. Eugene, OR: Wipf and Stock, 2010.

Volf, Miroslav. *Captive to the Word of God: Engaging the Scriptures for Contempory Theological Reflection*. Grand Rapids, MI: Wm. B. Eerdmans, 2010.

von Denffer, Ahmad. *'Ulūm al-Qur'ān: An Introduction to the Sciences of the Qur'ān*. Markfield, Leicestershire: Islamic Foundation, 2000.

Wadud, Amina. *Qur'an and Woman: Rereading the Sacred Text from a Woman's Perspective*. 2nd ed. New York: Oxford University Press, 1999.

West, M. L. *Hymns of Zoroaster: A New Translation of the Most Ancient Sacred Texts of Iran*. New York: I. B. Tauris, 2010.

Wolf, Laibl. *Practical Kabbalah: A Guide to Jewish Wisdom for Everyday Life*. New York: Three River Press, 1999.

Yogananda, Paramahansa. *The Yoga of Jesus: Understanding the Hidden Teachings of the Gospels*. Los Angeles: Self Realization, 2007.

Zwettler, Michael. "A Mantic Manifesto: The Sura of 'The Poets' and the Qur'anic Foundations of Prophetic Authority." In *Poetry and Prophecy: The Beginnings of a Literary Tradition*, edited by James L. Kugel. New York: Cornell University Press, 1990.

index

about the author

After a lengthy career in the United Church of Canada, **Brian Arthur Brown** is currently scholar-in-residence at the historic and progressive First Baptist Church of Niagara Falls, New York. Dr. Brown holds a bachelor's degree in classics from Dalhousie University in Halifax, a master's in theology from McGill University in Montreal, and a doctorate in ecclesiastical organizational behavior from the San Francisco Theological Seminary. He has done postdoctoral studies in executive leadership at Harvard University and is a current member of the Oxford Roundtable at Jesus College of Oxford University in England.

His first book was *The Sacramental Ministry to the Sick* (1968). Fifteen books since then have focused on bridging gaps between people and groups: French-English, Native-White, Canadian-American. Of late he has written on Jewish-Christian-Muslim relations in what he has described as the dysfunctional family of Abraham, Sarah and Hagar. His books include *Noah's Other Son: Bridging the Gap between the Bible and the Qur'an* and *Forensic Scriptures: Critical Analysis of Scripture and What the Qur'an Reveals about the Bible*.

He lives in Niagara Falls, Ontario, with his wife, Jenny, near their children and grandchildren, and within earshot of the thunderous falls. His website is www.BrianArthurBrown.com, from which he presents a monthly interfaith blog.

about the contributors

(In order of appearance)

Amir Hussain is the editor of the *Journal of the American Academy of Religion* and teaches theology at Loyola Marymount University in Los Angeles. His avocation is hockey and he personally embodies the interfaith and intercultural agendas as a Canadian Muslim teaching in an American Catholic university. He is the author of several books, including *Oil and Water: Two Faiths, One God.*

Ellen Frankel is the former CEO and editor-in-chief of the Jewish Publication Society in Philadelphia, and now serves as its first editor emerita. She is the author of ten published books, including *The Five Books of Miriam: A Woman's Commentary on the Torah,* and several libretti, including "The Golem Psalms" with composer Andrea Clearfield, and an opera, *Slaying the Dragon,* with composer Michael Ching, which premiered in Philadelphia in June 2012.

Marc Zvi Brettler is the Dora Golding Professor of Biblical Studies at Brandeis University in Boston. In addition to his many books and articles on the Hebrew Bible, he is the coeditor, with Adele Berlin, of *The Oxford Jewish Study Bible,* and also *The Jewish Annotated New Testament,* with Amy-Jill Levine.

Henry L. Carrigan Jr. is senior editor at Northwestern University Press near Chicago. A respected literary critic for *Atlanta Journal-Constitution, The Charlotte Observer, The Cleveland Plain Dealer, Orlando Sentinel, Christian Science Monitor,* and *Washington Post Book World,* he is a book reviewer for *Publishers Weekly, BookPage, Library Journal,* and *ForeWord.*

David Bruce, with doctorates from Fuller Theological Seminary and Saint Michael's College, is the author of the bestselling series, *Jesus 24/7.* He was a minister of the United Church of Canada for twenty-five years prior to his recent reception into the Roman Catholic Church. The latest book from this articulate biblical theologian is *The Resurrection of History* (2014), addressing a question of as much interest to many Jews and Muslims as to nearly all Christians.

Laleh Bakhtiar is the resident scholar at Kazi Publications (USA) in Chicago, where she is also the president of the Institute of Traditional Psychology. She is the author or coauthor of more than twenty-five books, and is the acclaimed translator of *The Sublime Quran* in English, in which she has recovered the inclusive spirit of the original.

Nevin Reda was the founding coordinator of the Muslim Studies Program at the University of Toronto's Emmanuel College in 2009. She contributes a theology of democracy in columns for *Al-Masry Al-Youm,* the most widely circulated Arabic newspaper in Egypt, where her models for leadership, based on feminist and minority verses in the Quran, have elicited a popular response.